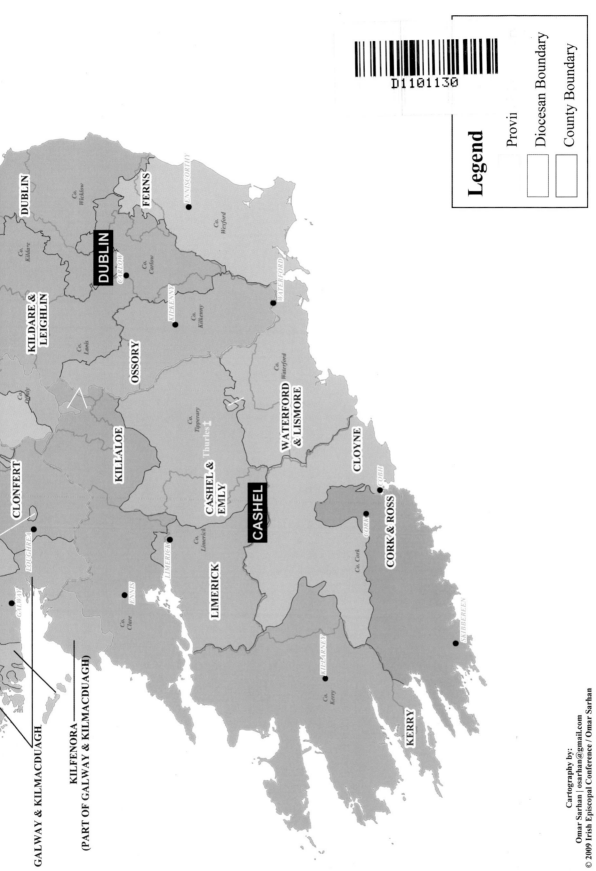

Legend

Provi[nces]
Diocesan Boundary
County Boundary

D1101130

DUBLIN
Co. Wicklow
FERNS
Co. Kildare
DUBLIN
ENNISCORTHY
Co. Wexford
Co. Carlow
KILDARE & LEIGHLIN
CARLOW
KILKENNY
Co. Kilkenny
OSSORY
Co. Laois
WATERFORD
Co. Offaly
Co. Waterford
WATERFORD & LISMORE
KILLALOE
Co. Tipperary
CLOYNE
CLONFERT
CASHEL & EMLY
Thurles †
CASHEL
COBH
LOUGHREA
GORK
CORK & ROSS
LIMERICK
Co. Limerick
Co. Cork
GALWAY
ENNIS
Co. Clare
LIMERICK
SKIBBEREEN
KILFENORA
(PART OF GALWAY & KILMACDUAGH)
KILLARNEY
GALWAY & KILMACDUAGH
Co. Kerry
KERRY

Cartography by:
Omar Sarhan | osarhan@gmail.com
© 2009 Irish Episcopal Conference / Omar Sarhan

# IRISH CATHOLIC DIRECTORY 2015

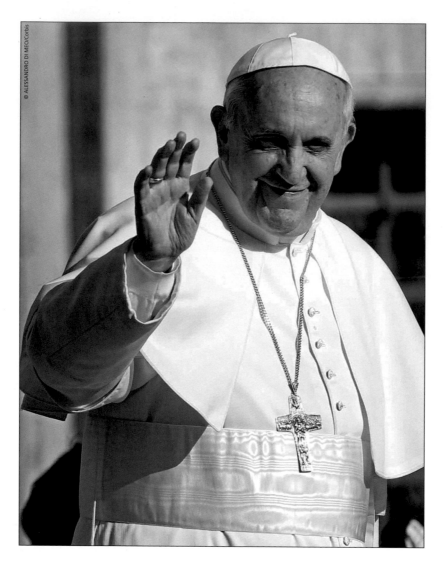

**FRANCIS**
BISHOP OF ROME
Vicar of Jesus Christ

Successor of the Prince of the Apostles, Supreme Pontiff of the Universal Church, Primate of Italy, Archbishop and Metropolitan of the Roman Province, Sovereign of the State of the Vatican City.

Servant of the Servants of God, Jorge Mario Bergoglio, born in Buenos Aires, Argentina on 17 December 1936; ordained priest on 13 December 1969. From 1973 to 1979 he was Argentina's Provincial superior of the Society of Jesus. He was ordained Auxiliary Bishop of Buenos Aires on 27 June 1992; became Archbishop of Buenos Aires in 1998 and created cardinal on 21 February 2001. He was elected pope on 13 March 2013 and inaugurated on 19 March 2013.

# IRISH
# CATHOLIC
# DIRECTORY
# 2015

PUBLISHED BY AUTHORITY
FOR THE HIERARCHY OF IRELAND

This publication
has been supported
by the generous
sponsorship
of

**Allianz**

VERITAS

Published for the Hierarchy by
Veritas Publications
7–8 Lower Abbey Street
Dublin 1
Ireland
publications@veritas.ie
www.veritas.ie

The publishers are not responsible for any
errors or omissions.

ISBN 978 1 84730 579 4

Cover design: Colette Dower, Veritas Publications
Design & Typesetting: Colette Dower, Veritas Publications
Printed in the Republic of Ireland
by Colour World Print Ltd, Kilkenny

*Veritas books are printed on paper made from the wood pulp of managed forests.
For every tree felled, at least one tree is planted, thereby renewing natural resources.*

# PREFACE

This is the twenty-fifth edition of the *Irish Catholic Directory*. Information for this edition was collected between August 2014 and November 2014. In general, all information comes from the organisation or community concerned.

Veritas has made every effort to ensure the accuracy and completeness of the information in the *Directory*. However, this information can only be as good as that supplied to us.

We would like to express our gratitude to all the bishops, diocesan secretaries, priests, brothers, sisters and lay people who have over the years supplied information, answered queries, chased details and checked proofs.

We are also indebted to the advertisers and sponsors, without whose support this publication would not be possible.

Finally, it may be appropriate to remind readers that the *Directory* is simply an orderly listing of personnel in the Church and related organisations. Our task is to make this listing as easy to use as possible. The *Directory* is not a statement of Church policy, nor an expression of precedence, and should not be taken as such.

# CONTENTS

2014 Review of the Pastoral Activities
of the Irish Episcopal Conference,
its Agencies, Councils and Initiatives                 8

The Roman Curia                                        13

Apostolic Nunciature                                   15

The Irish Episcopate                                   16
  The Hierarchy                                        16
  The Irish Episcopal Conference                       17

Archdioceses and Dioceses of Ireland                   24
*Archdioceses*
  Armagh                                               25
  Dublin                                               39
  Cashel and Emly                                      83
  Tuam                                                 93
*Dioceses*
  Achonry                                              100
  Ardagh and Clonmacnois                               104
  Clogher                                              110
  Clonfert                                             116
  Cloyne                                               120
  Cork and Ross                                        131
  Derry                                                140
  Down and Connor                                      151
  Dromore                                              165

Elphin                                                 170
Ferns                                                  176
Galway, Kilmacduagh and Kilfenora                      183
Kerry                                                  190
Kildare and Leighlin                                   201
Killala                                                209
Killaloe                                               213
Kilmore                                                221
Limerick                                               231
Meath                                                  240
Ossory                                                 249
Raphoe                                                 256
Waterford and Lismore                                  262

Personal Prelatures                                    270

Religious Orders and Congregations                     271
  Male Religious                                       271
  Communities of Religious Brothers                    290
  Communities of Religious Sisters                     291
  Institutes                                           297
  New Forms of Consecrated Life                        297

Seminaries and Houses of Study                         298

Retreat and Pastoral Centres                           300

**Organisations, Societies and Religious Periodicals**    **303**

   Organisations and Societies    303

   Religious Periodicals    313

**Marriage Tribunals**    **316**

**Chaplains**    **317**

   The Defence Forces Chaplaincy Service    317

   Prisons and Places of Detention in Ireland    317

   Britain    318

   Europe    319

   Australia    319

   United States of America    319

**General Information**    **320**

   Obituary List    320

   Ordinations    323

   Irish Council of Churches    324

   Ireland's Cardinals    328

   Statistics    329

   Catholic Archbishops and Bishops of Britain    332

   Forms of Ecclesiastical Address    335

   The Roman Pontiffs    336

**Index of Advertisers**    **339**

**Alphabetical List of Clergy in Ireland**    **340**

**Parish Index**    **433**

**General Index**    **444**

## ALL IRELAND STD DIALLING

All STD numbers in this Directory are listed with both the number and the local area code.

Callers from the Irish Republic to Northern Ireland simply **need to dial 048 followed by the 8-digit local number.**

# 2014 REVIEW OF THE PASTORAL ACTIVITIES OF THE IRISH EPISCOPAL CONFERENCE, ITS AGENCIES, COUNCILS AND INITIATIVES
## (for more information see www.catholicbishops.ie)

## JANUARY

The theme of Pope Francis' message for the World Day of Prayer for Peace on 1 January 2014 was 'Fraternity, the Foundation and Pathway to Peace'. Speaking at Mass in St Patrick's Cathedral in Armagh, Cardinal Brady said 'Effective policies are needed to secure for people, who are equal in dignity and rights, access to health, education and what they need to realise their potential and develop fully as a person'.

In a statement issued on 8 January, Church leaders encouraged politicians to sustain the momentum generated by the Haass talks.

A number of Irish bishops were part of an international group who visited the Holy Land in support of the local Church and the cause of peace. The delegation included Bishop William Crean, Bishop of Cloyne, Bishop Denis Nulty, Bishop of Kildare and Leighlin, and Mr Éamonn Meehan, Executive Director of Trócaire.

On 20 January, Bishop Denis Nulty launched Catholic Schools Week 2014 in St Dominic's College in Cabra, Dublin, on the theme 'Catholic Schools: Places of Faith and Learning'.

On 21 January, Archbishop Charles J. Brown, Apostolic Nuncio to Ireland, and Archbishop Diarmuid Martin welcomed the announcement that the government would re-open the Irish Embassy to the Holy See.

On 23 January, Archbishop Eamon Martin welcomed Pope Francis' message for World Communications Day 2014 on the theme 'Communication at the Service of an Authentic Culture of Encounter'.

On 26 January, RTÉ broadcast Mass from St Peter's Church, Drogheda, for Catholic Schools Week 2014. In his homily Archbishop Eamon said: 'In our Catholic schools, we help young people to become stronger followers of Jesus, and to find a clear direction in their lives despite all the conflicting and confusing messages that surround them.'

## FEBRUARY

Speaking on 1 February as part of the Irish Bishops' Drugs Initiative National Conference in Dublin, Archbishop Diarmuid Martin said: 'The Church must become the place where broken lives encounter the restoring of love of God through the life and witness of the Christian community.'

On 6 February, the Broadcasting Authority of Ireland (BAI) upheld a complaint made by the Catholic Communications Office on behalf of the Diocese of Meath. The complaint was in connection with an RTÉ Radio One Liveline broadcast on funeral guidelines which was transmitted on 14 August 2013. The BAI stated 'that the item did not meet the requirements for fairness in current affairs content and was not

presented with due accuracy and should have been rectified by the broadcaster'.

On 7 February, Cardinal Brady issued a statement of congratulations to Rev Michael Barry on his election as the new Moderator of the Presbyterian Church in Ireland.

On 13 February, ACCORD Catholic Marriage Care Service published figures for the year 2013 which indicated an increase in demand for its two key services – marriage preparation, and separately, marriage counselling.

On 19 February, the Irish Catholic Bishops' Councils for Immigrants and Emigrants jointly hosted a conference in Jury's Inn, Custom House Quay, Dublin, entitled 'Journeying Together: Challenges Facing the Migrant Today'. The keynote speaker was Archbishop Diarmuid Martin.

On 19 February, senior representatives of the Grand Orange Lodge of Ireland and the Royal Black Institution met with Roman Catholic clergy in Belfast. Among the attendees at the preliminary meeting, held at the Orange Institution's temporary headquarters, were the Grand Master of the Grand Orange Lodge of Ireland, Edward Stevenson; Sovereign Grand Master of the Royal Black Institution, Millar Farr; and the Bishop of Down and Connor, Bishop Noel Treanor.

On 25 February, Pope Francis appointed Bishop Donal McKeown, Auxiliary Bishop of Down and Connor, as Bishop of Derry.

On 26 February, Bishop Liam MacDaid issued a statement of welcome following the publication of Pope Francis' Letter to Families ahead of the Synod on the Family on the theme 'The Pastoral Challenges of the Family in the Context of Evangelisation'.

On 28 February, Fr Tom Deenihan, General Secretary of the Catholic Primary Schools Management Association, addressed the AGM of the CPSMA on the theme: 'Catholic Schools, Serving the Community with Dignity and Care'. In his address to the AGM in the Radisson Hotel, Dublin, Fr Deenihan said: 'It is important for Catholic schools to be aware of the risks that arise should they lose sight of the reasons why they exist.'

## MARCH

On 4 March, Bishop Brendan Leahy, Bishop of Limerick, published his Lenten message in which he urged Lenten sacrifice in support of those gripped by alcohol, drugs, gambling and pornography.

On 11 March, Archbishop Diarmuid Martin issued a statement in which he paid tribute to the late Christine Buckley RIP. Archbishop Martin said: 'Christine Buckley was a woman of courage. Her courage in coming forward, telling her story and advocating for change played a major role in exposing problems in

child protection in the Church and State.' Also on 11 March, the Irish Council for Prisoners Overseas made a presentation to the Oireachtas Committee on repatriation in which it outlined concerns and highlighted the importance of repatriation.

On 12 March, the Spring 2014 General Meeting of the Irish Catholic Bishops' Conference concluded in Maynooth. Subjects discussed by the bishops included: Synod of Bishops on the Family; The first year of the pontificate of Pope Francis; National Board for Safeguarding Children in the Catholic Church in Ireland; Lent and preparation for Holy Week and Easter; The Solemnity of St Patrick; Trócaire; Migration and the plight of children in Syria and direct provision; Canonisations of Blessed Pope John XXIII and Blessed Pope John Paul II; the 1,400th anniversary of St Columban; and appointments and anniversaries

On 13 March, the Bishops' Conference issued a statement regarding the questionnaire from the Synod on the Family in which they thanked the thousands of Irish people who responded. Bishops said: 'The responses to the Synod questionnaire identify the immense challenges faced by families in Ireland, including problems arising from severe financial hardship, unemployment and emigration, domestic violence, neglect and other forms of abuse, infidelity and constant pressures on 'family time' together. Some respondents expressed particular concern about the limited amount of State support for marriage and the family. These challenges form the context in which the Church in this country continues to proclaim to the world the "Gospel (Good News) of the family".'

On 14 March, bishops issued a message for the Solemnity of St Patrick in which they said: 'We pray through the intercession of our national patron, St Patrick, for the faith and well-being of the people of Ireland. As St Patrick's Day is a Holy Day of Obligation for Catholics in Ireland, the best way to honour him is to attend Mass.'

On 18 March, Veritas Publications announced that Evangelii Gaudium (The Joy of the Gospel), which was authored solely by Pope Francis, had proved to be a bestseller in Veritas bookshops with 11,000 copies sold across the north and south of Ireland.

On 22 March, Archbishop Diarmuid Martin extended his warmest congratulations to Marie Collins on her appointment by Pope Francis to the Pontifical Council for the Protection of Minors.

On 28 March, the Diocese of Cloyne and the Diocese of Kildare and Leighlin responded to the '24 Hours for the Lord' initiative called for by Pope Francis, by hosting twenty-four hours of prayer and reconciliation.

## APRIL

On 6 April, Bishop Donal McKeown, in his homily for the Mass of his episcopal installation as Bishop of Derry, said: 'In this springtime of our society and our churches in Ireland, there is much work to be done if the new season is to bear mellow fruitfulness. The ground needs to be tilled, the weeds removed, the new seed planted.'

On 8 April, Bishop Francis Duffy, Bishop of Kilmore, launched the updated 'Safeguarding Children: Policies and Procedures' for the Diocese of Ardagh and Clonmacnois. Speaking at the launch in St Mel's College, Longford Bishop Duffy said: 'The present level of awareness and action in ensuring that our Church is a safe place for children is the result of the bravery of those who called attention to our failures in the past.'

On 10 April, Archbishop Diarmuid Martin had a meeting with Pope Francis in Rome. Pope Francis was visiting an International Conference on Combating Human Trafficking, which Archbishop Martin attended.

On 16 April, Church leaders met with the Northern Ireland Secretary of State The Rt Hon Theresa Villiers MP who outlined her priorities for political progress in Northern Ireland. Those present were encouraged by Ms Villiers's acknowledgement of the important role Churches play in society in Northern Ireland.

On 17 April, in his Chrism Mass homily in Christ the King Cathedral, Mullingar, Diocese of Meath, His Excellency Archbishop Charles J. Brown, Apostolic Nuncio to Ireland, said: 'Let us also tonight thank God for the gift of the priesthood, for the men who have been called by Christ to serve the Church as priests … At times, it is not easy for them. And so, for your witness of faithfulness, you, the priests … have our sincere gratitude.'

On the same day in his Chrism Mass Homily in the Cathedral of the Assumption, Tuam, Archbishop Michael Neary said: 'Today we minister in a fractured world and at times do so as men who are ourselves disillusioned and disheartened. We endeavour to hear the silent cry of our people, share their distress, bring comfort and dignity to the deprived. The message of the Bible is that civilisations survive not by strength but by how they respond to the weak; not by wealth but by how they care for the poor; not by power but by their concern for the powerless.'

On 17 April, a special Holy Week and Easter feature was made available on www.catholicbishops.ie.

On 19 April, Bishop Noel Treanor, Bishop of Down and Connor, published a pastoral letter for Easter 2014 in which he said: 'We are Easter people: each year we receive in our parish churches the Easter candle. We salute the Paschal candle, representing the light of the Risen Christ, as the great Easter hymn, the Exultet, is proclaimed.'

Archbishop Diarmuid Martin offered a series of reflections as part of The Way of the Cross through Phoenix Park,

Dublin, on Good Friday, 18 April, saying: 'Holy Week is a journey. Many in these days go on pilgrimage and pilgrim walks. The fundamental walk of the Christian this week, however, is the interior walk with Jesus as he moves step by step to fulfilling the will of his Father.'

The Catholic Communications Office launched a special web feature on 22 April ahead of the canonisations of Blessed John XXIII and Blessed John Paul II on 27 April.

On 22 April, two students of the Pontifical Irish College in Rome – Reverend Marius O'Reilly (37) from Ballincollig in Cork, and Reverend Conor McCarthy (26) from Finaghy in Belfast – were ordained deacons by Bishop John Buckley in the Basilica of Santa Croce in Gerusalemme, Rome.

On 28 April, the Catholic Bishops of Northern Ireland published an open letter to all MLAs regarding the NI Assembly debate on 'Marriage Equality'. In the letter, bishops said: 'We ask you to reaffirm the unique value to children and society of the mutual and complementary roles of a mother and father … We ask you not to undermine the principle of equality by applying it inappropriately to two fundamentally different types of relationship … We therefore appeal to you to reject the forthcoming motion on what the motion describes, inappropriately, as "Marriage Equality".'

On 28 April, pilgrims from Ireland in Rome for the Canonisation of Blessed Popes John XXIII and John Paul II gave thanks to God at a special Mass of Thanksgiving which was concelebrated by Cardinal Seán Brady, Archbishop of Armagh and Primate of All Ireland, and Bishop Kieran O'Reilly, Bishop of Killaloe, in the Basilica of Santa Maria in Domnica.

## MAY

Bishop Liam MacDaid asked motorists, cyclists and pedestrians to take special care of themselves and their loved ones when using our road network in a statement issued on 2 May, ahead of the May Bank Holiday weekend in the Republic and in Northern Ireland.

In his homily at the annual Mass for all who died in 1916 at the Church of the Sacred Heart, Arbour Hill, Dublin, on 7 May, Bishop Eamonn Walsh said: 'We are gathered in a faith context to commemorate all who died in the 1916 Rising. We also remember those who made sacrifices, suffered lifelong consequences before and beyond on the journey towards Irish independence.'

Sunday, 11 May, was Vocations Sunday 2014, on the theme 'Vocations: Witness to the Truth'. Bishop McKeown was the principal celebrant of a special Mass which was broadcast on RTÉ One Television. In his homily Bishop McKeown said: 'To choose a life as a priest or religious in contemporary Ireland is a radical option, although a hugely fulfilling one.' The Bishop of Kildare and Leighlin, Bishop Denis Nulty, published a pastoral letter on vocations to coincide with Vocations Sunday. In his pastoral Bishop Nulty said: 'I believe that potential vocations are all around us – in our football clubs, in our bands, in our schools, in our colleges, in our families. Parents and friends need to encourage,

not discourage; young people need permission and reassurance to talk about and consider priesthood – my prayer is that this conversation will now begin.'

On 12 May, the National Board for Safeguarding Children in the Catholic Church in Ireland published its safeguarding reviews on the Archdiocese of Dublin, the Diocese of Meath, the Diocese of Killaloe, and the Diocese of Cloyne.

On 14 May, Pope Francis appointed Fr Kevin Doran as Bishop of Elphin. In his words of greeting to the faithful at the Cathedral of the Immaculate Conception in Sligo, Bishop-elect Doran said: 'I think my colleagues will know what I mean when I say that we are ordained to serve God's people, but it is often God's people who teach us how to be good priests. Now, I have to learn to be a bishop and I hope you will be my teachers.'

On 16 May, Bishop John McAreavey, Chair of the Council for Justice and Peace of the Irish Catholic Bishops Conference, called for social policy, North and South, to reflect the generosity that has been so evident in our local communities throughout the economic crisis of recent years.

On 17 May, Archbishop Diarmuid Martin delivered the homily in St Mary's Pro-Cathedral, Dublin, on the occasion of the 40th anniversary of the Dublin and Monaghan bombings, saying: 'We gather to pray, to mourn, and to remember. Our hope is that we will go away renewed ourselves in our commitment to those values which violence can never attain and to be witnesses to how truth and love alone bring fullness and meaning to life.'

On 18 May, the bishops issued a statement on the European and local elections 2014 in which they said: 'The Christian vision of the dignity of the human person is one in which the European Union finds its values reflected and supported. As Christians we are called to articulate the fundamental values of human life which can then find expression in political activity. We need to look at the impact of European policy on the pressing issues of youth employment and unemployment, social protection, income and working conditions, all of which have a major impact on family life.'

On 20 May, Archbishop Eamon Martin addressed the AGM of Soul Waves Radio on the theme of 'The New Media and the Work of Evangelisation'. As part of his address he offered ten principles to guide our presence as Church in the digital highways.

On 25 May, a concelebrated Mass for Healing and Reconciliation was celebrated at St Joseph's Church, Wilton, Cork. Following the Mass, Bishop John Buckley launched Towards Peace – the new spiritual support service specifically dedicated to survivors of abuse.

## JUNE

Cardinal Seán Brady ordained fifteen seminarians as deacons at Mass celebrated in the College Chapel of the national seminary in St Patrick's College, Maynooth, on 1 June.

Archbishop Diarmuid Martin ordained forty-eight-year-old Fr Seamus McEntee to the priesthood on 3 June.

On 3 June, the Safeguarding Service of the Archdiocese of Tuam facilitated the launch in Knock of the Towards Peace spiritual support service.

On 4 June, Archbishop Neary welcomed the announcement to establish a cross-departmental examination of the burial arrangements for children in mother and baby homes, whilst on 5 June, Archbishop Diarmuid Martin urged those responsible for running any of the mother and baby homes in Ireland, or any other person having information about mass graves, to give that information to the authorities.

On 8 June, Archbishop Michael Neary ordained Fr Seán Flynn for service in the Archdiocese of Tuam and on the same day Bishop John McAreavey celebrated the ordination Mass for Deacons Brian Fitzpatrick and Colum Murphy.

On 10 June, the second day of its Summer General Meeting, the Irish Catholic Bishops' Conference published a statement welcoming the Government's announcement of a commission of investigation into mother, and baby homes: 'It is important that the commission, and all of us, approach these matters with compassion, determination and objectivity. We need to find out more about what this period in our social history was really like and to consider the legacy it has left us as a people. Above all, we need to enable those who were directly affected to receive recognition and appropriate support. We therefore welcome the Government's intention that the commission of investigation will have the necessary legal authority to examine all aspects of life in the homes.'

On 11 June, the Summer General Meeting of the Irish Catholic Bishops' Conference concluded in the Columba Centre of St Patrick's College, Maynooth. The following topics were included on the press release issued at the end of the meeting: Statement of the Irish Catholic Bishops' Conference welcoming the commission of investigation into mother and baby homes; Launch of the *Irish Catholic Catechism for Adults*; Safeguarding Children; Vocations; Towards Peace spiritual support service; Liturgy on weekdays when the celebration of Mass is not possible; Presentation on behalf of the Commission of Bishops' Conferences of the European Union; Pope Francis meets members of the Pontifical Council Cor Unum; Trócaire – the overseas aid agency of the Catholic Church in Ireland; Supporting Marriage and Family; 45th Irish Church Music Summer School; Campaign to support young Irish emigrants; Call for prayer to mark the opening of the Synod on the Family in October; New Moderator of the Presbyterian Church and new President of the Methodist Church; Prayers for those suffering due to civil unrest in Iraq and Ukraine; Tributes to Bishop Christopher Jones and Bishop-elect Kevin Doran and Fr Joseph Dargan SJ RIP.

On 14 June, Bishop McAreavey asked the faithful to remember in prayer the Christian communities, and all civilians suffering from unrest in the Iraq and also in Ukraine. Bishop McAreavey asked for prayers to be included at Masses for peace in these two countries.

'Please, Thanks and I'm Sorry' were themes in an address by Archbishop Diarmuid Martin at a conference, 'Marriage and Family at the Heart of the Parish', hosted by the Bishops' Council for Marriage and the Family in Holy Cross Diocesan Centre, Dublin, on 14 June.

On 17 June, senior representatives of the Grand Orange Lodge of Ireland met with a delegation of Catholic clergy in Belfast, including Bishop of Down and Connor, Most Rev Noel Treanor. Among the attendees at the meeting were the Grand Master of the Grand Orange Lodge of Ireland, Edward Stevenson. Issues discussed included the Haass proposals, parading, and shared concerns regarding child poverty and educational underachievement in the province.

On 26 June, Maura Hyland, Director of Veritas, presented Pope Francis with a copy of the newly published *Irish Catholic Catechism for Adults*. Pope Francis thanked Ms Hyland and expressed his hope that it would promote the work of adult faith formation throughout the Church in Ireland.

On 29 June, Rev Dominic McGrattan was ordained to the priesthood for the Diocese of Down and Connor at a ceremony held in St Patrick's Church, Portaferry, by Most Rev Noel Treanor, Bishop of Down and Connor. On the same day Rev Stephen Gorman was ordained to the priesthood for the Diocese of Raphoe by Bishop Philip Boyce.

## JULY

On 1 July, Bishop McKeown led 365 pilgrims to Lourdes for his first visit to the Marian Shrine as Bishop of Derry. The theme for the 2014 Derry pilgrimage was 'The Joy of Conversion'.

On 2 July, the Council for Education of the Irish Episcopal Conference welcomed the publication by the Department of Education and Skills entitled: *Forum on Patronage and Pluralism in the Primary Sector: Progress to Date and Future Directions*.

Approximately two hundred people attended the 45th Irish Church Music Association summer school which took place in St Patrick's College, Maynooth, from 3 to 6 July 2014 on the theme 'The Joy of the Gospel'.

Cardinal Seán Brady, Archbishop of Armagh and Primate of All Ireland, and Bishop Michael Smith, Bishop of Meath, led the 2014 Festival of St Oliver Plunkett in Drogheda, County Louth, on 6 July.

The annual 'Anglophone Conference', which brings together child safeguarding experts and representatives from throughout the English-speaking Catholic Church, took place in the Pontifical Irish College in Rome during July and was co-hosted by the Irish Bishops' Conference and the Episcopal Conference of Chile.

On 9 July, the Holy See announced the appointment by Pope Francis of Dublin priest Mgr Paul Tighe to a new high profile committee tasked with reforming the Vatican media around the world.

The Episcopal Ordination of Fr Kevin Doran as Bishop of Elphin took place on 13 July in the Cathedral of the Immaculate Conception, Sligo. Also on 13 July Fr Seán Hyland was ordained for the Diocese of Kildare and Leighlin and Fr Barry Larkin was ordained for the Diocese of Ferns

On 22 July, Bishop John McAreavey called for prayers for peace in the Middle East and invited everybody to join in solidarity with all who are suffering in the Middle East and to pray, both personally and at Masses, for peace and justice in these lands.

Archbishop Michael Neary led the annual Reek Sunday pilgrimage on 26 July. In his homily on the summit of Croagh Patrick, Archbishop Neary said: 'In times past it was difficult to imagine the world without God. Today it is becoming a challenge to imagine the world with God.'

## AUGUST

On 13 August, Cardinal Seán Brady, President of the Irish Episcopal Conference, asked parishes to pray for peace in Iraq, especially on 15 August, the Feast of the Assumption of the Blessed Virgin Mary.

On 14 August, Bishop John Buckley called for prayers for those suffering from violence in Iraq, particularly those suffering for their religion.

The annual national public novena took place at the Basilica of Our Lady of Knock, Queen of Ireland, in County Mayo, from 14 until 22 August, on the theme 'Witness to Hope'.

Bishop Philip Boyce preached the homily for the annual Knock Shrine pilgrimage on 16 August saying: 'A pilgrimage is a journey in hope. Our vision and thoughts are directed to the goal of our journey. Our hope looks forward first of all to the shrine or place of apparition where we expect to come nearer to God.'

On 17 August, Bishop Kevin Doran celebrated Mass in the Cathedral of the Immaculate Conception, Sligo, which was broadcast live by RTÉ Raidió na Gaeltachta to mark Fleadh Cheoil na hÉireann in Sligo

On 24 August, St Patrick's College, Maynooth, welcomed fourteen new seminarians who commenced their formation for the priesthood at the National Seminary.

On 25 August, Pope Francis sent a telegram of condolence to Archbishop Diarmuid Martin following the death of former Taoiseach Albert Reynolds.

## SEPTEMBER

On 7 September, Archbishop Diarmuid Martin led two thousand pilgrims on the annual Dublin diocesan pilgrimage to Lourdes.

The guest of honour and preacher at the jubilee Mass in the Cathedral of Christ the King, Mullingar, on 7 September was Cardinal Timothy Dolan, Archbishop of New York. The celebration marked the 75th anniversary of the consecration of the cathedral of the Diocese of Meath. During his homily, Cardinal Dolan attributed his vocation in large part to the religious formation he received from the Irish Mercy Sisters.

On 8 September, the Feast of the Nativity of the Blessed Virgin Mary, the Holy Father Pope Francis accepted the resignation of His Eminence Cardinal Seán Brady as Archbishop of Armagh and Primate of All Ireland. The Coadjutor Archbishop of Armagh, His Grace Archbishop Eamon Martin (52), became the 116th Archbishop of Armagh and Primate of All Ireland in succession to St Patrick.

On 12 September, the Irish Council for Prisoners Overseas launched a social media awareness campaign entitled: 'Good to Know Before You Go.' The campaign asks young Irish emigrants to take care of themselves and each other, while respecting laws and customs when travelling, living and working abroad.

On 12 September, upon learning of the death of the Rev Ian Paisley, Lord Bannside, Bishop Noel Treanor said: 'Dr Paisley has left an indelible mark on the history of the relationship between the Unionist and Nationalist traditions on this island. I will hold his family and all those affected by his passing in my prayers at this time of loss.'

The inaugural Faith and Life Convention was held on 20 September in Our Lady and St Patrick's College, Knock, Belfast.

Bishops asked the faithful to support the worldwide day of prayer on Sunday, 28 September for the Synod of Bishops on the Family, and invited parishioners to pray Pope Francis' prayer to the Holy family.

On 28 September, it was announced that the first Synod for fifty years in Ireland had been convoked by Bishop Brendan Leahy, Bishop of Limerick, to take place in 2016.

On 30 September, upon receiving news of the tragic death of Sr Frances Forde and Sr Marie Duddy today, the Irish bishops in the plenary session of the autumn gathering of the Irish Episcopal Conference prayed for both the sisters and for their religious congregation.

## OCTOBER

On 1 October, the Autumn 2014 General Meeting of the Irish Catholic Bishops' Conference concluded in Maynooth. Archbishop Eamon Martin was elected as the new President of the Bishops' Conference. Topics discussed included: Mass of Thanksgiving for the work of the Conference (ii) Honouring Cardinal Seán Brady; Special discussion on the pastoral priorities of the Church in Ireland; Synod on the Family; World Communications Day 2015; *The Cry of the Earth – A Call to Action for Climate Justice*; Towards Healing – confidential helpline and counselling referral service; Child Safeguarding; Theme for Day for Life 2014: 'Protect and Cherish Life'; Conditions in Direct Provision Centres; Cura, the crisis pregnancy support service of the Catholic Church; Meeting of International Chaplains; Rosary Sunday; Prayers for persecuted Christians; Vocations (ii) Year for Consecrated Life 2015; October is Mission month and RTÉ's decision to cease broadcasting on its longwave transmitter.

On 1 October, bishops updated and published their 2009 document *The Cry of the Earth*, with supporting resources

for dialogue at parish level and a new title: *The Cry of the Earth: A Call to Action for Climate Justice*.

On 3 October, Fr Damian Mc Neice was announced as the the first Roman Catholic to hold the position of Chair of the Dublin Council of Churches.

Rosary Sunday was celebrated in parishes across Ireland on Sunday 5 October, the day on which the Church also celebrates its 'Day for Life 2014'. In his 'Day for Life' homily, Archbishop Eamon Martin said: 'Our annual Day for Life challenges all of us to examine our own attitudes and behaviour, and to ask: "what am I, personally, doing to build a culture of life?"'

During the morning debate at the Synod of Bishops in Rome on 7 October, Archbishop Diarmuid Martin stressed the importance of consulting married couples. He said parents, especially those in the poorer areas, have experienced all the economic and social difficulties which have affected Ireland during a dramatic economic crisis, yet they continue to live the daily realities of family relationships and commitment to the education of their children.

Ahead of the publication of Budget 2015 on Tuesday, 14 October, a network of seven Catholic social justice groups published a joint statement 'Promoting Real Recovery by Addressing Inequality', which appealed to Government to prioritise reducing inequality.

On 11 October, Bishop Denis Nulty, the new President of ACCORD, addressed delegates at the annual assembly saying: 'The heart is at the very centre of the ACCORD organisation. In the rebranding exercise as ACCORD replaced the former days of CMAC, the letters 'COR' at the centre of ACCORD were and remain essential to the identity, mission and ethos of our organisation.'

On 12 October, Cardinal Brady preached the homily at a Mass of Thanksgiving commemorating the death of St Columbanus in the Church of Santa Maria Sopra Minerva, Rome, at the opening of the jubilee year to mark the 1400th anniversary of the death of St Columbanus.

On 13 October, the Catholic Schools Partnership launched a new report entitled *Catholic Education at Second Level in the Republic of Ireland* in Presentation College, Clarence Mangan Road, Warrenmount, Dublin 8.

On 15 October, the Catholic Communications Office of the Irish Catholic Bishops' Conference welcomed the decision by RTÉ to postpone the closure of its longwave transmitter.

On 18 October, Archbishop Diarmuid Martin welcomed the publication of the final text at the closing of the Synod of Bishops in Rome. Archbishop Diarmuid Martin said the text must be read in the context of Pope Francis' extraordinary final remarks to the Synod, after which the pope received a five-minute standing ovation from those present.

World Mission Sunday was celebrated on 19 October on the theme 'That You May Have Life'. In his message for 2014 Pope Francis said: 'World Mission Day is a privileged moment when the faithful of various continents engage in prayer and concrete gestures of solidarity in support

of the young Churches in mission lands. It is a celebration of grace and joy.'

On 22 October, Bishop McKeown preached the homily at Mass to mark forty years of ACCORD in the Derry Diocese in the Church of Our Lady of Lourdes, Steelstown.

On 22 October, Archbishop Eamon Martin was the guest speaker at the 2014 Radharc Awards Ceremony in Dublin. He said: 'The spirit of Radharc is alive and well in Pope Francis who said, "The Church needs to be concerned for, and present in, the world of communication, in order to dialogue with people today and to help them encounter Christ".'

On 24 October, Pope Francis sent a message to those attending a weekend's assembly in the Diocese of Kilmore. The message was relayed to Bishop Leo O'Reilly through the office of the Apostolic Nuncio. The assembly took place in St Patrick's College, Cavan, on Saturday 25 and Sunday 26 October.

Diocesan Vocations Directors from around Ireland gathered for their annual conference in St Patrick's College, Maynooth, on 26 and 27 October on the theme 'I Will Make You Fishers of Men'. The conference was opened by Bishop McKeown, Bishop of Derry and Chairman of the Bishops' Conference Council for Vocations. The keynote speaker for the conference was Fr Stephen Langridge, a priest of the Diocese of Southwark (UK) and Chairman of the England and Wales Vocations Directors Conference.

Following a request for meetings over the impact of ongoing cuts in the welfare system on the most vulnerable, Church leaders met with the Chair of the Social Development Committee of the Northern Ireland Assembly, Alex Maskey MLA, and other representatives of Sinn Féin on 28 October.

On 30 October, the Catholic Schools Partnership issued an address by Fr Michael Drumm at a recent meeting of the Council of the Catholic Schools Partnership in which he called for balance in any amendment of employment equality laws.

## NOVEMBER

On 6 November, Archbishop Diarmuid Martin delivered the keynote address at the ICTR Annual Conference 2014 in the Ashling Hotel, Dublin.

On 11 November, bishops from across the continent of Europe visited Verdun as pilgrims to mark the centenary of the outbreak of the First World War. Two simple services of prayer were held at the Ossuaire de Douaumont and individual bishops laid votive lamps in the chapel of the Ossuaire where the bones of 130,000 unknown soldiers repose.

In his homily for the World Remembrance Day for Road Traffic Victims on 16 November, Bishop Liam MacDaid said: 'Prayer and reflection can change our driving behaviour, calm our aggression, remind us of the spiritual, moral and physical importance of what we are about to do.'

On 16 November, Archbishop Eamon Martin preached the homily at Mass to mark the beginning of Prisons Week in Northern Ireland saying: 'Today marks the beginning of Prisons Week and I invite you to think in a special way about those who are in our own prisons here in Ireland. I know that prison is society's way of punishing people for serious wrongdoing, and we ought never to forget the many victims of crime who have suffered, or give the impression that we excuse these crimes. Still, caring for our prisoners – and about the conditions in which they are being held – is a Christ-like thing to do.'

On 19 November, Bishop Kevin Doran published his first pastoral letter called 'A Future Full of Hope'. The focus of the pastoral letter was the shared contribution of parents, teachers, schools and parishes in the education of children including their education in faith.

On 21 November, Bishop Kirby issued a statement welcoming President Obama's change in the deportation system saying: 'The president's immigration accountability executive actions serve to underline the complexity of the problems surrounding migration. Our undocumented emigrants have faced great personal turmoil and pain as they have been prevented from participating in key moments of family life back home such as baptisms, marriages, and when a loved one is seriously ill or has died. Their family life existence in the United States has similarly been curtailed by being placed under the daily stress of constant fear of arrest and deportation.'

On 21 November, Archbishop Eamon Martin preached the homily at a concelebrated Mass in San Colombano Al Lambro, northern Italy, to mark the 1400th anniversary of the death of St Columbanus.

On 22 November, Pope Francis accepted the resignation, on the ground of age, of Archbishop Dermot Clifford as Archbishop of Cashel and Emly, and appointed Bishop Kieran O'Reilly SMA as Archbishop of Cashel and Emly.

On 23 November, Bishop John Buckley, Bishop of Cork and Ross, ordained Reverend Marius O'Reilly to the priesthood. It was the second ordination for the Diocese of Cork and Ross in 2014 with Fr Ben Hodnett ordained in June.

On 25 November, the Catholic Primary School Management Association welcomed the announcement by Ms Jan O'Sullivan TD, Minister for Education and Skills, that the recently restored Minor Works grant was to continue for the current academic school year.

On 25 November, Archbishop Eamon Martin launched a specially commissioned Advent calendar on the homepage of the Irish Catholic bishops' website www.catholicbishops.ie to coincide with the beginning of Advent.

**DECEMBER**

Trócaire launched their range of Christmas gifts for 2014. Each Trócaire gift is sourced locally and sustainably from the country where it is needed, so the gifts not only support families in the world's poorest places, they also help the local economy to grow.

On 1 December, Archbishop Diarmuid Martin made an appeal to parishioners to donate food to assist those most in need throughout the Archdiocese this Christmas. The Archbishop launched the appeal in all parishes following a request

from Crosscare for basic items for families. In the past twelve months Crosscare has had to set up four new food banks along the east coast. The following day Archbishop Martin issued a statement following the death of a homeless man on the streets of Dublin and announced that he would be making a diocesan property available for emergency homeless accommodation in Dublin city centre.

On 3 December, at a media conference in Maynooth, Bishop Liam MacDaid, chairman of the Council for Marriage and Family, along with Bishop Kevin Doran, Bishop of Elphin, officially launched the pastoral statement *The Meaning of Marriage* on behalf of the Irish Catholic Bishops' Conference. The pastoral statement advises the faithful that 'to redefine the nature of marriage would be to undermine it as the fundamental building block of our society. The Church seeks with others to reaffirm … that marriage should be reserved for the unique and complementary relationship between a woman and a man from which the generation and upbringing of children is uniquely possible.'

On 3 December, the Winter 2014 General Meeting of the Irish Catholic Bishops' Conference concluded in the Columba Centre, St Patrick's College, Maynooth. The following issues were discussed by the bishops during their meeting: Caring for our neighbour; Advent and the Sacrament of Reconciliation; Publication of the pastoral statement *The Meaning of Marriage*; Report on the Synod on the Family: 'marriage preparation should be understood as a life-long catechesis – or itinerary of faith – about the Sacrament of Marriage'; (i) Universal Year of Consecrated Life (ii) Vocations; Pastoral response to suicide; National Board for Safeguarding Children in the Catholic Church; Living conditions for asylum seekers in direct provision centres; The Peace Process in Northern Ireland; The Humanitarian crisis in Syria; Celebrating the 1400th anniversary of the death of St Columbanus; Appointments and retirements.

On 4 December, the Catholic Bishops of Northern Ireland announced, with regret, that the long-established relationship between the Catholic Church and the adoption services provider The Family Care Society (NI) would come to an end. The announcement followed the outcome of a judicial review of adoption law in Northern Ireland initiated by the Northern Ireland Human Rights Commission in 2011.

On 10 December, the bishops issued a statement to mark International Human Rights Day in which they called for the protection of human rights, and for the upholding of the dignity of the human person concerning people living in poverty, asylum seekers living in Ireland, other displaced people around the world, and for those subjected to human trafficking.

The Towards Peace spiritual support service for survivors of abuse was launched in the Diocese of Ferns on 10 December and in the Diocese of Kildare and Leighlin on 11 December.

In their joint Christmas message for 2014, the Archbishops of Armagh, Archbishop Eamon Martin and Archbishop Richard Clarke, said: 'As we pray for peace in the world, let us remember those who are forced to spend Christmas far from home because of man's inhumanity to man. We are forever grateful that many Christians and other people of good will do not stand idly by while their brothers and sisters live in fear. Many Church and humanitarian organisations reach out to help refugees across the world. Their work is an inspiring reminder of the compassionate love of Jesus for those least fortunate in our world. Let us continue to support their essential and life-saving services. But at the same time we also need to speak up loudly and often for the voiceless thousands who are not allowed to remain in peace and safety in the place they call home.'

On 19 December in Longford town, Bishop Francis Duffy, Bishop of Ardagh and Clonmacnois, reopened a restored St Mel's Cathedral five years after a devastating fire destroyed the interior of the building, most of its furnishings, fittings and the roof on Christmas Eve/Christmas morning in 2009. In his Christmas message, Bishop Treanor said: 'We all realise that the human family is confronted with massive challenges in our world: in national economies, in political governance, in respect for the inviolable dignity of human life, in care of creation, in care for immigrants, refugees and asylum seekers, in care for the poor and hungry, in care for the homeless, in responding to threats to security and privacy, in education to a humanism for the dawning age of the techno-sciences in the information society in a civilisation of increasing acceleration. These and other issues of our time send out a siren-call to Christians to unveil afresh the pertinence for the human family of the Christian perspective on life, on relationship to God, to creation and to the neighbour. Such, in part, is the call of our times, a time when many voices, in and out of tune, call for renewal in personal, religious and public life.'

In his homily for the first Midnight Mass in a restored St Mel's Cathedral, Bishop Colm O'Reilly, the retired Bishop of Ardagh and Clonmacnoise said: 'All Longford people, and many more from far and near, will remember how five years ago after the celebration of the First Mass of Christmas the lights went out here. This historic Cathedral was enveloped in a black pall of darkness that dimmed the light of the last four of our Christmases. Tonight we hear the words spoken by the Prophet Isaiah about a new light in the darkness, as if they were about us. After five years in darkness our Cathedral is again brilliantly lit to welcome all who have come here to celebrate the Birth of Jesus.'

On 25 December, Pope Francis delivered the traditional 'Urbi et Orbi' message to the faithful in St Peter's Square.

*For more information please see www.catholicbishops.ie. See also 'Irish Catholic Bishops' Conference' on Facebook and follow on Twitter @CatholicBishops.*

# THE ROMAN CURIA

## SECRETARIAT OF STATE

*Secretary of State:*
Cardinal Pietro Parolin

**First Section: General Affairs**
*Sostituto:*
Archbishop Giovanni Angelo Becciu
Palazzo Apostolico Vaticano,
Città del Vaticano 00120
Tel 66988-3913

**Second Section: Relations with States**
*Secretary:*
Archbishop Paul Richard Gallagher
Palazzo Apostolico Vaticano,
Città del Vaticano 00120
Tel 66988-3913

## CONGREGATIONS

**Congregation for the Doctrine of the Faith**
*Prefect:*
Cardinal Gerhard Ludwig Müller
*Secretary:* Archbishop Luis Francisco
Ladaria Ferrer (SJ)
Piazza del S. Uffizio 11, 00193 Roma
Tel 66988-3357/3413

**Congregation for the Oriental Churches**
*Prefect:*
Cardinal Leonardo Sandri
*Secretary:*
Archbishop Cyril Vasil (SJ)
Palazzo del Bramante,
Via della Conciliazione, 34, 00193 Roma
Tel 66988-4282

**Congregation for Divine Worship and the Discipline of the Sacraments**
*Prefect:* Cardinal Robert Sarah
*Secretary:* Archbishop Arthur Roche
Palazzo delle Congregazioni,
Piazza Pio XII, 10, 00193 Roma
Tel 66988-4316/4318

**Congregation for the Causes of Saints**
*Prefect:* Cardinal Angelo Amato (SDB)
*Secretary:* Archbishop Marcello Bartolucci
Palazzo delle Congregazioni,
Piazza Pio XII, 10, 00193 Roma
Tel 66988-4247

**Congregation for Bishops**
*Prefect:* Cardinal Marc Ouellet (PSS)
*Secretary:*
Archbishop Ilson de Jesus Montanari
Palazzo delle Congregazioni,
Piazza Pio XII, 10, 00193 Roma
Tel 66988-4217

**Congregation for Clergy**
*Prefect:*
Archbishop Beniamino Stella
*Secretary:*
Archbishop Jorge Carlos Patrón Wong
Palazzo delle Congregazioni,
Piazza Pio XII, 3, 00193 Roma
Tel 66988-4151

**Congregation for the Evangelisation of Peoples**
*Prefect:* Cardinal Fernando Filoni
*Secretary:*
Archbishop Savio Hon Tai-Fai (SDB)
Palazzo di Propaganda Fide, Piazza di
Spagna, 48, 00187 Roma
Tel 66987-9299

**Congregation for the Institutes of Consecrated Life and for Societies of Apostolic Life**
*Prefect:* Cardinal João Bráz de Aviz
*Secretary:* Archbishop José Rodríguez
Carballo (OFM)
Palazzo delle Congregazioni,
Piazza Pio XII, 3, 00193 Roma
Tel 66988-4128

**Congregation for Catholic Education**
*Prefect:* Cardinal Zenon Grocholewski
*Secretary:*
Archbishop Angelo Vincenzo Zani
Palazzo delle Congregazioni, Piazza Pio
XII, 3, 00193 Roma
Tel 66988-4167

## TRIBUNALS

**Apostolic Penitentiary**
*Major Penitentiary:*
Cardinal Mauro Piacenza
*Regent:*
Mgr Krzysztof Jósef Nykiel
Palazzo della Cancelleria,
Piazza della Cancelleria, 1, 00186 Roma
Tel 66988-7526/7523

**Supreme Tribunal of the Apostolic Signatura**
*Prefect:* Archbishop Dominique François
Joseph Mamberti
*Secretary:*
Archbishop Frans Daneels (OPraem)
Palazzo della Cancelleria,
Piazza della Cancelleria, 1, 00186 Roma
Tel 66988-7520

**Tribunal of the Roman Rota**
*Dean:* Mgr Pio Vito Pinto
Palazzo della Cancelleria,
Piazza della Cancelleria, 1, 00186 Roma
Tel 66988-7502

## PONTIFICAL COUNCILS

**Pontifical Council for the Laity**
*President:* Cardinal Stanislaw Rylko
*Secretary:* Bishop Josef Clemens
00120 Vatican City State
Tel 66988-7322/7141

**Pontifical Council for Promoting Christian Unity**
*President:* Cardinal Kurt Koch
*Secretary:* Bishop Brian Farrell (LC)
Via dell'Erba, 1, 00193 Roma
Tel 66988-3072/4271

**Pontifical Council for the Family**
*President:* Archbishop Vincenzo Paglia
*Secretary:* Bishop Jean Laffitte
Piazza S. Calisto, 16, 00153 Roma
Tel 66988-7243

**Pontifical Council for Justice and Peace**
*President:* Cardinal Peter Kodwo Appiah
Turkson
*Secretary:* Bishop Mario Toso (SDB)
00120 Vatican City State
Tel 66987-9911

**Pontifical Council 'Cor Unum'**
*Secretary:* Mgr Giovanni Pietro Dal Toso
*Undersecretary:*
Mgr Segundo Tejado Muñoz
00120 Vatican City State
Tel 66988-9411

## Pontifical Council for the Pastoral Care of Migrants and Itinerant People
*President:*
Cardinal Antonio Maria Vegliò
*Secretary:*
Bishop Joseph Kalathiparambil
00120 Vatican City State
Tel 66988-7193/7242

## Pontifical Council for Pastoral Assistance to Health Care Workers
*President:*
Archbishop Zygmunt Zimowski
*Secretary:* Mgr Jean-Marie Mate Musivi Mpendawatu
Via della Conciliazione, 3, 00193 Roma
Tel 66988-3138/4720

## Pontifical Council for Legislative Texts
*President:*
Cardinal Francesco Coccopalmerio
*Secretary:*
Bishop Juan Ignacio Arrieta Ochoa de Chinchetru
Palazzo delle Congregazioni, Piazza Pio XII, 10, 00193 Roma
Tel 66988-4008

## Pontifical Council for Inter-Religious Dialogue
*President:* Cardinal Jean-Louis Tauran
*Secretary*
Fr Miguel Ángel Ayuso Guixot (MCCJ)
Via dell'Erba, 1, 00193 Roma
Tel 66988-4321

## Pontifical Council for Culture
*President:*
Cardinal Gianfranco Ravasi
*Secretary:*
Bishop Barthélemy Adoukonou
00120 Vatican City State
Tel 66989-3811

## Pontifical Council for Social Communications
*President:*
Archbishop Claudio Maria Celli
*Secretary:* Mgr Paul Tighe
Palazzo S. Carlo,
00120 Vatican City State
Tel 66989-1800

## Pontifical Council for the Promotion of the New Evangelisation
*President:* Archbishop Salvatore Fisichella
*Secretary*:
Archbishop José Octavio Ruiz Arenas
Via della Conciliazione, 5, 00193 Roma
Tel 66986-9500

## OFFICES

### Apostolic Chamber/Camera
*Chamberlain of the Holy Church:*
Cardinal Jean-Louis Tauran
*Vice-Chamberlain*
Archbishop Giampiero Gloder
Palazzo Apostolico,
00120 Vatican City State
Tel 66988-3554/2139

### Administration of the Patrimony of the Apostolic See
*President:* Cardinal Domenico Calcagno
*Secretary:* Mgr Luigi Mistò
Palazzo Apostolico,
00120 Vatican City State
Tel 66989-3403

### Prefecture for the Economic Affairs of the Holy See
*President:* Cardinal Giuseppe Versaldi
*Secretary:* Mgr Lucio Ángel Vallejo Balda
Palazzo delle Congregazioni,
Largo del Colonnato, 3, 00193 Roma
Tel 66988-4263

### Synod of Bishops
*Secretary General:*
Cardinal Lorenzo Baldisseri
*Undersecretary:* Bishop Fabio Fabene
Palazzo del Bramante, Via della Conciliaziane, 34, 00193 Roma
Tel 66988-4821/4324

### Prefecture of the Papal Household
*Prefect:* Archbishop Georg Gänswein
*Regent:* Mgr Leonardo Sapienza (RCI)
00120 Vatican City State
Tel 66988-3114

### Office of Papal Charities
*Almoner of His Holiness:*
Archbishop Konrad Krajewski
00120 Vatican City State
Tel 66988-3135

### International Theological Commission
*President:*
Cardinal Gerhard Ludwig Müller
Palazzo delle Congr. per la Dottrina della Fede, Piazza del S. Uffizio, 11, 00193 Roma
Tel 66988-4727

### Pontifical Ecclesiastical Academy
*President:* Archbishop Giampiero Gloder
Piazza della Minerva, 74, 00186 Roma
Tel 66988201

### Vatican Apostolic Library
*Librarian*
Archbishop Jean-Louis Bruguès (OP)
Cortile del Belvedere,
00120 Vatican City State
Tel 66987-9411

### Vatican Secret Archives
*Archivist:* Bishop Jean-Louis Bruguès (OP)
*Prefect:* Bishop Sergio Pagano (B)
00120 Vatican City State
Tel 66988-3314

## COMMISSIONS AND COMMITTEES

### Pontifical Commission for Latin America
*President:*
Cardinal Marc Ouellet (PSS)
*Secretary Vice-President:*
Prof. Guzmán Carriquiry Lecour
00120 Vatican City State
Tel 66988-3131/3500

### Pontifical Commission for Sacred Archaeology
*President:* Cardinal Gianfranco Ravasi
*Secretary:* Mgr Giovanni Carrù
Via Napoleone III, 1, 00185 Roma
Tel 6446-5610

### Pontifical Biblical Commission
*President:*
Cardinal Gerhard Ludwig Müller
*Secretary:* Fr Pietro Bovati (SJ)
Palazzo delle Congr. per la Dottrina della Fede, Piazza del S. Uffizio, 11, 00193 Roma
Tel 66988-4682

### Pontifical Commission 'Ecclesia Dei'
*President:*
Cardinal Gerhard Ludwig Müller
*Secretary:* Archbishop Guido Pozzo
Palazzo delle Congr. per la Dottrina della Fede, Piazza del S. Uffizio, 11,
00193 Roma
Tel 66988-5213/5494

### Pontifical Commission for Reference on the Institute for Works of Religion
*President:* Cardinal Raffaele Farina (SDB)

### Pontifical Committee for Reference on the Organisation of the Economic-Administrative Structure of the Holy See
*President:* Dr Joseph F.X. Zahra

## INSTITUTIONS CONNECTED WITH HOLY SEE

### L'Osservatore Romano
*Director:* Prof. Giovanni Maria Vian
00120 Vatican City State
Tel 66988-3461

# APOSTOLIC NUNCIATURE

*Address:* The Apostolic Nunciature, 183 Navan Road, Dublin 7
Tel 01-8380577 Fax 01-8380276

*Papal Nuncio:* His Excellency Archbishop Charles John Brown, Titular Archbishop of Aquileia
Born 13 October 1959, New York, USA
Ordained priest 13 May 1989
Appointed Titular Archbishop of Aquileia 26 November 2011
Episcopal Consecration 6 January 2012
Appointed Apostolic Nuncio to Ireland 26 November 2011

*Counsellor:* Very Rev Mgr Amaury Medina Blanco

# THE IRISH EPISCOPATE

## THE HIERARCHY

### Archbishops

Most Rev Eamon Martin DD
Archbishop of Armagh
Primate of All Ireland
Ara Coeli, Armagh BT61 7QY
Tel 028-37522045 Fax 028-37526182
Email admin@aracoeli.com

Most Rev Diarmuid Martin DD
Archbishop of Dublin and Primate of
Ireland, Archbishop's House,
Drumcondra, Dublin 9
Tel 01-8373732 Fax 01-8369796

Most Rev Kieran O'Reilly DD
Archbishop Designate of Cashel and
Emly
Archbishop's House, Thurles, Co Tipperary
Tel 0504-21512 Fax 0504-22680
Email office@cashel-emly.ie

Most Rev Michael Neary DD
Archbishop of Tuam
Archbishop's House, Tuam, Co Galway
Tel 093-24166 Fax 093-28070
Email archdiocesetuam@eircom.net

### Retired Archbishops

His Eminence Seán Cardinal Brady DCL, DD
Retired Archbishop of Armagh
Ara Coeli, Armagh BT61 7QY

His Eminence Desmond Cardinal Connell DD
Retired Archbishop of Dublin
29 Iona Road, Glasnevin, Dublin 9

Most Rev Dermot Clifford DD
Retired Archbishop of Cashel and Emly
Archbishop's House, Thurles,
Co Tipperary

### Bishops

Most Rev Philip Boyce (OCD) DD
Bishop of Raphoe
Ard Adhamhnáin, Letterkenny, Co Donegal
Tel 074-9121208 Fax 074-9124872
Email raphoediocese@eircom.net

Most Rev Denis Brennan DD
Bishop of Ferns
Bishop's House, Summerhill, Wexford
Tel 053-9122177 Fax 053-9123436
Email adm@ferns.ie

Most Rev Raymond A. Browne DD
Bishop of Kerry
Bishop's House, Killarney, Co Kerry
Tel 064-6631168 Fax 064-6631364
Email admin@dioceseofkerry.ie

Most Rev John Buckley DD
Bishop of Cork and Ross
Diocesan Office, Bishop's House,
Redemption Road, Cork
Tel 021-4301717 Fax 021-4301557
Email secretary@corkandross.org

Most Rev William Crean DD
Bishop of Cloyne
Cloyne Diocesan Centre, Cobh, Co Cork
Tel 021-4811430 Fax 021-4811026
Email info@cloynediocese.ie

Most Rev Kevin Doran DD
Bishop of Elphin
St Mary's, Sligo
Tel 071-9162670/9162769
Fax 071-9162414
Email elphindo@eircom.net

Most Rev Martin Drennan DD
Bishop of Galway
Mount St Mary's, Taylor's Hill, Galway
Tel 091-563566 Fax 091-528536
Email galwaydiocese@eircom.net

Most Rev Francis Duffy DD
Bishop of Ardagh and Clonmacnois
St Michael's, Longford, Co Longford
Tel 043-3346432 Fax 043-3346833
Email ardaghdi@iol.ie

Most Rev Anthony Farquhar DD
Titular Bishop of Ermiana and Auxiliary
Bishop in Down and Connor
24 Fruithill Park, Belfast BT11 8GE
Tel 028-90624252
Email ajf@downandconnor.org

Most Rev Raymond Field DD
Titular Bishop of Ard Mor and
Auxiliary Bishop in Dublin
3 Castleknock Road,
Blanchardstown, Dublin 15
Tel 01-8209191 Fax 01-8209191
Email rf6275@eircom.net

Most Rev John Fleming DD, DCL
Bishop of Killala
Bishop's House, Ballina, Co Mayo
Tel 096-21518 Fax 096-70344
Email bishop@killaladiocese.org

Most Rev Séamus Freeman (SAC) DD
Bishop of Ossory
Sion House, Kilkenny
Tel 056-7762448 Fax 056-7763753
Email bishop@ossory.ie

Most Rev Brendan Kelly DD
Bishop of Achonry
Bishop's House, Ballaghaderreen,
Edmondstown, Co Roscommon
Tel 094-9860021 Fax 094-9860921
Email bishop@achonrydiocese.org

Most Rev John Kirby DD
Bishop of Clonfert
St Brendan's, Coorheen, Loughrea,
Co Galway
Tel 091-841560 Fax 091-841818
Email clonfert@iol.ie

Most Rev Brendan Leahy DD
Bishop of Limerick
Diocesan Office, Social Service Centre,
Henry Street, Limerick
Tel 061-315856 Fax 061-310186
Email office@ldo.ie

Most Rev John McAreavey DD, DCL
Bishop of Dromore
Bishop's House, 44 Armagh Road,
Newry, Co Down BT35 6PN
Tel 028-30262444 Fax 028-30260496
Email bishopofdromore@btinternet.com

Most Rev Liam MacDaid DD
Bishop of Clogher
Bishop's House, Monaghan
Tel 047-81019 Fax 047-84773
Email diocesanoffice@clogherdiocese.ie

Most Rev Donal McKeown DD
Bishop of Derry
Bishop's House
St Eugene's Cathedral
Francis Street, Derry BT48 9AP
Tel 028-71262302 Fax 028-71371960
Email office@derrydiocese.org

Most Rev Denis Nulty DD
Bishop of Kildare and Leighlin
Bishop's House, Carlow
Tel 059-9176725 Fax 059-9176850
Email bishop@kandle.ie

Most Rev Leo O'Reilly DD
Bishop of Kilmore
Bishop's House, Cullies, Co Cavan
Tel 049-4331496 Fax 049-4361796
Email bishop@kilmorediocese.ie

Most Rev Michael Smith DD, DCL
Bishop of Meath
Bishop's House, Dublin Road,
Mullingar, Co Westmeath
Tel 044-9348841/9342038
Fax 044-9343020
Email bishop@dioceseofmeath.ie

Most Rev Noël Treanor DD
Bishop of Down and Connor
Lisbreen, 73 Somerton Road,
Belfast, Co Antrim BT15 4DE
Tel 028-90776185 Fax 028-90779377
Email dccuria@downandconnor.org

Most Rev Eamonn Walsh DD, VG
Titular Bishop of Elmham and
Auxiliary Bishop in Dublin
Naomh Brid, Blessington Road,
Tallaght, Dublin 24
Tel/Fax 01-4598032
Email elmham@eircom.net

**Retired Bishops**
Most Rev Eamonn Casey DD
Retired Bishop of Galway
Diocesan Office,
Galway Cathedral, Galway

Most Rev Brendan Comiskey DD
Retired Bishop of Ferns
PO Box 40, Summerhill, Wexford

Most Rev Gerard Clifford DD
Retired Titular Bishop of Geron and
Auxiliary Bishop in Armagh
Annaskeagh, Ravensdale,
Dundalk, Co Louth

Most Rev Edward Daly DD
Retired Bishop of Derry
Gurteen, 9 Steelstown Road,
Derry BT48 8EU

Most Rev Joseph Duffy DD
Retired Bishop of Clogher
Bishop's House, Monaghan,
Co Monaghan

Most Rev Thomas Flynn DD
Retired Bishop of Achonry
St Michael's, Cathedral Grounds,
Ballaghaderreen, Co Roscommon

Most Rev Laurence Forristal DD
Retired Bishop of Ossory
Molassy, Freshford Road, Kilkenny

Most Rev Seamus Hegarty DD
Retired Bishop of Derry
Bishop's House, St Eugene's Cathedral,
Derry BT48 9AP

Most Rev Christopher Jones DD
Retired Bishop of Elphin
St Mary's, Sligo

Most Rev Francis Lagan DD
Retired Titular Bishop of Sidnascestre
and Retired Auxiliary Bishop in Derry
9 Glen Road, Strabane,
Co Tyrone BT82 8BX

Most Rev William Lee, DD, DCL
Retired Bishop of Waterford and Lismore
Bishop's House, John's Hill, Waterford

Most Rev John Magee DD
Retired Bishop of Cloyne
'Cormeen', Convent Hill,
Mitchelstown, Co Cork

Most Rev James Moriarty DD
Retired Bishop of Kildare and Leighlin
Bishop's House, Carlow
Most Rev William Murphy DD
Retired Bishop of Kerry
Bishop's House, Killarney, Co Kerry

Most Rev Donal Murray DD
Retired Bishop of Limerick
Limerick Diocesan Office,
Social Service Centre, Henry Street,
Limerick

Most Rev Fiachra Ó Ceallaigh DD
Retired Titular Bishop of Tre Taverne &
Retired Auxiliary Bishop in Dublin
19 St Anthony's Road,
Rialto, Dublin 8

Most Rev Colm O'Reilly DD
Retired Bishop of Ardagh and Clonmacnois
St Michael's, Longford,
Co Longford

Most Rev Dermot O'Mahony DD
Titular Bishop of Tiava and Retired
Auxiliary Bishop in Dublin
19 Longlands, Swords, Co Dublin

Most Rev Patrick J. Walsh DD
Retired Bishop of Down and Connor
6 Waterloo Park North,
Belfast BT15 5HW

Most Rev William Walsh DD
Retired Bishop of Killaloe
Westbourne, Ennis, Co Clare

## MITRED ABBOTS

Rt Rev Dom Mark Patrick Hederman (OSB)
Glenstal Abbey, Murroe, Co Limerick
Tel 061-386103

Rt Rev Dom Augustine McGregor (OCSO)
Mount Melleray Abbey,
Cappoquin, Co Waterford
Tel 058-54404

Rt Rev Dom Michael Ryan (OCSO)
Bolton Abbey, Moone, Athy,
Co Kildare
Tel 059-8624102

Rt Rev Dom Celsus Kelly (OCSO)
Our Lady of Bethlehem Abbey,
11 Ballymena Road, Portglenone,
Ballymena, Co Antrim BT44 8BL
Tel 028-25821211 Fax 028-25822310

Rt Rev Dom Richard Purcell (OCSO)
Mount St Joseph Abbey, Roscrea,
Co Tipperary
Tel 0505-25600

Rev Joseph Ryan (OCSO), Prior
Mellifont Abbey, Collon,
Co Louth
Tel 041-9826103

Rt Rev Dom Mark Ephrem Nolan (OSB)
Holy Cross Monastery,
119 Kilbroney Road,
Rostrevor, Co Down BT34 3BN
Tel 028-41739979

## THE IRISH EPISCOPAL CONFERENCE

*President*
His Grace Most Rev Eamon Martin
*Vice President*
His Grace Most Rev Diarmuid Martin
*Episcopal Secretary*
Most Rev Kieran O'Reilly
*Finance Secretary:* Most Rev John Fleming
*Executive Secretary*
Mgr Gearóid Dullea
Columba Centre, Maynooth, Co Kildare
Tel 01-5053000 Fax 01-6292360
Email ex.sec@iecon.ie
*Communications Director*
Mr Martin Long
Columba Centre, Maynooth, Co Kildare
Tel 01-5053000 Fax 01-6016401
Email mlong@catholicbishops.ie
*Executive Administrator of the
Commissions & Agencies of the Episcopal
Conference*
Mr Harry Casey
Columba Centre, Maynooth, Co Kildare
Tel 01-5053000 Fax 01-6016401
Email harry.casey@iecon.ie

**Standing Committee**
His Grace Most Rev Eamon Martin; His
Grace Most Rev Diarmuid Martin; His
Grace Most Rev Michael Neary; Most Rev
John Fleming; Most Rev Kieran O'Reilly;
Most Rev Seamus Freeman; Most Rev
Brendan Kelly; Most Rev Brendan Leahy;
Most Rev Leo O'Reilly; Most Rev Noël
Treanor; Most Rev Eamonn Walsh

## THE FIVE EPISCOPAL COMMISSIONS OF THE IRISH EPISCOPAL CONFERENCE

*An Episcopal Commission advises or
makes proposals/recommendations to the
Standing Committee and Plenary
Assembly of the Irish Episcopal
Conference. Councils and Agencies assist
the Episcopal Commissions, and the
Episcopal Conference itself, in attaining
their objectives. An Advisory Group/Body/
Committee to a Council of the Irish
Episcopal Conference advises the
relevant Council.*

**Episcopal Commission for Catholic
Education and Formation**
*Chaired by Most Rev Leo O'Reilly DD*

**Episcopal Commission for Pastoral Care**
*Chaired by Most Rev Eamonn Walsh DD*

**Episcopal Commission for Planning,
Communications and Resources**
*Chaired by His Grace Most Rev Eamon
Martin DD*

**Episcopal Commission for Social Issues
and International Affairs**
*Chaired by Most Rev Noël Treanor DD*

**Episcopal Commission for Worship,
Pastoral Renewal and Faith Development**
*Chaired by Most Rev Seamus Freeman DD*

*The Councils and Agencies of the Irish Episcopal Conference are clustered in five Departments corresponding to the five Episcopal Commissions. Details of several bodies which are linked to the Episcopal Conference are placed in square brackets and provided for your information.*

## DEPARTMENT OF CATHOLIC EDUCATION AND FORMATION

*Executive Secretary to the Episcopal Commission/Department*
Rt Rev Mgr James Cassin
Tel 01-5053014 Email jim.cassin@iecon.ie

## COUNCIL FOR CATECHETICS OF THE IRISH EPISCOPAL CONFERENCE

*Members of the Council*
Most Rev Brendan Leahy DD *(Chair)*
Most Rev William Crean DD, Rt Rev Mgr Dermot A. Lane, Rev Timothy Bartlett, Ms Marian Curran, Ms Fiona Dineen, Ms Maura Hyland, Rev Joseph McCann, Sr Anne Codd, Mr Gerry O'Connell, Ms Cora O'Farrell, Sr Marie McNamara
*Secretary of the Council of Catechetics:*
Ms Kate Liffey
Columba Centre, Maynooth, Co Kildare
Tel 01-5053000 Fax 01-6016401
Email catechetics@iecon.ie

## COUNCIL FOR DOCTRINE OF THE IRISH EPISCOPAL CONFERENCE

*Members of the Council*
Most Rev Michael Neary DD *(Chair)*;
Most Rev Philip Boyce DD;
Most Rev Martin Drennan DD
The Council for Doctrine works with the Theological Committee and the Bioethics Consultative Group on matters relating to faith and morals.

Columba Centre,
Maynooth, Co Kildare
Tel 01-5053000

**Bioethics Consultative Group**
*Secretary:* Rev Michael Shortall
St Patrick's College,
Maynooth, Co Kildare
Tel 01-7086165

## COUNCIL FOR ECUMENISM (AND DIALOGUE) OF THE IRISH EPISCOPAL CONFERENCE

*Members of the Council*
Most Rev Anthony Farquhar DD *(Chair)*;
Most Rev Brendan Leahy DD
Most Rev John McAreavey DD

**Advisory Committee on Ecumenism**
*Secretary:* Very Rev Kieran McDermott PP 'Emmaus', Main Street, Dundrum, Dublin 14
Tel 01-2984348

Advises the hierarchy on ecumenical affairs in Ireland and maintains contact with the Pontifical Council for Promoting Christian Unity, Rome. The committee has a membership of approximately 35, including the episcopal members, a priest representative from each diocese, and people chosen for their competence and experience in the ecumenical field.

## COUNCIL FOR EDUCATION OF THE IRISH EPISCOPAL CONFERENCE [WITH NORTHERN IRELAND COUNCIL FOR CATHOLIC EDUCATION (NICCE)]

The Council for Education articulates policy and vision for Catholic Education in Ireland, north and south, on behalf of the Episcopal Conference. It has responsibility for the forward planning necessary to ensure the best provision for Catholic Education in the country. It liaises with other Catholic Education Offices, the Department of Education and Skills and the Department of Education, Northern Ireland. The Council advises the Conference on all government legislation as applied to education. It responds to and acts as spokesperson for the Episcopal Conference on issues related to the work of education. It seeks also to develop long-term strategies in education for the Episcopal Conference

*Members of the Council for Education*
Most Rev Brendan Kelly *(Chairman)*
Most Rev Leo O'Reilly DD
Most Rev Donal McKeown DD
Most Rev Liam MacDaid DD
Rt Rev Mgr Dermot Lane,
Rev Michael Drumm,
Rev Tom Deenihan, Mr Ferdia Kelly
*Executive Secretary*
Rt Rev Mgr James Cassin
Council for Education of the IEC,
Columba Centre, Maynooth, Co Kildare
Tel 01-5053014
Email education@iecon.ie
*Administrative Assistant:* Ms Ann Maertens
Tel 01-5053027
Email ann.maertens@iecon.ie

*Northern Ireland Commission for Catholic Education (NICCE)*
Until 2005, there was no central body seeking to offer leadership across the Catholic education sector in NI. The 500+ 'Maintained' schools (nursery, primary and non-selective post-primary) were managed by CCMS (a statutory body) while the 32 Voluntary Grammar schools had a considerable degree of independence. The Northern Ireland Commission for Catholic Education (NICCE) was set up in 2005 by the

Trustees in order to provide co-ordination of the Catholic sector in a time of rapid change.

*Members of the Northern Ireland Commission for Catholic Education (NICCE) Diocesan Trustees*
Most Rev Donal McKeown DD *(Chair)*
Most Rev John McAreavey DD
Most Rev Noël Treanor DD

*Nominees from Religious and Lay Trusts*
Br Patrick Collier (FSC)
Sr Eithne Woulfe (SSL)
Prof Muredach Dynan

*In attendance*
Most Rev Patrick Walsh DD
His Grace Most Rev Eamon Martin DD
Canon Peter O'Reilly
Mr Gerry Lundy
Rev Timothy Bartlett
Rt Rev Mgr Jim Cassin

Northern Ireland Commission for Catholic Education (NICCE)
193-195 Donegall Street, Belfast BT1 2FL
Tel 0044-77-64349736
Email info@catholiceducation.org
Website info@catholiceducation-ni.com

**Catholic Education Service (CES)**
The Catholic Education Service (CES) is a national education service inspired by the gospel of Jesus Christ in support of the mission of Catholic education. CES was set up by the Irish Episcopal Conference (IEC) in association with the Conference of the Religious of Ireland (CORI).

The Catholic Education Service is a charity created by Deed of Trust. The Trustees of the CES are four Catholic Bishops who are Ordinaries of Catholic dioceses in Ireland and each representing one of the four ecclesiastical provinces of Ireland (Most Rev Leo O'Reilly DD, Most Rev John Buckley DD, Most Rev Seamus Freeman DD, Most Rev Brendan Kelly DD) and two Religious appointed by CORI (Sr Elizabeth Maxwell, IPVM and Rev David Corrigan, SM). The trustees of the CES are ex officio members of Catholic Education Service Committee (CESC).

**The Catholic Education Services Committee (CESC)** is a service incorporating a number of bodies as follows:
**The Catholic Schools' Partnership (CSP)** serves first and second level Catholic schools and colleges in the Republic of Ireland.
**The Trustee Support Service (TSS)** will serve Catholic schools and colleges in Northern Ireland.
CESC serves the formal education system at all levels as well as the non-formal and informal sectors. It aims to support a vibrant Catholic education sector in response to changing social, economic and political conditions in Ireland.

*Members of the Catholic Education Services Committee (CESC)*
Most Rev Seamus Freeman DD; Most Rev Francis Duffy DD; Most Rev Brendan Kelly DD; Most Rev Donal McKeown DD; Most Rev Diarmuid Martin DD; Most Rev Leo O'Reilly DD; Sr Brid Vallely; Fr Marc Whelan; Br Francis Manning (FSC); Sr Elizabeth Maxwell (IPVM); Br Cormac Commins (FSP); Sr Caitlin Conneely (RSM)
*Executive Secretaries:* Sr Eithne Woulfe; Rt Rev Mgr James Cassin
Catholic Education Service
Columba Centre, Maynooth, Co Kildare
Tel 01-5053014
Email education@iecon.ie

### Catholic Schools Partnership (CSP)
Catholic Schools Partnership was established in 2009 by the Irish Bishops Conference in co-operation with CORI. It aims to provide support for all the partners in Catholic education at first and second level in the Republic of Ireland. This includes patrons/trustees, management bodies including boards of management and teachers in Catholic schools.

The Partnership is overseen by a Council with members drawn from various stakeholders. The members of the Council are: Rev Michael Drumm *(Chair)*, Mr Gerry Bennett, Rt Rev Mgr James Cassin, Rev Peter Conaty, Rev Paul Connell, Rev Tom Deenihan, Sr June Farrelly, Sr Thomasina Finn, Ms Edwina Gottstein, Mr Justin Harkin, Ms Anne Kelleher, Bishop Brendan Kelly, Mr Ferdia Kelly, Ms Patricia Kieran, Ms Anne McDonagh, Mr Andrew McGrady, Ms Elaine Mahon, Mr Paul Meany, Bishop Leo O'Reilly, Ms Maria Spring and Sr Eithne Woulfe
New House, St Patrick's College, Maynooth, Co Kildare
Tel 01-5053164
Email office@catholicschools.ie
Website www.catholicschools.ie

### Association of Trustees of Catholic Schools (ATCS)
The Association of Trustees of Catholic Schools (ATCS) was established in September 2009. ATCS is a representative body for the 'Catholic Trustee Voice' in Irish education at primary and post-primary level. Its membership includes members of the Irish Episcopal Conference, representatives of various religious congregations, representatives of the recently established lay trusts, as well as the trustees of a number of other Catholic schools.

*Members of the ATCS Board*
Mr Gerry Bennett, Mr Paul Scanlon, Sr Ena Quinlan, Fr Tom Deenihan, Mr Declan Lawlor, Ms Eilis Humphreys, Ms Marie Griffin, Fr Brian Flannery, Sr Marie Carroll, Bishop Brendan Kelly, Ms Fiona Shanley, Sr Marie Celine, Ms Anna Gettings, Sr Concepta O'Brien, Mgr John O'Boyle

*Contact details:*
*Administrator:* Imelda Ashe
Association of Trustees of Catholic Schools (ATCS)
New House, Maynooth, Co Kildare
Tel 01-5053164
Email info@atcs.ie
*Chairperson:* Sr Marie Celine Clegg

### [Council of Management of Catholic Schools
*President:* Rev Paul Connell
*General Secretary:* Mr Ferdia Kelly
Secretariat of Secondary Schools,
Emmet House, Dundrum Road,
Milltown, Dublin 14
Tel 01-2838255 Fax 01-2695461
Email info@jmb.ie
Website www.jmb.ie

The Council of Management of Catholic Secondary Schools is the governing body for the Association of Management of Catholic Secondary Schools which promotes, advises and supports Catholic Voluntary Secondary Schools in Ireland. Founded in the 1960s, it adopted its present structure in 1972. Its membership includes a principal and chairperson of a Board of Management from each of its ten constituent regions. It also includes a representative of the Irish Episcopal Conference and a representative of CORI (Conference of Religious in Ireland). The Council cooperates and maintains links with other national and international groups interested in Catholic education. Its Secretariat provides a wide range of educational services and advice to its members.

### Catholic Primary School Management Association (CPSMA)
*Chair:* Mrs Maria Spring
Tel 087-2597004
*General Secretary:* Rev Tom Deenihan
New House, St Patrick's College, Maynooth, Co Kildare
Tel 01-6292462/1850-407200
Fax 01-6292654
Email info@cpsma.ie
Website www.cpsma.ie

The association represents the boards of management of all Catholic primary schools. Its standing committee has close links with the Episcopal Commission for Education.]

## DEPARTMENT OF PASTORAL CARE

*Executive Secretary to the Episcopal Commission/Department*
Rev Peter Murphy
Tel 01-5053107 Email peter.murphy@iecon.ie

## COUNCIL FOR MARRIAGE AND THE FAMILY OF THE IRISH EPISCOPAL CONFERENCE

*Members of the Council for Marriage and Family of the Irish Episcopal Conference*
Most Rev Liam MacDaid DD *(Chair)*
Most Rev Christopher Jones DD
Most Rev Colm O'Reilly DD
Most Rev Donal Murray DD
Rev Peter Murphy *(Secretary)*, Mr Gerry Mangan, Ms Breda McDonald, Very Rev Michael McGinnity, Sr Anne Codd, Ms Deirdre O'Rawe, Ms Trish Conway, Very Rev Kieran McDermott, Mr Pat Cunneen, Mrs Carmel Cunneen, Rev Mr John Taaffe, Mrs Máire Printer, Ms Elaine Mahon, Rev Mr Gabriel Corcoran, Mrs Finola Bruton, Mrs Gemma Rowley, Mr Francis Cousins, Mrs Madeleine McCully, Mr Tom McCully, Mr Denis Bradley, Mr John O'Malley and Mr Phil Butcher
Columba Centre, Maynooth, Co Kildare
Tel 01-5053000 Fax 01-6016401
Email columbacentre@iecon.ie

The purpose of the Council for Marriage and the Family is to assist the Bishops in their mission, specifically as it relates to marriage, families and family life.

## ACCORD

### Catholic Marriage Care Service
*President:* Most Rev Denis Nulty DD
*Vice President:* Most Rev Denis Brennan DD
*Coordinator of the work of ACCORD*
Mr Harry Casey
*National Chaplain:* Rev Peter Murphy
*Central Office:* Columba Centre, Maynooth, Co Kildare
Tel 01-5053112 Fax 01-6016410
Email admin@accord.ie
www.accord.ie
www.gettingmarried.ie

ACCORD, Catholic Marriage Care Service, is an Agency of the Irish Catholic Bishops' Conference. It has 55 centres located throughout the dioceses of Ireland. Its ministry is primarily concerned with supporting the sacrament of marriage by helping couples as they prepare for marriage and offering support to them in their marriage relationship. ACCORD's aim is to promote a better understanding of Christian marriage and to help couples initiate, sustain and enrich their commitment to one another and to family life. ACCORD's core services include Marriage Preparation and Marriage Counselling, Fertility Awareness and Wellbeing, Marriage Enrichment and Schools Programmes. For further information phone your local ACCORD Centre or ACCORD Central Office or visit *www.accord.ie* or *www.gettingmarried.ie.* or *www.accordni.com*

## CURA

**Pregnancy Counselling Service**
*President:* Most Rev Eamonn Walsh DD
*National Co-ordinator:* Ms Louise Graham
*National Office*
Columba Centre, Maynooth, Co Kildare
Tel 01-5053040 Fax 01-6292364
Email curacares@cura.ie
Website www.cura.ie

CURA is an agency of the Catholic
Church and was established in 1977 as a
caring service for those for whom their
pregnancy is or has become a crisis.

Services provided:
• Unplanned/crisis pregnancy support
  and counselling
• Pregnancy testing
• Post-abortion counselling support
• School Awareness Programme
• Support to mothers and fathers of a
  new baby.

Services available nationwide, see
www.cura.ie
National Helpline: 1850-622626
All services are free, confidential and non-
judgemental. Services are also available to
men and other family members.

## COUNCILS FOR EMIGRANTS AND IMMIGRANTS OF THE IRISH EPISCOPAL CONFERENCE

### EMIGRANTS (IECE)
The Irish Episcopal Council for Emigrants
(IECE) seeks to respond to the needs of
Irish emigrants prior to and following
departure. It is particularly committed to
addressing the needs of our most
vulnerable emigrants, especially the
elderly Irish emigrant community, the
undocumented in the United States and
Irish prisoners overseas. Working in
conjunction with the host Church, our
apostolates and sister organisations, the
IECE seeks to respond to the needs of
the Irish as an emigrant community.

*Members of the Council for Emigrants*
Most Rev John Kirby *(Chair)*
Most Rev Denis Brennan DD; Most Rev
Raymond Browne DD; Rev Paul Byrne
OMI, Rev Alan Hilliard, Rev Gerry French,
Fr Peter Rodgers (OFMCap), Sr Imelda
Wickham (PBVM) and Dr Patricia Kennedy
*Acting Director of IECE:* Mr Harry Casey
*Administrator:* Ms Bernadette Martin
Columba Centre, Maynooth, Co Kildare
Tel 01-5053155 Fax 01-6292363
Email bernie.martin@iecon.ie
emigrants@iecon.ie
Website www.catholicbishops.ie

**Irish Council for Prisoners Overseas is an outreach of IECE**
The Irish Council for Prisoners Overseas
(ICPO) is currently the only organisation
working on behalf of Irish prisoners
overseas and their families. Established
in 1985, the ICPO promotes social justice

and human dignity for Irish people in
prisons overseas and for their families.
ICPO provides information, support and
advocacy to Irish prisoners wherever they
are: it makes no distinction in terms of
religious faith, the nature of the prison
conviction or of a prisoner's status.
Casework, family support work, prison
visits and policy work comprise core
components of this work.

*Staff Maynooth:* Mr Brian Hanley, Ms
Catherine Jackson, Ms Bernadette Martin
*Volunteers Maynooth:* Sr Agnes Hunt, Ms
Eileen Boyle, Ms Joan O'Cléirigh and Sr
Anne Sheehy
*Staff London:* Rev Gerry McFlynn, Ms
Elizabeth Power, Ms Breda Power, Mr
Declan Ganly, Mr Russel Harland
*Volunteers London:* Sr Maureen McNally,
Sr Agnes Miller, Ms Kathleen Walsh, Ms
Jayne O'Connor, Sr Moira Keane, Ms
Marie Power
*Maynooth Office:* Columba Centre,
Maynooth, Co Kildare
Tel 01-5053156 Fax 01-6292363
Email icpo@iecon.ie
Website www.catholicbishops.ie
*London Office:* 50-52 Camden Square,
London NW1 9XB
Tel 0044-2074824148
Fax 0044-2074824815

[The Irish Chaplaincy in Britain
*Director:* Mr Eugene Dugan
Tel 0044-207-4825528 Fax 0044-207-4824815
Email prisoners@irishchaplaincy.org.uk
Website www.irishchaplaincy.org.uk]

### IMMIGRANTS (IECI)
The Irish Episcopal Council for
Immigrants (IECI) develops and fosters
initiatives for the pastoral care of
immigrants among the dioceses and
parishes of Ireland. It identifies
immigrant communities within a local
setting, recognises their needs and
develops pastoral outreach strategies to
engage with, support and integrate
immigrant communities into dioceses
and local parishes.

*Members of the Council for Immigrants*
Most Rev Raymond Field DD (*Chair*),
Mr Gerard Forde, Rev William Purcell,
Rev Cornelius Kelechi, Sr Julie Doran, Sr
Moira McDowall, Rev Patrick O'Hagan,
Rev Piotr Galus, Rev Brendan MacPartlin
and Rev Stanislaw Hajkowski
*Field Officer:* Dr Helen Young
Columba Centre, Maynooth, Co Kildare
Tel 01-5053009
Email helen.young@iecon.ie

## COUNCIL FOR HEALTHCARE

*Membership*
Most Rev Raymond Field DD (*Chair*);
Most Rev John Buckley DD;
Most Rev Ray Browne DD;
Most Rev Donal Murray DD;
Rev Peter Rodgers (OFMCap), Sr Helena
O'Donoghue (RSM), Very Rev Stephen

Foster (OSCam), Sr Marie Ryan, Sr Pat
O'Donovan (RSM) *(Secretary)*, Prof Tony
Fahey, Rev Prof Michael Mullaney, Rev
John Kelly, Rev Kevin O'Gorman (SMA),
Br Laurence Kearns (OH), Paul Caddell,
Dr Brendan Buckley.

*Secretary:* Sr Pat O'Donovan
c/o CORI Secretariat,
Saint Mary's, Bloomfield Avenue,
Donnybrook, Dublin 4
Tel 01-6677343/6677322
Email pat.odonovan@cori.ie
www.catholicbishops.ie/healthcare

## IRISH BISHOPS' DRUGS INITIATIVE

*Chair:* Ms Patricia Conway
*Vice Chair:* Most Rev Eamonn Walsh DD
*Community Development Worker:*
Mr Darren Butler
*Committee Members:* Sr Kathleen
Kelleher, Mr Chris Murphy, Mr David
Conway, Ms Gwen McKenna and Ms
Marion Rackard
Columba Centre, Maynooth, Co Kildare
Tel 01-5053044/086-8611531
Email ibdi@iecon.ie

The Irish Bishops' Drugs Initiative was
established in 1997 as a Church response
to the growing problem of drug/alcohol
misuse in Ireland. Its vision is to enable
parishes to use a pastoral response in
partnership with other service providers
to respond to the primary and secondary
prevention of drug/alcohol harms in
parish communities.

## OUTREACH TO PRISONERS

*Irish Prison Chaplains Team*
*Episcopal Liaison*
Most Rev Eamonn Walsh DD
*National Coordinator of Prison Chaplains*
Rev Ciarán Enright
Arbour Hill Prison, Dublin 7
Tel 01-6732990/6719333

There are at present twenty full-time
and five part-time chaplains working in
Irish prisons. The vision of the chaplaincy
is one that affirms the dignity of the
person and seeks to be a voice for those
deprived of their freedom. It is a vision
that urges us to take a prophetic stance
on issues of social justice and to
continue the exploration of Restorative
Justice as a valid alternative to
imprisonment.

## [CHAPLAINCY FOR DEAF PEOPLE

Rev Gerard Tyrrell *(Director)*
The National Chaplaincy for Deaf People
40 Lower Drumcondra Road, Dublin 9
Tel/Voice/TDD 01-8305744
Fax 01-8600284
Email gerard@ncdp.ie or office@ncdp.ie]

## DEPARTMENT OF PLANNING, COMMUNICATIONS AND RESOURCES

*Executive Secretary to the Episcopal Commission/Department*
Mr Paul Corcoran
Tel 01-5053000
Email paul.corcoran@iecon.ie

## COUNCIL FOR COMMUNICATIONS OF THE IRISH EPISCOPAL CONFERENCE

*Members of the Council*
His Grace Most Rev Eamon Martin DD (*Chair*)
Most Rev Eamonn Walsh DD
Most Rev Kieran O'Reilly DD
Mr Martin Long
Rev Timothy Bartlett
Rev Bill Kemmy
Ms Petra Conroy
Fr Fintan Monaghan
*Secretary:* Ms Maura Hyland
Veritas Company,
7-8 Lower Abbey Street, Dublin 1
Tel 01-8788177 Fax 01-8786507

### Catholic Communications Office
*Director:* Mr Martin Long
*Communications Officer*
Ms Brenda Drumm
*Editor of Intercom:* Mr Francis Cousins
*Communications Assistant*
Ms Marie Purcell
Columba Centre, Maynooth, Co Kildare
Tel 01-5053000 Fax 01-6016401
Email info@catholicbishops.ie
www.catholicbishops.ie
Twitter: @CatholicBishops
Facebook: Irish Catholic Bishops' Conference
YouTube: Irish Catholic Bishops' Conference
Audioboo:
www.audioboo.fm/IrishCatholicBishops

### Veritas Communications
*President:* Most Rev Joseph Duffy DD
*Chair:* Very Rev Ned Hassett
*Deputy Chair:* Mr Damian Byrne
*Director:* Ms Maura Hyland

Veritas advises the Episcopal Commission on Communications on matters related to communications. It has the following divisions:

*Veritas Company Ltd*
7-8 Lower Abbey Street, Dublin 1
Tel 01-8788177 Fax 01-8744913
Email sales@veritas.ie
Unit 309, Blanchardstown Centre,
Dublin 15
Tel 01-8864030 Fax 01-8864031
Email blanchardstownshop@veritas.ie
Carey's Lane, Cork
Tel 021-4251255 Fax 021-4279165
Email corkshop@veritas.ie

20 Shipquay Street,
Derry BT48 6DW
Tel 028-71266888 Fax 028-71365120
Email derryshop@veritas.ie
83 O'Connell Street,
Ennis, Co Clare
Tel 065-6828696 Fax 065-6820176
Email ennisshop@veritas.ie
13 Lower Main Street, Letterkenny,
Co Donegal
Tel 074-9124814 Fax-074-9122716
Email letterkennyshop@veritas.ie
13 Rue Du Bourg,
65100 Lourdes, France
Tel +33-562-422794
Email lourdesshop@veritas.ie
16-18 Park Street, Monaghan
Tel 047-84077 Fax 047-84019
Email monaghanshop@veritas.ie
Sallins Road, Naas, Co Kildare
Tel 045-856882 Fax 045-856871
Email naasshop@veritas.ie
40-41 The Mall, Newry,
Co Down BT34 1AN
Tel 028-30250321
Email newryshop@veritas.ie
Adelaide Street, Sligo
Tel 071-9161800 Fax 071-9160121
Email sligoshop@veritas.ie
*Veritas UK:* Veritas Warehouse,
14 Rosemount Business Park,
Ballycoolin, Dublin 15, Ireland
Tel 01926-451730 Fax 01926-451733
Email warehouse@veritas.ie

*Veritas Publications*
7-8 Lower Abbey Street, Dublin 1
Tel 01-8788177 Fax 01-8786507
Publishers of general religious books, liturgical texts in Irish and English, and catechetical texts.
*Director:* Ms Maura Hyland
*Manager of Publications*
Caitriona Clarke
*Commissioning Editor:* Donna Doherty
*Intercom Magazine*
Catholic Communications Office,
Columba Centre, Maynooth,
Co Kildare
Tel 01-5053000 Fax 01-6016401
*Editor:* Mr Francis Cousins
Email fcousins@catholicbishops.ie
*Subscriptions:* Mr Ross Delmar
Tel 01-8788177 Fax 01-8786507
Twitter @IntercomJournal

## COUNCIL FOR RESEARCH AND DEVELOPMENT OF THE IRISH EPISCOPAL CONFERENCE

*Members of the Council*
Most Rev Dermot Clifford DD (*Chair*)
Most Rev Kieran O'Reilly DD;
Prof Darach Turley; Ms Louise McCann;
Ms Ann Morash; Dr Brian Conway

### Council for Research and Development
*Social Researcher:* Mr Eoin O'Mahony
Tel 01-5053024 Fax 01-6016401
Email eoin.omahony@iecon.ie

The Council co-ordinates and assists in research projects approved or requested by the Episcopal Conference, its Agencies and Commissions. A social researcher is employed to devise research projects to explore and identify developmental needs and possibilities in relation to the Church in Ireland; the researcher offers a consultancy service and provides a data and information resource to members of the Conference.

## COUNCIL FOR FINANCE AND GENERAL PURPOSES OF THE IRISH EPISCOPAL CONFERENCE

*Episcopal Members of the Council*
Most Rev John Fleming DD (*Chair*);
Most Rev Michael Smith DD
Most Rev Francis Duffy DD
*Finance Manager:* Mr Paul Corcoran
Columba Centre, Maynooth, Co Kildare
Tel 01-5053000 Fax 01-6292360
Email finance@iecon.ie

The Finance and General Purposes Council is composed of three Episcopal members and four lay persons. The Council provides central administrative and accounting services for all the commissions and acts in an advisory capacity to the Episcopal Conference.

## DEPARTMENT OF SOCIAL ISSUES AND INTERNATIONAL AFFAIRS

*Executive Secretary to the Episcopal Commission/Department:* Mr Harry Casey
Tel 01-5053000
Email harry.casey@iecon.ie

## COUNCIL FOR EUROPEAN AFFAIRS OF THE IRISH EPISCOPAL CONFERENCE

*Members of the Council on European Affairs*
Most Rev Diarmuid Martin DD (*Chair*)
Most Rev Noël Treanor DD

### COMECE
19 Square de Meeûs, 1050 Bruxelles,
Belgium
Tel 32-(0)-22350510 Fax 0032-2-2303334
Email comece@comece.eu
Website www.comece.org

COMECE is a Commission of the Episcopal Conferences of the member countries of the European Community, with an office in Brussels.
*General Secretary:* Rev Patrick Daly
*Irish Episcopal Conference representative to COMECE*
Most Rev Noël Treanor DD

## COUNCIL FOR JUSTICE AND PEACE OF THE IRISH EPISCOPAL CONFERENCE

*Members of the Council*
Most Rev John McAreavey DD *(Chair)*
Most Rev Raymond Browne DD
*Research Co-ordinator:* Dr Nicola Brady
Columba Centre, Maynooth, Co Kildare
Tel 01-5053000 Fax 01-6016401
Email cjp@iecon.ie

The Council's role is to assist the Church in responding to the challenges facing it in the areas of human rights, social justice in Ireland and internationally, peace, including peace education, and world development. Its main activities are in research, education and information.

## COUNCIL FOR THE MISSIONS OF THE IRISH EPISCOPAL CONFERENCE

*Episcopal Members of the Council*
Most Rev Kieran O'Reilly DD *(Chair)*
Most Rev Leo O'Reilly DD

**National Mission Council**
*Chair:* Most Rev Kieran O'Reilly DD
*Secretary:* Rev Hugh McMahon (SSC)
IMU, 563 South Circular Road, Dublin 8
Tel 01-4923326/4923325 Fax 01-4923316
Email executive@imu.ie

**World Missions Ireland (Pontifical Mission Societies)**
*National Director*
Rev Maurice Hogan (SSC)
64 Lower Rathmines Road, Dublin 6
Tel 01-4972035
Email director@wmi.ie

Co-ordinates the activities of all national missionary bodies and acts as a forum for discussion on matters related to national mission policy.

## TRÓCAIRE

The Catholic Agency for World Development
*Board of Trustees*
His Grace Most Rev Eamon Martin
His Grace Most Rev Diarmuid Martin
His Grace Most Rev Dermot Clifford
His Grace Most Rev Michael Neary
Most Rev Noël Treanor
Most Rev John Kirby
Most Rev William Crean
*Executive Committee*
Most Rev William Crean *(Chair)*
*Executive Director*
Éamonn Meehan
*Director of International Department*
Caoimhe De Barra
*Director of Public Engagement*
Fintan Maher
*Head of Communications*
Michelle Hoctor
Maynooth, Co Kildare
Tel 01-6293333 Fax 01-6290661
Email info@trocaire.ie
Website http://www.trocaire.org

*Offices and Resource Centres:*
50 King Street, Belfast BT1 6AD
9 Cook Street, Cork
12 Cathedral Street, Dublin 1

Trócaire, the Catholic Agency for World Development, was established by the Irish bishops in 1973 to express the Church's concern for the needs and problems of the people of the developing nations. Trócaire's long-term development projects and emergency relief programmes in Africa, Asia, Latin America and the Middle East tackle the injustice of global poverty. In Ireland, through its education programmes and campaigning, Trócaire works to raise awareness about development issues and the principles of social justice involved.

## DEPARTMENT OF WORSHIP, PASTORAL RENEWAL AND FAITH DEVELOPMENT

*Executive Secretary to the Episcopal Commission/Department*
Vacant
Tel 01-5053000

## COUNCIL FOR PASTORAL RENEWAL AND ADULT FAITH DEVELOPMENT OF THE IRISH EPISCOPAL CONFERENCE

*Members of the Council*
Most Rev Seamus Freeman DD *(Chair)*
Most Rev Donal McKeown DD;
Most Rev Denis Nulty DD;
*Regional networks of diocesan personnel for pastoral renewal and adult faith development:* Rev Martin McAlinden, Ms Eileen Kelly, Ms Rosemary Lavelle and Ms Maureen Kelly
*Lay pastoral workers' network*
Ms Teresa Geraghty
*Ecclesial movements and associations of lay faithful:* Mr Seamus McDonald, Ms Anne Murray
*Youth and young adult ministry*
Mr Padraig Swan
*CORI and IMU*
Rev Peter Rodgers (OFMCap)
*Centres of theological and pastoral education and training*
Rev Dr Gareth Byrne

*Executive Staff of the Council*
*Research Assistant:* Ms Julieann Moran
Email julieann.moran@iecon.ie
Columba Centre, Maynooth, Co Kildare
Tel 01-5053025
Email pastoralrenewal@iecon.ie

The Council supports ongoing dialogue between the groups and agencies represented by its members. The fruits of these dialogues are brought to the Episcopal Commission for Worship, Pastoral Renewal and Faith Development, from where recommendations are presented to the Episcopal Conference.

On behalf of the Conference, the Council fosters a shared vision as well as pastoral priorities and strategies at national level. Areas for research, reflection and supportive action by the Council include evangelisation, adult faith development, parish development, lay discipleship and ministry, and the young Church.

**National Committee of Diocesan Youth Directors (NCDYD)**
Most Rev Donal McKeown DD *(Chair)*
96 Downview Park West,
Belfast BT15 5HZ
Tel 028-90781642

## COUNCIL FOR LITURGY OF THE IRISH EPISCOPAL CONFERENCE

*Episcopal Members of the Council for Liturgy*
Most Rev Martin Drennan DD *(Chair)*
Most Rev Brendan Kelly DD
Most Rev Philip Boyce DD
*Secretary:* Rev Danny Murphy
National Centre for Liturgy,
St Patrick's College,
Maynooth, Co Kildare
Tel 01-7083478 Fax 01-7083477
Email liturgy@spcm.ie
www.liturgy-ireland.ie

**National Centre for Liturgy**
St Patrick's College, Maynooth,
Co Kildare
Tel 01-7083478 Fax 01-7083477
*Director:* Rev Danny Murphy
Email liturgy@spcm.ie
www.liturgy-ireland.ie

The National Centre, relocated at Maynooth in 1996, houses the National Secretariat for Liturgy, offers programmes in liturgical formation at the Centre and elsewhere and provides an advisory service on liturgical matters.

**Advisory Committee on Church Music**
*Chair:* Prof Gerard Gillen
*Secretary:* Sr Moira Bergin
National Centre for Liturgy,
St Patrick's College, Maynooth,
Co Kildare
Tel 01-7083478 Fax 01-7083477
Email moira.bergin@spcm.ie

**Advisory Committee on Sacred Art and Architecture**
*Chair:* Mr Alexander White
*Secretary:* Rev Danny Murphy
National Centre for Liturgy,
St Patrick's College, Maynooth,
Co Kildare
Tel 01-7083478 Fax 01-7083477
Email danny.murphy@spcm.ie

**Coiste Comhairleach um an Liotúirge i nGaeilge**
*Cathaoirleach*
An Dr Marie Whelton
*Rúnaí:* An Canónach Seán Terry
Baile an Londraigh,
Cluain Uamha, Co Chorcai
Fón 021-4646779
Ephost jterry@eircom.net

**Schola Cantorum**
*Director:* Mr Gerard Lillis
St Finian's College, Mullingar,
Co Westmeath
Tel 044-9342906/086-2528029
Email scholacantorum@eircom.net
Website www.scholacantorum.ie

Established by the hierarchy in 1970 to provide specialised training in music for boys and girls within the framework of their general post-primary education.

Scholarships are awarded to students of good general and musical ability.

## COUNCIL FOR VOCATIONS OF THE IRISH EPISCOPAL CONFERENCE

*Members of the Council*
Most Rev Donal McKeown DD *(Chair)*
*National Co-ordinator for Vocations*
Rev William Purcell
Email info@vocations.ie

## COUNCIL FOR RELIGIOUS OF THE IRISH EPISCOPAL CONFERENCE

*Members of the Council for Religious of the IEC*
Most Rev Eamon Martin DD
Most Rev Diarmuid Martin DD
Most Rev Seamus Freeman DD
Most Rev John McAreavey DD

## COUNCIL FOR CLERGY OF THE IRISH EPISCOPAL CONFERENCE

*Episcopal Members of the Council*
Most Rev Philip Boyce DD *(Chair)*
Most Rev Donal McKeown DD
Most Rev Denis Nulty DD

Rev Oliver Treanor
Very Rev Stephen Farragher
Mrs Marie Hogan
Rev Leon Ó Giolláin SJ
Sr Consilio Rock (RSM)

**National Training Authority for the Permanent Diaconate**
Columba Centre, Maynooth, Co Kildare
Tel 01-5053000 Fax 01-6016401

## [NATIONAL BOARD FOR SAFEGUARDING CHILDREN IN THE CATHOLIC CHURCH IN IRELAND

*Chair:* Mr John B. Morgan
*Chief Executive Officer*
Ms Teresa Devlin
*Training Manager:* Mr Niall Moore
*Administrator:* Ms Ann Doyle
*Administrator:* Ms Imelda Ashe
National Board for Safeguarding Children in the Catholic Church in Ireland
New House, St Patrick's College,
Maynooth, Co Kildare
Tel 01-5053124 Fax 01-5053026
Email admin@safeguarding.ie

The National Board for Safeguarding Children in the Catholic Church in Ireland was established in 2006 in order to provide best practice advice and to monitor the safeguarding of children in the Catholic Church.

Over recent years there has been an increasing recognition of the existence of child abuse and growing acceptance of the potential risks to children from others working in positions of trust. Greater attention, therefore, has been paid to how church organisations ensure that the children with whom they are in contact are kept safe from harm.]

# ARCHDIOCESES AND DIOCESES OF IRELAND

Ireland is divided into four provinces: Armagh, Dublin, Cashel and Tuam, named from metropolitan sees. The areas covered by each province and diocese are described at the beginning of the entry for each diocese; a map of the ecclesiastical areas is printed on the front endpaper of this directory.

For ease of reference, the four archdioceses appear at the beginning of this section in the traditional order, but the individual dioceses appear in full alphabetical order regardless of province. Thus Achonry, from the Province of Tuam, starts the section, followed by Ardagh and Clonmacnois from the Province of Ardagh and so on.

The provinces and their suffragan sees are as follows:

**Province of Armagh**
Metropolitan See: Armagh
Suffragan Sees: Dioceses of Ardagh & Clonmacnois, Clogher, Derry, Down & Connor, Dromore, Kilmore, Meath, Raphoe.

*The Archbishop of Armagh is Primate of All Ireland.*

**Province of Dublin**
Metropolitan See: Dublin
Suffragan Sees: Dioceses of Ferns, Kildare & Leighlin, Ossory.

*The Archbishop of Dublin is Primate of Ireland.*

**Province of Cashel**
Metropolitan See: Cashel
Suffragan Sees: Dioceses of Cloyne, Cork & Ross, Kerry, Killaloe, Limerick, Waterford & Lismore.

**Province of Tuam**
Metropolitan See: Tuam
Suffragan Sees: Dioceses of Achonry, Clonfert, Elphin, Galway & Kilmacduagh with Kilfenora*, Killala.

*\*Kilfenora is in the Province of Cashel, but the Bishop of Galway and Kilmacduagh is its Apostolic Administrator.*

# ARCHDIOCESE OF ARMAGH

PATRONS OF THE ARCHDIOCESE
ST MALACHY, 3 NOVEMBER; ST PATRICK, 17 MARCH;
ST OLIVER PLUNKETT, 1 JULY

SUFFRAGEN SEES: ARDAGH AND CLONMACNOIS, CLOGHER, DERRY,
DOWN AND CONNOR, DROMORE, KILMORE, MEATH, RAPHOE

INCLUDES ALMOST ALL OF COUNTIES ARMAGH AND LOUTH
APPROX HALF OF COUNTY TYRONE
AND PARTS OF COUNTIES DERRY AND MEATH

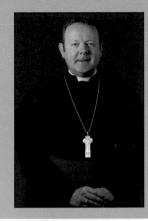

**Most Rev Eamon Martin DD**
Archbishop of Armagh;
Primate of All Ireland;
born 30 October 1961;
ordained priest 28 June 1987;
ordained Coadjutor Archbishop
21 April 2013; succeeded as
Archbishop of Armagh
8 September 2014.

Residence: Ara Coeli,
Cathedral Road,
Armagh BT61 7QY
Tel 028-37522045
Fax 028-37526182
Email admin@aracoeli.com
www.archdioceseofarmagh.com

## ST PATRICK'S CATHEDRAL, ARMAGH

The building of the new St Patrick's Cathedral lasted from St Patrick's Day 1840, when the foundation stone was laid, until its solemn consecration in 1904. There were occasional intermissions of the work, and one of the longest gaps occurred because of the Great Famine. Primate Crolly, who had initiated the building, became a victim of famine cholera, and, at his own wish, his body was laid to rest under the sanctuary of the unfinished cathedral.

For five years the low outline of the bare walls remained, but with the translation of Dr Paul Cullen to the See of Dublin, work was resumed under Primate Dixon. On Easter Monday 1854, tarpaulins and canvas covers were drawn from wall to wall to allow Mass to be celebrated in the unfinished building.

During the Famine cessation the original architect, Thomas J. Duff, died. The architect to take over from Duff's original Perpen-dicular Gothic design was J. J. McCarthy, destined to become one of the famous architects of the nineteenth century. In his anxiety to achieve a greater degree of classical purity, McCarthy drew up a continuation design in the old fourteenth-century Decorated Gothic. While critics may debate the wisdom of such a radical change when the building had reached a relatively advanced stage, the effect was undoubtedly to create an overall impression of massive grandeur.

The final impetus to complete the building came when Dr McGettigan was appointed (1870) to Armagh, and the solemn dedication took place in 1873.

Dr Logue, following Primate McGettigan's death, was to achieve the splendid interior decoration and the addition of the Synod Hall. He travelled to Rome and Carrara in search of precious marble for the reredos, pulpit and altar, and it was he also who achieved the decoration of the interior with mosaic. Under him, stained-glass windows were commissioned from Meyer in Germany. Cardinal Vanutelli represented Pope Pius X at the solemn consecration in 1904. A grand carillon was installed in 1924.

Vatican II's decree on Sacred Liturgy stressed the participation of the laity and hence greater visibility had to be afforded to the congregation. For this reason all the architects who submitted designs based their plans on the removal of the 1904 marble screens, which hindered visibility of the sanctuary from the sides. By raising, enlarging and opening the sanctuary area, the cathedral has, to a large extent, been restored to its original form.

With the removal of the rood screen, a new crucifix had to be placed at the sanctuary, and a specially commissioned 'Cross of Life' by Imogen Stuart was affixed to the right of the sanctuary.

The rededication took place in 1982, and a portion of St Malachy's relics from France, together with a relic of St Oliver Plunkett, was placed in the new altar. And so, the mortal remains of two of Armagh's most celebrated *comharbaí Phádraig* were carried back to the scene of their labours in more troubled times.

The most recent restoration project was completed in 2003 at a cost of £7.5 million, the majority of which was generously funded by parishioners and friends throughout the diocese and beyond. Funding was also received from both the Heritage Lottery Fund and the Environment and Heritage Service.

A unique, but now also an historical feature of the primatial cathedral, is the Cardinals' Hats. They are no longer conferred on new Cardinals. They were hung here and went deliberately untended so that their decay would represent the end of all earthly glory. The most recently hung (and last to be presented) is that of Cardinal Conway. Beside it are Cardinal Logue's and Cardinal O'Donnell's, while on the opposite side are the hats of Cardinals D'Alton and MacRory.

**His Eminence Cardinal Seán Brady DCL, DD**
Emeritus Archbishop of Armagh; born 1939; ordained priest 22 February 1964; ordained Coadjutor Archbishop 19 February 1995; installed Archbishop of Armagh 3 November 1996; created Cardinal 24 November 2007.
Residence: Parochial House, 86 Maydown Road, Tullysaran, Benburb, Co Tyrone BT71 7LN

**Most Rev Gerard Clifford DD, VG**
Titular Bishop of Geron and Former Auxiliary Bishop to the Archbishop of Armagh; born 1941; ordained priest 18 June 1967; ordained Bishop 21 April 1991
Residence: Annaskeagh, Ravensdale, Dundalk, Co Louth
Tel 042-9371012 Fax 042-9371013
Email gcliffrd@indigo.ie

## CHAPTER

*Dean:* Rt Rev Dean Colum Curry VG
*Archdeacon:* Rt Rev Francis Donnelly
*Canons:* Most Rev Gerard Clifford VG
Very Rev Michael Ward
Very Rev Patrick McDonnell
Rt Rev Christopher O'Byrne
Rt Rev Raymond Murray
Very Rev James Clyne
Very Rev Michael Crawley
Rt Rev James Carroll

## ADMINISTRATION

**Vicars General**
Most Rev Gerard Clifford DD, VG
Annaskeagh, Ravensdale, Dundalk, Co Louth
Tel 042-9371012 Fax 042-9371013
Email gcliffrd@indigo.ie
Rt Rev Dean Colum Curry PP, VG
4 Circular Road, Dungannon, Co Tyrone BT71 6BE
Tel 028-87722775
Very Rev Eugene Sweeney PP, VG, VF
Parochial House, 17 Eagralougher Road, Loughgall, Co Armagh BT61 8LA
Tel 028-38891231 Fax 028-38891827
Email esweeney64@btconnect.com

**Vicars Forane**
Very Rev Gerard Campbell PP, Kilkerley
Rt Rev Mgr James Carroll PP, Drogheda
Very Rev Malachy Conlon PP, Cooley
Very Rev John Connolly PP, Moy
Rt Rev Dean Colum Curry PP, VG, Dungannon
Very Rev Benedict Fee PP, Clonoe
Very Rev John Gates PP, Magherafelt
Very Rev Patick Hannigan PP, Killeeshil
Very Rev Gerard McAleer PP, Donaghmore
Very Rev Eamonn McCamley PP, Keady & Derrynoose
Rev Liam McKinney CC, Crossmaglen
Very Rev Aidan Murphy PP, Termonfechin
Very Rev Peter Murphy PP, Ardee & Collon
Very Rev Richard Naughton PP, Cloghogue
Rev Patrick Rushe, Chaplain, DKIT
Very Rev Eugene Sweeney PP, Loughgall

**Chancellor**
Very Rev Michael C. Toner PP
Ara Coeli, Cathedral Road, Armagh BT61 7QY
Tel 028-37522045 Fax 028-37526182
Email mtoner@aracoeli.com
diocesansecretary@aracoeli.com

**Diocesan Curia**
Very Rev Michael C. Toner PP
Diocesan Secretary
Email mtoner@aracoeli.com
diocesansecretary@aracoeli.com
Mr John McVey
Financial Administrator
Email jmcvey@aracoeli.com
Ara Coeli, Cathedral Road, Armagh BT61 7QY
Tel 028-37522045 Fax 028-37526182

**Archives**
*Director:* Mr Roddy Hegarty
Cardinal Tomás Ó Fiaich Memorial Library and Archive,
15 Moy Road, Armagh BT61 7LY
Tel 028-37522981 Fax 028-37511944
Email roddy.hegarty@ofiaich.ie

## CATECHETICS EDUCATION

**Catholic Primary School Managers' Association**
*Secretary:* Very Rev Malachy Conlon PP
Parochial House, Top Rath, Carlingford, Co Louth
Tel 042-9376105
Email malachykilkerley@eircom.net

**Council for Catholic Maintained Schools**
*Senior Management Officer*
Mr Stephen Walsh
1 Killyman Road, Dungannon
Co Tyrone BT71 6DE
Tel 028-87752116 Fax 028-87752783
Email stephen.walsh@ccmsschools.com

**Diocesan Advisers for Religious Education**
*Primary Schools*
Sr Elizabeth Wall
La Verna, St Clare's Convent, Newry, Co Down BT34 1PR
Tel 028-30253887
Email marylizwall@btinternet.com
*Post-Primary Schools*
Rev Declan O'Loughlin
Parochial House, 30 Newline, Killeavy, Newry, Co Down BT35 8TA
Tel 028-30889609
Email decoloughlin@yahoo.co.uk

## PASTORAL

**ACCORD**
*Drogheda Chairperson*
Mrs Sharon Duggan-Meehan
Verona, Cross Lane, Drogheda, Co Louth
Tel 041-9843860
Email accorddrogheda@eircom.net

*Armagh Chairperson*
Mr Denis Bradley
1 Tavanagh Avenue, Portadown, Co Armagh BT62 3AJ
Tel 028-38334781
Email armagh@accordni.com

*Dundalk Chairperson*
Ms Donna McLoughlin
St Patrick's, Roden Place, Dundalk, Co Louth
Tel 042-9331731
Email accorddundalk@eircom.net

**Apostolic Work Society**
*Diocesan President:* Ms Jean Hanratty
13 College Street, Armagh BT61 9BT
Tel 028-37522781

**Armagh Diocesan Pastoral Centre**
*Director:* Sr Rhoda Curran (RSM)
*Assistant Director:* Mr Joseph Purcell
The Magnet, The Demesne, Dundalk, Co Louth
Tel 042-9336393 Fax 042-9336432

**Armagh Diocesan Pastoral Council**
*Chairpersons:* Mr Martin Murray
Email martinmurray09@gmail.com
Mr Pearse O'Hanrahan
Email pearseohanrahan@eircom.net
*Secretary:* Mrs Sheila McEneaney
Email sheila.mceneaney@hotmail.com

**Charismatic Renewal**
Rt Rev Dean Colum Curry PP, VG
Parochial House, 4 Circular Road, Dungannon, Co Tyrone BT71 6BE
Tel 028-87722775

**Chokmah**
*Co-ordinator:* Rev Thomas Hamill
'Shekinah', 25 Wynnes Terrace, Dundalk, Co Louth
Tel 042-9331023
Email tomhamill@eircom.net

**Communications**
*Diocesan Officer:* Vacant

**Council of Priests**
*Chairman:* Rt Rev Mgr James Carroll PP, VF
Parochial House, 9 Fair Street, Drogheda, Co Louth
Tel 041-9838537
Email jcarlpp@eircom.net

**CURA**
17 Jocelyn Street, Dundalk, Co Louth
Tel 042-9337533
*Co-ordinator:* Ms Fidelma Callan

**Diocesan Safeguarding Committee**
*Chairperson:* Ms Edel O'Neill
Archdiocese of Armagh, Cathedral Road, Armagh BT61 7QY
*Designated Officer:* Mr Aidan Gordon
Tel 028-37525592

**Diocesan Safeguarding Office**
*Director and Designated Officer*
Mr Aidan Gordon
Email safeguardingdirector@archdioceseofarmagh.com
Tel 078-41101687
*Training Coordinator and Designated Officer:* Mrs Eleanor Kelly
Email ekelly@archdioceseofarmagh.com
Tel 075-84323138
*Admin Officer:* Mr Pierce Fox
Email pfox@archdioceseofarmagh.com
Archdiocese of Armagh, Catheral Road, Armagh BT61 7QY
Tel 028-37525592

**Ecumenism**
Very Rev Pádraig Murphy PP
Email pplordship@live.ie
Parochial House, Ravensdale, Dundalk, Co Louth
Tel 042-9371327 Fax 042-9371327
Very Rev Seán Dooley PP
Email seandooleyfriesian@btconnect.com
Parochial House, Tullyallen, Co Louth

**Fr Mathew Union**
*Diocesan Chairman*
Very Rev Seamus Rice PE
4 Ballymacnab Road, Armagh BT60 2QS
Email seamusrice@live.co.uk

**Knock Pilgrimage**
*Director:* Rev Benedict Fee PP, VF
Teaċ na h'Ard Croise,
3 Cloghog Road, Clonoe, Coalisland,
Co Tyrone BT71 5EH
Tel 028-87749184
Email frbennyfee@hotmail.com

**Legion of Mary**
*Armagh Curia President*
Ms Dympna McNamee
16 Springfield Crescent, Mullaghmore,
Dungannon, Co Tyrone BT70 1QU
Tel 028-87724178
*Drogheda Curia President*
Ms Elizabeth Molony
194 Meadow View, Drogheda, Co Louth
Tel 041-9830617
*Dundalk Curia President*
Mrs Patricia McGee
28 Aghameen Park, Muirhevnamor,
Dundalk, Co Louth
Tel 042-9329811

**Liturgy Commission**
*Chair:* Sr Mairead Ní Fhearáin
St Clare's Convent, 42 Madden Row,
Keady, Co Armagh BT60 3RW
Tel 028-37531252

**LMFM Community Radio**
Rt Rev Mgr James Carroll PP, VF
Parochial House, 9 Fair Street,
Drogheda, Co Louth

**Lourdes Pilgrimage**
*Director:* Very Rev Eamonn McCamley PP
34 Madden Row, Keady,
Co Armagh BT60 3RW
Tel 028-37531242

**Marriage Tribunal**
(See Marriage Tribunals section.)

**Pastoral Renewal & Family Ministry**
*Director:* Dr Tony Hanna
Email tonyhann@indigo.ie
*Diocesan Pastoral Worker:* Patrick Logue
Email patrickoprfm@gmail.com
Armagh Diocesan Pastoral Centre,
The Magnet, The Demesne,
Dundalk, Co Louth
Tel 042-9336649

**Pioneer Total Abstinence Association**
*Diocesan Director*
Very Rev Seamus Rice PE
4 Ballymacnab Road, Armagh BT60 2QS

**Polish Chaplaincy**
Rev Radoslaw Syzmoniak (SChr) CC
Parochial House, 6 Circular Road,
Dungannon, Co Tyrone BT71 6BE
Tel 028-37531620
Email rszymon@hotmail.com

**Pontifical Mission Societies**
*Diocesan Director*
Very Rev Vincent Darragh PE
81 Mullinahoe Road, Ardboe,
Dungannon, Co Tyrone BT71 5AU
Tel 028-86735774
Email vdarragh@aol.com

**Seminarian Liaison**
Very Rev Joseph McKeever PP
9 Newry Road, Crossmaglen, Newry,
Co Down BT35 9HH
Tel 028-30861208
Email jmckeever02@googlemail.com

**SPRED**
*Co-ordinator:* Ms Patricia Lennon
19 The Glen, Newry, Co Down BT35 8BS
Tel 028-30265353

**Travellers**
*Co-ordinator:* Vacant

**Vocations Commission**
*Vocations Director*
Very Rev Peter McAnelly Adm
42 Abbey Street, Armagh BT61 7DZ
Tel 028-31522802
Email p.mcanenly@btinternet.com

**Youth Commission (ADYC)**
*Chairperson:* Rev Brian White CC
Parochial House, Grianán Mhuire,
Main Street, Blackrock, Dundalk, Co Louth
*Director:* Mr Dermot Kelly
*Admin Officer:* Mr Pierce Fox
Archdiocese of Armagh, Cathedral Road,
Armagh BT61 7QY
Tel 028-37523084
Email armaghyouth@yahoo.co.uk

# PARISHES

*Mensal parishes are listed first. Other parishes follow alphabetically. Historical names are given in parentheses. Church titulars are in italics.*

## ARMAGH
*St Patrick's Cathedral, St Malachy,* Irish Street, *St Colmcille's,* Knockaconey *Immaculate Conception,* Tullysaran
Email armaghparish@btconnect.com
Very Rev Peter McAnelly Adm
Email p.mcanenly@btinternet.com
Rev Rory Coyle CC
Email rory_coyle@hotmail.com
Rev Thomas McHugh CC
Email thomasmch@gmail.com
Rev Biju Thomas CC
Email maliackalbiju@gmail.com
Parochial House, 42 Abbey Street,
Armagh BT61 7DZ
Tel 028-37522802 Fax 028-37522245
Rev Kevin Donaghy *(Priest in residence)*
St Patrick's Grammar School,
Cathedral Road, Armagh BT61 7QZ
Tel 028-37522018
Email kdonaghy480@c2kni.net
Parish Office: Cathedral Gate Lodge,
41a Cathedral Road, Armagh BT61 7QX
Tel 028-37522813

## DUNDALK, ST PATRICK'S
*St Patrick's, Roden Place*
*St Nicholas's, Church Street*
www.stpatricksparishdundalk.org
Email stpatricksparishdundalk@gmail.com
Very Rev Mark O'Hagan Adm
Email ohaganmark2@gmail.com

Rev Séamus Dobbin CC
Rev Magnus Ogbonna (MSP) CC
Email doziemsp@yahoo.com
Rev Garrett Campbell CC
Email frgarrettcampbell@gmail.com
Rev Des Branigan CC
Email desmond.branigan@gmail.com
Rev Mr Ben Ndubuisi, Permanent Deacon
Email maben4divine@yahoo.com
St Patrick's Presbytery, Roden Place,
Dundalk, Co Louth
Tel 042-9334648 Fax 042-9336355

## DUNDALK, HOLY REDEEMER
*Holy Redeemer*
www.redeemerparish.ie
Email holyredeemer@eircom.net
Very Rev Paul Montague Adm
Rev Neil O'Donoghue CC
Email padreodonoghue@gmail.com
Ard Easmuinn, Dundalk, Co Louth
Tel 042-9334259 Fax 042-9329073

## DUNDALK, ST JOSEPH'S
*St Joseph's*
Email dundalkoffice@redemptorists.ie
Very Rev Michael Cusack (CSsR) Adm
Rev Eamon Hoey (CSsR) CC
Email nedhoey@gofree.indigo.ie
Rev Patrick Sugrue (CSsR) CC
Rev Daniel Baragry (CSsR) CC
Email dan.baragry@redemptorists.ie
St Joseph's, St Alphonsus Road,
Dundalk, Co Louth
Tel 042-9334042 Fax 042-9330893

## DUNDALK, HOLY FAMILY
*Holy Family*
Email theholyfamily@eircom.net
Very Rev James O'Connell (SM) Adm
Email jimhoconnell@yahoo.co.uk
Rev Patrick Stanley (SM) CC
Email paddyholyfamily@gmail.com
Rev Francis Corry (SM) CC
Holy Family Parish, Dundalk, Co Louth
Tel 042-9336301 Fax 042-9336350

## DROGHEDA
*St Peter's, West Street*
*Our Lady of Lourdes, Hardman's Gardens*
www.saintpetersdrogheda.ie
Email stpetersadmin1@eircom.net
Rt Rev Mgr James Carroll PP
Parochial House,
9 Fair Street, Drogheda, Co Louth
Tel 041-9838537 Fax 041-9841351
Email jcarlpp@eircom.net
Rev Cathal Deveney CC
Email cathalarmagh@gmail.com
Very Rev Canon Patrick McDonnell PE
Rev Maciej Zacharek CC
Email zackarekmaciej@gmail.com
Our Lady of Lourdes Presbytery,
Hardman's Gardens, Drogheda, Co Louth
Tel 041-9831899
Rev Paul Murphy CC
Email pmurph12@tcd.ie
Rev Mr David Durrigan, Permanent Deacon
Email fuinneog@gmail.com
St Peter's Presbytery, 10 Fair Street,
Drogheda, Co Louth
Tel 041-9838239

## DUNGANNON (DRUMGLASS, KILLYMAN AND TULLYNISKIN)
*St Patrick's, Dungannon, St Malachy's Edendork, St Brigid's, Killyman, Sacred Heart, Clonmore*
www.parishofdungannon.com
Rt Rev Dean Colum Curry PP, VG
4 Circular Road, Dungannon,
Co Tyrone BT71 6BE
Tel 028-87722775
Email ccurry@btinternet.com
Rev Séamus White CC
Email seamuswhite@ymail.com
Rev Ryan McAleer CC
Email ryankmcaleer@hotmail.com
Rev Radoslaw Syzmoniak (SChr) CC
Tel 028-37531620
Email rszymon@hotmail.com
Rev Mr Andrew Hegarty, Permanent Deacon
Email andythegarty@gmail.com
Parochial House, 6 Circular Road,
Dungannon, Co Tyrone BT71 6BE
Tel 028-87722631
*Parish Office:* 4 Killyman Road,
Dungannon, Co Tyrone BT71 6DH
Tel/Fax 028-87726893
Email parishofdungannon@lycos.com

## ARDBOE
*Blessed Sacrament, Mullinahoe Immaculate Conception, Moortown*
Very Rev Seán McCartan PP
Parochial House, 19 Ardboe Road,
Moortown, Cookstown,
Co Tyrone BT80 0HT
Tel 028-86737236
Email seancmccartan@gmail.com
Very Rev Vincent Darragh PE
'Lisieux' 99 Loup Road,
Moneymore, Co Derry BT45 7ST
Tel 028-79418946
Email vdarragh@aol.com

## ARDEE & COLLON
*Nativity of Our Lady, Ardee St Catherine's, Ballapousta Mary Immaculate, Collon*
Website www.ardeeparish.com
Email ardee.collon@gmail.com
Very Rev Peter Murphy PP, VF
Tel 041-6850920 Fax 041-6850922
Very Rev John O'Leary PE, AP
Tel 041-6850920
Email jpoleary7@aol.com
Rev Anselm Emechebe (MSP) CC
Tel 041-6860080
Email aemechebe@yahoo.com
Rev Mr John Taaffe, Permanent Deacon
Email johntaaffe1@gmail.com
Parochial House, Moore Hall,
Ardee, Co Louth
Very Rev Stephen Duffy PE, AP
Parochial House, Collon, Co Louth
Tel 041-9826106
Email duffyst@hotmail.co.uk

## AUGHNACLOY (AGHALOO)
*St Mary's, Aughnacloy, St Brigid's, Killens, St Joseph's, Caledon*
Very Rev Gregory Carvill Adm
Parochial House, 19 Caledon Road,
Aughnacloy, Co Tyrone BT69 6HX
Tel 028-85557212
Email greg.carvill@gmail.com

Rev John McGoldrick (in residence)
Parochial House, 56 Minterburn Road,
Laireakean, Caledon, Co Tyrone BT68 4XH
Tel 028-37568288
Email minterburn@hotmail.com

## BALLINDERRY
*St Patrick's*
Very Rev Peter Donnelly PP
Parochial House,
130 Ballinderry Bridge Road, Coagh,
Cookstown, Co Tyrone BT80 0AY
Tel 028-79418244

## BALLYGAWLEY (ERRIGAL KIERAN)
*St Matthew's, Garvaghy, St Mary's, Dunmoyle, Immaculate Conception, Ballygawley, St Malachy's, Ballymacilroy*
Very Rev Michael Seery PP
Parochial House, 115 Omagh Road,
Ballygawley, Co Tyrone BT70 2AG
Tel 028-85568208
Very Rev Brian Hackett PE, AP
Parochial House, 31 Church Street,
Ballygawley, Co Tyrone BT70 2HA
Tel 028-85568219
Email brianhackett04@aol.com

## BERAGH
*Immaculate Conception, Beragh, St Malachy's, Seskinore, St Patrick's, Drumduff*
Very Rev Séamus McGinley PP
Parochial House, Beragh, Omagh,
Co Tyrone BT79 OSY
Tel 028-80758206
Email beraghparochial@btinternet.com

## BESSBROOK (KILLEAVY LOWER)
*SS Peter and Paul, Bessbrook, St Malachy, Camlough, Sacred Heart, Lislea, Immaculate Conception, Lissummon Road, Newry, Good Shepherd, Cloughreagh*
Rev Seán Larkin PP
Parochial House, 11 Chapel Road,
Bessbrook, Newry, Co Down BT35 7AU
Tel 028-30830206 Fax 028-30838154
Email larkinseanj@aol.com
Rev Aidan Dunne CC
Parochial House, 9 Chapel Road,
Bessbrook, Newry, Co Down BT35 7AU
Tel 028-30830272
Email fadunne@googlemail.com
Very Rev Robert McKenna PE, AP
Parochial House, 26 Newtown Road,
Camlough, Newry, Co Down BT35 7JJ
Tel 028-30830237 Fax 028-30837273
Email robert.mckenna3@btinternet.com
Rev Mr Philip Carder, Deacon
c/o Parochial House, 11 Chapel Road,
Bessbrook, Newry, Co Down BT35 7AU
Tel 028-30830206 Fax 028-30838154
Email philipcarder34@gmail.com

## CARLINGFORD AND CLOGHERNY
*St Michael's, Carlingford St Lawrence's, Omeath*
www.carlinnparish.com
Very Rev Brian MacRaois PP
Parochial House, Chapel Hill,
Carlingford, Co Louth
Tel 042-9373111 Fax 042-9373131
Email info@carlingford-omeath-parish.ie

Rev Christopher McElwee (IC) CC
Rev Oliver Stansfield (IC) *(priest in residence)*
Email ostansfield@gmail.com
Parochial House, Omeath, Co Louth
Tel 042-9375198

## CLOGHERHEAD
*St Michael's, Clogherhead, SS Peter and Paul, Walshestown*
www.clogherhead.com
Very Rev Martin McVeigh PP
Tel 041-9822438
Email clogherheadparish@hotmail.com
Very Rev William Murtagh PE, AP
Tel 041-9822224
Parochial House, Clogherhead,
Drogheda, Co Louth

## CLOGHOGUE (KILLEAVY UPPER)
*Sacred Heart, Cloghogue, St Joseph's, Meigh, St Michael's, Killean*
Very Rev Richard Naughton PP, VF
Mountain Lodge, 132 Dublin Road,
Newry, Co Down BT35 8QT
Tel 028-30262174 Fax 028-30262174
Very Rev Canon S. James Clyne PE, AP
24 Chapel Road, Killeavy, Newry,
Co Down BT35 8JY
Tel 028-30848222
Email clyne@eircom.net

## CLONOE
*St Patrick's, Clonoe, St Columcille's, Kingsland, St Brigid's, Brockagh*
Email clonoeparish@tiscali.co.uk
Very Rev Benedict Fee PP, VF
Teać na h'Ard Croise, 3 Cloghog Road,
Clonoe, Coalisland,
Co Tyrone BT71 5EH
Tel 028-87749184
Email frbennyfee@hotmail.com
Very Rev Kieran MacKeone PE, AP
Parochial House,
132 Washing Bay Road,
Coalisland, Dungannon,
Co Tyrone BT71 4QZ
Tel 028-87740376
Email kieran.mckeone@btinternet.com
Rev John McCallion CC
Parochial House,
140 Mountjoy Road,
Brocagh, Dungannon,
Co Tyrone BT71 5DY
Tel 028-87738381

## COAGH
*Our Lady's, Coagh SS Joseph and Malachy, Drummullan*
Very Rev Gerard Tremer Adm
Parochial House, 1 Convent Road,
Cookstown, Co Tyrone BT80 8QA
Tel 028-86763370
Email fr.gerard.tremer@cookstownparish.com
Rev Francis Coll CC
Parochial House, Hanover Square,
Coagh, Cookstown,
Co Tyrone BT80 0EF
Tel 028-86737212
Email gfcoll@talktalk.net

## COALISLAND

*Holy Family, Coalisland*
*St Mary & St Joseph, Coalisland,*
*St Mary's, Stewartstown*
Email coalislandparish@yahoo.co.uk
Very Rev Paul Byrne PP
Parochial House, 31 Brackaville Road,
Coalisland, Co Tyrone BT71 4NH
Tel 028-87740221 Fax 028-87746449
Email pauldbyrne@gmail.com
Rev Eugene O'Neill CC
5 Plater's Hill, Coalisland,
Co Tyrone BT71 4JZ
Tel 028-87740302
Email freoneill@btopenworld.com
Rev Mr Malachy McElmeel, Deacon
c/o Parochial House, 31 Brackaville Road,
Coalisland, Co Tyrone BT71 4NH
Tel 028-87740221 Fax 028-87746449
Email malachy.motability@gmail.com

## COOKSTOWN (DESERTCREIGHT AND DERRYLORAN)

*Holy Trinity, Cookstown, Sacred Heart,*
*Tullydonnell, St John's, Slatequarry,*
*St Laurán's, Cookstown*
Very Rev Gerard Tremer PP
Parochial House, 1 Convent Road,
Cookstown, Co Tyrone BT80 8QA
Email
fr.gerard.tremer@cookstownparish.com
Rev Emlyn McGinn CC
Email emlynmcginn@yahoo.com
Rev Seán McGuigan CC
Email sean.mcguigan.2009@nuim.ie
Parochial House, 3 Convent Road,
Cookstown, Co Tyrone BT80 8QA
Tel 028-86763293 Fax 028-86763490

## COOLEY

*St James's, Grange*
*Our Lady, Star of the Sea, Boher*
*St Anne's, Mullaghbuoy*
Very Rev Malachy Conlon PP, VF
Top Rath, Carlingford, Co Louth
Tel 042-9376105 Fax 042-9376075
Email malachycooley@eircom.net
Rev Thomas McNulty CC
Parochial House, Grange,
Carlingford, Co Louth
Tel 042-9376577
Email tommymcnulty37@gmail.com

## CROSSMAGLEN (CREGGAN UPPER)

*St Patrick's, Crossmaglen,*
*St Brigid's, Glassdrummond,*
*Sacred Heart, Shelagh*
Email uppercreggan@gmail.com
Very Rev Joseph McKeever PP
9 Newry Road, Crossmaglen,
Newry, Co Down BT35 9HH
Tel 028-30861208 Fax 028-30860163
Rev Liam McKinney CC, VF
Parochial House, 9a Newry Road,
Crossmaglen, Newry,
Co Down BT35 9HH
Tel 028-30868698 Fax 028-30860163
Email ltpmckinney@yahoo.com
Rev Bernard (Barney) King (SM) CC
Parochial House, Glassdrummond,
Crossmaglen, Newry, Co Down BT35 9DY
Tel 028-30861270
Email bconreen@gmail.com

Rev Mr Paul Casey, Deacon
c/o Parochial House, 9 Newry Road,
Crossmaglen, Newry, Co Down BT35 9HH
Tel 028-30861208
Email paulcasey2121@gmail.com

## CULLYHANNA (CREGGAN LOWER)

*St Patrick's, Cullyhanna*
*St Michael's, Newtownhamilton*
*St Oliver Plunkett's, Dorsey*
Very Rev Kevin Cullen PP
Parochial House, Tullynavall Road,
Cullyhanna, Newry, Co Down BT35 OPZ
Tel 028-30861235

## DARVER AND DROMISKIN

*St Peter's, Dromiskin, St Michael's, Darver*
Very Rev Patrick McEnroe PP
Darver, Readypenny, Dundalk,
Co Louth
Tel 042-9379147
Email patrickmmcenroe@eircom.net
Very Rev Liam Pentony PE, CC
Parochial House, Dromiskin,
Dundalk, Co Louth
Tel 042-9382877
Email frliampentony@gmail.com

## DONAGHMORE

*St Patrick's, Donaghmore*
*St John's, Galbally*
Very Rev Gerard McAleer PP, VF
Parochial House, 63 Castlecaulfield Road,
Donaghmore, Dungannon,
Co Tyrone BT70 3HF
Tel 028-87761327
Email donaghmoreparish@btinternet.com
Very Rev Patrick Breslan PE, AP
Parochial House, 55 Dermanaught Road,
Galbally, Dungannon,
Co Tyrone BT70 2NR
Tel 028-87758277

## DROMINTEE

*St Patrick's, Dromintee*
*Sacred Heart, Jonesboro*
Very Rev Dermot Maloney PP
Parochial House, 40 The Village,
Jonesboro, Newry, Co Down BT35 8HP
Tel 028-30849345
Email drominteeparish@btinternet.com

## DUNLEER

*St Brigid's, Dunleer,*
*St Finians's Dromin,*
*St Kevin's, Philipstown*
www.dunleerparish.ie
Very Rev G. Michael Murtagh PP
Parochial House, Old Chapel Lane,
Dunleer, Co Louth
Tel 041-6851278
Email gmmurtagh@eircom.net

## EGLISH

*St Patrick's*
Very Rev Michael Toner PP
Parochial House, 124 Eglish Road,
Dungannon, Co Tyrone BT70 1LB
Tel 028-37549661
Email parishofeglish@gmail.com

## FAUGHART

*St Brigid's, Kilcurry,*
*Most Holy Rosary, Brid-a-Crinn,*
*St Joseph's, Castletown*
Email phstbrigid@eircom.net
Very Rev Thomas Griffin (IC) PP
Rev Vinod Kurian (IC) CC
Email thennattil@hotmail.com
Parochial House, Kilcurry,
Dundalk, Co Louth
Tel 042-9334410/9333235

## HAGGARDSTOWN AND BLACKROCK

*St Fursey's Haggardstown*
*St Oliver Plunkett's, Blackrock*
Very Rev Pádraig Keenan PP
Parochial House, Chapel Road,
Haggardstown, Dundalk, Co Louth
Tel 042-9321621
Email pkredeemer@eircom.net
Rev Brian White CC
Grianán Mhuire, Main Street,
Blackrock, Dundalk, Co Louth
Tel 042-9322244
Email roadbowler@hotmail.com
Rev Mr Dermot Clarke, Deacon
c/o Parochial House, Chapel Road,
Haggardstown, Dundalk, Co Louth
Tel 042-9321621
Email dkclarke@eircom.net

## KEADY (DERRYNOOSE)

*St Patrick's, Keady, St Joseph's,*
*Derrynoose, St Joseph's, Madden*
Very Rev Eamonn McCamley PP, VF
Parochial House, 34 Madden Row, Keady,
Co Armagh BT60 3RW
Tel 028-37531242 Fax 028-37539627
Email info@keadyparish.net
Rev John McKeever CC
Email john_mckeever@yahoo.com
Rev Mr Martin Barlow, Permanent
Deacon
Email martin@thebarlows.biz
Parochial House, St Patrick Street, Keady,
Co Armagh BT60 3TQ
Tel 028-37531246 Fax 028-37530850
Very Rev Canon Michael Crawley PE, AP
Parochial House, 89 Derrynoose Road,
Derrynoose, Keady,
Co Armagh BT60 3EZ
Tel 028-37531222 Fax 028-37539397
Email michaelcrawley89@btinternet.com

## KILDRESS

*St Joseph's, Killeenan*
*St Mary's, Dunamore*
Very Rev Patrick Hughes PP
Parochial House, 10 Cloughfin Road,
Kildress, Cookstown,
Co Tyrone BT80 9JB
Tel 028-86751206
Email patrickhughes309@btinternet.com

## KILKERLEY

*Immaculate Conception*
Very Rev Gerard Campbell PP, VF
Parochial House, Kilkerley,
Dundalk, Co Louth
Tel 042-9333482
Email gerrycampbell65@gmail.com

## KILLCLUNEY
*St Patrick's, Baile Mhic an Aba,*
*St Michael's, Cladaí Móra,*
*St Mary's, Grainseach Mhór*
Very Rev Peter Kerr PP
Parochial House,
194 Newtown Hamilton Road,
Ballymacnab, Armagh BT60 2QS
Tel 028-37531641

## KILLEESHIL
*Assumption, Killeeshil, St Patrick's,*
*Aughnagar, St Joseph's, Ackenduff*
Very Rev Patrick Hannigan PP, VF
Parochial House, 65 Tullyallen Road,
Dungannon, Co Tyrone BT70 3AF
Tel 028-87761211
Email killeeshilparish@yahoo.co.uk

## KILMORE
*Immaculate Conception, Mullavilly,*
*St Patrick's, Stonebridge*
Email parishofkilmore@googlemail.com
www.parishofkilmore.com
Very Rev Oliver Brennan PP
Parochial House, 114 Battlehill Road,
Richhill, Co Armagh BT61 8QJ
Tel 028-38871661
Email olivervbrennan@eircom.net

## KILSARAN
*St Mary's, Kilsaran*
*St Nicholas, Stabannon*
Very Rev Phelim McKeown PP
Parochial House, Kilsaran,
Castlebellingham, Dundalk,
Co Louth
Tel 042-9372255
Email frphelim@eircom.net

## KNOCKBRIDGE
*St Mary's, Knockbridge*
Very Rev Gerard McGinnity PP
Parochial House, Knockbridge,
Dundalk, Co Louth
Tel 042-9374125
Email m.gmcg@hotmail.com

## LISSAN
*St Michael's*
Very Rev Patrick Hughes Adm
Parochial House, 10 Cloughfin Road,
Kildress, Cookstown,
Co Tyrone BT80 9JB
Tel 028-86751206
Email patrickhughes309@btinternet.com
Rev Oliver Breslan PE, AP
Parochial House, 2 Tullynure Road,
Cookstown, Co Tyrone BT80 9XH
Tel 028-86769921
Email oliverbreslan@btinternet.com

## LORDSHIP (AND BALLYMASCANLON)
*St Mary's, Ravensdale*
*St Mary's, Lordship*
*Our Lady of the Wayside, Jenkinstown*
www.lordship-ballymascanlon.org
Very Rev Pádraig Murphy PP
Parochial House, Ravensdale,
Dundalk, Co Louth
Tel 042-9371327
Email pplordship@live.ie

## LOUGHGALL
*Our Lady of Peace, Maghery*
*St Peter's, Collegeland*
*St Patrick's, Loughgall*
*St John's, Tartaraghan*
Very Rev Eugene Sweeney PP, VF
Parochial House,
17 Eagralougher Road,
Loughgall, Co Armagh BT61 8LA
Tel 028-38891231 Fax 028-38891827
Email esweeney64@btconnect.com

## LOUTH
*Our Lady of Immaculate Conception, Louth*
*Our Lady of the Snows, Stonetown*
Very Rev Seán Quinn PP
Parochial House, Louth Village,
Dundalk, Co Louth
Tel 042-9374285
Email sqparish@gmail.com

## MAGHERAFELT AND ARDTREA NORTH
*Assumption, Magherafelt*
*St John's, Milltown*
*St Patrick's Castledawson*
Email magherafeltparish@btinternet.com
www.magherafeltparish.org
Very Rev John Gates PP, VF
Parochial House, 30 King Street,
Magherafelt, Co Derry BT45 6AS
Tel 028-79632439
Email jgatesbrack@gmail.com
Rt Rev Mgr Canon Christopher O'Byrne
PE, AP
Parochial House, 12 Aughrim Road,
Magherafelt, Co Derry BT45 6AY
Tel 028-79634038
Email cobyrne@magherafeltparish.org
Very Rev Arthur McAnerney PE, AP
Parochial House, 10 Aughrim Road,
Magherafelt, Co Derry BT45 6AY
Tel 028-79632351
Email arthur.mcanerney@btinternet.com
Rev Mr Kevin Duffy, Deacon
Parochial House, 30 King Street,
Magherafelt, Co Derry BT45 6AS
Tel 028-79632439
Email kduffy37@yahoo.co.uk

## MELL
*St Joseph's*
Very Rev John McAlinden PP
Parochial House, Slane Road, Mell,
Drogheda, Co Louth
Tel 041-9838278
Email johnmcalinden@oceanfree.net

## MELLIFONT
*Our Lady of the Assumption, Tullyallen*
Very Rev Seán Dooley PP
Parochial House, Tullyallen,
Drogheda, Co Louth
Tel 041-9838520
Email seandooleyfriesian@btconnect.com
Very Rev Laurence Caraher PE, AP
The Ravel, School Lane, Tullyallen,
Drogheda, Co Louth
Tel 041-9834293
Email lacaraher@gmail.com

## MIDDLE KILLEAVY (NEWRY)
*St Mary's, Dromalane,*
*St Malachy's, Carnagat*
www.middlekilleavy.com
Email assumptionnewry@gmail.com
Very Rev Lawrence Boyle PP
'Glenshee', Dublin Road,
Newry, Co Down BT35 8DA
Tel 028-30262376
Rev Fergus Breslan CC
Email fr.fergusbreslin@btinternet.com
Rev Uduak Abara (MSP) CC
Email uduakabara@yahoo.co.uk
27 Woodhill, Monaghan Row, Newry,
Co Down BT35 8DL
*Parish sisters:* Sr Rita Dempsey (SMG),
Sr Marie Slacke (SMG)
Poor Servants of the Mother of God
Sisters, 15 Martin's Lane, Carnagat,
Newry, Co Down BT35 8JP
Tel 028-30268512
Email rdempsey.psmg@gmail.com

## MIDDLETOWN (TYNAN)
*St John's, Middletown*
*St Joseph's, Tynan*
Very Rev Seán Moore PP
Parochial House,
290 Monaghan Road,
Middletown, Co Armagh BT60 4HS
Tel 028-37568406
middletowntynanparish@hotmail.co.uk

## MONASTERBOICE
*Immaculate Conception, Tenure,*
*Nativity of Our Lady, Fieldstown*
Very Rev William Mulvihill PP
Parochial House, Monasterboice,
Drogheda, Co Louth
Tel 041-9822839
Rev Michael Hickey (CSSp) CC
Parochial House, Tenure,
Drogheda, Co Louth
Tel 041-6851281
Email michaelhickey01@eircom.net

## MONEYMORE (ARDTREA)
*SS John and Trea, Moneymore*
*St Patrick, Loup*
Very Rev Martin McArdle PP
Parochial House, 10 Springhill Road,
Moneymore, Magherafelt,
Co Derry BT45 7NG
Tel 028-86748242
Email ardtrea@btconnect.com

## MOY (CLONFEACLE)
*St John the Baptist, Moy*
*St Jarlath's, Clonfeacle*
www.clonfeacleparish.com
Email clonfeacle.parish@gmail.com
Very Rev John Connolly PP, VF
75 Clonfeacle Road,
Blackwatertown,
Dungannon, Co Tyrone BT71 7HP
Email connollyjm@btinternet.com
Very Rev John Hughes PE, CC
6 Jockey Lane, Moy
Dungannon, Co Tyrone BT71 7SR
Tel 028-87784240
Email revhughes135@btinternet.com

## MULLAGHBAWN (FORKHILL)
*St Mary's, Mullaghbawn*
*Our Lady, Queen of Peace, Aughanduff*
St Oliver Plunkett, Forkhill
Very Rev John Heagney PP
Parochial House, 9a Forkhill Road,
Mullaghbawn, Newry,
Co Down BT35 9RA
Tel 028-30888286
Email heagneyjh@aol.com

## NEWBRIDGE
*St James, Newbridge*
Very Rev John Fox PP
Parochial House, 153 Aughrim Road,
Toomebridge, Antrim BT41 3SH
Tel 028-79468277
Email newbridgechurch@googlemail.com

## POMEROY
*Assumption, Pomeroy,*
*Immaculate Conception, Altmore*
www.pomeroyparish.homestead.com
Very Rev David Moore PP
62A Main Street, Pomeroy,
Co Tyrone BT70 2QH
Tel 028-87757867
Email d.moore2323@btinternet.com

## PORTADOWN (DRUMCREE)
*St John the Baptist's, Garvaghy Road*
*St Patrick's, William Street*
www.drumcreeparish.com
Very Rev Michael O'Dwyer PP
Parochial House, 15 Moy Road,
Portadown, Co Armagh BT62 1QL
Tel 028-38350610
Email modppvf@fsmail.net
Rev Michael Sheehan CC
Parochial House, 11 Moy Road,
Portadown, Co Armagh BT62 1QL
Tel 028-38332218
Email frmichaelpsheehan@eircom.net

## TALLANSTOWN
*St Malachy's, Reaghstown,*
*St Medoc's, Clonkeen,*
*SS Peter and Paul, Tallanstown*
Very Rev Paul Clayton-Lea PP
Parochial House, Reaghstown,
Ardee, Co Louth
Tel 041-6855117
Email tallanstownparish@hotmail.com

## TANDRAGEE (BALLYMORE AND MULLAGHBRACK)
*St James's, Tandragee*
*St Patrick's, Ballyargan*
*St Joseph's, Poyntzpass*
*St James's, Markethill*
Very Rev Michael Woods PP
Parochial House, 40 Market Street,
Tandagree, Co Armagh BT62 2BW
Tel 028-38840442
Email parish57@btinternet.com
woodsmick@btinternet.com

## TERMONFECHIN
*Immaculate Conception, Termonfechin*
*The Assumption, Sandpit*
Very Rev Aidan Murphy PP, VF
Parochial House, Termonfechin,
Drogheda, Co Louth
Tel 041-9822121
Email termonfechinparish@eircom.net

## TERMONMAGUIRC (CARRICKMORE, LOUGHMACRORY & CREGGAN)
*St Colmcille's, Carrickmore*
*St Oliver Plunkett, Creggan*
*St Mary's, Loughmacrory*
Rev Sean O'Neill PP
Parochial House, 1 Rockstown Road,
Carrickmore, Omagh,
Co Tyrone BT79 9BE
Tel 028-80761207
Email termonmaguircparish@gmail.com
Very Rev Thomas Mallon PE, AP
Parochial House,
170 Loughmacrory Road, Loughmacrory,
Omagh, Co Tyrone BT79 9LG
Tel 028-80761230 Fax 028-80761131
Email mallontv@btinternet.com

## TOGHER
*St Columcille, Togher*
*St Finnian, Dillonstown*
*St Borchill, Dysart*
*St Mary's, Drumcar*
Very Rev Thomas Daly PP
Parochial House, Boicetown, Togher,
Drogheda, Co Louth
Tel 041-6852110
Very Rev Sean Quinn PE, AP
Parochial House, Dillonstown,
Dunleer, Co Louth
Tel 041-6863570
Email sjqdill@gmail.com

## WHITECROSS (LOUGHILLY)
*St Teresa's, Tullyherron*
*St Malachy's, Ballymoyer*
*St Brigid's, Carrickananney*
*St Laurence O'Toole, Belleeks*
Very Rev Malachy Murphy PP
Parochial House,
25 Priestbush Road, Whitecross,
Co Armagh BT60 2TP
Tel 028-37507214
Email malomurphy@googlemail.com

## INSTITUTIONS AND CHAPLAINCY SERVICES

**Aiken Military Barracks**
Barrack Street, Dundalk, Co Louth
Rev Bernard McCay-Morrissey OP
Tel 042-9332295
Email bernardmccaymorrissey@gmail.com

**Community School**
Ardee, Co Louth
Mr Seán Moran
Tel 041-6853313

**Cuan Mhuire**
Armagh Road, Newry, Co Down
Tel 028-30262429
(Bessbrook Parish Clergy)

**Dundalk Institute of Technology**
Dundalk, Co Louth
Very Rev Patrick Rushe
Dundalk Institute of Technology,
Dublin Road, Dundalk, Co Louth
Tel 042-9370224
Email patrickrushe@me.com

**Our Lady of Lourdes Hospital**
Drogheda, Co Louth
Rev Thomas Hogan CSsR
Our Lady of Lourdes Hospital,
Drogheda, Co Louth
Tel 041-9837601

**St Paul's High School**
Bessbrook, Co Armagh
Very Rev Dermot Maloney PP, VF
Parochial House, 40 The Village,
Jonesboro, Newry, Co Down BT35 8HP
Tel 028-3084945 (H) 028-30830309 (S)
Email drominteeparish@btinternet.com

*The following hospitals are served by parochial clergy:*
**Armagh Community Hospital**
Armagh
Tel 028-37522802 (Chaplain)

**Longstone Special Care Hospital**
Armagh
Tel 028-37522802 (Chaplain)

**Louth County Hospital**
Dundalk, Co Louth
Tel 042-9334648 (Chaplain)

**Mid-Ulster Hospital**
Magherafelt, Co Derry
Tel 028-79632351

**St Brigid's Hospital**
Ardee, Co Louth
Tel 041-6850920 (Chaplain)

**St Joseph's Hospital**
Ardee, Co Louth
Tel 041-6853313 (Chaplain)

**St Luke's Psychiatric Hospital, Armagh**
Armagh
Tel 028-37522802 (Chaplain)

**St Oliver Plunkett's Hospital**
Dundalk, Co Louth
Tel 042-9334259 (Chaplain)

**South Tyrone Hospital**
Dungannon, Co Tyrone
Tel 028-87722631 (Chaplain)

## PRIESTS OF THE DIOCESE ELSEWHERE

Very Rev Peter Clarke
Priest in Residence, 1A Rockstown Road,
Carrickmore, Omagh,
Co Tyrone BT79 9BE
Rev Patrick Coyle
c/o Ara Coeli, Armagh BT61 7QY
Tel 028-37522045
Rev Dominic Mallon
13 Richview Heights, Keady,
Co Armagh BT60 3SW
Rev Seán McEvoy
c/o Ara Coeli, Armagh BT61 7QY
Tel 028-37522045

## RETIRED PRIESTS

Very Rev John Bradley PE
8 Killymeal Road, Dungannon,
Co Tyrone BT71 6DP
Tel 028-87722183
Rev Desmond Corrigan
c/o Ara Coeli, Armagh BT61 7QY

Rev Harry Coyle
Moneymore Care Home,
Cookstown Road, Moneymore,
Co Derry BT45 7QF
Very Rev James Crowley PE
Parochial House, 60 Aughnagar Road,
Ballygawley, Dungannon,
Co Tyrone BT70 2HP
Tel 028-85568399
Rt Rev Archdeacon Francis Donnelly PE
64 Meadow Grove, Dundalk, Co Louth
Tel/Fax 042-9353264
Very Rev John Finn PE
Moorehall Lodge Nursing Home,
Hale Street, Ardee, Co Louth
Tel 041-6871942
Rev John Flanagan (SPS)
Fairfields Care Centre,
80a Fairhill Road, Cookstown,
Co Tyrone BT80 8DE
Very Rev Seán Hegarty PE
Greenpark Care Home,
15 Keady Road, Armagh BT60 4AA
Email dshegarty@btinternet.com
Very Rev Patrick Larkin PE
Parochial House, Jenkinstown,
Dundalk, Co Louth
Tel 042-9371328
Very Rev Kieran MacOscar PE
Parochial House, 10 Mullavilly Road,
Tandragee, Co Armagh BT62 2LX
Tel 028-38840840
Email revmacoscar@btinternet.com
Very Rev Patrick J. McCrory PE
Parochial House, Sixemilecross,
Omagh, Co Tyrone BT79 9NF
Tel 028-80758344
Email patrick.mccrory@btinternet.com
Very Rev Thomas McGeough PE
34 The Village, Moorehall Lodge,
Ardee, Co Louth
Tel 041-6857556
Email tmgeough12@gmail.com
Very Rev Patrick McGuckin PE
79 Reclain Road, Galbally, Dungannon,
Co Tyrone BT70 2PQ
Tel 028-87759692
Email frpmcguckin@hotmail.com
Very Rev Brendan McHugh PE
Anniscliff House, 41 Moneysharvin Road,
Maghera, Co Derry BT46 5HZ
Very Rev Brendan McNally PE
Moorehall Lodge Village,
Ardee, Co Louth
Tel 041-6855117
Very Rev James McNally PE
212 Staffordstown Road,
Toomebridge, Co Antrim BT41 3QT
Tel 028-79650260
Email sainttrea@btinternet.com
Rt Rev Mgr Raymond Murray PE
60 Glen Mhacaha, Cathedral Road,
Armagh BT61 8AF
Tel 028-37510821
Email raylmurray@tiscali.co.uk
Very Rev Christopher O'Brien PE
Haroldstown, Tobinstown,
Tullow, Co Carlow
Tel 059-9161633
Email revcobrien26@icloud.com
Very Rev Owen O'Donnell PE
Parochial House, Dunamore,
Cookstown, Co Tyrone
Tel 028-86751216
Email o.odonnell37@gmail.com

Very Rev Séamus Rice PE
4 Ballymacnab Road, Armagh BT60 2QS
Tel 028-37531620
Email seamusrice@live.co.uk
Very Rev James Shevlin PE
21 Village Green, Omeath, Co Louth
Email jamesshevlin@eircom.net

## RELIGIOUS ORDERS AND CONGREGATIONS

### PRIESTS

**AUGUSTINIANS**
St Augustine's Priory, Shop Street,
Drogheda, Co Louth
Tel 041-9838409 Fax 041-9831847
*Prior:* Rev Francis Aherne (OSA)
Email focal@eircom.net

**CISTERCIANS**
Mellifont Abbey, Collon, Co Louth
Tel 041-9826103 Fax 041-9826713
Email mellifontabbey@eircom.net
*Prior:* Br Andrew Considine
*Superior:* Rev Joseph Ryan

**DOMINICANS**
St Magdalen's, Drogheda, Co Louth
Tel 041-9838271 Fax 041-9832964
*Prior:* Rev Anthony McMullan (OP)

St Malachy's Priory, Dundalk, Co Louth
Tel 042-9334179/9333714
Fax 042-9329751
*Prior:* Rev Augustine Champion (OP)

**JESUITS**
Iona, 211 Churchill Park,
Portadown, Co Armagh BT62 1EU
Tel 028-38330366 Fax 028-38338334
*Superior:* Rev Brendan MacPartlin (SJ)
Email iona@jesuit.ie

**MARISTS**
Cerdon, Marist Fathers,
St Mary's Road, Dundalk, Co Louth
Tel 042-9334019
*Superior:* Rev Kevin Cooney (SM)

St Mary's College, Dundalk, Co Louth
Tel 042-9339984
*Principal:* Mr Con McGinley

(See also under parishes – Dundalk,
Holy Family)

**REDEMPTORISTS**
St Joseph's, Dundalk, Co Louth
Tel 042-9334042/9334762
Fax 042-9330893
*Superior*
Very Rev Michael Cusack (CSsR) PP
Email redsdalk@iol.ie
*Vicar-Superior*
Rev Eamonn Hoey (CSsR) CC

(See also under parishes – Dundalk,
St Joseph's)

**ROSMINIANS**
See under parishes – Faughart

**SERVITES**
Servite Priory, Benburb,
Co Tyrone BT71 7JZ
Tel 028-37548241
Retreat, conference and youth centre
*Prior:* Very Rev Gabriel Bannon (OSM)
*Provincial:* Very Rev Colm McGlynn (OSM)

## BROTHERS

**DE LA SALLE BROTHERS**
De La Salle College,
Dundalk, Co Louth
Tel 042-9331179 Fax 042-9330870
*Principal:* Ms Patricia O'Leary

**SAINT JOHN OF GOD NORTH EAST SERVICES**
St Mary's, Drumcar, Dunleer, Co Louth
Tel 041-6851211 Fax 041-6851529
Email admin.northeast@sjog.ie
*Director:* Ms Teresa Mallon
*Community Superior*
Br Ronan Lennon (OH)
Community: 4
*School Principal:* Mr Kevin Toale
Residential, day and community services
for children and adults with varying
degrees of intellectual disability.

## SISTERS

**CONGREGATION OF THE SISTERS OF MERCY**
Mill Street, Dundalk, Co Louth
Tel 042-9334200
*Leader:* Sr Margaret Tracey
Community: 12

Mile End, Avenue Road,
Dundalk, Co Louth
Tel 042-9330410
Community: 3

Bethany, 34 Point Road,
Dundalk, Co Louth
Tel 042-9331602

15 Cypress Gardens, Bay Estate,
Dundalk, Co Louth
Tel 042-9329315

6 Newry Road, Dundalk, Co Louth
Tel 042-9339285

Convent of Mercy,
Ardee, Co Louth
Tel 041-6853359
Community: 9

Dun Mhuire,
29 Convent Hill, Bessbrook,
Newry, Co Down BT35 7AW
Tel 028-30830258
*Leader:* Sr Kathleen O'Connor
Community: 4

58 Fairhill Road, Cookstown,
Co Tyrone BT80 8AG
Tel 028-86763363
Community: 5

Sisters of Mercy,
10 Killymeal Road, Dungannon,
Co Tyrone BT71 6DP
Tel 028-87722623

Sisters of Mercy,
90 Church View, Bessbrook,
Newry, Co Down BT35 78T
Tel 028-30837140

115 Oaklawns,
Dundalk, Co Louth
Tel 042-9334569

Convent Lodge,
Ein Karim, Hale Street,
Ardee, Co Louth

## DAUGHTERS OF CHARITY OF ST VINCENT DE PAUL
St Vincent's Retreat and Holiday Centre
Termonfeckin, Drogheda,
Co Louth
Tel 041-9822115
*Superior:* Sr Louise Coughlan
Community: 4
Pastoral work, Retreat & Holiday Centre

## DOMINICAN CONTEMPLATIVES
Monastery of St Catherine of Siena,
The Twenties, Drogheda, Co Louth
Tel 041-9838524
Email siena@eircom.net
www.dominicannuns.ie
http://dominicannunsireland.blogspot.com
*Prioress:* Sr M. Breda Carroll (OP)
Community: 20

## FRANCISCAN MISSIONARIES OF THE DIVINE MOTHERHOOD
Franciscan Friary, Laurence Street,
Droghega, Co Louth
Tel 041-9838554
Fax 041-9832535
Community: 3

## FRANCISCAN MISSIONARY SISTERS FOR AFRICA
Franciscan Convent, Mount Oliver,
Dundalk, Co Louth (Motherhouse)
Tel 042-9371123 Fax 042-9371159
Email mtofmsa20@gmail.com
Team Leadership
*Contact Person:* Sr Mary Ryan (FMSA)
Community: 35

## HOLY FAMILY OF BORDEAUX SISTERS
1-2 Wesleyan Mews, Church Street,
Magherafelt, Co Derry BT45 6NZ
Tel 028-79632529
*Contact:* The Sisters
Community: 2
Parish and pastoral work, art and retreat work

## MEDICAL MISSIONARIES OF MARY
Motherhouse, Beechgrove,
Drogheda, Co Louth
Tel 041-9837512 Fax 041-9839219
Email beechgroveadm@eircom.net
*Leader:* Sr Ursula Sharpe

MMM Nursing Facility
Áras Mhuire, Beechgrove,
Drogheda, Co Louth
Tel 041-9842222
*Administration:*
businessmanager@arasmhuire.com
*Pastoral Dept:*
pastoralcare@arasmhuire.com

Greenbank, Mell,
Drogheda, Co Louth
Tel 041-9831028
Email mmmgreenbankmell@eircom.net
Community: 4

13-14 Ashleigh Heights,
Drogheda, Co Louth
Tel 041-9830779/041-9830778
Email mmmashleigh@eircom.net
Community: 5

## MISSIONARIES OF CHARITY
19A Cathedral Road,
Armagh BT61 7QX
Tel 04837-528654
*Superior:* Sr Marie Stephen (MC)
Community: 4
Hostel for men

## NOTRE DAME DES MISSIONS (OUR LADY OF THE MISSIONS)
Pine Cottage, Dublin Road,
Dundalk, Co Louth
Community: 4
Pastoral work

## PRESENTATION SISTERS
Greenhills, Drogheda, Co Louth
Tel 041-9831420
Community: 4
School ministry
Our Lady's College, Greenhills
Tel 041-9831786 Fax 041-9832809
Email greenhillsconvent@yahoo.com

Primary Convent Primary School,
Ballymakenny Road,
Drogheda, Co Louth
Tel 041-9837119
Fax 041-9839425
Email presdrogheda.ias@eircom.net

103 Thomas Street, Portadown,
Co Armagh BT62 3AH
Tel 028-38332220
Email presentation103@hotmail.com
Community: 5
Cross community and pastoral ministry

28 Garvaghy Park,
Portadown, Co Armagh BT62 1HB
Tel 028-38335964
Email evetere1234@yahoo.com
Community: 3
School and pastoral ministry

## SACRED HEART SOCIETY
2 Convent Road,
Armagh BT60 4BJ
Tel 028-37522046 Fax 028-37518764
Community: 5
Education, pastoral work and youth work

*Linked with 2 Convent Road*
Gate Lodge, 4 Convent Road,
Armagh BT60 4BG
Email sr.nora.smyth@googlemail.com
Pastoral work and writing

## SISTERS OF ST CLARE
St Clare's Convent, Keady,
Co Armagh BT60 3RW
Tel 028-37531252
*Contact Person*
Sr Vera Kelly
Community: 7

St Clare's Convent,
4 The Brambles, Stewartstown Road,
Coalisland, Co Tyrone BT71 4SN
Tel 028-87746418
Community: 3

## ST JOHN OF GOD SISTERS
3 Tudor Grove, Mullaharlin Road,
Dundalk, Co Louth
Tel 042-9336422
Community: 1

## ST LOUIS SISTERS
266B Monaghan Road, Tynan,
Co Armagh BT60 4SQ
Tel 028-37568498
Community: 8

Dún Lughaidh, Dundalk, Co Louth
Tel 042-9335786
Community: 11
Dún Lughaidh Post-Primary School
Tel 042-9334474
Pupils: 700

137 Cedarwood Park,
Cox's Demesne, Dundalk, Co Louth
Tel 042-9339816
Community: 1

2 Mill Road, Dundalk, Co Louth
Tel 042-9335773
Community: 4

## EDUCATIONAL INSTITUTIONS

**Coláiste Rís**
Chapel Street, Dundalk, Co Louth
Tel 042-9334336 Fax 042-9338380
*Principal:* Mr Pádraig Hamill

**St Patrick's Academy**
37 Killymeal Road, Dungannon,
Co Tyrone BT71 6DS
Tel 028-87722668
Fax 028-87722745
*Principal:* Mr Fintan Donnelly

**St Patrick's Grammar School**
Cathedral Road, Armagh BT61 7QZ
Tel 028-37522018 Fax 028-37525930
*Principal:* Rev Kevin Donaghy
*Priest on Staff*
Rev John McGoldrick
Tel 028-37568288

**St Joseph's Convent Grammar School**
58 Castlecaulfied, Donaghmore,
Co Tyrone BT70 3HF
Tel 028-87761227
*Principal:* Mr Enda Cullen

**EDMUND RICE SCHOOLS TRUST**
St Joseph's Secondary School,
Newfoundwell, Drogheda, Co Louth
Tel 041-9837232
*Principal:* Mr David Madden

St Joseph's Primary School,
Sunday's Gate, Drogheda, Co Louth
Tel 041-9833620
*Principal:* Mr Paul Hussey

**EDMUND RICE SCHOOLS TRUST
NORTHERN IRELAND**
Christian Brothers' Primary School,
Greenpark, Keady Road,
Armagh BT60 4AB
Tel 028-37524354
Fax 028-37522308
*Principal:* Mr Nial P. Smyth

## CHARITABLE AND OTHER SOCIETIES

**Aras Mhuire**
Shambles Lane, Dungannon,
Co Tyrone BT70 1BW
Tel 028-87726852
Oratory and bookshop

**Avila Nursing Home**
Convent of Mercy, Convent Hill,
Bessbrook, Co Armagh BT35 7AW
Tel 028-30838969

**Armagh Diocesan Family Care Society**
Under the patronage and immediate
direction of the Archbishop and clergy
executive committee.
*Secretary:* John McVey
Ara Coeli, Armagh BT61 7QY
Tel 028-37522045

**Cuan Mhuire**
132 Armagh Road, Newry, Co Down
Tel 028-30269121
Alcohol counselling

**Family of God Community**
The Oratory, Carroll's Village,
Dundalk, Co Louth
Tel 042-9335851 Fax 042-9335566

**St Mary's Drumcar**
Residential and Day Training Centre
St Mary's, Drumcar, Co Louth
Tel 041-6851211/6851264

**SOS Prayer**
The Oratory, Carroll's Village,
Dundalk, Co Louth
Tel 042-9339888

# Working for a just world.

Charity No. CHY5883 (ROI) / XR10431 (NI)

## Trōcaire

Trócaire works in partnership with families and communities all over the developing world, helping people to help themselves.

We work to empower people so that they have an opportunity to lead lives with dignity, realise their potential and have hope for a brighter future.

Trócaire is deeply grateful for the support we receive from parishes and religious communities throughout the country.

Together, as Church, we are working to build a more just world.

**"For I was hungry and you gave me something to eat"**
Matthew 25:35

The Weldeanenia family, Ethiopia.
Photograph: Jeannie O'Brien

For further information, liturgical resources or to invite a Trócaire speaker to your parish, please contact the Church Officer at Maynooth.

Maynooth, Co. Kildare. Tel: (01) 629 3333
12 Cathedral Street, Dublin 1. Tel: (01) 874 3875
9 Cook Street, Cork. Tel: (021) 427 5622
50 King Street, Belfast, BT1 6AD. Tel: (028) 908 08030

**www.trocaire.org**
Trócaire is the overseas development agency of the Catholic Church in Ireland.

## Trōcaire
**Working for a just world.**

# ARCHDIOCESE OF DUBLIN

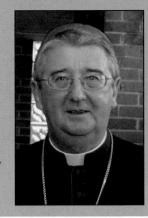

**Most Rev Diarmuid Martin DD**
Archbishop of Dublin and
Primate of Ireland
Born 8 April 1945; ordained priest
25 May 1969; ordained bishop by
Pope John Paul II 6 January 1999;
elevation to Dignity of
Archbishop and Apostolic Nuncio
March 2001; appointed Coadjutor
Archbishop of Dublin 3 May 2003;
Canonical/Liturgical Reception as
Coadjutor 30 August 2003;
succeeded as Archbishop of
Dublin 26 April 2004

Residence: Archbishop's House,
Drumcondra, Dublin 9
Tel 01-8373732 Fax 01-8369796

PATRONS OF THE ARCHDIOCESE
St Kevin, 3 June; St Laurence O'Toole, 14 November

SUFFRAGFEN SEES: KILDARE AND LEIGHLIN, FERNS, OSSORY

INCLUDES CITY AND COUNTY OF DUBLIN, NEARLY ALL OF COUNTY WICKLOW
AND PORTIONS OF COUNTIES CARLOW, KILDARE, LAOIS AND WEXFORD

## ST MARYS PRO-CATHEDRAL, DUBLIN

Though Catholic Dublin has not possessed a cathedral since the Reformation, for almost two hundred years now St Mary's Pro-Cathedral has served as the Mother Church of the Dublin arch-diocese. In that time it has won a special place in the hearts of the Dublin people, to whom it is known affectionately as 'The Pro'.

The Pro-Cathedral was born of the vision of Archbishop John Thomas Troy and brought to fruition thanks to the unstinting labours of its second administrator, Archdeacon John Hamilton. The parish of Saint Mary's, straddling the Liffey, was established in 1707 and a chapel dedicated to St Mary was opened in 1729. In 1797 Archbishop Troy successfully petitioned the Holy See to allow him take St Mary's as his *mensal* parish. He thereupon set about raising funds to build a 'dignified, spacious church' in a central location in the parish.

The site chosen was a building on Marlborough Street, opposite Tyrone House. Formerly the town house of the Earl of Annesley, it was purchased for £5,100 and a deposit was paid in 1803. However, it was not until 1814 that designs were publicly invited for the new church. A design of uncertain authorship, marked only with the letter 'P', for a church in the form of a Grecian Doric temple, was chosen as the winner. The only substantial alteration to the design was the erection of a dome.

The foundation stone was laid by Archbishop Troy in 1815. On the feast of St Laurence O'Toole in 1825, Archbishop Murray celebrated High Mass, to mark the dedication of the church to the 'Conception of the Virgin Mary', to a packed congregation, which included Daniel O'Connell. After the dedication, the interior embellishment of the church continued. Highlights included the alto relief representation of the Ascension by John Smyth; the high altar carved by Peter Turnerelli, and the marble statues of Archbishops Murray and Cullen by Thomas Farrell. Stained-glass windows, depicting Our Lady flanked by St Laurence O'Toole and St Kevin, were installed behind the sanctuary in 1886. The high point of liturgical embellishment was the generous benefaction by Edward Martyn, who endowed the Palestrina choir for male voices in 1902.

**Emeritus Archbishop**
**His Eminence Desmond Cardinal Connell**
born in Dublin 24 March 1926; ordained
priest 19 May 1951; ordained Archbishop
of Dublin 6 March 1988; created Cardinal
21 February 2001
*Address:* Archbishop's House,
Drumcondra, Dublin 9
Tel 01-8373732 Fax 01-8369796

**Most Rev Eamonn Walsh DD, VG**
Titular Bishop of Elmham;
Auxiliary Bishop of Dublin; ordained
Bishop 22 April 1990
*Residence:* Naomh Brid,
Blessington Road, Tallaght, Dublin 24
Tel/Fax 01-4598032

**Most Rev Raymond Field DD, VG**
Titular Bishop of Ard Mor;
Auxiliary Bishop of Dublin; ordained
Bishop 21 September 1997
*Residence:* 3 Castleknock Road,
Blanchardstown, Dublin 15
Tel/Fax 01-8209191

**Most Rev Dermot O'Mahony DD**
Titular Bishop of Tiava; former Auxiliary
Bishop of Dublin; ordained Bishop
13 April 1975
*Residence:* 19 Longlands,
Swords, Co Dublin
Tel 01-8401596 Fax 01-8403950

**Most Rev Fiachra Ó Ceallaigh DD, VG**
Titular Bishop of Tre Taverne; former
Auxiliary Bishop of Dublin; ordained
Bishop 17 September 1994
*Residence:* 19 St Anthony's Road, Rialto,
Dublin 8
Tel 01-4537495 Fax 01-4544966

**Episcopal Vicar with responsibility for
the deaneries of Howth, Fingal South
East and Fingal South West**
Rt Rev Mgr John Fitzpatrick PP
3 Glencarraig, Church Road,
Sutton, Co Dublin
Tel 01-8323147

**Episcopal Vicar with responsibility for
the deaneries of Bray, Donnybrook, Dun
Laoghaire and Wicklow**
Rt Rev Mgr Enda Lloyd Co-PP
Cluain Mhuire, Killarney Road,
Bray, Co Wicklow

**Episcopal Vicar with responsibility for
the deaneries of Cullenswood, North
City Centre and South City Centre**
Rt Rev Mgr Dermot A. Clarke
4 Griffith Avenue, Marino
Dublin 3

**Moderator of the Curia**
Very Rev Mgr Paul Callan VG
Archbishop's House,
Drumcondra, Dublin 9
Tel 01-8373732

**Office for Clergy**
Head of the Office for Clergy
Most Rev Eamonn Walsh DD, VG

**Vicar for Evangelisation and Ecumenism**
Very Rev Kieran McDermott
Holy Cross Diocesan Centre,
Clonliffe Road, Dublin 3
Tel 01-8379353

## CHAPTER

*Dean:* Most Rev Dermot O'Mahony DD
*Precentor:* Most Rev Eamonn Walsh DD, VG
*Chancellor:* Rt Rev Mgr James Ardle
Canon MacMahon
*Treasurer:* Rt Rev Mgr Owen Canon Sweeney
*Archdeacon of Dublin*
Ven Archdeacon Macarten Brady
*Archdeacon of Glendalough:*
Ven Archdeacon Kevin Lyon CC
*Prebendaries*
*Cullen:* Very Rev Martin Canon Cosgrove,
Moderator
Parochial House, Arklow, Co Wicklow
*Kilmactalway*
Very Rev James Canon Fingleton
279 Howth Road, Raheny, Dublin 5
*Swords:* Vacant
*Yago:* Very Rev Damian Canon O'Reilly Adm
Pro-Cathedral House,
83 Marlborough Street, Dublin 1
*St Audoen's*
Very Rev Bernard Canon Brady
61 Glasnevin Hill, Dublin 9
*Clonmethan*
Very Rev Walter Canon Harris PE
151 Clonsilla Road, Blanchardstown,
Dublin 15
*Wicklow*
Very Rev Erill D. Canon O'Connor
14 Clare Road, Drumcondra, Dublin 9
*Timothan:* Very Rev Patrick Canon Fagan PE
The Presbytery, Ballyboughal, Co Dublin
*Malahidert*
Very Rev Raymond T. Canon Molony
Presbytery No. 2, Thormanby Road,
Howth, Co Dublin
*Castleknock*
Very Rev Diarmuid Canon Connolly
4 Summerfield Lawn, Blanchardstown,
Dublin 15
*Tipper:* Rev John Canon Piert PC
The Presbytery, Johnstown,
Arklow, Co Wicklow
*Tassagard*
Very Rev Maurice Canon O'Moore PE
6 Richmond Avenue, Monkstown, Co Dublin
*Dunlavin*
Very Rev Francis Canon McDonnell
*Maynooth:* Very Rev Sean Canon Smith CC
The Presbytery, Newtownmountkennedy,
Co Wicklow
*Howth:* Very Rev John Canon Flaherty,
Moderator, Parochial House,
Sperrin Road, Drimnagh, Dublin 12
*Rathmichael*
Very Rev Ciarán Canon Holahan
11 Foxrock Court, Foxrock, Dublin 18
*Monmahenock*
Rt Rev Mgr Andrew P. Canon Boland PE
13 Griffith Avenue, Dublin 9
*Stagonilly:* Very Rev Peadar Canon Murney
25 Thomastown Road, Dun Laoghaire,
Co Dublin
*Tipperkevin, 1a pars*
Very Rev John Canon Fitzgibbon PE
The Presbytery, Chapel Road,
Lusk, Co Dublin
*Tipperkevin, 2a pars*
Very Rev James A. Canon Randles PE
Sacred Heart Residence, Sybil Hill Road,
Killester, Dublin 5
*Donaghmore, 1a pars*
Very Rev John Canon MacMahon PE
Holy Family Residence, Roebuck Road,
Dundrum, Dublin 14

*Donaghmore, 2a pars*
Very Rev Michael D. Canon Supple
Holy Family Residence, Roebuck Road,
Dublin 14

**Deaneries and Vicars Forane**
*Bray*
Very Rev Laurence Behan *(Moderator)* VF
Parochial House, St Fergal's,
Killarney Road, Bray, Co Wicklow
Tel 01-2768191
*Dun Laoghaire:* Vacant
*Wicklow:* Very Rev Martin Canon
Cosgrove *(Moderator)* VF
Parochial House, Arklow, Co Wicklow
Tel 0402-32294
*Donnybrook*
Very Rev Richard Behan *(Moderator)* VF
Presbytery No. 1, Ballinteer Avenue,
Dublin 16
*South City Centre*
Very Rev Patrick Boyle Adm, VF
87A St Stephen's Green, Dublin 2
Tel 01-4780616
*North City Centre*
Very Rev Donal Neary (SJ) PP, VF
Presbytery, Upper Gardiner Street, Dublin 1
Tel 01-8363411
*Cullenswood:* Very Rev John Canon
Flaherty VF *(Moderator)*
Parochial House, Sperrin Road, Dublin 12
Tel 01-4556103
*South Dublin:* Very Rev Martin Noone,
Moderator & Co-PP, VF
St Mary's Presbytery, Willbrook Road,
Dublin 14
Tel 01-4954554
*Tallaght*
Very Rev Patrick McKinley *(Moderator)* VF
68 Maplewood Road, Springfield,
Tallaght, Dublin 24
Tel 01-4513109
*Blessington*
Very Rev Gerard Tanham PP, VF
Parochial House, 1 Stanhope Place, Athy,
Co Kildare
Tel 059-8631781
*Fingal North:* Very Rev Eugene Taaffe PP, VF
Apt 2, The Presbytery, Balbriggan,
Co Dublin
Tel 01-6903391
*Finglas*
Very Rev Liam McClarey (SCA) PP, VF
Parochial House, Corduff,
Blanchardstown, Dublin 15
Tel 01-8213596
*Maynooth*
Very Rev Damian Farnon *(Moderator)* VF
St Cecilia's, New Road, Clondalkin,
Dublin 22
Tel 01-4592665
*Fingal South-East*
Very Rev Leo Philomin (OMI) PP
The Presbytery, Darndale, Dublin 17
*Fingal South-West*
Very Rev Patrick F. Carroll Co-PP, VF
124 New Cabra Road, Dublin 7
Tel 01-8385244
*Howth*
Very Rev Eoin McCrystal *(Moderator)* VF
12 Grangemore Grove, Donaghmede,
Dublin 5
Tel 01-8474652

## College of Consultors
Most Rev Eamonn Walsh DD, VG
Most Rev Raymond Field DD, VG
Rt Rev Mgr John Fitzpatrick, EV
Rt Rev Mgr Enda Lloyd EV
Very Rev Mgr Dermot A. Clarke EV
Rev Gareth Byrne, Council of Priests
Very Rev Kieran McDermott EV for
Evangelisation and Ecumenism
Very Rev Donal Neary (SJ) PP
Rt Rev Mgr Lorcan O'Brien Adm

## ADMINISTRATION

### Moderator of the Curia
Very Rev Mgr Paul Callan
Office of the Moderator,
Archbishop's House, Dublin 9
Tel 01-8379347

### Chancellor
Rt Rev Mgr John Dolan LCL
The Chancellery,
Archbishop's House, Dublin 9
Tel 01-8379253 Fax 8571650

### Ecclesiastical Censor
Rt Rev Mgr John Dolan
The Chancellery, Archbishop's House,
Dublin 9
Tel 01-8379253

### Diocesan Archivist
Ms Noelle Dowling
Holy Cross Diocesan Centre,
Clonliffe Road, Dublin 3
Tel 01-8379253

### Vicar for Religious
Sr Elizabeth Cotter
Archbishop's House, Dublin 9
Tel 01-8379253

### Financial Administrator
*Acting Financial Adminitrator:*
Ide Finnegan
Finance Secretariat,
Holy Cross Diocesan Centre,
Clonliffe Road, Dublin 3
Tel 01-8379253 Fax 01-8368393

### Master of Ceremonies to the Archbishop
Rev Damian McNeice
Diocesan Liturgical Resource Centre,
Holy Cross College, Clonliffe, Dublin 3
Tel 01-8379253 Ext 238

### Archbishop's Secretary
Mr Joseph Merrick
Archbishop's House, Drumcondra, Dublin 9
Tel 01-8373732 Fax 01-8369796

### *Vicar for Evangelisation and Ecumenism*
Very Rev Kieran McDermott
Holy Cross Diocesan Centre,
Clonliffe Road, Dublin 3
Tel 01-8373732

### *Child Safeguarding and Protection Service*
Tel 01-8360314 Fax 01-8842599
Email cps@dublindiocese.ie
Website www.cps.dublindiocese.ie
*Director:* Mr Andrew Fagan
Tel 01-8842590
*Priest Delegate:* Rev Richard Shannon

### *Child Safeguarding and Protection Training Co-ordinator*
Rev Paddy Boyle
Email p.boyle@dublindiocese.ie

### *Communications Office*
*Director:* Ms Annette O'Donnell
Tel 01-8360723 Fax 01-8360793
Email annetteodonell@dublindiocese.ie
Website www.dublindiocese.ie

### *Diocesan Office for Public Affairs*
*Director:* Vacant

### *Education*
*Director:* Ms Anne McDonagh
Tel 01-8379253 Fax 01-8368393
Email amcdonagh@dubcated.org
*Senior Education Specialists*
Ms Catherine Hennessy
Email chennessy@abhouse.org
Mr Declan Lawlor
Email dlawlor@abhouse.org

### *Finance*
*Acting Financial Administrator*
Ms Ide Finnegan ACMA
Email i.finnegan@abfinance.org

### *Diocesan Liturgical Resource Centre*
*Director:* Rev Pat O'Donoghue
Email pod@dublindiocese.ie

## DIOCESAN COMMITTEES

### Clerical Fund Society
Holy Cross Diocesan Centre,
Clonliffe Road, Dublin 3
Tel 01-8379253
*President:* The Archbishop of Dublin
*Vice-Presidents:* The Vicars General

### Standing Committee
*Chairperson:* Most Rev Eamonn Walsh DD
*Secretary:* Ms Ide Finnegan

### Commission on Parish Boundaries
c/o Archbishop's House,
Drumcondra, Dublin 9
Tel 01-8379253
*Chairperson:* Mr Willie Soffe
*Secretary:* Ms Anne Donnellan

### Common Fund Executive Committee
Holy Cross Diocesan Centre,
Clonliffe Road, Dublin 3
Tel 01-8379253
*Chairperson:* Very Rev Anthony Reilly
*Secretary:* Ms Ide Finnegan

### Finance Committee
Holy Cross Diocesan Centre,
Clonliffe Road, Dublin 3
Tel 01-8379253
*Chairperson:* Mr Jim McKenna
*Secretary:* Ms Ide Finnegan

## CATECHETICS EDUCATION

### Diocesan Advisers for Religious Education in Primary Schools
Education Secretariat,
Archbishop's House, Drumcondra, Dublin 9
Tel 01-8379253 Fax 01-8368393
Sr Anne Neylon, Ms Breda Holmes,
Ms Helen Leacy
*All at the Education Secretariat*

### Diocesan Advisors for Religious Education in Post-Primary Schools
Ms Anna Maloney

## LITURGY

### Commission for Sacred Art and Architecture & Historic Churches
*Chairperson:* Edward O'Shea
*Secretary:* Anne Donnellan

## PASTORAL

### ACCORD
Ms Barbara Gilroy (Dublin Director)
35 Harcourt Street, Dublin 2
Tel 01-4780866 Fax 01-4750462
Email admin@dublin.accord.ie

### Catholic Guides of Ireland
*Diocesan Chaplain:* Vacant

### CROSSCARE
**Catholic Social Care Agency, Dublin Archdiocese**
*Chairperson:* Mr Frank O'Connell
*Director:* Mr Conor Hickey
Holy Cross College, Clonliffe, Dublin 3
Tel 01-8360011 Fax 01-8367166

### Committee for the Continuing Formation of Priests
c/o Archbishop's House, Dublin 9
Tel 01-8375107

### Council of Priests
*President:* Most Rev Diarmuid Martin DD
*Chairperson:* Rev Gareth Byrne

### CÚNAMH
30 South Anne Street, Dublin 2
Tel 01-6710598

### CURA
16 Suffolk Street (3rd floor), Dublin 2
Tel 01-6778588

### Dublin Roman Catholic Diocesan Hospital Chaplains Association
*Chairperson of Committee:*
Rev John Kelly
Chaplain, Tallaght Hospital
Tel 01-4142482
Email john.kelly@amnch.ie

### Ecumenism
*Chairperson and Secretary*
Very Rev Kieran McDermott

**Knock Diocesan Pilgrimage**
*Director:* Very Rev David Lumsden PP
83 Tonlegee Drive, Edenmore,
Dublin 5
Tel 01-8480917

**Legion of Mary**
*Diocesan Chaplain:* Vacant

**Lourdes Diocesan Pilgrimage**
*Director:* Very Rev Martin Noone VF
Lourdes Pilgrimage Office,
Holy Cross College, Clonliffe, Dublin 3
Tel 01-8376820

**Marriage Tribunal**
(See Marriage Tribunals section)

**National Chaplaincy for Deaf People**
*Chaplain:* Rev Gerard Tyrrell
Tel 01-8305744
Email gerard@ncdp.ie
Website www.ncdp.ie

**Permanent Diaconate**
*Diocesan Director*
Very Rev John Gilligan Adm
*Assistant Directors*
Very Rev Joseph Mullan PP
Rev Noel Ryan
Holy Cross Diocesan Centre,
Clonliffe Road, Dublin 3
Tel 01-8087531

**Pontifical Mission Societies**
*Diocesan Director*
Very Rev Patrick Carroll PP
124 New Cabra Road, Dublin 7
Tel 01-8385244

**Travellers**
*Ministry to the Travelling People (Dublin Diocese):* Very Rev Derek Farrell PP
*Office:* St Laurence House,
6 New Cabra Road, Phibsboro, Dublin 7
Tel 01-8388874/087-2573857
Fax 01-8388901
Email partravs@iol.ie

**Vocations**
*Director:* Very Rev John Gilligan
Holy Cross College, Clonliffe,
Dublin 3
Tel 01-8379253

## PARISHES

*Mensal parishes are listed first. Other parishes follow alphabetically. Church titulars are in italics.*

**PRO-CATHEDRAL**
*St Mary's (Immaculate Conception)*
*Marlborough Street, Dublin 1*
Very Rev Damian F. Canon O'Reilly Adm
Rev Michael O'Grady CC
Rt Rev Mgr Francis Walsh PC
Rev Brendan Staunton (SJ) PC
*Parish Sister:* Sr Patricia Somers (RSC)
Pro-Cathedral House,
83 Marlborough Street, Dublin 1
Tel 01-8745441 Fax 01-8742406
Email procath@dublindiocese.ie
Website www.procathedral.ie

**WESTLAND ROW**
*St Andrew's, Westland Row, Dublin 2*
Very Rev John Gilligan Adm, VF
Tel 01-7005268(w)/8368746(h)
Email john.gilligan@dcu.ie
Rev Patrick Moran CC
Rev Jeremiah Markus PC
47 Westland Row, Dublin 2
Tel 085-2778177
Rev Patrick Gleeson *(Chaplain, Trinity College)*
48 Westland Row Tel 01-6767316
Trinity College Tel 01-8961260
Rev Egidijus Arnasius
48 Westland Row
Tel 01-6761030/087-7477554
Email arnasius@gmail.com
Rev Anthony Hou
Chaplain to the Chinese Community
*Parish Office:* Tel 01-6761270 Fax 01-6763544
Email westlandrow@dublindiocese.ie
Website www.saintandrewsparish.ie

**CITY QUAY**
*Immaculate Heart of Mary, Dublin 2*
Rev Pearse Walsh Adm
The Presbytery, City Quay, Dublin 2
*Parish Office:* Tel 01-6773073
Website jocityquayparish@gmail.com

**SEAN MCDERMOTT STREET**
*Our Lady of Lourdes,*
*Sean McDermott Street, Dublin 1*
Rev Richard Ebejer (SDB) Adm
Tel 01-8363358
Rev Cyril Odia (SDB) CC
72 Sean McDermott Street, Dublin 1
Rev Eugen Timpu, Chaplain to Romanian Community
*Parish Office:* Tel 01-8551259/086-8382631
Email seanmcdermott@dublindiocese.ie

**ARDLEA**
*St John Vianney, Ardlea Road,*
*Artane, Dublin 5*
Very Rev Hugh Hanley (SCJ), *(Moderator)*
Rev Michel Simo Temgo (SCJ) CC
Rev Marian Szalwa (SCJ) PC
Parochial House, St John Vianney,
Ardlea Road, Dublin 5
Tel 01-8474173
*Parish Sister:* Sr Nellie Barron (SJG)
*Parish Office:* Tel 01-8474123
Email st.jvianney@yahoo.ie

**ARKLOW**
(Grouped with the parish of Castletown)
*SS Mary and Peter, Arklow, Co Wicklow*
*Chapel of Ease: St David's, Johnstown,*
*Co Wicklow*
Very Rev Martin Canon Cosgrove
*(Moderator),* VF
Parochial House, Arklow, Co Wicklow
Tel/Fax 0402-32294
Email mfc53@indigo.ie
Rev Michael Murtagh Co-PP
2 St Mary's Terrace, Arklow, Co Wicklow
Tel 0402-41505
Very Rev John Canon Piert PC
The Presbytery, Johnstown, Arklow,
Co Wicklow
Tel 0402-31112

Rev Binoy Mathew Kombanathottathil (SVD) Co-PP
Presbytery No. 2, St Mary's Terrace,
Arklow, Co Wicklow
*Parish Office:* Tel/Fax 0402-31716
Email office@arklowparish.ie
www.arklowparish.ie

**ARTANE**
*Our Lady of Mercy, Brookwood Grove,*
*Dublin 5*
Rt Rev Mgr Alex Stenson PP
126 Furry Park Road, Killester, Dublin 5
Tel 01-8333793
Rev Brian Durnin CC
12 Brookwood Grove, Artane
Tel 01-8187996
*Parish Office*
Tel 01-8314297 Fax 01-8314054
Email ourladyofmercy.church@gmail.com

**ASHFORD**
*Church of the Most Holy Rosary, Co Wicklow*
Very Rev Eamonn Crosson Adm
Parochial House, Ashford, Co Wicklow
Tel/Fax 0404-40540

**ATHY**
*St Michael's, Co Kildare*
Very Rev Gerard Tanham PP
Parochial House, 1 Stanhope Place,
Athy, Co Kildare
Tel 059-8631781/087-2311947
Email gerardtanham@eircom.net
Rev Timothy Hannon CC
3 Stanhope Place, Athy
Tel 059-8631698
Very Rev Philip Dennehy PE
4 Stanhope Place, Athy
Tel 059-8631696
Email pdenn@eircom.net
Rev Brendan Kealy CC
12 Ashville, Athy, Co Kildare
Tel 087-9117575
Aine Egan PPW
5 Abbey Court, Properous Road, Clane,
Co Kildare
*Parish Office:* Tel 059-8638391
Email athyparishrc@eircom.net
Website www.stmichaelsathy.net

**AUGHRIM**
*The Most Sacred Heart, Co Wicklow*
Very Rev Martin Canon Cosgrove
*(Moderator),* VF
Parochial House, Arklow, Co Wicklow
Tel 0402-32294
Very Rev Edward Barry Co-PP
Parochial House, Aughrim, Co Wicklow
Tel 0402-36298

**AUGHRIM STREET**
*The Holy Family, Dublin 7*
Rev Patrick Madden Adm
Parochial House,
34 Aughrim Street, Dublin 7
Tel 01-8386571
Rev Gerard Young CC
Presbytery No 3, Most Sacred Heart Parish,
St Joseph's Road, Dublin 7
Mairin Keegan PPW
Email mairin.keegan@dublindiocese.ie

## AVOCA
*SS Mary and Patrick, Co Wicklow*
Very Rev Martin Canon Cosgrove PP
Parochial House, Arklow, Co Wicklow
Tel 0402-32294
Very Rev Diarmuid Byrne Co-PP
Parochial House, Avoca, Co Wicklow
Rev Thomas Coughlan (*Assistant Priest*) PC
The Presbytery, Avoca, Co Wicklow
Tel 0402-35204
Rev Sean O'Toole (retired)
Tel 0402-32153
*Parish Offices:* Avoca Tel 0402-35156
Templerainey Tel 0402-31943
Email Avoca avpar@eircom.net
Templerainey stjoseph@eircom.net

## AYRFIELD
*St Paul's, Dublin 13*
*Team Assistant:* Rev Niall McDermott
8 Slademore Close, Ard-na-Gréine,
Ayrfield, Dublin 13
Tel 01-8470685
Very Rev Thomas Colreavy *(Team Assistant)*
Very Rev Gerard Corcoran Co-PP
*Parish Office:* Tel 01-8160984
Email parishofficeayrfield@eircom.net
Website www.stpaulsparishayrfield.com

## BALALLY
*Church of the Ascension of The Lord, Dublin 16*
Rt Rev Mgr Dermot A. Lane DD, Co-PP
162 Sandyford Road, Dublin 16
Tel 01-2956165
Email dalane@eircom.net
*Team Assistant:* Rev Peter Byrne LC
The Presbytery, Hawthorns Road,
Co Dublin
Tel 01-2952869
*Parish Office:* Tel 01-2954296
Email parishofbalally@eircom.net
Website www.balallyparish.ie

## BALBRIGGAN
*SS Peter and Paul, Balbriggan, Co Dublin*
Very Rev Eugene Taaffe PP, VF
Apt 2, The Presbytery Parish of SS Peter & Paul, Dublin Road, Balbriggan, Co Dublin
Tel 01-6903391
Rev Paul Dunne CC
Apt 1 The Presbytery, Balbriggan,
Co Dublin
Tel 01-9680594
*Parish Pastoral Worker:* Niamh Morris
Tel 01-8412116
*Parish Office:* Tel 01-8412116 Fax 01-6904834
Email balbrigganparishoffice@gmail.com

## BALCURRIS
*St Joseph's, Ballymun*
Rev Eamon Sheridan (SSC) PP
Tel 01-8423865
Rev Gerard French (SSC)
Very Rev John Chute (SSC) CC
St Joseph's, Balcurris, Ballymun, Dublin 11
Tel 01-8423865
*Parish Office:* Tel 01-8423865

## BALDOYLE
*SS Peter and Paul, Dublin 13*
Very Rev Peter O'Connor Co-PP
The Presbytery, Baldoyle, Dublin 13
Tel 01-8322060
*Parish Office:* Tel 01-8324313
Email info@baldoyleparish.ie
Website www.baldoyleparish.ie

## BALLINTEER
*Ballinteer parish is now under the Team Ministry of Dundrum/Ballinteer/Meadowbrook*
*St John the Evangelist, Ballinteer Avenue, Dublin 16*
Very Rev Richard M. Behan, VF *(Moderator)*
Presbytery No 1, Ballinteer Avenue,
Dublin 16
Tel 01-4944448
Email rmfb@eircom.net
*Team Assistants*
Rev Charles Abba Donboyi
Rev Matthias E. Kulitunam
149 Ludford Road, Meadowbrook,
Ballinteer, Dublin 16
Tel 01-2987401
Rev Deacon Noel Ryan
*Parish Office:* Tel 01-4994203
Email parishoffice@ballinteer.dublindiocese.ie
Website www.ballinteer.dublindiocese.ie

## BALLYBODEN
*Our Lady of Good Counsel, Dublin 16*
Very Rev Flor O'Callaghan (OSA) PP
Tel 01-4944966
Rev Noel Hession (OSA) CC
Tel 01-4543356
Rev Dick Lyng (OSA) CC
St Augustine's, Taylors Lane,
Ballyboden, Dublin 16
*Parish Office:* Tel 01-4944966
Website www.ballybodenparish.com

## BALLYBRACK-KILLINEY
*SS Alphonsus and Columba, Co Dublin*
Very Rev Alex Conlan *(Moderator)*
Parochial House, Ballybrack, Co Dublin
Tel 01-2826404
Email alexconlan_ie@yahoo.com
Very Rev Michael A. O'Kelly Co-PP
39 Oakton Park, Ballybrack
Tel 01-2827282
*Parish Offices:* St Alphonsus & Columba
Tel 01-2820788
St Stephens Tel 01-2854512
Church of the Apostles Tel 01-2024804
Website
www.ballybrack-killiney-parish.org

## BALLYFERMOT
*Our Lady of the Assumption, Dublin 10*
Rev Richard Delahunty (CSsR) PP & Coordinator
Rev Cornelius Kenneally (CSsR) CC
Rev Stan Mellett (CSsR) CC
197 Kylemore Road, Ballyfermot,
Dublin 10
*Parish Office:* Tel 01-6264691
*Community:* Tel 01-5356977

## BALLYFERMOT UPPER
*St Matthew, Blackditch Road, Dublin 10*
Rev Joseph McDonald Adm
No 2, 148D Presbytery, Blackditch Road,
Dublin 10
Tel 01-6265119
Very Rev Seamus Ryan PE
No 1, 148B Presbytery, Blackditch Road,
Dublin 10
Tel 01-6265695 Fax 01-6230654
*Parish Office:* Tel 01-6265695 Fax 01-6230654
Website www.stmatthewsballyfermot.com

## BALLYGALL
*Our Mother of Divine Grace, Ballygall Road East, Dublin 11*
Very Rev Joseph Ryan Co-PP
41 Cremore Heights, St Canice's Road,
Glasnevin, Dublin 11
Tel 01-8573776
Rev Damian McNeice PC
4 Claremount Drive, Ballygall, Dublin 11
Tel 01-8087553
Very Rev Harry Gaynor Co-PP
112 Ballygall Road East, Glasnevin, Dublin 11
Tel 01-8342248
*Parish Office:* Tel 01-8369291
Email omdgballygallchurch@eircom.net
Website www.ballygallparish.ie

## BALLYMORE EUSTACE
*Immaculate Conception, Naas, Co Kildare*
Rt Rev Mgr John Wilson Adm
Parochial House, Ballymore Eustace,
Naas, Co Kildare
Tel 045-864114
Email jacw@gofree.indigo.ie
Rev James Prendiville CC
The Presbytery, Hollywood (via Naas),
Co Wicklow
Tel 045-864206
*Parish Office:* Tel 045-864114
Email hwparishoffice@gmail.com

## BALLYMUN/SILLOGUE
*Church of the Virgin Mary, Ballymun, Dublin 9*
Very Rev Declan Blake
Presbytery No. 2, Shangan Road,
Dublin 9
Tel 01-8421551/8621031
Rev Anthony Omolade
Presbytery, Silloge Road, Ballymun,
Dublin 11
Rev Deacon Steve Maher
*Parish Office:* 01-8421551/086-3455745
Website moelitreacha@eircom.net

## BALLYMUN ROAD
*Our Lady of Victories, Ballymun Road, Dublin 9*
Very Rev Colm Kenny Co-PP
137 Ballymun Road, Dublin 11
Tel 01-8376341
Rev Fintan Gavin PC
97 Ballymun Road, Dublin 9
Tel 01-8375440
Rev Patrick Sweeney PC
13 Home Farm Road, Drumcondra,
Dublin 9
Tel 01-8377402
*Assistant Priest:* Rev Eoin Murphy
25 The Haven, Glasnevin, Dubin 9
Tel 086-8831791
*Parish Office:* Tel 01-8420346
Email info@olv.ie

## BALLYROAN
*Ballyroan Parish is now under the Team Ministry of Rathfarnham/Churchtown/ Ballyroan*
Church of the Holy Spirit, Marian Road, Dublin 14
Very Rev Brendan Madden PP
67 Anne Devlin Park, Ballyroan, Dublin 14
Tel 01-4037536
*Parish Office:* Tel 01-4947303
Email ballyroanparish@gmail.com
Website www.ballyroanparish.ie

## BAWNOGUE
*Clondalkin/Rowlagh/Neilstown/ Deansrath/Bawnogue Grouping*
Church of the Transfiguration, Bawnogue, Clondalkin, Dublin 22
Very Rev Damian Farnon *(Moderator)*
Presbytery, Bawnogue, Clondalkin, Dublin 22
Tel 01-4519810
Email transfig2000@yahoo.com
www.bawnogueparish.com

## BAYSIDE
*Church of the Resurrection, Bayside, Dublin 13*
Very Rev Paul Ward PP
Parochial House, Bayside Square North, Sutton, Dublin 13
Tel 01-8323150
Email wardp@iol.ie
Rev Joe Kelly CC
5 Bayside Square East, Sutton, Dublin 13
Tel 01-8322305
Email gradyjoe1@eircom.net
Rev Christopher Sheridan CC
7 Bayside Square East, Sutton, Dublin 13
Tel 01-8322964
*Parish Office:* Tel 01-8323083
Email baysidercchurch@eircom.net
Website www.baysideparish.ie

## BEAUMONT
*(Grouped with the parishes of Larkhill, Whitehall, Santry & Kilmore Road West)*
Church of Nativity of Our Lord, Dublin 5
Very Rev Gerard Deegan Adm
Tel 01-8710013
Rev Dan An Nguyen CC
Presbytery, Montrose Park, Beaumont, Dublin 5
Tel 01-8476359
*Parish Office:*
Tel 01-8477740 Fax 01-8473209

## BEECHWOOD AVENUE
*Church of the Holy Name, Dublin 6*
Rev Bernard Kennedy MA, MSc, Adm
67 Edenvale Road, Dublin 6
Tel 01-4972165
Email b.kennedy@esatclear.ie
Rev Joseph Doran AP
Rev Paul Freeney PE
Parochial House, 43 Beechwood Avenue Upper, Ranelagh, Dublin 6
Tel 01-4972687
*Parish Office:* Tel 01-4967449
Email info@beechwoodparish.com
Website info@beechwoodparish.com

## BERKELEY ROAD
*St Joseph's, Dublin 7*
Rev David Donnellan (OCD) PP
Rev Patrick Keenan (OCD) CC
Tel 01-8306356/8306336
Rev Patrick Beecher (OCD) CC
The Presbytery, Berkeley Road, Dublin 7
*Parish Office:* Tel 01-8302071

## BLACKROCK
*St John the Baptist, Blackrock, Co Dublin*
Very Rev John Delany Adm
24 Barclay Court, Blackrock, Co Dublin
Tel 01-2832302
Very Rev Edward Conway PC
1 Maretimo Gardens West, Blackrock, Co Dublin
Tel 01-2882248
Email eddieconway@indigo.ie
*Parish Office:* Tel 01-2882104
Email saintjohnthebaptist@eircom.net

## BLAKESTOWN
*Blakestown Parish is now under the Team Ministry of Blakestown/Hartstown/ Huntstown/Mountview*
St Mary of the Servants, Dublin 15
Very Rev Liam Ó Cuív Co-PP
The Presbytery Blakestown, Clonsilla, Dublin 15
Tel 01-8210874
Email liamocuiv@yahoo.com
*Parish Office:* Tel 01-8210874
Email blakestownparish@dublindiocese.ie

## BLANCHARDSTOWN
*St Brigid's*
Very Rev Cyril Mangan Adm *(Adm Mulhuddart)*
Parochial House, Blanchardstown, Dublin 15
Tel 01-8213660
Rev John Casey (CSsR), CC
28 Broadway Road, Blanchardstown, Dublin 15
Tel 01-8213716
Email johnffcasey@eircom.net
Rev Patrick Guckian CC
44 Woodview Grove, Blanchardstown, Dublin 15
Tel 01-8262799
Kevin Mullaly PPW
8 Finglaswood Road, Finglas West, Dublin 11
*Parish Office:* Tel 01-8238354

## BLESSINGTON
*(Grouped with the parish of Valleymount)*
Church of Our Lady
Very Rev Timothy Murphy PP
The Presbytery, Main Street, Blessington, Co Wicklow
Tel 045-865442
Email office@blessington.info
*Our Lady of Mercy, Crosschapel*
Archdeacon Kevin Lyon CC
Parochial House, Crosschapel, Blessington, Co Wicklow
Tel 045-865215
Email lyonk@indigo.ie

*St Brigid's Church, Manor Kilbride*
Rev Paraic McDermott (CSSp) CC
The Presbytery, Manor Kilbride, Blessington, Co Wicklow
Tel 01-4582154
*Parish Office:* Tel/Fax 045-865327
Email office@blessington.info
Website www.blessington.info

## BLUEBELL
*Bluebell Parish is now under the Team Ministry of Inchicore (Mary Immaculate & St Michael's) & Bluebell*
Our Lady of the Wayside, Dublin 12
Rev Anthony Clancy (OMI)
Rev Peter Clucas (OMI)
Oblate Fathers House of Retreat, Inchicore, Dublin 8
Tel 01-4541117
*Parish Office:* Tel 01-4501040
Website www.oblateparishesindublin.ie

## BOHERNABREENA
*St Anne's, Dublin 24*
Very Rev Michael Hurley Adm
85 Tymon Crescent, Oldbawn, Dublin 24
Tel/Fax 01-4627080
Rev Piaras MacLochlainn CC
Parochial House, Bohernabreena, Dublin 1
Tel 01-4510986
*Parish Office:* Tel 01-4626893
Email bohernabreenaparish@eircom.net

## BONNYBROOK
*St Joseph's, Bonnybrook, Dublin 17*
Very Rev Joseph Jones *(Moderator)*
122 Greencastle Road, Dubin 17
Tel 01-8487657
Rev Frank Duggan CC
Parochial House No 2, Bonnybrook, Dublin 17
Tel 01-8485194
Deacon: Rev Jim Adams
c/o Parish Office
*Parish Office:* Tel 01-8485262

## BOOTERSTOWN
*Church of the Assumption*
Very Rev Cormac McIlraith Adm
52 Booterstown Avenue, Blackrock, Co Dublin
Tel 01-2882162
Rt Rev Mgr Seamus Conway PE
Parochial House, Booterstown, Co Dublin
Tel 01-2882889
*Parish Office:* Tel/Fax 01-2831593
Email info@booterstownparish.ie
Website www.booterstownparish.ie

## BRACKENSTOWN
*Swords/River Valley/Brackenstown Grouping*
St Cronan's
Very Rev Paul Thornton Adm
Parochial House, Brackenstown Road, Swords, Co Dublin
Tel 01-8401661
Rev Rajeev Thomas Njanackal CC
Parochial House, Brackenstown Road, Swords, Co Dublin
Tel 01-8408926
*Parish Office:* Tel 01-8401188
Email brackenstownparish@gmail.com
www.brackenstown.dublindiocese.ie

## BRAY (BALLYWALTRIM)
*St Fergal's, Bray, Co Wicklow*
Very Rev Laurence Behan *(Moderator)*, VF
Tel 01-2768191
Rev Hugh O'Donnell (OFM) *(Assistant)*
St Fergal's, Killarney Road,
Bray, Co Wicklow
Tel 01-2860980
*Parish Office:* Tel 01-2860980
Fax 01-2768196
Email info@stfergalsbray.ie
Website www.stfergalsbray.ie

## BRAY (HOLY REDEEMER)
*Holy Redeemer, Main Street,*
*Bray, Co Wicklow*
Rt Rev Mgr Enda Lloyd Co-PP, EV
Cluain Mhuire, Killarney Road,
Bray, Co Wicklow
Tel 01-2862026
Email padreenda@hotmail.com
Very Rev Robert Colclough Co-PP
'Shirley', Sidmonton Road,
Bray, Co Wicklow
Tel 01 2862955
Very Rev John O'Connell PE
53 Ardmore Wood, Herbert Road,
Bray, Co Wicklow
*Parish Office:* Tel 01-2868413
Email admin@holyredeemerbray.ie
Website www.holyredeemerbray.ie

## BRAY, PUTLAND ROAD
*Our Lady Queen of Peace*
Very Rev Joseph Whelan Co-PP
Parochial House, Putland Road, Bray,
Co Wicklow
Tel 01-2865723
*Team Assistant:* Rev Yusuf Bamai
c/o Parish Office
*Sacristy:* 01-2867303
Email secretary@queenofpeace.ie
*Parish Office:* Tel 01-2745497
*Villa Pacis – Parish Centre:* 01-2760045
Email villafas1@hotmail.com

## BRAY, ST PETER'S
*St Peter's, Little Bray, Co Wicklow*
Very Rev James Sheeran Co-PP
The Presbytery, Kilmacanogue, Co Wicklow
Tel 01-2862110
*In residence*
Very Rev Benedict Mulligan PE
42 Corke Abbey, Little Bray, Co Wicklow
Tel 01-2720224
*In residence*
Very Rev Edward Griffin (retired)
15 Connawood, Bray, Co Wicklow
Email stpeterslittlebray1@eircom.net

## BROOKFIELD
*St Aidan's, Brookfield Road*
Very Rev Jimmy McPartland Co-PP
1 Brookfield Road, Tallaght, Dublin 24
Email aodh@eircom.net
Tel 01-4590894

## CABINTEELY
*St Brigid's, Dublin 18*
Rev Arthur O'Neill Adm
1B Willow Court, Druid Valley,
Cabinteely, Dublin 18
Tel 087-2597520

Rt Rev Mgr Conor Ward *(Assistant)*
17 Prospect Lawn, The Park,
Cabinteely, Dublin 18
Tel 01-2850294
Rev Thomas O'Keeffe
20 Glen Avenue, The Park, Cabinteely
Tel 01-2853643

## CABRA
*Cabra Parish is now under the Team*
*Ministry of Cabra/Cabra West/Phibsboro*
*Christ the King, Dublin 7*
Very Rev Patrick F. Carroll Co-PP, VF
124 New Cabra Road, Dublin 7
Tel 01-8385244
Email pat47@eircom.net
Rev Thomas F. O'Shaughnessy *(Assistant*
*Priest)*
73 Annamoe Road, Dublin 7
Tel 01-8385626
*Parish Office:* Tel 01-8680804
Email christthekingchurch@eircom.net

## CABRA WEST
*Cabra West Parish is now under the Team*
*Ministry of Cabra/Cabra West/Phibsboro*
*Church of the Most Precious Blood, Dublin 7*
Very Rev John Greene *(Moderator)*
No 3 Presbytery, Dunmanus Court,
Cabra West, Dublin 7
Tel 01-8384325
*Parish Office:* Tel 01-8384418

## CASTLEDERMOT
*The Assumption, Castledermot, Co Kildare*
Very Rev Paul O'Driscoll Adm
Parochial House, Castledermot, Co Kildare
Tel 059-9144164
*Parish Office:* Tel/Fax 059-9144888

## CASTLEKNOCK
*Laurel Lodge/Carpenterstown/*
*Castleknock Grouping*
*Our Lady Mother of the Church*
*Castleknock, Dublin 15*
Very Rev Kieran Coghlan *(Moderator)*
6 Beechpark Lawn, Castleknock, Dublin 15
Tel 01-8212967/087-2425972
Rev Denis O'Connor (CSsR) CC
32 Auburn Drive, Dublin 15
Tel 01-8214003

## CASTLETOWN
*(Grouped with the parish of Arklow)*
*St Patrick's, Castletown, Co Wexford*
Very Rev Martin Canon Cosgrove
*(Moderator)*, VF
Parochial House, Arklow, Co Wicklow
Tel 0402-32294
Email mfc53@indigo.ie

## CELBRIDGE
*St Patrick's, Celbridge, Co Kildare*
Very Rev Paul Taylor PP
Tel 01-6275874
Rev Kevin Doherty CC
Parochial House, Celbridge, Co Kildare
Rev Douglas Zaggi PC
12 Coarsemoor Park, Staffon, Co Kildare
Tel 01-6012303
Rev Brian McKittrick CC
The Presbytery, Celbridge, Co Kildare
Tel 01-6274971
*Parish Office:* Tel 01-6288827
Email celbridgeparishoffice@gmail.com

## CHAPELIZOD
*Nativity of the BVM, Chapelizod, Dublin 20*
Rev Sean Mundow
The Presbytery, Chapelizod, Dublin 20
Tel 01-6264645/087-8195073
Rev Sean Mundow
The Presbytery, Chapelizod, Dublin 20
Tel 01-6264656

## CHERRY ORCHARD
*Most Holy Sacrament*
*Parish Team*
Very Rev Sean Duggan (CSsR) PP
Rev Patrick Reynolds (CSsR) CC
Email patcssr@yahoo.com
Presbytery, 103 Cherry Orchard Avenue,
Dublin 10
Tel 01-6267930
Rev Gerard O'Connor (CSsR) CC
52 Elmdale Park, Dublin 10
Tel 01-6267930

## CHURCHTOWN
*Churchtown Parish is now under the*
*Team Ministry of Rathfarnham/*
*Churchtown/Ballyroan*
*The Good Shepherd*
Very Rev Dermot Nestor Co-PP
Parochial House, Nutgrove Avenue,
Dublin 14
Tel 01-2985916
Very Rev Brian Edwards Co-PP
23 Oakdown Road, Dublin 14
Tel 01 2981744
*Emergencies:* Tel 087-2402585
*Parish Office:* Tel 01-2984642
Email info@goodshepherdchurchtown.ie
Website www.goodshepherdchurchtown.ie

## CLOGHER ROAD
*Clogher Parish is now under the Team*
*Ministry of Crumlin/Mourne Road/*
*Clogher Road*
*St Bernadette's*
Rev Melvyn Mullins
192 Sundrive Road, Dublin 12
Tel 01-4536988
Email mullins.melvyn@gmail.com
*Parish Office:* Tel 01-4733109
*Sacristy:* Tel 01-4535099
Email clogherroadparish@eircom.net
Website www.clogherroad.ie

## CLONDALKIN
*Clondalkin/Rowlagh/Neilstown/*
*Deansrath/Bawnogue Grouping*
*Immaculate Conception, Dublin 22*
Website www.clondalkin.dublindiocese.ie
Very Rev Damian Farnon *(Moderator)*
St Cecilia's, New Road, Clondalkin,
Dublin 22
Tel 01-4592665
Rev Padraig O'Sullivan Co-PP
St Columba Parish House, New Road,
Clondalkin, Dublin 22
Tel 01-4640441
Rev Seamus McEntee
St Mary's, New Road, Clondalkin,
Dublin 22

*Clonburris, Our Lady Queen of the Apostles*
Rev Shan O'Cuiv *(Team Assistant)*
c/o The Presbytery, Clonburris,
Clondalkin, Dublin 22
Tel 01-4573440
*Parish Office:* Tel 01-4640706

*Knockmitten*
Rev Desmond Byrne (CSSp) *(Team Assistant)*
45 Woodford Drive, Monastery Road,
Clondalkin, Dublin 22
Tel 01-4592323
*Parish Office:* Tel 01-4640706

## CLONSKEAGH
*Immaculate Virgin Mary of the Miraculous Medal, Bird Avenue, Dublin 14*
Very Rev William King PP
14 Rosemount Crescent,
Roebuck Road, Clonskeagh, Dublin 14
Tel 01-2697754
Rev James Larkin *(Assistant Priest)*
72 Bird Avenue, Clonskeagh, Dublin 14
Tel 01-2196869
*In residence:* Very Rev Maurice O'Shea PE
*Parish Office:* Tel/Fax 01-2837948
Email parishoffice@clonskeagh.org
Website www.clonskeaghparish.ie

## CLONTARF, ST ANTHONY'S
*St Anthony, Clontarf, Dublin 3*
Very Rev Larry White Co-PP
186 Clontarf Road, Clontarf, Dubin 3
Tel 01-8333394/086-4143888
Very Rev Patrick McManus *(Moderator)*
34 Dollymount Grove, Dublin 3
Tel 01-8057692/087-2371089
Rev Thomas McCarthy *(Team Assistant)*
119 The Stiles Road, Dublin 3
Tel 01-8338424
*Parish Office:* Tel 01-8333459
Email
saintanthonysclontarf@dublindiocese.ie
Website www.stanthonysclontarf.ie

## CLONTARF, ST JOHN'S
*St John the Baptist, Clontarf Road, Dublin 3*
Rev John Callanan (SJ) Co-PP
c/o St John the Baptist Church,
Clontarf Road, Dublin 3
Rev Martin Hogan Co-PP
187 Clontarf Road, Clontarf, Dublin 3
Tel 01-8338575
Very Rev Patrick McManus *(Moderator)*
34 Dollymount Grove, Dublin 3
Tel 01-8057692/087-2371089
*Parish Office:* Tel 01-8334606
Email sjtbclontarf@eircom.net
Website stjohnsclontarf.dublindiocese.ie

## CONFEY
*St Charles Borromeo, Leixlip, Co Kildare*
Rev Anthony O'Shaughnessy Adm
73 Newtown Park, Leixlip, Co Kildare
Tel 01-6244637
Rev Peter Clancy
75 Newtown Park, Leixlip, Co Kildare
Tel 01-6243533
*Parish Office:* Tel/Fax 01-6247410
Email confeyparish@gmail.com

## COOLOCK
*St Brendan's, Coolock Village, Dublin 5*
Rev John Hand (SM) *(Moderator)*
Email johnohand@eircom.net
*Superior:* Rev Joseph Rooney (SM)
Rev Kieran Butler (SM) PC
Rev Pat Byrne (SM) CC
The Presbytery, Coolock Village,
Dublin 5
Tel 01-8477133

*Parish Office:* Tel 01-8480102/01-8484799
*Parish Mobile:* 087-2269887
Email malachy@stbrendanscoolock.org
Website www.stbrendanscoolock.org

## CORDUFF
*St Patrick's, Corduff, Blanchardstown, Dublin 15*
Very Rev Liam McClarey (SAC) PP, VF
Parochial House, Corduff
Blanchardstown, Dublin 15
Tel 01-8213596
Email liammcclarey@eircom.net
Rev Joseph McLoughlin (SAC) CC
The Presbytery, Corduff,
Blanchardstown, Dublin 15
Tel 01-8215930
Email loughlinmc@hotmail.com

## CRUMLIN
*Crumlin Parish is now under the Team Ministry of Crumlin/Mourne Road/ Clogher Road*
*St Agnes*
Rev Paul Tyrrell Co-PP
41 St Agnes' Road, Crumlin, Dublin 12
Tel 01-6600075
Rev David Fleming Co-PP
94 Old County Road, Crumlin,
Dublin 12
Tel 01-4542308
Very Rev Mgr John F. Deasy *(Team Assistant)*
55 St Agnes' Road, Crumlin, Dublin 12
Tel 01-4550955
Rev Thomas Clowe (SDB)
45 St Teresa's Road, Crumlin,
Dublin 12
Rev Jimmy Fennell, Permanent Deacon
*Parish Office:* Tel 01-4555383
Fax 01-4652500
Email info@crumlinparish.ie
Website www.crumlinparish.ie

## DALKEY
*Assumption of BVM*
Very Rev Patrick Devitt Adm
No 1 Presbytery, Castle Street,
Dalkey, Co Dublin
Tel 01-2857773
Email paddy.devitt@materdei.dcu.ie
Rev Declan Gallagher CC
No 3 Presbytery, Castle Street,
Dalkey, Co Dublin
Tel 01-2859212
*Parish Office:* Tel 01-2859418
Email office@dalkeyparish.org
Website www.dalkeyparish.org

## DARNDALE-BELCAMP
*Our Lady Immaculate, Dublin 17*
Very Rev Leo Philomin (OMI) Co-PP
The Presbytery, Darndale, Dublin 17
Tel 086-7954706
Rev Edward Quinn (OMI) Co-PP
The Presbytery, Darndale, Dublin 17
Email nedqnn@gmail.com
*Parish Office:* Tel 01-8474547
Email parish@darndaleparish.ie
Website www.darndalebelcamp.ie

## DEANSRATH
*Clondalkin/Rowlagh/Neilstown/ Deansrath/Bawnogue Grouping*
Rev Brian Starken Co-PP
St Ronan's Presbytery, Deansrath,
Clondalkin, Dublin 22
Tel 01-4570380
Email stronansdeansrath@hotmail.com

## DOLLYMOUNT
*St Gabriel's, St Gabriel's Road, Dublin 3*
Very Rev Patrick McManus *(Moderator)*
34 Dollymount Grove, Clontarf, Dublin 3
Tel 01-8057692/087-2371089
Email frpatmcmanus@eircom.net
Rev Gareth Byrne *(Team Assistant)*
107 Mount Prospect Avenue,
Clontarf, Dublin 3
Tel 01-8339301
Rev Dermot Mansfield (SJ) *(Team Assistant)*
Manresa House, Clontarf Road, Dublin 3
Tel 01-8057209/087-6942844
*Parish Pastoral Worker:* Deirdre McDermott
Tel 087-6942844
*Parish Office:* Tel 01-8333602
Email stgabrielschurch@eircom.net

## DOLPHIN'S BARN/RIALTO
*(Grouped with the parish of Rialto)*
*Our Lady of Dolours, Dublin 8*
Very Rev Fergal MacDonagh *(Moderator)*
18 St Anthony's Road, Rialto, Dublin 8
Tel 01-4534469
Rev Gerard Fleming (SCA) CC
437 South Circular Road, Rialto, Dublin 8
Tel 01-4533268
Rev Gobezayehu Yilma Getachew
287 South Circular Road, Rialto, Dublin 8
Tel 01-4533490
*Parish Office:* Tel 01-4547271
Email dolphinsbarn@dublindiocese.ie

## DOMINICK STREET
*St Saviour's, Dublin 1*
Very Rev Edward Conway (OP) PP
Tel 01-8897610
Email stsaviours@eircom.net
Rev Tomasz Martynelis (OP) CC
Tel 01-8897610
Rev Cezary Binkiewicz (OP) CC
St Saviour's, Upper Dorset Street, Dublin 1
*Parish Office:* Tel 01-8897610
Email stsaviours@eircom.net
Website www.saintsavioursdublin.ie

## DONABATE
*St Patrick's*
Very Rev Joe Connolly PP
Parochial House, Donabate
Tel 01-8436011
Rev Patrick Reilly (OPraem) CC
13 Seaview Park, Portrane, Co Dublin
Tel 01-8436099
Rev Patrick Hannon PC
St Mary's, Donabate, Co Dublin
Tel 01-8434604
*Parish Office:* Tel/Fax 01-8434574 (9.30-12.00 noon)
Email stpatricksrcdonabate@gmail.com
Website www.donabateparish.ie

## DONAGHMEDE-CLONGRIFFIN-BALGRIFFIN
*Church of the Holy Trinity*
Very Rev Eoin McCrystal *(Moderator)*
12 Grangemore Grove, Donaghmede,
Dublin 13
Tel 01-8474652
Email epmcc@eircom.net
Very Rev Gerard Corcoran
Rev Deacon Gerard Reilly
*Parish Office*: Tel 01-8479822
Email info@holytrinity.ie
Website www.holytrinityparish.ie

## DONNYBROOK
*Church of the Sacred Heart, Dublin 4*
Rt Rev Mgr Lorcan O'Brien Adm
Parochial House,
Stillorgan Road, Dublin 4
Tel 087-2408975
Rev Conor Harper (SJ) CC
Parochial House,
Stillorgan Road, Dublin 4
Tel 01-2180244
Rev John Boyers PC
16 'Wilfield', Sandymount Avenue,
Ballsbridge, Dublin 4
Tel 087-1557887
*Parish Office*: Tel 01-2693903
Email mclarke@donnybrookparish.ie
Website www.donnybrookparish.ie

## DONNYCARNEY
*Our Lady of Consolation, Dublin 5*
Very Rev Peter Finnerty PP, VF
2 Maypark, Malahide Road,
Dublin 5
Tel 01-8313722
Rev John Ennis CC
1 Maypark, Malahide Road,
Dublin 5
Tel 01-8313033
*Parish Office*: Tel 01-8316016 (9 am-12 pm)
Rev Vasyl Kornitsky PC
Chaplain to Ukrainian Community
3 Maypark, Malahide Road, Dublin 5
Tel 01-5164752
Email info@donnycarneyparish.ie
Website www.donnycarneyparish.ie

## DONORE AVENUE
*St Teresa of the Child Jesus, Dublin 8*
Very Rev Cormac McNamara (SM) PP
Very Rev Sean McArdle (SM) CC
The Presbytery, 78A Donore Avenue,
Dublin 8
Tel 01-4542425
Email donoreavenue@dublindiocese.ie

## DRUMCONDRA
*Corpus Christi, Home Farm Road, Dublin 9*
Rt Rev Mgr Martin O'Shea Co-PP
23 Clare Road, Drumcondra,
Dublin 9
Tel 01-8378552
*Parish Office*: Tel 01-8360085
Email corpuschristi@eircom.net
Website
www.drumcondra.dublindiocese.ie

**DUBLIN AIRPORT** *see* **SWORDS**

## DUNDRUM
*Holy Cross, Dublin 14*
Very Rev Kieran McDermott Co-PP
Emmaus, Main Street, Dundrum,
Dublin 14
Tel 01-2984348
Email kieran.mcdermott@dublindiocese.ie
Rev John Bracken Co-PP
3 Sweetmount Drive, Dundrum, Dublin 14
Tel 01-2983557
Very Rev Mgr Donal O'Doherty PE
Holy Cross, Upper Kilmacud Road,
Dundrum, Dublin 14
Tel 01-2985264
Email 32donalodoherty@eircomm.net
Rev Deacon Gabriel Corcoran
*Parish Pastoral Worker*
Geraldine O'Keeffe
Tel 01-4240613
*Parish Office*: Tel 01-2983494
Email parishofficedundrum@eircom
Website www.holycrossdundrum.org

## DUN LAOGHAIRE
*St Michael's, Co Dublin*
Very Rev Paul Kenny PP
St Michael's Parochial House, 4 Eblana
Avenue, Dun Laoghaire, Co Dublin
Tel 01-2801505/087-7425862
Rev Patrick Monahan CC
'Renvyle', Corrig Avenue,
Dun Laoghaire, Co Dublin
Tel 01-2802100
Rev Aidan Carroll CC
'Carraig Donn', 23 Glenageary Woods,
Dun Laoghaire, Co Dublin
Tel 01-2807223
*Parish Office:* Tel 01-2804969
Email stmichdl2@eircom.net
Website www.dunlaoghaireparish.ie

## DUNLAVIN
*St Nicholas of Myra, Dunlavin, Co Wicklow*
Rev Douglas Malone Adm
The Presbytery, Dunlavin, Co Wicklow
Tel 045-401227
Rev Eamonn McCarthy CC
The Presbytery, Donard, Co Wicklow
Tel 045-404614
*Parish Office*: Tel 045-401871
Email parish10@eircom.net
Website www.dunlavinparish.ie

## EADESTOWN
*The Immaculate Conception,
Naas, Co Kildare*
Very Rev Micheál Comer Adm
The Presbytery, Eadestown,
Naas, Co Kildare
Tel 045-862187
Email eadestownparish@gmail.com

## EAST WALL-NORTH STRAND
*St Joseph's, Church Road, Dublin 3*
Very Rev Hugh Kavanagh Adm
Parochial House, 78 St Mary's Road,
East Wall, Dublin 3
Tel 01-8742320
Rev Francis Sunil Rosario PC
c/o Parish Office
*Parish Office*: Tel 01-8560980
Email stjosephsparish1941@gmail.com

## EDENMORE
*(Grouped with the parish of Grange Park)*
*St Monica's, Dublin 5*
Very Rev David Lumsden PP
83 Tonlegee Drive, Raheny, Dublin 5
Tel 01-8480917/087-2569873
Rev Ronnie Dunne *(priest in residence)*
60 Grange Park Grove, Raheny,
Dublin 5
Tel 086-4513904
Rev Anthony Power *(priest in residence)*
35 Grange Park Avenue
Tel 01-8480244
*Parish Office*: Tel 01-8471497
Email stmonicaedenmore@eircom.net

## ENNISKERRY/KILMACANOGUE (PART OF BRAY GROUPING)
*Immaculate Heart of Mary, Enniskerry,
Co Wicklow*
Very Rev Laurence Behan *(Moderator)*, VF
Very Rev John Wall Co-PP
Parochial House, Enniskerry,
Co Wicklow
Tel 01-2863506/087-2660821
Very Rev James Sheeran CC
The Presbytery, Kilmacanogue,
Bray, Co Wicklow
Tel 01-2862110
*Parish Office Enniskerry:* Tel 01-2760030
(10 am-1 pm, Mon-Fri)
*Parish Office Kilmacanogue*
Tel 01-2021882 (10 am-1 pm, Mon-Fri)
Email stmochonogs@eircom.net

## ESKER-DODDSBORO-ADAMSTOWN
*Esker-Doddsboro-Adamstown Parish is
now under the Team Ministry of Lucan/
Esker-Doddsboro-Adamstown/Lucan South
St Patrick's*
Rev John Hassett *(Moderator)*
127 Castlegate Way,
Adamstown, Co Dublin
Tel 01-6812088
Email hassettorama@gmail.com
Rev Michael Drumm PC
47 Westbury Drive, Lucan, Co Dublin
Tel 01-5031106
*Parish Office*: Tel 01-6281018
Email stpatrickschurchesker@eircom.net
Website www.stpatrickslucan.ie

## FAIRVIEW
*Church of the Visitation of BVM, Dublin 3*
Very Rev Antony Nallukunnel (OFM
Conv) PP
Rev Joseph Connick (OFM Conv) CC
Rev Aidan Walsh (OFM Conv) CC
Friary of the Visitation,
Fairview Strand, Dublin 3
Tel 01-8376000 Fax 01-8376021
*Parish Office*: Tel 01-8376000

## FINGLAS
*St Canice's, Dublin 11*
Very Rev Pádraig Ó Cochláin PP
5 The Lawn, Finglas, Dublin 11
Tel 01-8341894
Rev Gabriel O'Dowd CC
The Presbytery, St Margaret's,
Finglas, Dublin 11
Tel 01-8341009

Rev Michael Shiels CC
Tel 01-8341051
The Presbytery 1, St Canice's,
Finglas, Dublin 11
*Parish Office:* Tel 01-8343110
Fax 01-8646022
Email stcanices2@eircom.net
Website www.stcanicesfinglas.com

## FINGLAS WEST
*Church of the Annunciation, Dublin 11*
Very Rev Éamonn Cahill PP
4 The Lawn, Finglas West, Dublin 11
Tel 01-8341000
Rev Richard Shannon CC
7 Cardiff Castle Road, Finglas West,
Dublin 11
Tel 01-8343928
John Graham PPW
37 Old Fair Green, Dunboyne, Co Meath
Tel 087-2211963
Rev Rustico Tinkasiimire PC
10 Finglaswood Road, Finglas, Dublin 11
*Ministry with Travelling Community*
Rev Paddy Kelly (CSsR) CC
*Parish Office:* Tel 01-8341284

## FIRHOUSE
*Our Lady of Mount Carmel, Dublin 24*
Very Rev Peter Reilly Adm
Presbytery 1, Ballycullen Avenue,
Firhouse, Dublin 24
Tel 01-4599855
Rev Padraig B. Coleman (OFM) PC
Presbytery No 2, Ballycullen Avenue,
Firhouse, Dublin 24
Tel 01-4599899
*Parish Office:* Tel 01-4524702
Email
ourladyofmountcarmelchurch@eircom.net

## FOXROCK
*Our Lady of Perpetual Succour*
(All certs available 10.30 am–11.30 am)
Very Rev Frank Herron PP
Parochial House, Foxrock, Dublin 18
Tel 01-2893229
Rev Derek Smyth PhD CC
2 Kill Lane, Foxrock, Dublin 18
Tel 01-2894734
*Parish Office:* Tel 01-2893492/01-2898879
Email secretary@foxrockparish.ie
Website www.foxrockparish.ie

## FRANCIS STREET
*St Nicholas of Myra, Dublin 8*
Very Rev Martin Dolan Adm
The Presbytery, Francis Street, Dublin 8
Tel 01-4544861/086-4035318
*Parish Office:* Tel 01- 4542172
Email rita@francisstreetparish.ie
Website www.francisstreetparish.ie

## GARDINER STREET
*St Francis Xavier, Dublin 1*
Very Rev Donal Neary (SJ) PP, VF
Rev Fergus O'Donoghue (SJ) Parish
Chaplain
The Presbytery, Upper Gardiner Street,
Dublin 1
Tel 01-8363411
Email sfx@jesuit.ie
Website www.gardinerstparish.ie

## GARRISTOWN
*Garristown Parish is now under the Team
Ministry of Rolestown/ Garristown/The Naul
Church of the Assumption, Co Dublin*
Rev Thomas McGowan Co-PP
Parochial House, Garristown, Co Dublin
Tel 01-8354138
*Parish Office:* 01-8354138

## GLASNEVIN
*Our Lady of Dolours, Dublin 9*
Very Rev Richard Sheehy *(Moderator)*
50 Cremore Road, Glasnevin, Dublin 9
Tel 01-8373455
*Parish Office:* Tel 01-8379445

## GLASTHULE
*St Joseph's, Glasthule, Co Dublin*
Very Rev William Farrell CC
Parochial House, St Joseph's,
Glasthule, Co Dublin
Tel 01-2801226
Rev Denis Kennedy (CSSp) CC
St Joseph's Presbytery, Glasthule,
Co Dublin
Tel 01-2800403
*Parish Office:* Tel 01-6638604/5
Sacristy: 01-2800182
Email stjosephsglasthule@gmail.com
Website www.glasthuleparish.com

## GLENDALOUGH
*St Kevin's, Co Wicklow*
Very Rev Oliver Crotty Co-PP
Parochial House, Glendalough,
Co Wicklow
Tel 0404-45140
*Parish Office:* Tel 0404-45777
Email glendalough2007@eircom.net
Website www.glendalough.dublindiocese.ie

## GRANGE PARK
*(Grouped with the parish of Edenmore)
St Benedict's, Grange Park View, Dublin 5*
Very Rev David Lumsden PP
83 Tonlegee Drive, Raheny, Dublin 5
Tel 01-8480917/087-2569873
Rev Ronald Dunne CC
60 Grange Park Grove, Raheny, Dublin 5
Tel 086-4513904
Rev Tony Power CC
35 Grange Park Avenue
Tel 01-84802441/086-3905205
Email stmonicaedenmore@eircom.net

## GREENHILLS
*Church of the Holy Spirit, Dublin 12*
Very Rev Edward O'Farrell (CSSp) Adm
*(pro-tem)*
55 Fernhill Road, Greenhills, Dublin 12
Tel 01-4504040
Rev Roderick Curran (CSSp) CC
104 St Joseph's Road, Greenhills,
Dublin 12
Tel 01-4506617
*Parish Office:* Tel 01-4509191
Fax 01-4605287
Email greenhillsparish@eircom.net
Website holyspiritparishgreehills.ie

## GREYSTONES
*Church of the Holy Rosary, Co Wicklow*
Very Rev Liam Belton PP, VF
Parochial House, La Touche Road,
Greystones, Co Wicklow
Tel 01-2874278
Rev Denis Quinn *(priest in residence)*
The Presbytery, Kimberley Road,
Greystones, Co Wicklow
Tel 01-2877025
Rev Owen Lynch *(priest in residence)*
The Presbytery, Blacklion,
Greystones, Co Wicklow
Rev Carolus Gambogi CC
Parochial House, La Touche Road,
Greystones, Co Wicklow
Paul Thornton PPW
Tel 01-2819658
*Parish Office:* Tel 01-2874025
Email office@greystonesparish.com

## HADDINGTON ROAD
*St Mary's, Dublin 4*
Very Rev Fachtna McCarthy Adm
Parochial House, St Mary's,
Haddington Road, Dublin 4
Tel 01-6643295/086-3848432
Email frpfinn@stmaryshaddingtonroad.ie
Rev Michael Collins CC
Tel 01-6600075
Rev Pat Claffey (SVD) CC
Tel 085-7123675
Rev Eoin G. Cassidy PC
Tel 01-6688135
The Presbytery, Haddington Road,
Dublin 4
Email info@stmaryshaddingtonroad.ie
Website stmaryshaddingtonroad.ie

## HALSTON STREET AND ARRAN QUAY
*St Michan's, Halston Street, Dublin 7*
Very Rev Bryan Shortall (OFM Cap) PP
Capuchin Friary, Church Street, Dublin 7
Tel 01-8730599 Fax 01-8730250
Email halstonst@gmail.com
Rev Richard Hendrick (OFM Cap) CC
Capuchin Friary, Church Street, Dublin 7
Tel 01-8730599

## HAROLD'S CROSS
*Our Lady of the Rosary, Dublin 6W*
Very Rev Gerry Kane PP
213B Harold's Cross Road, Dublin 6W
Tel 01-4972816/086-8220956
Email gkane@ireland.com
*Parish Office:* Tel 01-4965055
Email enquiries@hxparish.ie
Website www.hxparish.ie

## HARRINGTON STREET
*St Kevin's, Dublin 8*
Very Rev Gerard Deighan Adm
Parochial House, Harrington Street,
Dublin 8
Tel 01-4751506
Rev Michael G. Nevin *(priest in residence)*
The Presbytery, Harrington Street,
Dublin 8
Tel 01-4789093

## HARTSTOWN

*Hartstown Parish is now under the Team Ministry of Blakestown/Hartstown/ Huntstown/Mountview*
*St Ciaran's, Dublin 15*
Rev Joseph Coyne *(Moderator)*
St Ciaran's, 36 Ashfield Lawn,
Huntstown, Dublin 15
Tel 01-8216447
*Parish Office:* Tel 01-8249651/01-8204777
Website www.st-ciarans-parish.ie

## HOWTH

*Church of the Assumption Howth, Co Dublin*
Rt Rev Mgr John V. Fitzpatrick
*(Moderator)* EV
3 Glencarrig, Church Road, Sutton,
Dublin 13
Tel 01-8323147
Rev Kilian Brennan Co-PP
Presbytery No 1, Thormanby Road,
Howth, Co Dublin
Tel 01-8232193
Email kilianbrennan@eircom.net
Rt Rev Mgr Brendan Houlihan PE
Parochial House, Mount Saint Mary's,
Thormanby Road, Howth, Dublin 13
Tel 01-8322036
Email assumptionhowth@eircom.net
Rev Raymond Canon Molony
Presbytery No 2, Thormanby Road
Tel 01-8322029
*Sacristy:* Tel 01-8397398
Email assumptionhowth@eircom.net

## HUNTSTOWN

*Sacred Heart of Jesus, Dublin 15*
Rev George P. Begley Co-PP
257 Pace Road, Littlepace, Dublin 15
Tel 01-8249651
*Parish Pastoral Worker*
Mr Clinton Maher
Tel 01-8218910

## INCHICORE, MARY IMMACULATE

*Inchicore/Bluebell Grouping*
*Mary Immaculate, Tyrconnell Road, Dublin 8*
Very Rev William Fitzpatrick (OMI) Co-PP
Rev Michael Guckian (OMI)
Rev Bernard Halpin (OMI)
Rev Patrick Carolan (OMI)
Oblate Fathers, House of Retreat,
Inchicore, Dublin 8
Tel 01-4541117
Website www.oblateparishesinchicore.ie

## INCHICORE, ST MICHAEL'S

*Inchicore/Bluebell Grouping*
*St Michael's, Emmet Road, Dublin 8*
Rev Louis McDermott (OMI) *(Moderator)*
Rev Dermot Mills (OMI)
52a Bulfin Road
Tel 01-4531660
Website www.stmichaelsinchicore.ie

## IONA ROAD

*St Columba's, Dublin 9*
Very Rev Patrick Jones Co-PP
'Marmion', 87 Iona Road, Dublin 9
Tel 01-8305651
Email saintcolumba@eircom.net
Website www.ionaroadparish.ie

## JAMES'S STREET

*St James's Church, Dublin 8*
Very Rev John Collins *(Moderator)*
The Presbytery,
James's Street, Dublin 8
Tel 01-4531143
Email roseo9@eircom.net
*Parish Office:*
Tel 01-4531143/087-1445888
Email jamesstreet@dublindiocese.ie

## JOBSTOWN

*St Thomas the Apostle*
Rev Derek Doyle Co-PP
The Presbytery, Jobstown, Tallaght,
Dublin 24
Tel 01-4610971
Email jobstownparish@gmail.com

## JOHNSTOWN-KILLINEY

*Our Lady of Good Counsel, Killiney,*
*Co Dublin*
Very Rev John Sinnott PP
56 Auburn Road, Killiney, Co Dublin
Tel 01-2856660/087-8122651
Rev Gerard Doyle CC
Tel 01-2852509
59 Auburn Road, Dun Laoghaire,
Co Dublin
*Parish Office:* Tel 01-2351416
Email johnstownparish@gmail.com
Website www.johnstownparish.org

## KILBARRACK-FOXFIELD

*St John the Evangelist, Greendale Road,*
*Kilbarrack, Dublin 5*
Very Rev Paul Lavelle PP
123 Foxfield Grove, Dublin 5
Tel 01-8328396
Rev Cathal Price *(priest in residence)*
54 Foxfield St John, Dublin 5
Tel 01-8323683
Email cathalprice@gmail.com
Rev Finbarr Neylan CC
*Parish Office:* Tel 01-8390433
Email info@kilbarrackfoxfieldparish.ie
Website www.kilbarrackfoxfieldparish.ie

## KILBRIDE AND BARNDARRIG

*St Mary's, Barndarrig, Co Wicklow*
Very Rev Michael Vincent Dempsey PP
The Presbytery, Barndarrig, Co Wicklow
Tel 0404-48130
Rev Anthony Scully CC
St Brigid's Presbytery, Brittas Bay,
Co Wicklow
Tel 0404-47177

## KILCULLEN

*Sacred Heart and St Brigid, Kilcullen*
Very Rev Niall Mackey Adm
Parochial House, Kilcullen, Co Kildare
Tel 045-481230
Email mclm@eircom.net
Rev Martin Harte CC
Presbytery, Kilcullen, Co Kildare
Tel 045-481222
*Parish Office:* Tel 045-480727
Email kilcullenparish@eircom.net
Website www.kilcullenparish.net

## KILLESTER

*St Brigid's, Howth Road, Dublin 5*
Rt Rev Mgr Alex Stenson PP
126 Furry Park Road, Dublin 5
Tel 01-8333793
*Parish Office:* Tel 01-8332974
Website www.killester.dublindiocese.ie

## KILLINARDEN

*Church of the Sacred Heart, Killinarden,*
*Tallaght, Dublin 24*
Very Rev Manus Ferry (MSC) PP
Rev John Finn (MSC) CC
The Presbytery, Killinarden, Tallaght,
Dublin 24
Tel 01-4522251
Email
sacredheartparishkillinarden@gmail.com
Website
www.sacredheartparishkillinarden.com

## KILL-O'-THE-GRANGE

*Holy Family, Kill Avenue,*
*Dun Laoghaire, Co Dublin*
Very Rev John D. Killeen PP
20 Abbey Court, Monkstown,
Co Dublin
Tel 01-2802533
Rev Michael O'Connor (CSSp) CC
Presbytery No 2, Church Grounds,
Kill Avenue, Dun Laoghaire, Co Dublin
Tel 01-2140863
*Parish Office:* Tel 01-2845299

## KILMACANOGUE see ENNISKERRY

## KILMACUD-STILLORGAN

*(Grouped with the parish of Mount Merrion)*
*St Laurence, Co Dublin*
Very Rev Tony Coote Adm *(Kilmacud &*
*Mount Merrion)*
79 The Rise, Mount Merrion, Co Dublin
Tel 01-2889879
Rev Conleth Meehan CC *(Kilmacud &*
*Mount Merrion)*
6 Allen Park Road, Stillorgan, Co Dublin
Tel 01-2880545
Rev Paddy O'Byrne CC
Presbytery No. 2, Church Grounds
Tel 01-2882257
Very Rev Brian O'Reilly PP
c/o Parish Office
Tel 087-7414857
*Parish Office:* Tel 01-2884009
Email kilmacudparish@eircom.net
Website www.kilmacudparish.com

## KILMORE ROAD WEST

*St Luke the Evangelist, Dublin 5*
Rev Patrick Littleton Adm
St Luke's, Kilbarron Road,
Kilmore West, Dublin 5
Tel 01-8486806
*Parish Office:* Tel 01-8488149

## KILNAMANAGH-CASTLEVIEW

*St Kevin's, Dublin 24*
Rev Michael Murphy
Presbytery No 1, Treepark Road,
Kilnamanagh, Dublin 24
Tel 01-4523805/086-2408188
Rev Fergus McGlynn CC
43 Chestnut Grove, Ballymount Road,
Dublin 24
*Parish Office:* Tel 01-4515570

Allianz (Ⅱ)

## KILQUADE
*St Patrick's, Kilquade, Co Wicklow*
Very Rev Liam Belton PP, VF
Parochial House, La Touche Road,
Greystones, Co Wicklow
Tel/Fax 01-2874278
Email liam.belton@gmail.com
Rev Eamonn Clarke CC
The Presbytery, Kilcoole, Co Wicklow
Tel 01-2876207
Rev Sean Smith CC
The Presbytery,
Newtownmountkennedy, Co Wicklow
Tel 01-2819253
Paul Thornton PPW
Tel 01-2017360
*Parish Office:* Tel 01-2819658
Email kilquadeparish@eircom.net
Website www.kilquadeparish.com

## KIMMAGE MANOR
*Church of the Holy Spirit, Kimmage Manor,*
*Whitehall Road, Dublin 12*
66 Rockfield Avenue, Dublin 12
Tel 01-4558316
Rev Thomas Hogan (CSSp) CC
Tel 01-4064377
Rev Edward O'Farrell (CSSp)
*Parish Office:* Tel 01-4064377
Email kimmagemanorparish@eircom.net
Website www.kimmagemanorparish.com

## KINSEALY
*(Grouped with the parishes of Malahide,*
*Yellow Walls & Portmarnock)*
*St Nicholas of Myra, Malahide Road,*
*Co Dublin*
Very Rev Martin O'Farrell Co-PP
'Aghadoe', Kinsaley Lane, Malahide,
Co Dublin
Tel 01-8461767
*Parish Office:* Tel 01-8460028

## KNOCKLYON
*St Colmcille, Idrone Avenue, Dublin 16*
Very Rev Eanna Ó hÓbáin (OCarm) PP
Rev Sean MacGiollarnáth (OCarm) CC
Rev Martin Parokkaran (OCarm) CC
Rev Michael Morrissey (OCarm) CC
Carmelite Presbytery, Idrone Avenue,
Knocklyon, Dublin 16
Tel 01-4941204
Email presbytery@knocklyonparish.ie
Website www.knocklyonparish.ie

## LARKHILL-WHITEHALL-SANTRY
*(Grouped with the parishes of Kilmore*
*Road West & Beaumont)*
*Holy Child, Thatch Road, Dublin 9*
Very Rev John Jones Adm
151 Swords Road, Whitehall, Dublin 9
Tel 01-8374887
Rev Bernard Collier CC
2 Knightswood, Coolock Lane,
Santry, Dublin 9
Tel 01-8425283
Rev Thomas Kearney CC
137 Shantalla Road, Whitehall, Dublin 9
Tel 01-8420260
*Parish Office:* Tel 01-8375274
Email whitehall@dublindiocese.ie
Website www.whitehall@dublindiocese.ie

## LAUREL LODGE-CARPENTERSTOWN
*St Thomas the Apostle, Castleknock,*
*Dublin 15*
Very Rev Kieran Coghlan *(Moderator)*
Rev Brendan Quinlan Co-PP
Presbytery, Church Grounds,
Laurel Lodge, Castleknock, Dublin 15
Tel 01-8208144
Rev Dan Joe O'Mahony (OFM Cap) PC
The Oratory, Blanchardstown Dublin 15
Tel 01-8200915/086-8090633
Email danjoe2006@gmail.com
*Parish Office:* Tel 01-8200915
Website www.laurellodgeparish.ie

## LEIXLIP
*Our Lady's Nativity, Co Kildare*
Rev John McNamara Adm
Parochial House, Old Hill, Leixlip,
Co Kildare
Tel 01-6245597
Rev Karl Fortune CC
No 1 Presbytery, 4 Old Hill,
Leixlip, Co Kildare
Tel 01-6243718
Rev Eladius Leonard Mutunzi PC
Presbytery No 2, 6 Old Hill, Leixlip,
Co Kildare
*Parish Office:* Tel 01-6243673/01-6245159
Email leixlip.parish@oln.ie
Website www.oln.ie

## LITTLE BRAY *see* BRAY, ST PETER'S

## LOUGHLINSTOWN
*St Columbanus, Dun Laoghaire*
Ver Rev Alex Conlan *(Moderator)*
Parochial House, Ballybrack, Co Dublin
Tel 01-2826404
Very Rev Michael O'Kelly Co-PP
39 Oakton Park, Ballybrack, Co Dublin
Tel 01-2827282
Email loughlinstownparish@eircom.net
Website www.loughlinstownparish.ie
*Parish Office:* Tel 01-2824085

## LUCAN
*Lucan Parish is now under the Team*
*Ministry of Lucan/Esker-Dodsboro-*
*Adamstown/Lucan South*
*St Mary's, Lucan, Co Dublin*
Very Rev Philip Curran Co-PP
231 Beech Park, Lucan, Co Dublin
Tel 01-6281756
Very Rev Thomas Kennedy Co-PP
14 Roselawn, Lucan, Co Dublin
Tel 01-6280205
*Parish Pastoral Worker:* Colette Kavanagh
Tel 087-7952330
*Parish Office:* Tel 01-6217041
Email parishoffice@stmarysparishlucan.ie
Website www.stmarysparishlucan.ie

## LUCAN SOUTH
*Lucan South Parish is now under the*
*Team Ministry of Lucan/Esker- Dodsboro-*
*Adamstown/Lucan South*
*Church of Divine Mercy, Balgaddy*
Very Rev Eamonn Bourke Co-PP
Parochial House, Foxdene Avenue,
Lucan, Dublin 22
Tel 01-4056858
Rev Joseph Raymond Otwey-Buabeng
*(Team Assistant)*
32 Earlsfort Road, Lucan, Dublin 22
Tel 01-6212560

Rev Deacon Joseph Walsh
*Parish Office:* Tel 01-4572900
Email churchdivinemercy@eircom.net
Website www.lucansouthparish.net

## LUSK
*St MacCullin's, Lusk, Co Dublin*
Very Rev Paul Hampson PP
Parochial House, Chapel Road,
Lusk, Co Dublin
Tel 01-8949229/087-2452161
*Parish Office:* Tel 01-8438421
Email luskparish@eircom.net
Website www.luskparish.ie

## MALAHIDE
*(Grouped with the parishes of Yellow*
*Walls, Kinsealy & Portmarnock)*
*St Sylvester's, Malahide, Co Dublin*
Very Rev Kevin Moore *(Moderator)*
Apartment No. 1, St Sylvester's Church,
Malahide, Co Dublin
Very Rev Gary Darby Co-PP
146 Seapark, Malahide, Co Dublin
Tel 01-8454172
Very Rev Frank Reburn Co-PP
11 Millview Court, Malahide, Co Dublin
Tel 01-8451902
Email fdreburn@hotmail.com
Very Rev Kevin Moore
*Parish Office:* Tel 01-8451244 Fax 01-8168539
Email stsylvesters@eircom.net
Website www.malahideparish.ie

## MARINO
*St Vincent de Paul, Griffith Avenue,*
*Dublin 9*
Very Rev Thomas Noone PP
69 Griffith Avenue, Dublin 9
Tel 01-8332864
Rev Joseph Ali PC
c/o The Sacristy, St Vincent de Paul Church,
Griffith Avenue, Dublin 9
Tel 01-8339756
Rev Paul Churchill PC
c/o Parish Office
*Parish Office:* Tel 01-8332772/087-2506786
Email info@marinoparish.ie
Website www.marinoparish.ie

## MARLEY GRANGE
*The Divine Word, 25/27 Hermitage Downs,*
*Rathfarnham, Dublin 16*
Rev Jim Mulherin (OSM) PP
Rev Camillus McGrane (OSM) CC
25–27 Hermitage Downs,
Marley Grange, Rathfarnham, Dublin 16
Tel 01-4944295
*Parish Office:* Tel 01-4944295 Fax 01-4941042
Email divine_word@ireland.com
Website www.marleygrangeparish.ie

## MAYNOOTH
*St Mary's, Maynooth, Co Kildare*
Very Rev Liam Rigney PhD, PP
Parochial House, Moyglare Road
Tel 01-6286220/087-2607377
Email liamrigney@eircom.net
Rev Paul Kelly CC
The Presbytery, 18 Straffan Way,
Maynooth, Co Kildare
Tel 01-6293018
*Parish Office:* Tel 01-5640012/
087-2048898/01-6293885
Email maynoothparishoffice@eircom.net
www.maynoothparish.dublindiocese.ie

## MEADOWBROOK

*Meadowbrook Parish is now under the
Team Ministry of Dundrum/Ballinteer/
Meadowbrook*
*St Attracta's Oratory, Dublin 16*
Very Rev John Ferris Co-PP
75 Ludford Drive, Dublin 16
Tel 01-2988746
*Assistant priests*
Rev Matthias E. Kulitunam
Tel 01-2987401
Rev Charles Abba Danboyi
c/o Parish Office
*Parish Office:* Tel 01-2980471
Email info@meadowbrookparish.ie
www.meadowbrookparish.ie

## MEATH STREET AND MERCHANTS QUAY

*St Catherine of Alexandria, Dublin 8*
*Church of the Immaculate Conception
(popularly known as Adam and Eve's)
4 Merchant's Quay, Dublin 8*
Rev Niall Coghlan (OSA) PP
St Catherine's Church, Meath Street,
Dublin 8
Tel 01-4543356
Rev Richard Goode (OSA)
The Presbytery, Meath Street, Dublin 8
*Parish Office*
Tel 01-4543356 Fax 01-4738303
Email meathst@hotmail.com
Website www.meathstreetparish.ie

## MERRION ROAD

*Our Lady Queen of Peace, Dublin 4*
Very Rev Fergus O'Connor (Opus Dei) PP
Email fc.oconnor@gmail.com
Rev James Hurley CC
Email jpatrickhurley@gmail.com
31 Herbert Ave., Merrion Road,
Dublin 4
Tel 01-2692001
*Parish Office:* Tel 01-2691825
Email info@merrionroadchurch.ie
Website www.merrionroadchurch.ie

## MILLTOWN

*SS Columbanus and Gall, Dublin 6*
Rt Rev Mgr Peter Bruscoe Adm
67 Ramleh Park, Milltown, Dublin 6
Tel 01-2196600
Rev Alan Mowbray (SJ) PC
Gonzaga Jesuit Community,
Sandford Road, Dublin 6
Tel 01-4972943
*Parish Office:* Tel 01-2196740/
01-2680041/087-9500334
Email milltownparishcentre@eircom.net
Website www.milltownparish.ie

## MONKSTOWN

*St Patrick's, Carrickbrennan Road*
Very Rev Michael Coady PP
Parochial House, Carrickbrennan Road,
Monkstown, Co Dublin
Tel 01-2802130/087-2401441
Email clovis78@eircom.net
Rev Deacon Eric Cooney
*Parish Office:* Tel 01-2807854
Email secretary@monkstownparish.ie
Website www.monkstownparish.ie

## MOONE

*Church of the Blessed Trinity*
Very Rev Francis McEvoy PP, VF
Parochial House, Crookstown,
Athy, Co Kildare
Tel 059-8624109
*Parish Office:* Tel 059-8623154
Email stlaurenceschurch@gmail.com
Wesbite www.narraghmoreparish.org

## MOUNT ARGUS

*St Paul of the Cross, Harold's Cross,
Dublin 6W*
Very Rev Frank Keevins (CP) PP
Tel 01-4992800
Rev Brendan McKeever (CP) PC
Rev Joe Kennedy (CP) PC
St Paul's Retreat, Mount Argus, Dublin 6W
Email secretary@mountargusparish.ie
Website www.mountargusparish.ie
*Parish Office:* Tel 01-4992000

## MOUNT MERRION

*St Therese, Mount Merrion, Co Dublin*
Very Rev Tony Coote Adm
79 The Rise, Mount Merrion, Co Dublin
Tel 01-2889879
Email tony.coote@gmail.com
Rev Conleth Meehan CC
6 Allen Park Road, Stillorgan, Co Dublin
Tel 01-2880545
Rev Patrick J. O'Byrne CC
188 Lower Kilmacud Road, Kilmacud,
Co Dublin
Tel 01-2981955
Very Rev Brian O'Reilly PP
*Parish Office:* Tel 01-2881271/01-2783804
Email mountmerrionparishoffice@eircom.net
Website www.mountmerrionparish.ie

## MOUNTVIEW

*Mountview Road Parish is now under the
Team Ministry of Blakestown/ Hartstown/
Huntstown/ Mountview*
*St Philip the Apostle, Blanchardstown,
Dublin 15*
Very Rev Patrick O'Byrne Co-PP
No. 2 The Presbytery, Mountview,
Blanchardstown, Dublin 15
Tel 01-8216380
Email pat.obyrne@yahoo.com
Email mountview@dublindiocese.ie
Website www.stphilipsmountview.ie

## MOURNE ROAD

*Mourne Road Parish is now under the
Team Ministry of Crumlin/Mourne Road/
Clogher Road*
*Our Lady of Good Counsel, Dublin 12*
Very Rev John Canon Flaherty *(Team
Moderator)*
Parochial House, Sperrin Road,
Drimnagh, Dublin 12
Tel 01-4556103
Rev David Brannigan Co-PP
89 Sperrin Road, Drimnagh, Dublin 12
Tel 01-4652418
Email copp@mourneroad.ie
Rev Jimmy Fennell, Permanent Deacon
*Parish Office:* Tel 01-4556105 Fax 01-4550133
Email mourneroadparish@eircom.net
Website www.mourneroad.ie

## MULHUDDART

Very Rev Seamus Connell Adm
24 The Court, Mulhuddart Wood,
Mulhuddart, Dublin 15
*Parish Office:* Tel 01-8205480
Email mulhudoffice@gmail.com

## NARRAGHMORE

*(Grouped with the parish of Moone)*
*SS Mary and Laurence, Co Kildare*
Very Rev Frank McEvoy PP, VF
Parochial House, Crookstown,
Athy, Co Kildare
Email stlaurencechurch@gmail.com
Website www.narraghmoreparish.org

## NAUL

*The Naul Parish is now under the Team
Ministry Rolestown/Garristown/The Naul*
*St Canice's, Damastown, Co Dublin*
*The Nativity of BVM, Naul*
*The Assumption of BVM, Ballyboughal*
Very Rev Denis M. Delaney *(Moderator)*
Parochial House, Naul, Co Dublin
Tel 01-8412932
Very Rev Patrick Canon Fagan PE
The Presbytery, Ballyboughal, Co Dublin
Tel 01-8433122

## NAVAN ROAD

*Our Lady Help of Christians, Dublin 7*
Very Rev John Scroope O'Brien Adm
Parochial House, 211 Navan Road,
Dublin 7
Tel 01-8681436
Rev Paul Coyle CC
194 Navan Road, Dublin 7
Tel 01-8383313/087-1186474
*Parish Office:* Tel 01-8380265
Email navanroadparish@eircom.net
Website www.navanroadparish.com

## NEILSTOWN

*St Peter the Apostle, Dublin 22*
Very Rev David Halpin Co-PP
The Presbytery, Neilstown,
Clondalkin, Dublin 22
Tel 01-6263920
Rev Abraham Pathackal George CC
32 Wheatfield Close,
Clondalkin, Dublin 22
Tel 01-6263920
*Parish Office:* Tel 01-4573546/085-7199087

## NEWCASTLE

*(Grouped with the parishes of Saggart,
Rathcool & Brittas)*
*St Finian's, Co Dublin*
Very Rev Enda Cunningham PP
St Mary's Parochial House,
Saggart, Co Dublin
Tel 01-4589209/087-1380695
Rev Aidan Kieran CC
No 1 the Glebe, Peamount Road,
Newcastle Lyons, Co Dublin
Tel 01-4589230/087-6397744
Rev Aloysius Zuribo CC
2 Carrigmore Place, Saggart, Co Dublin
Tel 087-9706309/01-4589209
Email aloysiuszuribo@yahoo.com

## NEWTOWNPARK
*The Guardian Angels, Blackrock, Co Dublin*
Very Rev Dermot Leycock PP
64 Newtownpark Avenue,
Blackrock, Co Dublin
Tel 01-2784860
Rev William Fortune PC
32 Newtownpark Avenue,
Blackrock, Co Dublin
Tel 01-2100337
*Parish Office:* Tel 01-2832988
Email newtownparkparish@eircom.net
Website www.newtownparkparish.com

## NORTH WALL-SEVILLE PLACE
*St Laurence O'Toole's (North Wall), Dublin 1*
Very Rev Colin Rothery Adm
Parochial House, 49 Seville Place, Dublin 1
Tel 01-8741625
Pauline O'Shea PPW
Tel 01-8783583/087-3199310
Email pauline.oshea@dublindiocese.ie
*Parish Office:* Tel 01-8744236

## NORTH WILLIAM STREET
*St Agatha's, Dublin 1*
Very Rev Brian Lawless Adm
Parochial House,
46 North William Street, Dublin 1
Tel 01-8556474
Email frbrian@stagathasparish.ie
*Parish Office:* Tel 01-8554078
Email office@stagathasparish.ie
Website www.stagathasparish.ie

## OLD BAWN (see TALLAGHT, OLDBAWN)

## PALMERSTOWN
*St Philomena's, Dublin 20*
Very Rev Anthony Reilly PP
Parochial House, Palmerstown, Dublin 20
Tel 01-6266254 Fax 01-6266255
Email reillya48@gmail.com
*Parish Office:* Tel 01-6260900/01-6266241
Email stphilomenasparish48@gmail.com
Website www.palmerstownparish.com

## PHIBSBOROUGH
*Phibsboro Parish is now under the Team Ministry of Cabra/Cabra West/Phibsboro*
*St Peter's, Dublin 7*
Very Rev Paschal Scallon (CM) Co-PP
St Peter's, Phibsboro, Dublin 7
Tel 01-8389708/8102566
*Parish Pastoral Worker:* Natasha Curran
Tel 01-8380170
Email info@stpetersphibsboro.ie
Website www.stpetersphibsboro.ie

## PORTERSTOWN-CLONSILLA
*St Mochta's, Porterstown, Dublin 15*
Very Rev John Daly PP
St Mochta's, Porterstown, Dublin 15
Tel 01-8213218 Fax 01-8213516
Rev Timothy Murphy, Permanent Deacon
Email frjohn@stmochtasparish.ie
Website www.stmochtasparish.ie

## PORTMARNOCK
*(Grouped with the parishes of Malahide, Yellow Walls & Kinsealy)*
*St Anne's, Portmarnock, Co Dublin*
Very Rev John Murphy Co-PP
St Anne's, Strand Road,
Portmarnock, Co Dublin
Tel/Fax 01-8461081

Very Rev Gary Darby
21 Wheatfield Grove, Portmarnock,
Co Dublin
*Parish Office*
Tel 01-8461561 Fax 01-8169802
Email stannes@portmarnockparish.ie
Website www.portmarnockparish.ie

## PRIORSWOOD
*St Francis of Assisi, Dublin 17*
Rev Jack Twomey (OFM Cap) PP *(Guardian)*
*Parish Office:* Tel 01-8474469
Fax 01-8487296
Email priorswoodparish@yahoo.ie
Website www.priorswoodparish.ie

## RAHENY
*Our Lady Mother of Divine Grace,
Howth Road, Dublin 5*
Very Rev Michael Cullen Adm
5 St Assam's Road West, Raheny, Dublin 5
Tel 01-8313806
*Parish Office:* Tel 01-8313232
Email oldgraheny@eircom.net

## RATHDRUM
*SS Mary and Michael, Co Wicklow*
Very Rev Derek Doyle *(Moderator)*
Parochial House, Rathdrum, Co Wicklow
Tel 0404-46229
Rev Moyison Irudayasamy (Assistant)
Presbytery No. 1, Rathdrum, Co Wicklow
Tel 0404-46214
*Parish Office:* Tel 0404 46517

## RATHFARNHAM
*Rathfarnham Parish is now under the
Team Ministry of Rathfarnham/
Churchtown/Ballyroan*
*The Annunciation, Dublin 14*
Very Rev Martin G. Noone VF *(Moderator)*
St Mary's Presbytery, Willbrook Road,
Rathfarnham, Dublin 14
Tel 01-4954554
Email martin.noone@dublindiocese.ie
Rev Kevin Rowan Co-PP
St Mary's Presbytery, Willbrook Road,
Rathfarnham, Dublin 14
Tel 01-4932390
*Parish Pastoral Worker:* Margaret Drew
Tel 01-4958695
*Parish Office:* Tel 01-4958695 Fax 01-4958696
Email rathfarnhamparish1@eircom.net

## RATHGAR
*Church of the Three Patrons,
Rathgar Road, Dublin 6*
Very Rev Joseph Mullan PP
49 Rathgar Road, Dublin 6
Tel 01-4971058
Rev Francis Sammon (SJ) CC
156B Rathgar Road, Dublin 6
Tel 01-4966042
Rev Gerry Moloney (CSsR) PC
Marianella, 75 Orwell Road,
Rathgar, Dublin 6
*Parish Office:* Tel 01-4972215
Email 3patrons@eircom.net
Website www.rathgarparish.ie

## RATHMINES
*Mary Immaculate, Refuge of Sinners,
Rathmines, Dublin 6*
Very Rev David Brough Adm
Tel 01-4969049
Rev John Galvin CC
Tel 01-4971531
52 Lower Rathmines Road, Dublin 6
*Parish Office:* Tel 01-4971531
Website www.rathminesparish.ie

## RIALTO/DOLPHIN'S BARN
*(Grouped with the parish of Dolphin's Barn)*
*Our Lady of the Holy Rosary of Fatima,
Rialto, Dublin 8*
Very Rev Fergal MacDonagh *(Moderator)*
18 St Anthony's Road, Rialto, Dublin 8
Tel 01-4534469
Very Rev Gerard Fleming (SAC) CC
437 South Circular Road, Rialto, Dublin 8
Tel 01-4533268
Rev Gobezayehu Yilma Getachew PC
287 South Circular Road, Rialto, Dublin 8
*Parish Office:* Tel 01-4539020
Website www.rialtoparish.com

## RINGSEND
*St Patrick's, Dublin 4*
Very Rev Ivan Tonge PP
St Patrick's, 2 Cambridge Road, Dublin 4
Tel 087-2726868
Rt Rev Mgr Daniel O'Connor PC
St Mary's, Irishtown Road, Dublin 4
*Parish Office:* Tel 01-6697429
Email
stpatrickschurchringsend@eircom.net
Website
www.stpatrickschurchringsend.com

## RIVERMOUNT
*St Oliver Plunkett, St Helena's Drive,
Dublin 11*
Very Rev Seamus Ahearne (OSA) PP
The Presbytery, 60 Glenties Park,
Finglas South, Dublin 11
Tel 01-8343722/087-6782746
Email seamus.ahearne@gmail.com
Rev Paddy O'Reilly (OSA)
Parochial House, St Helena's Drive,
Dublin 11
Tel 01-8343444/086 8279504
Email paddyforeilly@eircom.net

## RIVER VALLEY
*Swords/River Valley/Brackenstown
Grouping*
*St Finian's, Swords, Co Dublin*
Very Rev Desmond G. Doyle Co-PP
Parochial House, 1 River Valley Heights,
Swords, Co Dublin
Tel 01-8403400
Rev Eugene Rybansky, Team Assistant
and Chaplain to Slovakian Community
The Presbytery, 2 River Valley Heights,
Swords, Co Dublin
Tel 01-8404162
*Parish Office:* Tel 01-8409043
Website www.rivervalley.dublindiocese.ie

## ROLESTOWN-OLDTOWN

*Rolestown parish is now under the Team Ministry of Rolestown Garristown/The Naul*
*St Brigid's, Rolestown, Co Dublin*
Very Rev John F. Keegan Co-PP
Rolestown, Swords, Co Dublin
Tel 01-8401514
Rev John Carey Co-PP
Oldtown, Co Dublin
Tel 01-8433133
Email parishrolestown@gmail.com

## ROUNDWOOD

*St Laurence O'Toole, Co Wicklow*
Rev Peter Healy Co-PP
Parochial House, Roundwood,
Co Wicklow
Tel 01-2818149/087-2463876
*Parish Office:* Tel 01-2818384 (mornings)
Email roundwoodparish@eircom.net

## ROWLAGH AND QUARRYVALE

*Clondalkin/Rowlagh/Neilstown/*
*Deansrath/Bawnogue Grouping*
*Immaculate Heart of Mary, Clondalkin,*
*Dublin 22*
Very Rev David Halpin Co-PP
Rev Abraham Pathackal George (*Team Assistant*)
30 Wheatfield Close,
Clondalkin, Dublin 22
Tel 01-6263920
*Parish Office:* Tel/Fax 01-6261010
Email parishofrowlagh@eircom.net
Website
www.rowlaghandquarryvaleparish.com

## RUSH

*St Maur's, Rush, Co Dublin*
Very Rev Peter O'Connor PP
The Presbytery, Chapel Green,
Rush, Co Dublin
Tel 01-8437208
Mary Kirk PPW
Tel 087-3667645
Email rushparish@dublindiocese.ie
Website www.rushparish.dublindiocese.ie

## SAGGART/RATHCOOLE/BRITTAS

*(Grouped with the parish of Newcastle)*
*Nativity of the BVM, Co Dublin*
Very Rev Enda Cunningham PP
Rev Aloysius Zuribo CC
St Mary's Parochial House,
Saggart, Co Dublin
Tel 01-4589209
Rev Aidan Kieran CC
No 1 the Glebe, Peamount Road,
Newcastle Lyons, Co Dublin
Tel 01-4589230/087-6397744
Rev Michael Shortall PC
87 Beechwood Lawns,
Rathcoole, Co Dublin
Tel 01-4587187
Rev Michael McGowan PC
7 St Patrick's Crescent,
Rathcoole, Co Dublin
Tel 01-4589210
*Parish Pastoral Worker:* Sean O'Rourke
Tel 01-4589209

## SALLYNOGGIN

*Our Lady of Victories, Co Dublin*
Very Rev Padraig Gleeson Adm
Rev Michael Simpson CC
St Kevin's Presbytery, Pearse Street,
Sallynoggin, Co Dublin
Tel 01-2854667 Fax 01-2847024
*Parish Office:* Tel 01-2854667
Email sallynogginparish@eircom.net

## SANDYFORD

*St Mary's, Dublin 18*
Very Rev Andrew O'Sullivan (*Moderator*)
Parochial House, St Mary's,
Sandyford Village, Dublin 18
Tel 045-2956317
Very Rev Gerard Moore Co-PP
The Presbytery, St Mary's,
Sandyford, Dublin 18
Tel 01-2958933
*Parish Pastoral Worker:* Grainne Prior
*Parish Office:* Tel 01-2956414
Email office@sandyfordparish.org
Website www.sandyfordparish.org

## SANDYMOUNT

*St Mary's Star of the Sea, Dublin 4*
Very Rev John McDonagh Adm
'Stella Maris', 15 Oswald Road,
Sandymount, Dublin 4
Tel 01-6684265
Rev Martin Murnaghan CC
10 Cranfield Place, Sandymount,
Dublin 4
Tel 01-6676438
*Parish Office:* Tel 01-6683316
Fax 01-6683894
Email sandymountparish@eircom.net

## SHANKILL

*St Anne's, Co Dublin*
Very Rev John O'Connor (SAC) PP
St Benin's Parish, Dublin Road,
Shankill, Co Dublin
Tel 01-2824425
Email johnhenryoconnor@gmail.com
Rev Michael O'Dwyer (SAC) CC
Rev Eamonn Monson (SAC) CC
St Benin's, Dubin Road
Tel 01-2824425
*Supply:* Jose Maria Recondo
St Benin's, Dublin Road,
Shankill, Co Dublin
*Parish Office:* Tel 01-2822277
Email st.annes_parishoffice@yahoo.ie

## SILLOGE

*Holy Spirit, Silloge Road, Dublin 11*
*Virgin Mary, Shangan Road, Dublin 9*
Very Rev Declan Blake
Presbytery 2, Shangan Road, Dublin 9
Tel 01-8621031
Rev Anthony Omolade
No. 2 Presbytery, Silloge Road,
Ballymun, Dublin 11
*Parish Office:* Tel 01-8620586

## SKERRIES

*St Patrick's, Co Dublin*
Very Rev Richard Hyland PP
42 Strand Street, Skerries, Co Dublin
Tel 01-8491250
*Parish Office:* Tel 01-8492145
Email stpatrickschurchskerries@gmail.com

## SPRINGFIELD

*St Mark's, Maplewood Road,*
*Tallaght, Dublin 24*
Very Rev Patrick McKinley (*Moderator*)
68 Maplewood Road, Springfield,
Tallaght, Dublin 24
Rev Paul Ludden (*Team Assistant*)
70 Maplewood Road, Tallaght,
Dublin 24
Tel 01-4628336
Saule Cameron (PPW)
Tel 086-3592451
*Parish Office:* Tel 01-4620777
Email stmarkschurch@eircom.net
Website www.stmarksspringfield.com

## SRULEEN

*Sacred Heart, St John's Drive, Clondalkin,*
*Dublin 22*
Very Rev Michael Ruddy (SSCC) PP
Rev Pearse Mullen (SSCC) CC
Rev Eamon Aylward (SSCC) PC, CC (*priest in residence*)
Tel 087-0516625
*Parish Office:* Tel 01-4570032
Website www.sruleenparish.ie

## SUTTON

*Sutton/Howth/Baldoyle Grouping*
*St Fintan's, Greenfield Road, Dublin 13*
Rt Rev Mgr John V. Fitzpatrick (*Moderator*) EV
3 Glencarraig, Church Road, Sutton,
Dublin 13
Tel 01-8323147
Email jvf@eircom.net
Rev Liam Lacey Co-PP
8 Greenfield Road, Sutton, Dublin 13
Tel 01-8322396
Email liamflacey@gmail.com
*Parish Pastoral Worker:* James Daly MA
Email james.daly@dublindiocese.ie
*Parish Office:* Tel 01-8392001
Email office@stfintansparish.ie
Website www.stfintansparish.ie

## SWORDS

*Swords/River Valley/Brackenstown*
*Grouping*
*St Colmcille's, Co Dublin*
*(Dublin Airport Church, Our Lady Queen of Heaven is in this parish)*
Very Rev Michael Carey (*Moderator*)
5 Lissenhall Park, Seatown Road,
Swords, Co Dublin
Tel 01-8403378
Rev Peter McCarron Co-PP
18 Aspen Road, Kinsealy Court, Swords,
Co Dublin
Tel 01-8405948
*Parish Office:* Tel 01-8407277
Email stcolmcilleschurch@eircom.net
Website www.swordsparish.com

## TALLAGHT, DODDER
*St Dominic's, Dublin 24*
Rev Laurence Collins (OP) Adm
Rev Timothy Mulcahy (OP) CC
Presbytery, St Dominic's Road, Tallaght,
Dublin 24
Tel 01-4510620 Fax 01-4623223
*Parish Office:* Tel 01-4510620
Fax 01-4623223
Website www.stdominicsparishtallaght.ie

## TALLAGHT, OLDBAWN
*St Martin de Porres, Dublin 24*
Very Rev Michael Hurley Adm
The Presbytery, St Martin's, Aylesbury,
Dublin 24
Tel 01-4627080
Rev Piaras MacLochlainn CC
Rev Manoj Ponkattil CC
Rev Joseph Bharanikulangara CC and
Chaplain to Syro-Malabar Community
The Presbytery,
St Martin de Porres Parish,
Aylesbury, Dublin 24
Tel 01-4510160
*Pastoral Worker:* Breda Carroll
Blackhall, Calverstown,
Kilcullen, Co Kildare
Tel 085-1329895
Email stmartinsparish@eircom.net
*Parish Office:* Tel/Fax 01-4510160
Email stmartinsparish@eircom.net

## TALLAGHT, ST MARY'S
*St Mary's, Tallaght Village, Dublin 24*
Rev Donal Sweeney (OP) PP
Rev Robert Regula (OP) CC
*Church Apostolate*
Rev Eamon Moran (OP)
St Mary's Priory,
Tallaght, Dublin 24
Tel 01-4048100 Fax 01-4596784

## TALLAGHT, TYMON NORTH
*St Aengus's, Castletymon Road, Dublin 24*
Very Rev Benedict Moran (OP) PP
Dominican Community, St Aengus's,
Balrothery, Tallaght, Dublin 24
Tel 01-4513757
Email ben.moran25@gmail.com
Rev Pat Lucey (OP) CC
The Presbytery, St Aengus's,
Balrothery, Tallaght, Dublin 24
Tel 01-4528161
*Parish Office*
Tel 01-4513757 Fax 01-4624038
Email staenguschurch@eircom.net.
Website www.staengusparishtallaght.ie

## TEMPLEOGUE
*St Pius X, College Drive, Dublin 6W*
Very Rev Aquinas T. Duffy PP
23 Wainsfort Park,
Terenure, Dublin 6W
Tel 01-4900218
Email frduffy@eircom.net
Rev Deacon Gerard Larkin
*Parish Office*
Tel 01-4905284/087-9672258
Email info@stpiusx.ie
Website www.stpiusx.ie

## TERENURE
*St Joseph's, Dublin 6*
Very Rev Philip Bradley Adm
Parochial House, 83 Terenure Road East,
Dublin 6
Tel 01-4905520
Email fkmcdonnell@eircom.net
Rev Tom Dooley (SM) CC
4 Greenmount Road, Terenure,
Dublin 6
Tel 01-4904959
*Parish Office*: 01-4921755
Email stjosephterenure@eircom.net

## TRAVELLING PEOPLE
*Chapel of Ease, St Oliver's Park,
Clondalkin, Dublin 22*
Very Rev Derek Farrell PP
Tel 087-2573857
Email derek@ptrav.ie
Rev Paddy Kelly (CSsR) CC
6 New Cabra Road, Phibsborough,
Dublin 7
*Parish Office:* St Laurence House,
6 New Cabra Road, Phibsborough,
Dublin 7
Tel 01-8388874 Fax 01-8388901
Email into@ptrav.ie. www.ptrav.ie
Recommended Websites:
www.exchangehouse.ie
www.paveepoint.ie
www.stpetersphibsborough.com

## UNIVERSITY CHURCH
*Our Lady, Seat of Wisdom,
St Stephen's Green, Dublin 2*
Very Rev Patrick Boyle Adm
87A St Stephen's Green, Dublin 2
Tel 01-4780616
*Parish Chaplain*
Rev Raymond Kondowe PC
c/o Parish Office
*Parish Office*: Tel 01-4759674
Email newmanchurch@eircom.net
Website www.universitychurch.ie

## VALLEYMOUNT
*(Grouped with the parish of Blessington)*
*St Joseph's, Valleymount
Our Lady of Mount Carmel, Lacken*
Very Rev Timothy Murphy PP
The Presbytery, Main Street,
Blessington, Co Wicklow
Tel 045-865442
Rev Edward Downes CC
Parochial House, Cross,
Vallymount, Co Wicklow
Tel 045-867151

## WALKINSTOWN
*Assumption of the BVM, Dublin 12*
Very Rev John Jacob Adm
12 Walkinstown Road, Dublin 12
Tel 01-4502541
Rev Paul St John (SVD) CC
162 Walkinstown Road, Dublin 12
Tel 01-4501372
*Parish Sacristy*: Tel 01-4502649

## WHITEFRIAR STREET
*Our Lady of Mount Carmel,
Whitefriar Street, Dublin 2*
Very Rev Bernard Murphy (OCarm) PP
Carmelite Priory,
56 Aungier Street, Dublin 2
Tel 01-4758821
Email whitefriars@eircom.net

## WICKLOW
*St Patrick's, Wicklow, Co Wicklow*
Very Rev Donal Roche Adm
The Abbey, Wicklow, Co Wicklow
Tel 0404-671961 Fax 0404-69971
Rev Patrick O'Rourke (LC) CC
The Presbytery, St Patrick's Road,
Wicklow Town, Co Wicklow
*Parish Office:* Tel 0404-61699
Email parishofficewicklow@eircom.net

## WILLINGTON
*St Jude the Apostle, Orwell Park, Dublin 6W*
Very Rev Gregory O'Brien PP
2 Rossmore Road, Templeogue, Dublin 6W
Tel 01-4508432
*Parish Office*: Tel 01-4600127
Email judesparishoffice@eircom.net

## YELLOW WALLS, MALAHIDE
*(Grouped with the parishes of Malahide,
Kinsealy & Portmarnock)*
*Sacred Heart Church, Eastuary Road,
Malahide, Co Dublin*
Rev Frank Reburn Co-PP
11 Millview Court, Malahide, Co Dublin
Tel 01-8451902
Email fdreburn@hotmail.com
yellowwallsparish@gmail.com
Website www.yellowwallsparish.ie

# INSTITUTIONS AND THEIR CHAPLAINS

## COLLEGES

**Coláiste Mhuire Marino**
Griffith Avenue, Dublin 9
*Chaplain:* Vacant

**Dublin Institute of Technology**
Co-ordinator DIT Chaplaincy Service
*Chaplain:* Rev Alan Hilliard
Office Tel 01-4023639
Email alan.hilliard@dit.ie

**Dublin Institute of Technology,
Bolton Street**
Room 254, Bolton Street, Dublin 1
Tel 01-4023000 Fax 01-4023999
*Chaplain:* Rev Alan Hilliard
Office Tel 01-4023639
Email alan.hilliard@dit.ie

**Dublin Institute of Technology,
Kevin Street**
Room K251, Kevin Street, Dublin 2
Ms Fionnuala Walsh
Tel 01-4024568 Fax 01-4024999
Email fionnuala.walsh@dit.ie

**Dublin Institute of Technology, Cathal Brugha Street, Mountjoy Square and Grangegorman**
Room 25F, Cathal Brugha Street, Dublin 1
Room 239, Mountjoy Square,
Dublin 1
Tel 01-4023000 Fax 01-4024499
*Chaplain:* Mr Finbarr O'Leary
Tel 01-4024308, 01-4024112
Email finbarr.oleary@dit.ie

**Dublin Institute of Technology at Aungier Street**
Tel 01-4023000 Fax 01-4023003
Office Tel 01-4023050
Contact Co-ordinator of Chaplaincy

**Dublin Institute of Technology at Rathmines Road**
Tel 01-4023000 Fax 01-4023499
Contact Co-ordinator of Chaplaincy

**Dublin City University**
Very Rev Kevin Bartley, Chaplain
InterFaith Centre, Dublin 9
Tel 01-7005268 Fax 01-7005663
*Residence:* 30 Willow Park Crescent
Glasnevin, Dublin 11

**Institute of Technology**
Tallaght, Dublin 24
Tel 01-4042000
Sr Bernadette Purcell
Tel 01-4042615
Email bernadette.purcell@ittdublin.ie

**Mater Dei Institute of Education**
Tel 01-8086500
Mr Barrie McEntee

**National College of Art and Design**
100 Thomas Street, Dublin 8
*Chaplain:* Vacant

**St Patrick's College, Drumcondra**
Dublin 9
Tel 01-8842000
*Chaplain:* Rev Stephen Monaghan (CM)

**National University of Ireland, Maynooth (NUIM)**
Tel 01-7086000
Chaplaincy Service,
NUI Maynooth, Co Kildare
Tel 01-7083588
*Chaplains:* Mr Shay Claffey
Tel 01-7083588
Email seamus.claffey@nuim.ie
Ms Catherine Black
Tel 01-7083469
Email catherine.black@nuim.ie
*Executive Assistant:* Ms Susan Caldwell
Tel 01-7083320
Email chaplaincy@nuim.ie

**Trinity College, Dublin 2**
Rev Patrick Gleeson
Tel 01-6767316
48 Westland Row, Dublin 2
Rev Peter Sexton (SJ)
House 27 Trinity College, Dublin 2
Tel 01-8961260

**University College, Dublin**
Chaplains' Room, UCD, Belfield, Dublin 4
Tel 01-7168317
Rev John McNerney Tel 01-7164789
Rev Leon Ó Giolláin (SJ) Tel 01-7166495
*(office)*
*Chaplains' Residence:* St Stephen's, UCD
Belfield, Dublin 4 Tel 01-7161971

## DEFENCE FORCES

**Head Chaplain**
Rt Rev Mgr Eoin Thynne HCF
Tel 01-8042637
*Administrative Secretary:* Sgt Liam Bellew
Tel 01-8042638
Defence Forces Headquarters,
McKee Barracks, Blackhorse Avenue,
Dublin 7

**McKee Barracks**
Dublin 7
Tel 086-2256794
Rev Patrick Mernagh

**Cathal Brugha Barracks**
Rathmines, Dublin 6
Tel 01-8046484
Rev David Tyndall

**Casement Aerodrome**
Baldonnel, Co Dublin
Tel 01-4037536
Rev Jeremiah Carroll

**International Military Pilgrimage to Lourdes**
(Pelerinage Militaire Internationale)
*Director:* Rt Rev Mgr Eoin Thynne HCF
Tel 01-8042637

## HOSPITALS

**Baggot Street Hospital**
Baggot Street, Dublin 4
Vacant

**Beaumont Hospital**
Beaumont Road, Dublin 9
Tel 01-8377755
*Direct Line:* 01-8092815/8093229
Rev Eoin Hughes Tel 01-8477573
Rev Denis Sandham (OSCam)
Ms Jenny Cuypers

**Beaumont Convalescent Home**
Tel 8379186
Vacant

**Blackrock Clinic**
Blackrock, Co Dublin
Tel 01-2832222
Rev Gerard Byrne

**Blackrock Hospice**
Sweetman's Avenue, Blackrock,
Co Dublin
Tel 01-2064000
Sr Ann Purcell
Tel 01-2064024 – direct line

**Bloomfield**
Donnybrook, Dublin 4
Tel 01-4950021
Carmelite Fathers, Avila,
Morehampton Road, Dublin 4
Tel 01-6683091

**Bon Secours Hospital**
Glasnevin, Dublin 9
Tel 01-8065300
Rev Owen O'Sullivan (OFM Cap),
Sr Goretti Spillane, Ms Fionnuala Prunty,
Ms Patricia Nolan, Ms Eileen Kavanagh

**Cappagh National Orthopaedic Hospital**
Cappagh, Dublin 11
Tel 01-8341211
Appointment Pending

**Central Mental Hospital**
Dundrum
Tel 01-2989266
Rev Desmond O'Grady (SJ)

**Cherry Orchard Hospital**
Ballyfermot
Tel 01-6264702
Rev Patrick Cully (CSSp) (on behalf of the Holy Spirit Congregation)

**Children's Hospital**
Temple Street
Tel 01-8784200
Sr Julie Buckley, Ms Carmel Battigan

**Clonskeagh Hospital**
Vergemount, Dublin 6
Tel 01-2697877
Rev Jude Lynch (CSSp) (on behalf of the Holy Spirit Congregation)

**Connolly Hospital**
Blanchardstown, Dublin 15
Tel 01-8213844
Rev Martin Geraghty (OSCam)
Rev Anthony O'Riordan (SVD)
Tel 01-6465168
Ms Caroline Mullen

**Coombe Women's and Infant's University Hospital**
Dolphin's Barn, Dublin 8
Tel 01-4085200
Ms Philomena Power
Ms Catherine Dilworth

**Hermitage Medical Clinic**
Old Lucan Road, Lucan, Co Dublin
Tel 01-6459000
Appointment Pending

**Leopardstown Park Hospital**
Tel 01-2955055
Sr Annette Byrne
Ms Miriam Molan

**Mater Hospital**
Eccles Street, Dublin 7
Tel 01-8301122
Rev Vincent Xavier Kakkadampallil (OSCam), Rev John Philip Kakkarakunnel
Ms Catherine Ingoldsby, Ms Maire
Breathnach, Ms Margaret Sleator, Ms
Jackie Taylor

**Mater Private Hospital**
Dublin 7
Tel 01-8858888
Rev Kieran Dunne

**National Maternity Hospital**
Holles Street, Dublin 2
Tel 01-6373100
Sr Marion Ryan
Ms Eithne O'Reilly

**National Rehabilitation Hospital**
Rochestown Avenue,
Dun Laoghaire, Co Dublin
Tel 01-2854777
Rev Michael Kennedy (CSSp)

**Newcastle Hospital**
Tel 01-2819001
Very Rev Sean Canon Smith CC
The Presbytery, Newtownmountkennedy,
Co Wicklow
Tel 01-2819253

**Orthopaedic Hospital**
Castle Avenue, Clontarf
Tel 01-8332521
Very Rev Mícheál Hastings

**Our Lady's Children's Hospital**
Crumlin, Dublin 12
Tel 01-4096100
Rev John Dunphy, Ms Maria McGee

**Our Lady's Hospice**
Harold's Cross
Tel 01-4068700
Rev Brendan McKeever CP
Ms Elizabeth Coyle
Sr Helen Spragg (MMM)

**Peamount Hospital**
Newcastle, Co Dublin
Tel 01-6010300
Rev Jim Byrnes (CSSp)

**Rotunda Hospital**
Parnell Street, Dublin 1
Tel 01-8730700
Ms Anne Charlton

**Royal Hospital Donnybrook**
Morehampton Road, Dublin 4
Tel 01-4972844
Appointment Pending

**Royal Victoria Eye and Ear Hospital**
Adelaide Road, Dublin 12
Tel 01-6644600
Jesuit Community Milltown Park
Tel 01-2698411

**St Brendan's Hospital**
Upper Grangegorman, Dublin 7
Tel 01-8693000
Rev Piaras Ó Duill (OFMCap)
Tel 01-8730599

**St Bricin's Military Hospital**
Infirmary Road, Dublin 8
Tel 01-6776112
Rt Rev Mgr Eoin Thynne (HCF)

**St Columcille's Hospital**
Loughlinstown, Co Dublin
Tel 01-2825800
Rev Desmond Farren (MSC)
Ms Marianne Quinn

**St Francis Hospice, Raheny/
Blanchardstown**
Tel 01-8327535 (Raheny)
Tel 01-8294000 (Blanchardstown)
Rev Eustace McSweeney (OFMCap),
Rev Michael Duffy (OFMCap)
Capuchin Friary, Raheny, Dublin 5
Tel 01-8313886
Ms Marie Gribbin (Co-ordinating
Chaplain), Sr Anna Kennedy,
Sr Maire Brady

**St Ita's, Portrane**
Tel 01-8436337
Very Rev Joseph Connolly PP
Parochial House, Donabate, Co Dublin
Tel 01-8436011

**St James's Hospital**
James's Street, Dublin 8
Tel 01-4103000
Direct Line 01-4103659
Rev Brian Gough, Rev Jim Stapleton
(CSSp), Sr Joyce Cullinane, Sr Anne Kelly

**St John of God Hospital**
Stillorgan, Co Dublin
Tel 01-2771400
Rev Hugh Gillan (OH)

**St Joseph's Hospital**
Clonsilla
Tel 01-8217177
Chaplain: Vacant

**St Joseph's Hospital**
Springdale Road, Raheny, Dublin 5
Tel 01-8478433
Appointment pending

**St Loman's Hospital**
Ballyowen, Palmerstown, Dublin 20
Tel 01-6264077
Rev Jeremiah Lambe (CSSp)

**St Luke's Hospital**
Highfield Road, Rathgar, Dublin 6
Tel 01-4065000
Rev Tom O'Connor (OSCam)

**St Mary's Hospital**
Phoenix Park, Dublin 20
Tel 01-6250300
Rev John Agbaragba (CSSp)
Rev Azenda Ikyegh (CSSp)

**St Michael's Hospital**
Lower George's Street, Dun Laoghaire
Tel 01-2806901
Rev Thomas McDonald (CSSp)
Sr Margaret Hilliard

**St Patrick's Hospital**
James Street, Dublin 8
Tel 01-6775423
Chaplain: Vacant

**St Paul's (Autistic Children)**
Beaumont
Tel 01-8377673
Very Rev Gerard Deegan Adm
Tel 01-8477740

**St Vincent's Hospital**
Athy, Co Kildare
Tel 059-8643000
Very Rev Joseph O'Brien (OP)
Tel 059-8631573

**St Vincent's University Hospital**
Elm Park, Dublin 4
Tel 01-2214000
Direct Line 01-2094325
Rev Jim MacDonnell (CSSp), Rev Liam
Cuffe

**St Vincent's Private Hospital**
Tel 01-2638000
Rev John O'Keeffe (SJ), Ms Lucy Higgins,
Ms Pauline O'Dowd, Sr Mary Helen
Anthonythasan, Sr Yudith Anu (SSPS)

**St Vincent's, Fairview**
Tel 01-8375101
Mr Jim Owens
Sr Angela Burke

**Stewart's Hospital, Palmerstown**
Tel 01-6264444
Rev John Agbaragba (CSSp)
Rev Azenda Ikyegh (CSSp)

**St Colman's, Rathdrum**
Tel 0404-46109
Very Rev Derek Doyle
Tel 0404-46229

**Tallaght Hospital**
Tel 01-4142000
Roman Catholic Bleep: 2725
Director of Pastoral Care: Rev John Kelly
22 Nugent Road, Churchtown,
Dublin 14
Tel 01-4142482
Email john.kelly@amnch.ie
Pastoral Care Team: Ms Catherine Shirley,
Ms Eden Dela Druz, Ms Sally Phalan, Mr
Cathal O'Sullivan
Tel 01-4142485

## PRISONS

**Arbour Hill Prison**
Ard na Gaoithe, Arbour Hill, Dublin 7
Rev Ciaran Enright
Email ccenright@irishprisons.ie
Prison General Office: Tel 01-6719333

**Clover Hill Remand Centre**
Cloverhill Road, Clondalkin, Dublin 22
Rev John O'Sullivan (MSC)
Tel 01-6304586
Email jjosullivan@irishprisons.ie
Sr Margaret O'Donovan (DC)
Tel 01-6304584
Email mmodonovan@irishprisons.ie
Prison General Office: Tel 01-6304531/2

## Dóchas Centre Mountjoy Women's Prison
North Circular Road, Dublin 7
Sr Mary Mullins Tel 01-8858920
Email mtmullins@irishprisons.ie
Prison General Office 01-8858987

## Mountjoy Prison
North Circular Road, Dublin 7
Mrs Ruth Breen
Tel 01-8062843
Email rabreen@irishprisons.ie
Mark Davis
Tel 01-8062843
Rev Jimmy Kelly (OSM)
Tel 01-8062843
*Prison General Office:* Tel 01-8062800

## Saint Patrick's Institution
North Circular Road, Dublin 7
Tel 01-8062894
Miss Ruth Comerford
Email rmcomerford@irishprisons.ie
*General Office:* Tel 01-8062906

## Shelton Abbey
Arklow, Co Wicklow
Sr Patricia Egan (RSCJ)
Tel 0402-42321
*General Office:* Tel 0402-42300

## Training Unit
Glengariff Parade, Dublin 7
Sr Mairead Gahan LCM
Tel 01-8309612
Email gahanmairead@eircom.net
*Prison General Office:* Tel 01-8062881

## Wheatfield Prison
Cloverhill Road,
Clondalkin, Dublin 22
Sr Esther Murphy (RSC) Tel 01-6209447
Email esmurphy@irishprisons.ie
Sr Imelda Wickham (PBVM)
Tel 01-6209466
Email imwickham@irishprisons.ie
Sr Joan Kane (OSU) Tel 01-6209446
Email jakane@irishprisons.ie
Sr Kathleen Cunningham (DC)
Tel 01-6209466/7
*Prison General Office:* Tel 01-6209400

## PRIESTS ELSEWHERE IN THE DIOCESE

Rev Patrick Desmond
Apostolic Nunciature
The Lodge, Mount Sackville,
Chapelizod, Dublin 20
Tel 01-8214004
Rev Dermod McCarthy
RTÉ, Donnybrook, Dublin 4
Tel 01-2083237/087-2499719
Fax 01-2083974
Email mccartd@rte.ie
Rev Peter Murphy
Accord Catholic Marriage Care Service,
Columba Centre, Maynooth, Co Kildare

## PRIESTS WORKING OUTSIDE THE DIOCESE

Rev Adrian Crowley
c/o Archdiocese of Monrovia,
Liberia, West Africa
Rev Ian Evans
Chaplain, England
Rev John Kennedy (Congregation for the
Doctrine of the Faith)
Via del Mascherino 12,
00193 Roma, Italy
Very Rev Mgr Ciaran O'Carroll
Rector, Pontifical Irish College,
Via dei SS Quattro 1, 00184, Roma, Italy
Rt Rev Mgr Paul Tighe
Secretary of the Pontifical Council for
Social Communications, Vatican City

## RETIRED PRIESTS

Very Rev Denis T. Bergin
Ferndene Nursing Home,
Deansgrange Road,
Blackrock, Co Dublin
Very Rev Bernard Canon Brady
61 Glasnevin Hill, Dublin 9
Ven Archdeacon Macarten Brady
Sacred Heart Residence, Sybil Hill Road,
Killester, Dublin 5
Rev Noel Campbell
Ballysmutlan, Manor Kilbride,
Blessington, Co Wicklow
Rev John Carey
Sacred Heart Residence, Sybil Hill Road,
Killester, Dublin 5
Very Rev Patrick Carmody
16 Hazelgrove, Ardfert, Co Kerry
Rev Denis Carroll
85 Hillcrest Drive, Esker,
Lucan, Co Dublin
Very Rev Seamus Cassidy
Tavis, Kilmainham Wood,
Kells, Co Meath
Rt Rev Mgr Dermot Clarke EV
4 Griffith Avenue, Marino, Dublin 3
Very Rev Thomas Colreavy
28 Glentworth Park, Ard-na-Gréine,
Ayrfield, Dublin 13
Tel 01-8484836
Rev Diarmuid Connolly
4 Summerfield Lawn,
Blanchardstown, Dubin 15
Rev Michael Connolly
54 Wyattville Park,
Loughlinstown, Co Dublin
Rt Rev Mgr Seamus Conway
Parochial House, Booterstown, Co Dublin
Very Rev Philip Corcoran
542 River Forest Estate,
Leixlip, Co Kildare
Rev Edward Corry
Presbytery No. 2, Treepark Road,
Kilnamanagh, Dublin 24
Very Rev Patrick J. Culhane
138 Lucan Road, Chapelizod, Dublin 20

Rev Seamus F. Cullen
2 Ceol na Mara, Lower Main Street,
Rush, Co Dublin
Tel 01-8438024
Email scullen1@eircom.net
Rev Aidan D'Arcy
Little Sisters of the Poor, Sybil Hill,
Raheny, Dublin 5
Very Rev Philip Dennehy PE
4 Stanhope Place, Athy, Co Kildare
Very Rev Francis Dooley
76 Tritonville Road,
Sandymount, Dublin 4
Rev Cornelius Dowling
St Anthony's, 13 Richmond Grove,
Monkstown, Co Dublin
Tel 01-2800789
Email dowcpb@eircom.net
Very Rev Patrick Canon Fagan PE
The Presbytery, Ballyboughal,
Co Dublin
Very Rev James Canon Fingleton
279 Howth Road, Raheny, Dublin 5
Very Rev John Canon Fitzgibbon PE
The Presbytery, Chapel Road,
Lusk, Co Dublin
Very Rev Denis Foley
32 Walkinstown Road, Dublin 12
Very Rev Paul Freeney PE
Parochial House,
43 Upper Beechwood Avenue,
Ranelagh, Dublin 6
Very Rev Mgr Colm Gallagher
594 Howth Road, Raheny, Dublin 5
Very Rev J. Anthony Gaughan
56 Newtownpark Avenue, Blackrock,
Co Dublin
Rev Michael Geaney
7 Rockliffe Terrace,
Blackrock Road, Cork
Very Rev Edward Griffin
15 Connawood, Bray, Co Wicklow
Very Rev James Hannon
Our Lady's Manor, Bulloch Castle,
Dalkey, Co Dublin
Very Rev Walter Canon Harris PE
151 Clonsilla Road, Blanchardstown,
Dublin 15
Very Rev Mícheál Hastings
103 Mount Prospect Drive,
Clontarf, Dublin 3
Tel 01-8335255/087-2358634
Very Rev Liam Hickey
St Ciaran's, 1 Cherryfield Park,
Hartstown, Dublin 15
Very Rev Ciaran Holahan
11 Foxrock Court, Foxrock, Dublin 18
Rt Rev Mgr Brendan Houlihan
Parochial House, Mount Saint Mary's,
Howth, Co Dublin
Rev Cecil Johnston
8 Corrig Park, Dun Laoghaire,
Co Dublin
Tel 01-285594
Very Rev Thomas V. Kelly
Castlebar Road, Westport, Co Mayo
Very Rev Eugene Kennedy
7 Riverwood Vale, Castleknock,
Dublin 15
Email ekennedy@laurellodgeparish.ie

Rev Peter Kilroy
64 Cherbury Court,
Booterstown, Co Dublin
Rev Denis Laverty
Pro-Cathedral House,
83 Marlborough Street, Dublin 1
Rev John Lynch
Sacred Heart Residence, Sybil Hill Road,
Killester, Dublin 5
Rt Rev Mgr James Ardle Canon MacMahon
Sacred Heart Residence,
Sybil Hill Road, Killester, Dublin 5
Very Rev John Canon MacMahon
Holy Family Residence, Roebuck,
Dundrum, Dublin 14
Rev Christopher J. Madden, 'Lisieux',
196 Oakcourt Avenue, Palmerstown,
Dublin 20
Very Rev Patrick J. Mangan PE
Dun Mhuire, 44 Upper Beechwood Avenue,
Ranelagh, Dublin 6
Tel 01-4975180/087-9857264
Very Rev Val Martin
'Logatryna', Dunlavin, Co Wicklow
Rev Colm Mathews
Highfield Healthcare, Swords Road,
Dublin 9
Tel 01-8374444
Very Rev Eugene McCarney
Parochial House, Castletown,
Gorey, Co Wexford
Rev Padraig McCarthy
14 Blackthorn Court, Sandyford, Dublin 16
Very Rev Francis Canon McDonnell
c/o Parochial House,
83 Terenure Road East, Dublin 6
Rev Cornelius McGillicuddy
Sacred Heart Residence, Sybil Hill Road,
Killester, Dublin 5
Very Rev Raymond Canon Molony
Presbytery No 2, Thormanby Road,
Howth, Co Dublin
Tel 01-8222092
Very Rev Patrick B. Moore PE
Sandy Corner, Sallymount, Co Wicklow
Very Rev Seamus Moore PE
8 Herbert Avenue, Dublin 4
Rev John F. Moran
192 Navan Road, Dublin 7
Very Rev Benedict Mulligan PE
42 Corke Abbey, Little Bray, Co Wicklow
Very Rev Patrick Mulvey
Our Lady's Manor, Dalkey, Co Dublin
Very Rev Peadar Canon Murney
25 Thomastown Road, Dun Laoghaire,
Co Dublin
Tel 01-2856660
Very Rev Thomas Murphy
Tara Winthrop Private Clinic,
Nevinstown Lane, Pinnock Hill,
Swords, Co Dublin
Rev James Murray
9 Hillcrest Manor, Templeogue,
Dublin 6W
Very Rev Liam Murtagh
33 Grace Park Road,
Drumcondra, Dublin 9
Tel 087-2408416

Rev Sean Noone
The Presbytery, Pollathomas, Co Mayo
Rev James O'Brien
Sacred Heart Residence, Sybil Hill Road,
Killester, Dublin 5
Very Rev John O'Connell PE
53 Ardmore Wood, Herbert Road, Bray,
Co Wicklow
Very Rev Erill Canon O'Connor
14 Clare Road, Dublin 9
Tel 01-8372677
Very Rev Donal O'Doherty PE
Holy Cross, Upper Kilmacud Road,
Dundrum, Dublin 14
Rev Philip O'Driscoll
23 Barclay Court, Blackrock, Co Dublin
Very Rev Thomas O'Keeffe
20 Glen Avenue, The Park, Cabinteely,
Dublin 18
Very Rev Maurice Canon O'Moore PE
6 Richmond Avenue,
Monkstown, Co Dublin
Rev Sean O'Rourke
15 Seaview Park, Shankill, Co Dublin
Rev Padraig O'Saorai
Woodlands House Nursing Home,
Trim Road, Navan, Co Meath
Very Rev Maurice O'Shea PE
6 Beechpark Lawn, Castleknock,
Dublin 15
Rev Colm O'Siochru
Our Lady's Manor, Bulloch Castle,
Dalkey, Co Dublin
Rev Brian O'Sullivan
The Cottage, Glengara Park,
Glenageary, Dun Laoghaire,
Co Dublin
Rev John K. O'Sullivan
97 Kincora Avenue, Clontarf, Dublin 3
Rev Sean O'Toole
Presbytery, Sea Road Arklow
Tel 0402-32153
Email seanotoole@eircom.net
Rev Sean Quigley
The Presbytery, 48 Aughrim Street,
Dublin 7
Very Rev Leo Quinlan
'Carrefour', Jarretstown,
Dunboyne, Co Meath
Very Rev James A. Canon Randles PE
Sacred Heart Residence, Sybil Hill Road,
Killester, Dublin 5
Rev Henry Regan
Presbytery No. 1, Church Grounds,
Kill Avenue, Dun Laoghaire, Co Dublin
Very Rev Denis Ryan PE
Parochial House House,
1 Rossmore Road, Dublin 6W
Very Rev Patrick G. Ryan
Mounthaven Lodge Nursing Home,
Kilcock, Co Kildare
Rt Rev Mgr Richard Sherry PE
Presbytery No 2, Stillorgan Road,
Donnybrook, Dublin 4
Very Rev Patrick Shiel
74 Mount Drinan Avenue, Kinsealy
Downs, Swords, Co Dublin

Very Rev Mgr Thomas Stack PE
Apt 4, Maple Hall (adjoining church),
Milltown Road, Dublin 6
Very Rev John Stokes
44 Carlton Court, Swords, Co Dublin
Tel 01-8138566
Rev Michael D. Canon Supple
Holy Family Residence, Roebuck Road,
Dundrum, Dublin 14
Rt Rev Mgr Owen Canon Sweeney
Sacred Heart Residence, Sybil Hill Road,
Killester, Dublin 5
Rev Jeremiah Threadgold
Sacred Heart Residence, Sybil Hill Road,
Killester, Dublin 5
Rev Michael Wall
Sacred Heart Residence, Sybil Hill Road,
Killester, Dublin 5
Rev John M. Ward
1 Chestnut Grove, Ballymount Road,
Dublin 24

## PERSONAL PRELATURE

**OPUS DEI**
Harvieston, 22 Cunningham Road,
Dalkey, Co Dublin
Tel 01-2859877 Fax 01-2305059
*Vicar for Ireland:*
Rev Justin Gillespie DD

## RELIGIOUS ORDERS AND CONGREGATIONS

## PRIESTS

**AUGUSTINIANS**
St Augustine's, Taylor's Lane,
Ballyboden, Dublin 16
Tel 01-4241000 Fax 01-4939915
Email www.augustinians.ie
*Provincial:* Rev John Hennebry (OSA)
*Prior:* Rev Noel Hession (OSA)

St John's Priory, Thomas Street, Dublin 8
Tel 01-6770393/0415/0601
Fax 01-6713102 (Mission Office)/6770423
(House)
*Prior:* Rev Padraig A. Daly (OSA)

Orlagh Retreat Centre
Old Court Road, Dublin 16
Tel 01-4930932/4933315
Fax 01-4930987
Email orlagh@augustinians.ie
*Director:* Rev John Byrne (OSA)

(See also under parishes – Ballyboden,
Meath Street and Rivermount)

**BLESSED SACRAMENT CONGREGATION**
Blessed Sacrament Chapel,
20 Bachelors Walk, Dublin 1
Tel 01-8724597 Fax 01-8724724
Email sssdublin@eircom.net
*Superior:* Rev James Campbell (SSS)

**Allianz ⑪**

## CAMILLIANS
St Camillus, South Hill Avenue,
Blackrock, Co Dublin
Tel 01-2882873 Fax 01-2833380
*Superior:* Rev Denis Sandham

St Camillus,
11 St Vincent Street North, Dublin 7
Tel 01-8300365 (Residence)
Tel 01-8301122 (Mater Hospital)

## CAPUCHINS
Provincial Office
12 Halston Street, Dublin 7
Tel 01-8733205 Fax 01-8730294
Email capcurirl@eircom.net
*Provincial Minister*
Very Rev Adrian Curran (OFMCap)

St Mary of the Angels, Church Street,
Dublin 7
Tel (Parish) 01-8730925
Tel (Friary) 01-8730599/Fax 01-8730250
*Guardian:* Rev Bryan Shortall (OFMCap)

Capuchin Friary (Immaculate Heart of
Mary), Raheny, Dublin 5
Tel 01-8313886/8312805
*Guardian*
Rev Michael Burgess (OFMCap)

(See also under parishes – Halston Street
and Priorswood)

## CARMELITES (OCARM)
Provincial Office, Gort Muire,
Ballinteer, Dublin 16
Tel 01-2984014 Fax 01-2987221
*Provincial:* Rev Martin Kilmurray (OCarm)

Whitefriar Street Church,
56 Aungier Street, Dublin 2
Tel 01-4758821 Fax 01-4758825
Email whitefriars@eircom.net
*Prior:* Rev Brian McKay (OCarm)
*Parish Priest:* Rev Bernard Murphy (OCarm)

Terenure College, Terenure, Dublin 6W
Tel 01-4904621 Fax 01-4902403
Email admin@terenurecollege.ie
*Prior/Manager:* Rev Michael Troy (OCarm)
*Sub-Prior:* Rev Eoin Moore (OCarm)
*Principal (Senior School):*
Rev Richard Byrne (OCarm)
*Principal (Junior School):*
Rev Michael Troy (OCarm)

(See also under parishes – Knocklyon and
Whitefriar Street)

## CARMELITES (OCD)
53 Marlborough Road, Donnybrook,
Dublin 4
Tel 01-6617163/6601832 Fax 01-6683752
Email mmcgoldrickocd@gmail.com
Website www.ocd.ie
*Provincial:* Rev Michael McGoldrick (OCD)

St Teresa's, Clarendon Street, Dublin 2
Tel 01-6718466/6718127
*Prior:* Rev Christopher Clarke (OCD)

Avila, Bloomfield Avenue,
Morehampton Road, Dublin 4
Tel 01-6430200 Fax 01-6430281
Email avila@ocd.ie
*Prior:* Rev Vincent O'Hara (OCD)

Karmel Vocation Centre,
53/55 Marlborough Road, Dublin 4
Tel 01-6601832
*Prior:* Rev Edmund Smyth (OCD)

St Joseph's, Berkeley Road, Dublin 7
Tel 01-8306356/8306336
*Prior:* Rev David Donnellan (OCD) PP

## CISTERCIANS
Bolton Abbey, Moone, Co Kildare
Tel 059-8624102 Fax 059-8624309
Email info@boltonabbey.ie
Website www.boltonabbey.ie
*Abbot:* Rt Rev Dom Michael Ryan (OCSO)

## COMBONI MISSIONARIES
8 Clontarf Road, Dublin 3
Tel/Fax 01-8330051
Email combonimission@eircom.net
*Superior:* Rev Antonio Benetti (MCCJ)

## CONGREGATION OF THE PRIESTS OF THE SACRED HEART OF JESUS
Fairfield, 66 Inchicore Road, Dublin 8
Tel 01-4538655
Email scjdublin@eircom.net
House of Formation
*Superior and Formation Director:*
Rev John Kelly (SCJ)

(See also under parishes – Ardlea)

## CONGREGATION OF THE SACRED HEARTS OF JESUS AND MARY (SACRED HEARTS COMMUNITY)
*Provincialate:* Coudrin House,
27 Northbrook Road, Dublin 6
Tel 01-6604898
Email ssccdublin@eircom.net
Website www.sacredhearts.ie
Community 01-6686584 Fax 01-6686590
*Provincial:* Very Rev Derek Laverty (SSCC)

Sacred Heart Presbytery,
St John's Drive, Clondalkin, Dublin 22
Tel 01-4570032

(See also under parishes – Sruleen)

## DIVINE WORD MISSIONARIES
1 & 3 Pembroke Road, Dublin 4
Tel 01-6680904
*Praeses:* Rev Albert Escoto (SVD)
Email aesvd@hotmail.com
*Provincial:* Rev Patrick Byrne (SVD)
Email provincial@svdireland.com

133 North Circular Road, Dublin 7
Tel 01-8386743
*Praeses:* Rev John Feighery (SVD)

Maynooth, Co Kildare
Tel 01-6286391/2 Fax 01-6289184
*Rector:* Rev D. Vincent Twomey (SVD)
Email secretary@svdireland.com

## DOMINICANS
Provincial Office, St Mary's,
Tallaght, Dublin 24
Tel 01-4048118/4048114 Fax 01-4515584
Email provincialop@eircom.net
*Provincial:* Very Rev Gregory Carroll (OP)

St Mary's Priory, Tallaght, Dublin 24
Tel 01-4048100
Parish 01-4048188
*Prior:* Very Rev Donal Sweeney (OP) PP
Email dsyop@eircom.net

St Saviour's,
Upper Dorset Street, Dublin 1
Tel 01-8897610 Fax 01-8734003
Email stsaviours@eircom.net
*Prior:* Very Rev Edward Conway (OP) PP

St Dominic's,
Athy, Co Kildare
Tel 059-8631573 Fax 059-8631649
*Prior:* Very Rev Joseph O'Brien (OP)

Dominican Community,
47 Leeson Park, Dublin 6
Tel 01-6602427
*Superior:* Very Rev Bernard Treacy (OP)

(See also under parishes – Dominick
Street and three of the Tallaght parishes)

## FRANCISCANS (OFM)
Provincial Office, Franciscan Friary,
4 Merchant's Quay, Dublin 4
Tel 01-6742500 Fax 01-6742549
Email info@franciscans.ie
*Provincial:* Rev Hugh McKenna (OFM)
Email hughmck@gmail.com

Adam and Eve's, Merchants Quay,
Dublin 8
Tel 01-6771128 Fax 01-6771000
*Guardian:* Rev Brendan McGrath (OFM)

Franciscan House of Studies,
Dún Mhuire, Seafield Road,
Killiney, Co Dublin
Tel 01-2826760 Fax 01-2826993
Email dmkilliney@eircom.net
*Guardian:* Rev Kieran Cronin (OFM)

(See also under parishes – Merchants Quay)

## FRANCISCANS: ORDER OF FRIARS MINOR
Conventual (Greyfriars) (OFMConv)
The Friary of the Visitation of the BVM,
Fairview Strand, Fairview, Dublin 3
Tel 01-8376000 Fax 01-8376021

(See also under parishes – Fairview)

## HOLY SPIRIT CONGREGATION

Holy Spirit Provincialate, Temple Park,
Richmond Avenue South, Dublin 6
Tel 01-4977230/4975127 Fax 01-4975399
Email communications@spiritan.ie
*Provincial Leadership Team*
Rev Marc Whelan (CSSp) *(Provincial)*
Rev Brendan Carr (CSSp); Rev John
Kilcrann (CSSp); Rev Jude Lynch (CSSp)
*(Bursar);* Rev John Laizer (CSSp)

Spiritan Education Trust,
(Des Places Educational Association Ltd),
Kimmage Manor, Dublin 12
Tel 01-4997610
www.desplaces.ie
Rev Peter Conaty *(Chair)*
Awareness Education Services
Rev Tony Byrne (CSSp)
Tel/Fax 01-8388888
Email info@awarenesseducation.org

Spiritan Mission Resource and Heritage
Centre, Kimmage Manor, Dubin 12
*Manager:* Rev Brian O'Toole (CSSp)
Email archives@spiritan.ie

Holy Spirit Missionary College,
Kimmage Manor,
Whitehall Road, Dublin 12
Tel 01-4064300 Fax 01-4920062
Email reception@kimmagemanor.ie
*Community Leader*
Rev Daithí Kenneally (CSSp)

Kimmage Development Studies Centre,
Kimmage Manor, Dublin 12
Tel 01-4064386 Fax 01-4064388
Email info@kimmagedsc.ie
www.kimmagedsc.ie
*Director:* Dr Rob Kevlihan

Spiritan House – SPIRASI Project,
Spiritan Asylum Services Initiative,
213 North Circular Road, Dublin 7
Tel 01-8389664/8683504 Fax 01-8686500
*Director:* Mr Greg Straton
*Community Leader:* Rev John Laizer (CSSp)

Blackrock College, Blackrock, Co Dublin
Tel 01-2888681 Fax 01-2834267
Email info@blackrockcollege.com
*Community Leader:* Rev Tom Nash (CSSp)
*Principal:* Alan MacGinty

Willow Park
Tel 01-2881651 Fax 01-2783353
Email admin@willowparkschool.ie
*Principal Senior School:* Mr Hugh McGuire
*Principal Junior School:* Mr Jim Casey

St Mary's College, Rathmines, Dublin 6
Tel 01-4995760 Fax 01-4972621
Junior School Tel 01-4995721
Email junsec@stmarys.ie
Senior School Tel 4995700 Fax 01-4972574
Email sensec@stmarys.ie
*Community Leader*
Rev Richard Olin (CSSp)
*Principal Secondary School*
Mr Denis Murphy
*Principal Junior School*
Ms Mary O'Donnell

St Michael's College,
Ailesbury Road, Dublin 4
Tel 01-2189400 Fax 01-2698862
Email stmcoll@indigo.ie
*Principal:* Mr Tim Kelleher
*Principal Junior School:* Ms Lorna Heslin

Duquesne University,
Duquesne in Dublin, St Michael's,
1 Ailesbury Road, Ballsbridge, Dublin 4
Tel/Fax 01-2080940
www.duq.edu/ireland
*Resident Director:* Ms Laura K. Palilla
Email laurapalilla@gmail.com

Templeogue College,
Templeville Road, Dublin 6W
Tel 01-4903909 Fax 01-4920903
*Communty Leader*
Rev William Bradley (CSSp)
*Principal:* Ms Aoife O'Donnell
Tel 01-4905788
Email info@templeoguecollege.ie

(See also under parishes – Bawnogue,
Deansrath, Greenhills and Kimmage)

## JESUITS

Irish Jesuit Provincialate
Milltown Park, Sandford Road, Dublin 6
Tel 01-4987333 Fax 01-4987334
Email curia@jesuit.ie
*Provincial:* Rev Tom Layden (SJ)
*Assistant Provincial*
Rev Liam O'Connell (SJ)

Jesuit Communication Centre
Irish Jesuit Provincialate,
Milltown Park, Sandford Road, Dublin 6
Tel 01-4987347/01-4987348
*Director:* Ms Pat Coyle
Email coylep@jesuit.ie

Jesuit Curia Community,
Loyola House, Milltown Park,
Sandford Road, Dublin 6
Tel 01-2180276
Email loyola@jesuit.ie
*Superior & Guestmaster*
Rev Noel Barber (SJ)
*Minister:* Rev Liam O'Connell (SJ)

Belvedere College, Dublin 1
Tel 01-8586600 Fax 01-8744374
*Rector:* Rev Derek Cassidy (SJ)
Secondary day school
*Headmaster:* Mr Gerard Foley

Milltown Park, Sandford Road, Dublin 6
Tel 01-2698411/2698113
Fax 01-2600371
Email milltown@jesuit.ie
*Rector:* Rev William Callanan (SJ)

Milltown Institute of Theology and
Philosophy, Milltown Park, Dublin 6
Tel 01-2776300 Fax 01-2692528
Email info@milltown-institute.ie
*Rector & Acting President:* Associate
Prof. Rev Thomas R. Whelan (CSSp)

Lay Retreat Association of St Ignatius,
Milltown Park, Dublin 6
Tel 01-7072203
*Spiritual Director:* Rev Fergus O'Keefe (SJ)

25 Croftwood Park,
Cherry Orchard, Dublin 10
Tel 01-6267413

Gonzaga College,
Sandford Road, Dublin 6
Community Tel 01-4972943
Email gonzaga@s-j.ie
(College) Tel 01-4972931
Fax 01-4967769
Email (College) office@gonzaga.ie
Fax (Community) 01-4960849
Email (Community) gonzaga@jesuit.ie
*Rector:* Rev Myles O'Reilly (SJ)
*Minister:* Rev Kennedy O'Brien (SJ)
*Headmaster:* Mr Damon McCaul

Manresa House,
Dollymount, Dublin 3
Tel 01-8331352 Fax 01-8331002
Email manresa@jesuit.ie
*Rector:* Rev Michael Drennan (SJ)

Dominic Collins' House, Residence,
129 Morehampton Road, Dublin 4
Tel 01-2693075 Fax 01-2698462
*Vice-Superior:* Rev David Coghlan (SJ)

John Sullivan House,
House of Formation,
27 Leinster Road, Rathmines, Dublin 6
Tel 01-5242134
*Superior:* Rev Martin Curry (SJ)

35 Lower Leeson Street,
Dublin 2
Tel 01-6761248 Fax 01-7758598
*Superior:* Rev Brian Grogan (SJ)

Campion House, Residence,
28 Lower Hatch Street, Dublin 2
Tel 01-6383990 Fax 01-6762805
Email campion@jesuit.ie
*Superior:* Rev Patrick Hume (SJ)

(See also under parishes – Gardiner
Street)

## LEGIONARIES OF CHRIST

Leopardstown Road,
Foxrock, Dublin 18
Tel 01-2955902
Email ireland@legionaries.org
*Superior:* Rev Alejandro Fuentes (LC)

Clonlost Retreat and Youth Centre
Killiney Road, Killiney, Co Dublin
Tel 01-2350064
*Chaplain:* Rev Fergal O'Dúill (LC)

Dublin Oak Academy
Kilcroney, Bray, Co Wicklow
Tel 01-2863290 Fax 01-2865315
Email secretary@dublinoakacademy.com
*Director:* Rev Francisco Cepeda (LC)
*Chaplain:* Rev Matthew Schmitz (LC)

Woodlands Academy
Wingfield House, Bray, Co Wicklow
Tel 01-2866323 Fax 01-2864918
*Chaplain:* Rev Alejandro Fuentes (LC)

Faith and Family Centre,
Dal Riada House, Avoca Avenue,
Blackrock, Co Dublin
Tel 01-2889317
Email faithandfamilycentre@arcol.org
*Director:* Rev Aaron Vinduska (LC)

**MARIANISTS**
St Columba's, Church Avenue,
Ballybrack, Co Dublin
Tel 01-2858301
*Director:* Br James Contadino (SM)

St Laurence College,
Loughlinstown, Dublin 18
Tel 01-2826930
*Principal:* Mr Billy Redmond

**MARIST FATHERS**
Mount St Mary's, Milltown,
Dundrum Road, Dublin 14
*Regional Superior*
Rev Edwin McCallion (SM)
Tel 01-2698100/086-2597905
*Superior:* Rev Declan Marmion (SM)
Tel 01-2697322 (Residence)

Catholic University School,
89 Lower Leeson Street, Dublin 2
Tel 01-6762586
*Superior:* Rev Martin Daly (SM)

Chanel College, Coolock, Dublin 5
Tel 01-8480896/8480655
*Superior:* Rev Joseph Rooney (SM)

(See also under parishes – Coolock and
Donore Avenue)

**MILL HILL MISSIONARIES**
St Joseph's House, 50 Orwell Park,
Rathgar, Dublin 6
Tel 01-4127700 Fax 01-4127781
Email josephmhm@eircom.net
*Regional Superior*
Rev Michael Corcoran (MHM)
Tel 086-2239051
*Rector:* Rev Patrick Molloy (MHM)
*Vice Rector:* Rev Patrick O'Connell (MHM)
*Bursar:* Rev Patrick Murray
Email millhill@iol.ie

**MISSIONARIES OF AFRICA**
Provincialate, Cypress Grove Road,
Templeogue, Dublin 6W
Tel 01-4063965
Email provirl@indigo.ie
*Delegate Superior:* Rev P. J. Cassidy (MAfr)

Cypress Grove, Templeogue, Dublin 6W
Tel 01-4055263/4055264
Email provirl@indigo.ie
*Promotion Director*
Rev Jean Paul Cirhakarhula
*Superior:* Vacant

**MISSIONARIES OF THE SACRED HEART**
Provincialate,
65 Terenure Road West, Dublin 6W
Tel 01-4906622 Fax 01-4920148
*Provincial Leader*
Rev Joseph McGee (MSC)

Woodview House, Mount Merrion
Avenue, Blackrock, Co Dublin
Tel 01-2881644
*Leader:* Rev John Finn (MSC)

(See also under parishes – Killinarden)

**OBLATES OF MARY IMMACULATE**
Provincial Residence,
Oblates of Mary Immaculate House of
Retreat, Tyrconnell Road,
Inchicore, Dublin 8
Email omisec@eircom.net
*Provincial:* Very Rev Raymond Warren (OMI)

Oblate House of Retreat,
Inchicore, Dublin 8
Tel 01-4534408/4541805 Fax 01-4543466
*Superior:* Rev William Fitzpatrick (OMI)

170 Merrion Road, Ballsbridge, Dublin 4
Tel 01-2693658 Fax 01-2600597

Oblate Scholasticate, St Anne's,
Goldenbridge Walk, Inchicore, Dublin 8
Tel 01-4540841/4542955 Fax 01-4731903

(See also under parishes – Bluebell,
Darndale and the two Inchicore parishes)

**PALLOTTINES**
Provincial House, 'Homestead',
Sandyford Road, Dundrum, Dublin 16
Tel 01-2956180
*Provincial:* Rev Jeremiah Murphy (SAC)
*Rector/Vice-Provincial*
Rev Michael Irwin (SAC)
Email motherofdivinelove@gmail.com

(See also under parishes – Corduff and
Shankill)

**PASSIONISTS**
St Paul's Retreat,
Mount Argus, Dublin 6W
Tel 01-4992000 Fax 01-4992001
Email passionistmtargus@eircom.net
*Provincial:* Rev Pat Duffy (CP)

(See also under parish – Mount Argus)

**REDEMPTORISTS**
Liguori House,
75 Orwell Road, Rathgar, Dublin 6
Tel 01-4067100 Fax 01-4922654
Email provincial@redemptorists.ie
*Provincial:* Rev Michael G. Kelleher (CSsR)

Marianella,
75 Orwell Road, Rathgar, Dublin 6
Tel 01-4067100 Fax 01-4929635
*Superior:* Rev Con J. Casey (CSsR)

(See also under parishes – Ballyfermot
and Cherry Orchard)

**ROSMINIANS**
Clonturk House, Ormond Road,
Drumcondra, Dublin 9
Tel 01-6877014
*Provincial:* Rev David Myers (IC)
*Rector:* Rev Matt Gaffney (IC)

**SACRED HEART FATHERS**
**Congregation of the Priests of the
Sacred Heart of Jesus**
Fairfield, 66 Inchicore Road, Dublin 8
Tel 01-4538655
Email scjdublin@eircom.net
*Superior & Formation Director*
Rev John Kelly (SCJ)
*Promotions Director*
Rev James Lawless (SCJ)

St John Vianney, Ardlea Road, Dublin 5
Tel 01-8474123/8474173
Email jvianney@indigo.ie
Rev Hugh Hanley (SCJ) *(Moderator)*

(See also under parishes – Ardlea)

**ST COLUMBANS MISSIONARY SOCIETY**
St Columban's, Grange Road,
Donaghmede, Dublin 13
Tel 01-8476647
*Contact Person:* Rev Norman Jennings (SSC)
*In residence:* Rev Hugh MacMahon (SSC)
(Executive, Secretary, IMU)
*House of Studies:* St Columban's,
67-68 Castle Dawson, Rathcoffey Road,
Maynooth, Co Kildare
Tel 01-6286036
*Contact Person*
Rev Padraig O'Donovan (SSC)

(See also under parishes – Balcurris)

**ST PATRICK'S MISSIONARY SOCIETY**
21 Leeson Park, Dublin 6
Tel 01-4977897 Fax 01-4962812
*House Leader:* Rev Danny Gibbons (SPS)

**SALESIANS**
*Provincialate:* Salesian House,
45 St Teresa's Road, Crumlin, Dublin 12
Tel 01-4555787
Email (secretary) office@salesians.ie
*Provincial:* Very Rev Michael Casey (SDB)
Email ruanet1815@eircom.net
michael_casey@eircom.net
*Novitiate:* Tel 01-4555605
*Rector:* Rev Patrick Egan (SDB)

Salesian College, Maynooth Road,
Celbridge, Co Kildare
Tel 01-6275058/6275060 Fax 01-6272208
*Rector:* Rev Koenraad Van Gucht (SDB)
Secondary School Tel 01-6272166/6272200

Don Bosco House
12 Clontarf Road, Dublin 3
Tel 01-8336009/8337045
Rev Val Collier (SDB) *(Priest-in-charge)*

Rinaldi House
72 Seán McDermott Street, Dublin 1
Tel 01-8363358 Fax 01-8552320
*Rector:* Rev Val Collier (SDB)

(See also under parishes – Seán
McDermott Street)

**SALVATORIANS**
70 Charlestown Park, Dublin 11
Tel 01-8626255
Email liamsds@gmail.com
Rev Liam Talbot (SDS)

Room 420, Our Lady's Manor,
Bulloch Castle, Dalkey, Co Dublin
Tel 01-2718043
Email ericpowellsds@gmail.com
Rev Eric Powell (SDS)

**SERVITES**
Servite Priory, St Peregrine,
36 Grangewood Estate, Rathfarnham,
Dublin 16
Tel 01-4517115
*Prior:* Rev Tim Flynn (OSM)

Servite Oratory,
Rathfarnham Shopping Centre,
Dublin 14
Tel 01-4936300
*Director:* Rev Timothy M. Flynn (OSM)

Church of the Divine Word,
Marley Grange, 25-27 Hermitage Downs,
Rathfarnham, Dublin 16
Tel 01-4944295/4941064
*Prior:* Rev Liam Tracey (OSM)

(See also under parish – Marley Grange)

## SOCIETY OF AFRICAN MISSIONS
SMA House, 82 Ranelagh Road,
Ranelagh, Dublin 6
Tel 01-4968162/3 Fax 01-4968164
*Rector:* Rev John O'Brien (SMA)

(See also under parishes – Neilstown)

## SOCIETY OF ST PAUL
St Paul's House, Moyglare Road,
Maynooth, Co Kildare
Tel 01-6285933 Fax 01-6289330
Email book@stpauls.ie

## SONS OF DIVINE PROVIDENCE
Sarsfield House, Sarsfield Road,
Ballyfermot, Dublin 10
Tel 01-6266233/6266193
Email don-orion@clubi.ie
*Superior:* Rev Michael Moss (FDP)
Email mossmichael152@gmail.com

## VINCENTIANS
Provincial Office: St Paul's, Sybil Hill,
Raheny, Dublin 5
Tel 01-8510840/8510842 Fax 01-8510846
Email cmdublin@vincentians.ie
*Provincial:* Very Rev Eamon Devlin (CM)

St Joseph's, 44 Stillorgan Park,
Blackrock, Co Dublin
Tel 01-2886961
*Superior:* Very Rev Colm McAdam (CM)

All Hallows College,
Drumcondra, Dublin 9
Tel 01-8373745/6 Fax 01-8377642
Email info@allhallows.ie
*President:* Very Rev Patrick J. McDevitt (CM)
Ministry to Priests,
Missions and Retreat: Tel 01-8373745

St Vincent's College,
Castleknock, Dublin 15
Tel 01-8213051
*President/Superior*
Very Rev Peter Slevin (CM)

St Paul's, Raheny, Dublin 5
Tel 01-8314011/2 Fax 01-8316387
Email rmccm@eircom.net
Tel 01-8318113 (Community)
*Superior:* Very Rev Fergus Kelly (CM)

(See also under parishes – Phibsboro)

## BROTHERS

## ALEXIAN BROTHERS
47 Upper Drumcondra Road, Dublin 9
Tel 01-8375973
*Contact:* Br John Moran
Community: 4

## CHRISTIAN BROTHERS
Province Centre, Marino,
Griffith Avenue, Dublin 9
Tel 01-8073300 Fax 01-8073366
Email cbprov@edmundrice.ie
*Province Leader:* Br Edmund Garvey
Community: 8

St Helen's, York Road,
Dun Laoghaire, Co Dublin
Tel 01-2801214/2841656 Fax 01-2841657
*Community Leader:* Br Mark McDonnell
Community: 9

Christian Brothers' House,
Woodbrook, Bray, Co Wicklow
Tel 01-2821510
*Community Leader:* Br Pat Bowler
Community: 7

Christian Brothers; House,
Synge Street, Dublin 8
Tel 01-4751292/4755798 Fax 01-4761015
*Community Leader:* Br Dermot Ambrose
Community: 9

Adult Community Education Centre
D8CEC, Synge Street, Dublin 8
Tel 01-4054906
Email info@d8cec.com
*Acting CEO:* Rachel Morrissey

Christian Brothers' House,
10 Rosmeen Gardens, Dun Laoghaire,
Co Dublin
Tel 01-2802105
*Community Leader:* Br Colm Griffey
Community: 8

42 Glasnevin Avenue, Dublin 11
Tel 01-8623564
Community: 2

Christian Brothers' Residence,
St David's Park, Artane, Dublin 5
Tel 01-8317833
*Community Leader:* Br John Joe Linnane
Community: 4

Artane School of Music
Tel 01-8318929
*Administrator:* Joe Edge
*Musical Director:* Ronan O'Reilly
Email artaneband@gmail.com

Oratory of the Resurrection,
Artane, Dublin 5
Tel 01-8317833
*Director:* Br John Ledwidge

St Patrick's, Baldoyle, Dublin 13
Tel 01-8391287
Retirement home for brothers
*Community Leader:* Br Ferdi Foley
Community: 34

Christian Brothers' Monastery,
St Declan's, Nephin Road, Dublin 7
Tel 01-8389560
*Community Leader:* Br Leo Judge
Community: 7

Clareville, 89A Finglas Road,
Finglas, Dublin 11
Tel 01-8309811
*Community Leader:* Br Tom Connolly
Community: 5

Marino Institute of Education,
Griffith Avenue, Dublin 9
Tel 01-8057700 Fax 01-8335290
*President:* Dr Anne O'Gara

Christian Brothers, St Joseph's Community,
Marino Institute of Education,
Griffith Avenue, Marino, Dublin 9
Tel 01-8057790
*Community Leader:* Br Bart Walsh
Community: 7

242 North Circular Road, Dublin 7
Tel 01-8680454
*Community Leader:* Br Paddy McShane
Community: 5

Edmund Rice House,
North Richmond Street, Dublin 1
Tel 01-8556258 Fax 01-8555243
*Community Leader:* Br Pat Madigan
Community: 11

Emmaus, Lissenhall, Swords, Co Dublin
Tel 01-8401399/8402450
Fax 01-8408248
*Community Leader:* Br Tom Costello
Community: 4

Mainistir Aodhain, Collins Avenue West,
Whitehall, Dublin 9
Tel 01-8379953
*Community Leader:* Br Kieran Walsh
Community: 6

Christian Brothers, 8 Croftwood Grove,
Cherry Orchard, Ballyfermot, Dublin 10
Community: 3
Tel 01-6208920

Education Inclusion Initiative,
17 Synge Street, Dublin 8
Tel 01-4053868
*Co-ordinator:* Br Michael Murray
Email mmurray32@hotmail.com

The Life Centre,
57 Pearse Square, Dublin 2
Tel 01-6718894
Email lifecentreps@gmail.com
*Co-ordinator:* Helen Dooley

Cherry Orchard Life Centre, 61 Elmdale
Crescent, Cherry Orchard, Ballyfermot,
Dublin 10
Tel 01-6235832
*Co-ordinator:* Niamh Kearney
Email cherryolife@gmail.com

## DE LA SALLE BROTHERS
Provincialate, 121 Howth Road, Dublin 3
Tel 01-8331815 Fax 01-8339130
Email province@iol.ie
*Superior:* Br Patrick Collier
Community: 5

Beneavin College, Beneavin Road,
Finglas East, Dublin 11
Tel 01-8341410
*Headmaster:* Ms Aedeen Cassidy

Mount La Salle, Ballyfermot, Dublin 10
Tel 01-6264408
*Superior:* Br Ultan McDermott
Community: 9
De La Salle Primary School
*Principal:* Ms Naomi Plant
Tel 01-6267527 Schools
Fax 01-6236021

Ard Scoil La Salle,
Raheny Road, Dublin 5
Tel 01-8480055 Fax 01-8480082
*Principal:* Mr Colin Mythen

Benildus House,
160A Upper Kilmacud Road, Dublin 14
Tel 01-2981110
*Superior:* Br Ciarán Creedon
Community: 4

Benildus Pastoral Centre,
160A Upper Kilmacud Road, Dublin 14
Tel 01-2694195 Fax 01-2694168
*Director:* Mr Tom Farrell

St Benildus College, Upper Kilmacud
Road, Blackrock Co Dublin
Tel 01-2986539 Fax 01-2962710
*Headmaster:* Mr Martin Johnson

Hazelwood House,
160 Upper Kilmacud Road, Dublin 14
Tel 01-2985670
*Superior:* Br Patrick Marron
Community: 6

St John's Monastery,
Le Fanu Road, Dublin 10
Tel 01-6260867
*Superior:* Br Raymond McKeever
Community: 4

Secondary School
*Principal:* Ms Ann Marie Leonard
Tel/Fax 01-6264943

**FRANCISCAN BROTHERS**
49 Laurleen Estate,
Stillorgan, Co Dublin
Email franciscanbrs@eircom.net

**MARIST BROTHERS**
Marian College, Lansdowne Road,
Ballsbridge, Dublin 4
Tel 01-6683740
*Superior:* Br John Hyland
Community: 4
Secondary School

Moyle Park College,
Clondalkin, Dublin 22
Tel 01-4577683
*Superior:* Br Nicholas Smith
Community: 4
Secondary School

**PATRICIAN BROTHERS**
Patrician College,
35 Cardiffcastle Road,
Finglas West, Dublin 11
Tel 01-8342811
*Superior:* Br Dermot Dunne (FSP)
Community: 2

**PRESENTATION BROTHERS**
Provincial House,
Glasthule, Co Dublin
Tel 01-2842228
*Contact:* Br Ray Dwyer (FPM)
Community: 7

**SAINT JOHN OF GOD BROTHERS**
Saint John of God Hospital,
Stillorgan, Co Dublin
Tel 01-2771400 Fax 01-2881034
*Chief Executive:* Ms Emma Balmaine
Private psychiatric hospital
*Community Superior*
Br Laurence Kearns (OH)
Community: 11

St Joseph's Centre,
Crinken Lane, Shankill, Co Dublin
Tel 01-2823000 Fax 01-2823119
email stjosephs@sjog.ie
*Director:* Ms Brid O'Meara
Residential and day service for older
people

Cluain Mhuire,
Community Mental Health Services,
Newtownpark Avenue, Blackrock, Co Dublin
Tel 01-2172100 Fax 01-2833886
Email cms@sjog.ie
*Director:* Ms Clare Dempsey

Saint John of God Kildare Services,
St Raphael's, Celbridge, Co Kildare
Tel 01-6288161 Fax 01-6273614
Email admin.kildare@sjog.ie
*Director:* Ms Philomena Gray
*School Principal:* Mrs Kathy Waldron
Residential, day centre and community
services for children and adults with
varying degrees of intellectual disability

Saint John of God, Carmona Services,
Dunmore House,
111 Upper Glenageary Road,
Dun Laoghaire, Co Dublin
Tel 01-2852900 Fax 01-2851713
Email admin.carmona@sjog.ie
*Director:* Ms Pauline Bergin
*School Principal:* Marie Burke
Incorporating residential, day, enterprise
and community services for people with
intellectual disability.

St Augustine's School, Obelisk Park,
Carysfort Avenue, Blackrock, Co Dublin
Tel 01-2881771 Fax 01-2834117
Email staugustines@sjog.ie
*Director:* Ms Pauline Bergin
*Principal:* Mr John Kingston
Special National School

Saint John of God Lucena Clinic Services,
59 Orwell Road, Rathgar, Dublin 6
Tel 01-4923596 Fax 01-4928388
Email admin.lucena@sjog.ie
*Director:* Ms Clare Dempsey
*School Principal:* Mr John Condon
*Community Superior*
Br Finnian Gallagher (OH)
Community: 4
Child and adolescent psychiatric services

Saint John of God Menni Services,
Block A, Gleann na hEorna, Springfield,
Tallaght, Dublin 24
Tel 01-4686400 Fax 01-4686499
Email admin.menni@sjog.ie
*Director:* Ms Philomena Gray
*School Principal:* Ms Rita McCabe
Incorporating day services, residential
services (Tel 01-4731474), enterprises (Tel
01-4569320) and community services

Suzanne House, 6 Main Road,
Tallaght, Dublin 24
Tel 01-4521966 Fax 01-4525504
Email andrew.heffernan@sjog.ie
*Director:* Ms Philomena Gray
Respite service for children with terminal
illness and/or complex nursing needs

STEP, 30 Carmanhall Road,
Sandyford Industrial Estate, Dublin 18
Tel 01-2952379 Fax 01-2952371
Email step@sjog.ie
*Director:* Ms Pauline Bergin
Training centre and supported
employment

City Gate, 30 Carmanhall Road,
Sandyford Industrial Estate, Dublin 18
Tel 01-2952379 Fax 01-2952371
Email citygate@sjog.ie
*Director:* Ms Pauline Bergin
Housing Service

## SISTERS

**BLESSED SACRAMENT SISTERS**
91 Seabury Crescent, Malahide, Co Dublin
Tel 01-8451878
Community: 3

**BON SECOURS SISTERS (PARIS)**
Sisters of Bon Secours, Sacre Coeur,
1 Beechmount, Glasnevin Hill, Dublin 9
Tel 01-8065353
Community: 2
Hospital Ministry

Bon Secours Convent,
Glasnevin, Dublin 9
*Co-ordinator:* Sr Veronica Norton
Tel 01-8375111 Fax 01-8571020
Community: 10
Outreach Ministry

'Le Chéile', 9 St David's Terrace,
Glasnevin, Dublin 9
Tel 01-8370018
Community: 1
Pastoral Ministry

Sisters of Bon Secours, 9 Abbeyvale,
215 Botanic Avenue, Drumcondra,
Dublin 9
Tel 01-8373209
Community: 1
Hospital Ministry

Sisters of Bon Secours,
119 Esker Lawns, Lucan, Co Dublin
Tel 01-6217158
Community: 1
Parish Ministry

**BRIGIDINE SISTERS**
5 Sycamore Drive, Dundrum, Dublin 16
Tel 01-2988130
*Contact:* Sr Theresa Kilmurray
Community: 2
Clinical Pastoral Education, Parish
Ministry

7 Sycamore Drive,
Dublin 16
Tel 01-2966449
Community: 1
*Contact:* Sr Loretto Ryan
Community Work

2 Dartmouth Road, Dublin 6
Tel 01-6603027
Community: 2
Pastoral Work, Spiritual Direction

15 Gortmore Drive, Rivermount,
Finglas, Dublin 11
Tel 01-8642440
*Contact:* Sr Imelda Barry
Community: 1
Parish, Counselling

94 Moyville, Ballyboden, Dublin 16
Tel 01-7941596
Contact: Sr Anna Hennessy
Community: 1
Education and Parish Ministry

163 Park Drive Avenue, Castleknock,
Dublin 15
Tel 01-8200482
*Contact:* Sr Mary Slattery
Community: 1
Administration

## CARMELITES
Carmelite Monastery of the Immaculate
Heart of Mary, Delgany, Greystones,
Co Wicklow
Tel 085-8601794
Email
contact@carmelitemonasterydelgany.ie
*Prioress:* Sr Gwen Collins
Community: 8
Contemplatives, Mass & greeting cards,
candles and hermitage facilities.

Carmelite Monastery of St Joseph,
Upper Kilmacud Road, Stillorgan,
Blackrock, Co Dublin
Tel 01-2886089
Email contact@kilmacudcarmel.ie
www.kilmacudcarmel.ie
*Prioress:* Sr Mary Brigeen Wilson
Community: 12
Contemplatives, altar breads

Carmelite Monastery Star of the Sea,
Seapark, Malahide, Co Dublin
Tel 01-8454259
Email community@malahidecarmelites.ie
*Prioress:* Sr Attracta Hand
Community: 12
Contemplatives, cards, candles, honey (in
season) and rosettes for First
Communion and Confirmation
www.malahidecarmelites.ie

Carmelite Monastery of the Assumption,
Firhouse, Dublin 24
Tel 01-4526474
*Prioress:* Vacant
Community: 5
Contemplatives, needlework, scapulars,
cards and candles

Carmelite Monastery of the Immaculate
Conception, Roebuck, Dublin 14
Tel 01-2884732
Altar Breads
Email altarbreads@roebuckcarmel.com
www.roebuckcarmel.com
Email carmel@roebuckcarmel.com
*Prioress:* Sr Maria Maher
Community: 5
Contemplatives; altar breads supplied

## CARMELITE SISTERS FOR THE AGED AND INFIRM
Our Lady's Manor, Bullock Castle,
Dalkey, Co Dublin
Tel 01-2806993 Fax 01-2844802
Email ourladysmanor1@eircom.net
*Superior:* Sr Therese Eileen Mulvaney
Email sistereileen@eircom.net
*Administrator:* Sr Bernadette Murphy
Community: 5

## CHARITY OF NEVERS SISTERS
29 Hazelgrove Court,
Tallaght, Dublin 24
*Contact person:* Sr Rosaleen Cullen
Tel 01-4585654
Email rosaleencullen@upcmail.ie

91 Cherrywood,
Loughlinstown Drive,
Dun Laoghaire, Co Dublin
Tel 01-2824204

76 Cherrywood,
Loughlinstown Drive,
Dun Laoghaire, Co Dublin
Tel 01-2720453

66 Verschoyle Court, Dublin
Tel 01-6624815

17 Stephen's Place, Dublin
Tel 01-6768159
Email sisternoradowney@eircom.net

## CHARITY OF ST PAUL THE APOSTLE SISTERS
St Paul's Convent, Greenhills,
Dublin 12
Tel 01-4505358
Email marylyons2010@gmail.com
*Contact:* Sr Mary Lyons
Community: 4
Secondary school, parish work

129 Wainsfort Manor Drive, Terenure,
Dublin 6W
Tel 01-4908856
*Contact:* Sr Anne McLoughlin
Email annemcloughlin1958@yahoo.co.uk
Community: 2
Chaplaincy and education

Apt 6, 20 Highfield Road, Rathgar,
Dublin 6
Tel 01-4982867
*Contact:* Katherine Breene
Email katebre27@gmail.com
Community: 1
Education

## CLARISSAN MISSIONARY SISTERS OF THE BLESSED SACRAMENT
Our Lady of Guadalupe Residence for
Students, 28 Waltersland Road,
Stillorgan, Co Dublin
Tel/Fax 01-2886600
Email miscraidub@hotmail.com
www.guadaluperesidence.com
*Superior:* Sr Gabriela Luna

## CONGREGATION OF THE SISTERS OF MERCY
'Rachamim', 13/14 Moyle Park,
Convent Road, Clondalkin, Dublin 22
Tel 01-4673737 Fax 01-4673749
Email mercy@csm.ie
Website www.sistersofmercy.ie
*Congregational Leader:* Sr Margaret Casey

Mercy International Centre
64A Lower Baggot Street, Dublin 2
Tel 01-6618061
Email director@mercyinternational.ie
*Director:* Sr Mary Reynolds
Heritage tours, school tours, conference
facilities and pilgrimages to the tomb of
Ven. Catherine McAuley
Website www.mercyworld.org

*South Central Province*

*The Sisters of Mercy minister throughout
the diocese in pastoral and social work,
community development, counselling,
spirituality, education and health care,
answering current needs.*

St Mary's Convent, Arklow, Co Wicklow
Tel 0402-32675
Community: 1

1 & 2 Church Crescent, Athy, Co Kildare
Tel 059-8631361 Fax 059-8638180
Community: 9

2 Oak Lawn, Carlow Road,
Athy, Co Kildare
Tel 059-8638209
Community: 1

12 Park Avenue, Athy, Co Kildare
Tel 059-8634220
Community: 3

21 Shamrock Drive, Athy, Co Kildare
Tel 059-8632908
Community: 1

101/102 Rockfield Green,
Maynooth, Co Kildare
Tel 01-6291992 Fax 01-6016896
Community: 5

Mercy Convent, Beaumont, Dublin 9
Tel 01-8376741 Fax 01-8372770
Community: 11

18 Beverley Crescent,
Knocklyon, Dublin 16
Tel 01-4941232
Community: 1

St Anne's, Booterstown, Co Dublin
Tel 01-2882140
Community: 15
Province Archives

22A Camron Court, Cork Street, Dublin 8
Tel 01-4530498
Community: 2

St Brendan's Drive, Coolock, Dublin 5
Tel 01-8486420
Community: 12

Our Lady of Lourdes Hospital,
Rochestown Avenue, Dun Laoghaire,
Co Dublin
Tel 01-2851804 Fax 01-2355163
Community: 9

Sisters of Mercy, Convent of Mercy,
Eblana Avenue, Dun Laoghaire,
Co Dublin
Tel 01-2360686 Fax 01-2805470
Community: 22

23-26 The Paddocks, Kilmainham,
Dublin 8
Tel 01-4021727
Community: 7

81 Mackintosh Park,
Dun Laoghaire, Co Dublin
Tel-2851707
Community: 2

13 Emmet Crescent, Inchicore, Dublin 8
Tel 01-4163275
Community: 2

19 Emmet Crescent, Inchicore, Dublin 8
Tel 01-4163890
Community: 2

47 Emmet Crescent, Inchicore, Dublin 8
Tel 01-4538196
Community: 1

Mater Misericordiae, Eccles Street,
Dublin 7
Tel 01-8032237 Fax 01-8309070
Community: 20

8-9 Leo Street, Dublin 7
Tel 01-8858593
Community: 2

1 Oatfield Grove, Rowlagh, Clondalkin,
Dublin 22
Tel 01-6261114
Community: 3

Stella Maris, Convent Lane,
Rush, Co Dublin
Tel/Fax 01-8437347
Community: 3

40 Hillcourt Road, Glenageary, Co Dublin
Tel 01-2854729
Community: 2

14 Coolatree Close, Beaumont, Dublin 9
Tel 01-8377023
Community: 3

63 Kenilworth Park, Harolds Cross,
Dublin 6W
Tel 01-4452905
Community: 3

65 Kenilworth Park, Harolds Cross,
Dublin 6W
Tel 01-4929414
Community: 2

Glencree, 60 Knocklyon Road,
Templeogue, Dublin 16
Tel 01-4933027
Community: 4

90/91 The Park,
Beaumont Woods, Dublin 9
Tel 01-8570741
Community: 4

McAuley House,
Beaumont, Dublin 9
Tel 01-8379186 Fax 01-8373503
Community: 23

83/85 Silloge Park, Ballymun, Dublin 11
Tel 01-8547611
Community: 2

40 Gilford Road, Sandymount, Dublin 4
Tel/Fax 01-2601081
Community: 3

Sisters of Mercy, 14 Walnut Avenue,
Courtlands, Drumcondra, Dublin 9
Tel 01-8377602 Fax 01-8570684
Community: 4

Sisters of Mercy,
1 Charlemont, Griffith Avenue,
Dublin 9
Tel 01-8571246 Fax 01-8368149
Community: 3

Sisters of Mercy,
25 Cork Street, Dublin 8
Tel 01-4535262
Community: 6

11 Grangemore Road, Donaghmede,
Dublin 13
Tel 01-8482242
Community: 2

2 Charlemont,
Griffith Avenue, Dublin 9
Tel 01-4425896
Community: 2

Cuan Mhuire, Athy, Co Kildare
Tel 059-8631493
Community: 2

Knockfin, Laragh,
Glendalough, Co Wicklow
Tel 0404-45791
Community: 1

**CROSS AND PASSION CONGREGATION**
Cross and Passion Sisters,
3-5 Carberry Road, Glandore Road,
Dublin 9
Tel 01-8377256
Community: 6
Education, pastoral ministry

Cross and Passion Convent
22 Griffith Avenue, Marino,
Dublin 9
Tel 01-8336381
Community: 17
Nursing, care of elderly

Cross and Passion Convent,
41 Alderwood Green, Springfield,
Tallaght, Dublin 24
Tel 01-4511850
Community: 4
Pastoral ministry, school chaplaincy,
retreat work

Cross and Passion Convent,
13 Clare Road, Drumcondra, Dublin 9
Tel 01-8375511
Community: 3
Community development, pastoral
ministry, nursing

**DAUGHTERS OF CHARITY OF ST VINCENT
DE PAUL**
Provincialate, St Catherine's Provincial
House, Dunardagh, Blackrock,
Co Dublin
Tel 01-2882669/2882896 Fax 01-2834485
*Local Superior:* Sr Áine MacNamara
Community: 26
Administration and retreats

St Vincent's Centre,
Navan Road, Dublin 7
Tel 01-8384304
*Superior:* Sr Stella Bracken
Community: 5
Care, training and education of people
with intellectual disability

St Vincent's, North William Street,
Dublin 1
Tel 01-8552998
*Superior:* Sr Bridget O'Connor
Community: 7
Primary schools, parish and social work
Social Housing Project

77 Kilbarron Park,
Kilmore West, Dublin 5
Tel 01-8470648
*Superior:* Sr Patricia Walsh
Community: 5
Social and pastoral ministry

3 St Assam's Drive,
Raheny, Dublin 5
Tel 01-8312859
*Superior:* Sr Nuala Dolan
Community: 4
House of Residence for Sisters involved
in St Francis Hospice and child and family
services

St Louise's, Drumfinn Road,
Ballyfermot, Dublin 10
Tel 01-6264921
*Superior:* Sr Claire Sweeney
Community: 5
Education and parish work

St Joseph's Hospital,
Clonsilla, Co Dublin
Tel 01-8217177
*Superior:* Sr Anna Kennedy
Community: 10
Residential centre for women with
intellectual disability, work for social
justice

St Louise's, Glenmaroon,
Chapelizod, Dublin 20
Tel 01-8216166 Fax 01-8211991
Residential centre for girls with
intellectual disability.

St Michael's School for children with
special needs.
Tel 01-8201859

10 Henrietta Street, Dublin 1
Tel 01-8583063
*Superior:* Sr Frances Molloy
Community: 21
House of residence

Daughters of Charity Community
Services,
8/9 Henrietta Street, Dublin 1
(Specialised second chance education for
young people and adults)
Community Services
Tel 01-8874100 Fax 01-8723486

109 Mount Prospect Avenue,
Clontarf, Dublin 3
Tel 01-8338508
*Superior:* Sr Angela Doyle
Community: 17
House for retired sisters

St Teresa's, Temple Hill, Blackrock,
Co Dublin
Tel 01-2788205
*Superior:* Sr Bernadette McGinn
Community: 7
House of Residence

St Rosalie's, Portmarnock,
Co Dublin
Tel 01-8460132
Residential centre for people with
intellectual disability

St Catherine's, Knockmore Avenue,
Killinarden, Tallaght, Dublin 24
Tel 01-4516320
*Superior:* Sr Anne O'Neill
Community: 4
Parish and social work, after care,
chaplaincy

Seton House, 25 Northbrook Road,
Dublin 6
Tel 01-6687300
*Superior:* Sr Christina Quinn
Community: 6
House of residence

7 Belvedere Road, Dublin 1
Tel 01-8556719
*Superior:* Sr Áine Cahalan
Community: 5
House of residence, pastoral care

166 Navan Road, Dublin 7
Tel 01-8383801
*Superior:* Sr Marie Fox
Community: 3
House of residence for sisters involved in
parish work, and provides services for
people with intellectual disability

St Louise's, 16 Dalymount,
Phibsboro, Dublin 7
Tel 01-8680308
*Superior:* Sr Geraldine Henry
Community: 4
House of residence for sisters involved in
work with refugees, services for people
with intellectual disability, chaplaincy,
mission development

25 Killarney Street, Dublin 1
Tel 01-8366487
*Superior:* Sr Nora O'Sullivan
Community: 5
House of residence for sisters involved in
day care, prison chaplaincy, child and
family services, work with refugees

### DAUGHTERS OF THE CROSS OF LIÈGE
Beech Park Convent, Beechwood Court,
Stillorgan, Co Dublin
Tel 01-2887401/2887315 Fax 01-2881499
Email beech@eircom.net
*Superior:* Sr Anne Kelly
Community: 14

### DAUGHTERS OF THE HEART OF MARY
St Joseph's, Tivoli Road, Dun Laoghaire,
Co Dublin
Tel 01-2801204. Community: 8
Email heartofmary@eircom.net
Parish work; teaching; social work,
prayer groups
St Joseph's Primary School
Principal's Office: Tel 01-2803504

32 Brackenbush Road, Killiney, Co Dublin
Tel 01-2750917

### DAUGHTERS OF THE HOLY SPIRIT
88 Foxfield Road, Raheny,
Dublin 5
Tel 01-8312795
Community: 3
*Contact person:* Sr Teresa Buckley DHSp
Email tbuckley1929@yahoo.co.uk

9 Walnut Park, Drumcondra, Dublin 9
Tel 01-8371825
Community: 3
Pastoral ministry

### DAUGHTERS OF JESUS
17 Marino Green, Marino,
Dublin 3
Tel 01-8335530
*Contact:* Sister-in-charge

### DAUGHTERS OF MARY AND JOSEPH
65 Iona Road, Glasnevin, Dublin 11
Tel 01-8305640
Community: 6
Administration, pastoral, education

142 Chapelgate, St Alphonsus' Road,
Dublin 9
Tel 01-8827740
*Contact person:* Sr Brigid Devane
Community: 1
Parish pastoral

37 Bancroft Road, Tallaght, Dublin 24
Tel 01-4515321
Community: 5
Pastoral

Flat 7, 116 North Circular Road,
Dublin 7
Tel 01-8380525
*Contact person:* Sr Peggy McArdle
Community: 1
Community Development

### DAUGHTERS OF OUR LADY OF THE SACRED HEART
Provincial House, 14 Rossmore Avenue,
Templeogue, Dublin 6W
Tel 01-4903200 Tel/Fax 01-4903113
Email olshprov@eircom.net
*Provincial:* Sr Maireád Kelleher
Community: 4

50 Maplewood Road, Springfield,
Tallaght, Dublin 24
Tel 01-4512183
*Superior:* Sr Juliana O'Donoghue
Community: 2

### DAUGHTERS OF WISDOM
20 Grace Park Meadows,
Drumcondra, Dublin 9
Tel 01-8316508
Community: 2

### DISCIPLES OF THE DIVINE MASTER
Divine Master Centre, Newtownpark
Avenue, Blackrock, Co Dublin
Tel 01-2114949 *(community)*
01-2886414 *(Liturgical Centre)*
Fax 01-2836935
Email pddmdublin@eircom.net
*Sister-in-Charge:* Sr Brid Geraghty
Email bridpddm@eircom.net
Community: 4
Contemplative-apostolic, perpetual
adoration, Liturgical apostolate,
distributors and producers of high-
quality Liturgical art, vestments, church
goods, private retreats, prayer groups.

### DOMINICAN SISTERS
Generalate, 5 Westfield Road, Dublin 6
Tel 01-4055570/1/2/3 Fax 01-4055682
Email domgen@eircom.net
*Congregation Prioress*
Sr Helen Mary Harmey
Community: 4
*Congregaton Bursar:* Sr Brighde Vallely
*Congregation Archivist:* Sr Mary O'Byrne

Mary Bellew House,
Dominican Campus, Cabra, Dublin 7
Tel 01-8299797 Fax 01-8299799
Email marybellewhouse@gmail.com
*Prioress:* Sr Kathleen Fitzsimons
Community: 8

Novitiate, 71 Bancroft Park,
Tallaght, Dublin 24
Tel 01-4515130
Email domban@gmail.com
*Prioress:* Sr Kathleen Crowley
Community: 5
Varied ministries

Dominican Convent, 9 Elgin Road,
Ballsbridge, Dublin 4
Tel 01-4055570
*Contact person:* Sr Edel Murphy

St Mary's, Rectory Green,
Riverston Abbey, Cabra, Dublin 7
Tel 01-8683041
Email riverstonabbey@gmail.com
*Prioress:* Sr Áine Killen
Community: 7
Varied ministries

St Mary's, Cabra, Dublin 7
Tel 01-8380567 Fax 01-8682050
Email domcabra@eircom.net
*Prioress:* Sr Maria Maguire
Community: 14
Secondary School
Tel 01-8385282 Fax 01-8683003
Primary and secondary schools, Schools
for hearing-impaired, deaf girls (day and
boarding). Special schools for
emotionally disturbed children. Parish
work

Dominican Convent,
Sion Hill, Blackrock, Co Dublin
Tel 01-2886832/3
Email sionhillconvent@gmail.com
*Prioress:* Sr Lucina Montague
Community: 19
Varied ministries
Secondary School. Tel 01-2886791

St Mary's, 47 Mount Merrion Avenue,
Blackrock, Co Dublin
Tel 01-2888551
Email stmarysblackrock@yahoo.ie
Community: 4
Varied ministries

Dominican Convent, Convent Road,
Dun Laoghaire, Co Dublin
Tel 01-2801379 Fax 01-2302209
Email dldoms@eircom.net
*Prioress:* Sr Margaret Mary Ryder
Community: 12
Primary School. Tel 01-2809011
Education, varied ministries

Dominican Convent,
204 Griffith Avenue, Dublin 9
Tel 01-8379550 Fax 01-8571802
Email dsisters204@yahoo.ie
*Prioress:* Sr Marie Cunningham
Secondary School. Tel 01-8376080
Community: 12
Varied ministries

Dominican Sisters,
52 Newtownpark Ave,
Blackrock, Co Dublin
Tel 01-2833964
Email galldom@eircom.net
Community: 2

Dominican Convent,
Muckross Park, Donnybrook,
Dublin 4
Tel 01-2693018/2693707 Fax 01-2604041
Email muckrossconvent@eircom.net
*Prioress:* Sr Caitriona Geraghty
Community: 15
Varied ministries
Secondary school. Tel 01-2691096

St Catherine's,
2 Heather View Road,
Aylesbury, Tallaght, Dublin 24
Tel 01-4523462 Fax 01-4625636
Email domabury2@eircom.net
Community: 4
Education; varied ministries

1 Avonbeg Road,
Tallaght, Dublin 24
Tel 01-4514627
Email ruthpilkington@yahoo.co.uk
Community: 2
Pastoral

2 Croftwood Crescent,
Cherry Orchard, Ballyfermot,
Dublin 10
Tel 01-6231127
Email cherrydom@eircom.net
Community: 2
Education, varied ministries

93 Nephin Road,
Cabra, Dublin 7
Tel 01-8682054
Email domsis9395@gmail.com
Community: 5
Varied ministries

Dominican Sisters,
Santa Sabina House, Cabra, Dublin 7
Tel 01-8682666 Fax 01-8682667
Email santasabina@dominicansisters.com
*Prioress:* Sr Mary Daly
Community: 35
Varied ministries

Dominican Sisters,
St Mary's Convent, Wicklow
Tel 0404-67328 Fax 0404-65054
Email dcw@ecocentrewicklow.ie
Community: 7
Ecological centre, varied ministries

Dominican Sisters,
62 Ashington Avenue, Navan Road,
Dublin 7
Tel 01-8386304
Community: 3
Education and varied ministries

## FRANCISCAN MISSIONARIES OF THE DIVINE MOTHERHOOD
Emohruo, 2 Fonthill Abbey,
Ballyboden Road, Rathfarnham,
Dublin 14
Tel/Fax 01-4934275
Community: 3

St Francis Convent,
3/4 Fonthill Abbey, Ballyboden Road,
Rathfarnham, Dublin 14
Tel 01-4932537 Fax 01-4954846
Community: 4

## FRANCISCAN MISSIONARIES OF MARY
St Francis Convent, The Cloisters,
Mount Tallant Avenue,
Terenure, Dublin 6W
Tel 01-4908549
Email fmmcloisters@eircom.net
*Superior:* Sr Bernadette Reynolds
Community: 8
House of studies, pastoral work

Assisi, 36 Grange Abbey Drive,
Donaghmede, Dublin 13
Tel 01-8470591
*Superior:* Sr Mary Dunne
Community: 5
Social, pastoral work

97 St Lawrence Road, Clontarf,
Dublin 3
Tel 01-8332683/8332181
Email fmmclontarf@yahoo.co.uk
*Superior:* Sr Sheila Stewart
Community: 9
Pastoral, hospitality for missionary sisters

St Joseph's Convent, Old Road,
Hayestown, Rush, Co Dublin
Tel 01-8439308
*Superior:* Sr Theresa O'Flynn
Community: 17
Care of elderly sisters

FHM, 4 Muckross Drive,
Perrystown, Dublin 12
Tel 01-4562028
*Superior:* Sr Mary Dornan
Community: 4
Youth ministry, hospital chaplaincy

## FRANCISCAN MISSIONARIES OF ST JOSEPH
St Joseph's, 16 Innismore,
Crumlin Village, Dublin 12
Tel 01-4563445
Community: 3

## FRANCISCAN MISSIONARY SISTERS FOR AFRICA
Generalate, 34A Gilford Road,
Sandymount, Dublin 4
Tel 01-2838376 Fax 01-2602049
Email fmsagen@iol.ie
*Congregational Leader*
Sr Bridgette Cormack (FMSA)
Community: 4

34 Gilford Road, Sandymount, Dublin 4
Tel 01-2691923
*Contact person*
Sr Jeanette Watters (FMSA)
Community: 6

142 Raheny Road, Raheny, Dublin 5
Tel 01-8480852
Email fmsaraheny142@iol.ie
*Contact person:* Sr Úna Donnellan (FMSA)
Community: 5

**FRANCISCAN SISTERS**
3 St Andrew's Fairway, Lucan, Co Dublin
Tel 01-6108756
Email cearlsosf@gmail.com
Community: 4

**FRANCISCAN SISTERS OF THE IMMACULATE CONCEPTION**
Franciscan Sisters, 97/99 Riverside Park,
Clonshaugh, Dublin 17
Tel 01-8474214
Community: 2
Administration, pastoral ministry, nursing

**CONGREGATION OF OUR LADY OF CHARITY OF THE GOOD SHEPHERD**
245 Lower Kilmacud Road, Goatstown,
Dublin 14
Tel 01-2982699 Fax 01-2989033
Email rgsdublin@eircom.net
www.goodshepherdsisters.com
Community: 5
Provincialate

65 Taney Crescent, Goatstown, Dublin 14
Tel 01-2960235
Email rgstaney@gmail.com
Community: 3

63 Lower Séan McDermott Street,
Dublin 1
Tel 01-8711109 Fax 01-8366526
Email regionaloffice@olc.ie

Beechlawn Complex, High Park, Grace
Park Road, Drumcondra, Dublin 9
Nursing Home Tel 01-8369622
Community: 22

**HANDMAIDS OF THE SACRED HEART OF JESUS**
St Raphaela's, Upper Kilmacud Road,
Stillorgan, Co Dublin
Tel 01-2889963 Fax 01-2889536
*Superior*: Sr Patricia Lynch
Email trishaci@yahoo.com
Community: 8
Primary School. Tel 01-2886878
Secondary School. Tel 01-2888730
Students' residence. Tel 01-2887159
Fax 01-2889536

**HOLY CHILD JESUS, SOCIETY OF THE**
1 Stable Lane, Off Harcourt Street,
Dublin 2
Tel 01-4754053
Email stablelane@shcj.org
Community: 10

21 Grange Park Avenue,
Raheny, Dublin 5
Tel 01-8488961
Email shcjdub@gofree.indigo.ie
Community: 2

Convent of the Holy Child Jesus,
Kilmuire, Military Road, Killiney,
Co Dublin
Tel 01-2823089
Community: 4
Secondary School. Tel 01-2823120

Holy Child School,
Military Road, Killiney, Co Dublin
Tel 01-2823120
Email admin@holychildkilliney.ie

Holy Child Community School,
Sallynoggin, Co Dublin
Tel 01-2855334

**HOLY FAITH SISTERS**
Generalate, Aylward House,
Glasnevin, Dublin 11
Tel 01-8371426 Fax 01-8377474
Email aylward@eircom.net
*Superior General:* Sr Vivienne Keely

*Regional Superior:* Sr Rosaleen Cunniffe
Regional House,
25 Clare Road, Drumcondra, Dublin 9
Tel 01-8373569
Email ionahfs@eircom.net

Main Street, Celbridge, Co Kildare
Tel 01-6288267
Community: 2
Wellsprings Centre

183 Clontarf Road, Dublin 3
Tel 01-8338331
Community: 6
Holy Faith Secondary School
Tel 01-8332754
*Principal:* Ms Deirdre Gogarty
Parish ministry and education

Star of the Sea,
182 Clontarf Road, Dublin 3
Tel 01-8338252
Community: 4
Social work, faith development, prison
ministry, liturgy, third-level education,
All Hallows College

The Coombe, Dublin 8
Tel 01-4540244
Email coomconvent@eircom.net
Community: 10
Primary Education, Pastoral, NUI
Maynooth, counselling, pastoral work,
parish work Whitefriar Street

11 Drumcairn Green, Fettercairn,
Tallaght, Dublin 24
Tel 01-4513951
Community: 2
Counselling, parish work

12 Finglaswood Road, Dublin 11
Tel 01-8641551
Community: 1
Counselling

13 Wellmount Parade, Dublin 11
Tel 01-8640874
Community: 1
St John's Education Centre

14 Wellmount Parade, Dublin 11
Tel 01-8645153
Community: 1
Music ministry

St Michael's Secondary School
Tel 01-8341767
*Principal:* Mr John Barry

Holy Faith Sisters,
144 Cappagh Road, Finglas, Dublin 11
Tel 01-8643205
Community: 1
Ministry to Travellers, administration

Glasnevin, Dublin 11
Tel 01-8373427
*Resident Co-ordinator:* Sr Maura Keogh
Community: 30
Pastoral ministries; social work;
secondary and primary education
Margaret Aylward Centre for Faith and
Dialogue,
Holy Faith Convent, Glasnevin, Dublin 11
Tel 01-7979364
Marian House Nursing Home
Tel 01-8376165
Email marianhouse_hfc@yahoo.ie
St Mary's Secondary School Tel 01-8374413
*Principal:* Mrs Margaret Lennon
Mother of Divine Grace Primary School
Tel 01-8344000
*Principal:* Ms Eleanor Fahy

Greystones, Co Wicklow
Tel 01-2874081
Community: 4
Prayer, parish ministry, education
St David's Co-educational Secondary
School Tel 01-2874800/2874802
*Principal:* Mary O'Doherty
St Brigid's Primary School. Tel 01-2876113
*Principal:* Sr Kathleen Lyng

Credo, 1 Fairways Grove,
Griffith Road, Dublin 11
Tel 01-8348015
Community: 1
Pastoral work

2 Fairways Grove,
Griffith Road, Dublin 11
Tel 01-8533772
Community: 1
Holy Faith community service

Kilcoole, Co Wicklow
Tel 01-2874229
Community: 2
Parish ministry, faith development,
Justice, Luisne Spirituality Centre

St Brigid's Road, Killester, Dublin 5
Tel 01-8310009
Community: 7
Primary school, library work, pastoral
work

Haddington Place, Dublin 4
Tel 01-6681124
Community: 7
Parish ministry, prayer ministry,
counselling, education

18 Church Street, Skerries, Co Dublin
Tel 01-8491203
Community: 5
Pastoral work, liturgy, parish work,
administration

14 Main Road, Tallaght, Dublin 24
Tel 01-4515904
Community: 2
Faith development

11 Aylward Green, Finglas, Dublin 11
Tel 01-8646401
Community: 2
Pastoral support service, chaplaincy DCU,
club for people with disabilities

11 Johnstown Park, Ballygall Road East,
Dublin 11
Tel 01-864640
Community: 3
Parish ministry, spiritual direction,
liturgy, pastoral care

178-180 Clontarf Road, Dublin 3
Community: 8
Spiritual Direction, pastoral, healing
remedies, social justice, St John's
Education Support Centre, third-level
education, All Hallows College,
administration

Joseph's Cottage, Kippure East,
Manor Kilbride, Co Wicklow
Tel 0404-4507
Community: 1
Conservation work, parish work,
administration

30 Convent Court, Delgany, Co Wicklow
Primary school education
Community: 1

St Anne's Presbytery, Kilcarrig Avenue,
Fettercairn, Tallaght, Dublin 24
Tel 01-4141916
Community: 2
Parish work, Ruhana

## HOLY FAMILY OF BORDEAUX SISTERS
11 Arran Road, Drumcondra, Dublin 9
Tel 01-8370922
Contact: Sr Bernadette Deegan (Area
Councillor)
Community: 3
Hospitality, pastoral work, counselling,
spiritual direction

Holy Family of Bordeaux Sisters,
Irishtown, Clane, Co Kildare
Tel 01-6288459
Contact person: The Superior
Community: 4
Parish work, chaplaincy, adult religious
education, literacy and pastoral work

## INFANT JESUS SISTERS
Provincial House, 56 St Lawrence Road,
Clontarf, Dublin 3
Tel 01-8338930
Provincial: Sr Kitty Ellard
Email kittyijs@gmail.com
Tel 01-8339577
Community: 2

121 Tonlegee Road, Dublin 5
Tel 01-8472926
Community: 3
Pastoral ministry

140 Carrickhill Rise, Portmarnock,
Co Dublin
Tel 01-8461647
Community: 2
Pastoral ministry

16 Ard na Meala, Ballymun, Dublin 11
Tel 01-8426534
Community: 2
Pastoral ministry, youth ministry, social
work

7 Ard na Meala, Ballymun, Dublin 11
Pastoral ministry

54 Knowth Court, Poppintree,
Ballymun, Dublin 11
Pastoral ministry

2 Carrig Close, Poppintree,
Ballymun, Dublin 11
Pastoral ministry

1 Eccles Court, Dublin 7
Tel 01-8309004
Pastoral ministry

## JESUS AND MARY, CONGREGATION OF
Provincialate, 'Errew House',
110 Goatstown Road, Dublin 14
Provincial Offices: Tel 01-2993130
Direct line: Tel 01-2969150
Bursar's Office: Tel 01-2993140
Provincial Superior: Sr Mary Mulrooney
Tel 01-2969150
Email mulrooney.mary@gmail.com
Tel 01-2966059
Community: 5

Our Lady's Grove Community,
110 Goatstown Road, Dublin 14
Community: 5
Convent. Tel 01-2966104
Primary School. Pupils: 433
Secondary School. Pupils: 370

Home Farm Community, 'Errew House',
110 Goatstown Road, Dublin 14
Tel 01-2993665
Community: 3

## LA RETRAITE SISTERS
77 Grove Park, Rathmines, Dublin 6
Tel 01-4911771
Contact: Sr Avril O'Regan
Email avril@laretraite.ws

## LA SAINTE UNION DES SACRES COEURS
Teallach Mhuire, 41 Broadway Road,
Blanchardstown, Dublin 15
Tel 01-8214459
Leadership work base – Ireland
Hospitality

9 Tandy's Hill, Lucan, Co Dublin
Tel 01-6218863
Contact: Sr Rosemarie Madden
Parish work

126 Malahide Road,
Clontarf, Dublin 3
Tel 01-8332778
Community: 3
Pastoral work, literacy

14 Glenshane Grove,
Brookfield, Tallaght, Dublin 24
Tel 01-4527684
Community: 2
Teaching, pastoral work, travellers,
counselling

7 Summerfield Close,
Clonsilla Road, Dublin 15
Community: 1
Counselling, education

24 Esker Pines, Esker Lane,
Lucan, Co Dublin
Community: 1
Education

## LITTLE COMPANY OF MARY
Provincialate, Cnoc Mhuire,
29 Woodpark, Ballinteer Avenue,
Dublin 16
Tel 01-2987040 Fax 01 2961936
Province Leader: Sr Teresa Corby

40 Braemor Park,
Churchtown, Dublin 14
Tel 01-4904755/4904692/4904794/
4904795
Community: 23

14 Heather Lawn,
Marlay Wood, Dublin 16
Tel 01-4942324
Apostolic Community: 1
Apostolic community only

16 Heather Lawn,
Marlay Wood, Dublin 16
Tel 01-4947205
Apostolic Community: 1

Little Company of Mary,
12 The Avenue, Grange Manor,
Lucan, Co Dublin
Tel 01-6109360
Apostolic Community: 1

Little Company of Mary,
2 Esker Wood Grove, Lucan, Co Dublin
Tel 01-6210474
Apostolic Community: 1

Little Company of Mary,
64 Templeroan Avenue, Knocklyon,
Dublin 16
Tel 01-4957130
Apostolic Community: 1

Little Company of Mary,
45 Priory Way, Whitehall Road, Dublin 12
Tel 01-4907763
Community: 1

Little Company of Mary,
62 West Priory, Navan Road, Dublin 7
Tel 01-8386325
Community: 1

## LITTLE SISTERS OF THE ASSUMPTION
Administration Office,
42 Rathfarnham Road,
Terenure, Dublin 6W
Tel 01-4909850 Fax 01-4925740
Email pernet42@eircom.net
*Co-ordinators*
Sr Catherine Dunphy, Sr Carmel Molloy
Sisters work in family care and with local
community development groups

12 Convent Lawns, Ballyfermot, Dublin 10
Tel 01-6230898
Email conventlawnslsa@eircom.net

155 Swords Road, Whitehall, Dublin 9
Tel 01-8374894
Email lsas.155@gmail.com

11 The Covert, Woodfarm Acres,
Palmerstown, Dublin 20
Tel 01-6268556
Email littlesisters@eircom.net

8 Owendore Crescent,
Rathfarnham, Dublin 14
Tel 01-4931147
Email lasair@hotmail.com

Patrickswell Place, Finglas, Dublin 11
Tel 01-8342592
Email fagefinglas@yahoo.co.uk

Mount Argus, Assumption Convent,
Mount Argus Road, Dublin 6W
Tel 01-4977038
Email mountarguslsa@gmail.com

4 Oakdale, Oakton Park,
Ballybrack, Co Dublin
Tel 01-2821143
Email lsaballybrack@yahoo.ie

41 Liscarne Court, Rowlagh,
Clondalkin, Dublin 22
Tel 01-6263077
Email rowlaghlsa@gmail.com

14 Forestwood Avenue, Santry Avenue,
Dublin 9
Tel 01-8428016
Email lsaballymun@gmail.com

## LITTLE SISTERS OF THE POOR
Sacred Heart Residence,
Sybil Hill Road, Raheny, Dublin 5
Tel 01-8332308
*Provincial:* Sr Christine Devlin
*Superior:* Sr Miriam
Email msraheny@eircom.net
Community: 25
Nursing home for the elderly

Holy Family Residence,
Roebuck Road, Dublin 14
Tel 01-2832455
*Superior:* Sr Roseline
Community: 15
Nursing home for the elderly

St Brigid's Novitiate,
Roebuck Road, Dublin 14
Tel 01-2832536

## LORETO (IBVM)
Provincialate, Loreto House,
Beaufort, Dublin 14
Tel 01-4933827
Email provadmin@loreto.ie
*Provincial:* Sr Noelle Corscadden

Abbey House, Loreto Terrace,
Grange Road, Rathfarnham, Dublin 14
Tel 01-4932807
*Shared Community Leaders*
Sr Angela Powell, Sr Anna Brady
Community: 28
Primary School, Secondary Day School,
pastoral work

Loreto College and Junior School,
53 St Stephen's Green, Dublin 2
Tel 01-6618179/6618181

Loreto Community,
Nos 3, 6, 8, 9 Fort Ostman,
Old County Road, Crumlin, Dublin 12
Community: 4
*Co-Leaders*
Sr Máire Lagan, Sr Rosemary O'Connor
Loreto Secondary School. Tel 01-4542380
Senior Primary School. Tel 01-4541669
Junior Primary School. Tel 01-4541746
Loreto Centre Apartments, Crumlin Road
Tel 01-4541078
Community: 7
Personal and community development

Loreto Community, Bray, Co Wicklow
Tel 01-2862021
*Co-Leaders*
Sr Anne Mary Murphy, Sr Helen O'Riordan
Community: 9
Primary and secondary schools;
pastoral work

Nos 29/30 The Courtyard
Vevay Crescent
*Co-Leaders*
Sr Anne Mary Murphy, Sr Helen O'Riordan
Community: 2

Loreto Abbey, Dalkey, Co Dublin
Tel 01-2804331/2804416
Email lorcomdalkey@eircom.net
*Co-Leaders*
Sr Anne Mary Murphy, Sr Helen O'Riordan
Community: 7
Primary and secondary schools;
pastoral work

Teach Muire, Leslie Avenue,
Dalkey, Co Dublin
Tel 01-2800495
Email lorlesliedalkey@eircom.net
*Co-Leaders*
Sr Anne Mary Murphy, Sr Helen O'Riordan
Community: 4
Educational and pastoral work

Loreto Community,
Balbriggan, Co Dublin
Tel 01-8412796
*Team Leaders:* Sr Monica McElwee,
Sr Moira MacManus, Sr Mary O'Farrell
Community: 16
Secondary school; pastoral work

Loreto Education Trust, Foxrock, Dublin 18
Tel 01-2899956
Education and offices

Loreto Hall, 77 St Stephen's Green,
Dublin 2
Tel 01-4781816
*Co-Leaders*
Sr Ríonach Donlon, Sr Eileen Linehan
Community: 11
Pastoral work

The Apartments,
77 St Stephen's Green, Dublin 2
*Co-Leaders*
Sr Máire Lagan, Sr Rosemary O'Connor
Community: 5

Loreto, 13 Carrigmore Place, City West,
Saggart, Co Dublin
Tel/Fax 01-4589918
Also, 15 Carrigmore Place, City West,
Saggart, Co Dublin
Tel 01-4580780

Loreto, 22 Brookdale Drive,
River Valley, Swords, Co Dublin
*Co-Leaders*
Sr Máire Lagan, Sr Rosemary O'Connor
Community: 5
Tel 01-8405982
Secondary School, River Valley, Swords
Social and pastoral work

Loreto, 5 Greenville Road, Blackrock,
Co Dublin
Tel 01-2843171
*Co-Leaders*
Sr Anne Mary Murphy, Sr Helen O'Riordan
Community: 3
Education, social and pastoral work

Loreto, 20 Herberton Park,
Rialto, Dublin 8
Tel 01-4535048
Email lorialto@hotmail.com
*Co-Leaders*
Sr Ríonach Donlon, Sr Eileen Linehan
Community: 3
Social and pastoral work

265 Sundrive Road, Dublin 12
Tel 01-4541509
*Co-Leaders*
Sr Ríonach Donlon, Sr Eileen Linehan
Community: 3
Education and pastoral work

7/8/9/10 Stonepark Orchard,
Stonepark Abbey
Tel 01-4952110/4952111/4951444/4950155
Community: 10
Education and pastoral work

175, 176, 178, 184, 185 Prior's Gate,
Greenhills Road, Tallaght, Dublin 24

9, 11, 50, 52 New Bancrost Hall,
Tallaght Main Street, Dubin 24

64, 66, 68 Griffith Hall,
Glandore Road, Dublin 9

10 Loreto, Crescent, Rathfarnham,
Dublin 14

21, 30, 30 The Croft,
Parc na Silla Avenue, Loughlinstown,
Dublin 18

## MARIE AUXILIATRICE SISTERS
7 Florence Street,
Portobello, Dublin 8
Tel 01-4537622
*Contact Person:* Sr Máire Nally
Email maire.nally@gmail.com
Community: 4
Spiritual direction, social outreach,
education

Marie Auxiliatrice Sisters
130 Upper Glenageary Road,
Dun Laoghaire, Co Dublin
Tel 01-2857389
*Contact Person:* Sr Eileen Cartin
Email eileencartin@marieaux.org
Community: 2
Spiritual direction, social outreach,
counselling, prison ministry

## MARIE REPARATRICE SISTERS
29 Brackenstown Village,
Swords, Co Dublin
Tel 01-8406321
Email smrbtown@eircom.net
*Contact:* Sr Eileen Carroll
Community: 2
Hospital chaplaincy, spiritual direction/
retreats. House of welcome to parish
groups

9 St Andrew's Grove, Malahide,
Co Dublin
Tel 01-8455113
Email smrmal@eircom.net
*Contact:* Sr Elizabeth Dunne
Community: 2
Parish ministry, spiritual direction/
retreats

## MARIST SISTERS
Provincialate, 51 Kenilworth Square,
Rathgar, Dublin 6
Tel 01-4972196
Email secirl@eircom.net
*Leader – Ireland:* Sr Vera Magee
Community: 4

10 Cambridge Terrace,
Dartmouth Square, Dublin 6
Tel 01-6605332
Email maristcambridge@yahoo.ie
Community: 2
Justice, education

Sundrive Road, Crumlin, Dublin 12
Tel 01-4540778
Email sundrivesm@eircom.net
*Community Leader*
Sr Elizabeth Gilmartin
Community: 13
Primary school
Social work, youth work, health care,
adult education, Marist laity

185 Killarney Park, Bray, Co Wicklow
Tel 01-2863396
Email smbray@wicklowtoday.com
Community: 3
Social work, parish ministry

27 Grange Park Grove, Raheny, Dublin 5
Tel 01-8480232
Email raheny27@yahoo.ie
*Leader:* Sr Olive McVann
Community: 4
Parish Ministry, chaplaincy

## MEDICAL MISSIONARIES OF MARY
Congregational Centre,
Rosemount, Rosemount Terrace,
Booterstown, Blackrock, Co Dublin
Tel 01-2882722 Fax 01-2834626
Email rcsmmm@eircom.net

MMM Communications Department,
Rosemount Terrace, Booterstown,
Co Dublin
Tel 01-2887180 Fax 01-2834626
Email mmm@iol.ie

*European Area Leader*
Sr Dervilla O'Donnell
3 Danieli Road, Artane, Dublin 5
Tel 01-8316469
Email dervillaod@eircom.net

Réalt na Mara, 11 Rosemount Terrace,
Booterstown, Co Dublin
Tel 01-2832247
Email mmmrealtnamara@eircom.net
Community: 4

26 Malahide Road, Artane, Dublin 5
Tel 01-8310427
Email mmmartane@gmail.com
Community: 6

52 St Agnes Road, Crumlin, Dublin 12
Tel 01-4552692
Email mmmcrumlin@eircom.net
Community: 3

33 Templeville Drive
Templeogue, Dublin 6W
Tel 01-4991803
Email mmm.templeogue@upcmail.ie
Community: 3

177 Philipsburgh Avenue,
Marino, Dublin 3
Tel 01-8376336
Email mmmmarino@eircom.net
Community: 2

1 The Grange, Laurel Place,
Terenure Road West, Dublin 6W
Tel 01-4925263
Email mmmterenure@gmail.com
Community: 5

The Lodge, 1A School Avenue,
Killester, Dublin 5
Tel 01-8187552

Hillview, 2A St Margaret's Avenue,
Raheny, Dubin 5
Tel 01-8324221
Email mmmraheny@eircom.net
Community: 4

## MISSIONARIES OF CHARITY
223 South Circular Road, Dublin 8
Tel 01-4540163
*Superior:* Sr Edward (MC)
Community 4
Hostel For men

## MISSIONARY FRANCISCAN SISTERS OF THE IMMACULATE CONCEPTION
Assisi House, Navan Road, Dublin 7
Tel 01-8682216
Community: 3
*Contact:* Sr Philomena Conroy

## MISSIONARY SISTERS OF THE HOLY ROSARY
Generalate, 23 Cross Avenue,
Blackrock, Co Dublin
Tel 01-2881708/9 Fax 01-2836308
Email mshrgen@indigo.ie
*Superior General:* Sr Maureen O'Malley
Community: 8

Regional Administration, Drumullac,
41 Westpark, Artane, Dublin 5
Tel 01-8510010 Fax 01-8187494
Email mshrreg@eircom.net
*Regional Superior:* Sr Maura Garry
Community: 4

Holy Rosary Convent,
Brookville, Westpark,
Artane, Dublin 5
Tel 01-8480603/8481216
*Superior:* Sr Madeleine Aiker
House for sisters on leave from mission.
Pastoral, health care
Community: 12

Holy Rosary Convent,
48 Temple Road, Dartry, Dublin 6
Tel 01-4971918/4971094
*Superior:* Sr Teresa Stapleton
Pastoral, education, care of the elderly
Community: 25

Holy Rosary Sisters,
Glankeen, 9 Richmond Avenue South,
Dartry, Dublin 6
Tel 01-4977277
Pastoral, health care, care of elderly
Community: 9

Holy Rosary Sisters (Community)
11 Dalymount, Phibsboro, Dublin 7
Tel 01-8680381
Pastoral, educational, health care
Community: 7

Holy Rosary Sisters,
2 Grange Abbey Cresent, Baldoyle,
Dublin 13
Tel 01-8476219
Pastoral, health care, education
Community: 4

Holy Rosary Sisters,
72 Grange Park, Baldoyle,
Dublin 13
Tel 01-8390291
Regional administration, counselling
Community: 2

## MISSIONARY SISTERS OF OUR LADY OF APOSTLES
70b Shellbourne Road,
Ballsbridge, Dublin 4
Tel 01-6685796
Email olasrsdublin@gmail.com
No. of sisters: 5
House of studies

## MISSIONARY SISTERS OF ST COLUMBAN
St Columban's Convent,
Magheramore, Wicklow
Tel 0404-67348
Email colsrsmagheramore@eircom.net
*Community Leader:* Sr Rose Gallagher
Community: 50
Motherhouse, congregational nursing
home for sick and retired members

St Agnes Road, Crumlin, Dublin 12
Tel 01-4555435
Community: 8
Mission awareness

Apt C14, Killarney Court,
Killarney Street, Dublin 1
Tel 01-6577339
Community: 1
Parish ministry, work with migrants

Columban Sisters,
Parish House No. 1, Holy Spirit Parish,
Silloge, Ballymun, Dublin 11
Tel 01-8423696
Community: 3

Columban Sisters,
5/6 Grange Crescent, off Pottery Road,
Dun Laoghaire, Co Dublin
Tel 01-2853961/5167340
Community: 4

*Contact Person for above four houses*
Sr Nora Mary O'Driscoll
Columban Sisters,
5/6 Grange Crescent, off Pottery Road,
Dun Laoghaire, Co Dublin
Tel 01-2853961/5167340

## MISSIONARY SISTERS OF ST PETER CLAVER
Our Lady of the Angels
81 Bushy Park Road, PO Box 228,
Terenure, Dublin 6
Tel 01-4909360
*Superior:* Sr Lucyna Wisniowska
Email claver4@hotmail.com
Community: 4
Assist needy missions, especially those in
Africa

## MISSIONARY SISTERS SERVANTS OF THE HOLY SPIRIT
143 Philipsburgh Avenue,
Fairview, Dublin 3
Tel 01-8369383
Email sspsfairview1@gmail.com
*Community Leader:* Sr Joan Quirke
Community: 3

98 Foxfield Road,
Raheny, Dublin 5
Tel 01-8319011
*Community Leader:* Sr Yudith Anu
Community: 3

## NOTRE DAME DES MISSIONS
Upper Churchtown Road,
Leading to Sweetmount Avenue,
Dublin 14
Tel 01-2983308/2961628
Email ntrdame@hotmail.com
*Leader:* Sr Una Rutledge
Email srunarutledge@yahoo.co.uk
Community: 24
Community for retired sisters

Sisters of Our Lady of the Missions
5 Griffeen Glen Park,
Griffeen Valley, Lucan South,
Co Dublin
Tel 01-6219088
Shared Leadership
Community: 2
Education, pastoral work

## OUR LADY OF THE CENACLE
3 Churchview Drive,
Killiney, Co Dublin
Tel 01-2840175
Email cenacledublin@eircom.net
*Contact:* Cenacle Sisters
Community: 3
Retreats, spiritual direction, hospital
chaplain, facilitation days/ evenings of
prayer, pastoral work

## OUR LADY OF SION SISTERS
127 Griffith Avenue,
Drumcondra, Dublin 9
Tel 01-8573130
Website www.sistersofourladyofsion.org

## POOR CLARES
St Damian's, Simmonscourt Road,
Ballsbridge, Dublin 4
Fx 01-6685464
Email pccdamians@mac.com
Website www.pccdamians.ie
*Abbess/Contact:* Sr M. Patrice
Community: 8
Contemplatives
Rosary and Evening Prayer on Sundays at
4 pm
First Fridays, Evening Prayer and
Benediction at 4.30 pm

## POOR SERVANTS OF THE MOTHER OF GOD
St Mary's Convent, Manor House,
Raheny, Dublin 5
Tel/Fax 01-8317626

St Mary's Convent, 2 St John's,
Castledermot, Athy, Co Kildare
Tel 059-9144152
Community: 2

St Mary's Convent, Manor House,
Raheny, Dublin 5
Tel 01-8313652 Fax 01-8313299
Community: 10
Education, pastoral ministry

Maryfield Convent, Chapelizod,
Dublin 20
Tel 01-6264684/6265402
Fax 01-6233673
Community: 13
Home for elderly

216 Tonlegee Road,
Dublin 5
Tel 01-8478566
Community: 4
Care of the elderly, pastoral ministry

Providence, 2 Creighton Street, Dublin 2
Tel 01-6713130
Community: 2
Pastoral Ministry

Croí Mhuire, 120 Lucan Road,
Chapelizod, Dublin 20
Fax/Tel 01-6233734
Community: 2
Elderly and pastoral work

39 Glenayle Road, Dublin 5
Tel 01-8770700
Community: 4
Pastoral Ministry

Kairos Spirituality Centre,
125 Castlegate Way, Adamstown, Lucan,
Co Dublin
Tel 01-6822079
Community: 1
Pastoral Ministry

Cuan Mhuire, Old Mill,
Vicanstown Road, Athy, Co Kildare
Tel 059-8631090
Community: 1
Councelling Ministry

## CONGREGATION OF THE SISTERS OF NAZARETH
Nazareth House,
Malahide Road, Dublin 3
Tel 01-8338205 Fax 01-8330813
Email nazarethdublin@eircom.net
*Superior*: Sr Cornelia Walsh
Community: 17
*Regional Superior:* Sr Cora McHale
Tel 01-8332024 Fax 01-8334988
Home for elderly. Beds: 72

## PRESENTATION SISTERS
Lucan, Co Dublin
Tel 01-6280305
Community: 5
Home for missionaries on home leave
Mission Office Tel/Fax 01-6282467
*Contact:* Sr Josephine Murphy
Email pbvmmo@gofree.indigo.ie

69 Fortlawn Drive, Mountview,
Blanchardstown, Dublin 15
Tel 01-8119430
Email presfortlawn@eircom.net
*Contact:* Sr Mary Byrne
Interprovincial Community: 2
School and pastoral work

*Northern Province:*
George's Hill, Dublin 7
Tel 01-8746914
Community: 10
Presentation Convent Primary School
Tel/Fax 01-8733061
Email presghill@eircom.net
School and pastoral ministry

2/3 Castlebridge Estate,
Maynooth, Co Kildare
Tel 01-6289952
*Community Leader:* Sr Eithne Cunniffe
Community: 6
Scoil Mhuire Primary School
Tel 01-6280056 Fax 01-6282611
School and pastoral ministry

Apartment 2, Riverforest Court, Leixlip,
Co Kildare
Tel 01-6242538
Email presleixlip1@eircom.net
Community: 1

*South-East Province:*
Provincialate, 27 Wainsfort Drive,
Terenure, Dublin 6W
Tel 01-4929588 Fax 01-4929590
Email secretary@presprose.com
*Provincial:* Sr Margarita Ryan
Community: 1

Presentation Sisters,
Clondalkin, Dublin 22
Tel 01-4592656
*Local Leader:* Sr Concepta O'Brien
Community: 10
Scoil Mhuire Primary School,
Convent Road, Clondalkin, Dublin 22
Tel 01-4592766

Scoil Ide Primary School,
New Road, Clondalkin, Dublin 22
Tel 01-4592973
Scoil Aine Primary School
Tel 01-4591645
Coláiste Bríde Secondary School,
New Road, Clondalkin, Dublin 22
Tel 01-4591158

Presentation Sisters,
Warrenmount, Dublin 8
Tel 01-4113831
*Local Leader:* Sr Imelda Kane
Community: 14
Primary. Tel 01-4539547
Post Primary. Tel 01-4547520
Warrenmount CED Centre Ltd
Tel 01-4542622

7B Oliver Bond House, Dublin 8
Tel 01-6776702
*Contact:* Sr Brigid Phelan
Community: 2

17A South Earl Street, Dublin 8
*Contact:* Sr Imelda Wickham
Tel 01-4532239
Community: 1

41 O'Curry Road, Dublin 8
Tel 01-4542806
Community: 3

335 Dolphin House, Dublin 8
*Contact:* Sr Margaret Mary Healy
Tel 01-4540499
Community: 2

5 Foxdene Green, Balgaddy,
Lucan, Co Dublin
Tel 01-4574533
Community: 3

2 The Weavers,
Meath Place, Dublin 8
*Contact:* Sr Bernadette Flanagan
Community: 1

27 Mayfield Park,
Watery Lane, Dublin 22
Tel 01-4037316
*Contact:* Sr Kathleen Barrett
Community: 2

105 Tyrconnell Place,
Inchicore, Dublin 8
*Contact:* Sr Bernadette Purcell
Community: 1

42 Temple Hill Apartments,
Terenure Road West, Dublin 6W
Tel 086-3422227
*Contact:* Sr Una Trant
Community: 1

9A Kilmahuddrick Walk,
Clondalkin, Dubin 22
Tel 01-4576441
*Contact:* Sr Mary Brennan
Community: 2

## REDEMPTORISTINES
Monastery of St Alphonsus,
St Alphonsus Road, Dublin 9
Tel 01-8305723 Fax 01-8309129
*Superior:* Sr Gabrielle
Email gabrielle.fox@redemptorists.ie
Community: 16
Contemplatives

## RELIGIOUS OF CHRISTIAN EDUCATION
Provincial Office, 3 Bushy Park House,
Templeogue Road, Dublin 6W
Tel 01-4901668 Fax 01-4901101
*Provincial leader:* Sr Rosemary O'Looney

Community Residence,
4/5 Bushy Park House,
Templeogue Road, Dublin 6W
Tel 01-4905516
*Superior:* Sr Rosemary O'Looney

13 Oriel Street Lower, Dublin 1
Tel 087-6359057
Counselling

Our Lady's School,
Templeogue Road, Dublin 6W
Secondary School. Tel 01-4903241
*Principal:* Ms Pauline Meaney

## RELIGIOUS OF SACRED HEART OF MARY
Cormaria, 7 Bancroft Road,
Tallaght, Dublin 24
Tel 01-4515674
Community: 5
Ministry in local area

13/14 Huntstown Wood,
Mulhuddart, Dublin 15
Tel 01-8223566
Community: 3
Pastoral ministry, addiction, HIV
counselling

70 Upper Drumcondra Road, Dublin 9
Tel 01-8379898
Community: 4
Education, pastoral

72 Upper Drumcondra Road, Dublin 9
Tel 01-8368331
Community: 4
Spiritual direction, ministry in local area

## RELIGIOUS SISTERS OF CHARITY
Generalate, Caritas, 15 Gilford Road,
Sandymount, Dublin 4
Tel 01-2697833/2697935

Mary Aikenhead Heritage Centre,
Our Lady's Mount, Harold's Cross,
Dublin 6W
Tel 01-4910041

Office of the Cause,
Sisters of Charity, St Mary's,
Merrion Road, Dublin 4
Tel 086-4680427

Overseas and Development Office,
Sisters of Charity, St Mary's,
Merrion Road, Dublin 4
Tel 01-2604826

Provincialate, Provincial House,
Our Lady's Mount, Harold's Cross,
Dublin 6W
Tel 01-4973177

Marmion House, St Mary's,
185 Merrion Road, Dublin 4
Tel 01-2027223
Various Apostolic Ministries

St Anne's, 29 Thornville Drive,
Kilbarrack East, Dublin 5
Tel 01-8321112/8321114
Various Apostolic Ministries

Stanhope Street Convent,
Manor Street, Dublin 7
Tel 01-6779183
Various Apostolic Ministries

Stanhope Lodge,
Stanhope Green, Dublin 7
Tel 01-6704016
Various Apostolic Ministries

Convent of the Assumption,
76 Upper Gardiner Street, Dublin 1
Tel 01-8746431
Various Apostolic Ministries

Sisters of Charity, 3C Liberty House,
Railway Street, Dublin 1
Tel 01-8364269
Various Apostolic Ministries

St Monica's,
28/38 Belvedere Place, Dublin 1
Tel (Community) 01-8552317
Various Apostolic Ministries

Naomh Bríd Community,
28/38 Belvedere Place, Dublin 1
Tel 01-8557647
Various Apostolic Ministries

Our Lady of the Nativity, Lakelands,
Sandymount, Dublin 4
Tel 01-2692076/2603362
Various Apostolic Ministries

St Mary's, Donnybrook, Dublin 4
Tel 01-2600315/2600818
Various Apostolic Ministries

Mary Aikenhead House, St Mary's,
Donnybrook, Dublin 4
Tel 01-2693258
Various Apostolic Ministries

Sisters of Charity, Our Lady's Mount,
Harold's Cross, Dublin 6W
Ard Mhuire Community
Tel 01-4961488
Maranatha Community
Tel 01-4961423
Shandon community
Tel 01-4982614

4 Telford House, St Mary's,
Merrion Road, Dublin 4
Tel 01-2605495
Various Apostolic Ministries

Stella Maris Convent,
Baily, Co Dublin
Tel 01-8322228 Fax 01-8063469
Various Apostolic Ministries

Our Lady Queen of Ireland,
Walkinstown, Dublin 12
Tel 01-4503491
Various Apostolic Ministries

Sisters of Charity,
Seville Place, Dublin 1
Tel 01-8744179
Various Apostolic Ministries

Sisters of Charity, 95/97 Richmond Road,
Fairview, Dublin 3
Tel 01-8376874
Various Apostolic Ministries

Sisters of Charity,
1 Temple Street, Dublin 1
Tel 01-8745778/8745779

26 Park Avenue, Sandymount, Dublin 4
Tel 01-2604659
Various Apostolic Ministries

28 Park Avenue, Sandymount, Dublin 4
Tel 01-2604654
Various Apostolic Ministries

Providence,
St Mary's, Merrion Road, Dublin 4
Tel 01-2693450
Various Apostolic Ministries

Shalom,
St Mary's, Merrion Road, Dublin 4
Tel 01-2602775
Various Apostolic Ministries

386 Clogher Road,
Crumlin, Dublin 12
Tel 01-4169016/4169662
Various Apostolic Ministries

**ROSMINIANS (SISTERS OF PROVIDENCE)**
104a Griffith Court,
Fairview, Dublin 3
Tel 01-8375021
Email teresamolloy@eircom.net
*Contact Person:* Sr Teresa Molloy
Community: 2

**SACRED HEART SOCIETY**
76 Home Farm Road,
Drumcondra, Dublin 9
Tel 01-8375412  Fax 01-8375542
Email rscjirs@gmail.com
*Provincial Superior:* Sr Barbara Duffy
Email bpd@eircom.net

6 Achill Road, Drumcondra, Dublin 9
Tel 01-8360866
Email rochearscj@eircom.net
Community: 3
Adult education and pastoral work;
youth and pastoral ministry

*Linked with Achill Road:*
49 Philipsburgh Terrace, Marino, Dublin 3
Tel 01-8554018
Email lawlesse@hotmail.com

9 Clonshaugh Drive, Priorswood, Dublin 17
Tel 01-8474244 Fax 01-8488940
Email tdeasy@eircom.net
Community: 2
Parish work

10 Walnut Rise, Dublin 9
Tel/Fax 01-8844547
Email norabourke@eircom.net
Community: 3
Pastoral ministry, educational ministry

14 Merrion View Avenue, Dublin 4
Tel 01-2602533
Email dairne@eircom.net
Community: 2
Chairperson CH Board of Directors,
Facilitation, Literacy and ESOL tutor

Linked with Merrion View Avenue:
5 Redcourt Oaks, Seafield Road East,
Clontarf, Dublin 3
Educational trusteeships and voluntary
work

23 Castlelands Grove,
Dalkey, Co Dublin
Historical research; part-time university
teaching

Cedar House, Provincial Infirmary,
35 Mount Anville Park, Dublin 14
Tel 01-2831024/5 Fax 01-2831348
Email
cedarhouseadministration@eircom.net
Community: 12

36 Mount Anville Park,
Dublin 14
Tel 01-2880739
Community: 4
Work in provincial administration and
Cedar House

37/38 Mount Anville Park,
Dublin 14
Tel 01-2880708
Community: 4
Work in parish and community service,
translation

96 Mount Anville Wood,
Lower Kilmacud Road, Dublin 14
Tel 01-2880786 Fax 01-2789119
Email joanhutchinson@eircom.net
Community: 4
Work in provincial administration,
Mount Anville School, spiritual ministry

201 Lower Kilmacud Road,
Blackrock, Co Dublin
Tel 01-2834832 Fax 01-2104825
Community: 4
Work in provincial administration,
spiritual and parish ministry

107 Beechwood Lawn, Rochestown
Avenue, Dun Laoghaire, Co Dublin
Tel 01-2354933
Community: 2
Email silemac@eircom.net
Pastoral ministry

Sacred Heart Schools Network Ltd
Mount Anville Primary School,
Lower Kilmacud Road,
Blackrock, Co Dublin
Pupils: 467
Tel 01-2831148 Fax 01-2836395
Mount Anville Sacred Heart Education
Trust PJP
Mount Anville Secondary School
Convent of the Sacred Heart,
Mount Anville, Dublin 14
Pupils: 635
Tel 01-2885313/4 Fax 01-2832373
Mount Anville Junior and Montessori
School, Convent of the Sacred Heart,
Mount Anville, Dublin 14
Pupils: 420
Tel 01-2885313/4 Fax 01-2832373

**SACRED HEARTS OF JESUS AND MARY
(PICPUS) SISTERS**
Delegation House,
11 Northbrook Road, Ranelagh, Dublin 6
Tel 01-4910173 (Coordinator)
Tel 01-4974831 (Community)
Fax 01-4965551
Community: 4
*Contact:* Sr Angela O'Toole (SSCC)
Email aotoole70@gmail.com

Aymer House,
11 Northbrook Lane, Ranelagh, Dublin 6
Tel 01-4975614
Community: 4

**SACRED HEARTS OF JESUS AND MARY**
10 The Village,
Drumcondra Road Upper,
Drumcondra, Dublin 9
Tel 01-8040849

**SALESIAN SISTERS OF ST JOHN BOSCO**
Provincialate,
203 Lower Kilmacud Road,
Stillorgan, Co Dublin
Tel 01-2985188
*Provincial Superior:* Sr Mary Doran
Convent Tel 01-2985908
*Superior:* Sr Moira O'Sullivan
Community: 5
Parish ministry, provincial administration,
art therapy

38 Morehampton Road,
Donnybrook, Dublin 4
Tel 01-6684643
*Contact person:* Sr Anne O'Reilly
Community: 3
Mission promotion, working in resource
centre, President APTS

40 Morehampton Road,
Donnybrook, Dublin 4
Tel 01-6680012
*Superior:* Sr Jennifer Perkins
Community: 3
Hospital ministry, facilitators' training
course for youth retreats, Director of
Dominican Ecology Centre, Wicklow

91-95 Ashwood Road, Bawnoge,
Clondalkin, Dublin 22
Tel 01-4571792
*Superior:* Sr Gemma Beggan
Community: 5
Teaching and related activities

36 Glenties Park, Finglas South, Dublin 11
Tel 01-8345777
*Superior:* Sr Máire O'Byrne
Community: 4
Social and parish work, mission promotion

28 Hazelwood Crescent, Greenpark,
Clondalkin, Dublin 22
Tel 01-4123928
Superior: Sr Joan O'Brien
Community: 4
Parish work and school chaplaincy

**SISTERS OF ST CLARE**
St Clare's Convent,
Tel 01-4995100
63 Harold's Cross Road, Dublin 6W
*Contact:* Sr Dominic Savio Ward
Community: 11
Primary School

**ST JOHN OF GOD SISTERS**
34 Dornden Park,
Booterstown, Co Dublin
Tel 01-2698898
Community: 3
Community Project residence

39 St David's Wood, Malahide Road,
Artane, Dublin 5
Community: 3
Tel 01-8329798

**SISTERS OF ST JOSEPH OF CHAMBERY**
St Joseph's Convent,
Springdale Road, Raheny, Dublin 5
Tel 01-8478351
*Superior:* Sr Eileen Silke
Email esilke10@eircom.net
Community: 10
Care of the sick and pastoral activity

**SISTERS OF ST JOSEPH OF CLUNY**
Mount Sackville Convent,
Chapelizod, Dublin 20
Tel 01-8213134
Email clunyprov@sjc.ie
Website www.sjc.ie
*Provincial Superior:* Sr Rowena Galvin
Tel 01-8213134
*Superior:* Sr Maeve Guinan
Tel 01-8213134
Community: 43
Primary school; secondary day school;
nursing home

St Joseph of Cluny Convent,
Ballinclea Road, Killiney, Co Dublin
Tel 01-2851038
*Superior:* Sr Clare Little
Community: 9
Junior and secondary schools

Cluny House, 1 Beechwood Park,
Rathmines, Dublin 6
Tel 01-4971641
*Superior:* Sr Peggy McLoughlin
Community: 4

Parslickstown Drive,
Mulhuddart, Dublin 15
Tel 01-8217339
*Superior:* Sr Morag Collins
Community: 3
Education and pastoral ministry

**SISTERS OF ST JOSEPH OF LYON**
3 St Margaret's Avenue,
Raheny, Dublin 5
Tel 01-8325896
Email sistersofjoseph@oceanfree.net
*Contact Person:* Sr Marie Kiernan
*Community Coordinator*
Sr Marie Kiernan
Email sistersofstjosephlyon@eircom.net

**ST JOSEPH OF THE SACRED HEART
SISTERS**
St Joseph's Convent,
6 Farmleigh Avenue,
Stillorgan, Co Dublin
Tel 01-2781228 Fax 01-2782139
Sr Eileen Kirby

Sisters of St Joseph of the Sacred Heart,
25 Nutley Square, Donnybrook,
Dublin 4
Tel 01-2602306
Sr Eily Deasy

Sisters of St Joseph of the Sacred Heart,
27 Castlerosse View, Baldoyle, Dublin
Tel 01-8324508
Sr Theresa Herlihy

Sisters of St Joseph,
11 The Courtyard, Vevay Crescent,
Bray, Co Wicklow
Tel 01-2761288
Sr Briege Buckley

Sisters of St Joseph, 48 Seatown Villas,
Swords, Co Dublin
Tel 01-8907345
Sr Mary Kirrane

Sisters of St Joseph,
3 Carrigalea, Queens Park,
Monkstown, Co Dublin
Sr Clare Ahern

**ST LOUIS SISTERS**
St Louis Generalate,
3 Beech Court, Ballinclea Road,
Killiney, Dublin
Tel 01-2350304/2350309 Fax 01-2350345
*Institute Leader:* Sr Donna Hansen

St Louis Convent,
Charleville Road, Dublin 6
Tel 01-4975467
Community: 26
St Louis High School, Rathmines
Tel 01-4975458. Pupils: 750
St Louis Primary School, Rathmines
Tel 01-4976098. Pupils: 400
St Louis Infant School, Rathmines
Tel 01-4972188. Pupils: 350

Blakestown Road,
Mulhuddart, Dublin 15
Tel 01-8217432
Community: 6
Varied apostolates

7 Grosvenor Road, Rathgar, Dublin 6
Tel 01-4965485
Community: 7
Varied apostolates

8 Grosvenor Road, Rathgar, Dublin 6
Tel 01-4966631
Community: 6
Varied apostolates

38 Bushy Park Road, Terenure, Dublin 6
Tel 01-4900043
Community: 3
Varied apostolates

130 Beaufort Downs,
Rathfarnham, Dublin 16
Tel 01-4934194
Community: 5
Varied apostolates

17 Kilclare Crescent, Jobstown,
Tallaght, Dublin 24
Tel 01-4526344
Community: 1
Education

49 Moynihan Court,
Main Road, Tallaght Village, Dublin 24
Tel 01-4628386
Community: 4
Varied apostolates

**ST PAUL DE CHARTRES SISTERS**
Queen of Peace Centre,
Garville Avenue,
Rathgar, Dublin 6
Tel 01-4975381/4972366 Fax 01-4964084
Email spcqueen@eircom.net
*Regional Superior*
Sr Rose Margaret Nuval
Community: 6
Residences for the elderly

**URSULINES**
Generalate, 17 Trimleston Drive,
Booterstown, Co Dublin
Tel 01-2693503
*Congregational Leader:* Sr Mary McHugh
*Assistant:* Sr Anne Harte Barry

Ursuline Sisters, 24 Shrewsbury Wood,
Cabinteely, Dublin 18
Tel 01-2853706
Email urscab@eircom.net
Community: 2

St Ursula's, Sandyford, Dublin 18
Tel 01-2956881
*Contact Person:* Sr Finbarr Muckley
Community: 3
Pastoral ministry

5 Moynihan Court, Main Road, Tallaght,
Dublin 24
Tel 01-4148527
Sr Joan Kane
Community: 1
Pastoral Ministry

**URSULINES OF JESUS**
26 The Drive, Seatown Park,
Swords, Co Dublin
Tel 01-8404323
Email ujswords@eircom.net
*Contact Person:* Sr Mary McLoughney
Community: 2
Parish ministry, reflexology and
aromatherapy.

# EDUCATIONAL
# INSTITUTIONS

**Holy Cross College**
Clonliffe, Dublin 3
Tel 01-8375103

**All Hallows College**
Drumcondra, Dublin 9
Tel 01-8373745/8373746
Fax 01-8377642
*President:* Rev Patrick McDevitt (CM) PhD

**Marino Institute of Education**
Griffith Avenue, Dublin 9
Tel 01-8057700

**Mater Dei Institute of Education**
Clonliffe Road, Dublin 3
Tel 01-8086500 Fax 01-8370776
Email info@materdei.dcu.ie
Website www.materdei.ie
*Director:* Dr Andrew McGrady PhD
*Chair of Board:* Mr Eddie Sullivan

**The Milltown Institute of Theology and Philosophy**
Milltown Park, Dublin 6
Tel 01-2776300
*Rector/President*
Rev Dr Thomas R. Whelan (CSSp)
(See Seminaries and Houses of Study
section)

**St Patrick's College**
Drumcondra, Dublin 9
Tel 01-8842006
*President:* Dr Daire Keogh
*Chair of Board:* Prof. John Coolahan

**St Patrick's College**
Maynooth, Co Kildare
Tel 01-7084700 Fax 01-7083959
*President:* Rt Rev Mgr Hugh Connolly
(See Seminaries and Houses of Study
section)

**EDMUND RICE SCHOOLS TRUST**
Arklow CBS,
Coolgreaney Road, Arklow, Co Wicklow
Tel 0402-32564 Fax 0402-32564
*Principal:* Mr Peter Somers

St Brendan's College, Woodbrook, Bray,
Co Wicklow
Tel 01-2822317 (Principal)
Fax 01-2822616
Email info@saintbrendans.ie
*Principal:* Mr John Taylor

Coláiste Éanna,
Ballyroan, Dublin 16
Tel 01-4931767
Email secretary@colaiste.enna.ie
Principal: Mr Brendan McCauley

Clonkeen College, Clonkeen Road,
Blackrock, Co Dublin
Tel 01-2892709 Fax 01-2898260
Email reception@clonkeencollege.ie
*Principal:* Mr Edward Melly

Edmund Rice Schools Trust,
Meadow Vale, Clonkeen Road,
Blackrock, Co Dublin
Tel 01-2897511
*CE:* Mr Gerry Bennett

Scoil Colm,
Armagh Road, Crumlin, Dublin 12
Tel 01-4562622 Fax 01-4651889
Email scoilcolm1@gmail.com
*Principal:* Ms Claire Ní Chianáin

Drimnagh Castle Primary School,
Drimnagh Castle, Long Mile Road,
Dublin 12
Tel 01-4552066 (Principal)
Email
drimnaghcastle@primary.scoilnet.ie/blog/
*Principal:* Mr Eugene Duffy

Meánscoil Iognáid Rís,
Drimnagh Castle,
Long Mile Road, Dublin 12
Tel 01-4518316 (Principal)
Fax 01-4505401
Email dcbs@eircom.net
*Principal:* Mr John Devilly

Christian Brothers Secondary School,
James's Street, Dublin 8
Tel 01-4547756 Fax 01-4547856
*Principal:* Mr Paul McEntee
Email jamesstcbs123@outlook.ie

Oatlands Primary School,
Mount Merrion, Co Dublin
Tel 01-2887108
Email oatlandsprimary@eircom.net
*Principal:* Ms Ber O'Sullivan

Oatlands College,
Mount Merrion, Co Dublin
Tel 01-2888533/2880662
Email admin@oatlands.net
*Principal:* Ms Caroline Garrett

Coláiste Eoin, Bóthar Stigh Lorgan,
Baile an Bhóthair, Carraig Dubh,
Co Atha Cliath
Tel 01-2884002 Fax 01-2836896
Email eoincolaiste@eircom.net
*Principal:* Mr Finín Máirtín

Coláiste Íosagáin, Stillorgan Road,
Booterstown, Co Dublin
Tel 01-2884028
*Principal:* Ms Fíona Uí Uiginn

Scoil Íosagáin, Aughavannagh Road,
Dublin 12
Tel 01-4541821 Fax 01-4169930
*Principal:* Ms Mairéad Fanning

Scoil Treasa Naofa,
Donore Avenue, Dublin 8
Tel 01-4541899
Email scoiltreasanaofa@gmail.com
*Principal:* Ms Ann Marie Spillane

Scoil Sancta Maria,
Synge Street, Dublin 8
Tel 01-4784316
Email bscoilsynge.eircom.net
Website www.syngestreet.com
*Principal:* Mr Gerry Mooney

St Paul's Secondary School,
Synge Street, Dublin 8
Tel 01-4783998 Fax 01-4784154
Email syngestreetoffice@eircom.net
Website www.syngestreet.com
*Principal:* Mr Michael Minnock

Francis Street CBS (Primary),
Francis Street, Dublin 8
Tel 01-4531800
Email francisstcbs.ias@eircom.net
*Principal:* Ms Fiona Collins

Christian Brothers Secondary School,
Westland Row,
South Cumberland Street, Dublin 2
Tel 01-6614143 Fax 01-6763652
Email info@cbswestlandrow.ie
*Principal:* Ms Kate Byrne

Christian Brothers College,
Monkstown Park, Dun Laoghaire,
Co Dublin
Tel 01-2805854 Fax 01-2805907
Email cbcadmin@indigo.ie
*Principal:* Dr Gerard Berry

Coláiste Phádraig,
Roselawn, Lucan, Co Dublin
Tel 01-6282299 Fax 01-6282713
Email colaistelucan@eircom.net
*Principal:* Mr Tony Brady

St David's CBS Secondary School,
Malahide Road, Artane, Dublin 5
Tel 01-8315322 Fax 01-8311523
*Principal:* Mr Padraic Kavanagh

Scoil Chiaráin CBS Primary School,
Collins Avenue East, Dublin 5
Tel 01-8313072
Email scoilchiaraincbs.ias@eircom.net
*Principal:* Ms Ciara Harte

St Fintan's High School,
Sutton, Dublin 13
Tel 01-8324632
Email stfintanshs@eircom.net
*Principal:* Ms Mary Fox

St Kevin's College (CBS),
Ballygall Road East, Dublin 11
Tel 01-8371423
Email info@stkevinscollege.com
*Principal:* Mr Thomas J. Byrne

St Declan's Secondary School,
Nephin Road, Dublin 7
Tel 01-8380357
Email info@stdeclanscollege.ie
*Principal:* Mr Ciarán O'Hare

Gaelscoil Choláiste Mhuire,
4 Cearnóg Pharnell, Baile Átha Cliath 1
Tel 01-8729131 Fax 01-8788175
*Príomhoide:* An tUas S. Feiritéar

Coláiste Mhuire,
Bothar Ráth Tó, Baile Átha Cliath 7
Tel 01-8688996 Fax 01-8688998
Email runai@colaistemhuire.ie
*Príomhoide:* Tomás O'Murchú

St Vincent's CBS Primary School,
St Philomena's Road,
Glasnevin, Dublin 11
Tel 01-8302328
Email office@stvincentsprimary.com
*Principal:* Mr Edward Sewell

St Vincent's Secondary School,
Finglas Road, Glasnevin, Dublin 11
Tel 01-8304375 Fax 01-8309727
*Principal:* Mr John Horan

Scoil Mhuire Marino,
Griffith Avenue, Dublin 9
Tel 01-8336421 Fax 01-8338555
*Principal:* Mr Ben Dorney

St Joseph's CBS NS,
Fairview, Dublin 3
Tel 01-8336127
*Principal:* Ms Maureen Fitzpatrick

St Joseph's CBS Secondary School,
Fairview, Dublin 3
Tel 01-8531614 Fax 01-8531909
Email info@stjosephsfairview.ie
*Principal:* Mr Gerry Cullen

Ard Scoil Ris, Griffith Avenue,
Marino, Dublin 9
Tel 01-8332633 Fax 01-8331594
*Principal:* Mr Mark Neville

St Paul's Primary School,
North Brunswick Street, Dublin 7
Tel 01-8722167
Email brunnerprimary@gmail.com
*Principal:* Ms Ruth Coghlan

St Paul's CBS Secondary School,
North Brunswick Street, Dublin 7
Tel 01-8720781 Fax 01-8723160
Email brunneroffice@gmail.com
*Principal:* Mr Patrick McCormack

O'Connell Primary School,
North Richmond Street, Dublin 1
Tel 01-8557517
Email principal@oconnellprimary.ie
*Principal:* Mr Patsy O'Keeffe

O'Connell Secondary School CBS,
North Richmond Street, Dublin 1
Tel 01-8748307 Fax 01-8366616
Email secretary@oconnellschool.ie
*Principal:* Mr Gerry Duffy

St Laurence O'Toole Primary School,
Seville Place, Dublin 1
Tel 01-8363490
Email info@larriers.ie
Principal: Mr Mark Candon

Coláiste Choilm, Swords, Co Dublin
Tel 01-8401420 Fax 01-8400331
Email colchoilm.ias@eircom.net
*Principal:* Mr David Neville

St Aidan's CBS Secondary School,
Collins Avenue Extension, Whitehall,
Dublin 9
Tel 01-8377587 Fax 01-8376873
Email secretary@staidanscbs.ie
*Principal:* Mr Brendan Harrington

## EDUCATIONAL TRUSTS

**ERST – The Edmund Rice Schools Trust**
Meadow Vale, Clonkeen Road,
Blackrock, Co Dublin
Tel 01-2897511 Fax 01-2897540
Email reception@erst.ie
*CE:* Gerry Bennett

**LE CHÉILE SCHOOLS TRUST**
St Mary's, Bloomfield Avenue,
Donnybrook, Dublin 4
Tel 01-2375493 Fax 01-6602528
Email admin@lecheiletrust.ie
www.lecheiletrust.ie
*Education Officer:* Dr Eilís Humphreys
Tel 087-0509227
Email eilis@lecheiletrust.ie
*Faith and Ethos Development*
*Co-ordinator:* John Scally

**CEIST**
Ceist Education Office, Dublin Road,
Kildare Town, Co Kildare
Tel 01-6510350 Fax 01-6510180
Email info@ceist.ie
*CEO:* Dr Marie Griffin
Tel 01-6510350

**DEA – Spiritan Education Trust**
Des Places House, Kimmage Manor,
Whitehall Road, Kimmage, Dubin 12
Tel 01-4997610 Fax 01-4997060
Email reception@desplaces.ie

## CHARITABLE AND OTHER SOCIETIES

*Adoption Societies*

**CÚNAMH**
30 South Anne Street, Dublin 2
Tel 01-6779664
*Administrative Secretary:* Mr Jim Dwan
*Senior Social Worker:* Ms Julie Kerins

**St Brigid's Orphanage**
Holy Faith Convent, The Coombe,
Dublin 8
Tel 01-4542917/4540244
*Sister in Charge*
Sr M. Benignus McDonagh

**St Patrick's Guild**
203 Merrion Road, Dublin 4
Tel 01-2196551
*Director:* Sr Francis Fahy

*Travellers Family Care*

**Derralossary House**
Roundwood, Co Wicklow
Tel 01-2818355
Residential home for girls
Ballyowen Meadows
Tel 01-6235735
Exchange House Youth Service
61 Great Strand Street, Dublin 1
Tel 01-4546488
Training and employment programme
and youth work

*Hostels*

**Don Bosco House**
57 Lower Drumcondra Road, Dublin 9
Tel 01-8360696
Salesian hostel for homeless boys.
Priest in Charge: Rev V. Collier (SDB)
**Homeless Girls' Hostel**
Sherrard House,
19 Upper Sherrard Street, Dublin 1
Tel 01-8743742

**Iveagh Hostel**
Bride Road, Dublin 8
Tel 01-4540182

**Morning Star Hostel**
Morning Star Avenue,
Brunswick Street, Dublin 7
Tel 01-8723401

**Regina Coeli Hostel**
Morning Star Avenue,
Brunswick Street, Dublin 7
Tel 01-8723142

**St Vincent de Paul Night Shelter**
Back Lane, Dublin 8
Tel 01-4542181

*Housing*

**Catholic Housing Aid Society**
Grenville Street, Dublin 1
Tel 01-8741020
*Secretary:* Mrs Valerie Power
Flats for the aged

**Threshold**
21 Stoneybatter, Dublin 7
Tel 01-6353600/6786090
Website www.threshold.ie

*Other*

**Cuan Mhuire**
Athy, Co Kildare
Tel 059-8631493 Fax 059-8638765
Rehabilitation centre for alcoholics and
those with allied problems

**Irish School of Evangelisation (ISOE)**
9A Wyattville Park, Dun Laoghaire,
Co Dublin
*Contact:* Joe O'Callaghan
Tel 01-2827658
Email isoe@esatclear.ie
www.esatclear.ie/~isoe

**Our Lady's Choral Society**
(The Archdiocesan Choir)
*Director:* Rev Paul Ward
*Hon Secretary:* Lois Jarvis
Tel 01-2819363

**Society of St Vincent de Paul**
Dublin Office,
91-92 Sean McDermott Street, Dublin 1
Tel 01-8550022 Fax 01-8559168

## belltron

*Parish Services to Housebound Parishioners via WPAS Radio Link*
*Live Streaming Video of Chruch Services on the Internet*

## BELLS & CLOCKS

- Bells – Automation, Restoration & Re-hanging
- Survey, Maintenance and Replacement of Bell Support Structures
- Digital Electronic Bells & Carillons via speakers – (1000 hymns/peals)
- Tower Clocks – Hour Ringing – Westminster Chime
- Liturgical Calendar Event Programming

## COMMUNICATIONS

- The Parish Radio Link System
- Live Streaming Video of Church Serives on the Internet
- Sound & PA Amplification, Radio Microphones etc
- Audio Induction Loops for the Deaf
- Church Music Systems & Radio Remote Control

## ENGINEERING & BUILDING MAINTENANCE

- Bell Support Structure installation and restoration
- Water ingress protection. Guttering & drains – cleaning – repair
- Pointing and sealing of stone.  Roofing slates, tiles & flashing repairs
- Stone surface cleaning & restoration
- Lightning Protection: Dynasphere 3000 & Traditional systems
- Automation – Control of Heating, Lighting, Door opening etc
- Height Access for Surveys & Engineering reports
- Hoist Access to 75 mtrs – competitively priced

Installations by our Experienced, Highly Qualified and
Fully Insured Technical Team
Full Guarantees & After Sales Support
Contact Jim Doyle or Leo Brophy

Head Office: Dunleary House
83 Dublin Road, Sutton, Dublin 13
Tel/Fax 01-8392220 • Mobile 087-2538916
Email belltron@infatron.com • Website www.belltron.ie

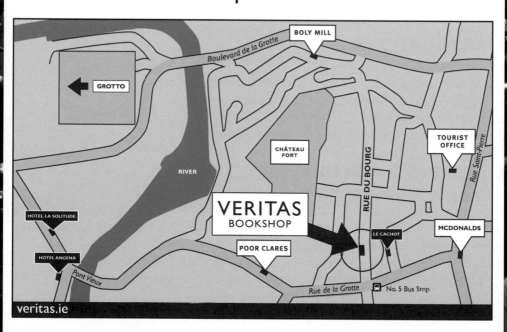

# Pioneer Total Abstinence Association of the Sacred Heart

**The Association has as its chief aim the promotion of temperance and sobriety; with prayer and self-sacrifice as its principal means. The members use their independence of alcohol to engage in good works and the organisation of counter attractions to drinking.**

**Central Spiritual Director:**
**Father Bernard McGuckian SJ**

**Monthly publication:**
*The Pioneer magazine*

**Dublin address:**
The Secretary
Pioneer Association
27 Upper Sherrard Street, Dublin 1
Tel: (01) 874 9464 • Fax: (01) 874 8485
Email: pioneer@jesuit.ie
Website: http://www.pioneerassociation.ie

# PONTIFICAL UNIVERSITY
## St Patrick's College, Maynooth

**Undergraduate Degree Programmes**
Baccalaureate in Divinity (BD)
Baccalaureate in Theology & Arts (BATh) CAO code MU001
Baccalaureate in Theology (BTh) CAO code MU002

*Northern Ireland applicants are eligible to apply for a student loan for the above programmes.*

*The latter two programmes qualify for the Republic of Ireland's Free Fees initiative for all eligible EU citizens and the Higher Education Grants Scheme where applicable.*

*Mature students are very welcome to apply to all of the above programmes.*

**BTh/BD Add-On Modes:** Students holding a Diploma in Theology or the equivalent may be admitted to the BTh or BD Add-on mode. The minimum duration of these programmes will be one academic year, and in the case of the BD, must be full-time. For further information, please contact the Admissions Office 00353 (1) 7084772.

**Postgraduate Programmes**
Postgraduate programmes available from Higher Diploma to Doctoral level.
Master's Degree programmes offered over one year or two years.
Affiliated programmes offered in centres around the country.

*Some Postgraduate programmes qualify for the Higher Education Grants scheme and tax relief where applicable.*

*OPEN DAYS: Last Friday and Saturday in November annually.*

*Information on all courses may be obtained from:*
The Admissions Office,
Pontifical University, St Patrick's College, Maynooth, Co Kildare
Tel +353-1-708 4772/3600/3892 • Fax +353-1-708 3441
Email admissions@spcm.ie • Website www.maynoothcollege.ie

# ARCHDIOCESE OF CASHEL AND EMLY

PATRON OF THE ARCHDIOCESE
ST AILBE, 12 SEPTEMBER

SUFFRAGEN SEES: CLOYNE, CORK AND ROSS, KERRY, KILLALOE,
LIMERICK, WATERFORD AND LISMORE

INCLUDES MOST OF COUNTY TIPPERARY AND PARTS OF COUNTY LIMERICK

**Most Rev Kieran O'Reilly (SMA) DD**
Archbishop of Cashel and Emly born 1952; ordained priest 17 June 1978; ordained Bishop of Killaloe 29 August 2010; Appointed Archbishop of Cashel and Emly 22 November 2014

Residence: Archbishop's House, Thurles, Co Tipperary
Tel 0504-21512 Fax 0504-22680
Email office@cashel-emly.ie
Website www.cashel-emly.ie

The Metropolitan Archdiocese of Cashel and Emly in mid-western Ireland is in the province of Munster. The then separate dioceses of Cashel and Emly were established in 1111 by the Synod of Rathbreasail. Cashel diocese was promoted to the status of a Metropolitan Province in 1152 at the Synod of Kells. Emly diocese was formally joined to Cashel in 1718. The incumbent Ordinary, Dermot Clifford, has been Archbishop of Cashel and Emly since 1988.

McMullen was the main builder, and J. C. Ashlin was responsible for the enclosing walls, railing and much of the finished work.

The cathedral has many beautiful features, including an impressive rose window, a free-standing baptistry and a magnificent altar. The prize possession of the cathedral is its exquisite tabernacle, the work of Giacomo dello Porta (1537–1602), a pupil of Michelangelo. This tabernacle, which belonged to the

Gesú (Jesuit) Church in Rome, was purchased by Archbishop Leahy and transported to Thurles.

The cathedral was extensively renovated and the sanctuary sympathetically remodelled on the occasion of its first centenary in 1979.

The most recent extensive conservation and renewal of the Cathedral, during 2001–2003, has restored the building to its original splendour.

## CATHEDRAL OF THE ASSUMPTION, THURLES

The Cathedral of the Assumption stands on the site of earlier chapels. The first church on this site was part of the Carmelite priory, which dates from the early fourteenth century.

Some time before 1730 George Mathew, Catholic proprietor of the Thurles Estate, built a chapel for the Catholics of Thurles beside the ruins of the Carmelite priory. It was known as the Mathew Chapel. In 1810 Archbishop Bray consecrated the new 'Big Chapel', which was more spacious and ornate than its humble predecessor.

Soon after his appointment as archbishop in 1857, Dr Patrick Leahy revealed his plan to replace the Big Chapel with 'a cathedral worthy of the archdiocese'. Building commenced in 1865, and the impressive Romanesque cathedral, with its façade modelled on that of Pisa, was consecrated by Archbishop Croke on 21 June 1879. The architect was J. J. McCarthy. Barry

**Most Rev Dermot Clifford PhD, DD**
Archbishop Emeritus of Cashel and Emly;
born 1939; ordained priest 22 February
1964; ordained Coadjutor Archbishop 9
March 1986; installed Archbishop of
Cashel and Emly 12 September 1988;
acted as Apostolic Administrator of
Cloyne, March 2009–January 2013;
Retired 22 November 2014
Residence: The Green, Holycross,
Thurles, Co Tipperary

## CHAPTER

*Dean*
Rt Rev Mgr Christy O'Dwyer
*Archdeacon*
Venerable Matthew McGrath, Tipperary
*Chancellor:* Vacant
*Precentor:* Vacant
*Treasurer:* Vacant
*Penitentiary*
Very Rev Canon Conor Ryan, Hospital
*Theologian*
Very Rev Canon Liam McNamara,
Ballybricken, Grange,
Kilmallock, Co Limerick
*Prebendaries*
*Newchapel*
Very Rev Canon Thomas J. Ryan, Murroe
*Lattin:* Vacant
*Killennellick*
Very Rev Canon Liam Ryan, Killenaule

## ADMINISTRATION

**College of Consultors**
Rt Rev Mgr Christy O'Dwyer PP
Venerable Matthew McGrath PP
Very Rev Nicholas J. Irwin PP
Very Rev John J. O'Rourke AP
Rev Celsus Tierney CC

**Vicars General**
Appointments pending

**Vicars Forane**
Very Rev Canon Thomas J. Ryan
Very Rev Canon Conor Ryan
Very Rev Canon Liam Ryan
Very Rev Canon Thomas F. Breen
Very Rev Canon Eugene Everard
Very Rev Canon John O'Neill

**Diocesan Planning Finance Committee**
*Secretary*
Venerable Matthew McGrath PP
Tel 062-51536
Very Rev George Bourke PP
Tel 0504-44227
Very Rev Conor Hayes PP
Tel 061-384213
Very Rev Nicholas J. Irwin PP
Tel 056-8834855
Very Rev John O'Keeffe PP
Tel 061-379172
Rev Thomas Lanigan-Ryan CC
Tel 062-80475

**Diocesan Archivist**
Rt Rev Mgr Christy O'Dwyer PP
Cashel, Co Tipperary
Tel 062-61127

**Diocesan Secretary/Chancellor**
Very Rev Nicholas J. Irwin PP
Archbishop's House, Thurles, Co Tipperary
Tel 0504-21512

## CATECHETICS EDUCATION

**Adult Religious Education**
Rev Thomas Dunne CC
Bothar Na Naomh,
Thurles, Co Tipperary
Tel 0504-22042

**Catechetics**
*Director:* Rev Patrick Coffey CC
Upperchurch, Thurles, Co Tipperary
Tel 0504-54181
*Assistant Director*
Very Rev Michael Kennedy PP
The Parochial House, New Inn,
Cashel, Co Tipperary
Tel 052-7462395

**Boards of Management of Primary
Schools**
*Education Secretary*
Very Rev John O'Keeffe PP
Birdhill, Killaloe, Co Tipperary
Tel 061-379172/087-2421678

## PASTORAL

**ACCORD**
Accord House, Cathedral Street,
Thurles, Co Tipperary
Tel 0504-22279
*Diocesan Director*
Rev Tomás O'Connell CC
Tel 0504-22505

**Adoption Society**
*Director:* Rev Celsus Tierney CC
Holy Cross Abbey, Holy Cross,
Thurles, Co Tipperary
Tel 0504-43118

**Charismatic Renewal**
*Adviser*
Very Rev Canon Denis Talbot AP
Galbally, Co Tipperary
Tel 062-37929

**Child Protection Delegate**
Mr Bill Meagher
Tel 087-7914517

**Cura**
Cura Centre, 20A Liberty Square,
Thurles, Co Tipperary
Tel 0504-26226

**Communications**
Very Rev Nicholas J. Irwin PP
The Parochial House, Gortnahoe,
Thurles, Co Tipperary
Tel 056-8834855

**Diocesan Counsellor**
Rev James Purcell CC
Diocesan Counselling Services,
Parish Centre, Friar Street,
Cashel, Co Tipperary
Tel 062-61199

**Ecumenism**
Archbishop's House,
Thurles, Co Tipperary
Tel 0504-21512

**Emigrant Commission**
Very Rev Loughlin Brennan PP
Liscreagh, Murroe, Co Limerick
Tel 061-386227

**Marriage Tribunal**
(See Marriage Tribunals section.)

**Pilgrimages**
*Director:* Rev Thomas Hearne CC
Bohermore, Cashel, Co Tipperary
Tel 062-61409

**Pioneer Total Abstinence Association**
*Diocesan Director*
Very Rev William Hennessy PP
Knocklong, Co Limerick
Tel 062-53114

**Social Services**
Thurles 0504-22169
*Director:* Rev Gerard Hennessy CC
Cathedral Presbytery, Thurles,
Co Tipperary
Tel 0504-22505

**Travellers**
*Chaplain*
Rev Daniel O'Gorman CC
Holycross House, Moyglass,
Fethard, Co Tipperary
Tel 052-6131343

**Vocations**
*Director:* Rev Joseph Walsh CC
Templemore, Thurles, Co Tipperary
Tel 0504-32890
Email
joewalsh05@eircom.net

**World Missions Ireland**
*Diocesan Director*
Very Rev Canon Eugene Everard PP
Templemore, Co Tipperary
Tel 0504-31684

## PARISHES

*Mensal parishes are listed first. Other parishes follow alphabetically. Church titulars are in italic.*

### THURLES, CATHEDRAL OF THE ASSUMPTION
Very Rev Martin Hayes Adm
Rev Gerard Hennessy CC
Rev Tomás O'Connell CC
Cathedral Presbytery, Thurles,
Co Tipperary
Tel 0504-22229/22779

### THURLES, SS JOSEPH AND BRIGID
Rev Thomas Dunne CC
Bóthar na Naomh Presbytery,
Thurles, Co Tipperary
Tel 0504-22042/22688

### ANACARTY
*St Brigid's, Anacarty*
*Immaculate Conception, Donohill*
Very Rev John Beatty PP
Anacarty, Co Tipperary
Tel 062-71104

### BALLINA
*Our Lady and St Lua, Ballina,*
*Mary, Mother of the Church, Boher*
Very Rev Edmond V. O'Rahelly PP
Ballina, Killaloe, Co Clare
Tel 061-376178

### BALLINAHINCH
*St Joseph's, Ballinahinch,*
*Sacred Heart, Killoscully*
Very Rev Robert Fletcher PP
Déalginis, Garraun Upper,
Ballinahinch, Birdhill,
via Killaloe, Co Clare
Tel 061-379862

### BALLINGARRY
*Assumption*
Very Rev Gerard Quirke PP
Ballingarry, Thurles, Co Tipperary
Tel 052-9154115

### BALLYBRICKEN
*St Ailbe's, Ballybricken,*
*Immaculate Heart of Mary, Bohermore*
Very Rev James Walton PP
Ballybricken, Grange, Kilmallock,
Co Limerick
Tel 061-351158

### BALLYLANDERS
*Assumption of BVM*
Very Rev Thomas O. Breen PP
Ballylanders, Kilmallock,
Co Limerick
Tel 062-46705

### BANSHA AND KILMOYLER
*Annunciation, Our Lady of the Assumption, Kilmoyler*
Very Rev Michael Hickey PP
Bansha, Co Tipperary
Tel 062-54132

### BOHERLAHAN AND DUALLA
*Immaculate Conception, Boherlahan*
*Our Lady of Fatima, Dualla*
Very Rev Joseph Egan PP
Boherlahan, Cashel, Co Tipperary
Tel 0504-41114
Rev Peter Brennan CC
Tel 0504-41215
Ballinree, Boherlahan,
Cashel, Co Tipperary

### BORRISOLEIGH
*Sacred Heart, Borrisoleigh*
Very Rev Liam Everard PP
Borrisoleigh, Thurles, Co Tipperary
Tel 0504-51259

### CAHERCONLISH
*Our Lady, Mother of the Church*
*Arch. O'Hurley Mem., Caherline*
Very Rev Roy Donovan PP
Caherconlish, Co Limerick
Tel 061-450730
Very Rev Patrick Currivan AP
Caherconlish, Co Limerick
Tel 061-351248

### CAPPAMORE
*St Michael's*
Very Rev Richard Browne PP
Cappamore, Co Limerick
Tel 061-381288

### CAPPAWHITE
*Our Lady of Fatima*
Very Rev Tadgh Furlong PP
Cappawhite, Co Tipperary
Tel 062-75427

### CASHEL
*St John the Baptist, Cashel*
*St Thomas the Apostle, Rosegreen*
Rt Rev Mgr Christy O'Dwyer PP
Bohereenglas, Cashel, Co Tipperary
Tel 062-61127
Rt Rev Mgr James Ryan AP
Bohermore, Cashel, Co Tipperary
Tel 062-61353
Rev Thomas Hearne CC
Bohermore, Cashel, Co Tipperary
Tel 062-61409
Rev James Purcell CC
Rosegreen, Cashel, Co Tipperary
Tel 062-61713
Rev Bernard Moloney
Cahir Road, Cashel, Co Tipperary
Tel 062-61443

### CLERIHAN
*St Michael's*
Very Rev Ailbe O'Bric PP
Clerihan, Clonmel, Co Tipperary
Tel 052-6135118

### CLONOULTY
*Church of St John the Baptist, Clonoulty*
*Church of Jesus Christ Our Saviour, Rossmore*
Very Rev Thomas F. Egan PP
Tel 0504-42494
Clonoulty, Cashel,
Co Tipperary

### DOON
*St Patrick's*
Very Rev Anthony Ryan PP
Doon, Co Limerick
Tel 061-380165

### DRANGAN
*Immaculate Conception, Visitation, Cloneen*
Very Rev Anthony Lambe PP
Drangan, Thurles, Co Tipperary
Tel 052-9152103

### DROM AND INCH
*St Mary's, Drom,*
*St Laurence O'Toole, Inch*
Very Rev Martin Murphy PP
Drom, Thurles, Co Tipperary
Tel 0504-51196

### EMLY
*St Ailbe's*
Very Rev James Kennedy PP
Emly, Co Tipperary
Tel 062-57111
Very Rev Seamus Rochford AP
Emly, Co Tipperary
Tel 062-57103

### FETHARD
*Holy Trinity, Fethard*
*Sacred Heart, Killusty*
Very Rev Canon Thomas F. Breen PP, VF
Fethard, Co Tipperary
Tel 052-6131178

### GALBALLY
*Christ the King, Galbally*
*Sacred Heart, Lisvernane*
Very Rev Canon John O'Neill PP, VF
Lisvernane, Aherlow,
Co Tipperary
Tel 062-56155
Very Rev Canon Denis Talbot AP
Galbally, Co Limerick
Tel 062-37929

### GOLDEN
*Blessed Sacrament, Golden*
*St Patrick's, Kilfeade*
Very Rev Patrick O'Gorman PP
Golden, Co Tipperary
Tel 062-72146

**GORTNAHOE**
*Sacred Heart, Gortnahoe*
*SS Patrick & Oliver, Glengoole*
Very Rev Nicholas J. Irwin PP
Tel 056-8834855
Very Rev John O'Rourke AP
Tel 056-8834128
Gortnahoe, Thurles, Co Tipperary

**HOLY CROSS**
*Holy Cross Abbey, Holy Cross*
*St Cataldus, Ballycahill*
Very Rev Thomas J. Breen PP
Holy Cross, Thurles, Co Tipperary
Tel 0504-43124
Rev Michael Mullaney
Ballycahill, Thurles, Co Tipperary
Tel 0504-26080
Rev Celsus Tierney CC
Holy Cross Abbey, Thurles, Co Tipperary
Tel 0504-43118

**HOSPITAL**
*St John the Baptist, Hospital*
*Sacred Heart, Herbertstown*
Very Rev Canon Conor Ryan PP, VF
Castlefarm, Hospital, Co Limerick
Tel 061-383108
Rev James Donnelly CC
Herbertstown, Hospital, Co Limerick
Tel 061-385104

**KILBEHENNY**
*St Joseph's, Kilbehenny,*
*St Patrick's, Anglesboro*
Very Rev Richard Kelly PP
Kilbehenny, Mitchelstown, Co Cork
Tel 025-24040

**KILCOMMON**
*St Patrick's, Kilcommon*
*St Joseph's, Hollyford*
*Our Lady of the Visitation, Rearcross*
Very Rev Daniel Woods PP
Kilcommon, Thurles, Co Limerick
Tel 062-78103
Rev Enda Brady CC
Hollyford, Co Tipperary
Tel 062-77104

**KILLENAULE**
*St Mary's, Killenaule*
*St Joseph the Worker, Moyglass*
Very Rev James O'Donnell PP
Killenaule, Co Tipperary
Tel 052-9156244
Rev Danny O'Gorman CC
Holycross House, Moyglass,
Fethard, Co Tipperary
Tel 052-6131343

**KILTEELY**
*SS Patrick & Brigid, Kilteely*
*St Bridget's, Dromkeen*
Very Rev Conor Hayes PP
Killeely, Co Limerick
Tel 061-384213

**KNOCKAINEY**
*Our Lady, Knockainey*
*St Patrick's, Patrickswell*
Very Rev Liam Holmes PP
Knockainey, Hospital, Co Limerick
Tel 061-383127
Rev Sean Fennelly CC
Barrysfarm, Hospital, Co Limerick
Tel 061-383565

**KNOCKAVILLA**
*Assumption, Knockavilla*
*St Bridget's, Donaskeigh*
Very Rev James Egan PP
Knockavilla, Dundrum, Co Tipperary
Tel 062-71157

**KNOCKLONG**
*St Joseph's, Knocklong*
*St Patrick's, Glenbrohane*
Very Rev William Hennessy PP
Knocklong, Co Limerick
Tel 062-53114
Very Rev John J. Ryan AP
Garryspillane, Kilmallock,
Co Limerick
Tel 062-53189

**LATTIN AND CULLEN**
*Assumption, Lattin*
*St Patrick's, Cullen*
Very Rev John Egan PP
Lattin, Co Tipperary
Tel 062-55240

**LOUGHMORE**
*Nativity of Our Lady, Loughmore*
*St John the Baptist, Castleiney*
Very Rev Padraig Corbett PP
Castleiney, Templemore, Co Tipperary
Tel 0504-31392
Very Rev Mgr Maurice Dooley AP
Loughmore, Templemore, Co Tipperary
Tel 0504-31375

**MOYCARKEY**
*St Peter's, Moycarkey*
*St James's, Two-Mile-Borris*
*Our Lady & St Kevin, Littleton*
Very Rev George Bourke PP
Moycarkey, Thurles, Co Tipperary
Tel 0504-44227
Rev Joseph Tynan CC
Ballydavid, Littleton,
Thurles, Co Tipperary
Tel 0504-44317

**MULLINAHONE**
*St Michael's*
Very Rev John McGrath PP
Mullinahone, Co Tipperary
Tel 052-9153152

**MURROE AND BOHER**
*Holy Rosary, Murroe*
*St Patrick's, Boher*
Very Rev Loughlin Brennan PP
Liscreagh, Murroe, Co Limerick
Tel 061-386227
Very Rev Canon Thomas J. Ryan AP, VF
Bohergar, Brittas, Co Limerick
Tel 061-352223

**NEW INN**
*Our Lady Queen, New Inn,*
*St Bartholomew's, Knockgrafton*
Very Rev Michael Kennedy PP
New Inn, Cashel, Co Tipperary
Tel 052-7462395

**NEWPORT**
*Most Holy Redeemer, Newport*
*Our Lady of the Wayside, Birdhill*
*Our Lady of Lourdes, Toor*
Very Rev John O'Keeffe PP
Birdhill, Killaloe, Co Tipperary
Tel 061-379172
Very Rev Joseph Delaney AP
Clonbealy, Newport, Co Tipperary
Tel 061-378126

**PALLASGREEN**
*St John the Baptist, Pallasgreen*
*St Brigid's, Templebraden*
Very Rev Pat Burns PP
Pallasgreen, Co Limerick
Tel 061-384114

**SOLOHEAD**
*Sacred Heart, Oola*
Very Rev John Morris PP
Solohead, Co Limerick
Tel 062-47614
Very Rev Canon Liam McNamara AP
Tipperary Town
Tel 062-82664

**TEMPLEMORE**
*Sacred Heart, Templemore*
*St Anne's, Clonmore*
*St James's, Killea*
Very Rev Canon Eugene Everard PP
Templemore, Co Tipperary
Tel 0504-31684
Rev Joe Walsh CC
Templemore, Co Tipperary
Tel 0504-32890
Rev Dominic Meehan CC
Templemore, Co Tipperary
Tel 0504-31492

**TEMPLETUOHY**
*Sacred Heart, Templetuohy*
*St Mary's, Moyne*
Very Rev Patrick Murphy PP
Templetuohy, Thurles, Co Tipperary
Tel 0504-53114
Very Rev John O'Connell AP
Moyne, Thurles, Co Tipperary
Tel 0504-45129

**TIPPERARY**
*St Michael's*
Venerable Matthew McGrath PP
St Michael's Street, Tipperary Town
Tel 062-51536
Rev Thomas Lanigan-Ryan CC
St Michael's Street, Tipperary Town
Tel 062-80475
Rev Edward Cleary CC
Knockinrawley, Tipperary
Tel 062-51242

## UPPERCHURCH

*Sacred Heart, Upperchurch*
*St Mary's, Drombane*
Very Rev Donal Cunningham PP
Upperchurch, Thurles, Co Tipperary
Tel 0504-54181
Rev Patrick Coffey CC
Upperchurch, Thurles, Co Tipperary
Tel 0504-54492

## INSTITUTIONS AND THEIR CHAPLAINS

**Cashel Community School**
Tel 062-61167
Rev Bernard Moloney

**Hospital Community School**
Tel 061-383565
Rev Sean Fennelly

**Vocational School, Thurles**
Tel 0504-22042
Rev Gerard Hennessy

**Vocational School, Tipperary Town**
Tel 062-51242
Rev Thomas Lanigan-Ryan

## PRIESTS OF THE DIOCESE ELSEWHERE

Rev John Littleton
The Priory Institute,
Tallaght Village, Dublin 24
Rev James O'Donoghue
Chaplain, Mid-Western Hospital,
37 Gouldavoher Estate, Dooradoyle,
Limerick

## RETIRED PRIESTS

Very Rev James Feehan
1 Castle Court, Thurles,
Co Tipperary
Tel 0504-24935
Very Rev Canon Denis O'Meara
Beechwood House Nursing Home,
Newcastlewest, Co Limerick
Rev Daniel J. Ryan
c/o Archbishop's House,
Thurles, Co Tipperary
Very Rev Liam Ryan DD
Cappamore, Co Tipperary
Very Rev Canon Liam Ryan PE, VF
Holycross, Thurles, Co Tipperary

## RELIGIOUS ORDERS AND CONGREGATIONS

## PRIESTS

**AUGUSTINIANS**
The Abbey, Fethard, Co Tipperary
Tel 052-31273
(Now amalgamated with Dungarvan,
Co Waterford)
*Bursar:* Rev Gerard Horan (OSA)

**BENEDICTINES**
Glenstal Abbey,
Murroe, Co Limerick
Tel 061-621000 Fax 061-386328
Email monks@glenstal.org
*Abbot*
Rt Rev Dom Mark Patrick Hederman (OSB)

**HOLY SPIRIT CONGREGATION**
Rockwell College,
Cashel, Co Tipperary
Tel 062-61444 Fax 062-61661
Email info@rockwell-college.ie
www.rockwell-college.ie
*Community Leader*
Rev Matthew J. Knight (CSSp)
Principal: Ms Audrey O'Byrne
Secondary Residential and Day Boys
School; Agricultural College

**PALLOTTINES**
Pallottine College, Thurles, Co Tipperary
Tel 0504-21202
*Rector:* Very Rev Emmet O'Hara (SAC)

## BROTHERS

**CHRISTIAN BROTHERS**
Christian Brothers Cowper Care,
Monastery Close, Templemore Road,
Thurles, Co Tipperary
Tel 0504-91152
*Community Leader:* Br Seamus Gill (CFC)
Community: 6

## SISTERS

**CONGREGATION OF THE SISTERS OF MERCY**
*The Sisters of Mercy minister throughout
the diocese in pastoral and social work,
community development, counselling,
spirituality, education and health care,
answering current needs.*

Sisters of Mercy, 28 Spafield Crescent,
Cashel, Co Tipperary
Tel 062-61402
Community: 1

Sisters of Mercy, 5 Slieve Chormac,
Áras na Rí, Old Road, Cashel, Co Tipperary
Tel 062-64574
Community: 2

Convent of Mercy, Newport, Co Tipperary
Tel 061-378145 Fax 061-378809
Community: 6

Convent of Mercy, Templemore,
Co Tipperary
Tel 0504-31427 Fax 0504-56078
Community: 11

1 Church Street,
Templemore, Co Tipperary
Tel 0504-32019
Community: 2

Sisters of Mercy, 1 Parkview Drive,
Thurles, Co Tipperary
Tel 0504-21137
Community: 2

Sisters of Mercy, Stanwix House,
Dublin Road, Thurles, Co Tipperary
Tel 0504-22320
Community: 3

Convent of Mercy, Tipperary Town
Tel 062-51218 Fax 062-52277
Community: 14

Convent of Mercy,
Knockinrawley, Tipperary Town
Tel/Fax 062-51120
Community: 4

Convent of Mercy, Cappamore,
Co Limerick
Tel/Fax 061-381268
Community: 3

Sisters of Mercy, Clonbealy,
Newport, Co Tipperary
Tel/Fax 061-378072
Community: 2

Convent of Mercy,
Doon, Co Limerick
Tel 061-380660 Fax 061-380263
Community: 10

**PRESENTATION SISTERS**
Presentation Sisters,
Thurles, Co Tipperary
Tel 0504-21250
*Local leader:* Sr Monica McGrath
Community: 24
Scoil Mhuire Primary School
Tel 0504-22331
Presentation Secondary School
Tel 0504-22291

Presentation Sisters,
The Commons, Thurles, Co Tipperary
Tel 052-9154781
Contact: Sr Miriam O'Byrne
Community: 2

Presentation Sisters, Hospital,
Co Limerick
Tel 061-383141
*Local Leader:* Sr Claude Meagher
Community: 7
Secondary School
St John The Baptist Community School
Tel 061-383283

Presentation Sisters,
14 Assumption Terrace, Ballingarry,
Thurles, Co Tipperary
Tel 052-9154118
*Contact:* Sr Patricia Wall
Community: 1
Presentation Secondary School
Tel 052-9154104

Presentation Sisters, Fethard,
Co Tipperary
Tel 052-6131225
*Local Leader:* Sr Maureen Power
Community: 10

Child care at St Bernard's group homes,
Rocklow Road, Fethard,
Co Tipperary
*Director:* Roisin Stewart
Tel 052-31141/31305/31392

Presentation Sisters,
16/17 Greenane Drive, Tipperary
Tel 062-80577
*Contact:* Sr Rosemary McCarthy
Community: 2

**URSULINES**
Ursuline Convent, Thurles, Co Tipperary
Tel 0504-21561
Email ursulinethurles@eircom.net
*Local Leader:* Sr Cecelia O'Dwyer
Community: 10
Scoil Aingeal Naofa Primary School
Tel 0504-22561 Fax 0504-20763
Email scoilangela@unison.ie
Secondary School
Tel 0504-22147 Fax 0504-22737
Email sec.uct@oceanfree.net
Website www.uct.ie

## EDUCATIONAL INSTITUTIONS

**St Patrick's College**
Thurles, Co Tipperary
Tel 0504-21201 Fax 0504-23735
Email office@stpats.ie
*President:* Very Rev Thomas Fogarty
*Registrar:* Ms Paula Hourigan

**EDMUND RICE SCHOOLS TRUST**
Bunscoil na mBráithre Criostaí Primary
School,
Doon, Co Limerick
Tel 061-380239 Fax 061-380060
Email dooncbsns@eircom.net
*Principal:* Br J. Dormer

Scoil Ailbhe Primary School,
Parnell Street, Thurles, Co Tipperary
Tel 0504-21448 Fax 0504-26094
Email reception@scoilailbhe.ie
*Principal:* Ms Miriam Anne Butler

Christian Brothers Secondary School,
Thurles, Co Tipperary
Tel 0504-22054 Fax 0504-23645
Email reception@cbsthurles.ie
*Principal:* Mr Tiernan O'Donnell

The Abbey School,
Tipperary Town
Tel 062-52299 Fax 062-52511
Email abbeyoffice@eircom.net
*Principal:* Mr John Kiely

## CHARITABLE AND OTHER SOCIETIES

**Apostolic Work Society**
Thurles Parish Centre, Cathedral Street,
Thurles, Co Tipperary
Tel 0504-22229 Fax 0504-22415
Email parishcentre@thurlesparish.ie
*President:* Mrs Anne Minihan
*Secretary:* Mrs Anna Maher

**Community Social Services Centres**
Rossa Street, Thurles, Co Tipperary
Tel 0504-22169

St Michael's Street, Tipperary Town
Tel 062-51622

Templemore, Co Tipperary
Tel 0504-31244
Sr Catherine Gannon

Cashel, Co Tipperary
Tel 062-61395

# WORLD MISSIONS
## IRELAND SPIRITUAL & PRACTICAL SUPPORT WORLDWIDE

## The work of the Pontifical Mission Societies

**The funds for projects we support from Ireland are sent directly to those projects in Africa, Asia & South America from the Irish National Office.**

▶ **World Missions Ireland** brings the prayers, solidarity and financial help of the Church in Ireland to Christian communities in other parts of the world, especially to those in greatest need.

▶ The **Mission Sunday Collection** in 2013 raised more than €1.5 million. In the past 10 years, **World Missions Ireland** has, through your generosity, made more than €30 million available to the establishment and growth of the Young Churches in mission lands.

▶ Please remember **World Missions Ireland** when you are making your will. Your donation can make a significant contribution to the establishment and growth of the Young Churches in mission lands by building churches & chapels, supporting seminarians & novices, and supporting children in the developing world both materially and spiritually. Please see our website (www.wmi.ie) for further information on the work that we do.

▶ Your excess Mass intentions can be an invaluable support to a native clergy in Africa, Asia and South America. If you have any excess Mass intentions, please consider sending them to **World Missions Ireland** for distribution abroad.

**What a gift can do:**

▶ **€50** will pay one month's food and accommodation for training a priest in Nigeria.

▶ **€250** will help a priest resettle a family following the devastation in the Philippines.

▶ **€400** will feed four children one meal every day for one year in Uganda.

▶ **€1,000** will buy an anti-malaria mosquito bed net for one hundred children in Malawi.

▶ **€2,500** will pay for the formation of a student to the priesthood in Sierra Leone.

▶ **€5,000** will cover the annual running costs of an orphanage in India.

▶ **€10,000** will build a mission church and train five catechists in Ecuador.

**WORLD MISSIONS, IRELAND**
64 Lower Rathmines Road,
Dublin 6, Ireland
T: +353 1 4972035 • F: +353 1 4960140
Email: director@wmi.ie • Web: www.wmi.ie
Charity number: CHY2318

# Sheridan
# Stained Glass

Sheridan Stained Glass has over 30 years
experience specialising in the conservation,
restoration, preservation and protection of
stained glass windows.
Our skilled team of artists and craftsmen are
well versed in the traditional techniques of
stained glass creation which places us in a
unique position as regards the conservation
and preservation of historic stained glass windows.

Our work is of the highest standard and can be
found in churches, cathedrals, convents and public,
private and commercial settings throughout
Ireland and abroad.

We are dedicated to the art of stained glass
and since our establishment have enjoyed
the trust and confidence of our clientele.

Sheridan Stained Glass, Newtown, Kells, Co.Kilkenny, Ireland
Studio: 056 7728384    Mobile: 087 2200877
joe@sheridanstainedglass.com    www.sheridanstainedglass.com

Sheridan Stained Glass Creations t/a Sheridan Stained Glass

# ARCHDIOCESE OF TUAM

PATRON OF THE ARCHDIOCESE
ST JARLATH, 6 JUNE

SUFFRAGEN SEES: ACHONRY, CLONFERT, ELPHIN, KILLALA,
UNITED DIOCESES OF GALWAY AND KILMACDUAGH

INCLUDES HALF OF COUNTY MAYO, HALF OF COUNTY GALWAY
AND PART OF COUNTY ROSCOMMON

**Most Rev Michael Neary DD**
Archbishop of Tuam;
born 15 April 1946;
ordained priest 20 June 1971;
ordained bishop 13 September
1992; installed Archbishop of
Tuam 5 March 1995.

Residence: Archbishop's House,
Tuam, Co Galway
Tel 093-24166 Fax 093-28070
Email
admin@tuamarchdiocese.org
Twitter Tuamarchdiocese
Facebook Tuam Archdiocese

## CATHEDRAL OF THE ASSUMPTION, TUAM

The Cathedral of the Assumption is the metropolitan cathedral of the Western Province.

Archbishop Oliver Kelly (1815–34) laid the foundation stone on 30 April 1827 – before Catholic Emancipation. The cathedral was dedicated on 18 August 1836 by Archbishop John MacHale (1834–81). It cost £14,204.

The cathedral is English-decorated Gothic in style, is cruciform in shape and has a three-stage West Tower. It was designed by architect Dominick Madden. Nineteen windows light the cathedral. It has seating capacity for 1,100 people.

Among the cathedral's notable features are its superbly cut Galway and Mayo limestone, its plaster-vaulted ceiling with heads and bosses, and its cantilevered oak organ loft. Its huge Oriel window has eighty-two compartments, is forty-two feet high and eighteen feet wide; it is the work of Michael O'Connor and was made in Dublin in 1832. Four large windows from the Harry Clarke studio also grace the cathedral. It has a very fine Compton organ with 1,200 pipes, a unique set of early nineteenth-century Stations of the Cross, recently restored, and a seventeenth-century painting of the Assumption by Carlo Maratta.

The sanctuary, as shown above, was completely redesigned in 1991 under the direction of the late Ray Carroll. The altar is Wicklow granite, and all the timberwork is by local craftsman Tom Dowd.

## CHAPTER

*Dean:* Rt Rev Mgr Dermot Moloney PE, VG
*Prebendaries*
Very Rev John Canon Cosgrove PP, VF
Castlebar
Very Rev Conal Canon Eustace PP, VF
The Parochial House, Ballinrobe, Co Mayo
Very Rev John Canon Fallon PP, Kilmaine,
Co Mayo
Very Rev Austin Canon Fergus PP
Mayo Abbey
Rt Rev Mgr John O'Boyle
Diocesan Resource Office, Tuam
Very Rev Joseph Canon O'Brien PP
Parochial House, Abbeyknockmoy,
Co Galway
Very Rev Padraig Canon O'Connor PP, VF
Mountbellew
Very Rev James Ronayne PP, VF, Clifden
Very Rev Brendan Canon Kilcoyne PP, VF,
Athenry
Rev James Canon Quinn CC
Taugheen, Claremorris
Very Rev Peter Canon Waldron PP
Keelogues, Ballyvary, Castlebar
Very Rev James Walsh AP
Kilmeena, Westport
Very Rev Des Canon Walsh PP
Lackagh, Co Galway
Very Rev John Canon Walsh PP
Parochial House, Aghamore, Ballyhaunis,
Co Mayo

**Honorary Canons**
Very Rev Eamon Concannon PE, Knock
Very Rev Joseph Cooney PE, Knock
Very Rev John D. Flannery PE, Milltown
Very Rev Anthony King PP, VF, Athenry
Very Rev Colm Kilcoyne PE, Castlebar
Very Rev Arthur Devine PE, Castlebar
Very Rev Martin Gleeson AP, Belclare
Very Rev Des Grogan PE
Partry, Claremorris
Very Rev Michael Goaley PE, Glenamaddy
Very Rev James Kelly AP, Tooreen
Very Rev Liam Kitt, Cleveland, Ohio
Very Rev Joseph Moloney PE, Tuam
Very Rev Martin Newell AP, Claran
Very Rev Colm Ó Ceannahbáin PE
An Tulach, Baile na hAbhann
Very Rev Kieran Waldron PE, Ballyhaunis
Venerable Patrick Williams PE
Kilkee, Co Clare

## ADMINISTRATION

**Vicar General**
Rt Rev Mgr Dermot Moloney PE, VG
5 Gold Cave Crescent,
Tuam, Co Galway
Tel 093-52946
Email dermotmol@eircom.net

**Chancellor**
Sr Mary Lyons RSM, JCD
Archbishop's House, Tuam
Tel 093-24166
Email chancellortuam@gmail.com

**Vicars Forane**
Very Rev Conal Canon Eustace VF
Very Rev Peter Gannon VF
Very Rev Brendan Canon Kilcoyne VF
Very Rev James Ronayne VF

Very Rev Padraic Canon O'Connor VF
Very Rev Charles McDonnell VF
Very Rev John Canon Cosgrove VF
Very Rev Fergal Cunnane VF

**Judicial Collegium for
Non-Matrimonial Cases**
Rev Michael Carragher (OP) JCD
Angelicum University, Rome
Rt Rev Mgr Michael Quinlan JCD, VG
Diocese of Salford, England
Rev Kevin Cahill JCD, Diocese of Ferns
Rev Paul Churchhill JCD
Archdiocese of Dublin
Rev Patrick Connolly JCD
Diocese of Clogher, University of Limerick

**Diocesan Secretary**
Rev Fintan Monahan
Archbishop's House, Tuam, Co Galway
Tel 093-24166
Email admin@tuamarchdiocese.org

**Council of Priests**
*Joint Chairpersons*
Very Rev Martin O'Connor PP
Tel 094-9364423
Email kilvineparish@gmail.com
Rev Stephen Farragher
Tel 094-9630006
Email stephenfarragher@gmail.com
*Secretary:* Rev Karl Burns, Westport
Tel 098-28871
Email karlburns07@gmail.com

## CATECHETICS EDUCATION

**Director of Adult Religious Education**
Rev Tod Nolan
Diocesan Resource Centre,
Bishop Street, Tuam, Co Galway
Tel 093-52284
Email todnolan@gmail.com

**Post-Primary Education**
*Director:* Rt Rev Mgr John O'Boyle
Diocesan Resource Centre,
Bishop Street, Tuam, Co Galway
Tel 093-52284
*Assistant Director:* Sr Margaret Buckley
Email secondaryre@tuamarchdiocese.org
Sisters of the Christian Retreat
Diocesan Resource Centre,
Bishop Street, Tuam, Co Galway
Tel 093-52284

**Advisory Council on
Catholic Second-level Education**
*Chairperson:* Sr Mary Corr
The Glebe, Tuam, Co Galway

**Post-Primary School Retreats and
Promotion of Universal Catechism**
*Director:* Rev Benny McHale CC
The Presbytery, New Line,
Athenry, Co Galway
Tel 091-844227

**Primary Catechetics**
*Director:* Mr John McDonagh
Diocesan Resource Centre,
Bishop Street, Tuam, Co Galway
Tel 093-52284
Email
primarycatechetics@tuamarchdiocese.org

**Primary Education**
*Director:* Rt Rev Mgr John O'Boyle
Diocesan Resource Centre,
Bishop Street, Tuam, Co Galway
Tel 093-52284

**CPSMA – Diocesan Committee**
*Chairperson:* Mr Frank Burns
Garrafrauns, Dunmore
Email frankburns1@eircom.net

**Child Protection Office**
*Director:* Rt Rev Mgr John O'Boyle
Diocesan Resource Centre,
Bishop Street, Tuam, Co Galway
Tel 093-52284
*Assistant Delegate:* Mrs Mary Trench
Robeen, Hollymount, Co Mayo
Email marytrench@gmail.com
Tel 087-9331679

**Safeguarding Children Committee**
*Chairperson:* Ms Maureen Walsh
*Co-ordinator of Training:* Fr Tod Nolan
*Designated Person:* Mgr John O'Boyle
*Designated Person:* Ms Mary Trench

## LITURGY

**Liturgical Commission, Sacred Art and
Sacred Music**
*Chairman:* Vacant
*Secretary:* Very Rev Michael Molloy PP
The Presbytery, Moore, Ballydangan,
Athlone, Co Westmeath
Tel 090-9673539
Email stmarysmoore@gmail.com

## PASTORAL

**ACCORD**
*Diocesan Directors*
Rev Conal Eustace PP
Ballinrobe, Co Mayo Tel 093-24342
Email eustaceconal@gmail.com
Rev James Ronayne PP
Clifden, Co Galway Tel 095-21251
Email clifdenparish@eircom.net
Very Rev Francis Mitchell Adm
Tuam, Co Galway Tel 093-24250
Email frfmitchell@gmail.com

**Archives**
*Archivist/Historian*
Very Rev Kieran Canon Waldron PE
Ballyhaunis
Tel 094-9630246
Email pkwaldron36@gmail.com

**Diocesan Pastoral Council**
*Chairperson:* Mrs Mary Trench
Email marytrench@gmail.com
Tel 087-9331679
*Secretary:* Mary Connell, Castlebar
Tel 086-6038483
Email mgallagherconnell@gmail.com

**Diocesan Youth Choir**
Ms Siobhán Bradley
Diocesan Resource Centre, Tuam
Tel 093-52284
Email youth@tuamarchdiocese.org

**Allianz (ⅲ)**

## Ecumenism
*Contact:* Very Rev Francis Mitchell Adm
The Presbytery, Tuam, Co Galway
Tel 093-24250
Email frfmitchell@gmail.com

## Emigrants
*Director:* Very Rev Gerard Burns PP
Orlando, Florida, USA
Email gerryosc@hotmail.com

## Family Ministry
www.thefamilycentre.com
*Director:* Mr Cathal Kearney
The Family Centre, Castle Street,
Castlebar, Co Mayo
Tel 094-9025900
Email cathalkearney@thefamilycentre.com

## Family Prayer Apostolate
*Director:* Mr Cathal Kearney
The Family Centre, Chapel Street,
Castlebar, Co Mayo
Tel 094-9025900
Email cathalkearney@thefamilycentre.com

## GMIT, Castlebar
*Chaplains:* Rev Pat Farragher
Castlebar, Co Mayo
Tel 094-9035748
Email farragherpat@gmail.com
Rev Daniel Caldwell
Tel 094-9043150

## Grandparents Pilgrimage
*Contact:* Ms Catherine Wiley
Tel 01-6625931
Email catherinewiley1@aol.com
www.nationalgrandparentspilgrimage.com

## Immigrants
Very Rev Stephen Farragher PP
Ballyhaunis, Co Mayo
Tel 094-9630006
Email stephenfarragher@gmail.com

## John Paul II Awards
Ms Siobhán Bradley
Diocesan Resource Centre, Tuam
Tel 093-52284
Email youth@tuamarchdiocese.org

## Knock Marriage Bureau
Canon Joe Cooney
Tel 094-9375933
Email jcooney25@gmail.com

## L'Arche
*National Chaplain:* Rev Fergal Cunnane PP
Dunmore, Co Galway
Tel 093-38124
Email fergcunnane@eircom.net

## Laity Commission
*Diocesan Representative*
*Secretary:* Ms Eileen Gildea
Riverview, Dunmore, Co Galway
*Chairperson:* Ms Teresa Carney, Castlebar

## Marriage Tribunal
(See Marriage Tribunals section.)

## Pastoral Councils Resource Person
*Director:* Rev Patrick Farragher
The Monastery, Chapel Street, Castlebar,
Co Mayo
Tel 094-9035748
Email farragherpat@gmail.com

## Pilgrimage Director
Mr John McLoughlin
3 Trinity Court, Tuam, Co Galway
Tel 087-7627910
Email johnb46@eircom.net

## Pioneer Total Abstinence Association
*Director:* Rev Seán Cunningham
The Presbytery, Castlebar, Co Mayo
Tel 094-9021844
Rev John O'Gorman PP
Menlough, Ballinasloe, Co Galway
Tel 090-9684818
Rev J. J. Cribben PP
Milltown, Co Galway
Tel 093-51609

## Polish Chaplain
Rev Krzysztof Sikora (SVD)
Knock Shrine, Co Mayo
Tel 094-9388100/087-3230382
Email lapulapu@op.pl

## Pontifical Mission Societies
*Diocesan Director*
Rev John McCormack (SMA) CC
The Parochial House, Breaffy,
Castlebar, Co Mayo
Tel 094-9022799

## Travellers
*Chaplain*
Very Rev Francis Mitchell Adm
Tuam, Co Galway
Tel 093-24250
Email frfmitchell@gmail.com

## Trócaire
Fr Michael Molloy PP
Moore, Ballydangan,
Athlone, Co Roscommon
Tel 090-9673539
Email stmarysmoore@gmail.com

## World Youth Day
*Contact:* Rev Tod Nolan, Tuam
Tel 093-52284
Email todnolan@gmail.com
Ms Siobhán Bradley
Tel 093-52284
Email youth@tuamarchdiocese.org

## Vocations Committee
*Contact:* Rev Fintan Monahan
Archbishop's House, Tuam, Co Galway
Tel 093-24166
Email admin@tuamarchdiocese.org
www.onelifeonecalloneresponse.com

## Youth
*Director of Youth Ministry*
Ms Siobhán Bradley
Diocesan Resource Centre, Bishop Street,
Tuam, Co Galway
Tel 093-52284
Email youth@tuamarchdiocese.org

## Youth – Diocesan Youth Council
*Chairperson:* Awaiting appointment
*Secretary:* Awaiting appointment
www.dyctuam.ie
www.facebook.com/tuamyouthministry

## PARISHES

*Mensal parishes are listed first. Other
parishes follow alphabetically. Historical
names are in parentheses.*

### TUAM (CATHEDRAL OF THE ASSUMPTION)
www.tuamparish.com
Very Rev Francis Mitchell Adm
Email fmitchell@eircom.net
Rev Shane Sullivan CC
Email osuilleabhain.shane@gmail.com
Rev Seán Flynn CC
Email keelogues@hotmail.com
Tuam, Co Galway
Tel 093-24250

### WESTPORT (AUGHAVAL)
www.westportparish.ie
Rev Charlie McDonnell Adm
Email frchaz@gmail.com
Rev Karl Burns CC
Westport, Co Mayo
Tel 098-28871 Fax 098-26900
Email karlburns07@gmail.com
Very Rev Patrick Gill AP
Lecanvey, Westport, Co Mayo
Tel 098-64808

### ABBEYKNOCKMOY
Very Rev Joseph Canon O'Brien PP
Abbey, Tuam, Co Galway
Tel 093-43510
Email joeobrienabbey@eircom.net
Rev Enda Howley CC
Parochial House, Ryehill,
Monivea, Co Galway
Tel 091-849019
Email eannahowley@eircom.net

### ACHILL
Very Rev Michael Gormally PP
Achill Sound, Achill, Co Mayo
Tel 098-45288
Rev Francis McGrath CC
Achill Sound, Achill, Co Mayo
Tel 098-45109
Email franciemcgrath@eircom.net

### AGHAMORE
Very Rev John Canon Walsh PP
Aghamore, Ballyhaunis, Co Mayo
Tel 094-9367024
Email johnwalsh05@eircom.net
Rev James Canon Kelly AP
Tooreen, Ballyhaunis, Co Mayo
Tel 094-9649002
Email frjameskelly@eircom.net

### ARAN ISLANDS
Very Rev Máirtín Ó Conaire (OCD) PP
Kilronan, Aran Islands, Co Galway
Tel 099-61221
Email oconaireocd@yahoo.com

### ATHENRY
www.athenryparish.ie
Very Rev Brendan Canon Kilcoyne PP, VF
Tel 091-844076
Email ppathenry@gmail.com
Rev Benny McHale CC
Tel 091-844169

**AUGHAGOWER**
Very Rev Jackie Conroy PP
Aughagower, Westport, Co Mayo
Tel 098-25057

**BALLA AND MANULLA**
Very Rev Denis Carney PP
Balla, Co Mayo
Tel 094-9365025
Email stcronansballa@eircom.net

**BALLINDINE (KILVINE)**
Very Rev Martin O'Connor PP
Ballindine, Co Mayo
Tel 094-9364423
Email kilvine@eircom.net

**BALLINLOUGH (KILTULLAGH)**
Very Rev Joseph Feeney PP
Ballinlough, Co Roscommon
Tel 094-9640155
Email frjoefeeney@eircom.net

**BALLINROBE**
Very Rev Conal Canon Eustace PP, VF
Ballinrobe, Co Mayo
Tel 094-9541085/9541784
Email eustaceconal@gmail.com

**BALLYHAUNIS (ANNAGH)**
Very Rev Stephen Farragher PP
Ballyhaunis, Co Mayo
Tel 094-9630006
Email stephenfarragher@gmail.com

**BEKAN**
www.bekan-parish.ie
Very Rev Brendan McGuinness PP
Bekan, Claremorris, Co Mayo
Tel 094-9380203
Email brendanmcguinness@eircom.net

**BURRISCARRA AND BALLINTUBBER**
www.ballintubberabbey.ie
Very Rev Michael Farragher PP
Carnacon, Claremorris, Co Mayo
Tel 094-9360205
Email frmichaelfarragher@gmail.com
Rev Francis Fahey CC
Ballintubber Abbey,
Claremorris, Co Mayo
Tel 094-9030934
Email btubabbey1@eircom.net

**CAHERLISTRANE (DONAGHPATRICK AND KILCOONA)**
Very Rev Pat O'Brien PP
Caherlistrane, Co Galway
Tel 093-55428
Email frpobrien@eircom.net

**CARNA (MOYRUS)**
Very Rev Padraic Standún PP
Carna, Co Galway
Tel 095-32232
Email pstandun@eircom.net

**CARRAROE (KILEEN)**
Very Rev Ciarán Blake PP
Carraroe, Co Galway
Tel 091-595452
Email blake.ciaran@gmail.com
Rev Eamon Ó Conghaile CC
Tiernea, Lettermore, Co Galway
Tel 091-551133
Email gorumna_1@eircom.net

**CASTLEBAR (AGLISH, BALLYHEANE AND BREAGHWY)**
Very Rev John Canon Cosgrove PP, VF
Tel 094-9021274
Email cbarpres@eircom.net
Rev Seán Cunningham CC
Email seancunn@eircom.net
Rev John Murray CC
Tel 094-9021253/1844
Castlebar, Co Mayo
Rev John McCormack (SMA) CC
Breaffy, Castlebar, Co Mayo
Tel 094-9022799
Email jmcsma@eircom.net
Rev Eugene O'Boyle, Hospital Chaplain, Tuam
Email eugeneoboyle@gmail.com
*Parish Co-ordinator:* Mrs Mary Connell
The Monastery, Castlebar, Co Mayo
Tel 094-9028473
Email mgallagherconnell@gmail.com

**CLARE ISLAND/INISHTURK**
Pastoral Care
Rev Karl Burns and priests of Westport Deanery
Tel 098-28871
Email karlburns07@gmail.com

**CLAREMORRIS (KILCOLMAN)**
Very Rev Peter Gannon PP
The Presbytery, Claremorris, Co Mayo
Tel 094-9362477
Email ganpete@eircom.net

**CLIFDEN (OMEY AND BALLINDOON)**
Very Rev James Canon Ronayne PP, VF
Clifden, Co Galway
Tel 095-21251
Email clifdenparish@eircom.net
Rev Anthony Neville CC
Claddaghduff, Co Galway
Tel 095-44668

**CLONBUR (ROSS)**
Very Rev Mícheál Mannion Adm
The Parochial House,
Clonbur, via Claremorris, Co Galway
Tel 094-9546304
Email michealmannion@gmail.com

**CONG AND NEALE**
Very Rev Patrick Gilligan PP
Cong, Co Mayo
Tel 094-9546030
Email patrickgilligan05@eircom.net

**CORRANDULLA (ANNAGHDOWN)**
Very Rev Hughie Loftus PP
Corrandulla, Co Galway
Tel 091-791125
Email newsletter@carrandullachurch.com
Rev Oliver McNamara CC
Annaghdown, Co Galway
Tel 091-791142

**CROSSBOYNE AND TAUGHEEN**
*For Administration*
Rev Martin O'Connor PP
Ballindine
Rev James Canon Quinn CC
Taugheen, Claremorris, Co Mayo
Tel 094-9362500
Email frjquinn@eircom.net

**CUMMER (KILMOYLAN AND CUMMER)**
Very Rev Patrick Mullins PP
Cummer, Tuam, Co Galway
Tel 093-41427
Email frpatrickmullins@eircom.net
Very Rev Martin Gleeson AP
Belclare, Tuam, Co Galway
Tel 093-55429
Email belclarechurch@eircom.net

**DUNMORE**
Very Rev Fergal Cunnane PP, VF
Dunmore, Co Galway
Tel 093-38124
Email fergcunnane@eircom.net

**GLENAMADDY (BOYOUNAGH)**
www.glenamaddychurch.ie
Very Rev Patrick Mooney PP
Glenamaddy, Co Galway
Tel 094-9659017
Email paddymooney@eircom.net
Email glenamaddynewsletter@hotmail.com

**HEADFORD (KILLURSA AND KILLOWER)**
Rev Raymond Flaherty Adm *(pro-tem)*
Headford, Co Galway
Tel 093-35448
Email rayflaherty@eircom.net
Very Rev Martin Canon Newell AP
Claran, Co Galway
Tel 093-35436
Email mnewell@eircom.net

**INISHBOFIN**
Rev Anthony Neville CC
Claddaghduff, Co Galway
Tel 095-44668

**ISLANDEADY**
www.islandeady.ie
Very Rev Patrick Donnellan PP
Islandeady, Castlebar, Co Mayo
Tel 094-9024125
Email patd@anu.ie

**KEELOGUES**
Very Rev Peter Canon Waldron PP
Keelogues, Ballyvary, Co Mayo
Tel 094-9031009
Email epwal@eircom.net

**KILCONLY AND KILBANNON**
Very Rev Michael Kenny PP
Kilconly, Tuam, Co Galway
Tel 093-47613
Email frmichael@eircom.net

**KILKERRIN AND CLONBERNE**
Very Rev Thomas Commins PP
Kilkerrin, Ballinasloe, Co Galway
Tel 094-9659212

**KILLERERIN**
Very Rev Tod Nolan PP
Killererin, Barnderg, Tuam, Co Galway
Tel 093-49222
Email todnolan@gmail.com

**KILMAINE**
Very Rev John Canon Fallon PP
Kilmaine, Co Galway
Tel 093-33378

## KILMEEN
Very Rev Iomar Daniels PP
Killoran, Ballinasloe, Co Galway
Tel 091-841758
Email idaniels@garbally.ie

## KILMEENA
Very Rev James Walsh AP
Kilmeena, Westport, Co Mayo
Tel 098-41270
*For Administration*
Rev Charlie McDonnell, Westport

## KNOCK
Very Rev Richard Gibbons PP
Email gibbonsrj@eircom.net
Rev Patrick Burke CC
Email scoruiocht@yahoo.com
Tel 094-9388100

## LACKAGH
Very Rev Des Canon Walsh PP
Turloughmore, Co Galway
Tel 091-797114
Email himselfdes@hotmail.com
Rev Bernard Shaughnessy CC
Coolarne, Turloughmore, Co Galway
Tel 091-797626
Email bjshaughnessy@eircom.net

## LEENANE (KILBRIDE)
Very Rev Kieran Burke PP
Leenane, Co Galway
Tel 095-42251
Email rathfran@gmail.com

## LETTERFRACK (BALLINAKILL)
Very Rev Ronnie Boyle PP
The Parochial House, Letterfrack,
Connemara, Co Galway
Tel 095-41053/087-2408171
Email ronnierobeen@eircom.net
ballinakillparish@eircom.net

## LOUISBURGH (KILGEEVER)
Very Rev Martin Long PP
Louisburgh, Co Mayo
Tel 098-66198
Email louisburghparish@eircom.net

## MAYO ABBEY (MAYO AND ROSSLEA)
Very Rev Austin Canon Fergus PP
Mayo Abbey, Claremorris, Co Mayo
Tel 094-9365086

## MENLOUGH (KILLASCOBE)
Very Rev John O'Gorman PP
Menlough, Ballinasloe, Co Galway
Tel 090-9684818
Email johncullmona@eircom.net

## MILLTOWN (ADDERGOLE AND LISKEEVEY)
Very Rev J. J. Canon Cribben PP
Milltown, Co Galway
Tel 093-51609

## MOORE
Very Rev Michael Molloy PP
Ballydangan, Athlone, Co Roscommon
Tel 090-9673539
Email stmarysmoore@gmail.com

## MOYLOUGH AND MOUNTBELLEW
Very Rev Padraig Canon O'Connor PP, VF
Mountbellew, Ballinasloe, Co Galway
Tel 090-9679235
Email patrickjaoc@eircom.net

## NEWPORT (BURRISHOOLE)
Very Rev Declan Carroll PP
Newport, Co Mayo
Tel 098-41123
Email frdeclan@eircom.net
Rev Nigel Woolen Adm (*pro-tem*)
Email abbaelgin@gmail.com

## PARKE (TURLOUGH)
c/o The Presbytery,
Castlebar, Co Mayo
Tel 094-9031314

## PARTRY (BALLYOVEY)
Very Rev John Kenny PP
Partry, Claremorris, Co Mayo
Tel 094-9543013
Email frjohnkenny@yahoo.ie

## ROBEEN
Very Rev Michael Murphy PP
Robeen, Hollymount, Co Mayo
Tel 094-9540026
Email mike.murphy@gmit.ie

## ROUNDFORT (KILCOMMON)
Very Rev Michael Murphy PP
Roundfort, Hollymount, Co Mayo
Tel 094-9540934
Email mike.murphy@gmit.ie

## ROUNDSTONE
Very Rev Jarlath Heraty PP (*pro-tem*)
Roundstone, Co Galway
Tel 095-35846

## SPIDDAL/KNOCK
Very Rev William Reilly PP
Knock, Inverin, Co Galway
Tel 091-593122
Email wreilly@eircom.net

## WILLIAMSTOWN (TEMPLETOHER)
*For Administration*
Very Rev Patrick Mooney PP
Glenamaddy Parish

## PRIESTS OF THE DIOCESE ELSEWHERE

Rev Gerry Burns
Orlando, Florida, USA
Rev Eamon Conway
Mary Immaculate College,
University of Limerick,
South Circular Road, Limerick
Tel 061-204353
Email eamonn.conway@gmail.com
Very Rev Seamus Cunnane
Grove House, Tuam, Co Galway
Rev Denis Gallagher
'Shraheens', Achill South, Achill, Co Mayo
Rev Thomas Gallagher
Cloughmore, Achill, Co Mayo
Rev John Gavin
c/o Archbishop's House, Tuam
Very Rev Gerard Needham
Louisburgh, Co Mayo
Very Rev James O'Grady
Headford, Co Galway
Rev Michael O'Malley
c/o Archbishop's House, Tuam
Rev Michael Whelan
c/o Archbishop's House, Tuam

## RETIRED PRIESTS

Very Rev Padraic Audley PE
An Cheathrú Rua, Co na Gaillimhe
Very Rev Eamonn Canon Concannon PE
Ballyhowley, Knock, Co Mayo
Very Rev Joseph Cooney PE
25 Carrowmore Meadows,
Knock, Co Mayo
Tel 094-9375933
Very Rev Arthur Devine PE
Abbeybreaffy Nursing Home,
Castlebar, Co Mayo
Very Rev John D. Canon Flannery PE
Cartron, Milltown, Co Galway
Very Rev John Garvey PE
Ballinrobe, Co Mayo
Very Rev Michael Canon Goaley
Glenamaddy, Co Galway
Very Rev Des Grogan PE
Partry, Co Mayo
Rev Paul Keane
Ballycrodick, Dunhill, Co Waterford
Very Rev Tony King PE
Westport, Co Mayo
Very Rev Sean Kilbane PE
Clonfad, Oldtown,
Athlone, Co Roscommon
Tel 090-9673527
Very Rev Colm Canon Kilcoyne
20 Rathbawn Drive, Castlebar, Co Mayo
Rev Christopher Kilkelly
c/o Archbishop's House, Tuam, Co Galway
Rev Dr Enda Lyons
Bermingham Road, Tuam, Co Galway
Rev Enda McDonagh
St Patrick's College, Maynooth,
Co Kildare
Tel 01-6285222
Very Rev John McCarthy
76 Carrowmore Meadows,
Knock, Co Mayo
Very Rev Joseph Moloney
Grove House, Vicar Street,
Tuam, Co Galway
Very Rev Máirtín Ó Lainn
Carraroe, Co Galway
Very Rev Kieran Waldron PE
Devlis, Ballyhaunis
Tel 094-9630246
Archdeacon Patrick Williams
6 Gort an Clochair, Kilkee, Co Clare

## RELIGIOUS ORDERS AND CONGREGATIONS

## PRIESTS

### OBLATES OF MARY IMMACULATE
Mazenod House, Churchfield,
Knock, Co Mayo
Tel 094-9388940

### ST PATRICK'S MISSIONARY SOCIETY (KILTEGAN FATHERS)
Main Street, Knock, Co Mayo
Tel 094-9388661
*House Leader*
Rev Gary Howley (SPS)

## BROTHERS

### ALEXIAN BOTHERS
Regional Residence
Churchfield, Knock, Co Mayo
Tel 094-9376996
Email alexianbros@eircom.net
*Community Leader*
Br Dermot O'Leary (CFA)
*Regional Leader:* Br Barry Butler (CFA)
Community: 3

### DE LA SALLE BROTHERS
St Gerald's College
Tel 094-9021383 Fax 094-9026157
*Headmaster:* Mr Daniel Hyland

### FRANCISCAN BROTHERS
Franciscan Brothers Generalate
Newtown, Mountbellew, Co Galway
Tel 090-9679295 Fax 090-9679687
Email franciscanbrs@eircom.net
*Minister General:* Br Peter Roddy

Corrandulla, Co Galway
Tel 091-791127
*Local Minister:* Br Conal Thomas
Community: 4

Clifden, Co Galway
Tel 095-21195
*Local Minister:* Br James Mungovan
Community: 3

Franciscan Brothers, Newtown,
Mountbellew, Co Galway
Tel 090-9679906
*Contact Person:* Br William Martyn
Community: 13

## SISTERS

### BENEDICTINE NUNS
Kylemore Abbey,
Kylemore, Connemara, Co Galway
Tel 095-52011
Email info@kylemoreabbey.ie
*Abbess:* Sr Máire Hickey (OSB)
Community: 12
Daily Liturgy: Morning Prayer – 7.15 am
weekdays; 8.30 am Sundays and Feasts.
Mass or Midday Prayer – 12.15 pm
weekdays; 11.30 am Sundays and Feasts.
Vespers – 6.00 pm in the Monastic Church.
Visitors welcome.
Visitor Destination, Abbey, Gothic
Church, Craft Shop, Restaurant, Pottery
Studio and 6-acre Victorian Walled
Garden open to visitors.
Soap and chocolate manufacturing by
the Benedictine Community.
Website www.kylemoreabbey.com

### BON SECOURS SISTERS (PARIS)
Sisters of Bon Secours, Drum,
Ballyhaunis Road, Knock, Co Mayo
Tel 094-9388439
*Contact:* Sr Felicitas O'Mahony
Community: 2
Prayer Ministry

99 Kilane View, Edenderry, Co Offaly
Tel 0405-33382
Community: 1
Community Health Ministry

### CARMELITES
Carmelite Monastery,
Tranquilla, Knock, Claremorris, Co Mayo
Email tranquillacarmel@eircom.net
*Prioress:* Sr Máire
Community: 16
Hidden life of prayer in the service of the
Church

### CHRISTIAN RETREAT SISTERS
'The Demense',
Mountbellew, Ballinasloe, Co Galway
Tel 090-9679311/9679939
*Contact:* Sr Assumpta Collins
Community: 5

Holy Rosary College Coeducational
Secondary School
Tel 090-9679222
Pupils: 547
Catechetical and pastoral ministry

### CONGREGATION OF THE SISTERS OF MERCY
Sisters of Mercy, The Glebe,
Tuam, Co Galway
Tel 093-25045
Community: 2

Convent of Mercy, Knock Road,
Ballyhaunis, Co Mayo
Tel 094-9630108
Community: 1

Teach Mhuire,
The Lawn, Castlebar, Co Mayo
Tel 094-9022141 Fax 094-9025266
Community: 3

Ard Bhride,
The Lawn, Castlebar, Co Mayo
Tel 094-9286410 Fax 094-9286404
Community: 30

Pontoon Road, Castlebar, Co Mayo
Tel 094-9025463 Fax 094-9026695
Community: 4

7 Chapel Street, Castlebar, Co Mayo
Tel 094-9021734
Community: 1

6 Riverdale Court, Castlebar, Co Mayo
Tel/Fax 094-9023622
Community: 1

Manor Court, Westport Road,
Castlebar, Co Mayo
Community: 4

1 Clareville, Claremorris, Co Mayo
Tel 094-9372654
Community: 1

Convent of Mercy,
Dunmore, Co Galway
Tel 093-38141 Fax 093-38567
Community: 5

Sisters of Mercy,
37, 38, 39, 40 St Jarlath's Court,
The Glebe, Tuam, Co Galway
Community: 3

Sisters of Mercy, Ruah, Cappanraheen,
Craughwell, Co Galway
Tel 091-876646
Community: 3

37 Michael Davitt Park,
Westport, Co Mayo
Tel 098-27137
Community: 2

Knock South, Cong, Co Mayo
Tel 094-9545833
Community: 1

7 Spencer Manor, Castlebar, Co Mayo
Tel 094-9035240
Community: 1

7 Liosdubh Court, Newport Road,
Castlebar, Co Mayo
Tel 094-9035240
Community: 1

50 An Sruthán,
Turlough Road, Castlebar, Co Mayo
Community: 1

Fern Hill (11, 14, 15, 16),
Knockranny, Westport, Co Mayo
Community: 4

33 Michael Davitt Park,
Westport, Co Mayo
Community: 1

The Octagon, Westport, Co Mayo
Community: 1

28 Firdomhnach Road,
The Glebe, Tuam, Co Galway
Community: 1

35 Gilmartin Road,
Tuam, Co Galway
Community: 1

New Street,
Ballinrobe, Co Mayo
Community: 1

### DAUGHTERS OF CHARITY OF ST VINCENT DE PAUL
St Mary's Hostel, Knock, Co Mayo
Tel 094-9388119
*Superior:* Sr Caitriona MacSweeney
Community: 7
Hostel for pilgrims

### FRANCISCAN SISTERS OF LITTLEHAMPTON
Eden, Knock, Co Mayo
Tel 094-9388302
*Leader:* Sr Stanislaus Geraghty
*Bursar:* Sr Ignatius Foley
Sr Benignus
Community: 3

### HOLY FAMILY SISTERS (ST EMILIE DE RODAT)
61 Carrowmore Meadows,
Knock, Co Mayo
Tel 094-9375288
*Contact:* Sr Josephine Harney
Community: 4

**LA SAINTE UNION DES SACRES COEURS**
57 Carrowmore Meadows,
Kiltimagh Road, Knock, Co Mayo
Community: 1
Pastoral

13 Glencarra, Kiltimagh Road,
Knock, Co Mayo
Community: 1
Pastoral

13 Carrowmore Drive, Knock, Co Mayo
Community: 1
Pastoral

**MISSIONARY SISTERS OF OUR LADY OF APOSTLES**
52 Elm Park, Claremorris, Co Mayo
Tel 094-9373569
Community: 4

**POOR SERVANTS OF THE MOTHER OF GOD**
SMG Sisters, Main Street,
Knock, Co Mayo
Community: 3
Pastoral Ministry

**PRESENTATION SISTERS**
Presentation Convent, St Joseph's, Tuam,
Co Galway
Tel 093-24111 Fax 093-25584
Email presjos@eircom.net
*Community Leader:* Sr Mary Gannon
Community: 22
Care of sick and elderly sisters, school
and pastoral ministry
Presentation Primary School
Tel 093-28324
Email clochard.ias@eircom.net

Presentation Convent,
Athenry, Co Galway
Tel 091-844077
*Community Leader:* Sr Evelyn Geraghty
Community: 10
School and pastoral ministry
Scoil Chroí Naofa Primary School
Tel 091-844510
Presentation College
Tel 091-844144 Fax 091-850862
Email pcathenry@hotmail.com

**ST JOSEPH OF THE SACRED HEART SISTERS**
14 Glencara, Kiltimagh Road,
Knock, Co Mayo
Sr Elizabeth McGoldrick

**ST LOUIS SISTERS**
Brooklodge,
Ballyhaunis Road, Knock, Co Mayo
Tel 094-9388020
Community: 5
Prayer ministry

**ST MARY MADELEINE POSTEL SISTERS**
'Fatima House', Kilkelly Road,
Knock, Co Mayo
*Apply:* Sister-in-charge
Tel 094-9388719
Community: 3

**URSULINES**
Ard Chiaráin Prayer Centre,
Shannonbridge, Co Roscommon
Tel 090-9674305/9674194
Email usac@eircom.net
Community: 3

## EDUCATIONAL INSTITUTIONS

**St Colman's College**
Claremorris, Co Mayo
Tel 094-9371442
*Principal:* Jimmy Finn
*Chaplain:* Rev Peter Gannon CC
Claremorris

**St Jarlath's College**
Tuam, Co Galway
Tel 093-24342
www.jarlaths.ie
*President:* Mr John Kelly
Tel 093-24248
Email presidentsjc@jarlaths.ie
*Chaplain:* Rev Fintan Monahan
Email fintanmonahan@jarlaths.ie
Tel 093-24166
Rev Shane Sullivan
Tel 093-24250
Email osuilleabhain.shane@gmail.com

**EDMUND RICE SCHOOLS TRUST**
St Patrick's Primary School,
Newport Road, Westport, Co Mayo
Tel 098-26450
*Principal:* Mr Stiofán Ó Moráin

Rice College, Castlebar Road,
Westport, Co Mayo
Tel 098-25698  Fax 098-26154
*Principal:* Ms Patricia Atkins

## CHARITABLE AND OTHER SOCIETIES

**ACCORD**
Shrine House, No 6 Bishop Street,
Tuam, Co Galway
Tel 093-24900/24776
*Contacts:* Rev Conal Eustace
Ms Anne Maguire
Mr Christopher Kelly
Castle Street, Castlebar
Tel 094-9022214

**Apostolic Work Society**
Branches at:
Abbeyknockmoy, Athenry, Achill,
Ballinrobe, Ballyhaunis, Barnaderg, Balla,
Belcarra, Brickens, Bekan, Castlebar,
Claremorris, Carnacon, Claran, Clifden,
Clonberne, Cortoon, Corofin,
Caherlistrane, Dunmore, Glenamaddy,
Headford, Kilkerrin, Knock, Kilconly,
Lavally, Leenane, Louisburgh, Monivea,
Mountbellew, Moylough, Newport,
Tooreen, Westport, Robeen, Roundfort,
Tuam, Tiernaul

**Cenacolo Community**
Our Lady of Knock,
Aughaboy, Knock, Co Mayo
*Contact:* Frank Walsh
Tel 087-9096007
Jean Ward
Tel 087-2687040
Email cenacolocommunityireland@yahoo.ie

**Flats for Newly Weds**
Tuam Community Council

**Homes for the Elderly**
Conference of St Vincent de Paul,
Castlebar

**Information Centres**
Tuam, Ballinrobe, Claremorris,
Glenamaddy, Castlebar, Westport

**Social Services Centres**
Dublin Road, Tuam
Tel 093-24577

Community Centre, Westport, Co Mayo
Tel 098-25669
*Contact:* Sr Agnes

Castle Street, Castlebar, Co Mayo
Tel 094-9021880
*Contact:* Sr Dolores

**Society of St Vincent de Paul**
Conferences at: Castlebar, Tuam,
Athenry, Westport, Dunmore,
Claremorris, Ballyhaunis, Ballinrobe,
Ballinlough, Headford, Monivea.

# DIOCESE OF ACHONRY

PATRONS OF THE DIOCESE
ST NATHY, 9 AUGUST; ST ATTRACTA, 12 AUGUST

INCLUDES PARTS OF COUNTIES MAYO, ROSCOMMON AND SLIGO

**Most Rev Brendan Kelly DD**
Bishop of Achonry;
born 20 May 1946;
ordained priest 20 June 1971;
ordained Bishop of Achonry
27 January 2008

Residence: Bishop's House,
Edmondstown,
Ballaghaderreen,
Co Roscommon
Tel 094-9860021
Fax 094-9860921
Email
bishop@achonrydiocese.org
Website www.achonrydiocese.org

## CATHEDRAL OF THE ANNUNCIATION AND ST NATHY, BALLAGHADERREEN

The building of the cathedral was begun in 1855 by Bishop Durcan. The architects were Messrs Hadfield & Goldie of Sheffield, while the Clerk of Works was Mr Charles Barker. It was completed in 1860.

The style is simple Gothic, known as Early English, of the Gothic Revival. The original intention was to have the roof fan-vaulted in wood and plaster, but it was abandoned owing to cost, and was finished in open timbers. The plan for a spire also had to be abandoned. This, however, was built in 1905 by Bishop Lyster, and a carillon of bells was installed.

The organ was built with continental pipes by Chestnutt of Waterford in 1925. The sanctuary was reconstructed to conform to the liturgical reforms of Vatican II in 1972. The baptistry in the left-hand Side Chapel was donated by Lydia Viscountess Dillon in memory of Charles Henry Viscount Dillon who died on 18 November 1865. The Apostles' Creed is carved on the baptistry lid.

There are commemorative plaques to former bishops of Achonry in the left-hand side Chapel: Bishops McNicholas, Durcan, Lyster and Morrisroe.

The window in the Lady Chapel has the inscription: 'This window to the Glory of God and Honour of the Blessed Virgin Mary was erected by united subscription of the Bishop, Clergy and 19 inhabitants of the Parish and neighbourhood to commemorate their respect and esteem for Charles Strickland and his wife Maria of Loughglynn and their zealous assistance in the erection of the Cathedral Church in 1860.' Charles Strickland was agent for Lord Dillon and was associated with the building of the neighbouring town of Charlestown and its church.

**Most Rev Thomas Flynn DD**
Bishop Emeritus of Achonry;
born 8 July 1931;
ordained priest 17 June 1956; ordained
Bishop of Achonry 20 February 1977;
retired 20 November 2007

Residence: St Michael's,
Cathedral Grounds,
Ballaghaderreen, Co Roscommon
Tel 094-9877808

## CHAPTER

*Dean*
Very Rev Michael Canon Joyce PE
Swinford
*Archdeacon*
Very Rev Patrick Canon Kilcoyne PP
Kiltimagh
Rt Rev Mgr Thomas Johnston PP, VG
Charlestown
Very Rev James Canon Finan CC
Collooney
Very Rev Patrick Canon Peyton PP
Collooney

## ADMINISTRATION

**Vicar General**
Rt Rev Mgr Thomas Johnston PP, VG
Charlestown, Co Mayo
Tel 094-9254315

**College of Consultors**
Rt Rev Mgr Thomas Johnston PP, VG
Very Rev Padraig Costello
Very Rev Thomas Towey
Very Rev Dermot Meehan
Very Rev James McDonagh

**Finance Committee**
*Chairman:* Mr Pat O'Connor
*Secretary:* Very Rev Martin Convey

**Vicars Forane**
Rev Gregory Hannan CC
Rev Martin Jennings

**Church Property Advisory Commission**
Very Rev Michael Canon Joyce PE
Swinford, Co Mayo
Tel 094-9384115

**Church Building Advisory Commission**
Rt Rev Mgr Thomas Johnston PP, VG
Charlestown, Co Mayo
Very Rev Joseph Caulfield PP
Gurteen, Co Sligo
Mr John Halligan
Charlestown, Co Mayo

**Historic Churches Advisory Committee**
*Chair*
Very Rev Patrick Canon Peyton PP
Tel 071-9167235
Very Rev Dermot Meehan PP
Tel 094-9252952

**Diocesan Communications Officer**
Very Rev Vincent Sherlock PP
Kilmovee, Ballaghaderreen, Co Mayo
Tel 094-9649137
Email vsherlock@achonrydiocese.org

## CATECHETICS EDUCATION

**Post-Primary Education**
*Secretary*
Very Rev Tomás Surlis DD
St Nathy's College, Ballaghaderreen,
Co Roscommon
Tel 094-9860010

**Primary Education**
*Secretary*
Rev Martin Henry CC
Ballaghaderreen, Co Roscommon
Tel 094-9860011

**Advisory Committee for Catholic Education**
*Contact*
Very Rev Martin Convey BSc, MLitt, PhD, PP
Straide, Foxford, Co Mayo
Tel 094-9031029

**Religious Education in Schools**
*Diocesan Religious Adviser*
*Primary:* Sr Regina Lydon
Tel 071-9183350
Sr Mary Richardson
Marist Convent, Tubbercurry, Co Sligo
Tel 071-9185018
*Post-Primary:* Rev Gerry Davey CC
Swinford, Co Mayo
Tel 094-9256401

## LITURGY

*Chairperson:* Vacant
*Secretary*
Very Rev Thomas Towey PP
Ballisodare, Co Sligo
Tel 071-9167467

## PASTORAL

**ACCORD**
*Director*
Very Rev Joseph Caulfield PP
Gurteen, Co Sligo
Tel 071-9182551

**Council of Priests**
*Chairman*
Very Rev Dermot Meehan PP
Swinford, Co Mayo
Tel 094-9252952
*Secretary*
Very Rev Vincent Sherlock PP
Kilmovee, Ballaghaderreen, Co Mayo
Tel 096-9649137

**Ecumenism**
*Director:* Very Rev John Durkan PP
Killasser, Swinford, Co Mayo
Tel 094-9251431

**Emigrants**
*Director*
Very Rev Vincent Sherlock PP
Kilmovee, Ballaghaderreen, Co Mayo
Tel 094-9649137

**Marriage Tribunal**
(See Marriage Tribunals section)

**Pastoral Centre**
Rt Rev Mgr Thomas Johnston PP, VG
St Nathy's Pastoral Centre,
Charlestown, Co Mayo
Tel 094-9254173

**Pioneer Total Abstinence Association**
*Spiritual Director*
Very Rev Joseph Gavigan PP
Ballaghaderreen, Co Roscommon
Tel 094-9860011

**Pontifical Mission Society**
*Diocesan Director*
Very Rev Peter Gallagher PP
Lavagh, Ballymote, Co Sligo
Tel 071-9184002

**Travellers**
*Chaplain*
Very Rev Patrick Canon Peyton PP
Collooney, Co Sligo
Tel 071-9167235

**Vocations**
*Director:* Very Rev Gabriel Murphy PP
Keash, Ballymote, Co Sligo
Tel 094-9381492

**Youth**
Rev Gerard Davey CC
Swinford, Co Mayo
Tel 094-9251143

## PARISHES

*The mensal parish is listed first. Other parishes follow alphabetically. Historical names are in parentheses. Church titulars are in italics.*

**BALLAGHADERREEN (CASTLEMORE AND KILCOLMAN)**
*Cathedral of The Annunciation & St Nathy*
*St Aidan, Monasteraden*
*SS John the Baptist & Colman,*
*Derrinacartha*
*Sacred Heart, Brusna*
Very Rev Joseph Gavigan PP
Rev Martin Henry CC
Rev Paul Kivlehan CC
The Presbytery, Ballaghaderreen,
Co Roscommon
Tel 094-9860011 Fax 094-9860350

## ACHONRY
*SS Nathy and Brigid, Achonry, Ballymote*
*Sacred Heart, Mullinabreena, Ballymote*
Very Rev Peter Gallagher PP
Lavagh, Ballymote, Co Sligo
Tel 071-9184002

## ATTYMASS
*St Joseph's*
Very Rev Thomas Mulligan PP
Attymass, Ballina, Co Mayo
Tel 096-45095 Fax 096-45375

## BALLISODARE
*St Brigid*
Very Rev Thomas Towey PP
Ballisodare, Co Sligo
Tel 071-9167467

## BALLYMOTE (EMLEFAD AND KILMORGAN)
*Immaculate Conception, Ballymote*
*St Joseph's, Doo*
Very Rev James McDonagh PP
Tel 071-9183361
Rev Greg Hannan CC
Tel 071-9189778
Ballymote, Co Sligo

## BOHOLA
*Immaculate Conception & St Joseph*
Very Rev Stephen O'Mahony PP
Bohola, Claremorris, Co Mayo
Tel 094-9384115

## BONNICONLON (KILGARVAN)
*Immaculate Heart of Mary*
Very Rev John Geelan PP
Parochial House, Bonniconlon,
Ballina, Co Mayo
Tel 096-45016

## BUNNINADDEN (KILSHALVEY, KILTURRA AND CLOONOGHILL)
*Sacred Heart, Bunninadden*
*Immaculate Heart of Mary, Killavil*
Very Rev Michael Reilly PP
Bunninadden,
Ballymote, Co Sligo
Tel 071-9183232
Fax 071-9189167

## CARRACASTLE
*St James', Carracastle*
*St Joseph's, Rooskey*
Very Rev Michael Quinn PP
Carracastle, Ballaghaderreen,
Co Mayo
Tel 094-9254301

## CHARLESTOWN (KILBEAGH)
*St James', Charlestown*
*St Patrick's, Bushfield*
Rt Rev Mgr Thomas Johnston PP, VG
Charlestown, Co Mayo
Tel 094-9254315

## COLLOONEY (KILVARNET)
*Assumption, Collooney*
*SS Fechin & Lassara, Ballinacarrow*
Very Rev Patrick Canon Peyton PP
Tel 071-9167235
Very Rev James Canon Finan CC
Tel 071-9167109
Collooney, Co Sligo

## COOLANEY (KILLORAN)
*Church of the Sacred Heart & St Joseph,*
*Coolaney*
Very Rev Patrick Holleran PP
Coolaney, Co Sligo
Tel 071-9167745

## CURRY
*Immaculate Conception, Curry*
*St Patrick's, Moylough*
Rev Leo Henry PP
Curry, Ballymote, Co Sligo
Tel 094-9254508

## FOXFORD (TOOMORE)
*St Michael's, Foxford*
*Assumption, Toomore*
*Attymachugh*
Very Rev Padraig Costello PP
Foxford, Co Mayo
Tel 094-9256131

## GURTEEN (KILFREE AND KILLARAGHT)
*St Patrick's, Gurteen*
*St Joseph's, Cloonloo*
*St Attracta's, Killaraght*
Very Rev Joseph Caulfield PP
Gurteen, Ballymote, Co Sligo
Tel 071-9182551 Fax 071-9182762

## KEASH (DRUMRAT)
*St Kevin, Keash*
*Our Lady of the Rosary, Culfadda*
Very Rev Gabriel Murphy PP
Keash, Ballymote, Co Sligo
Tel 071-9183334

## KILLASSER
*All Saints, Killasser*
*St Thomas', Callow*
Very Rev John Durkan PP
Killasser, Swinford, Co Mayo
Tel 094-9251431

## KILMOVEE
*Immaculate Conception, Kilmovee*
*St Joseph's, Urlaur*
Very Rev Vincent Sherlock PP
Kilmovee, Ballaghaderreen, Co Mayo
Tel 094-9649137
*St Celsus, Kilkelly*
*St Patrick's, Glann*
Rev John Maloney CC
Kilkelly, Co Mayo
Tel 094-9367031

## KILTIMAGH (KILLEDAN)
*Holy Family, Souls in Purgatory &*
*St Aidan*
Very Rev Patrick Canon Kilcoyne PP
Tel 094-9381198
Rev Patrick Lynch *(priest in residence)*
Tel 094-9381492
Kiltimagh, Co Mayo

## STRAIDE (TEMPLEMORE)
*SS Peter & Paul*
Very Rev Martin Convey PhD, PP
Straide, Foxford, Co Mayo
Tel 094-9031029

## SWINFORD (KILCONDUFF AND MEELICK)
*Our Lady Help of Christians, Swinford*
*St Luke's, Meelick*
*St Joseph's, Midfield*
Very Rev Dermot Meehan PP
Tel 094-9252952
Rev Gerard Davey CC
Tel 094-9253338
Swinford, Co Mayo

## TOURLESTRANE (KILMACTIGUE)
*St Attracta's, Tourlestrane*
*Our Lady of the Rosary, Kilmactigue*
*Sacred Heart, Loch Talt*
Very Rev John Glynn PP
Tourlestrane, Ballymote, Co Sligo
Tel 071-9181105

## TUBBERCURRY (CLOONACOOL)
*St John the Evangelist, Tubbercurry*
Rev Martin Jennings PP
Tubbercurry, Co Sligo
Tel 071-9185049
*St Michael's, Cloonacool*
Rev Dan O'Mahony CC
Cloonacool, Tubbercurry, Co Sligo
Tel 071-9185156
Rev Seamus Collery
St Attracta's Community School,
Tubbercurry, Co Sligo
Tel 071-9120184

## PRIESTS OF THE DIOCESE ELSEWHERE

Rev Eugene Duffy DD
Mary Immaculate College,
South Circular Road, Limerick
Tel 061-204968

## RETIRED PRIESTS

Very Rev Dermot Burns
Straide, Foxford, Co Mayo
Very Rev Farrell Cawley
Ballinacarrow, Co Sligo
Tel 086-0864347
Rt Rev Mgr John Doherty
*(priest in residence)*
Charlestown, Co Mayo
Tel 094-9255793
Very Rev Andrew Canon Johnston
c/o Innis Ree Lodge, Ballyleague,
Lanesborough, Co Roscommon
Tel 043-3327300
Very Rev Michael Canon Joyce PE
33 Fraunhill, Swinford, Co Mayo
Rev Pat Lynch
*(Priest in residence)*
Kiltimagh, Co Mayo
Tel 094-9381492
Very Rev Christopher Canon McLoughlin
Kilmactigue, Aclare, Co Sligo
Tel 071-9181007
*(Priest in residence, Tourlestrane Parish)*
Rt Rev Mgr Joseph Spelman
Sacred Heart Residence, Sybil Hill Road,
Raheny, Dublin 5
Tel 01-8332308

## RELIGIOUS ORDERS AND CONGREGATIONS

### SISTERS

#### CONGREGATION OF THE SISTERS OF MERCY
Convent of Mercy,
Collooney, Co Sligo
Tel/Fax 071-9167153
Community: 5

Tabor, Swinford, Co Mayo
Tel 094-9252197
Community: 3

21 Dun na Rí, Rathscanlon,
Swinford, Co Mayo
Community: 1

An Cheathrú Mhór, Cill Lasrach,
Swinford, Co Mayo
Community: 1

Convent of Mercy,
Ballymote, Co Sligo
Tel 071-9183350 Fax 071-9189177
Community: 5

Convent of Mercy,
Ballisodare, Co Sligo
Tel 071-9167279 Fax 071-9130538
Community: 5

Mercyville,
Ballaghaderren, Co Roscommon
Tel 094-9861193
Community: 3

Belgarrow, Sisters of Mercy,
Foxford, Co Mayo
Tel 094-9256573
Community: 2

Apt 4, Cormullen, Foxford, Co Mayo
Community: 1

#### MARIST SISTERS
Marist Convent,
Tubbercurry, Co Sligo
Tel 071-9185018
Email ms3tub@eircom.net
*Community Leaders:*
Sr Brendan Dodd, Sr Catherine Jordan
Community: 11
Parish ministry, Marist laity
Day care centre (For HSE – Western Region)

Marist Convent,
Charlestown, Co Mayo
Tel 094-9254133
Email maristch@eircom.net
Community: 4
Parish ministry, Marist laity

#### SISTERS OF ST JOSEPH OF THE APPARITION
St Joseph's Convent,
Dun Bríd, Ballymote, Co Sligo
Tel 071-9183973
Email stjsligo@eircom.net
*Contact:* Sr Teresa Cooney
Community: 10

#### ST JOSEPH OF THE SACRED HEART SISTERS
Sisters of St Joseph of Sacred Heart,
Killasser, Swinford, Co Mayo
Tel 094-9251265
Sr Margaret Maloney

#### ST LOUIS SISTERS
'Louisville', Cordarragh,
Kiltimagh, Co Mayo
Tel 094-9381205
Community: 6
Varied apostolates

St Louis Community School
Tel 094-9381228
Pupils: 650

## EDUCATIONAL INSTITUTIONS

**St Nathy's College**
Ballaghaderreen,
Co Roscommon
Tel 094-9860010 Fax 094-9860891
*President:* Very Rev Tomás Surlis DD
Rev Paul Kivlehan CC

**St Joseph Secondary School**
Foxford, Co Mayo
Tel 094-9256145 Fax 094-9256126
*Principal:* Eileen O'Brien
*Chaplain:* Very Rev Padraig Costello PP

## CHARITABLE AND OTHER SOCIETIES

**Hope House**
Foxford, Co Mayo
Tel 094-9256888 Fax 094-9256865
*Counsellors:* Sr Attracta Canny,
Sr Dolores Duggan
Treatment centre for addiction problems

**Fr Patrick Peyton Centre**
Attymass, Co Mayo
Tel 096-45374 Fax 096-45376
*Chaplain:* Fr Steve Gibson CSC

**Society of St Vincent de Paul**
*Contact:* Mr Liam McKibben
Swinford, Co Mayo
Tel 087-2522616

# DIOCESE OF ARDAGH AND CLONMACNOIS

PATRON OF THE DIOCESE
ST MEL, 7 FEBRUARY

INCLUDES NEARLY ALL OF COUNTY LONGFORD,
THE GREATER PART OF COUNTY LEITRIM
AND PARTS OF COUNTIES CAVAN, OFFALY, ROSCOMMON,
SLIGO AND WESTMEATH

**Most Rev Francis Duffy DD**
Bishop of Ardagh and
Clonmacnois;
born 21 April 1958;
ordained priest 20 June 1982;
ordained Bishop of Ardagh and
Clonmacnois 6 October 2013

Residence: St Michael's,
Longford,Co Longford
Tel 043-3346432
Fax 043-3346833
Email ardaghdi@iol.ie

## ST MEL'S CATHEDRAL, LONGFORD

On 19 May 1840, Bishop William O'Higgins laid the foundation stone of a new cathedral for the Diocese of Ardagh and Clonmacnois. The foundation stone was taken from the original Cathedral of St Mel at Ardagh. The preacher at that ceremony was the Archbishop of Tuam, Archbishop John MacHale. Four other bishops, one hundred and twenty priests and an estimated forty thousand people were present.

The architect of the cathedral was Mr John Benjamin Keane. The magnificent portico was not included in the original design. This was the work of another architect, Mr George Ashlin, and was not erected until 1883. Without any doubt Bishop O'Higgins influenced the original design, which reflected some of his own life experience, having been educated in Paris, Rome and having lived for a time in Vienna. The cathedral owes something in its design to the Madeleine in Paris, and the Pantheon and the Basilica of St John Lateran in Rome. Certainly something of the Lateran is to be seen in the attempt that was made to incorporate the bishop's house at the rear of the sanctuary.

Raising the money necessary to build the cathedral was an enormous challenge in poverty-stricken Ireland in the 1840s. Bishop O'Higgins travelled the length and breadth of the diocese and his appeals for help went well beyond the diocesan boundaries. He received great help, especially from the Dioceses of Elphin, Tuam and Meath, and contributions came from as far away as Belfast. A priest of the diocese toured North America and Canada to raise funds there.

By 1846 the walls, pillars and entire masonry were completed and the roof was the next stage in the building programme. Then the potato blight came and the Great Hunger. Work had to be suspended. Bishop O'Higgins would never see the great cathedral completed. He died in 1853.

Bishop John Kilduff, successor of Bishop O'Higgins, resumed work on the

cathedral. It was opened for worship in September 1856. Though the work was not complete, it was a time of great rejoicing. Present on that special day were Archbishop Dixon of Armagh and Archbishop Cullen of Dublin, and fourteen other bishops.

It was Bishop Bartholomew Woodlock who commissioned the erection of the impressive portico, with its huge Ionic columns. He was still bishop of the diocese in 1893 when the cathedral was consecrated on 19 May.

Since 1893 much additional work has been done. Bishop Hoare, successor of Bishop Woodlock, added a pipe organ and bell chimes. Later still, two beautiful stained-glass windows, the work of the Harry Clarke Studios in Dublin, were installed in the transepts. In the 1970s a major restyling of the sanctuary was undertaken.

On Christmas Morning 2009 St Mel's Cathedral was badly damaged by fire. The newly restored cathedral was opened at Christmas 2014

**Most Rev Colm O'Reilly DD**
Retired Bishop of Ardagh and
Clonmacnois; born 11 January 1935;
ordained priest 19 June 1960;
ordained Bishop of Ardagh and
Clonmacnois 10 April 1983;
retired 6 October 2013
Residence: Deanscurragh, Longford
Tel 043-3347831

## ST MEL'S DIOCESAN TRUST

Most Rev Francis Duffy (Chairman)
Rev Tom Murray (Secretary)
Rt Rev Mgr Patrick Earley
Rt Rev Mgr Bernard Noonan
Very Rev George Balfe
Very Rev Peter Brady
Very Rev Aidan Ryan
Very Rev Michael Bannon
Very Rev Bernard Hogan
Very Rev Peter Burke
Very Rev Liam Murray

## ADMINISTRATION

**Vicar General**
Rt Rev Mgr Bernard Noonan PP, VG

**Diocesan Chancellor**
Very Rev Michael Bannon PP, VF
Edgeworthstown, Co Longford
Tel 043-6671046

**College of Consultors**
Rt Rev Mgr Bernard Noonan PP, VG
Rev Peter Burke
Rev Tom Cox
Rev Owen Devaney
Rev James MacKiernan CC
Rev Tom Murray
Rev Peter Tiernan

**Vicars Forane**
Rt Rev Mgr Bernard Noonan PP, VG
Very Rev Francis Garvey PP
Very Rev Michael Bannon PP
Very Rev Simon Cadam PP

**Financial Administrator**
Rev Tom Murray
Diocesan Office, St Michael's, Longford
Tel 043-3346432 Fax 043-3346833

**Finance Committee**
*Chairman:* Most Rev Francis Duffy
*Members*
Very Rev Brian Brennan PP
Mr Frank Gearty, Solicitor
Mr Brian Loughran
Mr Michael Glennon
Rev Tom Murray
Mr Tom Mulligan

**Diocesan Archivist**
Rev Tom Murray
Diocesan Office, St Michael's, Longford
Tel 043-3346432 Fax 043-3346833

**Diocesan Secretary**
Rev Tom Murray
Diocesan Office, St Michael's, Longford
Tel 043-3346432 Fax 043-3346833
Email ardaghdi@iol.ie

## CATECHETICS EDUCATION

**Pastoral Renewal and Faith
Development**
Rev James MacKiernan CC
Boher, Ballycumber, Co Offaly
Tel 057-9336119

**Religious Education in Schools**
*Diocesan Advisers*
*Primary:* Rev Michael McGrath CC
Carrick-on-Shannon, Co Leitrim
Tel 071-9620347
Mr Peter Walsh, Abbeycartron, Longford
*Post-Primary:* Sr Una Purcell
Diocesan Office,
St Michael's, Longford
Tel 043-3346432

**Diocesan Council of Catholic Primary
School Managers' Association**
*Secretary:* Mrs Eileen Ward
Diocesan Office,
St Michael's, Longford
Tel 043-3346432

## LITURGY

**Church Music**
*Director:* Rev Turlough Baxter CC
St Mary's, Athlone, Co Westmeath
Tel 090-6472088

**Liturgy Commission**
*Secretary:* Rev Turlough Baxter CC
St Mary's, Athlone, Co Westmeath
Tel 090-6472088

**Sacred Art and Architecture Commission**
*Secretary:* Rev Sean Casey PP
Killoe, Co Longford
Tel 043-3323119

## PASTORAL

**ACCORD**
*Director:* Very Rev Patrick Murphy PP
Parochial House, Mohill, Co Leitrim
Tel 071-9631024

**Committee for Special Marriage
Preparation Procedures**
Rev Cathal Faughnan PP
Keadue, Boyle, Co Roscommon
Tel 071-9647212
Rev Thomas Healy Adm
The Presbytery, Longford
Tel 043-3346465
Very Rev Michael Bannon PP
St Mary's, Edgeworthstown, Co Longford
Tel 043-6671046

**Communications**
*Diocesan Counsellor*
Rev Tom Cox
Ferbane, Co Offaly
Tel 090-6454309

**Council of Priests**
*Chairman:* Rev James MacKiernan CC
Boher, Ballycumber, Co Offaly
Tel 057-9336119
*Secretary:* Rev Michael McGrath CC
Carrick-on-Shannon, Co Leitrim
Tel 071-9620347

**CURA**
Tel 0902-74272 (Centre)/1850-626260

**Ecumenism**
Rev Padraig Kelliher CC
The Presbytery, Longford
Tel 043-3346465

**Family Ministry**
Very Rev Patrick Murphy PP
Parochial House, Mohill, Co Leitrim
Tel 071-9631024
Sr Angela Clarkson
Teallach Iosa, St Mel's Road, Longford
Tel 043-3346827

**Marriage Tribunal**
(See Marriage Tribunals section.)

**Pilgrimage (Lourdes)**
*Director*
Rt Rev Mgr Bernard Noonan PP, VG
Moate, Co Westmeath
Tel 090-6481180

**Pioneer Total Abstinence Association**
*Diocesan Director*
Very Rev Michael Campbell PP
Abbeylara, Co Longford
Tel 043-6686270

**Pontifical Mission Societies**
*Diocesan Director*
Very Rev Aidan Ryan PP
Ballinahown, Athlone, Co Westmeath
Tel 090-6430124

**Safeguarding Children Diocesan
Committee**
Mr Sean Leydon, Mrs Trisha Nugent,
Mrs Roisin O'Doherty, Mr Liam
Faughnan, Mrs Evelyn Breen, Sr Una
Purcell, Rev Liam Murray, Rev Michael
Bannon, Philomena Lynch, Seamus
Mollaghan, Anita Allen

**Travellers**
*Chaplain:* Rev Nigel Charles Adm
The Presbytery, Killashee,
Co Longford
Tel 043-3345546

**Trócaire**
*Diocesan Director*
Very Rev Bernard Hogan PP
Drumlish, Co Longford
Tel 043-3324132

**Vocations**
*Director:* Very Rev Simon Cadam PP, VF
St Mary's, Granard, Co Longford
Tel 043-6686550

**Youth Commission**
*Diocesan Director:* Ms Anita Allen
St Mary's Youth Ministry Centre,
First Floor, St Mary's Hall,
Northgate Street, Athlone
Tel 090-6473358
Email info@aym.ie

## PARISHES

Mensal parishes are listed first. Other
parishes follow alphabetically. Historical
names are given in parentheses. Church
titulars are in italics.

**LONGFORD (TEMPLEMICHAEL, BALLYMACORMACK)**
*St Mel's Cathedral; St Anne's, Curry,
St Michael's, Shroid*
Rev Thomas Healy Adm
Rev Tom Murray CC
Rev Brendan O'Sullivan CC
Rev Padraig Kelliher CC
Rev Tony Gilhooly CC
The Presbytery, Longford
Tel 043-3346465

**ATHLONE**
*St Mary's, Athlone
Our Lady Queen of Peace, Coosan*
Rev Liam Murray Adm
Rev Declan Shannon CC
Rev Turlough Baxter CC
Rev Mark Bennett CC
Rev Krzysztof Przanowski CC *(Polish
Chaplaincy)*
Rev Thomas Kearney (SVD)
St Mary's, Athlone, Co Westmeath
Tel 090-6472088

**ABBEYLARA**
*St Bernard's, Abbeylara
St Mary's, Carra*
Very Rev Michael Campbell PP
Carra, Granard, Co Longford
Tel 043-6686270

**ANNADUFF**
*Immaculate Conception, Annaduff
Immaculate Conception, Drumsna*
Very Rev John Wall PP
Annaduff, Carrick-on-Shannon,
Co Leitrim
Tel 071-9624093

**ARDAGH AND MOYDOW**
*St Brigid's, Ardagh; Our Lady's, Moydow*
Very Rev Pat Lennon PP
Ardagh, Co Longford
Tel 043-6675006

**AUGHAVAS AND CLOONE**
*St Joseph's, Aughavas
St Stephen's, Rossan
St Mary's, Cloone*
Very Rev Peter Tiernan PP
Cloone, Co Leitrim
Tel 071-9636016

**BALLINAHOWN, BOHER AND POLLOUGH (LEMANAGHAN)**
*St Colmcille's, Ballinahown
St Manchain's, Ballycumber
St Mary's, Pollough*
Very Rev Aidan Ryan PP
Ballinahown, Athlone,
Co Westmeath
Tel 090-6430124
Rev James MacKiernan CC
Boher, Ballycumber, Co Offaly
Tel 057-9336119

**BALLYMAHON (SHRULE)**
*St Matthew's, Ballymahon*
Very Rev Padraig MacGowan PP
Ballymahon, Co Longford
Tel 090-6432253

**BORNACOOLA**
*St Michael's, Bornacoola
St Joseph's, Clonturk*
Very Rev Gerard O'Brien PP
Bornacoola, Carrick-on-Shannon,
Co Leitrim
Tel 071-9638229

**CARRICKEDMOND AND ABBEYSHRULE**
*(Taghshiney, Taghshinod & Abbeyshrule)
Sacred Heart, Carrickedmond
Our Lady of Lourdes, Abbeyshrule*
Very Rev Charles Healy PP
Carrickedmond, Colehill,
Co Longford
Tel 044-9357442

**CARRICK-FINEA (DRUMLUMMAN SOUTH AND BALLYMACHUGH)**
*St Mary's, Carrick
St Mary's, Ballynarry*
Very Rev Francis Gray PP
Carrick, Finea, Mullingar,
Co Westmeath
Tel 043-6681129

**CARRICK-ON-SHANNON (KILTOGHERT)**
*St Mary of the Assumption
Carrick-on-Shannon
Sacred Heart, Jamestown
St Patrick's, Gowel
St Joseph's, Leitrim*
Very Rev Francis Garvey PP, VF
Carrick-on-Shannon, Co Leitrim
Tel 071-9620118
Rev Merlyn Kenny CC
Tel 071-9620054
Rev Michael McGrath CC
Tel 071-9620347
St Mary's, Carrick-on-Shannon,
Co Leitrim

**CLOGHAN AND BANAGHER (GALLEN AND REYNAGH)**
*St Mary's, Cloghan
St Rynagh's Banagher*
Very Rev Michael Scanlon PP
Cloghan, Birr, Co Offaly
Tel 090-6457122
Rev Pierre Pepper CC
Banagher, Co Offaly
Tel 057-9151338

**CLONBRONEY**
*St James, Clonbroney
Holy Trinity, Ballinalee*
Very Rev Brian Brennan PP
Ballinalee, Co Longford
Tel 043-3323110

**CLOONE (CLOONE-CONMAICNE)**
*St Mary's, Cloone*
See Aughavas & Cloone

**COLMCILLE**
*St Colmcille's, Aughnacliffe
St Joseph's, Purth*
Very Rev Seamus McKeon PP
Aughnacliffe, Co Longford
Tel 043-6684118

**DROMARD**
*St Mary's, Legga; St Mary's, Moyne*
Very Rev Eamonn Corkery PP
Dromard, Moyne, Co Longford
Tel 049-4335248

**DRUMLISH**
*St Mary's, Drumlish
St Patrick's, Ballinamuck*
Very Rev Bernard Hogan PP
Drumlish, Co Longford
Tel 043-3324132
Rev Patsy McDermott CC
Ballinamuck, Co Longford
Tel 043-3324110

**DRUMSHANBO (MURHAUN)**
*St Patrick's, Drumshanbo*
Very Rev Peter Burke PP
Drumshanbo, Co Leitrim
Tel 071-9641010

**EDGEWORTHSTOWN (MOSTRIM)**
*St Mary of the Immaculate Conception*
Very Rev Michael Bannon PP, VF
St Mary's, Edgeworthstown,
Co Longford
Tel 043-6671046

**FENAGH**
*St Mary's, Foxfield*
See Mohill Parish

**FERBANE HIGH STREET AND BOORA (TISARAN AND FUITHRE)**
*Immaculate Conception, Ferbane
SS Patrick and Saran, Belmont
St Oliver Plunkett, Boora*
Very Rev Francis Murray PP
Tel 090-6454380
Rev Tom Cox CC
Tel 090-6454309
Ferbane, Co Offaly

## GORTLETTERAGH
*St Mary's, Gortletteragh*
*St Thomas', Fairglass*
*St Joseph's, Cornageetha*
Very Rev John Quinn PP
Gortletteragh,
Carrick-on-Shannon, Co Leitrim
Tel 071-9631074

## GRANARD
*St Mary's*
Very Rev Simon Cadam PP
St Mary's, Granard, Co Longford
Tel 043-6686550

## KEADUE, ARIGNA AND BALLYFARNON (KILRONAN)
*Nativity of the Blessed Virgin, Keadue*
*Immaculate Conception, Arigna*
*St Patrick's, Ballyfarnon*
Very Rev Cathal Faughnan PP
Keadue, Boyle, Co Roscommon
Tel 071-9647212

## KILCOMMOC (KENAGH)
*St Dominic's*
Very Rev Thomas Barden PP
Kenagh, Co Longford
Tel 043-3322127

## KILLASHEE
*St Patrick's, Killashee*
*St Brendan's, Clondra*
Rev Nigel Charles Adm
Parochial House, Killashee,
Co Longford
Tel 043-3345546

## KILLENUMMERY AND BALLINTOGHER (KILLENUMMERY AND KILLERY)
*St Mary's, Killenummery*
*St Michael's, Killavoggy*
*St Teresa's, Ballintogher*
Very Rev Vincent Connaughton PP
Killenummery, Dramahair,
via Sligo, Co Leitrim
Tel 071-9164125

## KILLOE
*St Mary's, Ennybegs*
*St Oliver Plunkett's, Cullyfad*
Very Rev Sean Casey PP
Ennybegs, Longford
Tel 043-3323119

## KILTUBRID
*St Brigid's, Drumcong*
*St Joseph's, Rantogue*
Very Rev Tomás Flynn PP
Drumcong, Carrick-on-Shannon
Co Leitrim
Tel 071-9642021

## LANESBORO (RATHCLINE)
*St Mary's, Lanesboro*
Very Rev Michael Reilly PP
Lanesboro, Co Longford
Tel 043-3321166

## LEGAN AND BALLYCLOGHAN (KILGLASS AND RATHREAGH)
*Nativity of the Blessed Virgin Mary, Lenamore*
*St Ann's, Ballycloghan*
Very Rev Peter Brady PP
Lenamore, Co Longford
Tel 044-9357404

## LOUGH GOWNA AND MULLINALAGHTA (SCRABBY AND COLMCILLE EAST)
*Holy Family, Lough Gowna*
*St Columba's, Mullinalaghta*
Very Rev PJ Fitzpatrick PP
Gowna, Co Cavan
Tel 043-6683120

## MOATE AND MOUNT TEMPLE (KILCLEAGH AND BALLYLOUGHLOE)
*St Patrick's, Moate; St Ciaran's, Castledaly*
*Corpus Christi, Mount Temple*
Rt Rev Mgr Bernard Noonan PP, VG
Tel 090-6481180
Rev Liam Farrell CC
Tel 090-6481189
Moate, Co Westmeath
Rev Patrick Kiernan CC
Mount Temple, Moate,
Co Westmeath
Tel 090-6481239

## MOHILL (MOHILL-MANACHAIN)
*St Patrick's, Mohill*
*St Joseph's, Gorvagh*
*St Mary's, Eslin Bridge*
*St Mary's, Foxfield*
Very Rev Patrick Murphy PP
Tel 071-9631024
Rev Sean Burke CC
Tel 071-9631097
Mohill, Co Leitrim

## MULLAHORAN AND LOUGHDUFF (DRUMLUMMAN NORTH)
*Our Lady of Lourdes, Mullahoran*
*St Joseph's, Loughduff*
Very Rev Owen Devaney PP
Mullahoran, Kilcogy via Longford,
Co Cavan
Tel 043-6683141

## NEWTOWNCASHEL (CASHEL)
*The Blessed Virgin*
Very Rev Gerard Brady PP
Newtowncashel, Co Longford
Tel 043-3325112

## NEWTOWNFORBES (CLONGUISH)
*St Mary's*
Very Rev Ciaran McGovern PP
Newtownforbes, Co Longford
Tel 043-3346805

## RATHOWEN (RATHASPIC, RUSSAGH & STREETE)
*St Mary's, Rathowen*
Rt Rev Mgr Patrick Earley
Rathowen, Mullingar,
Co Westmeath
Tel 043-6676044

## SHANNONBRIDGE (CLONMACNOIS)
*St Ciaran's, Shannonbridge*
*St Ciaran's, Clonfanlough*
Very Rev Francis O'Hanlon PP
Shannonbridge,
Athlone, Co Westmeath
Tel 090-9674125

## STREETE AND RATHOWEN
*St Mary's*
*See Rathown (Rathaspic and Rossagh)*
Rev Joseph McGrath
Parochial House,
Boherquill, Lismacaffney,
Mullingar, Co Westmeath

## PRIESTS OF THE DIOCESE ELSEWHERE

Rev George Balfe
Longford Road,
Rooskey, Co Leitrim
Rev Colman Carrigy
Clonee, Killoe, Co Longford
Rev Gerard Carroll
Ballinalee Road, Longford
Rev Liam Cuffe
Chaplaincy, St Vincent's Hospital,
Dublin 4
Rev Christy Stapleton
Rev Hugh Turbitt
c/o Diocesan Office, St Michael's,
Longford
Rev P. J. Hughes
On mission to Equador

## RETIRED PRIESTS

Very Rev Peter Beglan PE
The Presbytery,
Edgeworthstown, Co Longford

## RELIGIOUS ORDERS AND CONGREGATIONS

## PRIESTS

### FRANCISCANS
Franciscan Friary,
Athlone, Co Westmeath
Tel 090-6472095 Fax 090-6424713
Email athlonefriary@eircom.net
*Guardian:* Rev Gabriel Kinahan (OFM)

### MARIST FATHERS (SOCIETY OF MARY)
Rev Tim Kenny (SM)
Fermoyle, Lanesboro, Co Longord

## BROTHERS

### MARIST BROTHERS
Champagnat House, Athlone,
Co Westmeath
Tel 090-6476032
*Superior:* Br P.J. McGowan
Community: 4

Marist College, Athlone, Co Westmeath
Tel 090-6474491
Secondary pupils: 510

## SISTERS

### CONGREGATION OF THE SISTERS OF MERCY
Bracklin,
Edgeworthstown, Co Longford
Tel/Fax 043-71015
Community: 1

Sisters of Mercy,
Shalom, Edgeworthstown, Co Longford
Tel 043-71852 Fax 043-72989
Community: 3

Sisters of Mercy,
Manor Lodge, Dublin Road,
Edgeworthstown, Co Longford
Tel 043-6671102
Community: 1

Upper Main Street, Ballymahon,
Co Longford
Tel 090-6432532
Community: 5

7 Mill Street, Drumlish, Co Longford
Tel 043-29585
Community: 1

Sisters of Mercy, 2 Cnoc na Greine
Granard, Co Longford
Tel/Fax 043-6686633
Community: 2

Sisters of Mercy, 61 Cnoc na Greine,
Granard, Co Longford
Tel 043-6686563
Community: 1

Mount Carmel, Station Road,
Moate, Co Westmeath
Tel 090-6481912 Fax 090-6482803
Community: 3

Gort Mhuire, Knockdomney,
Moate, Co Westmeath
Tel/Fax 090-6482265
Community: 2

Shannagh Grove,
Mohill, Co Leitrim
Tel 071-9631064
Community: 2

St Michele, Curryline,
Newtownforbes, Co Longford
Tel 043-46326
Community: 1

19 Midara Gardens, Longford
Tel/Fax 043-3346702
Community: 1

6 Curryline, Newtownforbes,
Co Longford
Tel 043-41826
Community: 2

Sisters of Mercy, The Lodge,
Drumshanbo, Co Leitrim
Tel 071-9641308
Community: 3

7 Ard Michael Park,
Ballinalee Road, Longford
Tel 043-3334248
Community: 2

19 Cara Court,
Carrick-on-Shannon, Co Leitrim
Tel 071-9622582
Community: 1

107 Mostrim Oaks,
Edgeworthstown, Co Longford
Community: 1

Apartment 1, Boderg House,
Tearmonn Harbour, Clondra,
Co Longford
Community: 1

Bohermore, Ardagh, Co Longford
Community: 1

46 St Michael's Road, Longford
Community: 2

7 Oaklands Grove, Oaklands,
Ballinalee Road, Longford
Community: 1

10 St Mary's Terrace, Dublin Road,
Longford
Community: 1

108 Mostrim Oaks, Edgeworthstown,
Co Longford
Community: 1

Convent of Mercy, Longford
Community: 25

Sisters of Mercy,
8 St Patrick's Terrace,
Major Well Road, Longford
Community: 1

### LA SAINTE UNION DES SACRES COEURS
Our Lady's Bower, Athlone,
Co Westmeath
Tel 090-6472061/6472092
Fax 090-6474853
Community: 4

Secondary School (day)
Pupils: 650
*Principal:* Mr Noel Casey
Tel 090-6474777/6475524
Fax 090-6476356
Email bower@iol.ie

Mont Vista, House of the Sick,
Retreat Road, Athlone
Tel 090-6472887
*Sister in Charge:* Sr Evelyn Treacy
Sick and frail elderly, province ministry,
healthcare
Community: 18

Banagher,
Co Offaly
Tel 0509-51319
Email lsu1@eircom.net
Community: 7
Teaching, Parish care of the Sick
and Frail

11 Sonas Care Home,
Cloghanboy, Ballymahon Road,
Athlone, Co Westmeath
Community: 2

### MARIST SISTERS
Marist Convent
Carrick-on-Shannon, Co Leitrim
Tel 071-9620010
Email maristconventcarrick@eircom.net
*Co-ordinators:*
Sr Rita Durkin, Sr Imelda Layden
Community: 12

7 Summerhill Grove,
Carrick-on-Shannon, Co Leitrim
Tel 071-9621396
Email maristgrove7@gmail.com
Community: 2
Pastoral ministry in St Patrick's Hospital,
Marist laity

### POOR CLARES
Poor Clare Monastery of Perpetual
Adoration, Drumshanbo,
Co Leitrim
*Abbess:* Mother M. Angela McCabe
Community: 8
Contemplatives
Perpetual adoration of the Blessed
Sacrament
Small self-catering private retreat house
attached
Tel 071-9641308 Fax 071-9640789

### PRESENTATION SISTERS
Presentation Sisters Provincialate,
Garden Vale, Athlone,
Co Westmeath
Tel 090-6472186 Fax 090-6477617
Email presnpro@iol.ie
Administration of Northern Province of
Presentation Sisters
*Provincial Leader*
Sr Elizabeth Maxwell
Community: 5

### ST JOSEPH OF CLUNY SISTERS
St Joseph's Convent,
Main Street, Ferbane,
Co Offaly
Tel 090-6454324
Email stjf@eircom.net
*Superior:* Sr Helena Egan
Community: 6
Pastoral Ministry

## EDUCATIONAL INSTITUTIONS

**St Mel's College, Longford**
Tel 043-3346469
*Principal:* Mr Declan Rowley
*Priests on Teaching Staff:*
Rev Joe McGrath

**Athlone Institute of Technology**
Athlone, Co Westmeath
*Chaplain:* Rev Seamus Casey
Tel 090-6424400
*Res:* 11 Auburn Heights, Athlone,
Co Westmeath
Tel 090-6478318

## CHARITABLE AND OTHER SOCIETIES

**Apostolic Work Society**
Mrs Nuala Claffey
Ferbane, Co Offaly

**Knights of St Columbanus**
St Mary's Square,
Athlone, Co Westmeath

**Legion of Mary**
Centres at Longford, Athlone,
Carrick-on-Shannon, Granard, Mohill

**Our Lady's Nursing Home**
Edgeworthstown, Co Longford
Tel 043-6671007

**St Christopher's**
Battery Road, Longford
School for mentally handicapped

**St Hilda's**
Grace Park Road,
Athlone, Co Westmeath
School for mentally handicapped

**Social Service Council, Longford**
Tel 043-3346452

**Society of St Vincent de Paul**
*Longford:* Mr Cyril Hussey
*Athlone:* Mr Martin Fallon
*Carrick-on-Shannon:*
Mr Michael Duignan
*Mohill:* Mr Michael Burke
*Drumshanbo:* Mrs Bea Cullen
*Ferbane:* Mrs Breda Connolly
*Ballymahon:* Tel 085-1699437
*Granard:* Tel 085-1503985
*Edgeworthstown:* Tel 087-06788544

# DIOCESE OF CLOGHER

PATRON OF THE DIOCESE
ST MACARTAN, 24 MARCH

INCLUDES COUNTY MONAGHAN, MOST OF COUNTY FERMANAGH
AND PORTIONS OF COUNTIES TYRONE, DONEGAL, LOUTH AND CAVAN

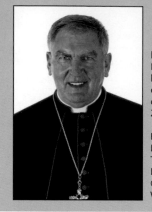

**Most Rev Liam S. MacDaid DD**
Bishop of Clogher;
born 19 July 1945;
ordained priest 15 June 1969;
ordained Bishop of Clogher
25 July 2010

Residence: Bishop's House,
Monaghan
Tel 047-81019 Fax 047-84773
Email diocesanoffice
@clogherdiocese.ie
Website www.clogherdiocese.ie

## ST MACARTAN'S CATHEDRAL, MONAGHAN

On Sunday, 3 January 1858, at a meeting of the Catholic inhabitants of the parish and vicinity of Monaghan, with the Bishop of Clogher, Dr Charles MacNally, presiding, it was formally resolved that a new Catholic church at Monaghan was urgently required. An eight-acre site was purchased by the bishop from Humphrey Jones of Clontibret for £800, and an architect, James Joseph McCarthy of Dublin, was employed to draw a design.

The style is French Gothic of the fourteenth century. In June 1861 the foundation stone was laid, and the work got underway the following year. Dr MacNally died in 1864, and work resumed under his successor, Dr James Donnelly, in 1865. The architect died in 1882 and was succeeded by William Hague, a Cavan man, who was responsible for the design of the spire and the gate-lodge. The work was completed in 1892, and the cathedral was solemnly dedicated on 21 August of that year.

Under the direction of Bishop Joseph Duffy, a radical rearrangement and refurbishing of the interior of the cathedral was begun in 1982 to meet the requirements of the revised liturgy. The artist responsible for the general scheme was Michael Biggs of Dublin, in consultation with local architect Gerald MacCann. The altar is carved from a single piece of granite from south County Dublin. The sanctuary steps are in solid Travertine marble. The sanctuary crucifix is by Richard Enda King; the cross is of Irish oak and the figure of Christ is cast in bronze. The Lady Chapel has a bronze Pietà by Nell Murphy, and the lettering of the Magnificat is by Michael Biggs.

The tabernacle, made of silver-plated sheet bronze and mounted on a granite pillar, has the form of a tent and was designed and made by Richard Enda King. In the chapel of the Holy Oils the aumbry was designed by Michael Biggs, while the miniature bronze gates were executed by Martin Leonard. The five great tapestries on the east walls of the cathedral are a striking feature of the renovation; they were designed by Frances Biggs and woven by Terry Dunne, both of Dublin.

**Most Rev Joseph Duffy DD**
Bishop Emeritus
born 3 February 1934; ordained priest 22
June 1958; ordained Bishop of Clogher 2
September 1979
*Residence:* Doire na gCraobh, Monaghan
Tel 047-62725
Email doirenagcraobh@gmail.com

## CHAPTER

*Dean:* Rt Rev Mgr Larry Duffy
*Archdeacon:* Rt Rev Mgr Peter O'Reilly
*Members*
Rt Rev Mgr Seán Cahill
Very Rev Macartan McQuaid
Very Rev Joseph Mullin
Very Rev John McKenna
Rt Rev Mgr Joseph McGuinness
Very Rev John McCabe
Very Rev Ramon Munster
Rt Rev Mgr Richard Mohan
Very Rev Patrick McHugh
Very Rev Shane McCaughey

## ADMINISTRATION

**Vicars General**
Rt Rev Mgr Larry Duffy
St Joseph's, Carrickmacross, Co Monaghan
Tel 042-9663200
Rt Rev Mgr Peter O'Reilly
1 Darling Street, Enniskillen,
Co Fermanagh BT74 7DP
Tel 028-66322627

**Chancellor**
Rt Rev Mgr Joseph McGuinness
Diocesan Office, Bishop's House,
Monaghan
Tel 047-81019
Email diocesanoffice@clogherdiocese.ie

**Council of Administration**
Bishop Joseph Duffy
Rt Rev Mgr Seán Cahill
Rt Rev Mgr Larry Duffy
Rt Rev Mgr Peter O'Reilly
Rt Rev Mgr Joseph McGuinness
Very Rev Canon Shane McCaughey

**Finance Committee**
*Chairman:* Most Rev Liam S. MacDaid
*Members*
Rt Rev Mgr Sean Cahill
Rt Rev Mgr Larry Duffy
Rt Rev Mgr Peter O'Reilly
Rt Rev Mgr Joseph McGuinness
*Financial Administrator*
Mrs Aileen Hughes
Bishop's House, Monaghan
Tel 047-81019 Fax 047-84773
Email diocesanoffice@clogherdiocese.ie

**Diocesan Secretary**
Rt Rev Mgr Joseph McGuinness
Diocesan Office, Bishop's House,
Monaghan
Tel 047-81019
Email diocesanoffice@clogherdiocese.ie

**Communications Officer & Co-ordinator
of Diocesan Website**
Rt Rev Mgr Joseph McGuinness
Diocesan Office, Bishop's House,
Monaghan
Tel 047-81019
Email diocesanoffice@clogherdiocese.ie

## CATECHETICS EDUCATION

**Adult Faith Development**
*Diocesan Adviser*
Very Rev Canon Macartan McQuaid
St Michael's College, Enniskillen,
Co Fermanagh BT74 6DE
Tel 028-66322935 Fax 028-66325128
Email mmcquaid@saintmichaels.org.uk

**Catholic Primary School Managers'
Association (RI)**
*Diocesan Council Secretary*
Very Rev Michael Daly PP
Broomfield, Castleblayney, Co Monaghan
Tel 042-9743617
Email dalyml@eircom.net

**Diocesan Education (NI)**
*Administrator:* Ms Suzette Bracken
Armagh/Clogher/Dromore Diocesan
Education Office,
1 Killyman Road, Dungannon
Co Tyrone BT71 6DE
Tel 028-87752116 Fax 028-87752783

**Religious Education**
*Diocesan Advisers*
*Primary:* Rev John Flanagan CC
Roslea, Enniskillen,
Co Fermanagh BT92 7LA
Tel 028-67751393
Ms Bridie Dolan
75 Dublin Road,
Enniskillen, Co Fermanagh BT74 6HN
Tel 028-66322805
*Post-Primary (NI):* Mrs Eileen Gallagher
St Michael's College,
Enniskillen, Co Fermanagh
(Friday 9.00am-5.00pm)
Tel 028-66328210
Email egallagher@stmichaels.org.uk
*Post-Primary (ROI):* Ms Claudine Marron
Parish Office, Park Street, Monaghan
Tel 085-8569916
Email claudinesh@eircom.net

## LITURGY

**Church Music**
*Director*
Rt Rev Mgr Joseph McGuinness Adm
Parochial House, Tyholland, Monaghan
Tel 047-85385 Fax 047-85051

**Diocesan Liturgy Commission**
*Chairman*
Rt Rev Mgr Joseph McGuinness Adm
Parochial House, Tyholland, Monaghan
Tel 047-85385 Fax 047-85051
*Secretary*
Very Rev Owen J. McEneaney Adm
Parochial House, Pettigo, Co Donegal
Tel 071-9861666

## PASTORAL

**ACCORD**
*Diocesan Directors:* Rev John Chester
St Joseph's Presbytery,
Park Street, Monaghan
Tel 047-81220 Fax 047-84004
Email
parishoffice@stjosephspresbytery.com

Rev David Donnelly
4 Darling Street, Enniskillen,
Co Fermanagh BT74 7DP
Tel 028-66322075 Fax 028-66322248
Email frmstfrancis@aol.com

**Council of Priests**
*Chairman*
Very Rev Canon Shane McCaughey
Shantonagh, Castleblayney, Co Monaghan
Tel 042-9745015
*Secretary:* Rev Kevin Duffy CC
Castleblayney, Co Monaghan
Tel 042-9740629
Email mucknoparish@eircom.net

**Ecumenism**
*Director:* Rt Rev Mgr Peter O'Reilly
1 Darling Street, Enniskillen,
Co Fermanagh BT74 7DP
Tel 028-66322627
Email pp@st-michaels.net

**Emigrants**
*Director:* Very Rev Lorcan Lynch CC
St Mary's, Clontibret, Co Monaghan
Tel 047-80631

**Immigrants**
Very Rev Canon Sean Clerkin PE
St Dympna's, Tydavnet, Co Monaghan
Tel 047-89402
Email sean.clerkin@eircom.net

**Lourdes Pilgrimage**
*Director*
Very Rev Canon Joseph Mullin PP, VF
Lisoneill, Lisnaskea,
Co Fermanagh BT92 0JE
Tel 028-67721342 Fax 028-67723773
*Assistant Director*
Very Rev Noel McGahan PP
Clogher, Co Tyrone BT76 0TQ
Tel 028-85549604

**Marriage Tribunal**
*Clogher Office of Armagh Regional
Marriage Tribunal*
Sr Elizabeth Fee
St Michael's Parish Centre,
28 Church Street, Enniskillen,
Co Fermanagh BT74 7EJ
Tel 028-66347860

**Pioneer Total Abstinence Association**
*Director:* Very Rev James McPhillips PP
Derrygonnelly, Co Fermanagh BT93 6HW
Tel 028-68641207
Email jimmymcp@eircom.net

**Pontifical Mission Societies**
*Diocesan Director:* Very Rev Brian Early PP
Scotstown, Co Monaghan
Tel 047-89204
Email bearly@eircom.net

**Travellers**
*Chaplain:* Rev Michael Jordan CC
Parochial House, Donaghmoyne,
Co Monaghan
Tel 042-9661586
Email michaeljordan@eircom.net

Allianz (ⅰ)

## Vocations

*Director and Chairman of Vocations Committee:* Rt Rev Mgr Seán Cahill VG
6 Boyhill Road, Maguiresbridge,
Enniskillen, Co Fermanagh BT94 4LN
Tel 028-67721258
Email seanpcahill1960@gmail.com

## Youth Ministry Co-ordinator

Mr Matthew McFadden
Clogher don Óige,
St Macartan's College, Monaghan
Tel 047-72784
Email info@clogherdonoige.com
Website www.clogherdonoige.com

## PARISHES

*The mensal parish is listed first. Other parishes follow alphabetically. In each case the postal name is given first, except where inappropriate, and the official name in parentheses. Church titulars are in italics.*

## MONAGHAN

*St Macartan's Cathedral, St Joseph's,*
*St Michael's*
Email parishoffice@stjosephspresbytery.com
Very Rev Patrick McGinn Adm
Rev John Chester CC
Email jchester@stjosephspresbytery.com
Rev Stephen Joyce CC
Email joyces@eircom.net
St Joseph's Presbytery, Park Street,
Monaghan
Tel 047-81220 Fax 047-84004

## ARNEY (CLEENISH)

*St Mary's, Arney*
*St Patrick's, Holywell*
*St Joseph's, Mullaghdun*
Very Rev Séamus Quinn PP
Belcoo East, Belcoo,
Co Fermanagh BT93 5FJ
Tel/Fax 028-66386225
Email ocoinne@gmail.com
Very Rev Canon John Finnegan PE
Arney, Enniskillen,
Co Fermanagh BT92 2AB
Tel 028-66348217
Email cleenish@btinternet.com

## AUGHNAMULLEN EAST

*Sacred Heart, Lough Egish*
*St Mary's, Carrickatee*
Very Rev Thomas Quigley PP
Latton, Castleblayney, Co Monaghan
Tel 042-9742212
Very Rev Canon Shane McCaughey
*(Priest in residence)*
Shantonagh, Castleblayney, Co Monaghan
Tel 042-9745015

## BALLYBAY (TULLYCORBET)

*St Patrick's, Ballybay*
*Holy Rosary, Tullycorbet*
*Our Lady of Knock, Ballintra*
Very Rev Laurence Flynn PP
Tel/Fax 042-9741032
Email contact@tullycorbetparish.com
Rt Rev Mgr Gerard McSorley PE
Tel/Fax 042-9741031
Ballybay, Co Monaghan

## BELLEEK-GARRISON (INIS MUIGHE SAMH)

*Our Lady, Queen of Peace, Garrison*
*St John the Baptist, Toura*
*St Joseph's, Cashelnadrea*
*St Patrick's, Belleek*
*St Michael's, Mulleek*
Very Rev Tiernach Beggan PP
Belleek, Enniskillen,
Co Fermanagh BT93 3FJ
Tel 028-68658229
Email belleekgarrison@btinternet.com
Rev John Kearns CC
Loughside Road, Garrison, Enniskillen,
Co Fermanagh BT93 4AE
Tel 028-68658238
Email kearnzie11578@hotmail.com
Rev Owen Gorman (OCDS) CC
506 Lattone Road, Carran West,
Garrison, Co Fermanagh BT93 4EL
Email fr.owengorman@yahoo.com
Very Rev Canon Patrick Lonergan PE
Garrison, Enniskillen,
Co Fermanagh BT93 4AE
Tel 028-68658234

## BROOKEBORO (AGHAVEA-AGHINTAINE)

*St Mary's, Brookeboro*
*St Joseph's, Coonian*
*St Mary's, Fivemiletown*
Very Rev Denis Dolan PP
Fivemiletown, Co Tyrone, BT75 OQP
Tel 028-89521291
Very Rev Canon Laurence Dawson PE
25 Teiges Hill, Brookeborough,
Co Fermanagh BT94 4EZ
Tel 028-89531770
Email dawson829@btinternet.com

## BUNDORAN (MAGH ENE)

*Our Lady, Star of the Sea, Bundoran*
*St Joseph's, The Rock, Ballyshannon*
Very Rev Canon Ramon Munster PP
Bundoran, Co Donegal
Tel 071-9841290 Fax 071-9841596
Email ppbundoran@eircom.net
Rt Rev Mgr Vincent Connolly PE
The Rock, Ballyshannon, Co Donegal
Tel 071-9851221
Email vconnolly51@gmail.com

## CARRICKMACROSS (MACHAIRE ROIS)

*St Joseph's, Carrickmacross*
*St Michael's, Corduff*
*St John the Evangelist, Raferagh*
Rt Rev Mgr Larry Duffy PP, VG
Tel 042-9664367
Email stjosephscarrickmacross@eircom.net
Rev Padraig McKenna CC
Tel 042-9661231
St Joseph's, Carrickmacross, Co Monaghan
Rev Brendan McCague CC
Corduff, Carrickmacross, Co Monaghan
Tel 042-9669456

## CASTLEBLAYNEY (MUCKNO)

*St Mary's, Castleblayney*
*St Patrick's, Oram*
Very Rev Canon Patrick McHugh PP
Tel 042-9740027
Rev Kevin Duffy CC
Tel 042-9740629
Rev Adrian Walshe CC
Tel 042-9740637
Email mucknoparish@eircom.net
Castleblayney, Co Monaghan

## CLOGHER

*St Patrick's, St Macartan's*
Very Rev Noel McGahan PP
25 Augher Road, Clogher,
Co Tyrone BT76 0AD
Tel 028-85549604
Email noelmcgahan@gmail.com
Very Rev Canon Laurence Dawson PE
25 Teiges Hill, Brookeborough,
Co Fermanagh BT94 4EZ
Tel 028-89531770
Email dawson829@btinternet.com

## CLONES

*Sacred Heart, Clones*
*St Macartan's, Aghadrumsee*
*St Alphonsus, Connons*
Rt Rev Mgr Richard Mohan PP
Clones, Co Monaghan
Tel 047-51048
Email clonesparish@eircom.net
Rev Cathal Deery CC
34 Lacky Road, Drumswords, Roslea,
Co Fermanagh BT92 7NQ
Tel 028-67751231
Email cdeery1966@gmail.com

## CLONTIBRET

*St Michael's, Annyalla*
*St Mary's, Clontibret*
*All Saints, Doohamlet*
Very Rev Paudge McDonnell PP
Annyalla, Castleblayney,
Co Monaghan
Tel 042-9740121
Email ppclontibretparish@eircom.net
Very Rev Lorcan Lynch CC
Clontibret, Co Monaghan
Tel 047-80631
Very Rev Canon Philip Connolly PE
Doohamlet Castleblayney,
Co Monaghan
Tel 042-9741239
Email fr.p.connolly@gmail.com

## CORCAGHAN (KILMORE AND DRUMSNAT)

*St Michael's, Corcaghan*
*St Mary's, Threemilehouse*
Very Rev Joseph McCluskey PP
Threemilehouse, Monaghan
Tel 047-81501
Email frmccluskey@gmail.com
Very Rev Thomas Coffey PE
Corcaghan, Monaghan
Tel 042-9744806

## DERRYGONNELLY (BOTHA)

*St Patrick's, Derrygonnelly*
*Sacred Heart, Boho*
*Immaculate Conception, Monea*
Very Rev Jimmy McPhillips PP
Derrygonnelly, Drumary,
Co Fermanagh BT93 6HW
Tel 028-68641207
Email jimmymcp@eircom.net
Very Rev John Finnegan PE
51 Arney Road, Mullymesker,
Enniskillen BT92 2AB
Tel 028-66348217

## DONAGH
*St Mary's, Glennan*
*St Patrick's, Corracrin*
Very Rev Hubert Martin PP
Glaslough, Monaghan
Tel 047-88120
Email donaghparish@emyvale.eu
Very Rev Canon Macartan McQuaid
*(Weekends only)*
Emyvale, Co Monaghan
Tel 087-2454705

## DONAGHMOYNE
*St Lastra's, Donaghmoyne*
*St Patrick's, Broomfield*
*St Mary's, Lisdoonan*
Very Rev Michael Daly PP
Broomfield, Castleblayney, Co Monaghan
Tel 042-9743617
Email dalyml@sky.com
Rev Michael Jordan CC
Parochial House, Donaghmoyne,
Co Monaghan
Tel 042-9661586
Email michaeljordan@eircom.net

## DROMORE
*St Davog's*
Very Rev Patrick MacEntee PP
Shanmullagh, Dromore, Omagh,
Co Tyrone BT78 3DZ
Tel 028-82898641
Email pmacentee@tiscali.co.uk
Very Rev Canon Thomas Breen PE
37 Esker Road, Dromore, Omagh,
Co Tyrone BT78 3LE
Tel 028-82898216

## EDERNEY (CÚL MÁINE)
*St Joseph's, Ederney*
*St Patrick's, Montiagh*
Very Rev Frank McManus PP
19 Ardvarney Road, Ederney, Enniskillen,
Co Fermanagh BT93 0DG
Tel 028-68631315
Email admin@culmaine.co.uk

## ENNISKILLEN
*St Michael's, Enniskillen*
*St Mary's, Lisbellaw*
Rt Rev Mgr Peter O'Reilly
1 Darling Street, Enniskillen,
Co Fermanagh BT74 7DP
Tel 028-66322627
Email pp@st-michaels.net
Rev David Donnelly CC
Rev Raymond Donnelly CC
4 Darling Street, Enniskillen,
Co Fermanagh BT74 7DP
Tel 028-66322075 Fax 028-66322248
Email parishcentre@st-michaels.net
Rev Joseph McVeigh *(priest in residence)*
Tattygar House, 4 Tattygar Road,
Lisbellaw, Co Fermanagh BT94 5GQ
Tel 028-66385232
Email mcveigh620@btinternet.com

## ERRIGAL TRUAGH
*Holy Family, Ballyoisin*
*St Patrick's, Clara*
*Sacred Heart, Carrickroe*
Very Rev Seán Nolan PP
St Joseph's, Emyvale, Monaghan
Tel/Fax 047-87152
Email tru@eircom.net

Very Rev Canon Macartan McQuaid
*(Weekends only)*
Emyvale, Monaghan
Tel 087-2454705

## ESKRA
*St Patrick's*
Very Rev Terence Connolly PP
178 Newtownsaville Road,
Omagh, Co Tyrone BT78 2RJ
Tel 028-82841306
Email terence.connolly1@btinternet.com

## FINTONA (DONACAVEY)
*St Laurence's*
Very Rev James Moore PP
Tel 028-82841907
Email frj1mmoore@gmail.com
Very Rev Canon Patrick Marron PE
Tel 028-82841239 Fax 028-82840302
Email pastoralcentrefintona@gmail.com
Fintona, Omagh,
Co Tyrone BT78 2NS

## INNISKEEN
*Mary, Mother of Mercy*
Very Rev Martin Treanor PP
Inniskeen, Dundalk, Co Louth
Tel 042-9378105
Email martintreanor@eircom.net
Rev Noel Conlon CC
Inniskeen, Dundalk, Co Louth
Tel 042-9378678

## IRVINESTOWN (DEVENISH)
*Sacred Heart, Irvinestown*
*St Molaise, Whitehill*
Very Rev Michael McGourty PP
Irvinestown, Enniskillen,
Co Fermanagh BT94 1EY
Tel 028-68628600
Email mmcgourty210@live.co.uk
Very Rev Canon Gerald Timoney PE
Irvinestown, Enniskillen,
Co Fermanagh BT94 1GD
Tel 028-68621329

## KILLANNY
*St Enda's*
Very Rev Martin Treanor PP
Inniskeen, Dundalk, Co Louth
Tel 042-9378105
Email martintreanor@eircom.net
Rev Martin O'Reilly CC
Killanny, Carrickmacross, Co Monaghan
Tel 042-9661452
Email frmartinkillany@hotmail.com

## KILLEEVAN (CURRIN, KILLEEVAN AND AGHABOG)
*St Livinus', Killeevan, St Mary's, Ture*
*Immaculate Conception, Scotshouse*
*St Mary's, Latnamard*
Very Rev Peter Corrigan PP
Shanco, Newbliss, Co Monaghan
Tel 047-54011
Email killeevanparish@eircom.net
Rev John F. McKenna CC
Scotshouse, Clones, Co Monaghan
Tel 047-56016
Email jmckenna420@live.ie

## LATTON (AUGHNAMULLEN WEST)
*St Mary's, Latton, St Patrick's, Bawn*
Very Rev Thomas Quigley PP
Latton, Castleblayney, Co Monaghan
Tel 042-9742212
Email tomquigleylatton@gmail.com

## LISNASKEA (AGHALURCHER)
*Holy Cross, Lisnaskea*
*St Mary's, Maguiresbridge*
Very Rev Canon Joseph Mullin PP, VF
Tel 028-67721342 Fax 028-67723773
Email jmullin68@yahoo.co.uk
Rev Eamon Bredin CC
Tel 028-67721324
Lisnaskea, Enniskillen,
Co Fermanagh BT92 0JE
Rt Rev Mgr Seán Cahill
18 Boyhill Road, Tattinderry,
Maguiresbridge, Enniskillen,
Co Fermanagh BT94 4LN
Tel 028-67721258
Email seanpcahill1960@gmail.com

## MAGHERACLOONE
*St Patrick's (The Rock Chapel),*
*Carrickasedge*
*SS Peter and Paul, Drumgossatt*
Very Rev Thomas Finnegan PP
Liscarnan, Magheracloone,
Carrickmacross, Co Monaghan
Tel 042-9663500
Email magheraclooneparish@eircom.net
Rev Philip Crowe (CSSp) CC
Drumgossatt, Carrickmacross,
Co Monaghan
Tel 042-9661388

## NEWTOWNBUTLER (GALLOON)
*St Mary's, Newtownbutler*
*St Patrick's, Donagh, Lisnaskea*
Very Rev Michael King PP
Tel 028-67738229
Email galloonparish@gmail.com
Very Rev Canon Edward Murphy PE
Tel 028-67738640
Newtownbutler, Enniskillen,
Co Fermanagh BT92 8JJ

## PETTIGO
*St Mary's, Pettigo*
*St Joseph's, Lettercran*
Very Rev Owen J. McEneaney Adm
Pettigo, Co Donegal
Tel 071-9861666
Lough Derg (See Charitable Societies)
Tel/Fax 071-9861518
Email pettigoparish@loughderg.org

## ROCKCORRY (EMATRIS)
*Holy Trinity, St Mary's, Corrawacan*
Very Rev Thomas Quigley PP
Latton, Castleblayney, Co Monaghan
Tel 042-9742212
Rev Jerry White (SSCC) CC
Sacred Hearts Community, Tanagh,
Cootehill, Co Cavan
Tel 049-5552188

## ROSLEA
*St Tierney's, Roslea*
*St Mary's, Magherarney*
Very Rev Canon John McCabe PP
Parochial House, Roslea,
Co Fermanagh BT92 7QY
Tel/Fax 028-67751227
Rev John Flanagan CC
Roslea, Enniskillen,
Co Fermanagh BT92 7QY
Tel 028-67751393
Rev Patrick Connolly (SPS) CC
Parochial House, Roslea,
Co Fermanagh BT92 7QY
Tel 028-67751393
Email rosleaparish@btinternet.com

## TEMPO (POBAL)
*Immaculate Conception, Tempo*
*St Joseph's, Cradien*
Very Rev John Halton PP
Tempo, Enniskillen,
Co Fermanagh BT94 3LY
Tel 028-89541344
Email johnhalton19@btinternet.com

## TRILLICK (KILSKEERY)
*St Macartan's, Trillick*
*St Mary's, Coa*
Very Rev Canon John McKenna PP
Trillick, Omagh, Co Tyrone BT78 3RD
Tel 028-89561350
Email john.mckenna35@btinternet.com
Very Rev Canon Thomas Marron PE
Trillick, Omagh, Co Tyrone BT78 3RD
Tel 028-89561217

## TYDAVNET
*St Dympna's, Tydavnet*
*St Mary's, Urbleshanny*
*St Joseph's, Knockatallon*
Very Rev Brian Early PP
Scotstown, Co Monaghan
Tel 047-89204 Fax 047-79772
Email bearly@eircom.net
Very Rev Canon Sean Clerkin PE
Tydavnet, Co Monaghan
Tel/Fax 047-89402
Email sean.clerkin@eircom.net

## TYHOLLAND
*St Patrick's*
Rt Rev Mgr Joseph McGuinness Adm
Tyholland, Monaghan
Tel 047-85385 Fax 047-85051
Email diocesanoffice@clogherdiocese.ie

## INSTITUTIONS AND THEIR CHAPLAINS

**Daughters of Our Lady of the Sacred Heart Convent**
Ballybay, Co Monaghan

**Finner Army Camp**
Ballyshannon, Co Donegal
Rev Alan Ward CF
Tel 071-9842294

**Monaghan General Hospital**
Priests of Monaghan parish
Tel 047-81220 Fax 047-84004

**St Davnet's Hospital, Monaghan**
Priests of Monaghan parish
Tel 047-81220 Fax 047-84004

**St Mary's Hospital**
Castleblayney, Co Monaghan
Priests of Castleblayney parish
Tel 042-9740027

**South West Acute Hospital, Enniskillen**
Priests of Enniskillen Parish
Tel 028-66322075 Fax 028-66322248

## PRIESTS OF THE DIOCESE ELSEWHERE

Rev Dr Patrick Connolly
Theology Department,
Mary Immaculate College,
South Circular Road, Limerick
Tel 061-204575 Fax 061-313632
Email patrick.connolly@mic.ul.ie
Rev Jeremiah Carroll
Archdiocese of Dublin/Defence Forces

*Study Leave/contact addresses*
Rev Ian Fee
Tullnacross, Donaghmoyne,
Castleblayney, Co Monaghan
Email ianfee1701@outlook.com
Rev Brendan Gallagher
c/o Clogher Diocesan Office,
Bishop's House, Monaghan
Tel 047-81019
Rev Benedict Hughes
Kellystown, Coolderry Road,
Carrickmacross, Co Monaghan
Rev Noel McConnell
64 The Green, Moyglare Hall,
Moyglare Road, Maynooth, Co Kildare

## RETIRED PRIESTS

Most Rev Joseph Duffy DD
Bishop Emeritus
Doire na gCraobh, Monaghan
Tel 047-62725
Email doirenagcraobh@gmail.com
Very Rev Canon Gerard Ferguson
Rockcorry, Co Monaghan
Tel 042-9742243
Rev Gerard Jennings
St Theresa's, Castleblayney Road,
Ballybay, Co Monaghan
Very Rev Liam Hughes PE
Inniskeen, Dundalk, Co Louth
Tel 042-9378338 Fax 042-9378988
Very Rev Edmond Maguire PE
Newtownbutler Road, Clones,
Co Monaghan
Tel 047-51160
Very Rev Canon Brian McCluskey PE
Apt 2, 2 Danesfort Park North,
Stranmillis Road, Belfast BT9 5RB
Tel 028-90683544
Rev Terence McElvaney
Church Square, Monaghan
Tel 047-82255
Very Rev Canon Gerard McGreevy PE
Magherarney, Smithboro, Co Monaghan
Tel 047-57011
Very Rev Canon Peter McGuinness PE
3 Castleross Retirement Village,
Carrickmacross, Co Monaghan
Tel 042-9690013

## RELIGIOUS ORDERS AND CONGREGATIONS

### PRIESTS

**PASSIONISTS**
St Gabriel's Retreat,
The Graan, Enniskillen, Co Fermanagh
Tel 028-66322272 Fax 028-66325201
*Superior:* Rev Brian D'Arcy (CP)
Email crccp@aol.com

**SACRED HEARTS COMMUNITY**
Cootehill, Co Cavan
Tel 049-5552188
Br Harry O'Gara (SSCC)
Email broharrysscc@gmail.com

Rockcorry, Co Monaghan
Rev Jerry White (SSCC)
Email jerrysscc@gmail.com

### SISTERS

**CONGREGATION OF THE SISTERS OF MERCY**
Northern Province, Provincial House,
74 Main Street, Clogher,
Co Tyrone BT76 0AA
Tel 028-85548127
Fax 028-85549459
*Provincial Leader:* Sr Ann Brady

11 Castlehill Gardens, Augher,
Co Tyrone BT77 0HA
Tel 028-85548157

St Brigid's, 2 Ballagh Road, Clogher,
Co Tyrone BT76 0HE
Tel 028-85548015

Convent of Mercy, 6 Belmore Street,
Enniskillen, Co Fermanagh
Tel 028-66322561
*Shared Leaders:* Srs Monica Gallagher &
Carmel McNally
Community: 21

Gate House, 72 Main Street, Clogher,
Co Tyrone BT76 0AA
Tel 028-85549545

Sisters of Mercy, 6 Gorminish Park,
Garrison, Co Fermanagh BT93 4GP
Tel 028-68659742

No. 16 The Grange,
Presentation Walk, Monaghan
Tel 047-84569

Buíochas, 29 The Commons, Bellanaleck,
Enniskillen, Co Fermanagh BT92 2BD
Tel 028-66349722

20 Crossowen Park,
Clogher, Co Tyrone BT76 0AT
Tel 028-85548139

St Faber's, 8 Castlecourt, Monea,
Co Fermanagh BT93 7AR
Tel 028-66341197

73 Scaffog Avenue, Sligo Road,
Enniskillen, Co Fermanagh BT74 7JJ
Tel 028-66327474

7 Friar's Park, Drumlyon, Enniskillen,
Co Fermanagh BT74 5NR
Tel 028-66320224

9 Devenish Crescent, Enniskillen,
Co Fermanagh BT74 4RB
Tel 028-66346754

Apt D3, Silver Hill Manor,
Enniskillen,
Co Fermanagh BT74 5JE

The Graan Stillpoint,
Derrygonnelly Road, Enniskillen,
Co Fermanagh BT74 5PB
Tel 028-66346817

30 Silver Hill Manor, Enniskillen,
Co Fermanagh BT74 5JE
Tel 028-66320792

No 19 The Sidings,
Breandrum, Enniskillen,
Co Fermanagh BT74 6GZ
Tel 028-66326836

Sisters of Mercy,
Laurel Hill Lodge,
Castleblayney, Co Monaghan
Tel 042-9740069

**DAUGHTERS OF OUR LADY OF THE
SACRED HEART**
Ballybay, Co Monaghan
Tel 042-9741068
*Superior:* Sr Mary Mallin
Community: 5
St Joseph's Nursing Home
*Superior:* Sr Kathleen McQuillan
Tel 042-9741141. Beds: 20
Community: 12

**ST LOUIS SISTERS**
St Louis Convent, Louisville, Monaghan
Tel 047-81411
Community: 23
Varied apostolates
Post-Primary School. Tel 047-81422
Pupils: 550
Primary School. Tel 047-81305
Pupils: 310
Infant School. Tel 047-82913
Pupils: 290

Our Lady's Community,
Louisville, Monaghan
Tel 047-82006
Community: 6
Varied apostolates

5 Lakeview, Monaghan
Tel 047-84122
Community: 1
Varied apostolates

St Raphael, 3 Lakeview, Monaghan
Tel 047-84719
Community: 1
Varied apostolates

173 Mullaghmatt, Monaghan
Tel 047-84110
Community: 2
Varied apostolates

Rowan Tree Court,
24 Mullach Glas Close, Monaghan
Tel 047-38685
Community: 1

Carrickmacross, Co Monaghan
Tel 042-9661247
Community: 17
Varied apostolates
Secondary. Tel 042-9661587/9661467
Pupils: 650

Iona House, Farney Street
Carrickmacross, Co Monaghan
Tel 042-9663326
Community: 3
Varied apostolates

15 Plás Fionnbara, Taillte an Chlochair,
Carrickmacross, Co Monaghan
Tel 042-9670126
Community: 2
Varied Apostolates

Clondergole, Clones, Co Monaghan
Tel 047-51136
Community: 1
Parish work

4 White Maple Drive,
Bundoran, Co Donegal
Tel 071-9829505
Community: 3
Varied apostolates

5 White Maple Drive,
Bundoran, Co Donegal
Tel 071-9841330
Community: 2
Varied apostolates

## EDUCATIONAL INSTITUTIONS

**St Macartan's College**
Monaghan, Co Monaghan
Tel 047-81642/83365/83367
Fax 047-83341
Email admin@stmacartanscollege.ie
*President*
Very Rev Canon Shane McCaughey BD
*Principal*
Mr Raymond McHugh BA, HDipEd, MSc

**St Michael's College**
Enniskillen, Co Fermanagh BT74 6DE
Tel 028-66322935
Fax 028-66325128
Email office@saintmichaels.org.uk
*Principal:* Mr Eugene McCullough
*Chaplain*
Very Rev Canon Macartan McQuaid
Email macqua743@gmail.com

## CHARITABLE AND OTHER SOCIETIES

**ACCORD**
St Macartan's College, Monaghan
Tel 047-83359
(10am-1pm Mon-Fri)

Ros Erne House,
8 Darling Street, Enniskillen,
Co Fermanagh BT74 7EW
Tel 028-66325696
(9am-5pm Mon-Fri)

**CURA**
7 The Grange, Plantation Walk,
Monaghan
Tel 047-83600
*Contact person:* Sr Brenda McCrudden

**Lough Derg, St Patrick's Purgatory**
Pettigo, Co Donegal
Tel 071-9861518 Fax 071-9861525
Email info@loughderg.org
*Prior:* Very Rev Owen J. McEneaney
Pilgrimage season, 1 June-15 August.
No advance booking or notice required.
Pilgrims arrive daily before 3 pm, having
fasted from midnight, and remain on the
island for two complete days of prayer
and penance.
One-day retreats before and after main
pilgrimage season.
School retreats also offered.
Tel for details and reservations.

**Veritas Bookshop & Christian Art Gallery**
Park Street, Monaghan
*Manager:* Ms Mary Flynn
Tel 047-84077

# DIOCESE OF CLONFERT

INCLUDES PORTIONS OF COUNTIES GALWAY, OFFALY AND ROSCOMMON

**Most Rev John Kirby DD**
Bishop of Clonfert;
born October 1938;
ordained priest 23 June 1963;
ordained Bishop of Clonfert
9 April 1988

Residence: Coorheen,
Loughrea, Co Galway
Tel 091-841560
Fax 091-841818
Email clonfert@iol.ie

## ST BRENDAN'S CATHEDRAL, LOUGHREA

St Brendan's Cathedral stands at the western extremity of the Diocese of Clonfert on the main highway from Dublin to Galway. The foundation stone of the cathedral was laid on 10 October 1897, and the fabric was completed in 1902. Plans were drawn by the Dublin architect William Byrne for a building in the neo-Gothic style, having a nave and an aspidal sanctuary, lean-to aisles and shallow transepts, with a graceful spire at the western end. Its dimensions were determined by the needs of the parish of Loughrea. While not impressive, its proportions are good, and despite a departure from the original plan by curtailment of the sanctuary, the overall effect is pleasing. The simplicity of the exterior, however, hardly prepares the visitor for the riches within.

It was due to two fortuitous circumstances that St Brendan's became a veritable treasure house of the Celtic Revival in sculpture, stained glass, woodcarving, metalwork and textiles.

The first circumstance was that the building of a Catholic cathedral was delayed for various reasons until close to the turn of the last century. The Irish Literary Renaissance was by then well advanced. When the building was completed in 1902, the Arts and Crafts movement was having effect.

The second circumstance was that of Edward Martyn's birth at the home of his maternal grandfather, James Smyth, in the parish of Loughrea. Martyn was an ascetic man and devoted his time and fortune to the development of every phase of the Irish revival, the Gaelic League, Sinn Féin, the Irish Literary Theatre, Irish music, church music and church art. With innate business acumen, he insured by personal donation and the financial support of the Smyth family that the new cathedral would reflect his views. The bishop, Dr John Healy, who was sensitive to the prevailing trend, accepted the challenge and assigned the project to the supervision of a young

curate in the parish, Fr Jeremiah O'Donovan, who was himself actively engaged in propaganda for Revival.

John Hughes was the foremost sculptor in the country at the time, and Bishop Healy commissioned him to do the modelling and carving. His work is found in the bronze figure of Christ on the reredos of the high altar and in the magnificent marble statue of the Virgin and Child. Michael Shortall, a student of Hughes in the Metropolitan School of Art, did the carvings on the corbels and executed the statue of St Brendan on the wall of the tower. His connection with the cathedral continued over twenty years, and he was responsible for carvings of incidents from the life and voyage of St Brendan carved on the capitals of the pillars.

The Yeats sisters, Lily and Elizabeth, along with their friend Evelyn Gleeson, set up the Dun Emer guild. They embroidered twenty-four banners of Irish saints for use in the cathedral. Jack B. Yeats and his wife Mary designed

these banners. With an economy of detail and richness of colour, they almost achieve the effect of stained glass. Mass vestments, embroidered with silk on poplin, also came from the same studio.

More than anything else, St Brendan's is famous for its stained glass. Martyn was particularly concerned about the quality of stained glass then available in Ireland. He was eager to set up an Irish stained-glass industry. He succeeded in having Alfred E. Childe appointed to the Metropolitan School of Art, and he later persuaded Sarah Purser to open a co-operative studio, where young artists could be trained in the technique of stained glass. This new studio, An Túr Gloinne, opened in January 1903, with Childe as manager, and so began the work of the Loughrea stained-glass windows. Over the next forty years, Childe, Purser and Michael Healy executed almost all the stained-glass windows in the cathedral, and it is these windows that have given St Brendan's its place in the Irish Artistic Revival.

## ADMINISTRATION

**Vicar General**
Rt Rev Mgr Cathal Geraghty PP, VG
St Brendan's Cathedral, Barrack Street,
Loughrea, Co Galway
Tel 091-841212

**Vicars Forane**
Very Rev Michael Finneran PP, VF
Very Rev Ciaran Kitching PP
Very Rev Martin McNamara PP

**Bishop's Secretary**
Ms Marcella Fallon
Coorheen, Loughrea, Co Galway
Tel 091-841560
Email clonfert@iol.ie

**Chancellor**
Rt Rev Mgr Cathal Geraghty PP, VG
St Brendan's Cathedral, Barrack Street,
Loughrea, Co Galway
Tel 091-841212

**College of Consultors**
Very Rev Michael Finneran PP, VF
Very Rev Ciaran Kitching PP
Very Rev John Garvey PP
Rt Rev Mgr Cathal Geraghty PP, VG
Very Rev Martin McNamara PP

**Diocesan Finance Committe**
Most Rev John Kirby DD
Rt Rev Mgr Cathal Geraghty PP, VG
Very Rev Martin McNamara PP
Mr Gerard McInerney
Mr Terry Doyle
Mr Patrick McDonagh
Mr Sean O'Dwyer
Mrs Nancy O'Gorman
Ms Marcella Fallon

**Diocesan Council of Priests**
*Chairman:* Very Rev Iomar Daniels PP
Leitrim, Loughrea, Co Galway
Tel 091-841758
*Secretary:* Very Rev Niall Foley PP
Mullagh, Loughrea, Co Galway
Tel 091-843119
*Members*
Most Rev John Kirby DD
Very Rev Michael Finneran PP, VF
Very Rev Ciaran Kitching PP
Very Rev Martin McNamara PP
Very Rev John Garvey PP
Rt Rev Mgr Cathal Geraghty PP, VG
Rev Bernard Costello
Rev Raymond Sweeney CC
Rev Thomas Shanahan (ODC)
Rev Patrick O'Keeffe (CSsR)

## CATECHETICS EDUCATION

**Adult Education**
Very Rev Ciaran Kitching PP
Killimor, Ballinasloe, Co Galway
Tel 090-9676151

**Catholic Primary School Managers' Association**
*Secretary:* Mr Eamon Lally
Gortnahorna, Clontuskert,
Ballinasloe, Co Galway
Tel 096-9643250

**Primary Schools**
*Diocesan Adviser*
Very Rev Declan McInerney
St Brendan Church, Eyrecourt,
Ballinasloe, Co Galway
Tel 090-9645080

## PASTORAL

**ACCORD**
*Director:* Very Rev John Garvey PP
St Michael's, Ballinasloe, Co Galway
Tel 090-9643916

**Legion of Mary**
*Diocesan Director*
Very Rev Patrick Conroy PP
Ballinakill, Loughrea, Co Galway
Tel 090-9745021

**Marriage Tribunal**
(See Marriage Tribunals section)

**Pilgrimages**
*Diocesan Director:* Rev Pat Conroy PP
Ballinakill, Loughrea, Co Galway
Tel 090-9745021

**Pioneer Total Abstinence Association**
*Diocesan Director*
Very Rev John Naughton PP
Clonfert Avenue, Portumna, Co Galway

**Pontifical Mission Societies**
*Diocesan Director*
Very Rev Brendan Lawless PP
Dunkellin Terrace,
Portumna, Co Galway
Tel 090-9741092

**Trócaire**
Very Rev Brendan Lawless PP
Dunkellin Terrace,
Portumna, Co Galway
Tel 090-9741092

**Vocations**
*Director:* Rev Iomar Daniels
St Andrew's Church, Leitrim,
Loughrea, Co Galway
Tel 091-841758

## PARISHES

*Mensal parishes are listed first. Other parishes follow alphabetically. Historical names are given in parentheses. Church titulars are in italics.*

**LOUGHREA, ST BRENDAN'S CATHEDRAL**
Rt Rev Mgr Cathal Geraghty PP, VG
Rev Sean Egan CC
Rev Aidan Costello CC
The Presbytery, Loughrea, Co Galway
Tel 091-841212

**BALLINASLOE, CREAGH AND KILCLOONEY**
*St Michael's, Ballinasloe*
*Our Lady of Lourdes, Creagh*
Very Rev John Garvey PP
Rev Dan O'Donovan CC
Very Rev Colm Allman
Tel 090-9643916

**AUGHRIM AND KILCONNELL**
*St Catherine's, Aughrim*
*Sacred Heart, Kilconnell*
Very Rev Gerard Geraghty PP
Aughrim, Ballinasloe, Co Galway
Tel 090-9673724/090-9686614

**BALLINAKILL**
*St Joseph's, Ballinakill*
*St Patrick's, Derrybrien*
Very Rev Pat Conroy PP
Ballinakill, Loughrea, Co Galway
Tel 090-9745021

**BALLYMACWARD AND GURTEEN (BALLYMACWARD AND CLONKEENKERRIL)**
*SS Peter and Paul*
*St Michael's*
Very Rev Raymond Sweeney PP
Ballymacward, Ballinasloe, Co Galway
Tel 090-9687614

**CAPPATAGLE AND KILRICKLE (KILLALAGHTAN AND KILRICKLE)**
*St Michael's, Cappatagle*
*Our Lady of Lourdes, Kilrickle*
Rt Rev Mgr Edward Stankard PP
Cappatagle, Ballinasloe, Co Galway
Tel 091-843017
Rev Joseph Long (SPS) CC
Kilrickle, Ballinasloe, Co Galway
Tel 091-843015

**CLONTUSKERT**
*St Augustine's*
Very Rev Michael Finneran PP, VF
Clontuskert, Ballinasloe, Co Galway
Tel 090-9642256

**CLOSTOKEN AND KILCONIERAN (KILCONICKNY, KILCONIERAN AND LICKERRIG)**
*Holy Family, Immaculate Conception*
Very Rev Benny Flanagan PP
Carrabane, Athenry, Co Galway
Tel 091-841103

**DUNIRY AND ABBEY (DUNIRY AND KILNELEHAN)**
*Holy Family*
Very Rev Abe Kennedy PP
Duniry, Loughrea, Co Galway
Tel 090-9745125
*Assumption*
Rev John Hickey CC
Abbey, Loughrea, Co Galway
Tel 090-9745217

**Allianz** ⑪

### EYRECOURT, CLONFERT AND MEELICK (CLONFERT, DONANAGHTA AND MEELICK)
*St Brendan's, St Francis*
Very Rev Declan McInerney PP
Eyrecourt, Ballinasloe, Co Galway
Tel 090-9675148

### FAHY AND QUANSBORO (FAHY AND KILQUAIN)
*Consoler of the Afficted, Christ the King*
Very Rev P. J. Bracken PP
Fahy, Eyrecourt, Ballinasloe,
Co Galway
Tel 090-9675116

### FOHENAGH AND KILLURE (FOHENAGH AND KILGERRILL)
*St Patrick's*
*St Teresa's*
Very Rev Christy McCormack PP
Fohenagh, Ahascragh,
Ballinasloe, Co Galway
Tel 090-9688623

### KILLIMOR AND TIRANASCRAGH (KILLIMORBOLOGUE AND TIRANASCRAGH)
*St Joseph's*
Very Rev Ciaran Kitching PP
Killimor, Ballinasloe, Co Galway
Tel 090-9676151

### KILNADEEMA AND AILLE (KILNADEEMA AND KILTESKILL)
*St Dympna's, St Mary's, Aille, Loughrea*
Very Rev Joseph Clarke PP
Kilnadeema, Loughrea, Co Galway
Tel 091-841201

### KILTULLA AND ATTYMON (KILLIMORDALY AND KILLTULAGH)
*SS Peter & Paul, Kiltulla,*
*St Mary's, Cloncagh,*
*St Iomar's, Killimordaly*
Very Rev Martin McNamara PP
Kiltulla, Athenry, Co Galway
Tel 091-848021
Rev Richard McMahon (CSsR) CC
Tel 091-848208

### LAWRENCETOWN AND KILTORMER (KILTORMER AND OGHILL)
*St Mary's, St Patrick's*
Very Rev Christopher O'Byrne PP
Lawrencetown, Ballinasloe, Co Galway
Tel 090-9685613

### LEITRIM AND BALLYDUGGAN (KILCOOLEY AND LEITRIM)
*St Andrew's, St Jarlath's, Ballyduggan*
Very Rev Iomar Daniels PP
St Andrew's Church, Leitrim,
Loughrea, Co Galway
Tel 091-841758

### LUSMAGH
*St Cronan's*
Very Rev Michael Kennedy PP
Lusmagh, Banagher, Co Offaly
Tel 0509-51358

### MULLAGH AND KILLORAN (ABBEYGORMICAN AND KILLORAN)
*St Brendan's*
*Our Lady of the Assumption*
Very Rev Niall Foley PP
Mullagh, Loughrea, Co Galway
Tel 091-843119

### NEW INN AND BULLAUN (BULLAUN, GRANGE AND KILLAAN)
*St Killian's, New Inn*
*St Patrick's, Bullaun*
Very Rev Pat Kenny PP
St Killian Church, New Inn,
Ballinasloe, Co Galway
Tel 090-9675819

### PORTUMNA (KILMALINOGUE AND LICKMOLASSEY)
*St Brigid's, SS Peter & Paul, Ascension*
Very Rev Brendan Lawless PP
Dunkellin Terrace,
Portumna, Co Galway
Tel 090-9741092

### TAGHMACONNELL
*St Ronan's*
Very Rev Sean Neylon PP
Taghmaconnell,
Ballinasloe, Co Galway
Tel 090-9683929

### TYNAGH
*St Lawrence's, Sacred Heart*
Very Rev Seamus Bohan PP
Tynagh, Loughrea, Co Galway
Tel 090-9745113

### WOODFORD
*St John the Baptist, St Brendan's*
Very Rev Kieran O'Rourke PP
Looscaun, Woodford, Co Galway
Tel 090-9749100

## INSTITUTIONS AND THEIR CHAPLAINS

**Emmanuel House of Providence**
Clonfert, Ballinasloe, Co Galway
*Director:* Mr Eddie Stones
*Chaplain:* Fr Michael Kennedy
Tel 057-9151552

**Portiuncula Hospital**
Ballinasloe, Co Galway
Tel 090-9648200
Rev Bernard Costello

**St Brendan's**
*Community Nursing Unit*
Loughrea, Co Galway
Tel 091-871200
Rt Rev Mgr Cathal Geraghty PP
Tel 091-841212

**St Brigid's Hospital**
Ballinasloe, Co Galway
Tel 090-9642117
Rev Bernard Costello

**Vocational School**
Loughrea, Co Galway
Tel 091-841919
Rev Iomar Daniels PP

**Vocational School**
New Inn, Co Galway
Tel 090-9675811
Very Rev Pat Kenny PP
Tel 090-9675819

## PRIESTS WORKING OUTSIDE THE DIOCESE

Rev Michael Byrnes
Galway Marriage Tribunal
Rev T. J. O'Connell
Kent, England

## RETIRED PRIESTS

Very Rev Sean Lyons
Dunkellin Terrace, Portumna, Co Galway
Rev Cathal Stanley
Dominic Street, Portumna, Co Galway
Tel 090-9759182
Rev Vivian Twohig
Millrace Nursing Home,
River Street, Ballinasloe, Co Galway
Tel 086-8116978
Rev Sean Slattery
Limerick
Rev John Naughton
Clonfert Avenue, Portumna, Co Galway

## RELIGIOUS ORDERS AND CONGREGATIONS

### PRIESTS

**CARMELITES (OCD)**
The Abbey,
Loughrea, Co Galway
Tel 091-841209
Fax 091-842343
*Prior:* Rev Willie Moran (OCD)

**REDEMPTORISTS**
St Patrick's, Esker,
Athenry, Co Galway
Tel 091-844007
Outside office hours 086-8440619
Fax 091-845698
*Superior*
Rev Brendan O'Rourke (CSsR)
*Vicar Superior*
Rev Patrick O'Keeffe (CSsR)

### SISTERS

**CARMELITES**
St Joseph's Monastery,
Mount Carmel, Loughrea, Co Galway
*Prioress:* Sr Mary Catharina Murphy
Community: 8
Contemplative order, primitive observance

## CONGREGATION OF THE SISTERS OF MERCY

Convent of Mercy, Loughrea, Co Galway
Tel 091-841354 Fax 091-847271
Community: 16

St Laurence's Fields,
Loughrea, Co Galway
Tel 091-842989
Community: 1

Sisters of Mercy,
Lake Road, Loughrea, Co Galway
Tel/Fax 091-847715
Community: 5

Beech Haven, Church Street,
Ballinasloe, Co Galway
Tel 090-9642191
Community: 4

Mount Pleasant,
Ballinasloe, Co Galway
Tel 090-9631695
Community: 4

'Cana', Garbally Drive,
Ballinasloe, Co Galway
Tel 090-9644570 Fax 090-9644834
Community: 4

7 Woodview, The Pines,
Ballinasloe, Co Galway
Tel 090-9644055
Community: 1

17 Hawthorn Crescent,
Ballinasloe, Co Galway
Tel 090-9644171
Community: 2

An Gairdín, Portumna, Co Galway
Tel 090-9741689
Community: 2

St Brendan's Convent of Mercy,
Eyrecourt, Co Galway
Tel 090-9675123
Community: 2

Sisters of Mercy, Bark Hill,
Woodford, Co Galway
Community: 1

5 College Crescent,
The Pines, Ballinasloe, Co Galway
Community: 1

## FRANCISCAN MISSIONARIES OF THE DIVINE MOTHERHOOD

Regional House,
Assisi, Harbour Road,
Ballinasloe, Co Galway
Tel 090-9648952
Community: 4

Franciscan Convent, Garbally Drive,
Ballinasloe, Co Galway
Tel 090-9642314/9648548
*Local Leader:* Sr Madeleine de Cruz
Community: 26

La Verna, Brackernagh,
Ballinasloe, Co Galway
Tel 090-9643679
Community: 3

St Clare's, Brackernagh,
Ballinasloe, Co Galway
Tel 090-9643986 Fax 090-9631757
Community: 3

Bethany, Brackernagh,
Ballinasloe, Co Galway
Tel 090-9643499
Community: 2

San Damiano, Ard Mhuire, Ballinasloe,
Co Galway
Community: 5

## EDUCATIONAL INSTITUTIONS

**Portumna Community School**
Portumna, Co Galway
*Chairman, BOM*
Very Rev P. J. Bracken BSc, HDE
Tel 090-9675116
*Chaplain:* Rev Abe Kennedy
St Molaise's, Portumna, Co Galway
Tel 090-9745125 (H)
Tel 090-9741053 (S)

**St Joseph's College**
Garbally Park, Ballinasloe, Co Galway
Tel 090-9642504 / 9642254
*President*
Very Rev Colm Allman BA, HDE

**St Raphael's College**
Convent of Mercy,
Loughrea, Co Galway
Tel 091-841062
*Chaplain:* Very Rev Pat Kenny PP

**Mercy College**
Woodford, Co Galway
Tel 090-9749076
*Chaplain:* Very Rev Kieran O'Rourke PP

# DIOCESE OF CLOYNE

PATRON OF THE DIOCESE
ST COLMAN, 24 NOVEMBER

COVERS MOST OF COUNTY CORK

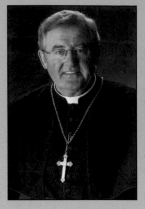

**Most Rev William Crean DD**
Bishop of Cloyne;
born 16 December 1951;
ordained priest 20 June 1976;
ordained Bishop of Cloyne
27 January 2013

Residence: Cloyne Diocesan
Centre, Cobh, Co Cork
Tel 021-4811430
Fax 021-4811026
Email info@cloynediocese.ie
website: www.cloynediocese.ie

## ST COLMAN'S CATHEDRAL, COBH

St Colman's Cathedral, overlooking Cobh, enshrines within its walls the traditions of thirteen centuries of the Diocese of Cloyne.

Built in the form of a Latin cross, its exterior is of Dalkey granite, with dressings of Mallow limestone. The style of architecture is French Gothic. The architects were Pugin (the Younger), Ashlin and Coleman.

The cathedral took forty-seven years to build (1868–1915). The total cost was £235,000. Of this, £90,000 was raised by the people of Cobh, with the remainder coming from the diocese and from collections in America and Australia.

The spire was completed in 1915 and the famous carillon and the clock were installed in 1916. The carillon – the largest in Britain and Ireland – has forty-nine bells and is tuned to the accuracy of a single vibration. This unusual instrument covers a range of four octaves and is played from a console located in the belfry, consisting of a keyboard and pedalboard. Inside, the cathedral has all the hallmarks of Gothic grandeur: the massive marble pillars, the beautiful arches, the capitals with their delicate carving of foliage, the shamrock design on the Bath Stone, and mellow, delicate lighting.

The carved panels over the nave arches give a history of the Church in Ireland from the time of St Patrick. The stained-glass windows in the northern aisle depict the parables of Christ, while those in the southern aisle depict the miracles of Christ. Overhead, in the clerestory, are forty-six windows, each having the patron of one of the forty-six parishes of the diocese. The high altar and its surround was designed by Ashlin. The pulpit is of Austrian oak. Towards the rear of the cathedral is the magnificent rose window, which depicts St John's vision of the throne of God. The organ was built by Telford and Telford, and has a total of 2,468 pipes.

**Most Rev John Magee DD**
Retired Bishop of Cloyne;
born 24 September 1936;
ordained priest 17 March 1962;
ordained Bishop of Cloyne 17 March 1987;
retired 24 March 2010
*Residence:* 'Carnmeen', Convent Hill,
Mitchelstown, Co Cork
Tel 025-41887

## CHAPTER

*Dean:* Rt Rev Mgr Eamonn Goold PP, VG
Midleton
*Archdeacon:* Vacant
*Chancellor:* Very Rev Seán Cotter PP
Charleville
*Prebendaries*
*Aghulter:* Very Rev Timothy O'Leary CC,
Mitchelstown
*Ballyhea:* Rt Rev Mgr Denis O'Callaghan
PE, Mallow
*Buttevant:* Vacant
*Cahirulton:* Very Rev Michael Harrington
PE, Buttevant
*Coole*
Very Rev Finbar Kelleher CC *(pro tem)*
Glanworth and Ballindangan
*Cooline:* Very Rev Patrick Twomey PE
Kildorrery
*Glanworth*
Very Rev Gerard Casey PP, VF
Mallow
*Inniscarra:* Vacant
*Kilmaclenine:* Rt Rev Mgr James
O'Donnell AP, Macroom
*Killenemer:* Vacant
*Subulter:* Very Rev John Terry PE
Kanturk
*Brigown:* Very Rev Mgr Denis Reidy PE,
Carrigtwohill
*Kilmacdonogh*
Very Rev Vincent O'Donohue PE
Blarney
*Donoughmore:* Vacant
*Laken*
Very Rev Patrick T. McSweeney PE,
Glantane
*Honorary Canons*
Very Rev Colman O'Donovan PE
Inniscarra
Very Rev Canon Thomas Browne PE
Youghal
Very Rev Donal O'Mahony PP
Cloyne
Very Rev Jackie Corkery PP, VF
Kanturk
Very Rev Donal Roberts PP, VF
Macroom
Very Rev Michael Fitzgerald PP, VF
Mitchelstown
Very Rev David Herlihy PP
Youghal

## ADMINISTRATION

**College of Consultors**
*Secretary*
Very Rev Canon Gerard Casey PP, VF
Mallow, Co Cork
Tel 022-21149

**Vicar General**
Rt Rev Mgr Eamonn Goold PP, VG
Midleton, Co Cork
Tel 021-4631750

**Episcopal Vicar for the Gaeltacht**
Very Rev Donal O'Brien PP
Ballyvourney, Co Cork
Tel 026-45042

**Financial Administrator**
Rt Rev Mgr Eamonn Goold PP, VG
Midleton
Tel 021-4631750
*Accountants:* Messrs Deloitte & Touche
6 Lapp's Quay, Cork

**Diocesan Administration**
*Diocesan Secretary for Primary Education*
Mr Dan Leo
Tel 086-8162370
*Diocesan Secretary for Second-level Education*
Vacant
*Diocesan Secretary for Canonical Affairs*
Very Rev William O'Donovan PP
Tel 058-59138

**Religious Education**
*Diocesan Director of Adult Faith Development:* Rev Seán Corkery
Mallow, Co Cork
Tel 086-2420240
*Education Commission Secretary:*
Sr Emmanuel Leonard
5 Ashgrove, Cluain Ard, Cobh, Co Cork
Tel 021-4815305
*Diocesan Advisers*
Very Rev Gerard Condon PP
Shanballymore, Mallow, Co Cork
Tel 022-25197
Sr Claire Fox
Darchno, Castleredmond,
Midleton, Co Cork
Tel 021-4631912

**Diocesan Secretary**
Rev James Moore
Cloyne Diocesan Centre, Cobh, Co Cork
Tel 021-4811430

**Administrative Secretary**
Mrs Eileen Greaney
Cloyne Diocesan Centre, Cobh, Co Cork
Tel 021-4811430
Email info@cloynediocese.ie

**Diocesan Archivist**
Pending Appointment

## LITURGY

**Cathedral Master of Ceremonies**
Rev Patrick O'Donoghue
Oliver Villa, Mount Crozier,
Cobh, Co Cork
Tel 021-4201623

**Church Music**
*Director:* Very Rev Gerard Coleman PP
Castlelyons, Co Cork
Tel 025-36372

## PASTORAL

**ACCORD**
*Diocesan Director*
Very Rev Michael Leamy PP
Main Street, Rathcormac, Co Cork
Tel 025-37667

**Communications**
*Diocesan Director*
Rev James Moore CC
Cloyne Diocesan Centre, Cobh, Co Cork
Tel 021-4811430

**Cura**
*Diocesan Director*
Very Rev Francis O'Neill PP
Ballyclough, Mallow, Co Cork
Tel 022-27650

**Diocesan Youth Services**
*Chairman:* Mr Noel O'Connor
*Director:* Mr Brian Williams
Mallow Community Youth Centre,
New Road, Mallow, Co Cork
Tel 022-53526

**Ecumenism**
*Secretary:* Very Rev Aquin Casey Adm
Ravenswood, Fermoy, Co Cork
Tel 025-31414

**Emigrant Apostolate**
*Diocesan Director*
Very Rev William O'Donovan PP
Conna, Co Cork
Tel 058-59138

**Immigrant Apostolate**
*Diocesan Director*
Rev Andrew Carvill CC
Ballynoe, Mallow, Co Cork
Tel 058-59269

**Marriage Tribunal**
(See also Marriage Tribunals section)
*Cork Regional Marriage Tribunal:*
*Officialis:*
Very Rev Gerard Garrett VJ

**Perpetual Eucharistic Adoration**
*Diocesan Directors*
Rev Eamonn McCarthy CC
53 Ros Álainn, Gurteenroe,
Macroom, Co Cork
Tel 085-8585308
Rev Patrick O'Donoghue CC
Oliver Villa, Mount Crozier,
Cobh, Co Cork
Tel 021-4201623

**Pilgrimage Director**
Very Rev Tobias Bluitt PP
Doneraile, Co Cork
Tel 022-24156

**Pioneer Total Abstinence Association**
*Dicoesan Director*
Rev Eamonn McCarthy CC
Macroom, Co Cork
Tel 085-8585308

**Pontifical Mission Societies**
*Diocesan Director*
Rev Micheál Leader CC
Cannon Field, Mallow, Co Cork
Tel 022-21382

**Prayer and Retreat Ministries**
*Facilitator:* Rev Eamonn Barry
St Colman's College, Fermoy, Co Cork
Tel 025-31622 Fax 025-31634

**Prayer Groups**
*Co-ordinator*
Very Rev Canon Michael Fitzgerald PP, VF
Mitchelstown, Co Cork
Tel 025-84090

**Travellers**
*Chaplain:* Very Rev Padraig Keogh PP
Milford, Co Cork
Tel 063-80038

**Trócaire**
Rev Tom McDermott CC
Cloghroe, Co Cork
Tel 021-4385163

**Vicar for Religious**
Very Rev Canon Sean Cotter PP
Charleville, Co Cork
Tel 063-81319

**Vocations**
*Director:* Rev Brian Boyle CC
Kanturk, Co Cork
Tel 029-50061
*Assistant Director:* Rev James Moore CC
Rushbrooke, Cobh, Co Cork
Tel 086-8694744

# PARISHES

*Mensal parishes are listed first. Other parishes follow alphabetically. Historical names are given in parentheses.*

**COBH, ST COLMAN'S CATHEDRAL**
*Sacred Heart, Rushbrooke*
*Sacred Heart, Ballymore*
Very Rev John McCarthy Adm
1 Cathedral Terrace, Cobh, Co Cork
Tel 021-4815619
Very Rev Liam Kelleher PE, CC
Tel 021-4816400
Rev James Killeen CC
Tel 021-4813601
Rev Peter O'Farrell CC
Tel 021-4855983
Cobh, Co Cork
Rev James Moore CC
Rushbrooke, Cobh, Co Cork
Tel 086-8694744
Rev Patrick O'Donoghue CC
Oliver Villa, Mount Crozier,
Cobh, Co Cork
Tel 021-4201623

**FERMOY**
*St Patrick's*
Very Rev Aquin Casey Adm
The Presbytery, Ravenswood,
Fermoy, Co Cork
Tel 025-31414
Rev Mark Hehir CC
Greenhill, Fermoy, Co Cork
Tel 025-33507
Rev P. J. O'Driscoll CC
Monument Hill, Fermoy, Co Cork
Tel 087-6490381

**AGHABULLOGUE**
*St John's, Aghabullogue*
*St Patrick's, Coachford*
*St Olan's, Rylane*
Very Rev Peadar Murphy PP
Aghabullogue, Co Cork
Tel 021-7334035
Rev Brendan Mallon CC
Coachford, Co Cork
Tel 021-7334059

**AGHADA**
*St Erasmus, Aghada*
*St Mary's, Saleen*
*St Mary's, Ballinrostig*
Very Rev Denis Kelleher PP
Church Road, Aghada, Co Cork
Tel 021-4661298
Rev Eamonn Kelleher CC
Jamesbrook, Midleton, Co Cork
Tel 021-4652456

**AGHINAGH**
*St John the Baptist, Bealnamorrive,*
*Rusheen, Ballinagree*
Very Rev John Ryan PP
Aghinagh, Coachford, Co Cork
Tel 026-48037

**BALLYCLOUGH**
*St John the Baptist, Ballyclough, Kilbrin*
Very Rev Francis O'Neill PP
Ballyclough, Mallow, Co Cork
Tel 022-27650
Rev Michael Campbell CC
Kilbrin, Kanturk, Co Cork
Tel 022-48169

**BALLYHEA**
*St Mary's*
Very Rev Patrick Linehan PP
Tel 063-81470

**BALLYMACODA AND LADYSBRIDGE**
*St Mary's, Ladysbridge*
*St Peter in Chains, Ballymacoda*
Very Rev David O'Riordan PP
Ladysbridge, Co Cork
Tel 021-4667173
Rev Kevin Mulcahy CC
Ballymacoda, Co Cork
Tel 024-98110

**BALLYVOURNEY**
*St Gobnait, Ballyvourney*
*Séipéal Ghobnatan, Cúil Aodha*
Very Rev Donal O'Brien PP
Tel 026-45042

**BANTEER (CLONMEEN)**
*St Fursey's, Banteer*
*St Nicholas', Kilcorney*
*St Joseph's, Lyre*
Very Rev William Winter PP
Banteer, Co Cork
Tel 029-56010

**BLARNEY**
*Immaculate Conception, Blarney*
*St Patrick's, Whitechurch*
*St Mary's, Waterloo*
Very Rev William Bermingham PP
Blarney, Co Cork
Tel 021-4385105
Rev Anthony Sheehan CC
5 Lavallin Drive, Whitechurch, Co Cork
Tel 021-4200184

**BUTTEVANT**
*St Mary's, Buttevant*
*St Mary's, Lisgriffin*
Very Rev Michael Fitzgerald PP
Buttevant, Co Cork
Tel 022-23195

**CARRIGTWOHILL**
*St Mary's*
Very Rev Anthony O'Brien PP
Tel 021-4883236
Rev James Greene CC
Tel 021-4853925
Carrigtwohill, Co Cork

**CASTLELYONS**
*St Nicholas', Castlelyons*
*St Mary's, Coolagown*
Very Rev Gerard Coleman PP
Castlelyons, Fermoy, Co Cork
Tel/Fax 025-36372

**CASTLEMAGNER**
*St Mary's*
Very Rev Michael Dorgan PP
Castlemagner, Mallow, Co Cork
Tel 022-27600

**CASTLETOWNROCHE**
*Immaculate Conception,*
*Castletownroche*
*Nativity of Our Lady, Ballyhooly*
Very Rev Patrick Scanlan PP
Castletownroche, Co Cork
Tel 022-26188
Very Rev Donal Broderick PE *(in residence)*
Ballyhooly, Co Cork
Tel 025-39148

**CHARLEVILLE**
*Holy Cross*
Very Rev Canon Seán Cotter PP
Tel/Fax 063-81319
Rev Tom Naughton CC
Tel 063-81437
Charleville, Co Cork

**CHURCHTOWN (LISCARROLL)**
*St Nicholas', Churchtown*
*St Joseph's, Liscarroll*
Very Rev Robin Morrissey PP
Churchtown, Mallow, Co Cork
Tel 022-23385

## CLONDROHID
*St Abina's, Clondrohid*
*St John the Baptist, Carriganimma*
Very Rev Anthony Wickham PP
Clondrohid, Macroom, Co Cork
Tel 026-41014

## CLOYNE
*St Colman's, Cloyne*
*Star of the Sea, Ballycotton*
*Immaculate Conception, Shanagarry*
*St Colmcille's, Churchtown South*
Very Rev Canon Donal O'Mahony PP
Cloyne, Midleton, Co Cork
Tel 021-4652597
Rev Joseph Rohan CC
Ballycotton, Midleton, Co Cork
Tel 021-4647899

## CONNA
*St Catherine's, Conna*
*St Catherine's, Ballynoe*
*St Mary's, Glengoura*
Very Rev William O'Donovan PP
Conna, Mallow, Co Cork
Tel 058 59138
Rev Andrew Carvill CC
Ballynoe, Mallow, Co Cork
Tel 058-59269

## DONERAILE
*The Nativity of the Blessed Virgin Mary, Doneraile*
*Christ the King, Shanballymore*
*St Joseph the Worker, Hazelwood*
Very Rev Tobias Bluitt PP
Tel 022-24156
Rev Aidan Crowley CC
Tel 022-24120
Doneraile, Co Cork

## DONOUGHMORE
*St Lachteen's, Stuake*
*St Joseph's, Fornaught*
Very Rev Jeremiah O'Riordan PP
Donoughmore, Co Cork
Tel 021-7337023
Very Rev Mortimer Downing PE *(in residence)*
Stuake, Donoughmore, Co Cork
Tel 021-7437815

## GLANTANE
*St Peter the Apostle, Dromahane*
*St John the Evangelist, Glantane*
*St Columba, Bweeng*
Very Rev Patrick Buckley PP
Dromahane, Mallow, Co Cork
Tel 022-21244
Rev Chris Donlon CC
Dromore, Mallow, Co Cork
Tel 022-21198
Rev Seán Horgan (MSC) CC *(Pro-tem)*
Glantane, Mallow, Co Cork
Tel 022-47158

## GLANWORTH AND BALLINDANGAN
*Holy Cross, Glanworth*
*Immaculate Conception, Ballindangan*
*Holy Family, Curraghagulla*
Very Rev Michael Corkery PP
Glanworth, Co Cork
Tel 025-38123
Very Rev Canon Finbar Kelleher CC *(Pro tem)*
Ballindangan, Mitchelstown, Co Cork
Tel 025-85563

## GRENAGH
*St Lachteen's, Grenagh*
*St Joseph's, Courtbrack*
Very Rev Micheál Ó Loingsigh PP
Grenagh, Co Cork
Tel 021-4886128

## IMOGEELA (CASTLEMARTYR)
*Sacred Heart, Mogeely*
*St Joseph's, Castlemartyr*
*St Peter's, Dungourney*
*St Lawrence's, Clonmult*
Very Rev John Cogan PP
Castlemartyr, Co Cork
Tel 021-4667133
Rev Finbarr O'Flynn CC
Dungourney, Co Cork
Tel 021-4668406

## INNISCARRA
*St Senan's, Cloghroe*
*St Mary's, Berrings*
*St Joseph's, Matehy*
Very Rev Donal Coakley PP
4 Upper Woodlands, Cloghroe, Co Cork
Tel 021-4385311
Rev Tom McDermott CC
Cloghroe, Blarney, Co Cork
Tel 021-4385163
Rev Gerard Coleman CC
Berrings, Co Cork
Tel 021-7332155

## KANTURK
*Immaculate Conception, Kanturk*
*St Joseph's, Lismire*
Very Rev Canon Jackie Corkery PP, VF
Tel 029-50192
Rev Brian Boyle CC
Tel 029-50061
Kanturk, Co Cork

## KILDORRERY
*St Bartholomew's, Kildorrery*
*St Molaga's, Sraharla*
Very Rev Michael Lomasney PP
Kildorrery, Co Cork
Tel 022-40703

## KILLAVULLEN
*St Nicholas', Kilavullen*
*St Crannacht's, Anakissa*
Very Rev Gerard Condon PP
Shanballymore, Mallow, Co Cork
Tel 022-25197
Very Rev Richard Hegarty PE, CC
Killavullen, Co Cork
Tel 022-26125

## KILLEAGH
*St John the Baptist, Killeagh*
*St Patrick's, Inch*
Very Rev Tim Hazelwood PP
Killeagh, Co Cork
Tel 024-95133

## KILNAMARTYRA
*St Lachtaín's, Kinamartyra*
*Renaniree Church*
Very Rev Richard Browne PP
Kilnamartyra, Macroom, Co Cork
Tel 026-40013

## KILWORTH
*St Martin's, Kilworth*
*Immaculate Conception, Araglin*
Very Rev Donal Leahy PP
Kilworth, Co Cork
Tel 025-27186

## LISGOOLD
*St John the Baptist, Lisgoold*
*Sacred Heart, Leamlara*
Very Rev Denis O'Hanlon PP
Lisgoold, Co Cork
Tel 021-4642363

## MACROOM
*St Colman's, Macroom*
*St John the Baptist, Caum*
Very Rev Canon Donal Roberts PP, VF
Tel 026-21068
Rt Rev Mgr James O'Donnell AP
Tel 026-41042
Rev Eamonn McCarthy CC
Tel 085-8585308
Rev Joseph O'Mahony CC
Tel 026-41092
Macroom, Co Cork

## MALLOW
*St Mary's, Mallow*
*Resurrection, Mallow*
Very Rev Canon Gerard Casey PP, VF
Tel 022-21149
Rev Micheál Leader CC
Tel 022-21382
Rev Paul Bennett CC
Tel 022-50626
Rev Patrick McCarthy CC
Tel 086-3831621
Rev Seán Corkery *(in residence)*
Tel 086-2420240
Bellevue, Mallow, Co Cork

## MIDLETON
*Holy Rosary, Midleton*
*St Colman's, Ballintotas*
Rt Rev Mgr Eamonn Goold PP, VG
Tel 021-4631750
Rev Tadhg O'Donovan CC
Tel 087-6292192
Rev Gerard Cremin CC
Tel 021-4631094
Rev Marek Pecak CC *(in residence)*
Tel 021-4634027
Midleton, Co Cork

**MILFORD**
*Assumption of BVM, Milford*
*St Michael's, Freemount*
*St Berchert's, Tullylease*
Very Rev Pádraig Keogh PP
Milford, Charleville, Co Cork
Tel 063-80038

**MITCHELSTOWN**
*Our Lady Conceived Without Sin,*
*Mitchelstown*
*Holy Family, Ballygiblin, Killacluig*
Very Rev Canon Michael Fitzgerald PP, VF
Tel 025-84090
Very Rev Canon Timothy O'Leary CC
Tel 025-84088
Rev Gabriel Burke CC
Tel 025-84077
Mitchelstown, Co Cork

**MOURNE ABBEY**
*St Michael the Archangel, Analeentha*
*St John the Baptist, Burnfort*
Very Rev Joseph O'Keeffe PP
Burnfort, Mallow, Co Cork
Tel 022-29920

**NEWMARKET**
*Immaculate Conception, Newmarket*
*Holy Spirit, Taur*
Very Rev Francis Manning PP
Newmarket, Co Cork
Tel 029-60999

**RATHCORMAC**
*Immaculate Conception, Rathcormac*
*St Bartholomew's, Bartlemy*
Very Rev Michael Leamy PP
Main Street, Rathcormac, Co Cork
Tel 025-37667
Very Rev Cornelius O'Donnell PE *(in residence)*
Rathcormac, Fermoy, Co Cork
Tel 025-36286

**ROCKCHAPEL AND MEELIN**
*St Joseph's, Meelin*
*St Peter's, Rockchapel*
Very Rev Denis Stritch PP
Meelin, Newmarket, Co Cork
Tel 029-68007

**SHANDRUM**
*St Joseph's, Shandrum*
*St Peter & Paul's, Dromina*
Very Rev Eugene Baker Adm
Dromina, Charleville, Co Cork
Tel 063-70207

**YOUGHAL**
*St Mary's, Our Lady of Lourdes, Holy*
*Family, Youghal; St Ita's, Gortroe*
Very Rev Canon David Herlihy PP
Tel 024-85012
Rev Patrick Winkle CC
Tel 024-92270
Rev Patrick Corkery CC
Tel 024-92336
Rev Damien Lynch CC
Tel 024-92456
Youghal, Co Cork

## PRIESTS OF THE DIOCESE ELSEWHERE

Rev Mgr Michael F. Crotty BA, JCL, D.Ecc.Hist
Section for Relations with States,
Secretariat of State,
00120 Vatican City
Tel 0039-06-69883546
Rev John Keane
Céilí Catholic Community,
Horseleap, Moate, Co Westmeath
Tel 057-9335922
Rev Thomas Lane
Mount Saint Mary's Seminary,
16300 Old Emmitsburg Road,
Emmitsburg,
Maryland 21727-7797, USA
Rev Daniel McCarthy CF
Office of the Chaplain,
James Stephen's Barracks,
Kilkenny City
Rev Danny Murphy
Director, National Centre for Liturgy,
St Patrick's College, Maynooth,
Co Kildare
Tel 01-7083478
Very Rev Mgr Joseph Murphy
Secretariat of State, (Section for Relations with States),
00120 Vatican City
Tel 0039-0669883193
Rt Rev Mgr James O'Brien
Congregation for Divine Worship and the Discipline of the Sacraments,
Vatican City 00120, Italy
Tel 0039-06-69884551
Fax 0039-06-69883499
Rev Donal O'Callaghan
Muintir Mhuire, Ballybutler,
Ladysbridge, Co Cork
Tel 024-98852
Rev Patrick Relihan
Pontificio Collegio Irlandese,
Via dei Santi Quattro 1,
00184 Rome
Tel 0039-06-772631

## RETIRED PRIESTS

Very Rev Donal Broderick PE
Ballyhooly, Co Cork
Tel 025-39148
Very Rev Canon Thomas Browne PE
Southabbey, Youghal, Co Cork
Tel 024-93199
Very Rev John Broderick PE
Killeagh, Co Cork
Tel 024-21841
Very Rev David Buckley PE
Lower Blue Pool, Kanturk, Co Cork
Tel 029-20676

Very Rev Mortimer Downing PE
Stuake, Donoughmore,
Co Cork
Tel 021-7437815
Very Rev Daniel Gould PE
Killavullen, Co Cork
Tel 022-26153
Rev James Hannon
Sandhill Road,
Ballybunion, Co Kerry
Dr Patrick Hannon
Emeritus Professor of Theology,
St Patrick's College, Maynooth,
Co Kildare
Tel 01-6285222
Very Rev Canon Michael Harrington PE
Charleville, Co Cork
Tel 063-21833
Very Rev Martin Heffernan PE, PhD
Skahardgannon,
Doneraile, Co Cork
Tel 022-24570
Very Rev Michael Madden PE
Ballycrennane,
Ballymacoda, Co Cork
Tel 024-98840
Very Rev Canon P. T. McSweeney PE
Nazareth House, Mallow, Co Cork
Tel 022-21561
Rt Rev Mgr Denis O'Callaghan PE
Mallow, Co Cork
Tel 022-21112
Very Rev Peadar O'Callaghan PE
Suaimhneas, Charleville, Co Cork
Tel 086-8054040
Very Rev Cornelius O'Donnell PE
Rathcormac, Fermoy, Co Cork
Tel 025-36286
Very Rev Canon Vincent O'Donohue PE
18 Kilcrea Park,
Magazine Road, Cork
Tel 021-4856881
Very Rev Canon Colman O'Donovan PE
1 Youghal Road, Midleton, Co Cork
Tel 021-4621617
Very Rev Stephen O'Mahony PE
Liscarroll, Mallow, Co Cork
Tel 022-48128
Rev Martin O'Riordan
Lisgoold, Co Cork
Tel 021-4642543
Very Rev Mgr Denis Reidy PE
Teach an tSagairt, Main Street,
Carrigtwohill, Co Cork
Tel 021-4533776
Very Rev Canon John Terry PE
Terriville, Ballylanders,
Cloyne, Co Cork
Tel 021-4646779
Very Rev Canon Patrick Twomey PE
Bellevue, Mallow, Co Cork
Tel 022-55632
Rev Denis Vaughan
45 The Oaks,
Maryborough Ridge,
Douglas, Cork

## RELIGIOUS ORDERS AND CONGREGATIONS

### SISTERS

**ADORERS OF THE SACRED HEART OF JESUS OF MONTMARTRE, OSB**
St Benedict's Priory,
The Mount, Cobh, Co Cork
Tel 021-4811354
*Prioress:* Mother Mary Vianney
Community: 7
Contemplative Benedictines
Residential retreats
*Contact person:* Guest Mistress

**BON SECOURS SISTERS (PARIS)**
38 Norwood Park,
Cobh, Co Cork
Tel 021-4815350
*Co-ordinator:* Sr Paschal Barry
Community: 5
Pastoral Ministry, Care of Elderly

Sisters of Bon Secours,
Bon Secours Convent,
Cobh, Co Cork
Tel 021-4811346
Community: 2
Care of Elderly

**CONGREGATION OF THE SISTERS OF MERCY**
'Trócaire', 6 Castleowen,
Blarney, Co Cork
Tel 021-4381745

Friaryville, Buttevant, Co Cork
Tel 022-23014

Charleville, Co Cork
Tel 063-81276 Fax 063-81830

Kanturk, Co Cork
Tel 029-50068 Fax 029-50332

Dan Corkery Place,
Macroom, Co Cork
Tel 026-42673

Holy Spirit Convent,
Bank Place, Mallow, Co Cork
Tel 022-21780

Convent of Mercy, Bathview,
Mallow, Co Cork
Tel 022-21395

3 Beechwood Grove,
Cluain Ard, Cobh, Co Cork
Tel 021-4815062

5 Ashgrove, Cluain Ard,
Cobh, Co Cork
Tel 021-4815305

41 Ivy Gardens,
Mallow, Co Cork
Tel 022-58036

Convent Bungalow,
Bathview, Mallow, Co Cork
Tel 022-31905

Billkit, Hume's Terrace,
Mallow, Co Cork
Tel 022-21414

Island Road, Longacre,
Newmarket, Co Cork

17 Bromley Court,
Midleton Co Cork

21 Whitepoint Avenue,
Rushbrooke, Co Cork
Tel 021-4811453

**INFANT JESUS SISTERS**
Bellevue, Mallow, Co Cork
Tel 022-43085
Community: 13
Retired sisters

**LITTLE COMPANY OF MARY**
Little Company of Mary, 'Lima',
College Road, Fermoy,
Co Cork
Tel 025-40627
Community: 1

**LORETO (IBVM)**
Loreto Sisters, Copperton,
Corrin View Estate,
Fermoy, Co Cork
Tel 025-33693
Community: 3
Secondary school, pastoral work

**MISSIONARIES OF CHARITY**
St Helen's Convent,
Blarney, Co Cork
Tel 021-4382041
*Superior:* Sr M. Francis (MC)
Community: 4
Residential Treatment Centre

**POOR SERVANTS OF THE MOTHER OF GOD**
St Aloysius' Convent,
Carrigtwohill, Co Cork
Tel 021-4883237 Fax 021-4883955
Community: 10
St Aloysius' Secondary School
Pastoral

**CONGREGATION OF THE SISTERS OF NAZARETH**
Nazareth House, Mallow, Co Cork
Tel 022-21561 Fax 022-21147
Email nazarethmallow@eircom.net
*Superior:* Sr Cataldus Courtney
Community: 9
Home for elderly. Beds: 84

**PRESENTATION SISTERS**
Presentation Convent,
Midleton, Co Cork
Tel 021-4631892
Team Leadership
Community: 12
Primary School Tel 021-4631593
St Mary's Secondary School
Tel 021-4631973

Presentation Primary School,
Doneraile, Co Cork
Tel 022-24512

Presentation Convent,
Fermoy, Co Cork
Tel 025-31248
Team Leadership
Community: 10
Primary School. Tel 025-31550

Presentation Lodge, College Road,
Fermoy, Co Cork
Tel 025-49928
Community: 1

Presentation Convent,
Front Strand, Youghal, Co Cork
Tel 024-93039
*Non-resident Leader*
Sr Mary John Staunton
Community: 5
Primary School. Tel 024-92700

Presentation Sisters, 'Darchno',
Castleredmond, Midleton, Co Cork
Tel 021-4631912
Community: 1

Presentation Primary School,
Mitchelstown, Co Cork
Tel 025-24264
Presentation Secondary School
Mitchelstown, Co Cork
Tel 025-24394

Nano Nagle Centre,
Presentation Sisters,
Ballygriffin, Mallow, Co Cork
Tel 022-26411 Fax 022-26953
Email enquiries@nanonaglebirthplace.ie
Community: 4
Website www.nanonaglebirthplace.ie

**ST JOSEPH OF THE SACRED HEART SISTERS**
Sisters of St Joseph of Sacred Heart,
Penola, 25B Harrison Place,
Charleville, Co Cork
Sr Maura Murphy

## EDUCATIONAL INSTITUTIONS

**St Colman's College (Diocesan College)**
Fermoy, Co Cork
Tel 025-31622 Fax 025-31634
Email stcolmansfermoy@eircom.net
*Priests on Staff*
Rev Eamonn Barry, Facilitator for Prayer
and Retreat Ministries (in residence)
Tel 025-31622/086-8157952

**EDMUND RICE SCHOOLS TRUST**
Midleton, Co Cork Secondary School
Tel 021-4631555 Fax 021-4631917
Email office@midletoncbs.ie
*Principal:* Mr Pat Hurley

Primary School, Baker's Road,
Charleville, Co Cork
Tel 063-89544
*Principal:* Mr. Jerry Murray

Secondary School, Baker's Road,
Charleville, Co Cork
Tel/Fax 063-81789 Staff 063-81669
Email charlevillecbs@gmail.com
*Principal:* Mr Maurice Keohane

Christian Brothers Secondary School,
Mitchelstown, Co Cork
Tel 025-24104 Fax 025-85153
Email cbssecmtown@gmail.com
*Principal:* Dr John A. Desmond

Nagle Rice Secondary School,
Doneraile, Co Cork
Tel 022-24500 Fax 022-24586
Email info@nrss.ie
*Principal:* Ms Bríd Lysaght

## CHARITABLE AND OTHER SOCIETIES

**St Mary's District Hospital**
Youghal, Co Cork

**County Hospital**
Mallow, Co Cork

**Society of St Vincent de Paul**
Conferences at: Ballyvourney,
Castlemartyr, Cobh, Fermoy, Doneraile,
Kanturk, Macroom, Mallow, Midleton,
Mitchelstown, Youghal, Carrigtwohill,
Lisgoold, Aghada, Charleville

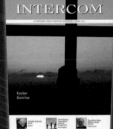

Wood carved

Fiberglass

7 Skerrif Road - Cullyhanna - Co Armagh
N Ireland - BT35 OJG
Tel: (028) 30861522  - Fax: (028) 30868352
From: ROI (048) 30861522 -   Mobile: 077 861 369 85

KEVIN KEARNEY
RELIGIOUS ARTICLES

Email: info@kevinkearney.net - Web : www.kevinkearney.net

# KNOCK

IRELAND'S NATIONAL MARIAN SHRINE
KNOCK, CO. MAYO, IRELAND
T: +353 (0) 94 93 88100    E: INFO@KNOCK-SHRINE.IE
W: WWW.KNOCK-SHRINE.IE

*"A Place of Welcome, Sanctuary and*
*Sacredness for all to gather in*
*Prayer and Worship"*

DAILY MASSES ~ CONFESSIONS ~ COUNSELLING
YOUTH MINISTRY ~ PRAYER GUIDANCE
KNOCK MUSEUM ~ CAFE LE CHEILE
GUIDED TOURS ~ PILGRIMAGE

*Novena to Our Lady of Knock*
Annually 14th - 22nd August
*Daily Ceremonies with Guest Speakers*
*Seminars & Workshops*
*Shop online at www.knock-shrine.ie/shop*

FOUNDED IN 1944
# The Abbey Stained Glass Studios

## ST MEL'S CATHEDRAL, LONGFORD

ABBEY STAINED GLASS STUDIOS HAVE BEEN COMMISSIONED TO SALVAGE THE
REMNANTS OF THE TWO TRANCEPT HARRY CLARKE STUDIOS STAINED GLASS
WINDOWS AFTER THE CATHEDRAL FIRE AND TO RECREATE THE MISSING AREAS
AND RESTORE THESE ARTISTIC TREASURES FOR FR TOM HEALY ADM

# CONTACT: WILLIE MALONE & KEN RYAN

## TELEPHONE (01) 677 7285

18 OLD KILMAINHAM, KILMAINHAM, DUBLIN 8
MOBILE: 087 738 9749

Email enquiries@asgs.ie          Website www.abbeystainedglassstudios.ie

# DIOCESE OF CORK AND ROSS

PATRON OF THE DIOCESE OF CORK
ST FINBARR, 25 SEPTEMBER

PATRON OF THE DIOCESE OF ROSS
ST FACHTNA, 14 AUGUST

INCLUDES CORK CITY AND PART OF COUNTY CORK

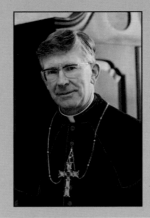

**Most Rev John Buckley DD**
Bishop of Cork and Ross;
born 1939;
ordained priest 1965;
ordained Titular Bishop of
Leptis Magna 29 April 1984 and
installed 6 February 1998

Residence:
Cork and Ross Offices,
Redemption Road, Cork
Tel 021-4301717
Fax 021-4301557

## CATHEDRAL OF ST MARY AND ST ANNE, CORK

The first cathedral on the site of the present Cathedral of St Mary and St Anne was the vision of Bishop Francis Moylan, who was Bishop of Cork from 1786 to 1815. The foundation stone was laid in 1799 and the cathedral was opened in 1808 as the parish church of the single parish then on the northside of the city – hence its local, popular name: the North Chapel. But in June 1820, the heat of the political climate struck the North Chapel when it was maliciously burned during the night.

Bishop John Murphy, one of the famous brewing family, wasted no time in calling a meeting to help restore the cathedral. The people of Cork generously rallied to the call.

The task of rebuilding was given to architect George Pain, who later designed Blackrock Castle, the court house and St Patrick's Church. The interior of the present-day cathedral, including the ornate ceiling, owes much to his creative gifts.

The next major alteration to the cathedral was undertaken in the 1870s when Canon Foley set about building the tower and the great Western Door – now the main door of the cathedral. The tower is higher than that of its more famous neighbour: St Anne's Church, Shandon, home of the much-played bells.

Almost a hundred years later, after the Second Vatican Council, Cornelius Lucey, then Bishop of Cork and Ross, added a further major extension at the other end of the cathedral. This included a completely new sanctuary and a smaller tower, and added capacity to the church, which served an area with a rapidly increasing population.

In 1994, major problems were discovered in the roof and other fabric of the building, which led to the closing of the cathedral for major refurbishment. The bishop, Michael Murphy, decided it was time to renovate the interior of the cathedral too. The task was entrusted to architect Richard Hurley, whose plan for the new interior saw a greater unity being achieved between the sanctuary and the rest of the floor area, and the new altar occupying the central place of prominence. The reordering and renovation was completed in 1996 at a cost of £2.5m and Bishop Murphy presided over its rededication – his last public function before he died a week later.

## CHAPTER

*Dean:* Very Rev Mícheál Ó Dalaigh
*Archdeacon:*
Venerable Kerry Murphy O'Connor
*Precentor:* Very Rev Canon James O'Donovan
*Treasurer:* Very Rev Canon Ted O'Sullivan
*Prebendaries*
*Kilbritain*
Very Rev Canon Bartholomew O'Mahony
*Desertmore*
Very Rev Canon Tadhg Ó Mathúna
*Kilnaglory:* Very Rev Canon Dan Crowley
*Holy Trinity*
Very Rev Canon Richard Hurley
*Kilbrogan*
Rt Rev Mgr Kevin O'Callaghan VG, VF
*Caherlag:* Very Rev Canon Donal Linehan
*Kilanully:* Very Rev Canon George Murphy
*Killaspugmullane*
Very Rev Canon Michael Murphy
*Liscleary:* Very Rev Canon Liam O'Regan
*St Michael:* Very Rev Canon Michael Riordan
*Inniskenny*
Very Rev Canon Vincent Hodnett
*Drimoleague*
Very Rev Canon Liam O'Driscoll

**Honorary Canons**
Very Rev Canon Liam Leader
Very Rev Canon Michael Crowley
Very Rev Canon Thomas Kelleher
Very Rev Canon John K. O'Mahony

## ADMINISTRATION

**Vicars General**
Rt Rev Mgr Kevin O'Callaghan PP, VG, VF
The Presbytery, Lissarda Co Cork
Tel 021-7336053
Rt Rev Mgr Aidan O'Driscoll PP, VG
Clonakilty, Co Cork
Tel 023-8833165

**Vicars Forane**
Rt Rev Mgr Kevin O'Callaghan PP, VG, VF

**Diocesan Secretary**
Rev Thomas Deenihan
Cork & Ross Offices,
Redemption Road, Cork
Tel 021-4301717
Email secretary@corkandross.org

## PASTORAL

**Catechetics**
*Primary:* Sr Geraldine Howard
North Presentation Convent, Cork
Tel 087-6115672
*Second-level:* Ms Mary Scriven
Cork and Ross Offices,
Redemption Road, Cork
Tel 021-4301717
Email catechetics@corkandross.org

**Child Protection**
*Diocesan Director:* Ms Cleo Yates
Diocesan Offices, Redemption Road, Cork
Tel 021-4301717
Email cleo.yates@corkandross.org

**CMCC Marriage Counselling**
*Director:* Dr Colm O'Connor
34 Paul Street, Cork
Tel 021-4275678 Fax 021-4270932
ACCORD, 5 Main Street, Bantry, Co Cork
Tel 027-50272

**CURA**
*Adm. Secretary:* Mrs Sue Curtin
Tel 021-4277544

**Diocesan Education Office**
Cork and Ross Offices,
Redemption Road, Cork
Tel 021-4301717 Fax 021-4301557
*Secretary for Education*
Rev Dr Tom Deenihan
*Secretary:* Ms Clare O'Leary
Email education@corkandross.org

**Immigrants**
Cois Tine, St Mary's, Pope's Quay, Cork
Tel 021-4557760
Email coistine@sma.ie
*Diocesan Chaplain to Polish Community*
Rev Piotr Galus
c/o St Augustine's,
Washington Street, Cork
Tel 021-4275390

**Marriage Tribunal**
(See Marriage Tribunals section)

**Parish Pastoral Development**
1 The Presbytery, Friar's Walk,
Ballyphehane, Cork
Tel 021-4537472
Email ppo@corkandross.org
*Director:* Rev Dr Charles Kiely
Email charles.kiely@corkandross.org
*Co-ordinator:* Sr Karen Kent
Email karen.kent@corkandross.org
*Co-ordinator of Liturgy:*
Rev Christopher Fitzgerald
Email liturgy@corkandross.org

**Pilgrimages**
*Director*
Very Rev Canon James O'Donovan PP
The Presbytery, Ballinlough, Cork
Tel 021-4292296

**Pontifical Mission Society**
Rev Pat Fogarty PP
The Presbytery, Carrigaline, Co Cork
Tel 021-4371684

## PARISHES

*The mensal parishes are listed first. Other
names follow alphabetically. Historical
names are given in parentheses.*

### CATHEDRAL OF ST MARY & ST ANNE
Very Rev Ted Sheehan Adm
Rev Tomás Walsh (SMA) AP
Cathedral Presbytery, Cork
Tel 021-4304325 Fax 021-4304204
*Parish Office:* Tel 021-4304325

### ST PATRICK'S CATHEDRAL, SKIBBEREEN
Very Rev Michael Kelleher Adm
Rev Chris O'Donovan
The Presbytery, Skibbereen, Co Cork
Tel 028-22878/22877
*Parish Office:* Tel 028-22828

### ARDFIELD AND RATHBARRY
Very Rev Patrick J. McCarthy Adm
Ardfield, Clonakilty, Co Cork
Tel 023-8840649

### AUGHADOWN
Very Rev Donal Cahill Adm
Lisheen, Skibbereen, Co Cork
Tel 028-38111

### BALLINCOLLIG
Very Rev George O'Mahony PP
Tel 021-4871206
Ballincollig, Co Cork
Rev James MacSweeney CC
64 Westcourt, Ballincollig, Co Cork
Tel 021-4870434
Rev David O'Connell CC
The Bungalow, St Mary & St John,
Ballincollig, Co Cork
Tel 021-4877161
*Parish Office:* Tel 021-4871206

### BALLINEASPAIG
Very Rev Canon Bartholomew O'Mahony PP
Tel/Fax 021-4346818
Very Rev Tom Clancy AP
Tel 021-4348588
Woodlawn, Model Farm Road,
Ballineaspaig, Cork
*Parish Office:* Tel 021-4344452

### BALLINHASSIG
Very Rev Kieron O'Driscoll PP
Barrett's Hill, Ballinhassig, Co Cork
Tel 021-4885104
*Parish Office:* Tel 021-4805062

### BALLINLOUGH
Very Rev Canon James O'Donovan PP
Tel 021-4292296
Very Rev Canon Michael Crowley PE
Tel 021-4292684
Ballinlough, Cork
*Parish Office:* Tel 021-4294332

### BALLINORA
Very Rev Declan Mansfield PP
Very Rev Canon Donal Linehan PE
Ballinora, Waterfall, near Cork
Tel 021-4873448

### BALLYPHEHANE
Very Rev Canon Michael Murphy PP
Tel 021-4965560
Rev Kazimierz Nawalaniec CC
Tel 021-4310835
*Parish Office:* Tel 021-4311244

### BANDON
Very Rev John Kingston PP
Tel 023-8854666
Rev Anthony O'Mahony CC
Tel 023-8865067
The Presbytery, Bandon, Co Cork
*Parish Office:* Tel 023-8841666

### BANTRY
Very Rev Martin Keohane PP
The Presbytery, Bantry, Co Cork
Tel 027-50096
Rev Sean Crowley CC
The Presbytery, Bantry, Co Cork
Tel 027-50193
*Parish Office:* Tel 027-56398

**BARRYROE**
Rt Rev Mgr Aidan O'Driscoll Adm
The Presbytery, Clonakilty, Co Cork
Tel 023-8833165
Rev Finbarr O'Leary
Lislevane, Bandon, Co Cork
Tel 023-8846171 Fax 023-8846914

**BLACKPOOL/THE GLEN**
Very Rev John O'Donovan PP
Hattons Alley, Blackpool, Cork
Tel 021-4501022
Rev Damien O'Mahony CC
1 Kilmorna Heights, Ballyvolane, Cork
Tel 021-4550425
*Parish Office:* Tel 021-4300518

**BLACKROCK**
Very Rev Kieran Twomey PP
1 Parochial House, Blackrock, Cork
Tel 021-2410519
Very Rev Canon Tadhg Ó Mathúna AP
2 Parochial House, Blackrock, Cork
Tel 021-4358025

**CAHERAGH**
Very Rev Daniel Pyburn PP
The Presbytery, Dromore, Bantry, Co Cork
Very Rev Michael O'Donovan AP
The Presbytery, Caheragh, Co Cork
Tel 028-31126

**CARRAIG NA BHFEAR**
Very Rev Michael Regan PP
Carraig na bhFear, Co Cork
Tel 021-4884119

**CARRIGALINE**
Very Rev Pat Fogarty PP
Tel 021-4371684
Rev Aidan Cremin CC
Tel 021-4372229
Rev Charles Nyhan CC
Cork Road, Carrigaline, Co Cork
Tel 021-4371860
*Parish Office:* Tel 021-4371109

**CASTLEHAVEN**
Very Rev Gerard Thornton (MSC) PP
Parish House, Union Hall,
Skibbereen, Co Cork
Tel 028-34940

**CLOGHEEN (KERRY PIKE)**
Very Rev Canon Liam O'Driscoll Adm
Rev Francis George AP
Church of the Most Precious Blood,
Clogheen, Co Cork
Tel 021-4392122
*Parish Office:* Tel 021-4210788

**CLONAKILTY AND DARRARA**
Rt Rev Mgr Aidan O'Driscoll PP, VG
Tel 023-8833165
Rev Edward J. Collins CC
Tel 023-8833100
The Presbytery, Clonakilty, Co Cork
Rt Rev Mgr Leonard O'Brien PE
O'Rahilly Street, Clonakilty, Co Cork
*Parish Office:* Tel 023-8834441

**CLONTEAD**
An tAth Tomás Ó Murchú SP
Riverstick, Kinsale, Co Cork
Tel 021-4771332

**COURCEYS**
Very Rev Michael O'Mahony PP
Ballinspittle, Co Cork
Tel 021-4778055

**CROSSHAVEN**
Very Rev Patrick Stevenson PP
The Presbytery
Most Rev Patrick Coveney AP
Crosshaven, Co Cork
Tel 021-4831218

**CURRAHEEN ROAD**
Very Rev Cristoír MacDonald PP
Very Rev Dean Micheál Ó Dálaigh AP
The Presbytery, Curraheen Road, Cork
Tel 021-4343535

**DOUGLAS**
Very Rev Canon Ted O'Sullivan PP
Parochial House, Douglas, Cork
Tel 021-4891265
Very Rev Canon Liam O'Regan AP
'Carraigin', Moneygourney, Douglas, Cork
Tel 021-4363998
*Parish Office:* Tel 021-4894128
*St Patrick's, Rochestown:*
Rev Pat O'Mahony (SMA) CC
St Patrick's Presbytery,
Rochestown Road, Cork
Tel 021-4892363
*Parish Office:* Tel 021-4896797

**DRIMOLEAGUE**
Very Rev Liam Crowley PP
Drimoleague, Co Cork
Tel 028-31133

**DUNMANWAY**
Very Rev Timothy Collins PP
Rev John O'Donovan CC
The Presbytery, Dunmanway, Co Cork
Tel 023-8845000
*Parish Office:* Tel 023-8856610

**ENNISKEANE AND DESERTSERGES**
Very Rev Tom Hayes PP
Parochial House, Enniskeane, Co Cork
Tel 023-8847769
*Parish Office:*
parishoffice@enniskeaneparish.ie

**FARRANREE**
Very Rev John Walsh PP
The Presbytery, Farranree, Cork
Tel 021-4393815/4210111
*Parish Office:* Tel 021-4932230

**FRANKFIELD-GRANGE**
Very Rev Christopher Fitzgerald PP
Tel 021-4361711
Rev Ben Hodnett CC
Tel 021-4362377
The Presbytery, Frankfield, Cork
*Parish Office:* Tel 021-4897379

**GLANMIRE**
Very Rev John Newman PP
Glanmire, Co Cork
Tel 021-4866307
Rev John Heinhold (SPS) CC
Springhill, Glanmire, Co Cork
Tel 021-4866306/086-1689292
*Parish Office:* Tel 021-4820654

**GLOUNTHAUNE**
Very Rev John Paul Hegarty PP
Glounthaune, Co Cork
Tel 021-4232881
Rev John Heinhold (SPS) CC
Tel 086-1689292
*Parish Office:* Tel 021-4353366

**GOLEEN**
Very Rev Alan O'Leary PP
The Presbytery, Schull, Co Cork
Tel 028-28898

**GURRANABRAHER**
Very Rev Kevin O'Regan PP
Rev Aidan Vaughan (OFMCap) CC
Ascension Presbytery,
Gurranabraher, Cork
Tel 021-4303655
*Parish Office:* Tel 021-4303655

**INNISHANNON**
Very Rev Finbarr Crowley PP
Innishannon, Co Cork
Tel 021-4775348
*Parish Office:* Tel 021-4776794

**KILBRITTAIN**
Very Rev Jerry Cremin Adm
Kilbrittain, Co Cork
Tel 023-8849637

**KILMACABEA**
Very Rev Patrick O'Sullivan (MSC) Adm
Leap, Co Cork
Tel 028-33177

**KILMEEN AND CASTLEVENTRY**
Very Rev John Collins PP
Rossmore, Clonakilty, Co Cork
Tel 023-8838630

**KILMICHAEL**
Very Rev Martin O'Driscoll Adm
Parochial House,
Inchigeelagh, Co Cork
Tel 028-49838
Rev Patrick O'Donovan CC
Parochial House, Tirelton,
Macroom, Co Cork
Tel 026-46012/086-2578065
*Parish Office:* Tel 085-8706204

**KILMURRY**
Very Rev Bernard Donovan PP
Cloughdubh, Crookstown, Co Cork
Tel 021-7336054
Rt Rev Mgr Kevin O'Callaghan AP, VG, VF
The Presbytery, Lissarda, Co Cork
Tel 021-7336053

## KINSALE
Very Rev Robert Young PP
Tel 021-4774019
Very Rev Canon John K. O'Mahony AP
Tel 021-4773700 Fax 021-4773821
Very Rev Canon Tom Kelleher PE
The Presbytery, Kinsale, Co Cork
*Parish Office:* Tel 021-4773821

## KNOCKNAHEENY/HOLLYHILL
Very Rev Greg Howard PP
The Presbytery, Knocknaheeny, Cork
*Parish Office:* Tel 021-4392459

## THE LOUGH
Very Rev Canon Vincent Hodnett PP
Tel 021-4273821
Rev Paul O'Donoghue CC
Tel 021-4322633
The Lough Presbytery,
St Finbarr's West, Cork

## MAHON
Very Rev Colin Doocey PP
1 The Presbytery,
Holy Cross Church, Mahon, Cork
Tel 021-2414624
Rev John P. O'Riordan (CSsR) CC
2 The Presbytery, Mahon, Cork
Tel 021-4515460
*Parish Office:* 021-4357040

## MONKSTOWN
Very Rev Sean O'Sullivan PP
Rev Con Cronin (SPS) CC
Monkstown, Co Cork
Tel 021-4863267
Rev John Galvin AP
Passage West, Co Cork

## MUINTIR BHÁIRE
Very Rev Gerard Galvin PP
Durrus, Co Cork
Tel 027-61013

## MURRAGH AND TEMPLEMARTIN
Very Rev Bernard Cotter PP
The Presbytery, Newcestown,
Bandon, Co Cork
Tel 021-743800
*Parish Office:* maighratha@gmail.com

## OVENS
Rev Liam Ó hÍcí PP
Ovens, Co Cork
Tel 021-4871180
Rt Rev Mgr Kevin O'Callaghan AP, VG, VF
The Presbytery, Lissarda, Co Cork
Tel 021-7336053

## PASSAGE WEST
Very Rev Sean O'Sullivan PP
New Parochial House,
Monkstown, Co Cork
Tel 021-4863267
Rev John Galvin AP
Tel 021-4841267
Rev Con Cronin (SPS) CC
Passage West, Co Cork

## RATH AND THE ISLANDS
Very Rev Michael Kelleher Adm
North Street, Skibbereen
Tel 028-22878
Rev Chris O'Donovan CC
Tel 028-22877
The Presbytery, Skibbereen, Co Cork
*Weekends:* Rev Peter Queally AP
Oiléan Cléire, Baltimore, Co Cork
Tel 028-39103

## ROSSCARBERY AND LISSAVAIRD
Very Rev John McCarthy PP
Rosscarbery, Co Cork
Tel 023-8848168

## SACRED HEART
Very Rev Terence O'Brien (MSC) PP
Sacred Heart Parish,
Western Road, Cork
Tel 021-4804120 Fax 021-4543823
*Parish Office:* Tel 021-4346711

## ST FINBARR'S SOUTH
Very Rev Canon Richard Hurley PP
South Presbytery, Dunbar Street, Cork
Tel 021-4272989

## ST JOSEPH'S (MAYFIELD)
Very Rev Myles McSweeney (*priest in charge*)
St Joseph's Presbytery, Mayfield, Cork
Tel 021-4501861
*Parish Office:* Tel 021-4503531

## ST JOSEPH'S (BLACKROCK ROAD)
Very Rev Noel O'Leary (SMA) PP
Rev John Horgan (SMA) AP
St Joseph's, Blackrock Road, Cork
Tel 021-4292871
*Parish Office:* Tel 021-4616327

## ST PATRICK'S
Very Rev Canon Dan Crowley PP
The Presbytery, Lower Road, Cork
Tel 021-4502696
Very Rev Canon Liam Leader AP
Tel 021-4500282
The Presbytery, Lower Road, Cork
*Parish Office:* Tel 021-4518191

## ST VINCENT'S, SUNDAY'S WELL
Very Rev Jack Harris (CM) PP
122 Sunday's Well Road, Cork
Tel 021-4304070 Fax 021-4300103
Email parishoffice@corkvinc.com

## SS PETER'S AND PAUL'S
Very Rev Patrick A. McCarthy PP
35 Paul Street, Cork
Tel 021-4276573

## SCHULL
Very Rev Alan O'Leary PP
The Presbytery, Schull
Tel 028-28171

## TIMOLEAGUE AND CLOGAGH
Very Rev Patrick Hickey Adm
The Presbytery, Clogagh,
Timoleague, Co Cork
Tel 023-8839114

## TOGHER
Very Rev Robert Brophy PP
The Presbytery, Togher, Cork
Tel 021-4316700
*Parish Office:* 021-4318899

## TRACTON ABBEY
Very Rev Canon George Murphy PP
Tel 021-4887105
Minane Bridge, Co Cork

## TURNER'S CROSS
Ven Archdeacon Kerry Murphy O'Connor PP
Tel 021-4312466
Rev Billy O'Sullivan CC
Tel 021-4313103
The Presbytery, Turner's Cross, Cork

## UIBH LAOIRE
Very Rev Martin O'Driscoll PP
Parochial House,
Inchigeela, Macroom, Co Cork
Tel 026-49838/087-2691432
Rev Pat O'Donovan CC
Parochial House, Tirelton,
Macroom, Co Cork
Tel 026-46012
*Parish Office:* Tel 087-1446958

## UPPER MAYFIELD
Very Rev Michael Keohane PP
The Presbytery, Our Lady Crowned,
Upper Mayfield, Cork
Tel 021-4503116
*Parish Office:* Tel 021-4551276

## WATERGRASSHILL
Very Rev Donal Cotter PP
Parochial House,
Watergrasshill, Co Cork
Tel 021-4889103
*Parish Office:* Tel 021-4513671

## WILTON, ST JOSEPH'S
Ver Rev Cormac Breathnach (SMA) PP
Rev John Gallagher (SMA) CC
St Joseph's, Wilton, Cork
Tel 021-4341362 Fax 021-4343940
*Parish Office:* smapcc@eircom.net

## INSTITUTIONS AND THEIR CHAPLAINS

### THIRD LEVEL COLLEGES

**Cork Institute of Technology**
*Chaplaincy Office:* 021-4326225
*Chaplaincy Base:* 3 Elton Lawn,
Rossa Avenue, Bishopstown, Cork
Tel 021-4326256
*Chaplain:* Rev Dr David McAuliffe
Tel 021-4346244
*Co-ordinator of Pastoral Care*
Ms Edel Dullea
Tel 021-4326778

Allianz (ⅲ)

**University College, Cork**
*Chaplaincy Office:* Iona,
College Road, Cork
Tel 021-4902459
*Chaplains:* Rev Marius O'Reilly
Rev Tom Forde (OFMCap)
Tel 021-4902704

## HOSPITALS

**Bandon District Hospital**
Bandon, Co Cork
Tel 023-8841403
*Chaplain:* Parish clergy, Bandon

**Bantry Hospital**
Bantry, Co Cork
Tel 027-50133
*Chaplain:* Parish clergy, Bantry

**Bon Secours Hospital**
College Road, Cork
Tel 021-4542807
*Chaplain:* Rev Patrick Flynn (OFMCap)
Tel 021-4546682
Mrs Pat Healy
Sr Claire O'Driscoll
Ms Anne Bermingham
Ms Catherine O'Regan

**Cork South Infirmary
Victoria Hospital Ltd**
Old Blackrock Road, Cork
Tel 021-4926100
*Chaplains*
Sr Catherine Quane
Tel 021-4926100
Rev Ray Riordan
Tel 021-4966555

**Cork University Hospital**
Wilton, Cork
Tel 021-4546400
*Chaplains*
Rev Michael Anthony Buckley
Tel 021-4546400
Rev Thomas Lyons
Tel 021-4546400/4922391
Rev Michael Forde
Tel 021-4546400

**District Hospital**
Skibbereen, Co Cork
Tel 028-21677
*Chaplain:* Parish Clergy

**Marymount Hospice**
Curraheen, Co Cork
Tel 021-4501201
*Chaplain:* Rev John Manley

**Mercy University Hospital**
Grenville Place, Cork
Tel 021-4271971
*Chaplain:* Rev Pierce Cormac

**Mount Carmel Hospital**
Clonakilty, Co Cork
Tel 023-8833205
*Chaplain:* Parish Clergy

**Sacred Heart Hospital**
Kinsale, Co Cork
Tel 021-4772202
*Chaplain:* Parish clergy, Kinsale

**St Anne's Hospital**
Shanakiel, Cork
Tel 021-4541901
*Chaplain:* Rev Francis George

**St Anthony's Hospital**
Dunmanway, Co Cork
Tel 023-8845102
*Chaplain:* Parish clergy, Dunmanway

**St Finbarr's Hospital**
Douglas Road, Cork
Tel 021-4966555
*Chaplains:* Rev Raymond Riordan
Tel 021-4966555
Sr Eleanor Redican
Tel 021-4966553

**St Gabriel's Hospital**
Schull, Co Cork
Tel 028-28120
*Chaplain:* Parish clergy, Schull

**St Joseph's Hospital**
Mount Desert, Lee Road, Cork
Tel 021-4541765

**St Mary's Orthopaedic Hospital**
Baker's Road, Cork
Tel 021-4303264
*Chaplains:* Parish clergy, Gurranabraher
Tel 021-4303655

**St Stephen's Hospital**
Glanmire, Co Cork
Tel 021-4821411
*Chaplain:* Rev Chris Coleman (MSC)

## Port

**Port Chaplaincy**
Rev Desmond Campion (SDB)
Tel 021-4378046

## PRISONS

**Cork Prison**
*Chaplain:* Rev David Murphy
Tel 021-4518820/087-6836567

## PRIESTS OF THE DIOCESE
ELSEWHERE

Rev Dr Pádraig Corkery
St Patrick's College,
Maynooth, Co Kildare
Tel 01-7083639
Rev Dr Gearóid Dullea
St Patrick's College, Maynooth,
Co Kildare
Rev Joseph O'Leary

1-38-16 Ekoda, Nakanoku, Tokyo,
16J0022 Japan
Rev Dr Noel O'Sullivan
St Patrick's College,
Maynooth, Co Kildare

## RETIRED PRIESTS

Rev James Good
Park View, Church Street, Douglas, Cork
Tel 021-4363913
Rev Edmund Keohan
The Bungalow, Turners Cross, Cork
Tel 021-4320592
Rev Michael O'Driscoll
Bushmount, Clonakilty, Co Cork
Tel 023-33991
Very Rev Jeremiah Hyde
The Presbytery, Kinsale, Co Cork
Rev Pat Walsh
Priests House, Aliohill, Enniskeane, Co Cork
Rev Patrick Keating
Drumoleague, Co Cork
Very Rev Tom Riordan
Willow Lawn, Ballinlough, Cork
Very Rev Canon Thomas Kelleher
The Presbytery, Kinsale, Co Cork
Rt Rev Mgr Leonard O'Brien
O'Rahilly Street, Clonakilty, Co Cork
Very Rev Timothy O'Sullivan
Villa Maria, Farnanes, Co Cork
Very Rev Canon Michael Riordan
Mount Desert, Lee Road, Cork
Rev Seosalmh Ó Cochláin
c/o Diocesan Office, Redemption Road,
Cork
Very Rev Denis Cashman
Ballincollig, Co Cork
Very Rev John Cotter PE
c/o Cork & Ross Offices,
Redemption Road, Cork

## RELIGIOUS ORDERS AND
CONGREGATIONS

### PRIESTS

**AUGUSTINIANS**
St Augustine's Priory,
Washington Street, Cork
Tel 021-4275398/4270410 Fax 021-4275381
*Prior:* Rev John Lyng (OSA)
*Bursar:* Rev Tom Sexton (OSA)

**CAPUCHINS**
Holy Trinity,
Fr Mathew Quay, Cork
Tel 021-4270827 Fax 021-4270829
*Guardian:* Rev Dermot Lynch (OFMCap)
*Vicar:* Rev Joseph Nagle (OFMCap)

Capuchin Community,
Monastery Road, Rochestown, Co Cork
Tel 021-4896244 Fax 021-4895915
*Guardian:* Br Paul O'Donovan (OFMCap)
*Vicar:* Rev John Manley (OFMCap)

St Francis Capuchin Franciscan College,
Rochestown, Co Cork
Tel 021-4891417 Fax 021-4361254

## CARMELITES (OCARM)
Carmelite Friary, Kinsale, Co Cork
Tel 021-4772138
Email kinsale@irishcarmelites.com
*Prior:* Very Rev Frank McAleese (OCarm)

## DOMINICANS
St Mary's, Pope Quay, Cork
Tel 021-4502267 Fax 021-4502307
*Prior:* Gerard Dunne (OP)
Email frgd@eircom.net

St Dominic's Retreat House,
Montenotte, Cork
Tel 021-4502520 Fax 021-4502712
*Prior:* Very Rev Benedict Hegarty (OP)
Email benedicthegarty@eircom.net

## FRANCISCANS
Franciscan Friary, Liberty Street, Cork
Tel 021-4270302 Fax 021-4271841
*Guardian:* Rev Bernard Jones (OFM)

## MISSIONARIES OF THE SACRED HEART
MSC Mission Support Centre,
PO Box 23, Western Road, Cork
Tel 021-4545704/4543988
Fax 021-4343587
*Director:* Rev Michael O'Connell (MSC)
Email info@mscmissioncentre.ie
www.mscireland.com

Western Road, Cork
Tel 021-4804120 Fax 021-4543823
*Leader:* Very Rev John Fitzgerald (MSC)
*Parish Priest*
Rev Terence O'Brien (MSC) PP

Carrignavor, Co Cork
Tel 021-4884404
*Leader:* Rev Dan O'Connor (MSC)

Myross Wood Retreat House,
Leap, Skibbereen, Co Cork
Tel 028-33118 Fax 028-33793
*Director & Leader*
Rev Michael Curran (MSC)

(See also Castlehaven Parish)

## REDEMPTORISTS
Scala, Castle Mahon House,
Castle Road, Blackrock, Cork
Tel 021-4358800 Fax 021-4359696
*Co-ordinator:* Rev Noel Kehoe (CSsR)

## ROSMINIANS
Rosmini House, Dunkereen,
Innishannon, Cork
Tel 021-4776268/4776923
Fax 021-4776268

## ST COLUMBAN'S MISSIONARY SOCIETY
No. 2 Presbytery,
Our Lady Crowned Church,
Mayfield Upper, Cork
Tel 021-4508610
Rev Patrick O'Herlihy (SSC)

## ST PATRICK'S MISSIONARY SOCIETY
Kiltegan House, 11 Douglas Road, Cork
Tel 021-4969371
*House Leader:* Rev Jim Barry (SPS)

## SOCIETY OF AFRICAN MISSIONS
St Joseph's Provincial House, Feltrim,
Blackrock Road, Cork
Tel 021-4292871 Fax 021-4292873
Email provincial@sma.ie
*Provincial:* Rev Michael McCabe (SMA)
*Superior:* Rev Colum P. O'Shea (SMA)

Wilton College, Cork
Tel 021-4541069/4541884
Fax 021-4541069
*Superior:* Rev John O'Keeffe (SMA)
*Bursar:* Rev Jarlath Walsh (SMA)

JPIC Office, SMA House, Wilton, Cork
Email justice@sma.ie
*Director:* Mr Gerry Forde

(See also under parishes – St Josephs
(Blackrock Road))

## VINCENTIANS
St Vincent's,
122 Sunday's Well Road, Cork
Tel 021-4304070/4304529 Fax 021-4300103
*Superior:* Very Rev Jack Harris (CM) PP

## BROTHERS

### BROTHERS OF CHARITY
Our Lady of Good Counsel, Lota,
Glanmire, Co Cork
Tel 021-4821012 Fax 021-4821711
*Chaplain:* Fr Paul Thettayil (IC)

### CHRISTIAN BROTHERS
Christian Brothers House,
Ard Mhuire, Fair Hill, Cork
Tel 021-4300879
Community: 4

Churchfield Community Trust,
109 Knockfree Avenue, Cork
Tel 021-4210348
Email cctrust@eircom.net
*Director:* Eileen O'Brien

Sunday's Well Life Centre,
6 Winter's Hill, Sunday's Well, Cork
Tel 021-4304391
Email corklifecentre@gmail.com
*Director:* Don O'Leary

### PRESENTATION BROTHERS
4 Lynbrook, Glasheen Road, Cork
Tel 021-4679007
*Contact:* Br Patrick Fitzgibbon (FPM)

Mardyke House, Cork
Tel 021-4272239
Community: 4
*Contact:* Br DePaul Hennessy (FPM)

Maiville, Turner's Cross, Cork
Tel 021-4272649
Community: 16
*Contact:* Br James O'Donovan (FPM)

Mount St Joseph,
Blarney Street, Cork
Tel 021-4392160
Community: 7
*Contact:* Br Bede Minehane (FPM)

## SISTERS

### BON SECOURS SISTERS (PARIS)
Bon Secours Convent, College Road, Cork
Tel 021-4542416 Fax 021-4542533
*Country Leader:* Sr Marie Ryan
*Co-ordinator:* Sr Martha Leamy
Email marthaleamy@gmail.com
Community: 12

Soilse Community
Mount Finbarr, Glasheen Road, Cork
Tel 021-4964804
*Contact:* Sr Columbanus Byrne
Community: 3

Cnoc Mhuire, Fernhurst,
College Road, Cork
Tel 021-4345410 Fax 021-4345491
*Co-ordinator:* Sr Maureen Condon
Community: 32
Pastoral, community, hospital and parish
ministry

Casa Maria, Fernhurst,
College Road, Cork
Tel 021-4345411
Community: 1
Pastoral and vocation ministry

3 Brookfield Villas, College Road, Cork
Tel 021-4545018
Community: 1

1 Aylsbury Lawn, Ballincollig, Co Cork
Tel 021-4872978
Community: 3
Parish and vocation ministry

20 Old Quarry,
Coolroe, Ballincollig, Co Cork
Tel 021-4810622
Community: 1
Parish ministry

St Enda's, College Road, Cork
Tel 021-4542750

### CONGREGATION OF THE SISTERS OF MERCY
Provincial Offices, Bishop Street, Cork
Tel 021-4975380 Fax 021-4915220
Email provincialoffice@mercysouth.ie
*Provincial:* Sr Miriam Kerrisk

13 Kempton Park, Ballyvolane, Cork
Tel 021-4551375

14 Kempton Park, Ballyvolane, Cork
Tel 021-4551371

49 Hollymount, Blarney Road, Cork
Tel 021-4302123

13 Ronayn's Court,
Rochestown Road, Cork

27 Ronayn's Court,
Rochestown Road, Cork

2 Rowan Hill, Mount Oval Village,
Rochestown, Cork
Tel 021-4366611

Arus Muire, 5 Somerton Drive,
Ballinlough, Cork

19 Sheraton Court,
Glasheen Road, Cork
Tel 021-4318092

144 Dun Eoin, Ballinrea Road,
Carrigaline, Co Cork
Tel 021-4919748
*Contact:* Sr Liz Murphy

2 Woodbrook Grove,
Bishopstown, Cork
Tel 021-4342286

St Marie's of the Isle,
Sharman Crawford Street, Cork
Tel 021-4316029

38 Sheares Street, Cork
Tel 021-4272982

9 Sharman Crawford Street, Cork

1 Kinloch Court, Bishopstown Avenue,
Model Farm Road, Cork
Tel 021-4345332

15 Sheraton Court,
Old Sheen Road, Cork
Tel 021-4315973

St Maries Bungalow, Convent Place,
Crosses Green, Cork
Tel 021-4318628

The Convent, Mercy Hospital,
Grenville Place, Cork
Tel 021-4271971

Convent of Our Lady Crowned,
Boherboy Road, Mayfield, Cork
Tel 021-4500080 Fax 021-4552267

'Lorg Dé', 27 St Joseph's Park,
Boherboy Road, Mayfield, Cork
Tel 021-4508519

38 Ard na Rí, Closes Green,
Farranree, Cork

5 Bellair Close, Douglas Road, Cork
Tel 021-2416120

11 Court Cairn,
Model Farm Road, Cork

79 Welwyn Road, Maryborough Woods,
Douglas, Cork

6 Belgard Downs, Rochestown Road,
Douglas, Cork
Tel 021-4890947

1 Sandymount Drive,
Glasheen Road, Cork
Tel 021-4541613

Cuan na Trócaire, 23 Benvoirlich Estate,
Bishopstown, Cork
Tel 021-4343371

Convent of Mercy, Winter's Hill, Kinsale,
Co Cork
Tel 021-4772165

Avila, Ard na Gaoithe Mór,
Bantry, Co Cork
Tel 027-50035

The Bungalow, Balindeasig,
Belgooly, Co Cork
Tel 021-4887954

Casa Maria Seskin, Bantry, Co Cork
Tel 027-51198

Schull, Co Cork
Tel 028-28189

'Tigh Amos', South Terrace,
Schull, Co Cork
Tel 028-28036

1 Park View, Church Hill,
Passage West, Co Cork
Tel 021-4863121

Arus Muire, McCurtain Hill, Scartagh,
Clonakilty, Co Cork
Tel 023-8833391

Mount Carmel Convent,
Clonakilty, Co Cork
Tel 023-8833072

Apt 1, Arus Muire, McCurtain Hill,
Scartagh, Clonakilty, Co Cork

Apt 2, Arus Muire, McCurtain Hill,
Scartagh, Clonakilty, Co Cork

Apt 3, Arus Muire, McCurtain Hill,
Scartagh, Clonakilty, Co Cork

Apt 4, Arus Muire, McCurtain Hill,
Scartagh, Clonakilty, Co Cork

Studio 26, Arus Muire, McCurtain Hill,
Scartagh, Clonakilty, Co Cork

2 The Drive, Priory Court,
Watergrasshill, Co Cork
Tel 021-4513949

## DAUGHTERS OF CHARITY OF ST VINCENT DE PAUL
St Louise's, Hollyhill House,
Harbour View Road,
Knocknaheeny, Cork
Tel 021-4392762
*Superior:* Sr Sheila Browne
Community: 8
Teaching, parish and social work

## FRANCISCAN MISSIONARIES OF ST JOSEPH
Convent of St Francis,
Blackrock Road, Cork
Tel 021-4317059
*Community Leader:* Sr Mary Coyne
Community: 11

## CONGREGATION OF OUR LADY OF CHARITY OF THE GOOD SHEPHERD
Baile an Aoire,
Leycester's Lane, Montenotte,
Cork
Tel 021-4551200 Fax 021-4550782
Email rgsbaile@eircom.net
Community: 9

'The Well',
Sunday's Well, Cork
Tel 021-4303216 Fax 021-4305250
Email rgsthewell@eircom.net
Community: 1

17 Killiney Heights,
Knockaheeny, Cork
Tel 021-4302660
Email janebmurphy@eircom.net
Community: 2

## INFANT JESUS SISTERS
10 Willow Drive, Muskerry Estate,
Ballincollig, Co Cork
Tel 021-4870625
Community: 2
Pastoral ministry

19 Cherry Walk, Muskerry Estate,
Ballincollig, Co Cork
Tel 021-4873599
Community: 1
Pastoral ministry

St Joseph's,
Model Farm Road, Cork
Tel 021-4342348
Community: 12
House for elderly sisters

## LA RETRAITE SISTERS
22 Salmon Weir,
Hanover Street, Cork
Tel 021-4251100/4276789
*Contact:* Sr Bridget Dunne
Email bridgetdunne@eircom.net

## LITTLE SISTERS OF THE ASSUMPTION
32 St Francis Gardens,
Thomas Davis Street,
Blackpool, Cork
Tel 021-4391407
Email lsablackpool@gmail.com

1 Ballinure Crescent, Mahon,
Blackrock, Cork
Tel 021-4358372
Email lsamahck@eircom.net
Professional services to the family

2–3 College View,
Old Youghal Road, Cork
Tel 021-2357070
Email lsacollegev@gmail.com

## MARIE REPARATRICE SISTERS
Regional House, 6 Knockrea Lawn,
Ballinlough Road, Cork
Tel 087-9860536
Email scoughlansmr@gmail.com
*Regional Superior*
Sr Stephanie Coughlan
7 Knockrea Lawn,
Ballinlough Road, Cork
Tel 021-2357070
Email smrknock@eircom.net
*Contact:* Sr Josephine Gleeson
Community: 4
Parish ministry, retreats, spiritual
direction

## MISSIONARY SISTERS OF THE HOLY ROSARY
7 The Circle, Broadale, Douglas, Cork
Tel 021-4362424
Healthcare, work with refugees
Community: 3

## MISSIONARY SISTERS OF OUR LADY OF APOSTLES
Ardfoyle Convent,
Ballintemple, Cork
Tel 021-4291851 Fax 021-4291105
Email prov@eircom.net
*Provincial:* Sr Mary Crowley
*Sister-in-Charge:* Sr Maura Cranney
Community: 57

## OUR LADY OF THE CENACLE
16 Mervue Lawn,
Ballyvolane, Cork
Tel 021-4508059
Email cenacle@iol.ie
*Contact:* Cenacle Sisters
Community: 2

## POOR CLARES
Poor Clare Colettine Monastery,
College Road, Cork
*Abbess:* Sr Colette-Marie O'Reilly
Community: 8
Contemplatives
Eucharistic Adoration: Daily 7 am-6 pm
Mass times: Monday-Friday 7.30 am
Saturday and Sunday 10 am
Rosary: Monday-Saturday 5.30 pm
Sunday Rosary, Evening Prayer and
Benediction: 5.00 pm

## PRESENTATION SISTERS
Presentation Provincial Office,
The Loft, Bessborough Centre,
Blackrock, Cork
Tel 021-4975190 Fax 021-4975192
Email swpres@eircom.net
*Provincial Leader:* Sr Sheila Kelleher

South Presentation Convent,
Douglas Street, Cork
Tel 021-4975042
Team Leadership
Community: 8

115 Cathedral Road, Cork
Tel 021-4393086
Community: 2

Christ King Convent,
Turner's Cross, Cork
Tel 021-4966552
*Non-resident Leader:* Sr Antonia Murphy
Community: 4
Christ King Girls' Secondary School
Tel 021-4961448

Presentation Convent,
Ballyphehane, Cork
Team Leadership
Tel 021-4321606
Community: 8
Primary School. Tel 021-4315724
Secondary School. Tel 021-4961765

18 The Orchards, Montenotte, Cork
Tel 021-4501456
Community: 2

North Presentation Convent,
Gerald Griffin Street, Cork
Tel 021-4302878
Team Leadership
Community: 17
Primary School Tel 021-4307132
An Gleann Primary School
Tel 021-4504877

Regina Coeli Convent, Farranree, Cork
Tel 021-4302770
*Non-resident Leader:* Sr Jo McCarthy
Community: 9
Aiséirí Chríost Primary School
Tel 021-4301383
Secondary School
Tel 021-4303330

25 Rosbarra, Deerpark,
Friar's Walk, Cork
Tel 021-4323321
Community: 2

Presentation Convent,
Bandon, Co Cork
Tel 023-8841476
Team Leadership
Community: 13
Primary School. Tel 023-8841809
Secondary School. Tel 023-8841814

Presentation Convent,
Crosshaven, Co Cork
Tel 021-4831189
Team Leadership
Community: 6
Primary School. Tel 021-4831646
Coláiste Mhuire Secondary School
Tel 021-4831604

Ardán Mhuire, Togher Road, Cork
Tel 021-4961471
Community: 2

7 Churchfield Terrace West,
Gurranabraher, Cork
Tel 021-4306640
Community: 3

7 Old Waterpark, Carrigaline, Co Cork
Tel 021-4372718
Community: 2

123 Comeragh Park,
The Glen, Cork
Tel 021-4504025
Community: 1

Dóchas, 21 Ashdene,
South Douglas Road, Cork
Tel 021-4897597
Community: 3

44 Castlemeadows,
Mahon, Cork
Tel 021-4515944
Community: 2

44 Ashbrook Heights, Lehenaghmore,
Togher, Cork
Tel 021-4320006
Community: 2

78 Grange Way, Douglas, Cork
Tel 021-4899704
Community: 1

5 Abbey View, Nano Nagle Walk,
Douglas Street, Cork
Tel 021-4322097
Community: 1

18 Convent View, Nano Nagle Walk,
Douglas Street, Cork
Tel 021-4915380
Community: 1

Apt 15, Ard na Rí, Closes Green,
Farranree, Cork
Tel 021-4909704
Community: 1

Apt 20, Ard na Rí, Closes Green,
Farranree, Cork
Tel 021-4397329
Community: 1

Apt 37, Ard na Rí, Closes Green,
Farranree, Cork
Tel 021-4309262
Community: 1

Apt 39, Ard na Rí, Closes Green,
Farranree, Cork
Tel 021-4309262
Community: 1

'Fallsway', Boreenmanna Road,
Ballinlough, Cork
Tel 021-4809008
Community: 2

## RELIGIOUS SISTERS OF CHARITY
St Vincent's Convent,
St Mary's Road, Cork
Tel 021-4211176/4211238
Various apostolic ministries

St Anthony's Convent, Vincent's Avenue,
St Mary's Road, Cork
Tel 021-4308162

**SACRED HEARTS OF JESUS AND MARY**
Blackrock, Cork
Tel 021-4936200
*Community Leader:* Sr Alexander

**URSULINES**
Ursuline Convent, Blackrock, Cork
Tel 021-4358663 Fax 021-4356077
Email corckucb@eircom.net
Community: 11
*Local Leader:* Sr Jean Browne
Primary School
Tel 021-4358476 Fax 021-4359073
Secondary School
Tel 021-4358012 Fax 021-4358012

58 Meadowgrove, Blackrock, Cork
Tel 021-4357249
Sr Máire O'Donohoe
Email mariefod55@eircom.net
Community: 1
Pastoral Ministry

## EDUCATIONAL INSTITUTIONS

**Christ the King Secondary School**
South Douglas Road, Cork
Tel 021-4961448 Fax 021-4314563

**Christian Brothers College, Cork**
Tel 021-4501653 Fax 021-4504113

**Coláiste Chríost Rí, Cork**
Tel 021-4274904 Fax 021-4964784

**Coláiste an Spioraid Naoimh**
Bishopstown, Cork
Tel 021-4543790 Fax 021-4543625

**Deerpark CBS**
St Patrick's Road, Cork
Tel 021-4962025 Fax 021-4311792

**EDMUND RICE SCHOOLS TRUST**
Scoil Mhuire Fatima
North Monastery, Cork
Tel 021-4305020
*Principal:* Mr Carl O'Brien

Christian Brothers Secondary School,
North Monastery, Cork
Tel 021-4301318 Fax 021-4307994
Email northmonastery.ias@eircom.net
*Principal:* Mr Mick Evans

Gaelcholáiste Mhuire (A.G.)
An Mhainistir Thuaidh, Corcaigh
Tel 021-4307579 Fax 021-4288011
Email info@gcm.ie
*Principal:* Dónal Ó Buachalla

Scoil Cholmcille, Blarney Street, Cork
Tel/Fax 021-4397000
Email blarneystreetcbs@gmail.com
*Principal:* Mr Billy Lynch

Deerpark CBS,
St Patrick's Road, Cork
Tel 021-4962025
Email deerparkcbs@eircom.net
*Principal:* Mr Kevin Barry

Christian Brothers College
Preparatory School,
Sidney Hill, Wellington Road, Cork
Tel 021-4500067
Email enquire@cbccork.ie
*School Head:* Mr Tony McCarthy

Christian Brothers College,
Sidney Hill, Wellington Road, Cork
Tel 021-4501653
Email enquire@cbccork.ie
*Principal:* Dr L. Jordan

**Mercy Heights Secondary School**
Skibbereen, Co Cork
Tel 028-21550 Fax 028-21451

**Mercy Sisters Secondary School**
Roscarbery, Co Cork
Tel 023-8848114 Fax 023-8848520

**Mount Mercy College**
Model Farm Road, Cork
Tel 021-4542366 Fax 021-4542709

**North Monastery,**
Our Lady's Mount, Cork
Tel 021-4301318 Fax 021-4309891

**Presentation College, Cork**
Tel 021-4272743 Fax 021-4273147

**Presentation Convent**
Bandon, Co Cork
Tel 023-8841814 Fax 023-8841385

**Presentation Convent Secondary School**
Crosshaven, Co Cork
Tel/Fax 021-4831604

**Presentation Secondary School**
Ballyphehane, Cork
Tel 021-4961765/4961767
Fax 021-4312864

**Regina Coeli Convent Secondary School**
Farranree, Cork
Tel 021-4303330 Fax 021-4303411

**Sacred Heart College**
Carrig na bhFear, Co Cork
Tel 021-4884104 Fax 021-4884442

**Sacred Heart Secondary School**
Clonakilty, Co Cork
Tel 023-8833737 Fax 023-8833908

**St Aloysius School, Cork**
Tel 021-4316017 Fax 021-4316007

**St Angela's College, Cork**
Tel 021-4500059 Fax 021-4504515

**St Fachtna's Secondary School**
Skibbereen, Co Cork
Tel 028-21454 Fax 028-21256

**St Francis Capuchin College,**
Rochestown, Co Cork
Tel 021-4891417 Fax 021-4361254

**St Vincent's Secondary School, Cork**
Tel 021-4307730 Fax 021-4307252

**Ursuline Convent Secondary School**
Blackrock, Cork
Tel/Fax 021-435801

# DIOCESE OF DERRY

PATRONS OF THE DIOCESE
ST EUGENE, 23 AUGUST; ST COLUMBA, 9 JUNE

INCLUDES ALMOST ALL OF COUNTY DERRY,
PARTS OF COUNTIES DONEGAL AND TYRONE
AND A VERY SMALL AREA ACROSS THE RIVER BANN IN COUNTY ANTRIM

**Most Rev Donal McKeown DD**
Bishop of Derry
Born 12 April 1950; ordained
priest 3 July 1977; appointed
Auxiliary Bishop of Down and
Connor 21 February 2001;
ordained Bishop 29 April 2001,
appointed Bishop of Derry 25
February 2014; installed 6 April
2014

Office Address:
Diocesan Offices,
St Eugene's Cathedral,
Francis Street, Derry BT48 9AP
Tel 028-71262302
Fax 028-71371960
Email office@derrydiocese.org

## ST EUGENE'S CATHEDRAL, DERRY

In the 1830s, following the Catholic Emancipation Act of 1829, the Catholic community of Derry was able to contemplate building a cathedral. In the summer of 1838, a number of Catholics of the city met with the then Bishop of Derry, Peter McLaughlin, to consider such a project. Over the next thirteen years a weekly collection was made in the city and eventually, on 26 July 1851, the foundation stone was laid by Bishop Francis Kelly.

The construction of the cathedral was sporadic as the funds became available over twenty-five years, and owing to the difficulty in raising money, it was agreed to postpone the building of the tower, belfry and spire until a later date. Due to the lack of funds in the diocese, the windows were initially all of plain glass, and it was only in later years that the stained glass was installed.

J. J. McCarthy (1817–1882) was the architect commissioned to design St Eugene's Cathedral. He was one of the most outstanding church architects in Ireland in his time and he designed many churches and convents all over the country, including St Patrick's Cathedral, Armagh, St Macartan's Cathedral, Monaghan and the Cathedral of the Assumption, Thurles.

The actual construction work took twenty-two years to complete, at a cost of £40,000. It was not until 1873 that the building was brought to a stage where it could be dedicated and used for liturgical celebrations. The cathedral was dedicated by Bishop Francis Kelly on 4 May 1873.

In 1899 it was decided to add a spire to the tower, which was estimated to cost £15,000. The spire was completed on 19 June 1903, and on 27 June the eight-foot-high granite cross was put in position by Fathers John Doherty and Lawrence Hegarty. The full complement of stained-glass windows was achieved in the Spring and Autumn of 1896 at a cost of £2,270. The ten bells of the cathedral first rang out on Christmas Eve, 1902.

St Eugene's was solemnly consecrated on 21 April 1936, the seventh cathedral in Ireland to be consecrated, and the event is celebrated annually on 21 April.

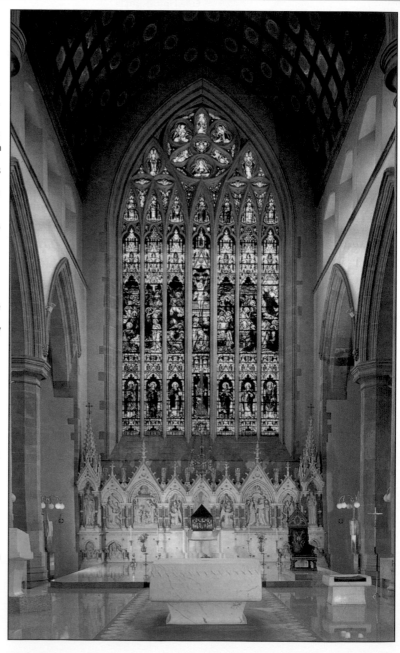

## Most Rev Seamus Hegarty DD
Retired Bishop of Derry;
born 1940;
ordained priest 19 June 1966;
ordained Bishop of Raphoe
28 March 1982;
appointed Bishop of Derry
1 October 1994;
installed 6 November 1994; retired as
Bishop of Derry 23 November 2011
Residence: Sappagh, Muff, Co Donegal

## Most Rev Francis Lagan DD
Retired Bishop of Sidnacestre and
Auxiliary Bishop of Derry; born 1934;
ordained priest 19 June 1960; ordained
Bishop 20 March 1988; Retired as
Auxiliary Bishop of Derry 6 May 2010
Residence: 9 Glen Road, Strabane,
Co Tyrone BT82 8BX
Tel 028-71884533 Fax 028-71884551
Email fblagan@gotadsl.co.uk

## Most Rev Edward Daly DD
Retired Bishop of Derry: born 1933;
ordained priest 16 March 1957; ordained
Bishop of Derry 31 March 1974; retired
as Bishop of Derry 26 October 1993
Residence: 9 Steelstown Road,
Derry BT48 8EU
Tel 028-71359809 Fax 028-71357098
Email Edward.Daly@btinternet.com

## ADMINISTRATION

### Vicars General
Rev Paul McCafferty VG
Rev Andrew Dolan VG

### Chancellor
Very Rev Francis Bradley PP

### College of Consultors
Rt Rev Mgr Joseph Donnelly PP, VF
Rt Rev Mgr Bryan McCanny PP
Very Rev Frank Bradley PP
Very Rev John Farren PP
Very Rev Michael Canny PP
Very Rev John Cargan PP
Very Rev Patrick McGoldrick CC

### Vicars Forane
*Derry City Deanery*
Very Rev Colum Clerkin PP, VF
*Co Derry Deanery*
Very Rev Kieran O'Doherty PP, VF
*Co Tyrone Deanery*
Rt Rev Mgr Joseph Donnelly PP, VF
*Inishowen Deanery*
Very Rev James McGonagle Adm, VF

### Diocesan Archives
*Archivists:* Most Rev Edward Daly DD
9 Steelstown Road,
Derry BT48 8EU
Tel 028-71359809
Email edward.daly@btinternet.com

## Derry Diocesan Trust
(St Columb's Diocesan Trust is Trustee of
the Derry Diocesan Trust)
*Director:* Most Rev Donal McKeown DD

Very Rev James McGonagle Adm, VF
Rev Aidan Mullan PP
Very Rev John Cargan PP
Very Rev Michael Canny PP
Ms Caroline McGonagle
Mr Shaun McElhinney
Ms Carmel McGilloway
Mr Tony Jackson
Ms Liz Hughes
*Secretary:* Teresa McMenamin

### Diocesan Office
*Bishop*
Most Rev Donal McKeown DD
Rev Paul McCafferty VG
*Administrative & Financial Secretary*
Ms Teresa McMenamin
Diocesan Offices,
St Eugene's Cathedral,
Francis Street, Derry BT48 9AP
Tel 028-71262302 Fax 028-71371960
Email office@derrydiocese.org

### Diocesan Notaries
Rev Kevin McElhennon PP
Very Rev Francis Bradley PP
Very Rev Colum Clerkin PP, VF
Rev Eamonn Graham PP

### Priest Penitentiary
Very Rev Kieran O'Doherty PP, VF
34 Moneysharvin Road, Swatragh
Co Derry BT46 5PY
Tel 028-79401236

## CATECHETICS EDUCATION

### Catholic Primary School Managers' Association
*Contact:* Rev Peter Devlin PP
Parochial House,
Malin, Co Donegal
Tel 074-9142022

### Catechetical Centre
Derry Diocesan Catechetical Centre,
The Gate Lodge, 2 Francis Street,
Derry BT48 9DS
Tel 028-71264087 Fax 028-71269090
Email ddcc@derrydiocese.org
*Acting Director:* Rev Paul Farren
*Adviser:* Miss Thérèse Ferry
*Youth Co-ordinator:* Niamh Moore
*Secretary:* Anne Marie Hickey

## LITURGY

### Diocesan Master of Ceremonies
Rev Peter O'Kane
Diocesan Pastoral Centre,
164 Bishop Street,
Derry BT48 6UJ
Tel 028-71362475

## PASTORAL

### ACCORD
*Derry Centre:* Diocesan Pastoral Centre,
164 Bishop Street, Derry BT48 6UJ
Tel 028-71362475 Fax 028-71260970
*Omagh Centre:* Mount St Columba
Pastoral Centre, 48 Brook Street, Omagh,
Co Tyrone BT78 5HD
Tel 028-82242439
*Maghera Centre:* Pastoral Centre,
159 Glen Road, Maghera
Tel 028-79642983
*Inishowen Centre:* Pastoral Centre
Church Road, Carndonagh, Co Donegal
Tel 074-9374103

### Chaplain to the Deaf
Rev Eamon Graham PP
42 Glenedra Road, Feeny,
Dungiven, Co Derry BT47 4TW
Tel 028-77781223

### Charismatic Renewal
*Director:* Rev Seamus Kelly PP
40 Derrynoid Road, Draperstown,
Co Derry BT45 7DN
Tel 028-79628376

### Columba Community
*Chaplain:* Rev Neal Carlin
St Anthony's, Dundrean,
Burnfoot, Co Donegal
Tel 074-9368370
Email sarce@eircom.net
Columba House, 11 Queen Street,
Derry BT48 7E6
Tel 028-71262407

### Communications
*Media Liaison Person:*
Very Rev Michael Canny PP
32 Chapel Road, Derry BT47 2BB
Tel 028-71342303
Email michaelcanny1958@gmail.com

### Ecumenism
*Director:* Rev Eamon McDevitt PP
78 Lisnaragh Road, Dunamanagh,
Strabane, Co Tyrone BT82 0QN
Tel 028-71398212

### Family Care Society (NI)
Colmcille House, 1A Millar Street,
Derry BT48 6SU
Tel 028-71368592

### Library/Museum
*Curators:* Rev John R. Walsh CC
Buncrana
Rev Brian McGoldrick PP
Doneyloop

### Marriage Tribunal
(See Marriage Tribunals section)

**LECKPATRICK (LECKPATRICK AND PART OF DONAGHEADY)**
*St Mary's, Cloughcor*
Rev Michael Porter PP
Parochial House,
447 Victoria Road,
Ballymagorry, Strabane,
Co Tyrone BT82 0AT
Tel 028-718802274 Fax 028-71884353
Email leckpatrick.rc@virgin.net

**LIFFORD (CLONLEIGH)**
*St Patrick's, Murlog*
Rev Edward Kilpatrick PP
Murlog, Lifford, Co Donegal
Tel 074-9142022
*Parish Office:* St Patrick's Church,
Murlog, Lifford, Co Donegal
Tel/Fax 074-9142001
Email clonleighparish@eircom.net

**LIMAVADY (DRUMACHOSE, TAMLAGHT, FINLAGAN AND PART OF AGHANLOO)**
*St Mary's, Irish Green Street*
Rt Rev Mgr Bryan McCanny PP
119 Irish Green Street, Limavady,
Co Derry BT49 9AB
Tel 028-77765649
Fax 028-77765290
Email parishoflimavady@btinternet.com
Rev James Devine CC
20 Loughermore Road,
Ogill, Ballykelly,
Co Derry BT49 9PD
Tel 028-77762721

**MAGHERA**
*St Patrick's, Glen*
Very Rev Patrick Doherty PP
159 Glen Road, Maghera,
Co Derry BT46 5JN
Tel 028-79642496 Fax 028-79644593
Email accordmaghera@btconnect.com
Rev Brian O'Donnell CC
157 Glen Road, Maghera,
Co Derry BT46 5JN
Tel 028-79642359
*Parish Office:* 159A Glen Road,
Maghera, Co Derry BT46 5JN
Tel 028-79642983

**MAGILLIGAN**
*St Aidan's*
Rev Francis O'Hagan PP
71 Duncrun Road, Bellarena,
Limavady, Co Derry BT49 0JD
Tel 028-77750226
Email frohagan@aol.com

**MALIN (CLONCA)**
*St Patrick's, Aghaclay*
Rev Peter Devlin PP
Malin, Co Donegal
Tel 074-9370615
Email pnd4680@eircom.net
Rev Charles Logue CC
Malin Head, Co Donegal
Tel 074-9370134

**MELMOUNT (MOURNE)**
*St Mary's, Melmount, Strabane*
Rev Michael Doherty PP
39 Melmount Road, Strabane,
Co Tyrone BT82 9EF
Tel 028-71882648
*Parish Office:* Melmount Parish Centre,
Melmount Road, Strabane,
Co Tyrone BT82 9EF
Tel 028-71383777 Fax 028-71886469
Email melparish@aol.com

**MOVILLE (MOVILLE LOWER)**
*St Mary's, Ballybrack*
Rev Patrick O'Hagan PP
Tel 074-9382057
Rev Patrick McGoldrick CC
Tel 074-9382102
Parochial House, Moville, Co Donegal
Email movilleparish@gmail.com

**NEWTOWNSTEWART (ARDSTRAW EAST)**
*St Eugene's, Glenock*
Rev Gerard Sweeney PP
41 Moyle Road, Newtownstewart,
Co Tyrone BT78 4AP
Tel 028-81661445 Fax 028-81662462
Email gerardsweeney@gmail.com

**OMAGH (DRUMRAGH)**
*St Mary's, Drumragh*
Rt Rev Mgr Joseph Donnelly PP, VF
52 Brook Street, Omagh,
Co Tyrone BT78 5HE
Tel 028-82243011 Fax 028-82252149
Email jopd@drumraghparish.com
Rev Dermot McGirr CC
48 Brook Street, Omagh,
Co Tyrone BT78 5HE
Tel 028-82242092
Rev Piotr Zimnoch CC
50 Brook Street, Omagh,
Co Tyrone BT78 5HE
*Parish Office:* 48 Brook Street,
Omagh, Co Tyrone BT78 5HE
Tel 028-82442092 Fax 028-82252149

**PLUMBRIDGE (BADONEY UPPER)**
*Sacred Heart*
Very Rev Brian Donnelly PP
Parochial House, Plumbridge,
Omagh, Co Tyrone BT79 8EF
Tel 028-81648283
Email bpdey@aol.co.uk

**SION MILLS**
*St Theresa's*
Rev Peter McLaughlin PP
143 Melmount Road, Sion Mills,
Strabane, Co Tyrone BT82 9EX
Tel 028-81658264

**STRABANE (CAMUS)**
*Immaculate Conception*
Rev Declan Boland PP
44 Barrack Street, Strabane,
Co Tyrone BT82 8HD
Tel 028-71883293 Fax 028-71882615
Email declan@strabaneparish.com

**STRATHFOYLE (STRATHFOYLE, ENAGH LOUGH)**
*St Oliver Plunkett*
Served by the Parish of Glendermot
Parochial House, Parkmore Drive,
Strathfoyle, Co Derry BT47 1XA
Tel 028-71342303

**SWATRAGH**
*St John the Baptist*
Very Rev Kieran O'Doherty PP, VF
34 Moneysharvin Road, Swatragh,
Maghera, Co Derry BT46 5PY
Tel 028-79401236
Email kodoherty@btinternet.com

**WATERSIDE (GLENDERMOTT)**
*St Columb's*
Very Rev Michael Canny PP
Rev Roland Colhoun CC
Rev Chris Ferguson CC
Rev Joseph Varghese CC
Parochial House, 32 Chapel Road,
Waterside, Derry BT47 2BB
Tel 028-71342303 Fax 028-71345495
Email secretary@watersideparish.net
Website www.watersideparish.org

## INSTITUTIONS AND THEIR CHAPLAINS

**Altnagelvin Hospital, Derry**
**Waterside General Hospital**
Rev Neil Farren PP
Rev Chris Ferguson CC
Parochial House, 32 Chapel Road,
Waterside, Derry BT47 2BB
Tel 028-71342303

**Community Hospital, Lifford**
Rev Edward Kilpatrick PP
Townparks, Lifford, Co Donegal
Tel 074-9142001

**District Hospital, Carndonagh**
Rev Con McLaughlin PP
Parochial House, Carndonagh
Tel 074-9174104

**Foyle Hospice**
Most Rev Edward Daly DD
9 Steelstown Road,
Derry BT48 8EU
Tel 028-71359809

**Gransha Hospital, Derry**
Rev Neil Farren PP
Rev Chris Ferguson CC
Parochial House, 32 Chapel Road,
Waterside, Derry BT47 2BB
Tel 028-71342303

**Magilligan Prison**
Point Road, Magilligan,
Limavady BT49 OLR, Co Derry
Rev Francis O'Hagan PP
Tel 028-77763311

**Nazareth House**
Fahan, Co Donegal
Rev Neil McGoldrick PP
Tel 074-9360151

**Allianz (ⅰ)**

Tyrone County Hospital, Omagh
Rev Kevin McElhennon PP

Tyrone and Fermanagh Hospital, Omagh
Rev Kevin McElhennon PP

University of Ulster
Magee College, Derry
Rev Brendan Collins CC
6 Victoria Place, Derry
Tel 028-71262302

## PRIESTS OF THE DIOCESE ELSEWHERE

Rev Manus Bradley
3690 Croissant Oscar,
Brossard, Quebec J4Y 2JB
Tel 00-1450-8127858
Rt Rev Mgr Brendan Devlin MA, DD
St Patrick's College,
Maynooth, Co Kildare
Tel 01-6285222
Rev Paul Fraser
c/o Our Lady Queen of Heaven,
111 Portsmouth Road, Frimley,
Camberley, Surrey GU16 7AA
Tel 01276-504876
Rev James McGrory
Armagh Regional Marriage Tribunal,
15 College Street,
Armagh BT61 9BT
Tel 028-37524537

## RETIRED PRIESTS

Rev Bernard Bryson PEm
Rev John Farrell PEm
Rev George McLaughlin PEm
Rev Colm Morris PEm
Rev John Ryder PEm
Rev Michael Keaveny PEm
Rev Michael Collins PEm
Rev John Doherty PEm
Rev Patrick Crilly PEm
Rev Joseph O'Conor PEm
Rt Rev Mgr Ignatius McQuillan PEm
Rev Michael McEldowney PEm
Rev Michael Mullan PEm
Rev Liam Donnelly PEm
Rev Seamus O'Connell PEm
Rev Brendan Doherty PEm

## RELIGIOUS ORDERS AND CONGREGATIONS

## PRIESTS

**CARMELITES (OCD)**
St Joseph's Retreat House,
Termonbacca, Derry BT48 9XE
Tel 028-71262512 Fax 028-71373589
*Prior:* Rev Sean Conlon (OCD)
Community: 4

**FRANCISCAN FRIARS OF THE RENEWAL (CFR)**
St Columba Friary,
Fairview Road, Derry BT48 8NU
Tel 028-71419980 Fax 028-71417652
*Local Servant (Superior)*
Rev Columba Jordan (CFR)

**SALVATORIANS**
'Naomh Mhuire',
Upper Slavery, Buncrana, Co Donegal
Tel 074-9322264
Rev Malachy McBride (SDS)

## BROTHERS

**CHRISTIAN BROTHERS**
20 Kevlin Road, Omagh,
Co Tyrone BT78 2LD
Tel 028-82242103
*Community Leader:* Br Tom Gough
Community: 3

## SISTERS

**CONGREGATION OF THE SISTERS OF MERCY**
Thornhill Convent,
121 Culmore Road, Derry BT48 8JF
Tel 028-71352209
Community: 4

3 Steelstown Road,
Derry BT48 8EU
Tel 028-71351432
Community: 3

22 Newtownkennedy Street,
Strabane, Co Tyrone BT82 8HT
Tel 028-71882269
Community: 7

8A Sheelin Park, Ballymagroarty,
Derry BT48 0PD
Tel 028-71260398
Community: 3

6 Ballycolman Road, Melmount,
Strabane, Co Tyrone BT82 9PH
Tel 028-71885913
Community: 3

60 Steelstown, Derry BT48 8JA
Tel 028-71352300

North Gate Lodge,
125 Culmore Road, Derry BT48 8JF
Tel 028-71350014

1 Lawrence Hill, Derry BT48 7NJ
Tel 028-71269854
Community: 5

19 Towncastle Road,
Strabane, Co Tyrone BT82 0AH
Tel 028-71419891

3 Milestone Way,
Fintona Road, Tattyreagh,
Omagh, Co Tyrone BT78 2LY
Sr Mary Daly RSM
Sr Maura Twohig PBVM

32 Berkeley Heights, Killyclogher,
Omagh, Co Tyrone BT79 7PR
Tel 028-82243329

44 Ballynagard Crescent,
Culmore, Derry BT48 8JR
Tel 028-71355776

31 Belmont Crescent,
Derry BT48 7RR
Tel 028-71358758

16 Papworth Avenue,
Derry BT48 8PT
Tel 028-71358827
Community: 6

27 Rockfield, Derry BT48 8AU
Tel 028-71350361

4 Culmore Park, Culmore Road,
Derry BT48 7AN
Tel 028-71350379

**CONGREGATION OF ST JOHN**
Sisters of St John
10 Belvoir Park, Culmore, Derry
Tel 028-71353414
*Prioress:* Sr Mary Magdalen

**CONGREGATION OF OUR LADY OF CHARITY OF THE GOOD SHEPHERD**
38 Dungiven Road, Waterside,
Derry BT47 6BW
Tel 028-71342429 Fax 028-71341711
Email rgsderry@hotmail.com
*Leader:* Sr Breda O'Connell
Community: 10

45 Virginia Court,
Gobnascale, Waterside,
Derry BT47 2DX
Tel 028-71345127 Fax 028-71312621
Email vircourt@yahoo.com
Community: 2

**HOLY FAMILY OF BORDEAUX SISTERS**
Holy Family Convent,
2a The High Street, Draperstown,
Co Derry BT45 7AA
Tel 028-79628030
*Contact:* Sr Rose Devlin
Community: 1
Pastoral work, urban and rural community development, community relations work, religious education of both able-bodied and disabled adults.

**LORETO (IBVM)**
Convent Grammar, Omagh BT78 1DL
Tel 028-82243633
Primary School,
Brookmount Road, Omagh
Tel 028-82243551

Allianz (Ⅲ)

Loreto Community, Coleraine,
Co Derry BT51 3JZ
Tel 028-70344426
*Co-Leaders*
Sr Mary Jo Corcoran, Sr Louise O'Sullivan
Community: 9
Loreto College, Coleraine BT51 3JZ
Tel 028-70343611

Loreto Sisters, 30 Buskin Way, Coleraine,
Co Derry BT51 3BD
Tel 028-70358065
Community: 2
Educational and pastoral work

**CONGREGATION OF THE SISTERS OF NAZARETH**
Nazareth House, Fahan,
Lifford, Co Donegal
Tel 074-9360113 Fax 074-9360561
*Superior:* Sr Bernadette O'Gorman
Community: 7
Home for aged. Residents: 48

Nazareth House Primary School
*Principal:* Mr Paul O'Hea
Tel 028-71280212
Pupils: 400

**SACRED HEART OF JESUS SISTERS**
119 Irish Green Street,
Limavady, Co Derry BT49 9AB
Tel 015047-68357
*Superior:* Sr Eileen McElhone
Community: 2
Pastoral ministry

## EDUCATIONAL INSTITUTIONS

**EDMUND RICE SCHOOLS TRUST NORTHERN IRELAND**
Christian Brothers Grammar School,
Kevlin Road, Omagh BT78 1LD
Tel 028-82243567 Fax 028-82240656
*Principal:* Mr Paul Brannigan

## CHARITABLE SOCIETIES

**St Vincent de Paul Diocesan Centre**
Ozanam House,
22 Bridge Street, Derry
Tel 028-71265489

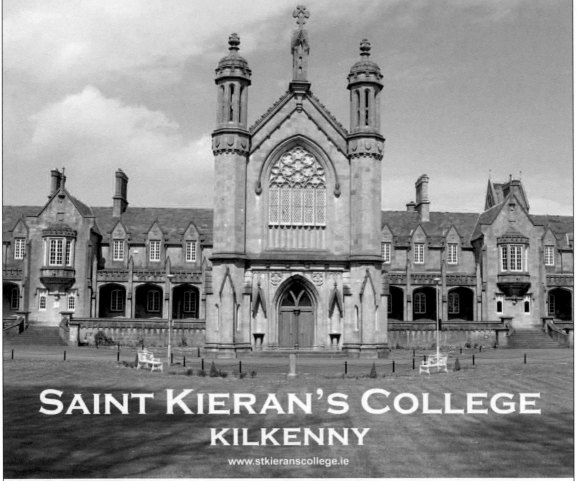

# SAINT KIERAN'S COLLEGE
## KILKENNY
www.stkieranscollege.ie

St Kieran's is a Catholic Diocesan College under the patronage of the Bishop of Ossory. It has two objectives: to provide a well-rounded education at second level and to further ongoing formation and education for third level and mature students. The College also provides facilities for the Co-Ordinator of the Ossory Diocesan Pastoral Council, the Director of Vocations, the Diocesan Archivist and the Director of Ossory Adult Faith Development.

■ **A SECONDARY SCHOOL** which models excellence in education to over 700 pupils, with a wide range of sporting and extracurricular activities.

■ **THEOLOGICAL STUDIES** which provides theological education and formation for those involved and taking positions of leadership at parish and diocesan level as well those who want to deepen their understanding of the faith.

■ **MAYNOOTH UNIVERSITY** which offers here off campus degree courses (First year First Arts and a BA in Local and community Studies) and a range of other initiatives for mature and evening students.

■ **THE KILKENNY RESEARCH & INNOVATION CENTRE** for research teams from Telecommunication Software and Systems Group in WIT and Carlow IT.

FOUNDED 1782

Further information:
The President, St Kieran's College, Kilkenny.
Tel: +353 (0)56 7721086  Email: president@stkieranscollege.ie

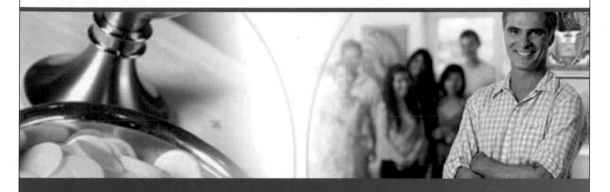

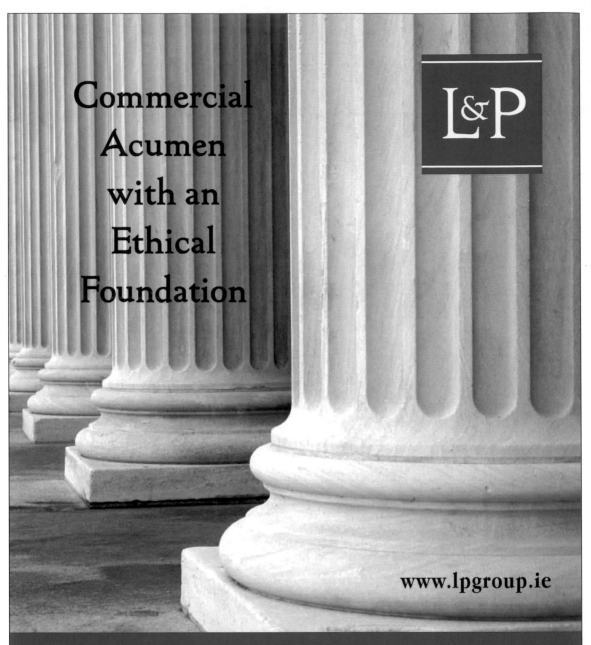

# DIOCESE OF DOWN AND CONNOR

PATRONS OF THE DIOCESE
ST MALACHY, 3 NOVEMBER; ST MACNISSI, 4 SEPTEMBER

INCLUDES COUNTY ANTRIM, THE GREATER PART OF COUNTY DOWN
AND PART OF COUNTY DERRY

**Most Rev Noel Treanor DD**
Bishop of Down and Connor;
ordained priest 13 June 1976;
ordained Bishop of Down and
Connor 29 June 2008

Residence: Lisbreen,
73 Somerton Road,
Belfast, Co Antrim BT15 4DE
Tel 028-90776185
Fax 028-90779377
Email
dccuria@downandconnor.org

## HISTORY OF THE DIOCESE

St Patrick does not provide many geographical details in his Confession about his sojourn in Ireland, yet a later tradition associated his work as a slave with Slemish in Co Antrim, his return as a missionary with Saul in Co Down and his burial place with Downpatrick.

In the course of his evangelisation of Ireland St Patrick ordained bishops to minister to local communities. Among those bishops was Mac Nissi, who, following his baptism by St Patrick, founded the church of Connor. However, by the sixth century, after Christianity had been well established, the monastic system was becoming the dominant form of ecclesiastical life. About 555 St Comgall founded a monastery at Bangor that was destined to become one of the most famous in Ireland. Monasteries were also founded in France, Switzerland and Italy, and these became influential centres for the conversion of many peoples. Other monasteries founded in the early centuries of Christianity in Down and Connor include those at Moville, Nendrum, Inch, Drumbo, Antrim and Comber. Some of these later adopted the Benedictine or Augustinian Rule.

The Norsemen cast greedy eyes on Irish monasteries, especially those near the coast, which could be easily attacked and plundered for silver and gold. Bangor fell victim to one such raid in 823, when many monks were killed and the shrine of St Comgall was destroyed. The loss of life and damage to buildings helped weaken the discipline and commitment of the monks. When St Malachy, the great reformer, became Abbot of Bangor in 1123, he found much of the abbey in ruins and the Rule being poorly observed.

In 1111, at the Synod of Rathbreasail, Ireland was at last given the diocesan territorial system that had been common in the western Church. Among the dioceses created were Connor for the Kingdom of Dalriada and Down for the Kingdom of Uladh. Though separate, these dioceses were united under St Malachy in 1124. He continued to reside at Bangor and pursue his reforms, but was driven from the monastery and forced to take refuge at Lismore. In 1129 he was appointed Archbishop of Armagh but because of local opposition, was not able to take control of the See until five years later. In 1137 he resigned and returned to the Diocese of Down, which was again separate from Connor. Invited by his fellow bishops to travel to Rome to obtain the pallia for the archbishops of Armagh and Cashel, Malachy set off in 1139 and visited St Bernard at Clairvaux. Though unsuccessful in his quest, he was appointed papal legate for Ireland. He left some monks at Clairvaux to be trained in the Cistercian way of life and they established the first Cistercian monastery at Mellifont in 1142. A second journey to Rome in 1148 to seek the pallia was cut short by his death on 2 November in the arms of St Bernard. The great Cistercian abbot later wrote Malachy's life story, which ensured that his fame spread widely on the Continent. Malachy was canonised in 1190.

In 1177 the Anglo-Norman adventurer, John de Courcy, carved out the Lordship of Ulster for himself and set up his base at Dunlethglaisse which he renamed Downpatrick. He took a keen interest in ecclesiastical affairs and brought Anglo-Norman Benedictine monks to the cathedral at Downpatrick. His wife founded the Cistercian Monastery at Greyabbey in the Ards Peninsula and he brought other Orders, such as the Premonstratensian and the Augustinian Canons to his territories.

In 1192 the Diocese of Dromore was cut off from Down to make provision for the native Irish, as the part that retained the name Down was by then regarded as Anglo-Norman. The Dioceses of Down and Connor continued to be administered separately until the fifteenth century. In 1439 Pope Eugene IV decided that, after the death of John Sely, the Bishop of Down, the two Sees should be united, and, although Sely was deprived of office three years later for misbehaviour, the Archbishop of Armagh resisted the union of the two dioceses for several years and it did not take place until 1453. In the 1220s the newly founded mendicant Orders, the Dominicans and Franciscans, established houses in the diocese. By the sixteenth century the Third Order of Franciscans had numerous friaries.

Robert Blyth, an English Benedictine, was Bishop of Down and Connor when Henry VIII demanded recognition as supreme Head of the Church. Blyth surrendered in 1539 and received a substantial pension. The Pope then deprived him of office and appointed in his place Eugene Magennis. Magennis also accepted the royal supremacy but later retracted his submission and was able to retain his See under Mary Tudor. The Franciscan pluralist, Miler McGrath, who succeeded in 1565 and accepted the royal supremacy in 1567, was deposed by Pope Gregory XIII in 1580 but had already been appointed Archbishop of Cashel by Queen Elizabeth. Two years later the Donegal Franciscan, Conor O'Devany, became bishop and after a lengthy episcopate of nearly thirty years was cruelly martyred in Dublin in 1612. (In 1992 he was one of the seventeen Irish martyrs beatified by Pope John Paul II)

During the upheavals of the seventeenth century and the harsh penal legislation of the early eighteenth century, the diocese was left vacant for long periods. After the death of Bishop Daniel Mackey in 1673 no appointment was made until Terence O'Donnelly became vicar apostolic in 1711. When O'Donnelly's successor, James O'Sheil, died in 1724 the See remained vacant until 1727. After the death of Bishop John Armstrong in 1739 all subsequent vacancies never lasted more than a year.

In 1825 William Crolly, who had been parish priest of Belfast for thirteen years, became bishop. Several of his predecessors had lived in or near Downpatrick but he chose to remain in the growing town which he rightly foresaw would become the largest in the diocese. Not only was Belfast geographically more central and convenient but its Catholic population soon dwarfed that of Downpatrick and of all other parishes in the diocese. By 1900 Catholics numbered 85,000 and represented just under a quarter of the city's population. The number of priests serving in it had greatly increased and religious orders of men and women had been brought in to care for the spiritual, educational and social needs of people.

The continued increase in the number of Catholics in and around Belfast accounts for the position Down and Connor holds as the second largest diocese in Ireland, with a population of approximately 300,000.

**Most Rev Anthony Farquhar DD**
Titular Bishop of Ermiana and Auxiliary Bishop of Down and Connor; ordained priest 13 March 1965; ordained Bishop 15 May 1983
Office: 73 Somerton Road,
Belfast BT15 4DE Tel 028-90776185
Residence: 24 Fruithill Park,
Belfast BT11 8GE Tel 028-90624252

**Most Rev Patrick J. Walsh DD**
Bishop Emeritus of Down and Connor; ordained priest 25 February 1956; ordained Titular Bishop of Ros Cré 15 May 1983; installed Bishop of Down and Connor 28 April 1991
Residence: 6 Waterloo Park North,
Belfast BT15 5HW
Tel 028-90778182

## CHAPTER

*Dean:* Rt Rev Brendan McGee
*Archdeacon:* Venerable Kevin Donnelly
*Members*
Very Rev Bernard Magee
Very Rev Noel Conway
Very Rev Hugh Starkey
Very Rev Robert Fullerton
Very Rev Brendan Murray
Very Rev George O'Hanlon
Very Rev Sean Rogan

*Honorary Canon*
Rt Rev Mgr Sean Connolly

## ADMINISTRATION

**Chancellor**
Very Rev Eugene O'Hagan *(Ad Interim)*
Lisbreen, 73 Somerton Road,
Belfast BT15 4DE
Tel 028-90776185 Fax 028-90779377

**Vicar General**
Rt Rev Mgr Sean Connolly VG
7 Tullyview, Loughguile,
Co Antrim BT44 9JY
Tel 077-39223280

**Diocesan Commission for Religious**
*Chairperson:* Rev Willie McGettrick (CSsR)
*Vice-Chair:* Sr Nuala Kelly DC
Tel 028-90445950

**Diocesan Safeguarding Office**
The Good Shepherd Centre,
511 Ormeau Road, Belfast BT7 3GS
Tel 028-90492798
Email cpodownconnor@gmail.com
*Diocesan Director for Safeguarding*
Mrs Barbara McDermott
*Diocesan Designated Officers*
Mr Andy Thomson
Mrs Barbara McDermott
*Development Consultant:* Mr Jim Tracey
*Training Consultant:* Mrs Imelda Henry
*Vetting & Barring Co-ordinator for the Catholic Church Northern Dioceses*
Mr Andrew Thomson
Tel 028-90492783
*Episcopal Vicar for Safeguarding*
Very Rev Peter Owens

**Consultors**
Most Rev Anthony J. Farquhar
Rt Rev Mgr Sean Connolly
Very Rev Brian Daly
Very Rev Sean Emerson
Very Rev John Forsythe
Very Rev Canon Sean Rogan
Very Rev Patrick Delargy
Very Rev Michael Spence
Rt Rev Mgr Colm McCaughan

**Episcopal Vicar for Clergy**
Rev Michael Spence

**Council of Priests**
*Chairman:* Very Rev John Forsythe PP
165 Antrim Road, Newtownabbey,
Co Antrim BT36 7QR
Tel 028-90832979
*Secretary:* Rev Gerard Fox
St Malachy's Seminary,
120 Cliftonville Road, Belfast BT14 6LA

**Judicial Vicar for Diocese of Down and Connor**
Very Rev Joseph Rooney JCL
The Good Shepherd Centre,
511 Ormeau Road, Belfast BT7 3GS
Tel 028-90491990 Fax 028-90491440

**Finance Committee**
*Chairman:* Most Rev Noel Treanor
*Secretary:* Ms Maria Morgan
*Members:* Most Rev Anthony Farquhar
Very Rev Eugene O'Hagan
Rev Joseph M. Glover
Mr Kevin Delaney
Mr Anthony Harbinson
Mr Charles Jenkins
Mr John B. McGuckian
Ms Alice Quinn

**Diocesan Financial Controller**
Rev Joseph M. Glover
Lisbreen, 73 Somerton Road,
Belfast BT15 4DE
Tel 028-90776185 Fax 028-90779377

**Diocesan Financial Administrator**
Ms Maria Morgan
Lisbreen, 73 Somerton Road,
Belfast BT15 4DE
Tel 028-90776185 Fax 028-90779377

**Diocesan Administration**
Mr Paul G. Shevlin *(Manager)*
Frances Doran, Brenda Dixon,
Shona Martin
Lisbreen, 73 Somerton Road,
Belfast BT15 4DE
Tel 028-90776185 Fax 028-90779377
Email dccuria@downandconnor.org

**Diocesan Property Administrator**
Mr David Gantley RICS
73 Somerton Road, Belfast BT15 4DE
Tel 028-90776185 Fax 028-90779377
Email dpa@downandconnor.org

**Seminary Fund Committee**
*Chairman:* Most Rev Noel Treanor
*Secretary:* Very Rev Michael Spence
Diocesan Seminary,
120 Cliftonville Road, Belfast BT14 6LA

**Media Liaison Officer**
Rev Edward McGee
Diocesan Seminary,
120 Cliftonville Road, Belfast BT14 6LA

**Diocesan Archivist**
Very Rev Canon George O'Hanlon
62 Coolkeeran Road, Armoy,
Ballymoney, Co Antrim BT53 8XN
Tel 028-20751121
*Assistant:* Rev Thomas McGlynn PP
St Agnes' Presbytery,
143 Andersonstown Road,
Belfast BT11 9BW
Tel 028-90615702

**Diocesan Secretary**
Rev Joseph M. Glover
Lisbreen, 73 Somerton Road,
Belfast BT15 4DE
Tel 028-90776185 Fax 028-90779377

## CATECHETICS AND EDUCATION

**Episcopal Vicar for Education**
Rev Timothy Bartlett
73 Somerton Road, Belfast BT15 4DE
Tel 028-90776185

**Catholic Schools Trustee Service**
*Director:* Mr Gerard Lundy
St Patrick's School, Donegall Street,
Belfast BT1 2SL
Tel 028-64349736

**CCMS Diocesan Education Office**
*Senior Management Officer*
Ms Susan Sullivan
160 High Street, Holywood,
Co Down BT18 9HT
Tel 028-90426972 Fax 028-90424255

**Diocesan Advisers in Religious Education**
*Positions to be filled*
511 Ormeau Road, Belfast BT7 3GS
Tel 028-90491886 Fax 028-90491440
Email readvisers@btconnect.com

## LITURGY

**Diocesan Commission on Liturgy**
*Chairman*
Very Rev Canon Robert Fullerton
501 Ormeau Road, Belfast BT7 3GR
Tel 028-90641064
*Secretary:* Rev Aidan McCaughan
2-4 Broughshane Road,
Ballymena, Co Antrim
Tel 028-25641515

## PASTORAL

**ACCORD Catholic Marriage Care Service**
*Regional Office*
*Administration Officer:* Ms Brenda Russell
Cana House, St Mary's Church,
Chapel Lane, Belfast BT1 1HH
Tel 028-90233002 Fax 028-90328113
Email info@accordni.com
www.accordni.com/www.accord-ni.co.uk
*Belfast*
Curran House, Twin Spires,
Northumberland Street, Belfast BT13 2JF
Tel 028-90339944
*Ballymena*
All Saints Parish Centre, 9 Cushendall Road,
Ballymena, Co Antrim
Tel 028-38334781

*Downpatrick*
*Appointments Secretary*
Mrs Sheila McPoland
99 Irish Street, Downpatrick,
Co Down BT30 6BS
Tel 028-44613435

**Down & Connor Office of the Armagh Regional Marriage Tribunal**
511 Ormeau Road, Belfast BT7 3GS
Tel 028-90491990 Fax 028-90491440
*Administrator*
Rev Joseph Rooney JCL

**Diocesan Ecumenical Commission**
*Secretary:* Rev Colin Grant
Aquinas Grammar School,
518 Ravenhill Road, Belfast BT6 0BY
Tel 028-90643939

**Pioneer Total Abstinence Association**
*Diocesan Director*
Rev Raymond McCullagh
1 Seafield Park South,
Portstewart BT55 7LH
Tel 028-70832066

**Pontifical Mission Societies**
*Diocesan Director*
Rev Conor McGrath
St Joseph's Presbytery,
56 Greystone Road, Antrim,
Co Antrim BT41 1JZ
Tel 028-94429103

**Vocations**
*Director:* Very Rev Kevin McGuckien
23 Hannahstown Hill,
Belfast BT17 0LT
Tel 028-90614567

**Diocesan Commission on Family Ministry**
*Secretary:* Very Rev Michael McGinnity
St Malachy's Parish, 24 Alfred Street,
Belfast BT2 8EN
Tel 028-90321713
Email familyministry.dc@btconnect.com

**Diocesan Social Affairs Commission**
*Director:* Rev Timothy Bartlett
73 Somerton Road,
Belfast BT15 4DE
Tel 028-90776185

**Diocesan Care Home**
Our Lady's Home,
68 Ard Na Va Road, Belfast BT12 6FF
*Secretary to Management Committee*
Mr Paul G. Shevlin
Tel 028-90325731 Fax 028-90236700

**Children's Home**
Glenmona Resource Centre
Glen Road, Belfast BT11 8BX
Tel 028-90301100
Director: Mr Liam Dumigan

**Diocesan Youth Commission (Living Youth)**
16 Chapel Lane, Belfast BT1 1HH
Tel 028-90232432
*Chairperson:* Ms Aine Lockhart
*Director:* Ms Pauline Dowd
Email info@livingyouthni.org

**Youth Link Training Offices**
Farset Enterprise Park,
683 Springfield Road, Belfast BT12 7DY
Tel 028-90323217
*Director:* Rev Patrick White
Email info@youthlink.org.uk

## PARISHES

*Mensal parishes are listed first. Other parishes follow alphabetically, city parishes first. Historical names are in parentheses.*

**THE CATHEDRAL (ST PETER'S)**
Very Rev Hugh Kennedy Adm
Very Rev Ciaran Dallat (*Assistant Priest*)
St Peter's Cathedral Presbytery,
St Peter's Square, Belfast BT12 4BU
Tel 028-90327573
Rev Paul Turley (CSsR)
Rev Alphonsus Doran (CSsR)
Clonard Monastery,
1 Clonard Gardens, Belfast BT13 2RL
Tel 028-90445950

**ST MARY'S**
Very Rev James A. Boyle (MHM) Adm
Rev James O'Donoghue (MHM) CC
Rev John Nevin (MHM)
St Mary's, Marquis Street, Belfast BT1 1JJ
Tel 028-90320482

**ST PATRICK'S**
Very Rev Michael Sheehan Adm
Dean Brendan McGee
Rev Dominic McGrattan CC
St Patrick's Presbytery,
199 Donegall Street, Belfast BT1 2FL
Tel 028-90324597

**HOLY FAMILY**
Very Rev Paul Strain Adm
Rev Paul Morely CC
Holy Family Presbytery,
Newington Avenue, Belfast BT15 2HP
Tel 028-90743119
Very Rev Canon Brendan Murray
(*Priest in residence*)
Apt 13 Downview Manor,
Belfast BT15 4JL

**ST COLMCILLE'S**
Very Rev Ciaran Feeney Adm
191 Upper Newtownards Road,
Belfast BT4 3JB
Tel 028-90654157

## CITY PARISHES

**CHRIST THE REDEEMER, LAGMORE**
Very Rev Martin Graham PP
81 Lagmore Grove, Dunmurry,
Belfast BT17 0TD
Tel 028-90309011

**CORPUS CHRISTI**
Very Rev Darach Mac Giolla Catháin PP
Corpus Christi Presbytery,
4-6 Springhill Grove, Belfast BT12 7SL
Tel 028-90246857
Very Rev Aidan Denny
10 New Barnsley Green, New Barnsley,
Belfast BT12 7HS
Tel 028-90328877

**DERRIAGHY**
Very Rev Paul Byrne PP
111 Queensway, Lambeg, Lisburn BT27 4QS
Tel 028-92662896

**GREENCASTLE**
Very Rev Anthony Alexander PP
824 Shore Road, Newtownabbey,
Co Antrim BT36 7DG
Tel 028-90370845

**HOLY CROSS**
Very Rev Gary Donegan (CP), Superior
Very Rev Eugene McCarthy (CP) PP
Rev Charles Cross (CP) CC
Rev Terence McGuckian (CP) CC
Rev Myles Kavanagh (CP) CC
Holy Cross Retreat, 432 Crumlin Road,
Ardoyne, Belfast BT14 7GE
Tel 028-90748231/2

**HOLY ROSARY**
Very Rev Patrick McKenna PP, VF
503 Ormeau Road, Belfast BT7 3GR
Tel 028-90642446
Very Rev Canon Robert Fullerton CC
Holy Rosary Presbytery,
501 Ormeau Road, Belfast BT7 3GR
Tel 028-90641064

**HOLY TRINITY**
Very Rev Brendan Smyth PP
Holy Trinity Presbytery,
26 Norglen Gardens, Belfast BT11 8EL
Tel 028-90590985/6

**THE NATIVITY**
Very Rev Patrick Sheehan PP
The Presbytery, Bell Steel Road,
Poleglass, Belfast BT17 0PB
Tel 028-90625739

**OUR LADY QUEEN OF PEACE, KILWEE**
Very Rev Rory Sheehan PP
Netherley Lodge,
130 Upper Dunmurry Lane,
Belfast BT17 0EW
Tel 028-90616300

**SACRED HEART**
Very Rev Martin Magill PP
Sacred Heart Presbytery,
1 Glenview Street, Belfast BT14 7DP
Tel 028-90351851

**ST AGNES'**
Very Rev Thomas McGlynn PP
143 Andersonstown Road,
Belfast BT11 9BW
Tel 028-90615702/90603951
Rev Robert Sloan CC
139 Andersonstown Road,
Belfast BT11 9BW
Tel 028-90613724

**ST ANNE'S**
Very Rev Feargal McGrady PP
St Anne's Parochial House,
Kingsway, Finaghy, Belfast BT10 0NE
Tel 028-90610112

**ST ANTHONY'S**
Very Rev Henry McCann PP
St Anthony's Presbytery,
4 Willowfield Crescent, Belfast BT6 8HP
Tel 028-90458158

**ST BERNADETTE'S**
Very Rev Paul Armstrong PP
28 Willowbank Park, Belfast BT6 0LL
Tel 028-90793023

**ST BRIGID'S**
Very Rev Edward O'Donnell PP
42 Derryvolgie Avenue, Belfast BT9 6FP
Tel 028-90665409

**ST GERARD'S**
Redemptorist Fathers
Very Rev Gerard Cassidy (CSsR) PP and
Rector
Rev Patrick McLoughlin (CSsR) CC
722 Antrim Road, Newtownabbey,
Co Antrim BT36 7PG
Tel 028-90774833/4

**ST JOHN'S**
Very Rev Anthony Fitzsimons PP
Very Rev Peter Forde PE
470 Falls Road, Belfast BT12 6EN
Tel 028-90321511
Very Rev Anthony McLaverty (priest in
residence)
470 Falls Road, Belfast BT12 6EN
Tel 028-90321102

**ST LUKE'S**
Very Rev Brian McCann PP
St Luke's Presbytery, Twinbrook Road,
Dunmurry, Co Antrim BT17 0RP
Tel 028-90619459

**ST MALACHY'S**
Very Rev Michael McGinnity PP
Rev Krzysztof Sanda (SCHR)
St Malachy's Presbytery,
24 Alfred Street, Belfast BT2 8EN
Tel 028-90321713

**ST MARY'S ON THE HILL**
Very Rev John Forsythe PP
Elmfield, 165 Antrim Road, Glengormley,
Newtownabbey, Co Antrim BT36 7QR
Tel 028-90832979
Rev Damian McCaughan CC
142 Carnmoney Road, Newtownabbey,
Co Antrim BT36 6JU
Tel 028-90832488
Very Rev Brendan Beagon CC
1 Christine Road, Newtownabbey,
Co Antrim BT36 6TG
Tel 028-90841507

**ST MATTHEW'S**
Very Rev Aidan Keenan PP
St Matthew's Presbytery, Bryson Street,
Newtownards Road, Belfast BT5 4ES
Tel 028-90457626

**ST MICHAEL'S**
Very Rev David Delargy PP
200 Finaghy Road North, Belfast BT11 9EG
Rev Eamon McCreave (OSM)
St Michael's Presbytery,
206 Finaghy Road North, Belfast BT11 9EG
Tel 028-90615174

**ST OLIVER PLUNKETT**
Very Rev Aidan Brankin PP
27 Glenveagh Drive, Belfast BT11 9HX
Tel 028-90618180

**ST PAUL'S**
Very Rev Anthony Devlin PP
Rev Antony Perumayan CC and Guardian
of the Syro-Malabar Catholics
St Paul's Presbytery, 125 Falls Road,
Belfast BT12 6AB
Tel 028-90325034
Rev Sean Keeney (CSsR) (Assistant Priest)
Clonard Monastery, Clonard Gardens,
Belfast BT13 2RL

**ST TERESA'S**
Very Rev Brendan Hickland PP
St Teresa's Presbytery, Glen Road,
Belfast BT11 8BL
Tel 028-90612855
Rev Aloysius Lumala (Assistant priest)
Very Rev Laurence McElhill PE (priest in
residence)
43B Glen Road, Belfast BT11 8BB

**ST VINCENT DE PAUL**
Very Rev Patrick Devlin PP
St Vincent de Paul Presbytery,
169 Ligoniel Road, Belfast BT14 8DP
Tel 028-90713401

**WHITEABBEY (ST JAMES'S)**
Very Rev Anthony Alexander PP
824 Shore Road,
Newtownabbey BT36 7DG
Very Rev Samuel Kerr (priest in residence)
463 Shore Road, Whiteabbey,
Newtownabbey, Co Antrim BT37 0AE
Tel 028-90365773

**WHITEHOUSE**
Very Rev Anthony Alexander PP
824 Shore Road,
Newtownabbey BT36 7DG

## COUNTRY PARISHES

**AGHAGALLON AND BALLINDERRY**
Very Rev Declan Mulligan PP
Parochial House, 5 Aghalee Road,
Aghagallon, Craigavon,
Co Armagh BT67 0AR
Tel 028-92651214

**AHOGHILL**
Very Rev Hugh J O'Hagan PP
Parochial House, 31 Ballynafie Road,
Ahoghill BT42 1LF
Tel 028-25871351

**ANTRIM**
Very Rev Sean Emerson PP
Parochial House, 3 Oriel Road,
Antrim BT41 4HP
Tel 028-94428016
Very Rev Felix McGuckin
5 Oriel Road, Antrim BT41 4HP
Tel 028-94428086
Rev Conor McGrath CC
St Joseph's Presbytery,
56 Greystone Road, Antrim BT41 1JZ
Tel 028-94429103

**ARMOY**
Very Rev Christopher Nellis PP
Parochial House, Armoy,
Ballymoney, Co Antrim BT53 8RL
Tel 028-20751205

**BALLINTOY**
Very Rev Brian Daly Adm
15 Moyle Road, Ballycastle,
Co Antrim BT54 6LB
Tel 028-20762223
Rev Hugh O'Kane (SMA) CC (priest in
residence)
53 Ballinlea Road, Ballycastle,
Co Antrim BT54 6JL
Tel 028-20762498

**BALLYCASTLE (RAMOAN)**
Very Rev Brian Daly PP
Parochial House, 15 Moyle Road,
Ballycastle, Co Antrim BT54 6LB
Tel 028-20762223
Rev Hugh O'Kane (SMA) CC
53 Ballinlea Road,
Ballycastle, Co Antrim BT54 6JL
Tel 028-20762498
Rev Barney McCahery (CSsR) CC
6 Market Street,
Ballycastle, Co Antrim BT54 6DP
Tel 028-20762202

**BALLYCLARE AND BALLYGOWAN**
Very Rev Eugene O'Hagan Adm
Parochial House, 69 Doagh Road,
Ballyclare, Co Antrim BT39 9BG
Tel 028-93342226

**BALLYGALGET**
Very Rev Patrick Mulholland PP
Parochial House, 9 Ballygalget Road,
Portaferry, Co Down BT22 1NE
Tel 028-42771212

**BALLYMENA (KIRKINRIOLA)**
Very Rev Patrick Delargy PP, VF
Venerable Archdeacon Kevin Donnelly
Rev Paul Symonds (on leave)
Rev Aidan McCaughan (priest in residence)
Parochial House,
4 Broughshane Road, Ballymena,
Co Antrim BT43 7DX
Tel 028-25641515 Fax 028-25631493

**BALLYMONEY AND DERRYKEIGHAN**
Very Rev Francis O'Brien PP
81 Castle Street, Ballymoney,
Co Antrim BT53 6JT
Tel 028-27662003

**BANGOR**
Very Rev Joseph Gunn PP, VF
St Comgall's Presbytery,
27 Brunswick Road, Bangor,
Co Down BT20 3DS
Tel 028-91465522
Rev Joseph Rooney (priest in residence)
45 Ballyholme Esplanade, Bangor,
Co Down BT20 5NJ
Tel 028-91465425

## BRAID
Very Rev Gabriel Lyons Adm
Parochial House, 119A Glenravel Road,
Martinstown, Co Antrim BT43 6QL
Tel 028-21758217

## CARNLOUGH
Very Rev Dermot McKay PP
51 Bay Road, Carnlough,
Ballymena, Co Antrim BT44 0HJ
Tel 028-28885220

## CARRICKFERGUS
Very Rev Peter Owens PP
Parochial House, 8 Minorca Place,
Carrickfergus, Co Antrim BT38 8AU
Tel 028-93363269

## CASTLEWELLAN (KILMEGAN)
Very Rev Denis McKinlay PP
Parochial House, 91 Main Street,
Castlewellan, Co Down BT31 9DH
Tel 028-43778259
Very Rev Canon Bernard Magee
41 Lower Square,
Castlewellan BT31 9DN
Tel 028-43770377

## COLERAINE
Very Rev Gregory Cormican PP
72 Nursery Avenue, Coleraine,
Co Derry BT52 1LR
Tel 028-70343156

## CROSSGAR (KILMORE)
Very Rev Eugene O'Neill PP
Parochial House, 4 Irish Street,
Killyleagh, Co Down BT30 9QS
Tel 028-44828211
Rev Patrick McCafferty CC
Parochial House, Crossgar,
Downpatrick, Co Down BT30 9EA
Tel 028-44830229
Rev Patrick McKenna CC
Teconnaught, 2 Drumnaconagher Road,
Crossgar BT30 9AN
Tel 028-44830342

## CULFEIGHTRIN
Very Rev Raymond Fulton PP
87 Cushendall Road, Ballyvoy,
Ballycastle, Co Antrim BT54 6QY
Tel 028-20762248

## CUSHENDALL
Very Rev Luke McWilliams PP
Parochial House,
28 Chapel Road, Cushendall,
Ballymena BT44 0RS
Tel 028-21771240

## CUSHENDUN
Very Rev Luke McWilliams PP
Parochial House, 28 Chapel Road,
Cushendall, Ballymena,
Co Antrim BT44 0RS
Tel 028-21771240
Very Rev James O'Kane PE, CC
21 Knocknacarry Avenue,
Cushenden, Co Antrim BT44 0NX
Tel 028-21761269

## DOWNPATRICK
Very Rev John Murray PP
Parochial House, 54 St Patrick's Avenue,
Downpatrick, Co Down BT30 6DN
Tel 028-44612443
Very Rev Liam Toland CC
29 Killough Road, Downpatrick,
Co Down BT30 6PX
Tel 028-44612443
Very Rev Finbar Glavin
Parochial House, 16 Ballykilbeg Road,
Downpatrick, Co Down BT30 8HJ
Tel 028-44613203
Very Rev Canon Noel Conway (priest in
residence)
23 Rathkeltair Road, Downpatrick,
Co Down BT30 6NL
Tel 028-44614777

## DRUMAROAD AND CLANVARAGHAN
Very Rev Peter Donnelly PP, VF (on leave)
Parochial House, 15 Drumaroad Hill,
Castlewellan, Co Down BT31 9PD
Tel 028-44811474

## DRUMBO
Very Rev Martin Kelly PP
Parochial House,
546 Saintfield Road, Carryduff,
Belfast BT8 8EU
Tel 028-90812238
Rev Brian Watters CC
79 Ivanhoe Avenue, Carryduff,
Belfast BT8 8BW
Tel 028-90817410

## DUNDRUM AND TYRELLA
Very Rev Robert Fleck PP
Parochial House, Dundrum,
Newcastle, Co Down BT33 0LU
Tel 028-43751212
Very Rev Maurice Henry PE, CC (priest in
residence)
Parochial House,
26 Tyrella Road, Ballykinlar,
Downpatrick, Co Down BT30 8DF
Tel 028-44851221

## DUNEANE
Very Rev Patrick McWilliams PP
103 Roguery Road, Moneyglass,
Toomebridge, Co Antrim BT41 3PT
Tel 028-79650225

## DUNLOY AND CLOUGHMILLS
Very Rev Liam Blayney (SPS) Adm
Parochial House,
14 Presbytery Lane, Dunloy,
Co Antrim BT44 9DZ
Tel 028-27657223

## DUNSFORD AND ARDGLASS
Very Rev Gerard McCloskey PP
Parochial House, Ardglass,
Co Down BT30 7TU
Tel 028-44841208

## GLENARIFFE
Very Rev David White PP
Parochial House, 182 Garron Road,
Glenariffe, Co Antrim BT44 0RA
Tel 028-21771249

## GLENARM (TICKMACREEVAN)
Very Rev Dermot McKay PP
Parochial House, 1 The Cloney, Glenarm,
Co Antrim BT44 0AB
Tel 028-28841246
Rev Michael McConville (Assistant Priest)
65 Moyle Road, Ballycastle,
Co Antrim BT54 6LG

## GLENAVY AND KILLEAD
Very Rev Colm McBride PP
Parochial House, 59 Chapel Road,
Glenavy, Crumlin, Co Antrim BT29 4LY
Tel 028-94422262
Rev Chris McGuinness (SPS) CC
Parochial House, Glenavy Road,
Crumlin, Co Antrim BT29 4LA
Tel 028-94452941

## GLENRAVEL (SKERRY)
Very Rev Gabriel Lyons PP
119A Glenravel Road, Martinstown,
Ballymena, Co Antrim BT43 6QL
Tel 028-21758217

## HANNAHSTOWN
Very Rev Kevin McGuckien PP
Parochial House, 23 Hannahstown Hill,
Belfast BT17 0LT
Tel 028-90614567
Rt Rev Mgr John Murphy (priest in
residence)
18 Rock Road, Lisburn,
Co Antrim BT28 3SU
Tel 028-92648244

## HOLYWOOD
Very Rev Stephen McBrearty PP
2A My Lady's Mile, Holywood,
Co Down BT18 9EW
Tel 028-90422167

## KILCLIEF AND STRANGFORD
Very Rev Peter O'Kane PP
Parochial House, Strangford,
Co Down BT30 7NL
Tel 028-44881206

## KILCOO
Very Rev Denis McKinlay Adm
91 Main Street, Castlewellan,
Co Down BT31 9DH
Very Rev Canon Sean Rogan PE (priest in
residence)
Parochial House, 121 Dublin Road,
Kilcoo, Co Down BT34 5HP
Tel 028-40630314

## KILKEEL (UPPER MOURNE)
Very Rev Sean Dillon PP
Parochial House, Greencastle Road,
Kilkeel, Co Down BT34 4DE
Tel 028-41762242
Very Rev Sean Cahill CC
Curates' Residence, Massforth,
152 Newry Road, Kilkeel,
Co Down BT34 4ET
Tel 028-41762257

Allianz (ⅲ)

**KILLOUGH (BRIGHT)**
Very Rev Peter O'Hare PP
16 Rossglass Road, Killough,
Co Down BT30 7QQ
Tel 028-44841221

**KILLYLEAGH**
Very Rev Eugene O'Neill PP
4 Irish Street, Killyleagh,
Co Down BT30 9QS
Tel 028-44828211

**KIRCUBBIN (ARDKEEN)**
Very Rev Patrick Neeson PP
46 Blackstaff Road, Ballycranbeg,
Kircubbin, Newtownards,
Co Down BT22 1AG
Tel 028-42738294

**LARNE**
Very Rev Aidan Kerr PP
Rev Michael McConville *(Assistant priest)*
Parochial House, 51 Victoria Road, Larne,
Co Antrim BT40 1LY
Tel 028-28273230/28273053

**LISBURN (BLARIS)**
Very Rev Dermot McCaughan PP
St Patrick's Presbytery, 29 Chapel Hill,
Lisburn, Co Antrim BT28 1EP
Tel 028-92662341
Rev Eamon Magorrian CC
Tel 028-92660206
Parochial House, 27 Chapel Hill, Lisburn,
Co Antrim BT28 1EP

**LOUGHGUILE**
Very Rev Robert Butler PP
Parochial House, 44 Lough Road,
Loughguile, Ballymena,
Co Antrim BT44 9JN
Tel 028-27641206
Very Rev Canon George O'Hanlon *(priest
in residence)*
62 Coolkeeran Road, Armoy,
Ballymoney, Co Antrim BT53 8XN
Tel 028-20751121

**LOUGHINISLAND**
Very Rev Kieran Whiteford PP
Parochial House, Loughinisland,
Downpatrick, Co Down BT30 8QH
Tel 028-44811661

**LOWER MOURNE**
Very Rev Sean Gilmore PP
Parochial House, 284 Glassdrumman Road,
Annalong, Newry, Co Down BT34 4QN
Tel 028-43768208

**NEWCASTLE (MAGHERA)**
Very Rev James Crudden PP
24 Downs Road, Newcastle,
Co Down BT33 0AG
Tel 028-43722401
Rev Colin Crossey CC
3 Donard Place, Newcastle, Co Down
BT33 0AJ
Tel 028-43722248

**NEWTOWNARDS**
Very Rev Martin O'Hagan PP
71 North Street, Newtownards,
Co Down BT23 4JD
Tel 028-91812137

**PORTAFERRY (BALLYPHILIP)**
Very Rev Patrick Mulholland PP
Parochial House, Portaferry,
Co Down BT22 1RH
Tel 028-42728234

**PORTGLENONE**
Very Rev Anthony Curran PP
St Mary's Presbytery, 12 Ballymena Road,
Portglenone, Co Antrim BT44 8BL
Tel 028-25821218

**PORTRUSH**
Very Rev Seamus O'Reilly (SPS) Adm
Parochial House, 111 Causeway Street,
Portrush, Co Antrim BT56 8JE
Tel 028-70823388

**PORTSTEWART**
Very Rev Austin McGirr PP, VF
Parochial House, 4 The Crescent,
Portstewart, Co Derry BT55 7AB
Tel 028-70832534
Rev Raymond McCullagh *(priest in
residence)*
1 Seafield Park South,
Portstewart BT55 7LH
Tel 028-70832066

**RANDALSTOWN**
Very Rev Con Boyle PP
Parochial House, 1 Craigstown Road,
Randalstown, Co Antrim BT41 2AF
Tel 028-94472640

**RASHARKIN**
Very Rev John J. Murray PP
Parochial House, 9 Gortahor Road,
Rasharkin, Ballymena,
Co Antrim BT44 8SB
Tel 028-29571212

**SAINTFIELD AND CARRICKMANNON**
Very Rev Anthony McHugh PP
Parochial House, 33 Crossgar Road,
Saintfield, Ballynahinch,
Co Down BT24 7JE
Tel 028-97510237

**SAUL AND BALLEE**
Very Rev Paul Alexander PP
10 St Patrick's Road,
Saul, Downpatrick, Co Down BT30 7JG
Tel 028-44612525

## INSTITUTIONS AND THEIR CHAPLAINS

## HOSPITALS

**City Group of Hospitals, Belfast**
Tel 028-90329241
Rev Gerard Fox
201 Donegall Street, Belfast BT1 2FL
Tel 028-90263473 *(chaplain's office)*

**Mater Hospital, Belfast**
Tel 028-90741211
Rev Dominic McGrattan CC
St Patrick's Presbytery,
199 Donegall Street, Belfast BT1 2FL
Tel 028-90324597

**Musgrave Park Hospital, Belfast**
Tel 028-90902000
Rev Adrian Eastwood (CM)
99 Cliftonville Road, Belfast BT14 6JQ
Tel 028-90751771

**Royal Victoria Hospital, Belfast**
Tel 028-90240503
Rev Robert Sloan CC
169B Glen Road, Belfast BT11 8BS

**Ulster Hospital, Dundonald**
Tel 028-90654157
Very Rev Ciaran Feeney Adm
Very Rev Martin O'Hagan PP
Very Rev Henry McCann PP
St Colmcille's Presbytery, 191 Upper
Newtownards Road, Belfast BT4 3JB

## PENAL INSTITUTIONS

**Maghaberry Prison**
Old Road, Ballinderry Upper, Lisburn,
Co Antrim BT28 2TP
*Pastoral Team:* Rev Frank Brady (SJ)
Br Brian Monaghan
Rev Gabriel Bannon
Sr Rosaleen McMahon
Tel 028-92614825
Prison General Office: 028-92611888

**Young Offenders' Detention Centre**
Hydebank Wood, Hospital Road,
Belfast BT8 8NA
*Co-ordinating Lead Chaplain of Catholic
Pastoral Team*
Very Rev Stephen McBrearty
Tel 028-90253666
Sr Oona, Sisters of Nazareth (Women
Prisoners)

## UNIVERSITIES

**Queen's University, Belfast**
Rev Gary Toman
The Chaplaincy, 28 Elmwood Avenue,
Belfast BT9 6AY
Tel 028-90669737

**University of Ulster, Coleraine**
Rev Raymond McCullagh
1 Seafield Park South, Portstewart,
Co Derry BT55 7LH
Tel 028-70832066

**University of Ulster, Jordanstown**
Rev Terence Howard (SJ)
Peter Faber House, 28 Brookvale Avenue,
Belfast BT14 6BW
Tel 028-90757615

## PRIESTS OF THE DIOCESE ELSEWHERE

Rev Peter Carlin
Padres de San Columbano
Apartado 073174, Lima 39, Peru
Rev Martin Henry
Rev Oliver Treanor
73 Somerton Road, Belfast BT15 4DE
Rev Gerard McFlynn
18 Maresfield Gardens,
London NW3 5SX
Rev Stephen Quinn
Carmelite Priory, Boars Hill,
Oxford OX1 5HB
Rev Vincent Cushnahan
St Paul University, Deschatelets
Residence, 175 Main Street, Ottawa,
Ontario K1S 1C3, Canada

## RETIRED PRIESTS

Rev Conleth Byrne
c/o 73 Somerton Road, Belfast BT15 4DE
Rev Colm Campbell
c/o Lisbreen, 73 Somerton Road,
Belfast BT15 4DE
Very Rev Harry Carlin
5 Fortwilliam Court, Belfast BT15 4DE
Tel 028-90772376
Rt Rev Mgr Sean Connolly VG
7 Tullyview, Loughguile,
Co Antrim BT44 9JY
Very Rev John Fitzpatrick
116 Strangford Road, Ardglass, BT30 7SS
Very Rev Padraic Gallinagh
'Polperro', 8 Beverley Close,
Newtownards BT23 7FN
Very Rev Frank Harper
32 Bryansford Avenue,
Newcastle BT33 0EQ
Very Rev Maurice Henry PE
28 Tyrella Road, Ballykinlar,
Co Down BT30 8DE
Tel 028-44851221
Very Rev John Hutton
Apt 2, Ceara Court, Windsor Avenue,
Belfast BT9 6EJ
Tel 028-90683002
Very Rev Donal Kelly
7 Knocksinna Park, Bray Road,
Foxrock, Dublin 18
Tel 01-2894170
Very Rev Sean McCartney
25 Alt-Min Avenue, Belfast BT8 6NJ
Rt Rev Mgr Colm McCaughan
3 Fortwilliam Demesne, Belfast BT15 4FD
Tel 028-90778111
Very Rev Francis McCorry
Our Lady's Home, 68 Ardnava Road,
Belfast BT12 6FF
Rt Rev Mgr Ambrose Macaulay
89a Maryville Park, Belfast BT9 6LQ
Very Rev Gerard McConville
68 Main Street, Portglenone BT44 8HS
Rev Gordon McKinstry
12 The Meadows, Randalstown,
Co Antrim BT41 2JB
Very Rev Brendan McMullan
26 Willowbank Park, Belfast BT6 0LL
Tel 028-90794440

Very Rev George McLaverty
518 Donegall Road, Belfast BT12 6DY
Very Rev Kevin McMullan
418 Oldpark Road, Belfast BT14 6QF
Tel 028-90748148
Very Rev Albert McNally
6 Hillside Avenue, Dunloy BT44 9DQ
Very Rev Patrick McVeigh
3 Broughshane Road, Ballymena,
Co Antrim BT43 7DX
Very Rev Vincent Maguire
26 Rodney Street, Portrush,
Co Antrim BT56 8LB
Very Rev John Moley
24 Mallard Road, Downpatrick,
Co Down BT30 6DY
Very Rev Michael Murray
c/o 73 Somerton Road, Belfast BT15 4DE
Very Rev Eamon O'Brien
No. 5 Hopecroft, Main Street,
Glenavy BT29 4LN
Very Rev Prof Martin O'Callaghan
c/o 73 Somerton Road, Belfast BT15 4DE
Rev John O'Connor
c/o Lisbreen, 73 Somerton Road,
Belfast BT15 4DE
Very Rev John O'Sullivan
6 Ferngrove Avenue, Aghagallon,
Craigavon BT67 0HA
Very Rev Gerard Patton
43 Head Road, Kilkeel,
Co Down BT34 4HX
Very Rev Jim Sheppard
189 Carrigenagh Road, Ballymartin,
Kilkeel, Co Down BT34 4GA
Very Rev Canon Hugh Starkey
40 Minerstown Road, Downpatrick,
Co Down BT30 8LR
Very Rev John Stewart
27F Windsor Avenue, Belfast BT9 6EE
Very Rev Daniel Whyte
53 Marlo Park, Bangor, Co Down BT19 6NL
Tel 078-12184624
Rev Desmond Wilson
6 Springhill Close, Belfast BT12 7SE
Tel 028-90326722

## RELIGIOUS ORDERS AND CONGREGATIONS

## PRIESTS

### CISTERCIANS
Our Lady of Bethlehem Abbey,
11 Ballymena Road, Portglenone,
Ballymena, Co Antrim BT44 8BL
Tel 028-25821211 Fax 028-25822795
Email celsus@bethabbey.com
Website www.bethlehemabbey.com
*Abbot:* Rt Rev Dom Celsus Kelly (OCSO)

### JESUITS
Peter Faber House, 28 Brookvale Avenue,
Belfast BT14 6BW
Tel 028-90757615
Fax 028-90747615
Email peter_faber@lineone.net
*Superior:* Rev Alan McGuckian (SJ)

### MILL HILL MISSIONARIES
St Mary's Parish, 25 Marquis Street,
Belfast BT1 1JJ
Tel 028-90320482
Rev James A. Boyle (MHM) Adm
Rev Jim O'Donoghue (MHM) CC
Rev John Nevin (MHM)

### PASSIONISTS
Holy Cross Retreat, Ardoyne,
Crumlin Road,
Belfast BT14 7GE
Tel 028-90748231 Fax 028-90740340
*Superior:* Rev Gary Donegan (CP)

Passionist Retreat Centre,
Tobar Mhuire, Crossgar,
Downpatrick, Co Down BT30 9EA
Tel 028-44830242 Fax 028-44831382
*Superior:* Rev John Friel (CP)

### REDEMPTORISTS
Clonard Monastery,
1 Clonard Gardens,
Belfast BT13 2RL
Tel 028-90445950 Fax 028-90445988
*Superior:* Rev Michael Murtagh (CSsR)

St Gerard's Parish,
722 Antrim Road, Newtownabbey,
Co Antrim BT36 7PG
Tel 028-90774833
Fax 028-90770923
*Superior & PP:* Rev Gerry Cassidy (CSsR)

### VINCENTIANS
99 Cliftonville Road,
Belfast BT14 6JQ
Tel 028-90751771 Fax 028-90740547
Email cmbelfast@ntlworld.co.uk
*Superior:* Very Rev Peter Gildea (CM)

## BROTHERS

### CHRISTIAN BROTHERS
An Dúnán, 210 Glen Road,
Belfast BT11 8BW
Tel 028-90611343
*Community Leader:* Br Brendan Prior
Community: 6

The Open Doors Learning Centre,
Barrack Street, Belfast BT12 4AH
Tel 028-90325867 Fax 028-90241013
*Coordinator:* Conor Kennedy
Email opendoorsbelfast@yahoo.co.uk

Westcourt Centre,
Barrack Street, Belfast BT12 4AH
Tel 028-90323009
*Project Manager:* Cormac McArt
Email westcourtcentre@btconnect.com

681 Crumlin Road,
Belfast BT14 7GD
Community: 4
Tel 028-90717694

## DE LA SALLE BROTHERS

De La Salle College,
Edenmore Drive, Belfast BT11 8LT
Tel 028-90508800
*Headmaster:* Ms Claire Whyte

De La Salle Brothers, Glanaulin,
141 Glen Road, Belfast BT11 8BP
Tel 028-90614848
Superior: Br Ailbe Mangan
*Community:* 5

La Salle Pastoral Retreat Centre,
Glanaulin, 141 Glen Road,
Belfast BT11 8BP
Tel 028-90501932 Tax 028-90501932

La Salle House, 4 Stream Street,
Downpatrick, Co Down BT30 6DD
Tel 028-44612996
*Superior:* Br Mark Jordan
Community: 5

St Patrick's Grammar School,
Downpatrick, Co Down BT30 6NJ
Tel 028-44619722
*Headmaster:* Mr Sean Sloan

Secondary School, Struell Road,
Downpatrick, Co Down BT30 6JR
Tel 028-44612520
*Headmaster:* Mr Barry Sharvin

Our Lady and St Patrick's Primary School,
Downpatrick, Co Down BT30 6JD
Tel 028-44612787
*Headmaster:* Mr Hugh Kelly

## SISTERS

### BON SECOURS SISTERS (PARIS)
52A Tullymore Gardens,
Belfast BT11 8ND
Tel 028-90625757
Community: 1
Pastoral ministry

### CONGREGATION OF THE SISTERS OF MERCY
Convent of Mercy, 2A Fruithill Park,
Belfast BT11 8GD
Tel 028-90616399

Convent of Mercy, Beechmount,
Ard Na Va Road, Belfast BT12 6FF
Tel 028-90319496
*Leader:* Sr Annie Jo Heduan
Community: 10

21 Ardglass Road,
Downpatrick, Co Down BT30 6JQ
Tel 028-44615645

27a Glenveagh Drive,
Belfast BT11 9HX
Tel 028-90602175
Community: 4

Mercy Convent, Whiteabbey,
453 Shore Road, Newtownabbey,
Co Antrim BT37 9SE
Tel 028-90863128

Convent of Mercy,
252 Limestone Road, Belfast BT15 3AR
Tel 028-90748830

Sisters of Mercy
616 Crumlin Road, Belfast BT14 7GL
Tel 028-90717112
Community: 3

23 Fortwilliam Fold,
Fortwilliam Park,
Belfast BT15 4AN
Tel 028-90371268

21 Camberwell Court,
Limestone Road, Belfast BT15 3BH
Tel 028-90286584

Sisters of Mercy, 24 Floral Park,
Glengormley, Co Antrim BT36 7RU
Tel 028-90878384

Sisters of Mercy, 2 Lever Street,
Ligoniel, Belfast BT14 8EF
Tel 028-90710529

Sisters of Mercy, Ballysillan House,
614 Crumlin Road, Belfast BT14 7GL
Tel 028-90715758
Community: 3

27 Wheatfield Gardens,
Belfast BT14 7HU
Tel 028-90715478

3 Ashgrove Lodge, Glengormley,
Newtownabbey, Co Antrim BT36 6WY
Tel 028-90843890

25 Camberwell Court,
Limestone Road, Belfast BT15 3BH
Tel 028-90290213

### CONGREGATION OF THE SISTERS OF SION
547 Ormeau Road, Belfast BT7 3JA
Tel 028-90643208
Email sionbelfast@hotmail.co.uk
Community: 3
Education, spirituality, counselling

### CROSS AND PASSION CONGREGATION
4 Innisfayle Road,
Belfast BT15 4ER
Tel 028-90774238
Community: 2
Adult education, ecumenical work,
healing ministries

St Teresa's Convent, 78 Glen Road,
Belfast BT11 8BH
Tel 028-90613955
Community: 4
Hospital chaplaincy and pastoral care,
ecumenical work, bereavement
counselling

Villa Pacis, 78A Glen Road,
Belfast BT11 8BH
Tel 028-90621766
*Sister-in-charge:* Sr Mary Sloan
Community: 13
Care of sick and elderly

Drumalis Retreat Centre,
47 Glenarm Road, Larne,
Co Antrim BT40 1DT
Tel 028-28276455/28272196
Fax 028-28277999
Email drumalis@btconnect.com
Community: 2

Cross and Passion Convent
120b Coast Road, Drains Bay,
Larne, Co Antrim
Tel 028-28279428
Community: 3
Prayer and Retreat work

Cross and Passion Convent,
3 Gort an Chlochair, Ballycastle,
Co Antrim BT54 6NU
Tel 028-20762228
Community: 2
Parish ministry, counselling

5c Easton Avenue, Cliftonville road,
Belfast BT14 6LL
Tel 028-90749507
Community: 2
Retreat work, Bosnia project, counselling
and facilitation

### DAUGHTERS OF CHARITY OF ST VINCENT DE PAUL
23 Glen Road, Belfast BT11 8BA
and
19 Upper Cavehill Road,
Belfast BT15 5EZ
Tel 028-9023052
*Superior:* Sr Mary Connaire
Community: 7
Pastoral work and education

St Louise's Comprehensive College,
468 Falls Road, Belfast BT 6EN
Tel 028-90325631

1c Grainne House
(for families in transition)
Newlodge, Belfast BT 2LA

### DOMINICAN SISTERS
St Catherine's, 133 Falls Road,
Belfast BT12 6AD
Tel 028-90327056
Email opfalls@dominicansisters.com
*Prioress:* Sr Catherine Campbell
Community: 14
Varied ministries
Grammar School. Tel 028-90320081
St Rose's High School. Tel 028-90240937

Dominican Convent,
Fortwilliam Park, Belfast BT15 4AP
Tel 028-90370008
Email ionas.house@btinternet.com
Community: 8
Varied ministries
Grammar School
Tel 028-90370298

## FAMILY OF ADORATION
63 Falls Road, Belfast BT12 4PD
Tel 01232-325668
Email adorationsisters@utv.net
*Superior:* Sr Molly Caldwell
Community: 4
A contemplative community with mission of adoration, making of altar breads

## CONGREGATION OF OUR LADY OF CHARITY OF THE GOOD SHEPHERD
25 Rossmore Drive,
Belfast BT7 3LA
Tel 028-90641346 Fax 028-90646360
Email 25rossmoredrive@gmail.com
*Leader:* Sr Cait O'Leary
Community: 20

Congregation of Our Lady of Charity of the Good Shepherd (Contemplative Sisters)
Lys Marie, 19 Rossmore Drive,
Belfast BT7 3LA
Tel 028-90491820
Fax 028-90493565
Email lysmariesisters@yahoo.com
*Leader:* Sr Esther Boyle
Community: 10

49 Knockbreda Park, Belfast BT6 0HD
Tel 028-90224236
Email franceslynch57@hotmail.com
Community: 1
Parish work

## MARIST SISTERS
22 St Peter's Place,
Belfast BT12 4SB
Tel 028-90247901
Community: 2
Parish ministry

Grosvenor House,
259 Grosvenor Road, Belfast BT12 4LL
Tel 028-90310383
Email marbelfast@yahoo.co.uk
Community: 2
Hostel for the homeless and hospital chaplaincy

## MISSIONARY SISTERS OF THE HOLY CROSS
86 Glen Road,
Belfast BT11 8BH
Tel 028-90614631 Fax 028-90614631
Email holycross3@sky.com
*Superior:* Sr Patricia Kelly
Email patkelly5@sky.com
Community: 4

## NOTRE DAME DES MISSIONS (OUR LADY OF THE MISSIONS SISTERS)
28 Niblock Oaks,
Co Antrim BT41 2DJ
Community: 2
Parish ministry

## POOR SERVANTS OF THE MOTHER OF GOD
The Convent,
15 Martin's Lane, Carnagat,
Newry, Co Down BT35 8PJ
Community: 2
Pastoral

## CONGREGATION OF THE SISTERS OF NAZARETH
Nazareth House Care Village,
516 Ravenhill Road,
Belfast BT6 0BX
Tel 028-90690600 Fax 028-90690601
*Superior:* Sr Mary Theresa Mallon
Community: 13
Home for the elderly. Beds: 70

Bethlehem Nursery School,
514 Ravenhill Road, Belfast BT6 0BW
Tel 028-90640406
Pupils: 50
St Michael's Primary,
516 Ravenhill Road, Belfast BT6 0BW
Tel 028-90491529. Pupils: 400

## PRESENTATION SISTERS
*Northern Province*
24 Ben Eden Green
Belfast BT15
*Contact Person:* Sr Camilla Flynn

## RELIGIOUS OF SACRED HEART OF MARY
100 Hillsborough Road, Lisburn,
Co Antrim BT28 1JU
Tel 01846-678501
Community: 4
Ministry in local area

28 Upper Green, Dunmurry,
Belfast BT17 0EL
Tel 01232-600792
Community 5
Ministry in local area and education

Sacred Heart of Mary Grammar School for Boys and Girls,
Rathmore, Finaghy, Belfast BT10 0LF
Pupils: 1,350
Tel 01232-610115
Email userid.rathmore@schools.class-ni.org.uk

## ROSMINIANS (SISTERS OF PROVIDENCE)
30A Deanby Gardens,
Belfast BT14 6NN
Tel 01232-756664
*Contact Person:* Sr Carmel Martin
Email sistercarmel1@utvinternet.com
Community: 2
Pastoral work

## SACRED HEARTS OF JESUS AND MARY
The Curragh Community,
2 Workman Avenue,
Belfast BT13 3SB
Tel 028-90312658

## ST CLARE SISTERS
St Clare's Convent, 43 Rosetta Park,
Belfast BT6 0DL
Tel 028-90694108
Community: 3

## ST LOUIS SISTERS
St Louis Grammar School, Kilkeel
Tel 016937-62747
Pupils: 590

St Louis Grammar School
Cullybackey Road, Ballymena,
Co Antrim BT43 5DW
Tel 01266-49534
Pupils: 989

14 Carndale Meadows, Carniny Road,
Ballymena BT43 5NX
Tel 028-25651683
Community: 1

21 Glenbawn Square, Poleglass,
Dunmurry, Belfast BT17 0TT
Tel 028-90225236
Community: 1

7 Riverdale Park Avenue,
Belfast BT11 9BP
Tel 028-90209074
Community: 1

22 Riverdale Park North,
Belfast BT11 9DL
Tel 028-90619375
Community: 1

Apartment 2 Hollycroft,
1-3 Inver Avenue, Belfast BT15 5DG
Tel 028-90721037
Community: 1

91 Hillhead Crescent,
Stewartstown Road, Belfast BT11 9FW
Tel 028-90621900
Community: 6
Varied Apostolates

49 Bracken Avenue,
Castlewellan Road,
Newcastle, Co Down BT33 0HG
Tel 028-43726282
Community: 3

## EDUCATIONAL INSTITUTIONS

**Aquinas College**
518 Ravenhill Road, Belfast BT6 0BY
Tel 028-90643939
*Principal:* Mr Barry Kelly
Priest on staff
Rev Colin Grant MA, STL, PGCE

**Our Lady and St Patrick's College**
Knock, Belfast BT5 7DQ
Tel 028-90401184
*Principal:* Mr Dermot G. Mullan MA, PGCE

**St Killian's College**
25 Tower Road, Carnlough,
Co Antrim BT44 0JS
Tel 028-2885202
*Principal:* Mr Jonathan Brady

**St Malachy's College**
Antrim Road, Belfast BT15 2AE
Tel 028-90748285
*Principal*
Mr Paul McBride
*Priest on Staff*
Very Rev Michael Spence BA, STL
*Resident Priest*
Rev Edward McGee (St Mary's University
College)

**St Mary's University College**
A College of Queen's University Belfast
191 Falls Road,
Belfast 12 6FE
Tel 028-90327678
*Principal*
Professor Peter Finn BA MSSc
*Priest Lecturers*
Rev Feidhlimidh Magennis MA, BD, LSS
(Dromore)
Rev Edward McGee BA, BD
Rev Paul Fleming BA, BD, STL
Rev Niall Coll BA, BD (Raphoe)

**EDMUND RICE SCHOOLS TRUST NORTHERN IRELAND**
Edmund Rice Schools Trust
Westcourt Centre
8-30 Barrack Street, Belfast BT12 4AH
*Education Officer:* Mr Kevin Burke
Tel 028-90333205
Email erstni@live.com

St Mary's Grammar School,
Glen Road, Belfast BT11 8NR
Tel 028-90294000 Fax 028-90294009
*Principal:* Mr John Martin

Christian Brothers' Secondary School,
Glen Road, Belfast BT11 8BW
Tel 028-90808050 Fax 028-90808055
*Principal:* Mr Tommy Armstrong

Edmund Rice College,
96-100 Hightown Road, Glengormley,
Newtownabbey, Belfast BT36 7AU
Tel 028-90848433/90840566
Fax 028-90844924
*Principal:* Mr Peter Friel

## CHARITABLE AND OTHER SOCIETIES

**Apostolic Work Society**
Xavier House,
156 Cliftonpark Avenue,
Belfast BT14 6DT
Tel 028-90351912
Email apostolic.work@btinternet.com
Office hours:
Monday-Wednesday 9.00 am-2.30 pm
Society for lay women
*President:* Mrs Anne Donaghy

**Legion of Mary**
14 Cliftonville Road,
Belfast BT14 6JX
Tel 028-90746626
*President:* Mr Joe Drew

**Morning Star House**
2-12 Divis Street, Belfast
Tel 028-90333500

**Regina Coeli Hostel**
8-10 Lake Glen Avenue,
Belfast BT11 8FE
Tel 028-90612473
Night shelter for destitute and homeless
women. Under the care of the Legion of
Mary

**Society of St Vincent de Paul**
196-200 Antrim Road,
Belfast BT15 2AJ
Tel 028-90351561
*Regional Administrator*
Ms Aileen Coney

**St Joseph's Centre for the Deaf**
321 Grosvenor Road,
Belfast BT12 4LP
Tel 028-90448211
The Centre provides a wide range of
facilities for the deaf.
*Co-ordinator:* Very Rev Patrick Devlin
*Northern Diocesan Lay Chaplain:*
Ms Denise Flack
Tel 078-77643961

# ST MARTIN APOSTOLATE

## 42 PARNELL SQUARE, DUBLIN 1

# *Religious Goods Supplies*

## *LITURGICAL & RELIGIOUS GOODS*

- *Mass Kits • Sick Call Sets and Pyxes*
- *Chalices • Ciboria • Communion Bowls*
- *Holy Water Containers and Sprinklers*
- *Thuribles*
- *Tabernacles suitable for Oratories or Prayer Rooms*
- *Statues*

The St Martin Apostolate are the agents for the
Slabbinck Vestment Company of Belgium.
Chasubles, overlay stoles, albs, altar cloths, etc.
A selection of Slabbinck Vestments are on display in our showrooms.
Catalogue available on request.

### *Visit our Showroom*

(HOURS: MONDAY-THURSDAY 10.00 AM-4.00 PM • LUNCH: 12.30 PM-2.15 PM)
PLEASE PHONE, WRITE OR FAX FOR DETAILS:
**Telephone (01) 874 5465/873 0147 • Fax (01) 873 1989**
**Email stmartin@iol.ie • Tel from UK 00353 1 8745465**
**www.stmartin.ie**

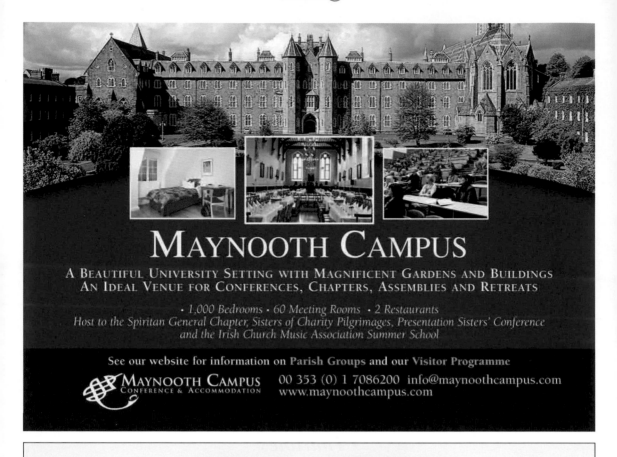

# MAYNOOTH CAMPUS

### A BEAUTIFUL UNIVERSITY SETTING WITH MAGNIFICENT GARDENS AND BUILDINGS
### AN IDEAL VENUE FOR CONFERENCES, CHAPTERS, ASSEMBLIES AND RETREATS

· 1,000 Bedrooms · 60 Meeting Rooms · 2 Restaurants
*Host to the Spiritan General Chapter, Sisters of Charity Pilgrimages, Presentation Sisters' Conference
and the Irish Church Music Association Summer School*

See our website for information on **Parish Groups** and our **Visitor Programme**

**MAYNOOTH CAMPUS** CONFERENCE & ACCOMMODATION    00 353 (0) 1 7086200  info@maynoothcampus.com
www.maynoothcampus.com

---

# CHURCH GOODS

CHURCH VESTMENTS • TABERNACLES • CHALICES • MASS KITS • ALTAR LINENS

UNIQUE RELIGIOUS ART PIECES FOR HOMES

BANNERS MADE TO ORDER • STATUES AND CRIBS

# Liturgical Centre

*pddm*

8 Castle Street, Athlone
Tel (090) 6492278 • Fax (090) 6492649

Newtownpark Avenue, Stillorgan, Dublin
Tel (01) 288 6414 • Fax (01) 283 6935

Email pddmdublin@eircom.net • Website www.pddm.org/ireland

# Michael McGowan

## CHURCH SUPPLIES

Dromod • Co. Leitrim
Tel (071) 9638357 • Fax (071) 9638528
Mobile (086) 256 1023
Email churchsupplies@eircom.net

*Suppliers of*
Votive Lights • Shrine Candles • Sanctuary Candles
Altar Candles • Oil Candles • Altar Wines
Vestments • Albs • Cruets • Silverware • Brassware
Charcoal • Incense • etc.
Mass Kits • Statues • Crib Sets
Restoration of all Brassware
Contractors for Furniture and Kneeler Padding

*Agent for*
**Lalor, Boramic and Duffy & Scott Church Candles**

## Fast – Free Delivery

# DIOCESE OF DROMORE

PATRONS OF THE DIOCESE
ST PATRICK, 17 MARCH; ST COLMAN, 7 JUNE

INCLUDES PORTIONS OF COUNTIES ANTRIM, ARMAGH AND DOWN

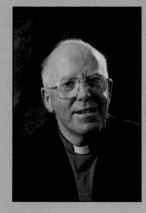

**Most Rev John McAreavey DD**
Bishop of Dromore; born 1949;
ordained priest 10 June 1973;
ordained Bishop of Dromore
19 September 1999

Residence:
Bishop's House,
44 Armagh Road,
Newry, Co Down BT35 6PN
Tel 028-30262444
Fax 028-30260496
Email
bishopofdromore@btinternet.com
Website dromorediocese.org

## ST PATRICK AND ST COLMAN'S CATHEDRAL, NEWRY

Newry cathedral was founded in 1825, at the centre of a growing and prosperous town. It symbolised, in many ways, the increasing confidence of the local Catholic population of the day, especially the newly emerging Catholic middle class.

The cathedral was designed by Thomas J. Duff, a prominent architect in the northern part of Ireland at the turn of the century. The building was dedicated in May 1829 by the then Irish Primate, Dr Curtis. It was believed to be the first major dedication ceremony in Ireland following the granting of Catholic Emancipation.

Originally, the cathedral was sparsely furnished, and it received its first significant interior decoration in 1851. The building was developed considerably between 1888 and 1891. During these years, its two transepts were added and a handsome bell tower erected. From 1904 to 1909, Bishop Henry O'Neill oversaw a further major phase of building. The main body of the church was extended in length by some forty feet and a new sanctuary was added. Much of the internal fabric of the cathedral, as we know it today, belongs to this period. Rich interior mosaic decoration was undertaken, side chapels were constructed and the cathedral's tubular organ was installed. The cathedral was solemnly consecrated in July 1925 – a century after its foundation! It enjoys the joint patronage of Ss Patrick and Colman.

Interior renovation was necessary in the wake of the Second Vatican Council. This work of extending and refurbishing the sanctuary area was undertaken by Bishop Francis Gerard Brooks from 1989 to 1990. It included the construction of the present marble altar, the rebuilding of the reredos of the former high altar, now in three parts, and the relocation of the bishop's chair to the front of the sanctuary. This work of renovation has earned widespread praise in the field of contemporary ecclesiastical architecture.

## CHAPTER

*Prebendaries*
*Saint Colman and Lann*
Very Rev Canon Francis Kearney PP
Annaclone
*Drumeragh*
Very Rev Canon Francis Boyle, Sàval
*Lanronan*
Rt Rev Mgr Aidan Hamill PP, VG
Shankill, St Peter's
*Aghaderg*
Very Rev Canon Liam Stevenson PP, VF
*Seapatrick*
*Clondallon*
Very Rev Canon Michael Hackett PP
Newry
*Kilmycon*
Very Rev Canon John Kearney Adm, VF
Warrenpoint
*Canon Penitentiary*
Very Rev Canon Francis Brown Adm,
Newry
*Downaclone*
Very Rev Canon Gerard McCrory PP
Magheradroll, Canon Theologian
*Retired Members, Honorary Canons:*
Very Rev Liam Boyle
Very Rev Arthur Byrne
Very Rev Anthony Davies
Very Rev Desmond Knowles
Very Rev Canon Cathal Jordan

## ADMINISTRATION

**Vicar General**
Rt Rev Mgr Aidan Hamill PP, VG
Parochial House, 70 North Street,
Lurgan, Co Armagh
Tel 028-38323161

**Chancellor/Diocesan Secretary**
Very Rev Gerald Powell PP
Parochial House, 4 Holymount Road
Laurencetown, Craigavon BT63 6AT
Co Armagh
Tel 028-40624236 Fax 028-40625440
Email gpowellpp@aol.com

**Council of Priests**
*Chairman*
Very Rev Canon Gerard McCrory
Church Street, Ballynahinch
Co Down BT24 8LP
Tel/Fax 028 97562410
*Secretary* Very Rev Peter McNeill PP
58 Ballydrumman Road,
Castlewellan, Co Down BT31 9UG
Tel 028 40650207 Fax 028 40650205
Email dromaradgooland@aol.co.uk

**Finance Council**
*Administrator and Secretary*
Rev Feidlimidh Magennis
St Mary's University College, Belfast
*Finance and Compliance Officer*
Mrs Rosaleen Conway
c/o Diocesan Office, Bishop's House,
44 Armagh Road, Newry,
Co Down BT35 6PN
Tel 028-30262444
Email finance@dromorediocese.org

*Members of Diocesan Finance Council*
*Chairman:* Most Rev John McAreavey
*Minute Secretary:* Agatha Larkin
Very Rev Canon Liam Stevenson
Very Rev Charlie Byrne
Mr Michael Gillen
Mr Cathal McHale
Ms Janette Burns

**Bishop's Secretary**
Miss Agatha Larkin
Bishop's House, Newry, Co Down
Tel 028-30262444

## CATECHETICS EDUCATION

**Diocesan Advisers for Religious Education**
*Primary Schools:* Sr Mercedes Coen
c/o Diocesan Office, Bishop's House,
44 Armagh Road, Newry,
Co Down BT35 6PN
Tel 028-30262444
*Post-Primary Schools:* Mrs Susan Morgan
c/o Diocesan Office, Bishop's House,
44 Armagh Road, Newry,
Co Down BT35 6PN
Tel 028-30262444

**Diocesan Education Committee**
*Chairman:* Rt Rev Mgr Aidan Hamill
70 North Street, Lurgan,
Co Armagh BT67 9AH
Tel 028-38323161

## LITURGY

**Music**
*Director:* Vacant

## PASTORAL

**ACCORD**
*Director:* Very Rev Michael Hackett
Cathedral Presbytery, Newry
Tel 028-30262586

**Adult Faith Development**
Rev Andrew McMahon
70 North Street, Lurgan, Co Armagh
BT67 9AH
Tel 028-38323161
Eail afmcmahon@hotmail.co.uk

**Chaplaincy to Deaf People**
*Contact:* Fr Colum Wright
10 Oaklands, Loughbrickland, Co Down
Email colum.wright@btinternet.com

**Communications**
*Press Officer:* Vacant
c/o Bishop's House, Newry, Co Down

**Dromore Clerical Provident Society**
*Contact:* Very Rev Brian Brown
26 Bottier Road, Moira, Craigavon,
Co Armgh BT67 0PE
Tel 028-92611347

**Ecumenism**
*Director:* Permanent Deacon Frank Rice
c/o Parochial House, Maypole Hill,
Dromore, Co Down BT25 1BQ
Email ricefa@aol.com

**Emigrant Services**
*Director:* Very Rev Patrick J. Murray PP
Maypole Hill, Dromore,
Co Down BT25 1BQ
Tel 028-92692218

**Immigrant Services**
Rev Krzysztof Kosciolek (SC) CC
Cathedral Presbytery, Newry
Tel 028-30262586

**Knock Diocesan Pilgrimage**
*Director:* Very Rev Jarlath Cushenan PP
17 Castlewellan Road, Hilltown,
Newry BT34 5UY
Tel 028-4063026

**Lourdes Diocesan Pilgrimage**
*Director:* Very Rev Jarlath Cushenan PP
17 Castlewellan Road, Hilltown, Newry,
Co Down BT34 5UY
Tel 028-40630206

**Marriage Tribunal**
Rev Peter C. McNeill
Diocesan Office, 44 Armagh Road,
Newry, Co Down BT35 6PN
Tel 028-30269836

**Pastoral Planning**
*Director:* Vacant

**Permanent Diaconate**
Rev John Byrne PP
The Presbytery, 11 Tullygally Road,
Craigavon, Co Armagh BT65 5BL
Tel 028-38341901

**Pioneer Total Abstinence Association**
*Diocesan Director:* Rt Rev Dean A. Davies
42 Old Killowen Road, Rostrevor,
Co Down BT34 3AD

**Pontifical Mission Societies and**
**Dromore/Lodwar Mission Project**
*Diocesan Director*
Rev Desmond Mooney CC
6 Derrymacash Road, Lurgan,
Craigavon BT66 6LG
Tel 028-38341356
Email mooneydesmond@googlemail.com

**Safeguarding Children**
Diocesan Offices, 44 Armagh Road,
Newry, Co Down BT35 6PN
*Designated person and Director*
Ms Patricia Carville
*Chair, Advisory Panel:* Mrs Aileen Oates
*Chair, Safeguarding Committee*
Mr Paul Carlin

**Special Needs Committee – Reachout**
Mrs Anne Loughlin
22 Dallan Hill, Warrenpoint
Tel 077-34330336

**Travellers**
*Chaplain:* Vacant

**Vocations**
*Director:* Rev Tony Corr CC
Cathedral Presbytery,
38 Hill Street, Newry BT34 1AT
Tel 028-30262586

**Youth**
*Chair Youth Commission*
Very Rev Canon Francis Brown
38 Hill Street, Newry BT34 1AT
Tel 028-30262586
*Director:* Ms Frances McNally
Pastoral Centre, The Mall, Newry
Tel 028-30833898
Email dromoreyd@btconnect.com

**Youth Ministry**
Ms Frances McNally
Pastoral Centre, The Mall, Newry
Tel 028-30833898
Email dromoreyd@btconnect.com

# PARISHES

*Since October 2012 the Diocese is divided into five Pastoral areas. The Parishes are set out below by Pastoral area.*

### Newry Pastoral Area
**NEWRY**
Very Rev Canon Francis Brown Adm
Very Rev Canon Michael Hackett PE
Rev Tony Corr CC
Rev Krzysztof Kosciolek (SC) CC
Rev Colum Murphy
Cathedral Presbytery, 38 Hill Street,
Newry BT34 1AT
Tel 028-30262586 Fax 028-30267505
Email newryparish@googlemail.com

### Pastoral Area of Clonallon
**ST PETER'S (WARRENPOINT)**
Very Rev Canon John Kearney Adm, VF
Parochial House, Great George's Street,
Warrenpoint, Co Down BT34 3NF
Tel 028-41754684 Fax 028-41754685
Rev Brendan Kearns CC
44 Church Street, Rostrevor,
Co Down BT34 3BB
Tel 028-41738277 Fax 028-41738315
*Parish Office:* Tel 028-41759981
Fax 028-41759980

**ST MARY'S (BURREN)**
Very Rev Charles Byrne
84 Milltown Street, Burren,
Warrenpoint, Co Down BT34 3PU
Tel 028-41772200
Email stmarysburren@btinternet.com
Rev Tom McAteer
91 Newry Road, Barnmeen,
Rathfriland, Co Down BT34 5AP
Tel 028-40630306 Fax 028-40631205

**ST PATRICK'S (MAYOBRIDGE)**
Very Rev Charles Byrne
84 Milltown Street, Burren,
Warrenpoint, Co Down BT34 3PU
Tel 028-41772200
Email stmarysburren@btinternet.com
Rev Tom McAteer
91 Newry Road, Barnmeen,
Rathfriland, Co Down BT34 5AP
Tel 028-40630306 Fax 028-40631205
Rev Marian Jachym (SC) CC
68 North Street, Lurgan,
Co Armagh BT67 9AH
Tel 028-38323161 Fax 028-38347927

**CLONDUFF (HILLTOWN)**
Very Rev Jarlath Cushenan PP
17 Castlewellan Road, Hilltown,
Newry, Co Down BT34 5UY
Tel/Fax 028-40630206

**DRUMGATH (RATHFRILAND)**
Very Rev Charles Byrne
84 Milltown Street, Burren, Warrenpoint,
Co Down BT34 3PU
Tel 028-41772200
Email stmarysburren@btinternet.com
Rev Tom McAteer
91 Newry Road, Barnmeen,
Rathfriland, Co Down BT34 5AP
Tel 028-40630306 Fax 028-40631205

**KILBRONEY (ROSTREVOR)**
Very Rev Canon John Kearney PP
Riverfields, Warrenpoint,
Co Down, BT34 3PU
Tel 028-41754684 Fax 028-41754685
Rev Brendan Kearns Adm
44 Church Street, Rostrevor,
Co Down BT34 3BB
Tel 028-41738277 Fax 028-41738315
*Office:* Tel 028-41739495
Email kilbroneyparish@hotmail.com

**SAVAL**
Very Rev Canon Francis Boyle PP
4 Shinn School Road, Newry
Co Down BT34 1PA
Tel 028-40630276

### Pastoral Area of Seapatrick
**AGHADERG**
Very Rev Colum Wright PP
10 Oaklands, Loughbrickland,
Co Down BT32 3NH
Tel 028-40623264 Fax 028-41759980
Email colum.wright@btinternet.com

**ANNACLONE**
Very Rev Canon Francis Kearney PP
17 Monteith Road, Annaclone,
Banbridge, Co Down BT32 5AQ
Tel 028-40671201
Email annacloneparish@fsmail.net

**DONAGHMORE**
Very Rev Colum Wright PP
10 Oaklands, Loughbrickland,
Co Down BT32 3NH
Tel 028-40623264 Fax 028-41759980
Email colum.wright@btinternet.com

**SEAPATRICK (BANBRIDGE)**
Very Rev Canon Liam Stevenson PP, VF
6 Scarva Road, Banbridge,
Co Down BT32 3AR
Tel 028-40662136
Rev Stephen Crossan CC
100 Dromore Street, Banbridge,
Co Down BT32 4DW
Tel 028-40622274 Fax 028-40622847
*Parish Office*
Tel 028-40624950 Fax 028-40626547
Email parishseapatrick@btconnect.com

**TULLYLISH**
Very Rev Gerald Powell PP
4 Holymount Road, Gilford,
Craigavon, Co Armagh BT63 6AT
Tel 028-40624236 Fax 028-40625440
Email gpowellpp@aol.com
*Parish Office:* Tel 028-40624236
Email tullylish.dromore@btinternet.com
Website www.tullylish.com

### Pastoral Area of Magheradroll
**DROMORE**
Very Rev Patrick J. Murray PP
Maypole Hill, Dromore,
Co Down BT25 1BQ
Tel 028-92692218
Email martinmcalinden@hotmail.com
Rev Frank Rice, Permanent Deacon
c/o Maypole Hill, Dromore,
Co Down BT35 1BQ

**DRUMGOOLAND**
Very Rev Peter C. McNeill PP
58 Ballydrumman Road,
Castlewellan, Co Down BT31 9UG
Tel 028-40650207 Fax 028-40650205
Email dromaradgooland@aol.co.uk

**DROMARA**
Very Rev Peter C. McNeill PP
58 Ballydrumman Road,
Castlewellan, Co Down BT31 9UG
Tel 028-40650207 Fax 028-40650205

**MAGHERADROLL (BALLYNAHINCH)**
Very Rev Canon Gerard McCrory PP
Church Street, Ballynahinch,
Co Down BT24 8LP
Tel/Fax 028-97562410
Email magheradrollrc.parish@nireland.com
Rev Desmond Loughran CC
Drumaness, Ballynahinch,
Co Down BT24 8NG
Tel 028-97561432
*Parish Office:* 028-97565429

### Pastoral Area of Shankill
**MAGHERALIN**
Very Rev Brian Brown PP
25 Bottier Road, Moira, Craigavon,
Co Armagh BT67 0PE
Tel 028-92611347
*Parish Office:* 028-92617435

**MOYRAVERTY (CRAIGAVON)**
Rev John Byrne PP
The Presbytery, 11 Tullygally Road,
Legahory, Craigavon BT65 5BL
Tel 028-38341901
Email johnbyrne5426@me.com
Rev Desmond Mooney CC
6 Derrymacash Road, Lurgan,
Craigavon BT66 6LG
Tel 028-38341356
Email mooneydesmond@googlemail.com
Very Rev Michael Maginn
The Presbytery, Tullygally Road,
Legahory, Craigavon BT65 5BY
Tel 028-38311872
Rev Gerry Heaney, Permanent Deacon
c/o The Presbytery, Tullygally Road,
Legahory, Craigavon BT65 5BL
*Parish Office:* Moyraverty,
10 Tullygally Road
Tel 028-38343013

## SEAGOE (DERRYMACASH)
Rev John Byrne PP
The Presbytery, 11 Tullygally Road,
Legahory, Craigavon BT65 5BL
Tel 028-38341901
Email johnbyrne5426@me.com
Rev Desmond Mooney CC
6 Derrymacash Road, Lurgan,
Craigavon BT66 6LG
Tel 028-38341356
Email mooneydesmond@googlemail.com
Very Rev Michael Maginn
The Presbytery, Tullygally Road,
Legahory, Craigavon BT65 5BY
Tel 028-38311872

## SHANKILL, ST PAUL'S (LURGAN)
Rt Rev Aidan Hamill PP, VG
Rev Andrew McMahon CC
Email afmcmahon@hotmail.co.uk
70 North Street, Lurgan,
Co Armagh BT67 9AH
Tel 028-38323161
Rev Conor McConville CC
Lisadell, 54 Francis Street,
Lurgan, Co Armagh BT66 6DL
Tel 028-38327173 Fax 028-38317974
Rev Brian Fitzpatrick
70 North Street, Lurgan,
Co Armagh BT67 9AH
Tel 028-38323161
Rev Josef Wozniak (SC) CC
68 North Street, Lurgan,
Co Armagh BT67 9AH
Tel 028-38323161 Fax 028-38347927
*St Paul's Parish Office:* Tel 028-38321289
Email parishsecretary@btinternet.com

## SHANKILL, ST PETER'S (LURGAN)
Rt Rev Mgr Aidan Hamill PP, VG
Rev Andrew McMahon CC
Email afmcmahon@hotmail.co.uk
70 North Street, Lurgan,
Co Armagh BT67 9AH
Tel 028-38323161
Rev Conor McConville CC
Lisadell, 54 Francis Street,
Lurgan, Co Armagh BT66 6DL
Tel 028-38327173 Fax 028-38317974
Rev Brian Fitzpatrick CC
70 North Street, Lurgan,
Co Armagh BT67 9AH
Tel 028-38323161
Rev Josef Wozniak (SC) CC
68 North Street, Lurgan,
Co Armagh BT67 9AH
Tel 028-38323161
Rev Kevin Devine, Permanent Deacon
c/o 70 North Street, Lurgan,
Co Armagh BT67 9AH
Email office@stpetersparishlurgan.org

## HOSPITALS AND THEIR CHAPLAINS

**Craigavon Area Hospital**
Co Armagh
*Chaplains:* Very Rev Michael Maginn PP
Sr Fiona Galligan

**District Hospital**
Lurgan and Portadown, Co Armagh
*Chaplain:* Very Rev Michael Maginn PP

**Hospice**
Southern Area Hospice Services,
St John's House, Courtenay Hill, Newry,
Co Down BT34 2EB
Tel 028-30267711 Fax 028-30268492
*Chaplain:* Sr Fiona Galligan

## PRIESTS OF THE DIOCESE ELSEWHERE

Rt Rev Mgr Hugh Connolly BA, DD
President, St Patrick's College,
Maynooth, Co Kildare
Very Rev Stephen Ferris
Keele University, England
Rev Matthew McConville
c/o Bishop's House
Rev Feidlimidh Magennis LSS
St Mary's University College, Belfast
Very Rev Martin McAlinden
Director of Pastoral Theology
St Patrick's College, Maynooth, Co Kildare

## RETIRED PRIESTS

Very Rev Liam Boyle
Carlingford Lodge Nursing Home,
Warrenpoint, Co Down
Very Rev Arthur Byrne
Castor's Bay Road, Lurgan
Very Rev P. G. Conway
Warrenpoint Road, Newry, Co Down
Very Rev John Joe Cunningham
Newcastle, Co Down
Very Rev Canon Anthony Davies
Killowen, Rostrevor
Rev Gerard Green
c/o Bishop's House, Newry, Co Down
Very Rev Canon Cathal Jordan
The Presbytery, 13 Tullygally Road,
Craigavon BT65 5BY
Very Rev Canon Desmond Knowles
Newry, Co Down
Very Rev Brendan McAteer
Warrenpoint, Co Down
Very Rev Arthur MacNeill
14 Ballyholland Road, Newry, Co Down
Very Rev Francis Molloy
Lurgan, Co Armagh
Very Rev Oliver Mooney
Newry, Co Down
Rev John Murtagh, Newry, Co Down
Very Rev James Poland
Rostrevor, Co Down

## RELIGIOUS ORDERS AND CONGREGATIONS

## PRIESTS

### BENEDICTINES
Holy Cross Monastery, 119 Kilbroney
Road, Rostrevor, Co Down BT34 3BN
Tel 028-41739979 Fax 028-41739978
*Prior:* Very Rev Dom Mark-Ephrem M.
Nolan (OSB)
Email benedictinemonks@btinternet.com
Website www.benedictinemonks.co.uk

### DOMINICANS
St Catherine's, Newry, Co Down BT35 8BN
Tel 028-30262178 Fax 028-30252188
*Prior:* Very Rev Joseph Ralph (OP)

### SOCIETY OF AFRICAN MISSIONS
Dromantine, Newry,
Co Down BT34 1RH
Tel 028-30821224 Fax 028-30821704
*Superior:* Rev Patrick O'Rourke (SMA)

Dromantine Retreat and Conference
Centre,
Newry, Co Down BT34 1RH
Tel 028-30821964 Fax 028-30821963
Email
admin@dromantineconference.com
Website www.dromantineconference.com
*Director:* Rev Paddy O'Rourke (SMA)

## SISTERS

### CARMELITES
Carmelite Monastery of Mary
Immaculate and St Therese,
42 Glenvale Road, Newry,
Co Down BT34 2RD
Fax 028/048-30252778
Email nuns@carmelitesglenvale.org
*Prioress:* Sr M. Carmel Clarke
Community: 4

### CONGREGATION OF THE SISTERS OF MERCY
Convent of Mercy, Catherine Street,
Newry, Co Down BT34 6JG
Tel 028-30262065/30264964
*Contact:* Sr Perpetua McArdle
Community: 11

Convent of Mercy, 3 Glenashley,
Rostrevor, Co Down BT34 3FW
Tel 028-41738356
Community: 2

14 Victoria Place, Lurgan,
Co Armagh BT67 9DL
Tel 028-38348602

89 North Street, Lurgan,
Co Armagh BT67 9AH
Tel 028-38347858

Convent of Mercy, 9 Queen Street,
Warrenpoint, Co Down BT34 3HZ
Tel 028-41752221

12 Cloghogue Heights, Newry,
Co Down BT35 8BA
Tel 028-30261628

Sisters of Mercy, Edward Street,
Lurgan, Co Armagh BT66 6DB
Tel 028-38322635
Community: 10

No 4 Ummericam Road, Silverbridge,
Newry, Co Down BT35 9PB
Tel 028-30860441

8 The Woodlands,
Lower Dromore Road,
Warrenpoint, Co Down BT34 6WL
Tel 028-41752383

17 Oakleigh Grove, Lurgan,
Co Armagh BT67 9AY
Tel 028-38347984

Convent of Mercy,
42 Antrim Road,
Lurgan, Co Armagh BT67 9BW
Tel 028-38347415

204 Drumglass, Craigavon,
Co Armagh BT65 5BB
Tel 028-38343447

Sisters of Mercy, 6 Portadown Road,
Lurgan, Co Armagh BT66 8QW
Tel 028-38327956

8 Parkhead Crescent, Newry,
Co Down BT35 8PE
Tel 028-30264615

5B Catherine Street, Newry,
Co Down BT35 6JG
Tel 028-30265342

1 Kildarragh Close,
Old Warrenpoint Road, Newry,
Co Down BT34 2SU
Tel 028-30267141

Sisters of Mercy, 49 Ardfreelan,
Rathfriland Road, Newry,
Co Down BT34 1CD
Tel 028-30250951

Sisters of Mercy, 2 Carrickree,
Bridle Loanan, Co Down BT34 3FA
Tel 028-41752347

27 Catherine Street, Newry,
Co Down, BT35 6JG
Tel 028-30833641

Rose Cottage,
14 Drumbanagher Wall Road,
Drumbanagher, Newry,
Co Down BT35 6LR
Tel 028-30821425

1 Dominican Court,
Newry, Co Down
Tel 028-30265184

Apt 4, Carlinn's Cove,
Warrenpoint Road, Rostrevor,
Co Down BT34 3GJ
Tel 028-41737751

6 Bracken Close,
Armagh Road, Newry,
Co Down BT35 6RW
Tel 028-30250630

## MISSIONARY FRANCISCAN SISTERS OF THE IMMACLATE CONCEPTION
28 Hawtorn Avenue,
Lurgan, Co Armagh BT66 6DU
Tel 028-38316958
Email elisegorman@btinternet.com

## MISSIONARY SISTERS OF THE ASSUMPTION
Assumption Convent,
34 Crossgar Road, Ballynahinch,
Co Down BT24 8EN
Tel 028-97561765 Fax 028-97565754
Email mail@assumption.org
*Superior:* Sr Ursula Hinchion
Email srursula@msassumption.org
Community: 8
Assumption Grammar School
Tel 028-97562250
Pupils: 840

## MISSIONARY SISTERS OF OUR LADY OF APOSTLES
Rostrevor, Newry, Co Down
Tel 028-41737653 Fax 028-417377656
Community: 4
Email olagreendale@hotmail.com
1 Greendale Crescent, Greenpark Road,
Rostrevor, Newry, Co Down BT34 3HF

## SISTERS OF ST CLARE
St Clare's Convent,
12 Ashgrove Avenue, Newry,
Co Down BT34 1PR
Tel 028-30252179
*Contact:* Sr Sheila Ryan
Community: 33
St Clare's Primary School, High Street,
Newry, Co Down BT34 1HD
Tel 028-30264909. Pupils: 665

St Clare's Convent,
75 Upper Damolly Road,
Newry, Co Down BT34 1QW
Tel 028-30268471
Community: 3
Sacred Heart Grammar School,
10 Ashgrove Avenue,
Newry, Co Down BT34 1PR
Tel 028-30264632. Pupils: 875

## EDUCATIONAL INSTITUTIONS
**St Colman's College (Diocesan College)**
Violet Hill,
Newry, Co Down
Tel 028-30262451
*Principal:* Mr Cormac McKinney
*Vice Principals:* Mr Aidan Henry,
Mr Michael Doyle
*Chaplain*
Very Rev Canon Michael Hackett

**EDMUND RICE SCHOOLS TRUST NORTHERN IRELAND**
St Colman's Abbey Primary School,
Courtenay Hill, Newry, Co Down BT34 2ED
Tel 028-30262175
Fax 028-30250648
Principal: Mr Eddie Sweeney

Abbey Christian Brothers' Grammar
School, 77a Ashgrove Road,
Newry, Co Down BT34 1QN
Tel 028-30263142 Fax 028-30262514
Principal: Mr D. McGovern

## CHARITABLE AND OTHER SOCIETIES
**ACCORD**
Cana House,
Newry Parish Pastoral Centre, The Mall,
Newry, Co Down
Tel 028-30263577

**Society of St Vincent de Paul**
Conferences at:
Ballynahinch (St Patrick's)
Banbridge (St Patrick's)
Craigavon (St Anthony's)
Dromore (St Colman's)
Gilford (St John's)
Hilltown (St John's)
Laurencetown (St Patrick's)
Lurgan (St Peter's)
Newry (Cathedral)
Newry (St Brigid's)
Rathfriland (St Marys)
Rostrevor (St Bronach's)
Warrenpoint (St Patrick's)

# DIOCESE OF ELPHIN

PATRONS OF THE DIOCESE
ST ASICUS, 27 APRIL; IMMACULATE CONCEPTION, 8 DECEMBER

INCLUDES PORTIONS OF COUNTIES ROSCOMMON, SLIGO,
WESTMEATH AND GALWAY

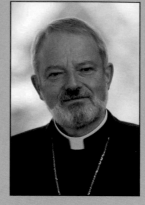

**Most Rev Kevin Doran MA, PhD**
Bishop of Elphin;
born 26 June 1953;
ordained priest 6 July 1977;
ordained Bishop of Elphin
13 July 2014

Residence: St Mary's,
Temple Street, Sligo
Tel 071-9150106
Fax 071-9162414
Email office@elphindiocese.ie

## CATHEDRAL OF THE IMMACULATE CONCEPTION, SLIGO

The 125-year-old cathedral church dominates the skyline of Sligo town. It was erected during the episcopate of Bishop Laurence Gillooly (1858–1895), whose knowledge of ecclesiastical architecture is imprinted on every stone.

The foundation stone was laid on 6 October 1868. It was designed by a renowned English architect, George Goldie, and was modelled on Normano-Romano-Byzantine style. It was acclaimed by an eminent architect as a 'poem in stone'. It is 275 feet long, with transepts and nave, and can accommodate 4,000 people. A square tower incorporating the main entrance to the cathedral is surmounted by a four-sided pyramidal spire which reaches a height of 210 feet. The stained-glass windows and the original high altar are magnificent works of art.

Although the cathedral was open for public worship in 1874, it wasn't until 1882 that all construction work was completed. The cathedral was finally consecrated on 1 July 1897 and dedicated in honour of the Immaculate Conception of the Blessed Virgin Mary.

The cathedral has undergone extensive renovations on two occasions since it was erected, including the remodelling of the sanctuary to comply with liturgical norms in 1970.

**Most Rev Christopher Jones DD**
Bishop Emeritus of Elphin;
born 3 March 1936;
ordained priest 21 June 1962;
ordained Bishop of Elphin
15 August 1994
Residence: St Mary's,
Temple Street, Sligo
Tel 071-9162670
Email christopherjones@elphindiocese.ie

## CHAPTER

*Castlerea*
Very Rev Canon Joseph Fitzgerald VF
*Athlone:* Very Rev Canon Liam Devine VG
*Roscommon*
Very Rev Canon Eugene McLoughlin VF
*Boyle:* Very Rev Canon Gerard Hanly VF
*Strandhill:* Very Rev Canon Niall Ahern
*Frenchpark:* Very Rev Canon Kevin Early
*Strokestown:* Very Rev Ciaran Whitney VF
*Sligo:* Very Rev Canon Thomas Hever VG

## ADMINISTRATION

**College of Consultors**
Very Rev Canon Eugene McLoughlin VF
Very Rev Canon Thomas Hever VG
Very Rev Canon Joseph Fitzgerald VF
Very Rev Ciaran Whitney VF
Very Rev Canon Gerard Hanly VF
Very Rev Canon Liam Devine VG
Very Rev Michael Duignan SThD, EV

**Vicars General**
Very Rev Canon Liam Divine PP, VG
Very Rev Canon Tom Hever Adm, VG

**Vicars Forane**
Very Rev Canon Eugene McLoughlin VF
Very Rev Canon Joseph Fitzgerald VF
Very Rev Ciaran Whitney VF
Very Rev Canon Gerard Hanly VF
Deaneries of Sligo and Athlone awaiting
appointment

**Finance Committee**
*Secretary*
Very Rev Michael Duignan SThD, EV
St Mary's, Temple Street, Sligo
Tel 071-9150106
Email chancellor@elphindiocese.ie

**Building Committee**
*Chairman*
Very Rev Raymond Milton PP
Knockcroghery, Co Roscommon

**Diocesan Secretary and Chancellor**
Very Rev Michael Duignan SThD, EV
St Mary's, Temple Street, Sligo
Tel 071-9150106
Email chancellor@elphindiocese.ie

**Secretary to the Bishop**
Ms Sheena Darcy
St Mary's, Temple Street, Sligo
Tel 071-9150106
Email bishopsecretary@elphindiocese.ie

## CATECHETICS EDUCATION

**Education (Post-Primary)**
*Episcopal Vicar*
Very Rev Michael Duignan SThD, EV
St Mary's, Temple Street, Sligo
Tel 071-9150106
Email chancellor@elphindiocese.ie

**Education (Primary)**
*Secretary*
Very Rev Christopher McHugh PP
Grange, Co Sligo
Tel 071-9163100

**Religious Instruction (Primary Schools)**
*Diocesan Director*
Sr Annette Duignan
Sisters of Mercy,
No. 1 St Patrick's Avenue, Sligo
Tel 071-9142731

## LITURGY

**Liturgical Music**
*Adviser Church Organ Music:*
Mr Charles O'Connor
Maugheraboy, Sligo
Tel 071-9145722

**Diocesan Magazine**
*The Angelus,* St Mary's, Sligo
Tel 071-9162670
*Editor:* Very Rev A. B. O'Shea PP
Sooey, via Boyle, Co Sligo
Tel 071-9165144
Email aboshea@eircom.net

## PASTORAL

**ACCORD**
*Director:* Rev James Murray CC
Carraroe, Sligo
Tel 071-9162136

**Adoption Society**
*Director*
Very Rev Canon Thomas Hever VG
Sligo Social Services,
Charles Street, Sligo
Tel 071-9145682

**Council of Priests**
*Chairman:* Very Rev John Cullen PP
Kiltoom, Athlone, Co Roscommon
Tel 090-6489105
*Secretary:* Rev Michael Duignan SThD
St Mary's, Temple Street, Sligo
Tel 071-9162670

**CURA**
*Co-ordinator:* Ms Geraldine Doherty
Sligo Social Services,
Charles Street, Sligo
Tel 071-9145682

**Diocesan Pastoral Council**
To be reconstituted in early 2015

**Ecumenism**
Rev Pat Lombard CC
St Mary's, Sligo
Tel 071-9162670

**Family Ministry**
*Director:* Very Rev Brian Conlon
Family Life Centre, Boyle,
Co Roscommon
Tel 071-9633000

**Marriage Tribunal**
(See Marriage Tribunals section)

**Pastoral Development**
*Director:* Dr Justin Harkin
Pastoral Development Office,
Church Grounds, St Coman's Club,
Abbey Street, Roscommon
Tel 087-6171526
Email justin@elphindiocese.ie

**Pilgrimage Directors (Lourdes)**
Rev Hugh McGonagle CC
7 Elm Park, Ballinode, Sligo
Tel 071-9143430
Very Rev Raymond Milton PP
Knockcroghery, Co Roscommon
Tel 090-6661127

**Pioneer Total Abstinence Association**
*Diocesan Director*
Very Rev Canon Liam Devine PP, VG
SS Peter and Paul, Athlone
Tel 090-6492171

**Pontifical Mission Societies**
*Diocesan Director*
Very Rev Ciaran Whitney PP, VF
Strokestown, Co Roscommon
Tel 071-9633027

**Social Services**
*Director:* Ms Christine McTaggart
Sligo Social Services, Charles Street, Sligo
Tel 071-9145682

**Travellers**
*Chaplain:* Rev John Carroll (SPS)
Cregg House, Rosses Point, Co Sligo
Tel 071-9177241

**Vocations to the Permanent Diaconate**
*Director:* Rev Michael Duignan SThD
St Mary's, Sligo, Co Sligo
Tel 071-9162670

**Vocations to the Priesthood**
*Directors:* Rev James Murray CC
Carraroe, Sligo, Co Sligo
Tel 071-9162136
Rev John Coughlan CC
Boyle, Co Roscommon
Tel 071-9662012

**Youth Ministry and Safeguarding Children**
*Diocesan Director*
Mr Frank McGuinness
St Mary's, Sligo, Co Sligo
Tel 087-9880690

# DIOCESE OF FERNS

PATRON OF THE DIOCESE
ST AIDAN, 30 JANUARY

INCLUDES ALMOST ALL OF COUNTY WEXFORD
AND PART OF COUNTY WICKLOW

**Most Rev Denis Brennan DD**
Bishop of Ferns
Ordained Bishop 23 April 2006

Residence: Bishop's House,
Summerhill, Wexford
Tel 053-9122177
Fax 053-9123436
Email adm@ferns.ie

## ST AIDAN'S CATHEDRAL, ENNISCORTHY

The foundation stone for St Aidan's Cathedral, Enniscorthy, was laid in 1843. The cathedral was designed by the architect Augustus Welby Northmore Pugin and is the largest church Pugin built in Ireland. The recent renovations of 1996 have restored to a great extent the original beautiful building as visualised by Pugin. The external stonework was executed by Irish stonemasons who were praised by Pugin. The restored stencilling of the interior gives some idea of what Pugin visualised for his churches.

Pugin, a Londoner, was as important an influence on the history of nineteenth-century English architecture as Frank Lloyd Wright was to be on American architecture. He was an extraordinarily gifted artist and designed ceramics, stained glass, wallpapers, textiles, memorial brasses, church plate, etc. His connection with the Diocese of Ferns came through the patronage of John, 16th Earl of Shrewsbury, Waterford and Wexford. Shrewsbury's wife was a native of Blackwater, Co Wexford. Her uncle, John Hyacinth Talbot, was the first Catholic MP for Co Wexford after Catholic Emancipation in 1829. A rich man through his marriage into the Redmond family, John Hyacinth Talbot introduced Pugin to Wexford, where through the patronage of the Talbot and Redmond family connections, he was to gain most of his Irish commissions.

Pugin was to die through overwork at the age of forty in 1852, but he has left a unique diocesan heritage to Ferns in his churches. His son and son-in-law, E.W. Pugin and George Ashlin, were to continue the building of Gothic Revival churches and monuments in Ireland.

**Most Rev Brendan Comiskey DD**
Retired Bishop of Ferns
PO Box 40, Summerhill, Wexford

## CHAPTER

Very Rev James B. Canon Curtis
Rt Rev Mgr Joseph L. Kehoe PA
Very Rev Nicholas Power
Very Rev Seamus De Val
Very Rev Thomas Curtis
Very Rev Felix Byrne
Very Rev Noel Hartley
Very Rev Lorenzo Cleary
Very Rev Tobias Kinsella
Very Rev Patrick C. O'Brien
Very Rev James Larkin
Very Rev John Sinnott

## ADMINISTRATION

**College of Consultors**
Rt Rev Mgr Joseph L. Kehoe PA
Rt Rev Mgr Denis Lennon PP, VF
Rt Rev Mgr Joseph McGrath VG, VF
Very Rev Patrick Cushen PP
Very Rev Noel Canon Hartley
Very Rev Denis Kelly
Very Rev William Howell PP, VF
Very Rev Brian Broaders
Very Rev Gerald O'Leary
Very Rev Hugh O'Byrne

**Vicar General**
Rt Rev Mgr Joseph McGrath VG, VF
New Ross, Co Wexford
Tel 051-447080

**Vicar for Clergy**
Rt Rev Mgr Denis Lennon PP, VF
39 Beechlawn, Clonard, Wexford
Tel 053-9124417

**Vicars Forane**
Very Rev Brian Broaders PP, VF
Rt Rev Mgr Joseph McGrath VG, VF
Rt Rev Mgr Denis Lennon PP, VF
Very Rev William Howell PP, VF

**Diocesan Finance Council**
Rt Rev Mgr Joseph McGrath VG, VF
Very Rev Patrick Cushen PP
Very Rev James Fegan Adm
Very Rev William Howell PP, VF
Mrs Catherine O'Gara
Mr Liam Gaynor
Mr John Murphy
Mr Patrick F. Dore
Ms Eleanor Furlong
Ms Pauline O'Neill
*Finance Officer and Chairman*
Mr Eugene Doyle

**Diocesan Archivist**
Very Rev Seamus Canon De Val
1 Irish Street, Bunclody, Co Wexford
Tel 053-9376140

**Diocesan Secretary & Chancellery**
Rev John Carroll
PO Box 40, Bishop's House,
Summerhill, Wexford
Tel 053-9124368
Email jc@ferns.ie

**Diocesan Pastoral Council**
*Co-ordinator:* Ms Maria Colfer
Ferns Diocesan Centre,
St Peter's College, Wexford
Tel 053-9145511
Email colfermaria@gmail.com

## CATECHETICS EDUCATION

**Catholic Primary School Management Association (CPSMA)**
Very Rev Francis Murphy PP
Kilmuckridge, Gorey, Co Wexford
Tel 053-9130116
Email fernsed@gmail.com

**Diocesan Adviser for Primary School Catechetics**
Rev Patrick Duffy CC
Kilmyshall, Enniscorthy, Co Wexford
Tel 053-9377188

**Director of Religious Education**
Sr Anna McDonagh
Ferns Diocesan Centre,
St Peter's College, Wexford
Tel 053-9145511

## PASTORAL

**Apostolic Work Society**
*Diocesan Director*
Very Rev Joseph Power PP
Kilrush, Bunclody, Enniscorthy,
Co Wexford
Tel 053-9377262

**Chaplain to Special Needs Groups**
Very Rev Tom Dalton PP
Riverchapel, Gorey, Co Wexford
Tel 053-9425241

**CORI (Ferns Branch)**
*Secretary:* Sr Teresa Walsh
Terrerath, New Ross, Co Wexford
Tel 051-428313
Email mshrterrerath@gmail.com

**Diocesan Mission Commission**
*Chairman:* Rt Rev Mgr Denis Lennon PP, VF
39 Beechlawn, Wexford
Tel 053-9124417

**Ecumenism**
*Director:* Rev James Murphy CC
St Brigid's, Rosslare, Co Wexford
Tel 053-9132118

**FDYS Youth Work Ireland**
*Director:* Mr Kieran Donohoe
Francis Street, Wexford
Tel 053-9123262

**Fatima Pilgrimage**
*Director:* Very Rev Thomas Doyle PP
Craanford, Gorey, Co Wexford
Tel 053-9428163

**House of Mission**
Rev Thaddeus Doyle
Shillelagh, Arklow, Co Wicklow
Tel 053-9429926

**Knock Pilgrimage**
*Director*
Very Rev Oliver Sweeney PP
Poulfur, Fethard-on-Sea, New Ross,
Co Wexford
Tel 051-397048

**Legion of Mary**
(Northern Curia)
Very Rev Seamus Canon De Val
1 Irish Street, Bunclody,
Co Wexford
Tel 053-9376140 (Southern Curia)
Very Rev Brendan Nolan PP
Our Lady's Island, Co Wexford
Tel 053-9131167

**Lourdes Pilgrimage**
*Director*
Rev Matthew Boggan CC
The Presbytery, Gorey, Co Wexford
Tel 053-942117

**Marriage Tribunal**
(See also Marriage Tribunals section)
*Ferns Diocesan Auditor for Dublin
Regional Marriage Tribunal*
Very Rev Kevin Cahill (DCL) PP
Rathangan, Duncormick,
Co Wexford
Tel 051-563104

**Our Lady's Island Pilgrimage**
*Director*
Very Rev Brendan Nolan PP
Our Lady's Island, Broadway,
Co Wexford
Tel 053-9131167

**Pioneer Total Abstinence Association**
*Diocesan Director*
Rev Robert McGuire CC
Galbally, Ballyhogue,
Enniscorthy, Co Wexford
Tel 053-9247882

**Pontifical Mission Societies**
*Diocesan Director*
Very Rev Hugh O'Byrne PP
Blackwater, Co Wexford
Tel 053-9127118

**St Aidan Retirement Fund**
*Chairman*
Very Rev Francis Murphy PP
Kilmuckridge, Gorey, Co Wexford
Tel 053-9130116

**St Joseph's Young Priests' Society**
*Diocesan Chaplain*
Right Rev Mgr Joseph McGrath PP, VF, VG
New Ross, Co Wexford
Tel 051-447080

**Travellers**
*Diocesan Co-ordinator*
Rev Thomas Orr CC
Traveller Resource Centre,
Mary Street, New Ross,
Co Wexford
Tel 051-422272

**Vocations**
*Director*
Very Rev James Finn PP
Crossabeg, Co Wexford
Tel 053-9159015

## PARISHES

*Mensal parishes are listed first. Other parishes follow alphabetically.*

**ENNISCORTHY, CATHEDRAL OF ST AIDAN**
Very Rev Richard Lawless Adm
Rev William Swan CC
St Aidan's, Enniscorthy,
Co Wexford
Tel 053-9235777
Fax 053-9237700

**WEXFORD**
Very Rev James Fegan Adm
Rev Michael O'Shea CC
Rev Aodhan Marken CC
Rev Brian Whelan CC
The Presbytery,
12 School Street, Wexford
Tel 053-9122055 Fax 053-9121724

**ADAMSTOWN**
Very Rev Robert Nolan PP
Adamstown, Enniscorthy,
Co Wexford
Tel 053-9240512

**ANNACURRA**
Very Rev James Hammel PP
Annacurra, Aughrim, Co Wicklow
Tel 0402-36119

**BALLINDAGGIN**
Very Rev John Sinnott PP
Ballindaggin, Enniscorthy,
Co Wexford
Tel 053-9388559
Rev Fintan Morris CC
Caim, Enniscorthy, Co Wexford
Tel 053-9255149

**BALLYCULLANE**
Very Rev William Byrne PP
Ballycullane, New Ross, Co Wexford
Tel 051-562123
Rev Michael A. Doyle CC
St Leonard's, Saltmills, New Ross,
Co Wexford
Tel 051-562135
Very Rev Sean Laffan CC
Gusserane, Co Wexford
Tel 051-562111

**BALLYGARRETT**
Very Rev James Butler PP
Ballygarrett, Gorey, Co Wexford
Tel 053-9427330

**BALLYMORE AND MAYGLASS**
Very Rev Martin Byrne PP
Ballymore, Killinick, Co Wexford
Tel 053-9158966

**BANNOW**
Very Rev James Kehoe PP
Carrig-on-Bannow,
Wellington Bridge, Co Wexford
Tel 051-561192
Rev Denis Browne
Ballymitty, Co Wexford
Tel 051-561128

**BLACKWATER**
Very Rev Hugh O'Byrne PP
Tel 053-9127118
Rev Kevin McDevitt *(priest in residence)*
Tel 053-9129288
Blackwater, Enniscorthy,
Co Wexford

**BREE**
Very Rev Michael Byrne PP
Bree, Enniscorthy, Co Wexford
Tel 053-9247843
Rev Robert McGuire CC
Galbally, Ballyhogue, Enniscorthy,
Co Wexford
Tel 053-9247814

**BUNCLODY**
*(Parish Office:* Tel/Fax 053-9376190)
Very Rev Laurence O'Connor PP
Bunclody, Enniscorthy, Co Wexford
Tel 053-9377319
Rev Patrick Duffy CC
Kilmyshall, Enniscorthy, Co Wexford
Tel 053-9377188

**CAMOLIN**
Very Rev Joseph Kavanagh PP
Camolin, Co Wexford
Tel 053-9383136
Rev Thomas Orr CC
Ballycanew, Gorey, Co Wexford
Tel 053-9427184

**CARNEW**
Very Rev Martin Casey PP
Woolgreen, Carnew, Co Wicklow
Tel 053-9426888
Rev Christopher Hayden CC
Coolfancy, Tinahely, Co Wicklow
Tel 0402-34725

**CASTLEBRIDGE**
Very Rev Walter Forde PP
Castlebridge, Co Wexford
Tel 053-9159769 Fax 053-9159158
Very Rev Denis Kelly Adm
Ballymore, Screen,
Enniscorthy, Co Wexford
Tel 053-9137140

**CLONARD**
*(Parish Office:* Tel 053-9123672
Fax 053-9146699)
Rt Rev Mgr Denis Lennon PP, VF
39 Beechlawn, Wexford
Tel 053-9124417
Rev James Cullen CC
6 Meadowvale, Coolcotts,
Wexford
Tel 053-9143932
Rev Barry Larkin CC
1 Clonard Park, Clonard,
Co Wexford
Tel 053-9147686

**CLONGEEN**
Very Rev Colm Murphy PP
Clongeen, Foulksmills, Co Wexford
Tel 051-565610

**CLOUGHBAWN AND POULPEASTY**
Very Rev Bernard Cushen PP
Clonroche, Enniscorthy,
Co Wexford
Tel 053-9244115

**CRAANFORD**
Very Rev Thomas Doyle PP
Craanford, Gorey, Co Wexford
Tel 053-9228163
Very Rev Felix Canon Byrne CC
Monaseed, Gorey, Co Wexford
Tel 053-9428207

**CROSSABEG AND BALLYMURN**
Very Rev James Finn PP
Crossabeg, Co Wexford
Tel 053-9159015

**CUSHINSTOWN**
Very Rev Martin Doyle PP
Cushinstown, Foulksmills,
Co Wexford
Tel 051-428347
Rev Odhrán Furlong CC
Rathgarogue, New Ross,
Co Wexford
Tel 051-424521

**DAVIDSTOWN AND COURTNACUDDY**
Very Rev James Nolan PP
Davidstown, Enniscorthy,
Co Wexford
Tel 053-9233382

**DUNCANNON**
Very Rev John P. Nolan PP
Duncannon, New Ross,
Co Wexford
Tel 051-389118

**FERNS**
Very Rev Patrick Cushen PP
Ferns, Enniscorthy, Co Wexford
Tel 053-9366152
Rev Richard Redmond CC
(Ballyduff) The Square, Ferns,
Enniscorthy, Co Wexford
Tel 053-9366162

**GLYNN**
Very Rev Patrick Stafford PP
Glynn, Enniscorthy, Co Wexford
Tel 053-9128115
Rev John Carroll CC
(Diocesan Secretary)
Barntown, Co Wexford
Tel 053-9120853

**GOREY**
Very Rev William Howell PP, VF
St Michael's, Gorey, Co Wexford
Tel 053-9421112
Rev William Flynn CC
Rev Matthew Boggan CC
Tel 053-9421117
St Patrick's, Gorey, Co Wexford

**HORESWOOD AND BALLYKELLY**
Very Rev Gerald O'Leary PP
Horeswood, Campile, Co Wexford
Tel 051-388129

**KILANERIN AND BALLYFAD**
Very Rev Donal Berney PP
Kilanerin, Gorey,
Co Wexford
Tel/Fax 0402-37120

**KILLAVENEY AND CROSSBRIDGE**
Very Rev Raymond Gahan PP
Killaveney, Tinahely,
Co Wicklow
Tel 0402-38188

**KILMORE AND KILMORE QUAY**
Very Rev Denis Doyle PP
Kilmore, Co Wexford
Tel 053-9135181
Rev James Doyle CC
Mulrankin, Co Wexford
Tel 053-9135166

**KILMUCKRIDGE (LITTER) AND MONAMOLIN**
Very Rev Francis Murphy PP
Kilmuckridge, Gorey, Co Wexford
Tel 053-9130116
Very Rev Seamus Canon Larkin (priest in residence)
Monamolin, Gorey, Co Wexford
Tel 053-9389223

**KILRANE AND ST PATRICK'S**
Very Rev Diarmuid Desmond PP
Kilrane, Co Wexford
Tel 053-9133128

**KILRUSH AND ASKAMORE**
Very Rev Joseph Power PP
Kilrush, Bunclody, Enniscorthy,
Co Wexford
Tel 053-9377262

**MARSHALLSTOWN AND CASTLEDOCKRELL**
Very Rev Daniel McDonald PP
Marshallstown, Enniscorthy,
Co Wexford
Tel 053-9388521

**MONAGEER**
Very Rev William Cosgrave PP
Monageer, Ferns, Enniscorthy,
Co Wexford
Tel 053-9233530
Rev Michael Byrne CC
Boolavogue, Ferns, Wexford
Tel 053-9366282

**NEWBAWN AND RAHEEN**
Very Rev James Furlong PP
Newbawn, Co Wexford
Tel 051-428227

**NEW ROSS**
Rt Rev Mgr Joseph McGrath PP, VF, VG
New Ross, Co Wexford
Tel 051-447080
Rev Tomás Kehoe CC
Tel 051-447086
Rev Roger O'Neill CC
Tel 051-447081
New Ross, Co Wexford

**OULART**
Very Rev Patrick Browne PP
Oulart, Gorey, Co Wexford
Tel 053-9136139
Rev Dermot Gahan CC
The Ballagh, Wexford
Tel 053-9136200

**OUR LADY'S ISLAND AND TACUMSHANE**
Very Rev Brendan Nolan PP
Our Lady's Island, Broadway,
Co Wexford
Tel 053-9131167

**OYLEGATE AND GLENBRIEN**
Very Rev James Cogley PP
Oylegate, Co Wexford
Tel 053-9138163

**PIERCESTOWN**
Very Rev John O'Reilly PP
Piercestown, Co Wexford
Tel 053-9158851
Rev James Moynihan CC
Murrintown, Wexford
Tel 053-9139136

**RAMSGRANGE**
Rt Rev Mgr Donald Kenny PP
Ramsgrange, New Ross,
Co Wexford
Tel 051-389148

**RATHANGAN AND CLEARIESTOWN**
Very Rev Kevin Cahill PP
Rathangan, Duncormick, Co Wexford
Tel 051-563104
Very Rev James Ryan (priest in residence)
Cleariestown, Co Wexford
Tel 053-9139110

**RATHNURE AND TEMPLEUDIGAN**
Very Rev Brian Broaders PP
Rathnure, Co Wexford
Tel 054-55122

**RIVERCHAPEL, COURTOWN HARBOUR**
Very Rev Thomas Dalton PP
Riverchapel, Courtown Harbour,
Gorey, Co Wexford
Tel 053-9425241

**ST SENAN'S, ENNISCORTHY**
Parish Office. Tel 053-9237611
Very Rev John Byrne Adm
Rev Patrick Banville CC
The Presbytery, Templeshannon,
Enniscorthy, Co Wexford
Tel 053-9237611

**TAGHMON**
Very Rev Seán Gorman PP
Taghmon, Co Wexford
Tel 053-9134123
Rev David Murphy CC
Caroreigh, Taghmon, Co Wexford
Tel 053-9134113

**TAGOAT**
Very Rev Matthias Glynn PP
Tagoat, Co Wexford
Tel 053-9131139
Rev James Murphy CC
St Brigid's, Rosslare, Co Wexford
Tel 053-9132118

**TEMPLETOWN AND POULFUR**
Very Rev Oliver Sweeney PP
Poulfur, Fethard-on-Sea,
New Ross, Co Wexford
Tel 051-397113

## INSTITUTIONS AND THEIR CHAPLAINS

**Community School**
Gorey, Co Wexford
Tel 053-9421000

**Vocational College Wexford**
Rev James Cullen CC
Caroreigh, Taghmon, Co Wexford
Tel 053-9134113

**Wexford General Hospital**
Tel 053-9142233
*Chaplain:* Rev Ken Quinn
General Hospital, Wexford
Tel 053-9142233

**Community School**
Ramsgrange
Tel 051-389211
Ms Maria McCabe

**St John of God Convent**
Newtown Road, Wexford
Rt Rev Mgr J. L. Kehoe PA
13 Priory Court, Spawell Road,
Wexford

**St John's Hospital**
Enniscorthy, Co Wexford
*Chaplain:* Rev Patrick Sinnott
Tel 053-9233228

## PRIESTS OF THE DIOCESE ELSEWHERE IN IRELAND

Rev Patrick Mernagh CF
McKee Barracks,
Blackhorse Avenue, Dublin 7
Rev Peter O'Connor
10 Cranfield Place, Dublin 4
Rev John Paul Sheridan
St Patrick's College,
Maynooth, Co Kildare

## PRIESTS OF THE DIOCESE ABROAD

Rev Thomas Brennan, USA
Rev Sean Devereux
Our Lady of Fatima Parish, Bwiam,
Roman Catholic Mission, PO Box 165,
Banjul, The Gambia, West Africa
Tel 00220-7878991
Email sean.devereux@gmail.com

## RETIRED PRIESTS

Very Rev James Byrne
Ballylannon, Wellingtonbridge,
Co Wexford
Rev James Cashman
11 Pinewood, Wexford
Very Rev Matthew L. Cleary
The Stables, Bridgetown, Co Wexford
Most Rev Brendan Comiskey (SSCC) DD
PO Box 40, Wexford

Very Rev James Curtis
3 Oldtown Court, Clongreen, Foulksmills,
New Ross, Co Wexford
Very Rev James B. Canon Curtis
Rathjarney, Drinagh, Co Wexford
Rev Thomas Canon Curtis
2 The Hollows, Lugduff, Tinahely,
Co Wicklow
Very Rev Seamus Canon De Val
1 Irish Streeet, Bunclody, Co Wexford
Very Rev Thomas Eustace
The Cools, Barntown, Wexford
Rev James Fitzpatrick
8 Alderbrook, Ferns,
Enniscorthy, Co Wexford
Very Rev John French
Horeswood, New Ross, Co Wexford
Tel 051-593196
Very Rev Noel Canon Hartley
10 Donovan's Wharf, Crescent Quay,
Wexford
Very Rev Richard Hayes
Collinstown, Duncormick, Co Wexford
Very Rev Aidan G. Jones
33 Twin Oaks, Clonattin,
Gorey, Co Wexford
Very Rev John Jordan
Kyle, Oulart, Gorey, Co Wexford
Rt Rev Mgr Joseph L. Kehoe PA
13 Priory Court, Spawell Road, Wexford
Tel 053-9180599
Very Rev Tobias Kinsella
Bloomfield Care Centre, Stocking Lane,
Rathfarnham, Dublin 16
Very Rev Seamus Canon Larkin
Monamolin, Gorey, Co Wexford
Tel 053-9389223
Very Rev Thomas McGrath
Cois Tra, Chapel Road,
Duncannon, Co Wexford
Very Rev Patrick Canon O'Brien
No 9 Bungalow, Chambersland,
New Ross, Co Wexford
Very Rev Anthony O'Connell
5 Parkside, Stoneybatter, Wexford
Very Rev Nicholas Canon Power
Moorfield, Rathaspeck, Co Wexford
Very Rev James Ryan
Cleariestown, Co Wexford

## RELIGIOUS ORDERS AND CONGREGATIONS

### PRIESTS

**AUGUSTINIANS**
St Augustine's Priory,
Grantstown, New Ross, Co Wexford
Tel 051-561119
*Superior:* Rev Aidan O'Leary (OSA)
Community: 1

Good Counsel College,
New Ross, Co Wexford
Tel 051-421363/421909 Fax 051-421909
*Prior:* Rev Sean MacGearailt (OSA)
*Bursar:* Rev Philip Kelly (OSA)

**CONVENTUAL FRANCISCANS**
The Friary, Wexford
Tel 053-9122758 Fax 053-9121499
*Guardian:* Rev Ciprian Budau (OFMConv)

## BROTHERS

**CHRISTIAN BROTHERS**
Christian Brothers' House,
Joseph Street, Wexford
Tel 053-45659
*Community Leader:* Br E. Kinsella
Community: 7

## SISTERS

**CARMELITES**
Mount Carmel Monastery,
New Ross, Co Wexford
Tel 051-421076
Email carmelites@eircom.net
*Prioress:* Sr Brenda Donovan
Community: 12
Contemplatives
Altar breads

**CONGREGATION OF THE SISTERS OF MERCY**
Convent of Mercy,
Clonard Road, Wexford
Tel 053-23024

Sisters of Mercy,
52 Westlands, Wexford
Tel 053-42917

Convent of Mercy, St Brigid's,
Rosslare Strand, Co Wexford
Tel 053-32104

Sisters of Mercy,
Lower South Knock,
New Ross, Co Wexford
Tel 051-425340

'Misericordia', 1 Tower Grove,
New Ross, Co Wexford
Tel 051-422027

The Lodge, 38 Irishtown, New Ross,
Co Wexford

**DAUGHTERS OF CHARITY OF ST VINCENT DE PAUL**
Cluain Mhuire, Gorey Road, Carnew,
Arklow, Co Wicklow
Tel 053-9426371
*Superior:* Sr Mary Crosbie
Community: 4
Residential housing for elderly, day care
centre, parish work

## FAMILY OF ADORATION
St Aidan's Monastery of Adoration,
Ferns, Co Wexford
Tel 053-9366634
Email staidansferns@eircom.net
*Superior:* Sr Dolores O'Brien
Community: 3
Contemplative life with adoration of the
Eucharist. 8 hermitages for private
retreats. Icon reproduction workshop.
The Centre for Contemplative Outreach
Ireland – Facilitating Centering Prayer
Retreats
Email contemplativeoutreachireland@
gmail.com

## LORETO (IBVM)
Loreto Community, Railway Road,
Gorey, Co Wexford
Tel 055-21257
*Shared Leaders*
Sr Chris Goodman, Sr Bridie Mullins
Community: 6
Primary School

Conabury,
11 Newtown Court, Wexford
Tel 053-43470
*Shared Leaders*
Sr Chris Goodman, Sr Bridie Mullins
Community: 3
Secondary School

## MISSIONARY SISTERS OF THE HOLY ROSARY
Parish House, Terrerath,
New Ross, Co Wexford
Tel 051-428313
Community: 3
Pastoral

## NOTRE DAME DES MISSIONS (OUR LADY OF THE MISSIONS SISTERS)
60 Pineridge,
Summerhill, Wexford
Tel 053-9143170
*Contact:* Sr Anna McDonagh
Community: 1
RE Adviser

## PERPETUAL ADORATION SISTERS
Perpetual Adoration Convent,
Bride Street, Wexford Town,
Co Wexford
Tel 053-9124134
Email adoration44@eircom.net
*Superior:* Sr M. Peter Leech
Community: 10
Perpetual adoration of the Blessed
Sacrament
Vestments, altar linen

## PRESENTATION SISTERS
Presentation Sisters, Wexford
Tel 053-9122504
*Superior:* Sr Grace Redmond
Community: 8
Secondary School
Tel 053-9124133 Fax 053-9124048

## ST JOHN OF GOD SISTERS
St John of God Congregational Centre,
1 Summerhill Heights, Wexford
Tel 053-9142396 Fax 053-9141500
Email stjohnogoffice@eircom.net
*Congregational Leader*
Sr Bríd Ryan

St John of God Convent,
Newtown Road, Wexford
Tel 053-9142276
*Resident Leader:* Sr Eileen Egan
Community: 28
Primary School, The Faythe, Wexford
Tel 053-9123105

St John of God Heritage Centre,
Sallyville, Newtown Road, Wexford
Tel 053-9146709

St John of God Convent, Ballyvaloo,
Blackwater, Co Wexford
Tel 053-9137576
Community: 5
Holiday and retreat house
Tel 053-9137160

St John of God Sisters,
26 The Orchard, Bellefield,
Enniscorthy, Co Wexford
Tel 053-9233079
Community: 2

St John of God Sisters,
Moorefield House, Loreto Village,
Enniscorthy, Co Wexford
Tel 053-9239734
Community: 3
Sheltered homes for the elderly

St John of God Sisters,
6 Parkside, Stoneybatter, Wexford
Tel 053-9146058
Community: 3

St John of God Sisters,
Ard Coilm, 15 Millpark,
Castlebridge, Co Wexford
Tel 053-9159862
Community: 2

St John of God Sisters,
1 Beechville, Clonard, Wexford
Tel 053-9142601
Community: 3

St John of God Sisters,
26 Mansfield Drive,
Coolcots, Wexford
Tel 053-9144427
Community: 2

St John of God Sisters,
2 Farnogue Drive,
Newlands, Wexford
Tel 053-9146149
Community: 3

St John of God Sisters,
Caritas, Glenbrook,
Newtown Road, Wexford
Tel 053-9143752
Community: 3

St John of God Sisters,
9 Farnogue Drive,
Newlands, Wexford
Tel 053-9140537
Community: 2

St John of God Sisters,
3 Cluain Aoibhinn,
Clonard, Wexford
Community: 3

## ST LOUIS SISTERS
Convent of St Louis,
Ramsgrange,
Co Wexford
Tel 051-389119
Community: 5
Varied apostolates

Ramsgrange Community School
New Ross, Co Wexford
Tel 051-389211
Pupils: 520

# EDUCATIONAL INSTITUTIONS

**St Peter's Diocesan College**
Tel 053-9142071
*Principal:* Mr Robert O'Callaghan
*Chaplain/Counsellor*
Rev Aodhan Marken

**EDMUND RICE SCHOOLS TRUST**
CBS Secondary School New Ross,
Mountgarret, New Ross,
Co Wexford
Tel 051-421384
Fax 051-425961
*Principal:* Mr Pat Rossiter

CBS Primary School,
Green Street, Wexford
Tel 053-41324
Email principal@cbsprimarywexford.com
*Principal:* Mr Jos Furlong

Coláiste Eamonn Rís,
Thomas Street, Wexford
Tel 053-41391
Fax 053-46803
Email admin@wexfordcbs.ie
Website www.wexfordcbs.ie
*Principal:* Mr Michael McMahon

St Mary's CBS,
Mill Park Road, Enniscorthy,
Co Wexford
Tel 053-9234330
Fax 053-9236424
Email admin@cbsenniscorthy.ie
*Principal:* Mr John Ryan

## CHARITABLE AND OTHER SOCIETIES

**Aiseiri**
Roxborough House,
Wexford
Tel 053-9141818

**Christian Media Trust**
Tel 053-9145176

**CURA**
Tel 053-9122255

**FDYS Youth Work Ireland**
Wexford
Tel 053-9123262/9123358

**Society of St Vincent de Paul**
17 Conferences in the Diocese of Ferns
*South Ferns President*
Ms Mary Dempsey
Ballinellard, Blackwater, Co Wexford
Tel 087-8313736
*North Ferns President*
Mr Edmund Roche
Woodbrook House, Ballinapierce,
Davidstown, Co Wexford
Tel 087-1413153

**Traveller Resource Centre**
Tel 051-422272

**Special Schools**
Our Lady of Fatima, Wexford
Tel 053-9123376
St John of God, Enniscorthy
Tel 053-9233419
St Patrick's, Enniscorthy
Tel 053-9233657
Dawn House, Wexford
Tel 053-9145351
Community Workshop
Enniscorthy Ltd
Tel 053-9233069
Community Workshop
New Ross Ltd
Tel 051-421956

# DIOCESE OF GALWAY, KILMACDUAGH AND KILFENORA

**Most Rev Martin Drennan DD**
Bishop of Galway;
born 2 January 1944;
ordained priest 16 June 1968;
ordained Auxiliary Bishop of
Dublin 21 September 1997;
installed Bishop of Galway
3 July 2005

Residence: Mount Saint Mary's,
Taylor's Hill, Galway
Tel 091-563566
Fax 091-568333
Email
galwaydiocese@eircom.net
Website www.galwaydiocese.ie

PATRONS OF THE DIOCESE
GALWAY – OUR LADY ASSUMED INTO HEAVEN, 15 AUGUST
KILMACDUAGH – ST COLMAN, 29 OCTOBER
KILFENORA – ST FACHANAN, 20 DECEMBER

INCLUDES PORTIONS OF COUNTIES GALWAY, MAYO AND CLARE
KILFENORA IS IN THE PROVINCE OF CASHEL BUT THE BISHOP OF GALWAY AND
KILMACDUAGH IS ITS APOSTOLIC ADMINISTRATOR

## CATHEDRAL OF OUR LADY ASSUMED INTO HEAVEN AND ST NICHOLAS, GALWAY

In 1484, the Church of St Nicholas in Galway became a collegiate church, with a warden and vicars. However, with the Reformation, after 1570, the Catholic people of Galway lost the right to practise their religion publicly. Mass was celebrated in private houses until the rigour of persecution moderated and a parish chapel was built in Middle Street about 1750. The Diocese of Galway was established in 1831, and the parish chapel became its pro-cathedral. A fund for the building of a more fitting cathedral was inaugurated in 1876 and was built up by successive bishops. In 1883 the Diocese of Kilmacduagh was joined with Galway, and the Bishop of Galway was made Apostolic Administrator of Kilfenora.

In 1941, Galway County Council handed over Galway Jail to Bishop Michael Browne as a site for the proposed new cathedral. The jail was demolished, and in 1949 John J. Robinson of Dublin was appointed architect for the new cathedral. Planning continued until 1957, when Pope Pius XII approved the plans submitted to him by Dr Browne. Cardinal D'Alton, the Archbishop of Armagh, blessed the site and the foundation stone on 27 October 1957. The construction, which began in February 1958, was undertaken by Messrs John Sisk Ltd of Dublin. The people of the diocese contributed to a weekly collection, and donations were received from home and abroad. The total cost, including furnishing, was almost one million pounds.

Pope Paul VI appointed Cardinal Richard Cushing, Archbishop of Boston, Pontifical Legate to dedicate the cathedral. The cathedral was dedicated on the Feast of the Assumption, 15 August 1965.

**Most Rev Eamonn Casey DD**
Born 1927; ordained priest June 1951; ordained Bishop of Kerry 9 November 1969; translated to Galway 19 September 1976; resigned 6 May 1992.
*Residence:* Carrigoran Nursing Home, Newmarket-on-Fergus, Co Clare

## CHAPTER

Rt Rev Mgr Malachy Hallinan PP, VG, VF
Sacred Heart Church, Galway
*Members*
Very Rev Canon William Cummins PP, Ennistymon, Co Clare
Very Rev Canon Michael Reilly PP, Castlegar, Galway
Very Rev Canon Patrick Callanan, Kilbeacanty
Very Rev Canon Francis Larkin AP, St Joseph's
Very Rev Canon Martin Moran PP, VF Killanin
Very Rev Canon Peter Rabbitte PP, VF The Cathedral
Very Rev Canon Joseph Delaney, Galway Clinic
Very Rev Canon Martin Downey, St Joseph's
Very Rev Canon Derek Feeney, Craughwell, Co Galway

## ADMINISTRATION

**Vicar General**
Rt Rev Mgr Malachy Hallinan PP, VG, VF
Church of the Sacred Heart,
Seamus Quirke Road, Galway
Tel 091-522713

**Vicars Forane**
Rt Rev Mgr Malachy Hallinan PP, VG, VF
Very Rev Canon Peter Rabbitte PP, VF
Very Rev Conor Cunningham PP, VF
Very Rev Canon Martin Moran PP, VF
Very Rev Thomas Marrinan PP, VF

**Chancellor**
Very Rev Ian O'Neill PP
Claregalway, Co Galway
Tel 091-798104

**Consultors**
Rt Rev Mgr Malachy Hallinan PP, VG, VF
Very Rev Canon Peter Rabbitte PP, VF
Very Rev Martin Glynn PP
Very Rev Ian O'Neill
Rev Barry Horan

**Finance Committee**
Most Rev Martin Drennan DD, Chairman
Rt Rev Mgr Malachy Hallinan PP, VG, VF
Mr John Rafferty
Rev Martin Whelan
Mr Thomas Kilgarriff, Secretary

**Financial Administrator**
Mr Thomas Kilgarriff
Diocesan Office, The Cathedral, Galway
Tel 091-563566

**Diocesan Development (Meitheal)**
*Director:* Mr Thomas Kilgarriff,
Diocesan Office, The Cathedral, Galway
Tel 091-563566
*Chairperson:* Most Rev Martin Drennan
*Members*
Rt Rev Mgr Malachy Hallinan PP, VG, VF
Mr Frank Canavan
Mr Prionsias Ó Máille
Mrs Breda Ryan
Mrs Dairin Coen
Mr Pat McCambridge

**Diocesan Secretary**
Rev Martin Whelan CC
Diocesan Office, The Cathedral, Galway
Tel 091-563566
Email galwaydiocesemw@eircom.net

## CATECHETICS EDUCATION

**Primary Education**
*Diocesan Adviser:* Sr Breda Coyne (RJM)
Diocesan Pastoral Centre, Árus De Brún,
Newtownsmith, Galway
Tel 091-575050
Mr Tom O'Doherty (Irish schools)
Tel 091-565066

## LITURGY

**Liturgical Committee**
*Chairperson:* Rev Alan Burke Adm
Parochial House, Oughterard,
Co Galway
Tel 091-552290
Email oughterclergy@gmail.com
*Members*
Sr Breda Coyne,
Mr Ray O'Donnell

**Sacred Music**
*Diocesan Director*
Mr Raymond O'Donnell MA, HDE, LTCL
Tel 091-563577/087-2241365
Fax 091-534881
Email music@galwaycathedral.ie

## PASTORAL

**ACCORD**
Árus de Brún, Newtownsmith, Galway
Tel 091-562331
*Diocesan Director*
Very Rev Michael McLoughlin PP
Parochial House, Moycullen, Co Galway
Tel 091-555106
Email accordgalway@eircom.net

**Apostolic Work Society**
*President:* Mrs Marie Dempsey
Cregboy, Claregalway, Co Galway
Tel 091-798125
Secretary: Mrs Eileen Flannery
102 Hazel Park, Newcastle, Galway
Tel 091-523845

**Brazilian Community**
*Chaplain:* Rev Kevin Keenan (SVD)
Main Street, Clarinbridge,
Co Galway
Tel 091-485777

**Catholic Primary School Managers' Association**
Diocesan Education Office
Pastoral Centre, Árus de Brún,
Newtownsmith, Galway
Tel 091-565066
Co-ordinator: Mr P. J. Callanan
Email pjcallanan65@eircom.net

**Child Protection Office**
Ms Ita O'Mahony
Diocesan Pastoral Centre,
Arús de Brún, Newtownsmith, Galway
Tel 091-575051
Email galwaydiocespo@eircom.net

**Communications Committee**
*Secretary:* Very Rev Diarmuid Hogan PP
Parochial House, Oranmore, Co Galway
Tel 087-1037452
Email dcogalway@gmail.com

**CURA**
Pastoral Centre, Árus de Brún,
Newtownsmith, Galway
Tel 091-562558
Email curagalway@eircom.net

**Diocesan Archivist**
Mr Tom Kilgarriff
Tel 091-563566
Email galwaydiocesetk@eircom.net

**Diocesan Pastoral Centre**
Árus de Brún, Newtownsmith, Galway
Tel 091-565066
*Acting Director:* Mrs Eileen Kelly
Email pastoraladministrator@eircom.net

**Diocesan Pilgrimage Committee**
*Pilgrimage Director*
Very Rev Canon Martin Moran PP
Rosscahill, Co Galway
Tel 091-550106

**Diocesan Youth Faith Development**
Diocesan Pastoral Centre,
Árus de Brún, Newtownsmith, Galway
Tel 091-565066

**Diocesan Youth Ministry**
*Co-ordinator:* Maura Garrihy
Email youthministry@galwaydiocese.ie

**Drug Misuse Prevention**
*Contact Person:* Very Rev David Cribbin
Parochial House, Kinvara, Co Galway
Tel 091-637154
Email david.cribbin@gmail.com

**Ecumenism**
Rev Barry Horan
Chaplaincy Department, NUI, Galway
Tel 091-495055
Email bdhoran@hotmail.com

**Emigrants Committee**
*Director*
Very Rev Gearóid Ó Griofa PP
Gort, Co Galway
Tel 091-631055
Email gogriofa@eircom.net
*Secretary*
Very Rev Canon Michael Reilly PP
Castlegar, Galway
Tel 091-751548
Email castlegaroffice@eircom.net

**Legion of Mary**
Annunciata House,
15 Fr Griffin Road, Galway
Tel 091-521871
*Contact:* Mr Bernard Finan
*Chaplain:* Rev Robert McNamara CC
Tel 091-524222
Email rmjmcn@hotmail.com

**Marriage Tribunal**
*Officials:* Rev Michael Byrnes
(see also Marriage Tribunals section)

**Missions Committee**
*Chairman*
Very Rev Canon Martin Downey PP
24 Presentation Road, Galway
Tel 091-562276
Email saintjosephs@eircom.net

**Diocesan Council of Priests**
Most Rev Martin Drennan
Rt Rev Mgr Malachy Hallinan PP, VG
Very Rev Canon Martin Moran PP, VF

*Members*
Rev Alan Burke *(Chairman)*
Very Rev Canon Peter Rabbitte
Rev Martin Whelan
Very Rev Michael McLoughlin
Very Rev Thomas Marrinan
Rev Conor Cunningham
Rev Barry Horan
Very Rev Canon Joseph Keogh PE
Rev Desmond Foley (OSA)
Rev Patrick O'Donohue *(Secretary)*
Very Rev Diarmuid Hogan
Rev Barry Hogg
Very Rev Ian O'Neill
Very Rev Martin Glynn

**Pioneer Total Abstinence Association**
*Diocesan Director*
Very Rev Canon Patrick Callanan PP
Kilbeacanty, Gort, Co Galway
Tel 091-631691

**Polish Community**
*Chaplain:* Rev Marek Cul (OP)
St Mary's Priory, Claddagh, Galway
Tel 091-582884
Email mcul@dominikanie.pl

**Pontifical Mission Societies**
*Diocesan Director*
Rev Patrick O'Donohue CC
129 Túr Uisce, Doughiska, Galway
Tel 091-756823
Email goodshepherdcuracy@gmail.com

**St Joseph's Young Priests' Society**
*Diocesan Chaplain:* Rev Sean Kilcoyne
Chaplain, Bon Secours Hospital,
Renmore, Galway
Tel 091-757711

**Trócaire**
*Diocesan Director*
Very Rev Thomas Brady PP
Parochial House, Renmore, Galway
Tel 091-751707
Email opcrenmore@gmail.com

**Vocations**
*Director:* Very Rev Ian O'Neill PP
Parochial House, Claregalway, Co Galway
Tel 091-798741
Email galwaypriesthood@gmail.com

# PARISHES

*Church titulars, if different from parish name, are in italics.*

**CATHEDRAL**
*Our Lady Assumed into Heaven and St Nicholas*
Very Rev Canon Peter Rabbitte PP, VF
Tel 091-563577
Rev Martin Whelan CC
18 University Road, Galway
Tel 091-524875/563577
Email info@galwaycathedral.ie

*City Parishes*

**BALLYBANE**
*St Brigid*
Very Rev John D. Keane
St Brigid's, Ballybane, Galway
Tel 091-755381
Email info@stbrigidsparishballybane.com

**GOOD SHEPHERD**
Very Rev Martin Glynn PP
Parochial House, Mervue, Galway
Tel 091-751721
Rev Patrick O'Donohue CC
129 Túr Uisce, Doughiska, Galway
Tel 091-756823
Email goodshepherdcuracy@gmail.com
Email goodshepherdgalway@gmail.com
Website www.goodshepherdgalway.com

**MERVUE**
*Holy Family*
Very Rev Martin Glynn PP
Mervue, Galway
Tel 091-751721
Email mervuechurch@gmail.com
Rev Michael Connolly CC
Curate's House, Walter Macken Road,
Mervue, Galway
Tel 091-456527
Email frmichaelc@hotmail.com

**RENMORE**
*St Oliver Plunkett*
Very Rev Thomas Brady PP
Parochial House, Renmore, Galway
Tel 091-751707
Email opcrenmore@gmail.com

**SACRED HEART CHURCH**
Rt Rev Mgr Malachy Hallinan PP, VG, VF
Church of the Sacred Heart
Seamus Quirke Road, Galway
Tel 091-522713
Email sacredheartgalway@eircom.net

**ST AUGUSTINE'S**
Very Rev John Hughes (OSA) PP
St Augustine's Priory,
St Augustine's Street, Galway
Tel 091-562524
Email jhughesosa@gmail.com

**ST FRANCIS**
Very Rev Eugene Barrett (OFM) PP
Rev Declan Timmons (OFM) CC
The Abbey, St Francis Street, Galway
Tel 091-562518
Email embarrett@eircom.net

**ST JOHN THE APOSTLE**
Very Rev Tadhg Quinn PP
St John the Apostle,
Knocknacarra, Galway
Tel 091-590059
Email tadhgknocknacarra@eircom.net
An tAthair Daithí Ó Murchú CC
8 The Links, Knocknacarra, Galway
Tel 091-590077
Email dgmurc@gmail.com

**ST JOSEPH'S**
Very Rev Canon Martin Downey PP
24 Presentation Road, Galway
Tel 091-562276
Very Rev Canon Francis Larkin AP
7 Presentation Road, Galway
Tel 091-449727
Email flarks@eircom.net

**ST MARY'S**
Very Rev Albert Leonard (OP) PP
Email aldleonard@gmail.com
Rev John O'Reilly (OP) CC
Rev Denis Murphy (OP) CC
Email murphydenis345@gmail.com
St Mary's Priory, The Claddagh, Galway
Tel 091-582884

**ST PATRICK'S**
Very Rev Patrick Whelan PP
St Patrick's Presbytery,
Forster Street, Galway
Tel 091-567994
Email pat5pat@eircom.net

**SALTHILL**
*Christ the King*
Very Rev Gerard Jennings PP
Tel 091-523413
Email salthillparish@eircom.net
Rev Michael Bailey (OFM) CC
Tel 091-526006
Email michaeljbailey@eirom.net
Rev Vivian Loughrey CC
Tel 091-523413
Email fvl@eircom.net
Curate's House, Monksfield,
Salthill, Galway

**TIRELLAN**
*Resurrection*
Very Rev Kevin Blade (MSC) PP
Rev Thomas Plower (MSC) CC
Church of the Resurrection,
Headford Road, Galway
Tel 091-762883
Email ballinfoyleparish@eircom.net

*Country Parishes*

**ARDRAHAN**
*St Teresa's*
Very Rev Joseph Roche PP
Ardrahan, Co Galway
Tel 091-635164
Email parishofardrahan@gmail.com

**BALLINDEREEN**
*St Colman's*
Very Rev David Cribbin PP
Ballindereen, Kilcolgan, Co Galway
Tel 091-796118
Email ballinderreenparish@eircom.net

**BALLYVAUGHAN**
*St John the Baptist*
Rev Richard Flanagan (SVD) Adm
Ballyvaughan, Co Clare
Tel 065-7077045
Email richardflanagan@me.com

**BEARNA**
*Mary Immaculate Queen*
Very Rev Des Forde PP
Bearna, Galway
Tel 091-590956
Email bearnaparish@eircom.net
Very Rev Dean Thomas Kyne AP
Réalt na Mara, Furbo, Co Galway
Tel 091-592457
Email realtnamara@hotmail.com

**CARRON AND NEW QUAY**
*St Columba's, Carron,*
*St Patrick's, New Quay*
Rev Colm Clinton (SPS) *(Administrator)*
New Quay, Co Clare
Tel 065-7078026
Email colmcc@gmail.com

**CASTLEGAR**
*St Columba's*
Very Rev Canon Michael Reilly PP
Castlegar, Co Galway
Tel 091-751548
Email castlegaroffice@eircom.net

**CLAREGALWAY**
*Assumption and St James*
Very Rev Ian O'Neill PP
Claregalway, Co Galway
Tel 091-798104
Email claregalwayparish@eircom.net

**CLARINBRIDGE**
*Annunciation of the BVM*
Rev Kevin Keenan (SVD) Adm
Main Street, Clarinbridge, Co Galway
Tel 091-485777
Email thebridgeparish@gmail.com

**CRAUGHWELL**
*St Colman's*
Very Rev Canon Derek Feeney PP
Craughwell, Co Galway
Tel 091-846057
Email derekfeeney@yahoo.co.uk

**ENNISTYMON**
*Our Lady and St Michael*
Very Rev Canon William Cummins PP
Ennistymon, Co Clare
Tel 065-7071063
Rev Henry Nevin (SDS) CC
Curate's House, Sea Park,
Lahinch, Co Clare
Tel 065-7081307
Email ennistymonparish@eircom.met

**GORT/BEAGH**
*St Colman's and St Ann*
Very Rev Thomas Marrinan PP, VF
Tel 091-631220
Email gortparish@eircom.net
Rev Gearóid Ó Griofa CC
Tel 091-631055
Gort, Co Galway
Email gogriofa@gmail.com

**KILBEACANTY/PETERSWELL**
*St Columba and St Thomas Apostle*
Very Rev Canon Patrick Callanan PP
Kilbeacanty, Gort, Co Galway
Tel 091-631691

**KILCHREEST**
*Nativity and Church of St Teresa*
Very Rev Joseph Roche *(priest in charge)*
Parochial House, Ardrahan, Co Galway
Tel 091-635164

**KILFENORA**
*St Fachanan's*
Very Rev Edward Crosby PP
Kilfenora, Co Clare
Tel 065-7088006
Email crosby32000@yahoo.com

**KINVARA**
*St Colman's*
Very Rev David Cribbin PP
Kinvara, Co Galway
Tel 091-637154
Email david.cribbin@gmail.com

**LETTERMORE**
*Naomh Colmcille*
Very Rev Michael Brennan PP
Lettermore, Co Galway
Tel 091-551169
Email miclbrennan@eircom.net

**LISCANNOR**
*St Brigid's*
Very Rev Denis Crosby PP
Liscannor, Co Clare
Tel 065-7081248
Email dcrosby@eircom.net

**LISDOONVARNA AND KILSHANNY**
*Corpus Christi*
Very Rev Conor Cunningham PP, VF
The Rectory, Lisdoonvarna, Co Clare
Tel 065-7074142
Email parishoffice@lisdoon.ie

**MOYCULLEN**
*Immaculate Conception*
Very Rev Michael McLoughlin PP
Moycullen, Co Galway
Tel 091-555106
Email moycullenparish@eircom.net
Website www.moycullenparish.com

**ORANMORE**
*Immaculate Conception*
Very Rev Diarmuid Hogan PP
Oranmore, Co Galway
Tel 091-794634
Email oranmorepp@gmail.com
*St Joseph's*
Very Rev Canon Richard Higgins AP
Maree, Oranmore, Co Galway
Tel 091-794113
Email mareechurch@eircom.net

**OUGHTERARD**
*Immaculate Conception*
Rev Alan Burke Adm
Oughterard, Co Galway
Tel 091-552290
Email oughterclergy@gmail.com

**ROSMUC**
*Séipéal an Ioncolnaithe*
Very Rev Michael Brennan PP *(priest in charge)*
Rosmuc, Co Galway
Tel 091-551169
Email miclbrennan@eircom.net

**ROSSCAHILL (KILLANIN)**
*Immaculate Heart of Mary*
Very Rev Canon Martin Moran PP, VF
Rosscahill, Co Galway
Tel 091-550106
Email frmmoran@eircom.net

**SHRULE**
*St Joseph's*
Very Rev Michael Crosby PP
Shrule, Galway
Tel 093-31262
Email crosby2@eircom.net

**AN SPIDÉAL**
*Cill Éinne*
An tAthair Seán McHugh PP
Teach an Sagairt, An Spidéal,
Co na Gaillimhe
Tel 091-553155
Email cilleinde@eircom.net

## INSTITUTIONS AND THEIR CHAPLAINS

**Brothers of Charity**
Kilcornan, Clarinbridge, Co Galway
Rev Martin Keane
Tel 091-796106

**Bon Secours Hospital**
Renmore, Galway
Rev Seán Kilcoyne
Tel 091-751534/757711

**Galway/Mayo Insititute of Technology**
Dublin Road, Galway
Rev Thomas Plower (MSC)
Tel 091-753161/757298

**Galway Clinic**
Doughiska, Galway
Chaplain's Office
Rev Joe Delaney

**Gort Community School**
Chaplain's Office
Tel 091-632163
Ms Orla Duggan

**Merlin Park University Hospital**
Chaplains Office
Tel 091-757631
Rev Michael Connolly
Mr Ray Gately

**NUI, Galway**
University Road, Galway
Chaplain's Office
Tel 091-495055
Rev Barry Horan
Email barry.horan@nuigalway.ie
Rev Ben Hughes
Email ben.hughes@nuigalway.ie

**St Enda's College**
Threadneedle Road, Salthill, Galway
Sr Pauline Uhlemann (RJM)
Tel 091-522458

**St Joseph's Secondary College**
Nun's Island, Galway
Priests of the Cathedral Parish
Tel 091-563577

**University Hospital**
Chaplain's Office
Tel 091-524222
Rev Robert McNamara
Email rmjmcn@hotmail.com
Rev Peter Joyce
Email frpeterjoyce@hotmail.com

## PRIESTS OF THE DIOCESE ELSEWHERE

Rev Hugh Clifford
Pontifical Irish College,
Via dei SS Quattro 1, 00184 Roma, Italy
Tel 0039-06-772631
Rev Patrick Connaughton
St Columban's, Dalgan Park,
Navan, Co Meath
Tel 046-21525
Rev Michael Conway
St Patrick's College, Maynooth, Co Kildare
Tel 01-6285222
Very Rev Enda Glynn
13 Lios Na Mara, Station Road,
Lahinch, Co Clare
Rev Frank Lee
5 Pine Grove, Moycullen, Co Galway
Tel 086-8308865
Rev Thomas Lyons
Cork University Hospital, Wilton, Cork
Tel 021-4546109
Rev Dr Murchadh O'Madagáin
310 Sarasota Street, Venice,
Florida FL 34285, USA
Tel 001-2394504345
Rev Gregory Raftery
An Der Tiefenriede 11, 3000,
Hanover 1, Germany

## RETIRED PRIESTS

Rev Michael Carney PE
c/o Diocesan Office, The Cathedral,
Galway
Tel 091-563566
Very Rev Dean Patrick Considine PE
Gort Mór, Rosmuc, Co na Gaillimhe
Tel 091-563566
Rev Tom Culloty PE
Ballydesmond, Mallow, Co Cork
Tel 087-2850824
Very Rev Canon Eamonn Dermody PE
Clarinbridge, Co Galway
Tel 091-796208
Very Rev Bernard Duffy PE
St Mary's Nursing Home,
Shantalla Road, Galway
Tel 091-540540
Rev Stephen Keane PE
Kilcolgan Nursing Home,
Kilcolgan, Co Galway
Tel 091-776446
Very Rev Canon Edward Kelly PE
No. 1 St Mary's College House,
Shantalla Road, Galway
Tel 091-586663
Very Rev Dean Michael Kelly PE
'Inchagill', Ballinamana Road,
Clarinbridge, Co Galway
Tel 086-8234027
Very Rev Canon Joseph Keogh PE
No. 4 St Mary's College House,
Shantalla Road, Galway
Tel 091-587773
Rev Dr James Mitchell
No. 2 St Mary's College House,
Shantalla Road, Galway
Tel 091-588750
Very Rev Leo Morahan PE
2 The Beeches, Louisburg, Co Mayo
Tel 098-66869
Very Rev Canon Michael Mulkerrins PE
Curate's Residence, Renmore, Galway
Tel 091-757859
Very Rev Dean Christopher O'Connor PE
Craughwell, Co Galway
Tel 091-846124
Very Rev Canon John O'Dwyer PE
20 Cloonarkin Drive,
Oranmore, Co Galway
Tel 091-484501
Rt Rev Mgr Seán O'Flaherty PE
Parkmore, Castlegar, Galway
Tel 091-764764
Very Rev Canon Richard Tarpey PE
Ennistymon, Co Clare
Tel 065-7071346

## PERSONAL PRELATURE

**Opus Dei**
Gort Ard University Residence,
Rockbarton North, Salthill, Galway
Tel 091-523846
Rev Charles Connolly
Rev Oliver Powell

## RELIGIOUS ORDERS AND CONGREGATIONS

### PRIESTS

**AUGUSTINIANS**
St Augustine's Priory, Galway
Tel 091-562524
www.augustinians.ie/galway
*Prior & Bursar:* Rev Desmond Foley (OSA)

**DOMINICANS**
St Mary's, The Claddagh, Co Galway
Tel 091-582884 Fax 091-581252
*Prior:* Very Rev Thomas Jordan (OP)
*Parish Priest:* Rev Albert Leonard (OP) PP

**FRANCISCANS**
The Abbey, 8 Francis Street, Galway
Tel 091-562518 Fax 091-565663
*Guardian:* Rev Patrick Younge (OFM)

**JESUITS**
St Ignatius Community & Church
27 Raleigh Row, Salthill, Galway
Tel 091-523707
Email galway@jesuit.ie
*Rector:* Rev Michael McGuckian (SJ)

Coláiste Iognáid, 24 Sea Road, Galway
Tel 091-501500 Fax 091-501551
Email colaisteiognaid@eircom.net
*Principal:* Ms Laoise Breathnach

**MISSIONARIES OF THE SACRED HEART**
Croí Nua, Rosary Lane,
Taylor's Hill, Galway
Tel 091-520960 Fax 091-521168
*Leader:* Rev Michael Screene (MSC)

**SALVATORIANS**
Parochial House,
Pairc Na Mara, Lahinch, Co Clare
Tel 065-7081307
Email henrynevinsds@hotmail.com
*Superior:* Rev Henry Nevin (SDS)

Ard Mhuire, Kilmoon,
Lisdoonvarna, Co Clare
Tel 086-1030261
Email seamusoduill@eircom.net
Rev Seamus O'Duill (SDS)

**SOCIETY OF AFRICAN MISSIONS**
Claregalway, Co Galway
Tel 091-798880 Fax 091-798879
Email smafathers@eircom.net
*Superior:* Rev Eamonn Finnegan (SMA)

### BROTHERS

**BROTHERS OF CHARITY**
Regional Office, Kilcornan Centre,
Clarinbridge, Co Galway
Tel 091-796389/796413
*Regional Leader:* Br Noel Corcoran
*Chaplain:* Rev Martin Keane
Community: 3

**CHRISTIAN BROTHERS**
Christian Brothers' House,
Mount St Joseph, Ennistymon, Co Clare
Tel 065-7071130

**Allianz ⑪**

12 Oldfield, Kingston, Galway
Tel 091-526705
*Community Leader:* Br Christy O'Carroll
Community: 4

**PATRICIAN BROTHERS**
Manor Drive, Kingston, Galway
Tel 091-523267
*Superior:* Br Niall Coll (FSP)
Community: 6

St Patrick's Primary School,
Market Street, Galway
Tel 091-568707. Pupils: 616
*Principal:* Mr Danny Whelan
Email sfoc@eircom.net

St Joseph's Patrician College,
Nun's Island, Galway
Tel 091-565980
Pupils: 775
*Principal:* Mr Ciarán Doyle

## SISTERS

**BON SECOURS SISTERS (PARIS)**
Sisters of Bon Secours,
5 Glenina Heights, Mervue, Galway
Tel 091-755979
Community: 2
Hospital ministry

**BRIGIDINE SISTERS**
27 Cuimín Mór,
Cappagh Road, Bearna, Co Galway
Tel 091-592234
*Contact:* Sr Margaret Coyle
Community: 1
Education

**CONGREGATION OF THE SISTERS OF MERCY**
Convent of Mercy,
St Vincent's, Newtownsmith, Galway
Tel 091-565519 Fax 091-564739
Community: 21

61 The Green,
College Road, Galway
Tel 091-564148
Community: 2

Convent of Mercy, Clochar Éinde,
An Spidéal, Gaillimh
Guthán 091-553288
Community: 3

Convent of Mercy,
Gort, Co Galway
Tel 091-631069 Fax 091-631482
Community: 8

Aisling Court,
Ballyloughaun Road, Renmore, Galway
Community: 4

Sisters of Mercy,
3 Greenview Heights, Inishannagh Park,
Newcastle, Galway
Tel 091-526126
Community: 1

146 Seacrest Road,
Knocknacarra, Galway
Tel 091-591685
Community: 2

Sisters of Mercy, 13 Beech Park,
Oranmore, Galway
Tel 091-794635
Community: 1

Sisters of Mercy, McAuley House,
7A Francis Street, Galway
Community: 3

17 Newtownsmith, Galway
Apt 1 Tel 091-563297
Apt 2 Tel 091-563698
Community: 2

Sisters of Mercy, Teaghlach Mhuire,
Ballyloughane Road, Renmore, Galway
Community: 41

13 Seaview Court,
College Road, Galway
Community: 1

St Anne's Lodge, Taylor's Hill Road,
Taylor's Hill, Galway
Tel 091-527710
Community: 1

147 Seacrest Road,
Knocknacarra, Galway
Tel 091-591598
Community: 1

19 Doughiska Road,
Merlin Park, Galway
Community: 2

**DAUGHTERS OF CHARITY OF ST VINCENT DE PAUL**
65 Shantalla Road, Galway
Tel 091-584410
*Superior:* Sr Patricia McLaughlin
Community: 4
SVP, pastoral work

**DOMINICAN SISTERS**
Dominican Convent,
Taylor's Hill, Galway
Tel 091-522124/523975
Email dominicancg@eircom.net
*Prioress:* Sr Caitríona Gorman
Community: 9
Varied ministries
Primary School. Tel 091-521517
Secondary School. Tel 091-523171

**FRANCISCAN MISSIONARIES OF MARY**
16 Tirellan Heights, Headford Road,
Galway
Tel 091-768272
*Superior:* Pending
Email fmmgalway@irishbroadband.net
Community: 5
Sisters involved in pastoral and social
work in parish

**JESUS AND MARY, CONGREGATION OF**
Convent of Jesus and Mary,
23 Lenaboy Gardens,
Salthill, Galway
Tel 091-524277
*Superior:* Sr Maria O'Toole
Community: 7
Sisters on staff of primary and post-
primary schools

Scoil Íde Primary School
Tel 091-522716. Pupils: 279
Salerno Post-Primary School
Tel 091-529500. Pupils: 544

Convent of Jesus and Mary,
229 Castlepark, Ballybane, Galway
Tel 091-764320
*Contact person*
Sr Mary Xavier McNamara
Community: 3

**LA RETRAITE SISTERS**
2 Distillery Road, Galway
Tel 091-524548
Community: 3

**LA SAINTE UNION DES SACRES COEURS**
Sarsfield Road,
Ballinasloe, Co Galway
Community: 2
Pastoral

8 Millrace Retirement Village,
Bridge Street, Ballinasloe, Co Galway
Community: 1

2 Boherbradagh House,
Coy's Boreen, Old Galway Road,
Loughrea, Co Galway
Community: 1
Healthcare

3 Dunclarin Court,
Athenry, Co Galway
Community: 1
Pastoral

10 Dún na Carraige,
Blackrock, Salthill, Galway
Community: 1
Leadership

Milltown, Dysart,
Ballinasloe, Co Galway
Community: 1
Pastoral

**LITTLE SISTERS OF THE ASSUMPTION**
25 Sea Road, Galway
Tel 091-583979
Email lsagalway@eircom.net

50 St Finbarr's Terrace,
Bohermore, Galway
Tel 091-568870

## POOR CLARES
St Clare's Monastery,
Nuns' Island, Galway
www.poorclares.ie
www.clairinibochta.ie
*Abbess:* Sr M. Paul
Community: 14
Contemplatives. Adoration of the
Blessed Sacrament. Altar breads

## PRESENTATION SISTERS
Presentation Convent,
Presentation Road, Galway
Tel 091-561067 Fax 091-562384
Email presroad@eircom.net
*Community Leader:* Sr Helen Hyland
Community: 18
School and pastoral ministry
Scoil Chroí Íosa, Primary School
Tel 091-525904
Pupils: 142
Presentation Secondary School
Tel 091-563495
Fax 091-561875
Email presgalpdp@eircom.net

Shantalla Road, Galway
Tel 091-522598
Email presshantalla@eircom.net
Community: 5
School and pastoral ministry
Scoil Bhride Primary School
Tel/Fax 091-525052
Email sns.ias@eircom.net

160 Corrib Park, Newcastle, Galway
Tel 091-581715
Community: 4
Counselling ministry

35/36 Coill Tíre, Doughiska, Galway
Tel 091-449027
Community: 5

## RELIGIOUS SISTERS OF CHARITY
Our Lady's Priory,
Clarinbridge, Co Galway
Tel 091-796254
Various apostolic ministries

## ASSOCIATION OF THE FAITHFUL
### FRATERNITY OF MARY IMMACULATE QUEEN
'Síiol Dóchas', Ballard, Barna, Galway
Tel/Fax 091-592196
Email miq@eircom.net

## EDUCATIONAL INSTITUTIONS
### Coláiste Einde, Gaillimh
Tel 091-522458/524904
*Principal:* Ms Deirbhle Quinn
*Chaplain's Office:* Tel 091-522458/524904
Sr Pauline Uhlemann (RJM)

### St Mary's College, Galway
Tel 091-522369/521984
*President:* Very Rev Barry Hogg BA, HDE
*Principal:* Mr Ciaran Murphy
*Chaplain:* Vacant
Email smcollege@eircom.net

### EDMUND RICE SCHOOLS TRUST
Scoil Mhainchín CBS Primary School,
Ennistymon, Co Clare
Tel 065-7071722
Email etynns@gmail.com
*Principal:* Ms Helen Sheridan

Meánscoil na mBráithre,
Ennistymon, Co Clare
Tel 065-7071349
Email cbsennistymon.las@eircom.net
*Principal:* Ms Mary Kennelly

## CHARITABLE AND OTHER SOCIETIES
### COPE Galway
(Crisis Housing, Caring Support) Ltd
3–5 Calbro House,
Tuam Road, Galway
Tel 091-778750
*Director:* Jacquie Horan
Cope provides emergency
accommodation for homeless persons
and families and women and children
experiencing domestic violence. It also
provides a community catering service in
Galway City and runs a day centre for
older people in Mervue.

### Society of St Vincent de Paul
Ozanam House,
St Augustine Street, Galway
Tel 091-563233/562254
*Acting Administrator*
Ms Madge McGreal

# DIOCESE OF KERRY

PATRON OF THE DIOCESE
ST BRENDAN, 16 MAY

INCLUDES COUNTY KERRY, EXCEPT KILMURRILY, AND PART OF COUNTY CORK

**Most Rev Raymond Browne DD**
Bishop of Kerry;
born 23 January 1957;
ordained priest 4 July 1982
ordained Bishop of Kerry
21 July 2013

Residence:
Bishop's House, Killarney,
Co Kerry
Tel 064-6631168
Fax 064-6631364
Email admin@dioceseofkerry.ie

## ST MARY'S CATHEDRAL, KERRY

The Cathedral of Our Lady of the Assumption, better known as St Mary's, was designed by Augustus Welby Pugin. The main part of the cathedral was built between 1842 and 1855. Work was suspended between 1848 and 1853 because of the Famine and the building was used as a shelter for victims of the Famine.

Between 1908 and 1912 the nave and side aisles were extended and the spire, sacristy and mortuary chapel were added.

In 1972/3 the cathedral was extensively renovated. The interior was reordered to meet the demands of the liturgical renewal that followed the Second Vatican Council.

**Most Rev William Murphy DD**
Retired Bishop of Kerry; born 6 June
1936; ordained priest 18 June 1961;
ordained Bishop of Kerry 10 September
1995; retired 2 May 2013
Residence: No. 2 Cathedral Place,
Killarney, Co Kerry
Tel 064-6631168 Fax 064-6631364
Email admin@dioceseofkerry.ie

## CHAPTER

Dean Sean Hanafin PP, VG
Tralee
Rt Rev Mgr Daniel O'Riordan PP
Castleisland
Very Rev Declan Canon O'Connor PP
Listowel
*Archdeacon:* Venerable Thomas Crean
Kenmare
Very Rev Larry Canon Kelly, Cahirciveen
Very Rev Thomas Canon Looney, Dingle
Very Rev Gearóid Canon Walsh,
Castletownbere
Very Rev Michael Canon Fleming
Killorglin
Very Rev Jack Canon Fitzgerald,
Millstreet

*Honorary Canons*
Very Rev Eoin Mangan, Knocknagoshel

*Retired Members*
Rt Rev Mgr Pádraig Ó Fiannachta
Very Rev Michael O'Doherty
Venerable Michael J. Murphy
Very Rev Denis O'Mahony
Very Rev Patrick Sheehan
Very Rev Seamus Linnane

*Retired Honorary Members*
Very Rev Patrick J. Horgan

## ADMINISTRATION

**College of Consultors**
Rt Rev Mgr Daniel O'Riordan
Dean Sean Hanafin PP, VG
Rev Gearóid Godley
Very Rev Michael Moynihan
Very Rev Declan O'Connor
Rev Kevin Sullivan
Very Rev Donal O'Neill
Very Rev Kieran O'Brien

**Vicar General**
Dean Sean Hanafin PP, VG
St John's, Tralee, Co Kerry
Tel 066-7122522

**Vicars Forane**
Dean Sean Hanafin PP, VG
Rt Rev Mgr Daniel O'Riordan
Venerable Thomas Crean
Very Rev Larry Canon Kelly
Very Rev Gearóid Canon Walsh
Very Rev Michael Canon Fleming
Very Rev Declan Canon O'Connor
Very Rev Thomas Canon Looney
Very Rev Liam Comer
Very Rev John Lawlor
Very Rev Kieran O'Brien
Very Rev Tadhg Fitzgerald

**Finance Council**
Rt Rev Mgr Daniel O'Riordan *(Chair)*,
Very Rev Donal O'Neill, Mr Liam Chute,
Ms Mary Harty, Mr Brian Durran, Rev
Gearóid Godley, Rev Bernard Healy
*(Secretary)*, Mr Patrick McElligott,
Ms Noeleen O'Sullivan, Ms Bridget
McGuire, Mr John Collins, Mr John
O'Connor, Mr Pádraig O'Sullivan,
Ms Rose O'Connor

**Foreign Missions Committee**
*Chairman:* Rev Gearóid Godley
John Paul II Pastoral Centre,
Rock Road, Killarney, Co Kerry
Tel 064-6630535 Fax 064-6631170

**Diocesan Archivist**
Ms Margaret de Brún
Diocesan Centre, Cathedral Walk,
Killarney, Co Kerry
Tel 064-6631168 Fax 064-6631364

**Diocesan Secretary**
Very Rev Donal O'Neill
Bishop's House, Killarney, Co Kerry
Tel 064-6631168 Fax 064-6631364
Email diosec@dioceseofkerry.ie

**Diocesan Communications Officer**
Ms Mary Fagan
Tel 087-1301555/066-7123787
Email maryfagan@dioceseofkerry.ie

**Property Committee**
*Chairman:* Mr Bill Looney
*Secretary:* Mr Willie Wixted
Diocesan Centre, Cathedral Walk,
Killarney, Co Kerry
Tel 064-6631168

## CATECHETICS EDUCATION

**Post-Primary Religious Education**
*Director:* Mr Tomás Kenny
John Paul II Pastoral Centre,
Rock Road, Killarney, Co Kerry
Tel 064-6632644 Fax 064-6631170

**Primary Religious Education**
*Director:* Sr Noreen Quilter
*Assistant Director:* Mr Kieran Coffey
c/o John Paul II Pastoral Centre,
Rock Road, Killarney, Co Kerry
Tel 064-6632644

**Primary School Management**
*Secretary:* Very Rev Donal O'Neill
Diocesan Office, Killarney, Co Kerry
Tel 064-6631168

## LITURGY

**Liturgical Committee**
*Chairman:*
Very Rev Canon Eoin Mangan PP
The Presbytery, Knocknagoshel,
Co Kerry
Tel 068-46107 Fax 068-46494
*Secretary:* Ms Eileen Burke

## PASTORAL

**Accord**
*Killarney Centre:* John Paul II Pastoral
Centre, Killarney, Co Kerry
Tel 064-6632644 Fax 064-6631170
Email jp2centre@eircom.net
*Director:* Very Rev Joseph Begley
*Tralee Centre:* St John's Pastoral Centre,
Castle Street, Tralee, Co Kerry
Tel 066-7122280
*Director:* Rev Francis Nolan

**Council of Priests**
*Chairman:* Very Rev Pádraig Walsh PP
*Secretary:* Very Rev Michael Moynihan PP

**CURA**
Tel 066-7127355

**Diocesan Pastoral Centre**
*Director:* Rev Gearóid Godley
John Paul II Pastoral Centre,
Rock Road, Killarney, Co Kerry
Tel 064-6632644 Fax 064-6631170

**Diocesan Pastoral Council**
*Chairman:* Mr Tony Darmody
*Secretary:* Mr Tomás Kenny
John Paul II Pastoral Centre,
Rock Road, Killarney, Co Kerry
Tel 064-6630508

**Diocesan Pastoral Strategic Plan**
*Co-ordinator:* Rev Gearoid Godley
John Paul II Pastoral Centre,
Killarney, Co Kerry
Tel 064-6630535

**Diocesan Safeguarding Children
Committee**
*Chairman:* Very Rev G. Canon Walsh
Castletownbere, Co Cork
Tel 027-70849
*Secretary:* Very Rev Donal O'Neill
Bishop's House, Killarney, Co Kerry
Tel 064-6685313
*Designated Officer:*
Mr Jim Sheehy
c/o Diocesan Office, Bishop's Path,
Killarney, Co Kerry
*Deputy Designated Officer:*
Very Rev Padraig Walsh
St Brendan's Presbytery,
Upper Rock Street, Tralee, Co Kerry

**Ecumenism**
*Secretary:* Very Rev Pat Crean-Lynch
The Presbytery, Ballymacelligott,
Tralee, Co Kerry
Tel 066-7137118 Fax 066-7137137

**Marriage Tribunal**
(See Marriage Tribunals Section)

**Pastoral Renewal Team**
Rev Gearóid Godley
Ms Frances Rowland
Ms Bernie McCaffrey
Pastoral Centre, Killarney, Co Kerry
Tel 064-6632644

**Pilgrimage Director**
Very Rev Nicholas Flynn PP
Killeentierna, Killarney, Co Kerry
Tel 066-9764141

**Pioneer Total Abstinence Association**
*Diocesan Director*
Very Rev Noel Spring PP
The Presbytery, Ballybunion, Co Kerry
Tel 068-27102 Fax 068-27153

**Pontifical Mission Societies**
*Diocesan Director:* Rev Gearóid Godley
John Paul II Pastoral Centre,
Killarney, Co Kerry
Tel 064-6630535 Fax 064-6631170

**Retreat Centre**
Ardfert, Co Kerry
*Director:* Very Rev Tadhg Fitzgerald
Tel 066-7134276 Fax 066-7133169

**Travellers**
*Chaplain:* Very Rev Luke Roche PP
Castlemaine, Co Kerry
Tel 066-9767322 Fax 066-9767467

**Vocations**
*Director:* Very Rev Liam Comer
*Assistant Director*
Very Rev Michael Moynihan

**Youth Director**
Mr Tim O'Donoghue
Diocesan Youth Office, The Friary,
Killarney, Co Kerry
Tel 064-6631748 Fax 064-6636770

## PARISHES

*The mensal parish is listed first. Other parishes follow alphabetically Historical names are given in parentheses. Church titulars are in italics.*

**KILLARNEY**
*St Mary's Cathedral, Killarney*
*Holy Spirit, Muckross*
*Resurrection, Park Road*
Very Rev Kieran O'Brien Adm, VF
Very Rev Jim Linehan CC
Rev Niall Howard CC
Very Rev Patrick Horgan *(Priest in residence)*
Killarney, Co Kerry
Tel 064-6631014 Fax 064-6631148

**ABBEYDORNEY**
*St Bernard's, Abbeydorney*
*St Mary's, Kilflynn*
Very Rev Denis O'Mahony PP
Abbeydorney, Co Kerry
Tel 066-7135146

**ADRIGOLE**
*St Fachtna's*
Very Rev Kieran O'Sullivan PP
Adrigole, Bantry, Co Cork
Tel 027-60006 Fax 027-60137

**ALLIHIES**
*St Michael's, Allihies,*
*St Michael's, Cahermore*
Very Rev Gearóid Walsh
Allihies, Bantry, Co Cork
Tel 027-70849 Fax 027-70557

**ANNASCAUL**
*Sacred Heart, Annascaul*
*St Mary's, Camp*
*St Joseph's, Inch*
Very Rev John Buckley PP
Annascaul, Co Kerry
Tel 066-9157103 Fax 066-9157221

**ARDFERT**
*St Brendan's, Ardfert*
*Sacred Heart, Kilmoyley*
Very Rev Tadhg Fitzgerald PP
Ardfert, Co Kerry
Tel 066-7134131 Fax 066-7134148

**BALLINSKELLIGS (PRIOR)**
*St Michael the Archangel, Ballinskelligs,*
*St Patrick's, Portmagee,*
*Sacred Heart and St Finan, The Glen*
Very Rev David Gunn PP
St Michael's, Ballinskelligs, Co Kerry
Tel 066-9479108 Fax 066-9479193

**BALLYBUNION**
*St John's*
Very Rev Noel Spring PP
Ballybunion, Co Kerry
Tel 068-27102 Fax 068-27153

**BALLYDESMOND**
*St Patrick's*
Very Rev Pádraig MacCarthaigh PP
Ballydesmond, Mallow, Co Cork
Tel 064-7751104 Fax 064-7751154

**BALLYDONOGHUE**
*St Teresa's*
Very Rev John Lawlor PP
Ballydonoghue, Lisselton, Co Kerry
Tel 068-47103 Fax 068-47230

**BALLYFERRITER**
*Uinseann Naofa, Baile an Fheitearaigh*
*Naomh Gobnait, Dún Chaoin*
*Séipéal na Carraige*
Very Rev Eugene Kiely PP
Tel 066-9156131
Very Rev Tomás Ó hIceadha AP
Tel 066-9156499
Ballyferriter West, Tralee, Co Kerry

**BALLYHEIGUE**
*St Mary's*
Very Rev Thomas Leane PP
Ballyheigue, Tralee, Co Kerry
Tel 066-7133110 Fax 066-7133114

**BALLYLONGFORD**
*St Michael the Archangel*
Very Rev Padraig Kennelly PP
Ballylongford, Co Kerry
Tel 068-43110 Fax 068-43187
*St Mary's*

**BALLYMACELLIGOTT**
*Immaculate Conception, Ballymacelligott*
*St Brendan's, Clogher*
Very Rev Pat Crean-Lynch PP
Ballymacelligott, Co Kerry
Tel 066-7137118 Fax 066-7137137

**BEAUFORT (TUOGH)**
*St Mary's, Beaufort*
*Our Lady of the Valley, The Valley*
Very Rev Donal O'Connor PP
The Presbytery, Beaufort, Co Kerry
Tel 064-6644128 Fax 064-6644130

**BOHERBUE/KISKEAM**
*Immaculate Conception, Boherbue*
*Sacred Heart, Kiskeam*
Very Rev Séamus Kennelly PP
Boherbue, Mallow, Co Cork
Tel 029-76151 Fax 029-76178

**BROSNA**
*St Carthage, Brosna*
*Our Lady of the Assumption, Knockaclarig*
Very Rev Anthony O'Sullivan PP
Brosna, Co Kerry
Tel 068-44112 Fax 068-44176

**CAHIRCIVEEN**
*Holy Cross, O'Connell Memorial,*
*Immaculate Conception, Filemore;*
*St Joseph's, Aghatubrid*
Very Rev Larry Canon Kelly
Cahirciveen, Co Kerry
Tel 066-9472210 Fax 066-9473130

**CAHIRDANIEL**
*St Crohan's, Mary Immaculate, Lohar*
*Most Precious Blood, Castlecove*
Very Rev Fergal Ryan PP
Cahirdaniel, Co Kerry
Tel 066-9475111 Fax 066-9475001

**CASTLEGREGORY**
*St Mary's, Castlegregory*
*St Brendan's, Cloghane*
Very Rev Michael Hussey PP
Castlegregory, Co Kerry
Tel 066-7139145 Fax 066-7139136

**CASTLEISLAND**
*SS Stephen and John*
Rt Rev Mgr Daniel O'Riordan PP
Castleisland, Co Kerry
Tel 066-7141241 Fax 066-7141273
*Our Lady of Lourdes*
*Immaculate Conception, Cordal*

**CASTLEMAINE**
*St Gobnait, Keel*
*St Carthage, Kiltallagh*
Very Rev Luke Roche PP
Castlemaine, Co Kerry
Tel 066-9767322 Fax 066-9767467

**CASTLETOWNBERE AND BERE ISLAND**
*Sacred Heart, Castletownbere*
*St Bartholomew, Rossmacowen*
*St Michael's, Bere Island*
Very Rev Gearóid Walsh
Castletownbere, Co Cork
Tel 027-70849 Fax 027-70047

**CAUSEWAY**
*St John the Baptist*
*SS Peter and Paul*
Very Rev Brendan Walsh PP
Causeway, Co Kerry
Tel 066-7131148 Fax 066-7131355

**DINGLE**
*St Mary's, Dingle*
*St John the Baptist, Lispole*
*Naomh Caitlín, Ceann Trá*
Very Rev Thomas Canon Looney SP, VF
Dingle, Co Kerry
Tel 066-9151208

**DROMTARIFFE**
*St John's, Dromagh*
*Presentation of the BVM, Derrinagree*
Very Rev Liam Comer PP, VF
Dromagh, Mallow, Co Cork
Tel 029-78096 Fax 029-78107

**DUAGH**
*St Brigid's, Duagh*
*Sacred Heart, Lyreacrompane*
Very Rev Patrick Moore PP
Duagh, Listowel, Co Kerry
Tel 068-45102 Fax 068-45149

**EYERIES**
*St Kentigern, Eyeries*
*Resurrection, Ardgroom*
Very Rev Daniel Broderick PP
Eyeries, Co Cork
Tel 027-74008 Fax 027-74090

**FIRIES**
*St Gertrude, Firies*
*Sacred Heart, Ballyhar*
Very Rev Tadhg O'Dochartaigh PP
Firies, Killarney, Co Kerry
Tel 066-9764122 Fax 066-9764046

**FOSSA**
*Christ, Prince of Peace*
Very Rev Brendan Harrington PP
Fossa, Killarney, Co Kerry
Tel 064-6631996 Fax 064-6631906

**GLENBEIGH**
*St James's, Glenbeigh*
*St Stephen's, Glencar*
Very Rev Jerry Keane PP
Glenbeigh, Co Kerry
Tel 066-9768209 Fax 066-9768225

**GLENFLESK**
*St Agatha, Glenflesk*
*Sacred Heart, Barraduff*
*Our Lady of the Wayside, Clonkeen*
Very Rev William Radley PP
St Agatha's Parish Centre, Headford,
Killarney, Co Kerry
Tel 064-7754008 Fax 064-7754458

**GLENGARRIFF (BONANE)**
*Sacred Heart, Glengarriff*
*St Fachtna's, Bonane*
Very Rev Michael Moynihan PP
Glengarriff, Co Cork
Tel 027-63045 Fax 027-63615

**KENMARE**
*Holy Cross, Kenmare*
*Our Lady of Perpetual Help,
Derreendaragh*
*Our Lady of the Assumption,
Templenoe*
Venerable Thomas Crean PP, VF
Kenmare, Co Kerry
Tel 064-6641352 Fax 064-6641925

**KILCUMMIN**
*Our Lady of Lourdes*
Very Rev Joseph Begley PP
Kilcummin, Killarney, Co Kerry
Tel 064-6643176

**KILGARVAN**
*St Patrick's*
Very Rev Donal O'Neill Adm
Rev Con Buckley
Kilgarvan, Co Kerry
Tel 064-6685313

**KILLEENTIERNA**
*Immaculate Conception, Currow*
*SS Thérèse & Colmcille, Currans*
Very Rev Nicholas Flynn PP
Killeentierna, Killarney, Co Kerry
Tel 066-9764141 Fax 066-9764862

**KILLORGLIN**
*St James, Killorglin*
*Our Lady, Star of the Sea, Cromane*
Very Rev Canon Michael Fleming PP, VF
Killorglin, Co Kerry
Tel 066-9761172 Fax 066-9761840

**KNOCKNAGOSHEL**
*St Mary's*
Very Rev Eoin Mangan PP
Knocknagoshel, Co Kerry
Tel 068-46107 Fax 068-46494

**LISTOWEL**
*St Mary's*
Very Rev Declan Canon O'Connor PP, VF
Listowel, Co Kerry
Tel 068-21188 Fax 068-23655

**LIXNAW**
*St Michael's, Lixnaw*
*Our Lady of the Assumption, Rathea*
*Our Lady of Fatima and St Senan,
Irremore*
Very Rev Maurice Brick PP
Tel 066-7132111 Fax 066-7132171
Rev Gerard O'Connell CC
Irremore, Listowel, Co Kerry
Tel 068-40244 Fax 068-40244

**MILLSTREET**
*St Patrick's, Millstreet*
*Our Lady of Lourdes, Ballydaly*
*Blessed Virgin Mary, Cullen*
Very Rev Jack Fitzgerald PP
Millstreet, Co Cork
Tel 029-70043 Fax 029-70919

**MILLTOWN**
*Sacred Heart, Milltown*
*Immaculate Conception, Listry*
Very Rev Gerard O'Leary PP
Milltown, Co Kerry
Tel 066-9767312 Fax 066-9767988

**MOYVANE**
*Assumption of the BVM, Moyvane*
*Corpus Christi, Knockanure*
Very Rev John Lucid PP
Moyvane, Listowel, Co Kerry
Tel 068-49308 Fax 068-49418

**RATHMORE**
*Christ the King, Knocknagree*
*St Joseph's, Rathmore*
*Our Lady of Perpetual Succour, Shrone*
*Holy Rosary, Gneeveguilla*
Very Rev Pat O'Donnell PP
Rathmore, Co Kerry
Tel 064-7758026 Fax 064-7758110
Rev Kevin McNamara CC
Gneeveguilla, Rathmore, Co Kerry
Tel 064-7756188 Fax 064-7756332

**SNEEM**
*St Michael, Sneem; St Brendan,
Glenlough; St Patrick, Tahilla*
Very Rev Liam O'Brien PP
Sneem, Co Kerry
Tel 064-6645141 Fax 064-6645941

**SPA**
*Church of the Purification, Churchill*
*St Joseph's, Fenit*
Very Rev Eamon Mulvihill PP
Fenit, Tralee, Co Kerry
Tel 066-7136145 Fax 066-7136327

**TARBERT**
*St Mary's*
Very Rev John Lawlor PP, VF
Tel 068-36111 Fax 068-36572

**TRALEE, ST BRENDAN'S**
*Our Lady and St Brendan, Rock Street*
Very Rev Pádraig Walsh PP
Rev Patsy Lynch CC
Rev Tomás O'Caoimh
St Brendan's, Tralee, Co Kerry
Tel 066-7125932 Fax 066-7127049

**TRALEE, ST JOHN'S**
*St John the Baptist, Castle Street, Tralee*
*Immaculate Conception, Rathass*
*St Brendan's, Curaheen*
Dean Sean Hanafin PP, VG
Rev Gerard Finucane
Rev Francis Nolan
Rev Bernard Healy CC
Rev Seámus Linnane AP
Rev Kevin Sullivan
St John's Presbytery, Tralee, Co Kerry
Tel 066-7122522 Fax 066-7122760
Email stjohnscastlestreet@eircom.net

**TUOSIST**
*St Kilian's, Lauragh*
*Dawros, Dawros*
Very Rev Martin Sheehan Adm
St Joseph's, Lauragh, Killarney, Co Kerry
Tel 064-6683107 Fax 064-6683577

**VALENTIA**
*Immaculate Conception, Knightstown*
*SS Derarca and Teresa, Chapeltown*
Very Rev John Shanahan PP
Valentia Island, Co Kerry
Tel 066-9476104 Fax 066-9476408

**WATERVILLE (DROMOD)**
*St Finian's, Dromod*
Our Lady of the Valley, Cillin Liath
Very Rev John Kerin PP
Tel 066-9474495 Fax 066-9474703

## INSTITUTIONS AND THEIR CHAPLAINS

**Ardfert Retreat Centre**
Rev Tomás O'Caoimh
Tel 066-7134276

**Boherbue Comprehensive School**
Mallow, Co Cork
Ms Fiona O'Donoghue
Tel 029-76032

**Castletownbere Community School,**
Co Cork
Ms Marie Murphy
Tel 027-70177/70026

**Causeway Comprehensive School**
Mr Paul Montgomery
Tel 066-7131197/7132513

**Coláiste na Sceilge**
Cahirciveen
Tel 066-9473335
*Chaplain:* Liam Egan

**Kenmare Pobalscoil Inbhear Scéine**
Ms Mairéad Hickey
Tel 064-6640846

**Killarney Community College**
Rev Niall Howard
Tel 064-6632764

**Killarney St Columbanus Home**
Sr Mary Boyle
Tel 064-6631018

**Killorglin Post-Primary Schools**
Parish Clergy
Tel 066-9761172

**Millstreet Community School**
Co Cork
Mr John Magee
Tel 029-70087/79028

**Listowel Presentation Convent**
Sr Eilis Daly
Tel 068-21452

**Our Lady of Fatima Home**
Oakpark, Tralee, Co Kerry
Tel 066-7125900
St John's Parish Clergy

**Pobalscoil Chorca Dhuibhne**
Dingle
Ms Una Ní Ghlíosáin
Tel 064-6640846

**Rathmore Community School**
Ms Yvonne O'Connor
Parish Clergy
Tel 064-6658027

**St Brendan's College**
Killarney, Co Kerry
Very Rev Joseph Begley PP
Very Rev Jim Linehan CC
Tel 064-6631021

**St Michael's College**
Listowel, Co Kerry
Parish Clergy
Tel 068-21049/21188

**Tarbert, Comprehensive School**
Listowel, Co Kerry
Sr Frances Day
Tel 068-36105/36177

**Tralee General Hospital**
Rev Teddy Linehan
Rev Martin Spillane
Mrs Mary Quinlan
Tel 066-7126222

**Tralee Institute of Technology**
Tralee, Co Kerry
Rev Kevin Sullivan
Tel 066-7145639/7135236

**Tralee Mercy Secondary Mounthawk**
Tel 066-7102550
Our Lady and St Brendan's Parish Clergy
Tel 066-7125932

## PRIESTS OF THE DIOCESE ELSEWHERE

Rev George Hayes
Collegio Pontificio Irlandese,
Via dei SS Quattro 1, 00184 Rome
Rev Liam Lovell
On Sabbatical
Rev Seamus McKenna BA, HDE
Cork Regional Marriage Tribunal,
The Lough, Cork
Tel 021-4963653
Rev Seamus O'Connell
St Patrick's College, Maynooth,
Co Kildare
Tel 01-6285222
Rev Richard O'Connor
Villa Maria Assunta,
Via Aurelia Antica 284,
00-165 Roma, Italy
Rev Anthony O'Reilly
Newry, Co Armagh
Rev Joseph Tarrant
On Sabbatical

## RETIRED PRIESTS

Rev Pat Ahern
St John's Parish Centre, Castle Street,
Tralee, Co Kerry
Very Rev Denis Costello
Fatima Home, Oakpark, Tralee, Co Kerry
Rev Jim Downey
Fatima Home, Oakpark, Tralee, Co Kerry

Very Rev Martin Hegarty
1 Track Road, Bridge Street,
Listowel, Co Kerry
Very Rev Roger Kelleher
9 St Emmet's Terrace, Killarney, Co Kerry
Very Rev Lawrence Kelly
Fatima Home, Oakpark, Tralee, Co Kerry
Very Rev John Kennelly
24 Ferndene, Greenville, Listowel, Co Kerry
Very Rev Denis Leahy
34 Knockmoyle Estate, Tralee, Co Kerry
Very Rev Noel Moran
Lahard, Milltown, Co Kerry
Archdeacon Michael J. Murphy
No 1 Cathedral Place, Killarney, Co Kerry
Very Rev Patrick Murphy
Fatima Home, Oakpark, Tralee, Co Kerry
Very Rev J. Nolan
36 Ashfield, Greenville, Listowel, Co Kerry
Rev Philip O'Connell
32 Knockmoyle Est, Tralee, Co Kerry
Very Rev Michael O'Dochartaigh
Ard an Aonaigh, Killarney, Co Kerry
Very Rev Canon Michael O'Doherty
No 1 Lynch Heights, Sun Hill,
Killorglin, Co Kerry
Rev Gearoid Ó Donnchadha
'An tSaoirse', Fenit, Tralee, Co Kerry
Rt Rev Mgr Pádraig Ó Fiannachta
An Diseart, Green Street, Dingle, Co Kerry
Very Rev Canon Denis O'Mahony
Killeagh, Farranfore, Co Kerry
Very Rev Denis Quirke
Fatima Home, Oakpark, Tralee, Co Kerry
Very Rev Canon P. Sheehan
'Shalom', Rossbeigh, Glenbeigh, Co Kerry
Rev Patrick Sugrue
Mastergeeha, Killarney, Co Kerry

## RELIGIOUS ORDERS AND CONGREGATIONS

### PRIESTS

**DOMINICANS**
Holy Cross, Tralee, Co Kerry
Tel 066-7121135/7129185
Fax 066-7180026
*Prior:* Very Rev Joseph Bulman (OP)

**FRANCISCANS**
Franciscan Friary, Killarney, Co Kerry
Tel 064-6631334/6631066
Fax 064-6637510
Email friary@eircom.net
*Guardian:* Rev Pádraig Breheny (OFM)

**OBLATES OF MARY IMMACULATE**
Department of Chaplaincy,
Tralee General Hospital, Co Kerry
Rev Edward Barrett
Tel 066-7126222

### BROTHERS

**CHRISTIAN BROTHERS**
Christian Brothers, 14 The Orchard,
Ballyrickard, Tralee, Co Kerry
Tel 066-71-3910
*Community Leader:* Br Daithi O'Connell
Community: 2

## PRESENTATION BROTHERS

Presentation Novitiate, Killarney,
Co Kerry
Tel 064-6631267
*Contact:* Br Barry Noel (FPM)
Community: 7

## SAINT JOHN OF GOD KERRY SERVICES

Cloonanorig, Monavalley,
Tralee, Co Kerry
Tel 066-7124333 Fax 066-7126197
Email kerry@sjog.ie
*Director:* Ms Pauline Bergin
Training and supported employment
service with back-up residential and
community services

St Mary of the Angels,
Beaufort, Co Kerry
Tel 064-44133 Fax 064-44302
Training, residential and community
services for people with an intellectual
disability

St Francis Special School,
Beaufort, Co Kerry
Tel 064-44452 Fax 064-24884
*School Principal:* Liam Twomey

## SISTERS

## BON SECOURS SISTERS (PARIS)

Bon Secours Convent, Strand Street,
Tralee, Co Kerry
Tel 066-7149800 Fax 066-7129068
*Co-ordinator:* Sr Teresita Hoare
Community: 7
Pastoral and hospital ministry

1 Cahermoneen, Tralee, Co Kerry
Tel 066-7127600
Community: 1
Pastoral ministry

5 Strand View Terrace, Tralee, Co Kerry
Tel 066-7181279
Community: 1

6 Strand Street, Tralee, Co Kerry
Tel 066-7194647
Community: 1
Hospital ministry

## CONGREGATION OF THE SISTERS OF MERCY

Mercy Lodge, Balloonagh,
Tralee, Co Kerry
Tel 066-7126336 Fax 066-7125901

St John's, Balloonagh, Tralee, Co Kerry
Tel 066-7121199/7122370

Mercy Convent, Rock Road,
Killarney, Co Kerry
Tel 064-6631040/6631916

Suaineas, Woodlawn Road,
Killarney, Co Kerry
Tel 064-6633660

7 Arbutus Drive,
Killarney, Co Kerry
Tel 064-6637484

11 Holy Cross Gardens,
Killarney, Co Kerry
Tel 064-6620554

21 The Grove, Mounthawk,
Tralee, Co Kerry
Tel 066-7189029

St Brigid's Convent, Greenville, Listowel,
Co Kerry
Tel 068-21557

Divine Providence, Castletownbere,
Co Cork
Tel 027-70061

'Mount St Michael', Rosscarbery, Co Cork
Tel 023-8848116

Pairc a Tobair, Rosscarbery, Co Cork
Tel 023-8848963

14 Brandon Place, Basin Road,
Tralee, Co Kerry
Tel 066-7144997

9 Carraig Lí, Killerisk, Tralee, Co Kerry
Tel 066-7121281

10 Carraig Lí, Killerisk, Tralee, Co Kerry
Tel 066-7192364

Goodwin House, The Mall,
Dingle, Co Kerry
Tel 066-9151943

Mercy Sisters, Aoibhneas,
103 Gort na Sidhe, Mounthawk,
Tralee, Co Kerry
Tel 066-7128056

7 Woodview, Moyderwell, Tralee,
Co Kerry
Tel 066-7118027

2 Carrigeendaniel Court, Caherslee,
Tralee, Co Kerry
Tel 066-7127517

1 St Brendan's Park, Tralee,
Co Kerry

## DAUGHTERS OF MARY AND JOSEPH

Fairways, Killowen, Kenmare, Co Kerry
Tel 064-6640755
*Contact Person:* Sr Helen Lane (DMJ)
Community: 1

## DOMINICAN SISTERS (KING WILLIAM'S TOWN)

Oak Park, Tralee, Co Kerry
Tel 066-71256641
Community: 5
Our Lady of Fatima Retirement Home
Tel 066-7125900 Fax 066-7180834
Email dominicansisterstralee@gmail.com
Beds: 66
Siena Court for Active Retired:
Bungalows: 10
*Contact Person:* Sr Teresa McEvoy OP
Email teresamcevoy@fatimahome.com

## FRANCISCAN MISSIONARIES OF THE DIVINE MOTHERHOOD

Sancta Chiara,
5 St Margaret's Road,
Killarney, Co Kerry
Tel 064-6626866 Fax 064-6626414
Community: 4

## INFANT JESUS SISTERS

Killarney Road,
Millstreet, Co Cork
Tel 029-70143
Community: 6
Retired sisters and pastoral ministry

7 Blackrock,
St Brendan's Road,
Tralee, Co Kerry
Tel 066-7124455
Community: 1
Teaching and pastoral ministry

## LITTLE COMPANY OF MARY

Park Road,
Killarney, Co Kerry
Tel 064-6671220 Fax 064-6671240
Community: 4

## PRESENTATION SISTERS

Teach na Toirbhirte,
Miltown, Co Kerry
Tel 066-9767387
*Non-resident Leader:* Sr Bríd Clifford
Community: 5
Primary School. Tel 066-9767626
Post-Primary School. Tel 066-9767168

Presentation Convent,
Killarney, Co Kerry
Tel 064-6631172
Team Leadership
Community: 10
Secondary School. Tel 064-6632209

Presentation Sisters,
25 Ballyspillane, Killarney, Co Kerry
Tel 064-6636389
Community: 2

Presentation Convent, Castle Street,
Tralee, Co Kerry
Tel 066-7122128
Team Leadership
Community: 14
Primary School. Tel 066-7123314
Secondary School. Tel 066-7122737

20 Baile and Toirín,
Killorglin, Co Kerry
Community: 1

Apt. 1, Presentation Convent,
Castle Street, Tralee, Co Kerry
Tel 066-7181627
Community: 1

Apt. 2, Presentation Convent,
Castle Street, Tralee, Co Kerry
Tel 066-7118539
Community: 1

Apt. 3, Presentation Convent,
Castle Street, Tralee, Co Kerry
Tel 066-7122828
Community: 1

Apt. 4, Presentation Convent,
Castle Street, Tralee, Co Kerry
Tel 066-7120641
Community: 1

Apt. 5, Presentation Convent,
Castle Street, Tralee, Co Kerry
Tel 066-7121827
Community: 1

Presentation Convent, Dingle, Co Kerry
Tel 066-9151194
Community: 1
Primary School. Tel 066-9151154

Presentation Convent,
Castleisland, Co Kerry
Tel 066-7141256
*Non-resident Leader*
Sr Elizabeth McMahon
Community: 10
Primary School. Tel 066-7141147
Secondary School. Tel 066-7141178

Presentation Convent,
Lixnaw, Co Kerry
Tel 066-7132138
*Non-resident Leader:* Sr Maureen Kane
Community: 7
Primary School. Tel 066-7132600

Presentation Convent,
Rathmore, Co Kerry
Tel 064-7758027
*Non-resident Leader:* Sr Margaret O'Brien
Community: 5
Primary School. Tel 064-7758499

48 Hawley Park, Tralee, Co Kerry
Tel 066-7122111
Community: 1

'Tigh na Féile', Ballygologue Road,
Listowel, Co Kerry
Tel 068-21156
Community: 1
Primary School. Tel 068-22294
Secondary School. Tel 068-21452
Nano Nagle Special School. Tel 068-21942

9 Beech Grove, Cahirdown,
Listowel, Co Kerry
Tel 068-53951
Community: 1

Mail Road, Cahirdown,Listowel, Co Kerry
Tel 068-22500
Community: 2

Presentation Sisters, 1 Glenard,
Mona Valley, Tralee, Co Kerry
Tel 066-7181318
Community: 1

7 Tamhnach Lí,
Monavalley, Tralee, Co Kerry
Tel 066-7180800
Community: 1

8 Tamhnach Lí,
Monavalley, Tralee, Co Kerry
Tel 066-7194174
Community: 1

9 Tamhnach Lí,
Monavalley, Tralee, Co Kerry
Tel 066-7195312
Community: 2

9 Woodbrooke Manor,
Monavalley, Tralee, Co Kerry
Tel 066-7185454
Community: 2

15 St Joseph's Gardens,
Millstreet, Co Cork
Tel 029-71655
Community: 1

31 St Joseph's Gardens,
Millstreet, Co Cork
Tel 029-71627
Community: 1

6 Meadowlands, Artigallivan, Headford,
Killarney, Co Kerry
Tel 064-7754030
Community: 1

20 Spring Well Gardens,
Ballyard, Tralee, Co Kerry
Tel 066-7102862
Community: 1

### SISTERS OF ST CLARE
St Clare's Convent, Kenmare, Co Kerry
Tel 064-6641385
Community: 3
St Clare's Primary. Pupils: 151
Kenmare Community School
Tel 064-6640846/7

### ST JOSEPH OF ANNECY SISTERS
St Joseph's Convent, Killorglin, Co Kerry
Tel 066-9761809 Fax 066-9761127
*Superior:* Sr Helena Lyne
Email margaret.lyne@talk21.com
Community: 4

St Joseph's Home for the Aged,
Killorglin, Co Kerry
Tel 066-9761124 (H)
Tel 066-9761808 (Patients)
Beds: 40

### ST JOSEPH OF THE SACRED HEART SISTERS
Sisters of St Joseph of Sacred Heart,
St Joseph's, Brosna Road,
Castleisland, Co Kerry
Tel 066-7141472
Sr Maryanne Sugrue

Sisters of St Joseph of Sacred Heart,
St Joseph's, 5 Allman's Terrace,
Killarney, Co Kerry
Tel 064-6623528
Sr Ellen Lane

## DIOCESAN SECONDARY SCHOOLS

**St Brendan's College (Diocesan College)**
Killarney, Co Kerry
Tel 064-6631021
*Principal:* Mr Sean Coffey

**St Michael's College**
Listowel, Co Kerry
Tel 068-21049
*Principal:* Mr John Mulvihill

## EDUCATIONAL INSTITUTIONS

**EDMUND RICE SCHOOLS TRUST**
Scoil Íognaid Rís, An Meall,
An Daingean, Co Kerry
Tel 066-9152157
Email sird@eircom.net
*Principal:* Róisín Uí Bheaglaoí

Scoil Mhuire na mBráithre,
Clounalour, Tralee, Co Kerry
Tel 066-7124029
*Principal:* Mr Denis Coleman

St Mary's CBS,
The Green, Tralee, Co Kerry
Tel 066-7145824
Fax 066-7129807
*Principal:* Ms Anne O'Callaghan
Email info@thegreen.ie

## CHARITABLE AND OTHER SOCIETIES

**Legion of Mary**
Dingle, Firies, Fossa, Glenflesk,
Kilcummin, Killarney, Killeentierna,
Knocknagree, Millstreet, Milltown,
Scartaglin, Tralee

**St Vincent de Paul**
Conferences at: Abbeydorney,
Annascaul, Ardfert, Ballybunion,
Ballyduff, Ballyferiter, Ballyheigue,
Ballylongford, Boherbue, Cahirciveen,
Castlemaine, Castlegregory, Castleisland,
Castletownbere, Dingle, Firies, Kenmare,
Killarney (four conferences), Killorglin,
Knocknagoshel, Listowel, Lixnaw,
Millstreet, Milltown, Moyvane,
Rathmore, Tralee (five conferences)

study
# theology
by distance
learning

## Certificate, Diploma, Higher Certificate and Degree Programmes

(also open to those studying without academic credit)

### Major Awards

Bachelor of Arts (Hons) in Theology (4 Years; NFQ Level 8)
Bachelor of Arts in Theology (3 Years; NFQ Level 7)
Higher Certificate in Theology (2 Years; NFQ level 7)

### Minor Awards

Diploma in Theology (1 Year; NFQ level 7)
Diploma in Philosophy (1 Year; NFQ level 7)
Diploma in Scripture (1 Year; NFQ level 7)
Certificate in Theology (1 Year; NFQ level 6)

(*NFQ = National Framework of Qualifications)
**All programmes are validated by the Institute of Technology Tallaght, Dublin**

Study theology in your own home
For further information call 01 404 8124
enquiries@prioryinstitute.com
www.prioryinstitute.com

## THE PRIORY INSTITUTE

Tallaght Village, Dublin 24

# ST. FINBARR'S
# ALTAR BREADS SUPPLIES LTD.

FARRANFERRIS,
REDEMPTION ROAD,
CORK.
TEL: 021 4300227 FAX: 021 4228199
EMAIL: altarbreads@nce.ie

SUPPLIERS OF

Altarbreads, votive candles, sanctuary candles, incense, charcoal, mass cards,
religious books, and Bog Oak religious goods.

OFFICE HOURS: 9.00AM-.5.00PM
AFTER HOURS TELEPHONE ANSWERING SERVICE AVAILABLE
COLLECTION AND POSTAL SERVICE AVAILABLE

# CHURCH FURNISHERS

SINCE 1972

**Bespoke Church Furnishers, Irish Contract Seating, have been meeting the needs of communities over the past 42 years through the innovtive design of high quality church furniture.**

To find out how we can take your project from concept to fruition contact us to discuss your specific requirements:

ICS Furniture
Dromod, Carrick-on-Shannon, Co.Leitrim, Ireland

Tel: +353 71 9638230 | Fax: +353 71 9638290
Email: info@icsfurniture.com | Web: www.icsfurniture.com

ST. KILLIANS
CANDLE BURNING SYSTEM
— For Cathedrals & Churches —
"The Light Of The World"
NO MORE UNPROTECTED FLAMES
With our patented glass system the flame is protected at all times. The candle itself is isolated in a uniquely designed glass and having burned for 90 minutes it extinguishes automatically allowing the waste wax to drop down into a tray of water.
NO MORE SMOKE OR SOOT DAMAGE
The persistent smoke and soot damage to church walls and ceilings caused by other candle burning systems have proved to be both costly and unsightly.
NO MORE UNSIGHTLY CANDELABRAS
People lighting candles can only place the candle into the patented glass provided thus ensuring that the candle stand is aesthetically attractive at all times.
ST ANTHONY PRAY FOR US
New Rental Scheme available from as little as €2 per week
Cahir Business Park, Cahir, Co. Tipperary, Ireland
PH: 00 353 52 7441945 FAX: 00 353 52 7441232
Michael Murphy PH: 00 353 87 2943193 Michael Barrett PH: 00 353 87 2716299
Email: info@saintkillians.ie Website: www.saintkillians.ie

# DIOCESE OF KILDARE AND LEIGHLIN

PATRONS OF THE DIOCESE
ST BRIGID, 1 FEBRUARY; ST CONLETH (KILDARE), 4 MAY;
ST LAZERIAN (LEIGHLIN) 18 APRIL

INCLUDES COUNTY CARLOW AND PARTS OF COUNTIES KILDARE, LAOIS,
OFFALY, KILKENNY, WICKLOW AND WEXFORD

**Most Rev Denis Nulty DD**
Bishop of Kildare and Leighlin
Born 1963;
ordained priest 1988;
ordained Bishop of Kildare &
Leighlin 4 August 2013

Residence:
Bishop's House, Carlow
Tel 059-9176725
Fax 059-9176850
Email bishop@kandle.ie

## CATHEDRAL OF THE ASSUMPTION, CARLOW

The ancient cathedrals of the Diocese of Kildare and Leighlin passed into Protestant usage in the period of the Reformation. Thus the cathedrals of Kildare and Old Leighlin stand on the sites of the ancient monasteries of St Brigid and St Laserian. Even before the Catholic Emancipation Act passed through the Westminster Parliament (1829), Bishop James Doyle OSA was working on the building of the Cathedral of the Assumption, Carlow. It is built on the site of and incorporates parts of the previous parish church of Carlow, which had been built in the 1780s by Dean Henry Staunton.

Carlow cathedral is not particularly large, having more the dimensions of a big parish church. The architectural work was begun by Joseph Lynch, but the final building is stamped with the design of Thomas Cobden, who replaced Lynch in 1829. Cobden gave the cathedral quite an elaborate exterior, with the obvious influence of the Bruges Town Hall tower. The cost of the building work was about £9,000. At its opening in November 1833, the interior decoration was incomplete. In fact, many elements were integrated over the following hundred years, sometimes adding to the mixture of styles.

The cathedral was consecrated on the occasion of its centenary, on 29 November 1933. A thorough reordering of the interior was completed in 1997, giving a very bright, welcoming, prayerful location for both diocesan and parish liturgical celebrations. The most notable elements are: the baptistry, the aumbry, the bishop's and president's chairs, and the Hogan statue of James Doyle, former Bishop of Kildare and Leighlin popularly known as JKL.

**Most Rev James Moriarty DD**
Retired Bishop of Kildare and Leighlin,
born 1936; ordained priest 1961; ordained
Bishop 22 September 1991; installed as
Bishop of Kildare & Leighlin on 31 August
2002; retired April 2010
Residence: 68 Clontarf Road, Dublin 3
Tel 01-8054738

## ADMINISTRATION

**Diocesan Website**
www.kandle.ie

**Vicar General**
Rt Rev Mgr John Byrne PP, VG
Dublin Road, Portlaoise, Co Laois
Tel 057-8621142

**Vicars Forane**
Very Rev Thomas Little PP, VF
(K&L South Deanery)
St Mary's Presbytery,
Brownshill Avenue, Carlow
Tel 059-9131559
Very Rev Mícheál Murphy PP, VF
(K&L West Deanery)
Mountmellick, Co Laois
Rev Paul Dempsey CC, VF
(K&L North Deanery)
The Presbytery, Ballymany,
Newbridge, Co Kildare
Tel 045-434069

**Episcopal Vicar for the Pastoral Care of
Priests**
Very Rev Andy Leahy PP
Tullow, Co Carlow
Tel 059-9180641

**Episcopal Vicar for Education and
Evangelisation**
Very Rev John Cummins
The Presbytery, Carlow
Tel 059-9131227

**Consultors**
Rt Rev Mgr Brendan Byrne, Chancellor
Rt Rev Mgr John Byrne PP, VG
Very Rev John Cummins Adm
Rev Paul Dempsey CC, VF
Very Rev Andy Leahy PP
Very Rev Thomas Little PP, VF
Very Rev Mícheál Murphy PP, VF

**Chancellor/Diocesan Secretary**
Rt Rev Mgr Brendan Byrne
Email brendan.byrne@kandle.ie
c/o Bishop's House, Carlow
Tel 059-9176725 Fax 059-9176850

**Diocesan Communications Liaison**
Very Rev Mícheál Murphy PP, VF
Tel 057-8679302
Email mfmurphy@eircom.net

**Diocesan Communications**
Rev Bill Kemmy
Tel 087-2308053
www.icatholic.ie

**Finance Committee**
*Chairperson:* Mrs Anna-May McHugh
Fallaghmore, Ballylinan, Athy, Co Kildare
*Recording Secretary:* Rosie Boyd
Bishop's House, Carlow
Tel 059-9176725 Fax 059-9176850
Email rosie@kandle.ie

**Churches and Buildings Committee**
*Chairman*
Very Rev Francis MacNamara PE, CC
Mountmellick, Co Laois
Tel 057-8624198
*Secretary:* Very Rev Denis Harrington PE
Clane, Co Kildare

**Director of Vocations & Permanent
Deacons**
Rev Ruairí Ó Domhnaill CC
77 Lakelands, Naas, Co Kildare
Tel 045-897470
Email vocations@kandle.ie

**Safeguarding Office**
*Diocesan Designated Liaison Person*
Ms Joan Treacy
c/o Bishop's House, Carlow
Tel 085-8021633
Email joantreacy@kandle.ie
*Deputy Designated Liaison Person*
Very Rev Mícheál Murphy PP, VF
11 Ashgrove, Mountmellick, Co Laois
Tel 057-8679302
Email mfmurphy@eircom.net
*Diocesan Safeguarding Co-ordinator*
Mr David Dwyer
c/o Bishop's House, Carlow
Tel 087-2874054
Email safeguarding@kandle.ie
*Diocesan Garda Vetting Administrator*
Rosie Boyd
c/o Bishop's House, Carlow
Tel 059-9176725
Email rosie@kandle.ie

**Archivist**
*Diocesan Archivist:* Bernie Deasy
Bishop's House, Carlow
Tel 059-9176725 Fax 059-9176850
Email bdeasy@carlowcollege.ie

## FAITH DEVELOPMENT SERVICES

**Faith Development Services**
Cathedral Parish Centre, College Street,
Carlow Town
Tel 059-9164084 Fax 059-9164020
Email fds@kandle.ie
*Primary Diocesan Advisor*
Ms Maeve Mahon
Email maeve.mahon@kandle.ie
*Post-Primary Diocesan Advisor*
Sr Anne Holton
Email anne.holton@kandle.ie
*Youth Ministry/Meitheal Co-ordinator*
Mr Robert Norton
Email robert.norton@kandle.ie
Ms Cathriona Kelly
Email cathriona.kelly@kandle.ie
*Pastoral Resource Person*
Ms Julie Kavanagh
Email julie.kavanagh@kandle.ie

**Church Music**
Rev Liam Lawton
Crossneen, Carlow Tel 059-9134548
Email liamlawtonireland@gmail.com

**Catholic Primary School Managers
Association**
*Chairman*
Very Rev Francis MacNamara PE, CC
Mountmellick, Co Laois
Tel 057-8624198

*Secretary:* Br Camillus Regan
c/o Bishop's House, Carlow
Tel 087-2244175
Email patbros@iol.ie

## PASTORAL

**ACCORD**
*Centre Directors*
Carlow: Very Rev John Cummins Adm
The Presbytery, Dublin Road, Carlow
Tel 059-9131227
Ms Mary Merrigan
Tel 059-9138738
*Portlaoise:* Ms Carmel Kelly
Tel 045-431394
Accord, Parish Office, Portlaoise, Co Laois
*Newbridge:* Very Rev Joseph McDermott PP
Station Road, Newbridge, Co Kildare
Tel 045-431741

**ALPHA**
Very Rev James O'Connell PP
Stradbally, Co Laois
Tel 057-8625132

**Conciliators**
Rt Rev Mgr John McDonald PP
Curragh Camp, Co Kildare
Tel 045-441369
Very Rev William O'Byrne PP
Kill, Co Kildare
Tel 045-878008
Ms Breda Parker
9 Moorepark, Newbridge, Co Kildare
Tel 045-431462
Mr Brian O'Sullivan
Drumcooley, Edenderry, Co Offaly
Tel 046-9731522 (W) 046-31435 (H)

**Ecumenism**
*Director:* Very Rev Tom Lalor PP
Leighlinbridge, Co Carlow
Tel 059-9721463
Rev Liam Morgan CC
Naas, Co Kildare
Tel 045-897260
Very Rev Liam Merrigan PP
Drogheda Street, Monasterevin, Co Kildare
Tel 045-525346

**Pioneer Total Abstinence Association**
*Diocesan Director*
Very Rev Mark Townsend PP
Daingean, Co Offaly
Tel 057-9362006

**Pontifical Mission Societies**
*Diocesan Director:* Rev Eddie Kavanagh CC
15 Lowtown Manor,
Robertstown, Co Kildare
Tel 045-890559

**Polish Chaplaincy**
Rev Tadeusz Durajczyk (SVD) CC
60 College Orchard, Newbridge, Co Kildare
Tel 086-2354320

**Prisons**
*Contact Priest:* Rev Eugene Drumm (SPS)
Portlaoise Prison, Portlaoise, Co Laois
Tel 057-8622549
Rev Tom Sinnott (MHM)
Midlands Prison, Portlaoise, Co Laois
Tel 057-8672222

## Travellers

*Chaplains*
Very Rev Thomas Dooley PP
Portarlington, Co Laois
Tel 057-8643004
Very Rev John Brickley PP
Sallins Road, Naas, Co Kildare
Tel 045-897260

## Youth Ministry

*Chairman:* Rev Liam Morgan CC
Sallins Road, Naas, Co Kildare
Tel 045-897260
*Meitheal Co-ordinator:* Mr Robert Norton
Email robert.norton@kandle.ie
Ms Cathriona Kelly
Faith Development Services,
Cathedral Parish Centre,
College Street, Carlow
Tel 059-9164084 Fax 059-9164020

## PARISHES

*Mensal parishes are listed first. Other parishes follow alphabetically. Historical names are given in parentheses. Church titulars are in italics.*

### CATHEDRAL, CARLOW

*Cathedral of the Assumption*
Email info@carlowcathedral.ie
Website www.carlowcathedral.ie
Very Rev John Cummins Adm
The Presbytery, Carlow
Tel 059-9131227 Fax 059-9130805
Email johncummins@kandle.ie
Rev Rory Nolan CC
The Presbytery, Carlow
Tel 059-9131227
Rev Martin Smith (SPS) CC
1 Green Road, Carlow
Tel 059-9142632
Permanent Deacon: Rev David O'Flaherty
Tel 059-9164086
Cathedral/Parish Shop & Office
Tel 059-9164087

### ASKEA

*Holy Family*
Email askeaparishcc@eircom.net
Very Rev Thomas Little Adm, VF
Browneshill Avenue, Carlow
Tel 059-9131559
Email tomlittle@eircom.net
Rev Sean Hyland CC
Tinryland, Co Carlow
Tel 059-9131212
Rev Alex Kochatt CC
The Presbytery, Askea, Carlow
Tel 059-9142565

### ABBEYLEIX

*Holy Rosary, Abbeyleix*
*St Patrick, Ballyroan*
Very Rev Gerard Ahern PP
Abbeyleix, Co Laois
Tel 057-8731135
Email aherngerard@eircom.net

### ALLEN

*Holy Trinity, Allen*
*St Brigid's, Milltown*
*Immaculate Conception, Allenwood*
Very Rev William Byrne PP
Allen, Kilmeague, Naas, Co Kildare
Tel 045-860135

Rev Edward Kavanagh CC
15 Lowtown Manor,
Robertstown, Naas, Co Kildare
Tel 045-890559

### ARLES

*Sacred Heart, Arles, St Anne's, Ballylinan*
*St Abban's, Maganey*
Very Rev Brian Kavanagh PP
Graiguecullen, Carlow
Tel 059-9179855
Very Rev Thomas O'Shea CC
Ballylinan, Athy, Co Kildare
Tel 059-8625261
Email tommieoshea1@eircom.net

### BALLINAKILL

*St Brigid's, Ballinakill*
*St Lazarian's, Knock*
Very Rev Seán Conlon Adm
Ballinakill, Co Laois
Tel 057-8733336

### BALLON

*SS Peter and Paul, Ballon*
*St Patrick's, Rathoe*
Very Rev Brendan Howard PP
Clonegal, Enniscorthy, Co Wexford
Tel 053-9377291
Rev Edward Whelan PE, CC
Ballon, Co Carlow
Tel 059-9159329

### BALLYADAMS

*St Joseph's, Ballyadams*
*St Mary's, Wolfhill*
*Holy Rosary, Luggacurren*
Very Rev Daniel Dunne PP
Tullamoy, Stradbally, Co Laois
Tel 059-8627123

### BALLYFIN

*St Fintan's*
Very Rev Pat Hennessy PP
Ballyfin, Portlaoise, Co Laois
Tel 057-8755227
Rev Joseph Brophy CC
Mountrath, Co Laois
Tel 057-8732234

### BALTINGLASS

*St Joseph's, Baltinglass*
*St Oliver's, Grange Con*
*St Mary's, Stratford*
Very Rev Thomas Dillon PP
Baltinglass, Co Wicklow
Tel 059-6482768
Email tfdb@eircom.net

### BALYNA

*St Mary's, Broadford,*
*St Patrick's Johnstownbridge,*
*St Brigid's, Clogherinchoe*
Email balynaparish@eircom.net
Website www.balynaparish.ie
Very Rev Gerard Breen PP
Broadford, Co Kildare
Tel 046-9551203

### BENNEKERRY

*St Mary's*
Very Rev Thomas Little PP, VF
St Mary's, Browneshill Avenue, Carlow
Tel 059-9131559
Email tomlittle@eircom.net
Rev Sean Hyland CC
Tinryland, Co Carlow
Tel 059-9131212

### BORRIS

*Sacred Heart, Borris*
*St Patrick's, Ballymurphy*
*St Forchan's, Rathanna*
Very Rev John O'Brien PP
Tel 059-9773128
Email john51@eircom.net
Very Rev Pierce Murphy
Borris, Co Carlow via Kilkenny
Tel 059-9773128

### CARAGH

*Our Lady and St Joseph, Caragh,*
Email parishoffice@caragh.net
Very Rev Joseph McDermott Adm
Chapel Lane, Newbridge, Co Kildare
Tel 045-431741

### CARBURY

*Holy Trinity, Carbury*
*Holy Family, Derrinturn*
Email carburyparish@eircom.net
Very Rev John Fitzpatrick PP
Carbury, Co Kildare
Tel 046-9553355

### CLANE

*SS Patrick and Brigid, Clane*
*Sacred Heart, Rathcoffey*
Email claneparish@eircom.net
Website www.claneparish.com
Very Rev Paul O'Boyle PP
Clane, Naas, Co Kildare
Tel 045-868249
Email oboylepaul@eircom.net
Permanent Deacon: Rev John Dunleavy
Tel 045-861393

### CLONASLEE

*St Manman's*
Very Rev Thomas O'Reilly Adm
Clonaslee, Co Laois
Tel 057-8648030

### CLONBULLOGUE

*Sacred Heart, Clonbullogue*
*St Brochan's, Bracknagh,*
*Immaculate Conception, Walsh Island*
Very Rev Gregory Corcoran PP
Rhode, Co Offaly
Tel 087-9402669
Permanent Deacon: Rev Gary Moore
Tel 046-9737579

### CLONEGAL

*St Brigid's, Clonegal*
*St Lasarian's, Kildavin*
Very Rev Thomas O'Byrne PP
Myshall, Co Carlow
Tel 059-9157635
Very Rev Joseph Fleming PE, CC
Clonegal, Enniscorthy, Co Wexford
Tel 053-9377298

### CLONMORE

*St Mary's, Ballyconnell*
*St Finian's, Kilquiggan*
*Our Lady of the Wayside, Clonmore*
*St Finian's Oratory, Killinure*
Very Rev James Gahan PP
Killinure, Tullow, Co Carlow
Tel 059-9156111
Email jkgahan@gmail.com
Rev Sean Maher CC
St Mary's, Ballyconnell, Tullow, Co Carlow
Tel 059-9156890

## COOLERAGH AND STAPLESTOWN
*Christ the King, Cooleragh,*
*St Benignus, Staplestown*
Email standco@eircom.net
Very Rev Jimmy Doyle PP
Cooleragh, Coill Dubh, Naas, Co Kildare
Tel 045-860281

## CURRAGH CAMP
*St Brigid's*
Rt Rev Mgr John McDonald PP
Tel 045-441369
Rev P. J. Somers (SDB)
Tel 045-441277
Email spj40@hotmail.com
Curragh Camp, Co Kildare

## DAINGEAN
*Mary Mother of God, Daingean*
*SS Peter and Paul, Kilclonfert*
*St Francis of Assisi and St Brigid,*
*Ballycommon; Oratory of the Immaculate*
*Conception, Cappincur*
Very Rev Mark Townsend PP
Tel 057-9362006
Rev Patrick O'Byrne PE, CC
Tel 057-9344161
Daingean, Co Offaly

## DOONANE
*St Abban's, Doonane*
*Blessed Virgin Mary, Mayo*
Very Rev Denis Murphy Adm
Tolerton, Ballickmoyler, Carlow
Tel 056-4442126

## DROICHEAD NUA/NEWBRIDGE
*St Conleth's, Newbridge*
*Cill Mhuire, Ballymany*
*St Eustace's, Dominican Church*
*Parish Office:* 045-431394
Email parishoffice@newbridgeparish.ie
Website www.newbridgeparish.ie
Very Rev Joseph McDermott PP
Tel 045-431741
Email jmcder@eircom.net
Rev Terence McGovern CC
Tel 045-433979
Rev Michat Cudzito
Chapel Lane, Droichead Nua, Co Kildare
Rev Paul Dempsey CC, VF
The Presbytery, Ballymany,
Droichead Nua, Co Kildare
Tel 045-434069
Rev Brian Reynolds (OP) CC
Droichead Nua, Co Kildare
Tel 045-431394
Permanent Deacon: Rev Jim Stowe
c/o Parish Office, Station Road,
Droichead Nua, Co Kildare
Tel 045-431394

## EDENDERRY
*St Mary's*
Very Rev P.J. McEvoy PP
Francis Street, Edenderry, Co Offaly
Tel 046-9731296
Rev Larry Malone *(in residence)*
Edenderry, Co Offaly
Tel 046-9732352
Permanent Deacon: Rev Paul Wyer
Tel 046-9733311

## EMO
*St Paul's, Emo; Sacred Heart, Rath*
Very Rev Thomas Dooley Adm
Patrick Street, Portarlington, Co Laois
Tel 057-8643004
Email frtomdooley@eircom.net
Rev Pat Hughes CC
Priest's House, Emo, Portlaoise, Co Laois
Tel 057-8646517

## GRAIGNAMANAGH
*Duiske Abbey, Graignamanagh*
*Our Lady of Lourdes,*
*Skeoughvosteen, Co Kilkenny*
Very Rev Gerald Byrne PP
Parochial House,
Graignamanagh, Co Kilkenny
Tel 059-9724238
*Abbey Centre:* 059-9724238

## GRAIGUECULLEN
*St Clare's, Graiguecullen*
*Holy Cross, Killeshin*
Email gkparish@gmail.com
www.graiguecullenkilleshin.com
Very Rev John Dunphy PP
Graiguecullen, Carlow
Tel 059-9141833
Email dunphiej@gmail.com
Permanent Deacon: Rev Joe O'Rourke
c/o Parish Office, Graiguecullen, Carlow
Tel 059-9141833

## HACKETSTOWN
*St Brigid's, Hacketstown*
*Our Lady, Killamoate*
*Church of the Immaculate Conception,*
*Knockanna*
*Church of Our Lady, Askinagap*
Rev James McCormack PP
Hacketstown, Co Carlow
Tel 059-6471257

## KILCOCK
*St Coca, Kilcock*
*Nativity of the BVM, Newtown*
Email stcocasparish@eircom.net
Website www.kilcockparish.net
Very Rev P. J. Byrne PP
Kilcock, Co Kildare
Tel 01-6287448
Rev Bogdan Wawrzaszek CC
Curate's House, Kilcock, Co Kildare
Tel 01-6287277

## KILDARE
*St Brigid's*
*Our Lady of Victories, Kildangan*
*Sacred Heart, Nurney*
*Parish Office:* 045-521352
Email arasbride@eircom.net
Website www.kildareparish.ie
Very Rev Adrian Carbery PP
26 Beech Grove, Kildare
Tel 045-521900
Rev Gaspar Habara CC
St Brigid's, Kildare
Tel 045-520347

## KILL
*St Brigid's, Kill*
*St Anne's, Ardclough*
Email killparish@eircom.net
Website www.killparish.ie
Very Rev William O'Byrne PP
Kill, Co Kildare
Tel 045-878008

Very Rev Matthew Kelly PE, CC
60 Hartwell Green, Kill, Naas, Co Kildare
Tel 045-877880

## KILLEIGH
*St Patrick's, Killeigh*
*St Joseph's, Ballinagar*
*St Mary's, Geashill*
Email killeighparish@eircom.net
Website www.killeigh.com
Very Rev John Stapleton PP
Killeigh, Co Offaly
Tel 057-9344161
Email johnstapleton@eircom.net
Rt Rev Mgr Thomas Coonan CC
Geashill, Co Offaly
Tel 057-9343517

## LEIGHLIN
*St Laserian's, Leighlin*
*St Fintan's, Ballinabranna*
Very Rev Thomas Lalor PP
Leighlinbridge, Co Carlow
Tel 059-9721463
Permanent Deacon: Rev Pat Roche
Leighlinbridge, Co Carlow
Tel 059-9722607

## MONASTEREVAN
*SS Peter and Paul, Monasterevan*
Very Rev Liam Merrigan PP
Tougher Road, Monasterevan, Co Kildare
Tel 045-525346

## MOUNTMELLICK
*St Joseph's, Mountmellick*
*St Mary's, Clonaghadoo*
Very Rev Mícheál Murphy PP, VF
11 Ashgrove, Mountmellick, Co Laois
Tel 057-8679302
Very Rev Francis MacNamara PE, CC
Tel 057-8624198
Very Rev Noel Dunphy PE, CC
Tel 057-8624141
Mountmellick, Co Laois

## MOUNTRATH
*St Fintan, Mountrath*
*Sacred Heart, Hollow*
Very Rev Patrick Hennessy PP
Ballyfin, Portlaoise, Co Laois
Tel 057-8755227
Rev Joe Brophy CC
Mountrath, Co Laois
Tel 057-8732234

## MUINEBHEAG/BAGENALSTOWN
*St Andrew's, Bagenalstown*
*St Patrick's Newtown*
*St Laserian's, Ballinkillen*
Email info@bagenalstownparish.ie
Website www.bagenalstownparish.ie
Very Rev Declan Foley PP
Tel 059-9721154
Email pdlfoley@gmail.com
Rev Declan Thompson (SPS) CC
Tel 059-9723886
Muinebheag, Co Carlow

## MYSHALL
*Exaltation of the Cross, Myshall*
*St Laserian's, Drumphea*
Very Rev Thomas O'Byrne PP
Myshall, Co Carlow
Tel 059-9157635
Email obyrneta@eircom.net

## NAAS
*Our Lady and St David, Naas*
*Irish Martyrs, Ballycane*
Very Rev John Brickley PP
Tel 045-897703
Rev Liam Morgan CC
Tel 045-897260
Sallins Road, Naas, Co Kildare
Rev P.J. Madden CC
Two-Mile-House, Naas, Co Kildare
Tel 045-876160
Rev Kevin Walsh CC
Tel 045-897150
Parochial House, Sallins, Co Kildare
Permanent Deacon: Rev Fergal O'Neill
Tel 045-879730

## PAULSTOWN
*The Assumption, Paulstown*
*Holy Trinity, Goresbridge*
Very Rev John McEvoy PP
Goresbridge, Co Kilkenny
Tel 059-9775180

## PORTARLINGTON
*St Michael's, Portarlington*
*St John the Evangelist, Killenard*
Very Rev Thomas Dooley PP
Patrick Street, Portarlington, Co Laois
Tel 057-8643004
Email frtomdooley@eircom.net
Rev Pat Hughes CC
Emo, Portlaoise, Co Laois
Tel 057-8646517

## PORTLAOISE
*SS Peter and Paul, Portlaoise*
*The Assumption, The Heath*
*The Holy Cross, Ratheniska*
Email info@portlaoiseparish.ie
Website www.portlaoiseparish.ie
Rt Rev Mgr John Byrne PP, VG
Parochial House, Portlaoise, Co Laois
Tel 057-8692153
Email jmbyrne@eircom.net
Rev Paddy Byrne CC
Annebrook, Stradbally Road,
Portlaoise, Co Laois
Tel 057-8661139
Email pmlb@eircom.net
Rev Eddie Lawlor (SPS) CC
1 Glendowns, Portlaoise, Co Laois
Tel 057-8622301
Rev Tom O'Connor CC
Rev George Augustine CC
Dublin Road, Portlaoise, Co Laois
Tel 057-8692153

## PROSPEROUS
*Our Lady and St Joseph, Prosperous*
Rev Joe O'Neill CC
Curate's House, Prosperous, Co Kildare
Tel 045-868187

## RAHEEN
*St Fintan's, Raheen*
*St Brigid's, Shanahoe*
Very Rev Jimmy Kelly PP
Raheen, Abbeyleix, Co Laois
Tel 057-8731182
Email jameskelly1@eircom.net

## RATHANGAN
*Assumption and St Patrick*
Very Rev Gerard O'Byrne PP
Rathangan, Co Kildare
Tel 045-524316
Email gerobyrne@eircom.net

## RATHVILLY
*St Patrick's, Rathvilly*
*St Brigid's, Talbotstown*
*Blessed Virgin Mary, Tynock*
Very Rev Michael Kelly (SPS) Adm
Rathvilly, Co Carlow
Tel 059-9161114
Rev Michael Moloney CC
Kiltegan, Co Wicklow
Tel 059-6473211

## RHODE
*St Peter's, Rhode*
*St Anne's, Croghan*
Website www.rhodeparish.ie
Very Rev Gregory Corcoran PP
Rhode, Co Offaly
Tel 046-9737010
Permanent Deacon: Rev Gary Moore
Tel 046-9737579

## ROSENALLIS
*St Brigid's*
Email rosenallisparish@eircom.net
Website www.rosenallis.com
Very Rev Thomas Walshe PP
Rosenallis, Portlaoise, Co Laois
Tel 057-8628513

## ST MULLINS
*St Moling's, Glynn*
*St Brendan's, Drummond*
Very Rev Edward Aughney Adm
Glynn, St Mullins via Kilkenny
Tel 051-424563

## SALLINS
*Our Lady of the Rosary & Guardian Angels*
Email sallinsparish@eircom.net
Very Rev John Brickley Adm
Sallins Road, Naas, Co Kildare
Tel 045-897703
Rev Kevin Walsh CC
Parochial House, Sallins, Co Kildare
Tel 045-897150

## STRADBALLY
*Sacred Heart, Stradbally*
*Assumption, Vicarstown*
*St Michael, Timahoe*
Very Rev James O'Connell PP
Very Rev Seán Kelly PE, CC
Stradbally, Co Laois
Tel 057-8625132/057-8625831

## SUNCROFT
*St Brigid's*
Email suncroftparish@eircom.net
Very Rev Barry Larkin PP
Suncroft, Curragh, Co Kildare
Tel 045-441586

## TINRYLAND
*St Joseph's*
Website www.tinryland.ie
Very Rev Thomas Little Adm
Brownshill Avenue, Carlow
Tel 059-9131559
Email tomlittle@eircom.net

Rev Sean Hyland CC
Tinryland, Carlow
Tel 059-9131212

## TULLOW
*Most Holy Rosary, Tullow*
*Immaculate Conception, Ardattin*
*St John the Baptist, Grange*
Email tullowparish@eircom.net
Website www.tullowparish.com
Very Rev Andy Leahy PP
Tullow, Co Carlow
Tel 059-9180641
Email andyolaoithe@eircom.net
Rev Padraig Shelley CC
Tullow, Co Carlow
Tel 059-9152159

## TWO-MILE-HOUSE
Very Rev John Brickley Adm
Sallins Road, Naas, Co Kildare
Tel 045-897703
Rev PJ Madden CC
Two-Mile-House, Naas, Co Kildare
Tel 045-876160

## INSTITUTIONS AND THEIR CHAPLAINS

**Abbeyleix District Hospital**
Very Rev Gerard Ahern PP
Tel 057-8731135

**Baltinglass District Hospital**
Very Rev Thomas Dillon PP
Tel 059-6482768

**County Hospital, Portlaoise**
Rt Rev Mgr John Byrne PP, VG
Portlaoise, Co Laois
Tel 057-8621142

**Curragh Camp**
Rt Rev Mgr John McDonald PP
Tel 045-441369

**Edenderry Hospital**
Very Rev P. J. McEvoy PP
Tel 046-9731296

**Institute of Technology, Carlow**
Rev Martin Smith (SPS)
Tel 059-9142632

**Midlands Prison**
Rev Tom Sinnott
Tel 057-8672222

**Portlaoise Prison**
Rev Eugene Drumm (SPS)
Tel 057-8622549

**Sacred Heart Hospital, Carlow**
Very Rev John Cummins Adm
Tel 059-9131227

**St Brigid's Hospital**
Shaen, Portlaoise, Co Laois
Rt Rev Mgr John Byrne PP
Tel 057-8621142

**St Dympna's Hospital, Carlow**
Very Rev John Cummins Adm
Tel 059-9131227

**St Fintan's Hospital, Portlaoise**
Rt Rev Mgr John Byrne PP, VG
Dublin Road, Portlaoise, Co Laois
Tel 057-8621142

**St Vincent's Hospital, Mountmellick**
Very Rev Michael Murphy PP, VF
Mountmellick, Co Laois
Tel 057-8679302

## PRIESTS OF THE DIOCESE ELSEWHERE

Very Rev Peter Cribbin
c/o Bishop's House, Dublin Road, Carlow
Very Rev Patrick Dunny
Wood Road, Graignamanagh, Co Kilkenny
Tel 059-9724518
Rev Paul McNamee
c/o Bishop's House, Dublin Road, Carlow
Rev Bill Kemmy (on sabbatical)
Arles, Co Carlow

## RETIRED PRIESTS

Very Rev Patrick Breen PE
Sue Ryder House, Ballyroan, Co Laois
Tel 057-8731071
Rt Rev Mgr Brendan Byrne PE
c/o Bishop's House, Carlow
Tel 059-9176725
Very Rev Charles Byrne
Holy Family Convent,
Newbridge, Co Kildare
Very Rev Patrick Daly PE
Braganza, Athy Road, Carlow
Very Rev John Fingleton PE
Hillview Nursing Home,
Tullow Road, Carlow
Tel 059-9139407
Very Rev Patrick Gaynor PE
Walsh Island, Geashill, Co Offaly
Very Rev Denis Harrington PE
Clane, Co Kildare
Tel 045-868224
Very Rev Patrick Kehoe PE
Droimnín Nursing Home, Brockley Park,
Stradbally, Co Laois
Tel 057-8641002
Very Rev Moling Lennon PE
364 Sundays Well, Naas, Co Kildare
Tel 045-888667
Very Rev Edward Moore PE
Marian House, Sallins Road,
Naas, Co Kildare
Very Rev Alphonsus Murphy PE
Carbury, Co Kildare
Tel 046-9553020
Very Rev Michael Noonan PE
Portarlington, Co Laois
Tel 057-8623431
Very Rev John O'Connell PE
Caragh, Co Kildare
Tel 045-875602
Very Rev Sean O'Laoghaire PE
Gowran Abbey Nursing Home,
Gowran, Co Kilkenny
Very Rev Philip O'Shea PE
Ballinakill, Garyhill, Co Carlow
Tel 059-9727425
Very Rev Denis O'Sullivan PE
Monasterevin, Co Kildare
Tel 045-525351

Very Rev Pat Ramsbottom PE
Gorman's Cottage, Cooleragh, Co Kildare
Tel 045-890744
Very Rev Colum Swan PE
32 Cherrygrove, Naas, Co Kildare
Tel 045-856274
Very Rev John Walsh PE
Rath, Portlaoise, Co Laois
Tel 057-8626401

## RELIGIOUS ORDERS AND CONGREGATIONS

## PRIESTS

**CAPUCHINS**
Capuchin Friary, 43 Dublin Street, Carlow
Tel 059-9142543 Fax 059-9142030
*Guardian*
Rev Christopher Twomey (OFMCap)
*Vicar:* Br John Wright (OFMCap)

**CARMELITES (OCARM)**
Carmelite Priory, White Abbey, Co Kildare
Tel 045-521391 Fax 045-522318
Email carmeliteskildare@gmail.com
*Prior:* Rev Anthony McDonald (OCarm)
*Bursar:* Rev Frederick Lally (OCarm)

**DOMINICANS**
Newbridge College,
Droichead Nua, Co Kildare
Tel 045-487200
*Prior:* Very Rev Joseph Dineen (OP)
Secondary School for Boys

**JESUITS**
Clongowes Wood College,
Clane, Co Kildare
Tel 045-868663/868202 Fax 045-861042
Email *(College)* reception@clongowes.ie
*(Community)* reception@clongowes.ie
*Rector:* Rev Michael Sheil (SJ)
*Headmaster:* Rev Leonard Moloney (SJ)
*Vice-Rector & Minister*
Rev Bernard McGuckian
Boarding School for Secondary Pupils

**ST PATRICK'S MISSIONARY SOCIETY**
St Patrick's, Kiltegan, Co Wicklow
Tel 059-6473600 Fax 059-6473622
Email spsoff@iol.ie (office)
*Society Leader:* Rev Victor Dunne (SPS)
*Assistant Society Leader*
Rev John Marren (SPS)
Fax *(Society Leader & Council)*
059-6473644

## BROTHERS

**CHRISTIAN BROTHERS**
Christian Brothers' House,
Friary's Road, Naas, Co Kildare
Tel 045-897884
*Commuity Leader:* Br P.J. McMahon
Community: 6

Christian Brothers' House,
Railway Street, Portlaoise, Co Laois
Tel 057-8621129
Community: 3

**PATRICIAN BROTHERS**
Delany House, Castledermot Road,
Tullow, Co Carlow
Tel 059-9151244 Fax 059-9152063
Email patbros@iol.ie
*Superior:* Br Bosco Mulhare (FSP)
Community: 2

10 Hawthorn Drive, Tullow, Co Carlow
Tel 059-9181727 Fax 059-9181728
*Superior:* Br Camillus Regan (FSP)
Community: 2

Newbridge, Co Kildare
Tel 045-431475 Fax 045-431505
*Superior:* Br James O'Rourke (FSP)
Community: 6
Monastery National School
Tel 045-432174
*Principal:* Mr John O'Donovan
Patrician Secondary School
Tel 045-432410
*Principal:* Mr Patrick O'Leary

Rathmoyle, Abbeyleix, Co Laois
Tel 057-8731229
Community: 2
Scoil Mhuire Primary School
*Superior:* Br Nicholas Leahy (FSP)

Patrician Brothers, Cavansheath,
Mountrath, Co Laois
Tel 057-8755964
*Superior:* Br Gerard Reburn (FSP)
Community: 2

Patrician Brothers
Shannon Road, Mountrath, Co Laois
Tel 057-8732260
*Superior:* Br Justin Madden (FSP)
Community: 2

The Irish Province has seven houses
in Kenya
*Regional Superior:* Br James Onunda (FSP)
Patrician Formation House,
PO Box 5064, via Eldoret, Kenya
Tel/Fax 0321-61134
Email pbroskam@africaonline.co.ke
Community: 9

## SISTERS

**BRIGIDINE SISTERS**
Brigidine Provincialate,
42 The Downs, Portlaoise, Co Laois
Tel/Fax 087-6922006
*Provincial Leader:* Sr Francesca Power
Community: 1

16 Mount Clare,
Graguecullen, Co Carlow
Tel 059-9135869
*Contact:* Sr Maureen O'Leary
Community: 1
Retired

Brigidine Convent, Tullow, Co Carlow
Tel 059-9151308
*Community Co-ordinator*
Sr Agnes Graham
Community: 15
Education, Parish Work, Pastoral Care
and Retired

Brigidine Sisters, Delany Court, New Chapel Lane, Tullow, Co Carlow
*Contact:* Sr Elizabeth Mary McDonald
Community: 8
Parish Work, Education

Teach Bhríde, Tullow, Co Carlow
Tel/Fax 059-9152465
Email teachbhride@eircom.net
*Contact:* Sr Carmel McEvoy
Community: 1
Holistic education centre

11 The Rise,
Ballymurphy Road, Tullow, Co Carlow
Tel 059-9152498
*Contact:* Sr Betty McDonald
Community: 1

1 Salem House,
Chantiere Gate, Portlaoise, Co Laois
Tel 057-8665516
*Contact:* Sr Angela Phelan
Community: 1

Carlow Road, Abbeyleix, Co Laois
Tel 057-8731467
Community: 2
*Contact:* Sr Mary Hiney
Parish, Adult education

Brigidine Convent, Castletown Road,
Mountrath, Co Laois
Tel 057-8732799
*Contact:* Sr Mary Sheedy
Community: 5
Parish and Pastoral Work

Brigidine Convent, Paulstown, Co Kilkenny
Tel 059-9726156
*Contact:* Sr Margaret Walsh
Community: 4

Solas Bhríde, 18 Dara Park, Kildare
Tel 045-522890 Fax 045-522212
*Contact:* Sr Mary Minehan
Community: 2
Education, spirituality centre

## CHARITY OF JESUS AND MARY, SISTERS OF
Ros Glas, Moore Abbey,
Monasterevan, Co Kildare
Tel 045-525478
*Superior:* Sr Mary-Anna Lonergan
Email maryannal@eircom.net
Community: 6
Residential centre transferred to Muiriesa Foundation

Grove House Community, Moore Abbey,
Monasterevin, Co Kildare
*Superior:* Sr Philomena Enright
Tel 087-2480738

## CONGREGATION OF THE SISTERS OF MERCY
*The Sisters of Mercy minister throughout the diocese in pastoral and social work, community development, counselling, spirituality, education and health care, answering current needs.*

St Leo's Convent of Mercy, Carlow
Tel 059-9131158 Fax 059-9142226
Community: 17

4 Pinewood Avenue, Rathnapish, Carlow
Tel 059-9140408
Community: 3

Convent of Mercy,
Monasterevan, Co Kildare
Tel/Fax 045-525372
Community: 2

St Helen's Convent of Mercy,
Naas, Co Kildare
Tel/Fax 045-897673
Community: 3

Convent of Mercy,
Rathangan, Co Kildare
Tel 045-524391
Community: 4

Convent of Mercy,
Leighlinbridge, Co Carlow
Tel 059-9721350 Fax 059-9721350
Community: 3

4 Lacken View, Naas, Co Kildare
Tel/Fax 045-874168
Community: 2

Parkmore, Baltinglass, Co Wicklow
Tel 059-6481561 Fax 059-6481561
Community: 2

59 Fr Byrne Park, Graiguecullen, Carlow
Tel 059-9141479
Community: 1

37 Lakelands, Naas, Co Kildare
Tel 045-875496
Community: 2

9 Spring Gardens, Naas, Co Kildare
Tel 045-876013
Community: 3

## DAUGHTERS OF MARY AND JOSEPH
3/4 Sycamore Road, Connell Drive,
Newbridge, Co Kildare
Tel 045-431842
Community: 3
Pastoral

## HOLY FAMILY OF BORDEAUX SISTERS
Holy Family Convent,
Droichead Nua, Co Kildare
Tel 045-431268
*Contact:* Sr Catherine Moran
Community: 28
Retired sisters, parish work, teaching English to non-nationals

'Sonas Chríost', Moorfield Park,
Droichead Nua, Co Kildare
Tel 045-431939
*Contact:* Sr Eileen Murphy
Community: 3
Sisters involved in community, parish work, chaplaincy to secondary school

5 Glen Barrow, Ballyfin Road,
Portlaoise, Co Laois
Tel 057-8620365
*Contact Person:* The Superior
Community: 3
Pastoral care of the sick, pastoral work and prison chaplaincy

## POOR CLARES
Poor Clare Colettine Monastery,
Graiguecullen, Carlow
Email poorclarescarlow@gmail.com
*Abbess:* Mother Rosario Byrne
Community: 11
Perpetual adoration, contemplatives

## PRESENTATION SISTERS
Generalate, Monasterevin, Co Kildare
Tel 045-525335/525503 Fax 045-525209
Email adminpresevin@eircom.net
www.presentationsistersunion.org
*Congregational Leader*
Sr Mary Deane

Presentation Sisters,
Nagle Community (Inter Provincial)
55 Kirwan Park, Mountmellick, Co Laois
Tel 057-8644005 Fax 057-8644372
Email presnagle@jmin.iol.ie
Community: 2
Justice ministry

Mount St Anne's
Retreat and Conference Centre,
Killenard, Portarlington, Co Laois
Tel 057-8626153 Fax 057-8626700
*Director:* Sr Roisin Gannon
Email msannes@iol.ie
Community: 3
Facilities available for seminars, conferences and meetings on request

Presentation Convent,
Ashbrook Gardens, Mountrath Road,
Portlaoise, Co Laois
Tel 057-8670877
*Community Leader*
Sr Maureen O'Rourke
School and counselling
Community: 10

Scoil Chroí Ró-Naofa Primary School
Tel/Fax 057-8621904
Scoil Mhuire Primary School
Tel 057-8621476
Scoil Chríost Rí Secondary School
Tel 057-8621441 Fax 057-8661437
Email scrport@eircom.net

17 Parnell Crescent, Knockmay,
Portlaoise, Co Laois
Tel 057-8620358
Community: 2
School and pastoral ministry

Presentation Convent, Kildare Town
Tel 045-521481
Community: 12
*Community Leader:* Sr Cecilia Molloy
School and pastoral ministry
Scoil Bhride Naofa Primary School
Tel 045-521799 Fax 045-530653
Email sbpp@eircom.net
Presentation Secondary School
Tel 045-521654 Fax 045-521090
Email psskprincipal@eircom.net

56 Oakley Park,
Tullow Road, Carlow
Tel 059-9143103
Community: 2
School ministry
Scoil Mhuire gan Smal Primary School
Tel 059-9142705 Fax 059-9140645
Email officesmns@eircom.net
Presentation College, Askea, Carlow
Tel 059-9143927 Fax 059-9140645
Email presentationcollege@eircom.net

Presentation Convent,
Bagenalstown, Co Carlow
Tel 059-9721263
Email presbagenalstown@eircom.net
*Community Leader:* Sr Kathleen Ryan
School and pastoral ministry
Community: 9
Queen of the Universe Primary School
Tel 059-9721075
Presentation/De La Salle Secondary
School
Tel 059-9721860 Fax 059-9722558
Email pdlsbc@eircom.net

Presentation Convent, Bridge Street,
Mountmellick, Co Laois
Tel 057-8624129
Community: 10
*Community Leader:* Sr Elizabeth Starken
School and pastoral ministry
St Joseph's Primary School
Tel/Fax 057-8624540
Email stjosephsgns.ias@eircom.net
St Mary's Community School
Tel 057-8624220 Fax 057-8644126
Email mountmellick@eircom.net

Shalom, Kilcock, Co Kildare
Tel 01-6287018 Fax 01-6287316
Email culnacille@eircom.net
*Community Leader*
Sr Clare Costello
Community: 34
Care of sick and elderly sisters
Scoil Choca Naofa Primary School
Tel 01-6287967
Email scoilchoca.ias@eircomm.net
Scoil Dara Secondary School
Tel 01-6287258 Fax 01-6284075
Email scoildara@eircom.net

Presentation Convent,
27 Abbeyfield, Kilcock, Co Kildare
Tel 01-6284579
Community: 5
*Community Leader:* Sr Genevieve Kilbane
Faith development, counselling and
pastoral ministry

2 Wolfe Tone Court,
Mountmellick, Co Laois
Tel 057-8679481
Community: 1

## ST JOHN OF GOD SISTERS
49 Blundell Wood, Edenderry, Co Offaly
Tel 046-9731582
Community: 1
St Mary's Primary School
Tel 0405-31424. Pupils: 606

St John of God Sisters,
1 Churchview Heights,
Edenderry, Co Offaly
Tel 046-9772717
Community: 2

## EDUCATIONAL INSTITUTIONS

**Carlow College (founded 1782)**
College Street, Carlow
Tel 059-9153200 Fax 059-9140258
Email infocc@carlowcollege.ie
Website www.carlowcollege.ie
*President*
Rt Rev Mgr Kevin O'Neill BA, MSc Ed
*Vice-President and Chaplain*
Rev Conn Ó Maoldhomhnaigh MA
*Bursar:* Vacant
*Priests on Staff*
Rev Dr Fergus Ó Fearghaill DSS
Rev Fintan Morris Lic.Eccl.Hist
Rev Dr Dermot Ryan DD
Rev Prof Michael Mullins
Sr Anne Holton (RSM) PhD

**St Mary's, Knockbeg College**
Knockbeg, Carlow
Tel 059-9142127 Fax 059-9134437
Email knockbegcollege@eircom.net
*Headmaster*
Mr Michael Carew
www.knockbegcollege.ie

**EDMUND RICE SCHOOLS TRUST**
St Mary's Academy, Station Road,
Carlow
Tel 0503-42419 Fax 0503-30922
Email principal@cbscarlow.ie
*Principal:* Mr Leo Hogan

Meánscoil Iognáid Rís,
Naas, Co Kildare
Tel 045-886402
Email admin@naascbs.ie
Website www.naascbs.ie
*Principal:* Mr Ben Travers

St Mary's Secondary School,
Borris Road, Portlaoise, Co Laois
Tel 057-8635041
Email portlaoisecbs@eircom.net
*Principal:* Ms Maura Murphy

## CHARITABLE AND OTHER SOCIETIES

**Apostolic Work Society**
*President:* Mrs Carmel Shortt
Glendara, Dublin Road, Clane,
Co Kildare
Tel 045-8688420

**Community Services**
St Catherine's
Community Services Centre,
St Joseph's Road, Carlow
Tel 059-9131354

# DIOCESE OF KILLALA

PATRON OF THE DIOCESE
ST MUREDACH, 12 AUGUST

INCLUDES PORTIONS OF COUNTIES MAYO AND SLIGO

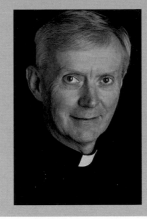

**Most Rev John Fleming DD, DCL**
Bishop of Killala;
born 16 February 1948;
ordained priest 18 June 1972;
ordained Bishop of Killala
7 April 2002

Residence: Bishop's House,
Ballina, Co Mayo
Tel 096-21518
Fax 096-70344
Email deocilala@eircom.net

## ST MUREDACH'S CATHEDRAL, BALLINA

In the lead-up to Catholic Emancipation and the erasing of restrictive laws on the building of Catholic places of worship, Killala diocese, one of the poorest in terms of resources and population, embarked on the massive project of building a new cathedral to replace the stone and thatch structure in Chapel Lane, which had served since 1740.

The project was first envisaged by the elderly Bishop Peter Waldron (1814–1835), but taken vigorously in hand by his coadjutor, Bishop John MacHale, who succeeded him for a short time before becoming Archbishop of Tuam.

In 1831 the first Mass was celebrated within the rough-hewn shell of the new cathedral. The architect was Dominick Madden, who designed Tuam cathedral. Because of financial restraints and the disruption caused by the Famine, several modifications of the design had to be made. It was not until 1853, some twenty-three years after the roofing of the main building, that work on the spire resumed. The entire work on the cathedral was completed in 1892.

The glory of the edifice is in the interior ceiling and overall design, modelled on the vaulting and ribbing of the Church of Santa Maria Sopra Minerva in Rome. The contract for the groining, plastering and stucco work was awarded to Arthur Canning, who undertook to have the bosses at the intersection of the rib mouldings, the centre over the intersections of the nave and transepts, the busts at the intersections of the groins of the naves and side aisles, and the crochets over the eastern windows 'executed by the first artists in the Kingdom'. How well he succeeded can be seen in the much-admired plasterwork of the cathedral ceiling, enhanced by the colour schemes and mosaics. The windows in the cathedral are the artistic treasuries of the building, all being the work of the Meyer studios of Munich, whose premises were destroyed by the Allied bombings in World War II.

The cathedral was completely renovated and refurbished in 2000, as part of a diocesan millennium project.

Photo: David Farrell, *The Western People, Ballina*

## CHAPTER

*Dean:* Vacant
*Chancellor*
Rt Rev Mgr Seán Killeen PP, VG
*Archdeacon:* Vacant
*Members*
Very Rev John George Canon MacHale
PP, VF
Rt Rev Mgr Kevin Loftus PP, VG

**Honorary Canon**
Very Rev Patrick Gallagher

## ADMINISTRATION

**Vicars General**
Rt Rev Mgr Seán Killeen VG
Cloghans, Ballina, Co Mayo
Rt Rev Mgr Kevin Loftus PP, VG
Easkey, Co Sligo
Tel 096-49011

**Vicars Forane**
Very Rev Michael Reilly PP, VF
Very Rev Michael Harrison PP, VF
Very Rev Gerard O'Hora VF
Very Rev John George Canon MacHale
PP, VF

**College of Consultors**
Most Rev John Fleming DD, DCL
Rt Rev Mgr Kevin Loftus PP, VG
Rt Rev Mgr Seán Killeen VG
Very Rev Michael Flynn PP
Very Rev Brian Conlon PP
Very Rev Michael O'Horo PP
Very Rev Edward Rogan AP
Very Rev Dr Michael Gilroy PP
Rev Liam Reilly CC

**Finance Secretary**
Very Rev Dr Michael Gilroy PP
Templeboy, Co Sligo
Tel 096-37802

**Diocesan Secretary**
Mrs Anne Forbes
Bishop's House, Ballina, Co Mayo
Tel 096-21518 Fax 096-70344
Email secretary@killaladiocese.org

## CATECHETICS EDUCATION

**Diocesan Advisers for Religious
Education**
*Primary:* Sr Patricia Lynott
*Post-Primary:* Mr Niall Loftus
Newman Institute, Cathedral Close,
Ballina, Co Mayo
Tel 096-72066

**Diocesan Education Council**
*Chairman:* Mr John Cummins

## LITURGY

**Church Music**
*Director:* Ms Regina Deacy
c/o The Pastoral Centre, Ballina, Co Mayo
Tel 096-70555

**Diocesan Liturgy and Music Commission**
*Chairman:* Very Rev Michael Flynn PP
Parochial House, Knockmore,
Ballina, Co Mayo
Tel 094-58108

## PASTORAL

**ACCORD**
*Director:* Very Rev Gerard O'Hora VF
The Pastoral Centre, Ballina, Co Mayo
Tel 096-70555

**Building Committee**
*Chairperson*
Rt Rev Mgr Seán Killeen PP, VG

**Child Protection Committee**
*Chairperson:* Mrs Anne Fleming

**Communications**
*Director:* Very Rev Gerard O'Hora VF

**Council of the Laity**
*Chairperson:* Peter McLoughlin

**Council of Priests**
*Chairperson*
Very Rev Dr Michael Gilroy PP
Templeboy, Co Sligo
Tel 096-47103
*Secretary:* Rev Liam Reilly CC
St Patrick's Presbytery, Ballina, Co Mayo
Tel 096-71360

**Diocesan Finance Committee**
*Chairman*
Most Rev John Fleming DD, DCL
*Secretary:* Ms Anne Forbes

**Ecumenism**
*Director:* Very Rev Anthony Gillespie PP
Dromore West, Co Sligo
Tel 096-47012

**Emigrants**
*Advisor:* Very Rev Michael Harrison PP, VF
Ballycastle, Co Mayo
Tel 096-43010

**Immigrants**
*Diocesan Representative*
Vacant

**Legion of Mary**
*Director:* Very Rev John Loftus, Co-Pastor
Tel 097-82350

**Marriage Tribunal**
(See Marriage Tribunals section)

**Pilgrimages**
*Director:* Rev Tom Doherty CC
Cathedral Presbytery, Ballina, Co Mayo
Tel 096-71365

**Pioneer Total Abstinence Association**
*Diocesan Director*
Very Rev Patrick Munnelly PP
Ardagh, Ballina, Co Mayo
Tel 096-31144

**Pontifical Mission Societies**
*Diocesan Director:* Rev Edward Rogan
Inver, Ballina, Co Mayo
Tel 097-84598

**Travellers**
*Chaplain:* Very Rev Michael Reilly PP, VF
Belmullet, Co Mayo
Tel 097-81426

**Trócaire**
*Secretary:* Rev Michael Nallen
Aughoose, Ballina, Co Mayo
Tel 097-87990

**Vocations**
*Director:* Rev Tom Doherty CC
Cathedral Presbytery, Ballina, Co Mayo
Tel 096-71365

**Youth Ministry**
*Co-ordinator:* Rev Francis Judge

## PARISHES

**BALLINA (KILMOREMOY)**
*St Muredach's Cathedral, St Patrick's*
Very Rev Gerard O'Hora PP, VF
Cathedral Presbytery, Ballina, Co Mayo
Tel 096-71365
Rev Tom Doherty CC
Cathedral Presbytery, Ballina, Co Mayo
Tel 096-71355
Rev Liam Reilly CC
St Patrick's Presbytery, Ballina, Co Mayo
*Parish Sister:* Sr Maureen McDonnell
Tel 096-71360

**BACKS**
*Christ the King*
Very Rev Michael Flynn PP
Knockmore, Ballina, Co Mayo
Tel 094-58108
*St Teresa's*
Rev Des Smith
Rathduff, Ballina, Co Mayo
Tel 096-21596

**ARDAGH**
Very Rev Patrick Munnelly PP
Ardagh, Ballina, Co Mayo
Tel 096-31144

**BALLYCASTLE (KILBRIDE AND
DOONFEENY)**
*St Bridget's, St Teresa's*
Very Rev Michael Harrison PP, VF
Ballycastle, Co Mayo
Tel 096-43010

**BALLYCROY**
*Holy Family*
Very Rev Christopher Ginnelly PP
Parochial House, Ballycroy,
Westport, Co Mayo
Tel 098-49134

**BALLYSOKEARY**
Very Rev James Corcoran PP
Cooneal, Ballina, Co Mayo
Tel 096-32242

**BELMULLET**
*Sacred Heart, Our Lady of Lourdes*
Very Rev Michael Reilly PP, VF
Belmullet, Co Mayo
Tel 097-81426

**CASTLECONNOR**
*St Joseph's*
Very Rev Desmond Kelly PP
Corballa, Ballina, Co Mayo
Tel 096-36266

**CROSSMOLINA**
*St Tiernan's, Holy Souls,*
*Our Lady of Mercy, St Mary's*
Very Rev Francis Judge PP
Crossmolina, Co Mayo
Tel 096-31677
Rev Gabriel Rosbotham CC
Chapel Road, Crossmolina, Co Mayo
Tel 096-31344
Rev Albert Slater CC
Keenagh, Ballina, Co Mayo
Tel 096-53018

**DROMORE-WEST (KILMACSHALGAN)**
Very Rev Anthony Gillespie PP
Dromore West, Co Sligo
Tel 096-47012

**EASKEY**
*St James's*
Rt Rev Mgr Kevin Loftus PP, VG
Easkey, Co Sligo
Tel 096-49011

**KILCOMMON-ERRIS**
Very Rev Michael Nallen PP
Aughoose, Ballina, Co Mayo
Tel 097-87990
Rev Joseph Hogan CC
Cornboy, Rossport, Ballina, Co Mayo
Tel 097-88939

**KILFIAN**
*Sacred Heart*
PP Vacant
Kilfian, Killala, Co Mayo
Tel 096-32420

**KILGLASS**
*Holy Family, Christ the King*
Very Rev Canon John George MacHale PP
Kilglass, Enniscrone, Ballina, Co Mayo
Tel 096-36191
Very Rev Edward Rogan, Assistant Priest
Enniscrone, Ballina, Co Mayo
Tel 096-36164

**KILLALA**
*St Patrick's*
Very Rev Patrick Hoban PP
Killala, Co Mayo
Tel 096-32176

**KILMORE-ERRIS**
*St Joseph's, Holy Family, Seven Dolours*
Very Rev John Loftus, Co-Pastor
Binghamstown,
Belmullet, Co Mayo
Tel 097-82350
Rev Kevin Hegarty, Co-Pastor
Carne, Belmullet, Co Mayo
Tel 097-81011

**KILTANE**
*Sacred Heart*
*St Pius X*
Very Rev James Cribbin, PP
Geesala, Bangor, Ballina, Co Mayo
Tel 097-86740

**LACKEN**
*St Patrick's*
Very Rev Brian Conlon PP
Carrowmore, Ballina, Co Mayo
Tel 096-34014

**LAHARDANE (ADDERGOOLE)**
*St Patrick's*
Very Rev John Reilly PP
Lahardane, Ballina, Co Mayo
Tel 096-51007

**MOYGOWNAGH**
*St Cormac's*
Very Rev Brendan Hoban PP
Moygownagh,
Ballina, Co Mayo
Tel 096-31288

**SKREEN AND DROMARD**
*St Adamnan's*
Very Rev Michael O'Horo PP
Skreen, Co Sligo
Tel 071-9166629

**TEMPLEBOY**
Very Rev Dr Michael Gilroy PP
Templeboy, Co Sligo
Tel 096-47103

## INSTITUTIONS AND THEIR CHAPLAINS

**An Coláiste**
Rossport, Ballina, Co Mayo
Tel 097-88940

**Convent of Mercy**
Belmullet, Co Mayo
Tel 097-81044
Rev Kevin Hegarty

**Convent of Jesus and Mary**
Enniscrone, Ballina, Co Mayo
Tel 096-36151
Rev Kieran Holmes CC

**Convent of Jesus and Mary**
Crossmolina, Co Mayo
Tel 096-30876/30877
Very Rev Francis Judge PP

**Distrist Hospital**
Ballina, Co Mayo
Tel 096-21166
Very Rev Gerard O'Hora

**District Hospital**
Belmullet, Co Mayo
Tel 097-81301
Very Rev John Loftus

**St Mary's Secondary School**
Ballina, Co Mayo
Tel 096-70333
Rev Liam Reilly CC

**Vocational School**
Easkey, Co Sligo
Tel 096-49021
Rt Rev Mgr Kevin Loftus

**Vocational School**
Ballina, Co Mayo
Tel 096-21472
Rev Tom Doherty

**Vocational School**
Crossmolina, Co Mayo
Tel 096-31236
Rev Gabriel Rosbotham CC

**Vocational School**
Belmullet, Co Mayo
Tel 097-81437
Rev Michael Nallen

**Vocational School**
Lacken Cross, Co Mayo
Tel 096-32177
Very Rev Brian Conlon PP

## PRIESTS OF THE DIOCESE ELSEWHERE

Very Rev Martin Keveny
Paroquia Sao Sebastiao,
Caixa Postal 94, CEP 77760-000
Colinas Do Tocantins, Brazil
Tel 63-8311427
Rev Aidan O'Boyle
Chicago

## RETIRED PRIESTS

Very Rev Michael Cawley
Newman Institute, Ballina, Co Mayo
Very Rev Michael Conway
Barr Trá, Enniscrone, Co Sligo
Rt Rev Mgr Patrick Gallagher
Cathedral Close, Ballina
Very Rev Gerard Gillespie
Rathball, Ballina, Co Mayo
Rev John Judge
c/o Pastoral Centre, Ballina, Co Mayo
Rt Rev Mgr Sean Killeen
Cloghans, Ballina, Co Mayo
Very Rev Patrick Tuffy
Culleens, Co Sligo

*Retired Priests (Other Dioceses)*
Very Rev Joseph Cahill (SSC)
Bohernasup, Ballina, Co Mayo
Rt Rev Mgr Patrick Fox
14 Amana Estate, Ballina, Co Mayo
Very Rev Leonard Taylor
Rathlee, Easkey, Co Sligo

## RELIGIOUS ORDERS AND CONGREGATIONS

## PRIESTS

**SPIRITUAL LIFE INSTITUTE**
Holy Hill Hermitage, Skreen, Co Sligo
Tel 071-66021
*Superior:* Sr Patricia McGowan
Community: 2

## BROTHERS

**MARIST BROTHERS**
Convent Hill, Ballina, Co Mayo
Tel 096-22342
*Superior:* Br Sebastian Davis
Community: 2

## SISTERS

**CONGREGATION OF THE SISTERS OF MERCY**
Sisters of Mercy, 'Bethany',
8/9 Rockwell Estate, Killala Road,
Ballina, Co Mayo
Tel 096-23066
Community: 7

Sisters of Mercy, 11 Drom Ard,
Church Road, Belmullet, Co Mayo
Tel 097-81044 Fax 097-20737
Community: 3

2 Hillside Rise, Mount Falcon,
Ballina, Co Mayo
Community: 1

Sisters of Mercy,
28 Moy Heights, Ballina, Co Mayo
Community: 2

**JESUS AND MARY, CONGREGATION OF**
Convent of Jesus and Mary,
Mullinmore Road,
Crossmolina, Co Mayo
Tel 096-30876/30877
*Contact person:* Sr Dolores McGee
*Headmistress:* Tel 096-31194/096-31597
Community: 4
Post-Primary Coeducational Day School
Tel 096-31131
Pupils: 421

Convent of Jesus and Mary,
Church Road, Enniscrone, Co Sligo
Tel 096-36151
*Superior:* Sr Goretti McGowan
Community: 6
Post-Primary, Coeducational School
Tel 096-36496
Pupils: 409

## EDUCATIONAL INSTITUTIONS

**St Muredach's College**
Ballina, Co Mayo
Tel 096-21298
*Principal:* Mr Leo Golden
Post-Primary Pupils: 400

**Newman Institute Ireland**
Centre for Pastoral Care,
Cathedral Place, Ballina, Co Mayo
Tel 096-72066
*Chancellor*
Most Rev John Fleming, DD, DCL
*Director:* Sr Attracta Tighe

## CHARITABLE AND OTHER SOCIETIES

**Council for the West**
(Parish Renewal and Development)
Asahi Business Park, Killala, Co Mayo
Tel 096-32014

**Society of St Vincent de Paul**
Ozanam House, Teeling Street,
Ballina, Co Mayo
Tel 096-72905

**St Joseph's Young Priests Society**
c/o Pastoral Centre, Ballina, Co Mayo
Tel 096-70555

**Legion of Mary**
c/o Pastoral Centre, Ballina, Co Mayo
Tel 096-70555

**ACCORD**
CMAC Centre
c/o Pastoral Centre, Ballina, Co Mayo
Tel 096-70555

# DIOCESE OF KILLALOE

PATRON OF THE DIOCESE
ST FLANNAN, 18 DECEMBER

INCLUDES PORTIONS OF COUNTIES CLARE, LAOIS, LIMERICK,
OFFALY AND TIPPERARY

**Diocesan Administrator**

Diocesan Office:
Westbourne, Ennis, Co Clare
Tel 065-6828638
Fax 065-6842538
Email office@killaloediocese.ie
Website www.killaloediocese.ie

## CATHEDRAL OF SS PETER AND PAUL, ENNIS

The church that now serves as the cathedral of the Diocese of Killaloe was originally built to serve as the parish church of Ennis. The diocese had not had a permanent cathedral since the Reformation. In 1828, Francis Gore, a Protestant landowner, donated the site for the new Catholic church. Dominick Madden, who also designed the cathedrals in Ballina and Tuam, was chosen as the architect.

The construction of the new church was a protracted affair. Shortly after the work began, the project ran into financial difficulties and was suspended for three years. Aided by generous donations from local Protestants, including Sir Edward O'Brien of Dromoland and Vesey Fitzgerald, the work began again in 1831. Progress was slow throughout the 1830s and there were many problems. In September 1837 there was a serious accident on the site when the scaffolding collapsed, killing two and seriously injuring two more. Finally, in 1842, the roof was on and the parish priest, Dean O'Shaughnessy, was able to say the first Mass inside the still-unfinished building.

On 26 February 1843, the new church was blessed and placed under the patronage of Saints Peter and Paul, by Bishop Patrick Kennedy. Fr Matthew, 'The Apostle of Temperance', preached the sermon.

Much still remained to be done on the project, but the Great Famine brought the work to a halt. After the Famine, the work recommenced. J. J. McCarthy, one of the leading church architects in nineteenth-century Ireland, was commissioned to oversee the interior decoration of the building. Much of this is still visible, including the internal pillars and arches and the organ gallery.

A local committee decided in 1871 to complete the tower and spire, but owing to financial difficulties, it was not until 23 October 1874 that the final stone was put in place.

In 1889 Dr Thomas McRedmond was appointed coadjutor bishop and he was consecrated in 1890. He had full charge of the diocese, owing to the illness of Bishop Flannery. Though he was already Parish Priest of Killaloe, the new bishop chose to make Ennis his home, remaining there after he succeeded to the office of diocesan bishop, on the death of Dr Flannery. The Parish Church of Ss Peter and Paul was thus designated the pro-cathedral of the diocese.

Major renovations were carried out in 1894. The present main entrance under the tower was constructed, a task that necessitated breaking through a six-foot-thick wall. The building was also redecorated. The improvements were under the direction of Joshua Clarke, father of the stained-glass artist Harry Clarke. The large painting of the Ascension, which dominates the sanctuary, the work of the firm Nagle and Potts, was also installed at this time. The building remained largely unchanged for the next eighty years. A new sacristy and chapter room were added in the 1930s, as were the pipe organ and chapter stalls for the canons.

Another major renovation was carried out in 1973 to bring the building into line with the requirements of the Second Vatican Council. The architect for the work was Andrew Devane and the main contractors were Ryan Brothers, Ennis. The artistic adviser was Enda King. The building was reopened after six months in December 1973. The Clare Champion reported: 'The main features of the renovation included new altar, ambo, new tabernacle on granite pillar, baptismal font located near sanctuary, new flooring. New heating system, new amplification system and complete reconstruction of the sanctuary.'

In 1990, 163 years after work on the building began, Bishop Harty named it The Cathedral of the Diocese. The solemn dedication of the cathedral and the altar took place on 18 November 1990. A fire at a shrine in the cathedral in October 1995 caused serious internal damage. The sanctuary had to be rebuilt and the building redecorated. The restoration was celebrated with Solemn Evening Prayer in November 1996.

In 2006 major repair and refurbishment was completed on the Cathedral spire.

**Most Rev William Walsh DD**
Retired Bishop of Killaloe;
born 1935; ordained priest 21 February
1959; ordained Bishop of Killaloe
2 October 1994
*Residence:* 'Camblin', College View,
Clare Road, Ennis, Co Clare
Tel 065-6842540

## CHAPTER

*Dean:* Vacant
*Archdeacon:* Venerable John F. Hogan AP
Ballycommon, Nenagh, Co Tipperary
*Chancellor:* Very Rev Brendan Canon
O'Donoghue AP, Shannon
*Precentor:* Vacant
*Treasurer:* Very Rev Patrick Canon Taaffe,
Ennis
*Members*
Very Rev Reuben Canon Butler AP,
Newmarket-on-Fergus
Very Rev Caimin Canon O'Carroll AP,
Barefield
Very Rev Seamus Canon Mullin AP,
Miltown Malbay

## COLLEGE OF CONSULTORS

Very Rev Pat Malone PP
Very Rev Albert McDonnell
Very Rev Michael Sheedy PP
Rev Sean Sexton
Rev Tom Ryan
Rev David Carroll
Rev Brendan Quinlivan
Rev Ger Nash

## ADMINISTRATION

**Killaloe Diocesan Office**
*Diocesan Chancellor*
Very Rev Albert McDonnell
Email a.mcdonnell@killaloediocese.ie
*Diocesan Secretary:* Rev Ger Nash
Email g.nash@killaloediocese.ie
*Diocesan Financial Administrator*
Mr John Lillis
Email jlillis@killaloediocese.ie
*Diocesan Office Administrator*
Ms Margaret Flynn
*Secretarial:* Ms Mary Brohan
Westbourne, Ennis, Co Clare
Tel 065-6828638 Fax 065-6842538
Email office@killaloediocese.ie
*Education Secretary:* Rev Gerry Kenny
Westbourne, Ennis, Co Clare
Tel 085-7858344
Sr Marie McNamara
Parish Pastoral Office,
c/o Westbourne, Ennis, Co Clare
Tel 065-6842235
Email kpastoral5@eircom.net

**Vicars General**
Pending

**Vicars Forane & Moderators of Clusters**
*Inis Cathaigh:* Rev Gerry Kenny PP
Kilkee, Co Clare
Tel 065-9056580

*South-East Clare:* Rev Pat Greed PP
Clonlara, Co Clare
Tel 061-354594
*Críocha Callan:* Very Rev Pat Larkin
Mullagh, Co Clare
Tel 065-7087012
*Radharc na nÓilean*
Very Rev Albert McDonnell
Kildysart, Co Clare
Tel 065-6832155
*Abbey:* Rev Tom Hogan
Cathedral, Ennis, Co Clare
Tel 065-6824043
*Imeall Boirne:* Rev Ger Nash
Crusheen, Co Clare
Tel 065-6827113
*Tradaree:* Rev Arnold Rosney
5 Drumgeely Avenue, Shannon, Co Clare
*East Clare:* Rev Donagh O'Meara PP
Ballyheafey, Killaloe, Co Clare
Tel 061-376766
*Odhrán:* Rev Brendan Moloney
Silvermines, Co Tipperary
Tel 067-25864
*Cronan:* Rev Michael Harding
Templemore Road, Roscrea
Tel 0505-21218
*Cois Deirge:* Rev Michael Cooney
Terryglass, Co Tipperary
Tel 067-22017
*Brendan:* Rev David Carroll
Parochial House, Birr, Co Offaly
Tel 057-9122028

**Finance Committee**
*Chairman:* Mr Aidan Spooner
*Recording Secretary:* Mr John Lillis
Mr David Williams
Rev Gerard Kenny PP
Ms Teresa Felle
Very Rev Caimin Canon O'Carroll AP
Mr Owen Smyth
Mr Des Leahy
Very Rev Albert McDonnell PP

**Killaloe Priests' Benevolent Fund**
*Secretary:* Mr John Lillis
c/o Westbourne, Ennis, Co Clare
Tel 065-6828638

**Killaloe Priests' Subsidy Fund**
*Secretary:* Mr John Lillis
c/o Westbourne, Ennis, Co Clare
Tel 065-6828638

**Killaloe Priests' Hospital Fund**
*Secretary:* Mr John Lillis
c/o Westbourne, Ennis, Co Clare
Tel 065-6828638 Fax 065-6842538

**Diocesan Archivist**
c/o Diocesan Chancellor
Westbourne, Ennis, Co Clare
Tel 065-6828638

**Diocesan Secretary (part-time)**
Rev Ger Nash
c/o Westbourne, Ennis, Co Clare
Tel 065-6828638

**Episcopal Vicars for Retired Priests**
Very Rev Tim O'Brien PP
Carrigatoher, Nenagh, Co Tipperary
Tel 067-31231
Very Rev Joe Hourigan PP
Lissycasey, Co Clare
Tel 065-6834145

## CATECHETICS EDUCATION

**Boards of Management**
*Primary Schools:* St Senan's Education
Office, Limerick Diocesan Office, Social
Service Centre, Henry Street, Limerick
Tel 061-317743
*Director:* Fiona Shanley

**Religious Education in Primary Schools**
*Directors:* Sr Essie Hayes
Ashe Road, Nenagh, Co Tipperary
Tel 067-33835
Mr Joe Searson
Mullagh, Co Clare
Tel 065-7087875/087-6762023
Rev Anthony McMahon CC
Parochial House, Nenagh, Co Tipperary
Tel 067-37134

**Religious Education in Post-Primary Schools**
*Directors:* Very Rev Tom Hogan PP
The Cathedral Presbytery,
Ennis, Co Clare
Tel 065-6824043
Sr Marie McNamara
Pastoral Office, Westbourne,
Ennis, Co Clare
Tel 065-6842235/086-8373922

## PASTORAL

**Diocesan Pastoral Planning Project**
*Co-ordinator:* Rev Anthony Casey PP
*Pastoral Worker in Liturgy, Prayer and
Spirituality:* Ms Maureen Kelly
*Pastoral Worker in Leadership and
Partnership – West:* Ms Marie O'Connell
Quin
45 Garden View, Creggaun na hilla,
Clarecastle, Co Clare
Tel 065-6847096
*Pastoral Worker in Leadership and
Partnership – East:* Ms Lorina Bourke
Pastoral Centre, Church Road, Nenagh,
Co Tipperary
Tel 067-37590

**Pastoral Office and Biblical Ministry**
Sr Marie McNamara
c/o Killaloe Diocesan Office,
Westbourne, Ennis, Co Clare
Tel 065-6842235
Email kpastoral5@eircom.net

**Diocesan Pastoral Council**
*Chairperson:* Mr Leonard Cleary
Ballyportry, Corofin, Co Clare
*Secretary:* Jean Gaynor
45 Garden View, Creggaun na Hilla,
Clarecastle, Co Clare

## ACCORD
*Director:* Rev Damien Nolan
Ennis ACCORD Centre,
7 Carmody Street Business Park,
Ennis, Co Clare
Tel 1850-585000
*Director:* Very Rev Willie Teehan
Nenagh Centre, Loretto House,
Kenyon Street, Nenagh, Co Tipperary
Tel 067-31272

## CURA
Barrack Street, Ennis, Co Clare
Tel 065-6829905/1850-58-5000

## Communications
*Director:* Rev Brendan Quinlivan
c/o Bishop's House, Westbourne,
Ennis, Co Clare
Tel 065-6828638/065-6869094

## Child Protection Committee
*Chairperson:* Mr Michael Culhane
Ballygreen, Garraunboy, Killaloe, Co Clare
*Delegates:*
Ms Cleo Yates, Director of Safeguarding
Tel 086-8096027
Rev Pat Malone
Assistant Director of Safeguarding
Tel 086-8096074

## Ecumenism
*Director:* Very Rev Dr Tom Corbett
Roscrea, Co Tipperary
Tel 0505-21108

## Lourdes Pilgrimage
*Director:* Very Rev Tom Ryan PP
Shannon, Co Clare
Tel 061-361257

## Marriage Tribunal
(See Marriage Tribunals section)

## Pastoral Care of Immigrants
Sr Maureen Haugh
c/o Bishop's House, Westbourne, Ennis,
Co Clare
Tel 065-6828638

## Pioneer Total Abstinence Association
*Diocesan Director:* Vacant

## Polish Chaplain
Rev Dariusz Plasek
Cathedral Presbytery, Ennis, Co Clare
Tel 065-6824043/087-7052157
Email dariuszplasek@ennisparish.com

## Pontifical Mission Societies
*Diocesan Director*
Very Rev Tom O'Halloran
Borrisokane, Co Tipperary
Tel 067-27105

## Ceifin, Centre for Values Led Change
*Founder/Director*
Rev Harry Bohan BA, MScEcon
172 Drumgeeley Hill,
Shannon, Co Clare

## Social Services
North Tipperary Community Services
Kenyon Street, Nenagh, Co Tipperary
Tel 067-31800
Clarecare
Harmony Row, Ennis, Co Clare
Tel 065-6828178

## Travellers
*Chaplain*
c/o Bishops House, Westbourne,
Ennis, Co Clare
Tel 065-6828638

## Vocations
*Director:* Rev Ignatius McCormack
St Flannan's College, Ennis, Co Clare
Tel 065-6828019/086-2777139

# PARISHES

*Parishes follow in cluster order. Historical names are given in parentheses. Church titulars are in italics.*

## ABBEY CLUSTER
### Ennis
*Cathedral: SS Peter & Paul*
Very Rev Tom Hogan PP
Tel 065-6869097/087-6446410
Rev Ger Fitzgerald CC
Tel 065-6824043/086-1697595
Rev Dariusz Plasek
Tel 065-6824043/087-7052157
Rev Brendan Quinlivan
Tel 065-6869094/087-2736310
Cathedral Presbytery, Ennis, Co Clare
Tel 065-6824043 Fax 065-6842541
*St Joseph's, Lifford*
Very Rev John McGovern Adm
Tel 065-6822166/086-3221210
St Joseph's Presbytery, 52 Kincora Park,
Lifford, Ennis, Co Clare
*Christ the King, Cloughleigh*
Rev Tom O'Gorman Adm
Tel 065-6840715/087-2285355
Cloughleigh Presbytery, 1 Shallee Drive,
Cloughleigh, Ennis, Co Clare
Tel 065-6840715/087-2285355
Very Rev Canon Patrick Taaffe AP
3 Cottage Gardens, Ennis, Co Clare
Tel 065-6891983/086-1731070
Rev Paddy Conway AP
Westbourne, Ennis, Co Clare
Tel 065-6849818/087-6831992
*Parish Sisters:* Sr Ann Boland
Tel 065-6844742/087-1369517
Sr de Montfort
Tel 065-6828024/086-1993838
Sr Betty Curtin
Tel 065-6868542/086-3715018

### Clarecastle (Clare Abbey)
*SS Peter & Paul, Clarecastle*
*St John the Baptist, Ballyea*
Very Rev Pat Malone PP
Church Drive, Clarecastle, Co Clare
Tel 065-6823011/086-8572023
Very Rev Harry Brady AP
10 Beechwood, Lissane,
Clarecastle, Co Clare
Tel 086-2349798

### Quin
*St Mary, Quin*
*St Stephen, Maghera*
*Pope John XXIII Memorial Church, Clooney*
Very Rev Michael Collins PP
Parish House, Quin, Co Clare
Tel 065-6825612/086-3475085
Rev Ignatius McCormack *(Assistant Priest)*
St Mary's, Quin, Co Clare
Tel 065-6839039/086-2777139

### Doora and Kilraghtis
*St Brecan, Doora*
*The Immaculate Conception, Barefield*
Rev Jerry Carey
Tig an tSagairt, 3 The Woods,
Cappahard, Tulla Road,
Ennis, Co Clare
Tel 065-6822225/086-2508444
Very Rev Caimin Canon O'Carroll AP
Barefield, Ennis, Co Clare
Tel 065-6821190/087-2521388

## INIS CHATHAIGH CLUSTER
### Carrigaholt & Cross (Kilballyowen)
*Blessed Virgin Mary, Carrigaholt*
*The Holy Spirit, Doonaha*
*Our Lady of Lourdes, Cross*
*St John the Baptist, Kilbaha*
Very Rev Michael Casey PP
Cross, Co Clare
Tel 065-9058008/086-0842216
Very Rev Patrick Culligan AP
Carrigaholt, Co Clare
Tel/Fax 065-9058043 Tel 087-9863865

### Doonbeg (Killard) & Kilkee
*Our Lady Assumed into Heaven, Doonbeg*
*St Senan, Bealaha*
*The Immaculate Conception & St Senan, Kilkee*
*St Flannan, Lisdeen*
Rev Gerry Kenny PP
Circular Road, Kilkee, Co Clare
Tel 065-9056580
Very Rev Joe Haugh AP
Bealaha, Doonbeg, Co Clare
Tel 065-9055022/087-2865434
Kilkee Parish Office, Circular Road,
Kilkee, Co Clare
Email office@kilkeeparish.com
www.kilkeeparish.com

### Killimer & Kilrush
*St Senan, Kilrush*
*St Senan, Knockerra*
*St Imy, Killimer*
*Little Senan Church, Monmore*
Very Rev Michael Sheedy PP
Toler Street, Kilrush, Co Clare
Tel 065-9051093/086-26203314
Rev Martin Blake CC
O'Gorman Street, Kilrush, Co Clare
Tel 065-9051016/087-9033682

### Cooraclare (Kilmacduane)
*St Senan, Cooraclare*
*St Mary, Cree*
Very Rev Tony Casey PP
Cooraclare, Co Clare
Tel 065-9059008/087-9936950
Very Rev Patrick Carmody AP
Cooraclare, Co Clare
Tel 065-9059010/086-3017371

**Kilmihil**
*St Michael*
Very Rev Peter O'Loughlin PP
Kilmihil, Co Clare
Tel 065-9050016/086-8250016

**Kilmurry McMahon**
*St Mary, Kilmurry McMahon*
*St Kerin, Labasheeda*
Rev Tom McGrath (MHM) PP
Labasheeda, Co Clare
Tel 065-6830126

**IMEALL BÓIRNE CLUSTER**
*Corofin*
*St Brigid, Corofin*
*St Joseph, Kilnaboy*
*St Mary, Rath*
Rev Damien Nolan
1a Laghtagoona, Corofin, Co Clare
Tel 065-6837178/086-8396636

**Crusheen (Inchicronan)**
*St Cronan, Crusheen*
*The Immaculate Conception, Ballinruan*
Rev Ger Nash
Parochial House, Crusheen, Co Clare
Tel 065-6827113/086-8576153

**Dysart & Ruan**
*St Mary's, Ruan*
*St Tola, Dysart*
Rev Pat O'Neill
Ruan, Co Clare
Tel 065-6827799/086-2612124

**Tubber (Kilkeedy)**
*St Michael, Tubber*
*All Saints, Boston*
Rev Seamus Nohilly (SMA)
Parochial House, Tubber, Co Clare
Tel 091-633124/085-1443021

**BRENDAN CLUSTER**
*Birr*
*St Brendan, Birr*
*Our Lady of the Annunciation, Carrig*
Very Rev David Carroll PP
Tel 057-9122028/086-3467909
Rev Patrick Gilbert (Chaplain)
Tel 087-2431956
The Presbytery, John's Mall, Birr, Co Offaly
Very Rev Anthony Cahir AP
5 Woodlands Park, Birr, Co Offaly
Tel 057-9120097/086-2612121
Rev Michael Reddan (SVD)
The Presbytery, John's Mall, Birr, Co Offaly
Tel 057-9121757/087-7599789

**Kilcolman**
*St Colman, Kilcolman*
*St Ita, Coolderry*
*St John, Ballybritt*
Very Rev Kieran Blake PP
Kilcolman, Sharavogue, Birr, Co Offaly
Tel/Fax 057-9120812/087-9302214

**Kinnitty**
*St Flannan, Kinnitty*
*St Luna, Cadamstown*
*St Finan Cam, Longford*
*St Molua, Roscomroe*
Very Rev Michael O'Meara PP
Kinnitty, Birr, Co Offaly
Tel 057-9137021/087-7735977

**Shinrone**
*St Mary, Shinrone*
*St Patrick, The Pike*
Very Rev Frank Meehan PP
Tel 0505-47167/087-2302413

**CRONAN CLUSTER**
*Roscrea*
*St Cronan, Roscrea*
*St John the Baptist, Camblin*
Very Rev Dr Tom Corbett Co-ordinator
Convent Hill, Roscrea, Co Tipperary
Tel 0505-21108/086-8418570
Rev Pat Treacy Co-PP
0505-21370/087-9798643
Rev Lorcan Kenny
Tel 0505-23637/087-6553402
Curate's House, Convent Hill,
Roscrea, Co Tipperary
Rev Michael Harding Co-PP
Templemore Road, Roscrea, Co Tipperary
Tel 0505-21218/086-2491941

**Kyle and Knock**
*St Molua, Ballaghmore*
*St Patrick, Knock*
Service provided by priests of Roscrea
Parish

**Dunkerrin**
*SS Mary & Joseph, Dunkerrin*
*St Joseph, Moneygall*
*Sacred Heart, Barna*
Very Rev Joe Kennedy PP
Monegall, Virr, Co Offaly
Tel 0505-45982/086-4072488
Rev Pat Deely
Dunkerrin, Birr, Co Offaly
Tel 0505-45982/086-8330225

**Bournea (Couraganeen)**
*St Patrick, Bournea*
*St Brigid, Clonakenny*
Service provided by priests of Roscrea
Parish
Very Rev Noel Kennedy AP
Bournea, Roscrea, Co Tipperary
Tel 0505-43211/086-3576775

**COIS DEIRIGE CLUSTER**
*Borrisokane*
*SS Peter & Paul, Borrisokane*
*St Michael the Archangel, Aglish*
Very Rev Tom O'Halloran PP
Borrisokane, Co Tipperary
Tel 067-27105

**Cloughjordan**
*St Michael & St John, Cloughjordan*
*St Flannan, Ardcroney*
*St Ruadhán, Kilruane*
Very Rev Tom Hannon PP
Templemore Road, Cloughjordan,
Co Tipperary
Tel 0505-42266/086-8768116

**Lorrha and Dorrha**
*St Ruadhan, Lorrha*
*Our Lady Queen of Ireland, Rathcabbin*
*Redwood Church*
Very Rev Pat Mulcahy PP
Lorrha, Nenagh, Co Tipperary
Tel 090-9747009/087-6329913

**Portroe (Castletown Arrha)**
*Blessed Virgin Mary*
Very Rev Tim O'Brien PP
Carrigatogher, Nenagh, Co Tipperary
Tel 067-31231/087-6548331
Rev Fergal O'Neill CC
Portroe, Nenagh, Co Tipperary
Tel 067-23105/087-6615975

**Puckane (Cloughprior and Monsea)**
*Our Lady & St Patrick, Puckane*
*St Mary's Church, Carrig*
Very Rev William McCormack PP
Puckane, Nenagh, Co Tipperary
Tel 067-24105/087-4168855
Venerable Archdeacon John F. Hogan AP
Ballycommon, Nenagh, Co Tipperary
Tel 067-24153/087-7536526

**Kilbarron and Terryglass**
*Immaculate Conception, Terryglass*
*St Barron, Kilbarron*
Very Rev Michael Cooney PP
Terryglass, Co Tipperary
Tel 067-22017/087-6548331
Email terryglasskilbarron@gmail.com

**Youghalarra (Burgess and Youghal)**
*Holy Spirit, Youghalarra*
*The Immaculate Conception, Ballywilliam*
Very Rev Timothy O'Brien PP
Carrigatoher, Nenagh, Co Tipperary
Tel 067-31231/087-2623922

**TRADAREE CLUSTER**
*Shannon*
*The Immaculate Mother of God, Shannon*
*SS John & Paul, Shannon*
Very Rev Tom Ryan PP
SS John & Paul Presbytery,
4 Dun na Rí, Shannon, Co Clare
Tel 061-364133/087-2349816
Rev Arnold Rosney CC
5 Drumgeely Avenue,
Shannon, Co Clare
Tel 061-471513/087-8598710
Very Rev Canon Brendan O'Donoghue AP
12 Tullyglass Square, Shannon, Co Clare
Tel 061-361257/086-8308153
Email office@shannonparish.ie
www.shannonparish.ie

**Sixmilebridge**
*St Finaghta, Sixmilebridge*
*St Mary's, Kilmurry*
Very Rev Harry Bohan PP
172 Drumgeely Hill, Shannon, Co Clare
Tel 061-713682/086-8223362
*Parish Office:* The Green,
Sixmilebridge, Co Clare
Tel 061-713682

**Newmarket-on-Fergus**
*BVM of the Rosary, Newmarket-on-Fergus*
*Our Lady of the Wells*
*St Conaire, Carrygarry*
Very Rev Tom Fitzpatrick PP
Tel 061-700883/087-2720187
Very Rev Reuben Canon Butler AP
Tel 061-368433/087-2425390
Newmarket-on-Fergus, Co Clare

## ODHRÁN CLUSTER
### Nenagh
*St Mary of the Rosary, Nenagh*
*St John the Baptist, Tyrone*
Very Rev Desmond Hillery PP
'Maryville', Church Street,
Nenagh, Co Tipperary
Tel 067-37130
Rev Gerard Jones CC
Tel 067-37131/087-2137238
Sr Clare Slattery, Parish Sister
Tel 067-31357/086-8349120
*Parish Office:* 067-37136

### Silvermines
*Our Lady of Lourdes, Silvermines*
*Our Lady of the Wayside, Ballinaclough*
Very Rev Brendan Moloney PP
Silvermines, Nenagh, Co Tipperary
Tel 067-25864/087-2907705

### Killanave and Templederry
*Immaculate Conception, Templederry*
*Our Lady of the Wayside, Killeen*
*Our Lady of the Wayside, Curreeney*
Very Rev Willie Teehan PP
Templederry, Co Tipperary
Tel 0504-52988/087-2347927
Very Rev Leo Long AP
Killeen, Ballinaclough,
Nenagh, Co Tipperary
Tel 067-25870/086-8353388

### Toomevara
*St Joseph, Toomevara*
*St Joseph, Ballinree*
*St Joseph, Gortagarry*
*St Joseph, Grennanstown*
Rev John Molloy PP
Toomevara, Co Tipperary
Tel 067-26023

## EAST CLARE CLUSTER
### Ogonnelloe & Bodyke (Kilnoe and Tuamgraney)
*St Molua, Ogonnelloe*
*St Mary, Ballybrohan*
*Our Lady Assumed into Heaven, Bodyke*
*St Joseph, Tuamgraney*
Very Rev Donagh O'Meara PP
Ballyheafey, Killaloe, Co Clare
Tel 061-376766/087-2322140

### Feakle & Killanena-Flagmount
*St Mary, Feakle*
*St Joseph, Kilclarin*
*St Mary, Killanena*
*St Mary, Flagmount*
Very Rev Joseph McMahon PP
Scariff, Co Clare
Very Rev James O'Brien AP
Feakle, Co Clare
Tel 061-924035/087-2665793

### Mountshannon (Clonrush)
*St Caimin, Mountshannon*
*St Flannan, Whitegate*
Very Rev John Jones PP
St Caimin's, Mountshannon, Co Clare
Tel 061-927213/086-1933479

### Scariff (Moynoe)
*Sacred Heart, Scariff*
*St Mary, Clonusker*
Very Rev Joseph McMahon PP
Scariff, Co Clare
Tel 061-921013

### Tulla
*SS Peter & Paul, Tulla*
*The Immaculate Conception, Drumcharley*
*St James, Knockjames*
Very Rev Martin O'Brien PP
Newline, Tulla, Co Clare
Tel 065-6835117/087-2504075
Rev Brendan Lawlor CC
2 Powerscourt, Tulla, Co Clare
Tel 065-6835284/087-9845417

### O'Callaghan's Mills
*St Patrick's, O'Callaghan's Mills*
*St Senan, Kilkishen*
*St Vincent de Paul, Oatfield*
Very Rev Donal Dwyer
O'Callaghan's Mills, Co Clare
Tel 065-6835148/086-1050090

### Broadford
*St Peter, Broadford*
*St Mary, Kilbane*
*St Joseph, Kilmore*
Very Rev John Bane PP
Parochial House, Broadford, Co Clare
Tel 061-473123/086-8246555

## RADHARC NA NÓILEAN CLUSTER
### Ballynacally (Clondegad)
*Our Lady of the Wayside, Lissycasey*
*Christ the King, Ballynacally*
Very Rev Joseph Hourigan PP
Lissycasey, Ennis, Co Clare
Tel 065-6834145/086-8170700
Very Rev Tom O'Dea AP
Ballynacally, Co Clare
Tel 065-6838135/086-8107475

### Kildysart & Coolmeen (Kilfidane)
*St Benedict, Coolmeen*
*St Mary, Cranny*
*St Michael, Kildysart*
Very Rev Albert McDonnell PP
Kildysart, Co Clare
Tel 065-6832155/085-7811823

## CRÍOCHA CALLAN CLUSTER
### Inch and Kilmaley
*St John the Baptist, Kilmaley*
*Our Lady of the Wayside, Inch*
*St Michael the Archangel, Connolly*
Very Rev Pat Larkin PP
Parochial House, Kilmaley, Co Clare
Tel 065-6839735/087-2300627
Very Rev Michael McLaughlin AP
Airfield, Inch, Ennis, Co Clare
Tel 065-6839332/086-2213025

### Kilnamona (Inagh)
*Immaculate Conception, Inagh*
*The Blessed Virgin Mary, Cloonanaha*
*St Joseph, Kilnamona*
Very Rev Sean Sexton PP
Kilnamona, Ennis, Co Clare
Tel 065-6829507/087-2621884

### Miltown Malbay (Kilfarboy)
*St Joseph, Miltown Malbay*
*St Mary, Moy*
Very Rev Seán Murphy PP
Tel 065-7084129
Very Rev Canon Seamus Mullin AP
Tel 065-7084003
Miltown Malbay, Co Clare

### Mullagh (Kilmurray-Ibrickane)
*Our Lady, Star of the Sea, Quilty*
*St Mary, Mullagh*
*The Most Holy Redeemer, Coore*
Very Rev Anthony McMahon PP
Carhuligane, Mullagh, Ennis, Co Clare
Tel 065-7087012/086-8243801
Email office@kibparish.ie
www.kibparish.ie

## SCÁTH NA SIONNAINE CLUSTER
### Castleconnell
*St Joseph, Castleconnell*
*St Patrick, Ahane*
Very Rev Brendan Kyne PP
The Spa, Castleconnell,
Co Limerick
Tel 061-377170/087-2025038
Rev Tom Whelan CC
Curate's House, Castleconnell,
Co Limerick
Tel 061-219482/087-2730299
Very Rev James Minogue AP
Castleconnell, Co Limerick
Tel 061-377166/087-6228674

### Clonlara (Doonas and Truagh)
*St Senan, Clonlara*
*Mary, the Mother of God, Truagh*
Very Rev Pat Greed PP
18 Churchfield, Clonlara, Co Clare
Tel 061-354594/086-6067003
Very Rev Brendan Cleary AP
17 Churchfield, Clonlara, Co Clare
Tel 061-354028/086-8484550

### Killaloe
*St Flannan, Killaloe*
*St Thomas, Bridgetown*
*Sacred Heart & St Lua, Garraunboy*
Very Rev James Grace PP
Killaloe, Co Clare
Tel 061-376137/087-6843315
Rev Patrick McMahon CC
Bridgetown, Co Clare
Tel 061-377158

## INSTITUTIONS AND THEIR CHAPLAINS

**Carrigoran House**
Newmarket-on-Fergus,
Co Clare
Tel 061-368100
Very Rev Tom Fitzpatrick
Tel 061-471406

**Community Hospital**
Kilrush, Co Clare
Tel 065-9051966
Very Rev Michael Sheedy PP, VG

**General Hospital, Ennis**
Acute Psychiatric Unit
Tel 065-6863218
Very Rev Tom Hogan Adm
Tel 065-6824043

**Cahercalla Community Hospital and Hospice**
Cahercalla, Ennis, Co Clare
Rev Tom Hogan
Tel 065-6824043

**Community Nursing Unit, Birr**
Co Offaly
Tel 057-9123200
Very Rev Anthony Cahir PP

**County Hospital, Nenagh**
Co Tipperary
Tel 067-31491
Very Rev Desmond Hillery PP

**District Hospital, Raheen**
Tuamgraney, Co Clare
Tel 061-923007
Rev Donagh O'Meara

**St Joseph's Hospital**
Ennis, Co Clare
Tel 065-6840666
Very Rev John McGovern Adm

**Welfare Home, Nenagh**
Co Tipperary
Tel 067-31893
Very Rev Desmond Hillery PP

**Welfare Home, Roscrea**
Co Tipperary
Tel 0505-21389
Very Rev Tom Corbett PP

**Regina House**
Kilrush, Co Clare
Tel 065-9051209
Very Rev Michael Sheedy PP, VG

**Community School, Roscrea**
Co Tipperary
Tel 0505-21454
Rev Lorcan Kenny

**St Anne's Community College**
Killaloe, Co Clare
Tel 061-376257
Veronica Molloy

**St Brendan's Community School**
Birr, Co Offaly
Tel 0509-20510
Rev Patrick Gilbert

**St Caimin's Community School**
Shannon, Co Clare
Tel 061-364211
Cora Guinnane

**Kilrush Community School**
Tel 065-9051359
Mr Karol Torpey

**St Joseph's Community College**
Kilkee, Co Clare
Tel 065-9056138
Mrs Ann Healy

**St Patrick's Comprehensive School**
Shannon, Co Clare
Tel 061-361428
Nuala Murray

**Kiladysart Community College**
Co Clare
Tel 065-6832300
Joanne O'Brien

## PRIESTS OF THE DIOCESE ELSEWHERE

Rev Michael Collins
St Patrick's College,
Maynooth, Co Kildare
Tel 01-7084700/087-6389847
Rev Pascal Hanrahan CF (RC)
St Michael's House,
Queens Avenue, Aldershot,
Hants GU11 2BY, UK
Tel 0044-1252316429/0044-7920593792
Mgr Seamus Horgan
Apostolic Nunciature,
PO Box 3604,
1099 Manila, Philippines
Tel 00632-5274271
Archbishop Eugene M. Nugent
Apostolic Nunciature, Villa Roma,
Ivandry BP 650, 101 Antananarivo,
Madagascar

## RETIRED PRIESTS

Very Rev Enda Burke
Cloughjordan, Co Tipperary
Very Rev John Donnelly
Rathcabban, Roscrea, Co Tipperary
Tel 057-9139072
Very Rev Paschal Flannery
Ballinderry, Nenagh, Co Tipperary
Tel 067-22916/086-2225099
Very Rev Seamus Gardiner
Portroe, Co Tipperary
Tel 067-23101/086-8392741
Very Rev Brian Geoghegan
Munnia, New Quay, Co Clare
Tel 087-2387067
Very Rev Oliver O'Doherty
The Presbytery, Church Road,
Nenagh, Co Tipperary
Very Rev JJ Rodgers
Killanena, Co Clare
Tel 061-925265
Very Rev Pat Sexton
5 Cottage Gardens, Station Road,
Ennis, Co Clare
Tel 065-6840828/087-2477814
Very Rev Tom Seymour
Church Road, Nenagh, Co Tipperary
Tel 067-31831/087-2889055
Very Rev John Slattery
30 Meadow Ville, Burke's Hill,
Birr, Co Offaly
Tel 087-3388899

## RELIGIOUS ORDERS AND CONGREGATIONS

### PRIESTS

**CISTERCIANS**
Mount Saint Joseph Abbey
Roscrea, Co Tipperary
Tel 0505-25600 Fax 0505-25610
Email info@msjroscrea.ie
Website www.msjroscrea.ie
*Abbot*
Rt Rev Dom Richard Purcell (OCSO)

**FRANCISCANS**
Franciscan Friary, Ennis, Co Clare
Tel 065-6828751 Fax 065-6822008
Email friars.ennis@eircom.net
*Guardian:* Rev Caoimhín Ó Laoide (OFM)

## BROTHERS

**CHRISTIAN BROTHERS**
Christian Brothers' House,
New Road, Ennis, Co Clare
Tel 065-6821471/6828469 (office)
*Community Leader:* Br Dan Healy
Community: 6

Christian Brothers' House,
Nenagh, Co Tipperary
Tel 067-31557
*Community Leader:* Br John Dooley
Community: 6

**PRESENTATION BROTHERS**
Presentation Brothers,
Birr, Co Offaly
Tel 0509-20247
*Contact:* Br Ultan Rohan (FPM)
Community: 4

## SISTERS

**SISTERS OF CHARITY OF THE INCARNATE WORD**
St Michael Convent, Carrigoran,
Newmarket-on-Fergus, Co Clare
Tel 061-368381
Community: 4
Carrigoran House, Retirement and
Convalescent Centre
Tel 061-368100 Fax 061-368170
Email info@carrigoranhouse.ie

**CONGREGATION OF THE SISTERS OF MERCY**
*The Sisters of Mercy minister throughout the diocese in pastoral and social work, community development, counselling, spirituality, education and health care, answering current needs.*

Mercy Sisters,
Garinis Clonroadmore, Ennis, Co Clare
Tel 065-6820768
Community: 2

St Xavier's, Ennis, Co Clare
Tel 065-6828024 Fax 065-6828776
Community: 19

1 Corovorrin Crescent, Ennis, Co Clare
Tel 065-6841375
Community: 5

7 Shalee Drive,
Cloughleigh, Ennis, Co Clare
Tel 065-6828894 Fax 065-6828892
Community: 5

8/9 Greendale, Clonroad, Ennis, Co Clare
Tel 065-6840385 Fax 065-6823869
Community: 6

5 & 6 Rosanore, Gort Road,
Ennis, Co Clare
Tel 065-6821554
Community: 4

Mercy Sisters, Killaloe, Co Clare
Tel 061-376138
Community: 5

Milltown Road, Kilkee, Co Clare
Tel 065-9056116
Community: 4

Convent of Mercy,
Kilkee Road, Kilrush, Co Clare
Tel 065-9051068
Community: 8

20 Sycamore Drive, Kilrush, Co Clare
Tel 065-9051957
Community: 2

31 Shannon Heights, Kilrush, Co Clare
Tel 065-9052354
Community: 2

64 Shannon Heights, Kilrush, Co Clare
Tel 065-9052789
Community: 2

Ashe Road, Nenagh, Co Tipperary
Tel 067-33835 Fax 067-34266
Community: 7

5 Dromin Court, Nenagh, Co Tipperary
Tel/Fax 067-31591
Community: 2

Spanish Point, Miltown Malbay, Co Clare
Tel 065-7084005 Fax 065-7084865
Community: 5

Tulla, Co Clare
Tel 065-6835118
Community: 4

1/2 Fergus Drive, Shannon, Co Clare
Tel 061-471637
Community: 5

St Mary's, Nenagh, Co Tipperary
Tel 067-31357 Fax 067-43586
Community: 15

33 Yewston Estate,
Nenagh, Co Tipperary
Tel 067-32830
Community: 4

St John's, Riverside, Birr, Co Offaly
Tel 057-9120891
Community: 7

McAuley Drive, Birr, Co Offaly
Tel 057-9121023 Fax 057-9121303
Community: 3

84 Aughanteeroe, Gort Road,
Ennis, Co Clare
Tel/Fax 065-6844533
Community: 3

10/11 Ardlea Close,
Clare Road, Ennis, Co Clare
Tel 065-6842399
Community: 5

## DAUGHTERS OF CHARITY OF ST VINCENT DE PAUL
St Vincent's, Woodstown House,
Lisnagry, Co Limerick
Tel 061-501490/332577
*Superior:* Sr Breege Fahy
Community: 4
St Vincent's Special School, day and
residential centre for people with
intellectual disability.

St Anne's Centre, Roscrea, Co Tipperary
Services for persons with intellectual
disability
Tel 0505-22046

## LA SAINTE UNION DES SACRES COEURS
LSU Sisters, 40 Cregaun,
Tobartaoscáin, Ennis, Co Clare
Community: 2
Education, pastoral, therapy

## POOR CLARES
Poor Clare Monastery,
Francis Street, Ennis, Co Clare
*Abbess:* Sr Gabrielle Murphy
Community: 11
Contemplative

## SACRED HEARTS OF JESUS AND MARY
The Convent, Sean Ross Abbey,
Roscrea, Co Tipperary
Tel/Fax 0505-21629
*Contact:* Sr Margaret Dobbin

St Anne's Special School (for children
with intellectual disabilities)
Sean Ross Abbey,
Roscrea, Co Tipperary
*School Principal:* Mr James McMahon
Tel 0505-21002

St Mary's,
Corville Road, Roscrea, Co Tipperary
Tel 0505-31599

## ST JOHN OF GOD SISTERS
St John of God Sisters,
19 Water Park View, Ennis Co Clare
Tel 065-6843579
Community: 1

## ST JOSEPH OF THE SACRED HEART SISTERS
7 Woodlands, Kilrush Road,
Ennis, Co Clare
Tel 065-6844742
Sr Anne Boland

57 Woodlands, Kilrush Road,
Ennis, Co Clare
Tel 065-6891178

## ST MARY MADELEINE POSTEL SISTERS
Park More Convent, Abbey Street,
Roscrea, Co Tipperary
Tel 0505-21038
*Local Superior:* Sr Marie Keegan
Community: 3

Mount Carmel Nursing Home,
Abbey Street, Roscrea, Co Tipperary
Tel 0505-21146
*Apply:* Matron
Community: 8

Ard Mhuire Convent, Parkmore,
New Line, Roscrea, Co Tipperary
*Regional Superior:* Sr M. Luke Minogue
Community: 3

## EDUCATIONAL INSTITUTIONS

### St Flannan's College (Diocesan College)
Ennis, Co Clare
Tel 065-6828019 Fax 065-6840644
*President*
Rev Joseph McMahon
Rev Ignatius McCormack

### EDMUND RICE SCHOOLS TRUST
Bunscoil na mBráithre,
New Road, Ennis, Co Clare
Tel 065-6822150 Fax 065-6823865
Email cbsennis@gmail.com
*Principal:* Mr Dara Glynn

Rice College, New Road,
Ennis, Co Clare
Tel 065-6822105 Fax 065-6824755
Email admin@ricecollege.ie
Website www.ricecollege.ie
*Principal:* Mr Louis Mulqueen

Nenagh CBS, Summer Hill,
Nenagh, Co Tipperary
Tel 067-32748
Email cbsnenagh@eircom.net
*Principal:* Ms Sheila Brophy

St Joseph's CBS Secondary School,
Summer Hill, Nenagh, Co Tipperary
Tel 067-34789 Fax 067-34967
Email reception@cbsnenagh.com
*Principal:* Mr Tony Slattery

## CHARITABLE AND OTHER SOCIETIES

### Apostolic Work Society
Diocesan Headquarters at Maria
Assumpta Hall, Station Road, Ennis,
Co Clare

### Birr Social Service Council
c/o 47 New Road, Birr, Co Offaly

### Clarecare
Clarecare, Harmony Row,
Ennis, Co Clare
Tel 065-6828178

**Clare Youth Advisory Service**
Carmody Street, Ennis, Co Clare
Tel 065-6845350

**Geriatric Centre**
Carrigoran House,
Newmarket-on-Fergus, Co Clare
Tel 061-368100

**Legion of Mary**
Headquarters at Maria Assumpta Hall,
Station Road, Ennis, Co Clare

**Mount Carmel Nursing home**
Parkmore, Abbey Street, Roscrea,
Co Tipperary
Tel 0505-21146

**North Tipperary Community Services**
Loreto House, Kenyon Street,
Nenagh, Co Tipperary
Tel 067-31800

**North Tipperary Youth Advisory Service**
c/o The Institute, Nenagh, Co Tipperary
Tel 067-32000

**Roscrea Community Service Centre**
Rosemary Street, Roscrea, Co Tipperary
Tel 0505-21498

**Schools for children with Special Needs**
*St Vincent's, Woodstown House,*
Lisnagry, Co Limerick
(Daughters of Charity)
Tel 061-501400

*St Anne's, residential and day school,*
Sean Ross Abbey,
Roscrea, Co Tipperary
Tel 0505-21187

*St Clare's, day school,*
Gort Road, Ennis, Co Clare
Tel 065-6821899

*St Anne's, day school,*
Ennis, Co Clare
Tel 065-6829072

**Society of St Vincent de Paul**
Conferences at: Birr, Castleconnell,
Clarecastle, Cloughjordan, Ennis, Kilrush,
Kilkee, Nenagh, Newmarket-on-Fergus,
Roscrea, Scariff/Tuamgraney and
Shannon

# DIOCESE OF KILMORE

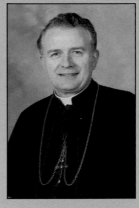

**Most Rev Leo O'Reilly DD**
Bishop of Kilmore;
born 1944;
ordained priest 15 June 1969;
ordained bishop 2 February
1997; installed as Bishop of
Kilmore 15 November 1998

Residence:
Bishop's House,
Cullies, Co Cavan
Tel 049-4331496
Fax 049-4361796
Email bishop@kilmorediocese.ie
Website www.kilmorediocese.ie

PATRONS OF THE DIOCESE
ST PATRICK, 17 MARCH; ST FELIM, 9 AUGUST

INCLUDES ALMOST ALL OF COUNTY CAVAN,
AND A PORTION OF COUNTIES LEITRIM, FERMANAGH, MEATH AND SLIGO

## CATHEDRAL OF ST PATRICK AND ST FELIM, CAVAN

The original cathedral of the diocese was situated about four miles south of Cavan in the present parish of Kilmore. Some time in the sixth century, St Felim had established a church there. Bishop Andrew MacBrady (1445–1455) rebuilt the ancient church of St Felim and received permission from Pope Nicholas V to raise it to the status of a cathedral. After the confiscation of the Cathedral of St Felim at Kilmore, the diocese had no cathedral for three hundred years. Bishop James Browne extended Cavan parish church and erected it into a cathedral in 1862. It was replaced by the new Cathedral of St Patrick and St Felim, built by Bishop Patrick Lyons in the years 1938–1942. The architects were W. H. Byrne & Son and the contractors John Sisk & Son. The cathedral cost £209,000 and was opened and dedicated in 1942. It was consecrated in 1947.

The cathedral is neo-classical in style with a single spire rising to 230 feet. The portico consists of a tympanum supported by four massive columns of Portland stone with Corinthian caps. The tympanum figures of Christ, St Patrick and St Felim were executed by a Dublin sculptor, George Smith. The twenty-eight columns in the cathedral, the pulpit on the south side and all the statues are of Pavinazetto marble and came from the firm of Dinelli Figli of Pietrasanta in Italy.

The fine work of George Collie can be seen in the Stations of the Cross and in the mural of the Risen Christ on the wall of the apse. Directly above the mural are twelve small windows, showing the heads of the twelve apostles. The High Altar is of green Connemara marble and pink Middleton marble, while the altar rails are of white Carrara marble. The apse has two side-chapels on the north and two on the south. The Blessed Sacrament is now reserved in the south chapel closest to the altar. The six splendid stained-glass windows in the nave and one in the south transept came from the studios of Harry Clarke.

## ADMINISTRATION

**College of Consultors**
Rt Rev Mgr Michael Cooke PP, VG, VF
Very Rev John Gilhooly PP
Very Rev Liam Kelly PP
Very Rev Michael Router PP, VF
Very Rev Sean Mawn PP, VF
Rev Charles Heerey
Rev Kevin Fay
Rev Donal Kilduff

**Vicar General**
Rt Rev Mgr Michael Cooke PP, VG, VF
Bridge Street, Belturbet, Co Cavan
Tel 049-9522109

**Council of Priests**
*Chairman:* Very Rev Liam Kelly PP
Bunnoe, Cootehill, Co Cavan
Tel 049-5553035
*Secretary:* Rev Donal Kilduff

**Vicars Forane**
Very Rev Oliver Kelly VF
Very Rev Sean Mawn PP, VF
Very Rev Michael Router PP, VF
Rt Rev Mgr Michael Cooke PP, VG, VF

**Finance Committee**
Rt Rev Mgr Michael Cooke PP, VG, VF
Very Rev Anthony Fagan PP
Very Rev Fintan McKiernan PP
Mrs Joan Quinn
Ms Carmel Denning
Mr John Boyle
Mr Kevin O'Connor
Mr Paul Kelly

**Financial Administrator**
Rev Donal Kilduff

**Chancellor/Diocesan Secretary**
Rev Donal Kilduff
Bishop's House, Cullies, Co Cavan
Tel 049-4331496 Fax 049-4361796
Email bishop@kilmorediocese.ie

**Bishop's Secretary**
Kathleen Conaty
Bishop's House, Cullies, Co Cavan
Tel 049-4331496 Fax 049-4361796
Email bishop@kilmorediocese.ie

**Diocesan Archivist**
Rev Donal Kilduff
Bishop's House, Cullies, Co Cavan
Tel 049-4331496 Fax 049-4361796

## CATECHETICS EDUCATION

**Catholic Primary School Managers' Association**
*Secretary:* Mrs Nancy Shiels
Kilmore Diocesan Pastoral Centre,
Cullies, Cavan
Tel 049-4375004 (ext 4) Fax 049-4327497
Email edsec@kilmorediocese.ie

**Diocesan Catechetical Advisers**
*Primary:* Sr Anna Smith
Sisters of Mercy, 2 Dún na Bó,
Willowfield Road, Ballinamore,
Co Leitrim
Tel 071-9645973
Mr Terence Leddy
Drumsilla, Butlersbridge, Co Cavan
*Second level:* Mrs Patricia Sheridan
Kells Road, Bailieborough,
Co Cavan

## LITURGY

*Pastoral Team:* Kilmore Diocesan Pastoral
Centre, Cullies, Cavan
Tel 049-4375004
*Advisor:* Very Rev Daniel Sheridan
Killeshandra, Co Cavan
Tel 049-4334179
Email danniedan88@gmail.com

**Church Music**
Kilmore Diocesan Pastoral Centre,
Cullies, Cavan
Tel 049-4375004

**Art, Architecture and Buildings**
*Chairman:* Very Rev Michéal Quinn

## PASTORAL

**Kilmore Diocesan Pastoral Centre**
Cullies, Cavan
*Director:* Mr Sean Coll
Tel 049-4375004 Fax 049-4327497
Email pastoralcentre@kilmorediocese.ie

**ACCORD**
Kilmore Diocesan Pastoral Centre
Tel 049-4375004
*Diocesan Director:* Ms Clare Carolan
*Chaplain:* Rev Paul Casey Adm
Magheranure, Cootehill, Co Cavan
Tel 049-5552163

**Apostolic Society**
*Diocesan President*
Ms Suzanna Tinnenny
Quivvy, Belturbet, Co Cavan
Tel 049-9522928
*Spiritual Director*
Rev John McMahon CC
Tel 071-9856987

**Communications**
*Diocesan Director:* Rev Donal Kilduff
Bishop's House, Cullies, Co Cavan
Tel 049-4331496 Fax 049-4361796

**Diocesan Pastoral Council**
*Chairperson:* Rev Maurice McMorrow
*Secretary:* Ms Nancy Shiels
Tel 049-4375004

**Ecumenism**
*Director:* Rev Andrew Tully CC
Ballyjamesduff, Co Cavan
Tel 049-8544410

**Eucharistic Adoration**
*Chairperson:* Rev Andrew Brady
Tel 049-8545160
*Chapain:* Rev John Cooney
Tel 046-9052129

**Family Ministry**
Rev Andrew Tully CC
Ballyjamesduff, Co Cavan
Tel 049-8544410

**Knock Pilgrimage**
*Director:* Very Rev Anthony Fagan
Killinkere, Virginia, Co Cavan
Tel 049-8547307

**Legion of Mary**
*Spiritual Director:* Rev Martin Gilcreest
Tel 049-4362014

**Lourdes Pilgrimage**
*Director:* Rev Kevin Fay
Lavey, Ballyjamesduff, Co Cavan
Tel 049-4330018

**Marriage Tribunal**
*Kilmore Office of Armagh Regional
Marriage Tribunal*
Sr Elizabeth Fee
Kilmore Diocesan Pastoral Centre,
Cullies, Cavan
Tel 049-4375004
Email tribunal@kilmorediocese.ie
St Michael's Parish Centre,
28 Church Street,
Enniskillen BT74 7EJ
Tel 028-66347860

**Pastoral Services**
*Director:* Rev Enda Murphy
Kilmore Diocesan Pastoral Centre,
Cullies, Cavan
Tel 049-4375004

**Safeguarding Children
Diocesan Committee**
*Chairperson:* Mr Christopher Dooley
*Director:* Sr Suzie Duffy
Kilmore Diocesan Pastoral Centre
Tel 049-4375004
*Designated Persons*
Sr Suzie Duffy
Kilmore Diocesan Pastoral Centre
Tel 049-4375004
Very Rev Sean Mawn VF
Ballinamore, Co Leitrim
Tel 071-9644039

**Permanent Diaconate**
*Director:* Rev Gabriel Kelly
Kinawley, Enniskillen,
Co Fermanagh
Tel 028-66348250

**Pioneer Total Abstinence Association**
*Diocesan Director:* Rev John Cusack CC
Ballinamore, Co Leitrim
Tel 071-9644050

**Pontifical Mission Societies**
*Diocesan Director*
Very Rev John McMahon PP
Knockbride, Bailieboro,
Co Cavan
Tel 042-9660112

**St Joseph's Young Priests' Society**
*Chaplain:* Very Rev Philip Brady CC
Cross, Mullagh, Via Kells, Co Meath
Tel 049-8547024
*Diocesan President:* Mr Pat Denning
Drumcave, Cavan
Tel 049-4331362

**Travellers**
*Chaplain:* Very Rev Sean McDermott PP
Carrigans, Ballinagh, Co Cavan
Tel 049-4367662

**Immigrants**
*Diocesan Representive:* Rev Rafal Siwek
The Presbytery, Cavan
Tel 049-4331404

**Vocations**
*Director:* Rev John Cusack
Ballinamore, Co Leitrim
Tel 071-9644050

# PARISHES

*Mensal parishes are listed first. Other parishes follow alphabetically. Historical names are given in parentheses. Church titulars appear in italics*

**CAVAN (URNEY AND ANNAGELLIFF)**
*Cathedral of SS Patrick and Felim, Cavan*
*St Clare's, Cavan*
*St Brigid's, Killygarry*
*St Aidan's, Butlersbridge*
Rev Kevin Donohoe Adm
Rev Ultan McGoohan CC
Rev Rafal Siwek CC
The Presbytery, Cavan
Tel 049-4331404/4332269 Fax 049-4332000
Information line 049-4371787
Email cavan@kilmorediocese.ie
Rev Sean Maguire CC
Butlersbridge, Co Cavan
Tel 049-4365266
Rev Darragh Connolly (priest in residence)
Tullacmongan, Cavan

**BAILIEBORO (KILLANN)**
*St Anne's, Bailieboro; St Anne's, Killann*
*St Patrick's, Shercock*
Very Rev Michael Router PP, VF
Bailieboro, Co Cavan
Tel 042-9665117
Email bailieboro@kilmorediocese.ie
Rev Oliver O'Reilly CC
Parochial House, Shercock, Co Cavan
Tel 042-9669127
Email shercockparish@gmail.com

**BALLAGHAMEEHAN**
*St Aidan's, Ballaghameehan*
*St Mary's, Rossinver*
*St Aidan's, Glenaniff*
*St Patrick's, Kiltyclogher*
Very Rev Pat Farrelly PP
Rossinver, Co Leitrim
Tel 071-9854022
Email rossinver@kilmorediocese.ie

**BALLINAGLERA**
*St Hugh's, Ballinaglera*
*St Columcill, Newbridge*
*Immaculate Conception, Doobally*
Very Rev Maurice McMorrow PP
Ballinaglera, Carrick-on-Shannon,
Co Leitrim
Tel 071-9643014
Email ballinaglera@kilmorediocese.ie

**BALLINAMORE (OUGHTERAGH)**
*St Patrick's Ballinamore,*
*St Mary's Aughnasheelin*
Very Rev Sean Mawn PP, VF
Ballinamore, Co Leitrim
Tel 071-9644039
Email ballinamore@kilmorediocese.ie
Rev John Cusack CC
Ballinamore, Co Leitrim
Tel 071-9644050

**BALLINTEMPLE**
*St Michael's, Potahee*
*St Mary's, Bruskey*
*St Patrick's, Aghaloora*
Very Rev Sean McDermott PP
Ballintemple, Ballinagh, Co Cavan
Tel 049-4337106
Email smcdcf@gmail.com
Rev Noel Boylan (priest in residence)
Parochial House, Carrigans,
Ballinagh, Co. Cavan
Tel 049-4367662

**BELTURBET (ANNAGH)**
*Immaculate Conception, Belturbet*
*St Patrick's, Drumalee*
*St Brigid's, Redhills*
Rt Rev Mgr Michael Cooke PP, VG
Bridge Street, Belturbet, Co Cavan
Tel 049-9522109
Email belturbet2@kilmorediocese.ie
Rev Charles Heerey CC
Fairgreen, Belturbet, Co Cavan
Tel 049-9522151
Email belturbet@kilmorediocese.ie
Rev Jason Murphy (priest in residence)
Killoughter, Redhills,
Co Cavan
Tel 047-55021
Email killatain1@hotmail.com

**CARRIGALLEN**
*St Mary's, Carrigallen*
*St Mary's, Drumeela*
*St Mary's, Drumreilly*
Very Rev Denis Murray PP
Carrigallen, Co Leitrim, via Cavan
Tel 049-4339610
Email carrigallen@kilmorediocese.ie

**CASTLERAHAN AND MUNTERCONNAUGHT**
*St Bartholomew's, Munterconnaught*
*St Mary's, Castlerahan*
*St Joseph's, Ballyjamesduff*
Very Rev Francis Kelleher PP
Knocktemple, Virginia, Co Cavan
Tel 049-8547435
Email frfkelleher@eircom.net
Very Rev Felim Kelly CC
Castlerahan, Ballyjamesduff, Co Cavan
Tel 049-8544150
Email castlerahan@kilmorediocese.ie
Rev Andrew Tully CC
Ballyjamesduff, Co Cavan
Tel 049-8544410
Email ballyjamesduff@kilmorediocese.ie

**CASTLETARA**
*St Mary's Ballyhaise,*
*St Patrick's, Castletara*
Very Rev Gerard Cassidy PP
Ballyhaise, Co Cavan
Tel 049-4338121
Email ballyhaise@kilmorediocese.ie

**COOTEHILL (DRUMGOON)**
*St Michael's, Cootehill*
*St Mary's, Middle Chapel*
*St Patrick's, Maudabawn*
Very Rev Owen Collins PP
Tel 049-5552120
Email cootehill@kilmorediocese.ie
Rev Paul Casey Adm
Tel 049-5552163
Cootehill, Co Cavan

**CORLOUGH AND DRUMREILLY**
*St Patrick's, Corlough,*
*St Brigid's, Corraleehan,*
*St Patrick's, Aughawillan*
Very Rev Thomas McManus PP
Corlough, Belturbet, Co Cavan
Tel 049-9523122
Email corlough@kilmorediocese.ie

**CROSSERLOUGH**
*St Patrick's, Kilnaleck*
*St Mary's, Crosserlough*
*St Joseph's, Drumkilly*
Very Rev Michael Quinn PP
Crosserlough, Co Cavan
Tel 049-4336122
Email crosserlough@kilmorediocese.ie

**DENN**
*St Matthew's, Crosskeys*
*St Matthew's, Drumavaddy*
Email crosskeys@kilmorediocese.ie
Very Rev Peter McKiernan PP
Crosskeys, Co Cavan
Tel 049-4336102

**DERRYLIN (KNOCKNINNY)**
*St Ninnidh's, Derrylin*
*St Mary's, Teemore*
Very Rev Fintan McKiernan PP
56 Mary Street, Derrylin,
Co Fermanagh BT92 9LA
Tel 028-67748315
Email derrylin@kilmorediocese.ie

**DRUMAHAIRE AND KILLARGUE**
*St Patrick's, Drumahaire*
*St Mary's, Newtownmanor*
*St Brigid's, Killargue*
Very Rev John McTiernan PP
Drumahaire, Co Leitrim
Tel 071-9164143
Email drumahaire@kilmorediocese.ie
Rev John Sexton *(Priest in residence)*
Killargue, Drumahaire,
Co Leitrim
Tel 071-9164131

**DRUMKEERIN (INISHMAGRATH)**
*St Brigid's, Drumkeerin*
*St Patrick's, Tarmon*
*St Brigid's, Creevalea*
Very Rev Gerard Alwill PP
Drumkeerin, Co Leitrim
Tel 071-9648025
Email drumkeerin@kilmorediocese.ie

**DRUMLANE**
*St Mary's, Staghall*
*St Patrick's, Milltown*
Very Rev Gerard Comiskey PP
Staghall, Belturbet,
Co Cavan
Tel 049-9522140
Email drumlaneparish@gmail.com

**GLENFARNE**
*St Michael's, Glenfarne*
*St Mary's, Brockagh*
Very Rev John Quinn Adm
West Barrs, Glenfarne,
Co Leitrim
Tel 071-9855134
Email glenfarne@kilmorediocese.ie

**KILDALLAN AND TOMREGAN**
*Our Lady of Lourdes, Ballyconnell*
*St Dallan's, Kildallan*
Very Rev Eamonn Lynch PP
Ballyconnell, Co Cavan
Tel 049-9526291
Email ballyconnell@kilmorediocese.ie

**KILLESHANDRA**
*St Brigid's, Killeshandra*
*Sacred Heart, Arva*
*Immaculate Conception, Coronea*
Very Rev Daniel Sheridan PP
Killeshandra, Co Cavan
Tel 049-4334179
Email danniedan88@gmail.com
Rev Donald Hannon CC
Arva, Co Cavan
Tel 049-4335246
Email arva@kilmorediocese.ie

**KILLINAGH AND GLANGEVLIN**
*St Patrick's, Killinagh*
*St Patrick's, Glangevlin*
*St Felim's, Gowlan*
Very Rev Charles O'Gorman PP
Blacklion, Co Cavan
Tel 071-9853012
Email blacklion@kilmorediocese.ie

**KILLINKERE**
*St Ultan's, Killinkere*
*St Mary's, Clanaphilip*
Very Rev Anthony Fagan PP
Killinkere, Virginia, Co Cavan
Tel 049-8547307
Email killinkere@kilmorediocese.ie

**KILMAINHAMWOOD AND MOYBOLOGUE**
*Sacred Heart*
*St Patrick's*
Very Rev John Cooney PP
Kilmainhamwood, Kells, Co Meath
Tel 046-9052129
Email kilmainhamwood@kilmorediocese.ie

**KILMORE**
*St Felim's, Ballinagh*
*St Patrick's, Drumcor*
Very Rev Peter Casey PP
Ballinagh, Co Cavan
Tel 049-4337232

**KINAWLEY/KILLESHER**
*St Mary's, Swanlinbar*
*St Naile's, Kinawley*
*St Patick's, Killesher*
*St Lasir's, Wheathill*
Very Rev Gabriel Kelly PP
Kinawley, Enniskillen,
Co Fermanagh BT92 4FH
Tel 028-66348250
Email kinawley@kilmorediocese.ie
Rev Bernard Fitzpatrick CC
Swanlinbar, Co Cavan
Tel 049-9521221/087-3899345
Email swanlinbar@kilmorediocese.ie

**KILSHERDANY AND DRUNG**
*Immaculate Conception, Drung*
*St Patrick's, Corick*
*St Mary's, Bunnoe*
*St Brigid's, Kill*
Very Rev Liam Kelly PP
Parochial House, Bunnoe,
Cootehill, Co Cavan
Tel 049-5553035
Email drung@kilmorediocese.ie
Rev Stefan Park (OSA) CC
Kill, Cootehill, Co Cavan
Tel 049-5553218
Email kill@kilmorediocese.ie

**KINLOUGH AND GLENADE**
*St Aidan's, Kinlough*
*St Patrick's, Tullaghan*
*St Michael's, Glenade*
*St Brigid's, Ballintrillick*
Very Rev Thomas M. Keogan PP
Kinlough, Co Leitrim
Tel 071-9841428
Email kinlough@kilmorediocese.ie

**KNOCKBRIDE**
*St Brigid's, Tunnyduff*
*St Brigid's, East Knockbride*
Very Rev John McMahon PP
Knockbride, Bailieboro, Co Cavan
Tel 042-9660112

**LARAGH**
*St Brigid's, Laragh*
*St Brigid's, Carrickallen*
*St Michael's, Clifferna*
Very Rev Brian Flynn PP
Laragh, Stradone, Co Cavan
Tel 049-4330142
Email laraghparish1@gmail.com
Rev Patrick V. Brady PE *(priest in residence)*
Clifferna, Stradone, Co Cavan
Tel 049-4330119

**LAVEY**
*St Dympna's, Upper Lavey*
*St Dympna's, Lower Lavey*
Very Rev Brian McElhinney PP
Lavey, Stradone, Co Cavan
Tel 049-4330125
Email lavey@kilmorediocese.ie
Rev Kevin Fay *(priest in residence)*
Lavey, Ballyjamesduff, Co Cavan
Tel 049-4330018
Email lavey1@kilmorediocese.ie

**MANORHAMILTON (KILLASNETT)**
*St Clare's, Manorhamilton*
*Annunciation, Mullies*
*St Osnat's, Glencar*
Very Rev Oliver Kelly PP, VF
Manorhamilton, Co Leitrim
Tel 071-9855042
Email manorhamilton@kilmorediocese.ie
Rev Tom Mannon CC
Glencar, Manorhamilton, Co Leitrim
Tel 071-9855433
Email glencar@kilmorediocese.ie

**MULLAGH**
*St Kilian's, Mullagh*
*St Mary's, Cross*
Very Rev John Gilhooly PP
Mullagh, via Kells, Co Meath
Tel 046-42208
Email mullagh@kilmorediocese.ie
Very Rev Philip Brady CC
Cross, Mullagh, Kells, Co Meath
Tel 049-8547024

**TEMPLEPORT**
*St Patrick's, Kilnavart,*
*St Mogue's, Bawnboy*
Very Rev John Phair PP
Kilnavart, Ballyconnell, Co Cavan
Tel 049-9526126
Email bawnboy@kilmorediocese.ie

**VIRGINIA (LURGAN)**
*Mary Immaculate, Virginia*
*St Patrick's, Lurgan*
*St Matthew's, Maghera*
Very Rev Dermot Prior PP
Virginia, Co Cavan
Tel 049-8547063
Email virginia@kilmorediocese.ie
Rev Loughlain Carolan CC
Virginia, Co Cavan
Tel 049-8547015

## INSTITUTIONS AND THEIR CHAPLAINS

**Bailieboro Community School**
*Chaplain:* Ms Mary Grimes
Tel 042-9665295

**Ballinamore Community School**
Ballinamore, Co Leitrim
*Visiting Chaplain:* Ms Ann Marie Madden
Email office@ballinamorecs.ie
Website www.ballinamorecs.ie

**Breifne College**
Cootehill Road, Cavan
*Catechist:* Rev Jason Murphy
Tel 049-4331735

**Carrigallen Vocational School**
*Visiting Chaplain:* Rev Denis Murray
Tel 049-4339640

**Cavan General Hospital**
Tel 049-4361399
Rev Martin Gilcreest
Rev Gerard Kearns

**Cavan Institute**
Cathedral Road, Cavan
*Chaplaincy and Pastoral Care*
Rev Ultan McGoohan
Tel 049-4332334

**Loreto College, Cavan**
Tel 049-4331354
*Visiting Chaplain:* Rev Kevin Fay

**Lough Allen College**
Drumkeerin, Co Leitrim
*Visiting Chaplain:* Rev Gerard Alwill
Tel 071-9648017

**Loughan House**
Blacklion, Co Cavan
*Visiting Chaplain*
Rev Charles O'Gorman
*General Office:* 071-9853059

**St Aidan's Comprehensive School**
Cootehill, Co Cavan
Tel 049-5552161
*Chaplain:* Mr Gabriel McQuillan

**St Aidan's High School**
Derrylin, Co Fermanagh
*Visiting Chaplain*
Rev Fintan McKiernan
Tel 028-67748337

**St Bricin's Vocational School**
Belturbet, Co Cavan
Tel 049-9522170

**St Clare's College**
Ballyjamesduff, Co Cavan
*Visiting Chaplain:* Rev Andrew Tully
Tel 049-8544410

**St Clare's Comprehensive School, Manorhamilton**
*Chaplain:* Rev John Sexton
Tel 071-9855060

**St Mogue's College**
Bawnboy, Co Cavan
*Visiting Chaplain:* Rev John Phair
Tel 049-9523112

**St Patrick's College, Cavan**
*Chaplain:* Rev Kevin Fay
Tel 049-4361888

**Virginia College**
Virginia, Co Cavan
*Visiting Chaplain:* Rev Loughlain Carolan
Tel 049-8547050

## PRIESTS OF THE DIOCESE ELSEWHERE

Rev Paul Prior
Director of Formation,
St Patrick's College, Maynooth,
Co Kildare
Rev John Murphy
Bailieborough Road, Virginia, Co Cavan
On sabbatical

## RETIRED PRIESTS

Rev Patrick Bannon
15 Lisdarn Heights, Cavan
Rev Raymond Brady
8 Earlsvale Road, Cavan
Tel 049-4380369
Rev P.J. Corrigan
Erne Hill, Beturbet, Co Cavan
Rev Eugene Clarke
5 Brookside, Farnham Road, Cavan
Tel 049-4331755
Rev Bernard Doyle
Kiltyclogher, Co Leitrim
Tel 071-9854302
Rev Colm Hurley
Killeshandra, Co Cavan
Tel 049-4334155
Rev Felim McGovern
The Presbytery, Cavan
Tel 049-4331404
Rev Patrick McHugh
Clontarf, Dublin 3
Rev Thomas McKiernan
Rosskeeragh, Belturbet, Co Cavan
Rt Rev Mgr Patrick J. McManus
Kilnaleck, Co Cavan
Tel 049-4336118
Rev Brian McNamara
Main Street, Derrylin,
Co Fermanagh BT92 9LA
Rev John O'Donnell
9 Rockview, Blacklion, Co Cavan
Rev Thomas Woods
Edenville, Kinlough, Co Leitrim

## RELIGIOUS ORDERS AND CONGREGATIONS

### PRIESTS

**NORBERTINE CANONS**
Abbey of the Most Holy Trinity and
St Norbert, Kilnacrott Abbey,
Ballyjamesduff, Co Cavan
Tel 049-8544416
Fax 049-8544909
Email kilnacrottabbeytrust@eircom.net
*Prelate Administrator*
Rt Rev William M. Fitzgerald (OPraem)

### SISTERS

**CONGREGATION OF THE SISTERS OF MERCY**
Church Street,
Belturbet, Co Cavan
Tel 049-9522110

No. 4 Oriel Lodge, Church Sreet,
Belturbet, Co Cavan
Tel 049-9524657

17 Castlemanor,
Billis, Cavan, Co Cavan
Tel 049-4379267

Sisters of Mercy,
2 Castle View, Manorhamilton,
Co Leitrim
Tel 071-9855401

No 2 Dun na Bo, Willowfield Road,
Ballinamore, Co Leitrim
Tel 071-9645973
Community: 4

No 16 Dun na Bo, Willowfield Road,
Ballinamore, Co Leitrim
Tel 071-9644006
Community: 4

No. 16 Drumnavanagh, Cavan, Co Cavan
Tel 049-4365941

Station Road, Cootehill, Co Cavan
Tel 049-5552490

**LORETO (IBVM)**
Loreto Post-Primary School
Tel 049-4331354

**MISSIONARY SISTERS OF THE HOLY ROSARY**
Cavan Town
Tel 049-4332735/4332733
Fax 049-4362077
Centre for mission education
co-ordination
Pastoral, care of the elderly
Community: 28

27 Cherrymount,
Keadue, Cavan Town
Tel 049-4372936
Pastoral, healthcare
Community: 2

**SISTERS OF ST CLARE**
St Clare's Convent, Cavan
Tel 049-4331134
Community: 3
Primary School. Pupils: 550
Tel 049-4332671

## EDUCATIONAL INSTITUTIONS

**St Clare's College**
Ballyjamesduff, Co Cavan
Tel 049-8544551
Fax 049-8544081
*Principal:* Ms Teresa Donlon
*Visiting Chaplain:* Rev Andrew Tully
Tel 049-8544410

**Ballinamore Community School**
Ballinamore, Co Leitrim
Tel 071-9644049
*Principal:* Mr Padraig Leyden
*Visiting Chaplain:* Ms Ann Marie Madden
Email office@ballinamorecs.ie
Website www.ballinamorecs.ie

**St Patrick's College**
Cullies, Co Cavan
Tel 049-4361888
Email stpats@kilmorediocese.ie
*Principal:* Mr Christopher Rowley
*Chaplain:* Rev Kevin Fay

# *Welcome to Tranquillity*

*Emmaus, Ennis Lane, Lissenhall, Swords, Co Dublin*
*Telephone (01) 8700050 • Fax (01) 8408248*
*Email emmauscentre@emmauscentre.ie*

**Emmaus** *provides an excellent location*
*For both Adult & School Retreat Programmes.*

*Emmaus hosts a comprehensive range of Seminars,*
*Workshops, Chapters and Parish Renewal days. We also offer a quality,*
*relaxed and peaceful setting for Jubilee and Private Celebrations.*

*Our facilities include 62 en-suite guest rooms, 13 meeting rooms,*
*Private chapel, 2 prayer rooms, private dining rooms*
*and extensive grounds for quiet Reflection,*
*and all Located close to the M1& Dublin International Airport.*

*For up to date information on all our Retreats/Seminars*
*Call us on 01-8700050*

*Or log onto our website for a complete listing of Retreats/Seminars on*
*www.emmauscentre.ie*
*Email emmauscentre@emmauscentre.ie*

# THE NATIONAL BIBLE SOCIETY OF IRELAND
## And Bestseller Bookshop

We stock a wide range of Bibles, Theology, Prayer & Spirituality, Liturgical and Children's books. Mail Order welcome. All major credit cards accepted. Online ordering available via the Society's website www.biblesociety.ie

*We aim for the widest possible effective distribution of the Holy Scriptures, both at home and worldwide.* We support projects in many countries, including translation in India, distribution in Ghana and Scriptures for the visually impaired in the Philippines. Please contact us for more information.

Contact: Ms Judith Wilkinson, Chief Executive
41 Dawson Street, Dublin 2
Tel (01) 677 3272  Fax (01) 671 0040
Email info@biblesociety.ie • Website www.biblesociety.ie
Charity No. CHY1592

*Serving All Irish Churches with the Holy Scriptures*
Under the patronage of Most Rev Diarmuid Martin, Archbishop of Dublin, and other Church leaders.

# My First Holy Communion

## *Every child needs this book!*

Written, illustrated, designed,
published and printed in Ireland!

Through beautiful,
colourful images and
stories, this premium
quality hardback
presents the wonderful
gift of the Catholic faith
in an appealing and
comprehensive way to
children (and adults!)
who are preparing for
first Holy Communion.
*Now just released in Irish,
'Mo Chéad Chomaoineach
Naofa,' with Nihil Obstat
from Bishop Donal
McKeown of Derry.*

€18 plus €5 P&P. **Special bulk offer:** Just €10 per book including free delivery,
based on boxes of minimum 25 books – a great idea for Parish Pastoral Councils,
Schools, Parents Committees or local groups to sponsor. Please post cheque
payable to 'Clonmacnois Press', 4 Aran Centre, Blessington, Co. Wicklow.
Tel (045) 900 742 | www.clonmacnoispress.com

# Digital Church Organs & Digital Pianos
## SALES • SERVICE • HIRE

Yamaha digital piano

Viscount Organ

Allen Organ

Digital Organs & Pianos, both large and small, have been the choice for over 850 churches in Ireland since Jeffers started installing these instruments over 40 years ago. Churches are still choosing these instruments today benifiting from the reasonable purchase and maintainence costs yet enjoying the realistic Pipe Organ & Piano sound and versitility of the most up to date digital technology from some of the worlds leading companies in this field. Please contact us to find out more.

## JEFFERS MUSIC COMPANY LTD, BANDON, CO CORK

087-2559922 • www.jeffersmusic.ie • info@jeffersmusic.ie

# DIOCESE OF LIMERICK

PATRONS OF THE DIOCESE
ST MUNCHIN, 3 JANUARY; ST ITA, 15 JANUARY

INCLUDES THE GREATER PART OF COUNTY LIMERICK, PART OF COUNTY CLARE
AND ONE TOWNLAND IN COUNTY KERRY

**Most Rev Brendan Leahy DD**
Bishop of Limerick;
born 28 March 1960;
ordained priest 5 June 1986;
ordained Bishop of Limerick
14 April 2013

Dioesan Office: Social Service
Centre, Henry Street, Limerick
Tel 061-315856 Fax 061-310186
Email bishop@ldo.ie
Website
www.limerickdiocese.org

## ST JOHN'S CATHEDRAL, LIMERICK

Since the twelfth century, a church dedicated to St John has stood in the area of Limerick city known as Garryowen. The earliest reference to the first church comes from the year 1205 when the Cathedral Chapter of the Diocese of Limerick was founded by Bishop Donatus O'Brien, Bishop of Limerick from 1195 to 1207. In the document of foundation, the revenues from the Church of St John were given to the Archdeacon of Limerick. This medieval church was replaced by a penal church, which in turn was supplanted by the parish church of St John in the middle of the eighteenth century. With an increase in population in the area around Garryowen, it was decided to build a new church to accommodate the estimated 15,000 parishioners of St John's. An appeal for funds was so well received that the decision was made to abandon the plans for a parish church and build a cathedral for the diocese instead.

Designed by Philip Charles Hardwick, a contemporary and associate of Pugin, St John's Cathedral is revival Gothic in the early English style. It was opened for worship in 1861 and consecrated in 1894 by Cardinal Logue. The spire, standing at 308 feet, 3 inches, is the tallest in Ireland and was built between 1878 and 1883.

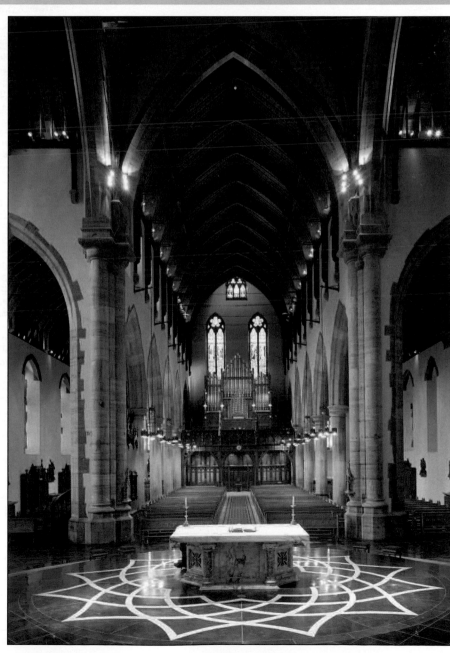

**Most Rev Donal Murray DD**
Bishop Emeritus
born 29 May 1940; ordained priest 22
May 1966; ordained bishop 18 April
1982; installed as Bishop of Limerick 24
March 1996; retired December 2009

## CHAPTER

*Dean:* Very Rev Anthony Canon Mullins PP
*Archdeacon:* Vacant
*Theologian*
Very Rev Donough Canon O'Malley
*Penitentiary*
Very Rev Garrett Canon Bluett
*Chancellor*
Very Rev Frank Canon Duhig PP, VF
*Precentor*
Very Rev James Canon Ambrose PP
*Prebendaries and Canons*
*Dysart*
Very Rev John Canon O'Shea PP, VF
*Croagh:* Very Rev James Canon Neville
*Effin*
Very Rev James Canon Costello PP
*Killeedy*
Very Rev Donal Canon McNamara PP, VF
*Athnitt:* Vacant
*Tullybrackey*
Very Rev Anthony Canon O'Keeffe PP, VF
*Ardcanny*
Very Rev Alphonsus Canon Cullinan PP
*St Munchin's*
Rt Rev Mgr Michael Lane
*Kilpeacon:* Vacant
*Donaghmore*
Rt Rev Mgr Daniel Neenan PP
*Ballycahane*
Very Rev William Canon Fitzmaurice PP

## COLLEGE OF CONSULTORS

Very Rev Éamonn Fitzgibbon
Very Rev Muiris O'Connor
Very Rev Alphonsus Cullinan PP
Very Rev Michael O'Shea
Very Rev John Donworth
Very Rev Paul Finnerty

## ADMINISTRATION

**Episcopal Vicars**
*Episcopal Vicar for Pastoral Care of Priests*
Very Rev Muiris O'Connor

*Episcopal Vicar for Pastoral Planning*
Very Rev Éamonn Fitzgibbon

*Episcopal Vicar for Administration*
Very Rev Paul Finnerty

**Council of Priests**
Most Rev Brendan Leahy
Very Rev Paul Finnerty
Very Rev Éamonn Fitzgibbon
Very Rev Muiris O'Connor
Rt Rev Mgr Daniel Neenan PP
Very Rev Donal Canon McNamara PP, VF
Very Rev David Gibson
Very Rev Alphonsus Canon Cullinan PP
Very Rev John Keating
Very Rev Joseph Shire
Very Rev Michael O'Shea
Very Rev Adrian Egan (CSsR)
Very Rev John Donworth

**Diocesan Secretary/Moderator of the Curia**
Rev Paul Finnerty
Diocesan Office,
Social Service Centre,
Henry Street, Limerick
Tel 061-315856 Fax 061-310186
Email paul@ldo.ie
Website www.limerickdiocese.org
*Finance Manager:* Mr Tony Sadlier
*Secretarial Staff:* Margaret Dalton
*Diocesan Spokesperson:* Rev Paul Finnerty
*Finance and Synod Administrator*
Karen Kiely

**Diocesan Archivist**
David Bracken
Diocesan Office,
Social Service Centre,
Henry Street, Limerick
Tel 061-315856

## DIOCESAN PASTORAL COUNCIL

Pending

## CATECHETICS EDUCATION

**Primary Level Religious Education**
*Director:* Rev Sean Harmon
c/o Limerick Diocesan Pastoral Centre,
St Michael's Courtyard,
Denmark Street, Limerick
Tel 061-400133
Email sean@ldo.ie
Ms Fiona Dineen
Tel 061-315856
Email fionad@ldo.ie

**Second Level Religious Education**
*Adviser:* Vacant
c/o Limerick Diocesan Pastoral Centre,
St Michael's Courtyard,
Denmark Street, Limerick
Tel 061-400133

**Primary Education Secretary**
Ms Fiona Shanley
St Senan's Education Office,
Social Service Centre,
Henry Street, Limerick
Tel 061-317742 Fax 061-310186
Email fiona@ldo.ie
*Secretarial Staff*
Linda Fleming Email linda@ldo.ie
Gwen O'Sullivan Email gwen@ldo.ie
Donna Noonan Email sseo@ldo.ie
*Faith Development Co-ordinator:*
Lorraine Buckley
Tel 061-400133
Email lorraine@ldpc.ie

## LITURGY

**Liturgical Group**
*Director:* Rev Derek Leonard

## PASTORAL

**ACCORD**
Limerick City Centre:
St Munchin's College, Corbally, Limerick
Email accordlimerick@eircom.net
www.accord.ie
*Director:* Rev Joseph Shire PP
Ballyagran, Kilmallock, Co Limerick
Tel 063-82028
Enquiries: Tel 061-343000
Fax 061-350000
*Administrator:* Ms Katrina Quilligan
Newcastle West Centre:
Parish Centre, Newcastle West,
Co Limerick
*Contact:* Helen Ahern
Tel 069-61000 (Mon-Fri 10.00am-1.00pm)
*Spiritual Director*
Very Rev Frank Canon Duhig PP, VF
St Ita's Presbytery,
Newcastle West, Co Limerick
Tel 069-62141/087-6380299

**Apostleship of the Sea, Foynes**
*Director and Port Chaplain*
Very Rev Anthony Canon O'Keeffe PP, VF
Shanagolden, Co Limerick
Tel 069-60112

**Charismatic Renewal Groups**
*Liaison Priest:* Rev Damian Ryan PP
Manister, Co Limerick
Tel 061-397335/087-2274412

**Communications**
*Director:* Rev Paul Finnerty
Diocesan Office, Social Services Centre,
Henry Street, Limerick
Tel 061-315856

**CURA**
*Helpline:* Tel 061-318207
*Administrator:* Ms Anne Finucane

**Limerick Diocesan Pastoral Centre**
St Michael's Courtyard,
Denmark Street, Limerick
Tel 061-400133 Fax 061-400601
Email reception@ldpc.ie
http://www.limerickdiocese.org/ldpc/
*Director:* Rev Chris O'Donnell

**Ecumenism**
*Director:* Rev Frank O'Connor
Cathedral House, Cathedral Place,
Limerick
Tel 061-414624

**Emigrant Apostolate**
*Director:* Vacant

**Apostolate of the Laity**
*Adviser:* Very Rev Noel Kirwan PP
Cathedral House, Cathedral Place,
Limerick
Tel 061-414624

**Diocesan Representative on the National Council for the Laity**
*Diocesan Representative*
Ms Mary Sadlier
Rockfield, Crecora, Co Limerick
Tel 061-301044

**Marriage Encounter Movement**
Very Rev Liam Enright PP
Cratloe, Co Clare
Tel 061-357196/087-2546335
Email leppcrat@iol.ie

**Marriage Tribunal**
*Contact:* Mrs Jean Ryan
Diocesan Offices, Social Service Centre,
Henry Street, Limerick
*Office hours:* Tuesday 2.00-5.00 pm
Thursday 9.00-5.00 pm
Tel 061-315856 Fax 061-310186
Email office@ldo.ie

**Military Chaplain**
Rev Seamus Madigan
Sarsfield Barracks, Limerick
Tel 061-316817

**Pioneer Total Abstinence Association**
*Spiritual Director:* Vacant

**Pilgrimage**
*(Lourdes) Director*
Very Rev Donal Canon McNamara PP
St Munchin's, Clancy Strand,
Limerick
Tel 061-455635/087-2402518
Email donal@donalmcnamara.com

**Pre-Marriage Courses**
*Contact:* ACCORD
Limerick City Centre
Tel 061-343000 Fax 061-350000
Newcastle West Parish Centre
Tel 069-61000

**Pontifical Mission Societies**
*Diocesan Director*
Very Rev Thomas Crawford PP
Glin, Co Limerick
Tel 068-23897/087-2218078
Email tdec@eircom.net

**Safeguarding Children**
*Director of Safeguarding/Designated Person:* Ger Crowley
Email ger@ldo.ie
*Safeguarding Children Co-ordinator:*
Margaret Dalton
Email margaret@ldo.ie
*Safeguarding Children Training Co-ordinator:* Aoife Walsh
Email awalsh@ldpc.ie

**Social Service Council**
*General Manager:* Mr Brian Ryan
Henry Street, Limerick
Tel 061-314111/314213

**Travelling Community**
*Diocesan Chaplain*
Very Rev Joseph Shire
Kilmallock, Co Limerick
Tel 087-6924563
Email taylor@eircom.net

**Trócaire**
*Director:* Very Rev Derek Leonard PP
St Nicholas Presbytery, Westbury,
Limerick
Tel 061-340614
Email derekleonard@eircom.net

**Vocations**
*Director:* Rev Leslie McNamara
Cathedral House, Cathedral Place,
Limerick
Tel 061-414624
Email lesliemcnamara@eircom.net

**Youth Apostolate**
*Director:* Rev Chris O'Donnell
Limerick Diocesan Pastoral Centre,
St Michael's Courtyard,
Denmark Street, Limerick
Tel 061-400133 Fax 061-400601
Email codonnell@ldpc.ie

# PARISHES

*Mensal and city parishes are listed first.
Other parishes follow alphabetically.
Church titulars are in italics.*

**ST JOHN'S**
*St John's Cathedral*
Very Rev Noel Kirwan Adm
Rev Frank O'Connor CC
Rev Leslie McNamara
Cathedral House,
Cathedral Place, Limerick
Tel 061-414624/087-2589279
Fax 061-316570
Email stjohnsparishlk@eircom.net

**ST JOSEPH'S**
*St Joseph's*
Sacristy: 061-313401 (10.00 am-1.00 pm)
Very Rev Oliver Plunkett
7 Crescent Avenue, Limerick

**ST MICHAEL'S**
*St Michael's*
Very Rev Leo McDonnell
Cathedral House,
Cathedral Place, Limerick
Tel 061-413315 (church)

**ST MARY'S**
*St Mary's*
Sacristy: 061-416300
Very Rev Donough Canon O'Malley PP
Tel 061-414092/086-2586908
Rev John O'Byrne AP
Tel 085-7491268
St Mary's, Athlunkard Street, Limerick

**ST MUNCHIN'S AND ST LELIA'S**
*St Munchin's and St Lelia's*
Sacristy: 061-455133
Email stmunchinspresbytery@eircom.net
St Lelia's, Ballynanty
Tel 061-328577
Very Rev Donal Canon McNamara PP
Clancy Strand, Limerick
Tel/Fax 061-455635
Email donal@donalmcnamara.com
Rev Patrick Seaver CC
4 Glenview Terrace, Farranshone,
Limerick
Tel 061-328838
Email patseaver@hotmail.com

**ST PATRICK'S**
*St Patrick's & St Brigid's*
Very Rev David Gibson PP
St Patrick's, Dublin Road, Limerick
Tel 061-415397/087-2547707
Fax 061-417152

**ST PAUL'S**
*St Paul's*
Very Rev John Leonard PP, VF
The Presbytery, 10 St Nessan's Park,
Dooradoyle, Limerick
Tel 061-302729
Rev Noel Murphy CC
14 Springfield Drive, Dooradoyle,
Limerick
Tel 061-304508

**ST SAVIOUR'S**
*St Saviour's*
Very Rev Jordan O'Brien (OP) PP
St Saviour's, Glentworth Street, Limerick
Tel 061-412333 Fax 061-311728
Email oplimerick@eircom.net

**OUR LADY QUEEN OF PEACE**
*Our Lady Queen of Peace*
Sacristy: 061-467676
Very Rev Patrick O'Sullivan PP
'Elm View', Roxboro Road, Limerick
Tel 061-410846/087-2237501

**OUR LADY OF LOURDES**
*Our Lady of Lourdes*
Very Rev Patrick O'Sulliven PP
Lourdes House, Childers Road, Limerick
Tel 061-467676

**OUR LADY OF THE ROSARY**
*Holy Rosary*
Very Rev William Walsh PP
8 Merval Crescent, Clareview, Limerick
Tel/Fax 061-453026
Very Rev Thomas Ryan CC
Gleneden, North Circular Road, Limerick
Tel 061-329448
Parish mobile 087-2997733

**HOLY FAMILY**
*Holy Family*
Very Rev Patrick Hogan PP
334 O'Malley Park, Southill, Limerick
Tel 061-414248
Email pkfhogan@yahoo.co.uk

# DIOCESE OF MEATH

PATRON OF THE DIOCESE
ST FINIAN, 12 DECEMBER

INCLUDES THE GREATER PART OF COUNTIES MEATH, WESTMEATH AND OFFALY,
AND A PORTION OF COUNTIES LONGFORD, LOUTH, DUBLIN AND CAVAN

**Most Rev Michael Smith DCL, DD**
Bishop of Meath;
born 1940;
ordained priest 1963;
consecrated Bishop 29 January
1984; Co-adjutor Bishop of
Meath 10 October 1988;
succeeded 16 May 1990

Residence: Bishop's House,
Dublin Road,
Mullingar, Co Westmeath
Tel 044-9348841 Fax 044-9343020
Email bishop@dioceseofmeath.ie
Website www.dioceseofmeath.ie

## CATHEDRAL OF CHRIST THE KING, MULLINGAR

As the Penal Laws began to be relaxed, Bishop Patrick Plunkett was appointed Bishop of Meath in 1778. He was to spend the next forty-nine years of his life restoring and rebuilding the diocese. He had no cathedral, but providing one was not his immediate priority. Towards the end of his time as bishop, work began on the magnificent new Church of St Mary in Navan. This was opened in 1830 and was considered the Cathedral Church of the Diocese. In 1870 Bishop Thomas Nulty decided to locate the

bishop's residence in Mullingar, and the parish church there was designated Cathedral Church of the Diocese. It had been built in 1828 but was quite small.

On his appointment as bishop in 1900, Matthew Gaffney called a public meeting to discuss the building of a cathedral for the Diocese of Meath. This meeting adopted the following resolution: 'The Diocese of Meath not having a cathedral nor the parish of Mullingar a suitable church, be it resolved that a church be built in Mullingar which will fulfil this double purpose.' A building fund was established, and £15,000 was subscribed

at this first meeting – a very sizeable sum at that time. It was not until the day of his consecration as bishop in 1929 that Thomas Mulvany was able to announce the decision to proceed with the project. Ralph A. Byrne, chief architect with William H. Byrne & Son, Dublin, prepared plans, which were accepted. Work began in 1932, and the Cathedral of Christ the King was opened for worship in September 1936. It was consecrated on 30 August 1939, the debt having been cleared. In recent years, a major renovation, including the replacement of the roof, has been completed.

## ADMINISTRATION

Diocesan website
www.dioceseofmeath.ie

**Vicars General**
Rt Rev Mgr Dermot Farrell PP, VG
Parochial House, Dunboyne, Co Meath
Tel 01-8255342
Rt Rev Mgr Seán Heaney AP, VG
Parochial House, Tullamore, Co Offaly
Tel 057-9321587 Fax 057-9351510

**Vicars Forane**
Very Rev John Byrne PP, VF
Parochial House, Kells, Co Meath
Tel 046-9240213 Fax 046-9293475
Very Rev Joseph Clavin PP, VF
Parochial House,
Dunshaughlin, Co Meath
Tel 01-8259114 Fax 01-8011614
Very Rev Richard Matthews PP, VF
Parochial House, Killucan, Co Westmeath
Tel 044-9374127
Very Rev Patrick Keary PP, VF
Parochial House, Clara, Co Offaly
Tel 057-9331170 Fax 057-9330100
Very Rev Patrick Moore PP, VF
Parochial House,
Castlepollard, Co Westmeath
Tel 044-9661126 Fax 044-9661881
Very Rev Andrew Doyle PP, VF
Parochial House, Durhamstown,
Bohermeen, Navan, Co Meath
Tel 046-9073805
Very Rev Denis McNelis PP, VF
Parochial House, Laytown, Co Meath
Tel 041-9827258
Very Rev Patrick O'Connor PP, VF
Parochial House, Athboy, Co Meath
Tel 046-9432184 Fax 046-9430021

**College of Consultors**
Most Rev Michael Smith DD, DCL
Rt Rev Mgr Seán Heaney AP, VG
Rt Rev Mgr Dermot Farrell PP, VG
Very Rev John Byrne PP, VF
Very Rev Joseph Clavin PP, VF
Very Rev Richard Matthews, PP, VF
Very Rev Patrick Keary PP, VF
Very Rev Patrick Moore PP, VF
Very Rev Andrew Doyle PP, VF
Very Rev Denis McNelis PP, VF
Very Rev Patrick O'Connor PP, VF
Rev Paul Crosbie CC

**Diocesan Secretary**
Rev Paul Crosbie
Bishop's House, Dublin Road, Mullingar,
Co Westmeath
Tel 044-9348841 Fax 044-9343020
Email paul@dioceseofmeath.ie

**Secretary**
Mrs Irene Connaughton
Bishop's House, Dublin Road, Mullingar,
Co Westmeath
Tel 044-9348841 Fax 044-9343020
Email secretary@dioceseofmeath.ie

## EDUCATION

**Diocesan Office for Primary Education**
Rev Brendan Ludlow CC
Parochial House, Ratoath, Co Meath
Tel 01-8256207
Email cpsma@dioceseofmeath.ie

**Post-Primary Religious Education**
*Diocesan Director:* Mr Seán Wright
The Whinnies, Tierworker,
Kells, Co Meath
Tel 042-9665547 Fax 042-9666969
Email ppdd@eircom.net

**Primary Religious Education**
*Diocesan Advisers*
David Gavin
Helen Kiernan
Sr Annette O'Brien
Antoinette Shaw
Josephine Taylor
Bishop's House, Dublin Road, Mullingar,
Co Westmeath
Tel 044-9348841

## LITURGY

**Liturgical Commission**
*Chairman:* Very Rev Joseph McEvoy PP
Parochial House, Moynalty,
Kells, Co Meath
Tel 046-9244305
Email josephus@indigo.ie
*Secretary:* Mr James Walsh
18 Beechgrove, Laytown, Co Meath

## PASTORAL

**ACCORD**
*Secretary, Mullingar Centre*
Ms Mary Timmins
Tel 044-9348707
*Secretary, Navan Centre*
Ms Mary McCabe
Tel 046-9023146
*Secretary, Tullamore Centre*
Ms Michelle Cleary
Tel 057-9341831
www.dioceseofmeath.ie/marriage

**Apostolic Work Society**
*Mullingar Branch*
*Chaplain*
Rev Joseph Naikarakudy (MI) CC
Cathedral House, Mullingar,
Co Westmeath
Tel 044-9348338
*Navan Branch*
*Chaplain:* Rev Stephen Kelly CC
St Mary's, Navan, Co Meath
Tel 046-9027518

**Chaplain to Polish Community**
Rev Janusz Lugowski
Mount Rivers, Kells Road,
Navan, Co Meath
Tel 087-9538786

**Council of Priests**
*Chairman:* Very Rev Denis McNelis PP, VF
Parochial House, Laytown, Co Meath
Tel 041-9827258
*Secretary:* Rev Brendan Ludlow CC
Parochial House, Ratoath, Co Meath
Tel 01-8256207

**Dowdstown House (Blowick Conference Centre)**
Dowdstown House,
Navan, Co Meath
Tel 046-9021407 Fax 046-9073091
*Director:* Sr Elma Peppard
*Family Ministry Co-ordinators*
Sr Rose King, Sr Rose Sloan

**Ecumenism**
*Secretary:* Very Rev William Coleman PP
Parochial House, Rochfortbridge,
Co Westmeath
Tel 044-9222107

**Fr Matthew Union**
*Secretary:* Very Rev Séamus Houlihan PP
Parochial House,
Nobber, Co Meath
Tel 046-9052197

**Knock Pilgrimage**
*Director:* Very Rev Martin Halpin PP
Parochial House, Ballinabrackey,
Kinnegad, Co Westmeath
Tel 046-9739015

**Laity Commission**
*Diocesan Representative*
Mrs Molly Buckley
Moylena, Clara Road,
Tullamore, Co Offaly
Tel 0506-41357

**Lourdes Pilgrimage**
*Director*
Very Rev Joseph Gallagher PP
Parochial House, Tullamore, Co Offaly
Tel 057-9321587

**Marriage Tribunal**
(See Marriage Tribunals section)

**Pioneer Total Abstinence Association**
Very Rev Seamus Houlihan PP
Parochial House, Nobber,
Co Meath
Tel 046-9052197

**Pontifical Mission Societies**
*Diocesan Director*
Very Rev Gerard Stuart PP
Parochial House, Ratoath, Co Meath
Tel 01-8256207

**Safeguarding Resource Team**
Mrs Sandra Neville
Email neville.sandra@gmail.com
Mrs Joan Walshe
Email joan.walshe@yahoo.co.uk

**Travellers**
*Chaplain:* Very Rev Patrick O'Connor PP, VF
Parochial House Athboy, Co Meath
Tel 046-9432184

**Vocations and Youth**
*Directors:* Rev Joseph Campbell CC
St Mary's, Drogheda, Co Louth
Tel 041-9834958
Rev Shane Crombie CC
Parochial House, Tullamore, Co Offaly
Tel 057-9321587
Email vocations@dioceseofmeath.ie

# PARISHES

*Mensal parishes are listed first. Other parishes follow alphabetically.*

**MULLINGAR,**
*Cathedral of Christ the King*
*St Paul's, Mullingar*
*Assumption, Walshestown*
*Immaculate Conception, Gainstown*
*Little Flower and Our Lady of Good Counsel, Brotenstown*
Very Rev Padraig McMahon Adm
Rev Michael Kilmartin CC
Rev Paul Crosbie CC
Rev Joseph Naikarakudy (MI) CC
Cathedral House, Mullingar,
Co Westmeath
Tel 044-9348338/9340126
Fax 044-9340780
Email cathedral@dioceseofmeath.ie
Website www.mullingarparish.ie

**NAVAN**
*St Mary's; St Oliver's*
Very Rev Declan Hurley Adm
Rev Stephen Kelly CC
Rev Kevin Heery CC
Rev Louis Illah CC
St Mary's, Navan, Co Meath
Tel 046-9027518
Fax 046-9071774
Email stmarysnavan@eircom.net
Website www.navanparish.ie

**ARDCATH**
*St Mary's, Ardcath*
*St John the Baptist, Clonalvy*
Very Rev Brendan Ferris PP
Parochial House, Curraha, Co Meath
Tel 01-8350136
www.ardcath.com

**ASHBOURNE-DONAGHMORE**
*Immaculate Conception, Ashbourne*
*St Patrick, Donaghmore*
*Parish Office:* Tel/Fax 01-8353149
Email ashdon@indigo.ie
Website www.ashbourneparish.ie
Very Rev Derek Darby PP
54 Brookville, Ashbourne, Co Meath
Tel 01-8350547
Rev Michael Hinds CC
Parochial House, Ashbourne, Co Meath
Tel 01-8350406

**ATHBOY**
*St James', Athboy*
*St Lawrence, Rathmore*
*Naomh Pádraig, Rathcairn*
Very Rev Patrick O'Connor PP, VF
Parochial House, Athboy, Co Meath
Tel 046-9432184 Fax 046-9430021
Email naomhjames@gmail.com
Website www.athboyparish.ie

**BALLINABRACKEY**
*Assumption, Ballinabrackey*
*Trinity, Castlejordan*
Very Rev Martin Halpin PP
Parochial House, Ballinabrackey,
Kinnegad, Co Westmeath
Tel/Fax 046-9739015
Email mhalpin@eircom.net

**BALLYNACARGY**
*The Nativity, Ballynacargy*
*St Michael, Sonna*
Very Rev John Nally PP
Parochial House, Ballynacargy,
Co Westmeath
Tel 044-9373923

**BALLIVOR**
*St Columbanus*
Very Rev Mark Mohan PP
Parochial House, Ballivor, Co Meath
Tel/Fax 046-9546488
Parish email
ballivorkildalkeyparish@eircom.net
Website www.ballivorkildalkey.ie

**BALLYMORE**
*The Holy Redeemer, Ballymore*
*St Brigid's, Boher*
Very Rev Philip Smith PP
Parochial House, Ballymore, Mullingar,
Co Westmeath
Tel 044-9356212
Email ballymoreparish@hotmail.com

**BEAUPARC**
*The Assumption, Beauparc*
*The Assumption, Kentstown*
Very Rev James Lynch PP
Parochial House,
Kentstown, Navan, Co Meath
Tel 041-9825276 Fax 041-9825252
Email kentstownchurch1854@gmail.com
Website www.beauparcparish.ie
Very Rev Peter Farrelly AP
Parochial House, Beauparc,
Navan, Co Meath
Tel 046-9024114
Email peterfarrelly@eircom.net

**BOHERMEEN**
*St Ultan's, Bohermeen*
*St Cuthbert's, Boyerstown*
*Christ the King, Cortown*
Very Rev Andrew Doyle PP, VF
Durhamstown, Bohermeen,
Navan, Co Meath
Tel 046-9073805
Email bohermeenparish1@gmail.com

**CARNAROSS**
*St Ciaran, Carnaross*
*Sacred Heart, Mullaghea*
Rt Rev Mgr John Hanly PP
Parochial House, Carnaross,
Kells, Co Meath
Tel 046-9245904

**CASTLEPOLLARD**
*St Michael's, Castlepollard*
*St Michael's, Castletown*
*St Mary's, Finea*
Very Rev Patrick A. Moore PP, VF
Parochial House, Castlepollard,
Co Westmeath
Tel 044-9661126/087-2510855
Fax 044-9661881
Email fr.patrick.moore@gmail.com
Rev Sean Connaughton (SSC)
Castletown-Finea, Co Westmeath
Tel 043-6681141

**CASTLETOWN-GEOGHEGAN**
*St Michael, Castletown-Geoghegan*
*St Stephen, Tyrrellspass*
*St Peter, Raheenmore*
Rev Barry Condron PP
Tyrrellspass, Co Westmeath
Tel 044-9223115
Email tyrrellspass1@eircom.net
Rev Benny Bohan
Parochial House,
Castletown-Geoghegan, Co Westmeath
Tel 044-9226118
Email castletown8@eircom.net

**CASTLETOWN-KILPATRICK**
*St Patrick's, Castletown-Kilpatrick*
*St Colmcille's, Fletcherstown*
Very Rev Martin McErlean PP
Parochial House, Castletown-Kilpatrick,
Navan, Co Meath
Tel 046-9055789
*Office:* Tel 046-9054142

**CLARA**
*St Brigid's, Clara*
*Sts Peter & Paul, Horseleap*
Very Rev Patrick Keary PP, VF
Parochial House, Clara, Co Offaly
Tel 057-9331170 Fax 057-9330100
Email claraparish@eircom.net

**CLONMELLON**
*Sts Peter & Paul, Clonmellon*
*St Bartholomew, Killallon*
Very Rev Sean Garland PP
Parochial House, Clonmellon
Navan, Co Meath
Tel 046-9433124
Email clonmellonparish@eircom.net

**COLLINSTOWN**
*St Mary's, Collinstown*
*St Feichin's, Fore*
Very Rev Patrick Donnelly PP
Parochial House, Collinstown,
Co Westmeath
Tel 044-9666326

## Irish Catholic Directory 2014

*21st May 2014.* A copy of the above came in here at the beginning of the year intended for the LIBRARY. But (as far as I know) it never reached the Library. It is an item which should be there. If anyone knows where the stray is now I would appreciate if it could be placed on the library desk.

*Thank you,*
*G. McNicholas.*

## COOLE (MAYNE)
*Immaculate Conception, Coole*
*St John the Baptist, Whitehall*
Very Rev Oliver Skelly PP
Parochial House, Coole, Co Westmeath
Tel 044-9661191
Email cooleparish@gmail.com
Website coolemayneparish.ie

## CURRAHA
*St Andrew's*
Very Rev Brendan Ferris PP
Parochial House, Curraha, Co Meath
Tel 01-8350136
Website www.currahaparish.ie

## DELVIN
*Assumption, Delvin*
*St Livinus, Killulagh*
Very Rev Seamus Heaney PP
Parochial House, Delvin, Co Westmeath
Tel 044-9664127
Email info@delvinparish.ie
Website www.delvinparish.ie

## DONORE
*Nativity, Donore*
*Nativity, Rosnaree*
Rev Anthony Gonoude Adm
Parochial House, Donore,
Drogheda, Co Louth
Tel 041-9823137
Email donoreparish@iolfree.ie

## DROGHEDA, HOLY FAMILY
Very Rev David Bradley PP
The Presbytery, Ballsgrove,
Drogheda, Co Louth
Tel 041-9831991
Email holyfamilyballsgrove@eircom.net
Website www.holyfamilydrogheda.ie

## DROGHEDA, ST MARY'S
Very Rev Philip Gaffney PP
Email gaffney.phil21@gmail.com
Rev Joseph Campbell CC
Email frjoecampbell@gmail.com
St Mary's, Drogheda, Co Louth
Tel 041-9834958 Fax 041-9845144
*Parish Office:* Tel 041-9834587
Email stmarysdrogheda@gmail.com
Website www.stmarysdrogheda.ie

## DRUMCONRATH
*Sts Peter & Paul, Drumconrath*
*Sts Brigid & Patrick, Meath Hill*
Very Rev Finian Connaughton PP
Parochial House, Drumconrath,
Navan, Co Meath
Tel 041-6854146
Email drumconrathparish@topmail.ie
Website www.drumconrathparish.ie

## DRUMRANEY
*Immaculate Conception, Drumraney*
*Immaculate Conception, Tang*
*Immaculate Conception, Forgney*
Very Rev Oliver Devine PP
Drumraney, Athlone, Co Westmeath
Tel 044-9356207
Email oliver_devine@eircom.net

Rev Jerry Murphy (SSC) CC
St Mary's, Tang,
Ballymahon, Co Longford
Tel 0906-432214

## DULEEK
*St Cianan, Duleek*
*St Thérèse, Bellewstown*
Very Rev John Conlon PP
Parochial House, Duleek, Co Meath
Tel 041-9823205
Email duleekparish@eircom.net
Website www.duleek.net

## DUNBOYNE
*SS Peter & Paul, Dunboyne*
*St Brigid & Sacred Heart, Kilbride*
Rt Rev Mgr Dermot Farrell PP, VG
Parochial House, Dunboyne, Co Meath
Tel 01-8255342 Fax 01-8252321
Email dunboynekilbride.parish@gmail.com
Website www.dunboynekilbrideparish.org
Rev Ciaran Clarke CC
2 Orchard Court, Dunboyne, Co Meath
Rev Gabriel Flynn DD, PC
1 Orchard Court, Dunboyne, Co Meath
Tel 01-8255342/8086554
Email gabriel.flynn@materdei.dcu.ie

## DUNDERRY
*Assumption, Dunderry*
*Assumption, Robinstown*
*Assumption, Kilbride*
Very Rev Noel Horneck PP
Parochial House, Dunderry,
Navan, Co Meath
Tel 046-9431433 Fax 046-9431474

## DUNSHAUGHLIN
*Sts Patrick & Seachnall, Dunshaughlin*
*St Martin, Culmullen*
Very Rev Joseph Clavin PP, VF
Parochial House, Dunshaughlin,
Co Meath
Tel 01-8259114 Fax 01-8011614
Rev Colm Browne CC
St Martin's, Culmullen, Drumree,
Co Meath
Tel 01-8241976
Email dunshaughlinparish@eircom.net
Website
www.dunshaughlin-culmullenparish.ie

## DYSART
*St Patrick's, Dysart*
*Assumption, Loughanavalley*
Very Rev Philip O'Connor PP
Parochial House, Dysart, Mullingar,
Co Westmeath
Tel 044-9226122
Email dysart.parish@gmail.com

## EGLISH
*St James, Eglish*
*St John the Baptist, Rath*
Very Rev John Moorhead PP
Parochial House, Eglish, Birr, Co Offaly
Tel 057-9133010
Website www.eglishdrumcullen.com

## ENFIELD
*St Michael, Rathmolyon*
*Assumption, Jordanstown*
Very Rev Michael Whittaker PP
The Presbytery, Enfield, Co Meath
Tel 046-9541282
Email michaeljwhittaker@gmail.com
Rev Timothy Mejida
Parochial House, Rathmolyon, Co Meath
Tel 046-9555212
Email tmejida@yahoo.com
Website www.enfieldparish.ie

## GLASSON–TUBBERCLAIRE
*Immaculate Conception, Tubberclaire*
Very Rev Seamus Mulvany PP
Parochial House, Tubberclaire-Glasson,
Athlone, Co Westmeath
Tel 090-6485103
Email tubberclairchurch@gmail.com
Website www.tubberclairchurch.com

## JOHNSTOWN
*Nativity, Johnstown*
*Assumption, Walterstown*
Very Rev Michael Cahill PP
Parochial House, Johnstown,
Navan, Co Meath
Tel 046-9021731
Email johnsnavan@eircom.net

## KELLS
*Columcille, Kells*
*Immaculate Conception, Girley*
Very Rev John Byrne PP, VF
Email jplowebyrne@eircom.net
Rev Liam Malone CC
Parochial House, Kells, Co Meath
Tel 046-9240213 Fax 046-9293475
Email info@kellsparish.ie
Website www.kellsparish.ie

## KILBEG
*Nativity of Our Lady, Kilbeg*
*St Michael, Staholmog*
Very Rev Séamus Houlihan Adm
Parochial House, Kilbeg, Kells, Co Meath
Tel 046-9246604

## KILBEGGAN
*St James, Kilbeggan*
*St Hugh, Rahugh*
Very Rev Brendan Corrigan PP
Parochial House, Harbour Road,
Kilbeggan, Co Westmeath
Tel 057-9332155
Email info@kilbegganparish.ie
Website www.kilbegganparish.ie

## KILCLOON
*St Oliver Plunkett, Kilcloon*
*The Assumption, Batterstown*
*Little Chapel of the Assumption, Kilcock*
Very Rev Stan Deegan PP
Parochial House, Batterstown,
Dunboyne, Co Meath
Tel 01-8259267
Eail kilcloonparish@gmail.com

## KILCORMAC
*Nativity of the Blessed Virgin Mary, Kilcormac*
*St Brigid, Mountbolus*
Very Rev Michael Walsh PP
Parochial House, Kilcormac, Co Offaly
Tel 057-9135989
Very Rev Edmond Daly AP
Mount Bolus, Tullamore, Co Offaly
Tel 057-9354035
Website
www.kilcormackillougheyparish.com

## KILDALKEY
*St Dympna's*
Very Rev Mark Mohan PP
Parochial House, Ballivor, Co Meath
Tel 046-9546488
Parish email
ballivorkildalkeyparish@eircom.net
Website www.ballivorkildalkey.ie

## KILLUCAN
*St Joseph's, Rathwire*
*St Brigid's, Raharney*
Very Rev Richard Matthews PP, VF
Parochial House, Killucan, Co Westmeath
Tel 044-9374127
Email killucanparish@eircom.net

## KILMESSAN
*Nativity of Our Lady, Kilmessan*
*Assumption, Dunsany*
Very Rev Terence Toner PP
Parochial House, Kilmessan, Co Meath
Tel 046-9025172
Email terencetoner@eircom.net

## KILSKYRE
*St Alphonsus Liguori, Kilskyre*
*Assumption, Ballinlough*
Very Rev John Brogan PP
Parochial House, Kilskyre, Kells, Co Meath
Tel 046-9243623
Email kilskyreparish1@eircom.net
Website www.kilskyreballinlough.ie

## KINGSCOURT
*Immaculate Conception, Kingscourt*
*St Joseph's, Corlea*
*Our Lady of Mount Carmel, Muff*
Very Rev Gerard MacCormack PP
Parochial House, Kingscourt, Co Cavan
Tel 042-9667314 Fax 042-9668141
Email info@kingscourtparish.ie
Website www.kingscourtparish.ie

## KINNEGAD
*Assumption, Kinnegad*
*St Agnes, Coralstown*
*St Finian, Clonard*
Very Rev Thomas Gilroy PP
Rev Emmanuelle Abuh
Parochial House, Kinnegad, Co Meath
Tel 044-9375117
Rt Rev Mgr Eamonn Marron PE
Parochial House, Raharney, Co Westmeath
Tel 044-9374271
Email kinnegadparish@eircom.net
Website www.kinnegadparish.ie
*Parish Office:* 044-9391030
Fridays 10.00 am-4.00 pm

## LAYTOWN-MORNINGTON
*Sacred Heart, Laytown*
*Star of the Sea, Mornington*
Very Rev Denis McNelis PP, VF
Parochial House, Laytown, Co Meath
Tel 041-9827258
Website www.sacredheartlaytown.com
Rt Rev Mgr William Cleary AP
Star of the Sea, Mornington, Co Meath
Tel 041-9827384 Fax 041-9827324
Email mgtparish@eircom.net
Website www.morningtonchurch.com

## LOBINSTOWN
*Holy Cross*
Very Rev Michael Sheerin PP
Parochial House, Lobinstown,
Navan, Co Meath
Tel 046-9053155
Email frmlsheerin@eircom.net

## LONGWOOD
*Assumption, Longwood*
*Assumption, Killyon*
Very Rev Patrick Kearney PP
Parochial House, Longwood, Co Meath
Tel 046-9555009

## MILLTOWN
*St Matthew, Milltown*
*St Matthew, Empor*
*St Patrick, Moyvore*
Very Rev William Fitzsimons PP
Parochial House, Milltown,
Rathconrath, Co Westmeath
Tel 044-9355106

## MOUNTNUGENT
*St Brigid, Mountnugent*
*Sts Brigid & Fiach, Ballinacree*
Very Rev Oliver J. Devine PP
Parochial House, Mountnugent, Co Cavan
Tel 049-8540123
Email froliverdevine@eircom.net

## MOYNALTY
*Assumption, Moynalty*
*Assumption, Newcastle*
Very Rev Joseph McEvoy PP
Parochial House, Moynalty,
Kells, Co Meath
Tel 046-9244305
Email moynaltyparish@eircom.net
Website www.moynaltyparish.ie

## MOYNALVEY
*Nativity, Moynalvey*
*Assumption, Kiltale*
Very Rev David Brennan Adm
Parochial House, Moynalvey,
Summerhill, Co Meath
Tel 046-9557031
Email mknotices@gmail.com
Website www.moynalveykiltaleparish.com

## MULTYFARNHAM
*St Nicholas, Multyfarnham*
*St Patrick's, Leney*
Very Rev Gerry Boyle PP
Parochial House, Multyfarnham,
Co Westmeath
Tel 044-9371124

## NOBBER
*St John the Baptist*
Very Rev Séamus Houlihan PP
Parochial House, Nobber, Co Meath
Tel 046-9052197
Email nobberparish@eircom.net

## OLDCASTLE
*St Brigid, Oldcastle*
*St Mary, Moylough*
Very Rev Ray Kelly PP
Parochial House, Oldcastle, Co Meath
Tel 049-8541142 Fax 049-8542865
Email oldcastle@gmail.com
Website www.oldcastle.myparish.eu

## ORISTOWN
*St Catherine, Oristown*
*St John the Baptist, Kilberry*
Very Rev John O'Brien PP
Parochial House, Oristown,
Kells, Co Meath
Tel 046-9054124
Email oristownparish@eircom.net
Website www.oristownparish.com

## RAHAN
*St Carthage, Killina*
*St Patrick, The Island*
*St Colman, Mucklagh*
Very Rev Martin Carley PP
Parochial House, Killina, Rahan,
Tullamore, Co Offaly
Tel/Fax 057-9355917
Email rahanparish@gmail.com
Website www.rahanparish.ie

## RATHKENNY
*Sts Louis & Mary, Rathkenny*
*St Patrick, Rushwee*
*St Brigid, Grangegeeth*
Very Rev John Hogan Adm
Parochial House, Rathkenny, Co Meath
Tel 046-9054138
Email johnhogan_ie@yahoo.com
Website www.rathkennyparish.ie

## RATOATH
*Holy Trinity*
Very Rev Gerard Stuart PP
Parochial House, Ratoath, Co Meath
Tel 01-8256207 Fax 01-8256662
Email ratoathparish@eircom.net
Website www.ratoathparish.ie
Rev Brendan Ludlow CC
35a Moatlands, Ratoath, Co Meath
Tel 01-8256207

## ROCHFORTBRIDGE
*Immaculate Conception, Rochfortbridge*
*Sacred Heart, Meedin*
*St Joseph, Milltownpass*
Very Rev William Coleman PP
Parochial House, Rochfortbridge,
Co Westmeath
Tel 044-9222107
Email rochfortbridgeparish@eircom.net

**Allianz ⓘ**

## SKRYNE

*St Colmcille, Skryne*
*Immaculate Conception, Rathfeigh*
Very Rev Thomas O'Mahony PP
Parochial House, Skryne, Tara, Co Meath
Tel 046-9025152
Email thomasomahony03@gmail.com
Very Rev Joseph Gleeson PE
Rathfeigh, Tara, Co Meath
Tel/Fax 041-9825159
Website
www.skryneandrathfeighparish.ie

## SLANE

*St Patrick, Slane*
*Assumption, Monknewtown*
Very Rev Joseph Deegan PP
Parochial House, Slane, Co Meath
Tel 041-9824249
Email parochialhouse@slaneparish.com
Website www.slaneparish.com

## STAMULLEN

*St Patrick, Stamullen*
*St Mary's, Julianstown*
Very Rev Declan Kelly PP
Preston Hill, Stamullen, Co Meath
Tel/Fax 01-8412647
Parish Email secsj@eircom.net
Rev Robert McCabe CF
Gormanston Military Camp,
Gormanston, Co Meath
Tel 01-8413990
Email robertmccabe@dioceseofmeath.ie
www.militarychaplaincy.ie

## SUMMERHILL

*Our Lady of Lourdes, Dangan*
*Assumption, Coole*
Very Rev Michael Meade PP
Rev David O'Hanlon CC
Parochial House, Summerhill, Co Meath
Tel 046-9557021
Email coolsummerhillparish@gmail.com
Website www.summerhillparish.ie

## TAGHMON

*Assumption, Taghmon*
*St Joseph, Turin*
Very Rev Declan Smith PP
Parochial House, Taghmon,
Mullingar, Co Westmeath
Tel 044-9372140

## TRIM

*St Patrick, Trim*
*St Brigid, Boardsmill*
Very Rev Seán Henry PP
Rev Declan Kelly CC
Email declanoppkelly@gmail.com
Parochial House, Trim, Co Meath
Tel 046-9431251
Parish email spcctrim@eircom.net

## TUBBER

*Holy Family, Tubber*
*St Thomas the Apostle, Rosemount*
Very Rev Tony Gavin Adm
Rosemount, Moate, Co Westmeath
Tel 090-6436110
Email frtonygavin@eircom.net

## TULLAMORE

*Assumption, Tullamore*
*St Colmcille, Durrow*
Very Rev Joseph Gallagher PP
Rt Rev Mgr Seán Heaney AP, VG
Email heaneysean@eircom.net
Rev Shane Crombie CC
Email frshane@gmail.com
Parochial House, Tullamore, Co Offaly
Tel 057-9321587
Email tullamoreparishsecretary@gmail.com
Website www.tullamoreparish.ie

## INSTITUTIONS AND THEIR CHAPLAINS

**St Loman's Hospital**
Mullingar, Co Westmeath
Tel 044-9340191

**Longford & Westmeath General Hospital**
Mullingar, Co Westmeath
Tel 044-9340221
Priests of the parish

**Our Lady's Hospital**
Navan, Co Meath
Tel 046-9021210
Priests of the parish

**Tullamore General Hospital**
Tullamore, Co Offaly
Tel 057-9321501
Priests of the parish

## PRIESTS OF THE DIOCESE ELSEWHERE

Rev Anthony Draper DD
All Hallows College,
Drumcondra, Dublin 9
Tel 01-373745
Email tdraper@allhallows.ie
Rev Ronan Drury
St Patrick's College, Maynooth, Co Kildare
Tel 01-6285222
Rev Mark English
c/o Bishop's House, Dublin Road,
Mullingar, Co Westmeath
Email markjpenglish@gmail.com
Rev Dwayne Gavin
Centre Culturel Irlandais,
5 Rue des Irlandais, 75005 Paris, France
Rev David Hanratty
Tierhogar, Portarlington, Co Laois
Tel 057-8645719
Rev Thomas O'Connor DD
St Patrick's College, Maynooth, Co Kildare
Tel 01-6285222

## RETIRED PRIESTS

Very Rev Ray Brady
c/o Bishop's House, Mullingar
Very Rev Eamonn Butler PE
10 Lynn Heights, Mullingar, Co Westmeath
Tel 044-9344008
Very Rev Patrick Casey PE
5 St Mary's Terrace, Bishopsgate Street,
Mullingar, Co Westmeath
Tel 044-9342746
Very Rev Michael V. Daly PE
35 Herbert Place, Navan, Co Meath
Tel 046-9093935

Rt Rev Mgr Edward Dunne PE
Knightsbridge Nursing Home,
Trim, Co Meath
Very Rev Andrew Farrell PE
Knightsbridge Nursing Home,
Trim, Co Meath
Very Rev Sean Fay PE
Knightsbridge Nursing Home,
Trim, Co Meath
Very Rev Edward Flynn PE
Multyfarnham Retirement Village,
Co Westmeath
Very Rev Joseph Garvey PE
Beaufort House, Navan, Co Meath
Very Rev Lauri Halpin PE
Knightsbridge Nursing Home,
Trim, Co Meath
Very Rev John Kiernan PE
Kilberry, Navan, Co Meath
Rev Barney Maxwell PE
Empor, Ballymacargy, Co Westmeath
Very Rev Patrick A. Mackin PE
Bohermeen, Navan, Co Meath
Tel 046-9021439
Email frpatmack@gmail.com
Very Rev Frank McNamara PE
Newbrook Nursing Home,
Mullingar, Co Westmeath
Very Rev Matthew Mollin PE
4 St Finbar, Maryfield, Chapelizod,
Co Dublin
Tel 01-6268851
Very Rev Colm Murtagh PE
1 Greenville, Kildalkey, Co Meath
Tel 046-9435133
Very Rev Eamonn O'Brien PE
Newbrook Nursing Home,
Mullingar, Co Westmeath
Very Rev Gerard Rice PE
Moyglare Nursing Home, Maynooth,
Co Kildare
Rt Rev Mgr Thomas Woods DD
Newbrook Nursing Home,
Mullingar, Co Westmeath

## PERSONAL PRELATURE

**OPUS DEI**
Lismullin Conference Centre
Navan, Co Meath
Tel 046-9026936
Rev James Gavigan, Chaplain

## RELIGIOUS ORDERS AND CONGREGATIONS

## PRIESTS

**BENEDICTINE MONKS OF PERPETUAL ADORATION**
Silverstream Priory
Stamullen, Co Meath
Tel 01-8417142
Email prior@cenacleosb.org
*Prior:* Very Rev Dom Mark Daniel Kirby (OSB)
Rev Dom Benedict Maria Andersen
2 novices, 2 postulants
Community Email info@cenacleosb.org
Monastery Website http://cenacleosb.org/
Vocations Website
http://cenacleosb.org/vocations/
Vultus Christi Weblog
http://vultus.stblogs.org/

## CAMILLIANS
St Camillus Community,
Killucan, Co Westmeath
Tel 044-74115
*Superior:* Rev Frank Monks (OSCam)
Nursing Centre
Tel 044-74196

## CARMELITES (OCARM)
Carmelite Priory,
Moate, Co Westmeath
Tel 090-6481160/6481398
Fax 090-6481879
Email carmelitemoate@eircom.net
*Prior:* Rev Martin Ryan (OCarm)

## FRANCISCANS
LaVerna Friary,
Gormanston, Co Meath
Tel 01-8412203 Fax 01-8412685
Email friary@gormanstoncollege.ie
*Guardian:* Rev Ulic Troy (OFM)

Franciscan Abbey,
Multyfarnham, Co Westmeath
Tel 044-9371114/9371137
Fax 044-9371387
*Guardian:* Rev Liam McCarthy (OFM)

## HOLY SPIRIT CONGREGATION
Spiritan Missionaries,
Ardbraccan, Navan, Co Meath
Tel 046-9021441
*Community Leader*
Rev Peter Conaty (CSSp)

## ST COLUMBAN'S MISSIONARY SOCIETY
St Columban's, Dalgan Park,
Navan, Co Meath
Tel 046-9021525
*Regional Director:* Rev Patrick Raleigh (SSC)
*Regional Vice-Director*
Rev Padraig O'Donovan (SSC)

St Columban's Retirement Home,
Dalgan Park, Navan, Co Meath
Tel 046-9021525
*Director:* Rev Bernard Mulkerins (SSC)

## SALESIANS
Salesian House,
Warrenstown, Drumree, Co Meath
Tel 01-8259761
Community 01-8259894
Fax 01-8240298
*Rector:* Rev P. J. Nyland (SDB)

## SOCIETY OF ST PAUL
St Paul Book Centre,
Castle Street, Athlone, Co Westmeath
Tel/Fax 090-6492882
Email saintpaul_books@yahoo.com

# BROTHERS

## CHRISTIAN BROTHERS
St Joseph's, Kells, Co Meath
Tel 046-9240239
*Community Leader:* Br Michael Keane
Community: 4

Edmund Rice Centre
Bective Street, Kells, Co Meath
Tel 046-9240239

## FRANCISCAN BROTHERS
The Monastery, Clara, Co Offaly
Tel 057-9331130
*Local Minister:* Br Charles Conway
Community: 5

# SISTERS

## BLESSED SACRAMENT SISTERS
Marian Hostel, High Street,
Tullamore, Co Offaly
Tel 057-9321182
Tel 057-9351371 (Convent)
Community: 3
Hostel for women
Day centre for children with mental
handicap. Tel 057-9323774
Activation and resource centre for
people with special needs.
Tel 057-9351629

## CHARITY OF JESUS AND MARY SISTERS
St Mary's Convent, South Hill, Delvin,
Co Westmeath
Tel 044-64108/9 Fax 044-64488
*Contact:* Sr Kathleen O'Connor
Community: 3
Residential centre transferred to
Muiriesa Foundation

Aisling, Mitchelstown,
Delvin, Co Westmeath
Tel 044-64379
*Contact:* Sr Kathleen O'Connor
Community: 2

## CONGREGATION OF THE SISTERS OF MERCY
St Mary's Convent of Mercy, Athlumney,
Navan, Co Meath
Tel 046-9021271
*Facilitator:* Sr Consilio Rock
Community: 8

Sisters of Mercy,
6 Meadowlands, Athboy, Co Meath
Tel 046-9430085

Sisters of Mercy,
3 St Brigid's Court, Connaught Street,
Athboy, Co Meath
Tel 046-9430047

Convent of Mercy, Charlestown,
Clara, Co Offaly
Tel 057-9331184

202 Ballsgrove,
Drogheda, Co Louth
Tel 041-9830160

38 Congress Avenue,
Drogheda, Co Louth
Tel 041-9837876

Convent of Mercy, Kells, Co Meath
Tel 046-9240159
Community: 11

Sisters of Mercy
1 Circular Road, Kells, Co Meath
Tel 046-9249381

Cill na Gréine, Convent of Mercy,
Kells, Co Meath
Tel 046-9252536

Sisters of Mercy,
13 Grand Priory, Kells, Co Meath
Tel 046-9249027

Convent of Mercy, Tullamore Road,
Kilbeggan, Co Westmeath
Tel 057-9332161
*Leader:* Sr Sacred Heart Beirne
Community: 5

Convent of Mercy,
Kilcormac, Co Offaly
Tel 057-9335007
Community: 4

Sisters of Mercy, Ard Aoibhinn
Mount Bolus, Co Offaly
Tel 057-9354867

Sisters of Mercy, Loughcrew,
Laytown, Co Meath
Tel 041-9827432
Community: 2

29 Green Road,
Mullingar, Co Westmeath
Tel 044-9341680

10 College Court, College Street,
Mullingar, Co Westmeath
Tel 044-9330768

St Joseph's,
Leighsbrook, Navan, Co Meath
Tel 046-9071760
Community: 6

Sisters of Mercy,
Mount Carmel, 15 Aylesbury Lodge,
Navan, Co Meath
Tel 046-9071757
Community: 5

Sisters of Mercy, 4 Ferndale,
Navan, Co Meath
Tel 046-9023844

Sisters of Mercy, Sacre Coeur,
The Commons, Navan, Co Meath
Tel 046-9021970

Sisters of Mercy,
Rochfortbridge, Co Westmeath
Tel 044-9222130

Main Street,
Rochfortbridge, Co Westmeath
Tel 044-9222461

Convent of Mercy, Trim, Co Meath
Tel 046-9431264
Shared Leadership
Community: 12

Sisters of Mercy,
1 Mornington Way, Trim, Co Meath
Tel 046-9437025 Fax 046-9437025
Community: 4

Convent of Mercy,
St Joseph's, Tullamore, Co Offaly
Tel 057-9321221
Community: 33
*Leaders:* Sr Madeleine Gavigan, Sr Elma Peppard, Sr Agnes Heffernan

Sisters of Mercy, 130 Arden Vale,
Tullamore, Co Offaly
Tel 057-9352733

Sisters of Mercy, 47 Tara Crescent,
Clonminch, Tullamore, Co Offaly
Tel 057-9322150

69 Carne Hill, Johnstown,
Navan, Co Meath
Tel 046-9091772

42 Blackcastle Estate,
Navan, Co Meath

Sisters of Mercy,
Blackfriary, Trim, Co Meath
Tel 046-9437759

Sisters of Mercy,
5 Headfort Road, Kells, Co Meath
Tel 046-9249775
Community: 3

6 Friars Park, Trim, Co Meath
Tel 046-9437037
Community: 3

Sisters of Mercy, 133 College Hill,
Irishtown, Mullingar, Co Westmeath
Tel 044-9335303

St Colmcille's, Laytown, Co Meath
Tel 041-9887904
Community: 4

20 The Crescent, Athlumney,
Navan, Co Meath
Tel 046-9088940

135 Droim Liath, Collins Lane,
Tullamore, Co Offaly
Tel 057-9361133

No. 2 Bishopsgate Street,
Mullingar, Co Westmeath
Tel 044-9396721

Apartment 6, Knightsbridge Village,
Longwood Road, Trim, Co Meath
Tel 046-9486028

38 Cill Bán, Collins Lane,
Tullamore, Co Offaly
Tel 057-9361422

1 Oakfield, Church Road,
Tullamore, Co Offaly

Harbour Road,
Kilbeggan, Co Westmeath
Tel 057-9332147

No. 6 The Carmelite Centre,
Moate, Co Westmeath
Tel 090-6466525

3 Roselawn, High Street,
Tullamore, Co Offaly
Tel 057-9352077

**FRANCISCAN MISSIONARIES OF OUR LADY**
Franciscan Convent, Ballinderry,
Mullingar, Co Westmeath
Tel 044-9352000
*Superior:* Sr Cecilia Cody
Email ceciliacody1@gmail.com
Commmunity: 4

**HOLY FAMILY OF ST EMILIE DE RODAT**
Arden Road,
Tullamore, Co Offaly
Tel 057-9321577
*Superior:* Sr Mary-Paul English
Email mpe1809@eircom.net
Community: 7

**LORETO (IBVM)**
Loreto Community,
St Michael's, Navan,
Co Meath
Tel 046-9021740
Email loretonavan@eircom.net
*Co-Leaders*
Sr Máire Lagan, Sr Rosemary O'Connor
Community: 13
Loreto Secondary School
Tel 046-9023830
Day Care Centre

Loreto Sisters, Athlumney Road,
Navan, Co Meath
Tel 046-9073423
Community: 2
Education

Anam Aras, Laytown, Co Meath
Tel 041-9828952
Superior: Sr Julie Clinton
Retreat centre

**MEDICAL MISSIONARIES OF MARY**
Bruach na Mara,
Bettystown, Co Meath
Tel 041-9827207
Email mmmbettystown@eircom.net

**MISSIONARY SISTERS OF THE HOLY ROSARY**
Holy Rosary Convent,
Coast Road, Bettystown, Co Meath
Tel 041-9827362
Community: 4
Pastoral

**PRESENTATION SISTERS**
Killina, Rayan, Tullamore, Co Offaly
Tel 057-9355920
*Community Leader:* Sr Joan Bland
Community: 6
School and pastoral ministry
Scoil Naomh Seosamh Primary School
Tel 056-9355790
Presentation Secondary School
Tel 057-9355706

**VISITATION SISTERS**
Visitation Sisters,
Dublin Road, Drogheda, Co Louth
Tel 041-9838184
*Superior*
Sr Josephine Thérèse Gallagher
Email visitationstamullen@gmail.com
Community: 3

# EDUCATIONAL INSTITUTIONS

**Diocesan Office for Post-Primary Schools**
*Director:* Mr Liam Murphy BA, HDE
Moatlands, Navan, Co Meath
Tel 046-9021847

**St Finian's College**
Mullingar, Co Westmeath
Tel 044-9348313 Fax 044-9345275
*President:* Rev Paul Connell PhD
Tel 044-9348672
*Chaplain:* Very Rev Gerry Boyle PP

**St Mary's Diocesan School**
Beamore Road,
Drogheda, Co Louth
Tel Office: 041-9837581
Staff: 041-9838001 Fax 041-9841151
*Principal:* Mr Jim Brady
*Chaplain:* Rev Joseph Campbell CC

**St Patrick's Classical School**
Mount Rivers, Moatlands,
Navan, Co Meath
Tel 046-9021847
*Principal:* Mr Colm O'Rourke
*Chaplain:* Mr Mark Donnelly

**Coláiste Choilm**
Tullamore, Co Offaly
Tel 057-9351756
*Headmaster:* Mr Colin Roddy
*Chaplain:* Rev Shane Crombie CC

**Boyne Community School**
Trim, Co Meath
Tel 046-9431358
*Principal:* Ms Elizabeth Cahill
*Chaplain:* Ms Aoife Daly

**Ashbourne Community School**
Ashbourne, Co Meath
Tel 01-8353066
*Principal:* Ms Aine O'Sullivan
*Chaplain:* Ms Frances Gildea

**St Peter's College**
Dunboyne, Co Meath
Tel 01-8252552
*Principal:* Ms Maureen Murray
*Chaplain:* Mr John Tighe

**St Ciaran's Community School**
Kells, Co Meath
Tel 046-9241551
*Principal:* Mr Francis Lafferty
*Chaplain:* Mr Sean Wright

**Athboy Community School**
Athboy, Co Meath
Tel 046-9487894
*Principal:* Mr Anthony Leavy
*Chaplain:* Mr Joe Tynan

**Ratoath College**
Jamestown, Ratoath, Co Meath
Tel 01-8254102
*Acting Principal*
Ms Oonagh Prendergast
*Chaplain:* Rev P.J. Nyland (SDB)

EDMUND RICE SCHOOLS TRUST
St Mary's Primary School,
Mullingar, Co Westmeath
Tel 044-9341517
*Principal:* Mrs Bernie McVeigh

Coláiste Mhuire Secondary School,
Mullingar, Co Westmeath
Tel 044-9344743
*Principal:* Mr Joe O'Meara

## CHARITABLE AND OTHER SOCIETIES

**Bethany Pastoral Care**
Cathedral Social Services Centre,
Mullingar, Co Westmeath
Tel 087-6309808

**Parish Community Centre**
Bishopsgate Street,
Mullingar, Co Westmeath
Tel 044-9343432

**Society of St Vincent de Paul**
Ozanam Holiday Home, Mornington,
Co Meath
Tel 041-9827924

# DIOCESE OF OSSORY

Patron of the Diocese
St Kieran, 5 March

INCLUDES MOST OF COUNTY KILKENNY
AND PORTIONS OF COUNTIES LAOIS AND OFFALY

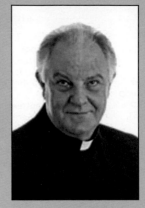

**Most Rev Seamus Freeman (SAC) DD**
Bishop of Ossory;
born 23 February 1944;
ordained priest 12 June 1971;
Consecrated Bishop of Ossory
2 December 2007

Residence: Blessed Felix House,
Tilbury Place, James's Street,
Kilkenny
Tel 056-7762448
Fax 056-7763753
Email bishop@ossory.ie
Website www.ossory.ie

## ST MARY'S CATHEDRAL, KILKENNY

At the end of the twelfth century, during the Episcopate of Felix O'Dulany, Kilkenny replaced Aghaboe as the seat of the Bishops of Ossory. The building of the new cathedral – dedicated to St Canice – began early in the thirteenth century by Hugh de Rous, the first Anglo-Norman Bishop of Ossory (1202–18). The commencement date is generally given as 1210, with completion c. 1270.

With the defeat of the Confederation by Oliver Cromwell, St Canice's Cathedral reverted to Protestant hands, leaving the Roman Catholics without a cathedral. A small chapel in St Mary's parish, St James's Chapel – built c. 1700 – just outside St James's Gate, functioned as a cathedral until its replacement by St Mary's Cathedral, which became available for use in 1857.

William Kinsella, appointed Bishop of Ossory in 1829, initiated the building of St Mary's Cathedral. William Deane Butler, the architect for St Kieran's College and the parochial church of Ballyragget, was the chosen architect. His neo-Gothic style marked a new and ambitious phase in church architecture. This reflected the newfound confidence of Irish Catholics, which only as recently as 1829 had become fully emancipated and enjoyed the same rights as their Protestant peers.

The site chosen for the new cathedral was occupied by Burrell's Hall, a Georgian-style house. This residence had been the early home of St Kieran's College, established in 1782 – the first Irish Catholic Academy in a country 'awakening from the penal laws'. Subscribers from St Mary's parish pledged over £1,500, including £100 from Bishop Kinsella and £20 from Fr Theobald Matthew. Money was also raised by door-to-door and street collections, by the sale of site materials and by bank loans. Work began on the site in April 1843. By the time Bishop Kinsella died in December 1845, the foundations had been fully laid and the walls of the cathedral were up to seven feet high.

The new Bishop, Edmond Walsh, assisted by Fr Robert O'Shea and an active lay committee, continued the project. They kept it going throughout the famine years, providing much-needed work locally. The cost of the original building was estimated at £25,000, funded by diocesan collections and bank loans. The grand opening took place on 4 October 1857.

The cathedral has been described as being 'of pure Gothic design, built entirely of chiselled limestone and cruciform in shape'. The tower, originally designed for St Kieran's College, rises to a height of 186 feet. The high altar of Italian marble was purchased in Italy. The relics of Saints Cosmos and Damian and of St Clement were brought to Kilkenny from Rome. The relic of St Victoria came later. A statue of the Madonna by the acclaimed Italian sculptor Giovanni Maria Benzoni stands on the left of the sanctuary.

During Bishop Brownrigg's time (1884–1929), a new sacristy and chapter room were added to the cathedral structure. The centre porch and organ gallery were also remodelled and central heating was installed. James Pearse, the father of Patrick and William Pearse, erected the marble altar rails and the Sacred Heart altar, which stands at the right-hand side of the sanctuary. The cost was about £8,000. The refurbished cathedral was reopened on 9 April 1899.

Less than thirty years later, Bishop Patrick Collier carried out further work on the cathedral. The cost of this work, which amounted to £28,000, was borne by the faithful of Ossory. Later, during the Episcopacy of Peter Birch, the cathedral was again reordered to bring it into line with the perceived requirements of the Second Vatican Council.

At present, St Mary's Cathedral is undergoing a complete reordering initiated by Bishop Séamus Freeman SAC, under the supervision of a conservation architect. A newly established Blessed Sacrament Chapel, in the basement beneath the main sanctuary, continues the cathedral tradition of ongoing prayer which was at the heart of its foundation. Since its inception, the cathedral has served the faithful of the parish of St Mary's, the City of Kilkenny, the Diocese of Ossory and beyond. The reordering of our cathedral is a work in hand, and when completed will continue the tradition of St Mary's Cathedral – a place of worship, prayer, faith formation and welcome.

St Mary's Cathedral dominates the landscape of Kilkenny city and environs. It stands not only as a reminder of the faith and growing confidence of a far-off generation, but also of the continuing faith of a people united around their bishop in the heart of the Diocese of Ossory.

**Most Rev Laurence Forristal DD**
Retired Bishop of Ossory
Born 5 June 1931; ordained priest
21 December 1955; ordained Titular
Bishop of Rotdon and Auxiliary Bishop
of Dublin 20 January 1980; installed
Bishop of Ossory 13 September 1981;
Retired 14 September 2007
*Residence*
Molassy, Freshford Road, Kilkenny
Tel/Fax 056-7777928/087-2330369
Email laurenceforristal@ossory.ie

## CHAPTER

*Dean:* Very Rev Seamus McEvoy Adm
*Archdeacon*
Venerable Archdeacon Patrick Grace
*Members*
Very Rev Patrick Canon Dalton PP, VF
Very Rev Patrick Canon Duggan PE
Very Rev Laurence Canon Dunphy
Very Rev Brian Flynn PE
Very Rev Peter Canon Grant PE
Very Rev Thomas Canon Murphy PE
Very Rev Seán Canon O'Doherty PP
Rt Rev Mgr Michael Ryan PP, VG
*Honorary Members*
Very Rev Patrick Canon Brennan
Very Rev James Canon Carrigan
Rt Rev Mgr Thomas Maher
Very Rev Robert Canon Raftice

## ADMINISTRATION

**Vicars General**
Rt Rev Mgr Michael Ryan PP, VG

**Chancellor**
Very Rev William Dalton
c/o Diocesan Office, James's Street,
Kilkenny
Tel/Fax 056-7725287

**College of Consultors**
Rt Rev Mgr Michael Ryan PP, VG
Very Rev Dean Seamus McEvoy Adm
Rt Rev Mgr Kieron Kennedy
Very Rev Joseph Delaney
Very Rev Daniel Carroll
Rev Dermot Ryan
Very Rev Patrick Canon Dalton VF
Very Rev Anthony O'Connor
Very Rev Laurence Wallace

**Vicars Forane**
Very Rev Patrick Canon Dalton PP, VF
Very Rev Richard Scriven PP, VF
Very Rev Laurence Wallace PP, VF

**Financial Administrator**
Very Rev John Lalor
c/o Diocesan Office, James's Street,
Kilkenny
Tel 057-8735122
Email johnlalor@eircom.net

**Diocesan Secretary**
Mrs Frances Lennon
Diocesan Office, James's Street, Kilkenny
Tel 056-7762448 Fax 056-7763753
Email admin@ossory.ie

**Diocesan Finance**
Mrs Sheila Walshe
Diocesan Office, James's Street, Kilkenny
Email sheilawalshe@ossory.ie

**Finance Committee**
*Chairman:* Mr Geoffrey Meagher
Slievenamon, Granges Road, Kilkenny
Tel 056-7762092
*Secretary:* Mrs Joan Mahon
Diocesan Office, James's Street, Kilkenny
Tel 056-7762448

**Episcopal Vicars**
*Primary Education*
Very Rev Patrick Canon Dalton PP, VF
*Family and Social Affairs*
Rt Rev Mgr Kieron Kennedy
*Retired Priests*
Rev Thomas O'Toole

**Diocesan Pastoral Co-ordinator**
Very Rev Daniel Bollard PP
Thomastown, Co Kilkenny
Tel 056-7724279/087-6644858
Email dbollard@eircom.net

**Buildings and Properties Committee**
*Chairman:* Mr John Norris
Rathpatrick, Slieverue, Co Kilkenny
Tel 051-832495
*Secretary:* Mrs Frances Lennon
Diocesan Office, James's Street, Kilkenny
Tel 056-7762448

**Diocesan Clerk of Works**
Mr Joe Meagher
Edenvale Close, Kilkenny
Tel 087-2448041

## CATECHETICS EDUCATION

**Diocesan Advisers for Religious Education**
*Primary Education:* Sr Maria Comerford
Convent of Mercy, Callan, Co Kilkenny
Tel 087-2350719
Email mgcomerford@hotmail.com
*Post Primary:* Sr Louise Phelan
Convent of Mercy, Callan, Co Kilkenny
Tel 056-7725223/086-3404730

**Catholic Primary School Managers Association**
*Chairperson:* Mrs Maureen Daly
Granges Road, Kilkenny
*Secretary*
Very Rev Patrick Canon Dalton PP
Gowran, Co Kilkenny
Tel 056-7726128/086-8283478
Fax 056-7726134
Email pdalton@iolfree.ie

## LITURGY

**Liturgy Chairman**
Very Rev Richard Scriven PP, VF
The Rower, Thomastown, Co Kilkenny
Tel 087-2420033
Email rscriven@eircom.net

## PASTORAL

**Adult Faith Formation**
*Director:* Rev Dr Dermot Ryan
St Kieran's College, Kilkenny
Tel 056-7721086/086-6097483

**Vocations**
*Director:* Rev William Purcell
St Kieran's College, Kilkenny
Tel 056-7721086/087-6286858

**Safeguarding Children**
*Director of Safeguarding*
Sr Ena Kennedy
Safeguarding Office, Waterford Road, Kilkenny
Tel 056-7721685
Email safeguarding@ossory.ie

**Advisory Committee on Housing Elderly People**
*Chairman:* Very Rev Liam Cassin PP
Hugginstown, Co Kilkenny
Tel 087-2312354/056-7768678

**Chaplain to the Deaf**
Very Rev Daniel Carroll
St Fiacre's Gardens, Bohernatonish Road,
Loughboy, Kilkenny
Tel 056-7764400/087-9077769
Fax 056-7770173
Email dancarroll@ossory.ie

**Chaplain to the Travelling Community**
Rev Sean O'Connor
St John's Presbytery, Kilkenny
Tel 056-7756889/086-3895911
Email seanoconnor@ossory.ie

**Communications**
*Director:* Very Rev Daniel Carroll
St Fiacre's Gardens, Bohernatonish Road,
Loughboy, Kilkenny
Tel 056-7764400 Fax 056-7770173
Email dancarroll@ossory.ie

**Council of Priests**
*Chairman:* Very Rev Martin Delaney
Tel 0505-46213/086-2444594
Email delaneymartin@eircom.net

**Diocesan Forum Co-ordinator**
Sr Helen Maher
St Kieran's College, Kilkenny
Tel 056-7789714
Email diocesanforum@ossory.ie

**Ossory Diocesan Pastoral Council**
*Chairperson*
Rt Rev Mgr Michael Ryan PP, VG

**Middle Deanery Pastoral Council**
*Chairperson:* Ms Gemma Mulligan

**Southern Deanery Pastoral Council**
*Chairperson:* Mr Paschal Grace

**Northern Deanery Pastoral Council**
*Chairperson:* Mrs Kathleen Maher

**ACCORD**
Seville Lodge, Callan Road, Kilkenny
Tel 056-7722674
*Chaplain:* Rev Kieran O'Shea
Tel 086-8272828

**CURA**
Tel 056-7722739 Fax 056-7770240
*Co-ordinator:* Mrs Ann Coyne
*Chaplain:* Rev Sean O'Connor
Tel 086-3895911

**Ecumenism**
Very Rev James Murphy PP
St Canice's Presbytery, Dean Street,
Kilkenny
Tel 056-7752991/087-2609545
Email jimmurphy@ossory.ie

**Emigrant Commission**
Very Rev Laurence Wallace PP
Muckalee, Ballyfoyle, Co Kilkenny
Tel 056-4441271/087-2326807
Fax 056-4440007
Email muckalee@ossory.ie

**Lourdes Pilgrimage**
*Director:* Very Rev M. A. O'Connor PP
Glenmore, via New Ross, Co Kilkenny
Tel 051-880213/087-2517766

**Marriage Tribunal**
(See Marriage Tribunals section)

**Ossory Adoption and Referral Services**
Information and Guidance in all matters
in relation to adoption
Tel 056-7721685
Ms Mary Curtin, Social Service Centre,
Waterford Road, Kilkenny
Tel 056-7721685

**Ossory Priests Fraternal Fund**
*Administrator:* Mr James Kelly
Talbot's Inch, Freshford Road, Kilkenny
Tel 087-2455842

**Ossory Priests Society**
*Administrator:* Mrs Maura Joyce
Talbot's Inch, Freshford Road, Kilkenny
Tel 056-7765617

**Ossory Youth**
Desart Hall, New Street, Kilkenny
Tel 056-7761200 Fax 056-7752385
*Chairman:* Padraig Fleming
*CEO:* Ms Mary Mescal

**Pioneer Total Abstinence Association**
*Diocesan Director*
Very Rev Thomas Murphy PP
Ballyragget, Co Kilkenny
Tel 056-8833123/086-8130694

**Pontifical Mission Societies**
*Diocesan Director:* Very Rev John Lalor PP
Camross, Co Laois
Tel 057-8735122

## PARISHES

*Kilkenny city parishes are listed first.*
*Other parishes follow alphabetically.*
*Church titulars are in italics.*

**ST MARY'S**
*St Mary's Cathedral*
Rt Rev Mgr Kieron Kennedy Adm
Tel 056-7721253/087-2523521
Email kieronkennedy@ossory.ie
Rev William Purcell (*Parish Team*)
Tel 056-7721253/087-6286858
Email wpurcell@eircom.net
St Mary's Cathedral, Kilkenny
*Parish sister:* Sr Maria Comerford

**ST JOHN'S**
*St John the Evangelist, Holy Trinity,*
*St John the Baptist*
Email stjohns@ossory.ie
Website www.stjohnskilkenny.com
Very Rev Francis Purcell
Tel 056-7721072/086-6010001
Fax 056-7722209
Email jfpurcell@eircom.net
Rev Sean O'Connor
Tel 056-7756889/086-3895911
Fax 056-7722209
Email seanoconnor@ossory.ie
St John's Presbytery, Kilkenny

**ST CANICE'S**
*St Canice's*
Very Rev James Murphy PP
St Canice's Presbytery, Dean Street,
Kilkenny
Tel 056-7752991/087-2609545
Fax 056-7721533
Email jimmurphy@ossory.ie
Rev Kieran O'Shea CC
St Canice's Presbytery, Granges Road,
Kilkenny
Tel 056-7752994/086-8272828
Email kieranoshea@ossory.ie

**ST PATRICK'S**
*St Patrick's, St Fiacre's, St Joseph's*
Very Rev Daniel Carroll PP
Tel 087-9077769/056-7764400
Email dancarroll@ossory.ie
Rev Liam Taylor
Tel 056-7764400/086-8180954
Email liamtaylor@ossory.ie
Rev Roderick Whearty
Tel 056-7764400/086-8133661
St Fiacre's Gardens, Bohernatownish
Road, Loughboy, Kilkenny
Tel 056-7764400 Fax 056-7770173
Email stpatricksparish@ossory.ie
Website www.patricksparish.com

**AGHABOE**
*Immaculate Conception, St Canice*
Very Rev Noel Maher PP
Clough, Ballacolla, Portlaoise, Co Laois
Tel 057-878513 Fax 057-8738909
Email nmaher@eircom.net

**AGHAVILLER**
*St Brendan's, Stoneyford,*
*St Brendan's, Newmarket*
*Holy Trinity*
Very Rev Liam Cassin PP
Hugginstown, Co Kilkenny
Tel/Fax 056-7768693/087-2312354
Email liamcassin@ossory.ie
Very Rev Peter Hoyne PE
Newmarket, Hugginstown, Co Kilkenny
Tel/Fax 056-7768678

**BALLYCALLAN**
*Queen of Peace, St Molua, St Brigid*
Parish email ballycallan@ossory.ie
Very Rev Lorcan Moran PP
Ballycallan, Co Kilkenny
Tel 056-7769564/086-8550521

**BALLYHALE**
*St Martin of Tours, Our Lady of the*
*Assumption, All Saints*
Very Rev Benedict O'Callaghan (OCarm) PP
Ballyhale, Co Kilkenny
Tel/Fax 056-7768686
Email knockcar@hotmail.com

**BALLYRAGGET**
*St Patrick's, Assumption of BVM*
Very Rev Eamonn O'Gorman PP
Tel 087-2236145
Very Rev Thomas Canon Murphy PE
Tel 056-8833123/086-8130694
Email tommurphy@ossory.ie
Ballyragget, Co Kilkenny

**BORRIS-IN-OSSORY**
*St Canice, Assumption, St Kieran*
Very Rev John Robinson PP
Borris-in-Ossory, Portlaoise, Co Laois
Tel 0505-41148/087-2431412
Fax 0505-41148
Email robjon@eircom.net

**CALLAN**
*Assumption, All Saints, Nativity of BVM*
Very Rev William Dalton PP
Callan, Co Kilkenny
Tel 056-7725287/086-8506215
Fax 056-7725287
Email williamdalton@ossory.ie
Website
www.callanparish@irishchurch.net

**CAMROSS**
*St Fergal*
Very Rev John Lalor PP
Camross, Portlaoise, Co Laois
Tel/Fax 0502-35122/087-6888711
Email johnflalor@eircom.net

**CASTLECOMER**
*Immaculate Conception*
Rt Rev Mgr Michael Ryan PP
Tel 056-4441262/086-3693863
Fax 056-4441969
Rev Joseph Campion (SAC) CC
Tel 056-4441263/086-1775172
Email josecampion@yahoo.co.uk
Castlecomer, Co Kilkenny
Parish email castlecomer@ossory.ie

**CASTLETOWN**
*St Edmund*
Very Rev William Hennessy PP
Castletown, Portlaoise, Co Laois
Tel 0502-32622/087-8736155
Fax 0502-32622

**CLARA**
*St Coleman*
Very Rev Laurence O'Keeffe PP
Clifden Villa, Clifden, Co Kilkenny
Tel 056-7726560/087-2258443
Fax 056-7726558
Email larryokeeffe@ossory.ie
Parish email clara@ossory.ie

**CLOGH**
*St Patrick's, Sacred Heart*
Very Rev Martin Tobin PP
Clogh, Castlecomer, Co Kilkenny
Tel 056-4442135/086-2401278
Fax 056-4442135
Email martintobin@ossory.ie

**CONAHY**
*St Coleman, Our Lady of Perpetual Help*
Very Rev Eamonn O'Gorman PP
Conahy, Jenkinstown, Co Kilkenny
Tel 056-7767657/087-2236145
Email 1eamonnogorman@eircom.net

**DANESFORT**
*St Michael the Archangel, Holy Cross, Kells*
*Holy Cross, Cuffesgrange*
Very Rev Kieran Cantwell PP
Danesfort, Co Kilkenny
Tel 056-7727137/087-2661228
Fax 056-7727137
Email info@irelandescorted.com

**DUNAMAGGAN**
*St Leonard, St Eoghan*
Very Rev Nicholas Flavin PP
Dunamaggan, Co Kilkenny
Tel 056-7728173/087-2257498
Fax 056-7728173
Email naflavin@eircom.net

**DURROW**
*Holy Trinity, St Tighearnach*
Very Rev Seán Canon O'Doherty PP
Durrow, Portlaoise, Co Laois
Tel 057-8736156
Rev Thomas McGree CC
Durrow, Portlaoise, Co Laois
Tel 057-8736155/087-7619235
Fax 057-8736226

**FERRYBANK**
*Sacred Heart*
Very Rev James Crotty PP
Tel/Fax 051-832787
Email jimcrotty@ossory.ie
Rev Raymond Dempsey CC
Tel 051-832577/087-2859682
Fax 051-832577
Email 1dempseyr@gmail.com
Ferrybank, Waterford
Website www.ferrybankparish.com

**FRESHFORD**
*St Lachtain, St Nicholas*
Very Rev Patrick Comerford PP
Freshford, Co Kilkenny
Tel 056-8832461/086-1038430
Email patcomerford@ossory.ie

**GALMOY**
*Immaculate Conception*
Very Rev Thomas Coyle PP
Galmoy, Crosspatrick, via Thurles,
Co Kilkenny
Tel 056-8831227/087-7668969
Fax 056-8831227
Email tjcoyle@eircom.net

**GLENMORE**
*St James*
Very Rev Thomas O'Toole PP
Glenmore, via New Ross, Co Kilkenny
Tel 051-880213/087-2240787
Email tm5-tle@eircom.net

**GOWRAN**
*Assumption*
Very Rev Patrick Canon Dalton PP, VF
Gowran, Co Kilkenny
Tel 056-7726128/086-8283478
Fax 056-7726134
Email pdalton@iolfree.ie

**INISTIOGE**
*St Columcille, Assumption, St Brendan*
Very Rev Richard Scriven PP
The Rower, Inistioge, Co Kilkenny
Tel 051-423619/087-2420033
Fax 051-423619

**JOHNSTOWN**
*St Kieran, St Michael*
Very Rev Francis Maher PP
Johnstown via Thurles, Co Kilkenny
Tel 056-8831219/087-2402487
Fax 056-8831219
Email frankmaher@ossory.ie

**KILMACOW**
*St Senan*
Very Rev Anthony O'Connor PP
Tel/Fax 051-885269/087-2517766
Email maoc1@eircom.net
Very Rev Brian Flynn PE
Tel 051-885122/087-2828391
Email brianflynn@ossory.ie
Email kilmacowparish@ossory.ie
Kilmacow, via Waterford, Co Kilkenny

**LISDOWNEY**
*St Brigid, St Munchin, St Fiacre*
Very Rev Patrick O'Farrell PP
Lisdowney, Ballyragget, Co Kilkenny
Tel 056-8833138/087-2353520
Fax 056-8833701
Email patofarrell@ossory.ie
Parish email lisdowney@ossory.ie

**MOONCOIN**
*Assumption, St Kevin, St Kilgoue*
Very Rev Peter Muldowney PP
Mooncoin, Co Kilkenny
Tel 051-895123/086-9131080
Fax 051-895123
Email peter.muldowney@hotmail.com

**MUCKALEE**
*St Brendan, St Brigid, St Joseph*
Very Rev Laurence Wallace PP, VF
Muckalee, Ballyfoyle, Co Kilkenny
Tel 056-4441271/087-2326807
Fax 056-4440007
Email wallace@eircom.net
Rev John Delaney CC
Coon, Carlow
Tel 056-4443116/086-8596321
Fax 056-4443283
Email jondel@eircom.net
Parish email muckalee@ossory.ie

**MULLINAVAT**
*St Beacon, St Paul*
Very Rev Liam Barron PP
Tel 051-898108/087-2722824
Fax 051-898108
Mullinavat, via Waterford, Co Kilkenny
Email liambarron@ossory.ie

**RATHDOWNEY**
*Holy Trinity, Our Lady, Queen of the Universe*
Very Rev Martin Delaney PP
Rathdowney, Portlaoise, Co Laois
Tel 0505-46282/086-2444594
Email delaneymartin@eircom.net
Email rathdowney@ossory.ie

**ROSBERCON**
*Assumption, St David, St Aidan*
Very Rev Daniel Cavanagh PP
Rosbercon, New Ross, Co Wexford
Tel 051-421515/087-2335432
Fax 051-425093
Email danieljcavanagh@eircom.net
Very Rev Michael Norton PE
Rosbercon, New Ross, Co Wexford
Tel 051-420333/087-2580496
Fax 051-420333

**SEIR KIERAN**
*St Kieran*
Very Rev Dean Seamus McEvoy Adm
Seir Kieran, Clareen, Birr, Co Offaly
Tel 0509-31080/086-2634093

**SLIEVERUE**
*Assumption*
Very Rev Thomas Corcoran PP
Slieverue, Co Kilkenny
Tel 051-832773/087-6886678
Fax 051-832773
Email tomjcorcoran1@gmail.com
Parish email slieverue@ossory.ie
Website www.slieverue.com

**TEMPLEORUM**
*Assumption*
Very Rev Paschal Moore PP
Piltown, Co Kilkenny
Tel 051-643112/087-2408078
Fax 051-644911
Email paschalmoore@eircom.net
Rev Richard Brennan (SPS) CC
38 Owning House, Owning,
Piltown, Co Kilkenny
Tel 085-1185866

**THOMASTOWN**
*Assumption*
Very Rev Daniel Bollard PP
Tel/Fax 056-7724279/087-6644858
Email dbollard@eircom.net
Rev Mark Condon CC
Tel 056-7793191/086-6005402
Email markcondon123@gmail.com
Thomastown, Co Kilkenny
Parish email thomastown@ossory.ie

**TULLAHERIN**
*St Bennet, St Kieran*
Very Rev Patrick Canon Dalton PP
Tel 056-7726128/086-8283478
Email patdalton@iolfree.ie
Very Rev Patrick Canon Duggan PE
Tel 056-7727140/087-6644858
Fax 056-7727755
Bennetsbridge, Co Kilkenny
Email patduggan@ossory.ie

**TULLAROAN**
*Assumption*
Very Rev Patrick Guilfoyle PP
Tullaroan, Co Kilkenny
Tel 056-7769141/087-6644858
Fax 056-7769141
Email guilfoylepat@eircom.net

**URLINGFORD**
*Assumption, St Patrick*
Very Rev Oliver Maher PP
Urlingford, Co Kilkenny
Tel 056-8831121/086-8323010
Email olivermaher@ossory.ie

**WINDGAP**
*St Nicholas, Windgap*
*St Nicholas, Tullahought*
Very Rev Nicholas Flavin PP
Windgap, Co Kilkenny
Tel/Fax 051-648111
Email napflavin@eircom.net

## INSTITUTIONS AND THEIR CHAPLAINS

**Aut Even Hospital**
Aut Even, Kilkenny
Priests of St Canice's Parish
Tel 056-7721523/087-9335663

**City Vocational School, Kilkenny**
Rev William Purcell
Tel 056-7721253/087-6286858
Email wpurcell@eircom.net

**Community School**
Castlecomer, Co Kilkenny
Ms Edel O'Connor
Tel 056-4441447

**Abbey Community College**
Ferrybank, Waterford
Ms Claire Bolger
Tel 051-832930

**District Hospital**
Castlecomer, Co Kilkenny
Rt Rev Mgr Michael Ryan
Tel 056-4441262/086-3034155

**Orthopaedic Hospital**
Kilcreene, Kilkenny
Priests of St Mary's Parish
Tel 056-7721253 Ext 180/181

**St Canice's Hospital, Kilkenny**
Priests of St John's Parish
Tel 056-7721072

**St Columba's Hospital**
Thomastown, Co Kilkenny
Very Rev Daniel Bollard
Tel 056-7724279/087-6644858

**St Luke's Hospital, Kilkenny**
Rev Patrick Carey
Tel 056-7785000/7771815/087-2599087
Email paddycarey@ossory.ie

**Stephen Barracks, Kilkenny**
Rev Daniel McCarthy
Tel 056-7761852

## PRIESTS OF THE DIOCESE ELSEWHERE

*In Ireland*
Rt Rev Mgr James Cassin
St Patrick's College, Maynooth, Co Kildare
Tel 01-6285222/086-2380984
Email jamescassin@ossory.ie

*Abroad*
Rt Rev Mgr Liam Bergin
St Brigid's Parish, 841 East Broadway,
Boston, MA 02127, USA
Tel 001-617-4477770
Email lbergin@ossory.ie

Rev John Duggan
St John and Paul Church,
341 South Main Street,
Coventary RI R102816-5987, USA
Tel 001-401-8275022
Rev Dr Thomas Norris
Spiritual Director,
Pontificio Collegio Irlandese,
Via dei SS Quattro 1, 00184 Rome, Italy
Email thomas.norris@spcm.ie

## RETIRED PRIESTS

Very Rev Patrick Canon Brennan
Gathabawn, Via Thurles, Co Kilkenny
Tel 056-8832110
Very Rev James Canon Carrigan
Ballacolla, Portlaoise, Co Laois
Tel 0502-34016
Rev John Condon
Piltown, Co Kilkenny
Tel 086-8394615
Very Rev Joseph Delaney
Strathmore Nursing Home,
Callan, Co Kilkenny
Tel 086-8206730
Very Rev James Dollard
Donoughmore, Johnstown, Co Kilkenny
Very Rev Liam Dunne
The Forge, Martin's Lane,
Upper Main Street, Arklow, Co Wicklow
Tel 0402-32779
Very Rev Laurence Canon Dunphy
Urlingford, Co Kilkenny
Tel 087-2300849
Very Rev Eamon Foley
Clara, Co Kilkenny
Tel 087-7828784
Venerable Archdeacon Patrick Grace
Inistioge, Co Kilkenny
Tel 056-7758429/086-8817628
Very Rev Patrick Canon Grant
Ballyragget, Co Kilkenny
Tel 056-8833120
Rt Rev Mgr Thomas Maher
Archersrath Nursing Home, Kilkenny
Tel 056-7790137
Very Rev Robert Canon Raftice
St Joseph's Home, Ferrybank, Waterford
Tel 051-833006/086-0614682
Very Rev Donal Walsh
Tinnahinch, Graiguenamanagh,
Co Kilkenny
Tel 059-9725550
Most Rev Thomas White
Abbey Nursing Home, Gowran, Co Kilkenny
Tel 056-7726500

## RELIGIOUS ORDERS AND CONGREGATIONS

## PRIESTS

**CAPUCHINS**
Capuchin Friary, Friary Street,
Kilkenny
Tel 056-7721439 Fax 056-7722025
*Guardian:* Rev Sean Donohoe (OFMCap)
*Vicar:* Rev Terence Harrington (OFMCap)

**CARMELITES (OCARM)**
Carmelite Priory, Knocktopher,
Co Kilkenny
Tel 056-7768675
Email knockcar@indigo.ie
*Prior*
Rev Benedict O'Callaghan (OCarm) PP

**DOMINICANS**
Black Abbey, Kilkenny, Co Kilkenny
Tel 056-7721279 Fax 056-7721297
*Prior:* Very Rev James Donleavy (OP)

**MILL HILL MISSIONARIES**
St Joseph's, Mill Hill Missionaries,
Waterford Road, Kilkenny
Tel 056-7721482 Fax 056-7751490
*Rector:* Rev Maurice McGill (MHM)
Email mcgillmhm@yahoo.com

## BROTHERS

**BROTHERS OF CHARITY**
St Vincent's Brothers' Community,
Ferrybank, Waterford
Tel 051-832180 Fax 051-833490
*Community Leader:* Br Joseph Killoran
Email
jkilloran@waterford.brothersofcharity.ie
Community: 3

**CHRISTIAN BROTHERS**
Christian Brothers,
Edmund Rice House,
Westcourt, Callan, Co Kilkenny
Tel 056-7725141
*Community Leader*
Br Denis Vaughan
Community: 6

Edmund Rice Centre,
Callan, Co Kilkenny
Tel 056-7725993

Christian Brothers, Chapel Lane,
Callan, Co Kilkenny
Tal 056-7706939
Community: 2

**DE LA SALLE BROTHERS**
De La Salle Monastery,
Castletown, Portlaoise, Co Laois
Tel 057-8732359 (residence)
Fax 057-8732925
*Superior:* Br Stephen Deignan
Community: 11

Miguel House, Castletown,
Portlaoise, Co Laois
Tel 057-8732136 Fax 057-8756648
*Superior:* Br David O'Riordan
Community: 19
House for retired brothers

La Salle Pastoral Centre,
Castletown, Portlaoise,
Co Laois
Tel 057-8732442 Fax 057-872925
*Director:* Mr Derek Doherty
Retreat centre

# DIOCESE OF RAPHOE

PATRON OF THE DIOCESE
ST EUNAN, 23 SEPTEMBER

INCLUDES THE GREATER PART OF COUNTY DONEGAL

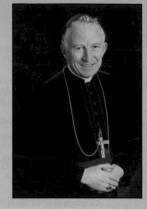

**Most Rev Philip Boyce
(OCD) DD**
Bishop of Raphoe;
born 25 January 1940;
ordained priest 17 April 1966;
ordained Bishop of Raphoe
1 October 1995

Residence: Ard Adhamhnáin,
Letterkenny, Co Donegal
Tel 074-9121208
Fax 074-9124872
Email
raphoediocese@eircom.net
Website www.raphoediocese.ie

## ST EUNAN'S CATHEDRAL, LETTERKENNY

The old cathedral of Raphoe passed into Protestant hands at the Reformation. In the eighteenth century the Catholic bishops came to live in Letterkenny. A church was built circa 1820 and, having been extended by Bishop Patrick McGettigan, was used as a pro-cathedral. Bishop McDevitt (1871–1879) thought of building a new cathedral, and Lord Southwell promised a site, but it was not until 1891, when Bishop O'Donnell was in office, that actual building began. The cathedral was completed in 1901. Besides overseeing the cathedral project, Bishop O'Donnell had the task of providing a house for the bishop and priests of the cathedral parish.

The main benefactors were Fr J.D. McGarvey PP, Killygarvan, and Mr Neil Gillen of Airdrie. Various priests of the diocese spent considerable time fund-raising in Britain, the US and Canada. The style is Gothic, with some Hiberno-Romanesque features, and the building is of white Mountcharles sandstone. The cathedral dominates the Letterkenny skyline. Among the artistic features to be noted are the 'Drumceat' window, by Michael Healy (North Transept); the pulpit, by Messrs Pearse (Patrick Pearse's family); the Great Arch, with its St Columba and St Eunan columns; and, outside, the fine statue of Bishop O'Donnell, by Doyle of Chelsea.

Remodelling of the cathedral took place in 1985, with the addition of an altar table and chairs; great care was taken to preserve the style and materials of the original altar. Bishop Hegarty promoted this tasteful restoration work, which left intact the architectural character of the building.

Allianz (ⅱ)

## CHAPTER

*Dean:* Very Rev Dean John Silke PE
Portnablagh
*Archdeacon*
Ven Archdeacon William McMenamin PE
Raphoe
*Members*
Very Rev Canon Denis McGettigan PP
Raphoe
Very Rev Canon John Gallagher PE
Ardara
Very Rev Canon Austin Laverty PP, VF
Ardara
Very Rev Canon John Silke PE
Portnablagh
Very Rev Canon Francis McAteer PP
Carrick
Very Rev Canon James Friel PE
Rathmullan

## ADMINISTRATION

**Vicar General**
Rt Rev Mgr Daniel Carr PP, VG, VF
St Johnston, Lifford, Co Donegal
Tel 074-9148203

**Diocesan Chancellor/Diocesan Secretary**
Rev Michael McKeever
Diocesan Office, Ard Adhamhnáin,
Letterkenny, Co Donegal
Tel 074-9121208 Fax 074-9124872
Email raphoediocese@eircom.net

**College of Consultors**
Rt Rev Mgr Daniel Carr PP, VG, VF
St Johnston
Very Rev Kieran McAteer PP
Stranorlar
Rev Eamonn Kelly Adm, VF
Letterkenny
Very Rev Francis McLoone PP
Killymard
Very Rev Cathal Ó Fearraí PP, VF
Ballyshannon
Rev Donnchadh O'Baoill CC
Cnoc Fola

**Vicars Forane**
Rt Rev Mgr Daniel Carr PP, VG, VF
St Johnston
Very Rev Canon Austin Laverty PP, VF
Ardara
Very Rev Cathal Ó Fearraí PP, VF
Ballyshannon
Rev Eamonn Kelly Adm, VF
Letterkenny
Very Rev Martin Collum PP, VF
Rathmullan
Very Rev Michael Herrity PP, VF
Annagry

**Financial Administrators**
Rt Rev Mgr Daniel Carr PP, VG, VF
Mrs Carmel Doherty
Ard Adhamhnáin,
Letterkenny, Co Donegal

**Finance Committee**
Bishop Philip Boyce, Rt Rev Mgr Daniel
Carr, Mr Noel O'Connell, Mrs Mary Foley,
Mr John McCreadie, Mr Peadar Murphy,
Mrs Carmel Doherty *(Secretary),*
Ms Siobhan Logue, Mr Conal Boyle,
Mr Seán Ó Longáin

**Building Committee**
Very Rev Canon Austin Laverty PP, VF
Very Rev Canon John Gallagher PE

**Diocesan Archives**
Faíche Ó Dónaill Building
Ard Adhamhnáin, Letterkenny,
Co Donegal
Tel 074-9161109
Email raphoearchives@eircom.net

## CATECHETICS EDUCATION

**Religious Education in Primary Schools**
*Co-ordinator*
Very Rev Aodhan Cannon PP
Dungloe, Co Donegal
Tel 074-9521008

**Religious Education in Secondary Schools**
Mount Carmel House of Prayer,
Drumkeen, Co Donegal
Tel 074-9134167
Sr Susan Evangelist Taegue

## LITURGY

**Perpetual Eucharistic Adoration**
*Diocesan Director*
Very Rev Patrick Dunne
Parochial House, Kilmacrennan,
Letterkenny
Tel 074-9139018

## PASTORAL

**ACCORD**
*Letterkenny area:* Pastoral Centre,
Monastery Ave, Letterkenny
Tel 074-9122218
*Chairperson:* Mrs Marie Ferry
*Treasurer:* Mrs Betty Clancy
*Secretary:* Mrs Sheila Leeper
*Chaplain:* Rev Eamonn Kelly
Open Monday–Friday 10.00 am-1.00 pm
LoCall 1850-201878

**Child Safeguarding Office**
Pastoral Centre, Monastery Avenue,
Letterkenny, Co Donegal
Tel 074-9125669
Email cporaphoediocese@eircom.net

**Director of Pastoral Development**
Grainne Doherty
Pastoral Centre,
Letterkenny, Co Donegal
Tel 074-9121853/087-9119426

**Ecumenism**
*Diocesan Director*
Very Rev Canon Francis McAteer PP
Carrick, Co Donegal
Tel 074-9739008

**Family Ministry Centre**
The Pastoral Centre,
Letterkenny, Co Donegal
Tel 074-9121853 Fax 074-9128433

**Fatima Pilgrimage**
*Director:* Very Rev James Sweeney PP
Bruckless, Co Donegal
Tel 074-9737015

**Knock Pilgrimage**
*Director:* Rev Michael McKeever
Church Hill, Co Donegal
Tel 074-9137057

**Lourdes Pilgrimage**
*Director:* Very Rev Patrick McHugh PP
Parochial House, Termon,
Co Donegal
Tel 074-9139016/074-9125090 *(Lourdes office)*

**Marriage Tribunal**
*(See also Marriage Tribunals section)*
*Secretary:* Kathleen Kelly
*Officialis:* Vacant
*Assistants:* Vacant
Rev Eamonn McLaughlin
Rev John Joe Duffy
The Pastoral Centre, Letterkenny,
Co Donegal
Tel 074-9121853

**Pioneer Total Abstinence Association**
*Diocesan Director*
Very Rev Canon James Friel PE
Rathmullan, Co Donegal
Very Rev James Sweeney PP
Bruckless, Co Donegal
Tel 074-9737015

**Raphoe Diocesan Directory**
Rev Michael McKeever
Ard Adhamhnáin, Letterkenny,
Co Donegal
Tel 074-9121208
Fax 074-9124872
Email raphoediocese@eircom.net

**Religious Broadcasting**
*Diocesan Director*
Very Rev Patrick Dunne PP
Parochial House, Kilmacrennan,
Letterkenny
Tel 074-9139018

**Vocations**
*Directors:* Rev Joseph O'Donnell CC
Parochial House,
Mountcharles, Co Donegal
Tel 074-9735009
Rev Gerard Cunningham CC
Parochial House, Fintown
Tel 074-9546107
Rev Rory Brady
1 Cathedral Place,
Letterkenny, Co Donegal
Tel 074-9125182

**World Missions Ireland**
*Diocesan Director*
Very Rev Canon Francis McAteer PP
Parochial House, Carrick, Co Donegal
Tel 074-9739008

## PARISHES

*The mensal parish is listed first. Other parishes follow alphabetically. Historical names are given in parentheses.*

**LETTERKENNY (CONWAL AND LECK)**
*Cathedral of St Eunan and St Columba*
Very Rev Eamonn Kelly Adm
Rev Eamonn McLaughlin CC
Rev Stephen Gorman CC
Parochial House, Letterkenny,
Co Donegal
Tel 074-9121021 Fax 074-9122707
Email steunanscathedral@eircom.net
Letterkenny General Hospital
Rev Martin Chambers
2 Chaplain's House, Knocknamona,
Letterkenny, Co Donegal
Tel 074-9125090
Rev Shane Gallagher
1 Chaplain's House, Knocknamona,
Letterkenny, Co Donegal
Tel (Hospital) 074-9125888

**ANNAGRY**
Very Rev Michael Herrity PP
Annagry, Co Donegal
Tel 074-9548111

**ARDARA**
Very Rev Canon Austin Laverty PP, VF
Tel 074-9541135
Rev Liam Boyle CC
Tel 087-0562452
Ardara, Co Donegal
Rev Philip Daly CC
Kilclooney, Co Donegal
Tel 074-9545114

**AUGHANINSHIN**
Very Rev Brian Quinn PP
Ballyraine, Letterkenny, Co Donegal
Tel 074-9127600
Rev James Gillespie CC
Carnamuggagh Lower,
Letterkenny, Co Donegal
Tel 074-9122608

**BALLINTRA (DRUMHOLM)**
Very Rev Seamus Dagens PP
Ballintra, Co Donegal
Tel 074-9734016

**BALLYSHANNON (KILBARRON)**
Very Rev Cathal Ó Fearraí PP, VF
Tel 071-9851295
Rev Hugh Hanlon (MSC) CC
Tel 071-9851090

**BRUCKLESS (KILLAGHTEE)**
Very Rev James Sweeney PP
Bruckless, Co Donegal
Tel 074-9737015

**BURTONPORT (KINCASSLAGH)**
Very Rev Pat Ward PP
Burtonport, Co Donegal
Tel 074-9542006
Rev Francis Ferry CC
Arranmore Island, Co Donegal
Tel 074-9520504
www.kincasslagh.ie

**CARRICK (GLENCOLMCILLE)**
Very Rev Canon Francis McAteer PP
Carrick, Co Donegal
Tel 074-9739008
Rev Paul McGeehan CC
Glencolmcille, Co Donegal
Tel 074-9730888

**CARRIGART (MEEVAGH)**
Very Rev Charles Byrne PP
Carrigart, Co Donegal
Tel 074-9155154

**CLOGHAN (KILTEEVOGUE)**
Very Rev Lorcan Sharkey PP
Cloghan, Lifford, Co Donegal
Tel 074-9133007

**DONEGAL TOWN (TAWNAWILLY)**
Very Rev William Peoples PP
Tel 074-9721026
Donegal Town, Co Donegal
Rev Danny McBrearty CC
Parochial House, Clar
Tel 074-9721093

**DRUMOGHILL (RAYMOCHY)**
Very Rev Martin Cunningham PP
Drumoghill, Co Donegal
Tel 074-9157169

**DUNFANAGHY (CLONDAHORKEY)**
Very Rev Martin Doohan PP
Dunfanaghy, Co Donegal
Tel 074-9136163
Rev Jonathan Flood CC
Cleeslough, Co Donegal
Tel 074-9138011

**DUNGLOE (TEMPLECRONE AND LETTERMACAWARD)**
Very Rev Aodhan Cannon PP
Tel 074-9521008
Rev Nigel Ó Galláchóir CC
Tel 074-9522194
Dungloe, Co Donegal
Rev Mark Byrne (SOLT)
Leitirmacaward, Co Donegal
Tel 074-9544102

**FALCARRAGH**
Very Rev Denis Quinn PP
Falcarragh, Co Donegal
Tel 074-9135196

**GLENSWILLY (GLENSWILLY AND TEMPLEDOUGLAS)**
Very Rev Hugh Sweeney PP
Glenswilly, New Mills, Letterkenny,
Co Donegal
Tel 074-9137020

**GLENTIES (INISKEEL)**
Very Rev Patrick Prendergast PP
Glenties, Co Donegal
Tel 074-9551117
Rev Gerard Cunningham CC
Fintown, Donegal Town, Co Donegal
Tel 074-9546107

**GORTAHORK (TORY ISLAND)**
Very Rev Seán Ó Gallchóir PP
Tel 074-9135214
Rev Kieran Creagh (CP) CC
Tory Island, Co Donegal
Tel 074-9135505
Rev Paul Gallagher CC (Tory Island)
Falcarragh, Co Donegal
Tel 074-9165356

**GWEEDORE**
Very Rev Pádraig Ó Baoighill PP
Tel 074-9531310
Rev Brian O'Fearraigh CC
Tel 074-9531947
Derrybeg, Letterkenny
Rev Donnchadh Ó Baoill CC
Bun-a-leaca, Letterkenny,
Co Donegal
Tel 074-9531155

**INVER**
Very Rev Seamus Gallagher PP
Frosses, Co Donegal
Tel 074-9736006
Rev Joseph O'Donnell CC
Mountcharles, Co Donegal
Tel 074-9735009

**KILCAR**
Very Rev Edward Gallagher PP
Kilcar, Co Donegal
Tel 074-9738007

**KILLYBEGS**
www.killybegsparish.com
Very Rev Colm O'Gallchoir PP
Killybegs, Co Donegal
Tel 074-9731030

**KILLYMARD**
Very Rev Francis McLoone PP
Killymard, Co Donegal
Tel 074-9721929

**KILMACRENNAN**
Very Rev Patrick Dunne PP
Kilmacrennan, Co Donegal
Tel 074-9139018

**NEWTOWNCUNNINGHAM & KILLEA**
Very Rev Ciaran Harkin PP
Parochial House,
Newtowncunningham,
Lifford, Co Donegal
Tel 074-9156138

## RAMELTON (AUGHNISH)
Very Rev Michael Carney PP
Ramelton, Co Donegal
Tel 074-9151304

## RAPHOE
www.parishofraphoe.com
Very Rev Canon Denis McGettigan PP
Raphoe, Lifford, Co Donegal
Tel 074-9145647
Rev Philip Kemmy CC
Convoy, Lifford, Co Donegal
Tel 074-9147238
Rev John Boyce
Drumkeen, Ballybofey,
Co Donegal
Tel 074-9134005

## RATHMULLAN (KILLYGARVAN AND TULLYFERN)
www.mrparishes.ie
Very Rev Martin Collum PP
Rathmullan, Co Donegal
Tel 074-9158156
Rev Adrian Gavigan CC
Milford, Co Donegal
Tel 074-9153236
Very Rev Michael Sweeney AP
Glenvar
Tel 074-9150014

## ST JOHNSTON (TAUGHBOYNE)
Rt Rev Mgr Daniel Carr PP, VG, VF
St Johnston, Lifford, Co Donegal
Tel 074-9148203

## STRANORLAR
www.stranorlarparish.com
Very Rev Kieran McAteer PP
Parochial House, Ballybofey,
Co Donegal
Tel 074-9131135
Rev John Joe Duffy CC
Parochial House, Stranorlar,
Co Donegal
Tel 074-9131157

## TAMNEY (CLONDAVADDOG)
Very Rev Patrick McGarvey PP
Fanavolty, Kindrum,
Letterkenny, Co Donegal
Tel 074-9159007
Rev Mariusz Semla CC
Tamney, Letterkenny,
Co Donegal
Tel 074-9159015

## TERMON (GARTAN AND TERMON)
Very Rev Patrick McHugh PP
Termon, Letterkenny,
Co Donegal
Tel 074-9139016
Rev Michael McKeever CC
Church Hill, Letterkenny,
Co Donegal
Tel 074-9137057
www.gartantermonparish.ie

## INSTITUTIONS AND THEIR CHAPLAINS

**General Hospital**
Letterkenny, Co Donegal
Tel 074-9125888
Rev Martin Chambers
c/o General Hospital, Letterkenny
or 2 Chaplain's House,
Knocknamona, Letterkenny
Rev Shane Gallagher
1 Chaplain's House,
Knocknamona, Letterkenny

**Letterkenny Institute of Technology**
Letterkenny, Co Donegal
Tel 074-9124888
Rev John Boyce

**St Conal's Hospital**
Letterkenny, Co Donegal
Tel 074-9121022
Canon John Gallagher
Rev Martin Chambers

**St Joseph's Hospital**
Stranorlar, Co Donegal
Tel 074-9131038
Parochial clergy Stranorlar

## PRIESTS OF THE DIOCESE ELSEWHERE

Rev Patrick Bonner
Church of St Patrick, 55 Grand Street,
Newburgh, NY 12550
Tel 845-5610885
Rev Joseph Briody
St John's Seminary, 127 Lake Street,
Brighton, MA 02135, USA
Rev Niall Coll
St Mary's College, Belfast
Rt Rev Mgr Kevin Gillespie
Congregation for the Clergy, Rome
Rev Brendan McBride
St Philip's Church, 725 Diamond Street,
San Francisco, California, 94114
Rev Damien McGroarty
c/o Diocesan Office, Letterkenny

## RETIRED PRIESTS

Very Rev Connell Cunningham PE
Carrick, Co Donegal
Rev Thomas Curran
Glenview House, College Road,
Letterkenny, Co Donegal
Tel 074-9127617
Rev Anthony Griffith
Rushbrook, Laghey, Co Donegal
Tel 074-9734021
Very Rev Daniel O'Doherty PE
Ballyheerin, Fanad, Co Donegal
Very Rev John J. Silke PhD
'Stella Maris', Portnablagh,
Co Donegal
Tel 074-9136122
Very Rev Seamus L. Gallagher PE
Glenlee, Killybegs, Co Donegal
Tel 074-9732729

Very Rev Kevin O'Doherty PE
Nazareth House, Fahan, Co Donegal
Very Rev Desmond Sweeney PE
17 Meadowvale, Ramelton
Tel 074-9151085
Very Rev Michael Connaghan PE
6 Fields Court, Kilmacrennan,
Co Donegal
Tel 074-9119871
Very Rev Canon James Friel PE
Massreagh, Rathmullen, Co Donegal
Tel 074-9158306
Canon William McMenamin PE
'St Columba's', Meeting House Street,
Raphoe, Co Donegal
Tel 074-9144834
Very Rev Dermot McShane PE
St John's Point, Dunkineeley,
Co Donegal
Very Rev Seamus Meehan PE
Main Street, Dungloe, Co Donegal
Tel 074-9521895
Very Rev Canon John Gallagher PE
Ardara, Co Donegal
Tel 074-9541318

## RELIGIOUS ORDERS AND CONGREGATIONS

### PRIESTS

**CAPUCHINS (OFMCAP)**
Capuchin Friary, Ard Mhuire,
Creeslough, Letterkenny, Co Donegal
Tel 074-9138005 Fax 074-9138371
*Guardian*
Rev Silvester O'Flynn (OFMCap)
*Vicar*
Br Bernard McAllister (OFMCap)

**FRANCISCANS (OFM)**
Franciscan Friary, Rossnowlagh,
Co Donegal
Tel 072-9851342 Fax 072-9852206
Email franciscanfriary@eircom.net
*Guardian*
Rev Feargus McEveney (OFM)

**SALVATORIANS**
Saint John's House, West Rock,
Ballyshannon, Co Donegal
Tel 071-9851541
Rev Gerard Daly (SDS)

### SISTERS

**CONGREGATION OF THE SISTERS OF MERCY**
Convent of Mercy, Donegal Town,
Co Donegal
Tel 074-9721175
Shared leadership
Community: 4

Convent of Mercy,
15 Blackrock Drive, Ballybofey,
Co Donegal
Tel 074-9132721

St Catherine's,
Ballyshannon, Co Donegal
Tel 071-9851268
Community: 16

Dia Linn, Gortnamucklagh,
Glenties, Co Donegal
Tel 074-9551125

Convent of Mercy,
Carnmore Road, Dungloe,
Co Donegal
Tel 074-9521209

Sisters of Mercy,
Ceoil na Coille, Stranorlar,
Lifford, Co Donegal
Tel 074-9131245
Family Enrichment Centre
Dromboe Avenue, Stranorlar
Tel 074-9131245

Convent of Mercy, Windy Hall,
Letterkenny, Co Donegal
Tel 074-9122729
Community: 3

Sisters of Mercy,
St Anne's Convent,
Ballyshannon, Co Donegal
Tel 071-9852737
Community: 3

Sisters of Mercy,
No. 1 McCloskey Close,
Glenties, Co Donegal
Tel 074-9551713

Sisters of Mercy,
15 Taobh na Cille,
Moville, Co Donegal

Glór na Mara, West End,
Bundoran, Co Donegal
Tel 071-9833899

2 Marina View, Dinglei Coush,
Bundoran, Co Donegal
Tel 071-9829832

The Lodge, Glór na Mara,
West End, Bundoran, Co Donegal
Tel 071-9841818

35 Brookfield Manor,
Donegal Town, Co Donegal
Tel 074-9725996

**LORETO (IBVM)**
Loreto Community, Letterkenny,
Co Donegal
Tel 074-9122896
*Team Leaders:* Sr Moira MacManus,
Sr Monica McElwee, Sr Mary O'Farrell
Community: 11
Loreto Primary School
Tel 074-9122896
Loreto Secondary School
Tel 074-9124237

## NEW FORMS OF CONSECRATED LIFE

**THE SPIRITUAL FAMILY THE WORK OF CHRIST (FSO)**
Bishop's House, Ard Adhamhnáin,
Letterkenny, Co Donegal
Tel 074-9124898
Email lk@thework-fso.org
Website www.thework-fso.org
*Superior:* Sr Nellie Baerts FSO
Community: 2

## EDUCATIONAL INSTITUTIONS

**Coláiste Ailigh**
Carnamuggagh, Letterkenny,
Co Donegal
Tel 074-9125943
*Príomh-Óid*
Mr Michael Gibbons
*Séiplineadh*
Ms Annmarie Canning

**Coláiste Cholmcille**
Ballyshannon, Co Donegal
Tel 071-9858288/9851369/9852459
*Principal:* Mr Jimmy Keogh
*Chaplain:* Ms Pauline Kilfeather

**Coláiste Phobail Cholmcille**
Oileán Thoraigh, Co Dhún na nGall
Tel 074-9165448
*Príomh-Óide:* Máire Clár Nic Mhathúna
*Séiplineach:* Rev Kieran Creagh CP

**Rosses Community School**
Dungloe, Co Donegal
Tel 074-9521122
*Principal:* Mr John Gorman
*Chaplain:* Rev Nigel Ó Gallchóir CC

**Comprehensive School**
Glenties, Lifford, Co Donegal
Tel 074-9551172
Fax 074-9551664
*Principal:* Mrs Frances Bonner
*Chaplain:* Vacant

**Institute of Technology, Letterkenny**
*Director:* Mr Paul Hannigan
Tel 074-9124888
*Chaplain:* Rev John Boyce

**Loreto Convent Secondary School**
Letterkenny, Co Donegal
Tel 074-9121850
*Principal:* Mrs Susan Kenny
*Chaplain:* Parish Clergy

**Loreto Community School**
Milford, Co Donegal
Tel 074-9153253
Fax 074-9153518
*Principal:* Mr Andrew Kelly
Tel 074-9153399
*Chaplain:* Mr John Lynch

**Pobalscoil Chloich Cheannfhaola**
Falcarragh,
Letterkenny, Co Donegal
Tel 074-9135424/9135231
Fax 074-9135019
*Príomh-Oide:* Ms Maeve Sweeney
*Séiplineach:* Rev Paul Gallagher CC

**Pobalscoil Ghaoth Dobhair**
Derrybeg,
Letterkenny, Co Donegal
Tel 074-9531040
*Príomh-Oide:* Mr Noel Ó Gallchóir
*Séiplineach:* Rev Brian O'Fearraigh CC

**St Columba's College**
Stranorlar, Co Donegal
Tel 074-9131246
*Principal:* Ms Maeve Scully
*Chaplain:* Parish Clergy

**St Eunan's College**
Letterkenny, Co Donegal
Tel 074-9121143
*Principal:* Mr Chris Darby
*Chaplain:* Rev Rory Brady

**Vocational Schools**
*Arranmore Island, Co Donegal*
Tel 074-9520747
*Principal:* Mrs Mary Doherty
*Chaplain:* Rev Francis Ferry CC

*Ballinamore, Co Donegal*
Tel 074-9546133 Fax 074-9546256
*Principal:* Ms Fiona Bonner
*Chaplain:* Rev Gerard Cunningham CC
Fintown, Donegal Town, Co Donegal

*Carrick, Co Donegal*
Tel 074-9739071 Fax 074-9739265
*Principal:* Mr Pádráig Ó Léime
*Chaplain:* Very Rev Eddie Gallagher PP
Kilcar, Co Donegal

*Abbey Vocational School,*
Donegal Town, Co Donegal
Tel 074-9721105 Fax 074-9722851
*Principal:* Mrs Geraldine Diver
*Chaplain:* Rev Joseph O'Donnell CC

*Gairm Scoil Catríona,*
Killybegs, Co Donegal
Tel/Fax 074-9731491
*Principal:* Ms Anne Marie Luby

*Errigal College,*
Letterkenny, Co Donegal
Tel 074-9121047/9121861
Fax 074-9121861
*Acting Principal:* Mr Charlie Cannon
*Chaplain:* Rev Eamonn Kelly Adm

*Mulroy College,*
Milford, Co Donegal
Tel 074-9153346
*Principal:* Ms Fiona Temple
*Chaplain:* Rev Adrian Gavigan CC
Milford, Co Donegal

Allianz (ⁱⁱ)

*Deele College,*
Raphoe, Co Donegal
Tel 074-9145493
*Principal:* Mr Joe Boyle
*Chaplain:* Very Rev Denis McGettigan PP

*Finn Valley College,*
Stranorlar, Co Donegal
Tel 074-9131684 Fax 074-9131355
*Principal:* Mr Alan Thompson

## CHARITABLE AND OTHER SOCIETIES

**Ards Friary Retreat and Conference Centre**
*Manager:* Mr Benito Conangelo
Tel 074-9138909
Email info@ardsfriary.ie
Website www.ardsfriary.ie

**Society of St Vincent de Paul**
North West Region Council,
The Diamond, Raphoe, Co Donegal
Tel/Fax 074-9173933
Email svpnorthwest@eircom.net

**St Mura's Adoption Society**
The Pastoral Centre, Monastery Avenue,
Letterkenny, Co Donegal
Tel 074-9122047
Mr Seamus Gallagher
Breda Gallinagh
*Secretary:* Kathleen Kelly

**Trócaire**
Very Rev Aodhan Cannon PP
Parochial House, Dungloe,
Co Donegal
Tel 074-9521008

# DIOCESE OF WATERFORD AND LISMORE

PATRONS OF THE DIOCESE
ST OTTERAN, 27 OCTOBER; ST CARTHAGE, 15 MAY;
ST DECLAN, 24 JULY

INCLUDES COUNTY WATERFORD
AND PART OF COUNTIES TIPPERARY AND CORK

**Rt Rev Mgr Nicholas O'Mahony**
Diocesan Administrator of Waterford and Lismore
born 30 June 1942;
ordained priest 11 June 1967;

Office Address: Bishop's House, John's Hill, Waterford
Tel 051-874463
Fax 051-852703
Email waterfordlismore@eircom.net

## CATHEDRAL OF THE MOST HOLY TRINITY, WATERFORD

The Cathedral of the Most Holy Trinity, Barronstrand Street, Waterford is the oldest Roman Catholic cathedral in Ireland. The work began in 1793 with the Protestant Waterford man, John Roberts, as architect. Roberts also designed the Church of Ireland cathedral.

Over the years, additions and alterations have been made. Most of the present sanctuary was added in the 1830s; the apse and a main altar in 1854. The beautiful baldachin, which is supported by five Corinthian columns, was erected in 1881.

The carved oak Baroque pulpit, the chapter stalls and bishop's chair, designed by Goldie and Sons of London and carved by Buisine and Sons of Lille, were installed in 1883.
The stained-glass windows, mainly by Meyer of Munich, were installed between 1883 and 1888.

The Stations of the Cross, which are attached to the columns in the cathedral, are nineteenth-century paintings by Alcan of Paris. The cut-stone front was built in 1892–1893 for the centenary of the cathedral.

In 1977, a new wooden altar was placed in the redesigned sanctuary. The Belgian walnut panels of the base of the altar were originally part of the altar rails at St Carthage's Church, Lismore.

There are many plaques in the cathedral. One of them commemorates fourteen famous Waterford men: Luke Wadding OFM; Peter Lombard; Patrick Comerford OSA; James White; Michael Wadding SJ: Peter Wadding SJ; Thomas White; Paul Sherlock SJ; Ambrose Wadding SJ; Geoffrey Keating; Luke Wadding SJ; Stephen White SJ; Thomas White SJ and Bonaventure Barron OFM.

Ten Waterford Crystal chandeliers were presented by Waterford Crystal in 1979.

In 1993 the Bicentenary of the Cathedral was celebrated.

**Most Rev William Lee DD**
Retired Bishop of Waterford and Lismore
born 1941;
ordained priest 19 June 1966;
ordained Bishop of Waterford and
Lismore 25 July 1993;
retired 1 October 2013
*Residence:* 5 The Brambles,
Ballinakill Downs, Waterford
Tel 051-821485

## CHAPTER

Right Rev Mgr Dean John Shine AP
Tramore
Right Rev Mgr Nicholas O'Mahony PP
Tramore
Very Rev Gregory Power PE
St Mary's, Clonmel
Right Rev Mgr Michael Olden PE
Waterford
Very Rev Martin Slattery AP
Cathedral, Waterford
Very Rev Canon Daniel O'Connor PE
Dungarvan
Very Rev Canon William Ryan PP, VF
Dungarvan
Very Rev Canon Brendan Crowley PP, VF
SS Peter & Paul's, Clonmel
Very Rev Canon Edmond Cullinan PP, VF
Carrick-on-Suir

**College of Consultors**
Right Rev Mgr Nicholas O'Mahony PP
Very Rev Canon Brendan Crowley PP, VF
Very Rev Patrick Fitzgerald PP
Very Rev Liam Power PP
Very Rev Edmond Hassett Adm

## ADMINISTRATION

**Diocesan Administrator**
Right Rev Mgr Nicholas O'Mahony PP
Parochial House, Tramore,
Co Waterford
Tel 051-381525

**Chancellor**
Very Rev Gerard Chestnutt PP
Sacred Heart Presbytery, The Folly,
Waterford
Tel 051-878429

**Diocesan Development Committee**
Right Rev Mgr Nicholas O'Mahony,
Diocesan Administrator
Right Rev Mgr John Shine PE
Very Rev Matthew Cunningham AP
Very Rev Michael Cullinan PP
Very Rev Milo Guiry PP
Rev Richard O'Halloran CC

**Diocesan Finance Committee**
Right Rev Mgr Nicholas O'Mahony,
Diocesan Administrator
Mr Anthony Brophy
Very Rev Gerard Chestnutt PP
Very Rev Canon Brendan Crowley PP, VF
Sr June Fennelly
Mr Michael Holland
Mr Frank Kelly
Very Rev Gerard Langford PP
Mr David McCarthy
Mr Frank O'Regan
Mr Sean Ryan
Mr Tim Walsh

**Diocesan Financial Administrator**
Very Rev Gerard Chestnutt PP
Sacred Heart Presbytery, The Folly,
Waterford
Tel 051-878429

**Diocesan Building Projects Committee**
Right Rev Mgr Nicholas O'Mahony PP
Very Rev Richard Doherty AP
Very Rev Patrick Fitzgerald PP
Very Rev Thomas Flynn PP
Mr Michael J. Maguire BE, CEng, MIEI

**Diocesan Common Fund Committee**
Very Rev Raymond Liddane AP
Very Rev Garret Desmond PP
Very Rev Joseph Flynn PP
Very Rev Martin Keogh PP
Very Rev Canon William Ryan PP, VF

**Diocesan Retirement Fund Committee**
Right Rev Mgr Nicholas O'Mahony,
Diocesan Administrator
Very Rev Gerard Chestnutt PP
Very Rev Richard Doherty AP
Very Rev Martin Keogh PP
Very Rev Canon Brendan Crowley PP, VF
Very Rev Paul Waldron Adm

**Diocesan Secretary**
Very Rev Gerard Chestnutt PP
Sacred Heart Presbytery, The Folly,
Waterford
Tel 051-878429

**Episcopal Vicar for Retired Priests**
Very Rev John Kiely PP
Cappoquin, Co Waterford
Tel 058-54216

## CATECHETICS EDUCATION

**Catechetics**
*Primary Schools Religious Education:*
Sr Antoinette Dilworth
St John's Pastoral Centre, John's Hill,
Waterford
Tel 051-874199
Sr De Lourdes Breen
Presentation Sisters, 158 Larchville,
Waterford
Tel 051-355496

Very Rev Edmond Hassett Adm
Strandside South, Abbeyside,
Dungarvan, Co Waterford
Tel 058-42036
Rev Richard O'Halloran CC
Portlaw, Co Waterford
Tel 051-387227
Very Rev Paul Waldron Adm
Holy Family Presbytery, Waterford
Tel 051-350023

*Director Post-Primary Schools Religious
Education:* Sr Antoinette Dilworth
St John's Pastoral Centre, John's Hill,
Waterford
Tel 051-874199

**Catholic Primary School Managers'
Association**
*Secretary:* Very Rev Paul Waldron Adm
Holy Family Presbytery,
Luke Wadding Street, Waterford
Tel 051-350023
*Chairman:* Mr Michael O'Shea
West Street, Lismore, Co Waterford

## LITURGY

**Assistant to Parishes**
Ms Mary Dee
St John's Pastoral Centre,
John's Hill, Waterford
Tel 051-874199

**Diocesan Liturgy Committee**
Very Rev Canon William Ryan PP
Very Rev Paul Waldron Adm
Mr Noel Casey
Ms Deirdre Moore
Ms Mary Dunphy
Ms Anna Fennessey

## PASTORAL

**ACCORD**
*Director:* Very Rev Liam Power PP
St John's Pastoral Centre, John's Hill
Waterford
Tel 051-874199
Rev Raymond Reidy CC
Church of the Resurrection,
Fethard Road, Clonmel, Co Tipperary
Tel 052-6123239

**Charismatic Groups**
Very Rev Patrick Gear PP
Ballyneale, Carrick-on-Suir,
Co Tipperary
Tel 051-647011

**CURA**
St John's Pastoral Centre, John's Hill,
Waterford
Tel 051-876452

**Diocesan Archivist**
Bishop's House, John's Hill, Waterford
Tel 051-874463

**Ecumenism**
*Director*
Very Rev Canon Edmond Cullinan PP, VF
Parochial House, Chapel Street,
Carrick-on-Suir, Co Tipperary
Tel 051-640168

**Emigrant Bureau**
*Director:* Very Rev Michael Enright PE
Priest's Road, Tramore, Co Waterford
Tel 087-2371546

**Family Ministry**
*Director:* Ms Ann O'Farrell
Family Ministry Office,
St John's Pastoral Centre,
John's Hill, Waterford
Tel 051-874199/858772

**Historic Churches Advisory Committee**
Mr Eamonn McEneaney
Very Rev Canon William Ryan PP, VF
Very Rev Michael Walsh PE
Tel 051-874463

**Marriage Tribunal**
*Diocesan Official:* Rt Rev Mgr John Shine AP
Tramore, Co Waterford
Tel 051-381531
(See also Marriage Tribunals section)

**Media Spokesperson**
Very Rev Liam Power PP
St John's Pastoral Centre, John's Hill
Waterford
Tel 051-874199

**Ministry to Polish Community**
Rev Emil Adler
St Anne's Presbytery, Convent Hill,
Waterford
Tel 087-4182223

**Pastoral Development**
Very Rev Liam Power PP
St John's Pastoral Centre, John's Hill
Waterford
Tel 051-874199

**Pilgrimage**
*Director:* Very Rev Conor Kelly PP
Ring, Dungarvan, Co Waterford
Tel 058-46125

**Pioneer Total Abstinence Association**
*Diocesan Director:* Vacant

**Pontifical Mission Societies**
*Diocesan Director*
Very Rev Sean O'Dwyer PE
Clonmel Road, Cahir, Co Tipperary
Tel 087-4184213

**Travellers**
*Chaplain:* Very Rev Paul Murphy PP
St John's Presbytery, New Street,
Waterford
Tel 051-874271

**Trócaire**
*Diocesan Director*
Very Rev Conor Kelly PP
Ring, Dungarvan, Co Waterford
Tel 058-46125

**Youth Ministry**
Edmund Rice Youth & Community
Centre, Manor Street,
Waterford
Tel 051-872710

## PARISHES

*City parishes are listed first. Other parishes follow alphabetically. Italics denote church titulars where they differ from parish names.*

**TRINITY WITHIN AND ST PATRICK'S**
*Holy Trinity Cathedral*
Very Rev Paul Waldron Adm
Holy Family Presbytery,
Luke Wadding Street,
Waterford
Tel 051-350023
Very Rev Martin Slattery AP
Apt 5, Luke Wadding Suites,
Adelphi Wharf, Waterford
Tel 051-311561
*Sacristy:* Tel 051-875166

**ST JOHN'S**
Very Rev Paul Murphy PP
Rev Thomas Burns
Rev Robert Grant CC
St John's Presbytery, New Street,
Waterford
Tel 051-874271
*Sacristy:* Tel 051-875849

**SS JOSEPH AND BENILDUS**
*SS Joseph & Benildus, Newtown*
*St Mary, Ballygunner*
Very Rev Liam Power PP
30 Viewmount Park,
Waterford
Tel 051-873073
Very Rev Raymond Liddane AP
Newtown, Waterford
Tel 051-874284
Rev John Treacy CC
14 Heathervue Road, Knockboy,
Waterford
Tel 051-843207
*Sacristy:* Tel 051-878977

**BALLYBRICKEN**
*Holy Trinity Without*
Very Rev Michael Mullins PP
Rev Michael O'Brien
Rev Emil Adler
St Anne's Presbytery, Convent Hill,
Waterford
Tel 051-855819
*Sacristy:* Tel 051-874519

**HOLY FAMILY**
Very Rev Thomas Rogers PP
Holy Family Presbytery,
Luke Wadding Street, Waterford
Tel 051-375274

**ST PAUL'S**
Very Rev Patrick Fitzgerald PP
Parochial House, Lisduggan,
Waterford
Tel 051-372257
*Sacristy:* Tel 051-378073

**SACRED HEART**
Very Rev Gerard Chestnutt PP
The Presbytery, The Folly,
Waterford
Tel 051-878429
Sacristy: Tel 051-873792
Very Rev Sean Melody AP
Sacred Heart Presbytery,
21 The Folly, Waterford
Tel 051-873759

**ST SAVIOUR'S**
Very Rev Declan Corish (OP) PP
Rev Martin Crowe (OP) CC
St Saviour's Priory, Kilbarry,
Waterford
Tel 051-376032 Fax 051-376581

**ABBEYSIDE**
*St Augustine, Abbeyside*
*St Laurence, Ballinroad*
*St Vincent de Paul, Garranbane*
Very Rev Edmond Hassett Adm
Strandside South, Abbeyside,
Dungarvan, Co Waterford
Tel 058-42036
Very Rev Richard Doherty AP
Abbeyside, Dungarvan, Co Waterford
Tel 058-42379

**AGLISH**
*Our Lady of the Assumption, Aglish*
*St James, Ballinameela*
*St Patrick, Mount Stuart*
Very Rev Gerard O'Connor PP
Aglish, Cappoquin, Co Waterford
Tel 024-96287

**ARDFINNAN**
*Holy Family, Ardfinnan*
*St Nicholas, Grange, Ballybacon Church*
Very Rev Robert Power Adm
Ardfinnan, Clonmel, Co Tipperary
Tel 052-7466216

## ARDMORE
*St Declan, Ardmore*
*Our Lady of the Assumption, Grange*
Very Rev Michael Guiry PP
Ardmore, Youghal, Co Waterford
Tel 024-94275

## BALLYDUFF
*St Michael*
Very Rev Gerard McNamara PP
Ballyduff, Co Waterford
Tel 058-60227

## BALLYLOOBY
*Our Lady & St Kieran, Ballylooby*
*St John the Baptist, Duhill*
Very Rev James Denmead PP
Ballylooby, Cahir, Co Tipperary
Tel 052-7441489

## BALLYNEALE AND GRANGEMOCKLER
*St Mary, Ballyneale*
*St Mary, Grangemockler*
Very Rev Patrick Gear PP
Ballyneale, Carrick-on-Suir, Co Tipperary
Tel 051-640148

## BALLYPOREEN
*Our Lady of the Assumption*
Very Rev Joseph Flynn PP
Ballyporeen, Cahir, Co Tipperary
Tel 052-7467105

## BUTLERSTOWN
*St Mary*
Very Rev Patrick Fitzgerald PP *(priest in charge)*
Parochial House, Lisduggan, Waterford
Tel 051-372257

## CAHIR
*St Mary*
Very Rev Gerard Langford PP
Parochial House, Cahir, Co Tipperary
Tel 052-7441404

## CAPPOQUIN
*St Mary's*
Very Rev John Kiely PP
Tel 058-54216
Very Rev Robert Arthure AP
Tel 058-54221
Cappoquin, Co Waterford

## CARRICKBEG
*St Molleran, Carrickbeg*
*St Bartholomew, Windgap*
Very Rev Thomas Flynn PP
Carrickbeg, Carrick-on-Suir, Co Tipperary
Tel 051-640340

## CARRICK-ON-SUIR
*St Nicholas, Carrick-on-Suir*
*St Patrick, Faugheen*
Very Rev Canon Edmond Cullinan PP, VF
Parochial House, Carrick-on-Suir,
Co Tipperary
Tel 051-640168

Rev Richard Geoghegan CC
The Presbytery, Carrick-on-Suir,
Co Tipperary
Tel 051-640080

## CLASHMORE
*St Cronan, Clashmore*
*St Bartholomew, Piltown*
Very Rev Maurice O'Gorman PP
Clashmore, Co Waterford
Tel 024-96110

## CLOGHEEN
*St Mary, Clogheen*
*Our Lady of the Assumption, Burncourt*
Very Rev Patrick Butler PP
Parochial House, Clogheen, Cahir,
Co Tipperary
Tel 052-7465268

## CLONMEL, ST MARY'S
*St Mary*
Very Rev Peter Ahearne PP *(priest in charge)*
Rathronan, Clonmel, Co Tipperary
Tel 052-6121891
Very Rev. William Meehan PP
Tel 052-6122954
Rev Patrick Hayes CC
Tel 052-6121952
St Mary's, Clonmel, Co Tipperary

## CLONMEL, ST OLIVER PLUNKETT
*St Oliver Plunkett*
Very Rev Michael Hegarty (IC) PP
Very Rev James Pollock (IC) AP
Cooleens, Glenconnor, Clonmel,
Co Tipperary
Tel 052-6125679

## CLONMEL, SS PETER AND PAUL'S
*SS Peter and Paul's,*
*Church of the Resurrection*
Very Rev Canon Brendan Crowley PP, VF
SS Peter and Paul's, Clonmel,
Co Tipperary
Tel 052-6126292
Rev Raymond Reidy (SPS) CC
Church of the Resurrection,
Fethard Road, Clonmel, Co Tipperary
Tel 052-6123239
Rev Slawomir Jarzab CC
22 Gladstone Street, Clonmel,
Co Tipperary
Tel 052-6122138

## DUNGARVAN
*St Mary*
Very Rev Canon William Ryan PP, VF
Parochial House, Dungarvan,
Co Waterford
Tel 058-42374
Rev John Harris CC
Tel 058-42384
Rev Matthew Cooney (OSA)
The Presbytery, Dungarvan, Co Waterford

## DUNHILL
*Sacred Heart, Dunhill*
*Immaculate Conception, Fenor*
Rt Rev Mgr Nicholas O'Mahony PP (priest in charge)
Priest's Road, Tramore, Co Waterford
Tel 051-381525

## KILGOBINET
*St Gobnait, Kilgobinet*
*St Anne, Colligan*
*St Patrick, Kilbrian*
Very Rev Michael Kennedy PP
Parochial House, Colligan, Dungarvan,
Co Waterford
Tel 058-41629

## KILLEA (DUNMORE EAST)
*Holy Cross, Killea*
*St John the Baptist, Crooke*
*St Nicholas, Faithlegg*
Very Rev Brian Power PP
Dunmore East, Co Waterford
Tel 051-383127

## KILROSSANTY
*St Brigid, Kilrossanty*
*St Anne, Fews*
Very Rev John Delaney PP
Parochial House, Kilrossanty,
Kilmacthomas, Co Waterford
Tel 051-291985

## KILSHEELAN
*St Mary, Gambonsfield*
*St John the Baptist, Kilcash*
Very Rev William Carey PP
Tel 052-6133118
Rev James O'Donoghue CC
Tel 052-6133292
Kilsheelan, Clonmel, Co Tipperary

## KNOCKANORE
Very Rev Patrick T. Condon PP
Knockanore, Tallow, Co Waterford
Tel 024-97140

## LISMORE
*St Carthage*
Very Rev Michael Cullinan PP, VF
Parochial House,
Lismore, Co Waterford
Tel 058-54246

## MODELIGO
*Our Lady of the Assumption, Modeligo*
*St John the Baptist, Affane*
Priest in charge:
Very Rev John Kiely
Cappoquin, Co Waterford
Tel 058-54216

## NEWCASTLE AND FOURMILEWATER
*Our Lady of the Assumption, Newcastle*
*Our Lady & St Laurence, Fourmilewater*
Very Rev Garrett Desmond PP
Newcastle, Clonmel, Co Tipperary
Tel 052-6136387

## NEWTOWN
*All Saints, Newtown*
*St Mary, Saleen, Kill Church*
Very Rev Martin Keogh PP
Parochial House, Newtown,
Kilmacthomas, Co Waterford
Tel 051-294261
Very Rev William Callanan AP
Kill, Co Waterford
Tel 051-292212

## PORTLAW
*St Patrick, Portlaw*
*St Nicholas, Ballyduff*
Very Rev Michael O'Byrne PP
Kilmeaden, Co Waterford
Tel 051-384117
Rev Richard O'Halloran CC
Portlaw, Co Waterford
Tel 051-387227

## POWERSTOWN
*St John the Baptist, Powerstown*
*St John the Baptist, Lisronagh*
Very Rev Peter Ahearne PP
Rathronan, Clonmel,
Co Tipperary
Tel 052-6121891

## RATHGORMACK
*SS Quan & Broghan, Clonea*
*Sacred Heart, Rathgormack*
Rev Bernard Hughes (IC) (priest in
charge)
Rathgormack, Carrick-on-Suir,
Co Waterford
Tel 051-646006

## RING AND OLD PARISH
*Nativity of the BVM*
*St Nicholas*
Very Rev Conor Kelly PP
Ring, Dungarvan, Co Waterford
Tel 058-46125

## STRADBALLY
*Exaltation of the Holy Cross, Stradbally*
*St Anne, Ballylaneen, Faha Church*
Very Rev Jeremiah Condon PP
Stradbally, Kilmacthomas,
Co Waterford
Tel 051-293133

## TALLOW
*Immaculate Conception*
*Priest in Charge*
Very Rev Gerard McNamara PP
Ballyduff Upper,
Co Waterford
Tel 058-60227

## TOURANEENA
*St Mary, Touraneena, Nire Church*
Very Rev Cornelius Kelleher PP
Tournaneena, Ballinamult,
Clonmel, Co Tipperary
Tel 058-47138

## TRAMORE
*Holy Cross, Tramore*
*Our Lady, Carbally*
Right Rev Mgr Nicholas O'Mahony PP
Parochial House, Tramore,
Co Waterford
Tel 051-381525
Rt Rev Mgr John Shine AP
Priest's Road, Tramore,
Co Waterford
Tel 051-381531
Rev Michael Toomey CC
Priest's Road, Tramore,
Co Waterford
Tel 051-386642

## INSTITUTIONS AND THEIR CHAPLAINS

**Bon Sauveur Services**
Carriglea, Dungarvan, Co Waterford
Tel 058-41322 Fax 058-41432
Email bonsav@eircom.net

**University Hospital, Waterford**
Tel 051-873321
*Chaplains:* Rev Art McCoy (OFM)
Rev Ailbe Ó Murchú (OFM)
Rev Isidore Cronin (OFM)

**South Tipperary General Hospital**
*Chaplain:* Very Rev Thomas Coffey (IC)
Tel 052-6177000

**Waterford Institute of Technology**
*Chaplain:* Rev David Keating
10 Claremont, Cork Road, Waterford
Tel 051-378878

## PRIESTS OF THE DIOCESE ELSEWHERE

Very Rev Michael Kennedy
Ballylaneen, Kilmacthomas,
Co Waterford
Very Rev Paul F. Murphy (CF)
Chaplain's House, Dún Uí Mhaoilíosa,
Renmore, Galway
Tel 091-751156
Very Rev Michael O'Connor
c/o St John's Pastoral Centre,
John's Hill, Waterford
Email mnoc@iol.ie
Rev Charles Scanlan
Ballinwillin, Lismore, Co Waterford
Tel 058-54282

## RETIRED PRIESTS

Very Rev Eanna Condon PE
St Mary's, Clonmel, Co Tipperary
Tel 052-6127870
Very Rev Matthew Cunningham PE
Care Choice Nursing Home,
The Burgery, Dungarvan,
Co Waterford

Rev James Curran
61 Tournane Court, Dungarvan,
Co Waterford
Tel 058-45177
Very Rev Michael Enright PE
Priest's Road, Tramore, Co Waterford
Tel 087-2371546
Very Rev Michael Farrell PE
Padre Pio Nursing Home,
Cappoquin, Co Wateford
Very Rev Patrick Fitzgerald PE
Priest's House, Ballinameela,
Cappagh, Co Waterford
Tel 058-68021
Very Rev Francis Lloyd PE
The Presbytery, Dungarvan,
Co Waterford
Very Rev Finbarr Lucey PE
Ardmore, Youghal, Co Cork
Tel 024-94177
Very Rev James Mulcahy PE
St John's Pastoral Centre,
John's Hill, Waterford
Tel 051-858306
Rt Rev Mgr Michael Olden PE
'Woodleigh', Summerville Avenue,
Waterford
Tel 051-874132
Very Rev Canon Daniel O'Connor PE
The Presbytery, Dungarvan,
Co Waterford
Tel 058-42381
Very Rev Sean O'Dwyer PE
Clonmel Road, Cahir,
Co Tipperary
Tel 087-4184213
Very Rev Gregory Power PE
St Mary's, Clonmel, Co Tipperary
Tel 052-6182690
Very Rev Patrick Canon Quealy PE
Care Choice Dungarvan, The Burgery,
Dungarvan, Co Waterford
Tel 058-40200
Very Rev Michael J. Ryan PE
Clonmel Road, Cahir,
Co Tipperary
Tel 052-7443004
Very Rev Michael F. Walsh PE
Ballinarrid, Bonmahon,
Co Waterford
Tel 051-292992

## RELIGIOUS ORDERS AND CONGREGATIONS

### PRIESTS

**AUGUSTINIANS**
St Augustine's Priory, Dungarvan,
Co Waterford
Tel 058-41136  Fax 058-44534
*Prior:* Rev Tony Egan (OSA)

St Augustine's College,
Dungarvan, Co Waterford
Tel 058-41140/41152 Fax 058-41152

Allianz (⚺)

Duckspool House (Retirement
Community)
Abbeyside, Dungarvan,
Co Waterford
Tel 058-23784

## CISTERCIANS
Mount Melleray Abbey,
Cappoquin, Co Waterford
Tel 058-54404 Fax 058-52140
Email mountmellerayabbey@eircom.net
*Claustral Prior*
Br Boniface McGinley (OCSO)
*Abbot:* Vacant

## DOMINICANS
Bridge Street, Waterford
Tel 051-875061 Fax 051-858093
*Prior:* Very Rev Richard Walsh (OP)

Ballybeg, Waterford
Tel 051-376032 Fax 051-376581
*Prior and Parish Priest*
Very Rev Declan Corish (OP) PP

## FRANCISCANS
Franciscan Friary, Clonmel,
Co Tipperary
Tel 052-6121378 Fax 052-6125806
Email clonmel@eircom.net
*Vicar:* Rev Larry Mulligan (OFM)

Franciscan Friary,
Lady Lane, Waterford
Tel 051-874262 Fax 051-843062
Email waterfordfriary@eircom.net
*Guardian:* Rev Ailbe O'Murchú (OFM)

## ROSMINIANS
Rosminian House of Prayer,
Glencomeragh, Kilsheelan,
Co Tipperary
Tel 052-6133181
*Rector:* Rev Michael Melican (IC)

St Joseph's Doire na hAbhann
Tickincor, Clonmel, Co Tipperary
Tel 052-26914 Fax 052-26915
Residential centre for children in care

(See also under parishes – St Oliver
Plunkett)

# BROTHERS

## CHRISTIAN BROTHERS
Christian Brothers' House,
Brú na Cruinne, Carrick-on-Suir,
Co Tipperary
Tel 051-640335 Fax 051-642605
Email brunacruinne@eircom.net
*Community Leader:* Br Sean O'Dugain
Community: 3

Mount Sion, Waterford
Tel 051-879580 Fax 051-841578
Community: 3

International Heritage Centre & Chapel
Mount Sion, Barrack Street,
Waterford
Tel 051-874390 Fax 051-841578

## DE LA SALLE BROTHERS
De La Salle College, Newtown,
Waterford
Tel 051-875294 Fax 051-841321
Email delasall@iol.ie
*Superior:* Br Amedy Hayes
Community: 6
Secondary School
*Headmaster:* Mr Gearoid O'Brien

De La Salle Brothers
25 Patrick Street, Waterford
Tel 051-874623
Community: 3
*Superior:* Br Francis McCallig
St Stephen's Primary School
*Principal:* Mr Paudge Morris
Tel 051-871716

## PRESENTATION BROTHERS
Glór na hAbhann, Ballinamona Lower,
Old Parish, Dungarvan,
Co Waterford
Tel 058-46904
*Contact:* Br John Hunt (FPM)
Community: 3

# SISTERS

## BON SAUVEUR SISTERS
Carriglea, Dungarvan, Co Waterford
Tel 058-45884 Fax 058-45891
Email lbscarriglea@eircom.net
*Superior:* Sr Mary Fitzgerald
Community: 5
Pastoral Ministry to Carriglea Cairde
Service – Residential and day care services
for persons with an intellectual disability

## CARMELITES
St Joseph's Carmelite Monastery, Tallow,
Co Waterford
Tel 058-56205
Email carmeltallow@eircom.net
*Superior:* Sr Teresa Gibbons
Community: 6
Contemplatives

## CISTERCIANS
St Mary's Abbey, Glencairn, Lismore,
Co Waterford
Tel 058-56168 Fax 058-56616
Email glencairnabbey@eircom.net
*Abbess:* Sr Marie Fahy
Tel 058-56197
Email mbfahy@eircom.net
Community: 31
Monastic

## CONGREGATION OF THE SISTERS OF MERCY
Convent of Mercy, Cahir,
Co Tipperary
Tel 052-7441294

Teach Bride, Convent Road,
Townspark, Cahir, Co Tipperary
Tel 052-7443809

St Mary's Mount Anglesby,
Clogheen, Co Tipperary
Tel 052-7465255

Greenhill, Carrick-on-Suir,
Co Tipperary
Tel 051-640059

Springwell, Pill Road,
Carrick-on-Suir, Co Tipperary
Tel 051-642870

12 Comeragh View,
Carrick-on-Suir, Co Tipperary
Tel 051-645012

10 Ash Park, Carrick-on-Suir,
Co Tipperary
Tel 051-640814

Apartment 1, William Street,
Carrick-on-Suir, Co Tipperary
Tel 051-642576

21 Heywood Heights,
Clonmel, Co Tipperary
Tel 052-6125235

31 Willow Park,
Clonmel, Co Tipperary
Tel 052-6128903

32 Willow Park,
Clonmel, Co Tipperary
Tel 052-6125809

Convent of Mercy, Church Street,
Dungarvan, Co Waterford
Tel 058-41293/41337

1 Park Lane Drive, Abbeyside,
Dungarvan, Co Waterford
Tel 058-48795

22 Blackrock Court, Youghal Road,
Dungarvan, Co Waterford
Tel 058-48286

16 Blackrock Court, Youghal Road,
Dungarvan, Co Waterford
Tel 058-45713

17 Blackrock Court, Youghal Road,
Dungarvan, Co Waterford
Tel 058-44865

11 Blackrock Court, Youghal Road,
Dungarvan, Co Waterford
Tel 058-24656

3 Marine View, Youghal Road,
Dungarvan, Co Waterford

Convent of Mercy,
Military Road, Waterford
Tel 051-74161/77909

Coolock House,
Grange Park Road, Waterford
Tel 051-878710

17/18 Bromley Close,
Ardkeen Village, Waterford
Tel 051-857684

2 Chestnut Grove,
Waterford
Tel 051-373542

93 Clonard Park,
Ballybeg, Waterford
Tel 051-379110

7 Aisling Court,
Hennessy's Road, Waterford
Tel 051-874592

5 Cul Rua, Portlaw,
Co Waterford
Tel 051-387125

**CONGREGATION OF OUR LADY OF
CHARITY OF THE GOOD SHEPHERD**
Virginia Crescent, Hennessy's Road,
Waterford
Tel 051-874294 Fax 051-855940
Email rgswat33@hotmail.co.uk
*Leader:* Sr Bríd Mullins
Community: 15

Good Shepherd Sisters,
37 Clonard Park, Ballybeg,
Waterford
Email rgsanna02@eircom.net
Community: 1

**LITTLE COMPANY OF MARY**
36 Willowbrook,
Tallow, Co Waterford
Tel 058-55962
Apostolic community: 1

**LORETO (IBVM)**
Loreto Secondary School,
Clonmel, Co Tipperary
Tel 052-21402
Community: 2

**PRESENTATION SISTERS**
Presentation Sisters, Chapel Street,
Carrick-on-Suir, Co Tipperary
Tel 051-640069
*Contact:* Sr Immaculata Buckley

Presentation Sisters,
Clonmel, Co Tipperary
Tel 052-6121538
*Local Leader:* Sr Marie Stella Mangan
Community: 22
Primary school, Secondary school

Presentation Sisters,
Youghal Road,
Dungarvan, Co Waterford
Tel 058-41359
*Local Leader:* Sr Gertrude Howley
Community: 9
Primary School

Presentation Sisters, 158 Larchville,
Waterford
Tel 051-355496
*Contact:* Sr de Lourdes Breen
Community: 4

Presentation Sisters,
81 Treacy Park, Carrick-on-Suir,
Co Tipperary
Tel 051-641733
Community: 5

Presentation Sisters,
50 Cathal Brugha Place,
Dungarvan, Co Waterford
Tel 058-45582
Community: 3

11 Convent Lodge,
Mitchell Street, Dungarvan,
Co Waterford
*Contact:* Sr Martina O'Callaghan

**RELIGIOUS SISTERS OF CHARITY**
Star of the Sea,
Tramore, Co Waterford
Tel 051-381308
Various apostolic ministries

**ST JOHN OF GOD SISTERS**
9 The Cloisters, John's Hill,
Waterford
Tel 051-874370
Community: 2

St John of God Sisters,
41 Grange Cove, Waterford
Tel 051-855585
Community: 3

**URSULINES**
Ursuline Convent,
Waterford
Tel 051-874068
Email ursuline94@eircom.net
*Local Leader:* Sr Barbara Burke
Community: 10
Primary School
Tel 051-873788/852855
Fax 051-852855
Secondary School
Tel 051-876121 Fax 051-879022
18 Shannon Drive,

Avondale, Waterford
Tel 051-854680
Email ursulinesisterswd@eircom.net
Community: 2

1 St Anne's,
Ursuline Court, Waterford
Tel 051-857015
Email onestannes@eircom.net
Community: 2

## EDUCATIONAL INSTITUTIONS

**EDMUND RICE SCHOOLS TRUST**
Scoil Náisiúnta Mhuire na mBráithre,
Carrick-on-Suir, Co Tipperary
Primary School
Tel 051-641333
*Principal:* Mr Denis Cotter

CBS Secondary School
Mount St Nicholas, Carrick-on-Suir,
Co Tipperary
Tel 051-640522
Email cbscarrickonsuir@eircom.net
*Principal:* Mr Billy O'Farrell

Ardscoil na mBráithre,
Kickham Street, Clonmel,
Co Tipperary
Tel 052-24459 Fax 052-25320
Email info@cbshighschoolclonmel.ie
*Principal:* Ms Karen Steenson

Scoil na mBráithre,
Mitchell Street, Dungarvan,
Co Waterford
Secondary School
*Principal:* Mr Paul Sheehan
Tel 058-41185Fax 058-48512

Mount Sion Primary School,
Barrack Street, Waterford
Tel 051-377947 Fax 051-358304
Email office.mountsion@gmail.com
*Principal:* Mr Michael Walsh

Mount Sion CBS Secondary School,
Barrack Street, Waterford
Tel 051-377378Fax 051-376468
Staff Tel 051-877456
Email mountsionsecondary@yahoo.ie
*Principal:* Mr John McArdle

Waterpark College Secondary School
Park Road, Waterford
Tel 051-874445
Fax 051-874040
Email waterparkcollege@eircom.net
Website www.waterparkcollege.com
*Principal:* Mr T. Beecher

Ardscoil na Mara,
Tramore, Co Waterford
Tel 051-395124
Email office@ardscoilnamara.ie
Website www.ardscoilnamara.ie
*Principal:* Mr Padraig Cawley

## ST JOHN'S
## PASTORAL CENTRE

**St John's Pastoral Centre**
John's Hill, Waterford
Tel 051-874199 Fax 051-843107
Email stjohnspastoralcentre@eircom.net
*Administrator:* Ms Mary Dee

## CHARITABLE AND OTHER
## SOCIETIES

**Apostolic Work Society**
*President of Diocesan Council*
Vacant
Centres at Dungarvan, Cappoquin,
Carrick-on-Suir, Kilmacthomas, Dunmore
East, Clogheen, Clonmel

**Hostels**
Men's Hostel, Ozanam House,
Lady Lane, Waterford
(St Vincent de Paul)

## BENEDICTINES (OSB)

*Archdiocese of Cashel and Diocese of Emly*

Attached to the Benedictine Congregation of the Annunciation, Belgium.

**Glenstal Abbey**
Murroe, Co Limerick
Tel 061-621000
Fax 061-386328
Email monks@glenstal.org

*Abbot:* Rt Rev Dom Mark Patrick Hederman
*Prior*
Very Rev Brendan Coffey
*Sub-Prior*
Right Rev Dom Christopher Dillon
*Abbot 1992-2008*
Right Rev Dom Christopher Dillon
*Abbot 1980-92*
Right Rev Dom Celestine Cullen
*Headmaster*
Br Martin Browne
*Guestmaster*
Rev Christopher Dillon
*Novice Master*
Rev Columba McCann

*Directors of Associates and Oblates*
Rev David Conlon
Rev Columba McCann
Rev Anselm Barry
Rev Cuthbert Brennan
Rev Alan Crawford
Rev Bonaventure Dunne
Rev William Fennelly
Br Ciarán Forbes
Rev Basil Forde
Rev Senan Furlong
Br Denis Hooper
Br Anselm Hurt
Rev Anthony Keane
Br Cyprian Love
Rev Fintan Lyons
Rev Joseph McGilloway
Br Timothy McGrath
Br Pádraig McIntyre
Rev James McMahon
Rev Luke MacNamara
Rev Brian Murphy
Rev Placid Murray
Rev Paul Nash
Rev Andrew Nugent
Rev John O'Callaghan
Br Colmán Ó Clabaigh
Br Emmaus O'Herlihy
Br Cillian Ó Sé
Rev Henry O'Shea
Rev Simon Sleeman
Rev Philip Tierney

*Diocese of Dromore*

Attached to the Benedictine Congregation of St Mary of Monte Oliveto.

**Benedictine Monks**
Holy Cross Monastery,
119 Kilbroney Road,
Rostrevor, Co Down BT34 3BN
Tel 028-41739979
Fax 028-41739978
Email benedictinemonks@
btinternet.com
Website
www.benedictinemonks.co.uk

*Prior*
Very Rev Dom Mark-Ephrem M. Nolan

Rev D. Eric M. Loisel
Rev D. Thierry M. Marteaux
D. Benoît M. Charlet
D. Pascal M. Jouy
D. Joshua M. Domenzain Canul

## BENEDICTINE MONKS OF PERPETUAL ADORATION OF THE MOST HOLY SACRAMENT (OSB)

*Diocese of Meath*

**Silverstream Priory**
Stamullen, Co Meath
Tel 01-8417142
Email prior@cenacleosb.org
*Prior:* Very Rev Dom Mark Daniel Kirby
Rev Dom Benedict Maria Andersen

## BLESSED SACRAMENT CONGREGATION (SSS)

*Provincial*
Rev Peter Dowling
62 Langlands Road, Govan,
Glasgow G51 3BD, Scotland
Tel 0044-141-4451416
Email petdowling1@aol.com

*Archdiocese of Dublin*

**Blessed Sacrament Chapel**
20 Bachelors Walk, Dublin 1
Tel 01-8724597
Fax 01-8724724
Email sssdublin@eircom.net

*Superior*
Rev James Campbell

Rev Renato Esoy
Rev James Hegarty
Br Andrew McTeigue
Rev Raphael O'Halloran

## CAMILLIANS (OSCam)
### Order of St Camillus

Anglo-Irish Province

*Archdiocese of Dublin*

**St Camillus**
South Hill Avenue,
Blackrock, Co Dublin
Tel 01-2882873/2833380

*Superior:* Rev Denis Sandham
*(Chaplain to Beaumont Hospital)*

Rev Suresh Babu
Rev Jayan Joseph *(Chaplain to St Luke's Hospital)*
Rev Tom O'Connor

**St Camillus**
11 St Vincent Street North,
Dublin 7
Tel 01-8300365 (residence)
Tel 01-8301122 (Mater Hospital)

*Superior & Provincial*
Rev Stephen Forster
Tel 01-8304635

Br Camillus McHugh
Rev Tomy Paradiyil
Rev John Philip *(Chaplain to Mater Hospital)*
Rev Vincent Xavier *(Chaplain to Mater Hospital)*
4 St Vincent Street North,
Dublin 7

*Diocese of Meath*

**St Camillus**
Killucan, Co Westmeath
Tel 044-74196 (nursing centre)
Tel 044-74115 (community)
Fax 044-74309

*Superior:* Rev Frank Monks
Email fmonks@libero.it

Rev Andrew Carroll
Rev Martin Geraghty *(Chaplain to Connolly Memorial Hospital, Blanchardstown)*
Rev Nik Houlihan
Rev Suneesh Mathew
Br Augustine McCormack
Rev Joseph Naikaruddy
Br John O'Brien

## CAPUCHINS (OFM Cap)

Province of Ireland

Includes nine friaries in Ireland, Vice-Provinces in South Africa and Zambia, and custodies in South Korea and New Zealand.

*Archdiocese of Dublin*

**Provincial Office**
12 Halston Street, Dublin 7
Tel 01-8733205 Fax 01-8730294
Email capcurirl@eircom.net

*Provincial Minister*
Very Rev Adrian Curran
*Guardian:* Br Pius Higgins

Rev Richard Hendrick
Rev Paul Murphy

**Capuchin Friary**
Church Street, Dublin 7
Tel 01-8730599
Fax 01-8730250

*Guardian:* Rev Bryan Shortall
(PP Halston Street Parish)
*Vicar:* Br Kevin Crowley

Br Bosco Connolly
Rev Piaras Ó Dúill
Rev Dan Joe O'Mahony
Rev Angelus O'Neill
Rev Owen O'Sullivan
*(Assigned)*
Rev Peter Rodgers
Rev Kieran Shorten

**Capuchin Friary**
Station Road,
Raheny, Dublin 5
Tel 01-8313886
Fax 01-8511498

*Guardian:* Rev Michael Burgess
*Vicar:* Rev Eustace McSweeney

Rev Philip Baxter
Br Martin Bennett
Rev Anthony Boran
Br Oliver Brady
Rev Michael Duffy
Rev Sean Kelly
Rev Pádraig Ó Cuill

**Capuchin Friary**
Clonshaugh Drive,
Priorswood, Dublin 17
Tel 01-8474469
Fax 01-8487296

*PP & Guardian*
Rev Jack Twomey

Br Ignatius Galvin

*Diocese of Cork & Ross*

**Capuchin Friary**
Holy Trinity,
Fr Mathew Quay, Cork
Tel 021-4270827
Fax 021-4270829

*Guardian:* Rev Dermot Lynch
*Vicar:* Rev Joseph Nagle

Rev Tom Forde
Rev Edwin Flynn
Rev Patrick Flynn
Br John Hickey
Rev Michael Murphy
Rev Desmond McNaboe
Rev Brendan O'Mahony
Rev Aidan Vaughan

**St Francis Capuchin Friary**
Rochestown, Co Cork
Tel 021-4896244
Fax 021-4895915

*Guardian:* Br Paul O'Donovan
*Vicar:* Rev John Manley

Br Felix Carroll
Br Albert Cooney
Br Hugh Davis
Br Jeremy Heneghan
Rev Kevin Kiernan
Rev Anthony O'Keeffe
Rev Kenneth Reynolds

**St Francis Capuchin Franciscan College**
Rochestown, Co Cork
Tel 021-4891417
Fax 021-4361254

*Principal*
Mr Diarmaid Ó Mathúna

*Diocese of Kildare & Leighlin*

**Capuchin Friary**
43 Dublin Street, Carlow
Tel 059-9142543
Fax 059-9142030

*Guardian*
Rev Christopher Twomey
*Vicar:* Br John Wright

Rev Alexius Healy
Rev Leo McAuliffe
Br Philip Tobin

*Diocese of Ossory*

**Capuchin Friary**
Friary Street, Kilkenny
Tel 056-7721439
Fax 056-7722025

*Guardian*
Rev Sean Donohoe
*Vicar*
Rev Terence Harrington

Rev Benignus Buckley
Rev Philip Connor
Br Joseph Gallagher
Rev James Harrington

*Diocese of Raphoe*

**Capuchin Friary**
Ard Mhuire, Creeslough,
Letterkenny, Co Donegal
Tel 074-9138005
Fax 074-9138371

*Guardian*
Rev Silvester O'Flynn
*Vicar*
Br Bernard McAllister

Rev Brian Browne *(Assigned)*
Br Vianney Holmes
Rev Flannan Lynch
Rev Patrick Lynch
Rev James Ryan
Rev William Ryan

*Vice-Province of Zambia*

**Capuchin Franciscans Vice-Provincialate**
Post Net Box 147, P/Bag E891,
Lusaka, Zambia
Tel 00260-1250269
Fax 00260-1252828
Email capzam@iconnect.zm

*Vice-Province of South Africa*

**Capuchin Franciscans**
PO Box 118,
Howard Place 7450,
South Africa
Tel 00272-16370026
Fax 00272-16370014
Email capadmin@iafrica.com

*Custody of South Korea*

**Capuchin Franciscans**
Hyochang-Dong 5-40,
Yong San-Gu, Seoul,
South Korea 140120
Tel 0082-2-7015727
Fax 0082-2-7176128
Email capdelkor@yahoo.com

*Custody of New Zealand*

**Capuchin Franciscans**
Holy Cross Friary,
PO Box 21082, 14 Lavelle Road,
Henderson, Auckland 1008,
New Zealand
Tel 0064-9-8388663
Fax 0064-9-8387114
Email auck@capuchins.org.nz

For further details concerning
the Missions contact:

**Capuchin Mission Office**
Church Street, Dublin 7
Tel 01-8731022
Fax 01-8740478

# CARMELITES (OCarm)

Irish Province

*Archdiocese of Dublin*

**Provincial Office and Carmelite Community**
Gort Muire, Ballinteer,
Dublin 16
Tel 01-2984014 Fax 01-2987221

*Provincial*
Very Rev Martin Kilmurray
Email
mkilmurray@gortmuire.com
*Assistant Provincial*
Rev Patrick Staunton
Email
pstaunton@gortmuire.com

*Prior:* Rev Joseph Mothersill
*Bursar:* Rev Fintan Burke
*Sub-Prior:* Rev Simon Nolan

Rev Albert Breen
Rev Michael Cremin
Rev Christopher Crowley
Rev P.J. Cunningham
Rev Liam Fennell
Rev Thomas Fives
Rev Patrick Gallagher
Rev Lovemore Gutu
Rev Charles Hoey
Rev Brian Kiernan
Rev Martin Kilmurray
Rev Anthony McKinney
Rev Robert Manik
Rev Fergus O'Loan
Rev Patrick Mullins
Rev James Murray
Br Vito Saracino
Rev Patrick Staunton

**Whitefriar Street Church**
56 Aungier Street, Dublin 2
Tel 01-4758821
Fax 01-4758825
Email whitefriars@eircom.net

*Prior:* Rev Brian McKay
*Sub-Prior:* Rev Martin Baxter
*Bursar:* Rev Dermot Kelly
*Parish Priest*
Rev Bernard Murphy

Rev Donal Byrne
Rev Daniel Callaghan
Rev Christopher Conroy
Rev Patrick (Alan) Fitzpatrick
Rev Patrick Graham
Rev Thomas Higgins
Rev Desmond Kelly
Rev Jarlath O'Hea
Rev David Twohig

**Terenure College**
Terenure, Dublin 6W
Tel 01-4904621
Fax 01-4902403
Email admin@terenurecollege.ie

*Prior/Manager*
Rev Michael Troy
*Sub-Prior:* Rev Eoin Moore
*Principal Senior School*
Rev Richard Byrne
*Principal Junior School*
Rev Michael Troy

Rev P.J. Breen
Rev James Eivers
Rev John Madden
Rev Christopher O'Donnell
Rev Francis O'Gara
Rev David Weakliam

**St Colmcille's**
The Presbytery,
Idrone Avenue,
Knocklyon, Dublin 16
Tel 01-4941204/4944986
Fax 01-4946842
Email presbytery@
knocklyonparish.ie

*Parish Priest/Prior*
Rev Eanna Ó hÓbáin

Rev Seán MacGiollarnáth CC
Rev Michael Morrissey CC
Rev Martin Parokkaran CC

*Diocese of Cork & Ross*

**Carmelite Friary**
Kinsale, Co Cork
Tel 021-4772138
Email
kinsale@irishcarmelites.com

*Prior*
Rev Frank McAleese
*Bursar*
Rev Stan Hession

Rev Robert Kelly

*Diocese of Kildare & Leighlin*

**Carmelite Priory**
White Abbey,
Co Kildare
Tel 045-521391
Fax 045-522318
Email
carmeliteskildare@gmail.com

*Prior*
Rev Anthony McDonald
*Bursar*
Rev Frederick Lally

Rev Aloysius Ryan
Rev Patrick Smyth

*Diocese of Meath*

**Carmelite Priory**
Moate, Co Westmeath
Tel 090-6481160/6481398
Fax 090-6481879
Email
carmelitemoate@eircom.net

*Prior*
Rev Martin Ryan
*Sub-Prior*
Rev Jaison Kuthanapillil
*Bursar*
Rev Peter Kehoe

Rev Bernard O'Reilly

Allianz (ⅱ)

*Diocese of Ossory*

**Carmelite Priory**
**(Knocktopher/Ballyhale)**
Knocktopher, Co Kilkenny
Tel 056-7768675
Fax 056-7768237
Email knockcar@indigo.ie

*Prior/Parish Priest*
Rev Benedict O'Callaghan PP
*Bursar:* Rev Laurence Lynch

Rev Philip Brennan

## CARMELITES (OCD)

Anglo-Irish Province

The Province has five
communities in Ireland and
thirteen overseas including
five in Nigeria.

*Provincial*
Rev Michael McGoldrick
53 Marlborough Road,
Donnybrook, Dublin 4
Tel 01-6617163/6601832
Fax 01-6683752
Email
mmcgoldrickocd@gmail.com
Website www.ocd.ie

*Archdiocese of Dublin*

**St Teresa's**
Clarendon Street, Dublin 2
Tel 01-6718466/6718127
Fax 01-6718462

*Prior*
Very Rev Christopher Clarke
Email stteresa@ocd.ie

Rev Michael Brown
Rev Joe Glynn
Rev Michéal MacLaifeartaigh
Rev Desmond McCaffrey
Rev Nicholas Madden
Rev Paul O'Sullivan

**Avila**
Bloomfield Avenue,
Morehampton Road, Dublin 4
Tel 01-6430200 Fax 01-6430281
Email avila@ocd.ie

*Prior:* Rev Vincent O'Hara

Rev Stanislaus Callanan
Rev Eugene McCaffrey
Rev James Noonan
Br Noel O'Connor
Rev Tom Stone

**Karmel**
53/55 Marlborough Road,
Dublin 4
Tel 01-6601832

*Prior:* Rev Edmund Smyth

Rev Joseph Birmingham
Rev Liam Ó Bréartúin
Rev Herman Doolan

**St Joseph's**
Berkeley Road, Dublin 7
Tel 01-8306356/8306336
Fax 01-8304681

*Prior*
Rev David Donnellan PP

Rev Patrick Beecher
Rev Peter Cryan
Rev Patrick Keenan CC
Rev Richard Young

*Diocese of Clonfert*

**The Abbey**
Loughrea, Co Galway
Tel 091-841209
Fax 091-842343

*Prior:* Rev Willie Moran

Rev Bernard Cuffe
Rev Cronan Glynn
Rev Ambrose McNamee
Rev Anthony Parsons
Rev Tom Shanahan

*Diocese of Derry*

**St Joseph's Carmelite**
**Retreat Centre**
Termonbacca,
Derry BT48 9XE
Tel 028-71262512
Fax 028-71373589

*Prior:* Rev Sean Conlon

Rev Jeremiah Fitzpatrick
Rev John McNamara

## CISTERCIAN ORDER (OCSO)

The mother house of the
Cistercian Order is the Arch-
abbey of Citeaux, Côte d'Or,
France.

*Archdiocese of Armagh*

**Mellifont Abbey**
Collon, Co Louth
Tel 041-9826103
Fax 041-9826713
Email
mellifontabbey@eircom.net

*Superior:* Rev Joseph Ryan
*Prior:* Br Andrew Considine

Br Brian Berkeley
Rev Dom Bernard Boyle
Rev William Cullinan
Br Brendan Garry
Br Thomas Maher
Rev Laurence McDermott
Rev Alphonsus O'Connor
Br Cornelius Ogwu
Br Ifunanya Onwe

*Archdiocese of Dublin*

**Bolton Abbey**
Moone, Co Kildare
Tel 059-8624102
Fax 059-8624309
Email info@boltonabbey.ie
Website www.boltonabbey.ie

*Abbot*
Rt Rev Dom Michael Ryan
*Prior:* Br Anthony Jones
*Guestmaster*
Br Francis McLean
*Novice Director*
Rev Ambrose Farrington

Rev Martin Garry
Rev Eoin de Bhaldraithe
Br Alberic Turner
Br Brian O'Dowd

*Diocese of Down & Connor*

**Our Lady of Bethlehem Abbey**
11 Ballymena Road,
Portglenone, Ballymena,
Co Antrim BT44 8BL
Tel 028-25821211
Fax 028-25822795
Email celsus@bethabbey.com
www.bethlehemabbey.com

*Abbot*
Rt Rev Dom Celsus Kelly

*Prior*
Rev Martin Dowley
*Sub-Prior*
Rt Rev Dom Charles Kaweesi

Br Michael McCourt
Br Finbar McLoughlin
Rev Aelred Magee
Rev Francis Morgan
Rev Chrysostom O'Connell
Br Vianney O'Donnell
Br Columba O'Neill
Rev Finnian Owens
Rev Philip Scott
Br Joseph Skehan

*Diocese of Killaloe*

**Mount Saint Joseph Abbey**
Roscrea, Co Tipperary
Tel 0505-25600 Fax 0505-25610
Email info@msjroscrea.ie
www.msjroscrea.ie

*Abbot*
Rt Rev Dom Richard Purcell
*Prior*
Rev Dom Laurence Walsh

Rev Kevin Daly
Rev Peter Garvey
Rev Eanna Henderson
Rev Robert Kelly
Rev Gabriel McCarthy
Br John McDonnell
Rev Aodhán McDunphy

Br Laurence Molloy
Rev Anthony O'Brien
Rev Liam O'Connor
Rev Ciaran Ó Sabhaois
Rev Colmcille O'Toole
Br Vladimir Tkachenko
Br Malachy Thompson
Br Dominic Tobin
Br Oliver Tyrrell

*Diocese of Waterford &
Lismore*

**Mount Melleray Abbey**
Cappoquin,
Co Waterford
Tel 058-54404 Fax 058-52140
Email mountmellerayabbey@
eircom.net

*Claustral Prior*
Br Boniface McGinley

Rev Michael Ahern
Br Camillus Canning
Rev Denis Collins
Br Seamus Corrigan
Br Edmund Costine
Rev Bonaventure Cumiskey
Br Donal Davis
Br John Dineen
Rev Kevin Fogarty
Rev Ignatius Hahessy
Rev Columban Heaney
Rt Rev Augustine McGregor
Br Declan Murphy
Rev Alphonsus O'Connell
Rev Denis Luke O'Hanlon
Rev Celestine O'Leary
Rev Vincent O Maidin
Rev Patrick Ryan

## COMBONI MISSIONARIES (MCCJ)

Verona Fathers

*Provincial:* Rev Martin Devenish
Comboni Missionaries,
London Road, Sunningdale,
Berks SL5 OJY, UK

*Archdiocese of Dublin*

**8 Clontarf Road**
Clontarf, Dublin 3
Tel/Fax 01-8330051
Email
combonimission@eircom.net

*Superior:* Rev Antonio Benetti

## Congregation of the Sacred Hearts of Jesus and Mary (SSCC)

### Sacred Hearts Community

*Archdiocese of Dublin*

**Provincialate**
Coudrin House,
27 Northbrook Road,
Dublin 6
Tel 01-6604898 (Provincialate)
Email ssccdublin@eircom.net
Tel 01-6686584 (Community)
Fax 01-6686590
Website
www.sacred-hearts.net

*Provincial*
Very Rev Derek Laverty
Tel 01-6473750
Email
dereklaverty2005@yahoo.co.uk
*Provincial Secretary*
Sheila O'Dowd

Most Rev Brendan Comiskey DD
Rev Michael F. Foley
Tel 01-6473759
Email
michaelffoley@eircom.net
Br Anthony McMorrow
Tel 01-6473754
Rev Andy Wafer
Tel 01-6473755
Email waferandy@gmail.com
Rev Franciscus Xaverius Sri
Waluyo
Tel 01-6473756

**Sacred Heart Presbytery**
St John's Drive,
Clondalkin,
Dublin 22
Tel 01-4570032

Rev Michael Ruddy
Email mikeruddy@eircom.net
Rev Eamon Aylward
Email ssccmoz@eircom.net
Rev Pearse Mullen
Email
pearsepmullen@yahoo.com

*Diocese of Clogher*

**Cootehill**
Co Cavan
Tel 049-5552188

Rev Jerry White
Email jerryssccc@gmail.com
Br Harry O'Gara
Email broharryssccc@gmail.com
Rev Kieran Murtagh
Email
kieranpmurtagh@yahoo.com

**Rockcorry**
Co Monaghan

Rev Jerry White CC
Email jerryssccc@gmail.com

## DIVINE WORD MISSIONARIES (SVD)

Irish & British Province

Each Province of the Society is independent. When members are assigned to work in the missions, they automatically become members of the territory to which they are assigned and are no longer members of the Irish British Province.

*Archdiocese of Dublin*

**1 & 3 Pembroke Road,**
Dublin 4
Tel 01-6680904
*Praeses:* Rev Albert Escoto
Email aesvd@hotmail.com

*Provincial:* Rev Patrick Byrne
Email
provincial@svdireland.com

Rev Pat Claffey
Rev Liam Dunne
Rev Gaspar Habara
Rev Tom Kearney
Rev Binoy Mathew
Rev John McAteer
Rev Oliver O'Connor
Rev John Owen
Rev Noel Ruane
Rev Bart Parys

**133 North Circular Road,**
Dublin 7
Tel 01-8386743
*Praeses*
Rev John Feighery

Rev Henry Barlage
Rev Patrick Lee
Rev Anthony O'Riordan
Rev Paul St John
Rev Finbarr Tracey

**Maynooth**
Co Kildare
Tel 01-6286391/2
Fax 01-6289184
Email
secretary@svdireland.com

*Rector*
Rev D. Vincent Twomey
*Provincial Treasurer*
Rev Jega Susai

Rev Brendan Casey
Rev Daniel Daly
Rev Tadeusz Durajczyk
Rev Richard Kelly
Rev Francis Kom
Rev Gerard McCarthy
Rev George Millar
Rev Jim Perry

## Divine Word School of English
Tel 01-6289512
Fax 01-6289748
Email dwse@eircom.net

*Director*
Mr Michael Fitzgerald

*Diocese of Elphin*

**Donamon Castle**
Roscommon
Tel 090-6662222
Fax 090-6662511
pathogansvd@gmail.com

*Rector*
Very Rev Patrick Hogan

Rev Tony Coote
Rev Norman Davitt
Br Brendan Fahey
Rev Larry Finnegan
Rev Richard Flanagan
Rev Charles Guthrie
Rev Michael Joyce
Rev Kevin Keenan
Rev Jerry Lanigan
Rev Peter Maloney
Br Gerhard Osthues
Rev Michael Reddan
Rev Krzysztof Sikora

**Creggs**
(Kilbegnet & Glinsk)
Tel 090-6662222
pathogansvd@gmail.com

*Parish Priest*
Rev John McCarthy

*British District*

**London**
8 Teignmouth Road,
London, NW2 4HN
Tel 020-84528430

*Praeses*
Rev Phelim Jordan

Rev Michael Egan
Rev Brian Gilmore

Rev Martin McPake
Rev Kevin O'Toole

**Bristol**
St Mary-on-the-Quay
Presbytery,
20 Colston Street,
Bristol BS1 5AE
Tel 0117-9264702

*Parish Priest*
Rev Nicodemus Lobo Ratu

Rev John Bettison
Rev Kieran Fitzharris

## DOMINICAN ORDER (OP)

### Order of Preachers

Irish Province

*Archdiocese of Dublin*

**Provincial Office**
St Mary's, Tallaght, Dublin 24
Tel 01-4048118/4048114
Fax 01-4515584
Email provincialop@eircom.net

*Provincial*
Very Rev Gregory Carroll
*Provincial Bursar and
Provincial Secretary*
Rev Tom Monahan
*Children Protection Officer*
Rev Vincent Travers

**Dominican Community**
St Mary's Priory
Tallaght, Dublin 24
Tel 01-4048100
Parish 01-4048188
Email
parish@stmarys-tallaght.ie
Retreat House
Tel 01-4048189/8123/8191
Fax 01-4596080
Email domretreat@eircom.net

*Prior*
Very Rev Donal Sweeney PP
Email dsyop@eircom.net

Rev Wilfrid Harrington
Rev Paschal Tiernan
Rev Luke Dempsey
Rev Hugh Fenning
Rev Philip Gleeson
Rev Donagh O'Shea
Rev Thomas O'Flynn
Rev Brian McKevitt
Rev Philip McShane
Br Martin Cogan
Rev Donal Roche
Br Eamonn Moran
Br Michael Neenan
Br James Ryan
Rev Gerard Norton
Rev Séamus Touhy
Rev Robert Regula CC
Rev Atanasio Flores

**St Saviour's**
Upper Dorset Street, Dublin 1
Tel 01-8897610
Fax 01-8734003
Email stsaviours@eircom.net

*Prior*
Very Rev Edward Conway PP

Rev Clement Greenan
Rev Edward Foley
Rev Liam Walsh
Rev Diarmuid Clifford
Rev Martin Boyle
Rev John Harris
Rev Tomasz Martynelis
Rev Bernard McCay-Morrissey
Rev Cezary Binkiewicz

Rev Terence Crotty
Rev Brian Doyle
Rev Colm Mannion
Br David McGovern
Br Damian Polly
Br Ronan Connolly
Br Patrick Desmond
Br Daragh McNally
Br Conor McDonough
Br Eoin Casey
Br Kevin O'Reilly
Br Matthew Farrell
Br Philip Mulryne
Br Jesse Maingot
Br Ronan O'Dubhghaill

**47 Leeson Park**
Dublin 6
Tel 01-6602427

*Superior*
Very Rev Bernard Treacy

Rev Ambrose O'Farrell
Rev Andrew Allen

**St Aengus's**
Tymon North, Balrothery,
Tallaght, Dublin 24
Tel 01-4513757
Fax 01-4624038

*Superior*
Very Rev Benedict Moran PP
Email ben.moran25@gmail.com

Rev Pat Lucey CC

**St Dominic's**
St Dominic's Road,
Tallaght, Dublin 24
Tel 01-4510620
Fax 01-4623223

*Superior*
Very Rev Laurence Collins Adm
Email collinsl1@eircom.net

Rev Timothy Mulcahy CC

**St Dominic's**
Athy, Co Kildare
Tel 059-8631573
Fax 059-8631649

*Prior:* Very Rev Joseph O'Brien
Email joeobop@eircom.net

Rev Ignatius Candon
Rev Gerard O'Keeffe
Rev Andrew Kane
Rev John Heffernan
Rev Dominic O'Connor
Rev John Walsh

*Archdiocese of Armagh*

**St Malachy's**
Dundalk, Co Louth
Tel 042-9334179/9333714
Fax 042-9329751

*Prior*
Rev Augustine Champion

Rev Bede McGregor
Rev Ronan Cusack
Rev Gabriel Harty

**St Magdalen's**
Drogheda, Co Louth
Tel 041-9838271
Fax 041-9832964

*Prior:* Rev Anthony McMullan

Rev Humbert O'Brien
Rev Joseph Heffernan

*Diocese of Cork & Ross*

**St Mary's**
Pope Quay, Cork
Tel 021-4502267
Fax 021-4502307

*Prior:* Rev Gerard Dunne
Email frgd@eircom.net

Rev Robert Talty
Rev Finian Lynch
Rev Simon Roche
Rev Adrian Farrelly
Rev Martin MacCarthy
Rev David Barrins
Rev Maurice Colgan
Rev Stephen Hutchinson
Rev Denis Keating
Rev Dermot Brennan

**St Dominic's Retreat House**
Montenotte, Co Cork
Tel 021-4502520
Fax 021-4502712

*Prior*
Very Rev Benedict Hegarty
Email
benedicthegarty@eircom.net

Br James Beausang
Br Thomas Casey
Rev Stephen Cummins
Rev Frank Downes
Rev Archie Byrne

*Diocese of Dromore*

**St Catherine's**
Newry, Co Down BT35 8BN
Tel 028-30262178
Fax 028-30252188

*Prior:* Very Rev Joseph Ralph

Br Mark McGreevy
Rev Stephen Tumilty
Rev Noel McKeown
Rev Denis Murphy

*Diocese of Elphin*

**Holy Cross**
Sligo, Co Sligo
Tel 071-9142700
Fax 071-9146533

*Prior*
Very Rev Donal Mehigan

Rev Anthony Morris
Rev Sean Cunningham

*Diocese of Galway*

**St Mary's**
The Claddagh, Co Galway
Tel 091-582884 Fax 091-581252

*Prior:* Very Rev Thomas Jordan
Email jordan.tom34@gmail.com

Rev Terence McLoughlin
Rev John O'Reilly
Br Christopher O'Flaherty
Rev Denis Murphy
Rev Marek Cul
Rev Albert Leonard PP

*Diocese of Kerry*

**Holy Cross**
Tralee, Co Kerry
Tel 066-7121135/7129185
Fax 066-7180026

*Prior:* Very Rev Joseph Bulman

Rev Placid Nolan
Rev James Duggan
Rev John O'Rourke
Rev Krzysztof Kupczakiewicz

*Diocese of Kildare & Leighlin*

**Newbridge College**
Droichead Nua, Co Kildare
Tel 045-487200 Fax 045-487234
Email
newbridgepriory@ireland.com
Secondary School for Boys

*Prior:* Very Rev Joseph Dineen

Rev Raymond O'Donovan
Rev Brian Reynolds
Rev Edmund Murphy
Rev Benedict MacKenna
Rev Thomas McCarthy
Rev Michael Commane
Rev Laurence Kelly
Rev Peter Collins
Rev Louis Hughes
Re Luuk Jansen
Rev Matthew Martinez

*Diocese of Limerick*

**St Saviour's**
Glentworth Street, Limerick
Tel 061-412333
Fax 061-311728

*Prior*
Very Rev Jordan O'Brien PP

Rev Vincent Kennedy
Rev Brendan Clifford
Rev Thomas Brodie

*Diocese of Ossory*

**Black Abbey**
Kilkenny, Co Kilkenny
Tel 056-7721279
Fax 056-7721297

*Prior:* Very Rev James Donleavy

Rev Dominic Browne
Rev Finbar Kelly
Rev Alan O'Sullivan
Rev Joseph Kavanagh

*Diocese of Waterford & Lismore*

**St Saviour's**
Bridge Street, Waterford
Tel 051-875061 Fax 051-858093

*Prior:* Very Rev Richard Walsh

Rev Raymond Collins
Rev Canice Murphy

**St Saviour's**
Ballybeg, Waterford
Tel 051-376032 Fax 051-376581

*Superior*
Very Rev Declan Corish PP

Rev Martin Crowe CC

*Rome*

**Convent of SS Xystus and Clement**
Collegio San Clemente,
Via Labicana 95, 00184 Roma,
Italy
Tel 0039-06-7740021

*Prior*
Rev John M. Cunningham
Email priore@
basilicasanclemente.com

Rev Michael Carragher
Rev Ciaran Dougherty
Rev Fergus Ryan
Rev Michael Dunleavy

*Lisbon*

**Convento dos Padres Dominicanos Irlandeses**
Praceta Infante D. Henrique,
No 34, l-Dto, Rua do Murtal
San Pedro do Estoril, 2765-531
Estoril, Portugal
Tel 351-21-4673771

*Superior and Parish Priest*
Rev David Walker PP
Email stmarys@netcabo.pt

**FRANCISCAN ORDER (OFM)**

Province of Ireland

Provincial Office,
Franciscan Friary,
4 Merchant's Quay, Dublin 8
Tel 01-6742500 Fax 01-6742549
Email info@franciscans.ie

*Provincial*
Rev Hugh McKenna
Email hughmck@gmail.com

*Vicar Provincial*
Rev Kieran Cronin
Dún Mhuire, Seafield Road,
Killiney, Co Dublin
Tel 01-2826760
Email kierancronin@eircom.net
*Secretary of the Province*
Rev Joseph MacMahon
Email info@franciscans.ie

**Allianz** Ⓜ

## Archdiocese of Dublin

**Adam & Eve's**
4 Merchant's Quay, Dublin 8
Tel 01-6771128
Fax 01-6771000

*Guardian*
Rev Brendan McGrath
*Vicar:* Br Niall O'Connell

Rev Patrick Hudson
Br Philip Lane
Rev Angelus Lee
Rev Gearóid Ó Conaire
Br Stephen O'Kane
Rev Jude O'Riordan
Rev Fintan O'Shea
(3 The Millhouse, Steelworks,
Foley Street, Dublin 1)
Rev Joseph Walsh

**Franciscan House of Studies**
Dún Mhuire, Seafield Road,
Killiney, Co Dublin
Tel 01-2826760 Fax 01-2826993
Email dmkilliney@eircom.net

*Guardian:* Rev Kieran Cronin
*Vicar:* Rev Patrick Conlan

Rev Ronald Bennett
Rev Pádraig Coleman
(Firhouse)
Rev Francis Cotter
Rev John Dalton
(4 McSweeney House,
Berkeley Road, Dublin 7)
Rev Ignatius Fennessy
Rev Hugh O'Donnell
Rev Maelisa Ó Huallacháin
Rev Paschal Slevin

## Diocese of Ardagh & Clonmacnois

**Franciscan Friary**
Friary Lane, Athlone,
Co Westmeath
Tel 090-6472095
Fax 090-6424713

*Guardian*
Rev Gabriel Kinahan
*Vicar:* Rev Patrick Lynch

Br David Connolly
Rev Séamus Donohoe
Br Vincent Finnegan
Rev Liam Kelly
Br Salvador Kenny
Rev Ralph Lawless

## Diocese of Cork & Ross

**Franciscan Friary**
Liberty Street, Cork
Tel 021-4270302
Fax 021-4271841

*Guardian*
Rev Bernard Jones
*Vicar*
Rev Edward O'Callaghan

Rev Michael Nicholas
Rev Michael Holland
Rev John Bosco O'Byrne
Rev Iain Duggan
Rev Oswald Gill
Rev Oscar O'Leary
Rev Ambrose O'Mahony
Rev Christopher Regan
Rev John O'Brien

## Diocese of Galway

**The Abbey**
8 Francis Street,
Galway
Tel 091-562518
Fax 091-565663
Email
galwayabbeyofm@eircom.net

*Guardian:* Rev Patrick Younge
*Vicar, Parish Priest*
Rev Eugene Barrett

Rev Michael Bailey CC
*(Curate's Residence,
Monksfield, Salthill, Galway)*
Rev Colin Garvey
Rev Egbert O'Dea
Rev Peter O'Grady
Br Martin Thompson
Rev Declan Timmons CC

## Diocese of Kerry

**Franciscan Friary**
Killarney, Co Kerry
Tel 064-6631334/6631066
Fax 064-6637510
Email friary@eircom.net

*Guardian*
Rev Pádraig Breheny
*Vicar:* Rev Hilary Steblecki

Rev P.J. Brady
Rev Christopher Connelly
Br Seán Murphy

## Diocese of Killaloe

**Franciscan Friary**
Ennis, Co Clare
Tel 065-6828751
Fax 065-6822008
Email friars.ennis@eircom.net

*Guardian*
Rev Caoimhín Ó Laoide
*Vicar/Novice Master*
Rev Francis McGrath

Rev Joseph Condren
Rev James Hasson
Rev Cletus Noone
Br Elzear O'Brien

## Diocese of Meath

**LaVerna Friary**
Gormanston, Co Meath
Tel 01-8412203
Fax 01-8412685

*Guardian:* Rev Ulic Troy
*Vicar:* Rev Malcom Timothy

Rev Laurence Brady
Rev Edward Burke
Rev Augustine Hughes
Br Kevin McKenna
Rev Fiachra Ó Ceallaigh
Br Gerard Phayer

**Franciscan Abbey**
Multyfarnham,
Co Westmeath
Tel 044-9371114/9371137
Fax 044-9371387

*Guardian:* Rev Liam McCarthy
*Vicar:* Rev Eamonn O'Driscoll

Rev Sean Cassin
Rev Philip Forker
Rev John Kealy
Rev Lomán Mac Aodha
Rev Diarmaid Ó Riain

## Diocese of Raphoe

**Franciscan Friary**
Rossnowlagh, Co Donegal
Tel 072-9851342
Fax 072-9852206
Email
franciscanfriary@eircom.net

*Guardian*
Rev Feargus McEveney
*Vicar:* Rev Pius McLaughlin

Rev Richard Callanan
Rev Florian Farrelly
Rev Vincent Gallogley
Rev Seán Gildea
Rev Paschal McDonnell

## Diocese of Waterford & Lismore

**Franciscan Friary**
Clonmel, Co Tipperary
Tel 052-6121378
Fax 052-6125806
Email clonmel@eircom.net

**Filial House of Waterford**
*Vicar:* Rev Larry Mulligan

Rev Br Isidore Cronin
Rev John Harty
Rev Thomas Russell

**Franciscan Friary**
Lady Lane, Waterford
Tel 051-874262 Fax 051-843062
Email
waterfordfriary@eircom.net
*Chaplaincy*
Tel 051-842244

*Guardian*
Rev Ailbe Ó Murchú
*Vicar*
Rev Richard Kelly

Rev Brian Allen
Rev Patrick Cogan
*(15 Orchard Drive, Ursuline
Court, Waterford/
Tel 087-236039/Respond!
Office Tel 051-876865)*

Rev David Collins
Rev Henry Houlihan
Rev Ultan McCaffrey
Rev Art McCoy
Rev Peter Baptist O'Toole
Br Nicholas Shanahan
Rev Bonaventure Ward

## Other Individual Addresses

Rev Pádraig B. Coleman
Presbytery 2, Ballycullen Ave,
Firhouse, Dublin 24
Rev William Hoyne
Hermanos Franciscanos, Iglesia
Parroquial 'Dios con Nostros',
1a Av, 5a-6a Calles, Monzana
10, Elmezquital,
Zana 12,
10102 Guatemala City,
Guatemala
Rev Crispin Keating
5225 North Himes Avenue,
Tampa, Fl 33614-6623, USA
Rev Aidan McGrath
Curia Generalizia dei Frati
Minori, Via S. Maria Mediatrice
25, 00165 Roma, Italy
Most Rev Fiachra Ó Ceallaigh
'St Cecilia's', 19 St Anthony
Road, Rialto, Dublin 8
Rev Adrian Peelo
Old Mission San Luis Rey,
4050 Mission Avenue,
Oceanside,
CA 92057-6497, USA

*Franciscan Communities Abroad*

**St Anthony's Parish**
*(English-Speaking Chaplaincy)*
23/25 Oudstrijderslaan,
1950 Kraainem, Belgium
Tel 0032-2-7201970
Fax 0032-2-7255810

Rev Patrick Power *(Provincial
Delegate/Parish Priest)*
Rev Brendan Scully *(Associate
Pastor)*

**Collegio S. Isidoro**
Via degli Artisti 41,
00187 Roma, Italy
Tel 0039-06-4885359
Fax 0039-06-4884459
Email
collegio_s_isidoro@libero.it

*Guardian*
Rev Micheál MacCraith

Rev Louis Brennan
Rev John O'Keeffe

**Franciscan Missionaries in**
Zimbabwe
*Custos:* Rev Emmanuel Musara

Rev Nicholas Banhwa
Br Tawanda Chirigo
Rev Walter Gallahue
Rev James Hasson

Rev Maxwell Jaya
Br Raymond Kondo
Br Francis Lembani
Rev Fanuel Magwidi
Rev Thomas Makamure
Br Naison Manjovha
Rev Liam McCarthy
Br Albert Mhari
Br Linous Mukumbuzi
Rev Xavier Mukupo
Br Salicio Mukuwe
Br Onward Murape
Br Juniper O'Brien
Br Stephen O'Kane *(Collegio S. Isidoro, Rome)*
Br Stephen Office
Br Ndabaningi Sithole
Br Patience Tigere
Rev Alfigio Tunha
Br Clemence Wiziki

## CONVENTUAL FRANCISCANS (OFMConv)

Provincial Delegation Office
St Patrick's Friary
26 Cornwall Road, Waterloo,
London SE1 8TW, England
Tel 020-79288897

*Provincial Custos:* Very Rev
Peter Damian Massengill

*Archdiocese of Dublin*

**Friary of the Visitation of the BVM**
Fairview Strand, Dublin 3
Tel 01-8376000 Fax 01-8376021

Rev Antony Nallukunnel PP
Rev Joseph Connick CC
Rev Patrick Griffin
Rev Aidan Walsh
Rev James McInerney

*Diocese of Ferns*

**The Friary**
Wexford
Tel 053-9122758 Fax 053-9121499

Rev Ciprian Budau *(Guardian)*
Rev Fritz O'Kelly
Rev Aquino Maliakkal

## FRANCISCAN FRIARS OF THE RENEWAL (CFR)

Community of the Franciscan
Friars of Renewal
*Community Servant*
Rev John-Paul Overlette
St Felix Friary, 15 Trinity Plaza,
Yonkers, NJ 10701
Tel 001-914-4767279

*Vocation Contact*
Rev Gabriel Kyte
St Pio Friary,
Sedgefield Terrace, Westgate,
Bradford BD1 2RU, UK
Tel 01274-721989
Fax 01274-740038

*Diocese of Derry*

**St Columba Friary**
Fairview Road, Derry BT48 8NU
Tel 028-71419980
Fax 028-71417652
*Local Servant (Superior)*
Rev Columba Jordan

Rev Thomas Cacciola
Br Patrick Crowley
Br Andre Manders
Br Seraphim Roycourt

*Diocese of Limerick*

**St Patrick Friary**
64 Delmege Park, Moyross,
Limerick
Tel 061-458071 Fax 061-457626
*Local Servant (Superior)*
Rev Charles-Benoit Reche

Br Frantisek Chloupek
Rev Bernard Murphy
Br Damien Novak
Rev Lawrence Schroedel

## HOLY SPIRIT CONGREGATION (CSSp)

Province of Ireland

*Archdiocese of Dublin*

**Holy Spirit Provincialate**
Temple Park, Richmond
Avenue South, Dublin 6
Tel 01-4975127/4977230
Fax 01-4975399
Website www.spiritan.ie

*Provincial Leadership Team*
Rev Marc Whelan *(Provincial)*
Rev Brendan Carr
Rev John Kilcrann
Rev John Laizer
Rev Jude Lynch *(Provincial Bursar)*

*Communications Manager*
Mr Peter O'Mahony
Email communications@
spiritan.ie

**Safeguarding Office**
Mr Liam Lally *(Designated person)*
Tel 087-6709461
Email liam.lally@spiritan.ie
Ms Jane Ferguson *(Support person for survivors and their families)*
Tel 087-7405936
Email jane.ferguson@spiritan.ie

**Holy Spirit Education Office**
(Des Places Educational
Association Ltd)
Kimmage Manor, Dublin 12
Tel 01-4997610
www.desplaces.ie
Rev Peter Conaty *(Chair)*
Awareness Education Services
Rev Tony Byrne
Tel/Fax 01-8388888
Email
info@awarenesseducation.org

**Spiritan Mission Resource and Heritage Centre**
Kimmage Manor, Dublin 12
*Manager:* Rev Brian O'Toole
Email archives@spiritan.ie

**Holy Spirit Missionary College**
Kimmage Manor,
Whitehall Road, Dublin 12
Tel 01-4064300 Fax 01-4920062
Email
reception@kimmagemanor.ie

*Community Leader*
Rev Daithí Kenneally

Rev Enzo Agnoli
Rev Savino Agnoli
Rev Raphael Annan
Rev Joseph Beere *(Bursar)*
Rev Kevin A. Browne
Br Albert Buckley
Rev Christopher Burke
Rev James Byrnes
Rev Francis Caffrey
Rev Brian Carey
Rev Michael Casey
Rev Seán Casey
Bishop Michael J. Cleary
Rev Patrick Cleary
Rev William Cleary
Rev Martin J. Collins
Rev Timothy Connolly
Rev Kevin Corrigan
Rev James Corry
Rev Noel Cox
Rev Patrick Cully
Rev James Daly
Rev Anthony Darragh
Rev Patrick Donovan
Rev Dermot Doran
Rev Brendan Duggan
Rev Colm Duggan
Rev James F. Duggan
Rev James Duncan
Rev Bartholomew Egan
Rev John Egan
Rev Hugh Fagan
Rev Thomas Farrelly
Rev John A. Finucane *(Concern)*
Rev John Fitzpatrick
Rev Seamus Fleming
Rev Reginald Gillooly
Rev Edward Grimes
Rev Austin Healy
Rev Brendan Heeran
Rev Anthony Heerey
Rev John Hogan
Rev Gregory Iwuozor
Rev William Jenkinson
Rev Michael Kane
Rev John (Seán) Kealy
Rev Patrick James Kelly
Rev Patrick Joseph Kelly
Rev John Joe King
Rev Jeremiah Lambe
Rev Owen Lambert
Rev Francis Laverty
Rev Patrick Leddy
Rev Anthony Little
Rev Jude Lynch
Rev Liam Martin
Rev James McCaffrey
Rev Charles McCarthy
Rev Michael McCarthy

Rev Martin McDonagh
Rev Peter J. McEntire
Rev Leo McGarry
Rev Patrick McGlynn
Rev Laurence McHugh
Rev Brian McLaughlin
Rev Walter McNamara
Rev James J. McNulty
Samson Mann *(Scholastic)*
Rev Henry Moloney
Rev John Moriarty
Rev James Morrow
Rev Noel Moynihan
Rev Frank Mulloy
Rev Henry Mullin
Rev Michael Mulvihill
Rev James Murphy
Rev Patrick Murphy
Rev Marino Nguekam
Rev William Nugent
Rev Brendan J. O'Brien
Rev Valentine O'Brien
Rev John (Seán) O'Connell
Rev Vincent O'Connell
Rev Anthony O'Farrell
Rev Eddie O'Farrell
Rev Vincent O'Grady
Rev Michael O'Looney
Rev Noel O'Meara
Rev Hugh O'Reilly
Bishop John C. O'Riordan
Rev Sean O'Shaughnessy
Rev Desmond L. O'Sullivan
Rev James Peters
Rev Joseph Prendergast
Rev Michael B. Reynolds
Rev Denis Robinson
Rev Edvaldo Rodrigues Da
Silva
Rev Gerard Ryan
Rev Patrick J. Ryan
Rev Joseph Sheehan
Rev Terence Smith
Rev Jim Stapleton
Rev Brian Starken
Rev Paul Walsh
Rev William Walsh
Rev Patrick A. Whelan
Rev Tom Whelan

**Kimmage Development Studies Centre**
Kimmage Manor, Dublin 12
Tel 01-4064386
Fax 01-4064388
Email info@kimmagedsc.ie
www.kimmagedsc.ie

*Director:* Dr Rob Kevlihan

**Church of the Holy Spirit**
Kimmage, Dublin 12
Tel 01-4558316
www.kimmagemanorparish.com

**Church of the Holy Spirit**
Greenhills, Dublin 12
Tel 01-4504040
www.holyspiritparishgreenhills.ie

Rev Roderick Curran CC
Rev Thomas Hogan CC
Rev Edward O'Farrell

**Blackrock College**
Blackrock, Co Dublin
Tel 01-2888681 Fax 01-2834267
www.blackrockcollege.com
Email
info@blackrockcollege.com

*Community Leader*
Rev Tom Nash
*Principal:* Alan MacGinty

Rev Vincent Browne
Rev Patrick Dundon
Rev Norman Fitzgerald
Rev Denis J. Gavin
Rev Brian M. Gogan
Rev Joseph A. Gough
Rev Myles Healy
Rev Liam Kehoe
Rev Malachy Kilbride
Rev Thomas McDonald
Rev James McDonnell
Rev Hyacinth Nwakuna
Rev Cormac Ó Brolcháin
Rev Richard J. Thornton
Br Conleth Tyrrell

**Willow Park**
Tel 01-2881651 Fax 01-2783353
Email
admin@willowparkschool.ie

*Principal Senior School*
Mr Hugh McGuire
*Principal Junior School*
Mr Jim Casey

**St Mary's College**
Rathmines, Dublin 6
Community Tel 01-4995760
Fax 01-4972621
www.stmarys.ie
Junior School Tel 01-4995721
Email junsec@stmarys.ie
Senior School Tel 01-4995700
Fax 01-4972574
Email sensec@stmarys.ie

*Community Leader*
Rev Richard Olin
*Principal Secondary School*
Mr Denis Murphy
*Principal Junior School*
Ms Mary O'Donnell

Rev Michael J. Buckley
Br Ignatius Curry
Rev Michael Duggan
Rev Francis Toochukwu
Ekwomadu
Rev John P. Flavin
Rev Leo Layden
Rev Brian O'Toole

**St Michael's College**
Ailesbury Road, Dublin 4
Tel 01-2189400 Fax 01-2698862
www.stmichaelscollege.com
Email stmcoll@indigo.ie

*Principal:* Mr Tim Kelleher
*Principal Junior School*
Ms Lorna Heslin

**Duquesne University**
Duquesne in Dublin,
St Michael's, 1 Ailesbury Road,
Ballsbridge, Dublin 4
Tel/Fax 01-2080940
www.duq.edu/ireland
*Resident Director:*
Ms Laura K. Palilla
Email laurapalilla@gmail.com

**Spiritan House**
**Spiritan Asylum Services**
**Initiative (SPIRASI)**
213 North Circular Road,
Dublin 7
Tel 01-8389664/8683504
Fax 01-8686500
www.spirasi.ie
Mr Greg Straton (*Director,*
*SPIRASI*)
*Community Leader*
Rev John Laizer

Rev Brendan Foley
Rev Michael Fillie
Br Liam Sheridan

**Templeogue College**
Templeville Road, Dublin 6W
Tel 01-4903909 Fax 01-4920903
www.templeoguecollege.ie
Email
info@templeoguecollege.ie

*Community Leader*
Rev William Bradley
*Principal:* Ms Aoife O'Donnell

Rev James Delaney
Rev Séamus Galvin
Rev Thomas Raftery
Rev Noel Redmond
Rev Patrick Reedy
Rev Desmond Reid

**Church of the Transfiguration**
Presbytery, Bawnogue,
Clondalkin, Dublin 22
Tel 01-4519810
www.bawnogueparish.com

**Parish of St Ronan's**
Deansrath, Clondalkin,
Dublin 22
Tel 01-4570380

Rev Brian Starken

**Newlands Institute for**
**Counselling**
2 Monastery Road, Clondalkin,
Dublin 22
Tel 01-4594573

Rev Ronan Grimshaw
Rev Patrick Coughlan

*Archdiocese of Cashel and*
*Diocese of Emly*

**Rockwell College**
Cashel, Co Tipperary
Tel 062-61444 Fax 062-61661
www.rockwell-college.ie
Email info@rockwell-college.ie

Secondary Residential and Day
School

*Community Leader*
Rev Matthew J. Knight
*Principal:* Ms Audrey O'Byrne

Br Gerard Cummins
Rev Colm Cunningham
Rev Tom Cunningham
Rev Patrick Downes
Rev Bernard M. Frawley
Rev Gerard Griffin
Rev James Hurley
Rev William Kingston
Rev Jeremiah Kirwin (*Bursar*)
Rev Michael Malone
Rev Patrick McGeever
Rev John Meade
Rev Michael Moore
Rev Noel Murphy (*Promotions*)
Rev Peter Queally
Rev Samuel Udogbo

*Diocese of Elphin*

**Spiritan Community**
Ballintubber, Castlerea,
Co Roscommon
Tel 094-9655226

*Community Leader*
Rev Joseph Poole
Rev Patrick O'Toole

*Diocese of Meath*

**Spiritan Missionaries**
Ardbraccan, Navan, Co Meath
Tel 046-9021441

*Community Leader*
Rev Peter Conaty

Rev Brian Murtagh
Erasmus Manwa (*Scholastic*)

*Rome*

**Clivo di Cinna 195, 00136**
Roma, Italy
Tel +39-06-3540461
Fax +39-06-35450676

*Superior General*
Most Rev John Fogarty

# JESUITS (SJ)
# SOCIETY OF JESUS

Irish Province

*Archdiocese of Dublin*

**Irish Jesuit Provincialate**
Milltown Park,
Sandford Road, Dublin 6
Tel 01-4987333 Fax 01-4987334
Email curia@jesuit.ie

*Provincial:* Rev Tom Layden
*Assistant Provincial*
Rev Liam O'Connell

**Jesuit Centre for Faith and**
**Justice**
26 Upper Sherrard Street,
Dublin 1
Tel 01-8556814 Fax 01-8364377
Email info@jcfj.ie
www.jcfj.ie
*Director:* Rev John K. Guiney

**Jesuit Communication Centre**
Irish Jesuit Provincialate,
Milltown Park,
Sandford Road, Dublin 6
Tel 01-4987347/4987348
*Director:* Ms Pat Coyle
Email coylep@jesuit.ie
*Irish Jesuit News*
amdg@jesuit.ie
jcc@jesuit.ie
pwandrews@gmail.com

**Jesuit Curia Community**
Loyola House, Milltown Park,
Sandford Road, Dublin 6
Tel 01-2180276
Email loyola@jesuit.ie

*Superior & Guestmaster*
Rev Noel Barber
*Minister:* Rev Liam O'Connell

Rev James Culliton
Rev Peter Sexton
*Residing elsewhere:*
Rev James Hayes

Applications for *retreats* to
Rev Finbarr Lynch SJ
Manresa House, Dollymount,
Dublin 3
Tel 01-8331352

Enquiries in respect of *foreign*
*missions* to Rev Director, Jesuit
Foreign Missions,
28 Upper Sherrard Street,
Dublin 1
Tel 01-8366509
Fax 01-8366510

**St Francis Xavier's**
Upper Gardiner Street,
Dublin 1
Tel 01-8363411 Fax 01-8555624
Email sfxcommunity@jesuit.ie
Parish church and residence

*Superior*
Rev Fergus O'Donoghue
*Vice-Superior*
Rev Patrick Carberry
*Minister:* Br Tom Phelan
*Parish Priest*
Very Rev Donal Neary PP

Rev Kieran Barry-Ryan
Rev Derek Cassidy
Br Eamonn Davis
Rev Richard D'Souza
Rev Paul Farquharson
Rev Frank Keenan
Rev Mícheál Mac Gréil
Br Martin Murphy
Rev John O'Holohan
Rev Fergus O'Keefe
Rev Kevin O'Rourke
Rev James Smyth
Rev Brendan Staunton
Rev Tomasz Szymczyk

*Residing Elsewhere*
Rev Brian Lennon
Rev Peter McVerry
Rev Neil O'Driscoll

**Belvedere College**
Great Denmark Street, Dublin 1
*Community resides in SFX
Gardiner Street*

Secondary day school
Tel 01-8586600 (College)
Fax 01-8744374
*Rector:* Rev Derek Cassidy
*Headmaster:* Mr Gerard Foley

**35 Lower Leeson Street**
Dublin 2
Tel 01-6761248 Fax 01-7758598
Residence

*Superior:* Rev Brian Grogan
*Vice-Superior*
Rev Edmond Grace

Rev Gerard Bourke (JPN)
Rev Hugh P. Duffy
Rev Philip Fogarty
Rev Michael O. Gallagher
Rev Kevin Laheen
Hun-June, Peter Lee *(Scholastic)*
Rev John Looby
Br Gerard Marks
Rev James Moran
Rev Conall Ó Cuinn

*Residing Elsewhere*
Rev Ronan Geary
Rev Francis Sammon

*Sacred Heart Messenger* – a
Jesuit Publication
37 Lower Leeson Street,
Dublin 2
Tel 01-6767491
*Editor:* Rev John Looby
*Manager:* Ms Cecilia West
Email manager@messenger.ie

*Sacred Space*
*Director:* Rev Piaras Jackson
Website www.sacredspace.ie

**Campion House Residence**
28 Lower Hatch Street,
Dublin 2
Tel 01-6383990 Fax 01-6762805
Email campion@jesuit.ie

*Superior:* Rev Patrick Hume
*Provincial:* Rev Tom Layden

Rev John O'Keeffe
Rev Michael O'Sullivan

**Manresa House**
Dollymount, Dublin 3
Tel 01-8331352 Fax 01-8331002
Email manresa@jesuit.ie
Retreat House

*Rector:* Rev Michael Drennan
*Director of Retreat House*
Rev Piaras Jackson
*Plant Manager*
Br Joseph Ward

Rev Brendan Comerford
Br Peter Doyle
Rev Patrick Greene
Rev Peter Hannan
Rev Finbarr Lynch
Rev Dermot Mansfield

Rev Thomas Morrissey
Rev Laurence Murphy
Rev Ciary Quirke
Rev Jan Van de Poll (NER)

*Residing Elsewhere*
Rev Kevin O'Higgins

**Dominic Collins' House
Residence**
129 Morehampton Road,
Dublin 4
Tel 01-2693075
Fax 01-2698462
*Vice-Superior*
Rev David Coghlan

Rev David Tuohy

**Milltown Park**
Sandford Road,
Dublin 6
Tel 01-2698411/2698113
Fax 01-2600371
Email milltown@jesuit.ie

*Rector*
Rev William Callanan
*Vice-Rector:* Rev Thomas Casey
*Plant Manager*
Br John Adams

Rev Paul Andrews
Rev Fergal Brennan
Rev Liam Browne
Rev John Dooley
Rev Brendan Duddy
Br George Fallon
Rev David Gaffney
Rev Henry Grant
Rev John Guiney
Rev John K. Guiney
Rev Conor Harper
Rev James Kelly
Rev Colm Lavelle
Br John Maguire
Rev William Mathews
Br James McCabe
Rev Dermot McKenna
Rev Raymond Moloney
Rev Brian O'Leary
Rev Hugh O'Neill
Rev Stephen Redmond

*Residing Elsewhere*
Br James Dunne
Rev Patrick Heelan
Br Brendan Hyland
Rev Bartholomew Kiely

**Lay Retreat Association of
St Ignatius**
Milltown Park, Dublin 6
Tel 01-2698411/2180274
Lay apostolate for the
promotion of retreats in
different locations

Mr John Callaghan
Tel 01-8370778

*Spiritual Director*
Rev Fergus O'Keefe
Tel 01-7072203

**Milltown Institute of
Theology and Philosophy**
Milltown Park,
Sandford Road, Dublin 6
Tel 01-2776300
Fax 01-2692528
Email
info@milltown-institute.ie

*Rector and Acting President*
Associate Prof. Rev Thomas R.
Whelan (CSSp)
*Professor of Theology at
Milltown Institute*
Vacant

**Gonzaga College**
Sandford Road, Dublin 6
Tel 01-4972943 (community)
Fax 01-4960849 (community)
Tel 01-4972931 (college)
Fax 01-4967769
Email
*(Community)* gonzaga@jesuit.ie
*(College)* office@gonzaga.ie

*Rector*
Rev Myles O'Reilly
*Minister*
Rev Kennedy O'Brien
*Headmaster*
Mr Damon McCaul

Rev Joseph Brennan
Rev John Callanan
Rev Alan Mowbray
Rev Edward O'Donnell
Rev Desmond O'Grady
Rev Colin Warrack

**John Sullivan House**
House of Formation,
27 Leinster Road, Rathmines,
Dublin 6

*Superior:* Rev Martin Curry
Tel 01-5242134
*Minister:* Rev Leon Ó Giolláin

Rev Malasi S. Killenga (AOR)
Kamil Slawínski (PMH)
*(Scholastic)*
Jae-wook Anselmus Lee
*(Scholastic)*

25 Croftwood Park
Cherry Orchard, Dublin 10
Tel 01-6267413

Rev Gerard O'Hanlon
Rev William Toner

*Archdiocese of Armagh*

**Iona**
211 Churchill Park
Portadown, BT62 1EU
Tel 028-38330366
Fax 028-38338334
Email iona@jesuit.ie

*Superior*
Rev Brendan MacPartlin
Rev Michael Bingham *(Prov Brit)*
Rev Proinsias Mac Brádaigh

*Diocese of Down & Connor*

**Peter Faber House**
28 Brookvale Avenue
Belfast BT14 6BW
Tel 028-90757615
Fax 028-90747615
Email
peter_faber@lineone.net

*Superior:* Rev Alan McGuckian

Rev Patrick Davis
Rev Terence Howard
Rev Brendan McManus

*Diocese of Galway*

**St Ignatius Community &
Church**
27 Raleigh Row, Salthill,
Galway
Tel 091-523707
Email galway@jesuit.ie

*Rector*
Rev Michael McGuckian
*Minister*
Rev Enda O'Callaghan

Rev Paul Brassil (ZAM)
Rev Gerard Clarke
Rev Charles Davy
Rev Anthony Farren (CHN)
Rev John Humphreys
Rev Paul Tonna (MAL)

*Residing Elsewhere*
Rev Dermot Cassidy
Rev Connla O Duláine

**Coláiste Iognáid**
24 Sea Road, Galway
College Tel 091-501550
Fax 091-501551
Email
colaisteiognaid@eircom.net

*Secondary School Principal*
Ms Mary Joyce
*Scoil Iognaid (National School)*
*Principal:* Ms Laoise Breathnach
Tel 091-584491

*Diocese of Kildare & Leighlin*

**Clongowes Wood College**
Clane, Co Kildare
Tel 045-868663/868202
Fax 045-861042
Email *(College)*
reception@clongowes.net
*(Community)*
reception@clongowes.net
Secondary Boarding School

*Rector:* Rev Michael Sheil
*Headmaster*
Rev Leonard Moloney
Email hm@clongowes.net
*Vice-Rector & Minister*
Rev Bernard McGuckian
*Sub-Minister*
Br Charles Connor

Rev Bruce Bradley
Rev Finbarr Clancy
Niall S. Leahy *(Scholastic)*
Rev Vincent Murphy
Rev Dermot Murray
Rev William Reynolds

*Residing Elsewhere*
Rev Patrick Crowe

*Diocese of Limerick*

**Crescent College
Comprehensive**
Dooradoyle, Limerick
*(Community)*
Tel 061-229655 Fax 061-229013
Email dooradoyle@jesuit.ie
*(College)*
Email ccadmin.ias@eircom.net
Comprehensive Day School for
Boys and Girls

*Superior*
Rev Declan Murray
*Minister:* Rev James Maher
Rev Anthony O'Riordan
*Headmaster:* To be appointed

*Jesuits temporarily outside
Ireland*

Correspondence to
Irish Jesuit Provincialate
Milltown Park,
Sandford Road, Dublin 6
Tel 01-4987333
Email curia@jesuit.ie

Rev Brendan Carmody
Rev Kevin Casey
Rev James Corkery
Edward Cosgrove *(Scholastic)*
Shane Daly *(Scholastic)*
Rev John Dardis
Rev Cathal Doherty
Rev Ashley Evans
Rev Michael P. Gallagher
Rev Donal Godfrey
Rev Timothy Healy
Rev Niall F.X. Leahy
Rev Brian MacCuarta
Rev James Murphy
Rev Dermot O'Connor
Rev Richard O'Dwyer
Rev Patrick Riordan
Rev Patrick Sheary
Rev Patrick Tyrrell
Rev Gerard Whelan

## LEGIONARIES OF CHRIST
(LC)

*Archdiocese of Dublin*

**Community**
Leopardstown Road,
Foxrock, Dublin 18
Tel 01-2955902
Email ireland@legionaries.org

*Superior*
Rev Alejandro Fuentes

*Vocations Director*
Rev Fergal O'Dúill
Email foduill@legionaries.org
*Regnum Christi*
Rev Aaron Vinduska
Email
avinduska@legionaries.org

**Clonlost Retreat and Youth
Centre**
Killiney Road,
Killiney, Co Dublin
Tel 01-2350064
Day school retreats,
pre-confirmation retreats,
Creidim Leadership
Programme

*Chaplain:* Rev Fergal O'Duill

**Dublin Oak Academy**
Kilcroney, Bray,
Co Wicklow
Tel 01-2863290 Fax 01-2865315
Email secretary@
dublinoakacademy.com

*Director:* Rev Francisco Cepeda
*Chaplain*
Rev Matthew Schmitz

**Woodlands Academy**
Wingfield House, Bray
Co Wicklow
Tel 01-2866323
Fax 01-2864918

*Chaplain*
Rev Alejandro Fuentes

**Faith and Family Centre**
Dal Riada House,
Avoca Avenue, Blackrock,
Co Dublin
Tel 01-2889317
Email
faithandfamilycentre@arcol.org

Marriage Enrichment days,
Spiritual retreats, Evenings of
Reflection, Family days, Faith
development programmes and
personal spiritual direction

*Director:* Rev Aaron Vinduska
Email
avinduska@legionaries.org

## MARIANISTS (SM)
Society of Mary

**Provincial Headquarters**
4425 West Pine Boulevard,
St Louis, MO 63108-2301,
USA
Tel 314-533-1207

*Provincial*
Rev Martin Solma

*Archdiocese of Dublin*

**St Columba's**
Church Avenue, Ballybrack,
Co Dublin
Tel 01-2858301
Residence for religious and
candidates; religious centre

*Director:* Br James Contadino
Email jimcontadino@yahoo.co.uk

Rev Michael Reaume
Br Fred Rech
Br Gerry McAuley

**St Laurence College**
Loughlinstown, Dublin 18
Tel 01-2826930
Coeducational Secondary Day
School

*Principal:* Mr Billy Redmond

## MARIST FATHERS (SM)
Society of Mary

*Archdiocese of Dublin*

**Marist Regional Office**
Mount St Mary's,
Dundrum Road, Milltown,
Dublin 14
Tel 01-2698100/086-2597905
Email edwinmcc@hotmail.com

*Regional Superior*
Rev Edwin McCallion
*Regional Secretary*
Margery Ging
Email margeryging@gmail.com

**Mount St Mary's, Milltown,**
Dundrum Road, Dublin 14
Tel 01-2697322

*Superior:* Rev Declan Marmion

Rev Brendan Bradshaw
Cherryfield Lodge,
Hilltown Park, Ranelagh,
Dublin 6
Rev P. J. Byrne
Rev Sean Fagan
Rev Liam Forde
Rev Denis Green
Rev Frank Hennigan
Rev Des Hunt
Rev Thomas Tuohy

**St Brendan's Parish**
Coolock Village, Dublin 5
Tel 01-8484799

*Moderator:* Rev John Hand
*Superior:* Rev John Harrington

Rev David Corrigan
Rev Edwin McCallion

**Chanel Community**
Coolock, Dublin 5
Tel 01-8477133

*Superior:* Rev Joseph Rooney

Rev Kieran Butler PC
Rev Thomas Butler
Rev P. G. Byrne
Rev Tony Malone
Rev Ray Staunton

**Chanel College**
Coolock, Dublin 5
Tel 01-8480655/8480896

*Headmaster*
Mr Declan Mowlds

**St Teresa's**
Donore Avenue, Dublin 8
Tel 01-4542425/4531613

*Parish Priest*
Rev Cormac McNamara PP

Rev Tom Dalzell
Rev Bobby Kelly CC
Rev Sean McArdle CC

**Catholic University School**
89 Lower Leeson Street,
Dublin 2
Tel 01-6762586

*Headmaster:* Rev Martin Daly

*Archdiocese of Armagh*

**Cerdon**
Marist Fathers, St Mary's Road,
Dundalk, Co Louth
Tel 042-9334019

*Superior:* Rev Kevin Cooney

Rev Jim Johnston
Rev James McElroy
Rev Joseph McKenna
St Peter's Nursing Home,
Castlebellingham Village,
Co Louth
Rev Michael Maher
Rev Patrick Meehan
Rev John Mulligan
'Cois Abhainn',
Moore Hall Lodge, Co Louth

**St Mary's College**
Dundalk, Co Louth
Tel 042-9339984

*Principal:* Mr Con McGinley

**Holy Family Parish**
Parochial House,
Dundalk, Co Louth
Tel 042-9336301

*Superior*
Rev James O'Connell Adm

Rev Frank Corry CC
Rev Edmund Duffy
Rev Patrick Stanley CC

*Marist Fathers elsewhere in Ireland*

*Armagh*
Rev Bernard (Barney) King CC
Glassdrummond, Crossmaglen,
Newry, Co Down

*Dublin*
Rev Tom Dooley CC,
4 Greenmount Road,
Terenure
Rev Martin Daly
C.U.S., 89 Lr Leeson Street,
Dublin 2

*Ardagh & Clonmacnois*
Rev Tim Kenny
Fermoyle, Lanesboro,
Co Longord

*Marist Fathers outside Ireland*

Rev Aidan Carvill, Australia
Rev Larry Duffy, Rome
Rev John Hannan,Rome
Rev Laurence Hannan, Fiji
Rev Patrick Muckian,
Philippines
Rev Paddy O'Hare, France
Archbishop Adrian Smith,
Honiara, Solomon Islands
Rev Paul Walsh, London
Rev Martin McAnaney, Paris
Rev Roger McCarrick, Fiji
Rev Seamus McMahon,
Australia
Rev Rory Mulligan, Norway
Rev Jim Ross, Fiji

## MILL HILL MISSIONARIES (MHM)

*Archdiocese of Dublin*

**St Joseph's House**
50 Orwell Park,
Rathgar, Dublin 6
Tel 01-4127700
Email josephmhm@eircom.net

*Regional Superior*
Rev Michael Corcoran
Tel 01-4127773/4127735/
086-2239051
millhillregional@eircom.net
*Rector:* Rev Patrick Molloy
*Vice Rector*
Rev Patrick O'Connell
*Bursar:* Rev Patrick Murray
Email millhill@iol.ie

Rev Matthew Dunne
Rev Lawrence English
Rev Christopher Fox
Rev Noel Hanrahan
Rev Denis Hartnett
Rev Bartholomew Hayes

Rev Ray Hogan
Rev Paddy Neville
Rev Sean O'Brien
Rev Christopher O'Connor
Rev Daniel O'Connor
Rev Patrick J. Ryan
Rev Fachtna Staunton

*Diocese of Down & Connor*

**St Mary's Parish**
25 Marquis Street,
Belfast BT1 1JJ
Tel 028-90320482

Rev James A. Boyle Adm
Rev John J. Courtney
Rev John Nevin
Rev Jim O'Donoghue CC

*Diocese of Ossory*

**St Joseph's**
Mill Hill Missionaries,
Waterford Road, Kilkenny
Tel 056-7721482
Fax 056-7751490

*Rector:* Rev Maurice McGill
Email mcgillmhm@yahoo.com
*Vice-Rector and Editor of
Advocate:* Rev Jim O'Connell
Email jimocmhm@eircom.net
*Organising Secretary*
Rev Maurice Crean
mcreanmhm@eircom.net

Rev Gerald Doyle
Rev Donal Harney

*Elsewhere in Ireland*

Rev Lorenzo Bracken
Rev Terence Gogarty
Rev Tom Keane
Rev Thomas Keogan
Rev Hugh Lee
Rev Roger McGorty
Rev Tom McGrath
Rev Anthony Murphy
Rev Michael O'Brien
Rev Kevin O'Rourke
Rev Kevin Reynolds
Rev Thomas Sinnott
Rev Joseph P. Whelan

*Generalate*

**Mill Hill Missionaries**
1 Colby Gardens,
Cookham Road,
Maidenhead SL6 7GZ, England
Tel 0044-1628-789752

*Superior General*
Very Rev Anthony Chantry

## MISSIONARIES OF AFRICA (White Fathers)

Province of Europe
Irish Sector

*Archdiocese of Dublin*

**Provincialate**
Cypress Grove Road,
Templeogue, Dublin 6W
Tel 01-4055263 (House)
Tel 01-4063965 (Delegate
Superior)
Tel 01-4055510 (Treasurer)
Email provirl@indigo.ie

*Delegate Superior*
Rev P. J. Cassidy
*Provincial Treasurer*
Rev Neil Loughrey

**Cypress Grove**
Templeogue, Dublin 6W
Tel 01-4055263/4055264
Tel 01-4055526 (Promotion)
Email provirl@indigo.ie
House of promotion/retired
priests and brothers/studies

*Superior:* Vacant
*Promotion Director:*
Rev Jean Paul Cirhakarhula
*Mite Boxes:* Br Tim Murphy

Rev Thomas Bradley
Rev Eugene Lewis
Rev Jim McTiernan

*Working in Provinces other
than Africa*

Rev Ian Buckmaster
Rev James Greene
Br Raymond Leggett
Rev Michael O'Sullivan
Rev Charles Timoney

*Working in Dioceses in Ireland*

Rev James Browne

## MISSIONARIES OF THE SACRED HEART (MSC)

The Missionaries of the Sacred
Heart is a congregation of 16
provinces. Members of the
Irish Province work in
England, USA, South Africa,
Venezuela and Russia.

*Archdiocese of Dublin*

**Provincialate**
65 Terenure Road West,
Dublin 6W
Tel 01-4906622 Fax 01-4920148

*Provincial Leader*
Rev Joseph McGee

**Woodview House**
Mount Merrion Avenue,
Blackrock, Co Dublin
Tel 01-2881644 (community)

*Leader:* Rev John Finn

Rev John Bennett
Rev Eugene Clarkson
Rev Daniel Cleary
Rev Con O'Connell
Rev Patrick Courtney
Rev Joseph Falloon
Rev Desmond Farren
Rev John McCarthy
Rev Martin McNamara
Rev Liam O'Brien
Rev Tadhg Ó Dálaigh
Rev John O'Sullivan
Rev Patrick Sheehan
Rev David Smith

**Sacred Heart Parish**
Killinarden, Tallaght, Dublin 24
Tel 01-4522251

Rev Manus Ferry PP
Rev John Finn

**Formation House**
Rev Michael Serrage
Rev Diarmuid Ó Murchú
56 Mulvey Park, Dundrum,
Dublin 16
Tel 01-2951856

*Diocese of Cork & Ross*

**MSC Mission Support Centre**
PO Box 23,
Western Road, Cork
Tel 021-4545704/4543988
Fax 021-4343587
info@mscmissioncentre.ie
www.mscireland.com

Rev Michael O'Connell

**Western Road**
Cork
Tel 021-4804120
Fax 021-4543823

*Leader:* Rev John Fitzgerald
*Parish Priest*
Rev Terence O'Brien

Rev Charles Conroy
Rev Jeremiah Daly
Rev Roger Duggan
Rev John Kevin Fleming
Rev Tim Gleeson
Br Donal Hallissey
Rev Donncha Mac Cárthaigh
Rev Jim Mannix
Rev Donal McCarthy
Rev Alan Neville
Rev Thomas O'Brien
Rev Michael O'Connell
Rev Michael Whelan

**Carrignavar**
Co Cork
Tel 021-4884044

*Leader:* Rev Dan O'Connor

Rev Patrick Breen
Rev Christopher Coleman
Rev William Fleming
Rev Seán Horgan
Rev Thomas Jordan
Rev Daniel O'Neill

**Myross Wood Retreat House**
Leap, Skibbereen, Co Cork
Tel 028-33118
Fax 028-33793

*Leader & Director*
Rev Michael Curran

Rev Timothy Cullinane
Rev Dominic Duffy
Rev Brendan Hanley
Rev Daniel O'Brien

**Castlehaven Parish**
Parish House,
Union Hall, Skibbereen,
Co Cork
Tel 028-34940

*Parish Priest*
Rev Gerard Thornton PP

**Leap-Glandore Parish**
Parish House, Leap,
Skibbereen, Co Cork
Tel 028-33177

*Parish Priest*
Áth Pádraig Ó Súilleabháin PP

*Diocese of Galway*

**'Croí Nua'**
Rosary Lane,
Taylor's Hill, Galway
Tel 091-520960
Fax 091-521168

*Leader*
Rev Michael Screene

Rev Eamon Donohoe
Rev Patrick Kelly
Rev Thomas Mulcahy
Rev Michael Smyth
Rev Augustine O'Brien

**Parish of the Resurrection**
Ballinfoyle,
Headford Road,
Galway
Tel 091-762883

*Parish Priest*
Rev Kevin Blade PP

Rev Thomas Plower

## NORBERTINE CANONS (OPraem)

*Diocese of Kilmore*

**Abbey of the Most Holy**
Trinity and St Norbert
Kilnacrott Abbey,
Ballyjamesduff, Co Cavan
Tel 049-8544416
Fax 049-8544909
Email kilnacrottabbeytrust
@eircom.net

*Prelate Administrator*
Rt Rev William M. Fitzgerald

Rev Paul Madden
Rev Oliver Martin
Rev Kilian Mitchell
Br Kevin O'Brien
Rt Rev Kevin Smith
Rev Terry Smyth

*Priests working elsewhere in Ireland*
Rev Joseph O'Donohoe
Rev Pat Reilly

## OBLATES OF MARY IMMACULATE (OMI)

*Archdiocese of Dublin*

**Provincial Residence**
Oblates of Mary Immaculate
House of Retreat,
Tyrconnell Road, Inchicore,
Dublin 8
Tel 01-4541160/4541161
Fax 01-4541138
Email omisec@eircom.net

*Provincial*
Very Rev Raymond Warren
*Provincial Treasurer*
Rev Liam Griffin
*Provincial Secretary*
Angela Malone

**Oblate House of Retreat**
Inchicore, Dublin 8
Tel 01-4534408/4541805
Fax 01-4543466

*Superior*
Rev William Fitzpatrick Co-PP
*Moderator of Pastoral Area of Inchicore/Bluebell*
Very Rev Bernard Halpin

Rev Anthony Boyhan
Rev Paul Byrne
Rev Connie Campbell
Rev Edward Carolan
Rev Eugene Clerkin
Rev Peter Daly
Rev William Fitzpatrick
Br Francis Flanagan
Br Patrick Flanagan
Rev Michael Guckian
Rev Richard Haslam
Rev Eoghan Haughey
Rev James Hyland
Rev Sean Hynes
Rev Gerard Kenny
Rev Peter McCluskey
Rev Vincent Mulligan
Rev John Murphy
Rev Kevin O'Connor
Rev Desmond O'Donnell
Rev Joseph O'Melia
Rev John Poole
Rev Eamon Reilly
Rev Thomas Scully

**170 Merrion Road**
Ballsbridge, Dublin 4
Tel 01-2693658
Fax 01-2600597

Rev Charles O'Connor
Rev Conor Murphy

**Oblate Scholasticate**
St Anne's,
Goldenbridge Walk,
Inchicore, Dublin 8
Tel 01-4540841/4542955
Fax 01-4731903

Rev Michael Hughes
Rev Thomas McCabe
Rev Raymond Warren

**Inchicore**
St Michael's Parish
52a Bulfin Road,
Inchicore, Dublin 8
Tel 01-4531660
Fax 01-4548191

Rev L. McDermott
Rev D. Mills

**Bluebell Parish**
Our Lady of the Wayside
118 Naas Road,
Bluebell, Dublin 12
Tel 01-4501040
Email
olowbluebell@oceanfree.net

Rev Peter Clucas
Rev Anthony Clancy
Br M. Moore

**Darndale Parish**
The Presbytery,
Darndale, Dublin 17
Tel 01-8474547
Fax 01-8479295
Email omiddale@eircom.net

*Superior*
Very Rev Leo Philomin Co-PP

Rev Edward Quinn Co-PP

*Archdiocese of Tuam*

**Mazenod House**
Churchfield, Knock,
Co Mayo
Tel 094-9388940

Rev Martin O'Keeffe

*Diocese of Kerry*

**Department of Chaplaincy**
Tralee General Hospital,
Tralee, Co Kerry
Tel 066-7126222

Rev Edward Barrett

## PALLOTTINES (SAC) Society of the Catholic Apostolate

The Pallottine houses in
Ireland and Britain are united
in the Irish Province, as are the
houses in Kenya, Tanzania,
Rome, Argentina and the
USA.

*Archdiocese of Dublin*

**Provincial House**
'Homestead', Sandyford Road,
Dundrum, Dublin 16
Tel 01-2956180/2954170
Email
motherofdivinelove@gmail.com

*Provincial*
Very Rev Jeremiah Murphy
*Rector/Vice Provincial*
Rev Michael Irwin
Email mirwin99@eircom.net
*Provincial Bursar/Secretary
for Missions:* Rev John Kelly
Email
pallbursar@oceanfree.net
*Director of Formation*
Rev Michael Irwin
*Provincial Secretary*
Rev John O'Connor PP

Rev John Coen
Rev John Howlett
Rev Michael Kiely
Rev Donal McCarthy *(Archivist)*
Rev Ned O'Brien
Br Tony Doherty

*Attached to Provincial House*
Rev Patrick Murray,
Ashborough Lodge,
Milltown, Co Kerry
Rev Gerard Fleming CC
437 South Circular Road,
Dolphin's Barn, Dublin 8
Tel 01-4533268

**St Anne's**
Shankill, Co Dublin
Rev John O'Connor PP
*(Provincial Secretary)*
St Benin's, Dublin Road,
Shankill, Co Dublin
Tel 01-2824425

Rev Michael O'Dwyer CC
Rev Eamonn Monson CC
St Benin's, Dublin Road,
Shankill, Co Dublin
Tel 01-2824381

**St Patrick's**
Corduff, Blanchardstown,
Dublin 15
Tel 01-8213596/8215930

Rev Liam McClarey PP
Rev Joseph McLoughlin CC

*Archdiocese of Cashel and Diocese of Emly*

**Pallottine College**
Thurles, Co Tipperary
Tel 0504-21202

*Rector:* Very Rev Emmet O'Hara

Rev Patrick Dwyer
Rev Roger Rafter
Rev John Bergin
Rev Philip Barry
Rev William Hanly
Rev Louis Sisti
Rev John Joseph O'Brien
Rev Martin Mareja
Rev John Sweeney

*Attached to Pallottine College*
Rev Vincent Kelly
18 Silvercourt,
Silversprings, Cork
Rev Joseph Campion
9 Donaguile,
Castlecomer, Co Kilkenny

## PASSIONISTS (CP)
## Congregation of the Passion

Province of St Patrick: houses in Ireland, Scotland and Paris; missions in Africa.

*Archdiocese of Dublin*

**St Paul's Retreat**
Mount Argus, Dublin 6W
Tel 01-4992000 Fax 01-4992001
Email
passionistsmtargus@eircom.net
Provincial Office
Tel 01-4992050 Fax 01-4992055
passionistprov@eircom.net

*Provincial:* Rev Pat Duffy
*Superior:* Rev Bernard Lowe

Rev Kenneth Brady
Br Martin Denny
Rev Ralph Egan
Rev Frank Keevins
Rev Anselm Keleghan
Rev Joseph Kennedy
Rev Brian Mulcahy
Br Vincent McCaughey
Rev Brendan McDermott
Rev Sylvius McGaughey
Rev Brendan McKeever
Rev Nicholas O'Grady
Rev Patrick Rogers
Rev James Sheridan
Rev Patrick Sheridan
Rev Paul Francis Spencer
Rev Ignatius Waters

Applications for missions and retreats to Rev Superior of any of our local Communities

*Diocese of Clogher*

**St Gabriel's Retreat**
The Graan, Enniskillen,
Co Fermanagh
Tel 028-66322272
Fax 028-66325201

*Superior:* Rev Brian D'Arcy

Rev Victor Donnelly
Rev Arthur McCann
Rev Dermot O'Carroll
Rev Anthony O'Leary

*Diocese of Down & Connor*

**Passionist Retreat Centre**
Tobar Mhuire, Crossgar,
Downpatrick,
Co Down BT30 9EA
Tel 028-44830242
Fax 028-44831382

*Superior:* Rev John Friel

Rev Ephrem Blake
Rev Mel Byrne

**Holy Cross Retreat**
Ardoyne, Crumlin Road,
Belfast BT14 7GE
Tel 028-90748231
Fax 028-90740340

*Superior*
Rev Gary Donegan

Rev Charles Cross
Rev Myles Kavanagh
Rev Salvian Maguire
Rev Eugene McCarthy PP
Rev Terence McGuckin

*Scotland*

**St Mungo's Retreat**
52 Parson Street,
Glasgow G4 0RX, Scotland
Tel 141-552-1823
Fax 141-553-1838

*France*

**St Joseph's Church**
50 Avenue Hoche,
75008 Paris
Tel 33-1-42272856
Fax 33-1-42278649

*Botswana*

**Passionist Community**
Forest Hill, PO Box 1216
Gaborone
Tel 267-3904382
Fax 267-3951693

*Republic of South Africa*

**Passionist Community**
PO Box 1395, Wingate 0153,
Republic of South Africa
Tel 27-11-3161852
Fax 27-11-3163763

## REDEMPTORISTS (CSSR)
## Congregation of the Most Holy Redeemer

The Irish Province of the Redemptorists is a complete province, with one dependent.
Vice-Province in Brazil, eleven other members assigned to the Province of CEBU/Philippines, one member assigned to the Province of Bangalore, India, and four members in a new mission in Mozambique.

*Archdiocese of Dublin*

**Liguori House**
75 Orwell Road, Rathgar,
Dublin 6
Tel 01-4067100 Fax 01-4922654
provincial@redemptorists.ie
Provincial administration

*Provincial*
Rev Michael G. Kelleher
*Provincial Vicar*
Rev Brendan O'Rourke
*2nd Provincial Consultor*
Rev Peter Burns
*Delegate for Finance & Development*
Mr Denis Mahoney

*Secretary to the Provincial*
Ms Ann-Marie Cartwright
*Designated Officer, Child Safeguarding:* Mr Phil Mortell
Tel 061-327184/087-2252415
*Delegate for the Proclamation of the Word*
Rev Ciarán O'Callaghan
*Youth/Young Adult Ministry contact person*
Rev Noel Kehoe
Tel 021-4358800

*Human Resources Delegate*
Mr Phil Mortell

**Marianella/Liguori House**
75 Orwell Road,
Rathgar, Dublin 6
Tel 01-4067100 Fax 01-4929635
Outside office hours
086-0514292
Mission house

*Superior:* Rev Con J. Casey
*Vicar-Superior*
Rev Ciarán O'Callaghan

Rev John Casey
Rev John F. Corbett
Rev Peter Flannery
Rev Raphael Gallagher
Br Nicholas Healy
Rev Thomas Hogan
Rev Patrick Horgan
Rev Michael Kelleher
Rev Patrick Kelly Jnr

Rev Brendan McConvery
Br Anthony McCrave
Rev Clement MacMánuis
Rev Gerard Moloney
Rev Pat O'Connell
Rev Denis O'Connor
Rev Martin Ryan
Rev George Wadding

**Most Holy Sacrament Parish**
Cherry Orchard, Dublin 10
Tel 01-6267930

*Co-ordinator*
Rev Gerry O'Connor CC
Rev Patrick Reynolds CC
Rev Seán Duggan PP

**Redemptorist Communications**
75 Orwell Road, Dublin 6
Tel 01-4922488

*Editor:* Rev Gerard Moloney

**Ballyfermot Assumption Parish**
197 Kylemore Road,
Ballyfermot, Dublin 10
Parish Tel 01-6264691
Community Tel 01-5356977

Rev Richard Delahunty PP & Coordinator
Rev Cornelius Kenneally CC
Rev Stan Mellett CC

*Archdiocese of Armagh*

**St Joseph's**
St Alphonsus Road,
Dundalk, Co Louth
Tel 042-9334042/9334762
Fax 042-9330893
Mission house, parish and formation

*Superior & PP*
Rev Michael Cusack PP
*Vicar-Superior*
Rev Eamonn Hoey CC

Rev Dan Baragry *(Formator)*
Rev Peter Burns
Rev Cathal Cumiskey
Br Patrick Doherty
Rev Louis Eustace
Rev Laurence Gallagher
Rev Philip Hearty
Rev Patrick Kelly Snr
Br Dermot McDonagh
Rev Brian McGrath
Rev Anthony Mulvey
Rev Joseph Naughton
Rev Tony Rice *(Formator)*
Rev Patrick Sugrue CC
Rev Richard Tobin

*Diocese of Clonfert*

**St Patrick's**
Esker, Athenry, Co Galway
Tel 091-844007 Fax 091-845698
Outside office hours 086-8440619
Mission house, retreat house
and Youth Village

*Superior*
Rev Brendan O'Rourke
*Vicar Superior*
Rev Patrick O'Keeffe

Rev James Buckley
Rev Thomas Byrne
Br James Casey
Rev Flann Daffy
Rev Séamus Devitt
Rev Patrick Egan
Rev Anthony Flannery
Rev Brian Foley
Br Augustine Forrie
Rev Michael Heagney
Rev Vincent Kavanagh
Br John Long
Rev Denis Luddy
Rev Edward Lynch
Rev Richard McMahon
Rev Dermot O'Connor
Rev Michael O'Flynn

*Diocese of Cork & Ross*

**Scala**
Castlemahon House,
Castle Road, Blackrock, Cork
Tel 021-4358800
Fax 021-4359696
*Co-ordinator:* Rev Noel Kehoe

Rev Michael Forde
Rev John Hanna
Rev John P. O'Riordan CC
Mahon Parish,
2 The Presbytery, Mahon, Cork

*Diocese of Down & Connor*

**Clonard Monastery**
1 Clonard Gardens,
Belfast, BT13 2RL
Tel 028-90445950
Fax 028-90445988
Mission house

*Superior:* Rev Michael Murtagh
*Vicar:* Rev William McGettrick

Rev Edmond Creamer
Rev Johnny Doherty
Rev Alphonsus Doran
Rev Philip Dunlea
Br Michael Gilleece
Rev Brendan Keane
Rev Sean Keeney
Rev Barney McCahery
Rev Sean Moore
Rev Brendan Mulhall
Rev Pat O'Connor
Rev Gerard Reynolds
Rev Paul Turley
Rev Peter Ward

**St Gerard's Parish**
722 Antrim Road,
Newtownabbey,
Co Antrim BT36 7PG
Tel 028-90774833
Fax 028-90770923

*Superior & PP*
Rev Gerry Cassidy

Rev Pat McLaughlin CC

*Diocese of Limerick*

**Mount Saint Alphonsus**
South Circular Road, Limerick
Tel 061-315099 Fax 061-315303
Mission House

*Superior:* Rev Adrian Egan
*Vicar Superior*
Rev Seamus Enright

Rev Kevin Browne
Rev Peter Byrne
Br Seamus Campion
Rev John Goode
Rev John Lucey
Rev David McNamara
Rev Joseph McLoughlin
Rev Derek Meskell
Rev James Murphy
Rev Brian Nolan
Rev James O'Connor
Rev Michael G. O'Connor
Rev John J. Ó Ríordáin
Rev Patrick Walsh

**St Clement's College**
Laurel Hill Avenue,
South Circular Road, Limerick
Tel 061-315878/318749 (staff)
Tel 061-310294 (students)
Fax 061-316640
Secondary school for boys

*Principal:* Mr Vincent Foley

*Province of Cebu (Philippines)*

**PO Box 280,**
6000 Cebu City,
Philippine Islands
Tel +63-32-2536341/2536315

*Provincial*
Rev Cruzito Manding

*Province of Bangalore (India)*

**Redemptorist Community**
R.C. Church, Morrispet PO,
Tenali, Guntur DT 522 202,
Andhra Pradesh, India
Tel +91-8644-223382

Rev Martin Cushnan

*Vice-Province of Fortaleza
(Brazil)*

**Missionarios Redentoristas**
Caixa Postal 85
60,001-970 Fortaleza
Est. do Ceara, Brazil
Tel +55-8532232016

*Vice-Provincial*
Rev Eridian Gonçalves de Lima

*Mission in Rome*

**Via Merulana 31**
CP 2458, 00185 Roma-PT158,
Italy
Tel 0039-06-494901
Rev Eamonn Breslin *(Archives)*
Rev Seán Cannon
*(Alphonsian Academy)*
Rev Brendan Kelly
*(Administration)*
Rev Martin McKeever
*(Alphonsian Academy)*

*Mission in Siberia*

**Redemptorysci**
Box 878, 650099 Kemerovo,
Sibir, Russia
Tel +7-3842-256335

Rev Anthony Branagan

*Mission in Mozambique/
Malawi*

**Santa Maria dei Monti
Mission**
Furancungo, Mozambique,
Africa

Rev John Bermingham (Dublin
Prov)
Rev Brian Holmes (Fortaleza
V-Prov)
Rev José Carlos Júnior
(Fortaleza V-Prov)
Rev Michael Dempsey (Dublin
Prov)
Rev Derek Ryan (Dublin Prov)
*Contact:* c/o Provincial, Dublin

## ROSMINIANS (IC)
### Institute of Charity

Irish Region of the Gentili
Province

*Archdiocese of Dublin*

**Clonturk House**
Ormond Road,
Drumcondra, Dublin 9
Tel 01-6877014

*Provincial:* Rev David Myers
*Secretary:* Rev James Browne
*Vocations Director*
Rev James Browne
*Mission Secretary*
Rev Frank Quinn
*Rector:* Rev Matt Gaffney

Rev Donal Sullivan
Rev Thomas Hubbort
Rev Gerald Cunningham
Rev Sean Walsh
Rev Tom Griffin
Rev John Mullen
Rev William Stuart
Br Jim Kane

Br Joseph Gardner
Br Terence O'Donnell
Br Eamon Fitzpatrick

**Rosminian Mission
Development Office**
Clonturk House,
Ormond Road,
Drumcondra, Dublin 9
Tel 01-6877014

*Archdiocese of Armagh*

**Faughart Parish**
St Brigid's, Kilcurry,
Dundalk, Co Louth
Tel 042-9334410

*Parish Priest*
Rev Christopher McElwee
Rev Bernard Hughes
Rev James Pollock

*Diocese of Cork & Ross*

**Rosmini House**
Dunkereen,
Innishannon, Co Cork
Tel 021-4776268/4776923
Fax 021-4776268

Rev Matthew Corcoran
Rev Seamus McKenna
Rev Polachan Thettayil

*Diocese of Waterford &
Lismore*

**St Joseph's**
Doire na hAbhann,
Tickincar, Clonmel,
Co Tipperary
Tel 052-6126914
Fax 052-6126915

Rev Tom Coffey
Rev P. J. Fegan
Rev Thomas Marley

**Rosminian House of Prayer**
Glencomeragh House,
Kilsheelan,
Co Tipperary
Tel 052-6133181

*Rector*
Rev Michael Melican

Rev Pat Pierce

**St Oliver Plunkett's Parish**
Cooleens, Glenconnor,
Clonmel, Co Tipperary
Tel 052-6125679

Rev Michael Hegarty PP
Rev Vinod Kurian Thennatil

*Enquiries concerning the
missions to:* Rev Frank Quinn
Clonturk House,
Ormond Road,
Drumcondra, Dublin 9

Rev Sean O'Dowd
Rev Ciaran O'Flynn
Rev Ray Reidy
Rev Martin Reilly
Rev Martin Spillane
Rev Declan Thompson

*Retired*

Rev John Flanagan
Rev James Regan

## SALESIANS (SDB)

The Irish Province includes
Ireland and Malta.

*Archdiocese of Dublin*

**Provincialate**
Salesian House,
45 St Teresa's Road,
Crumlin, Dublin 12
Tel 01-4555787
Email (secretary)
ofice@salesians.ie

*Provincial*
Very Rev Michael Casey
Email ruanet1815@eircom.net
michael_casey@eircom.net

**Salesian House**
45 St Teresa's Road,
Crumlin, Dublin 12
Tel 01-4555605
House of residence

*Rector*
Rev Patrick Egan
*Vice-Rector*
Rev Peter Coffey
*Provincial Secretary*
Rev Patrick Egan

Rev Hugh Boyle
Rev Thomas Clowe CC
Rev Thomas Dunne
Rev John Finnegan
Rev John Foster
Br Colum Maguire
Rev Florence McCarthy
Rev Raymond McIntyre
Rev Alan Mowles
Rev Michael Ross
Rev Michael Scott
Rev James Somers

**Rinaldi House**
72 Sean McDermott Street,
Dublin 1
Tel 01-8363358
Fax 01-8552320

*Rector:* Rev Val Collier
*Vice-Rector and Bursar*
Rev John Quinn

Rev Charles Cunningham
Rev Richard Ebejer Adm
Br Sean Feeney
Rev Hugh O'Donnell
Rev James O'Halloran
Rev Cyril Odia CC

**Don Bosco Houses**
12 Clontarf Road, Dublin 3
Tel 01-8336009/8337045

*Priest-in-Charge*
Rev Val Collier

**Our Lady of Lourdes Parish**
Seán McDermott Street,
Dublin 1
Tel 01-8363554

Rev Richard Ebejer Adm

**Salesian College**
Maynooth Road,
Celbridge, Co Kildare
Tel 01-6275058/60
Fax 01-6272208
Secondary School
Tel 01-6272166/6272200

*Rector*
Rev Koenraad Van Gucht
*Bursar:* Rev A. McEvoy

Rev Arulanandam Alphonse
Br Dominic Binh
Br Paul Binh
Rev John Butler
Rev Patrick Hennessy *(Vice-Rector)*
Rev Eunan McDonnell

*Diocese of Limerick*

**Salesian College**
Pallaskenry, Co Limerick
Tel 061-393105 Fax 061-393298
Secondary and agricultural
schools
Salesian Mission Office
Tel 061-393223
Fax 061-393021

*Rector:* Very Rev Daniel Carroll
*Vice-Rector & Bursar*
Br Padraig McDonald
*Mission Procurator*
Rev Dan Devitt

Rev Michael Browne
Br Lukasz Burnicki
Br Patrick Coye
Rev Joseph Harrington
Rev Lukasz Nawrat

**Salesian House**
Milford, Castletroy, Limerick
Tel 061-330268/330914
Student hostel and parish

*Rector:* Very Rev John Horan
*Vice-Rector, Bursar and
Chaplain, University of
Limerick:* Rev John Campion

Rev John Fagan
Rev Martin Loftus
Rev Bob Swinburne PP

*Diocese of Meath*

**Salesian House**
Warrenstown,
Drumree, Co Meath
Tel 01-8259761
Community 01-8259894
Fax 01-8240298

*Rector:* Rev P. J. Nyland
*Bursar:* Br James O'Hare

Rev Patrick Brewster
Br Colm Kennedy
Rev George McCaughey

*Elsewhere in Ireland*
Rev Desmond Campion
*(Chaplain Naval Service,
Haulbowline, Cobh, Cork)*
Rev G. Dowd *(Chaplain,
Custume Barracks, Athlone)*
Rev P.J. Healy (Chaplain,
Mount Carmel Nursing Home,
Roscrea, Co Tipperary)
Rev Patrick J. Somers (Chaplain,
The Curragh, Co Kildare)
Rev Gerard O'Neill (Chaplain,
Collins Barracks, Cork)
Rev Tomasz Grzegorzewski CC
Aughrim, Carrick-on-Shannon,
Co Roscommon

## SALVATORIANS (SDS)

*Superior:* Rev Henry Nevin

**Parochial House**
Pairc Na Mara,
Lahinch, Co Clare
Tel 065-7081307
Email
henrynevinsds@hotmail.com

*Archdiocese of Dublin*

Rev Liam Talbot
70 Charlestown Park, Dublin 11
Tel 01-8626255
Email liamsds@gmail.com
Rev Eric Powell
Room 420, Our Lady's Manor,
Bulloch Castle, Dalkey,
Co Dublin
Tel 01-2718043
Email ericpowellsds@gmail.com

*Diocese of Derry*

Rev Malachy McBride
'Naomh Mhuire',
Upper Slavery, Buncrana,
Co Donegal
Tel 074-9322264

*Diocese of Galway*

Rev Seamus O'Duill
Ard Mhuire, Kilmoon,
Lisdoonvarna, Co Clare
Tel 086-1030261
Email
seamusoduill@eircom.net

*Diocese of Raphoe*

Rev Gerard Daly
Saint John's House,
West Rock, Ballyshannon,
Co Donegal
Tel 071-9851541

## SERVITES (OSM) Order of Friar Servants of Mary

*Provincial*
Rev Colm McGlynn
Servite Priory, Benburb,
Co Tyrone BT71 7JZ
Northern Ireland
Tel 028-37548241

Province of the Isles

*Archdiocese of Dublin*

**Servite Priory**
St Peregrine,
36 Grangewood Estate,
Rathfarnham, Dublin 16
Tel 01-4517115

*Prior:* Rev Tim Flynn

Rev Jimmy Kelly *(Chaplain,
Mountjoy Prison)*

**Servite Oratory**
Rathfarnham
Shopping Centre, Dublin 14
Tel 01-4936300

*Director:* Rev Timothy M. Flynn

**Church of the Divine Word**
Marley Grange,
25–27 Hermitage Downs,
Rathfarnham, Dublin 16
Tel 01-4944295/4941064
Fax 01-4941069

*Prior:* Rev Liam Tracey

Rev Camillus McGrane CC
Rev Jim Mulherin PP

*Archdiocese of Armagh*

**Servite Priory**
Benburb, Dungannon,
Co Tyrone, BT71 7JZ
Northern Ireland
Tel 028-37548241
Tel 01861-548241/548533
Retreat, Conference Centre
and youth centre

*Prior:* Very Rev Gabriel Bannon

Rev Damian Kilbride
Rev Sean Lennon

Rev Eamonn McCreave
Rev Colum McDonnell
Rev Colm McGlynn
Rev Dermot McNeice
Very Rev Raymond O'Connell
Rev Eoin O'Malley
Rev Bernard Thorne
Br Eugene Traynor
Br Joe Whelan

*Outside Ireland*

Br Patrick Gethins (OSM)
St Mary's Priory,
264 Fulham Road,
London SW10 9EL, England

## SOCIETY OF AFRICAN MISSIONS (SMA)
### Societas Missionum Ad Afros

*Diocese of Cork & Ross*

**African Missions**
Provincial House
Feltrim, Blackrock Road, Cork
Tel 021-4292871
Fax 021-4292873
Email provincial@sma.ie

*Provincial*
Rev Michael McCabe
*Vice Provincial*
Rev Malachy Flanagan
*Provincial Councillor*
Rev Maurice Henry

**African Missions**
Blackrock Road, Cork
Tel 021-4292871

*Superior*
Rev Colum P. O'Shea
*Vice-Superior*
Rev Edward O'Connor
*Bursar:* Rev Edward O'Connor
*Provincial Bursar*
Rev Malachy Flanagan
*Assistant Bursar*
Mr Paul Murphy
*Provincial Archivist*
Rev Edmund M. Hogan
*Provincial Development Officer*
Rev Martin Kavanagh
*Director of Communications*
Rev Martin Kavanagh
*JPIC Director*
Mr Gerry Forde

Rev Anthony J. Butler
Rev Tim Carroll
Rev John Casey
Rev John Clancy
Rev Denis Collins
Rev Bernard Cotter
Br Patrick Dowd
Rev Thomas Faherty
Rev James Fegan
Br Thomas Fitzgerald
Rev John Flynn
Rev Francis Furey

Rev William Ghent
Rev Hugh Harkin
Rev James Higgins
Rev Michael Igoe
Rev Patrick Jennings
Rev Eamonn Kelly
Rev James Kirstein
Rev Sean Lynch
Rev Joseph Maguire
Rev Patrick McGovern
Rev Francis Meehan
Rev Gerard Murray
Rev Daniel Murphy
Rev Fionnbarra O'Cuilleanáin
Rev Martin O'Hare
Rev James O'Hea
Rev Con O'Leary
Rev Eugene O'Riordan
Rev Alberto Olivoni
Rev John Quinlan
Rev Desmond Smith
Rev Oscar Welsh

**SMA House**
Wilton, Cork
Tel 021-4541069/4541884

*Superior:* Rev John O'Keeffe
*Bursar:* Rev Jarlath Walsh

Rev Daniel Cashman
Rev Francis Coltsmann
Rev James Conlon
Rev Thomas Furlong
Rev Thomas Gorman
Rev Terence Gunn
Most Rev Patrick Harrington
(Retired Bishop)
Rev John Horgan
Rev Thomas Kearney
Rev Maurice Kelleher
Rev William Kennedy
Rev Angelo Lafferty
Rev Cornelius Murphy
Rev Denis O'Sullivan
Rev Leo Silke

**St Joseph's**
African Missions Parish
Blackrock Road, Cork
Tel 021-4293325
Email smapar@oceanfree.net

Rev John Horgan AP
Rev Noel O'Leary PP

**St Joseph's Parish**
Wilton, Cork
Tel 021-4341362
Fax 021-4343940

Rev Cormac Breathnach PP
Rev John Gallagher CC

**JPIC Office**
SMA House, Wilton, Cork
Email justice@sma.ie

*Director:* Mr Gerry Forde

*Archdiocese of Dublin*

**SMA House**
82 Ranelagh Road,
Ranelagh, Dublin 6
Tel 01-4968162/3
Fax 01-4968164

*Superior*
Rev John O'Brien
*Bursar*
Rev Owen McKenna

Rev John Bowe
Rev Thomas Curran
Rev Joseph Egan

*Also in Dublin*
Rev Sean Healy
Social Justice Ireland,
Arena House, Arena Road,
Sandyford, Dublin 18
Tel 01-2130724
www.socialjustice.ie
Rev Thomas McNamara
Religious Formation
Programme, Loretto House,
Dublin
Rev Kevin O'Gorman
St Patrick's College,
Maynooth, Co Kildare

*Diocese of Galway*

**SMA House**
Claregalway, Co Galway
Tel 091-798880
Fax 091-798879
Email smafathers@eircom.net

*Superior*
Rev Eamonn Finnegan

Rev Brendan Dunning
Rev Thomas Fenlon
Rev Valentine Hynes
Rev Alphonsus Kelly
Rev Eugene McLoughlin
Rev Kieran Morahan
Rev Michael Nohilly
Rev Daniel O'Neill
Rev Gerard Sweeney

*Diocese of Dromore*

**Dromantine College**
Dromantine, Newry,
Co Down BT34 1RH
Tel 028-30821224
Fax 028-30821704

*Superior*
Rev Patrick O'Rourke
*Bursar:* Rev Peter Thompson
*Leadership Team*
Rev Patrick O'Rourke and
Rev John Denvir

Rev Lee Cahill
Rev Edward Deeney
Rev Kevin Mulhern
Rev John Travers

**Dromantine Retreat and Conference Centre**
Dromatine College,
Newry, Co Down BT34 1RH
Tel 028-30821964
Fax 028-30821963
Email admin@
dromantineconference.com
www.dromatineconference.com
*Accommodation:*
40 single en suite rooms,
30 double en suite rooms,
8 conference rooms

*Director:* Rev Paddy O'Rourke

*Temporary diocesan work in Ireland*

Rev Michael Kidney
Rev Patrick Lynch
Rev John McCormack
Rev Francis McGrath
Rev Seamus Nohilly
Rev Hugh O'Kane
Rev Patrick O'Mahony
Rev Thomas Walsh

*Retired in Ireland outside SMA houses*

Rev Michael Boyle
Rev Edward Casey
Rev Martin Costello
Rev Sean Kilbane
Rev Vincent Lawless
Rev Patrick Mackle

**Church of Our Lady of the Rosary and St Patrick**
61 Blackhorse Road,
Walthamstow,
London E17 7AS,
England
Tel 20-85203647

Very Rev John Brown PP
Rev Kevin Conway

*Rome*

**Generalate**
Via della Nocetta 111,
00164 Rome, Italy
Tel 06-6616841
Fax 06-66168490
Email smaroma@smainter.org

*Superior General*
Rev Fachtna O'Driscoll
*Anglophone Secretary*
Steve Philips (Lay Associate,
USA)
*Bursar General*
Rev Didier Eloi Lawson

*Seconded to US Province*

Rev Patrick Kelly

## SOCIETY OF ST PAUL (SSP)

The Society of St Paul in Ireland operates exclusively through the mass media.

*Archdiocese of Dublin*

**Society of St Paul**
Moyglare Road,
Maynooth, Co Kildare
Tel 01-6285933 Fax 01-6289330
Email book@stpauls.ie

*Diocese of Meath*

**St Paul Book Centre**
Castle Street,
Athlone, Co Westmeath
Tel/Fax 090-6492882
Email
saintpaul_books@yahoo.com

## SONS OF DIVINE PROVIDENCE (FDP)

The Irish Foundation is part of the Missionary English-speaking Delegation of 'Mary Mother of the Church'.

*Regional Superior*
Rev Malcolm Dyer
c/o Via Etruria 6, 00183 Rome, Italy
*Local Co-ordinator*
Rev Philip Kehoe
25 Lower Teddington Road,
Kingston-on-Thames, Surrey
Tel 208-9775130

*Archdiocese of Dublin*

**Sarsfield House**
Sarsfield Road,
Ballyfermot, Dublin 10
Tel 01-6266193/6266233
Fax 01-6260303
Email don-orion@clubi.ie

*Superior:* Rev Michael Moss
Email
mossmichael152@gmail.com
Rev John Perrotta
Email jperrotta16@yahoo.ie

## VINCENTIANS (CM)

Vincentian communities of the Irish Province are established in Ireland and England.

*Archdiocese of Dublin*

**Provincial Office**
St Paul's, Sybil Hill,
Raheny, Dublin 5
Tel 01-8510840/8510842
Fax 01-8510846
Email
cmdublin@vincentians.ie
www.vincentians.ie

*Provincial*
Very Rev Eamon Devlin

## All Hallows Institute for Mission and Ministry

Drumcondra, Dublin 9
Tel 01-8373745/6
Fax 01-8377642
Email info@allhallows.ie

*President*
Very Rev Patrick J. McDevitt

Seminary/Pastoral Ministry/
Pastoral Leadership

**St Paul's**
Raheny, Dublin 5
Tel 01-8314011/2 (college)
Tel 01-8318113 (community)
Fax 01-8316387
Secondary School

*Superior*
Very Rev Fergus Kelly

Rev Simon Clyne
Rev Joseph Cunningham
Rev Thomas Davitt
Rev Michael Dunne
Rev Aidan Galvin
Rev Joseph McCann
Rev Richard McCullen
Rev James McCormack
Rev Patrick McDevitt
Rev Bernard Meade
Rev Brendan Steen

**Phibsboro**
St Peter's, Dublin 7
Tel 01-8389708/8389841
Email vinphibs@iol.ie

*Superior*
Very Rev Paschal Scallon Co-PP

Rev Desmond Beirne
Rev John Concannon
Rev Sean Farrell
Rev Patrick Hughes
Rev Aidan McGing
Rev Stephen Monaghan
Rev Mark Noonan
Rev Kevin Scallon (*Ministry to Priests*) Tel 01-8389708

**St Joseph's**
44 Stillorgan Park,
Blackrock, Co Dublin
Tel 01-2886961

*Superior*
Very Rev Colm McAdam

Rev Patrick Collins
Rev Francis MacMorrow

**St Vincent's College**
Castleknock,
Dublin 15
Tel 01-8213051
Secondary Day School for Boys

*President/Superior*
Very Rev Peter Slevin

Rev Stanislaus Brindley
Rev Eugene Curran
Rev John Gallagher
Rev Michael McCullagh
Rev Cornelius Nwaogwugwu
Rev Eamon Raftery

*Diocese of Cork & Ross*

**St Vincent's**
122 Sunday's Well Road, Cork
Tel 021-4304070/4304529
Fax 021-4300103
Email
parishoffice@corkvins.com

*Superior*
Very Rev Jack Harris PP

Rev Timothy Casey
Rev Roderic Crowley

*Diocese of Down & Connor*

**99 Cliftonville Road**
Belfast BT14 6JQ
Tel 028-90751771
Fax 028-90740547
Email cmbelfast@ntlworld.co.uk

*Superior:* Very Rev Peter Gildea

Rev Adrian Eastwood
Rev James Rafferty

## COMMUNITIES OF RELIGIOUS BROTHERS

*In this section, details of each community's main house are given, followed by a list of the dioceses in which the community is present. For more information on houses in particular dioceses, please see the entry for the appropriate diocese.*

## ALEXIAN BROTHERS (CFA)

Anglo-Irish Province

**Regional Residence**
Churchfield, Knock,
Co Mayo
Tel 094-9376996
Email alexianbros@eircom.net

*Regional Leader*
Br Barry Butler

Dublin, Tuam

## BROTHERS OF CHARITY

St Joseph's Region

**Regional Office**
Regional Administration
Kilcornan Centre,
Clarinbridge, Co Galway
Tel 091-796389/796413
Fax 091-796352
Email bronoelcorcoran@
galway.brothersofcharity.ie

*Regional Leader*
Br Noel Corcoran

Cork & Ross, Galway,
Limerick, Ossory

## CHRISTIAN BROTHERS (CFC)

European Province

**Province Centre**
Marino, Griffith Avenue,
Dublin 9

Leadership Team
*Province Leader*
Br Edmund Garvey
*Deputy Leader*
Br Dominic Sassi
*Councillor:* Br Liam Deasy
*Councillor:* Br Chris Glavey
*Councillor:* Br Paul Hendrick

Cashel & Emly, Dublin, Cork,
Derry, Down & Connor, Ferns,
Galway, Kerry, Kildare &
Leighlin, Killaloe, Limerick,
Meath, Ossory, Waterford &
Lismore

As of 1 September 2008, The Edmund Rice Schools Trust became Trustees of the 97 schools previously under the trusteeship of the Christian Brothers. The Company is established for the following charitable objects: to ensure and foster the advancement of education and to further the aims and purposes of Catholic Education in the Edmund Rice tradition in colleges, schools and other educational projects in Ireland owned or operated by the Company in accordance with the religion and education philosophy of the Company as stated in the Edmund Rice Schools Trust Charter, and so that they may continue to provide Catholic education in the spirit and tradition of Blessed Edmund Rice into the future for the people of Ireland.

## DE LA SALLE BROTHERS (FSC)

**Provincialate**
121 Howth Road, Dublin 3
Tel 01-8331815
Fax 01-8339130
Email province@iol.ie

*Provincial*
Br Francis Manning

Armagh, Dublin, Tuam, Down & Connor, Ossory, Waterford & Lismore

## FRANCISCAN BROTHERS (OSF)

Franciscan Brothers of the Third Order Regular

A branch of the Regular Third Order of Penance of St Francis of Asissi, with communities in East Africa and the USA as well as Ireland.

**Generalate**
Mountbellew, Co Galway
Tel 090-9679295
Fax 090-9679687
Email franciscanbrs@eircom.net

*Minister General*
Br Peter Roddy
*Assistant General*
Br Michael Burke
*Councillors*
Br Sean Conway
Br Boniface Kyalo
Br Conal Thomas
*Procurator General*
Br Conal Thomas

*Bursar General*
Br Gerald Smith
*Secretary General*
Br Conal Thomas

Dublin, Tuam, Meath

## MARIST BROTHERS (FMS)

The Marist Brothers in Ireland are part of the province of West Central Europe principally involved in education.

**Provincialate**
Sophiaweg 4
NL-6523 NJ Nijmegen
Netherlands
Email provincial@maristen.nl

*Provincial Superior*
Br Brendan Geary

Dublin, Ardagh & Clonmacnois, Killala

## PATRICIAN BROTHERS (FSP)

Brothers of St Patrick
**Delany Place**
18 Boomerang Road,
The Entrance, NSW 2261,
Australia

*Superior General*
Br Jerome Ellens
*Vicar:* Br Paul O'Keeffe

*Councillors*
Br Felim Ryan
Br George Mangara

Dublin, Kildare & Leighlin, Galway

## PRESENTATION BROTHERS (FPM)

**Generalate**
Mount St Joseph,
Blarney Street, Cork
Tel 021-4392160
Fax 021-4398200
Email generalate@
presentationbrothers.org

*Congregation Leader*
Br Martin Kenneally

**Provincial House**
Glasthule, Dun Laoghaire,
Co Dublin
Tel 01-2842228
Email aiprovince@
presentationbrothers.org

*Province Leader*
Br Andrew Hickey

Dublin, Cork & Ross, Kerry, Killaloe, Waterford & Lismore

## SAINT JOHN OF GOD BROTHERS (OH)

Hospitaller Order of Saint John of God

West European Province of Saint John of God (Great Britain, Ireland, Malawi)

**Provincial Curia**
Hospitaller Order of Saint John of God, Granada, Stillorgan, Co Dublin
Tel 01-5333313
Fax 01-2831274
Email provincial@sjog.ie

*Provincial*
Br Donatus Forkan (OH)

**Saint John of God House Ministries**
Hospitaller House,
Stillorgan, Co Dublin
Tel 01-5333300
Fax 01-2831257
*Group Chief Executive*
John Pepper

*Regional Office (UK)*
St Bede's House, Morton Park,
Darlington CL1 4XZ,
Co Durham, England
Tel +44-1325-373700
Fax +44-1325-373707
*Chief Executive:* Bridget Doogan

Saint John of God Communty Services
*Chief Executive*
Bernadette Shevlin
Email
bernadette.shevlin@sjog.ie

Armagh, Dublin, Kerry

## COMMUNITIES OF RELIGIOUS SISTERS

*In this section, details of each community's main house are given, followed by a list of the dioceses in which the community is present. For more information on houses in particular dioceses, please see the entry for the appropriate diocese.*

## ADORERS OF THE SACRED HEART OF JESUS OF MONTMARTRE (OSB)

**St Benedict's Priory**
The Mount, Cobh, Co Cork
Tel/Fax 021-4811354

*Prioress*
Mother Mary Vianney

Cloyne

## AUGUSTINIAN SISTERS

**'Villa Nova' Prayer House**
Grangecon, Co Wicklow
Tel 045-403874

*Contact:* Sr Mary Bernard

Kildare & Leighlin

## BENEDICTINE NUNS (OSB)

**Kylemore Abbey**
Kylemore, Connemara,
Co Galway
Tel 095-52011
Email info@kylemoreabbey.ie

*Abbess:* Sr Máire Hickey

Tuam

## BLESSED SACRAMENT SISTERS

**Blessed Sacrament Convent**
High Street,
Tullamore, Co Offaly
Tel 057-9351371
Email rsstlm@eircom.net

Dublin, Meath

## BON SAUVEUR SISTERS

**Carriglea**
Dungarvan, Co Waterford
Tel 058-45884 Fax 058-45891
Email lbscarriglea@eircom.net

*Superior:* Sr Mary Fitzgerald

Waterford & Lismore

## BON SECOURS SISTERS (Paris)

**Leadership Office**
College Road, Cork
Tel 021-4543310
Fax 021-4542533

*Country Leader:* Sr Marie Ryan
Email mryan@congregation.
bonsecours.ie

Dublin, Tuam, Cloyne, Cork &
Ross, Down & Connor, Galway,
Kerry

Sisters are also working in
Peru and Tanzania and South
Africa

## BRIGIDINE SISTERS
### Sisters of St Brigid

**Brigidine Generalate**
Albert Park, 52 Beaconsfield
Parade, Victoria 3206,
Australia

*Congregational Leader*
Sr Louise Cleary

Dublin, Galway, Kildare &
Leighlin

## CARMELITE MONASTERIES

*Archdiocese of Dublin*

**Carmelite Monastery of the
Immaculate Conception**
Roebuck, Dublin 14
Tel 01-2884732
Altar Breads
Email altarbreads@
roebuckcarmel.com
Email
carmel@roebuckcarmel.com

*Prioress:* Sr Maria Maher

**Carmelite Monastery of the
Assumption**
Firhouse, Dublin 24
Tel 01-4526474

*Prioress:* Vacant

**Carmelite Monastery of the
Immaculate Heart of Mary**
Delgany,
Co Wicklow
Tel 085-8601794
Email contact@carmelite
monasterydelgany.ie

*Prioress:* Sr Gwen Collins

**Carmelite Monastery Star of
the Sea**
Seapark, Malahide,
Co Dublin
Tel 01-8454259
Email community@
malahidecarmelites.ie
www.malahidecarmelites.ie

*Prioress:* Sr Attracta Hand

**Carmelite Monastery of St
Joseph**
Upper Kilmacud Road,
Stillorgan, Blackrock,
Co Dublin
Tel 01-2886089
Email
contact@kilmacudcarmel.ie
www.kilmacudcarmel.ie

*Prioress*
Sr Mary Brigeen Wilson

*Archdiocese of Tuam*

**Carmelite Monastery**
Tranquilla, Knock,
Claremorris, Co Mayo
Email
tranquillacarmel@eircom.net

*Prioress:* Sr Máire

*Diocese of Clonfert*

**St Joseph's Monastery**
Mount Carmel, Loughrea,
Co Galway
Email theholychild1@eircom.net

*Prioress*
Sr Mary Catharina Murphy

*Diocese of Dromore*

**Carmelite Monastery**
42 Glenvale Road, Newry,
Co Down BT34 2RD
Fax 028/048-30252778
Email
nuns@carmelitesglenvale.org

*Prioress:* Sr M. Carmel Clarke

*Diocese of Ferns*

**Mount Carmel Monastery**
New Ross, Co Wexford

*Prioress:* Sr Brenda Donovan

*Diocese of Waterford &
Lismore*

**St Joseph's Carmelite
Monastery**
Tallow, Co Waterford
Tel 058-56205
Email carmeltallow@eircom.net

*Prioress:* Sr Teresa Gibbons

## CARMELITE SISTERS FOR THE AGED AND INFIRM

**Our Lady's Manor**
Bulloch Castle,
Dalkey, Co Dublin
Tel 01-2806993 Fax 01-2844802
Email
ourladysmanor1@eircom.net

*Superior*
Sr Therese Eileen Mulvaney
Email sistereileen@eircom.net
*Administrator*
Sr Bernadette Murphy

Dublin

## SISTERS OF CHARITY OF THE INCARNATE WORD

**Carrigoran House**
Newmarket-on-Fergus,
Co Clare
Tel 061-368100 Fax 061-368170
Email info@carrigoranhouse.ie

*Administrator*
Sr Christina Murphy

Killaloe

## CHARITY OF JESUS AND MARY SISTERS

**Anglo-Irish Province**
Moore Abbey
Monasterevin, Co Kildare
Tel 045-525478

*Contact*
Sr Mary-Anna Lonergan
Email maryanna1@eircom.net
*Provincial Superior*
Sr Elizabeth Roche
108 Spring Road, Letchworth,
Hertfordshire SG6 3B
Tel 0462-675694

Our residential centres have
been transferred to Muiriesa
Foundation since 1 January
2012

Kildare & Leighlin, Meath

## CHARITY OF NEVERS SISTERS

**29 Hazelgrove Court**
Tallaght, Dublin 24
*Contact person*
Sr Rosaleen Cullen
Tel 01-4585654
Email
rosaleencullen@upcmail.ie

Dublin

## SISTERS OF CHARITY OF OUR LADY MOTHER OF MERCY

**St Andrew's**
3 Avonmore Road,
Raheen, Limerick
Tel 061-229935

Limerick

## CHARITY OF ST PAUL THE APOSTLE SISTERS

**St Paul's Convent**
Greenhills, Dublin 12
Tel 01-4505358

*Superior:* Sr Mary Lyons
Email
marylyons2010@gmail.com

Dublin, Limerick

## CHRISTIAN RETREAT SISTERS

**'The Demense'**
Mountbellew, Ballinasloe,
Co Galway
Tel 090-9679311/9679939

*Contact:* Sr Assumpta Collins
Email assumptahrc@gmail.com

*Superior General*
Sr Rose Marie Prongue
17 Rue Du Couvent, 25210 Les
Fontenelles, France

Tuam

## CISTERCIANS

**St Mary's Abbey**
Glencairn, Lismore,
Co Waterford
Tel 058-56168 Fax 058-56616
Email
glencairnabbey@eircom.net

*Abbess:* Sr Marie Fahy

Waterford & Lismore

## CLARISSAN MISSIONARY SISTERS OF THE BLESSED SACRAMENT

**Our Lady of Guadalupe
Residence for Students**
28 Waltersland Road,
Stillorgan, Co Dublin
Tel/Fax 01-2886600
Email misclaridub@hotmail.com
www.guadaluperesidence.com

*Superior:* Sr Gabriela Luna

Dublin

## CONGREGATION OF THE SISTERS OF MERCY

The Congregation of the Sisters of Mercy is an International Congregation. It has 2,114 members currently serving in Ireland, Britain, Brazil, Kenya, South Africa, Peru, Nigeria, Zambia and the US.

**Congregational Leadership Team**
Sr Margaret Casey
*(Congregational Leader)*
Sr Patricia O'Donovan
Sr Cecilia Cadogan
Sr Scholasticah Nganda
Sr Marie Louise White

**Congregational Offices**
'Rachamim',
13/14 Moyle Park, Convent Road, Clondalkin, Dublin 22
Tel 01-4673737 Fax 01-4673749
Email mercy@csm.ie
Website www.sistersofmercy.ie

The Northern Province comprising the dioceses of Raphoe, Derry, Down & Connor, Armagh, Dromore, Clogher, Kilmore, Meath and the regions of Nigeria and Zambia.

*Provincial:* Sr Ann Brady

Sr Paula Carron
Sr Mary Conway
Sr Agnes Crowley
Sr Jean Kelly

Provincial Office
74 Main Street, Clogher,
Co Tyrone BT76 0AA
Tel 028-85548127
Fax 028-85549459
Email mercy@mercynth.org

**The Western Province**
Comprising the dioceses of Killala, Achonry, Elphin, Galway, Tuam, Clonfert, Ardagh & Clonmacnois.

*Provincial:* Sr Caitlín Conneely

Sr Anna Burke
Sr Breege Donohoe
Sr Mary Glynn
Sr Juliet Walsh

Provincial Office
Caoineas, Society Street,
Ballinasloe, Co Galway
Tel 090-9645202
Fax 090-9645203
Email caoineas@smwestprov.ie

**The South Central Province**
Comprising the dioceses of Dublin, Cashel & Emly, Kildare & Leighlin, Killaloe, Limerick.

*Provincial:* Sr Peggy Collins

Sr Frances Minahan
Sr Margaret Corkery
Sr Mary Margaret Costigan
Sr Clare Gunning

Provincial Office, Oldtown, Sallins Road, Naas, Co Kildare
Tel 045-876784 Fax 045-871509
Email provoffice@mercyscp.ie

**The Southern Province**
Comprising the dioceses of Cork & Ross, Cloyne, Kerry, Ferns, Ossory, Waterford & Lismore.
*Provincial:* Sr Miriam Kerrisk
Sr Clare O'Reilly
Sr Nora Anne Lombard
Sr Veronica Mangan
Sr Nora Flynn

Provincial Office
Bishop Street, Cork
Tel 021-4975380
Fax 021-4915220
provincialoffice@mercysouth.ie

## CROSS AND PASSION CONGREGATION

**Province Office,**
299 Boarshaw Road, Middleton, Manchester M24 2PF
Tel 0161-6553184
Fax 0161-6533666

*Province Leader*
Sr Máire Ní Shúilleabháin

Dublin, Down & Connor

## DAUGHTERS OF CHARITY OF ST VINCENT DE PAUL

**St Catherine's Provincial House**
Dunardagh, Blackrock,
Co Dublin
Tel 01-2882669/2882896/2882660 Fax 01-2834485
*Local Superior*
Sr Áine MacNamara
*Provincial Superior*
Sr Goretti Butler

Armagh, Dublin, Tuam, Cork & Ross, Down & Connor, Ferns, Galway and Killaloe

## DAUGHTERS OF THE CROSS OF LIÈGE

**Daughters of the Cross**
Beech Park Convent,
Beechwood Court, Stillorgan,
Co Dublin
Tel 01-2887401/2887315
Fax 01-2881499
Email beechpark@eircom.net
*Superior:* Sr Anne Kelly
Dublin

## DAUGHTERS OF THE HEART OF MARY

St Joseph's
Tivoli Road, Dun Laoghaire,
Co Dublin
Tel 01-2801204
Dublin

## DAUGHTERS OF THE HOLY SPIRIT

**88 Foxfield Road**
Raheny, Dublin 5
Tel 01-8312795

*Contact person*
Sr Teresa Buckley DHSp

*Provincial Superior*
Sr Mary Regina Bond
Provincial House,
103 Harlestone Road,
Northhampton,
NN5 7AQ, England

Dublin

## DAUGHTERS OF JESUS

*Provincial Superior*
55 Nightingale Road,
Rickmansworth,
Herts WD3 7BU, England
Tel 01923-897386

Dublin

## DAUGHTERS OF MARY AND JOSEPH

*Leadership Team*
Email dmjirishregion@eircom.net

Dublin, Kerry, Kildare & Leighlin, Ossory

## DAUGHTERS OF OUR LADY OF THE SACRED HEART

**Provincial House**
14 Rossmore Avenue,
Templeogue, Dublin 6W
Tel 01-4903200
Tel/Fax 01-4903113
Email olshprov@eircom.net

*Provincial:* Sr Mairead Kelleher

Dublin, Clogher

## DAUGHTERS OF WISDOM (LA SAGESSE)

35 The Park
Strandhill Road, Sligo
Tel 071-9154019
*Co-ordinator*
Sr Maureen Seddon

Dublin, Elphin

## DISCIPLES OF THE DIVINE MASTER

**Newtownpark Avenue,**
Blackrock, Co Dublin
Tel 01-2114949/2886414
Fax 01-2836935

*Regional Superior*
Sr Brid Geraghty
Email bridpddm@eircom.net
www.pddm.org/ireland

Dublin, Elphin

## DOMINICAN CONTEMPLATIVES

**Monastery of St Catherine of Siena**
The Twenties, Drogheda,
Co Louth
Tel 041-9838524
Email siena@eircom.net

*Prioress*
Sr M. Breda Carroll OP

Armagh

## DOMINICAN SISTERS (King William's Town)

**Our Lady of Fatima Convent**
Oakpark, Tralee, Co Kerry
Tel 066-7125641/066-7125900
Fax 066-7180834
Email teresamcevoy@fatimahome.com

*Contact:* Sr Teresa McEvoy OP

Kerry

## DOMINICAN SISTERS

**Mission Area Office**
Mary Bellew House,
Dominican Campus, Cabra,
Dublin 7
Tel 01-8299700 Fax 01-8299799
Email regionop@gmail.com

*Mission Area Prioress*
Sr Martina Phelan OP

Dublin, Down & Connor,
Galway

## FAMILY OF ADORATION SISTERS

**St Aidan's Monastery**
Ferns, Co Wexford
Tel 053-9366634
Email staidansferns@eircom.net

*Superior:* Sr Dolores O'Brien

Ferns, Down & Connor

## FRANCISCAN MISSIONARIES OF THE DIVINE MOTHERHOOD

**Regional House**
Assisi, Harbour Road,
Ballinasloe, Co Galway
Tel 090-9642320
Fax 090-9642648

*Regional Leader*
Sr Anne O'Brien
Email anne4@gofree.indigo.ie

Dublin, Armagh, Clonfert, and Kerry

*Diocese of Ardagh & Clonmacnois*

**Poor Clare Monastery of Perpetual Adoration**
Drumshanbo, Co Leitrim

*Abbess*
Mother M. Angela McCabe

*Diocese of Cork & Ross*

**Poor Clare Colettine Monastery**
College Road, Cork

*Abbess*
Sr Colette-Marie O'Reilly

*Diocese of Galway*

**St Clare's Monastery**
Nuns' Island, Galway

*Abbess*
Sr M. Paul

*Diocese Kildare & Leighlin*

**Poor Clare Colettine Monastery**
Graiguecullen, Carlow

*Abbess*
Mother Rosario Byrne

*Diocese of Killaloe*

**Poor Clare Monastery**
Francis Street,
Ennis, Co Clare

*Abbess*
Sr Gabrielle Murphy

## POOR SERVANTS OF THE MOTHER OF GOD

**Generalate**
Maryfield Convent,
Mount Angelus Road,
Roehampton SW15 4JA,
England
Tel 0208-7884351

*General:* Sr Mary Whelan

*Local Leader (Dublin region North)*
Sr Margaret O'Sullivan
Email mosul5@eircom.net
*Local Leader (Dublin region West)*
Sr Helen Coughlan
Email
helencoughlan@yahoo.com
*Local Leader (outside Dublin)*
Sr Caitriona Walsh
Email trionawalsh@eircom.net

Dublin, Tuam, Cloyne, Down & Connor, Limerick

## CONGREGATION OF THE SISTERS OF NAZARETH

**Nazareth House**
Malahide Road, Dublin 3
Tel 01-8332024
Fax 01-8334988
Email
regional.ie@nazarethcare.com

*Regional Superior*
Sr Cora McHale

Dublin, Cloyne, Derry, Down and Connor, Elphin

## PRESENTATION SISTERS

**Generalate**
Monasterevin, Co Kildare
Tel 045-525335/525503
Fax 045-525209
Email
adminpresevin@eircom.net
Website www.
presentationsistersunion.org

*Congregational Leader*
Sr Mary Deane

Armagh, Dublin, Cashel,
Tuam, Ardagh & Clonmacnois,
Cloyne, Cork and Ross, Ferns,
Galway, Kerry, Kildare and
Leighlin, Limerick, Meath,
Ossory, Waterford & Lismore

## PRESENTATION OF MARY SISTERS

**4 Lower John Street,**
Sligo
Tel 071-9160740

*Superior:* Sr Elenita Baguio
Email
elenitabpm@hotmail.com

Elphin

## REDEMPTORISTINES

**Monastery of St Alphonsus**
St Alphonsus Road, Dublin 9

*Superior:* Sr Gabrielle
Email
gabrielle.fox@redemptorists.ie

Dublin

## RELIGIOUS OF CHRISTIAN EDUCATION

**Provincial Office**
3 Bushy Park House,
Templeogue Road, Dublin 6W
Tel 01-4901668 Fax 01-4901101
Email rodyolooney@yahoo.co.uk

*Provincial Superior*
Sr Rosemary O'Looney

Dublin

## RELIGIOUS OF SACRED HEART OF MARY

**13/14 Huntstown Wood,**
Mulhuddart, Dublin 15
Tel 01-8223566

*Contact person*
Sr Regina King

Dublin, Down & Connor,
Ossory

## RELIGIOUS SISTERS OF CHARITY

**Generalate**
Caritas, 15 Gilford Road,
Sandymount, Dublin 4
Tel 01-2697833/2697935

Provincialate, Provincial House,
Our Lady's Mount,
Harold's Cross, Dublin 6W
Tel 01-4973177

Dublin, Cork & Ross, Galway,
Ossory, Waterford & Lismore

## ROSMINIANS (SISTERS OF PROVIDENCE)

**104a Griffith Court**
Fairview, Dublin 3
Tel 01-8375021

Dublin, Down & Connor

## SACRED HEART SOCIETY

**Provincial Administration Office**
76 Home Farm Road,
Drumcondra, Dublin 9
Tel 01-8375412 Fax 01-8375542

*Provincial Secretary*
Email rscjirs@gmail.com
*Provincial Superior*
Sr Barbara Duffy

Armagh, Dublin

## SACRED HEARTS OF JESUS AND MARY (PICPUS)

**Delegation House**
11 Northbrook Road
Ranelagh, Dublin 6
Tel 01-4910173 (Coordinator)
Tel 01-4974831 (Community)
Fax 01-4965551

*Contact*
Sr Angela O'Toole SSCC

Dublin

## SACRED HEARTS OF JESUS AND MARY

**Blackrock**
Cork
Tel 021-4936200

*Community Leader*
Sr Alexander MacLean

Dublin, Cork & Ross, Down & Connor, Killaloe

## SALESIAN SISTERS OF ST JOHN BOSCO

**Provincialate**
203 Lower Kilmacud Road,
Stillorgan, Co Dublin
Tel 01-2985188
Email prov@salsisdb.iol.ie

*Provincial Superior*
Sr Mary Doran

Dublin, Limerick

## SISTERS OF ST CLARE

**St Clare's Generalate**
63 Harold's Cross Road,
Dublin 6W
Tel 01-4966880/4995135
Fax 01-4966388
Email annedkelly@yahoo.com

*Abbess General:* Sr Anne Kelly

Armagh, Dublin, Down &
Connor, Dromore, Kerry, Kilmore

*Regional Superior*
Sr Mercedes Coen
St Clare's Convent,
Keady, Co Armagh BT60 3RW
Tel/Fax 028-37530554

## ST JOHN OF GOD SISTERS

**St John of God Congregational Centre**
1 Summerhill Heights, Wexford
Tel 053-9142396
Fax 053-9141500
Email stjohnogoffice@eircom.net

*Congregational Leader*
Sr Bríd Ryan

Dublin, Ferns, Kildare &
Leighlin, Killaloe, Ossory,
Waterford & Lismore

## ST JOSEPH OF ANNECY SISTERS

**St Joseph's Convent**
Killorglin, Co Kerry
Tel 066-9761809
Fax 066-9761127
Email margaret.lyne@talk21.com

*Superior:* Sr Helena Lyne

Kerry

## ST JOSEPH OF THE APPARITION SISTERS

**St Joseph's Convent**
Dun Bríd, Ballymote, Co Sligo
Tel 071-9183973
Email stjsligo@eircom.net

Achonry

## SISTERS OF ST JOSEPH OF CHAMBERY

**St Joseph's Convent**
Springdale Road, Raheny,
Dublin 5
Tel 01-8478351 (Convent)
Email esilke10@eircom.net
*Superior:* Sr Eileen Silke
Email esilke10@eircom.net
*Regional Superior*
Sr Sarah Goss

Dublin

## ST JOSEPH OF CLUNY SISTERS

Mt Sackville Convent
Chapelizod, Dublin 20
Tel 01-8213134 Fax 01-8224002
Email clunyprov@sjc.ie
Website www.sjc.ie

*Provincial Superior*
Sr Rowena Galvin

Dublin, Ardagh & Clonmacnois

## ST JOSEPH OF LYON SISTERS

3 St Margaret's Avenue,
Raheny, Dublin 5
Tel 01-8325896

*Contact:* Sr Marie Kiernan

Dublin

## ST JOSEPH OF THE SACRED HEART SISTERS

**Granagh**
Kilmallock, Co Limerick
Tel 061-399027

*Regional Leader*
Sr Margaret O'Sullivan

Dublin, Tuam, Achonry, Cloyne,
Killaloe, Limerick, Kerry

## ST LOUIS SISTERS

**St Louis Regional House**
60 Ard Easmuinn,
Dundalk, Co Louth
Tel 042-9334752/9334753
Fax 042-9334651
Email regionalate@stlouisirl.ie

*Regional Leader*
Sr Anne Kavanagh

Armagh, Dublin, Tuam,
Achonry, Clogher, Down &
Connor, Ferns

## ST MARY MADELEINE POSTEL SISTERS

**Park More Convent**
Abbey Street, Roscrea,
Co Tipperary
Tel 0505-21038

*Local Superior*
Sr Marie Keegan

Tuam, Killaloe

## ST PAUL DE CHARTRES SISTERS

**Queen of Peace Centre**
Garville Avenue,
Rathgar, Dublin 6
Tel 01-4975381/4972366
Fax 01-4964084
Email spcqueen@eircom.net

*Regional Superior*
Sr Rose Margaret Nuval

Dublin

## URSULINES

**Ursuline Generalate**
17 Trimleston Drive,
Booterstown, Co Dublin
Tel 01-2693503
Email angemer@eircom.net
Website www.ursulines.ie

*Congregational Leader*
Sr Mary McHugh
*Assistant:* Sr Anne Harte Barry

Dublin, Tuam, Cashel & Emly,
Cork & Ross, Elphin,
Waterford & Lismore

## URSULINES OF JESUS

**26 The Drive**
Seatown Park,
Swords, Co Dublin
Tel 01-8404323

*Delegated Councillor*
Sr Hilary Brown
St Ursula's Convent,
11 Amhurst Park, Stamford Hill,
London N16 5DH, England
Tel 020-88020256
Email supgb@dircon.co.uk

Dublin

## VISITATION SISTERS

**Monastery of the Visitation**
Dublin Road,
Drogheda, Co Louth
Tel 041-9838184

*Sister in Charge:* Sr Josephine
Thérèse Gallagher
Email visitationstamulen
@gmail.com

Meath

## INSTITUTES

## LAY SECULAR INSTITUTES

Lay secular institutes come
under the jurisdiction of the
Sacred Congregation for
Religious Secular Institutes as
laid down by the Apostolic
Constitution, *Provida Mater
Ecclesia.*

**Caritas Christi**
Secular institute of pontifical
right founded in 1937 for
laywomen.

*Priest Assistant*
Rev Finian Lynch (OP)
St Mary's Priory,
Pope's Quay, Cork
Tel 021-4502267
Fax 021-4502307
Email simonrop@eircom.net

*Priest Assistant for Dublin*
Rev Gregory Carroll (OP)
St Mary's Priory,
Tallaght, Dublin 24
Tel 01-4048118
Fax 01-4515584
Email gregcop@eircom.net

*Contacts:* www.ccinfo.org
Brigid Tel 086-4002414
Kathleen Tel 087-9005767

**Columba Community**
Private association of the
faithful involved in prayer,
Christian teaching, counsel,
reconciliation and healing and
rehabilitation from drugs and
alcohol.

Columba House,
11 Queen Street,
Derry BT48 7EG
Tel 028-71262407
Email columbacommunity@
hotmail.com
Website
www.columbacommunity.com

*Spiritual Director*
Rev Neal Carlin
*Treasurer:* Ms Kathleen Devlin
*Contact:* Tommy McCay

**Servitium Christi**
A Secular Institute of
Pontifical right for women in
the Eucharistic Family of St
Peter Julian Eymard (also
includes the Congregation of
the Blessed Sacrament).

*Enquiries:* Mary Keane
58 Moyne Road,
Ranelagh, Dublin 6

## Society of Madonna della Strada

Founded in Austria in 1936 for
single or widowed laywomen;
membership worldwide.

*Enquiries:* Mary C. Peyton
18 Rock Road, Lisburn,
Co Antrim BT28 3SU
Tel Lisburn 92648244
Email mary.peyton@talktalk.net

## NEW FORMS OF CONSECRATED LIFE

Next to already existing
institutes of consecrated life
new forms of evangelical life
spring up, 'through which
God in his goodness enriches
the Church, enabling her to
follow her Lord in a constant
outpouring of generosity and
attentive to God's invitation
revealed through the signs of
the times' (John Paul II)
(Annuario Pontificio p1646).

**The Spiritual Family
The Work of Christ Familia
Spiritualis Opus (FSO)**
Family of consecrated life.
Pontifical Right. Founded in
Belgium in 1938 by Julia
Verhaeghe. It consists of a
Priests' Community and of a
Sisters' Community of
Consecrated Women. The
nucleus of The Work is made
up of members in the strict
sense who are consecrated to
the Sacred Heart of Jesus in a
'Holy Covenant in the three
evangelical counsels'. They
strive to unite a life of prayer
with the apostolic life, and so
have a positive influence on
faith in society. They follow
above all the example of St
Paul, imitating his love for
Christ and His Body, the
Church. They seek to help
with the new evangelisation
as spiritual fathers and
mothers in a spirit of unity
and respectful
complementarity. They are
joined by members in a wider
sense, and by lay faithful who
are spiritually associated with
the Work of Christ.

*Enquiries*
Sr Nellie Baerts FSO
Bishop's House,
Ard Adhamhnáin,
Letterkenny, Co Donegal
Tel 074-9124898
Email lk@thework-fso.org
www.thework-fso.org

Raphoe

# SEMINARIES AND HOUSES OF STUDY

## SEMINARIES

### PONTIFICAL IRISH COLLEGE, ROME

Founded in 1628 the Irish National College in Rome provides formation to seminarians and priests for the diocesan priesthood in Ireland and beyond.
Via dei SS Quattro 1, 00184 Roma, Italy
Tel 003906-772631 Fax 003906-77263323
Email ufficio@irishcollege.org
www.irishcollege.org
*Rector:* Rev Ciarán O'Carroll DEcclesHist
*Vice-Rector*
Rev George Hayes B.Comm, BD, JCL
*Spiritual Director*
Rev Tom Norris BPhil, DD
*Director of Formation*
Rev Hugh Clifford BSc, BD, STL

### ST PATRICK'S COLLEGE, MAYNOOTH

Founded in 1795, the National Seminary for Ireland and Pontifical University, Maynooth, Co Kildare
Tel 01-7084700 Fax 01-7083959
Email president@spcm.ie
*College Officers*
*President*
Rt Rev Mgr Hugh Connolly BA, DD
*Financial Officer*
Ms Fidelma Madden ACA, AITI
*Registrar and Supervisor of Examinations*
Rev Professor Michael Mullaney
*Directors of Formation*
Rev Paul Prior
Rev Michael Collins
*Dean of Faculty of Theology*
Rev Dr Padraig Corkery BSc, STD (CUA), LSS, HDE
*Dean of Faculty of Philosophy*
Dr Michael Dunne
*Librarian:* Cathal McCauley
*Archivist:* Ms Susan Leyden BA, HDip (Archival Studies)
*Acting Director of Human Resources*
Rosaleen McCarthy

Pontifical University Courses:
*Professors/Department Heads*
*Canon Law*
Rev Professor Michael Mullaney
*Systematic Theology*
Rev Professor Declan Marmion (SM)
*Ecclesiastical History*
Professor Salvador Ryan
*Liturgy:* Rev Professor Liam Tracey (OSM) STB, SLD, DipMar, DipPastoral Theology
*Moral Theology:* Rev Dr Padraig Corkery, BSc, STD (CUA)
*Sacred Scripture*
Rev Professor Seamus O'Connell BSc, LSS
*Faith and Culture*
Rev Professor Michael A. Conway

### MILLTOWN INSTITUTE OF THEOLOGY AND PHILOSOPHY

Milltown Park, Sandford Road, Ranelagh, Dublin 6
Tel 01-2776300
Fax 01-2692528
Email info@milltown-institute.ie
www.milltown-institute.ie
Founded in 1968.
An Ecclesiastical Faculty, a recognised College of the NUI, and a designated institution of HETAC.
*Patron:* Most Rev Diarmuid Martin, Archbishop of Dublin
*Chancellor*
Very Rev Adolfo Nicolás (SJ)
*Vice-Chancellor*
Very Rev Thomas Layden (SJ)
*Rector of Ecclesiastical Faculty*
Dr Thomas R. Whelan
*Acting President*
Dr Thomas R. Whelan
*Dean of Theology*
Dr Thomas Whelan (CSSp)
*Registrar:* Dr Thomas Whelan (CSSp)
*Editor, Milltown Studies*
Dr Joseph Egan (SMA)
*Assistant to the President*
Mr Philip FitzPatrick
Email pfitzpatrick@milltown-institute.ie
*Librarian:* Ms June Rooney
*Financial Advisor:* Mr Patrick Lally

Allianz ⑪

## HOUSES OF STUDY

*For details see Religious Orders and Congregations Section*

**Augustinians (OSA)**
*Prior:* Rev John Lyng OSA
St Augustine's, Ballyboden, Dublin 16
Tel 01-4241000 Fax 01-4939915

**Camillians (OSCam)**
St Camillus, South Hill Avenue,
Blackrock, Co Dublin
Tel 01-2882873/2833380

**Carmelites (OCarm)**
*Prior:* Rev Joseph Mothersill
Gort Muire, Ballinteer, Dublin 16
Tel 01-2984014 Fax 01-2987221
Email gortmuire@gortmuire.com

**Divine Word Missionaries (SVD)**
Divine Word Missionaries,
Maynooth, Co Kildare
Tel 01-6286391/2
Fax 01-6289184
Email dv.twomcy@may.ie

**Dominicans (OP)**
St Mary's Priory, Tallaght, Dublin 24
Tel 01-4048100
The Priory Institute
Tel 01-4048124 Fax 01-4626084
Email enquiries@prioryinstitute.com

St Saviour's Priory, Upper Dorset Street,
Dublin 1
Tel 01-8897610 Fax 01-8734003
Email stsaviours@eircom.net

Dominican Biblical Institute,
Upper Cecil Street, Limerick
Tel 061-490600 Fax 061-468604
Email info@dbclimerick.ie

**Franciscans (OFM)**
Dún Mhuire, Seafield Road,
Killiney, Co Dublin
Tel 01-2826760 Fax 01-2826993
Email dmkilliney@eircom.net

**Missionaries of Africa (White Fathers)**
Cypress Grove, Templeogue, Dublin 6W
Tel 01-4055263
*Contact Person:* Rev P. J. Cassidy
Email provirl@indigo.ie

**Oblates (OMI)**
St Anne's, Goldenbridge Walk, Inchicore,
Dublin 8
Tel 01-4540841

Mona,
12 Tyrconnell Road, Inchicore, Dublin 8
Rev Patrick Carolan (OMI)
Rev Liam Griffin (OMI)

**Redemptorists (CSsR)**
St Jopseph's Monastery,
St Alphonsus Road,
Dundalk, Co Louth

**Salesians (SDB)**
St Catherine's Centre, North Campus,
Maynooth, Co Kildare
Tel 01-6286111 Fax 01-6286268
Email sdbmaynooth@iol.ie
Members part of Celbridge community

## SPECIAL INSTITUTES OF EDUCATION

**Dominican Biblical Institute**
Dominic Street & Cecil Street Upper,
Limerick
*Moderator:* Rev Gerard Norton (OP)
Tel 061-490600
061-490606 (administration)
Fax 061-468604
www.dbil.ie
enquiries@dbil.ie

**IMU Mission Institute**
St Columban's, Dalgan Park, Navan,
Co Meath
Tel 046-9021525 Fax 046-9022799
Email imuinst@eircom.net
*Director:* P. Dooher (SSC)

**Irish School of Ecumenics
Trinity College Dublin**
Confederal School of Religions,
Peace Studies and Theology,
ISE-LI Building,
Trinity College, Dublin 2
*Contact:* Prof. Gillian Wylie, Head of ISE
Tel 01-8964770 Fax 01-6725024
Email isedir@tcd.ie
www.tcd.ie/ise

**Irish School of Ecumenics
Trinity College Dublin**
Confederal School of Religions,
Peace Studies and Theology,
683 Antrim Road, Belfast BT15 4EG
Tel 028-90775010 Fax 028-90373986
Email isedir@tcd.ie
www.tcd.ie/ise

**Mater Dei Institute of Education**
Clonliffe Road, Dublin 3
Tel 01-8086500 Fax 01-8370776
Email info@materdei.dcu.ie
www.materdei.ie
Director: Dr Andrew G. McGrady
Tel 01-8086504
Email andrew.mcgrady@materdei.dcu.ie

**Redemptoris Mater Archdiocesan
Missionary House of Formation**
(Archdiocese of Armagh)
Founded in 2012 by Cardinal Brady to
form priests for the New Evangelisation
who are both diocesan and missionary.
The vocations come from the
communities of the Neocatechumenal
Way and, upon ordination, will be
incardinated in the Archdiocese of
Armagh, but with a willingness to serve
the New Evangelisation anywhere in the
world where there is a need, in
communion with the Archbishop of
Armagh.

5 Bothar Na Dara, Lis Na Dara Estate,
Dundalk, Co Louth
Tel 042-9338862
Email seminary@redmatarmagh.ie
Web www.redmatarmagh.ie
*Rector:* Rev Giuseppe Pollio
*Vice-Rector:* Rev Neil Xavier O'Donoghue
*Spiritual Director:* Rev Brendan Scully

## Association of Primary Teaching Sisters

7/8 Lower Abbey Street, Dublin 1
*President:* Sr Mary Collins
*Secretary/Treasurer:* Sr Margaret Ivers
Tel 01-8781986 Fax 01-8781986
Email srmarycollins@eircom.net

Aims to unite its members through their religious consecration to share in the mission of the Church by ensuring Catholic education in schools and fostering the Christian message; to facilitate communication and liaison to improve the educational opportunity of children in primary schools.

## Catholic Boy Scouts of Ireland (see Scouting Ireland)

## Catholic Grandparents Association

Castlebar Street, Westport, Co Mayo
Tel 098-24877
Email
info@catholicgrandparentsassociation.com
Website
www.catholicgrandparentsassociation.com
*Founder:* Catherine Wiley
*President:* Maire Printer
*Patrons*
Archbishop Michael Neary (Ireland)
Bishop John Hine (England)

## Catholic Guides of Ireland (Banóglaigh Catoilicí na hÉireann)

*Chief Commissioner:* Cecilia Browne
*Assistant Chief Commissioner*
Phil McKeever
*National Treasurer:* Philomena Dawson
*National Secretary:* Phil Dempsey
*National Chaplain:* Rev Eamonn McCamley
*National Office Co-ordinator*
Laura Saunders
*National Office:* 12 Clanwilliam Terrace, Grand Canal Quay, Dublin 2
Tel 01-6619566 Fax 01-6765691
Email nat.office@girlguidesireland.ie
www.girlguidesireland.ie

The Catholic Guides of Ireland (CGI) is a voluntary nationwide association open to all girls and women. It is organised on a diocesan basis, providing challenging indoor and outdoor activities which encourage the overall development of the individual. CGI through the Council of Irish Guiding Associations (CIGA) is a member of the World Association of Girl Guides and Girl Scouts (WAGGGS). CGI's youth programmes are available for 5-18 year olds at local community level. There are also opportunities for volunteer adult leadership, who receive training and support for this role.

## Catholic Nurses Guild of Ireland

*National President:* Ms Breda Murphy
Ballyshane, Inishtigue, Kilkenny
*National Vice-President*
Sr Brid Commins, 29 Green Road, Mullingar, Co Westmeath
*National Secretary and Contact*
Ms Marie Shinnick
19 Ashford Estate, The Lough, Cork

*National Treasurer:* Ms Mary Mulcahy
9 Beauparc Downs, Monkstown Valley, Co Dublin
*Headquarters:* Central Catholic Library, 74 Merrion Square, Dublin 2
Tel 01-6761264

The Guild is a response to the Vatican's Decree on the Apostolate of the Laity. Its role is to promote the social, educational, professional and spiritual development of its members so as to help them to work effectively in the service of life. There are several branches of the Guild active throughout Ireland.

## Catholic Communications Office

*Director:* Mr Martin Long
*Communications Officer:* Ms Brenda Drumm
*Editor of Intercom:* Mr Francis Cousins
*Communications Assistant*
Ms Marie Purcell
Columba Centre, Maynooth, Co Kildare
Tel 01-5053000 Fax 01-6016401
Email info@catholicbishops.ie
www.catholicbishops.ie
Twitter: @CatholicBishops
Facebook: Irish Catholic Bishops' Conference
YouTube: Irish Catholic Bishops' Conference
Audioboo:
www.audioboo.fm/IrishCatholicBishops

## CatholicIreland.net

St Mary's, Bloomfield Avenue, Donnybrook, Dublin 4
Tel 01-6077150 Fax 01-6319755
Email info@catholicireland.net
www.catholicireland.net;
www.gettingmarried.ie
*Editor:* Vacant
*Chief Executive:* Mr Tony Bolger

CatholicIreland.net is an organisation whose aim is to promote the Catholic faith using modern communications like the world wide web. The site is a dynamic and attractive internet portal, which gathers and disseminates a wealth of quality information and resources, including the times of all masses in Ireland to support believers and to reach out to others, in Ireland and throughout the world. Catholic Ireland is part of Church Support Group. Supplies only daily online Catholic news for Ireland.

## Catholic Primary School Management Association (CPSMA)

*Chairperson:* Mrs Maria Spring
11 The Enclosure, Oldtown Demesne, Naas, Co Kildare
Tel 045-879235 Fax 045-879270
*General Secretary:* Ms Eileen Flynn
*Assistant General Secretary*
Ms Margaret Gorman
*Office Manager:* Ms Linda Gorman
New House, St Patrick's College, Maynooth, Co Kildare
Tel 01-6292462/1850-407200
Fax 01-6292654
Email info@cpsma.ie
Website www.cpsma.ie

## Catholic Historical Society of Ireland

*Secretary:* Dáire Keogh
*Treasurer:* Colm Lennon
*Conference Secretary:* Mary Ann Lyons

*Editor (Contact):* Dr Thomas O'Connor
Tel 01-7083926 Fax 01-7083314
Email thomas.oconnor@nuim.ie
www.archivium-hibernicum.ie

Founded in 1911, its annual journal *Archivium Hibernicum* publishes documents and studies dealing with Irish ecclesiastical history and Irish history in general. The society also organises an annual public conference and sponsors a lecture programme.

## Catholic Men and Women's Society of Ireland

*Patron:* Most Rev Donal Murray, Bishop of Limerick
*President:* Mr Eamon Hennessy
Tel 045-525165
*Hon Secretary:* Mr Ken Butterworth
Tel 087-1257132
*Hon Treasurer:* Ms Esther Brady
Tel 045-522094
*National Chaplain*
Very Rev Liam Merrigan PP
Monasterevin, Co Kildare
Tel 045-525346

The Society strives for the personal development of its members through spiritual, intellectual, social and physical activities. The basic unit is called the branch. The society is organised at national level by the governing body, the National Council.

## CEIST

*Chairperson, Board of Directors*
Mr Bernard Keeley
*CEO:* Dr Marie Griffin
CEIST Ltd, Dublin Road, Kildare Town, Co Kildare
Tel 01-6510350 Fax 01-6510180
Email info@ceist.ie
www.ceist.ie

CEIST: Catholic Education – An Irish Schools Trust is a collaborative trustee body for the voluntary secondary schools of the following congregations:
• Presentation Sisters
• Sisters of the Christian Retreat
• Congregation of the Sisters of Mercy
• Missionaries of the Sacred Heart
• Daughters of Charity

CEIST Ltd was incorporated in May 2007
*Vision:* A compassionate and just society inspired by the life and teachings of Jesus Christ.

*Mission Statement:* To provide a holistic education in the Catholic tradition
*Values:* Promoting spiritual and human development, achieving quality in teaching and learning, showing respect for every person, creating community and being just and responsible.

## Central Catholic Library

*Chairman:* Rev Noel Barber (SJ)
*Librarian:* Dr Teresa Whitington
74 Merrion Square, Dublin 2
Tel 01-6761264
Email catholiclibrary@imagine.ie
www.catholiclibrary.ie

Nationally important collection (founded 1922 by Fr Stephen Brown) of over 50,000 books with reference, research and lending departments. Emphasis on theology, scripture, spirituality, Church history, etc., but also on Irish history and culture (including Gaelic); literature and foreign languages (including important Dante collection), biography, history, travel; an extensive collection on art and architecture; and the philosophy, religion and sociology books of the old Central Students Library (for loan). Some pre-1800 titles. Runs of 400 journals (from 1814) in these areas. A voluntary subscription library, with an annual fee for borrowing rights; the reference and research departments are open to the public. Managed by an elected council, the library relies on public support for its continued existence and welcomes new members. Open: Mon-Fri 11.00-18.00; Saturday 11.00-15.00.

## Charismatic Renewal Movement
Emmanuel, 3 Pembroke Park, Ballsbridge, Dublin 4

The Charismatic Renewal Movement seeks to foster spiritual renewal under the inspiration of the Holy Spirit and to promote Christian unity. There are over 450 prayer groups in Ireland which are open to all. The movement maintain an office at 'Emmanuel'. Tel 01-6670570 NSC, Box 2434, Dublin 4. All telephone messages will be returned. The office is manned on Tuesday and Thursday 10.30am to 12.30pm

*Office of the National Service Committee for Catholic Charismatic Renewal in Ireland*
*Chairperson:* Marie Beirne
Tel 071-9624404
*Liaison Bishop to Charismatic Renewal:*
Bishop Martin Drennan
Email nsc@iol.ie

## Christian Life Communities
35/36 Lower Leeson Street, Dublin 2
Tel 01-6471096
Email clc@jesuit.ie
www.jesuit.ie/clc

CLC is a worldwide lay association which has special links with the Society of Jesus. Founded in 1563 as the 'Sodality of Our Lady', it has changed radically since the Second Vatican Council. Members of CLC are helped to integrate their faith and daily living through the carism of the Spiritual Exercises of St Ignatius of Loyola. They meet on a regular basis, in groups of between six and ten, thereby getting support from each other. This form of spirituality, supported by the Group, leads to a sense of mission, which is rooted in the whole quality of presence which we bring to the world in which we live.

At present there are more than twenty thousand members in over 50 countries in every continent.

*For more information, contact:*
Fr Michael Gallagher (SJ)
Tel 01-7758596
Email mgallagher@jesuit.ie

## Church Resources/Church Telecom/Staffroom.ie
St Mary's, Bloomfield Avenue, Donnybrook, Dublin 4
Tel 01-6077150 Fax 01-6319755
Email info@churchresources.ie
www.churchresources.ie
www.churchresources.co.uk
*Chief Executive:* Mr Tony Bolger

Church Resources exists to combine the purchasing power of church organisations, including parishes, schools, religious congregations, care facilities and all other ministries and Church-related groups, to achieve financial savings on their everyday essential purchases. The savings that each group makes can then be used to finance their ministry activity. In the process this activity attracts a small commission from each of Church Resources' suppliers, which is in turn used to finance the maintenance and expansion of catholicireland.net and gettingmarried.ie. Part of Church Support Group.

## ChurchServices.tv
St Mary's, Bloomfield Avenue, Donnybrook, Dublin 4
Tel 01-6077150 Fax 01-6319755
Email info@churchservices.tv
www.churchservices.tv

ChurchServices.tv provides live video streaming from Cathedrals, Churches, or any other location via the internet. The video streaming can come from a permanent installation or from a one-off broadcast from a conference or any other single event. Video documentaries or other video material can also be streamed from ChurchServices.tv. Recording facilities to cater for online replay or to download a permanent copy of a service available. Part of Church Support Group.

## Communion and Liberation
*Contact:* Margaret Biondi
Tel 01-4973361
Email info@clireland.com
www.clireland.com

An international movement founded by Mgr Luigi Giussani in Italy in 1954 and approved by the Church. It is present in over seventy countries throughout the world. The essence of its charism is the announcement of the Incarnation of Christ who is present in the here and now and can be encountered in the unity of his people which is the Church.

## Concern Worldwide
*Office:* Camden Street, Dublin 2
Tel 01-4177700 Fax 01-4757362
Email info@concern.net
www.concern.net
*Chief Executive:* Mr Dominic MacSorley
*Chairperson:* Tom Shipsey
*Secretary:* Siobhan Toale

Concern Worldwide is an international humanitarian organisation dedicated to tackling poverty and suffering in the world's poorest countries. We work in partnership with the very poorest people in these countries, directly enabling them to improve their lives, as well as using our knowledge and experience to influence decisions made at a local, national and international level that can significantly reduce extreme poverty.

## Conference of Religious of Ireland
'St Mary's', Bloomfield Avenue, Donnybrook, Dublin 4,
Tel 01-6677322 Fax 01-6689460
Email secretariat@cori.ie
Website www.cori.ie
*Director General*
Rev Peter Rodgers (OFMCap)
*President:* Sr Noelle Corscadden (IBVM)
*Vice-President:* Rev Gregory Carroll (OP)

The Conference is a voluntary coming together of religious. Among its objectives are: to promote the spiritual and religious welfare of the congregations of Irish religious; to foster an ever-increasing effectiveness in the apostolate of the congregations; to effect a closer cooperation between congregations and with all members of the Church; to provide appropriate and official representation with civil government and bishops.

## Council of Irish Adoption Agencies
The Council of Irish Adoption Agencies (CIAA) was established in 1961. Membership of the CIAA is open to all adoption agencies which are accredited by the Adoption Authority of Ireland and to all HSE adoption services.

The aims of the CIAA are to:
- ensure that all its members operate to the highest professional standards;
- advocate on the basis of best practice in all aspects of adoption;
- inform and highlight adoption issues;
- influence adoption policies;
- campaign for changes in adoption legislation;
- contribute to the development of services for all those concerned with adoption.

The Council of Irish Adoption Agencies may be contacted at ciadoptionagencies@gmail.com or via our website http://councilofirishadoptionagencies.com

## Council of Management of Catholic Secondary Schools
*President:* Fr Paul Connell
*General Secretary:* Mr Ferdia Kelly
Secretariat of Secondary Schools
Emmet House, Dundrum Road, Dublin 14
Tel 01-2838255 Fax 01-2695461
Email info@secretariat.ie
www.jmb.ie

The Council of Management of Catholic Secondary Schools (CMCSS) is the governing body for the Association of Management of Catholic Secondary Schools (AMCSS) which promotes, advises and supports Catholic Voluntary Secondary Schools in Ireland. Founded in the 1960s, it adopted its present structure in 1972. Its membership includes a principal and a Board of Management chairperson from each of its ten constituent regions. It also includes a representative of the Irish Episcopal Conference and a representative of the Conference of Religious in Ireland (CORI). The Council cooperates and maintains links with other national and international groups interested in Catholic education. Its Secretariat provides a wide range of educational services and advice to its members.

**CPRSI (See Cúnamh)**

**Cumann na Sagart**
*Uachtarán:* An tAth Seamus Ó hÉanaigh SP
Dealbhna, Co na hIarmhí
Guthán 044-9664127
Email info@delvinparish.ie
*Rúnaí:* An tAth Tadhg Furlong
Ceapach na bhFaoiteach,
Co Thiobraid Arann
Guthán 062-75427

Is é aidhm an Chumainn ná dúchas creidimh na tíre a chothú, agus tacaíocht a thabhairt do shagairt a bhfuil an Ghaeilge in úsáid acu. Tugtar faoin aidhm seo a chur i gcrích: (a) trí léachtaí ag tionól bliantúil ina bpléitear gné éigin den dúchas creidimh; (b) trí fhoilseacháin liotúirge, scrioptúir, diagachta agus cultúir dhúchais; (c) trí chomhoibrú le pobal gach deoise tré mhean Ionadaí an Deoise, agus trí imeachtaí éagsúla fríd an tír; (d) trí chomhoibriú le heagrais eile chun traidisiún dúchasach an phobail logánta a chothú, go háirithe i gcomórtas *Glór na nGael*. Tá suíomh idirlín ag Cumann na Sagart www.cumannnasagart.ie

**Cúnamh (formerly Catholic Protection and Rescue Society of Ireland) (CPRSI)**
*Secretary/Principal Social Worker*
Julie Kerins, BSocSc, CQSW, MSocSC
30 South Anne Street, Dublin 2
Tel 01-6779664
Email info@cunamh.com
www.cunamh.com

Cúnamh is an accredited adoption agency providing pre and post-natal counselling for pregnant women, their partners and families, short-term foster care and adoption. Cúnamh provides support and advice for adoptive parents and their children. An information and trace service for adult adopted persons, birth parents and other birth relatives is also provided.

**CURA Pregnancy Counselling Service**
*President:* Most Rev Éamonn Walsh DD
*National Co-ordinator:* Louise Graham
*National Office:* Columba Centre,
Maynooth, Co Kildare
Tel 01-5053040/1 Fax 01-6292364
Email curacares@cura.ie
www.cura.ie
National Helpline: 1850-622626

CURA is an agency of the Irish Catholic Bishops' Conference and was established in 1977 as a caring, counselling and support service for those whose pregnancy is or has become a crisis.
Cura services:
• Crisis or unplanned pregnancy support and counselling
• Pregnancy testing
• Counselling and support after an abortion
• Support to mothers and fathers of a new baby
• Cura Schools Awareness Programme.

Services are free, confidential and non-judgemental.
All services also available to men and other family members.

**Dialogue Ireland Trust**
7/8 Lower Abbey Street, Dublin 1
Tel 01-8309384/087-2396229
Fax 01-8744913
*Director:* Mike Garde
Email info@dialogueireland.org
http://dialogueireland.wordpress.com

The Dialogue Ireland Trust was established to promote awareness and understanding of 'cultism'. Dialogue Ireland Trust is an independent organisation at the service of Irish Society. Our mission is to provide advice and information and to alert the public to the challenge cultism poses to our mental health and our democratic freedoms. A specific area addressed is our schools programme directed at 6th years at Secondary School as a preparation for third level.

**Eco-Congregation Ireland**
Eco-Congregation aims to encourage churches to celebrate the gift of Gods creation, to recognise the interdependence of all creation and to care for it in their life and mission and through the members personal lifestyles
*Communications Officer:* Fiona Murdoch
Email info@ecocongregationireland.com
Website www.ecocongregationireland.com
Tel 086-1706923
*Roman Catholic Representative*
Catherine Brennan SSL
Email catherinebrennanssl@eircom.net
Tel 087-2599071

**ERST – Edmund Rice School Trust**
*Chairperson, Board of Directors*
Mr Pat Diggins
*Chief Executive:* Mr Gerry Bennett
*Co-ordinator of Ethos:* Mr Tony McCann
*Co-ordinator of Governance Services*
Ms Helen O'Brien
*Finance/Property Officer*
Ms Louise Callaghan
Meadow Vale, Clonkeen Road
Blackrock, Co Dublin
Tel 01-2897511 Fax 01-2897540
Email reception@erst.ie
www.erst.ie

The Edmund Rice Schools Trust, an independent lay company based in Dublin, ensure that the schools in the former Christian Brother Network (currently 96) will continue to provide a Catholic education into the future, in the spirit and tradition of Blessed Edmund Rice, for the people of Ireland.
ERST was incorporated in May 2008.
*Vision:* Promoting full personal and social development in caring Christian communities of learning and teaching.
*Mission Statement:* To provide Catholic Education in the Edmund Rice tradition.

The five keys elements of an Edmund Rice Schools Trust School are:
• Nurturing faith, Christian spirituality and Gospel-based values;
• Promoting partnership in the school community;
• Excelling in teaching and learning;
• Creating a caring school community;
• Inspiring transformational leadership.

**Equestrian Order of the Holy Sepulchre of Jerusalem, Lieutenancy of Ireland**
*Lieutenant*
Charles A. Kelly KCSS, GCHS
Beachmount, Kilkelly Road,
Swinford, Co Mayo
Tel 094-9251061
Email charlesakellyswinford@gmail.com
*Grand Prior:* Cardinal Séan Brady
Archbishop of Armagh
*Secretary:* Ivan J. Healy KCHS
39 Ashdale Road, Terenure, Dublin 6

The Lieutenancy of All Ireland of the Equestrian Order of the Holy Sepulchre of Jerusalem was established in July 1986. The venue for investitures is St Patrick's College, Maynooth, Co Kildare.

**Equipes Notre-Dame (Teams of Our Lady)**
Tony and Breda Preston
Tel 01-6270633
Email mapreston@eircom.net
Rev Gerard Cassidy (CSsR)
Email ireland@teams-transatlantic.org
www.equipes-notre-dame.ie

An international movement of spirituality for married couples which has received official recognition from the Pontifical Council for the Laity. A team consists of five or six couples and a priest, and meets once a month. United by the sacrament of marriage, the couples seek, by deepening their spirituality, to strengthen their faith and increase their love. Informal evenings are arranged for couples wishing to know more about the movement.

**Evangelical Catholic Initiative**
72 Hillcourt Road,
Glenageary, Co Dublin
Tel 01-2854863
Email evancat@eircom.net
*Secretary:* Paddy Monaghan
60 Shore Road, Rostrevor,
Co Down BT34 3AA
Tel 028-41738801
Email boylecb@aol.com
*Secretary:* Eugene Boyle

ECI is an initiative for a New Evangelisation, comprised of Catholic Christians who are evangelical by conviction and committed to a personal relationship with Jesus Christ. It seeks to promote the kingdom of God under the guidance and empowering of the Holy Spirit, through working for a Christ-centred, biblically based renewal in the Catholic Church, through fostering reconciliation and unity among Christians and through building up Jewish/Christian relationships.

Email for a new document 'What is the Kerygma?', which sets out the core of the Catholic faith.

## Family and Media Association
*Chairman:* Dr Ivo O'Sullivan PhD
*Contact:* Donal O'Sullivan, Executive
Tel 086-3309724
*Development Officer*
Email info@fma.ie
www.familyandmedia.ie

Aims: to promote respect by the media for Christian values, especially those relating to the family; to seek high standards of honesty, decency, fairness and truthfulness in the media; to promote effective dialogue between the media and the public; to promote public understanding of the functioning and power of the media, and to assess and enhance the value of the media to the individual, the family and the community.

## The Family of God
The Oratory, Carroll Village,
Dundalk, Co Louth
Tel 042-9335566
Email fogoratory@eircom.net
*Contact:* Mr Teddy Lambe

The community was founded in Ireland in 1979. The community is non-residential and it is essentially a lay organisation although priests, religious and sisters are welcome to become associate members. The community is committed to a lifestyle of prayer, service and evangelisation. It is a registered charity in Ireland and Northern Ireland. The community has been recognised as a Private Association of the Faithful since July 1995 and it is a council member of the Catholic Fraternity, an international association of Catholic communities formally recognised by the Pontifical Council for the Laity.

## Father Matthew Union
*President:* Most Rev Thomas A. Finnegan
*Spiritual Director*
Most Rev Francis McKiernan
*Secretary:* Rev Seán Moore CC
Parochial House, Carnmore Drive,
Newry, Co Down Tel 01693-68512

An organisation of priests interested in promotion of temperance. Its branches operate on a diocesan basis. The Union works in liaison with Catholic and interdenominational temperance groups, with Alcoholics Anonymous and with the Irish National Council on Alcoholism.

## Focolare Movement
*National Centre:* Focolare Centre,
Curryhills, Prosperous, Co Kildare
Tel 045-840410/840420
Email focolare@focolare.ie,
czmdublin@eircom.net
*Contact:*
Ms Juanita Majury/Mr David Hickey

*Dublin Centres*
20 Ramleh Close, Milltown, Dublin 6
Tel 01-2698081
Email ramleh@focolare.ie
*Contact:* Ms Catherine Burke

8 Clareville Road, Harold's Cross,
Dublin 6 Tel 01-4922709
*Contact:* Aurelio Cerviño Alcayaga
Email focmdublin@eircom.net
www.focolare.org

An international movement founded by Chiara Lubich in 1943, at Trent in Northern Italy. Subsequently approved by the Church, its principal aim is to help bring about the fulfilment of the prayer of Jesus 'That All may be One'.

## Irish Biblical Association
*President:* Dr Bradford Anderson
Email brad.anderson@dcu.ie
*Vice President:* Dr Benjamin Wold
Email WOLDB@tcd.ie
*Secretary:* Bernadette Baker
Email irishbiblical@gmail.com
*Treasurer:* Ms Diane Corkery
Email dcorkery@stpats.ie
www.irish-biblical-association.com

The IBA was established in 1966. The aims of the association are to: (a) assist the Irish Church in its work of understanding and proclaiming the word of God; (b) promote the scientific study of the Bible and related branches of learning; (c) organise conferences, study groups and lectures on biblical subjects; (d) support the publication of scientific studies on the scripture; (e) contribute to articles on biblical matters which will be of assistance in promoting a general biblical apostolate.

The association publishes an annual periodical, the Proceedings of the Irish Biblical Association. The members of the Irish Biblical Association are engaged professionally with and/or take a personal interest in the Jewish and Christian Scriptures. The Irish Biblical Association welcomes new members. There are two kinds of membership, ordinary and associate. Associate members are those interested in supporting and taking part in the events arranged by the IBA. Ordinary membership is for people with a post-graduate qualification in biblical studies.

Membership is accepted at the annual AGM in the spring and in the meantime prospective members are, of course, welcome in our meetings and can be on our mailing list.

## The Irish Chaplaincy in Britain
*(For details, see Episcopal Commissions and Advisory Bodies and Chaplains)*

## Irish Church Music Association (Cumann Ceol Eaglasta na hÉireann)
National Centre for Liturgy,
St Patrick's College,
Maynooth, Co Kildare
*Chairperson:* Rev Turlough Baxter
St Mary's, Athlone, Co Westmeath
Tel 090-6472088
Email enquiries@
irishchurchmusicassociation.com
www.irishchurchmusicassociation.com

An association for the promotion of church music. Activities include the publication of music, the organisation of regional meetings of church musicians and an annual summer school. A newsletter is issued regularly.

## Irish College, Paris
Founded in 1578
5 Rue des Irlandais, 75005-Paris
*Rector:* Rt Rev Mgr Brendan P. Devlin
*Communicating Secretary*
Dr Thomas O'Connor
Maynooth College, Co Kildare
Tel 01-6285222
Email history.department@nuim.ie

The college is now vested in the Fondation Irlandaise, a trust for the education of Irish people and their accommodation in Paris. The college also hosts a full scale cultural centre. Visitors' rooms are periodically available to Irish people on application to the administrator, Ms Sheila Pratschke.
Tel 00-331-58 52 10 30
*Resident Chaplain:* Rev David Bracken
Tel 00-331-58 52 10 89

## Irish Council of Churches
Inter-Church Centre,
48 Elmwood Avenue, Belfast BT9 6AZ
Tel 028-90663145
Email info@churchesinireland.com
www.churchesinireland.com
*(For details, see General Information section)*

## Irish Episcopal Council for Emigrants
Columba Centre,
Maynooth, Co Kildare
Tel 01-5053155  Fax 01-6292363
*Chair:* Most Rev John Kirby
*Administration:* Ms Bernie Martin
Email emigrants@iecon.ie

## Irish Episcopal Commission for Liturgy
*National Secretary:* Rev Danny Murphy
National Centre for Liturgy
St Patrick's College,
Maynooth, Co Kildare
Tel 01-7083478 Fax 01-7083477
Email liturgy@spcm.ie

## The Irish Pilgrimage Trust
Kilcuan, Clarinbridge, Co Galway
Tel 091-796622 Fax 091 796916
Email info@irishpilgrimagetrust.com
*Chairman:* James White
*Honorary Treasurer:* Damian McNicholl
*Contact:* National Co-ordinator
Bernadette Connolly (for further
information and application forms)
Email bconnolly@irishpilgrimagetrust.com

The Irish Pilgrimage Trust is a voluntary
organisation which brings young people
with special needs to Lourdes at Easter
time. The helpers pay their own fares
and raise the funds for the young
people. The Irish Pilgrimage Trust has a
holiday house, Kilcuan, in Clarinbridge,
Co Galway, which caters for groups with
special needs. The trust has also recently
opened a holiday house in Kilrane,
Rosslare Harbour, Co Wexford.
*For further details contact*
Tel 091-796622

## Irish Hospitalité of Our Lady of Lourdes
(Affiliated to Hospitalité Notre Dame de
Lourdes)
Ely House, 8 Ely Place, Dublin 2
*President:* Ms Máire Ní Bhain
*Secretary/Contact Person*
Ms Deirdre O'Sullivan
26 Vernon Street, Dublin 8
Tel 01-6570138
Email deirdreosullivan@gmail.com
*Treasurer*
Mr Gerard Bennett
*Spiritual Director*
Rev Vincent Mulligan (OMI)

Founded in 1930, under the patronage
of the Archbishop of Dublin. An
organisation of people, from all walks of
life, who are dedicated to working with
the sick in Lourdes.

## Irish Inter-Church Meeting
Inter-Church Centre,
48 Elmwood Avenue,
Belfast BT9 6AZ
Tel 028-90663145
Email info@churchesinireland.com
www.churchesinireland.com
*Co-Chairs:* Cardinal S. Brady
Rev G. O'Donnell
*Executive Officer:* Mr M. McCullagh
*Secretary:* Very Rev K. McDermott
*Treasurer:* Mr E. Fleming KCSG
*Administrator:* Ms K. Kelly

## Irish Inter-Church Meeting
Church in Society Forum
*Chairperson:* Ms E. Gallagher

## Irish Inter-Church Meeting
Theology Forum
*Chairpersons:* Bishop B. Leahy and
Ms G. Kingston

## Irish Missionary Union (IMU)
*Headquarters:* 29 Westland Square,
Dublin 2
Tel 01-4923326/4923325/4923337
Fax 01-4923316
Email executive@imu.ie
*President, Executive Council*
Rev Michael Corcoran (MHM)
*Vice President:* Dr Vincent Kenny (VMM)
*Executive Secretary*
Fr Hugh McMahon (SSC)
*Contact Person*
Fr Hugh McMahon (SSC)
Email executive@imu.ie

The Irish Missionary Union is a
collaborative network of Missionary
Groups that promotes the
understanding, development and
sharing of Mission and strives to be a
prophetic voice in society. It promotes
the call of all Christians to Mission, and
supports those sent to witness to the
gospel of Jesus Christ and the reign of
God in other cultures. The IMU runs: The
IMU Mission Institute; The IMU Religion
Formation Ministry Programme.

## IMU Mission Institute
*Director:* Rev Patrick Dooher (SSC)
St Columban's, Dalgan Park, Navan
Tel 046-9021525 Ext 332
Fax 046-9073726/9022799
Email imuinst@eircom.net
www.imudalganpark.com

General renewal programme for priests
and sisters. Centre for Theology and
Ecology

## Irish School of Ecumenics, Trinity College, Dublin
Ireland's Centre for Reconciliation
Studies
*Head of ISE:* Professor Gillian Wylie
Confederal School of Religions, Peace
Studies and Theology
ISE-LI Building,
Trinity College, Dublin 2
Tel 01-8964770 Fax 01-6725024
683 Antrim Road, Belfast BT15 4EG
Tel 028-90775010 Fax 028-90373986
Email isedir@tcd.ie
www.tcd.ie/ise

The Irish School of Ecumenics, Trinity
College Dublin, is located in Dublin and
Belfast. It is committed to the study and
promotion of dialogue, peace and
reconciliation in Ireland and around the
world. It is recognised for its
interdisciplinary approach to taught
courses and research, drawing on the
fields of politics, sociology, ethics,
theology and religion. Applied research
is at the heart of all work undertaken at
ISE, where students engage with crucial
issues currently facing governments,
religions, NGOs and peace organisations.

The MPhil courses in Intercultural
Theology and Interreligious Studies,
International Peace Studies and the
Postgraduate Diploma in Conflict and

Dispute Resolutions Studies are based in
Dublin, while the MPhil course in
Conflict Resolution and Reconciliation is
based in Belfast. Research degrees
(M.Litt and PhD) can also be supervised
within the School. Please use the
website: www.tcd.ie/ise to find detailed
information about our taught courses,
research, and up-to-date news and
events. Please note that applications
should be made online at
http://www.tcd.ie/ise/postgraduate/
Apply.php

## Irish School of Evangelisation – ISOE
The ISOE is an Association of Christ's
Faithful [Can 298] founded in 1994 to
promote initiatives of the 'New
Evangelisation' e.g. Life in the Spirit
Seminars/Retreats. The ISOE is a member
of the "Catholic Bible Federation" and is
affiliated with 'TINE' in Ireland and
'Evangelisation 2000' in Rome.

*Contact:* Joe O'Callaghan, 9A Wyattville
Park, Dun Laoghaire, Co Dublin
Tel 01 2827658
Email isoe@esatclear.ie
www.esatclear.ie/~isoe

## Irish Theological Association
*Secretary:* Tony McNamara
66 Foxfield Avenue, Raheny, Dublin 5
Tel 087 2903493
Email mctony@eircom.net
Email russelc@tcd.ie
www.theology.ie

Founded in 1965, the object of the
association is to promote theological
studies, and for this purpose it organises
conferences and meetings for discussion,
lectures and the general exchange of
ideas.

## Jesuit Communication Centre
Irish Jesuit Provincialate, Milltown Park,
Sandford Road, Dublin 6
Tel 01-4987370
*Communications Manager*
Ms Pat Coyle
Email jcc@jesuit.ie
www.jesuit.ie

## Jesus Caritas Fraternity of Priests
*National Responsible:* Fr Liam Ó Cuiv
St Mary of the Servants,
Blakestown Way, Blakestown,
Dublin 15
Tel 01-8210874/086-2342170
Email liamocuiv@yahoo.com

An international association of priests
who, following the spirituality of Charles
de Foucauld, try to help one another to
live their priesthood through mutual
support, in their presence to Jesus in
daily Eucharistic adoration, in the Gospel
and in his people. The Fraternity is the
largest priestly fraternity in the country
and has a presence in most dioceses.

## Kairos Communications Ltd
*Director:* Fr Finbarr Tracey (SVD)
Tel 01-6286007 Fax 01-6286511
Email info@kairoscomms.ie

Kairos Communications Ltd, is the media arm of Divine Word Missionaries, Ireland. Established in 1973, Kairos is now one of the biggest Christian communications facilities in Europe. Equipped with its own studios and outside broadcast facilities, it produces masses/services for RTÉ television and radio from all parts of the country on a monthly and weekly basis. Other religious productions for RTÉ television include the daily 'iWitness' and Angelus. On the education front Kairos works closely with St Patrick's College, Maynooth (Pontifical University), and the National University of Ireland, Maynooth (NUIM). Courses running at the moment include: BA in Media Studies (NUIM); MA in Radio and Television Production (NUIM), BA in Multimedia (NUIM).

## Knights of St Columbanus
*Supreme Secretary*
Ely House, 8 Ely Place, Dublin 2
Tel 01-6761835 Fax 01-6762839
Email koc@iol.ie
www.knightsofstcolumbanus.ie

Organised into twelve Provincial Areas throughout Ireland. A member of Unum Omnes (International Federation of Catholic Men), based in Rome, since 1966. Foundation member of the International Alliance of Catholic Knights, which has 2.6 million members in Europe, Africa, Australasia and America.

## Knock Shrine Pilgrimages
Promoting Knock Shrine, Co Mayo, as a place of pilgrimage. For details and dates of ceremonies and/or assistance in organising a pilgrimage or school tour to Knock, please contact:

*Secretary:* Knock Shrine Office,
Knock, Co Mayo
Tel 094-9388100 Fax 094-9388295
Email info@knock-shrine.ie
www.knock-shrine.ie

*Secretary:* Knock Shrine Pilgrimages,
Veritas Bookshop, 7–8 Lower Abbey Street, Dublin 1 Tel/Fax 01-8733356
Email dublinoffice@knock-shrine.ie

*Secretary:* Knock Shrine Pilgrimages,
76/77 Little Catherine Street, Limerick
Tel 061-419458 Fax 061-405178
Email limerickoffice@knock-shrine.ie

*Secretary:* Knock Shrine Pilgrimages,
14 King Street, Belfast BT1 1HY
Tel 028-90311652
Email knockshrinebelfast@gmail.com

## Lay Fraternity of Blessed Charles de Foucauld
*Enquiries:* Seán Ryan
146 Norwood Park, Limerick
Tel 087-6157867

Composed of small groups of lay people, married or single, who, after the example of Charles de Foucauld, seek to follow the way of Jesus present to them in the Gospel, in the Eucharist, and in their fellow men and women.

## Legion of Mary
*President:* Síle Ní Chochláin
*Secretary:* Mr Patrick Fay
Concilium Legionis Mariae,
International Centre of the Legion of Mary, De Montfort House, Morning Star Avenue, Brunswick Street, Dublin 7
Tel 01-8723153/8725093 Fax 01-8726386
Email concilium@legionofmary.ie
www.legionofmary.ie

Catholic lay organisation for men and women. Its members are engaged in charitable and apostolic work.

## Life in the Eucharist Team
Blessed Sacrament Chapel
20 Bachelors Walk, Dublin 1
*Contact:* Rev Jim Campbell (SSS)
Mary Keane *(Secretary)*
Tel 01-8724597 Fax 01-8724724
Email sssdublin@eircom.net
www.blessedsacramentuki.org

A team of dedicated trained lay people under the direction of a priest who, through weekend or evening seminars, lead participants into a fuller awareness of the Eucharist as a living experience in daily life. It is a source of nourishment for new and existing ministers of the Eucharist and Adoration groups. Lay people interacting with lay people from personal experience.

## Lough Derg
*(For details, see Diocese of Clogher)*

## Marriage Encounter
*Ecclesial Leadership Team*
Mike and Rose Curtin
Robin's Nest, Kilmallock Road,
Kildorrery, Co Cork
Tel 022-40809
Email michaelcurtin.curtin@gmail.com
Rev Gabriel Burke
4 Carrig Downs, Carrigtwohill, Co Cork
Tel 021-4883867
Email frgabiburke@gmail.com
www.marriageencounter.ie

Worldwide Marriage Encounter is a movement dedicated to the renewal of Matrimony, Priesthood and Religious Life. It provides the opportunity for participants to reflect upon their vocation in a private and positive way. It is for those who are committed to living out their sacrament in a dedicated way. Weekends are held all over Ireland. The Marriage Encounter weekend is not a retreat or counselling workshop, rather

it is an enriching experience based on deepening communication skills within the marriage relationship, within parishes and within religious communities.

## National Association of Christian Brothers Past Pupils Unions
*National Officers*
*President:* Sean O'Callaghan
56 Park Court, Ballyvolane, Cork
*Secretary/Contact Person:* John Cooley,
73 Lansdowne Road, Belfast BT15 44B
Tel 028-90777491
Email johncooley50@hotmail.com
*Treasurer:* Richard Cruise
44 Granitefield, Cabinteely, Dublin 18

Established in 1976. The Association meets quarterly, generally in Dublin. Its aims include: co-operating with regional, national and international bodies of Past Pupils' Unions of Christian Brothers and with other organisations whose objectives and aims are similar in purpose and intent with those of the Association; promoting the cause of Blessed Edmund Rice with a view to canonisation; assisting the Edmund Rice Schools in their efforts to ensure that the tradition of Christian education as maintained by the Edmund Rice Schools Trust will not be lost, materially diluted or obscured; preserving and fostering the national heritage.

## National Association Executive of Primary Diocesan Advisors
*Chairperson:* Mr David Gavin
*Secretary:* Ms Fiona Dineen
Limerick Diocesan Advisory Service,
Limerick Diocesan Pastoral Centre,
St Michael's Courtyard,
Denmark Street, Limerick
Tel: 061-400133
Email fionad@ldo.ie

The National Association of Primary Diocesan Advisors in Religious Education is a national organisation whose members support, educate and resource the partners in religious education at a primary school level in Ireland.

Membership of the Association is open to all full-time or part-time primary Diocesan Advisers. Associate membership is open to others who work in the area of Religious Education in primary schools.

The association aims to:
- support individual members in their work.
- provide a forum for discussion and debate.
- offer further formation and education for the members.
- review nationally the work of religious education in the Primary School and to actively encourage continual evaluation of progress.
- liaise with other agencies involved in the field of Religious Education.

- articulate nationally the needs of Religious Education at primary level.
- foster co-operation between the three partners involved in Religious Education – home, school and parish.

The association holds an Annual Conference and a minimum of two other meetings during the year. It is represented and organised by an executive, which is elected by the membership and holds office for three years. Members of the Executive represent the Association at the Catholic Primary School Management Association, the Episcopal Commission on Catechetics, and the Consultation Group for the National Primary School Programme.

### National Association of Healthcare Chaplains
*Members of The NAHC Executive Committee 2014/2015*
*Chairperson:* Rev Brian Gough
NAHC Office, PO Box 10858, Blackrock, Co Dublin
Tel 01-2782693
Secretary: Ms Margaret Naughton
*Treasurer:* Ms Renée Dilworth

*Republic of Ireland Members*
*HSE Dublin/Mid-Leinster*
Rev Brian Gough, Ms Renée Dilworth
*HSE Western:* Fr James O'Donoghue
*HSE Dublin/North-Eastern*
Marie Gribbon
*HSE Southern*
Ms Margaret Naughton,
Br Isidore Cronin, Rev Jenny Crowley

*Northern Ireland Members*
*Southern H&SS Board:* Vacant
*Eastern H&SS Board:* Vacant
*Western H&SS Board:* Vacant

*Hierarchy Representative*
Most Rev Raymond Field DD
*Secretary to the Executive*
Danielle Browne
NAHC, PO Box 10858,
Blackrock, Co Dublin
Tel/Fax 01-2782693
Email nahc@eircom.net
Website www.nahc.ie

National Association of Healthcare Chaplains is a support organisation for Chaplains working in hospitals and other healthcare facilities. The Executive is composed of representatives from each of the HSE areas.

### National Centre for Liturgy
St Patrick's College, Maynooth, Co Kildare
Tel 01-7083478 Fax 01-7083477
Email liturgy@spcm.ie
www.liturgy-ireland.ie
*(For details, see Episcopal Commissions and Advisory Bodies)*

### National Chaplaincy for Deaf People
Deaf Village Ireland, Ratoath Road, Cabra, Dublin 7
Tel 01-8305744 Fax 01-8600284
*Director of Services (National)*
Rev Fr Gerard Tyrrell
Email gerard@ncdp.ie
*Chaplain (Leinster & Connaught)*
Ms Frankie Berry
Email frankie@ncdp.ie
*Chaplain (North of Ireland)*
Denise Flack
Tel 0044 78 77643961
Email denise@ncdp.ie
*Chaplain (Munster)*
John Patrick Doherty
Email johnpatrick@ncdp.ie
*Administrator:* Annie Egan
Email office@ncdp.ie

The Chaplaincy gives a sacramental and pastoral service to the Deaf Community. This organisation seeks to increase awareness among priests and the wider church community of the pastoral needs of the Deaf Community. It also promotes an interest in the apostolate at diocesan level.

### National Mission Council of Ireland
563 South Circular Road, Dublin 8
Tel 01-4923326, 4923325 Fax 01-4923316
Email executive@imu.ie
*(For details, see Episcopal Commissions)*

### Order of Malta, Ireland
Services provided include

*First Aid Training Services*
Courses in Occupational First Aid, Basic First Aid, Manual Handling, Defibrillation Training (AED) and Refresher courses can be provided at your premises, a local venue or at our Training Centre in Ballsbridge, Dublin 4

*Malta Services Drogheda*
Provision of education and training to people with physical and learning disabilities on a daily basis. The service is run in partnership with the Health Service Executive.

*Malta-Share, Lisnaskea, Co Fermanagh, N Ireland*
Holidays for older people, respite care facilities for people with disabilities.

*General Community Care activities include:*
Day care, supper clubs for the elderly. Pilgrimages to Knock and Lourdes and an International Camp for Young People with disabilities.

*International*
Many Order of Malta projects are supported particularly the Holy Family Maternity Hospital, Bethlehem, Palestine.

*President:* Adrian FitzGerald
*CEO:* Rosemary Keogh
St John's House,
32 Clyde Road, Ballsbridge, Dublin 4
Tel 01-6140031 Fax 01-6685288
Email chancellery@orderofmalta.ie
www.orderofmalta.ie

### Order of Malta Ambulance Corps
Provides a range of first aid, ambulance and emergency care services at major national and local level events in most of the principal cities and towns throughout the island of Ireland. As part of the major emergency plans it provides assistance to the statutory services, drawing on its fleet of over 150 ambulances and vehicles, ranging from minibuses, 4WD support vehicles to full accident and emergency ambulances. It also provides youth development services through Order of Malta Cadets – a National Youth Organisation.

*Hospitaller:* Brendan Lawlor
St John's House,
32 Clyde Road, Dublin 4
Tel 01-6140033/6 Fax 01-6685288
Email info@orderofmalta.ie
www.orderofmalta.ie

### Pax Christi – International Catholic Movement for Peace (Irish Section)
*National President*
Most Rev John Kirby
*Chairperson*
Mr Bryan Maguire
*Vice-Chairperson*
Sr Margaret Ivers
*Treasurer*
Ms Brenda Farrell
*General Secretary*
Mr Tony D'Costa
*Headquarters*
52 Lower Rathmines Road, Dublin 6
Tel 01-4965293
Email tdc2@paxchristi.ie

Pax Christi is an international Catholic peace movement, with national sections in four continents. Its international office is in Belgium. Its activities are mainly related to the issues of security and disarmament; human rights; East-West contacts; North-South relations; peace education; peace spirituality; non-violence; faith, dialogue and reconciliation. Pax Christi has consultative status at the United Nations, UNESCO and the Council of Europe.

### People's Eucharistic League
Blessed Sacrament Chapel
20 Bachelors Walk, Dublin 1
*Contact:* Rev Jim Campbell

An association of men and women with special devotion to the Holy Eucharist. Founded by St Peter Julian Eymard, members are associated with the apostolate of the Congregation of the blessed Sacrament. Members undertake to spend one hour per month in prayer before the Blessed Sacrament.

Allianz (ⁱⁱⁱ)

## Pioneer Total Abstinence Association of the Sacred Heart
*Information Officer:* Ms Róisín Fulham
*Central Spiritual Director*
Rev Bernard J. McGuckian (SJ)
27 Upper Sherrard Street, Dublin 1
Tel 01-8749464 Fax 01-8748485
Email pioneer@jesuit.ie
www.pioneerassociation.ie

The Association has as its chief aim the promotion of temperance and sobriety, with prayer and self-sacrifice as its principal means. The members use their independence of alcohol to engage in good work and the organisation of counter-attractions to drinking.

*(For details of spiritual directors see dioceses)*

## The Radharc Trust
*Trustees:* Peter Dunn, Peter Kelly, Phil Donnelly, Miriam Dunn, Donna Doherty
*Director:* Peter Dunn
18 Newbridge Ave, Sandymount, Dublin 4
Tel 01-2755909/087-2520158
Email mail@radharc.ie
peter@radharc.ie
www.radharc.ie
www.radharcfilms.com

The Radharc Film Archive contains over 400 documentary films, made by a group of Dublin priests and lay people for Irish Television from 1961 to 1996. Filmed in over 75 countries they looked at life from a religious, social and cultural point of view. They were among the most popular programmes on Irish Television during that time and won many awards at home and abroad for the quality and integrity of their work.

The films are one of the most important and substantial collections held by the IFI Irish Film Archive with copies in the RTÉ library and archive. They are readily available on DVD for educational and entertainment purposes as are clips for professional use. Visit the websites or contact the Radharc Trust for more details.

## Regnum Christi
*Contact:* Rev Aaron Venduska (LC)
The Faith and Family Centre,
Avoca Avenue, Blackrock, Co Dublin
Tel 01-2889317
Email faithandfamilycentre@arcol.org
www.regnumchristi.org

Regnum Christi is an apostolic movement whose specific charism is to know, live and preach Christ's commandment of love. Through the formation of its members it seeks to support the ministry of the local dioceses and parish life. The areas of apostolate include: youth and family work, missions, educational and catechetical works.

## Religious Press Association
*Chairperson and Public Relations Consultant:* Garry O'Sullivan, Journalist,
c/o 36 Lower Leeson Street, Dublin 2
Email garryos@yahoo.ie
*Treasurer:* Lillian Webb 66 Roseville,
Naas, Co Kildare Tel 045-866160

Association of editors of religious papers and magazines in Ireland. Seeks to improve the quality of and develop the influence of the religious press.

## Retreats Ireland
*Secretary:* Sr Breda Ahearn (CP)
Tearmann Spirituality Centre,
Brockagh, Glendalough, Co Wicklow
Tel 0404-45639
Email bredaahearn@eircom.net
Paddy O'Rourke
Dromantine Retreat and Conference Centre
Email paddyorourke38@yahoo.com
*President:* Roisin Gannon
Mount St Anne's, Killenard,
Portarlington, Co Laois
Email roisingannon@eircom.net
Pius McLaughlin
La Verna, Franciscan Friary,
Rossnowlagh, Co Donegal
Email piusmcl@hotmail.com
*Treasurer:* Margaret Prendergast
Glendalough Hermitage Centre,
Glendalough, Co Wicklow
Email mqtmprendergast@eircom.net
*Executive Committee Members 2014*
Peter Conaty (CSSp)
An Tobar, Ardbraccan, Navan, Co Meath
Email peter.conaty@spiritan.ie
Mary O'Shea
Ballyvaloo, Retreat Centre, Blackwater,
Enniscorthy, Co Wexford
Email maryossJg@gmail.com

The aim of Retreats Ireland is to promote retreat work, to provide an information service, to offer training programmes, to encourage mutual support and co-operation in the context of retreat and pastoral centres in Ireland.

## RNN (Religious News Network)
36 Lower Leeson Street, Dublin 2
Tel 01-7758515 Fax 01-6767493
Email info@rnn.ie
*Director:* Eileen Good
Tel 01-7758516
Email eileengood@rnn.ie
*Production Administrator:* Jeanann Cox
Tel 01-7758515
Email jeanann@rnn.ie
*Editor:* Miriam Gormally
Email miriam@rnn.ie
www.rnn.ie

RNN is a new syndication service of religious and social affairs, supplying more than 30 local, community and hospital radio stations throughout Ireland with live and recorded news, reaction stories and features. The service is funded by the religious congregations (CoRI) and the Church of Ireland.

## Saint Joseph's Young Priests Society
*President:* Mr George Dee
23 Merrion Square, Dublin 2
Tel 01-6762593 Fax 01-6762549
Email sjyps@eircom.net
www.stjosephsyoungpriestssociety.com

An Irish lay organisation founded in 1895 with branches in every diocese in Ireland. Its members promote vocations to the priesthood and religious life and assist students financially, at home and abroad.

## School Chaplains Association (Cumann na Seiplineach Scoile)
*Chairperson:* Mr Sean Wright
St Ciaran's CS, Kells, Co Meath
Tel 046-9241551
Email ppdd@eircom.net
*Vice-chairperson*
Anne Loughman
St Colmcilles CS, Dublin
Tel 087-6874658
Email anneloughmann@hotmail.com
www.schoolchaplains.ie

## Scouting Ireland
*Chief Scout*
Michael John Shinnick
*National Secretary*
Mr Sean Farrell
*National Treasurer*
Ms Annette Byrne
*Communications Commissioner*
Mr Jimmy Cunningham
*CEO:* Mr John Lawlor
National Office, Larch Hill,
Dublin 16
Tel 01-4956300 Fax 01-4956301
Email questions@scouts.ie
www.scouts.ie

The aim of Scouting Ireland is to encourage the physical, intellectual, character, emotional, social and spiritual development of young people so they may achieve their full potential and, as responsible citizens, to improve society.

Scouting Ireland has a 32-county membership of 40,000 including 60,000 adult volunteers. It provides young people with opportunities to take part and lead a progressive programme through fun, friendship and challenge.

## Secular Franciscan Order
*National President:* Colm MacConfhaola
*National Headquarters*
C/o Mary Tiernan SFO
3 St Mary's Terrace, Chapelizod, Dublin 20
Tel 01-6262264
Email sfohq@eircom.net
*Contact:* Mary Tiernan

An Order of lay people who seek to follow Christ in their everyday life in the footsteps of St Francis of Assisi (going from gospel to life and life to gospel).

**Society of St Vincent de Paul –
National Office**
*National President*
Mr Geoff Meagher
*National Secretary*
Andy Heffernan
*Headquarters:* SVP House,
91-92 Sean MacDermott Street,
Dublin 1
Tel 01-8386990
Email info@svp.ie
Website www.svp.ie

An international lay organisation, which
endeavours to alleviate need and
redress situations which cause it. Its
principal work is visiting people in their
homes, but it also provides holidays,
hostels for the homeless, youth clubs,
housing for the elderly, and good-as-
new shops.

**The Teresian Association**
St Patrick's Cottage,
21 Beaufield Park,
Stillorgan, Co Dublin
Tel 01-2056937
Email irelandta@eircom.net

The Teresian Association is an
International Association of the Faithful
for lay Christians, present today in 30
countries. It was started in 1911 by Saint
Pedro Poveda, a Spanish diocesan priest,
canonised by Pope John Paul II in
Madrid on 4 May 2003. It aims to help
transform society through education
and culture in the light of the Gospel. Its
members are women and men who,
according to their specific calling, live
out their vocation of Christian lay
people in society, working in
educational, cultural and professional
areas. They witness to Gospel values in
all they do and are involved in a wide
variety of areas across society. Their
particular focus, however, is education
at all levels and in its broadest sense.
Members do this through the way they
live their professional, occupational and
family lives. The Association supports
and sustains a number of non-
governmental organisations and
collaborates with Church programmes
and other institutions. It also runs a
number of educational centres in
different countries, including the
Teresian School in Dublin.

The Teresian School,
*(Pre-School, Kindergarten, Junior and
Secondary School)*
12 Stillorgan Road,
Dublin 4
Tel 01-2691376 Fax 01-2602878
Email school@teresian.ie

**Trócaire**
*Lenten Campaigns Organiser*
Nicola Perrin
*Church Officers*
Kate McQuillan, Hannah Evans
*Press and Communications*
Michelle Hoctor
Tel 01-6293333 Fax 01-6290661
Email info@trocaire.ie
Website www.trocaire.org
*Offices and Resource Centres*
12 Cathedral Street, Dublin 1
9 Cook Street, Cork
50 King Street, Belfast BT1 6AD
*(For details, see Episcopal Commissions)*

**Tuesday's Child**
74 North Parade, Belfast,
Co Antrim BT7 2GJ
Tel 028-90646104/07545-452362
Email info@tuesdayschild.ie
Website www.tuesdayschild.ie
*Chairperson:* Orla Sheehan

Tuesday's Child is a voluntary
humanitarian organisation dedicated to
helping children and families living in
areas of war, extreme poverty and social
injustice. We also give witness to the
global war of evil raging against babies
and children around the world and
encourage prayer for their protection.
Tuesday's Child partners with Catholic
missionaries in project areas. We take no
salaries and administration costs from
monies raised/donations received.
Everything we do is All Through Mary
for Jesus.

**Veritas Communications**
Veritas House,
7-8 Lower Abbey Street, Dublin 1
Tel 01-8788177 Fax 01-8786507
*(For details, see Episcopal Commissions)*

**Veritas Company Ltd**
Veritas House,
7-8 Lower Abbey Street, Dublin 1
Tel 01-8788177 Fax 01-8744913
*(For details, see Episcopal Commissions)*

**Veritas Publications**
Veritas House,
7-8 Lower Abbey Street, Dublin 1
Tel 01-8788177 Fax 01-8786507
*(For details, see Episcopal Commissions)*

**Viatores Christi**
8 New Cabra Road,
Phibsboro, Dublin 7
Tel 01-8689986 Fax 01-8689891
Email info@viatoreschristi.com
Website www.viatoreschristi.com

A voluntary Catholic lay missionary
association. Recruits, prepares and
facilitates the placement of people who
wish to work overseas, for one year or
more, in areas of need such as Africa,
South America, Asia and parts of
Canada, USA and Europe. Viatores Christi
offers a 6 month part-time preparation
programme.

**Vocations Ireland**
St Mary's, Bloomfield Avenue,
Donnybrook, Dublin 4
*Director:* Ms Anne Marie Gallagher
Tel 01-6689954/086-7820149
Email info@vocationsireland.com
Website www.vocationsireland.com

Vocations Ireland presents Religious life
as a creative opportunity to live the
mission of Christ in today's world. It
provides information about missionary
and religious life as well as support,
resources and in-service opportunities
for those in vocation ministry. It also
provides personal accompaniment and
discernment programmes for prospective
candidates.

**Volunteer Mission Movement**
VMM,
The Priory, John Street West,
Dublin 8
Tel 01-3664421
*Contact:* Dr Vincent Kenny,
Chief Executive, VMM
Email vincent@vmminternational.org
Email mission@vmminternational.org
Website www.vmminternational.org

The VMM is an international lay, mission
organisation, founded in 1969. VMM
currently have 65 professional
volunteers currently working in East
Africa and Central America. Following
completion of their overseas contract,
they are enouraged to maintain their
Christian commitment through working
for change within their home
community.

**World Missions, Ireland –
The work of the Pontifical Mission
Societies**
*National Director*
Fr Maurice Hogan (SSC)
64 Lower Rathmines Road, Dublin 6
Tel 01-4972035/4972422
Fax 01-4960140
Email director@wmi.ie
Website www.wmi.ie
Registered Charity Number: CHY 2318

World Missions Ireland is the work of
four Pontifical Mission Societies giving
spiritual and material help to Young
Churches: Society for the Propagation of
the Faith; Society of St Peter Apostle;
Society of Missionary Children (Holy
Childhood); Pontifical Missionary Union.

**Young Christian Workers (Saotharaithe
Ógra Críostaí)**
*National Co-ordinator*
Ms Vicky Rattigan
Email vicky@ycw.ie
*Development Worker:* Gellért Merza
*National Chaplain:* Rev Eoin McCrystal
YCW National Office,
11 Talbot Street, Dublin 1
Tel 01-8780291
Email info@ycw.ie
Website www.ycw.ie

The Young Christian Workers is an international youth movement which values the dignity and worth of each young person. It enables its members to challenge social exclusion and take action to bring about change in their home, their workplace and their social life. Many useful skills are acquired through attendance at weekly meetings, socials, international exchanges and training weekends. YCW IMPACT! 'Change through Action' Programme is aimed at young people in the 16-18 age group. A starter pack for working with young people aged 18 plus and a media resource complete with accompanying DVD are also available at our national office. YCW handbook also available to assist in the formation of YCW groups and provide a practical experience of the See, Judge, Act Method. For further details on retreats and events check our website: www.ycw.ie.

## RELIGIOUS PERIODICALS

## PUBLICATION OF THE IRISH CATHOLIC BISHOPS' CONFERENCE

**Intercom**
*Editor:* Mr Francis Cousins
Columba Centre, St Patrick's College
Maynooth, Co Kildare
Tel 01-5053000
Email fcousins@catholicbishops.ie
Website www.catholicbishops.ie
Twitter @IntercomJournal
A pastoral and liturgical resource for people in ministry, published by the Veritas Group, an agency of the Irish Catholic Bishops' Conference. Publiched ten times a year.
*Subscriptions:* Ross Delmar
7-8 Lower Abbey Street, Dublin 1
Tel 01-8788177 Fax 01-8786507
Email ross.delmar@veritas.ie

## OTHER RELIGIOUS PERIODICALS

**Africa**
*Editor:* Rev Tim Redmond (SPS)
Email africa@spms.ie
*Manager:* Rev Sean Deegan
Tel 059-6473600 Fax 059-6473529
Email office@spms.ie
International family mission magazine with topical articles on Christianity today; Bible reflections; youth and children's features. Nine issues per year. Published by St Patrick's Missionary Society, Kiltegan, Co Wicklow

**African Missionary**
*Editor:* Rev Martin Kavanagh SMA
Magazine with news of the lives and activities of SMA and OLA members in Africa and elsewhere. Three issues per year (including Calendar issue). Distributed free to supporters. Published by the Society of African Missions, Blackrock Road, Cork
Tel 021-4616318 Fax 021-4292873
Email publications@sma.ie
www.sma.ie

**Alive!**
*Editor:* Rev Brian McKevitt (OP)
Free 16-page Catholic tabloid paper with news, features, interviews. Available free for distribution by parishes, churches, shops, praesidia, etc. nationwide.
Circulation: 240,000
Published monthly from
St Mary's Priory, Tallaght, Dublin 24
*Contact:* Breda
Tel 01-4048187
Email alivepaper@gmail.com

**Being One**
*Editor:* Rev Brendan Leahy
Focolare Centre, Prosperous, Co Kildare
Tel 045-840430
Email beingone@eircom.net
Published three times a year.

**Bulletin of St Vincent de Paul**
*Editor:* Tom MacSweeney
Published quarterly by the Society of St Vincent de Paul in Ireland at National Office, SVP House, 91-92 Sean MacDermot Street, Dublin 1
Tel 01-8386990 Fax 018387355
Email editorbulletin@svp.ie
www.svp.ie

**Catholic Voice Newspaper**
*Editor:* Anthony Murphy
PO Box 11559, Dublin 1
Tel 059-8627268
Email editor@catholicvoice.ie
Tabloid 28 pages. Rrp €1/£1

**Church of Ireland Gazette**
*Editor:* Rev Canon Ian Ellis
Office: 3 Wallace Avenue, Lisburn, Co Antrim BT27 4AA
Tel 028-92675743
Email gazette@ireland.anglican.org
The Church of Ireland Gazette is an editorially independent weekly newspaper.

**Daystar**
*Editor:* Sr Ann McColl
Email annca7349@yahoo.co.uk
*Contact:* Sr Nora Bergin
Published bi-annually by the Franciscan Missionary Sisters for Africa
Mount Oliver, Dundalk, Co Louth
Tel 042-9358900 Fax 042-9371159
Email norabergin@yahoo.ie
*Regional Leader*
Sr Ann McColl
Moredun Convent, Alexandra Drive, Renfrew PA4 8UB, Scotland
Tel 0044-141-5615588
Email annca7349@yahoo.co.uk

**Doctrine and Life**
*Editor:* Rev Bernard Treacy (OP)
Published ten times a year by Dominican Publications, 42 Parnell Square, Dublin 1
Tel 01-8721611 Fax 01-8731760
Email subscriptions@dominicanpublications.com

**The Far East**
*Editor:* Rev Cyril Lovett (SSC)
Full colour, emphasis on Christian mission and related topics.
Circulation: 100,000 in Ireland and Britain. Published seven times a year by the Missionary Society of St Columban, St Columban's, Navan, Co Meath
Tel 046-9098272 Fax 046-9071297
Email editorfareast@columban.com
www.columban.com
*Manager:* Rev Noel Daly

## Foilseacháin Ábhair Spioradálta

Bunaíodh 1957
*Eagarthóir:* Frainc Mac Brádaigh (SJ)
*Eagarthóir Chúnta is Feidhmeanach*
*Riaracháin:* Martina Mhic an Phríora
Ephost antimire@gmail.com
*Bainistíocht:* Comhchoiste Timire & FS,
37 Sr Líosain Íocht, Baile Átha Cliath 2
Fón 01-7758502

## The Furrow

*Editor:* Rev Ronan Drury
Published monthly by
The Furrow Trust, St Patrick's College,
Maynooth, Co Kildare
Tel 01-7083741 Fax 01-7083908
Email furrow.office@may.ie
www.thefurrow.ie

## Irish Catholic

*Managing Editor:* Mr Garry O'Sullivan
Published weekly by The Agricultural
Trust, The Irish Catholic is Ireland's
largest and best selling Catholic
Newspaper since 1888
Irish Farm Centre, Blubell, Dublin 12
Tel 01-4276400 Fax 01-4276450
Email news@irishcatholic.ie,
advertising@irishcatholic.ie

## Irish Theological Quarterly

*Editor-in-Chief:* Rev Declan Marmion
*Secretary:* Prof Salvador Ryan
*Review Editor:* Rev Liam Tracey
*Business Manager:* Ms Fidelma Madden
Published by members of the Faculty of
Theology, St Patrick's College, Maynooth,
Co Kildare
Tel 01-7083496 Fax 01-6289063
Email itq.editor@may.ie

## Maria Legionis

(Journal published quarterly by the
Legion of Mary)
Presentata House,
263 North Circular Road, Dublin 7
Tel 01-8387770
Email marialegionis@eircom.net

## Medical Missionaries of Mary

*Editor:* Sr Carol Breslin (MMM)
*Healing & Development* yearbook plus
calendar, supplementary newsletters
Easter and Christmas, available from
MMM Communications, Rosemount
Terrace, Booterstown, Co Dublin
Tel 01-2887180 Fax 01-2834626
Email mmm@iol.ie
www.mmmworldwide.org

## Milltown Studies

*Editor:* Dr Joseph Egan (SMA)
Milltown Institute of Theology and
Philosophy, Milltown Park, Dublin 6
Tel 01-2776300 Fax 01-2692528
Email mseditor@milltown-institute.ie

## New Liturgy

*Editor:* Rev Patrick Jones
Bulletin of the National Secretariat,
Irish Episcopal Commission for Liturgy,
published quarterly at the
National Centre for Liturgy,
St Patrick's College,
Maynooth, Co Kildare
Tel 01-7083478 Fax 01-7083477
Email liturgy@spcm.ie
www.liturgy-ireland.ie

## Non-Subscribing Presbyterian Magazine

*Editor:* Rev Dr A. D. G. Steers
223 Upper Lisburn Road,
Belfast BT10 0LL
Tel 028-90947850
Email nspresb@hotmail.com

## Pioneer

*Editor:* Fr Bernard J. McGuckian (SJ)
*Sub-editor:* Ms Róisín Fulham
Published monthly by Pioneer Total
Abstinence Association,
27 Upper Sherrard Street, Dublin 1
Tel 01-8749464 Fax 01-8748485
Email pioneer@jesuit.ie
www.pioneerassociation.ie

## Presbyterian Herald

*Editor:* Sarah Harding
Published monthly by Presbyterian
Church in Ireland, Assembly Buildings,
2–10 Fisherwick Place,
Belfast BT1 6DW
Tel 028-90322284
Email herald@presbyterianireland.org
www.presbyterianireland.org

## Proceedings of the Irish Biblical Association

Published by IBA Publications
*Contact:* Noel Fitzpatrick
16 Granville Park, Blackrock, Co Dublin
Email njfitzpatrick712@gmail.com

## Reality

*Editor:* Rev Gerard R. Moloney (CSsR)
*Marketing:* Paul Copeland
Published monthly by Redemptorist
Communications, 75 Orwell Road,
Rathgar, Dublin 6
Tel 01-4922488 Fax 01-4927999
Email info@redcoms.org
www.redcoms.org

## Religious Life Review

*Editor:* Rev Thomas McCarthy (OP)
Published six times a year by
Dominican Publications,
42 Parnell Square, Dublin 1
Tel 01-8587103
Fax 01-8731760
Email thomasnewbridge@gmail.com

## Sacred Heart Messenger

*Editor:* Rev John Looby (SJ)
*Operations & Marketing Manager*
Cecilia West
Official publication of the Apostleship of
Prayer, published monthly by Messenger
Publications at
37 Lower Leeson Street, Dublin 2
Tel 01-6767491
Fax 01-6767493
Email sales@messenger.ie
www.messenger.ie

## An Sagart

*Eagarthóir*
An Mgr Pádraig Ó Fiannachta
Foilsítear ceithre uair sa bhliain ag
An Sagart, An Díseart, An Daingean,
Trá Lí, Co Chiarraí
Tel 066-915000
Ephost pof@ansagart.ie
www.ansagart.ie
Síntiús Bliana €15

## The Salesian Bulletin

*Editor:* Rev Pat Egan (SDB)
Salesian House, St Teresa's Road,
Crumlin, Dublin 12
Tel 01-4555787
Email office@salesians.ie
homepage.eircom.net/~sdbmedia
*Subscriptions*
Rev Dan Devitt (SDB)
Salesian Missions, PO Box 50,
Pallaskenry, Co Limerick
Tel 061-393223 Fax 061-393354
Published quarterly for the Salesians of
Don Bosco by Salesian Bulletin.

## Scripture in Church

*Editor in Chief*
Rev Martin McNamara (MSC)
Published quarterly by
Dominican Publications,
42 Parnell Square, Dublin 1
Tel 01-8721611 Fax 01-8731760
Email
subscriptions@dominicanpublications.com

## The Sheaf

Formerly *St Joseph's Sheaf*
*Editor:* Dominic Dowling FCII KCHS
St Joseph's Young Priests Society
23 Merrion Square, Dublin 2
Tel 01-6762593
Fax 01-6762549
Email sjyps@eircom.net
and jddowling@eircom.net
Its purpose is twofold:
(a) to foster vocations to priesthood and
religious life
(b) to promote the vocation of the laity.
www.thesheaf.vpweb.ie

**Spirituality**
*Editor:* Rev Tom Jordan (OP)
Published six times a year by
Dominican Publications,
42 Parnell Square, Dublin 1
Tel 01-8721611 Fax 01-8731760
Email
tom.jordan@dominicanpublications.com
Website
www.dominicanpublications.com

**The St Anthony Brief**
*Editor:* Br Stephen O'Kane (OFM)
Email ctsok@yahoo.com
Published every two months by the
Franciscan Missionary Union,
8 Merchant's Quay, Dublin 8
Tel 01-6777651 Fax 01-6777293

**St Joseph's Advocate**
*Editor:* Fr Jim O'Connell (MHM)
Tel 056 7753631
Published quarterly by Mill Hill Missionaries,
St Joseph's, Waterford Road, Kilkenny
Tel 056-7721482 Fax 056-7751490
Email jimocmhm@eircom.net

**St Martin Magazine**
*Editor:* Rev Diarmuid Clifford (OP)
Published monthly by St Martin
Apostolate,42 Parnell Square, Dublin 1
Tel 01-8745464/8730147 Fax 01-8731989
From UK 00-353-1-8745465
Email stmartin@iol.ie
Personal email dcop@eircom.net

**Studies – An Irish Quarterly Review**
*Editor:* Rev Bruce Bradley (SJ)
Published by the Irish Jesuits,
35 Lower Leeson Street, Dublin 2
Tel 01-6766785 Fax 01-7758598
Email studies@jesuit.ie
Website www.studiesirishreview.ie

**Timire an Chroí Naofa**
Bunaíodh 1911
*Eagarthóir*
Frainc Mac Brádaigh (SJ)
*Eagarthóir Chúnta is Feidhmeanach*
*Riaracháin:* Martina Mhic an Phríora
Ephost antimire@gmail.com
*Bainistíocht:* Comhchoiste Timire & FS,
37 Sr Líosain Íocht, Baile Átha Cliath 2
Fón 01-7758502

**The Universe Catholic Weekly**
*Editor:* Joseph Kelly
The Universe Media Group Ltd,
Ground Floor, Alberton House,
St Mary's Parsonage,
Manchester M3 2WJ, UK

# MARRIAGE TRIBUNALS

By Decree dated 24 March 1975, the Irish Episcopal Conference decided to establish four Regional Marriage Tribunals of first instance to be located at Armagh, Dublin, Cork and Galway. This decree was formally approved by the Supreme Tribunal of the Apostolic Signatur on 6 May 1975. In accordance with the terms of the Roman rescript, the Episcopal Conference, in a decision of 30 September 1975, determined the Regional Tribunals would come into effect on 1 January 1976. From that date they replaced all previous diocesan marriage tribunals.

By the same process which established in Ireland Regional Marriage Tribunals of first instance, the Episcopal Conference set up a sole Appeal Tribunal, located in Dublin, to hear cases on appeal from each of the four Regional Tribunals. It also came into effect on 1 January 1976. Its personnel and administration are wholly distinct from the Dublin Regional Marriage Tribunal.

## NATIONAL MARRIAGE APPEAL TRIBUNAL

Columba Centre, Maynooth, Co Kildare
Tel 01 5053119 Fax 01-5053122
*Judicial Vicar*
Rev Michael Smyth (MSC), STL, JUD
*Administrator:* Mrs Stephanie Walpole
*Vice Officialis*
Rt Rev Mgr Joseph Donnelly PP, VF
*Associate Judges*
Very Rev Canon Eugene Mangan PP (Kerry), Very Rev Gerard McNamara PP (Limerick), Rt Rev Mgr John Shine BD, LCL, LPh, PP, (Waterford and Lismore), Very Rev Patrick Gill AP,
Very Rev John Canon O'Boyle BA,
Very Rev Patrick Williams AP,
Very Rev S.J. Clyne PP, VF,
Rev Patrick Connolly DCL,
Rev Brendan Kilcoyne LCL,
Rev Michael Mullaney DCL,
Rev Brian Flynn PP,
Rev John Whelan (OSA),
Mr Michael V. O'Mahony,
Rev Seán O'Neill,
Very Rev Francis Maher PP,
Rev Lorcan Moran PP,
Rt Rev Mgr Gerard Dolan PP, LCL,
Very Rev Patrick Canon Twomey PE
Most Rev William Walsh DD
*Defenders of the Bond*
Sr Máirín McDonagh (RJH),
Rev Michael Bannon
Rev Gabriel Kelly, Rev Kevin O'Gorman
*Correspondence to:* Administrator

## REGIONAL MARRIAGE TRIBUNALS

### ARMAGH REGIONAL MARRIAGE TRIBUNAL

*Regional Office:* 15 College Street, Armagh BT61 9BT
Tel 028-37524537 Fax 028-37528763
Email armthq@btconnect.com
*Judicial Vicar*
Rev Dr James J. McGrory JCD
*Presiding Judges*
Rev Dr James J. McGrory JCD
Sr Carmel Maguire JCL
Rev Joseph Rooney JCL
*Correspondance to*
Mrs Marie Kelly, Secretary
*Contact Person for Constituent Dioceses*
*Armagh:* Rev John McKeever LLB, STL;
Rev Eugene O'Neill
*Clogher:* Sr Elizabeth Fee
*Derry:* Rev Peter O'Kane JCL
*Down & Connor:* Rev Joseph Rooney JCL
*Dromore:* Rev Peter C. McNeill
*Kilmore:* Sr Elizabeth Fee
*Raphoe:* Rev Eamonn McLaughlin;
Rev John Joe Duffy

### DUBLIN REGIONAL MARRIAGE TRIBUNAL

Diocesan Offices,
Archbishop's House, Dublin 9
Tel 01-8379253 Fax 01-8368309
Email dublinrmt@eircom.net
*Judicial Vicar:* Rev Paul Churchill
*Judges*
Rev Kilian Byrne LCL (Kildare and Leighlin)
Rev Kevin Cahill DCL (Ferns)
Sr Mary Grennan LCL (PBVM)
Rev Brian Kavanagh LCL (Dublin)
Rev William Richardson PhD, JCD (Dublin)
Mgr Alex Stenson DCL (Dublin)
Rev Tom Dowd
*Defenders of the Bond*
Very Rev Laurence Collins (OP)
Mr Paul MacKay
*Advocates:* Mrs Pamela van de Poll
*Tribunal Assistants*
Maeve Cotter, Collette Nugent,
Jane O'Donoghue, Mary O'Kane,
Carolyn O'Toole
*Correspondence to:* The Rev Judicial Vicar
*Constituent Dioceses:* Dublin, Ferns, Kildare and Leighlin, Meath, Ossory

### CORK REGIONAL MARRIAGE TRIBUNAL

Tribunal Offices, The Lough, Cork
Tel 021-4963653 Fax 021-4314149
*Judicial Vicar*
Very Rev Gerard Garrett LCL, MCL, LLM
Email ggarrett.tribunal@eircom.net
*Associate Judicial Vicar*
Vacant
*Judge:* Very Rev Seamus McKenna BA, HDE, LCL
Email smckenna.tribunal@eircom.net
*Constituent Dioceses*
Cashel, Cloyne, Cork and Ross, Kerry, Limerick, Waterford and Lismore
*Correspondence to:* Mrs Marlies Ferriter, (Administrator)
Email mferriter.tribunal@eircom.net

### GALWAY REGIONAL MARRIAGE TRIBUNAL

7 Waterside, Woodquay, Galway
Tel 091-565179 Fax 091-563512
Email 7waterside@eircom.net
*Judicial Vicar:* Very Rev Michael Byrnes BA JCL
Mairéad Uí Mhurchadha
*Correspondence to the Administrator:* Nicola Burke
*Constituent Dioceses:* Tuam, Achonry, Ardagh and Clonmacnois, Clonfert, Elphin, Galway, Killala, Killaloe

# CHAPLAINS

## THE DEFENCE FORCES CHAPLAINCY SERVICE

*Head Chaplain*
Rt Rev Mgr Eoin Thynne HCF
Defence Forces Headquarters,
McKee Barracks, Blackhorse Avenue,
Dublin 7
Tel 01-8042637
Email mgreointhynne@gmail.com
*Administration Secretary*
Sgt Liam Bellew
Defence Forces Headquarters,
McKee Barracks, Blackhorse Avenue,
Dublin 7
Tel 01-8042638
Email liam.bellew@defenceforces.ie

### Aiken Barracks
Dundalk, Co Louth
Tel 042-9331759
Rev Bernard McCay-Morrissey CF
Email
bernardmccaymorrissey@gmail.com

### Casement Aerodrome
Baldonnel, Co Dublin
Tel 01-4037536
Rev Jeremiah Carroll CF
Email jerryzulu@eircom.net

### Cathal Brugha Barracks
Rathmines, Dublin 6
Tel 01-8046484
Rev David Tyndall CF
Email davidwtyndall@yahoo.ie

### Collins Barracks (Cork)
Tel 021-4502734
Rev Gerard O'Neill CF
Email frgerryoneill@eircom.net

### Curragh Camp
Co Kildare
Rt Rev Mgr John McDonald CF
Tel 045-441369
Email frjohnmcdonald@gmail.com
Rev P.J. Somers CF
Tel 045-441277
Email somerspj@gmail.com

### Custume Barracks
Athlone, Co Westmeath
Tel 090-6421277
Rev Gerard Dowd CF
Email gerard.dowd@yahoo.co.uk

### Finner Camp
Bundoran, Co Donegal
Tel 071-9842294
Rev Alan Ward CF
Email awardcf@gmail.com

### Gormanston Camp
Co Meath
Tel 01-8413990
Rev Robert McCabe CF
Email frbobmac@gmail.com

### McKee Barracks
Dublin 7
Tel 086-2256794
Rev Patrick Mernagh CF
Email pat.mernagh@defenceforces.ie

### The Naval Base
Haulbowline, Co Cork
Tel 021-4378046
Rev Desmond Campion (SDB) CF
Email campiond@eircom.net

### Renmore Barracks
Galway
Tel 091-751156
Rev Paul Murphy CF
Email papamurfi@gmail.com
Tel 086-2326851

### Saint Bricin's Hospital
Infirmary Road, Dublin 7
Tel 01-8042637
Rt Rev Mgr Eoin Thynne HCF

### Sarsfield Barracks
Limerick
Tel 061-316817
Rev Seamus Madigan CF
Email seamusmadigan@hotmail.com
Tel 086-8441609

### James Stephens Barracks
Kilkenny
Tel 056-7761852
Rev Dan McCarthy CF
Tel 086-8575155
Email danielmaccarthy@eircom.net

### International Military Pilgrimage to Lourdes (Pèlerinage Militaire International)
*Director:* Rt Rev Mgr Eoin Thynne HCF
Defence Forces Headquarters,
McKee Barracks, Blackhorse Avenue,
Dublin 7
Tel 01-8042637

## PRISONS AND PLACES OF DETENTION IN IRELAND

*There are fourteen prisons or places of detention in the Republic of Ireland*

### Liason Bishop between Prison Chaplains and the Bishops' Conference
Bishop Eamonn Walsh
'Naomh Brid,' Blessington Road
Tallaght, Dublin 24
Tel 01-4598032
Email elmham@eircom.net

### National Co-ordinator of Prison Chaplains in the Republic of Ireland
Rev Ciaran Enright
Arbour Hill Prison, Dublin 7
Tel 01-4724030
Email ccenright@irishprisons.ie

### Arbour Hill Prison
Ard na Gaoithe,
Arbour Hill, Dublin 7
Rev Ciaran Enright
Tel 01-4724030
Email ccenright@irishprisons.ie
Prison General Office Tel 01-4724019

### Castlerea Prison
Castlerea, Co Roscommon
Margaret Connaughton
Tel 094-9625278
Email maconnaugh@irishprisons.ie
Prison General Office Tel 094-9625213

### Cloverhill Remand Prison
Cloverhill Road,
Clondalkin, Dublin 22
Rev John O'Sullivan (MSC)
Tel 01-6304586
Email jjosullivan@irishprisons.ie
Prison General Office Tel 01-6304531/2

### Cork Prison
*Awaiting appointment*
Rathmore Road, Cork
Prison General Office Tel 021-45188000

### Dóchas Centre Mountjoy Women's Prison
North Circular Road, Dublin 7
Sr Mary Mullins
Tel 01-8858920
Email mtmullins@irishprisons.ie
Prison General Office Tel 01-8858987

**Limerick Prison**
Mulgrave Street, Limerick
Awaiting appointment
Prison General Office Tel 061-204700

**Loughan House**
Blacklion, Co Cavan
Awaiting appointment
General Office Tel 071-9836000

**Midlands Prison**
Dublin Road, Portlaoise, Co Laois
Vera Mc Hugh
Tel 057-8672221
Email vamchugh@irishprisons.ie
Rev Tom Sinnott (MHM)
Tel 057-8672222
Email tgsinnott@irishprisons.ie
Prison General Office Tel 057-8672110

**Mountjoy Prison**
North Circular Road, Dublin 7
Rev Jimmy Kelly OSM
Tel 01-8062843
Email jxkelly@irishprisons.ie
Michael Loughnane
Email mjloughnane@irishprisons.ie
Mr Mark Davis
Tel 01-8062846
Email mcdavis@irishprisons.ie
Prison General Office Tel 01-8062800

**Portlaoise Prison**
Dublin Road, Portlaoise, Co Laois
Rev Eugene Drumm
Tel 057-8621318
Email eadrum@irishprisons.ie
General Office Tel 057-8621318

**Saint Patrick's Institution**
North Circular Road, Dublin 7
Ms Ruth Comerford
Tel 01-8858945
Email rmcomerfor@irishprisons.ie
General Office Tel 01-8062906

**Shelton Abbey**
Arklow, Co Wicklow
Sr Margaret O'Donovan
Email mmodonovan@irishprisons.ie
General Office Tel 040-242300

**Training Unit**
Glengarrif Parade, Dublin 7
Awaiting appointment
Prison General Office Tel 01-8062881

**Wheatfield Prison**
Cloverhill Road, Clondalkin, Dublin 22
Sr Joan Kane (OSU)
Tel 01-6209446
Email jakane@irishprisons.ie
Sr Esther Murphy (RSM)
Tel 01-6209447
Email esmurphy01@irishprisons.ie
Sr Kathleen Cunningham *(Part-time)*
Email ktcunningh@irishprisons.ie
Tel 01-6209446/7
Sr Imelda Wickham (PBVM) *(Part-time)*
Tel 01-6209466
Email imwickham@irishprisons.ie
Prison General Office Tel 01-6209400

*There are three Prisons and Places of Detention in Northern Ireland, administered by the Northern Ireland Office (Use prefix (048) from Republic)*

**HMP Maghaberry**
Old Road, Ballinderry Upper,
Lisburn, Co Antrim, BT28 2TP
Tel 028-92614825
*Pastoral Team*
Br Brian Monaghan
Email bmonaghan@btinternet.com
Rev Frank Brady (SJ)
Email frank.brady@dojni.x.gsi.gov.uk
Rev Gabriel Bannon
Email gabriel.bannon@dojni.x.gsi.gov.uk
Rev Brian Lennon
Email brian.lennon@dojni.x.gsi.gov.uk
Sr Rosaleen McMahon
Email macmahon2000@yahoo.co.uk
Fr John McCallion
Email revtrad@btinternet.com
Tel 02892 614825

**HMP Magilligan**
Point Road, Magilligan,
Limavaddy BT49 OLR, Co Derry
Rev Francis O'Hagan
Email www.frohagan@aol.com
Prison General Office Tel 028-77763311

**Hydebank Young Offenders' Centre**
Hydebank Wood, Hospital Road,
Belfast BT8 8NA, Co Antrim
Tel 028-90253666
*Pastoral Team*
Rev Stephen McBrearty
Email smc02@hotmail.com
Sr Oonah Hanrahan
Email oonahhanrahan2002@yahoo.co.uk

## BRITAIN

**Irish Chaplaincy in Britain**
*Director:* Mr Eugene Dugan
50–52 Camden Square
London NW1 9XB
Tel 0044-2074825528
Fax 0044-2074824815
Email info@irishchaplaincy.org.uk
*Trustees:* Mr John Walsh (Chair),
Mgr Canon Tom Egan (Hon. Treasurer)

## SPECIALISED APOSTOLATES

**Irish Chaplaincy Prisoners**
*Irish Council for Prisoners Overseas (ICPO)*
50–52 Camden Square, London NW1 9XB
Tel 0044-2074824148
Email prisoners@irishchaplaincy.org.uk

**Irish Chaplaincy Traveller Equality**
50–52 Camden Square
London NW1 9XB
Tel 0044-2074825525
Email travellers@irishchaplaincy.org.uk

**Irish Chaplaincy Seniors**
50–52 Camden Square
London NW1 9XB
Tel 0044-2074823274
Email seniors@irishchaplaincy.org.uk

For all news, events and details please see www.irishchaplaincy.org.uk

## EUROPE

**Brussels**
Rev Vincent Gallogley (OFM)
23/25 Ave des Anciens Combattants,
1950 Kraainem, Belgium
Tel 0032-2-7201970
Fax 0032-2-7255810

**Copenhagen**
Rev Patrick Shiels (CSSR)
Skt Annae Kirke, Hans Bogbinders Alle 2,
2300 Copenhagen S, Denmark
Tel 0045-31-582102

**Lisbon**
Rev Gus Champion
St Mary's, Rua do Murtal 368
San Pedro do Estoril
2765 Estoril, Portugal
Tel 00-351-1-4673771 *(Residence)*
Tel 00-351-1-4681676 *(Parish)*

**Luxembourg**
Rev Eamonn Breslin
European Parish, 34 Rue des Capucins,
Luxembourg BP 175
Tel 00352-470039 Fax 00352-220859

**Munich**
Rev Chetus Cohace
Landsberger Strasse 39,
80399 Munich, Germany
Email englischsprachige-
mission.muenchen@erzbistum-
muenchen.de
Tel 0049-89-5003580
Fax 0049-89-50035826
Website
www.englishspeking-mission-munic.de

**Paris**
Rev Tom Scanlon (CP)
Rev Anthony Behan (CP)
St Joseph's Church,
50 Avenue Hoche, 75008 Paris, France
Tel 0033-1-42272856
Fax 0033-1-42278649
Rev Sean Maher
Irish College, Paris, 5 Rue des Irlandais,
75005 Paris, France
Tel 0033-1-58521030 *(College)*
Email dechurley@eircom.net

**Rome**
Rev Raphael Gallagher (CSSR)
Redentoristi, Via Merulana 31,
CP2458, Rome, Italy Tel 0039-6-494932
Email rgallagher@alfonsiana.edu

## AUSTRALIA

**Sydney**
Rev Tom Devereux OMI
Parish of St Patrick's,
2 Wellington St, Bondi, NSW 2026
Tel 0061-02-93651195
Fax 0061-02-93654002
Mobile 0061-04-07347301
Email stpatbon@bigpond.net.au

## UNITED STATES OF AMERICA

*Director:* Rev Brendan McBride
Irish Immigration Pastoral Centre
5340 Geary Boulevard #206,
San Francisco, CA 94121
Tel 001-4157526006
Fax 001-4157526910
Email nationaloffice@usairish.org
Cellphone 001-4157609818
*Administrator:* Ms Geri M. Garvey
Irish Apostolate USA
1005 Downs Drive,
Silver Spring, MD 20904
Tel/Fax 001-3013843375
Email administrator@usairish.org

**Boston**
*Irish Pastoral Centre*
*Executive Director:* Sr Marguerite Kelly
953 Hancock Street,
Quincy, MA 02170
Tel 001-617-4797404
Fax 001-617-4790541
Email ipcboston@yahoo.com
*Chaplain:* Rev John McCarthy
15 Rita Road, Dorchester, MA 02124
Tel 001-617-4797404
Fax 001-617-4790541
Cellphone 001-617-4121331
Email jmccarthyipc@yahoo.com

**Chicago**
*Chicago Irish Immigrant Support*
*Chaplain:* Rev Michael Leonard
3525 S. Lake Park Avenue,
Chicago, IL 60653
Tel 312-5348445
Fax 312-5348446
Email irishoverhere@sbcglobal.net
Website www.ci-is.com

**Ocean City, Maryland**
*(Open June–September)*
*Irish Student Outreach*
*Co-ordinator:* William Ferguson
13701 Sailing Rd, Ocean City, MD 21842
Tel 001-410-2500362
001-443-7837893
Email wfergus4@aol.com

**Milwaukee**
Irish Immigrant Service of Milwaukee
John Gleeson, 2133 Wisconsin Ave,
Milwaukee, WI 53233-1910
Tel 001-414-3458800
Email gleeson@uwm.edu
Website www.ichc.net

**New York**
*Project Irish Outreach*
*Co-ordinator:* Patricia O'Callaghan
1011 First Avenue, New York NY 10022
Tel 001-212-3171011
Fax 001-212-7551526
Email patricia.ocallaghan@archny.org

*Aisling Irish Community Centre*
990 McLean Avenue, Yonkers, NY 10704
*Chaplain:* Sr Christine Hennessey
Tel 001-914-2375121
Fax 001-914-2375172
Email Sr.Christine.Hennessy@archny.org,
aislingirishcc@mindspring.com
Website www.aislingirishcenter.org

**Philadelphia**
*Philadelphia Immigration Resource Centre*
*Executive Director:* Siobhan Lyons
7 South Cedar Lane
Upper Darby, PA 19082 2816
Tel 001-610-7896355 Fax 001-7896352
Email irishimmigration@aol.com
Website www.irishimmigrants.org

**San Diego**
*Irish Outreach San Diego Inc.*
Bernadette Cashmann
2725 Congress Street 2G,
San Diego, CA 92110
Tel 001-619-2911630
Email irishsd@sbcglobal.net
Website www.irishoutreachsd.org

**San Francisco**
*Irish Immigration Pastoral Centre*
Celine Kennelly
5340 Geary Boulevard #206,
San Francisco, CA 94121
Tel 001-415-7526006
Fax 001-415-7526910
Email iipc@pacbell.net
Website www.sfiipc.org
Cellphone 001-415-7605762

**Seattle**
*Seattle Immigration Support Group*
*Chairman:* James Cummins
5819 St Andrews Drive, Mukileto,
WA 98275
Tel 001-425-2445147
Email siisg@irishclub.org

# GENERAL INFORMATION

## OBITUARY LIST

*Beata mortui qui in Domino moriuntur*
Rv 14:13

## PRIESTS AND BROTHERS

Bambrick, Thomas (SM) 16 May 2014
Barret, Paul (OFMCap) 8 February 2014
Barrett, Martin (Killala) 19 June 2014
Beausang, Sean (CFC) 22 July 2014
Bennett, Seán (CSsR) 28 September 2013
Boland, Andrew P. (Dublin) 20 September 2014
Boland, John (OFMCap) 3 January 2014
Boyhan, Matt (CFC) 25 November 2013
Brady, John (SJ) 15 April 2014
Breen, Simeon (OFMCap) 7 December 2013
Brilley, Joseph (Meath) 28 September 2014
Burke, John DeSales (FPM) 23 December 2013
Burke, Liam (SMA) 29 October 2013
Burns, Dan (Cork & R.) 9 April 2014
Butler, Anthony J. (SMA) 16 October 2014
Cahill, David (SDB) 6 December 2013
Carton, Francis (OCSO) 24 June 2014
Christy, Myles (Dublin) 13 February 2014
Coen, Michael (OCD) 6 May 2014
Cogan, Mícheál (Cloyne) 28 March 2014
Costelloe, Liam (OFM) 23 January 2014
Curtin, Cornelius (CM) 3 July 2014
Dargan, Joseph (SJ) 1 June 2014
Dempsey, Canon Joseph (Limerick) 4 October 2014
Desmond, Bartholomew (Cloyne) 4 July 2014
Diamond, Mark (Killala) 12 August 2014
Dillon, Sean (SPS) 24 October 2013
Dolan, James (MHM) 15 July 2014
Doyle, Declan (Dublin) 12 February 2014
Doyle, Denis (Kildare & L.) 19 May 2014
Doyle, John Baptist (CSSp) 30 April 2014
Drohan, Dermot (CFC) 19 August 2014
Duffy, James (Declan) (FMS) 22 April 2014
Dunphy, Aengus (OCSO) 8 February 2014
Dwan, Martin (SPS) 18 April 2014

Earley, Tom (CFC) 7 February 2014
Farragher, John Peter (Seán) (CSSp) 12 December 2013
Fay, Ambrose (CP) 10 May 2014
Fennelly, John (Tuam) 23 December 2013
Finan, Andrew (Achonry) 2 February 2014
Flood, Aloysius (CSSp) 7 December 2013
Foley, George (SSCC) 19 July 2014
Flynn, Robert (Achonry) 9 July 2014
Foley William (SMA) 30 July 2014
Forde, Nicholas (OMI) 13 June 2014
Gallagher, Louis (OCD) 24 May 2014
Garvey, Kieran (OFMCap) 9 July 2013
Gavin, Camillus (CFC) 16 November 2013
Gavin, Thomas P. (Meath) 23 September 2014
Geoghegan, M. Anthony (CSSp) 29 December 2013
Giles, Seamus (Meath) 8 December 2013
Gleeson, Ignatius (OFM) 25 January 2014
Hanratty, Oliver (Dublin) 24 April 2014
Haran, Cyril (Elphin) 25 June 2014
Harris, James Dominic (OP) 22 February 2014
Haughey, Peter Francis (OSA) 5 March 2014
Hayes, Sean (SMA) 15 July 2014
Hegarty, Patrick (Killala) 11 December 2013
Henry, Seamus (Ossory) 25 February 2014
Heverin, Seamus (Killala) 12 December 2013
Hogan, Flannan (OCSO) 3 July 2014
Holmes, Samuel (Ardagh & Cl.) 23 September 2014
Horgan, Conny (CFC) 18 February 2014
Hughes, Paul (OCarm) 15 May 2014
Hughes, Peter (CSSp) 16 July 2014
Hughes, Solanus (OFM) 22 August 2012
Hurley, Ivan (CSsR) 28 May 2014
Ingoldsby, Thomas (SDB) 20 October 2013
Jennings, Joseph (SM) 18 November 2013
Jones, Joseph (MHM) 11 July 2014
Kearney, Brendan (SJ) 24 February 2014
Kearney, Larry (SPS) 12 October 2013
Keegan, Patrick (CSSp) 10 October 2013

Kelly, Edward (Kildare & L.) 24 November 2013
Kelly, Michael (Limerick) 17 January 2014
Kelly, Robert (SM) 15 September 2014
Kelly, Terence (Armagh) 6 January 2014
Kennedy, Seraphin (OFM) 11 February 2014
Kenny, Martin (Armagh) 27 May 2014
Kenny, Thomas (SDB) 12 April 2014
Kerrane, John (Meath) 30 June 2014
King, Alexis (Martin) (OFM) 13 September 2013
Kirby, Canon Brendan (Ferns) 2 June 2014
Langan, William (OCarm) 6 June 2014
Linehan, Diarmuid (Cork & R.) 29 September 2014
Macaulay, Jeremiah (Ardagh & Cl.) 9 February 2014
MacCourt, Aloysius (Armagh) 20 February 2014
MacGurnaghan, Joseph (Down & C.) 26 February 2014
Maguire, Niall (OCSO) 23 January 2014
Manning, Seán (Galway) 22 January 2014
Martyn, Fidelis (OSF) 8 March 2014
McDermott, Sean (OMI) 19 October 2013
McDonald, Matthew (OFM) 24 September 2013
McEgan, Michael (SMA) 18 June 2014
McEvoy, Eddie (CFC) 26 April 2014
McGale, Harry (OCD) 8 June 2014
McGrady, Colm (Down & C.) 19 August 2014
McGuane, Joseph (Cloyne) 12 December 2013
McGuinness, T. J. (Dromore) 29 June 2014
McHenry, Francis (OSB) 29 July 2014
McKenna, Kevin (Derry) 25 April 2014
McMullan, Alexander (Down & C.) 23 April 2014
Meade, Noel (OP) 4 March 2014
Meaney, Anthony (OCarm) 19 March 2014
Moloney, Mgr John (Dublin) 8 March 2014
Moran, Joseph (Tuam) 17 January 2013
Moran, Patrick J. (OSA) 9 July 2014

Mullahy, Thomas (SMA) 5 December 2013

Murphy O'Connor, Jerome James (OP) 11 November 2013

Murphy, Fiacre (CFC) 30 December 2013

Murray, James (Dublin) 22 April 2014

Naughten, Patrick (Clonfert) 13 February 2014

Neville, Edward (OFMCap) 19 March 2014

Nugent, Sean (Waterford & L.) 10 September 2014

O'Brien, Juniper (OFM) 13 October 2013

O'Callaghan, Liam (SMA) 5 April 2014

O'Connor, Charles (SJ) 3 February 2014

O'Connor, David (CSSp) 30 November 2013

O'Connor, Michael (OSB) 10 February 2014

O'Connor, Thomas (CFC) 15 February 2014

O'Donovan, John (Killaloe) 2 November 2014

O'Donovan, William (OMI) 27 February 2014

O'Dwyer, Malachy Jeremiah (OP) 13 June 2014

O'Gorman, William (Limerick) 23 August 2014

O'Keeffe, Philip (Cloyne) 9 August 2014

O'Mahony, Ultan (FSP) 5 December 2013

O'Neill, Denis (SPS) 12 November 2013

O'Reilly, Phil (CFC) 15 September 2013

O'Riordan, Timothy (Waterford & L.) 12 November 2013

O'Rourke, John (Elphin) 3 June 2014

O'Shea, Patrick (MSC) 25 October 2013

O'Sullivan, Martin (OFMCap) 29 September 2013

Pidgeon, James (OH) 18 July 2014

Polke, Desmond (Derry) 21 May 2014

Power, William (CSsR) 23 October 2013

Reid, Alexander (CSsR) 22 November 2013

Rocks, Edward (CSsR) 20 July 2014

Ryan, Edmund (SAC) 3 December 2013

Ryan, Sean (SMA) 22 February 2014

Sheedy, Cyril (CSSp) 11 February 2014

Slater, Jack (MHM) 4 November 2013

Surlis, Paul (Achonry) 30 May 2014

Sutton, Malachy (OCSO) 23 March 2014

Tighe, Sebastian (OFM) 22 September 2013

Tinsley, Ambrose (OSB) 24 September 2013

Toohey, Seamus (Dublin) 19 October 2014

Treanor, Eamon (Armagh) 17 March 2014

Tuohy, Timothy (Killaloe) 26 July 2014

Tynan, Matt (CFC) 11 August 2014

Tynan, Seán (Ardagh & Cl.) 5 February 2014

Vaughan, Timothy (SPS) 21 March 2014

Walsh, Alphonsus (CSsR) 20 September 2013

Walsh, Martin (SMA) 29 July 2014

Walsh, Thomas (CSsR) 15 May 2014

Ward, Canon Michael (Armagh) 24 October 2014

Watters, Enda (CSSp) 13 March 2014

White, Con (Cork & R.) 13 October 2013

Whittle, Joseph (SDB) 11 March 2014

Woods, Brendan (SJ) 28 May 2014

Young, Patrick F. (Kilmore) 6 February 2014

## SISTERS

Altman, Margaret Mary (Daughters of Charity) 5 January 2014

Andrews, Benedict (Mercy) 3 December 2013

Bellew, Patricia (IBVM) 8 December 2013

Barrett, Canice (Presentation) 1 July 2014

Bourke, Mary Finian (Religious Sisters of Charity) 25 August 2014

Breen, Maol Íosa (Mercy) 21 July 2014

Brehony, Assumpta (Mercy) 17 August 2014

Brehony, Avellino (Mercy) 26 March 2014

Brosnan, Mary (Poor Servants of the Mother of God) 27 March 2014

Buckley, Catherine Mary (Presentation) 14 August 2014

Buckley, Eucharia (Presentation) 21 June 2014

Butler, Mary Lelia (Religious Sisters of Charity) 26 March 2014

Byrne, Antoinette (Little Sisters of the Poor) 23 April 2014

Byrne, Elizabeth (Charity of Jesus and Mary Sisters) 6 August 2014

Carew, Ellen (Presentation) 14 August 2014

Carroll, Dolores (Mercy) 23 July 2014

Casey, Bridie (Daughters of Charity) 11 June 2014

Claffey, Anne (St Joseph of Cluny Sisters) 4 March 2014

Clarke, Carmelita (Mercy) 13 June 2014

Close, Margaret (OP) 18 May 2014

Coffey, Finbarr (Mercy) 22 January 2014

Cogan, Margaret (Marist) 18 June 2014

Connaughton, Mary (Mercy) 7 February 2014

Coogan, Patricia (OP) 1 September 2014

Cooley, Anne (St Joseph of Cluny Sisters) 16 May 2014

Cooney, Ita (Mercy) 7 March 2014

Corrigan, Elizabeth (FMM) 10 August 2014

Cosgrave, Mary Thomasina (Religious Sisters of Charity) 20 June 2014

Coughlan, Ann (Mercy) 10 March 2014

Coyne, Helena (Mercy) 14 December 2013

Cullen, Stanislaus (IBVM) 19 March 2014

Cunney, Rita Mary (OP) 5 February 2014

Curran, Kevin (Presentation) 3 July 2014

Curran, Labouré (Presentation) 18 July 2014

Darcy, Mary (Mercy) 10 December 2013

Deevy, Colman (Mercy) 14 July 2014

Delaney, Elizabeth (St Joseph of Cluny Sisters) 28 November 2013

Delany, Inez (OP) 14 December 2013

Dempsey, Mary Bernard (Carmelites) 6 October 2013

Devery, Felicitas (Brigidine) 31 January 2014

Dillon, Clare (Cistercians) 11 November 2013

Doherty, Annunciata (Mercy) 22 January 2014

Dolan, Norbert (Mercy) 4 May 2014

Doyle, Catherine (IBVM) 6 December 2013

Doyle, Catherine (Mercy) 20 November 2013

Duggan, Maura (OP) 6 April 2014

Duignan, Ursula (Mercy) 18 March 2014

Dunning, Aquin (Mercy) 3 March 2014

Enright, Rosalie (MSHR) 8 August 2014

Faherty, Attracta (Mercy) 29 December 2013

Fahie, Teresa (Congregation of Our Lady of Charity of the Good Shepherd) 10 March 2014

Feeney, Rosa (OP) 26 November 2013

Finn, Catherine (Kathleen) (Society of the Sacred Heart) 14 February 2014

Fitzgerald, Elizabeth (Cistercians) 13 July 2014

Fitzgerald, Francis (Cistercians) 1 March 2014

Fitzgibbon, Lelia (Congregation of Our Lady of Charity of the Good Shepherd) 26 November 2014

Flannery, Assumpta (Mercy) 1 October 2013

Fleming, Finbar (Mercy) 4 October 2013

Flynn, Philomena (IBVM) 17 December 2013

Funge, Clare (IBVM) 8 October 2013

Geraghty, Mary (Presentation) 11 June 2014

# THE ROMAN PONTIFFS

Information includes the name of the Pope, in many cases his name before becoming Pope, his birth-place or country of origin, the date of accession to the Papacy, and the date of the end of reign which, in all but a few cases, was the date of death. Double dates record the day of election and coronation.
Source: *Annuario Pontificio*

**St Peter** (Simon Bar-Jona) of Bethsaida, in Galilee, Prince of the Apostles, who received from Jesus Christ supreme pontifical power to be transmitted to his successors, resided first at Antioch, then at Rome, where he was martyred in the year 64 or 67, having governed the Church from that city for twenty-five years.
**St Linus**, Tuscany, 67-76
**St Anacletus** (Cletus), Rome, 76-88
**St Clement**, Rome 88-97
**St Evaristus**, Greece, 97-105
**St Alexander I**, Rome, 105-25
**St Sixtus I**, Rome, 115-25
**St Telesphorus**, Greece, 125-36
**St Hyginus**, Greece, 136-40
**St Pius I**, Aquilea, 140-55
**St Anictus**, Syria, 155-66
**St Soter**, Campania, 166-75
**St Eleutheius**, Nicopolis in Epirus, 175-89

*Up to the time of St Eleutherius, the years indicated for the beginning and end of pontificates are not certain. Also, up to the middle of the eleventh century, there are some doubts about the exact days and months given in chronological tables.*

**St Victor I**, Africa, 189-99
**St Zephyrinus**, Rome, 199-217
**St Callistus I**, Rome, 217-22
**St Urban I**, Rome, 222-30
**St Pontian**, Rome, 21 July 230 to 28 Sept 235
**St Anterus**, Greece, 21 Nov 235 to 3 Jan 236
**St Fabian**, Rome, 10 Jan 236 to 20 Jan 250
**St Cornelius**, Rome, Mar 251 to June 253
**St Lucius I**, Rome, 12 May 254 to 2 Aug 254
**St Stephen I**, Rome, 12 May 254 to 2 Aug 257
**St Sixtus II**, Greece, 30 Aug 257 to 6 Aug 258
**St Dionysius**, birthplace unknown, 22 July 259 to 26 Dec 268
**St Felix I**, Rome, 5 Jan 269 to 30 Dec 274
**St Eutychian**, Luni, 4 Jan 275 to 7 Dec 283
**St Caius**, Dalmatia, 17 Dec 283 to 22 Apr 296
**St Marcellinus**, Rome, 30 June 296 to 25 Oct 304
**St Marcellus I**, Rome, 27 May 308 or 26 June 308 to 16 Jan 309
**St Eusebius**, Greece, 18 Apr 309 or 310 to 17 Aug 309 or 310
**St Melchiades** (Miltiades), Africa, 2 July 311 to 11 Jan 314
**St Sylvester I**, Rome, 31 Jan 314 to 31 Dec 335

*Most of the popes before St Sylvester I were martyrs.*

**St Marcus**, Rome, 18 Jan 336 to 7 Oct 336
**St Julius I**, Rome, 6 Feb 337 to 12 Apr 352
**Liberius**, Rome, 17 May 352 to 24 Sept 366
**St Damasus I**, Spain, 1 Oct 366 to 11 Dec 384
**St Siricius**, Rome, 15 or 22 or 29 Dec 384 to 26 Nov 399
**St Anastasius I**, Rome, 27 Nov 399 to 19 Dec 401
**St Innocent I**, Albano, 22 Dec 401 to 12 Mar 417
**St Zozimus**, Greece, 18 Mar 417 to 26 Dec 418
**St Bonifice I**, Rome, 28 or 29 Dec 418 to 4 Sept 422
**St Celestine I**, Campania, 10 Sept 422 to 27 July 432
**St Sixtus III**, Rome, 31 July 432 to 19 Aug 440
**St Leo I** (the Grant), Tuscany, 29 Sept 440 to 10 Nov 461
**St Hilary**, Sardinia, 19 Nov 461 to 29 Feb 468
**St Simplicius**, Tivoli, 3 Mar 468 to 10 Mar 483
**St Felix III (II)**, Rome, 13 Mar 483 to 1 Mar 492

*He should be called Felix II, and his successors of the same name should be numbered accordingly. The discrepancy in the numerical designation of popes named Felix was caused by the erroneous insertion in some lists of the name of St Felix of Rome, a martyr.*

**St Gelasius I**, Africa, 1 Mar 492 to 21 Nov 496
**Anastasius II**, Rome, 24 Nov 496 to 19 Nov 498
**St Symmachus**, Sardinia, 22 Nov 498 to 19 July 514
**St Hormisdas**, Frosinone, 20 July 514 to 6 Aug 523
**St John I**, Martyr, Tuscany, 13 Aug 523 to 18 May 526
**St Felix IV (III)**, Samnium, 12 July 526 to 22 Sept 530
**Boniface II**, Rome, 22 Sept 530 to 17 Oct 532
**John II**, Rome, 2 Jan 533 to 8 May 535

*John II was the first pope to change his name. His given name was Mercury.*

**St Agapitus I**, Rome, 13 May 535 to 22 Apr 536
**St Silverius**, Martyr, Campania, 1 or 8 June 536 to 11 Nov 537 (d. 2 Dec 537)

*St Silverius was violently deposed in March 537 and abdicated on 11 Nov 537. His successor, Vigilius, was not recognised as pope by all the Roman clergy until his abdication.*

**Vigilius**, Rome, 29 Mar 537 to 7 June 555

**Pelagius I**, Rome, 16 Apr 556 to 4 Mar 561
**John III**, Rome, 17 July 561 to 13 July 574
**Benedict I**, Rome, 2 June 575 to 30 July 579
**Pelagius II**, Rome, 26 Nov 579 to 7 Feb 590
**St Gregory I** (the Great), Rome, 3 Sept 590 to 12 Mar 604
**Sabinian**, Blera in Tuscany, 13 Sept 604 to 22 Feb 606
**Bonifcace III**, Rome, 19 Feb 607 to 12 Nov 607
**St Boniface IV**, Abruzzi, 25 Aug 608 to 8 May 615
**St Deusdedit** (Adeodatus I), Rome, 19 Oct 615 to 8 Nov 618
**Boniface V**, Naples, 23 Dec 619 to 25 Oct 625
**Honorius I**, Campania, 27 Oct 625 to 12 Oct 638
**Severinus**, Rome, 28 May 640 to 2 Aug 640
**John IV**, Dalmatia, 24 Dec 640 to 12 Oct 642
**Theodore I**, Greece, 24 Nov 642 to 14 May 649
**St Martin I**, Martyr, Todi, July 649 to 16 Sept 655 (in exile from 17 June 653)
**St Eugene I**, Rome, 10 Aug 654 to 2 June 657

*St Eugene I was elected during the exile of St Martin I, who is believed to have endorsed him as pope.*

**St Vitalian**, Segni, 30 July 657 to 27 Jan 672
**Adeodatus II**, Rome, 11 Apr 672 to 17 June 676
**Donus**, Rome, 2 Nov 676 to 11 Apr 678
**St Agatho**, Sicily, 27 June 678 to 10 Jan 681
**St Leo II**, Sicily, 17 Aug 682 to 3 July 683
**St Benedict II**, Rome, 26 June 684 to 8 May 685
**John V**, Syria, 23 July 685 to 2 Aug 686
**Conon**, birthplace unkown, 21 Oct 686 to 21 Sept 687
**St Sergius I**, Syria, 15 Dec 687 to 8 Sept 701
**John VI**, Greece, 30 Oct 701 to 11 Jan 705
**John VII**, Greece, 1 Mar 705 to 18 Oct 707
**Sisinnius**, Syria, 15 Jan 708 to 4 Feb 708
**Constantine**, Syria, 25 Mar 708 to 9 Apr 715
**St Gregory II**, Rome, 19 May 715 to 11 Feb 731
**St Gregory II**, Syria, 18 May 731 to Nov 741
**St Zachary**, Greece, 10 Dec 741 to 22 Mar 752

**Stephen II (III)**, Rome, 26 Mar 752 to 26 Apr 757

*After the death of St Zachary, a Roman priest named Stephen was elected but died (four days later) before his consecration as Bishop of Rome, which would have marked the beginning of his pontificate. Another Stephen was elected to succeed Zachary as Stephen II. (The first pope with this name was St Stephen 254-7). The ordinal III appears in parentheses after the name of Stephen II because the name of the earlier elected but deceased priest was included in some lists. Other Stephens have double numbers.*

**St Paul I**, Rome, Apr (29 May) 757 to 28 June 767

**Stephen III (IV)**, Sicily, 1 (7) Aug 768 to 24 Jan 772

**Adrian I**, Rome, 1 (9) Feb 772 to 25 Dec 795

**St Leo III**, Rome, 26 (27) Dec 795 to 12 June 816

**Stephen IV (V)**, Rome, 22 June 816 to 24 Jan 817

**St Paschal I**, Rome, 25 Jan 817 to 11 Feb 824

**Eugene II**, Rome, Feb (May) 824 to Aug 827

**Valentine**, Rome, Aug 827 to Sept 827

**Gregory IV**, Rome, 827 to Jan 844

**Sergius II**, Rome, Jan 844 to 27 Jan 847

**St Leo IV**, Rome, Jan (10 Apr) 847 to 17 Jan 855

**Benedict III**, Rome, July (29 Sept) 855 to 17 Apr 858

**St Nicholas I (the Great)**, Rome, 24 Apr 858 to 13 Nov 867

**Adrian II**, Rome, 14 Dec 867 to 14 Dec 872

**John VIII**, Rome, 14 Dec 872 to 16 Dec 882

**Marinus I**, Gallese, 16 Dec 882 to 15 May 884

**St Adrian III**, Rome, 17 May 884 to Sept 885

**Stephen V (VI)**, Rome, Sept 885 to 14 Sept 891

**Formosus**, Portus, 6 Oct 891 to 4 Apr 896

**Boniface VI**, Rome, Apr 896 to Apr 896

**Stephen VI (VII)**, Rome, May 896 to Aug 897

**Romanus**, Gallese, Aug 897 to Nov 897

**Theodore II**, Rome, Dec 897 to Dec 897

**John IX**, Tivoli, Jan 898 to Jan 900

**Benedict IV**, Rome, Jan (Feb) 900 to July 903

**Leo V**, Ardea, July 903 to Sept 903

**Sergius III**, Rome, 29 Jan 904 to 14 Apr 911

**Anastasius III**, Rome, Apr 911 to June 913

**Landus**, Sabina, July 913 to Feb 914

**John X**, Tossignano (Imola), Mar 914 to May 928

**Leo VI**, Rome, May 928 to Dec 928

**Stephen VII (VIII)**, Rome, Dec 928 to Feb 931

**John XI**, Rome, Feb (Mar) 931 to Dec 935

**Leo VII**, Rome, 3 Jan 936 to 13 July 939

**Stephen VIII (IX)**, Rome, 14 July 939 to Oct 942

**Marinus II**, Rome, 30 Oct 942 to May 946

**Agapitus II**, Rome, 10 May 946 to Dec 955

**John XII** (Octavius), Tusculum, 16 Dec 955 to 14 May 964 (date of his death)

**Leo VIII**, Rome, 4 (6) Dec 963 to 1 Mar 965

**Benedict V**, Rome, 22 May 964 to 4 July 966

*Confusion exists concerning the legitamcy of claims to the pontificate by Leo VII and Benedict V. John XII was deposed on 4 Dec 963 by a Roman council. If this deposition was invalid, Leo was an antipope. If the deposition of John was valid, Leo was the legitimate pope and Benedict was an antipope.*

**John XIII**, Rome, 1 Oct 965 to 6 Sept 972

**Benedict VI**, Rome, 19 Jan 973 to June 974

**Benedict VII**, Rome, Oct 974 to 10 July 983

**John XIV** (Peter Campenora), Pavia, Dec 983 to 20 Aug 984

**John XV**, Rome, Aug 985 to Mar 996

**Gregory V** (Bruno of Carinthia), Saxony, 3 May 996 to 18 Feb 999

**Sylvester II** (Gerbert), Auvergne, 2 Apr 999 to 12 May 1003

**John XVII** (Siccone), Rome, June 1003 to Dec 1003

**John XVIII** (Phasianus), Rome, Jan 1004 to July 1009

**Sergius IV** (Peter), Rome, 31 July 1009 to 12 May 1012

*The custom of changing one's name on election to the papacy is generally considered to date from the time of Sergius IV. Before his time, several popes had changed their names. After his time, this became a regular practice, with few exceptions, e.g. Adrian VI and Marcellus II.*

**Benedict VIII** (Theophylactus), Tusculum, 18 May 1012 to 9 Apr 1024

**John XIX** (Rosmanus), Tusculum, Apr (May) 1024 to 1032

**Benedict IX** (Theophylactus), Tusculum, 1032-44

**Sylvester III** (John), Rome, 20 Jan 1045 to 10 Feb 1045

*Sylvester III was an antipope if the forcible removal of Benedict IX in 1044 was not legitimate.*

**Benedict IX** (second time), 10 Apr 1045 to 1 May 1045

**Gregory VI** (John Gratian), Rome, 5 May 1045 to 20 Dec 1046

**Clement II** (Suitger, Lord of Morsleben and Homburg), Saxony, 24 (25) Dec 1046 to 9 Oct 1047

*If the resignation of Benedict IX in 1045 and his removal at the December 1046 synod were not legitimate, Gregory VI and Clement II were antipopes.*

**Benedict IX** (third time), 8 Nov 1047 to 17 July 1028 (d. c.1055)

**Damasus II** (Poppo), Bavaria, 17 July 1028 to 9 Aug 1028

**St Leo IX** (Bruno), Alsace 12 Feb 1049 to 19 Apr 1054

**Victor II** (Gebhard), Swabia, 16 Apr 1055 to 28 July 1057

**Stephen IX (X)** (Frederick), Lorraine, 3 Aug 1057 to 29 Mar 1058

**Nicholas II** (Gerard), Burgundy, 24 Jan 1059 to 27 July 1061

**Alexander II** (Anselmo da Baggio), Milan, 1 Oct 1061 to 21 Apr 1073

**St Gregory VII** (Hildebrand), Tuscany, 22 Apr (30 June) 1073 to 25 May 1085

**Bl Victor III** (Dauferius; Desiderius), Benevento, 24 May 1086 to 15 Sept 1087

**Bl Urban II** (Otto di Lagery), France, 12 Mar 1088 to 29 July 1099

**Paschall II** (Raniero), Ravenna, 13 (14) Aug 1099 to 21 Jan 1118

**Gelasius II** (Giovanni Caetani), Gaeta, 24 Jan (10 Mar) 1118 to 28 Jan 1119

**Callistus II** (Guido of Burgundy), Burgundy, 2 (9) Feb 1119 to 13 Dec 1124

**Honorius II** (Lamberto), Fiagnano (Imola), 15 (21) Dec 1124 to 13 Feb 1130

**Innocent II** (Gregorio Paperschi), Rome, 14 (23) Feb 1130 to 24 Sept 1143

**Celestine II** (Guido), Città di Castello, 26 Sept (3 Oct) 1143 to 8 Mar 1144

**Lucius II** (Gerardo Caccianemici), Bologna, 12 Mar 1144 to 15 Feb 1145

**Bl Eugene III** (Bernardo Paganelli di Montemagno), Pisa, 15 (18) Feb 1145 to 8 July 1153

**Anastasius IV** (Corrado), Rome, 12 July 1153 to 3 Dec 1154

**Adrian IV** (Nicholas Breakspear), England, 4 (5) Dec 1154 to 1 Sept 1159

**Alexander III** (Rolando Bandinelli), Siena, 7 (20) Sept 1159 to 30 Aug 1181

**Lucius III** (Ubaldo Allucingoli), Lucca, 1 (6) Sept 1181 to 25 Sept 1185

**Urban III** (Uberto Crivelli), Millan, 25 Nov (1 Dec) 1185 to 20 Oct 1187

**Gregory VIII** (Alberto de Morra), Benevento, 21 (25) Oct 1187 to 17 Dec 1187

**Clement III** (Paolo Scolari), Rome, 19 (20) Dec 1187 to Mar 1191

**Celestine III** (Giacinto Bobone), Rome, 30 Mar (14 Apr) 1191 to 8 Jan 1198

**Innocent III** (Lotario dei Conti di Segni), Anagni, 8 Jan (22 Feb) 1198 to 16 July 1216

**Honorius III** (Cencio Savelli), Rome, 18 (24) July 1216 to 18 Mar 1227

**Gregory IX** (Ugolino, Count of Segni), Anagni, 19 (21) Mar 1227 to 22 Aug 1241

**Celestine IV** (Goffredo Castiglioni), Milan, 25 (28) Oct 1241 to 10 Nov 1241

**Innocent IV** (Sinibaldo Fieschi), Genoa, 25 (28) June 1243 to 7 Dec 1254

**Alexander IV** (Rinaldo, Count of Segni) Anagni, 12 (20) Dec 1254 to 25 May 1261

**Urban IV** (Jacques Pantaléon), Troyes, 29 Aug (4 Sept) 1261 to 2 Oct 1264

**Clement IV** (Guy Foulques or Guido le Gros), France, 5 (15) Feb 1265 to 29 Nov 1268

**Bl Gregory X** (Teobaldo Visconti), Piacenza, 1 Sept 1271 (27 Mar 1272) to 10 Jan 1276

**Bl Innocent V** (Peter of Tarentaise), Savoy, 21 Jan (22 Feb) 1276 to 22 June 1276

**Adrian V** (Ottobono Fieschi), Genoa, 11 July 1276 to 18 Aug 1276

Collins, Timothy, Very Rev, PP
The Presbytery,
Dunmanway, Co Cork
Tel 023-8845000
(*Dunmanway*, Cork & R.)

Collum, Martin, Very Rev, PP, VF
Rathmullan, Co Donegal
Tel 074-9158156
(*Rathmullan*, Raphoe)

Colreavy, Thomas, Very Rev
(Retired priest)
Team Assistant, St Pauls,
28 Glentworth Park,
Ard-na-Gréine,
Ayrfield, Dublin 13
Tel 01-8484836
(*Ayrfield*, Dublin)

Coltsmann, Francis (SMA)
SMA House, Wilton, Cork
Tel 021-4541069/4541884

Comer, Liam, Very Rev, PP, VF
Dromagh, Mallow, Co Cork
Tel 029-78096
(*Dromtariffe*, Kerry)

Comer, Micheál, Very Rev, Adm
The Presbytery, Eadestown,
Naas, Co Kildare
Tel 045-862187
(*Eadestown*, Dublin)

Comerford, Brendan (SJ)
Manresa House,
Dollymount, Dublin 3
Tel 01-8331352

Comerford, Patrick, Very Rev, PP
Freshford, Co Kilkenny
Tel 056-8832461/
086-1038430
(*Freshford*, Ossory)

Comiskey, Brendan (SSCC), Most Rev, DD
Coudrin House, 27
Northbrook Road, Dublin 6
Tel 01-6473751/6686590

Comiskey, Brendan, Most Rev, DD
Retired Bishop of Ferns,
PO Box 40, Summerhill,
Wexford
(Ferns, retired)

Comiskey, Gerard, Very Rev, PP
Staghall, Belturbet,
Co Cavan
Tel 049-9522140
(*Drumlane*, Kilmore)

Commane, Michael (OP)
Newbridge College,
Droichead Nua, Co Kildare
Tel 045-487200

Commins, Thomas, CC
Kilkerrin, Ballinasloe,
Co Galway
Tel 094-9659212
(*Kilkerrin and Clonberne*,
Tuam)

Conaghan, Michael, Very Rev, PE
6 Fields Court,
Kilmacrennan, Co Donegal
Tel 074-91198711
(Raphoe, retired)

Conaty, Eamonn (SSC), Very Rev, PP
Ballinameen, Boyle,
Co Roscommon
Tel 071-9668104
(*Ballinameen (Kilnamanagh and Estersnow)*, Elphin)

Conaty, Peter (CSSp)
Community Leader,
Spiritan Missionaries,
Ardbraccan,
Navan, Co Meath
Tel 046-9021441

Concannon, Eamonn, Very Rev Canon, PE
Ballyhowley, Knock,
Co Mayo
(Tuam, retired)

Concannon, John (CM)
St Peter's, Phibsboro,
Dublin 7
Tel 01-8389708/8389841

Condon, Eanna, Very Rev, PE
St Mary's, Clonmel,
Co Tipperary
Tel 052-6127870
(Waterford & L., retired)

Condon, Gerard, Very Rev, PP
Diocesan Advisor for
Religious Education,
Shanballymore, Mallow,
Co Cork
Tel 022-25197
(*Killavullen*, Cloyne)

Condon, Jeremiah, Very Rev, PP
Stradbally, Kilmacthomas,
Co Waterford
Tel 051-293133
(*Stradbally*, Waterford & L.)

Condon, John
Piltown, Co Kilkenny
Tel 086-8394615
(Ossory, retired)

Condon, Joseph, Very Rev, PP
Ballymabin, Dunmore East,
Co Waterford
(Waterford & L.)

Condon, Mark, CC
Thomastown, Co Kilkenny
Tel 056-7793191/086-
6005402
(*Thomastown*, Ossory)

Condon, Patrick T., Very Rev, PP
Knockanore, Tallow,
Co Waterford
Tel 024-97140
(*Knockanore*, Waterford & L.)

Condon, Sean
Cathedral House,
Cathedral Place, Limerick
Tel 061-414624
(Limerick, retired)

Condren, Joseph (OFM)
Franciscan Friary, Ennis,
Co Clare
Tel 065-6828751

Condron, Barry, PP
Tyrrellspass, Co Westmeath
Tel 044-9223115
(*Castletown-Geoghegan*,
Meath)

Conlan, Alex, Very Rev
(Moderator)
Parochial House, Ballybrack,
Co Dublin
Tel 01-2826404
(*Ballybrack-Killiney,
Loughlinstown*, Dublin)

Conlan, Anthony
Chaplain,
St Vincent's University
Hospital
Elm Park, Dublin 4
Tel 01-2694533
(Dublin)

Conlan, Patrick (OFM)
Vicar,
Franciscan House of Studies,
Dún Mhuire, Seafield Road,
Killiney, Co Dublin
Tel 01-2826760

Conlon, Brian, Very Rev, PC
Director,
Boyle Family Life Centre,
Knocknashee, Boyle,
Co Roscommon
Tel 071-9663000
Parish: Cootehall, Boyle,
Co Roscommon
Tel 071-9667004
(*Cootehall*, Elphin)

Conlon, Brian, Very Rev, PP
Carrowmore,
Ballina, Co Mayo
Tel 096-34014
(*Lacken*, Killala)

Conlon, David (OSB)
Glenstal Abbey, Murroe,
Co Limerick
Tel 061-386103

Conlon, John, Very Rev, PP
Parochial House, Duleek,
Co Meath
Tel 041-9823205
(*Duleek*, Meath)

Conlon, Malachy, Very Rev, PP, VF
Top Rath, Carlingford,
Co Louth
Tel 042-9376105
(*Cooley*, Armagh)

Conlon, Noel, CC
Inniskeen, Dundalk,
Co Louth
Tel 042-9378678
(*Inniskeen*, Clogher)

Conlon, Sean (OCD)
Prior,
St Joseph's Carmelite
Retreat Centre,
Termonbacca,
Derry BT48 9XE
Tel 028-71262512

Conlon, Seán, Very Rev, Adm
Ballinakill, Co Laois
Tel 057-8733336
(*Ballinakill*, Kildare & L.)

Connaughton, Finian, Very Rev, PP
Parochial House,
Drumconrath, Navan,
Co Meath
Tel 041-6854146
(*Drumconrath*, Meath)

Connaughton, P. Aloysius (SSC)
St Columban's, Dalgan Park,
Navan, Co Meath
Tel 046-9021525

Connaughton, Patrick
St Columban's, Dalgan Park,
Navan, Co Meath
Tel 046-9021525
(Galway)

Connaughton, Sean (SSC)
Castletown Finea,
Co Westmeath
Tel 043-6681141
(Meath)

Connaughton, Vincent, Very Rev, PP
Killenummery, Dromahair,
via Sligo, Co Leitrim
Tel 071-9164125
(*Killenummery and
Ballintogher*, Ardagh & Cl.)

Connell, Desmond, His
Eminence Cardinal
Emeritus Archbishop of
Dublin,
Archbishop's House,
Drumcondra, Dublin 9
Tel 01-8373732
(Dublin)

Connell, Paul, PhD
President,
St Finian's College,
Mullingar, Co Westmeath
Tel 044-9348672
(Meath)

Connell, Seamus, Very Rev, Adm
24 The Court,
Mulhuddart Wood,
Mulhuddart, Dublin 15
Tel 01-8205480

Connell, Seamus (SSC)
Padres de San Columbano,
Apartado 073/074,
Lima 39, Peru

Connelly, Christopher (OFM)
Franciscan Friary, Killarney,
Co Kerry
Tel 064-6631334/6631066

Connick, Joseph (OFMConv),
CC
Friary of the Visitation,
Fairview Strand, Dublin 3
Tel 01-8376000
(*Fairview*, Dublin)

Connolly, Charles, (Opus Dei)
Gort Ard University
Residence
Rockbarton North, Galway
Tel 091-523846

Connolly, Darragh
(priest in residence)
Tullacmongan, Cavan
(*Cavan (Urney and
Annagelliff)*, Kilmore)

Connolly, Dermot (SPS)
St Patrick's, Kiltegan,
Co Wicklow
Tel 059-6473600

Connolly, Diarmuid, Very Rev
Canon
4 Summerfield Lawn,
Blanchardstown, Dublin 15
(Dublin, retired)

Connolly, Hugh, Rt Rev Mgr,
BA, DD, President,
St Patrick's College,
Maynooth, Co Kildare
Tel 01-6285222
(Dromore)

Connolly, John, Very Rev, PP,
VF
75 Clonfeacle Road,
Blackwatertown,
Dungannon,
Co Tyrone BT71 7HP
(*Moy (Clonfeacle)*, Armagh)

Connolly, Joseph, Very Rev, PP
Parochial House, Donabate,
Co Dublin
Tel 01-8436011
(*Donabate*, Dublin)

Connolly, Michael
54 Wyattville Park,
Loughlinstown, Co Dublin
(Dublin, retired)

Connolly, Michael, CC
Curate's House, Walter
Macken Road,
Mervue, Galway
Tel 091-456527
(*Mervue*, Galway)

Connolly, Patrick (SPS), CC
Parochial House, Roslea,
Co Fermanagh BT92 7QY
Tel 028-67751393
(*Roslea*, Clogher)

Connolly, Patrick, Dr
Theology Department,
Mary Immaculate College,
South Circular Road,
Limerick
Tel 061-204575
(Clogher)

Connolly, Peter, Very Rev, PP
(On sick leave)
Kilgevrin,
Milltown, Go Galway
(Tuam)

Connolly, Philip, Very Rev
Canon, PE
Doohamlet, Castleblayney,
Co Monaghan
Tel 042-9741239
(*Clontibret*, Clogher)

Connolly, Sean, Rt Rev Mgr,
VG
7 Tullyview, Loughguile,
Co Antrim BT44 9JY
(Down & C., retired)

Connolly, Stan (SPS)
St Patrick's, Kiltegan,
Co Wicklow
Tel 059-6473600

Connolly, Terence, Very Rev,
PP
178 Newtownsaville Road,
Omagh, Co Tyrone BT78 2RJ
Tel 028-82841306
(*Eskra*, Clogher)

Connolly, Timothy (CSSp)
Holy Spirit Missionary
College, Kimmage Manor,
Dublin 12
Tel 01-4064300

Connolly, Vincent, Rt Rev
Mgr, PE
The Rock,
Ballyshannon, Co Donegal
Tel 071-9851221
(*Bundoran (Magh Ene)*,
Clogher)

Connor, Philip (OFMCap)
Capuchin Friary,
Friary Street, Kilkenny
Tel 056-7721439

Conroy, Charles (MSC)
Western Road, Cork
Tel 021-4804120

Conroy, Christopher (OCarm)
Whitefriar Street Church,
56 Aungier Street, Dublin 2
Tel 01-4758821

Conroy, Jackie, Very Rev, PP
Aughagower, Westport,
Co Mayo
Tel 098-25057
(*Aughagower*, Tuam)

Conroy, Michael (SPS)
St Patrick's, Kiltegan,
Co Wicklow
Tel 059-6473600

Conroy, Patrick, Very Rev, PP
Ballinakill, Loughrea,
Co Galway
Tel 090-9745021
(*Ballinakill*, Clonfert)

Conry, Anthony
Brazil
(Elphin)

Considine, Patrick, Very Rev
Dean, PE
Gort Mór, Rosmuc,
Co na Gaillimhe
Tel 091-563566
(Galway, retired)

Convey, Martin, Very Rev, BSc,
MLitt, PhD, PP
Straide, Foxford, Co Mayo
Tel 094 9031029
(*Straide*, Achonry)

Conway, Alan, Very Rev, PP
Ballinafad, Boyle,
Co Roscommon
Tel 071-966606
(*Ballinafad (Aghanagh)*,
Elphin)

Conway, Brian (SPS)
Chaplain,
Sligo General Hospital, The
Mall, Sligo
Tel 071-9171111
(Elphin)

Conway, Bernard (SPS)
On temporary diocesan
work

Conway, Eamon
Head of Department of
Theology & Religious
Studies, Mary Immaculate
College, University of
Limerick, South Circular
Road, Limerick
Tel 061-204353
(Limerick)

Conway, Edward, Very Rev, PC
1 Maretimo Gardens West,
Blackrock, Co Dublin
Tel 01-2882248
(*Blackrock*, Dublin)

Conway, Edward (OP), Very
Rev, PP
Prior, St Saviour's,
Upper Dorset Street,
Dublin 1
Tel 01-8897610
(*Dominick Street*, Dublin)

Conway, Kevin (SMA)
Church of Our Lady of the
Rosary and St Patrick,
61 Blackhorse Road,
Walthamstow,
London E17 7AS, UK

Conway, Michael
St Patrick's College,
Maynooth, Co Kildare
Tel 01-6285222
(Galway)

Conway, Michael, Very Rev
Barr Trá, Enniscrone,
Co Sligo
(Killala, retired)

Conway, Noel, Very Rev
(priest in residence)
23 Rathkeltair Road,
Downpatrick,
Co Down BT30 6NL
Tel 024-4461477
(*Downpatrick*, Down & C.)

Conway, Paddy, AP
c/o Westbourne, Ennis,
Co Clare
Tel 065-6849818/
087-6831992
(*Abbey Cluster (Ennis)*,
Killaloe)

Conway, Patrick (SSC)
c/o Bishop's Residence,
Westbourne,
Ennis, Co Clare
Tel 065-6828638

Conway, Patrick G., Very Rev
Warrenpoint Road, Newry,
Co Down
(Dromore, retired)

Conway, Seamus, Rt Rev Mgr,
PE
Parochial House,
Booterstown Avenue,
Co Dublin
(Dublin, retired)

Cooke, Michael, Rt Rev Mgr,
PP, VG, VF
Bridge Street, Belturbet,
Co Cavan
Tel 049-9522109
(*Belturbet (Annagh)*,
Kilmore)

Coonan, Thomas, Rt Rev Mgr,
CC
Geashill, Co Offaly
Tel 057-9343517
(*Killeigh*, Kildare & L.)

Cooney, Brendan (SPS)
Laragh, Castleblayney,
Co Monaghan

Cooney, John, Very Rev, PP
Kilmainhamwood, Kells,
Co Meath
Tel 046-9052129
(*Kilmainhamwood and
Moybologue*, Kilmore)

Cooney, Joseph, Very Rev, PE
25 Carrowmore Meadows,
Knock, Co Mayo
Tel 094-9375933
(Tuam, retired)

Cooney, Kevin (SM)
Superior,
Cerdon, Marist Fathers,
St Mary's Road,
Dundalk, Co Louth
Tel 042-9334019

Cooney, Matthew (OSA)
The Presbytery, Dungarvan,
Co Waterford
(*Dungarvan*, Waterford & L.)

Cooney, Michael, CC
Presbytery 1,
Thormanby Road, Howth,
Co Dublin
Tel 01-8323193
(*Howth*, Dublin)

Cooney, Michael, Very Rev, PP
Terryglass, Nenagh,
Co Tipperary
Tel 067-22017/087-6548331
(*Kilbarron and Terryglass*,
Killaloe)

Cooney, Thomas (OSA)
St John's Priory,
Thomas Street, Dublin 8
Tel 01-6770393

Coote, Tony (SVD)
Donamon Castle,
Roscommon
Tel 090-6662222

Coote, Tony, Very Rev, Adm
79 The Rise, Mount Merrion,
Co Dublin
Tel 01-2889879
(*Kilmacud, Mount Merrion*,
Dublin)

Corbett, John F. (CSsR)
Marianella/Liguori House,
75 Orwell Road, Rathgar,
Dublin 6
Tel 01-4067100

Corbett, Padraig, PP
Castleiney, Templemore
Co Tipperary
Tel 0504-31392
(*Loughmore*, Cashel & E.)

Corbett, Tom, Very Rev Dr,
Co-ordinator
Convent Hill, Roscrea,
Co Tipperary
Tel 0505-21108/086-8418570
Chaplain, Welfare Home,
Roscrea, Co Tipperary
Tel 0505-21389
(*Cronan Cluster (Roscrea)*,
Killaloe)

Corcoran, Gerard, Very Rev,
Co-PP
c/o St Pauls,
Ayrfield, Dublin 13
Tel 01-8160984
c/o Church of the Holy
Trinity, Donaghmede,
Dublin 13
Tel 01-8479822
(*Ayrfield, Donaghmede-
Clongriffin-Balgriffin*,
Dublin)

Corcoran, Gregory, Very Rev,
PP
Rhode, Co Offaly
Tel 087-9402669/
046-9737010
(*Clonbullogue, Rhode*,
Kildare & L.)

Corcoran, James, Very Rev, PP
Cooneal, Ballina, Co Mayo
Tel 096-32242
(*Ballysokeary*, Killala)

Corcoran, Matthew (IC)
Rosmini House, Dunkereen,
Innishannon, Co Cork
Tel 021-4776268/4776923

Corcoran, Michael (MHM)
St Joseph's House,
50 Orwell Park, Rathgar,
Dublin 6
Tel 01-4127773/086-2239051

Corcorcan, Patrick (SM)
Chanel Community,
Coolock, Dublin 5
Tel 01-8477133

Corcoran, Philip, Very Rev, PE
542 River Forest Estate,
Leixlip, Co Kildare
(Dublin, retired)

Corcoran, Thomas, Very Rev,
PP
Slieverue, Co Kilkenny
Tel 051-832773/087-6886678
(*Slieverue*, Ossory)

Corish, Declan (OP), PP
St Saviour's Priory, Kilbarry,
Waterford
Tel 051-376032
(*St Saviour's*, Waterford &
L.)

Corkery, Eamonn, Very Rev,
PP
Dromard, Moyne,
Co Longford
Tel 049-4335248
(*Dromard*, Ardagh & Cl.)

Corkery, Jackie, Very Rev
Canon, PP, VF
Kanturk, Co Cork
Tel 029-50192
(*Kanturk*, Cloyne)

Corkery, James (SJ)
c/o Irish Jesuit Provincialate,
Milltown Park,
Sandford Road, Dublin 6
Tel 01-4987333

Corkery, Michael, Very Rev, PP
Glanworth, Co Cork
Tel 025-38123
(*Glanworth*, Cloyne)

Corkery, Pádraig, Dr
St Patrick's College,
Maynooth, Co Kildare
Tel 01-7083639
(Cork & R.)

Corkery, Patrick, CC
Youghal, Co Cork
Tel 024-92336
(*Youghal*, Cloyne)

Corkery, Seán
Diocesan Advisor for
Religious Education
(Primary)
Director of Adult Faith
Formation
(priest in residence)
Bellevue, Mallow, Co Cork
Tel 086-2420240
(*Mallow*, Cloyne)

Cormac, Pierce
Chaplain,
Mercy University Hospital,
Grenville Place, Cork
Tel 021-4271971
(Cork & R.)

Cormican, Gregory, Very Rev,
PP
72 Nursery Avenue,
Coleraine,
Co Derry BT52 1LR
Tel 028-70343156
(*Coleraine*, Down & C.)

Corr, Sean (SSC)
38 Washingbay Road,
Coalisland,
Co Tyrone BT71 4PU

Corr, Tony, CC
Director of Vocations,
Cathedral Presbytery,
38 Hill Street,
Newry BT34 1AT
Tel 028-30262586
(*Newry Pastoral Area*,
Dromore)

Corrigan, Brendan, Very Rev,
PP
Parochial House,
Harbour Road, Kilbeggan,
Co Westmeath
Tel 057-9332155
(*Kilbeggan*, Meath)

Corrigan, David (SM)
St Brendan's Parish,
Coolock Village, Dublin 5
Tel 01-8484799

Corrigan, Desmond
c/o Ara Coeli,
Armagh BT61 7QY
(Armagh, retired)

Corrigan, Desmond (SMA)
Director, Dromantine
Retreat and Conference
Centre,
Dromantine College,
Newry, Co Down BT34 1RH
Tel 028-30821219

Corrigan, Kevin (CSSp)
Holy Spirit Missionary
College,
Kimmage Manor, Dublin 12
Tel 01-4064300

Corrigan, Patrick J.
Erne Hill, Belturbet,
Co Cavan
(Kilmore, retired)

Corrigan, Peter, Very Rev, PP
Shanco, Newbliss,
Co Monaghan
Tel 047-54011
(*Killeevan*, Clogher)

Corry, Edward
Presbytery 2, Treepark Road,
Kilnamanagh, Dublin 24
(Dublin, retired)

Corry, Francis (SM), CC
Holy Family Parish, Dundalk,
Co Louth
Tel 042-9336301
(*Dundalk, Holy Family*,
Armagh)

Corry, James (CSSp)
Holy Spirit Missionary
College,
Kimmage Manor, Dublin 12
Tel 01-4064300

Cosgrave, William, Very Rev,
PP
Monageer, Ferns,
Enniscorthy, Co Wexford
Tel 053-9233530
(*Monageer*, Ferns)

Cosgrove, John, Very Rev
Canon, PP, VF
Castlebar, Co Mayo
Tel 094-9021274
(*Castlebar (Aglish, Ballyheane
and Breaghwy)*, Tuam)

Cosgrove, Martin, Very Rev
Canon (Moderator), PP, VF
Parochial House, Arklow,
Co Wicklow
Tel 0402-32294
(*Arklow, Aughrim, Avoca,
Castletown*, Dublin)

Costello, Aidan, CC
The Presbytery, Loughrea,
Co Galway
Tel 091-841212
(*Loughrea, St Brendan's
Cathedral*, Clonfert)

Costello, Bernard
Chaplain of Portuincula and
St Brigid's hospitals, Creagh,
Ballinasloe, Co Galway
Tel 090-9644360
(Clonfert)

Costello, David
c/o The Missionary Society
of St James the Apostle,
24 Clark Street, Boston,
MA 02109, USA
(Limerick)

Costello, Denis, Very Rev
Fatima Home, Oakpark,
Tralee, Co Kerry
(Kerry, retired)

Costello, James, Very Rev
Canon, VF
Bruff, Kilmallock,
Co Limerick
Tel 061-382555
(*Bruff/Meanus/Grange*,
Limerick)

Costello, Martin (SMA)
Retired in Ireland outside
SMA houses

Costello, Maurice
Main Street, Rathkeale,
Co Limerick
Tel 069-63452
(Limerick, retired)

Costello, Padraig, Very Rev, PP
Chaplain, St Joseph's
Secondary School,
Foxford, Co Mayo
Tel 094-9860010
Parish: Foxford, Co Mayo
Tel 094-9256131
(*Foxford*, Achonry)

Costelloe, Morgan
Our Lady's Manor,
Bullock Harbour,
Dalkey, Co Dublin
Tel 01-2718007
(Dublin, retired)

Costelloe, Patrick,
Mount Sarto, Lower Park,
Corbally, Limerick
Tel 061 342276/086 244 4528
(Limerick, retired)

Cotter, Bernard (SMA)
African Missions,
Blackrock Road, Cork
Tel 021-4292871

Cotter, Bernard, Very Rev, PP
The Presbytery,
Newcestown,
Bandon, Co Cork
Tel 021-7438000
(*Murragh and
Templemartin*, Cork & R.)

Cotter, Donal, Very Rev, PP
Parochial House,
Watergrasshill,
Co Cork
Tel 021-4889103
(*Watergrasshill*, Cork & R.)

Cotter, Francis (OFM)
Franciscan House of Studies,
Dún Mhuire, Seafield Road,
Killiney, Co Dublin
Tel 01-2826760

Cotter, John, Very Rev, PF
c/o Cork & Ross Offices,
Redemption Road, Cork
(Cork & R., retired)

Cotter, Seán, Very Rev Canon,
PP
Charleville, Co Cork
Tel 063-81319
(*Charleville*, Cloyne)

Coughlan, John, CC
Boyle, Co Roscommon
Tel 071-9662012
(*Boyle*, Elphin)

Coughlan, Patrick (CSSp)
Newlands Institute for
Counselling,
2 Monastery Road,
Clondalkin, Dublin 22
Tel 01-4594573

Coughlan, Thomas, PC
SS Mary and Patrick Parish,
The Presbytery, Avoca,
Co Wicklow
Tel 0402-35204
(*Avoca*, Dublin)

Coughlan, Thomas, Very Rev,
PP
Effin, Kilmallock,
Co Limerick
Tel 063-71314
(*Effin/Garrienderk*, Limerick)

Coulter, Charles (SSC)
St Columban's Retirement
Home, Dalgan Park,
Navan, Co Meath
Tel 046-9021525

Courtney, John J. (MHM)
St Mary's Parish,
25 Marquis Street,
Belfast BT1 1JJ
Tel 028-90320482

Courtney, Patrick (MSC)
Woodview House,
Mount Merrion Avenue,
Blackrock, Co Dublin
Tel 01-2881644

Coveney, Patrick, Most Rev,
AP
Crosshaven, Co Cork
Tel 021-4831218
(*Crosshaven*, Cork & R.)

Cox, Noel (CSSp)
Holy Spirit Missionary
College, Kimmage Manor,
Whitehall Road, Dublin 12
Tel 01-4064300

Cox, Seamus, Very Rev
Ballyleague, Co Roscommon
(Elphin, retired)

Cox, Tom, CC
Ferbane, Co Offaly
Tel 090-6454309
(*Ferbane High Street &
Boora (Tisaran & Fuithre)*,
Ardagh & Cl.)

Coyle, Harry
Moneymore Care Home,
Cookstown Road,
Moneymore,
Co Derry BT45 7QF
(Armagh, retired)

Coyle, Mark (OFMCap)
Capuchin Friary,
Ard Mhuire, Creeslough,
Letterkenny, Co Donegal
Tel 074-9138005

Coyle, Patrick
(elsewhere in the Diocese)
c/o Ara Coeli,
Armagh BT61 7QY
Tel 028-37522045
(Armagh)

Coyle, Paul, CC
194 Navan Road, Dublin 7
Tel 01-8383313/087-1186474
(*Navan Road*, Dublin)

Coyle, Peter (SPS)
St Patrick's, 21 Leeson Park,
Dublin 6
Tel 01-4977897

Coyle, Rory, CC
Parochial House,
42 Abbey Street,
Armagh BT61 7DZ
Tel 028-37522802
(*Armagh*, Armagh)

Coyle, Thomas, Very Rev, PP
Galmoy, Crosspatrick,
via Thurles, Co Kilkenny
Tel 056-8831227/
087-7668969
(*Galmoy*, Ossory)

Coyne, Joseph (Moderator)
St Ciaran's,
36 Ashfield Lawn,
Huntstown, Dublin 15
Tel 01-8216447
(*Hartstown*, Dublin)

Crawford, Alan (OSB)
Glenstal Abbey, Murroe,
Co Limerick
Tel 061-386103

Crawford, Thomas, Very Rev,
PP, VF
Glin, Co Limerick
Tel 068-26897
(*Glin*, Limerick)

Crawley, Michael, Very Rev
Canon, PE, AP
Parochial House,
89 Derrynoose Road, Keady,
Co Armagh BT60 3EZ
Tel 028-3751222
(*Keady (Derrynoose)*,
Armagh)

Creagh, Kieran, CP, CC
Tory Island, Co Donegal
Tel 074-9135505
(*Gortahork (Troy Island)*,
Raphoe)

Creamer, Edmond (CSsR)
Clonard Monastery,
1 Clonard Gardens,
Belfast BT13 2RL
Tel 028-90445950

Crean, Jack (OSA)
Duckspool House
(Retirement Community),
Abbeyside, Dungarvan,
Co Waterford
Tel 058-23784

Crean, Martin (OSA)
The Abbey, Fethard,
Co Tipperary
Tel 052-6131273

Crean, Maurice (MHM)
Organising Secretary,
St Joseph's,
Freshford House, Kilkenny
Tel 056-7721482

Crean, Thomas, Venerable
Archdeacon PP, VF
Kenmare, Co Kerry
Tel 064-6641352
(*Kenmare*, Kerry)

Crean, William, Most Rev, DD
Bishop of Cloyne,
Cloyne Diocesan Centre,
Cobh, Co Cork
Tel 021-4811430
(Cloyne)

Crean-Lynch, Pat, Very Rev, PP
The Presbytery,
Ballymacelligott, Tralee,
Co Kerry
Tel 066-7137118
(*Ballymacelligott*, Kerry)

Cremin, Aidan, CC
Cork Road, Carrigaline,
Co Cork
Tel 021-4372229
(*Carrigaline*, Cork & R.)

Cremin, Gerard, CC
Midleton, Co Cork
Tel 021-4631094
(*Midleton*, Cloyne)

Cremin, Jerry, Very Rev, Adm
Kilbrittain, Co Cork
Tel 023-8849637
(*Kilbrittain*, Cork & R.)

Cremin, Michael (OCarm)
Gort Muire, Ballinteer,
Dublin 16
Tel 01-2984014

Cribben, J. J., Very Rev Canon,
PP
Milltown, Co Galway
Tel 093-51609
(*Milltown (Addergole and
Liskeevey)*, Tuam)

Cribbin, David, Very Rev, PP
Ballindereen, Kilcolgan,
Co Galway
Tel 091-796118
Parochial House, Kinvara,
Co Galway
Tel 091-637154
(*Ballindereen, Kinvara*,
Galway)

Cribbin, James, Very Rev, PP
Geesala, Bangor,
Ballina, Co Mayo
Tel 097-86740
(*Kiltane*, Killala)

Cribbin, Peter, Very Rev
c/o Bishop's House,
Dublin Road, Carlow
(Kildare & L.)

Crilly, Oliver, PP
230b Mayogall Road, Clady,
Portglenone,
Co Derry BT44 8NN
Tel 028-25821190
(*Greenlough*, Derry)

Crilly, Patrick, PEm
35 Rocktown Lane,
Knockloughrim,
Magerafelt,
Co Derry BT45 8QF
(Derry, retired)

Cristóbal, Jimenez A. (SJ)
Jesuit Community,
27 Leinster Road,
Rathmines, Dublin 6
Tel 01-4970250

Crombie, Shane, CC
Parochial House, Tullamore,
Co Offaly
Tel 057-9321587
(*Tullamore*, Meath)

Cronin, Con (SPS), CC
Monkstown, Co Cork
Tel 021-4863267
Passage West, Co Cork
(*Monkstown, Passage West*,
Cork & R.)

Cronin, Isidore (OFM)
Franciscan Friary, Clonmel,
Co Tipperary
Tel 052-6121378

Cronin, Kieran (OFM)
Guardian
Franciscan House of Studies,
Dún Mhuire, Seafield Road,
Killiney, Co Dublin
Tel 01-2826760

Cronin, Tony (SPS)
St Patrick's, Kiltegan,
Co Wicklow
Tel 059-6473600

Crosbie, Paul, CC
Cathedral House, Mullingar,
Co Westmeath
Tel 044-9348338/9340126
(*Mullingar*, Meath)

Crosby, Denis, Very Rev, PP
Liscannor, Co Clare
Tel 065-7081248
(*Liscannor*, Galway)

Crosby, Edward, PP
Parochial House, Kilfenora,
Co Clare
Tel 065-7088006
(*Kilfenora*, Galway)

Crosby, Michael, Very Rev, PP
Shrule, Galway
Tel 093-31262
(*Shrule*, Galway)

Cross, Charles (CP), CC
Holy Cross Retreat,
432 Crumlin Road, Ardoyne,
Belfast BT14 7GE
Tel 028-90748231/2
(*Holy Cross*, Down & C.)

Crossan, Stephen, CC
100 Dromore Street,
Banbridge,
Co Down BT32 4DW
Tel 028-40622274
(*Seapatrick (Banbridge)*,
Dromore)

Crossey, Colin, CC
3 Donard Place, Newcastle,
Co Down BT33 0AJ
Tel 028-43722248
(*Newcastle (Maghera)*,
Down & C.)

Crosson, Eamonn, Very Rev,
Adm
Parochial House, Ashford,
Co Wicklow
Tel 0404-40540
(*Ashford*, Dublin)

Crotty, James, Very Rev, PP
Ferrybank, Waterford
Tel 051-832787/086-8317711
(*Ferrybank*, Ossory)

Crotty, Michael F., Rev Mgr,
BA, JCL, D.ECC Hist.
Sections for Relations With
States, Secretariat of State,
00120 Vatican City
Tel 0039 06 698 83546
(Cloyne)

Crotty, Oliver, Very Rev, Co-PP
Parochial House,
Glendalough, Co Wicklow
Tel 0404-45140
(*Glendalough*, Dublin)

Crotty, Terence (OP)
St Saviour's,
Upper Dorset Street,
Dublin 1
Tel 01-8897610

Crowe, Martin (OP), CC
St Saviour's Priory, Kilbarry,
Waterford
Tel 051-376581
(*St Saviour's*, Waterford &
L.)

Crowe, Patrick (SJ)
Clongowes Wood College,
Clane, Co Kildare
Tel 045-868663/868202

Crowe, Philip (CSSp), CC
Drumgossatt,
Carrickmacross,
Co Monaghan
Tel 042-9661388
(*Magheracloone*, Clogher)

Crowe, Richard
St Paul's Nursing Home,
Dooradoyle, Limerick
(Limerick, retired)

Crowley, Adrian
c/o Archdiocese of
Monrovia, Liberia,
West Africa
(Dublin)

Crowley, Aidan, CC
Doneraile, Co Cork
Tel 022-24120
(*Doneraile*, Cloyne)

Crowley, Brendan, CC
Parochial House, Burt,
Lifford, Co Donegal
Tel 074-9368155
(*Fahan (Burt, Inch and
Fahan)*, Derry)

Crowley, Brendan, Very Rev
Canon, PP, VF
SS Peter and Paul's,
Clonmel, Co Tipperary
Tel 052-6126292
(*Clonmel, SS Peter and
Paul's*, Waterford & L.)

Crowley, Christopher (OCarm)
Provincial Office and
Carmelite Community
Gort Muire, Ballinteer,
Dublin 16
Tel 01-2984014

Crowley, Dan, Very Rev
Canon, PP
The Presbytery,
Lower Road, Cork
Tel 021-4502696
(*St Patrick's*, Cork & R.)

Crowley, Finbarr, PP
Innishannon, Co Cork
Tel 021-4775348
(*Innishannon*, Cork & R.)

Crowley, James, Very Rev, PE
Parochial House,
60 Aughnagar Road,
Ballygawley, Dungannon,
Co Tyrone BT70 2HP
Tel 028-85568399
(Armagh, retired)

Crowley, Kevin (OFMCap)
Vicar, Capuchin Friary,
Church Street, Dublin 7
Tel 01-8730599

Crowley, Liam, PP
Drimoleague, Co Cork
Tel 028-31133
(*Drimoleague*, Cork & R.)

Crowley, Michael, Very Rev
Canon, PE
Ballinlough, Cork
Tel 021-4292684
(*Ballinlough*, Cork & R.)

Crowley, Patrick (SSC)
St Columban's Retirement
Home, Dalgan Park, Navan,
Co Meath
Tel 046-9021525

Crowley, Roderic (CM)
St Vincent's, 122 Sunday's
Well Road, Cork
Tel 021-4304070/4304529

Crowley, Sean, CC
The Presbytery,
Bantry, Co Cork
Tel 027-50193
(*Bantry*, Cork & R.)

Crudden, James, Very Rev, PP
24 Downs Road, Newcastle,
Co Down BT33 0AG
Tel 028-43722401
(*Newcastle (Maghera)*,
Down & C.)

Cryan, Gerard, BA, HDE, STB,
L Eccl Hist
(priest in residence)
St Mary's, Sligo
Tel 071-9162670/9162769
College of the Immaculate
Conception, Summerhill,
Sligo
Tel 071-9160311
(Elphin)

Cryan, Peter (OCD)
St Joseph's, Berkeley Road,
Dublin 7
Tel 01-8306356/8306336

Cudzito, Michat
Chapel Lane, Droichead
Nua, Co Kildare
Tel 045-434069
(*Droichead Nua/Newbridge*,
Kildare & L.)

Cuffe, Bernard (OCD)
The Abbey, Loughrea,
Co Galway
Tel 091-841209

Cuffe, Liam
Chaplain,
St Vincent's Hospital,
Elm Park, Dublin 4
Tel 01-2094325
(Ardagh & Cl.)

Cul, Marek (OP)
St Mary's, The Claddagh,
Co Galway
Tel 091-582884

Culhane, Patrick J., Very Rev
138 Lucan Road, Chapelizod,
Dublin 20
(Dublin, retired)

Cullen, Celestine (OSB), Rt Rev
Dom
Glenstal Abbey,
Murroe, Co Limerick
Tel 061-386103

Cullen, James
6 Meadowvale, Coolcotts,
Wexford
Tel 053-9143932
(*Clonard*, Ferns)

Cullen, John, Very Rev, PP
Kiltoom, Athlone,
Co Roscommon
Tel 090-6489105
(*Kiltoom*, Elphin)

Cullen, Kevin, Very Rev, PP
Parochial House,
Tullynaval Road,
Cullyhanna, Newry,
Co Down BT35 0PZ
Tel 028-30861235
(*Cullyhanna (Creggan
Lower)*, Armagh)

Cullen, Laurence, Very Rev, PP
Geevagh, Boyle,
Co Roscommon
Tel 071-9647107
(*Geevagh*, Elphin)

Cullen, Michael, Very Rev,
Adm
5 St Assam's Road West,
Raheny, Dublin 5
Tel 01-8313806
(*Raheny*, Dublin)

Cullen, Seamus
2 Ceol Na Mara,
Lower Main Street,
Rush, Co Dublin
Tel 01-8438024
(Dublin, retired)

Culligan, Patrick, Very Rev
Carrigaholt, Co Clare
Tel 065-9058043/
087-9863865
(*Carrigaholt and Cross*,
Killaloe)

Cullinan, Alphonsus, Very Rev
Canon, PP
Lower Main Street,
Rathkeale, Co Limerick
Tel 061-63133
(*Rathkeale*, Limerick)

**Allianz (ⅲ)**

Cullinan, Edmond, Very Rev
Canon, PP, VF
Parochial House,
Chapel Street,
Carrick-on-Suir, Co Tipperary
Tel 051-640168
(*Carrick-on-Suir*, Waterford
& L.)

Cullinan, William (OCSO)
Mellifont Abbey,
Collon, Co Louth
Tel 041-9826103

Cullinane, Michael, Very Rev,
PP, VF
Parochial House, Lismore,
Co Waterford
Tel 058-54246
(*Lismore*, Waterford & L.)

Cullinane, Timothy (MSC)
Myross Wood Retreat
House, Leap, Skibbereen,
Co Cork
Tel 028-33118

Culliton, James (SJ)
Jesuit Curia Community,
Loyola House,
Milltown Park,
Sandford Road, Dublin 6
Tel 01-2180276

Culloty, Tom, PE
Ballydesmond,
Mallow, Co Cork
Tel 087 2850824
(Galway, retired)

Cully, Patrick (CSSp)
Cherry Orchard Hospital,
Ballyfermot, Dublin 10
Tel 01-6264702
Holy Spirit Missionary
College, Kimmage Manor,
Dublin 12
Tel 01-4064300

Cumiskey, Bonaventure
(OCSO)
Mount Melleray Abbey,
Cappoquin, Co Waterford
Tel 058-54404

Cumiskey, Cathal (CSsR)
St Joseph's, Dundalk,
Co Louth
Tel 042-9334042/9334762

Cummings, Daniel
30 Knapton Road,
Dun Laoghaire, Co Dublin
Tel 01-2804353
(Opus Dei)

Cummins, John, Very Rev,
Adm
Episcopal Vicar for
Education & Evangelisation,
The Presbytery,
Dublin Road, Carlow
Tel 059-9131227
(*Cathedral, Carlow*, Kildare
& L.)

Cummins, Stephen (OP)
Ennismore Retreat Centre,
Ennismore, Montenotte,
Cork
Tel 021-4502520

Cummins, William, Very Rev
Canon, PP
Parochial House,
Ennistymon, Co Clare
Tel 065-7071063
(*Ennistymon*, Galway)

Cunnane, Fergal, PP, VF
Dunmore, Co Galway
Tel 093-38124
(*Dunmore*, Tuam)

Cunningham, Charles (SDB)
Rinaldi House,
72 Sean McDermott Street,
Dublin 1
Tel 01-8363358

Cunningham, Colm (CSSp)
Rockwell College, Cashel,
Co Tipperary
Tel 062-61444

Cunningham, Connell, Very
Rev, PE
Carrick, Co Donegal
(Raphoe, retired)

Cunningham, Conor, PP, VF
The Rectory, Lisdoonvarna,
Co Clare
Tel 065-7074142
(*Lisdoonvarna and
Kilshanny*, Galway)

Cunningham, Donal, Very
Rev, PP
Upperchurch, Thurles,
Co Tipperary
Tel 0504-54181
(*Upperchurch*, Cashel & E.)

Cunningham, Enda, Very Rev,
PP
St Mary's Parochial House,
Saggart, Co Dublin
Tel 01-4589209/087-1380695
(*Saggart*, Dublin)

Cunningham, Gerald (IC)
Clonturk House,
Ormond Road,
Drumcondra, Dublin 9
Tel 01-6877014

Cunningham, Gerard, CC
Director of Vocations,
Fintown, Donegal Town,
Co Donegal
Tel 074-9546107
(*Glenties*, Raphoe)

Cunningham, John Joe, Very
Rev
Newcastle, Co Down
(Dromore, retired)

Cunningham, John M. (OP)
Prior, Convent of SS Xystus
and Clement,
Collegio San Clemente,
Via Labicana 95,
00184 Roma
Tel 0039-06-7740021

Cunningham, Joseph (CM),
Very Rev
St Paul's, Raheny, Dublin 5
Tel 01-8314011/2/3

Cunningham, Martin, Very
Rev, PP
Drumoghill, Co Donegal
Tel 074-9157169
(*Drumoghill (Raymochy)*,
Raphoe)

Cunningham, Matthew, Very
Rev, PE
Care Choice Nursing Home,
The Burgery, Dungarvan,
Co Waterford
(Waterford & L., retired)

Cunningham, PJ (OCarm)
Gort Muire, Ballinteer,
Dublin 16
Tel 01-2984014

Cunningham, Seán, CC
The Presbytery, Chapel
Street, Castlebar,
Co Mayo
Tel 094-9021844
(*Castlebar (Aglish,
Ballyheane and Breaghwy)*,
Tuam)

Cunningham, Sean (OP)
Holy Cross, Sligo, Co Sligo
Tel 071-9142700

Cunningham, Tom (CSSp)
Rockwell College,
Cashel, Co Tipperary
Tel 062-61444

Curran, Adrian (OFMCap),
Very Rev
Provincial Minister,
Provincial Office,
12 Halston Street, Dublin 7
Tel 01-8733205

Curran, Anthony, Very Rev,
PP,
St Mary's Presbytery,
12 Ballymena Road,
Portglenone,
Co Antrim BT44 8BL
Tel 028-25821218
(*Portglenone*, Down & C.)

Curran, Colum, Very Rev
(priest in residence)
Parochial House,
Glenavy Road, Crumlin,
Co Antrim BT29 4LA
Tel 028-94422278
(*Glenavy and Killead*, Down
& C.)

Curran, Eugene (CM)
St Vincent's College,
Castleknock, Dublin 15
Tel 01-8213051

Curran, James
61 Tournane Court,
Dungarvan, Co Waterford
Tel 058-45177
(Waterford & L., retired)

Curran, Matthew (OSA)
St Augustine's,
Taylor's Lane,
Balyboden, Dublin 16
Tel 01-4241000

Curran, Michael (MSC)
Leader & Director,
Myross Wood Retreat
House, Leap, Skibbereen,
Co Cork
Tel 028-33118
Parish House, Union Hall,
Skibbereen, Co Cork
Tel 028-34940
(*Castlehaven*, Cork & R.)

Curran, Michael, Very Rev, PE
c/o Bishop's House,
John's Hill, Waterford
(Waterford & L., retired)

Curran, Philip, Very Rev, Co-PP
231 Beech Park, Lucan,
Co Dublin
Tel 01-6281756
(*Lucan*, Dublin)

Curran, Roderick (CSSp), CC
104 St Joseph's Road,
Greenhills, Dublin 12
Tel 01-4506617
(*Greenhills*, Dublin)

Curran, Thomas
Glenview House,
College Road, Letterkenny,
Co Donegal
Tel 074-9127617
(Raphoe, retired)

Curran, Thomas (SMA)
SMA House,
82 Ranelagh Road,
Ranelagh, Dublin 6
Tel 01-4968162/3

Currivan, Patrick, Very Rev, AP
Caherconlish, Co Limerick
Tel 061-351248
(*Caherconlish*, Cashel & E.)

Curry, Colum, Rt Rev Dean,
PP, VG
Parochial House,
4 Circular Road,
Dungannon,
Co Tyrone BT71 6BE
Tel 028-87722775
(*Dungannon (Drumglass,
Killyman and Tullyniskin)*,
Armagh)

Curry, Martin (SJ)
Superior,
John Sullivan House,
House of Formation,
27 Leinster Road,
Rathmines, Dublin 6
Tel 01-5242134

Curtin, Tim, Very Rev, PP
Kilcolman, Ardagh,
Co Limerick
Tel 069-60126
(*Coolcappa*, Limerick)

Curtis, James, Very Rev
3 Oldtown Court,
Clongreen, Foulksmills,
New Ross, Co Wexford
(Ferns, retired)

Curtis, James B., Very Rev
Canon
Rathjarney, Drinagh,
Co Wexford
(Ferns, retired)

Curtis, Thomas, Very Rev
Canon
2 The Hollows, Lugduff,
Tinahely, Co Wicklow
(Ferns, retired)

Cusack, John, CC
Ballinamore, Co Leitrim
Tel 071-9644050
(Ballinamore (Oughteragh),
Kilmore)

Cusack, Michael (CSsR) Adm
St Joseph's,
St Alphonsus Road,
Dundalk, Co Louth
Tel 042-9334042
(Dundalk, St Joseph's,
Armagh)

Cusack, Ronan (OP), Very Rev
St Malachy's, Dundalk,
Co Louth
Tel 042-9334179

Cushen, Bernard, Very Rev, PP
Clonroche, Enniscorthy,
Co Wexford
Tel 053-9244115
(Cloughbawn and
Poulpeasty, Ferns)

Cushen, Patrick, Very Rev, PP
Ferns, Enniscorthy,
Co Wexford
Tel 053-9366152
(Ferns, Ferns)

Cushenan, Jarlath, Very Rev,
PP
17 Castlewellan Road,
Hilltown, Newry BT34 5UY
Tel 028-40630206
(Clonduff (Hilltown),
Dromore)

Cushnahan, Vincent, CC
St Paul University,
Deschatelets Residence,
175 Main Street, Ottawa,
Ontario KIS IC3, Canada
(Down & C.)

Cushnan, Martin (CSsR)
Redemptorist Community,
R.C. Church,
Morrispet P.O., Tenali,
Guntur DT 522 202,
Andhra Pradesh, India
Tel 0091-8644-223-382

Cussen, Joseph, Very Rev, PP
'Lisieux', Glenfield Road,
Kilmallock, Co Limerick
Tel 063-98061
(Bulgaden/Martinstown,
Limerick)

Cussen, Michael, Very Rev, PP,
VF
Ballybrown, Clarina,
Co Limerick
Tel 061-353711
(Patrickswell/Ballybrown,
Limerick)

## D

D'Arcy, Aidan, CC
2 Knightswood,
Coolock Lane, Santry,
Dublin 9
Tel 01-8428283
(Larkhill-Whitehall-Santry,
Dublin)

D'Arcy, Brian (CP)
Superior,
St Gabriel's Retreat,
The Graan, Enniskillen,
Co Fermanagh
Tel 028-66322272

D'Arcy, Paul A. (SMA)
Provincial Secretary,
African Missions,
Blackrock Road, Cork
Tel 021-4292871

D'Souza, Darryl (SDB)
c/o Salesian House,
45 St Teresa's Road,
Crumlin, Dublin 12
Tel 01-4555605
(India)

D'Souza, Richard (SJ)
St Francis Xavier's
Upper Gardiner Street,
Dublin 1
Tel 01-8363411

Daffy, Flannan (CSsR)
St Patrick's, Esker, Athenry,
Co Galway
Tel 091-844007

Dagens, Seamus, Very Rev, PP
Ballintra, Co Donegal
Tel 074-9734016
(Ballintra, Raphoe)

Dallat, Ciaran, Very Rev, AP
St Peter's Cathedral
Presbytery,
St Peter's Square,
Belfast BT12 4BU
Tel 028-90327573
(The Cathedral (St Peter's),
Down & C.)

Dalton, John (OFM)
4 McSweeney House,
Berkeley Road, Dublin 7
Tel 01-2826760

Dalton, Patrick, Very Rev
Canon, PP, VF
Gowran, Co Kilkenny
Tel 056-7726128/
086-8283478
(Gowran, Tullaherin, Ossory)

Dalton, Thomas, Very Rev, PP
Riverchapel,
Courtown Harbour,
Gorey, Co Wexford
Tel 053-9425241
(Riverchapel, Courtown
Harbour, Ferns)

Dalton, William, Very Rev, PP
Callan, Co Kilkenny
Tel 056-7725287/
086-8506215
(Callan, Ossory)

Daly, Brian, Very Rev, PP
Parochial House,
15 Moyle Road, Ballycastle,
Co Antrim BT54 6LB
Tel 028-20762223
Administration Ballintoy
(Ballintoy, Ballycastle
(Ramoan), Down & C.)

Daly, Daniel (SVD)
Maynooth, Co Kildare
Tel 01-6286391/2

Daly, Edmond, Very Rev, AP
Mount Bolus, Tullamore,
Co Offaly
Tel 057-9354035
(Kilcormac, Meath)

Daly, Edward, Most Rev, DD
Retired Bishop of Derry,
9 Steelstown Road,
Derry BT48 8EU
Tel 028-71359809
(Derry)

Daly, Gabriel (OSA)
St Augustine's,
Taylor's Lane,
Balyboden, Dublin 16
Tel 01-4241000

Daly, Gerard (SDS)
Saint John's House,
West Rock, Ballyshannon,
Co Donegal
Tel 071-9851541

Daly, James (CSSp)
Holy Spirit College,
Kimmage Manor,
Whitehall Road,
Dublin 12
Tel 01-4064300

Daly, Jeremiah (MSC)
Western Road, Cork
Tel 021-4804120

Daly, John, Very Rev, PP
St Mochta's, Porterstown,
Dublin 15
Tel 01-8213218
(Porterstown-Clonsilla,
Dublin)

Daly, John, Very Rev, PP
Bruff, Kilmallock,
Co Limerick
Tel 087-8180815
(Bruff/Meanus/Grange,
Limerick)

Daly, Kevin (OCSO)
Mount Saint Joseph Abbey,
Roscrea, Co Tipperary
Tel 0505-25600

Daly, Martin (SM)
Catholic University School,
89 Lower Leeson Street,
Dublin 2
Tel 01-6762586

Daly, Martin J., Very Rev
On sabbatical
(Dublin)

Daly, Michael V., Very Rev, PE
35 Herbert Place, Navan,
Co Meath
Tel 046-9093935
(Meath, retired)

Daly, Michael, Very Rev, PP
Broomfield, Castleblayney,
Co Monaghan
Tel 042-9743617
(Donaghmoyne, Clogher)

Daly, Noel (SSC)
St Columban's, Dalgan Park,
Navan, Co Meath
Tel 046-9021525

Daly, Pádraig A. (OSA)
Prior, St John's Priory,
Thomas Street, Dublin 8
Tel 01-6770393/0415/0601

Daly, Patrick, Very Rev, PE
Braganza, Athy Road,
Carlow
(Kildare & L., retired)

Daly, Peter (OMI)
Oblate House of Retreat,
Inchicore, Dublin 8
Tel 01-4534408/4541805

Daly, Philip, CC
Kilclooney, Co Donegal
Tel 074-9545114
(Ardara, Raphoe)

Daly, Thomas, Very Rev, PP
Parochial House,
Boicetown, Togher,
Drogheda, Co Louth
Tel 041-6852110
(Togher, Armagh)

Dalzell, Tony (SM)
St Teresa's, Donore Avenue,
Dublin 8
Tel 01-4542425/4531613
(Donore Avenue, St Teresa's,
Dublin)

Danaher, Michael (OSA)
St Augustine's Priory,
O'Connell Street, Limerick
Tel 061-415374

Daniels, Iomar, Very Rev, PP
St Andrew's Church,
Leitrim, Loughrea,
Co Galway
(Leitrim and Ballyduggan
(Kilcooley and Leitrim),
Clonfert)
Killoran, Ballinasloe,
Co Galway
Tel 091-841758 for both
parishes
(Kilmeen, Tuam)

Darby, Derek, PP
54 Brookville, Ashbourne,
Co Meath
Tel 01-8350547
(*Ashbourne-Donaghmore*,
Meath)

Darby, Gary, Co-PP
146 Seapark, Malahide,
Co Dublin
Tel 01-8454172
21 Wheatfields Grove,
Portmarnock, Co Dublin
(*Malahide, Portmarnock*,
Dublin)

Dardis, John (SJ)
c/o Irish Jesuit Provincialate,
Milltown Park,
Sandford Road, Dublin 6
Tel 01-4987333

Darragh, Anthony (CSSp)
Holy Spirit Missionary
College,
Kimmage Manor, Dublin 12
Tel 01-4064300

Darragh, Vincent, Very Rev,
PE, AP
'Lisieux', 99 Loup Road,
Moneymore,
Co Derry, BT45 7ST
Tel 028-79418946
(*Ardboe*, Armagh)

Davern, Richard, CC
Ballyduane, Clarina,
Co Limerick
Tel 061-353529
(*Mungret/Crecora*, Limerick)

Davey, Gerard, CC
Swinford, Co Mayo
Tel 094-9253338
(*Swinford (Kilconduff and
Meelick)*, Achonry)

Davies, Anthony, Very Rev
Canon
Killowen, Rostrevor
(Dromore, retired)

Davies, Dean A.,
42 Old Killowen Road,
Rosstrevor,
Co Down BT34 3AD

Davis, Patrick (SJ)
Peter Faber House,
28 Brookvale Avenue,
Belfast BT14 6BW
Tel 028-90757615

Davitt, Norman (SVD)
Donamon Castle,
Roscommon
Tel 090-6662222

Davitt, Thomas (CM)
St Paul's, Raheny, Dublin 5
Tel 01-8314011/2/3

Davy, Charles (SJ)
St Ignatius Community &
Church, 27 Raleigh Row,
Salthill, Galway
Tel 091-523707

Dawson, Laurence, Very Rev
Canon, PE
25 Teiges Hill,
Brookeborough,
Co Fermanagh BT94 4EZ
Tel 028-89531770
(*Brookeboro (Aghavea-
Aghintaine), Clogher*,
Clogher)

de Bhaldraithe, Eoin (OCSO)
Bolton Abbey, Moone,
Co Kildare
Tel 059-8624102

de Burca, Peadar, Very Rev
Kilmeedy, Co Limerick
Tel 063-87008
(Limerick, retired)

De Lima, Eridian Goncalves
(CSsR)
Missionaries Redentoristas,
Caixa Postal 85,
60,000-970 Fortaleza,
Est. do Ceara, Brazil
Tel +55-8532232016

De Val, Seamus, Very Rev
Canon
1 Irish Street, Bunclody,
Co Wexford
Tel 053-9376140
(Ferns, retired)

Deasy, Declan (OSA)
St Augustine's Priory,
St Augustine's Street,
Galway
Tel 091-562524

Deasy, John F., Very Rev Mgr,
(Team Assistant)
55 St Agnes' Road, Crumlin,
Dublin 12
Tel 01-4550955
(*Crumlin*, Dublin)

Deegan, Gerard, Adm
Presbytery, Montrose Park,
Beaumont, Dublin 5
Tel 01-8710013
(*Beaumont*, Dublin)

Deegan, Joseph, Very Rev, PP
Parochial House, Slane,
Co Meath
Tel 041-9824249
(*Slane*, Meath)

Deegan, Sean (SPS)
Director of Promotion,
St Patricks,
Kiltegan, Co Wicklow
Tel 059-6473600

Deegan, Stan, Very Rev, PP
Parochial House,
Batterstown, Dunboyne,
Co Westmeath
Tel 01-8259267
(*Kilcloon*, Meath)

Deely, Pat
Dunkerrin, Birr, Co Offaly
Tel 0505-45982/087-6329913
(*Dunkerrin*, Killaloe)

Deeney, Edward (SMA)
Dromantine College,
Dromantine, Newry,
Co Down BT34 1RH
Tel 028-30821224

Deenihan, Thomas
Cork & Ross Offices,
Redemption Road, Cork
Tel 021-4301717
(Cork & R.)

Deery, Cathal, CC
34 Lacky Road, Drumswords,
Roslea,
Co Fermanagh BT92 7NQ
Tel 028-67751231
(*Clones*, Clogher)

Deighan, Gerard, Very Rev,
Adm
Parochial House,
Harrington Street, Dublin 8
Tel 01-4751506
(*Harrington Street*, Dublin)

Delahunty, Richard (CSsR),
Very Rev, PP
The Presbytery,
197 Kylemore Road,
Ballyfermot, Dublin 10
Tel 01-6264789

Delaney, Denis M., Very Rev
(Moderator)
Parochial House, Naul,
Co Dublin
Tel 01-8412932
(*Naul*, Dublin)

Delaney, James (CSSp)
Templeogue College,
Templeville Road,
Dublin 6W
Tel 01-4903909

Delaney, Joe, Very Rev Canon
Chaplain's Office,
Galway Clinic,
Doughiska, Galway
Tel 091-785000
(Galway)

Delaney, John, CC
Coon, Carlow
Tel 056-4443116/
086-8596321
(*Muckalee*, Ossory)

Delaney, John, Very Rev, PP
Parochial House, Kilrossanty,
Kilmacthomas,
Co Waterford
Tel 051-291985
(*Kilrossanty*, Waterford & L.)

Delaney, Joseph, Very Rev
Strathmore Nursing Home,
Callan, Co Kilkenny
Tel 086-8206730
(Ossory, retired)

Delaney, Joseph, Very Rev, AP
Clonbealy, Newport,
Co Tipperary
Tel 061-378126
(*Newport*, Cashel & E.)

Delaney, Martin, Very Rev, PP
Rathdowney, Co Laois
Tel 0505-46282
(*Rathdowney*, Ossory)

Delany, John, Very Rev, Adm
24 Barclay Court,
Blackrock, Co Dublin
Tel 01-2832302
(*Blackrock*, Dublin)

Delargy, David, Very Rev, PP
200 Finaghy Road North,
Belfast BT11 9EG
Tel 028-90615174
(*St Michael's*, Down & C.)

Delargy, Patrick, Very Rev, PP,
VF
Parochial House,
4 Broughshane Road,
Ballymena,
Co Antrim BT43 7DX
Tel 028-25641515
(*Ballymena (Kirkinriola)*,
Down & C.)

Dempsey, Luke (OP)
Dominican Community,
St Mary's Priory, Tallaght,
Dublin 24
Tel 01-4048100

Dempsey, Michael (CSsR)
Santa Maria dei Monti
Mission, Furancungo,
Mozambique, Africa
c/o Marianella/Liguori House
75 Orwell Road,
Rathgar, Dublin 6
Tel 01-4067100

Dempsey, Michael Vincent,
Very Rev, PP
The Presbytery, Barndarrig,
Co Wicklow
Tel 0404-48130
(*Kilbride and Barndarrig*,
Dublin)

Dempsey, Paul, CC, VF
The Presbytery, Ballymany,
Droichead Nua, Co Kildare
Tel 045-434069
(*Droichead Nua/Newbridge*,
Kildare & L.)

Dempsey, Raymond, CC
Ferrybank, Waterford
Tel 051-832577/087-2859682
(*Ferrybank*, Ossory)

Denmead, James, CC
Ballylooby, Cahir,
Co Tipperary
Tel 052-7441489
(*Ballylooby*, Waterford & L.)

Dennehy, Philip, Very Rev, PE
4 Stanhope Place, Athy,
Co Kildare
Tel 059-8631696
(Dublin, retired)

Denny, Aidan, Very Rev
10 New Barnsley Green,
New Barnsley,
Belfast BT12 7HS
Tel 028-90328877
(*Corpus Christi*, Down & C.)

Denvir, John (SMA)
Dromantine College,
Dromantine,
Newry, Co Down BT34 1RH

Dermody, Eamonn, Very Rev
Canon, PE
Clarinbridge, Co Galway
Tel 091-796208
(Galway, retired)

Desmond, Diarmuid, Very Rev,
PP
Kilrane, Co Wexford
Tel 053-9133128
(Kilrane and St Patrick's,
Ferns)

Desmond, Garrett, Very Rev,
PP
Newcastle, Clonmel,
Co Tipperary
Tel 052-6136387
(Newcastle and
Fourmilewater, Waterford &
L.)

Desmond, Patrick
The Lodge, Mount Sackville,
Chapelizod, Dublin 20
Tel 01-8214004
(Dublin)

Devaney, Owen, Very Rev, PP
Mullahoran,
Kilcogy via Longford,
Co Cavan
Tel 043-6683141
(Mullahoran and Loughduff,
Ardagh & Cl.)

Deveney, Cathal, CC
Our Lady of Lourdes
Presbytery,
Hardman's Gardens,
Drogheda, Co Louth
Tel 041-9831899
(Drogheda, Armagh)

Devenish, Martin (MCCJ)
Provincial, Comboni
Missionaries, London Road,
Sunningdal, Berks Sl5 OJY,
UK

Devereux, Sean
Our Lady of Fatima Parish,
Bwiam, Roman Catholic
Mission, PO Box 165, Banjul,
The Gambia, West Africa
Tel 00220-7878991
(Ferns)

Devine, Arthur, Very Rev, PE
Abbeybreaffy Nursing
Home, Castlebar, Co Mayo
(Tuam, retired)

Devine, James, CC
20 Loughermore Road,
Ogill, Ballykelly,
Co Derry BT49 9PD
Tel 028-77762721
(Limavady, Derry)

Devine, Liam, Very Rev Canon,
PP, VG
SS Peter and Paul's, Athlone
Tel 090-6492171
(Athlone, SS Peter and
Paul's, Elphin)

Devine, Oliver J., Very Rev, PP
Parochial House,
Mountnugent, Co Cavan
Tel 049-8540123
(Mountnugent, Meath)

Devine, Oliver, Very Rev, PP
Drumraney, Athlone,
Co Westmeath
Tel 044-9356207
(Drumraney, Tang, Meath)

Devine, Robert
(priest in residence)
Crossroads, Killygordon,
Co Donegal
Tel 074-9149194
(Killygordon (Donaghmore),
Derry)

Devitt, Dan (SDB)
Mission Procurator,
Salesian College,
Pallaskenry, Co Limerick
Tel 061-393313

Devitt, Patrick, Adm
No. 1 Prebytery,
Castle Street, Dalkey,
Co Dublin
Tel 01-2857773
(Dalkey, Dublin)

Devitt, Séamus (CSsR)
St Patrick's, Esker,
Co Galway
Tel Tel 091-844007

Devlin, Anthony, Very Rev, PP
St Paul's Presbytery,
125 Falls Road,
Belfast BT12 6AB
Tel 028-90325034
(St Paul's, Down & C.)

Devlin, Brendan, Rt Rev Mgr,
MA, DD
St Patrick's College,
Maynooth, Co Kildare
Tel 01-6285222
(Derry)

Devlin, Eamon (CM), Very Rev
Provincial, Provincial Office,
St Paul's, Sybil Hill,
Raheny, Dublin 5
Tel 01-8510840/8510842

Devlin, Patrick, PP
St Vincent de Paul
Presbytery,
169 Ligoniel Road,
Belfast BT14 8DP
Tel 028-90713401
(St Vincent de Paul, Down &
C.)

Devlin, Peter, PP
Parochial House,
Malin, Co Donegal
Tel 074-9370615
(Malin (Clonca), Derry)

Diggin, Fintan, PP
Parochial House, Cleagh,
Clonmany, Co Donegal
Tel 074-9376264
(Clonmany, Derry)

Dillon, Christopher (OSB), Rt
Rev Dom
Glenstal Abbey, Murroe,
Co Limerick
Tel 061-621000

Dillon, Sean, Very Rev, PP
Parochial House,
Greencastle Road, Kilkeel,
Co Down BT34 4DE
Tel 028-41762242
(Kilkeel (Upper Mourne),
Down and C.)

Dillon, Thomas, Very Rev, PP
Baltinglass, Co Wicklow
Tel 059-6482768
(Baltinglass, Kildare & L.)

Dineen, Joseph (OP)
Prior, Newbridge College,
Driochead Nua, Co Kildare
Tel 045-487200

Dobbin, Séamus, CC
St Patrick's Presbytery,
Roden Place, Dundalk,
Co Louth
Tel 042-9334648
(Dundalk, St Patrick's,
Armagh)

Dodd, Michael (SSC)
St Columban's, Dalgan Park,
Navan, Co Meath
Tel 046-9021525

Doherty, Brendan, PEm,
4 Garvagh Road, Kilrea,
Co Derry BT51 5QP
Tel 028-29540343
(Derry, retired)

Doherty, Cathal (SJ)
Irish Jesuit Provincialate,
Milltown Park,
Sandford Road, Dublin 6
Tel 01-4987333

Doherty, George, CC
Glebe, Linsfort, Buncrana,
Co Donegal
Tel 074-9361126
(Buncrana, Derry)

Doherty, John (CSsR)
Clonard Monastery,
1 Clonard Gardens,
Belfast BT13 2RL
Tel 028-90445950

Doherty, John, PEm
Parochial House,
447 Victoria Road,
Ballymagorry, Strabane,
Co Tyrone BT82 0AT
Tel 028-718802274
(Derry, retired)

Doherty, John, Rt Rev Mgr
(priest in residence),
Charlestown, Co Mayo
Tel 094-9255793
(Achonry, retired)

Doherty, Kevin, CC
Parochial House, Celbridge,
Co Kildare
Tel 01-6288827
(Celbridge, Dublin)

Doherty, Michael, PP
39 Melmount Road,
Strabane,
Co Tyrone, BT82 9EF
Tel 028-71882648
(Melmount, Derry)

Doherty, Patrick, Very Rev, PP
159 Glen Road, Maghera,
Co Derry BT46 5JN
Tel 028-79642496
(Maghera, Derry)

Doherty, Richard, Very Rev,
AP
Abbeyside, Dungarvan,
Co Waterford
Tel 058-42379
(Abbeyside, Waterford & L.)

Doherty, Sean (SSC)
St Columban's Retirement
Home, Dalgan Park, Navan,
Co Meath
Tel 046-9021525

Doherty, Tom, CC
Cathedral Presbytery,
Ballina, Co Mayo
Tel 096-71365

Dolan, Andrew, PP, VG
25 Ballynease Road,
Bellaghy, Magherafelt,
Co Derry BT45 8JS
Tel 028-79386259
(Bellaghy (Ballyscullion),
Derry)

Dolan, Denis, Very Rev, PP
Fivemiletown,
Co Tyrone BT75 OQP
Tel 028-89521291
(Brookeboro, Clogher)

Dolan, Gerard, Rt Rev Mgr, PP
St Columba's, Rosses Point,
Co Sligo
Tel 071-9177133
(Rosses Point, Elphin)

Dolan, John, Rt Rev Mgr, LCL
The Chancellery,
Archbishop's House,
Dublin 9
Tel 01-8379253
(Dublin)

Dolan, Joseph (SSC)
St Columban's, Dalgan Park,
Navan, Co Meath
Tel 046-9021525

Dolan, Martin, Adm
The Presbytery,
Francis Street, Dublin 8
Tel 01-4544861/086-4035318
(Francis Street, Dublin)

Dollard, James, Very Rev
Donoughmore, Johnstown,
Co Kilkenny
(Ossory, retired)

Donaghy, Kevin
(priest in residence)
St Patrick's Grammar School,
Cathedral Road,
Armagh BT61 7QZ
Tel 028-37522018
(Armagh)

Donegan, Gary, Very Rev (CP)
Superior, Holy Cross Retreat,
432 Crumlin Road,
Ardoyne,
Belfast BT14 7GE
Tel 028-90748231/2
(Holy Cross, Down & C.)

Donleavy, James (OP)
Black Abbey, Kilkenny,
Co Kilkenny
Tel 056-7721279

Donlon, Chris, CC
Dromore, Mallow, Co Cork
Tel 022-21198
(Glantane, Cloyne)

Donnellan, David (OCD), PP
Prior,
St Joseph's, Berkeley Road,
Dublin 7
Tel 01-8306356/8306336
(Berkeley Road, Dublin)

Donnellan, Patrick, Very Rev,
PP
Islandeady, Castlebar,
Co Mayo
Tel 094-9024125
(Islandeady, Tuam)

Donnelly, Brian, PP
Parochial House,
Plumbridge, Omagh,
Co Tyrone BT79 8EF
Tel 028-81648283
(Plumbridge (Badoney
Upper), Derry)

Donnelly, David CC
4 Darling Street,
Enniskillen,
Co Fermanagh BT74 7DP
Tel 028-66322075
(Enniskillen, Clogher)

Donnelly, Francis, Rt Rev
Archdeacon, PE
64 Meadow Grove,
Dundalk, Co Louth
Tel 042-9353264
(Armagh, retired)

Donnelly, Gerald, Very Rev
Canon
Ballygar, Co Galway
(Elphin, retired)

Donnelly, James
Herbertstown, Hospital,
Co Limerick
Tel 061-385104
(Hospital, Cashel & E.)

Donnelly, John, Very Rev
Rathcabbin, Roscrea,
Co Tipperary
Tel 057-9139072
(Killaloe, retired)

Donnelly, Joseph, Rt Rev Mgr,
PP, VF
52 Brook Street, Omagh,
Co Tyrone BT78 5HE
Tel 028-82243011
(Omagh, Derry)

Donnelly, Kevin, Venerable
Archdeacon
Parochial House,
4 Broughshane Road,
Ballymena,
Co Antrim BT43 7DX
Tel 028-25641515
(Ballymena (Kirkinriola),
Down & C.)

Donnelly, Liam, PEm
20 Loughermore Road,
Ogill, Ballykelly,
Co Derry BT49 9PD
Tel 028-77762721
(Derry, retired)

Donnelly, Michael, Very Rev,
PP
Drumcliff, Sligo
Tel 071-9142779
(Drumcliff/Maugherow,
Elphin)

Donnelly, Mícheál, CC, Adm
The Presbytery, Castlerea,
Co Roscommon
Administration Fairymount
Fairymount, Castlerea,
Co Roscommon
Tel 094-9620039
(Castlerea, Fairymount
(Tibohine), Elphin)

Donnelly, Patrick, PP
Parochial House,
Collinstown, Co Westmeath
Tel 044-9666326
(Collinstown, Meath)

Donnelly, Peter, Very Rev, PP,
VF
Parochial House,
15 Drumaroad Hill,
Castlewellan,
Co Down BT31 9PD
Tel 028-44811474
(Drumaroad and
Clanvaraghan, Down & C.)

Donnelly, Peter, Very Rev, PP,
VF
Parochial House,
130 Ballinderry Bridge Road,
Coagh, Cookstown,
Co Tyrone BT80 0AY
Tel 028-79418244
(Ballinderry, Armagh)

Donnelly, Raymond CC
4 Darling Street, Enniskillen,
Co Fermanagh BT74 7DP
Tel 028-66322075
(Enniskillen, Clogher)

Donnelly, Victor (CP)
St Gabriel's Retreat,
The Graan, Enniskillen,
Co Fermanagh
Tel 028-66322272

Donohoe, Eamon (MSC)
'Croí Nua', Rosary Lane,
Taylor's Hill, Galway
Tel 091-520960

Donohoe, Kevin, Adm
The Presbytery, Cavan
Tel 049-4331404
(Cavan (Urney and
Annagelliff), Kilmore)

Donohoe, Patrick (SSC)
Columban Sisters,
Magheramore, Co Wicklow

Donohoe, Séamus (OFM)
Franciscan Friary,
Friary Lane,
Athlone, Co Westmeath
Tel 090-6472095

Donohoe, Sean (OFMCap)
Capuchin Friary,
Friary Street, Kilkenny
Tel 056-7721439

Donohoe, Steve (SPS)
St Patrick's, Main Street,
Knock, Co Mayo
Tel 094-9388661

Donovan, Bernard, Very Rev,
PP
Cloughdubh, Crookstown,
Co Cork
Tel 021-7336054
(Kilmurry, Cork & R.)

Donovan, Patrick (CSSp)
Holy Spirit Missionary
College, Kimmage Manor,
Dublin 12
Tel 01-4064300

Donovan, Roy, PP
Caherconlish, Co Limerick
Tel 061-450730
(Caherconlish, Cashel & E.)

Donworth, John, Very Rev, PP
Kildimo, Co Limerick
Tel 061-394134/087-2237501
(Kildimo and Pallaskenry,
Limerick)

Doocey, Colin, Very Rev, PP
1 The Presbytery,
Holy Cross Church,
Mahon, Cork
Tel 021-2414624
(Mahon, Cork & R.)

Doody, Patrick (CSSp)
22 Glenquin Manor,
Knockane Road,
Newcastle West,
Co Limerick
Tel 069-77473

Doohan, Martin, Very Rev, PP
Dunfanaghy,
Co Donegal
Tel 074-9136163
(Dunfanaghy, Raphoe)

Doohan, Michael (SSC)
St Columban's, Dalgan Park,
Navan, Co Meath
Tel 046-9021525

Dooher, Patrick G. (SSC)
St Columban's, Dalgan Park,
Navan, Co Meath
Tel 046-9021525

Doolan, Herman (OCD)
53/55 Marlborough Road,
Dublin 4
Tel 01-6601832

Dooley, Francis Desmond,
Very Rev
75 Tritonville Road,
Sandymount, Dublin 4

Dooley, John (SJ)
Milltown Park,
Sandford Road, Dublin 6
Tel 01-2698411/2698113

Dooley, Maurice, Rt Rev Mgr,
AP
Loughmore, Templemore,
Co Tipperary
Tel 0504-31375
(Loughmore, Cashel & E.)

Dooley, Seán, Very Rev, PP
Parochial House, Tullyallen,
Drogheda, Co Louth
Tel 041-9838520
(Mellifont, Armagh)

Dooley, Thomas, Very Rev, PP,
Adm
Patrick Street,
Portarlington, Co Laois
Tel 057-8643004
Administration Emo
(Emo, Portarlington, Kildare
& L.)

Dooley, Tom (SM), CC
4 Greenmount Road,
Terenure, Dublin 6
Tel 01-4904959
(Terenure, Dublin)

Doran, Dermot (CSSp)
Holy Spirit Missionary
College,
Kimmage Manor,
Whitehall Road, Dublin 12
Tel 01-4064300

Doran, Fonsie (CSsR)
Clonard Monastery,
1 Clonard Gardens,
Belfast BT13 2RL
Tel 028-90445950

Doran, Joseph, AP
Parochial House,
43 Beechwood Avenue
Upper,
Ranelagh, Dublin 6
Tel 01-4967449
(Beechwood Avenue,
Dublin)

Doran, Kevin, Most Rev, MA,
PhD
Bishop of Elphin
St Mary's, Temple Street,
Sligo
Tel 071-9150106
(Elphin)

Doran, Senan (OSA)
St Augustine's,
Taylor's Lane,
Balyboden, Dublin 16
Tel 01-4241000

Dorgan, Michael, Very Rev, PP
Castlemagner, Mallow,
Co Cork
Tel 022-27600
(*Castlemagner*, Cloyne)

Dorr, Donal (SPS)
St Patrick's, 21 Leeson Park,
Dublin 6
Tel 01-4977897

Dougherty, Ciarán (OP)
Collegio San Clemente,
Via Labicana 95,
00184 Roma
Tel 0039-06-7740021

Dowd, G. (SDB)
Chaplain, Custume Barracks,
Athlone
Tel 0902-21277

Dowd, Gerard, CF
Chaplain, Custume Barracks,
Athlone, Co Westmeath
Tel 090-6421277
(Elphin)

Dowd, Thomas
Ely University Centre,
10 Hume Street, Dublin 2
Tel 01-6767420
(Opus Dei)

Dowley, Martin (OCSO)
Prior,
Our Lady of Bethlehem
Abbey, 11 Ballymena Road,
Portglenone, Ballymena,
Co Antrim BT44 8BL
Tel 028-25821211

Dowling, Cornelius
St Anthony's,
13 Richmond Grove,
Monkstown, Co Dublin
Tel 01-2800789
(Dublin, retired)

Dowling, Peter (SSS)
62 Langlands Road,
Govan, Glasgow G51 3BD
Scotland
Tel 0044-141-4451416

Dowling, Sean (OSA)
St Augustine's Priory,
Washington Street, Cork
Tel 021-275398

Downes, Edward, CC
Parochial House,
St Joseph's Parish Cross,
Valleymount, Co Wicklow
Tel 045-867151
(*Valleymount*, Dublin)

Downes, Frank (OP)
St Dominic's Retreat House,
Montenotte, Co Cork
Tel 021-4502520

Downes, Patrick (CSSp)
Rockwell College, Cashel,
Co Tipperary
Tel 062-61444

Downes, Teddy, CC,
Parochial House, Cross,
Valleymount,
Co Wicklow
Tel 045-867151
(*Valleymount*, Dublin)

Downey, James (OSA)
St Patrick's College and
Church, Via Piemonte 60,
00187 Rome, Italy
Tel 00396-4203121

Downey, Jim
Fatima Home, Oak Park
Tralee, Co Kerry
(Kerry, retired)

Downey, John, CC
36 Moneyneena Road,
Draperstown, Magherafelt,
Co Derry BT45 7DZ
Tel 028-79628375
(*Ballinascreen*
(*Draperstown*), Derry)

Downey, Martin, Very Rev
Canon, PP
24 Presentation Road,
Galway
Tel 091-562276
(*St Joseph's*, Galway)

Downing, Mortimer, Very Rev,
PE
(priest in residence)
Stuake, Donoughmore,
Co Cork
Tel 021-7437815
(Cloyne, retired)

Doyle, Andrew, Very Rev, PP
Durhamstown, Bohermeen,
Navan, Co Meath
Tel 046-9073805
(*Bohermeen*, Meath)

Doyle, Bernard
Kiltyclogher, Co Leitrim
Tel 071-9854302
(Kilmore, retired)

Doyle, Brian (OP)
St Saviour's,
Upper Dorset Street,
Dublin 1
Tel 01-8897610

Doyle, Derek, Very Rev
(Moderator)
Parochial House,
Rathdrum, Co Wicklow,
Tel 0404-46229
(*Rathdrum*, Dublin)

Doyle, Denis, Very Rev, PP
Kilmore, Co Wexford
Tel 053-9135181
(*Kilmore*, Ferns)

Doyle, Desmond G., Co-PP
Parochial House, 1 River
Valley Heights,
Swords, Co Dublin
Tel 01-8403400
(*River Valley*, Dublin)

Doyle, Gerald (MHM)
St Joseph's,
Mill Hill Missionaries,
Waterford Road, Kilkenny
Tel 056-7721482

Doyle, Gerard, CC
59 Auburn Road,
Dun Laoghaire, Co Dublin
Tel 01-2852509
(*Johnstown-Killiney*, Dublin)

Doyle, James, CC
Mulrankin,
Co Wexford
Tel 053-9135166
(*Kilmore and Kilmore Quay*,
Ferns)

Doyle, Jimmy, Very Rev, PP
Cooleragh,
Coill Dubh, Naas, Co Kildare
Tel 045-860281
(*Cooleragh and
Staplestown*, Kildare & L.)

Doyle, Martin, Very Rev, PP
Cushinstown,
Foulksmills, Co Wexford
Tel 051-428347
(*Cushinstown*, Ferns)

Doyle, Michael A., CC
St Leonard's, Saltmills,
New Ross, Co Wexford
Tel 051-562135
(*Ballycullane*, Ferns)

Doyle, Noel (SSC)
St Columban's, Dalgan Park,
Navan, Co Meath
Tel 046-9021525

Doyle, Owen (SSC)
St Columban's, Dalgan Park,
Navan, Co Meath
Tel 046-9021525

Doyle, Thaddeus
Shillelagh, Arklow,
Co Wicklow
Tel 053-9429926
(Ferns)

Doyle, Thomas, Very Rev, PP
Craanford, Gorey,
Co Wexford
Tel 053-9428163
(*Craanford*, Ferns)

Draper, Anthony, DD
All Hallows College,
Drumcondra, Dublin 9
Tel 01-373745
(Meath)

Drennan, Martin, Most Rev,
DD
Bishop of Galway,
Mount Saint Mary's,
Taylor's Hill, Galway
Tel 091-563566
(Galway)

Drennan, Michael (SJ)
Rector, Manresa House,
Dollymount, Dublin 3
Tel 01-8331352

Drumm, Eugene (SPS)
On temporary diocesan
work

Drumm, Michael, PC
47 Westbury Drive, Lucan,
Co Dublin
Tel 01-5031106
(*Esker-Doddsboro-
Adamstown*, Dublin)

Drumm, Michael
Columba Centre, St Patrick's
College, Maynooth
(Elphin)

Drury, Ronan
St Patrick's College,
Maynooth, Co Kildare
Tel 01-6285222
(Meath)

Duddy, Brendan (SJ)
Milltown Park,
Sandford Road, Dublin 6
Tel 01-2698411/2698113

Duffy, Aquinas T., Very Rev,
PP
23 Wainsfort Park, Terenure,
Dublin 6W
Tel 01-4900218
(*Templeogue*, Dublin)

Duffy, Bernard, Very Rev, PE
St Mary's Nursing Home,
Shantalla Road, Galway
Tel 091-540540
(Galway, retired)

Duffy, Dominic (MSC)
Myross Wood Retreat
House, Leap, Skibbereen,
Co Cork
Tel 028-33118

Duffy, Eddie (SM)
Holy Family Parish,
Parochial House, Dundalk,
Co Louth
Tel 042-9336301

Duffy, Eugene, DD
Mary Immaculate College,
South Circular Road,
Limerick
Tel 061-204968
(Achonry)

Duffy, Francis, Most Rev, DD
Bishop of Ardagh and
Clonmacnois,
St Michael's, Longford,
Co Longford
Tel 043-3346432
(Ardagh & C.)

Duffy, Hugh P. (SJ)
35 Lower Leeson Street,
Dublin 2
Tel 01-6761248

Duffy, John Joe, CC
Assistant, Marriage Tribunal,
The Pastoral Centre,
Letterkenny,
Co Donegal
Tel 074-9121853
Parish: Parochial House,
Stranorlar, Co Donegal
Tel 074-9131157
(*Stranorlar*, Raphoe)

Duffy, Joseph, Most Rev, DD
Bishop Emeritus,
Doire na gCraobh,
Monaghan
Tel 047-62725
(Clogher)

Duffy, Kevin, CC
Castleblayney,
Co Monaghan
Tel 042-9740629
(Castleblayney (Muckno),
Clogher)

Duffy, Larry (SM)
Rome

Duffy, Larry, Rt Rev Mgr
St Joseph's, Carrickmacross,
Co Monaghan
Tel 042-9663200
(Carrickmacross (Machaire
Rois), Clogher)

Duffy, Michael (OFMCap)
Capuchin Friary,
Station Road, Raheny,
Dublin 5
Tel 01-8313886

Duffy, Michael (SSC)
St Columban's Retirement
Home, Dalgan Park, Navan,
Co Meath
Tel 046-9021525

Duffy, Pat (CP)
Provincial, St Paul's Retreat,
Mount Argus, Dublin 6W
Tel 01-4992050

Duffy, Patrick, CC
Kilmyshall, Enniscorthy,
Co Wexford
Tel 053-9377188
(Bunclody, Ferns)

Duffy, Stephen, Very Rev, PE,
AP
Parochial House, Collon,
Co Louth
Tel 041-9826106
(Ardee & Collon, Armagh)

Duggan, Brendan (CSSp)
Holy Spirit Missionary
College, Kimmage Manor,
Whitehall Road, Dublin 12
Tel 01-4064300

Duggan, Colm (CSSp)
Holy Spirit Missionary
College,
Kimmage Manor, Whitehall
Road, Dublin 12
Tel 01-4064300

Duggan, Frank
Parochial House No. 2,
Bonnybrook, Dublin 17
Tel 01-8485194
(Bonnybrook, Dublin)

Duggan, Iain (OFM)
Franciscan Friary,
Liberty Street, Cork
Tel 021-4270302

Duggan, James (OP)
Holy Cross, Tralee,
Co Kerry
Tel 066-7121135/29185

Duggan, James F. (CSSp)
Holy Spirit Missionary
College, Kimmage Manor,
Dublin 12
Tel 01-4064300

Duggan, John
St John and Paul Church,
341 South Main Street,
Coventary RI R102816-5987,
USA
(Ossory)

Duggan, John, Very Rev, PP
Castlemahon, Co Limerick
Tel 069-72108/086-2600464
(Mahoonagh, Limerick)

Duggan, Michael (CSSp)
St Mary's College,
Rathmines, Dublin 6
Tel 01-499 5760

Duggan, Patrick, Very Rev
Canon, PE
Bennetsbridge, Co Kilkenny
Tel 056-7727140/087-
6644858
(Tullaherin, Ossory)

Duggan, Roger (MSC)
Western Road, Cork
Tel 021-4804120

Duggan, Seán (CSsR), Very
Rev, PP
Presbytery, 103 Cherry
Orchard, Dublin 10
Tel 01-6267930
(Cherry Orchard, Dublin)

Duhig, Frank, Very Rev Canon,
PP, VF
St Ita's Presbytery,
Newcastle West, Co Limerick
Tel 069-62141/087-6380299
Adm, Monagea Parish
(Monagea, Newcastle West,
Limerick)

Duignan, Michael, Very Rev,
SThD, EV
Diocesan Secretary &
Chancellor, St Mary's,
Temple Street, Sligo
Tel 071-9150106
(Elphin)

Dullea, Gearóid, Dr
St Patrick's College,
Maynooth, Co Kildare
(Cork & R.)

Duncan, James (CSSp)
Holy Spirit Missionary
College, Kimmage Manor,
Whitehall Road, Dublin 12
Tel 01-4064300

Dundon, Patrick (CSSp)
Blackrock College,
Blackrock, Co Dublin
Tel 01-2888681

Dunlea, Philip (CSsR)
Clonard Monastery,
1 Clonard Gardens,
Belfast BT13 2RL
Tel 028-90445950

Dunleavy, John (SMA)
African Missions,
Claregalway, Co Galway
Tel 091-798880

Dunleavy, Michael, Very Rev
(OP)
Convent of SS. Xystus and
Clement,
Collegio San Clemente,
Via Labicana 95, 00184
Roma
Tel 0039-06-7740021

Dunne, Aidan, CC
Parochial House,
9 Chapel House,
Bessbrook, Newry,
Co Down BT35 7AU
Tel 028-30830272
(Bessbrook (Killeavy Lower),
Armagh)

Dunne, Bonaventure (OSB)
Glenstal Abbey, Murroe,
Co Limerick
Tel 061-386103

Dunne, Daniel, Very Rev, PP
Tullamoy, Stradbally,
Co Laois
Tel 059-8627123
(Ballyadams, Kildare & L.)

Dunne, Edward, Rt Rev Mgr,
PE
Knightsbridge Nursing
Home, Trim, Co Meath
(Meath, retired)

Dunne, Gerard (OP)
Prior,
St Mary's, Pope Quay, Cork
Tel 021-4502267

Dunne, Liam (SVD)
1 & 3 Pembroke Road,
Dublin 4
Tel 01-6680904

Dunne, Liam, Very Rev
The Forge, Martin's Lane,
Upper Main Street, Arklow,
Co Wicklow
Tel 0402-32779
(Ossory, retired)

Dunne, Matthew (MHM)
St Joseph's House,
50 Orwell Park, Rathgar,
Dublin 6
Tel 01-4127700

Dunne, Michael (CM)
St Paul's College, Raheny,
Dublin 5
Tel 01-8318113

Dunne, Patrick, Very Rev, PP
Parochial House,
Kilmacrennan, Letterkenny
Co Donegal
Tel 074-9139018
(Kilmacrennan, Raphoe)

Dunne, Paul, CC
Apt 1 The Presbytery,
Balbriggan, Co Dublin
Tel 01-9680594
(Balbriggan, Dublin)

Dunne, Ronald, CC
(priest in residence)
60 Grange Park Grove,
Raheny, Dublin 5
Tel 086-4513904
(Edenmore, Grange Park,
Dublin)

Dunne, Thomas (SDB)
Salesian House,
45 St Teresa's Road,
Crumlin, Dublin 12
Tel 01-4555605

Dunne, Thomas, CC
Bóthar na Naomh
Presbytery,
Thurles, Co Tipperary
Tel 0504-22042/22688
(Thurles, SS Joseph and
Brigid, Cashel & E.)

Dunne, Victor (SPS)
Society Leader, St Patrick's
Kiltegan, Co Wicklow
Tel 059-6473600

Dunning, Brendan (SMA)
SMA House,
Claregalway, Co Galway
Tel 091-798880

Dunny, Patrick, Very Rev
Wood Road,
Graignamanagh,
Co Kilkenny
Tel 059-9724518
(Kildare & L.)

Dunphy, John, Very Rev
On sabbatical
(Dublin)

Dunphy, John, Very Rev, Adm
Graiguecullen, Co Carlow
Tel 059-9141833
(Graiguecullen, Kildare & L.)

Dunphy, Laurence, Very Rev
Canon
Urlingford, Co Kilkenny
Tel 087-2300849
(Ossory, retired)

Dunphy, Noel, Very Rev, PE,
CC
Mountmellick, Co Laois
Tel 057-8624141
(Mountmellick, Kildare & L.)

Dunphy, Paul
Two-Mile-House,
Naas, Co Kildare
Tel 045-876160
(Naas, Kildare & L.)

Durajczyk, Tadeusz (SVD), CC
Polish Chaplaincy,
60 College Orchard,
Newbridge, Co Kildare
Tel 0862354320

Durkan, John, Very Rev, PP
Killasser, Swinford, Co Mayo
Tel 094-9251431
(Killasser, Achonry)

Durnin, Brian, CC
12 Brookwood Grove,
Artane, Dublin 5
Tel 01-8187996
(Artane, Dublin)

Fennelly, Sean
Barrysfarm, Hospital,
Co Limerick
Tel 061-383565
(*Knockainey*, Cashel & E.)

Fennelly, William (OSB)
Glenstal Abbey, Murroe,
Co Limerick
Tel 061-386103

Fennessy, Ignatius (OFM)
Franciscan House of Studies,
Dún Mhuire, Seafield Road,
Killiney, Co Dublin
Tel 01-2826760

Fenning, Hugh (OP)
St Mary's Priory, Tallaght,
Dublin 24
Tel 01-4048100

Fergus, Austin, Very Rev
Canon, PP
Mayo Abbey, Claremorris,
Co Mayo
Tel 094-9365086
(*Mayo Abbey (Mayo and Rosslea)*, Tuam)

Ferguson, Chris, CC
Parochial House,
32 Chapel Road, Waterside,
Derry BT47 2BB
Tel 028-71342303
(*Waterside (Glendermott)*,
Derry)

Ferguson, Gerard, Very Rev
Canon, PE
Rockcorry, Monaghan
Tel 042-9742243
(Clogher, retired)

Ferris, Brendan, PP
Parochial House, Curraha,
Co Meath
Tel 01-8350136
(*Ardcath*, Meath)

Ferris, John, Co-PP
75 Ludford Drive,
Dundrum, Dublin 16
Tel 01-2988746
(*Meadowbrook*, Dublin)

Ferris, Stephen, Very Rev, PP
Keele University, England
(Dromore)

Ferry, Francis, CC
Arranmore Island,
Co Donegal
Tel 074-9520504
(*Burtonpont (Kincasslagh)*,
Raphoe)

Ferry, Manus (MSC), Very Rev,
PP
Sacred Heart Parish,
Killinarden, Tallaght,
Dublin 24
Tel 01-4522251
(*Killinarden*, Dublin)

Field, Raymond, Most Rev,
DD, VG
Titular Bishop of Ard Mor
and Auxiliary Bishop of
Dublin,
3 Castleknock Road,
Blanchardstown, Dublin 15
Tel 01-8209191
(Dublin)

Fillie, Michael (CSSp)
Spiritan House,
213 North Circular Road,
Dublin 7
Tel 01-8389664/8683504

Finan, James, Very Rev Canon,
CC
Colloney, Co Sligo
Tel 071-9167109
(*Collooney (Kilvarnet)*,
Achonry)

Fingleton, James, Very Rev
Canon
279 Howth Road, Raheny,
Dublin 5
(Dublin, retired)

Fingleton, John, Very Rev, PE
Hillview Nursing Home,
Tullow Road, Carlow
Tel 059-9139407
(Kildare & L., retired)

Finn, John, Very Rev, PE
Moorehall Lodge Nursing
Home, Hale Street, Ardee,
Co Louth
Tel 041-6871942
(Armagh, retired)

Finn, John (MSC), CC
The Presbytery, Killinarden,
Tallaght, Dublin 24
Tel 01-4522251
(*Killinarden*, Dublin)

Finn, Tony (OSA)
Rector Ecclesiae, St Patrick's
College and Church,
Via Piemonte 60,
00187 Rome, Italy
Tel 00396-4203121

Finn, William (OCD)
St Teresa's,
Clarendon Street, Dublin 2
Tel 01-6718466/6718127

Finnegan, Eamonn (SMA)
Superior, SMA House,
Claregalway, Co Galway
Tel 091-798880

Finnegan, John (SDB)
Salesian House,
45 St Teresa's Road,
Crumlin, Dublin 12
Tel 01-4555605

Finnegan, John, Very Rev
Canon, PE
51 Arney Road,
Mullymesker, Enniskillen,
Co Fermanagh BT92 2AB
Tel 028-66348217
(*Arney (Cleenish)*,
*Derrygonnelly (Botha)*,
Clogher)

Finnegan, Larry (SVD)
Donamon Castle,
Roscommon
Tel 090-6662222

Finnegan, Thomas, Very Rev,
PP
Liscarnan, Magheracloone,
Carrickmacross,
Co Monaghan
Tel 042-9663500
(*Magheracloone*, Clogher)

Finneran, Michael, Very Rev,
PP, VF
Clontuskert, Ballinasloe,
Co Galway
Tel 090-9642256
(*Clontuskert*, Clonfert)

Finnerty, Liam (OCD)
Prior, The Abbey, Loughrea,
Co Galway
Tel 091-841209

Finnerty, Paul
Diocesan Secretary and
Spokesperson,
Diocesan Office,
Social Service Centre,
Henry Street, Limerick
Tel 061-315856
(Limerick)

Finnerty, Peter, Very Rev, PP,
VF
2 Maypark, Malahide Road,
Dublin 5
Tel 01-8313722
(*Donneycarney*, Dublin)

Finucane, Gerard
St John's Presbytery, Tralee,
Co Kerry
Tel 068-7122522
(*Tralee, St John's*, Kerry)

Finucane, John A. (CSSp)
Holy Spirit Missionary
College, Kimmage Manor,
Dublin 12
Tel 01-4064300

Fitzgerald, Brendan
St Barnabas Church,
409 East 241 Street,
Bronx, New York 10470 USA

Fitzgerald, Christopher, Very
Rev PP
The Presbytery,
Frankfield, Cork
Tel 021-4361711
(*Frankfield-Grange*, Cork &
R.)

Fitzgerald, Dan (SSC)
St Columban's Retirement
Home, Dalgan Park, Navan,
Co Meath
Tel 046-9021525

Fitzgerald, Ger, CC
Cathedral Presbytery,
Ennis, Co Clare
Tel 065-6824043/
086-1697595
(*Abbey Cluster (Ennis)*,
Killaloe)

Fitzgerald, Jack, Very Rev
Canon, PP
Millstreet, Co Cork
Tel 029-70043
(*Millstreet*, Kerry)

Fitzgerald, John, Very Rev
(MSC)
Western Road, Cork
Tel 021-4804120

Fitzgerald, John, Very Rev, PP
Abbeydorney, Co Kerry
Tel 066-7135146
(*Abbeydorney*, Kerry)

Fitzgerald, John, Very Rev, PP
Parish Administrator
Rockhill, Bruree,
Co Limerick
087-6522746
(*Rockhill/Bruree*, Limerick)

Fitzgerald, Joseph, Very Rev
Canon, PP, VF
Castlerea, Co Roscommon
Tel 094-9620040
(*Castlerea (Kilkeevan)*,
Elphin)

Fitzgerald, Michael, Very Rev,
PP, VF
Buttevant, Co Cork
Tel 022-23195
(*Buttevant*, Cloyne)

Fitzgerald, Michael, Very Rev
Canon, PP, VF
Mitchelstown, Co Cork
Tel 025-84090
(*Mitchelstown*, Cloyne)

Fitzgerald, Michael (OSA),
St Augustine's,
Taylor's Lane,
Ballyboden, Dublin 16
Tel 01-4241000

Fitzgerald, Norman (CSSp)
Blackrock College,
Blackrock, Co Dublin
Tel 01-288 8681

Fitzgerald, Patrick, Very Rev,
PE
Priest's House, Ballinameela,
Cappagh, Co Waterford
Tel 058-68021
(Waterford & L., retired)

Fitzgerald, Patrick, Very Rev,
PP
(priest in charge)
Parochial House, Lisduggan,
Waterford
Tel 051-372257
(*Butlerstown*, Waterford &
L.)

Fitzgerald, Tadhg, Very Rev,
PP
Ardfert, Co Kerry
Tel 066-7134131
Ardfert Retreat Centre
Tel 066-7134276
(*Ardfert*, Kerry)

Allianz (ⅠⅠ)

Fitzgerald, William (OPraem), Rt Rev
Prelate Administrator,
Abbey of the Most Holy Trinity and St Norbert,
Kilnacrott Abbey,
Ballyjamesduff, Co Cavan
Tel 049-8544416
(Kilmore)

Fitzgibbon, Éamonn, Rt Rev, VG
Ballyduane, Clarina,
Co Limerick
Tel 087-6921191
(Limerick)

Fitzgibbon, John, Very Rev Canon, PE
Parochial House,
Chapel Road, Lusk,
Co Dublin
Tel 01-8438023
(Dublin, retired)

Fitzmaurice, William, Very Rev Canon, PP
Croom, Co Limerick
Tel 061-397231
(Banogue, Croom, Limerick)

Fitzpatrick, Bernard, CC
Swanlinbar, Co Cavan
Tel 049-9521221/087-3899345
(Kinawley/Killeher, Kilmore)

Fitzpatrick, Brian, CC
70 North Street, Lurgan,
Co Armagh, BT67 9AH
Tel 028-38323161
(Shankill, St Paul's & St Peter's (Lurgan), Dromore)

Fitzpatrick, James
8 Alderbrook Ferns,
Enniscorthy, Co Wexford
(Ferns, retired)

Fitzpatrick, Jeremiah (OCD)
St Joseph's Carmelite Retreat Centre,
Termonbacca,
Derry BT48 9XE
Tel 028-71262512

Fitzpatrick, John (CSSp)
Holy Spirit Missionary College, Kimmage Manor,
Whitehall Road, Dublin 12
Tel 01-4064300

Fitzpatrick, John, Very Rev
116 Strangford Road,
Ardglass BT30 7SS
(Down & C., retired)

Fitzpatrick, John, Very Rev, PP
Carbury, Co Kildare
Tel 046-9553355
(Carbury, Kildare & L.)

Fitzpatrick, John V., Rt Rev Mgr, EV
(Moderator)
3 Glencarrig, Church Road,
Sutton, Dublin 13
Tel 01-8323147
(Howth, Sutton, Dublin)

Fitzpatrick, P.J., Very Rev, PP
Gowna, Co Cavan
Tel 043-6683120
(Lough Gowna and Mullinalaghta, Ardagh & Cl.)

Fitzpatrick, Patrick (Alan) (OCarm)
Whitefriar Street Church,
56 Aungier Street, Dublin 2
Tel 01-4758821

Fitzpatrick, Tom, Very Rev, PP
Newmarket-on-Fergus,
Co Clare
Tel 061-700883/087-2720187
(Newmarket-on-Fergus, Killaloe)

Fitzpatrick, William (OMI), Co-PP
Superior, Oblate Fathers,
House of Retreat,
Inchicore, Dublin 8
Tel 01-4541117
(Inchicore, Mary Immaculate, Dublin)

Fitzsimons, Anthony, Very Ref, PP
470 Falls Road, Belfast, BT12 6EN
Tel 028-90321511
(St John's, Down & C.)

Fitzsimons, Patrick, Very Rev Canon
Holy Family Residence,
Roebuck, Dundrum,
Dublin 14
(Dublin, retired)

Fitzsimons, William, Very Rev, PP
Parochial House, Milltown,
Rathconrath, Co Westmeath
Tel 044-9355106
(Milltown, Meath)

Fives, Thomas (OCarm)
Gort Muire, Ballinteer,
Dublin 16
Tel 01-2984014

Flaherty, John, Very Rev Canon, VF
(Team Moderator)
Parochial House,
Sperrin Road, Drimnagh,
Dublin 12
Tel 01-4556103
(Mourne Road, Dublin)

Flaherty, Raymond, Adm (pro-tem)
Headford, Co Galway
Tel 093-35448
(Headford (Killursa and Killower), Tuam)

Flanagan, Benny, Very Rev, PP
Carrabane, Athenry,
Co Galway
Tel 091-841103
(Clostoken and Kilconieran, Clonfert)

Flanagan, Eamon (CM)
St Paul's College, Raheny,
Dublin 5
Tel 01-8318113

Flanagan, John (SPS)
Fairfields Care Centre,
80A Fairhill Road,
Cookstown,
Co Tyrone BT80 8DE
(Armagh, retired)

Flanagan, John, CC
Roslea, Enniskillen,
Co Fermanagh BT92 7QY
Tel 028-67751393
(Roslea, Clogher)

Flanagan, Joseph (SSC)
St Columban's, Dalgan Park,
Navan, Co Meath
Tel 046-9021525

Flanagan, Malachy (SMA)
Vice Provincial,
African Missions, Feltrim,
Blackrock Road, Cork
Tel 021-4292871
Provincial Bursar,
Blackrock Road, Cork

Flanagan, Padraig, (SPS)
St Patrick's, Kiltegan,
Co Wicklow
Tel 059-6473600
(Kiltegan, Kildare and L.)

Flanagan, Richard (SVD), Adm
Ballyvaughan, Co Clare
Tel 065-7077045
(Ballyvaughan, Galway)

Flannery, Anthony (CSsR)
St Patrick's, Esker, Athenry,
Co Galway
Tel 091-844007

Flannery, John D., Very Rev Canon, PE
Cartron, Milltown,
Co Galway
(Tuam, retired)

Flannery, Paschal, Very Rev
Ballinderry, Nenagh,
Co Tipperary
Tel 067-22916/086-2225099
(Killaloe, retired)

Flannery, Peter (CSsR)
Marianella/Liguori House,
75 Orwell Road, Dublin 6
Tel 01-4067100

Flavin, John P. (CSSp)
St Mary's College,
Rathmines, Dublin 6
Tel 01-4995760

Flavin, Nicholas, Very Rev, PP
Dunamaggan, Co Kilkenny
Tel 056-7728173/087-2257498
Windgap, Co Kilkenny
Tel 051-648111
(Dunamaggan, Windgap, Ossory)

Fleck, Robert, Very Rev, PP
Parochial House,
Dundrum, Newcastle,
Co Down BT33 0LU
Tel 028-43751212
(Dundrum and Tyrella, Down & C.)

Fleming, David, Co-PP
94 Old County Road,
Crumlin, Dublin 12
Tel 01-4542308
(Crumlin, Dublin)

Fleming, Gerard (SAC), CC
437 South Circular Road,
Rialto, Dublin 8
Tel 01-4533268
(Dolphin's Barn/Rialto, Dublin)

Fleming, John Kevin (MSC)
Western Road, Cork
Tel 021-4804120

Fleming, John, Most Rev, DD, DCL
Bishop of Killala,
Bishop's House, Ballina,
Co Mayo
Tel 096-21518
(Killala)

Fleming, Joseph, Very Rev, CC
Clonegal, Enniscorthy,
Co Wexford
Tel 053-9377298
(Clonegal, Kildare & L.)

Fleming, Kevin (SSC)
St Columban's, Dalgan Park,
Navan, Co Meath
Tel 046-9021525
(Meath)

Fleming, Michael, Very Rev Canon, PP, VF
The Presbytery, Killorglin,
Co Kerry
Tel 066-9761172
(Killorglin, Kerry)

Fleming, Paul, BA, BD, STL
St Mary's University College,
191 Falls Road,
Belfast 12 6FE
Tel 028-90327678
(Down & C.)

Fleming, Seamus (CSSp)
Holy Spirit Missionary College,
Kimmage Manor, Dublin 12
Tel 01-4064300

Fleming, William (MSC)
Carrignavar, Co Cork
Tel 021-4884044

Fletcher, Robert, CC
Dealginis, Garraun Upper,
Ballinahinch, Birdhill,
via Killaloe, Co Clare
Tel 061-379862
(Ballinahinch, Cashel & E.)

Flood, Jonathan, CC
Cleeslough, Co Donegal
Tel 074-9138011
(Dunfanaghy (Clondahorkey), Raphoe)

Allianz (⏸)

Flores, Atanasio (OP)
Dominican Community,
St Mary's Priory, Tallaght,
Dublin 24
Tel 01-4048100

Flynn, Brian, Very Rev, PP
Laragh, Stradone, Co Cavan
Tel 049-4330142
(*Laragh*, Kilmore)

Flynn, Brian, Very Rev, PE
Kilmacow, via Waterford,
Co Kilkenny
Tel 051-885122/087-2828391
(*Kilmacow*, Ossory)

Flynn, Edward, Very Rev, PE
Multyfarnham Retirement
Village, Co Westmeath
(Meath, retired)

Flynn, Edwin (OFMCap)
Holy Trinity,
Fr Mathew Quay, Cork
Tel 021-4270827

Flynn, Gabriel, DD, PC
1 Orchard Court, Dunboyne,
Co Meath
Tel 01-8255342/8086554
(*Dunboyne*, Meath)

Flynn, Joe (SPS)
Tearmann Spirituality
Centre, Brockagh,
Glendalough, Co Wicklow
Tel 0404-45208

Flynn, John (SMA)
African Missions,
Blackrock Road, Cork
Tel 021-4292871

Flynn, Joseph, Very Rev, PP
Ballyporeen, Cahir,
Co Tipperary
Tel 052-7467105
(*Ballyporeen*, Waterford &
L.)

Flynn, Laurence, Very Rev, PP
Ballybay, Co Monaghan
Tel 042-9741032
(*Ballybay*, Clogher)

Flynn, Michael, Very Rev, PP
Christ the King Church,
Knockmore, Ballina,
Co Mayo
Tel 094-58108
(*Backs*, Killala)

Flynn, Nicholas, Very Rev, PP
Killeentierna, Killarney,
Co Kerry
Tel 066-9764141
(*Killeentierna*, Kerry)

Flynn, Patrick (OFMCap)
Holy Trinity,
Fr Mathew Quay, Cork
Tel 021-4270827

Flynn, Paul (OSA)
Assigned to the Anglo-
Scottish Province of the
Augustinians

Flynn, Seán, CC
Tuam, Co Galway
Tel 093-24250
(*Tuam (Cathedral of the
Assumption)*, Tuam)

Flynn, Thomas, Most Rev, DD
Bishop Emeritus of Achonry
St Michael's, Cathedral
Grounds, Ballaghaderreen,
Co Roscommon
Tel 094-9877808
(Achonry)

Flynn, Thomas, Very Rev, PP
Carrickbeg, Carrick-on-Suir,
Co Tipperary
Tel 051-640340
(*Carrickbeg*, Waterford & L.)

Flynn, Tim (OSM)
Prior, Servite Priory,
St Peregrine,
36 Grangewood Estate,
Rathfarnham, Dublin 16
Tel 01-4517115

Flynn, Timothy (OSM)
Director, Servite Oratory,
Rathfarnham Shopping
Centre, Dublin 14
Tel 01-4936300

Flynn, Tomás, Very Rev, PP
Drumcong,
Carrick-on-Shannon,
Co Leitrim
Tel 071-9642021
(*Kiltubrid*, Ardagh & Cl.)

Flynn, William, CC
St Patrick's, Gorey,
Co Wexford
Tel 053-9421117
(*Gorey*, Ferns)

Fogarty, Finbarr Declan (OSA)
On assignment in USA

Fogarty, John (CSSp), Most
Rev
Superior General,
Clivo di Cinna 195,
00136, Roma, Italy
Tel 0039-06-3540461

Fogarty, Kevin (OCSO)
Mount Melleray Abbey,
Cappoquin, Co Waterford
Tel 058-54404

Fogarty, Pat, Very Rev, PP
Cork Road, Carrigaline,
Co Cork
Tel 021-4371684
(*Carrigaline*, Cork & R.)

Fogarty, Philip (SJ)
35 Lower Leeson Street,
Dublin 2
Tel 01-6761248

Fogarty, Thomas, Very Rev
President,
St Patrick's College, Thurles,
Co Tipperary
Tel 0504-21201
(Cashel & E.)

Foley, Brendan (CSSp)
Spiritan House,
213 North Circular Road,
Dublin 7
Tel 01-8389664/8683504

Foley, Brian (CSsR)
St Patrick's, Esker, Athenry,
Co Galway
Tel 091-844007

Foley, Declan, Very Rev, PP
Bagenalstown, Co Carlow
Tel 059-9721154
(*Muinebheag/Bagenalstown*,
Kildare & L.)

Foley, Denis, Very Rev, PE
32 Walkinstown Road,
Dublin 12
(Dublin, retired)

Foley, Dermot (SPS)
Tearmann Spirituality
Centre, Brockagh,
Glendalough, Co Wicklow
Tel 0404-45208

Foley, Desmond (OSA)
Prior & Bursar,
St Augustine's Priory, St
Augustine's Street, Galway
Tel 091-562524

Foley, Eamon, Very Rev, PE
Clara, Co Kilkenny
Tel 087-7828784
(Ossory, retired)

Foley, Edward (OP)
St Saviour's,
Upper Dorset Street,
Dublin 1
Tel 01-8897610

Foley, Joseph
Convent Street,
Abbeyfeale, Co Limerick
(*Abbeyfeale*, Limerick)

Foley, Michael F. (SSCC)
Coudrin House,
27 Northbrook Road,
Dublin 6
Tel 01-6686584/01-6686590

Foley, Niall, BSc, BD, HDE
Vice-President,
St Joseph's College,
Garbally Park, Ballinasloe,
Co Galway
Tel 090-9642504/9642254
(Clonfert)

Forbes, John, Very Rev, PP
Parochial House,
Gortin, Omagh,
Co Tyrone BT79 8PU
Tel 028-81648203
(*Gortin*, Derry)

Forde, Basil (OSB)
Glenstal Abbey, Murroe,
Co Limerick
Tel 061-386103

Forde, Denis, Very Rev
Tigh an tSagairt,
Clogheen, Cork
(Cork & R.)

Forde, Des, Very Rev, PP
Parochial House,
Bearna, Galway
Tel 091-590956
(*Bearna*, Galway)

Forde, Liam (SM)
Mount St Mary's,
Dundrum Road, Milltown,
Dublin 14
Tel 01-2697322

Forde, Michael (CSsR)
Scala, Castlemahon House,
Castle Road, Blackrock, Cork
Tel 021-4358800

Forde, Peter, Very Rev, PE
470 Falls Road, Belfast BT12
6EN
Tel 028-90321511
(*St John's*, Down & C.)

Forde, Tom (OFMCap)
Chaplain,
Holy Trinity,
Fr Mathew Quay, Cork
Tel 021-4270827

Forde, Walter, Very Rev, PP
Castlebridge, Co Wexford
Tel 053-9159769
(*Castlebridge*, Ferns)

Forker, Philip (OFM)
Franciscan Abbey,
Multyfarnham, Co
Westmeath
Tel 044-9371114/9371137

Forristal, Laurence, Most Rev,
DD
Retired Bishop of Ossory,
Molassy, Freshford Road,
Kilkenny
Tel 056-7777928/
087-2330369
(Ossory)

Forristal, Leonard (SPS)
St Patrick's, Kiltegan,
Co Wicklow
Tel 059-6473600

Forster, Stephen (MI)
Superior and Provincial,
St Camillus,
4 St Vincent Street North
Dublin 7
Tel 01-8300365

Forsythe, John, Very Rev, PP
Elmfield, 165 Antrim Road,
Glengormley,
Newtownabbey,
Co Antrim, BT36 7QR
Tel 028-90832979
(*St Mary's on the Hill*, Down
& C.)

Fortune, Finbarr (OSA)
St John's Priory,
Thomas Street, Dublin 8
Tel 01-6770393

Fortune, Karl, CC
No 1 Presbytery,
4 Old Hill, Leixlip, Co Kildare
Tel 01-6243718
(*Leixlip*, Dublin)

Fortune, William, PC
32 Newtownpark Avenue,
Blackrock, Co Dublin
Tel 01-2100337
(*Newtownpark*, Dublin)

Foster, John (SDB)
Salesian House,
45 St Teresa's Road,
Crumlin, Dublin 12
Tel 01-4555605

Fox, Christopher (MHM)
St Joseph's House,
50 Orwell Park, Rathgar,
Dublin 6
Tel 01-4127700

Fox, Gerard
St Malachy's Seminary,
120 Cliftonville Road,
Belfast BT14 6LA
(Down & C.)

Fox, John, Very Rev, PP
Parochial House,
153 Aughrim Road,
Toomebridge,
Antrim BT41 3SH
Tel 028-79468277
(*Newbridge*, Armagh)

Fox, Patrick, Rt Rev Mgr
14 Amana Estate,
Ballina, Co Mayo
(retired)

Fraser, Paul
c/o Our Lady Queen of
Heaven,
111 Portsmouth Road,
Frimley, Camberley,
Surrey GU16 7AA
Tel 01276-504876
(Derry)

Frawley, Bernard M. (CSSp)
Rockwell College, Cashel,
Co Tipperary
Tel 062-61444

Freeman, Seamus (SAC), Most
Rev, DD
Bishop of Ossory,
Blessed Felix House,
Tilbury Place, James's Street,
Kilkenny
Tel 056-7762448
(Ossory)

Freeney, Paul, Very Rev, PE
Parochial House,
43 Upper Beechwood
Avenue, Ranelagh, Dublin 6
Tel 01-4972687
(Dublin, retired)

French, Gerry (SSC)
St Joseph's, Balcurris,
Ballymun, Dublin 11
Tel 01-8423865
(*Balcurris*, Dublin)

French, John, Very Rev
Horeswood, New Ross,
Co Wexford
Tel 051-593196
(Ferns, retired)

Friel, James, Very Rev Canon,
PE
Massreagh, Rathmullan,
Co Donegal
Tel 074-9158306
(Raphoe, retired)

Friel, John (CP)
Superior,
Passionist Retreat Centre,
Tobar Mhuire, Crossgar,
Co Down BT30 9EA
Tel 028-44830242

Fuentes, Alejandro (LC)
Superior,
Leopardstown Road,
Foxrock, Dublin 18
Tel 01-2955902
Chaplain,
Woodlands Academy,
Wingfield House, Bray,
Co Wicklow
Tel 01-2866323

Fullerton, Robert, Very Rev
Canon
501 Ormeau Road,
Belfast BT7 3GR
Tel 028-90641064
(*Holy Rosary*, Down & C.)

Fulton, Raymond, Very Rev,
PP
87 Cushendall Road,
Ballyvoy, Ballycastle,
Co Antrim BT54 6QY
Tel 028-20762248
(*Culfeightrin*, Down & C.)

Fulton, William (SSC)
St Patrick's, Kiltegan,
Co Wicklow
Tel 059-6473600

Furey, Francis (SMA)
African Missions,
Blackrock Road, Cork
Tel 021-4292871

Furlong, James, Very Rev, PP
Newbawn, Co Wexford
(*Newbawn and Raheen*,
Ferns)

Furlong, Odhrán, CC
Rathgarogue, New Ross,
Co Wexford
Tel 051-424521
(*Cushinstown*, Ferns)

Furlong, Senan (OSB), Very
Rev
Glenstal Abbey, Murroe,
Co Limerick
Tel 061-621000

Furlong, Shem (OSA)
St Augustine's Priory,
Washington Street, Cork
Tel 021-4275398/4270410

Furlong, Tadgh, Very Rev, PP
Cappawhite, Co Tipperary
Tel 062-75427
(*Cappawhite*, Cashel & E.)

Furlong, Thomas (SMA)
SMA House, Wilton, Cork
Tel 021-4541069/4541884

## G

Gaffney, David (SJ)
Milltown Park,
Sandford Road, Dublin 6
Tel 01-2698411/2698113

Gaffney, Matthew (IC)
Rector, Clonturk House,
Ormond Road,
Drumcondra, Dublin 9
Tel 01-6877014

Gaffney, Philip, Very Rev, PP
St Mary's, Drogheda,
Co Louth
Tel 041-9834958
(*Drogheda, St Mary's*,
Meath)

Gahan, Dermot, CC
The Ballagh, Wexford
Tel 053-9136200
(*Oulart*, Ferns)

Gahan, James, Very Rev, PP
Killinure, Tullow,
Co Carlow
Tel 059-9156111
(*Clonmore*, Kildare & L.)

Gahan, Raymond, Very Rev,
PP
Killaveney, Tinahely,
Co Wicklow
Tel 0402-38188
(*Killaveney and Crossbridge*,
Ferns)

Gallagher, Brendan
(On study leave)
c/o Clogher Diocesan Office,
Bishop's House, Monaghan
Tel 047-81019
(Clogher)

Gallagher, Colm, Very Rev Mgr
594 Howth Road, Raheny,
Dublin 5
(Dublin, retired)

Gallagher, Declan, CC
No. 3 Prebytery,
Castle Street, Dalkey,
Co Dublin
Tel 01-2859212
(*Dalkey*, Dublin)

Gallagher, Denis
'Shraheens', Achill South,
Achill, Co Mayo
(Tuam)

Gallagher, Edward, Very Rev,
PP
Kilcar, Co Donegal
(*Kilcar*, Raphoe)

Gallagher, Edward, Adm
St Columba's Presbytery,
18 Pump Street,
Derry BT48 6JG
Tel 028-71262301
(*Derry City*, Derry)

Gallagher, Edward, Very Rev,
PP
Kilcar, Co Donegal
Tel 074-9738007
(*Kilcar*, Raphoe)

Gallagher, John (CM)
St Vincent's College,
Castleknock, Dublin 15
Tel 01-8213051

Gallagher, John, (SMA), CC
St Joseph's Parish, Wilton,
Cork
Tel 021-4341362
(*Wilton, St Joseph's*, Cork)

Gallagher, John Vincent (SSC)
St Columban's Retirement
Home, Dalgan Park, Navan,
Co Meath
Tel 046-9021525

Gallagher, John, Very Rev
Canon, PE
Ardara, Co Donegal
Tel 074-9541318
(Raphoe, retired)

Gallagher, Joseph, Very Rev,
PP
Parochial House, Tullamore,
Co Offaly
Tel 057-9321587
(*Tullamore*, Meath)

Gallagher, Laurence (CSsR)
St Joseph's, Dundalk,
Co Louth
Tel 042-9334042/9334762

Gallagher, Michael O. (SJ)
35 Lower Leeson Street,
Dublin 2
Tel 01-6761248

Gallagher, Michael P. (SJ)
Irish Jesuit Provincialate,
Milltown Park,
Sandford Road, Dublin 6
Tel 01-4987333

Gallagher, Patrick (OCarm)
Gort Muire, Ballinteer,
Dublin 16
Tel 01-2984014

Gallagher, Patrick, Rt Rev Mgr
Cathedral Close, Ballina,
Co Mayo
(Killala, retired)

Gallagher, Paul, CC
Falcarragh, Co Donegal
Tel 074-9165356
(*Gortahork (Tory Island)*,
Raphoe)

Gallagher, Peter, Very Rev, PP
Lavagh, Ballymote,
Co Sligo
Tel 071-9184002
(*Achonry*, Achonry)

Gallagher, Raphael (CSsR)
Marianella/Liguori House,
75 Orwell Road, Rathgar,
Dublin 6
Tel 01-4067100

Gallagher, Seamus L., Very
Rev, PE
Glenlee, Killybegs,
Co Donegal
Tel 074-9732729
(Raphoe, retired)

Gallagher, Seamus, Very Rev, PP
Frosses, Co Donegal
Tel 074-9736006
(*Inver*, Raphoe)

Gallagher, Shane, CC
1 Chaplain's House,
Knocknamona, Letterkenny,
Co Donegal
Tel 074-9125888 (Hospital)
(*Letterkenny (Conwal and Leck)*, Raphoe)

Gallagher, Thomas
Cloughmore, Achill,
Co Mayo
(Tuam)

Gallinagh, Padraic, Very Rev
'Polperro', 8 Beverley Close,
Newtownards BT23 7FN
(Down & C., retired)

Gallogley, Vincent (OFM)
Franciscan Friary,
Rossnowlagh, Co Donegal
Tel 072-9851342

Galus, Piotr
Diocesan Chaplain to Polish
Community,
c/o St Augustine's,
Washington Street, Cork
Tel 021-4275390
(Cork & R.)

Galvin, Aidan (CM)
St Paul's College, Raheny,
Dublin 5
Tel 01-8318113

Galvin, Gerard, Very Rev, PP
Durrus, Co Cork
Tel 027-61013
(*Muintir Bháire*, Cork & R.)

Galvin, John, AP
Passage West, Co Cork
Tel 021-4841267
(*Monkstown*, Cork & R.)

Galvin, John, CC
c/o Parish Office, 52 Lower
Rathmines Road,
Dublin 6
Tel 01-4971531
(*Rathmines*, Dublin)

Galvin, Séamus (CSSp)
Templeogue College,
Templeville Raod,
Dublin 6W
Tel 01-490 3909

Gambogi, Carolus, CC
Parochial House,
La Touche Road,
Greystones, Co Wicklow
(*Greystones*, Dublin)

Gannan, John
Churchfield Presbytery,
Knock, Co Mayo
(*Knock*, Tuam)

Gannon, John J., Very Rev, PP
Elphin, Co Roscommon
Tel 071-9635058
(*Elphin*, Elphin)

Gannon, Peter, Very Rev., CC,
VF
The Presbytery, Claremorris,
Co Mayo
Tel 094-9362477
(*Claremorris (Kilcolman)*,
Tuam)

Gardiner, Seamus, Very Rev
Portroe, Nenagh,
Co Tipperary
Tel 067-23101/086-8392741
(Killaloe, retired)

Garland, Sean, Very Rev, PP
Parochial House,
Clonmellon, Navan,
Co Meath
Tel 046-9433124
(*Clonmellon*, Meath)

Garrett, Gerard, Very Rev, VJ
Cork Regional Marriage
Tribunal,
The Lough, Cork
Tel 021-4963653
(Limerick)

Garry, Martin (OCSO)
Bolton Abbey, Moone,
Co Kildare
Tel 059-8624102

Garvey, Colin (OFM)
The Abbey,
8 Francis Street, Galway
Tel 091-562518

Garvey, Francis, Very Rev, PP,
VF
Carrick-on-Shannon,
Co Leitrim
Tel 071-9620118
(*Carrick-on-Shannon*,
Ardagh & Cl.)

Garvey, John, Very Rev, PP
St Michael's, Creagh,
Ballinasloe, Co Galway
Tel 090-9643916
(*Ballinasloe, Creagh and
Kilclooney*, Clonfert)

Garvey, John, Very Rev, PE
Ballinrobe,
Co Mayo
(Tuam, retired)

Garvey, Joseph, Very Rev, PE
Beaufort House,
Navan, Co Meath
(Meath, retired)

Garvey, Peter (OCSO)
Mount Saint Joseph Abbey
Roscrea, Co Tipperary
Tel 0505-25600

Garvey, Thomas
Cloverhill, Co Roscommon
(Elphin, retired)

Gates, John, Very Rev, PP, VF
Parochial House,
30 King Street, Magherafelt,
Co Derry BT45 6AS
Tel 028-79632439
(*Magherafelt and Ardtrea
North*, Armagh)

Gaughan, J. Anthony, Very
Rev, PE
56 Newtownpark Avenue,
Blackrock, Co Dublin
Tel 01-2833897
(Dublin, retired)

Gavigan, Adrian, CC
Millford, Co Donegal
Tel 074-9153236
(*Rathmullan (Killygarvan
and Tullyfern)*, Raphoe)

Gavigan, James
30 Knapton Road,
Dun Laoghaire, Co Dublin
Tel 01-2804353
(Opus Dei)

Gavigan, James (SSC)
St Columban's Retirement
Home, Dalgan Park, Navan,
Co Meath
Tel 046-9021525

Gavigan, Joseph, Very Rev, PP
The Presbytery,
Ballaghaderreen,
Co Roscommon
Tel 094-9860011
(*Ballaghaderreen
(Castlemore & Kilcolman)*,
Achonry)

Gavin, Denis J. (CSSp)
Blackrock College,
Blackrock, Co Dublin
Tel 01-2888681

Gavin, Dwayne
Centre Culturel Irlandais,
5 Rue des Irlandais
75005 Paris, France
(Meath)

Gavin, Fintan, Rev PC
97 Ballymun Road,
Dublin 9
Tel 01-8375440
(*Ballymun Road*, Dublin)

Gavin, John
c/o Archbishop's House,
Tuam
(Tuam)

Gavin, Tony, Very Rev, Adm
Parochial House,
Rosemount, Co Westmeath
Tel 090-6436110
(*Tubber*, Meath)

Gayer, Pat (OSA)
St John's Priory,
Thomas Street, Dublin 8
Tel 01-6770393

Gaynor, Harry, Very Rev, Co-
PP
112 Ballygall Road East,
Glasnevin, Dublin 11
Tel 01-8342248
(*Ballygall*, Dublin)

Gaynor, Patrick, Very Rev, PE
Walsh Island, Geashill,
Co Offaly
Tel 057-8649510
(Kildare & L., retired)

Geaney, Michael
3 Hillview Cross,
Douglas Road, Cork
(Dublin, retired)

Gear, Patrick, Very Rev, PP
Ballyneale, Carrick-on-Suir,
Co Tipperary
Tel 051-640148
(*Ballyneale and
Grangemockler*, Waterford
& L.)

Geary, Ronan (SJ)
(residing elsewhere)
35 Lower Leeson Street,
Dublin 2
Tel 01-6761248

Geelan, John, Very Rev, PP
Parochial House,
Bonniconlon,
Ballina, Co Mayo
Tel 096-45016
(*Bonniconlon*, Achonry)

Geoghegan, Brian, Very Rev
Munnia, New Quay,
Co Clare
Tel 087-2387067
(Killaloe, retired)

Geoghegan, Richard, CC
The Presbytery,
Carrick-on-Suir, Co Tipperary
Tel 051-640080
(*Carrick-on-Suir*, Waterford
& L.)

George, Francis, AP
Church of the Most Precious
Blood, Clogheen, Co Cork
Tel 021-4392122
(*Clogheen (Kerry Pike)*, Cork
& R.)

Geraghty, Cathal, Rt Rev Mgr,
PP, VG
Chancellor, The Presbytery,
Barrack Street, Loughrea,
Co Galway
Tel 091-841212
(*Loughrea, St Brendan's
Cathedral*, Clonfert)

Geraghty, Gerard, Very Rev,
PP
Aughrim, Ballinasloe,
Co Galway
Tel 090-9673724/090-
9686614
(*Aughrim and Kilconnell*,
Clonfert)

Geraghty, Martin (MI)
St Camillus, Killucan,
Co Westmeath
Tel 044-74196/044-74115

Gesla, Marceli (OFM)
Chaplain to Polish
Community,
Franciscan Friary, Killarney,
Co Kerry
Tel 064-6631334/6631066

Ghent, William (SMA)
African Missions,
Blackrock Road, Cork
Tel 021-4292871

Gibbons, Danny (SPS)
House Leader, St Patrick's,
21 Leeson Park, Dublin 6
Tel 01-4977897

Gibbons, Richard, Very Rev, PP
Knock, Co Mayo
Tel 094-9388100
(*Knock*, Tuam)

Gibson, David, Very Rev, PP
St Patrick's, Dublin Road,
Limerick
Tel 061-415397/087-2547707
(*St Patrick's*, Limerick)

Gibson, Steve (CSC)
Fr Patrick Peyton Centre,
Attymass, Co Mayo
Tel 096-45374
(Tuam)

Gilbert, Patrick
The Presbytery, John's Mall,
Birr, Co Offaly
Tel 057-9120098/
087-2431956
Chaplain, St Brendan's
Community School,
Birr, Co Offaly
Tel 0509-20510
(*Birr*, Killaloe)

Gilcreest, Martin
Spiritual Director, Legion of
Mary
Tel 049-4362014
Chaplain, Cavan General
Hospital
Tel 049-4361399
(Kilmore)

Gildea, Peter (CM), Very Rev
Superior,
99 Cliftonville Road,
Belfast BT14 6JQ
Tel 028-90751771

Gildea, Seán (OFM)
Franciscan Friary,
Rossnowlagh, Co Donegal
Tel 072-9851342

Gilhooly, Anthony, CC
The Presbytery, Longford
Tel 043-3346465
(*Longford (Templemichael,
Ballymacormack)*, Ardagh &
Cl.)

Gilhooly, John, Very Rev, PP
Mullagh, via Kells, Co Meath
Tel 046-42208
(*Mullagh*, Kilmore)

Gill, Oswald (OFM)
Franciscan Friary,
Liberty Street, Cork
Tel 021-4270302

Gill, Patrick, Very Rev, AP
Lecanvey, Westport,
Co Mayo
Tel 098-64808
(*Westport (Aughaval)*,
Tuam)

Gillan, Hugh (OH)
St John of God Hospital,
Stillorgan, Co Dublin
Tel 01-2771400
(Dublin)

Gillespie, Anthony, Very Rev,
PP
Dromore West, Co Sligo
Tel 096-47012
(*Dromore-West
(Kilmacshalgan)*, Killala)

Gillespie, Gerard, Very Rev, PE
Rathball, Ballina, Co Mayo
(Killala, retired)

Gillespie, James, CC
Carnamuggagh Lower,
Letterkenny, Co Donegal
Tel 074-9122608
(*Aughaninshin*, Raphoe)

Gillespie, Kevin, Rt Rev Mgr
Congregation for the
Clergy, Rome
(Raphoe)

Gilligan, John, Very Rev, Adm
47 Westland Row, Dublin 2
Tel 01-7005268(w)/
8368746(h)
Director of Vocations,
Holy Cross College
Clonliffe, Dublin 3
Tel 01-8379253
(*Westland Row*, Dublin)

Gilligan, Patrick, Very Rev, PP
Cong, Co Mayo
Tel 094-9546030
(*Cong and Neale*, Tuam)

Gillooly, Dominick, Very Rev,
PP
St Anne's, Sligo
Tel 071-9145028
(*Sligo, St Anne's*, Elphin)

Gillooly, Reginald (CSSp)
Holy Ghost Missionary
College, Kimmage Manor,
Dublin 12
Tel 01-4064300

Gilmore, John (SSC)
St Columban's, Dalgan Park,
Navan, Co Meath
Tel 046-9021525

Gilmore, John, PP
11 Church Road,
Aghyaran, Castlederg,
Co Tyrone BT81 7XZ
Tel 028-81670728
(*Aghyaran
(Termonamongan)*, Derry)

Gilmore, Sean, Very Rev, PP
Parochial House,
284 Glassdrumman Road,
Annalong,
Newry, Co Down BT34 4QN
Tel 028-43768208
(*Lower Mourne*, Down & C.)

Gilroy, Michael, Very Rev Dr,
PP
Templeboy, Co Sligo
Tel 096-47103
(*Templeboy*, Killala)

Gilroy, Thomas, Very Rev, PP
Parochial House, Kinnegad,
Co Westmeath
Tel 044-9375117
(*Kinnegad*, Meath)

Gilsenan, Michael CC
St Mary's, Clontibert,
Co Monaghan
Tel 047-80631

Gilton, Michael, CC
48 Aughrim Street,
Dublin 7
Tel 01-8386176
(*Aughrim Street*, Dublin)

Ginnelly, Christopher, Very
Rev, PP
Parochial House, Ballycroy,
Westport, Co Mayo
Tel 098-49134
(*Ballycroy*, Killala)

Glavin, Finbar, Very Rev
Parochial House,
16 Ballykilbeg Road,
Downpatrick,
Co Down BT30 8HJ
Tel 028-44613203
(*Downpatrick*, Down & C.)

Gleeson, Joseph, Very Rev, PE
Rathfeigh, Tara, Co Meath
Tel 041-9825159
(*Skryne*, Meath)

Gleeson, Martin, Very Rev, AP
Belclare, Tuam, Co Galway
Tel 093-55429
(*Cummer (Kilmoylan and
Cummer)*, Tuam)

Gleeson, Padraig, Adm
St Kevin's Presbytery,
Pearse Street, Sallynoggin,
Co Dublin
Tel 01-2854667
(*Sallynoggin*, Dublin)

Gleeson, Patrick
48 Westland Row,
Dublin 2
Tel 01-6767316
Chaplain, Trinity College
Dublin 2
Tel 01-8961260
(*Westland Row*, Dublin)

Gleeson, Philip (OP)
St Mary's Priory, Tallaght,
Dublin 24
Tel 01-4048100

Gleeson, Tim (MSC)
Western Road, Cork
Tel 021-4804120

Glennon, Francis, Very Rev, PP
Cams, Roscommon
Tel 090-6626275
(*Cloverhill*, Elphin)

Glover, Joseph M.
c/o Lisbreen,
73 Somerton Road,
Belfast BT15 4DE
(Down & C.)

Glynn, Cronan (OCD)
The Abbey, Loughrea,
Co Galway
Tel 091-841209

Glynn, Enda, Very Rev
(elsewhere in the diocese)
c/o 13 Lios Na Mara,
Station Road, Lahinch,
Co Clare
(Galway)

Glynn, Joe (OCD)
St Teresa's,
Clarendon Street, Dublin 2
Tel 01-6718466/6718127

Glynn, John, Very Rev, PP
Parochial House,
Tourlestrane, Ballymote,
Co Sligo
Tel 071-9181105
(*Tourlestrane (Kilmactigue)*,
Achonry)

Glynn, Martin, Very Rev, PP
Parochial House, Mervue,
Galway
Tel 091-751721
(*Good Shepherd, Mervue*,
Galway)

Glynn, Matthias, Very Rev, PP
Tagoat, Co Wexford
Tel 053-9131139
(*Tagoat*, Ferns)

Glynn, Michael
Chaplain,
Convent of Mercy,
Mullaghmore, Co Sligo
Tel 071-9166345
(Elphin)

Goaley, Michael, Very Rev
Canon
Glenamaddy, Co Galway
(Tuam, retired)

Godfrey, Donal (SJ)
Irish Jesuit Provincialate,
Milltown Park,
Sandford Road, Dublin 6
Tel 01-4987333

Godley, Gearóid
John Paul II Pastoral Centre,
Rock Road, Killarney,
Co Kerry
Tel 064-6632644
(Kerry)

Gogan, Brian M. (CSSp)
Blackrock College,
Blackrock, Co Dublin
Tel 01-2888681

Gogarty, Terence (MHM)
(elsewhere in Ireland)

Gonoude, Anthony, Adm
Parochial House, Donore,
Drogheda, Co Louth
Tel 041-9823137
(*Donore*, Meath)

Good, James
Park View, Church Street,
Douglas, Cork
Tel 021-4363913
(Cork & R., retired)

Goode, John (CSsR)
Mount Saint Alphonsus,
Limerick
Tel 061-315099

Goode, Richard (OSA)
The Presbytery, Meath
Street, Dublin 8
Tel 01-4543356
(*Meath Street and
Merchant's Quay*, Dublin)

Goold, Eamonn, Rt Rev Mgr,
PP, VG
Midleton, Co Cork
Tel 021-4631750
(*Midleton*, Cloyne)

Gorevan, Patrick
Harvieston,
Cunningham Road,
Dalkey, Co Dublin
Tel 01-2859877
(Opus Dei)

Gormally, Michael, Very Rev,
PP
Achill Sound, Achill,
Co Mayo
Tel 098-45288
(*Achill*, Tuam)

Gorman, Owen, (OCDS), CC
506 Lattone Road,
Carran West, Garrison,
Co Fermanagh BT93 4EL
(*Belleek-Garrison (Inis
Muighe Samh)*, Clogher)

Gorman, Seán, Very Rev, PP
Taghmon, Co Wexford
Tel 053-9134123
(*Taghmon*, Ferns)

Gorman, Stephen, CC
Parochial House,
Letterkenny, Co Donegal
Tel 074-9121021
(*Letterkenny (Conwal and
Leck)*, Raphoe)

Gorman, Thomas (SMA)
SMA House, Wilton, Cork
Tel 021-4541069/4541884

Gormley, Joseph, PP
Parochial House,
St Mary's, Creggan,
Derry BT48 9QE
Tel 028-71263152
(*St Mary's, Creggan*, Derry)

Gough, Brian
Chaplain,
St James's Hospital,
James's Street, Dublin 8
Tel 01-4103659/4162023
(Dublin)

Gough, Joseph A. (CSSp)
Blackrock College,
Blackrock, Co Dublin
Tel 01-2888681

Gould, Daniel, Very Rev, PE
Killavullen, Co Cork
Tel 022-26153
(Cloyne, retired)

Grace, Edmond (SJ)
Vice-Superior,
35 Lower Leeson Street,
Dublin 2
Tel 01-6761248

Grace, James, Very Rev, PP
Killaloe, Co Clare
Tel 061-376137/087-6843315
(*Killaloe*, Killaloe)

Grace, John (OSA)
On assignment in USA

Grace, Ned (SPS)
St Patrick's, Kiltegan,
Co Wicklow
Tel 059-6473600

Grace, Patrick, Venerable
Archdeacon
Inistioge, Co Kilkenny
Tel 056-7758429/
086-8817628
(Ossory, retired)

Graham, Eamon, PP
42 Glenedra Road,
Feeny, Dungiven,
Co Derry BT47 4TW
Tel 028-77781223
(*Banagher*, Derry)

Graham, Martin, Very Rev, PP
81 Lagmore Grove,
Dunmurry, Belfast BT17 0TD
Tel 028-90309011
(*Christ the Redeemer,
Lagmore*, Down & C.)

Graham, Patrick (OCarm)
Whitefriar Street Church,
56 Aungier Street, Dublin 2
Tel 01-4758821

Grant, Colin, MA, STL, PGCE
Diocesan Ecumenical
Commission,
Aquinas Grammar School,
518 Ravenhill Road,
Belfast BT6 0BY
Tel 028-90643939
(Down & C.)

Grant, Henry (SJ)
Milltown Park,
Sandford Road, Dublin 6
Tel 01-2698411/2698113

Grant, Patrick, Very Rev
Canon, PE
Ballyragget, Co Kilkenny
Tel 056-8833120
(Ossory, retired)

Grant, Robert, CC
St John's Presbytery,
New Street, Waterford
Tel 051-874271
(*St John's*, Waterford & L.)

Gray, Francis, Very Rev, PP
Carrick, Finea,
Mullingar, Co Westmeath
Tel 043-6681129
(*Carrick-Finea*, Ardagh & Cl.)

Greed, Pat, Very Rev, PP
18 Churchfield,
Clonlara, Co Clare
Tel 061-354594/086-6067003
(*Clonlara*, Killaloe)

Green, Denis (SM)
Mount St Mary's, Dundrum
Road, Milltown, Dublin 14
Tel 01-2697322

Green, Gerard
c/o Bishop's House, Newry,
Co Down
(Dromore, retired)

Greenan, Clement (OP)
St Saviour's,
Upper Dorset Street,
Dublin 1
Tel 01-8897610

Greenan, Thomas (SPS)
Kiltegan Leader, St Patrick's
Kiltegan, Co Wicklow
Tel 059-6473600

Greene, James (White Fathers)
c/o Cypress Grove Road,
Templeogue, Dublin 6W
Tel 01-4055263

Greene, James, CC
Carrigtwohill, Co Cork
Tel 021-4853925
(*Carrigtwohill*, Cloyne)

Greene, John, Very Rev
(Moderator)
No. 3 Presbytery,
Dunmanus Court,
Cabra West, Dublin 7
Tel 01-8384325
(*Cabra West*, Dublin)

Greene, Patrick (SJ)
Manresa House,
Dollymount, Dublin 3
Tel 01-8331352

Grenham, Thomas (SPS)
Tearmann Spirituality
Centre,
Brockagh, Glendalough,
Co Wicklow
Tel 0404-45208

Griffin, Edward, Very Rev
10 Connawood, Bray,
Co Wicklow
(Dublin, retired)

Griffin, Eugene (SSC)
(Limerick, retired)

Griffin, Gerard (CSSp)
Rockwell College,
Cashel, Co Tipperary
Tel 062-61444

Griffin, Liam (OMI)
Oblates of Mary Immaculate
House of Retreat,
Tyrconnell Road, Inchicore,
Dublin 8
Tel 01-4541160/4541161

Griffin, Pat
Ashborough Lodge, Lyre,
Milltown, Co Kerry
(Kerry, retired)

Griffin, Patrick (OFMConv)
Friary of the Visitation,
Fairview Strand, Dublin 3
Tel 01-8376000

Griffin, Philip
Nullamore, Richmond
Avenue South, Dublin 6
Tel 01-4971239
(Opus Dei)

Griffin, Thomas (IC), PP
Parochial House,
Kilcurry,
Dundalk, Co Louth
Tel 042-9334410
(*Faughart*, Armagh)

Griffith, Anthony
Rushbrook, Laghey,
Co Donegal
Tel 074-9734021
(Raphoe, retired)

Grimes, Edward (CSSp)
Holy Ghost Missionary
College,
Kimmage Manor, Dublin 12
Tel 01-4064300

Grimshaw, Ronan (CSSp)
Newlands Institute for
Counselling,
2 Monastery Road,
Clondalkin, Dublin 22
Tel 01-4594573

Grogan, Brian (SJ)
Superior, 35 Lower Leeson
Street, Dublin 2
Tel 01-6761248

Grogan, Desmond, Very Rev
Canon, PE
Partry, Claremorris,
Co Mayo
Tel 094-9543013
(Tuam, retired)

Grzegorzewski, Tomasz (SDB),
CC
Aughrim,
Carrick-on-Shannon
Co Roscommon

Guckian, Michael (OMI)
Oblate Fathers,
House of Retreat, Inchicore,
Dublin 8
Tel 01-4541117
(*Inchicore, Mary
Immaculate*, Dublin)

Guckian, Patrick, CC
44 Woodview Grove,
Blanchardstown, Dublin 15
Tel 01-8262799
(*Blanchardstown*, Dublin)

Guilfoyle, Patrick, Very Rev,
PP
Tullaroan, Co Kilkenny
Tel 056-7769141/087-
6644858
(*Tullaroan*, Ossory)

Guiney, John K. (SJ)
Milltown Park, Sandford
Road, Dublin 6
Tel 01-2698411/2698113

Guiry, Michael, Very Rev, PP
Ardmore, Youghal,
Co Waterford
Tel 024-94275
(*Ardmore*, Waterford & L.)

Gunn, David, PP
St Michael's, Ballinskelligs
Co Kerry
Tel 066-9479108
(*Ballinskelligs*, Kerry)

Gunn, Joseph, Very Rev, PP, VF
St Comgall's Presbytery,
27 Brunswick Road, Bangor,
Co Down BT20 3DS
Tel 028-91465522
(*Bangor*, Down & C.)

Gunn, Terence (SMA)
SMA House, Wilton, Cork
Tel 021-4541069/4541884

Guthrie, Charles (SVD)
Donamon Castle,
Roscommon
Tel 090-6662222

Gutu, Lovemore (OCarm)
Provincial Office and
Carmelite Community,
Gort Muire, Ballinteer,
Dublin 16
Tel 01-2984014

### H

Haan, Karl, CC
33 Glen Road, Garvagh,
Co Derry BT51 5DB
Tel 028-29558342
(*Garvagh*, Derry)

Habara, Gaspar (SVD)
1 & 3 Pembroke Road,
Dublin 4
Tel 01-6680904

Hackett, Brian, Very Rev, PE, AP
Parochial House,
31 Church Street,
Ballygawley,
Co Tyrone BT70 2HA
Tel 028-85568219
(*Ballygawley (Errigal Kieran)*, Armagh)

Hackett, Michael, Very Rev
Canon, PE
(Assistant Priest)
Cathedral Presbytery,
38 Hill Street,
Newry BT34 1AT
Tel 028-30262586
(*Newry Pastoral Area*, Dromore)

Hahessy, Ignatius (OCSO)
Mount Melleray Abbey,
Cappoquin, Co Waterford
Tel 058-54404

Hallinan, Malachy, Rt Rev
Mgr, PP, VG, VF
Church of the Sacred Heart,
Seamus Quirke Road,
Galway
Tel 091-522713
(*Sacred Heart Church*, Galway)

Halpin, Bernard (OMI)
Oblate Fathers,
House of Retreat,
Inchicore, Dublin 8
Tel 01-4541117
(*Inchicore, Mary Immaculate*, Dublin)

Halpin, David, Very Rev, Co-PP
30 Wheatfield Close,
Clondalkin, Dublin 22
Tel 01-6263920
(*Rowlagh and Quarryvale*, Dublin)

Halpin, Lauri, Very Rev, PE
Knightsbridge Nursing
Home, Trim, Co Meath
(Meath, retired)

Halpin, Martin, Very Rev, PP
Parochial House,
Ballinabrackey, Kinnegad,
Co Westmeath
Tel 046-9739015
(*Ballinabrackey*, Meath)

Halpin, Rory (SJ)
Crescent College
Comprehensive, Dooradoyle,
Limerick
Tel 061-480920

Halton, John, Very Rev, PP
Tempo, Enniskillen,
Co Fermanagh BT94 3LY
Tel 028-89541344
(*Tempo*, Clogher)

Hamill, Aidan, Rt Rev Mgr, PP, VG
70 North Street, Lurgan,
Co Armagh BT67 9AH
Tel 028-38323161
(*Shankill, St Paul's & St Peter's (Lurgan)*, Dromore)

Hamill, Thomas
'Shekinah',
25 Wynnes Terrace,
Dundalk, Co Louth
Tel 042-9331023
(Armagh)

Hammel, James, Very Rev, PP
Annacurra, Aughrim,
Co Wicklow
Tel 0402-36119
(*Annacurra*, Ferns)

Hampson, Paul, PC
Parochial House,
Chapel Road, Lusk,
Co Dublin
Tel 01-8949229/087-2452161
(*Lusk*, Dublin)

Hanafin, Sean, Dean, PP, VG
St John's Presbytery, Tralee,
Co Kerry
Tel 066-7122522
(*Tralee, St John's*, Kerry)

Hand, John (SM)
(Moderator)
The Presbytery,
Coolock Village, Dublin 5
Tel 01-8484799
(*Coolock*, Dublin)

Hanley, Brendan (MSC)
Myross Wood Retreat
House, Leap, Skibbereen,
Co Cork
Tel 028-33118

Hanley, Hugh, Very Rev (SCJ)
(Moderator)
Parochial House,
St John Vianney,
Ardlea Road, Dublin 5
Tel 01-8474173
(*Ardlea*, Dublin)

Hanley, Michael, Very Rev, PP
Kilfinane Co Limerick
Tel 063-91016/086-8595733
(*Kilfinane*, Limerick)

Hanlon, Hugh, (MSC), CC
Ballyshannon, Raphoe
Tel 071-9851090
(*Ballyshannon (Kilbarron)*, Raphoe)

Hanlon, Joseph, Very Rev
(Assistant Priest)
St Mary's Presbytery,
Willbrook Road,
Rathfarnham, Dublin 14
Tel 01-4932390
(*Rathfarnham*, Dublin)

Hanly, Gerard, Very Rev
Canon, PP, VF
Boyle, Co Roscommon
Tel 071-9662218
(*Boyle*, Elphin)

Hanly, John, Rt Rev Mgr, PP
Parochial House, Carnaross,
Kells, Co Meath
Tel 046-9245904
(*Carnaross*, Meath)

Hanly, William (SAC)
Pallottine College, Thurles,
Co Tipperary
Tel 0504-21202

Hanna, John (CSsR)
Scala, Castlemahon House,
Castle Road, Blackrock, Cork
Tel 021-4358800

Hannan, Greg, CC
Ballymote, Co Sligo
Tel 071-9189778
(*Ballymote (Emlefad and Kilmorgan)*, Achonry)

Hannan, John (SM)
Rome

Hannan, Laurence (SM)
Fiji

Hannan, Peter (SJ)
Manresa House,
Dollymount, Dublin 3
Tel 01-8331352

Hannigan, Patrick, Very Rev, PP, VF
Parochial House,
65 Tullyallen Road,
Dungannon,
Co Tyrone BT70 3AF
Tel 028-87761211
(*Killeeshil*, Armagh)

Hannon, Donald, CC
Arva, Co Cavan
Tel 049-4335246
(*Killeshandra*, Kilmore)

Hannon, James
Sandhill Road, Ballybunion,
Co Kerry
(Cloyne, retired)

Hannon, James, Very Rev
Our Lady's Manor, Bulloch
Castle, Dalkey, Co Dublin
(Dublin, retired)

Hannon, Martin
30 Knapton Road,
Dun Laoghaire, Co Dublin
Tel 01-2804353
(Opus Dei)

Hannon, Patrick, Dr
Emeritus Professor of
Theology,
St Patrick's College,
Maynooth, Co Kildare
Tel 01-6285222
(Cloyne, retired)

Hannon, Patrick, PC,
St Mary's, Donabate,
Co Dublin
Tel 01-8434604
(*Donabate*, Dublin)

Hannon, Raymond
(Dublin, retired)

Hannon, Timothy, CC
3 Stanhope Place, Athy
Tel 059-8631698
(*Athy*, Dublin)

Hannon, Tom, Very Rev, PP
Templemore Road,
Cloughjordan,
Co Tipperary
Tel 0505-42266/0868768116
(*Cloughjordan*, Killaloe)

Hanrahan, Noel (MHM)
St Joseph's House,
50 Orwell Park,
Rathgar, Dublin 6
Tel 01-4127700

Hanrahan, Paschal, CF (RC)
St Michael's House,
Queens Avenue,
Aldershot,
Hants GU11 2BY, UK
Tel 0044-1252-316429/
0044-7920-593792
(Killaloe)

Hanratty, David
Tierhogar, Portarlington,
Co Laois
Tel 057-8645719
(Meath)

Hanratty, Malachy (SSC)
St Columban's, Dalgan Park,
Navan, Co Meath
Tel 046-9021525

Hanratty, Oliver
The Bungalow,
Crescent Road, Rogerstown,
Rush, Co Dublin
(Dublin, retired)

Hanson, Frederick (SSC)
St Columban's
Retirement Home,
Dalgan Park, Navan,
Co Meath
Tel 046-9021525

Harding, Michael, Co-PP
Templemore Road, Roscrea,
Co Tipperary
Tel 0505-21218
(*Cronan Cluster (Roscrea)*,
Killaloe)

Hargaden, Joseph (SCC)
Kilkenny, retired

Harkin, Ciarán, Very Rev, PP
Parochial House,
Newtowncunningham,
Lifford, Co Donegal
Tel 074-9156138
(*Newtowncunningham &
Killea*, Raphoe)

Harkin, Dermott, CC
7 Cloonty Road, Drumquin,
Omagh, Co Tyrone BT78
4TG
Tel 028-81661235
(*Castlederg (Ardstraw West
and Castlederg)*, Derry)

Harkin, Hugh (SMA)
African Missions,
Blackrock Road, Cork
Tel 021-4292871

Harmon, Sean
Director, Primary Level
Religious Education,
c/o Limerick Diocesan
Pastoral Centre,
St Michael's Courtyard,
Denmark Street, Limerick
Tel 061-400133
(Limerick)

Harney, Donal (MHM)
St Joseph's,
Freshford House, Kilkenny
Tel 056-7721482

Harper, Conor (SJ), CC
Parochial House,
Stillorgan Road, Dublin 4
Tel 01-2180244
(*Donnybrook*, Dublin)

Harper, Frank, Very Rev
32 Bryansford Ave,
Newcastle BT33 0EQ
(Down & C., retired)

Harrington, Brendan, Very
Rev, PP
Fossa, Killarney, Co Kerry
Tel 064-6631996
(*Fossa*, Kerry)

Harrington, Denis, Very Rev,
PE
Clane, Naas, Co Kildare
Tel 045-868224
(Kildare & L., retired)

Harrington, James (OFMCap)
Vicar, Capuchin Friary,
Friary Street, Kilkenny
Tel 056-7721439

Harrington, John (SM), PC
Superior,
St Brendan's Parish,
Coolock Village, Dublin 5
Tel 01-8484799
(*Coolock*, Dublin)

Harrington, Joseph (SDB)
Salesian College,
Pallaskenry, Co Limerick
Tel 061-393313

Harrington, Michael, Very Rev
Canon, PE
Charleville, Co Cork
Tel 063-21833
(Cloyne, retired)

Harrington, Patrick
Retired Bishop,
SMA House, Wilton, Cork
Tel 021-4541069/4541884

Harrington, Terence
(OFMCap)
Capuchin Friary,
Friary Street, Kilkenny,
Tel 056-7721439

Harrington, Wilfred (OP)
St Mary's Priory, Tallaght,
Dublin 24
Tel 01-4048100

Harris, Derek (SSC)
44 Harbour View, Howth,
Co Dublin
Tel 01-8395161

Harris, Jack (CM), PP
122 Sunday's Well Road,
Cork
Tel 021-4304070/4304529
(*St Vincent's, Sunday's Well*,
Cork & R.)

Harris, John (OP)
St Saviour's,
Upper Dorset Street,
Dublin 1
Tel 01-8897610

Harris, John, CC
The Presbytery, Dungarvan,
Co Waterford
(*Dungarvan*, Waterford)

Harris, Walter, Very Rev
Canon, PE
151 Clonsilla Road,
Blanchardstown, Dublin 15
Tel 01-8213716
(Dublin, retired)

Harrison, Michael, Very Rev,
PP, VF
Ballycastle, Co Mayo
Tel 096-43010
(*Ballycastle (Kilbride and
Doonfeeny)*, Killala)

Harrison, Michael (SSC)
St Columban's, Dalgan Park,
Navan, Co Meath
Tel 046-9021525

Harte, Martin, CC
Presbytery,
Kilcullen, Co Kildare
Tel 045-481222
(*Kilcullen*, Dublin)

Hartley, Noel, Very Rev Canon
10 Donovan's Wharf,
Crescent Quay, Wexford
(Ferns, retired)

Hartnett, Denis (MHM)
St Joseph's House,
50 Orwell Park, Rathgar,
Dublin 6
Tel 01-4127700

Harty, Gabriel (OP)
St Malachy's, Dundalk,
Co Louth
Tel 042-9334179/9333714

Harty, John (OFM)
Franciscan Friary, Clonmel,
Co Tipperary
Tel 052-6121378

Haslam, Richard (OMI)
Oblate House of Retreat,
Inchicore, Dublin 8
Tel 01-4534408/4541805

Hassett, Edmond, Very Rev,
Adm
Strandside South,
Abbeyside,
Dungarvan, Co Waterford
Tel 058-42036
(*Abbeyside*, Waterford & L.)

Hassett, John,
(Moderator)
127 Castlegate Way,
Adamstown, Co Dublin
Tel 01-62812088
(*Esker-Doddsboro-
Adamstown*, Dublin)

Hasson, Eugene, PP
164 Greencastle Road,
Omagh,
Co Tyrone BT79 7RU
Tel 028-81648474
(*Greencastle*, Derry)

Hasson, Gerald (CSSp), CC
Aghadowney, Coleraine
(*Coleraine*, Derry)

Hasson, James (OFM)
Franciscan Friary, Ennis,
Co Clare
Tel 065-6828751

Hastings, Mícheál, Very Rev
103 Mount Prospect Drive,
Clontarf, Dublin 3
Tel 01-8335255/087-2358634
(Dublin, retired)

Haugh, Joseph, Very Rev
Bealaha, Doonbeg,
Co Clare
Tel 065-9055022/
087-2603314
(*Doonbeg and Killard*,
Killaloe)

Haughey, Eoghan (OMI)
Oblate House of Retreat,
Inchicore, Dublin 8
Tel 01-4534408/4541805

Hayden, Chris
Coolfancy, Tinahely,
Co Wicklow
Tel 0402-34725
(*Carnew*, Ferns)

Hayden, Desmond
(working outside the
diocese)
Ampleforth Abbey,
York YO62 4EN, UK
(Dublin)

Hayes, Bartholomew (MHM)
St Joseph's House,
50 Orwell Park, Rathgar,
Dublin 6
Tel 01-4127700

Hayes, Colm, Very Rev
15 St Patrick's Terrace, Sligo
(Elphin, retired)

Hayes, Conor, Very Rev, CC
Kilteely, Co Limerick
Tel 061-384213
(*Kilteely*, Cashel & E.)

Hayes, George
Collegio Pontificio Irlandese,
Via dei SS Quattro 1,
00184 Rome, Italy
(Kerry)

Hayes, James (SJ)
(residing elsewhere)
c/o Loyola House,
Milltown Park,
Sandford Road, Dublin 6
Tel 01-2180276

Hayes, Martin, Very Rev, Adm
Cathedral Presbytery,
Thurles, Co Tipperary
Tel 0504-22229/22779
(*Thurles, Cathedral of the
Assumptio*n, Cashel & E.)

Hayes, Noel (SPS)
St Patrick's, Kiltegan,
Co Wicklow
Tel 059-6473600

Hayes, Patrick, CC
St Mary's, Clonmel,
Co Tipperary
Tel 052-6121952
(*Clonmel, St Mary's*,
Waterford & L.)

Hayes, Richard, Very Rev
Collinstown, Duncormack,
Co Wexford
(Ferns, retired)

Hayes, Tom, Very Rev, PP
Parochial House,
Enniskeane, Co Cork
Tel 023-8847769
(*Enniskeane and
Desertserges*, Cork & R.)

Hazelwood, Timothy, Very
Rev, PP
Killeagh, Co Cork
Tel 024-95133
(*Killeagh*, Cloyne)

Heagney, John, Very Rev, PP
Parochial House,
9a Forkhill Road,
Mullaghbawn, Newry,
Co Down BT35 9RA
Tel 028-30888286
(*Mullaghbawn (Forkhill)*,
Armagh)

Heagney, Michael (CSsR)
St Patrick's, Esker, Athenry,
Co Galway
Tel 091-844007

Healy, Alexius (OFMCap)
St Anthony's Capuchin
Friary, 43 Dublin Street,
Carlow
Tel 059-9142543

Healy, Austin (CSSp)
Kimmage Manor,
Whitehall Road, Dublin 12
Tel 01-4064300

Healy, Bernard, CC
St John's Presbytery,
Tralee, Co Kerry
Tel 066-7122522
(*Tralee, St John's*, Kerry)

Healy, Charles, PP
Carrickedmond, Colehill
Co Longford
Tel 044-9357442
(*Carrickedmond And
Abbeyshrule*, Ardagh & Cl.)

Healy, Myles (CSSp)
Blackrock College,
Blackrock, Co Dublin
Tel 01-2888681
(*Greenhills*, Dublin)

Healy, Patrick J. (SDB)
Chaplain, Mount Carmel
Nursing Home,
Roscrea, Co Tipperary

Healy, Peter, Rev, Co-PP
Parochial House,
Roundwood, Co Wicklow
Tel 01-2818149/087-2463876
(*Roundwood*, Dublin)

Healy, Sean (SMA)
Social Justice Ireland,
Arena House
Arena Road, Sandyford,
Dublin 18
Tel 01-2130724

Healy, Thomas, Adm
The Presbytery, Longford
Tel 043-3346465
(*Longford (Templemichael,
Ballymacormack)*, Ardagh &
Cl.)

Healy, Timothy (SJ)
Irish Jesuit Provincialate,
Milltown Park,
Sandford Road, Dublin 6
Tel 01-4987333

Heaney, Columban (OCSO)
Mount Melleray Abbey,
Cappoquin, Co Waterford
Tel 058-54404

Heaney, Seamus, Very Rev, PP
Parochial House, Delvin,
Co Westmeath
Tel 044-9664127
(*Delvin*, Meath)

Heaney, Seán, Rt Rev Mgr, AP,
VG
Parochial House,
Tullamore, Co Offaly
Tel 057-9321587/
057-9351510
(*Tullamore*, Meath)

Hearne, Thomas, CC
Bohermore, Cashel,
Co Tipperary
Tel 062-61409
(*Cashel*, Cashel & E.)

Hearty, Philip (CSsR)
St Joseph's, St Alphonsus
Road,
Dundalk, Co Louth
Tel 042-9334042/9334762

Hederman, Mark Patrick
(OSB), Rt Rev Dom
Abbot, Glenstal Abbey,
Murroe, Co Limerick
Tel 061-621000

Heelan, Patrick (SJ)
(Residing elsewhere)

Heeran, Brendan (CSSp)
Holy Ghost Missionary
College,
Kimmage Manor, Dublin 12
Tel 01-4064300

Heerey, Anthony (CSSp)
Holy Spirit Missionary
College,
Kimmage Manor,
Whitehall Road, Dublin 12
Tel 01-4064300

Heerey, Charles, CC
Fairgreen, Belturbet,
Co Cavan
Tel 049-9522151
(*Belturbet (Annagh)*,
Kilmore)

Heery, Kevin, CC
St Mary's, Navan, Co Meath
Tel 046-9027518/046-
9071774
(*Navan*, Meath)

Heffernan, John (OP)
St Dominic's, Athy,
Co Kildare
Tel 059-8631573

Heffernan, Joseph (OP)
St Magdalen's, Drogheda,
Co Louth
Tel 041-9838271

Heffernan, Martin, Very Rev,
PE, PhD
Skahardgannon, Doneraile,
Co Cork
Tel 022-24570
(Cloyne, retired)

Hegarty, Benedict (OP), Very
Rev, Prior,
St Dominic's Retreat House,
Montenotte, Co Cork
Tel 021-4502520

Hegarty, Ciarán
(on study leave)
c/o The Presbytery,
30A Deanby Gardens,
Belfast BT14 6NN
Tel 028-90745140
(Down & C.)

Hegarty, James (SSS)
Blessed Sacrament Chapel,
20 Bachelors Walk, Dublin 1
Tel 01-8724597

Hegarty, John Paul, Very Rev,
PP
Glounthaune, Co Cork
Tel 021-4232881
(*Glounthaune*, Cork & R.)

Hegarty, Kevin, Very Rev
Carne, Belmullet, Co Mayo
Tel 097-81011
(*Kilmore-Erris*, Killala)

Hegarty, Martin, Very Rev, PP
1 Track Road, Bridge Street,
Listowel, Co Kerry
(Kerry, retired)

Hegarty, Michael (IC), Very
Rev, PP
St Oliver Plunkett's Parish,
Cooleens, Clonmel,
Co Tipperary
Tel 052-6125679
(*Clonmel, St Oliver Plunkett*,
Waterford & L.)

Hegarty, Peter (SPS)
On temporary diocesan
work

Hegarty, Richard, Very Rev,
PE, CC
Killavullen, Co Cork
Tel 022-26125
(*Killavullen*, Cloyne)

Hegarty, Seamus, Most Rev,
DD
Retired Bishop of Derry
Sappagh, Muff, Co Donegal
(Derry)

Hegarty, Seán, Very Rev, PE
Greenpark Care Home,
15 Keady Road,
Armagh, BT60 4AA
(Armagh, retired)

Hehir, Mark, CC
Greenhill, Fermoy, Co Cork
Tel 025-33507
(*Fermoy*, Cloyne)

Heinhold, John (SPS), CC
Springhill, Glanmire,
Co Cork
Glounthaune, Co Cork
Tel 021-4866306/086-
1689292
(*Glanmire, Glounthaune*,
Cork & R.)

Henderson, Eanna (OCSO)
Mount Saint Joseph Abbey,
Roscrea, Co Tipperary
Tel 0505-25600

Hendrick, Richard (OFMCap),
CC
Capuchin Friary,
Church Street, Dublin 7
Tel 01-8730599
(*Halston Street and Arran
Quay*, Dublin 7)

Heneghan, James (CSSp)
(Chaplain to Brazilian
Community)
12 Abbeyville, Roscommon
Tel 090-6627978
(*Roscommon*, Elphin)

Heneghan, Kieran (SSC)
Knock, Co Mayo

Hennebry, John (OSA)
Provincial, St Augustine's
Taylor's Lane, Ballyboden,
Dublin 16
Tel 01-4241000

Hennessy, Gerard, CC
Cathedral Presbytery,
Thurles, Co Tipperary
Tel 0504-22505
(*Thurles, Cathedral of the
Assumption*, Cashel & E.)

Hennessy, Patrick (SDB)
Salesian College,
Maynooth Road, Celbridge,
Co Kildare
Tel 01-6275058/60

Hennessy, Patrick, Very Rev,
PP
Ballyfin, Portlaoise, Co Laois
Tel 057-8755227
(*Mountrath*, Kildare & L.)

Hennessy, William, Very Rev,
PP
Castletown, Portlaoise,
Co Laois
Tel 0502-32622/087-8736155
(*Castletown*, Ossory)

Hennessy, William, Very Rev,
PP
Knocklong, Co Limerick
Tel 062-53114
(*Knocklong*, Cashel & E.)

Hennigan, Frank (SM)
Mount St Mary's, Dundrum
Road, Milltown, Dublin 14
Tel 01-2697322

Henry, Denis, Co-PP
1A Ballydowd Grove, Lucan,
Co Dublin
Tel 01-2955541
(*Lucan*, Dublin)

Henry, Leo, BA, HDE, PP
Curry, Ballymote, Co Sligo
Tel 094-925408
(*Curry*, Achonry)

Henry, Martin
St Patrick's College,
Maynooth, Co Kildare
Tel 01-6285222
(Down & C.)

Henry, Martin, CC
The Presbytery,
Ballaghaderreen,
Co Roscommon
Tel 094-9860011
(*Ballaghaderreen
(Castlemore and Kilcolman*),
Achonry)

Henry, Maurice (SMA)
Provincial Councillor,
African Missions,
Provincial House, Feltrim,
Blackrock Road, Cork
Tel 021-4292871

Henry, Maurice, Very Rev, PE
28 Tyrella Road, Ballykinlar,
Downpatrick,
Co Down BT30 8DE
Tel 028-44851221
(Down & C., retired)

Henry, Seán, Very Rev, PP
Parochial House, Trim,
Co Meath
Tel 046-9431251
(*Trim*, Meath)

Heraty, Jarlath, PP (pro-tem)
Roundstone, Co Galway
Tel 095-35846
(*Roundstone*, Tuam)

Herlihy, David, Very Rev
Canon, PP
Youghal, Co Cork
Tel 024-85012
(*Youghal*, Cloyne)

Herrity, Michael, Very Rev, PP
Annagry, Co Donegal
Tel 074-9548111
(*Annagry*, Raphoe)

Herron, Frank, Very Rev, PP
Parochial House, Foxrock,
Dublin 18
Tel 01-2893229
(*Foxrock*, Dublin)

Hession, Noel (OSA), CC
Prior, St Augustine's,
Taylor Lane, Ballyboden,
Dublin 16
Tel 01-4543356
(*Ballyboden*, Dublin)

Hession, Stan (OCarm)
Carmelite Friary, Kinsale,
Co Cork
Tel 021-772138

Hever, Thomas, Very Rev
Canon, Adm, VG
Director, Adoption Society,
Sligo Social Services,
Charles Street, Sligo
Tel 071-9145682
Administration
St Mary's, Temple Street,
Sligo
Tel 071-9162670/9162769
(*Sligo, St Mary's*, Elphin)

Hickey, Jeremiah (OSA)
St Augustine's Priory,
O'Connell Street, Limerick
Tel 061-415374

Hickey, John (SSC)
Catholic Rectory, Abbey,
Loughrea, Co Galway
Tel 0909-745217

Hickey, John, CC
Abbey, Loughrea,
Co Galway
Tel 090-9745217
(*Duniry and Abbey*,
Clonfert)

Hickey, Liam, Very Rev
St Ciaran's,
1 Cherryfield Park,
Hartstown, Dublin 15
Tel 01-8214863
(Dublin, retired)

Hickey, Michael (CSSp), CC
Parochial House, Tenure,
Drogheda, Co Louth
Tel 041-6851281
(*Monasterboice*, Armagh)

Hickey, Michael, Very Rev, PP
Bansha, Co Tipperary
Tel 062-54132
(*Bansha and Kilmoyler*,
Cashel & E.)

Hickland, Brendan, Very Rev,
PP
St Teresa's Presbytery,
Glen Road, Belfast BT11 8BL
Tel 028-90612855
(*St Teresa's*, Down & C.)

Higgins, James (SMA)
African Missions,
Blackrock Road, Cork
Tel 021-4292871

Higgins, Richard, Very Rev
Canon, AP
Maree, Oranmore,
Co Galway
Tel 091-794113
(*Oranmore*, Galway)

Higgins, Thomas (OCarm)
Whitefriar Street Church,
56 Aungier Street, Dublin 2
Tel 01-4758821

Hillery, Desmond, Very Rev,
PP
'Maryville', Church Street,
Nenagh, Co Tipperary
Tel 067-37130
(*Nenagh*, Killaloe)

Hilliard, Alan
Chaplain, DIT
206 Ballymun Road,
Ballymun, Dublin 9
Tel 01-4023639
(Dublin)

Hinds, Michael, CC
Parochial House, Ashbourne,
Co Meath
Tel 01-8350406
(*Ashbourne-Donaghmore*,
Meath)

Hoban, Brendan (SSC)
Alcoholic Advisory Board,
St Columban's, Dalgan Park,
Navan, Co Meath
Tel 046-9021525

Hoban, Brendan, Very Rev, PP
Moygownagh, Ballina,
Co Mayo
Tel 096-31288
(*Moygownagh*, Killala)

Hoban, Patrick, Very Rev, PP
Killala, Co Mayo
Tel 096-32176
(*Killala*, Killala)

Hodnett, Ben, CC
The Presbytery,
Frankfield, Cork
Tel 021-4362377
(*Frankfield-Grange*, Cork &
Ross.)

Hodnett, Vincent, Very Rev
Canon, PP
The Lough Presbytery,
St Finbarr's West, Cork
Tel 021-4273821
(*The Lough*, Cork & R.)

Hoey, Charles (OCarm)
Provincial Office and
Carmelite Community,
Gort Muire, Ballinteer,
Dublin 16
Tel 01-2984014

Hoey, Eamonn, (CSsR), CC
St Joseph's,
St Alphonsus Road,
Dundalk, Co Louth
Tel 042-9334042
(*Dundalk, St Joseph's*,
Armagh)

Hogan, Bernard, Very Rev, PP
Drumlish, Co Longford
Tel 043-3324132
(*Drumlish*, Ardagh & Cl.)

Hogan, Diarmuid, Very Rev,
PP
Parochial House, Oranmore,
Co Galway
Tel 091-794634/087-1037452
(*Oranmore*, Galway)

Hogan, Donal (SSC)
Designated Officer
St Columban's, Dalgan Park,
Navan, Co Meath
Tel 046-9021525

Hogan, Edmund M. (SMA)
African Missions,
Blackrock Road, Cork
Tel 021-4292871

Hogan, John, CC
St Mary's, Drogheda,
Co Louth
Tel 041-9834958
(*Drogheda, St Mary's*,
Meath)

Hogan, John (CSSp)
Holy Ghost Missionary
College, Kimmage Manor,
Dublin 12
Tel 01-4064300

Hogan, John F., Venerable
Archdeacon, AP
Ballycommon, Nenagh,
Co Tipperary
Tel 067-24153/087-7536526
(*Puckane (Cloughprior and
Monsea*), Killaloe)

Hogan, Joseph, CC
Cornboy, Rossport, Ballina,
Co Mayo
Tel 097-88939
(*Kilcommon-Erris*, Killala)

Hogan, Martin, Co-PP
187 Clontarf Road, Clontarf,
Dublin 3
Tel 01-8338575
(*Clontarf, St John's*, Dublin)

Hogan, Maurice (SSC)
Society Archivist,
St Columban's,
Dalgan Park, Navan,
Co Meath
Tel 046-9021525

Hogan Patrick (SVD), Very
Rev, PC
Rector, Donamon Castle,
Roscommon
Tel 090-6662222
(*Creggs (Glinsk And
Kilbegnet*), Elphin)

Hogan, Patrick, Very Rev, PP
334 O'Malley Park,
Southill, Limerick
Tel 061-414248
(*Holy Family*, Limerick)

Hogan, Ray (MHM)
St Joseph's House,
50 Orwell Park, Rathgar,
Dublin 6
Tel 01-4127700

Hogan, Thomas (CSSp), CC
Church of the Holy Spirit,
Kimmage Manor,
Whitehall Road, Dublin 12
Tel 01-4064377
(*Kimmage Manor*, Dublin)

Hogan, Thomas (CSsR)
Marianella/Liguori House,
75 Orwell Road, Rathgar,
Dublin 6
Tel 01-4067100

Hogan, Tom, Very Rev, PP
Cathedral Presbytery,
O'Connell Street,
Ennis, Co Clare
Tel 065-6869097/087-
6446410
(*Abbey Cluster (Ennis*),
Killaloe)

Hogg, Barry, Very Rev
President, St Mary's College,
Galway
Tel 091-522458/524904
(Galway)

Holahan, Ciarán, Very Rev, PP
11 Foxrock Court, Foxrock,
Dublin 18
Tel 01-2893229
(Dublin, retired)

**Allianz ⑪**

Holland, Michael (OFM)
Franciscan Abbey, Liberty
Street, Cork
Tel 021-4270302

Holleran, Patrick, Very Rev, PP
Coolaney, Co Sligo
Tel 071-9167745
(*Coolaney (Killoran)*,
Achonry)

Holloway, Sean (SSC)
St Columban's Retirement
Home, Dalgan Park, Navan,
Co Meath
Tel 046-9021525

Holmes, Brian (CSsR)
Santa Maria dei Monti
Mission, Furancungo,
Mozambique, Africa
c/o Marianella,
75 Orwell Road,
Rathgar, Dublin 6
Tel 01-4067100

Holmes, Kieran
Chaplain, Convent of Jesus
and Mercy, Enniscrone,
Ballina, Co Mayo
Tel 096-36151
(Killala)

Holmes, Liam, Very Rev, PP
Knockaney, Hospital,
Co Limerick
Tel 061-383127
(*Knockaney*, Cashel & E.)

Holmes, Vianney (OFMCap)
Vicar, Capuchin Friary,
Ard Mhuire, Creeslough,
Letterkenny, Co Donegal
Tel 074 9138005

Horan, Barry
Chaplain's Office,
NUI Galway,
University Road, Galway
Tel 091-495055
(Galway)

Horan, Gerard (OSA)
Bursar, The Abbey, Fethard,
Co Tipperary
Tel 052-31273

Horan, John (SDB), Very Rev
Rector, Salesian House,
Milford, Castletroy,
Limerick
Tel 061-330268/330914

Horgan, John (SMA), AP
St Joseph's,
Blackrock Road, Cork
Tel 021-4292871/021-4293325
(*St Joseph's (Blackrock
Road)*, Cork & R.)

Horgan, Patrick (CSsR)
Marianella/Ligouri House,
75 Orwell Road, Rathgar,
Dublin 6
Tel 01-4067100

Horgan, Patrick, Very Rev
(priest in residence)
Killarney, Co Kerry
Tel 064-31014
(*Killarney*, Kerry)

Horgan, Seamus, Mgr
Apostolic Nunciature,
PO Box 3604, 1099 Manila,
Philippines
Tel 00632-527-4271
(Killaloe)

Horgan, Seán (MSC), CC (pro-
tem)
Glantane, Mallow, Co Cork
Tel 022-47158
(*Glantane*, Cloyne)

Horneck, Noel, Very Rev, PP
Parochial House, Dunderry,
Navan, Co Meath
Tel 046-9431433
(*Dunderry*, Meath)

Hou, Anthony
Chaplain to Chinese
Community,
Westland Row, Dublin 2
Tel 01-6761270
(*Westland Row*, Dublin)

Houlihan, Brendan, Rt Rev
Mgr, PE
Parochial House,
Mount Saint Mary's,
Thormanby Road, Howth,
Co Dublin
(Dublin, retired)

Houlihan, Henry
Franciscan Friary, Lady Lane,
Waterford
Tel 051-874262

Houlihan, Nik (MI)
St Camillus, Killucan,
Co Westmeath
Tel 044-74115

Houlihan, Séamus, Very Rev,
PP, Adm
Administration
Parochial House, Kilbeg,
Kells, Co Meath
Tel 046-9246604
Parish Priest
Parochial House,
Nobber, Co Meath
Tel 046-9052197
(*Kilbeg, Nobber*, Meath)

Hourigan, Joseph, Very Rev,
PP
Lissycasey, Ennis,
Co Clare
Tel 065-6834145
(*Ballynacally*, Killaloe)

Howard, Brendan, Very Rev,
PP
Clonegal, Enniscorthy,
Co Wexford
Tel 053-9377291
(*Ballon*, Kildare & L.)

Howard, Greg
The Prebytery,
Knocknaheeny, Cork
Tel 021-4392459
(*Knocknaheeny*, Cork & R.)

Howard, Niall, CC
Killarney, Co Kerry
Tel 064-6631014
(*Killarney*, Kerry)

Howard, Patrick, Very Rev
Athlacca, Kilmallock,
Co Limerick
Tel 063-90540
(Limerick, retired)

Howard, Terence (SJ)
Peter Faber House,
28 Brookvale Avenue,
Belfast BT14 6BW
Tel 028-90757615

Howell, William, Very Rev, PP,
VF
St Michael's, Gorey,
Co Wexford
Tel 053-9421112
(*Gorey*, Ferns)

Howlett, John (SAC)
Provincial House,
'Homestead', Sandyford
Road, Dundrum, Dublin 16
Tel 01-2956180/2954170

Howley, Enda, CC
Parochial House, Ryehill,
Monivea, Galway
Tel 091-849019
(*Abbeyknockmoy*, Tuam)

Howley, Gary (SPS)
House Leader, St Patrick's,
Main Street, Knock,
Co Mayo
Tel 094-9388661

Hoyne, Peter, Very Rev, PE
Newmarket, Hugginstown,
Co Kilkenny
Tel 056-7768678
(*Aghaviller*, Ossory)

Hoyne, William (OFM)
Hermanos Franciscanos,
Iglesia Parroquial 'Dios con
Nostros',
1a Av, 5a-6a Calles,
Manzana 10,
Elmezquital, Zana 12,
10102 Guatemala City,
Guatemala

Hubbort, Thomas (IC)
Clonturk House,
Ormond Road,
Drumcondra, Dublin 9
Tel 01-6877014

Hudson, Patrick (OFM)
Adam and Eve's,
4 Merchant's Quay,
Dublin 8
Tel 01-6771128

Hughes, Augustine (OFM)
Franciscan College,
Gormanston, Co Meath
Tel 01-8412203

Hughes, Ben
Chaplain, NUI Galway,
University Road, Galway
Tel 091-495055

Hughes, Benedict
(On study leave)
Kellystown, Coolderry Road,
Carrickmacross,
Co Monaghan
Tel 086-3864907
(Clogher)

Hughes, Bernard (IC)
(priest in charge)
Rathgormack,
Carrick-on-Suir,
Co Waterford
Tel 051-646006
(*Rathgormack*, Waterford &
L.)

Hughes, Eoin
Chaplain,
Beaumont Hospital,
Beaumont Road, Dublin 9
Tel 01-8477573
(Dublin)

Hughes, John (OSA), Very Rev,
PP
St Augustine's Priory,
St Augustine's Street,
Galway
Tel 091-562524
(*St Augustine's*, Galway)

Hughes, John, Very Rev, PE,
CC
6 Jockey Lane, Moy,
Dungannon,
Co Tyrone BT71 7SR
Tel 028-87784240
(*Moy (Clonfeacle)*, Armagh)

Hughes, Liam, Very Rev, PE
Inniskeen, Dundalk,
Co Louth
Tel 042-9378338
(Clogher, retired)

Hughes, Louis (OP)
Newbridge College,
Droichead Nua, Co Kildare
Tel 045-487200

Hughes, Martin
(Team Assistant)
447 The Oaks,
Belgard Heights
Tallaght, Dublin 24
Tel 01-4519399
(Dublin)

Hughes, Michael (OMI)
Oblate Scholasticate,
St Anne's,
Goldenbridge Walk,
Inchicore, Dublin 8
Tel 01-4540841/4542955

Hughes, Pat, CC
Priest's House, Emo,
Portlaoise, Co Laois
Tel 057-8646517
(*Emo, Portarlington*, Kildare
& L.)

Hughes, Patrick (CM)
St Peter's, Phibsboro,
Dublin 7
Tel 01-8389708

Hughes, Patrick, Very Rev, PP, Adm
Parochial House,
10 Cloughfin Road,
Kildress, Cookstown,
Co Tyrone BT80 9JB
Administration Kildress
Tel 028-86751206
(*Kildress, Lissan*, Armagh)

Hume, Patrick (SJ)
Superior, Campion House
Residence, 28 Lower Hatch
Street, Dublin 2
Tel 01-6383990

Humphreys, John (SJ)
St Ignatius Community &
Church, 27 Raleigh Row,
Salthill, Galway
Tel 091-523707

Humphries, Seamus (OSA)
St Augustine's Priory,
Dungarvan, Co Waterford
Tel 058-41136

Hunt, Anselm (OSB)
Abbot, Glenstal Abbey,
Murroe, Co Limerick
Tel 061-386103

Hunt, Des (SM)
Mount St Mary's,
Dundrum Road, Milltown,
Dublin 14
Tel 01-2697322

Hurley, Colm
Killeshandra, Co Cavan
Tel 049-4334155
(Kilmore, retired)

Hurley, Declan, Very Rev, Adm
St Mary's, Navan,
Co Meath
Tel 046-9027518/9071774
(*Navan*, Meath)

Hurley, James, CC
31 Herbert Avenue,
Merrion Road, Dublin 4
Tel 01-2692001
(*Merrion Road*, Dublin)

Hurley, James (CSSp)
Rockwell College, Cashel,
Co Tipperary
Tel 062-61444

Hurley, Michael C., Very Rev
Canon, PP, VF
Killeshandra, Co Cavan
Tel 049-4334155
(*Killeshandra*, Kilmore)

Hurley, Michael, Very Rev,
Adm
85 Tymon Crescent,
Oldbawn, Dublin 24,
Tel 01-4627080
(*Bohernabreena, Tallaght,
Oldbawn*, Dublin)

Hurley, Patrick (SSC)
St Columban's Retirement
Home, Dalgan Park,
Navan, Co Meath
Tel 046-9021525

Hurley, Richard, Very Rev
Canon, PP
South Presbytery,
Dunbar Street, Cork
Tel 021-4272989
(*St Finbarr's South*, Cork &
R.)

Hurley, Thomas, Very Rev
Templeglantine,
Co Limerick
Tel 068-84021
(Limerick, retired)

Hussey, Michael, Very Rev, PP
Castlegregory, Co Kerry
Tel 066-7139145
(*Castlegregory*, Kerry)

Hutchinson, Stephen (OP),
Very Rev
St Mary's, Pope Quay, Cork
Tel 021-4502267

Hutton, John, Very Rev
Apt 2, Ceara Court,
Windsor Avenue,
Belfast BT9 6EJ
Tel 028-90683002
(Down & C., retired)

Hyde, Jeremiah, Very Rev
The Presbytery, Kinsale,
Co Cork
(Cork & R., retired)

Hyland, James (OMI)
Oblate House of Retreat,
Inchicore, Dublin 8
Tel 01-4534408/4541805

Hyland, Richard, Very Rev, PP
42 Strand Street, Skerries,
Co Dublin
Tel 01-8491250
(*Skerries*, Dublin)

Hyland, Sean, CC
Tinryland, Co Carlow
Tel 059-9131212
(*Askea, Bennekerry,
Tinryland*, Kildare & L.)

Hynes, James (OFM)
98 Bld de Montpernasse,
95014 Paris, France

Hynes, Sean (OMI)
Oblate House of Retreat,
Inchicore, Dublin 8
Tel 01-4534408/4541805

Hynes, Valentine (SMA)
SMA House, Claregalway,
Co Galway
Tel 091-798880

---

**I**

Igoe, Michael (SMA)
African Missions,
Blackrock Road, Cork
Tel 021-4292871

Illah, Louis, CC
St Mary's, Navan, Co Meath
Tel 046-9027518/
046-9071774
(*Navan*, Meath)

Inharjanto, Anselmus (SCJ)
Sacred Heart Fathers,
Fairfield, 66 Inchicore Road,
Dublin 8
Tel 01-4538655

Irudayasamy, Moyison, AP
Presbytery No. 1,
Rathdrum, Co Wicklow
Tel 0404-46214
(*Rathdrum*, Dublin)

Irwin, Charles, Very Rev, BD,
HDE
President,
St Munchin's College,
Corbally, Limerick
Tel 061-348922
(Limerick)

Irwin, Edwin, Very Rev, PP
Cloncagh, Ballingarry,
Co Limerick
Tel 069-83006
(*Knockaderry and Cloncagh*,
Limerick)

Irwin, John
c/o Diocesan Offices,
St Eugene's Cathedral,
Francis Street,
Derry BT48 9AP
(Derry)

Irwin, Michael (SAC)
Rector and Vice-Provincial,
'Homestead',
Sandyford Road, Dundrum,
Dublin 16
Tel 01-2956180/2954170

Irwin, Michael (SSC)
(priest in residence)
Kilcornan, Co Limerick
Tel 061-393113
(*Kilcornan*, Limerick)

Irwin, Nicholas J., Very Rev, PP
Diocesan
Secretary/Chancellor,
Archbishop's House,
Thurles, Co Tipperary
Tel 0504-21512
The Parochial House,
Gortnahoe, Thurles,
Co Tipperary
Tel 056-8834855
(*Gortnahoe*, Cashel & E.)

Issac, Sunil (SCJ)
Sacred Heart Fathers,
Fairfield, 66 Inchicore Road,
Dublin 8
Tel 01-4538655

Iwuozor, Gregory (CSSp)
Holy Ghost Missionary
College, Kimmage Manor,
Dublin 12
Tel 01-4064300

---

**J**

Jachym, Marian (SC), CC
68 North Street, Lurgan,
Co Armagh, BT67 9AH
Tel 028-38323161
(*St Patrick's (Mayobridge)*,
Dromore)

Jackson, Piaras (SJ)
Director of Retreat House,
Manresa House,
Dollymount, Dublin 3
Tel 01-8331352
Director Sacred Space

Jacob, John, Very Rev, Adm
12 Walkinstown Road,
Dublin 12
Tel 01-4502541
(*Walkinstown*, Dublin)

Jarzab, Slawomir, CC
22 Gladstone, Clonmel,
Co Tipperary
Tel 052-6122138
(*Clonmel, Ss Peter and
Paul's*, Waterford & L.)

Jansen, Luuk (OP)
Newbridge College,
Droichead Nua, Co Kildare
Tel 045-487200

Jenkinson, William (CSSp)
Holy Spirit Missionary
College,
Kimmage Manor,
Whitehall Road, Dublin 12
Tel 01-4064300

Jennings, Gavan
Harvieston,
Cunningham Road, Dalkey,
Co Dublin
Tel 01-2859877
(Opus Dei)

Jennings, Gerard
St Theresa's,
Castleblayney Road,
Ballybay, Co Monaghan
(Clogher, retired)

Jennings, Gerard, Very Rev, PP
Curate's House,
Monksfield, Salthill, Galway
Tel 091-523413
(*Salthill*, Galway)

Jennings, Martin, Very Rev, PP
Tubbercurry, Co Sligo
Tel 071-9185049
(*Tubbercurry (Cloonacool)*,
Achonry)

Jennings, Norman (SSC)
St Columban's,
Grange Road,
Donaghemede, Dublin 13
Tel 01-8476647

Jennings, Patrick (SMA)
African Missions,
Blackrock Road, Cork
Tel 021-4292871

**Allianz ⑪**

Johnston, Andrew, Very Rev
Canon
c/o Innis Ree Lodge,
Ballyleague, Lanesborough,
Co Roscommon
Tel 043-3327300
(Achonry, retired)

Johnston, Anthony
8 Corrig Park,
Dun Laoghaire, Co Dublin
Tel 01-2805594
(Dublin, retired)

Johnston, Cecil
8 Corrig Park,
Dun Laoghaire, Co Dublin
Tel 01-2805594
(Dublin, retired)

Johnston, Jim (SM)
Cerdon, Marist Fathers,
St Mary's Road, Dundalk,
Co Louth
Tel 042-9334019

Johnston, Thomas, Rt Rev
Mgr, PP, VG
Charlestown, Co Mayo
Tel 094-9254315
(Charlestown (Kilbeagh),
Achonry)

Jones, Aidan G., Very Rev
33 Twin Oaks,
Clonattin, Gorey,
Co Wexford
Tel 053-9481848
(Ferns, retired)

Jones, Bernard (OFM)
Guardian, Franciscan Friary,
Liberty Street, Cork
Tel 021-4270302

Jones, Christopher, Most Rev,
DD
Bishop Emeritus of Elphin,
St Mary's,
Temple Street, Sligo
Tel 071-9162670
(Elphin)

Jones, Gerard, CC
The Presbytery, Nenagh,
Co Tipperary
Tel 067-37131/087-2137238
(Nenagh, Killaloe)

Jones, John (SPS)
Dysart, Mullingar,
Co Westmeath

Jones, John, Very Rev, Adm
151 Swords Road,
Whitehall, Dublin 9
Tel 01-8374887
(Larkhill-Whitehall-Santry,
Dublin)

Jones, John, Very Rev, PP
St Caimin's, Mountshannon,
Co Clare
Tel 061-927213/086-1933479
(Mountshannon, Killaloe)

Jones, Joseph
(Moderator)
122 Greencastle Road,
Dublin 17
Tel 01-8487657
(Bonnybrook, Dublin)

Jones, Patrick, Very Rev, Co-PP
'Marmion', 87 Iona Road,
Dublin 9
Tel 01-8305651
(Iona Road, Dublin)

Jordan, Cathal, Very Rev
Canon
The Presbytery,
13 Tullygally Road,
Craigavon BT65 5BY
(Dromore, retired)

Jordan, Columba (CFR)
St Columba Friary,
Fairview Road,
Derry, BT48 8NU
Tel 028-71419980

Jordan, John, Very Rev, PP
Kyle, Oulart,
Gorey, Co Wexford
(Ferns, retired)

Jordan, Michael, CC
Parochial House,
Donaghmoyne,
Co Monaghan
Tel 042-9661586
(Donaghmoyne, Clogher)

Jordan, Phelim (SVD)
8 Teignmouth Road,
London NW2 4HN
Tel 020-84528430

Jordan, Thomas (MSC)
Carrignavar, Co Cork
Tel 021-4884044

Jordan, Thomas (OP), Very
Rev
Prior, St Mary's,
The Claddagh, Co Galway
Tel 091-582884

Joseph, Jayan (OSCam)
Chaplain,
St James's Hospital
St Camillus, South Hill Ave,
Blackrock, Co Dublin

Joyce, Michael (SVD)
Donamon Castle,
Roscommon
Tel 090-6662222

Joyce, Michael, Very Rev
Dean, PE
33 Fraunhill, Swinford,
Co Mayo
(Achonry, retired)

Joyce, Peter
Chaplain, University
Hospital, Galway
Tel 091-524222
(Galway)

Joyce, Stephen, CC
St Joseph's Presbytery,
Park Street, Monaghan
Tel 047-81220
(Monaghan, Clogher)

Judge, Francis, Very Rev, PP
Crossmolina, Ballina
Co Mayo
(Crossmolina, Killala)

Judge, John
c/o Pastoral Centre, Ballina,
Co Mayo
(Killala, retired)

Júnior, José Carlos (CSsR)
Santa Maria dei Monti
Mission, Furancungo,
Mozambique, Africa
c/o Marianella/
Liguori House,
75 Orwell Road,
Rathgar, Dublin 6
Tel 01-4067100

## K

Kakkadampallil, Vincent
Xavier (OSCam)
Chaplain, Mater Hospital,
Eccles Street, Dublin 7
Tel 01-8301122
(Dublin)

Kalema, Godfrey
Team Assistant, Holy
Redeemer Parish,
Herbert Road, Bray,
Co Dublin
Tel 01-2868413
(Bray, Holy Redeemer,
Dublin)

Kamau, Bosco (SPS)
Councillor, St Patrick's
Kiltegan, Co Wicklow
Tel 059-6473600

Kane, Andrew (OP)
St Dominic's, Athy,
Co Kildare
Tel 059-8631573

Kane, Gerry, Very Rev, PP
213B Harold's Cross Road,
Dublin 6W
Tel 01-4972816/086-8220956
(Harold's Cross, Dublin)

Kane, Michael
Claremount Nursing Home,
Claremorris, Co Mayo
(Tuam, retired)

Kane, Michael (CSSp)
Holy Ghost Missionary
College, Kimmage Manor,
Dublin 12
Tel 01-4064300

Kane, Michael (SPS)
St Patrick's, Kiltegan,
Co Wicklow
Tel 059-6473600

Kavanagh, Brian, PP
Graiguecullen, Carlow
Tel 059-9179855
(Arles, Kildare & L.)

Kavanagh, Dermot (CSSp)
Ballybeg, Rathnew,
Co Wicklow
Tel 0404-69774

Kavanagh, Edward, CC
15 Lowtown Manor,
Robertstown,
Naas, Co Kildare
Tel 045-890559
(Allen, Kildare & L.)

Kavanagh, Hugh, Very Rev,
Adm
Parochial House, 78 St
Mary's Road,
East Wall, Dublin 3
Tel 01-8742320
(East Wall-North Strand,
Dublin)

Kavanagh, Joseph (OP)
Black Abbey, Kilkenny,
Co Kilkenny
Tel 056-7721279

Kavanagh, Joseph, Very Rev,
PP
Camolin, Co Wexford
Tel 053-9383136
(Camolin, Ferns)

Kavanagh, Mark (SSC)
St Columban's
Retirement Home,
Dalgan Park, Navan,
Co Meath
Tel 046-9021525

Kavanagh, Martin (SMA)
African Missions,
Blackrock Road, Cork
Tel 021-4292871

Kavanagh, Myles (CP), CC
Holy Cross Retreat, 432
Crumlin Road,
Ardoyne, Belfast BT14 7GE
Tel 028-90748231/2
(Holy Cross, Down & C.)

Kavanagh, Vincent (CSsR)
St Patrick's, Esker, Athenry,
Co Galway
Tel 091-844007

Kaweesi, Charles (OCSO), Rt
Rev Dom
Sub-Prior, Our Lady of
Bethlehem Abbey,
11 Ballymena Road,
Portglenone, Ballymena,
Co Antrim BT44 8BL
Tel 028-25821211

Kealy, Brendan, CC
12 Ashville, Athy, Co Kildare
Tel 087-9117575
(Athy, Dublin)

Kealy, John (OFM)
Franciscan Abbey,
Multyfarnham,
Co Westmeath
Tel 044-9371114/9371137

Kealy, John (Seán)(CSSp)
Holy Spirit Missionary
College, Kimmage Manor,
Whitehall Road, Dublin 12
Tel 01-4064300

Keane, Anthony (OSB)
Glenstal Abbey, Murroe,
Co Limerick
Tel 061-621000

Keane, Brendan (CSsR)
Clonard Monastery,
1 Clonard Gardens,
Belfast, BT13 2RL
Tel 028-90445950

Keane, Jerry, Very Rev, PP
Glenbeigh, Co Kerry
Tel 066-9768209
(Glenbeigh, Kerry)

Keane, John
Céili Catholic Community,
Horseleap, Moate,
Co Westmeath
Tel 057-9335922
(Cloyne)

Keane, John D., Very Rev
St Brigid's, Ballybane,
Galway
Tel 091-755381
(Ballybane, Galway)

Keane, Martin
Chaplain,
Brothers of Charity,
Kilcornan, Clarinbridge,
Co Galway
Tel 091-796106
(Galway)

Keane, Paul
Ballycrodick, Dunhill,
Co Waterford
(Tuam, retired)

Keane, Richard, CC
(part-time study leave)
Gortboy, Newcastle West,
Co Limerick
Tel 069-77090/087-9552729
(Newcastle West, Limerick)

Keane, Stephen, PE
Kilcolgan Nursing Home,
Kilcolgan, Co Galway
Tel 091-776446
(Galway, retired)

Keane, Tom (MHM)
(elsewhere in Ireland)

Keaney, Charles, PP
Chapelfield,
59 Laurel Hill, Coleraine,
Co Derry BT51 3AY
Tel 028-70343130
(Coleraine, Derry)

Kearney, Derek (SMA)
On sabbatical

Kearney, Francis, Very Rev
Canon, PP
17 Monteith Road,
Annaclone, Banbridge,
Co Down BT32 5AQ
Tel 028-40671201
(Annaclone, Dromore)

Kearney, John, Very Rev
Canon, Adm, PP,VF
Administration St Peter's
Great George's Street,
Warrenpoint,
Co Down, BT34 3NF
Parish Priest
Riverfields, Warrenpoint,
Co Down, BT34 3PU
Tel 028-41754684
(St Peter's (Warrenpoint),
Kilbroney (Rostrevor),
Dromore)

Kearney, Patrick, Very Rev, PP
Parochial House, Longwood,
Co Meath
Tel 046-9555009
(Longwood, Meath)

Kearney, Stephen
(priest in residence)
Knockmoyle, Omagh,
Co Tyrone
Tel 028-82252643
(Killyclogher, Derry)

Kearney, Thomas (SVD)
St Mary's Athlone,
Co Westmeath
Tel 090-6472088
(Athlone, Ardagh & Cl.)

Kearney, Thomas, CC
137 Shantalla Road,
Whitehall, Dublin 9
Tel 01-8420260
(Larkhill-Whitehall-Santry,
Dublin)

Kearney, Tom (SVD)
1 & 3 Pembroke Road,
Dublin 4
Tel 01-6680904

Kearns, Brendan, CC
44 Church Street, Rostrevor,
Co Down BT34 3BB
Tel 028-41738277
(St Peter's (Warrenpoint),
Kilbroney (Rostrevor),
Dromore)

Kearns, Gerard
Cavan General Hospital
Tel 049-4361399
(Kilmore)

Kearns, John (SPS)
On temporary diocesan
work

Kearns, John, CC
Loughside Road, Garrison,
Enniskillen
Co Fermanagh BT93 4AE
Tel 028-68658238
(Belleek-Garrison (Inis
Muighe Samh), Clogher)

Kearny, Nicholas (OSA)
St John's Priory,
Thomas Street, Dublin 8
Tel 01-6770393/0415/0601

Keary, Patrick, Very Rev, PP,
VF
Horseleap, Co Offaly
Tel 057-9335922
(Meath)

Keating, Andy (SPS)
St Patrick's, Kiltegan,
Co Wicklow
Tel 059-6473600

Keating, Crispin (OFM)
5225 North Himes Avenue,
Tampa, Fl 33614-6623, USA

Keating, David
Chaplain, Waterford
Institute of Technology,
10 Claremont, Cork Road,
Waterford
Tel 051-378878
(Waterford & L.)

Keating, Denis (OP)
St Mary's, Pope Quay, Cork
Tel 021-4502267

Keating, John, Very Rev, PP
Raheenagh, Ballagh,
Co Limerick
Tel 069-85014
(Killeedy, Limerick)

Keating, Patrick, Very Rev, PP
Drimoleague
(Cork & R., retired)

Keaveny, Michael, PEm
53 Brisland Road, Eglinton,
Co Derry BT47 3EA
Tel 028-71810234
(Derry, retired)

Keegan, John F., Very Rev, Co-
PP
Rolestown, Swords,
Co Dublin
Tel 01-8401514
(Rolestown-Oldtown,
Dublin)

Keenan, Aidan, Very Rev, PP
St Matthew's Presbytery,
Bryson Street,
Newtownards Road,
Belfast BT5 4ES
Tel 028-90457626
(Portglenone, Down & C.)

Keenan, Brian (SM)
CUS Community,
89 Lower Leeson Street,
Dublin 2
Tel 01-6762586

Keenan, Frank (SJ)
St Francis Xavier's,
Upper Gardiner Street,
Dublin 1
Tel 01-8363411

Keenan, Kevin (SVD), PP
Main Street, Clarinbridge,
Co Galway
Chaplain to Brazilian
Community
Tel 091-485777
(Clarinbridge, Galway)

Keenan, Pádraig, Very Rev, PP
Parochial House,
Chapel Road,
Haggardstown,
Dundalk, Co Louth
Tel 042-9321621
(Haggardstown and
Blackrock, Armagh)

Keenan, Patrick (OCD), CC
The Presbytery,
Berkeley Road, Dublin 7
Tel 01-8306356/8306336
(Berkeley Road, Dublin)

Keeney, Sean (CSsR)
Clonard Monastery,
1 Clonard Gardens,
Belfast, BT13 2RL
(St Paul's, Down & C.)

Keevins, Frank (CP), Very Rev,
PP
St Paul's Retreat,
Mount Argus, Dublin 6W
Tel 01-4992000
(Mount Argus, Dublin)

Kehoe, James, Very Rev, PP
Carrig-on-Bannow,
Wellington Bridge,
Co Wexford
Tel 051-561192
(Bannow, Ferns)

Kehoe, Joseph L., Rt Rev Mgr,
PA
13 Priory Court, Spawell
Road, Wexford
Tel 053-9180599
(Ferns, retired)

Kehoe, Liam (CSSp)
Blackrock College,
Blackrock, Co Dublin
Tel 01-2888681

Kehoe, Noel (CSsR)
Co-ordinator, Scala,
Castlemahon House,
Castle Road, Blackrock,
Cork
Tel 021-4358800

Kehoe, Patrick, Very Rev, PE
Droimnín Nursing Home,
Brockley Park,
Stradbally, Co Laois
Tel 057-8641002
(Kildare & L., retired)

Kehoe, Peter, (OCarm), Very
Rev
Bursar, Carmelite Priory,
Moate, Co Westmeath
Tel 090-6481160/6481398

Kehoe, Philip (FDP)
25 Lower Teddington Road,
Kingston-on-Thames, Surrey
Tel 208-9775130

Kehoe, Tomás, CC
New Ross, Co Wexford
Tel 051-447086
(New Ross, Ferns)

Keleghan, Anselm (CP)
St Paul's Retreat,
Mount Argus, Dublin 6W
Tel 01-4992000

Kelleher, Cornelius, Very Rev,
PP
Tournaneena, Ballinamult,
Clonmel, Co Tipperary
Tel 058-47138
(Tournaneena, Waterford &
L.)

Kelleher, Denis, Very Rev, PP
Church Road, Aghada,
Co Cork
Tel 021-4661298
(*Aghada*, Cloyne)

Kelleher, Eamonn, CC
Jamesbrook, Midleton,
Co Cork
Tel 021-4652456
(*Aghada*, Cloyne)

Kelleher, Finbar, Very Rev
Canon, CC (pro-tem)
Ballindangan, Mitchelstown,
Co Cork
Tel 025-85563
(*Glanworth and
Ballindangan*, Cloyne)

Kelleher, Francis, Very Rev, PP
Knocktemple, Virginia,
Co Cavan
Tel 049-8547435
(*Castlerahan and
Munterconnaught*, Kilmore)

Kelleher, Liam, Very Rev, PE,
CC
Cobh, Co Cork
Tel 021-4816400
(*Cobh, St Colman's
Cathedral*, Cloyne)

Kelleher, Maurice (SMA)
SMA House, Wilton, Cork
Tel 021-4541069/4541884

Kelleher, Michael, Very Rev,
Adm
The Presbytery, Skibbereen,
Co Cork
Tel 028-22878/22877
(*St Patrick's Cathedral,
Skibbereen, Rath and the
Islands*, Cork & R.)

Kelleher, Michael G. (CSsR)
Marianella/Liguori House,
75 Orwell Road, Rathgar,
Dublin 6
Tel 01-4067100

Kelleher, Roger, Very Rev
9 St Emmet's Terrace,
Killarney, Co Kerry
(Kerry, retired)

Kelleher, Thomas, Very Rev
Canon, PE
The Presbytery, Kinsale,
Co Cork
(Cork & R., retired)

Kelliher, Padraig, CC
The Presbytery, Longford
Tel 043-3346465
(*Longford*, Ardagh & Cl.)

Kelly Jnr, Patrick (CSsR)
Marianella, 75 Orwell Road,
Dublin 6
Tel 01-4067100

Kelly Snr, Patrick (CSsR)
St Joseph's, Dundalk,
Co Louth
Tel 042-9334042/9334762

Kelly, Brendan (CSsR), Adm
Via Merulana 31, CP 2458,
00185 Roma-PT158, Italy
Tel 0039-06-494901

Kelly, Brendan, Most Rev, DD
Bishop of Achonry,
Bishop's House,
Edmondstown,
Ballaghaderreen,
Co Roscommon
Tel 094-9860021
(Achonry)

Kelly, Celsus (OCSO), Rt Rev
Dom
Abbot, Our Lady of
Bethlehem Abbey,
11 Ballymena Road,
Portglenone, Ballymena,
Co Antrim BT44 8BL
Tel 028-25821211

Kelly, Conor, Very Rev, PP
Ring, Dungarvan,
Co Waterford
Tel 058-46125
(*Ring*, Waterford & L.)

Kelly, David (OSA)
Dublin North

Kelly, Declan, CC
Parochial House,
Trim, Co Meath
Tel 046-9431251
(*Trim*, Meath)

Kelly, Declan, Very Rev, PP
Preston Hill, Stamullen,
Co Meath
Tel 01-8418066
(*Stamullen*, Meath)

Kelly, Denis, Very Rev, Adm
Ballymore, Screen,
Enniscorthy, Co Wexford
Tel 053-9137140
(*Castlebridge*, Ferns)

Kelly, Dermot (OCarm)
Bursar,
Whitefriar Street Church
56 Aungier Street, Dublin 2
Tel 01-4758821

Kelly, Desmond (OCarm)
Whitefriar Street Church,
56 Aungier Street, Dublin 2
Tel 01-4758821

Kelly, Desmond, Very Rev, PP
Corballa, Ballina,
Co Mayo
Tel 096-36266
(*Castleconnor*, Killala)

Kelly, Donal, Very Rev
7 Knocksinna Park,
Bray Road, Foxrock,
Dublin 18
Tel 01-2894170
(Down & C., retired)

Kelly, Eamonn (SMA)
African Missions,
Blackrock Road, Cork
Tel 021-4292871

Kelly, Eamonn, Adm, VF
Parochial House,
Letterkenny, Co Donegal
Tel 074-9121021
Chaplain,
Errigal College, Letterkenny,
Co Donegal
Tel 074-9121047/9121861
(*Letterkenny*, Raphoe)

Kelly, Edward, Very Rev
Canon, PE
No. 1 St Mary's College
House,
Shantalla Road, Galway
Tel 091-586663
(Galway, retired)

Kelly, Felim, Very Rev, CC
Castlerahan, Ballyjamesduff,
Co Cavan
Tel 049-8544150
(*Castlerahan and
Munterconnaught*, Kilmore)

Kelly, Fergus, Very Rev (CM)
Superior, St Paul's, Raheny,
Dublin 5
Tel 01-8314011/14012/18113

Kelly, Finbar (OP)
Black Abbey, Kilkenny,
Co Kilkenny
Tel 056-7721279

Kelly, Gabriel, Very Rev, PP
Kinawley, Enniskillen,
Co Fermanagh BT92 4FH
Tel 028-66348250
(Kinawley/Killesher, Kilmore)

Kelly, Gilbert
Ballycarron House, Golden,
Co Tipperary
(Dublin, retired)

Kelly, James (SJ)
Milltown Park,
Sandford Road, Dublin 6
Tel 01-2698411/2698113

Kelly, James, Canon, AP
Tooreen, Ballyhaunis,
Co Mayo
Tel 094-9649002
(*Aghamore*, Tuam)

Kelly, Jimmy (OSM)
Chaplain, Mountjoy Prison,
c/o Servite Priory,
St Peregrine,
36 Grangewood Estate,
Rathfarnham, Dublin 16
Tel 01-4517115

Kelly, Jimmy, Very Rev, PP
Raheen, Abbeyleix,
Co Laois
Tel 057-8731182
(*Raheen*, Kildare & L.)

Kelly, Joe, CC
5 Bayside Square East,
Sutton, Dublin 13
Tel 01-8322305
(*Bayside*, Dublin)

Kelly, John
Director of Pastoral Care,
Tallaght Hospital,
22 Nugent Road,
Churchtown, Dublin 14
Tel 01-4142482
(Dublin)

Kelly, John (SAC)
Bursar/Secretary for
Missions,
Provincial House,
'Homestead',
Sandyford Road, Dundrum,
Dublin 16
Tel 01-2956180/2954170

Kelly, John (SCJ)
Superior & Formation
Director,
Sacred Heart Fathers,
Fairfield, 66 Inchicore Road,
Dublin 8
Tel 01-4538655

Kelly, Larry, Very Rev Canon,
PP, VF
Cahirciveen, Co Kerry
Tel 066-9472210
(*Cahirciveen*, Kerry)

Kelly, Laurence (OP)
Newbridge College,
Droichead Nua,
Co Kildare
Tel 045-487200

Kelly, Lawrence, Very Rev
Fatima Home, Oakpark,
Tralee, Co Kerry
(Kerry, retired)

Kelly, Liam (OFM)
Franciscan Friary, Friary
Lane,
Athlone, Co Westmeath
Tel 090-6472095

Kelly, Liam, Very Rev, PP
Chairman, Council of Priests,
Bunnoe, Cootehill, Co Cavan
Parish: Parochial House,
Bunnoe, Cootehill, Co Cavan
Tel 049-5553035
(*Kilsherdany and Drung*,
Kilmore)

Kelly, Martin, Very Rev, PP
Parochial House,
546 Saintfield Road,
Carryduff, Belfast BT8 8EU
Tel 028-90812238
(*Drumbo*, Down & C.)

Kelly, Matthew, Very Rev, PE,
CC
60 Hartwell Green, Kill,
Naas, Co Kildare
Tel 045-877880
(*Kill*, Kildare & L.)

Kelly, Michael
Crumlin, Dublin 12
Tel 01-4542308
(Dublin)

Kelly, Michael (SPS)
St Patrick's, Kiltegan,
Co Wicklow
Tel 059-6473600

Kelly, Michael (SPS), Very Rev, Adm
Rathvilly, Co Carlow
Tel 059-9161114
(*Rathvilly*, Kildare & L.)

Kelly, Michael, Very Rev Dean, PE
'Inchagill',
Ballinamana Road,
Clarinbridge, Co Galway
Tel 086-8234027
(Galway, retired)

Kelly, Oliver, Very Rev, PP, VF
Manorhamilton, Co Leitrim
Tel 071-9855042
(*Manorhamilton*, Kilmore)

Kelly, Paddy (CSSR), CC
c/o Parish of Travelling People,
St Laurence House,
6 New Cabra Road,
Phibsborough, Dublin 7
(*Firhouse*, Dublin)

Kelly, Patrick (MSC)
'Croí Nua', Rosary Lane,
Taylor's Hill, Galway
Tel 091-520960

Kelly, Patrick (SMA)
Seconded to US Province

Kelly, Patrick (SPS)
Tearmann Spirituality Centre, Brockagh,
Glendalough,
Co Wicklow
Tel 0404-45208

Kelly, Patrick, Very Rev Canon, PE
Athea, Co Limerick
Tel 068-42107
(*Athea*, Limerick)

Kelly, Patrick Joseph (CSSp)
Holy Spirit Missionary College, Kimmage Manor,
Whitehall Road, Dublin 12
Tel 01-4064300

Kelly, Paul, Very Rev, CC
The Presbytery,
18 Straffan Way,
Maynooth, Co Kildare
Tel 01-6293018
(*Maynooth*, Dublin)

Kelly, Philip (OSA)
Bursar,
Good Counsel College,
New Ross, Co Wexford
Tel 051-421182

Kelly, Ray, Very Rev, PP
Parochial House,
Oldcastle, Co Meath
Tel 049-8541142
(*Oldcastle*, Meath)

Kelly, Richard (OFM)
Vicar, Franciscan Friary,
Lady Lane, Waterford
Tel 051-874262

Kelly, Richard (SVD)
Maynooth, Co Kildare
Tel 01-6286391/2

Kelly, Richard, Very Rev, PP
Kilbehenny, Mitchelstown,
Co Cork
Tel 025-24040
(*Kilbehenny*, Cashel & E.)

Kelly, Robert (OCarm)
Carmelite Friary,
Kinsale, Co Cork
Tel 021-4772138

Kelly, Robert (OCSO)
Mount Saint Joseph Abbey,
Roscrea, Co Tipperary
Tel 0505-25600

Kelly, Seamus, PP
40 Derrynoid Road,
Draperstown,
Co Derry BT45 7DN
Tel 028-79628376
(*Ballinascreen (Draperstown)*, Derry)

Kelly, Sean (OFMCap)
Capuchin Friary,
Station Road, Dublin 5
Tel 01-8313886

Kelly, Seán, Very Rev, PE, CC
Stradbally, Co Laois
Tel 057-8625831
(*Stradbally*, Kildare & L.)

Kelly, Stephen CC
Chaplain,
St Mary's, Navan, Co Meath
Tel 046-9027518/9071774
(*Navan*, Meath)

Kelly, Thomas V., Very Rev
Castlebar Road, Westport,
Co Mayo
(Dublin, retired)

Kelly, Vincent (SAC)
(attached to Pallottine College, Thurles)
18 Silvercourt,
Silversprings, Cork

Kemmy, Bill
Diocesan Communications,
c/o Bishops House, Carlow
Tel 087-2308053
(Kildare & L.)

Kemmy, Philip, CC
Parochial House, Convoy
Tel 074-9147238
(*Convoy*, Raphoe)

Kenneally, Cornelius (CSsR), CC
The Presbytery,
197 Kylemore Road,
Ballyfermot, Dublin 10
Tel 01-6264789
(*Ballyfermot*, Dublin)

Kenneally, Daithí (CSSp)
Community Leader,
Kimmage Manor,
Whitehall Road, Dublin 12
Tel 01-4064300

Kenneally, David (SSC)
Regional Bursar,
St Columban's, Dalgan Park,
Navan, Co Meath
Tel 046-9021525

Kennedy, Abe, Very Rev, PP
Duniry, Loughrea,
Co Galway
Tel 090-9745125
(*Duniry & Abbey (Duniry & Kilnelehan)*, Clonfert)

Kennedy, Bernard, MA, MSc, Adm
67 Edenvale Road, Dublin 6
Tel 01-4972165
(*Beechwood Avenue*, Dublin)

Kennedy, David, Very Rev
Clonlusk Doon, Co Limerick
(Limerick, retired)

Kennedy, Denis, (CSSp), CC
St Joseph's Presbytery,
Glasthule, Co Dublin
Tel 01-2800403
(*Glasthule*, Dublin)

Kennedy, Eugene
7 Riverwood Vale,
Carpenterstown,
Castleknock, Dublin 15
(Dublin, retired)

Kennedy, Hugh, Very Rev, Adm
Cathedral Presbytery,
St Peter's Square,
Belfast BT12 4BU
Tel 028-90327573
(*The Cathedral (St Peter's)*, Down & C.)

Kennedy, James, PP
Emly, Co Tipperary
Tel 062-57111
(*Emly*, Cashel & E.)

Kennedy, Joe, Very Rev, PP
Moneygall, Birr, Co Offaly
Tel 0505-45982/086-4072488
(*Dunherrin*, Killaloe)

Kennedy, John
(Congregation for the Doctrine of the Faith)
Via del Mascherino 12,
00193 Roma, Italy
(Dublin)

Kennedy, Joseph (CP), PC
St Paul's Retreat,
Mount Argus, Dublin 6W
Tel 01-4992000
(*Mount Argus*, Dublin)

Kennedy, Joseph, Very Rev
Glenfield Road, Kilmallock,
Co Limerick
(Limerick, retired)

Kennedy, Kieron, Rt Rev Mgr, Adm
St Mary's Cathedral,
Kilkenny
Tel 056-7721253/
087-2523521
(*St Mary's*, Ossory)

Kennedy, Michael (CSSp)
Chaplain, NRH,
Rochestown Avenue,
Dun Laoghaire, Co Dublin
Tel 01-2355272

Kennedy, Michael, Very Rev
Ballylaneen, Kilmacthomas,
Co Waterford
(Waterford & L.)

Kennedy, Michael, Very Rev, PP
Lusmagh,
Banagher, Co Offaly
Tel 0509-51358
(*Lusmagh*, Clonfert)

Kennedy, Michael, Very Rev, PP
Parochial House,
New Inn, Cashel,
Co Tipperary
Tel 052-7462395
(*New Inn*, Cashel & E.)

Kennedy, Michael, Very Rev, PP
Parochial House, Colligan,
Dungarvan, Co Waterford
Tel 058-41629
(*Kilgobinet*, Waterford & L.)

Kennedy, Noel, Very Rev, PP
Bournea, Roscrea,
Co Tipperary
Tel 0505-43211/086-3576775
(*Bournea*, Killaloe)

Kennedy, Thomas, Very Rev, Co-PP
14 Roselawn, Lucan,
Co Dublin
Tel 01-6280205
(*Lucan*, Dublin)

Kennedy, Vincent (OP)
St Saviour's,
Glentworth Street, Limerick
Tel 061-412333

Kennedy, William (SMA)
SMA House, Wilton, Cork
Tel 021-4541069/4541884

Kennelly, John, Very Rev
24 Ferndene, Greenville,
Listowel, Co Kerry
(Kerry, retired)

Kennelly, Pádraig, PP
Ballylongford, Co Kerry
Tel 068-43110
(*Ballylongford*, Kerry)

Kennelly, Séamus, Very Rev, PP
Boherbue, Mallow,
Co Cork
Tel 029-76151
(*Boherbue/Kiskeam*, Kerry)

Kenny, Colm, Very Rev, Co-PP
137 Ballymun Road,
Dublin 11
Tel 01-8376341
(*Ballymun Road*, Dublin)

Kenny, Donald, Rt Rev Mgr, PP
Ramsgrange, New Ross,
Co Wexford
Tel 051-389148
(*Ramsgrange*, Ferns)

Kenny, Gerard, PP
Circular Road, Kilkee,
Co Clare
Tel 065-9056580
(*Doonbeg (Killard) & Kilkee*,
Killaloe)

Kenny, Gerard (OMI)
Oblate House of Retreat,
Inchicore, Dublin 8
Tel 01-4534408/4541805

Kenny, John, Very Rev, PP
Partry, Claremorris,
Co Mayo
Tel 094-9543013
(*Partry (Ballyovey)*, Tuam)

Kenny, Lorcan
Curates House, Convent Hill,
Roscrea, Co Tipperary
Tel 0505-21454
Chaplain, The Valley,
Roscrea, Co Tipperary
Tel 0505-23637/087-6553402
(*Cronan Cluster (Roscrea)*,
Killaloe)

Kenny, Merlyn CC
St Mary's,
Carrick-on-Shannon,
Co Leitrim
Tel 071-9620054
(*Carrig-on-Shannon*, Ardagh
& Cl.)

Kenny, Michael, Very Rev, PP
Kilconly, Tuam, Co Galway
Tel 093-47613
(*Kilconly and Kilbannon*,
Tuam)

Kenny, Pat, Very Rev, PP
St Killian Church, Newinn,
Ballinasloe, Co Galway
Tel 090-9675819
(*New Inn and Bullaun*,
Clonfert)

Kenny, Paul, PP
St Michael's Parochial
House, 4 Eblana Avenue,
Dun Laoghaire, Co Dublin
Tel 01-2801505/087-7425862
(*Raheny*, Dublin)

Kenny, Tim (SM)
Fermoyle, Lanesboro,
Co Longford

Keogan, Thomas (MHM)
(elsewhere in Ireland)

Keogan, Thomas M., Very Rev,
PP
Kinlough, Co Leitrim
Tel 071-9841428
(*Kinlough and Glenade*,
Kilmore)

Keogh, Joseph, Very Rev
Canon, PE
No. 4 St Mary's College
House,
Shantalla Road, Galway
Tel 091-587773
(Galway, retired)

Keogh, Martin, Very Rev, PP
Parochial House, Newtown,
Kilmacthomas,
Co Waterford
Tel 051-294261
(*Newtown*, Waterford & L.)

Keogh, Pádraig, Very Rev, PP
Milford, Charleville,
Co Cork
Tel 063-80038
(*Milford*, Cloyne)

Keohan, Edmund
The Bungalow,
Turners Cross, Cork
Tel 021-4320592
(Cork & R., retired)

Keohane, Martin, Very Rev, PP
The Presbytery, Bantry,
Co Cork
Tel 027-50096
(*Bantry*, Cork & R.)

Keohane, Michael, Very Rev,
PP
The Presbytery,
Our Lady Crowned,
Upper Mayfield, Cork
Tel 021-4503116
(*Upper Mayfield*, Cork & R.)

Kerin, John, Very Rev, PP
Our Lady of the Valley, Cillin
Liath, Killarney,
Co Kerry
Tel 066-9474495
(*Waterville*, Kerry)

Kerr, Aidan, Very Rev, PP
Parochial House,
51 Victoria Road, Larne,
Co Antrim BT40 1LY
Tel 028-28273230/28273053
(*Larne*, Down & C.)

Kerr, Peter, Very Rev, PP
Parochial House,
194 Newtown Hamilton
Road, Ballymacnab,
Armagh BT60 2QS
Tel 028-37531641
(*Killcluney*, Armagh)

Kerr, Samuel, Very Rev
(priest in residence)
463 Shore Road,
Whiteabbey,
Newtownabbey,
Co Antrim BT37 0AE
Tel 028-90365773
(*Whiteabbey (St James's)*,
Down & C.)

Kett, Patrick J., Very Rev
27 Huntsgrove, Ashbourne,
Co Meath
(Dublin, retired)

Keveny, Martin, Very Rev
Paroquia Sao Sebastiao,
Caixa Postal 94,
CEP 77760-000,
Colinas Do Tocantins, Brazil
Tel 63-8311427
(Killala)

Kidney, Michael (SMA)
Temporary diocesan work in
Ireland

Kiely, Bartholomew (SJ)
c/o Irish Jesuit Provincialate,
Milltown Park,
Sandford Road, Dublin 6
Tel 01-4987333

Kiely, Charles, Dr
Director, Parish Pastoral
Development,
1 The Presbytery,
Friar's Walk,
Ballyphehane, Cork
Tel 021-4537472
(Cork & R.)

Kiely, Eugene, Very Rev, PP
Ballyferriter West,
Tralee, Co Kerry
Tel 066-9156131
(*Ballyferriter*, Kerry)

Kiely, John, Very Rev, PP
Cappoquin, Co Waterford
Tel 058-54216
(*Cappoquin*, Waterford & L.)

Kiely, Michael (SAC)
Provincial House,
'Homestead',
Sandyford Road, Dundrum,
Dublin 16
Tel 01-2956180/2954170

Kieran, Aidan, CC
No. 1 the Glebe,
Peamount Road,
Newcastle Lyons, Co Dublin
Tel 01-4589230/087-6397744
(*Newcastle,
Saggart/Rathcoole/Brittas*,
Dublin)

Kiernan, Brian (OCarm)
Gort Muire, Ballinteer,
Dublin 16
Tel 01-2984014

Kiernan, John, Very Rev, PE
Kilberry, Navan, Co Meath
(Meath, retired)

Kiernan, Kevin (OFMCap)
St Francis Capuchin Friary,
Rochestown, Co Cork
Tel 021-4896244

Kiernan, Patrick, CC
Mount Temple, Moate,
Co Westmeath
Tel 090-6481239
(*Moate and Mount Temple*,
Ardagh & Cl.)

Kiggins, Thomas (SPS)
St Patrick's, Kiltegan,
Co Wicklow
Tel 059-6473600

Kilbane, Seán (SMA), Very
Rev, PE
Clonfad, Oldtown, Athlone,
Co Roscommon
Tel 090-9673527
(Tuam, retired)

Kilbride, Damian (OSM)
Servite Priory, Benburb,
Dungannon,
Co Tyrone BT71 7JZ
Tel 028-37548241

Kilbride, Malachy (CSSp)
Blackrock College,
Blackrock, Co Dublin
Tel 01-2888681

Kilcoyne, Brendan, Very Rev
Canon, PP, VF
St Mary's Presbytery,
Athenry,
Co Galway
Tel 091-844076
(*Athenry*, Tuam)

Kilcoyne, Colm, Very Rev
Canon, PE
20 Rathbawn Drive,
Castlebar, Co Mayo
(Tuam, retired)

Kilcoyne, Patrick, Very Rev
Canon, PP
Kiltimagh, Co Mayo
Tel 094-9381198
(*Kiltimagh (Killedan)*,
Achonry)

Kilcoyne, Seán
Chaplain,
Bon Secours Hospital,
Renmore, Galway
Tel 091-751534/757711
(Galway)

Kilcrann, John (CSSp)
Temple Park, Richmond
Avenue South, Dublin 6
Tel 01-4975127/4977230

Kilduff, Donal, CC
Bishop's House,
Cullies, Co Cavan
Tel 049-4331496
(Kilmore)

Kilkelly, Christopher
c/o Archbishop's House,
Tuam, Co Galway
(Tuam, retired)

Kilkenny, Thomas (SSC)
Castlerea, Co Roscommon

Killeen, James, CC
Cobh, Co Cork
Tel 021-4813601
(*Cobh, St Colman's
Cathedral*, Cloyne)

Killeen, John D., Very Rev, PP
20 Abbey Court,
Abbey Road, Monkstown
Co Dublin
Tel 01-2802533
(*Kill-O'-The-Grange*, Dublin)

Killeen, Seán, Rt Rev Mgr, VG
Cloghans, Ballina, Co Mayo
(Killala, retired)

Killenga, Malasi S. (AOR)
John Sullivan House of
Formation,
27 Leinster Road,
Rathmines, Dublin 6
Tel 01-5242134

Kilmartin, Michael, CC
Cathedral House, Mullingar,
Co Westmeath
Tel 044-9348338/9340126
(*Mullingar*, Meath)

Kilmurray, Martin (OCarm),
Very Rev
Provincial, Provincial Office
and Carmelite Communi,
Gort Muire, Ballinteer,
Dublin 16
Tel 01-2984014

Kilpatrick, Edward, PP
Orchard Park, Murlog,
Lifford, Co Donegal
Tel 074-9142022
(*Lifford (Clonleigh)*, Derry)

Kilroy, Peter
64 Cherbury Court,
Booterstown, Co Dublin
(Dublin, retired)

Kinahan, Gabriel (OFM)
Guardian, Franciscan Friary,
Friary Lane, Athlone,
Co Westmeath
Tel 090-6472095

King, Anthony, Very Rev,
Canon, PE
Westport, Co Mayo
(Tuam, retired)

King, Bernard (SM), CC
Parochial House,
Glassdrummond,
Crossmaglen, Newry,
Co Down BT35 9DY
Tel 028-30861270
(*Crossmaglen (Creggan
Upper)*, Armagh)

King, John Joe (CSSp)
Holy Ghost Missionary
College,
Kimmage Manor, Dublin 12
Tel 01-4064300

King, Jude (OSA)
Augustinian Retreat Centre,
Old Court Road,
Dublin 16
Tel 01-4930932

King, Michael, Very Rev, PP
Newtownbutler, Enniskillen,
Co Fermanagh BT92 8JJ
Tel 028-67738229
(*Newtownbutler*, Clogher)

King, William, Very Rev, PP
14 Rosemount Crescent,
Roebuck Road, Clonskeagh,
Dublin 14
Tel 01-2697754
(*Clonskeagh*, Dublin)

Kingston, John, Very Rev, PP
The Presbytery, Bandon,
Co Cork
Tel 023-8854666
(*Bandon*, Cork & R.)

Kingston, William (CSSp)
Rockwell College, Cashel,
Co Tipperary
Tel 062-61444

Kinsella, Tobias, Very Rev
Bloomfield Care Centre,
Stocking Lane,
Rathfarnham, Dublin 16
(Ferns, retired)

Kirby, John, Most Rev, DD
Bishop of Clonfert,
Coorheen, Loughrea,
Co Galway
Tel 091-841560
(Clonfert)

Kirstein, James (SMA)
African Missions,
Blackrock Road, Cork
Tel 021-4292871

Kirwan, Joseph (OSA)
St John's Priory,
Thomas Street, Dublin 8
Tel 01-6770393

Kirwan, Noel, Very Rev, Adm,
VF
St John's Cathedral,
Cathedral House, Cathedral
Place, Limerick
Tel 061-414624/087-2589279
(*St John's*, Limerick)

Kirwin, Jeremiah M (CSSp)
Rockwell College, Cashel,
Co Tipperary
Tel 062-61444

Kitching, Ciaran, Very Rev, PP
St Joseph's
Killimor, Ballinasloe,
Co Galway
Tel 090-9676151
(*Killimor & Tiranascragh*,
Clonfert)

Kitt, Liam, Very Rev
Cleveland, Ohio
(Tuam)

Kivlehan, Paul, CC
The Presbytery,
Ballaghdereen,
Co Roscommon
Tel 094-9860011
(*Ballaghaderreen
(Castlemore and Kilcolman)*,
Achonry)

Knight, Matthew J. (CSSp)
Community Leader,
Rockwell College, Cashel,
Co Tipperary
Tel 062-61444

Knowles, Desmond, Very Rev
Canon
Newry, Co Down
(Dromore, retired)

Kochatt, Alex CC
The Presbytery,
Askea, Carlow
Tel 059-9142565
(*Askea*, Kildare & L.)

Kom, Francis (SVD)
Maynooth, Co Kildare
Tel 01-6286391/2

Kombanathottathil, Binoy
Mathew (SVD), Co-PP
Presbytery No. 2,
St Mary's Terrace,
Arklow, Co Wicklow
Tel 0402-31716
(*Arklow*, Dublin)

Kondowe, Raymond, PC
c/o Parish Office,
87B St Stephen's Green,
Dublin 2
Tel 01-4759674
(*University Church*, Dublin)

Kornitsky, Vasil
Chaplain to Ukranian
Community,
3 Maypark, Malahide Road,
Dublin 5
Tel 01-5164752
(*Donnycarney*, Dublin)

Kosciolek, Krzysztof (SC), CC
Cathedral Presbytery,
38 Hill Street,
Newry BT34 1AT
Tel 028-30262586
(*Newry Pastoral Area*,
Dromore)

Kowalski, Wojciech (SJ)
Jesuit Community,
27 Leinster Road,
Rathmines, Dublin 6
Tel 01-4970250

Krawiec, Jaroslaw (OP)
St Saviour's,
Upper Dorset Street,
Dublin 1
Tel 01-8897610

Kulitunam, Matthias E.
149 Ludford Road,
Meadowbrook,
Ballinteer, Dublin 16
Tel 01-2987401
(*Ballinteer, Meadowbrook*,
Dublin)

Kupczakiewicz, Krzysztof (OP)
Holy Cross, Tralee, Co Kerry
Tel 066-7121135/7129185

Kuthanapillil, Jaison (OCarm)
Carmelite Priory, Moate,
Co Westmeath
Tel 090-6481160/6481398

Kuzmicki, Ireneusz, CC
Curate's Residence,
Abbey Street, Roscommon
Tel 090-6626189
(*Roscommon*, Elphin)

Kyne, Brendan, Very Rev, PP
The Spa, Castleconnell,
Co Limerick
Tel 061-377170/086-1050090
(*Castleconnell*, Killaloe)

Kyne, Thomas, Very Rev Dean,
AP
Réalt na Mara, Furbo,
Co Galway
Tel 091-592457
(*Barna*, Galway)

Kyne, Valentine (SSC)
Alcoholic Advisory Board,
St Columban's
Dalgan Park, Navan,
Co Meath
Tel 046-9021525

## L

Lacey, Liam, Co-PP
8 Greenfield Road, Sutton,
Dublin 13
Tel 01-8322396
(*Sutton*, Dublin)

Laffan, Sean, Very Rev, CC
Gusserane, Co Wexford
Tel 051-562111
(*Ballycullane*, Ferns)

Lafferty, Angelo (SMA)
SMA House,
Wilton, Cork
Tel 021-4541069/4541884

Lagan, Francis, Most Rev, DD
Retired Bishop of
Sidnacestre and Auxiliary
Bishop of Derry,
9 Glen Road, Strabane,
Co Tyrone BT82 8BX
Tel 028-71884533
(Derry)

Lagan, Hugh (SMA)
Further studies, Maryland,
USA

Lagan, Patrick
Parochial House,
St Eugene's Cathedral,
Derry BT48 9AP
Tel 028-71262894/71365712

Laheen, Kevin (SJ)
35 Lower Leeson Street,
Dublin 2
Tel 01-6761248

Laizer, John (CSSp)
Holy Spirit Provincialate,
Temple Park,
Richmond Avenue South,
Dublin 6
Tel 01-4975127/4977230
Community Leader,
Spiritan House,
213 North Circular Road,
Dublin 7
Tel 01-8389664/8683504

Lally, Fredrick (OCarm)
Bursar, Carmelite Priory,
White Abbey, Co Kildare
Tel 045-521391

Lalor, Eddie (SPS), CC
Dublin Road, Portlaoise,
Co Laois
Tel 057-8622301
(*Portlaoise*, Kildare & L.)

Lalor, John, Very Rev, PP
Camross, Portlaoise,
Co Laois
Tel 0507-8735122
(*Camross*, Ossory)

Allianz (ll)

Lalor, Thomas, Very Rev, PP
Leighlinbridge, Co Carlow
Tel 059-9721463
(*Leighlin*, Kildare & L.)

Lambe, Anthony, Very Rev, PP
Drangan, Thurles,
Co Tipperary
Tel 052-9152103
(*Drangan*, Cashel & E.)

Lambe, Jeremiah (CSSp)
Holy Ghost Missionary
College, Kimmage Manor,
Dublin 12
Tel 01-4064300

Lambert, Owen (CSSp)
Holy Ghost Missionary
College, Kimmage Manor,
Dublin 12
Tel 01-4064300

Lane, Daniel, Very Rev, DD, PP
Ballingarry, Co Limerick
Tel 069-68141/087-2533030
(*Ballingarry and Granagh*,
Limerick)

Lane, Dermot A., Rt Rev Mgr,
Co-PP
162 Sandyford Road,
Dublin 16
Tel 01-2956165
(*Balally*, Dublin)

Lane, Michael, Rt Rev Mgr
2 Meadowvale, Raheen,
Limerick
Tel 061-228761/087-2544450
(Limerick, retired)

Lane, Michael, Very Rev
Shrakovee, Clonlara,
near Limerick
(Limerick, retired)

Lane, Thomas
Mount Saint Mary's
Seminary,
16300 Old Emmitsburg
Road, Emmitsburg,
Maryland 21727-7797, USA
(Cloyne)

Langford, Gerard, Very Rev,
PP
Parochial House,
Cahir, Co Tipperary
Tel 052-7441404
(*Cahir*, Waterford & L.)

Lanigan-Ryan, Thomas, CC
St Michael's Street,
Tipperary Town,
Co Tipperary
Tel 062-80475
(*Tipperary*, Cashel & E.)

Lanigan, Jerry (SVD)
Donamon Castle,
Roscommon
Tel 090-6662222

Larkin, Aidan (SSC)
St Columban's, Dalgan Park,
Navan, Co Meath
Tel 046-9021525

Larkin, Barry, CC
1 Clonard Park,
Clonard, Co Wexford
Tel 053-9147686
(*Clonard*, Ferns)

Larkin, Barry, Very Rev, PP
Suncroft, Curragh,
Co Kildare
Tel 045-441586
(*Suncroft*, Kildare & L.)

Larkin, Francis, Very Rev
Canon, AP
7 Presentation Road,
Co Galway
Tel 091-449727
(*St Joseph's*, Galway)

Larkin, James, AP
72 Bird Avenue,
Clonskeagh, Dublin 14
Tel 01-2196869
(*Clonskeagh*, Dublin)

Larkin, Pat, Very Rev, PP
Parochial House, Kilmaley,
Co Clare
Tel 065-6839735/087-
2300627
(*Inch and Kilmaley*, Killaloe)

Larkin, Patrick, Very Rev, PE
Parochial House,
Jenkinstown,
Dundalk, Co Louth
Tel 042-9371328
(Armagh, retired)

Larkin, Seamus, Very Rev
Canon
(priest in residence)
Monamolin,
Gorey, Co Wexford
Tel 053-9389223
(Ferns, retired)

Larkin, Seán, PP
Parochial House,
11 Chapel Road, Bessbrook,
Newry, Co Down BT35 7AU
Tel 028-30830206
(*Bessbrook (Killeavy Lower)*,
Armagh)

Lavelle, Colm (SJ)
Milltown Park,
Sandford Road, Dublin 6
Tel 01-2698411/2698113

Lavelle, Paul, Very Rev, PP
123 Foxfield Grove, Dublin 5
Tel 01- 8390433
(*Kilbarrack-Foxfield*, Dublin)

Laverty, Austin, Very Rev
Canon, PP, VF
Ardara, Co Donegal
Tel 074-9541135
(*Ardara*, Raphoe)

Laverty, Denis
Pro-Cathedral House,
83 Marlborough Street,
Dublin 1
Tel 01-8745441
(Dublin, retired)

Laverty, Derek (SSCC), Very
Rev
Provincial,
Coudrin House,
27 Northbrook Road,
Dublin 6
Tel 01-6686584/01-6686590

Laverty, Francis (CSSp)
Holy Spirit Missionary
College,
Kimmage Manor, Dublin 12
Tel 01-406 4300

Lavin, Peadar, Very Rev Canon
3 Slinagee, Golf Links Road,
Roscommon
(Elphin, retired)

Lawless, Brendan, Very Rev,
PP
Dunkellin Terrace,
Portumna,
Co Galway
Tel 090-9741092
(*Portumna (Kilmalinogue &
Lickmolassey)*, Clonfert)

Lawless, Brian, Very Rev, Adm
Parochial House,
St Agatha's Parish,
46 North William Street,
Dublin 1
Tel 01-8556474
(*North William Street*,
Dublin)

Lawless, James (SCI)
Promotions Director,
Sacred Heart Fathers,
Fairfield, 66 Inchicore Road,
Dublin 8
Tel 01-4538655

Lawless, Ralph (OFM)
Franciscan Friary,
Friary Lane, Athlone,
Co Westmeath
Tel 090-6472095

Lawless, Richard, Adm
St Aidan's Cathedral,
Enniscorthy, Co Wexford
Tel 053-9235777
(Ferns)

Lawless, Vincent (SMA)
Dromantine Retreat and
Conference Centre
Dromatine College,
Newry, Co Down BT34 1RH
Tel 028-30821219
(Retired in Ireland outside
SMA houses)

Lawlor, Brendan, CC
2 Powerscourt, Tulla,
Co Clare
Tel 065-6835284/087-
9845417
(*Tulla*, Killaloe)

Lawlor, Eddie (SPS), CC
1 Glendowns, Portlaoise,
Co Laois
Tel 057-8622301
(*Portlaoise*, Kildare & L.)

Lawlor, John, Very Rev, PP, VF
St Mary's,
Tarbert, Co Kerry
Tel 068-36111
(*Tarbert*, Kerry)

Lawton, Liam
Crossneen, Carlow
Tel 059-9134548
(Kildare & L.)

Lawton, Patrick, Very Rev, PP
Shandrum, Charleville,
Co Cork
Tel 063-70016
(*Shandrum*, Cloyne)

Layden, Leo (CSSp)
St Mary's College,
Rathmines, Dublin 6
Tel 01-4995760

Layden, Thomas (SJ)
Campion House Residence,
28 Lower Hatch Street,
Dublin 2
Tel 01-6383990

Leader, Liam, Very Rev Canon,
AP
The Presbytery,
Lower Road, Cork
Tel 021-4500282
(*St Patrick's*, Cork & R.)

Leader, Micheál, CC
Cannon Field,
Mallow, Co Cork
Tel 022-21382
(*Mallow*, Cloyne)

Leahy, Andy, Very Rev, PP
Episcopal Vicar for the
Pastoral Care of Priests,
Tullow, Co Carlow
Tel 059-9180641
(*Tullow*, Kildare & L.)

Leahy, Brendan, Most Rev, DD
Bishop of Limerick,
Social Service Centre,
Henry Street, Limerick
Tel 061-315856
(Limerick)

Leahy, Denis, Very Rev
34 Knockmoyle Est,
Tralee, Co Kerry
(Kerry, retired)

Leahy, Donal, Very Rev, PP
Kilworth, Co Cork
Tel 025-27186
(*Kilworth*, Cloyne)

Leahy, Michael (OSA)
St Augustine's Priory,
Washington Street, Cork
Tel 021-2753982

Leahy, Niall F.X. (SJ)
Irish Jesuit Provincialate,
Milltown Park,
Sandford Road, Dublin 6
Tel 01-4987333

Leahy, Niall S. (SJ)
Clongowes Wood College,
Clane, Co Kildare
Tel 045-868663/868202

Leahy, Thomas (SPS), CC
Ballinaheglish,
Co Roscommon
Tel 090-6662229
(*Cloverhill (Oran)*, Elphin)

Leamy, Michael, Very Rev, PP
Main Street, Rathcormac,
Co Cork
Tel 025-37667
(*Rathcormac*, Cloyne)

Leane, Thomas, Very Rev, PP
Ballyheigue, Tralee,
Co Kerry
Tel 066-7133110
(*Ballyheigue*, Kerry)

Leddy, Patrick (CSSp)
Holy Ghost Missionary
College,
Kimmage Manor, Dublin 12
Tel 01-4064300

Lee, Angelus (OFM)
Adam & Eve's,
4 Merchant's Quay, Dublin 8
Tel 01-6771128

Lee, Francis,
5 Pine Grove, Moycullen,
Co Galway
Tel 086-8308865
(Galway, retired)

Lee, Hugh (MHM), CC
Curraghboy, Athlone,
Co Roscommon
Tel 090-6488143
(*Kiltoom*, Elphin)

Lee, Patrick (SVD)
133 North Circular Road,
Dublin 7
Tel 01-8386743

Lee, William, Most Rev, DD
Retired Bishop of Waterford
and Lismore,
5 The Brambles,
Ballinakill Downs,
Waterford
Tel 051-821485
(Waterford & L.)

Lennon, Brian (SJ)
St Francis Xavier's,
Upper Gardiner Street,
Dublin 1
Tel 01-8363411
(Zam-Mal)

Lennon, Denis, Rt Rev Mgr,
PP, VF
39 Beechlawn, Clonard,
Wexford
Tel 053-9124417
(*Clonard*, Ferns)

Lennon, James, CC
(Hexham & Newcastle)
Castledockrell, Ballycarney,
Enniscorthy, Co Wexford
Tel 053-9388569
(*Marshallstown*, Ferns)

Lennon, Moling, Very Rev, PE
364 Sundays Well, Naas,
Co Kildare
Tel 045-888667
(Kildare & L., retired)

Lennon, Pat, Very Rev, PP
Ardagh, Co Longford
Tel 043-6675006
(*Ardagh and Moydow*,
Ardagh & Cl.)

Lennon, Patrick (OSA)
Duckspool House,
(Retirement Community),
Abbeyside, Dungarvan,
Co Waterford
Tel 058-23784

Lennon, Sean (OSM)
Servite Priory, Benburb,
Dungannon,
Co Tyrone, BT71 7JZ
Tel 028-37548241

Leogue, John, Very Rev, PP
Athleague, Co Roscommon
Tel 090-6663338
(*Athleague*, Elphin)

Leonard, Albert (OP), Very
Rev, PP
St Mary's Priory, The
Claddagh, Galway
Tel 091-582884
(*St Mary's*, Galway)

Leonard, Derek, Very Rev, PP
St Nicholas' Presbytery,
Westbury, Limerick
Tel 061-340614
(*St Nicholas'*, Limerick)

Leonard, John, Very Rev, PP,
VF
The Presbytery,
10 St Nessan's Park,
Dooradoyle, Limerick
Tel 061-302729
(*St Paul's*, Limerick)

Lewis, Eugene (White Fathers)
Cypress Grove, Templeogue,
Dublin 6W
Tel 01-4055263/4055264

Leycock, Dermot, Very Rev, PP
64 Newtownpark Avenue,
Blackrock, Co Dublin
Tel 01-2784860
(*Newtownpark*, Dublin)

Liddane, Raymond, Very Rev,
AP
Newtown, Waterford
Tel 051-874284
(*SS Joseph and Benildus*,
Waterford & L.)

Linehan, Donal, Very Rev
Canon, PE
Ballinora, Waterfall,
near Cork
Tel 021-4873448
(*Ballinora*, Cork & R.)

Linehan, Jim, Very Rev, CC
St Brendan's College,
Killarney, Co Kerry
Tel 064-6631021
Parish
Killarney, Co Kerry
Tel 064-6631014
(*Killarney*, Kerry)

Linehan, Patrick, Very Rev, PP
Ballyhea
Tel 063-81470
(*Ballyhea*, Cloyne)

Linnane, Seámus, Very Rev,
AP
St John's Presbytery,
Tralee, Co Kerry
Tel 066-7122522
(*Tralee, St John's*, Kerry)

Liston, Micheál, Very Rev
Canon
Chaplain to Gaelscoileanna,
21 Sullane Crescent, Raheen
Heights, Limerick
Tel 087-2314804
(Limerick)

Little, Anthony G. (CSSp)
Holy Spirit Missionary
College,
Kimmage Manor, Whitehall
Road, Dublin 12
Tel 01-4064300

Little, Thomas, Very Rev, PP,
VF,
Brownshill Avenue, Carlow
Tel 059-9131559
(*Tinryland*, Kildare & L.)

Littleton, John
(Elsewhere in the Diocese)
The Priory Institute,
Tallaght Village, Dublin 24
(Cashel & E.)

Littleton, Patrick, Adm
St Luke's, Kilbarron Road,
Kilmore West, Dublin 5
Tel 01-8486806
(*Kilmore Road West*, Dublin)

Lloyd, Enda, Rt Rev Mgr, EV,
Co-PP
Cluain Mhuire,
Killarney Road,
Bray, Co Wicklow
Tel 01-2862026
(*Bray (Holy Redeemer)*,
Dublin)

Lloyd, Francis, Very Rev, PE
The Presbytery, Dungarvan,
Co Waterford
(Waterford & L., retired)

Loftus, Hughie, Very Rev, PP
Corrandulla, Co Galway
Tel 091-791125
(*Corrandulla (Annaghdown)*,
Tuam)

Loftus, John, Very Rev, Co-
Pastor
Binghamstown, Belmullet
Co Mayo
Tel 097-82350
(*Kilmore-Erris*, Killala)

Loftus, Kevin, Rt Rev Mgr, PP,
VG
St James's,
Easkey, Co Sligo
Tel 096-49011
(*Easkey*, Killala)

Loftus, Martin (SDB)
Salesian House, Milford,
Castletroy, Limerick
Tel 061-330268

Logue, Charles, CC
Malin Head, Co Donegal
Tel 074-9370134
(*Malin (Clonca)*, Derry)

Loisel, D. Eric M. (OSB)
Benedictine Monks,
Holy Cross Monastery,
119 Kilbroney Road,
Rostrevor,
Co Down BT34 3BN
Tel 028-41739979

Lomasney, Michael, Very Rev,
PP
Kildorrery, Co Cork
Tel 022-40703
(*Kildorrery*, Cloyne)

Lombard, Patrick, CC
St Mary's, Sligo
Tel 071-9162670/9162769
(*Sligo, St Mary's*, Elphin)

Lonergan, Patrick, Very Rev
Canon, PE
Garrison, Enniskillen,
Co Fermanagh BT93 4AE
Tel 028-68658234
(*Belleek-Garrison*, Clogher)

Long, Derrick (SSC)
St Columban's Dalgan Park,
Navan, Co Meath
Tel 046-9021525

Long, Joseph (SPS), CC
Kilrickle, Ballinasloe,
Co Galway
Tel 091-843015
(*Cappatagle and Kilrickle*,
Clonfert)

Long, Leo
Killeen, Ballinaclough,
Nenagh,
Co Tipperary
Tel 067-25870/086-8353388
(*Killanave and Templederry*,
Killaloe)

Long, Martin, Very Rev, PP
Louisburgh, Co Mayo
Tel 098-66198
(*Louisburgh (Kilgeever)*,
Tuam)

Long, Michael (SPS)
Tearmann Spirituality
Centre,
Brockagh, Glendalough,
Co Wicklow
Tel 0404-45208

Looby, John (SJ)
35 Lower Leeson Street,
Dublin 2
Tel 01-6761248
(Editor, Sacred Heart
Messenger)
Tel 01-6767491

Looney, Thomas, Very Rev
Canon, SP, VF
Dingle, Co Kerry
Tel 066-9151208
(*Dingle*, Kerry)

Loughran, Desmond, CC
Drumaness, Ballynahinch,
Co Down BT24 8NG
Tel 028-97561432
(*Magheradroll*
(*Ballynahinch*), Dromore)

Loughran, Malachy (OSA)
St Augustine's Priory,
Shop Street,
Drogheda, Co Louth
Tel 041-9838409

Loughran, Terence, Adm
Cappagh, Askeaton,
Co Limerick
Tel 069-63432
(*Kilcornan*, Limerick)

Loughrey, Neil (White
Fathers)
Provincial Treasurer,
Provincialate,
Cypress Grove Road,
Templeogue, Dublin 6W
Tel 01-4055510

Loughrey, Vivian, CC
Curate's House,
Monksfield, Salthill, Galway
Tel 091-523413
(*Salthill*, Galway)

Lovell, Liam
On sabbatical
(Kerry)

Lovett, Cyril (SSC)
(Editor, Far East Magazine),
St Columban's,
Dalgan Park, Navan,
Co Meath
Tel 046-9021525

Lowe, Bernard (CP)
Superior, St Paul's Retreat,
Mount Argus, Dublin 6W
Tel 01-4992000

Lucey, Finbarr, Very Rev, PP
Ardmore, Youghal
Co Cork
Tel 024-94177
(Waterford & L.)

Lucey, John (CSsR)
Mount Saint Alphonsus,
Limerick
Tel 061-315099

Lucey, Pat (OP), CC
The Presbytery, St Aengus's,
Balrothery,
Tallaght, Dublin 24
Tel 01-4528161
(*Tallaght, Tymon North*,
Dublin)

Lucid, John, Very Rev, PP
Moyvane, Listowel,
Co Kerry
Tel 068-49308
(*Moyvane*, Kerry)

Ludden, Paul
(Team Assistant)
70 Maplewood Road,
Tallaght, Dublin 24
Tel 01-4628336
(*Springfield*, Dublin)

Luddy, Denis (CSsR)
St Patrick's,
Esker, Athenry, Co Galway
Tel 091-844007

Ludlow, Brendan, CC
35a Moatlands, Ratoath,
Co Meath
Tel 01-8256207
(*Ratoath*, Meath)

Lugowki, Janusz
Chaplain to Polish
Community,
Mount Rivers, Kells Road,
Navan, Co Meath
Tel 087-9538786
(Meath)

Lumala, Aloysius, AP
43b Glen Road,
Belfast BT11 8BB
Tel 028-90613949
(*St Teresa's*, Down & C.)

Lumsden, David, Very Rev, PP
Director, Knock Diocesan
Pilgrimage,
83 Tonlegee Drive,
Raheny, Dublin 5
Tel 01-8480917/087-2569873
(*Edenmore, Grange Park*,
Dublin)

Lynch, Damien CC
Chaplain, Coláiste na
Troinoide
Youghal, Co Cork
Tel 024-92456
(*Youghal*, Cloyne)

Lynch, Dermot (OFMCap)
Holy Trinity,
Fr Mathew Quay, Cork
Tel 021-4270827

Lynch, Dermot (SJ)
St Ignatius Community &
Church, 27 Raleigh Row,
Salthill, Galway
Tel 091-523707

Lynch, Eamonn, Very Rev, PP
Ballyconnell, Co Cavan
Tel 049-9526291
(*Kildallan and Tomregan*,
Kilmore)

Lynch, Edward (CSsR)
St Patrick's, Esker, Athenry,
Co Galway
Tel 091-844007

Lynch, Finbarr (SJ)
Manresa House,
Dollymount, Dublin 3
Tel 01-8331352

Lynch, Finian (OP)
St Mary's, Pope Quay, Cork
Tel 021-4502267

Lynch, Flannan (OFMCap)
Capuchin Friary,
Ard Mhuire, Creeslough,
Letterkenny, Co Donegal
Tel 074-9138005

Lynch, Francis (OP), CC
Parochial House, Castlefin,
Lifford, Co Donegal
Tel 074-9146251
(*Doneyloop (Urney and
Castlefinn)*, Derry)

Lynch, James (SJ)
St Ignatius Community &
Church,
27 Raleigh Row, Salthill,
Galway
Tel 091-523707

Lynch, James, Very Rev, PP
Parochial House, Kentstown
Navan, Co Meath
Tel 041-9825276
(*Beauparc*, Meath)

Lynch, John
Sacred Heart Residence,
Sybil Hill Road, Killester,
Dublin 5
(Dublin, retired)

Lynch, Jude (CSSp)
Clonskeagh Hospital,
Vergemount, Dublin 6
Tel 01-2697877
Bursar, Holy Spirit
Provincialate,
Temple Park,
Richmond Avenue South,
Dublin 6
Tel 01-4975127/4977230

Lynch, Laurence (OCarm)
Carmelite Priory,
Knocktopher, Co Kilkenny
Tel 056-7768675
(*Knocktopher/Ballyhale*,
Ossory)

Lynch, Lorcan, Very Rev, CC
St Mary's, Clontibret,
Co Monaghan
Tel 047-80631
(*Clontibret*, Clogher)

Lynch, Owen
(priest in residence)
The Presbytery, Blacklion,
Greystones, Co Wicklow
(Dublin, retired)

Lynch, Patrick (OFM)
Vicar, Franciscan Friary,
Friary Lane, Athlone,
Co Westmeath
Tel 090-6472095

Lynch, Patrick (OFMCap)
Capuchin Friary,
Ard Mhuire, Creeslough,
Letterkenny, Co Donegal
Tel 074-9138005

Lynch, Patrick (SMA)
(On temporary diocesan
work in Ireland)

Lynch, Patrick, Very Rev, PE
(priest in residence)
Kiltimagh, Co Mayo
(Achonry, retired)

Lynch, Patsy, CC
St Brendan's, Tralee,
Co Kerry
Tel 066-7125932
(*Tralee, St Brendan's*, Kerry)

Lynch, Sean (SMA)
African Missions,
Blackrock Road, Cork
Tel 021-4292871

Lyng, Dick (OSA), CC
Provincial Secretary,
St Augustine's,
Taylor's Lane,
Ballyboden, Dublin 16
Tel 01-4241000
(*Ballyboden*, Dublin)

Lyng, John (OSA)
Prior, St Augustine's Priory,
Washington Street, Cork
Tel 021-4275398/4270410

Lyon, Kevin, Archdeacon, CC
Archdeacon of
Glendalough,
Parochial House,
Crosschapel, Blessington,
Co Wicklow
Tel 045-865215
(*Blessington*, Dublin)

Lyons, Enda, Dr
Bermingham Road, Tuam,
Co Galway
(Tuam, retired)

Lyons, Fintan (OSB)
Glenstal Abbey, Murroe,
Co Limerick
Tel 061-386103

Lyons, Gabriel, Very Rev, PP
119A Glenravel Road,
Martinstown, Ballymena,
Co Antrim BT43 6QL
Tel 028-21758217
Administration Braid
(*Braid, Glenravel (Skerry)*,
Down & C.)

Lyon, Kevin, Rev Archdeacon,
CC,
Parochial House,
Crosschapel,
Blessington, Co Wicklow
Tel 01-865215
(*Blessington*, Dublin)

Lyons, Seán, Very Rev, PE
Dunkellin Terrace,
Portumna, Co Galway
(Clonfert, retired)

Lyons, Thomas
Chaplain,
Cork University Hospital,
Wilton, Cork
Tel 021-4546400/4922391/
4546109
(Galway)

## M

MacAodh, Lomán (OFM)
Franciscan Abbey,
Multyfarnham,
Co Westmeath
Tel 044-9371114/9371137

Macaulay, Ambrose, Rt Rev
Mgr
89a Maryvile Park,
Belfast BT9 6LQ
(Down and C., retired)

MacBradaigh, Proinsias (SJ)
Superior,
Arrupe Community,
127 Shangan Road,
Ballymun, Dublin 9
Tel 01-8625345

MacCárthaigh, Donncha
(MSC)
Western Road, Cork
Tel 021-4804120

MacCarthaigh, Pádraig, Very
Rev, PP
The Presbytery,
Ballydesmond, Mallow,
Co Cork
Tel 064-7751104
(Ballydesmond, Kerry)

MacCarthy, Martin (OP)
St Mary's, Pope Quay, Cork
Tel 021-4502267

MacCormack, Gerard, Very
Rev, PP
Parochial House, Kingscourt,
Co Cavan
Tel 042-9667314
(Kingscourt, Meath)

MacCraith, Micheál (OFM)
Guardian, Collegio S.
Isidoro, Via degli Artisti 41,
00187 Roma, Italy
Tel 0039-06-4885359

MacCuarta, Brian (SJ)
c/o Irish Jesuit Provincialate,
Milltown Park,
Sandford Road,
Dublin 6
Tel 01-4987333

MacDaid, Liam S., Most Rev,
DD
Bishop of Clogher,
Bishop's House,
Monaghan
Tel 047-81019
(Clogher)

MacDonagh, Fergal, Very Rev
(Moderator)
18 St Anthony's Road,
Rialto, Dublin 8
Tel 01-4534469
(Dolphin's Barn/Rialto,
Dublin)

MacDonald, Criostoír, Very
Rev, PP
The Presbytery,
Curraheen Road
Tel 021-4343535
(Curraheen Road, Cork & R.)

MacEntee, Patrick, Very Rev,
PP
Shanmullagh,
Dromore, Omagh,
Co Tyrone BT78 3DZ
Tel 028-82898641
(Dromore, Clogher)

MacGearailt, Sean (OSA)
Prior,
Good Counsel College,
New Ross, Co Wexford
Tel 051-421182

MacGiolla Catháin, Darach, PP
Corpus Christi Presbytery,
4-6 Springhill Grove,
Belfast BT12 7SL
Tel 028-90246857
(St Luke's, Down & C.)

MacGiollarnáth, Sean,
(OCarm), CC
Carmelite Presbytery,
Idrone Avenue, Knocklyon,
Dublin 16
Tel 01-4941204
(Knocklyon, Dublin)

MacGowan, Padraig, Very
Rev, PP
Ballymahon, Co Longford
Tel 090-6432253
(Ballymahon, Ardagh & Cl.)

MacGréil, Mícheál (SJ)
St Francis Xavier's,
Upper Gardiner Street,
Dublin 1
Tel 01-8363411

MacHale, Brendan (SSC)
St Columban's,
Dalgan Park, Navan,
Co Meath
Tel 046-9021525

MacHale, John George, Very
Rev Canon, PP, VF
Kilglass, Enniscrone,
Ballina, Co Mayo
Tel 096-36191
(Kilglass, Killala)

Macken, Walter
Ely University Centre,
10 Hume Street, Dublin 2
Tel 01-6767420
(Opus Dei)

MacKenna, Benedict (OP)
Newbridge College,
Droichead Nua, Co Kildare
Tel 045-487200

MacKeone, Kieran, Very Rev,
PE, AP
Parochial House,
132 Washing Bay Road,
Coalisland, Dungannon,
Co Tyrone BT71 4QZ
Tel 028-87740376
(Clonoe, Armagh)

Mackey, Niall, Very Rev, Adm
Parochial House,
Kilcullen, Co Kildare
Tel 045-481230
(Kilcullen, Dublin)

MacKiernan, James, CC
Boher, Ballycumber,
Co Offaly
Tel 057-9336119
(Ballinahown, Boher &
Pollough (Lemanaghan),
Ardagh & Cl.)

Mackin, Patrick A., Very Rev,
PE
Bohermeen, Navan,
Co Meath
Tel 046-9021439
(Meath, retired)

Mackle, Patrick (SMA)
Retired in Ireland outside
SMA houses

MacLaifeartaigh, Micheál
(OCD)
St Teresa's,
Clarendon Street,
Dublin 2
Tel 01-6718466/6718127

MacLochlainn, Piaras, CC
Parochial House,
Bohernabreena,
Dublin 24
Tel 01-4510986
(Bohernabreena, Tallaght,
Oldbawn, Dublin)

MacMahon, Hugh (SSC)
IMU Exective Secretary
St Columban's,
Grange Road,
Donaghmede, Dublin 13
Tel 01-8476647

MacMahon, James Ardle, Rt
Rev Mgr, Canon,
Chancellor
Sacred Heart Residence,
Sybil Hill Road, Killester,
Dublin 5
(Dublin, retired)

MacMahon, John, Very Rev
Canon, PE
Holy Family Residence,
Roebuck Road, Dundrum,
Dublin 14
(Dublin, retired)

MacMahon, Joseph (OFM)
Secretary of the Province,
Provincial Office,
La Verna, Gormanston,
Co Meath
Tel 01-8020951

MacMánuis, Clement (CSsR)
Marianella/Liguori House,
75 Orwell Road, Dublin 6
Tel 01-4067100

MacMorrow, Francis (CM)
St Joseph's,
44 Stillorgan Park,
Blackrock, Co Dublin
Tel 01-2886961

MacNamara, Francis, Very
Rev, PE, CC
Mountmellick, Co Laois
Tel 057-8624198
(Mountmellick, Kildare & L.)

MacNamara, Henry (OSA)
St Patrick's College and
Church,
Via Piemonte 60,
00187 Rome, Italy
Tel 00396-4203121

MacNamara, Luke (OSB)
Glenstal Abbey, Murroe,
Co Limerick
Tel 061-386103

MacNamara, Vincent (SPS)
St Patrick's, 21 Leeson Park,
Dublin 6
Tel 01-4977897

MacNeill, Arthur, Very Rev
14 Ballyholland Road,
Newry, Co Down
(Dromore, retired)

MacOscar, Kieran, Very Rev,
PE
Parochial House,
10 Mullavilly Road,
Tandragee,
Co Armagh BT62 2LX
Tel 028-38840840
(Armagh, retired)

MacPartlin, Brendan (SJ)
Superior,
Iona, 211 Churchill Park,
Portadown BT62 1EU
Tel 028-38330366

MacRaois, Brian, Very Rev, PP
Parochial House, Chapel Hill,
Carlingford, Co Louth
Tel 042-9373111
(Carlingford and Clogherny,
Armagh)

MacSuibhne, Domhnall (OP),
Very Rev, PP
Prior, St Mary's,
The Claddagh, Co Galway
Tel 091-582884
(The Claddagh, Galway)

MacSweeney, James, CC
64 Westcourt, Ballincollig,
Co Cork
Tel 021-4870434
(Ballincollig, Cork & R.)

Madden, Brendan, Very Rev,
PP
67 Anne Devlin Park,
Ballyroan, Dublin 14
Tel 01-4037536
(Ballyroan, Dublin)

Madden, Christopher J.,
Lisieux
196 Oakcourt Avenue,
Palmerstown, Dublin 20
(Dublin, retired)

Madden, John (OCarm)
Terenure College, Terenure,
Dublin 6W
Tel 01-4904621

Madden, Laurence, Very Rev, PP
Ardagh, Co Limerick
Tel 069-76121/087-2286450
(*Ardagh and Carrickerry*, Limerick)

Madden, Michael, Very Rev, PE
Ballycrennane, Ballymacoda, Co Cork
Tel 024-98840
(Cloyne, retired)

Madden, Nicholas (OCD)
St Teresa's,
Clarendon Street, Dublin 2
Tel 01-6718466/6718127

Madden, Paul (OPraem)
Abbey of the Most Holy Trinity and St Norbert,
Kilnacrott Abbey,
Ballyjamesduff, Co Cavan
Tel 049-8544416

Madden, Patrick, Very Rev, Adm
Parochial House,
34 Aughrim Street, Dublin 7
Tel 01-8386571
(*Aughrim Street*, Dublin)

Madden, Peter, PP
50 Tobermore Road,
Desertmartin,
Magherafelt,
Co Derry BT45 5LE
Tel 028-79632196
(*Desertmartin*, Derry)

Madden, PJ, CC
Two-Mile-House,
Naas, Co Kildare
Tel 045-876160
(*Naas, Two-Mile-House*, Kildare & L.)

Madigan, Martin, Very Rev
Hamilton's Terrace, Glin,
Co Limerick
Tel 087-9418568
(Limerick, retired)

Madigan, Seamus
Chaplain,
Sarsfield Barracks, Limerick
Tel 061-316817
(Limerick)

Magee, Aelred (OCSO)
Our Lady of Bethlehem Abbey,
11 Ballymena Road,
Portglenone, Ballymena,
Co Antrim BT44 8BL
Tel 028-25821211

Magee, Bernard, Very Rev Canon
41 Lower Square,
Castlewellan BT31 9DN
Tel 028-43770377
(*Castlewellan (Kilmegan)*, Down & C.)

Magee, Gerard
Cistercian Monastery,
Portglenone
(Down & C.)

Magee, John, Most Rev, DD
Retired Bishop of Cloyne,
'Carnmeen', Convent Hill,
Mitchelstown, Co Cork
Tel 025-41887
(Cloyne)

Magennis, Feidlimidh, LSS
St Mary's University College, Belfast
(Dromore)

Magill, Martin, Very Rev, PP
Sacred Heart Presbytery,
1 Glenview Street,
Belfast BT14 7DP
Tel 028-90351851
(*Sacred Heart*, Down & C.)

Magill, Neil (SSC)
St Columban's, Dalgan Park,
Navan, Co Meath
Tel 046-9021525

Maginn, Michael, Very Rev
The Presbytery,
Tullygally Road, Legahory,
Craigavon BT65 5BY
Tel 028-38311872
(*Seagoe (Derrymacash)*, Dromore)

Magorrian, Eamon, CC
Parochial House,
27 Chapel Hill, Lisburn,
Co Antrim BT28 1EP
Tel 028-92660206
(*Lisburn (Blaris)*, Down & C.)

Maguire, Edmond, Very Rev, PE
Newtown Butler Road,
Clones, Co Monaghan
Tel 047-51160
(Clogher, retired)

Maguire, James (OSA)
St Augustine's Priory,
Washington Street, Cork
Tel 021-2753982

Maguire, Joseph (SMA)
African Missions,
Blackrock Road, Cork
Tel 021-4292871

Maguire, Salvian (CP)
Holy Cross Retreat,
Ardoyne,
Belfast BT14 7GE
Tel 028-90748231

Maguire, Sean, CC
Butlersbridge, Co Cavan
Tel 049-4365266
(*Cavan (Urney and Annagelliff)*, Kilmore)

Maguire, Vincent, Very Rev
26 Rodney Street,
Portrush,
Co Antrim BT56 8LB
(Down and C., retired)

Maher, Francis, Very Rev, PP
Johnstown via Thurles,
Co Kilkenny
Tel 056-8831219/
087-2402487
(*Johnstown*, Ossory)

Maher, James (SJ) Minister,
Crescent College Comprehensive,
Dooradoyle, Limerick
Tel 061-480920

Maher, Michael (SM)
Cerdon, Marist Fathers,
St Mary's Road, Dundalk,
Co Louth
Tel 042-9334019

Maher, Noel, Very Rev, PP
Clough, Ballacolla,
Portlaoise, Co Laois
Tel 057-878513
(*Aghaboe*, Ossory)

Maher, Oliver, Very Rev, PP
Urlingford, Co Kilkenny
Tel 056-8831121/
086-8323010
(*Urlingford*, Ossory)

Maher, Sean, CC
St Mary's,
Ballyconnell, Tullow,
Co Carlow
Tel 059-9156890
(*Clonmore*, Kildare & L.)

Maher, Thomas, Rt Rev Mgr
Archersrath Nursing Home,
Kilkenny
Tel 056-7790137
(Ossory, retired)

Mailey, Anthony, CC
Parochial House,
Quigley's Point, Co Donegal
Tel 074-9383008
(*Iskaheen (Iskaheen & Upper Moville)*, Derry)

Maliakkal, Aquino (OFMConv)
The Friary, Wexford
Tel 053-9122758

Mallon, Brendan, CC
Coachford, Co Cork
Tel 021-7334059
(*Aghabullogue*, Cloyne)

Mallon, Dominic
13 Richview Heights, Keady,
Co Armagh BT60 3SW
(Armagh)

Mallon, Thomas, Very Rev, PE, AP
Parochial House,
170 Loughmacrory Road,
Loughmacrory,
Omagh, Co Tyrone BT79 9LG
Tel 028-80761230
(*Termonmaguirc (Carrickmore, Loughmacrory & Creggan)*, Armagh)

Malone, Douglas, Adm
The Presbytery, Dunlavin,
Co Wicklow
Tel 045-401227
(*Dunlavin*, Dublin)

Malone, Larry
(priest in residence)
Edenderry, Co Offaly
Tel 046-9732352
(*Edenderry*, Kildare & L.)

Malone, Liam, CC
Parochial House, Kells,
Co Meath
Tel 046-9240213
(*Kells*, Meath)

Malone, Michael (CSSp)
Rockwell College, Cashel,
Co Tipperary
Tel 062-61444

Malone, Pat, Very Rev, PP
Church Drive, Clarecastle,
Co Clare
Tel 065-6823011/
086-8572023
(*Clarecastle (Clare Abbey)*, Killaloe)

Malone, Tony (SM)
Chanel College, Coolock,
Dublin 5
Tel 01-8480655/8480896

Maloney, Dermot, Very Rev, PP
Parochial House,
40 The Village,
Jonesboro, Newry,
Co Down BT35 8HP
Tel 028-30849345
(*Dromintee*, Armagh)

Maloney, John, CC
Curate's House, Kikelly,
Co Mayo
Tel 094-9367031
(*Kilmovee*, Achonry)

Maloney, Peter (SVD)
Donamon Castle,
Roscommon
Tel 090-6662222

Mandi, Josephat
Parish Chaplain,
287 South Circular Road,
Dublin 8
Tel 01-4533490
(*Dolphin's Barn*, Dublin)

Manding, Cruzito (CSsR)
Provincial, PO Box 280,
6000 Cebu City,
Philippine Islands
Tel 0063-32-2536341/
2536315

Mangan, Cyril, Very Rev, Adm
Parochial House,
Blanchardstown, Dublin 15
Tel 01-8213660
(*Blanchardstown*, Dublin)

Mangan, Eoin, Very Rev Canon, PP
The Prebytery,
Knockagoshel, Co Kerry
Tel 068-46107
(*Knocknagoshel*, Kerry)

Mangan, Patrick J., Very Rev, PE
Dún Mhuire,
44 Beechwood Avenue Upper, Dublin 6
Tel 01-4975180/
087-9857264
(Dublin, retired)

Mangan, Thomas, Very Rev, PP
Donaghmore, Co Limerick
Lifford Avenue, Limerick
Tel 061-313898
(*Donaghmore/Knockea*, Limerick)

Manik, Robert (OCarm)
Gort Muire, Ballinteer, Dublin 16
Tel 01-2984014

Manley, John (OFMCap)
St Francis Capuchin Friary, Rochestown, Co Cork
Tel 021-4896244

Mann, Robert (SCJ), Very Rev
On sabbatical
(Dublin)

Manning, Francis, Very Rev, PP
Newmarket, Co Cork
Tel 029-60999
(*Newmarket*, Cloyne)

Mannion, Colm (OP)
(study leave)
St Saviour's, Upper Dorset Street, Dublin 1
Tel 01-8897610

Mannion, Francis (SSC)
St Columban's
Retirement Home,
Dalgan Park, Navan,
Co Meath
Tel 046-9021525

Mannion, John, CC
Killoran, Ballinasloe,
Co Galway
Tel 090-9627120
(*Mullagh and Killoran*, Clonfert)

Mannion, Michéal, Very Rev, PP, Adm
Parochial House,
Clonbur, via Claremorris,
o Galway
Tel 094-9546304
(*Clonbur (Ross)*, Tuam)

Mannion, Tom, CC
Glencar, Manorhamiliton,
Co Leitrim
Tel 071-9855433
(*Manorhamilton (Killasnett)*, Kilmore)

Mannix, Jim (MSC)
Western Road, Cork
Tel 021-4804120

Mansfield, Declan, Very Rev, Adm
Ballinora, Waterfall,
near Cork
Tel 021-4873448
(*Ballinora*, C. & Ross)

Mansfield, Dermot (SJ)
(Team Assistant)
Maressa House,
Clontarf Road, Dublin 3
Tel 01-8057209/087-6942844
(*Dollymount*, Dublin)

Mareja, Martin (SAC)
Pallottine College,
Thurles, Co Tipperary
Tel 0504-21202

Marken, Aodhan, CC
Chaplain/Counsellor,
St Peter's Diocesan College,
Wexford
Tel 053-9142071
Parish: The Presbytery,
12 School Street, Wexford
Tel 053-9122055
(*Wexford*, Ferns)

Markus, Jeremiah, PC
47 Westland Row, Dublin 2
Tel 085-2778177
(*Westland Row*, Dublin)

Marley, Thomas (IC)
St Joseph's, Doire na hAbhann,
Tickincor, Clonmel,
Co Tipperary
Tel 052-6126914

Marmion, Declan (SM)
Superior, Mount St Mary's,
Dundrum Road, Milltown,
Dublin 14
Tel 01-2697322

Marren, John (SPS)
Assistant Society Leader,
St Patrick's
Kiltegan, Co Wicklow
Tel 059-6473600

Marrinan, Thomas, Very Rev, PP, VF
Gort, Co Galway
Tel 091-631220
(*Gort/Beagh*, Galway)

Marron, Eamonn, Rt Rev Mgr, PE
Parochial House, Raharney,
Co Westmeath
Tel 044-9374271
(*Kinnegad*, Meath)

Marron, Patrick, Very Rev Canon, PE
Fintona, Omagh,
Co Tyrone BT78 2NS
Tel 028-82841239
(*Fintona*, Clogher)

Marron, Thomas, Very Rev Canon, PE
Trillick, Omagh,
Co Tyrone BT78 3RD
Tel 028-89561217
(*Trillick*, Clogher)

Marsden, David (SCJ)
Sacred Heart Fathers,
Fairfield, 66 Inchicore Road,
Dublin 8
Tel 01-4538655

Marteaux, D. Thierry (OSB)
Benedictine Monks,
Holy Cross Monastery,
119 Kilbroney Road,
Rostrevor,
Co Down BT34 3BN
Tel 028-41739979

Martin, Diarmuid, Most Rev, DD
Archbishop of Dublin and Primate of Ireland,
Archbishop's House,
Drumcondra, Dublin 9
Tel 01-8373732
(Dublin)

Martin, Eamon, Most Rev, DD
Archbishop of Armagh,
Primate of All Ireland,
Ara Coeli, Cathedral Road,
Armagh BT61 7QY
Tel 028-37522045
(Armagh)

Martin, Hubert, Very Rev, PP
Glaslough, Monaghan
Tel 047-88120
(*Donagh*, Clogher)

Martin, Liam (CSSp)
Holy Spirit Missionary College, Kimmage Manor,
Dublin 12
Tel 01-4064300

Martin, Oliver (OPraem)
Abbey of the Most Holy Trinity and St Norbert,
Kilnacrott,
Ballyjamesduff, Co Cavan
Tel 049-8544416

Martin, Valentine, Very Rev, PP
Logatryna, Dunlavin,
Co Wicklow
(Dublin, retired)

Martinez, Matthew (OP)
Newbridge College,
Droichead Nua, Co Kildare
Tel 045-487200

Martynelis, Tomasz (OP), CC
St Saviour's, Upper Dorset Street, Dublin 1
Tel 01-8897610
(*Dominick Street*, Dublin)

Mathew, Binoy (SVD)
1 & 3 Pembroke Road,
Dublin 4
Tel 01-6680904

Mathew, Suneesh (OSCam)
St Camillus, Killucan,
Co Westmeath
Tel 044-74196/74115

Mathews, Colm
Highfield Healthcare,
Swords Road, Dublin 9
Tel 01-8374444
(Dublin, retired)

Massengill, Peter Damian (OFMConv), Very Rev
Provincial Delegation Office,
St Patrick's Friary,
26 Cornwall Road,
Waterloo, London SE1 8TW,
England
Tel 020-79288897

Maszkiewicz, Jaroslaw, CC
10 Ashford, Monksland,
Athlone, Co Westmeath
Tel 090-6493262
(*Athlone, SS Peter and Paul's*, Elphin)

Mathews, William (SJ)
Milltown Park,
Sandford Road, Dublin 6
Tel 01-2698411/2698113

Matthews, Richard, Very Rev, PP, VF
Parochial House, Killucan,
Co Westmeath
Tel 044-9374127
(*Killucan*, Meath)

Mawn, Sean, Very Rev, PP, VF
Ballinamore, Co Leitrim
Tel 071-9644039
(*Ballinamore (Oughteragh)*, Kilmore)

Maxwell, Barney
Empor, Ballymacargy,
Co Westmeath
(Meath, retired)

McAdam, Colm (CM), Very Rev
St Joseph's,
44 Stillorgan Park,
Blackrock, Co Dublin
Tel 01-2886961

McAleer, Brendan, Very Rev, PP
Parochial House,
Garristown, Co Dublin
Tel 01-8354138
(*Garristown*, Dublin)

McAleer, Gerard, Very Rev, PP, VF
Parochial House,
63 Castlecaulfield Road,
Donaghmore, Dungannon,
Co Tyrone BT70 3HF
Tel 028-87761327
(*Donaghmore*, Armagh)

McAleese, Frank (OCarm)
Carmelite Friary,
Kinsale, Co Cork
Tel 021-772138

McAlinden, John, PP
Parochial House,
Slane Road, Mell,
Drogheda, Co Louth
Tel 041-983 8278
(*Mell*, Armagh)

McAlinden, Martin, Very Rev
Director of Pastoral Theology,
St Patrick's College,
Maynooth, Co Kildare
(Dromore)

McAnaney, Martin (SM)
Paris

McAnenly, Peter, Very Rev,
Adm
Parochial House,
42 Abbey Street,
Armagh BT61 7D2
Tel 028-37522802
(*Armagh*, Armagh)

McAnerney, Arthur, Very Rev,
PE, AP
Parochial House,
10 Aughrim Road,
Magherafelt,
Co Derry BT45 6AY
Tel 028-79632351
(*Magherafelt and Ardtrea
North*, Armagh)

McArdle, Martin, Very Rev, PP
Parochial House,
10 Springhill Road,
Moneymore, Magherafelt,
Co Derry BT45 7NG
Tel 028-86748242
(*Moneymore (Ardtrea)*,
Armagh)

McArdle, Sean (SM), CC
The Presbytery,
78A Donore Avenue,
Dublin 8
Tel 01-4542425
(*Donore Avenue*, Dublin)

McAreavey, John, Most Rev,
DD
Bishop of Dromore,
Bishop's House,
44 Armagh Road, Newry,
Co Down BT35 6PN
Tel 028-30262444
(Dromore)

McAteer, Brendan, Very Rev
Warrenpoint,
Co Down
(Dromore, retired)

McAteer, Francis, Very Rev
Canon, PP
Parochial House, Carrick,
Co Donegal
Tel 074-9739008
(*Carrick (Glencolmcille)*,
Raphoe)

McAteer, John (SVD)
1 & 3 Pembroke Road,
Dublin 4
Tel 01-6680904

McAteer, Kieran, Very Rev, PP
Parochial House,
Ballybofey,
Co Donegal
Tel 074-9131135
(*Stranorlar*, Raphoe)

McAteer, Tom
91 Newry Road, Barnmeen,
Rathfriland,
Co Down BT34 5AP
Tel 028-40630306
(*St Mary's (Burren), St
Patrick's (Mayobridge),
Drumgath (Rathfriland)*,
Dromore)

McAuliffe, David, Dr
Chaplaincy Base, Cork
Institute of Technology,
3 Elton Lawn, Rossa Avenue,
Bishopstown, Cork
Tel 021-4346244
(Cork & R.)

McAuliffe, Desmond, Very
Rev, PP
Rockhill, Bruree,
Co Limerick
Tel 063-90515/087-2336476
(*Rockhill/Bruree*, Limerick)

McAuliffe, James (SPS)
St Patrick's, Kiltegan,
Co Wicklow
Tel 059-6473600

McAuliffe, Leo (OFMCap)
St Anthony's Capuchin
Friary,
43 Dublin Street, Carlow
Tel 059-9142543

McBrearty, Danny, CC
Parochial House, Clar,
Co Donegal
Tel 074-9721093
(*Donegal Town
(Tawnawilly)*, Raphoe)

McBrearty, Stephen, Very Rev,
PP
2A My Lady's Mile,
Holywood,
Co Down BT18 9EW
Tel 028-90422167
(*Holywood*, Down & C.)

McBride, Brendan
St Philip's Church,
725 Diamond Street,
San Francisco,
California, 94114
(Raphoe)

McBride, Colm, Very Rev, PP
Parochial House,
59 Chapel Road,
Glenavy, Crumlin,
Co Antrim, BT29 4LY
Tel 028-94422262
(*Glenavy And Killead*, Down
& C.)

McBride, Malachy (SDS)
'Naomh Mhuire',
Upper Slavery,
Buncrana, Co. Donegal
Tel 074-9322264

McCabe, John, Very Rev
Canon, PP
Parochial House, Roslea,
Co Fermanagh BT92 7QY
Tel 028-67751227
(*Roslea*, Clogher)

McCabe, Michael (SMA)
Provincial, African Missions,
Provincial House,
Feltrim, Blackrock Road,
Cork
Tel 021-4292871

McCabe, Robert, CF
Gormanston Military Camp,
Gormanston, Co Meath
Tel 01-8413990
(*Stamullen*, Meath)

McCabe, Thomas (OMI)
Oblate Scholasticate,
St Anne's,
Goldenbridge Walk,
Inchicore, Dublin 8
Tel 01-4540841/4542955

McCafferty, Patrick, CC
Parochial House, Crossgar,
Downpatrick,
Co Down BT30 9EA
Tel 028-44830229
(*Crossgar (Kilmore)*, Down &
C.)

McCafferty, Paul
Derry Diocesan Office,
St Eugene's Cathedral,
Francis Street,
Derry BT48 9AP
Tel 028-71262302
(Derry)

McCaffrey, Desmond (OCD)
St Teresa's,
Clarendon Street, Dublin 2
Tel 01-6718466/6718127

McCaffrey, Eugene (OCD)
Avila, Bloomfield Avenue,
Morehampton Road,
Dublin 4
Tel 01-6430200

McCaffrey, James (CSSp)
Holy Spirit Missionary
College, Kimmage Manor,
Dublin 12
Tel 01-4064300

McCaffrey, Ultan (OFM)
Franciscan Friary, Lady Lane,
Waterford
Tel 051-874262

McCague, Brendan, CC
Corduff, Carrickmacross,
Co Monaghan
Tel 042-9669456
(*Carrickmacross*, Clogher)

McCahery, Barney (CSsR), CC
6 Market Street, Ballycastle,
Antrim BT54 6DP
Tel 028-20762202
(*Ballycastle (Ramoan)*, Down
& C.)

McCallion, Edwin (SM)
Regional Superior, Marist
Regional Office,
Mount St Mary's, Dundrum
Road, Milltown, Dublin 14
Tel 01-2698100/086-2597905

McCallion, John, CC
Parochial House,
140 Mountjoy Road,
Brocagh, Dungannon,
Co Tyrone BT71 5DY
Tel 028-87738381
(*Clonoe*, Armagh)

McCamley, Eamonn, Very Rev,
PP, VF
Parochial House,
34 Madden Row, Keady,
Co Armagh BT60 3RW
Tel 028-30531242
(*Keady (Derrynoose)*,
Armagh)

McCann, Arthur (CP)
St Gabriel's Retreat,
The Graan, Enniskillen,
Co Fermanagh
Tel 028-66322272

McCann, Brian, Very Rev, PP
St Luke's Presbytery,
Twinbrook Road, Dunmurry,
Co Antrim BT17 0RP
(*St Luke's*, Down & C.)

McCann, Columba (OSB)
Novice Master,
Glenstal Abbey, Murroe,
Co Limerick
Tel 061-621000

McCann, Henry, Very Rev, PP
St Anthony's Presbytery,
4 Willowfield Crescent,
Belfast BT6 8HP
Tel 028-90458158
(*St Anthony's*, Down & C.)

McCann, Joseph (CM)
St Paul's, Raheny, Dublin 5
Tel 01-8314011/2/3

McCanny, Bryan, Rt Rev Mgr,
PP
119 Irish Green Street,
Limavady,
Co Derry BT49 9AB
Tel 028-77729759
(*Limavady*, Derry)

McCarney, Eugene, Very Rev,
PE
Parochial House,
Castletown, Gorey,
Co Wexford
Tel 0402-37115
(Dublin, retired)

McCarney, Henry (SPS)
St Patrick's, Kiltegan,
Co Wicklow
Tel 059-6473600

McCarrick, Roger (SM)
Fiji

McCarron, Peter, Co-PP
18 Aspen Road,
Kinsealy Court, Swords,
Co Dublin
Tel 01-8405948
(*Swords*, Dublin)

McCartan, Seán, Adm
Parochial House,
19 Ardboe Road, Moortown,
Cookstown,
Co Tyrone BT80 0HT
Tel 028-86737236
(*Ardboe*, Armagh)

McCarthy, Berchmans
(OFMCap)
St Francis Capuchin Friary,
Rochestown, Co Cork
Tel 021-4896244

McCarthy, Brian
Castleville Study Centre,
Golf Links Road, Castletroy,
Limerick
Tel 061-331223
(Opus Dei)

McCarthy, Charles (CSSp)
Holy Spirit Missionary
College, Kimmage Manor,
Whitehall Road, Dublin 12
Tel 01-4064300

McCarthy, Daniel, CF (Cloyne)
Chaplain,
Stephen's Barracks, Kilkenny
Tel 056-7761852
(Ossory)

McCarthy, Dermod
Pastoral Care Facilitator,
RTÉ, Donnybrook, Dublin 4
Tel 01-2083237/087-2499719
(Dublin)

McCarthy, Donal (MSC)
Western Road, Cork
Tel 021-4804120

McCarthy, Donal (SAC)
Archivist,
Provincial House,
'Homestead',
Sandyford Road, Dundrum,
Dublin 16
Tel 01-2956180/2954170

McCarthy, Eamonn, CC
53 Ros Álainn,
Gurteenroe, Macroom,
Co Cork
Tel 085-8585308
(Macroom, Cloyne)

McCarthy, Eamonn, CC
The Presbytery, Donard,
Co Wicklow
Tel 045-404614
(Dunlavin, Dublin)

McCarthy, Eugene (CP), Very
Rev, PP
Holy Cross Retreat,
432 Crumlin Road, Ardoyne,
Belfast BT14 7GE
Tel 028-90748231/2
(Holy Cross, Down & C.)

McCarthy, Fachtna, Adm
Parochial House, St Mary's,
Haddington Road, Dublin 4
Tel 01-6643295/086-3848432
(Haddington Road, Dublin)

McCarthy, Florence (SDB)
Salesian House,
45 St Teresa's Road,
Crumlin, Dublin 12
Tel 01-4555605

McCarthy, Gabriel (OCSO)
Mount Saint Joseph Abbey,
Roscrea, Co Tipperary
Tel 0505-25600

McCarthy, Gerard (SVD)
Maynooth, Co Kildare
Tel 01-6286391/2

McCarthy, John
Irish Pastoral Centre,
953 Hancock Street, Quincy,
Massachusetts CO2170, USA
Tel 001-617479740
(Limerick)

McCarthy, John (MSC)
Woodview House,
Mount Merrion Avenue,
Blackrock, Co Dublin
Tel 01-2881644

McCarthy, John (SVD), PP
Donamon Castle,
Co Roscommon
Tel 090-6662222
(Creggs (Glinsk and
Kilbegnet), Elphin)

McCarthy, John, Very Rev,
Adm
1 Cathedral Terrace,
Cobh, Co Cork
Tel 021-4815619
(Cobh, St Colman's
Cathedral, Cloyne)

McCarthy, John, Very Rev
76 Carrowmore Meadows,
Knock, Co Mayo
(Tuam, retired)

McCarthy, John, Very Rev, PP
Rosscarbery, Co Cork
Tel 023-8848168
(Rosscarbery and Lissavaird,
Cork & R.)

McCarthy, Liam (OFM)
Guardian, Franciscan Abbey,
Multyfarnham,
Co Westmeath
Tel 044-9371114/9371137

McCarthy, Michael (CSSp)
Holy Spirit Missionary
College, Kimmage Manor,
Dublin 12
Tel 01-4064300

McCarthy, Patrick A., Very
Rev, PP
35 Paul Street, Cork
Tel 021-4276573
(SS Peter and Paul, Cork &
R.)

McCarthy, Patrick J., Very Rev,
Adm
Ardfield, Clonakilty, Co Cork
Tel 023-8840649
(Ardfield and Rathbarry,
Cork & R.)

McCarthy, Patrick, CC
Mallow, Co Cork
Tel 086-3831621
(Mallow, Cloyne)

McCarthy, Thomas
(Team Assistant)
119 The Stiles Road,
Dublin 3
Tel 01- 8338424
(Clontarf, St Anthony's,
Dublin)

McCarthy, Thomas (OP)
Newbridge College,
Droichead Nua, Co Kildare
Tel 045-487200

McCarthy, Vincent (OSA)
Duckspool House,
Abbeyside, Dungarvan,
Co Waterford
Tel 058-23784

McCartney, Sean, Very Rev, PP
25 Alt-Min Avenue,
Belfast BT8 6NJ
(Down & C., retired)

McCathy, Anthony (OParem)
Abbey of the Most Holy
Trinity and St Norbert,
Kilnacrott,
Ballyjamesduff, Co Cavan
Tel 049-8544416

McCaughan, Aidan
(priest in residence)
Parochial House,
2-4 Broughshane Road,
Ballymena,
Co Antrim BT43 7DX
Tel 028-25641515
(Ballymena (Kirkinriola),
Down & C.)

McCaughan, Colm, Rt Rev
Mgr
3 Fortwilliam Demesne,
Belfast BT15 4FD
Tel 028-90778111

McCaughan, Damian, CC
142 Carnmoney Road,
Newtownabbey,
Co Antrim BT36 6JU
Tel 028-90832488
(St Mary's on the Hill, Down
& C.)

McCaughan, Dermot, Very
Rev, PP
St Patrick's Presbytery,
29 Chapel Hill, Lisburn,
Co Antrim BT28 1EP
Tel 028-92662341
(Lisburn (Blaris), Down & C.)

McCaughey, George (SDB)
Salesian House,
Warrenstown, Drumree,
Co Meath
Tel 01-8240298

McCaughey, Michael M., PP
St Patrick's, Buncrana road,
Pennyburn, Derry BT48 7QL
Tel 028-71262360
(The Three Patrons, Derry)

McCaughey, Shane, Very Rev
Canon
(priest in residence)
Shantonagh, Castleblayney,
Co Monaghan
Tel 042-9745015
(Aughnamullen East,
Clogher)

McCay-Morrissey, Bernard
(OP)
St Saviour's,
Upper Dorset Street,
Dublin 1
Tel 01-8897610

McClarey, Liam Very Rev,
(SAC), PP, VF
Parochial House Corduff,
Blanchardstown, Dublin 15
Tel 01-8213596
(Corduff, Dublin)

McCloskey, Gerard, Very Rev,
PP
Parochial House, Ardglass,
Co Down BT30 7TU
(Dunsford and Ardglass,
Down & C.)

McCluskey, Brian, Very Rev
Canon, PE
Apt 2,
2 Danesfort Park North,
Stranmillis Road,
Belfast BT9 5RB
Tel 028-90683544
(Clogher, retired)

McCluskey, Joseph, Very Rev,
PP
Threemilehouse, Monaghan
Tel 047-81501
(Corcaghan, Clogher)

McCluskey, Peter (OMI)
Oblate House of Retreat,
Inchicore, Dublin 8
Tel 01-4534408/4541805

McConnell, Noel
(On study leave)
64 The Green, Moyglare Hall,
Moyglare Road, Maynooth,
Co Kildare
(Clogher)

McConvery, Brendan (CSsR)
Marianella/Liguori House,
75 Orwell Road, Rathgar,
Dublin 6
Tel 01-4067100

McConville, Conor, CC
Lisadell, 54 Francis Street,
Lurgan,
Co Armagh BT66 6DL
(Shankill, St Paul's & St
Peter's (Lurgan), Dromore)

McConville, Gerard, Very Rev
68 Main Street,
Portglenone BT44 8HS
(Down & C., retired)

McConville, Matthew
c/o Bishop's House,
44 Armagh Road,
Newry, Co Down
(Dromore)

McConville, Michael, AP
65 Moyle Road, Ballycastle,
Co Antrim, BT54 6LG
Tel 028-28273230
(Glenarm (Tickmacreevan),
Larne, Down & C.)

McCormack, Christy
Fohenagh, Ahascragh,
Ballinasloe, Co Galway
Tel 090-9688623
(*Fohenagh and Killure*,
Clonfert)

McCormack, Ignatius, AP
St Mary's, Quin, Co Clare
Tel 065-6839039/
086-2777139
(*Quin*, Killaloe)

McCormack, James (CM)
St Paul's College, Raheny,
Dublin 5
Tel 01-8314011/2

McCormack, James, PP
Hacketstown, Co Carlow
Tel 059-6471257
(*Hacketstown*, Kildare & L.)

McCormack, John (SMA), CC
Parochial House,
Breaffy, Castlebar,
Co Mayo
Tel 094-9022799
(*Castlebar (Aglish,
Ballyheane and Breaghwy)*,
Tuam)

McCormack, Martin (SDB), CC
Salesian House, Milford,
Castletroy, Limerick
Tel 061-330268
(*Our Lady Help of Christians*,
Limerick)

McCormack, William, Very
Rev, PP
Puckane, Nenagh,
Co Tipperary
Tel 067-24105/087-4168855
(*Puckane (Cloughprior and
Monsea)*, Killaloe)

McCormick, Diarmuid, CC
Kilkishen, Co Clare
Tel 061-367193
(*O'Callaghan's Mills*,
Killaloe)

McCorry, Francis, Very Rev
Our Lady's Home,
68 Ardnava Road,
Belfast BT12 6FF
(Down & C., retired)

McCoy, Art (OFM)
Franciscan Friary,
Lady Lane, Waterford
Tel 051-874262

McCrann, Christopher, CC
Knocknahur, Sligo
Tel 071-9128470
(*Strandhill/Ransboro*, Elphin)

McCreave, Eamon (OSM)
St Michael's Presbytery,
200 Finaghy Road North,
Belfast BT11 9EG
Tel 028-90615174
(*St Michael's*, Down & C.)

McCrory, Gerard, Very Rev
Canon, PP
Church Street, Ballynahinch,
Co Down BT24 8LP
Tel 028-97562410
(*Magheradroll
(Ballynahinch)*, Dromore)

McCrory, Patrick, J., Very Rev,
PE
Parochial House,
Sixemilecross, Omagh,
Co Tyrone BT79 9NF
Tel 028-80758344
(Armagh, retired)

McCrossan, Oliver (SSC)
St Columban's,
Dalgan Park, Navan,
Co Meath
Tel 046-9021525

McCrystal, Eoin, Very Rev
(Moderator), VF
12 Grangemore Grove,
Donaghmede, Dublin 13
Tel 01-8474652
(*Donaghmede-Clongriffin-
Balgriffin*, Dublin)

McCullagh, Michael (CM),
Very Rev, PP
St Peter's, Phibsboro,
Dublin 7
Tel 01-8389708
(*Phibsboro*, Dublin)

McCullagh, Raymond
(*priest in residence*)
1 Seafield Park South,
Portstewart,
Co Derry BT55 7LH
Tel 028-70832066
(*Portstewart*, Down & C.)

McCulloch, Robert (SSC)
Collegio San Colombano,
Corso Trieste 57,
00198 Roma

McCullen, Richard (CM)
St Paul's College, Raheny,
Dublin 5
Tel 01-8318113

McDermott, Brendan (CP)
St Paul's Retreat,
Mount Argus, Dublin 6W
Tel 01-4992000

McDermott, Joseph, Very Rev,
PP
c/o Parish Office,
Station Road, Newbridge,
Co Kildare
Tel 045-431741
(*Droichead Nua/Newbridge*,
Kildare & L.)

McDermott, Kieran, Very Rev,
Co-PP
'Emmaus', Main Street,
Dundrum, Dublin 14
Tel 01-2984348
(*Dundrum*, Dublin)

McDermott, Laurence (OCSO)
Mellifont Abbey,
Collon, Co Louth
Tel 041-9826103

McDermott, Louis (OMI)
(Moderator)
52a Bulfin Road,
Dublin 8
Tel 01-4531660
(*Inchicore, St Michael's*,
Dublin)

McDermott, Niall, Adm
St Pauls,
8 Slademore Close,
Ard-na-Gréine,
Ayrfield, Dublin 13
Tel 01-8470685
(*Ayrfield*, Dublin)

McDermott, Noel, CC
91 Ervey Road, Eglinton,
Co Derry BT47 3AU
Tel 028-71810235
(*Faughanvale*, Derry)

McDermott, Paraic, (CSSp), CC
The Presbytery,
Manor Kilbride, Blessington,
Co Wicklow
Tel 01-4582154
(*Blessington*, Dublin)

McDermott, Patsy, CC
Ballinamuck, Co Longford
Tel 043-3324110
(*Drumlish*, Ardagh & Cl.)

McDermott, Sean, Very Rev,
PP
Ballintemple, Ballinagh,
Co Cavan
Tel 049-4337106
(*Ballintemple*, Kilmore)

McDermott, Thomas
Cloghroe, Blarney
Co Cork
Tel 021-4385163
(*Inniscarra*, Cloyne)

McDevitt, Eamon, PP
78 Lisnaragh Road,
Dunamanagh, Strabane,
Co Tyrone BT82 0QN
Tel 028-71398212
(*Dunamanagh
(Donagheady)*, Derry)

McDevitt, John
c/o Diocesan Offices,
St Eugene's Cathedral,
Francis Street,
Derry BT48 9AP
(Derry)

McDevitt, Kevin
(*priest in residence*)
Blackwater, Enniscorthy,
Co Wexford
Tel 053-9129288
(*Blackwater*, Ferns)

McDevitt, Patrick (CM), Very
Rev
President, All Hallows
Institute for Mission
and Ministry,
Drumcondra, Dublin 9
Tel 01-8373745/6
St Paul's, Raheny, Dublin 5
Tel 01-8314011/2

McDevitt, Vincent (CSSp), CC
Caltra, Ballinasloe
Co Galway
Tel 090-9678125
(*Ahascragh (Ahascragh and
Caltra)*, Elphin)

McDonagh, Brendan (SPS)
On temporary diocesan
work

McDonagh, Donald (SPS)
St Patricks, Main Street,
Knock, Co Mayo
Tel 094-9388661

McDonagh, Enda
St Patrick's College,
Maynooth, Co Kildare
Tel 01-6285222
(Tuam, retired)

McDonagh, James, Very Rev,
PP
Ballymote, Co Sligo
Tel 071-9183361
(*Ballymote (Emlefad and
Kilmorgan)*, Achonry)

McDonagh, John, Very Rev, PP
'Stella Maris',
15 Oswald Road,
Sandymount, Dublin 4
Tel 01-6684265
(*Sandymount*, Dublin)

McDonagh, Martin, (CSSp)
Holy Spirit Missionary
College, Kimmage Manor,
Dublin 12
Tel 01-406 4300

McDonagh, Sean (SSC)
(Research JPIC)
St Columban's, Dalgan Park,
Navan, Co Meath
Tel 046-9021525

McDonald, Anthony (OCarm)
Prior, Carmelite Priory,
White Abbey, Co Kildare
Tel 045-521391

McDonald, Daniel, Very Rev,
PP
Marshallstown, Enniscorthy,
Co Wexford
Tel 053-9388521
(*Marshallstown*, Ferns)

McDonald, John, CC
3 Stanhope Place, Athy,
Co Kildare
Tel 059-8631698
(*Athy*, Dublin)

McDonald, John, Rt Rev Mgr,
PP
Curragh Camp, Co Kildare
Tel 045-441369
(*Curragh Camp*, Kildare & L.)

McDonald, Joseph, Adm
No 2, 148D Presbytery,
Blackditch Road, Dublin 10
Tel 01-6265119
(*Ballyfermot Upper*, Dublin)

McDonald, Joseph
56 Auburn Road, Killiney,
Co Dublin
Tel 01 2856660/087 8122651
(*Johnstown-Killiney*, Dublin)

McDonald, Thomas (CSSp)
Blackrock College,
Blackrock, Co Dublin
Tel 01-2888681

McDonnell, Albert, Very Rev,
PP
Diocesan Chancellor,
Killaloe Diocesan Office,
Westbourne, Ennis, Co Clare
Tel 065-6828638
Kildysart, Co Clare
Tel 065-6832155/
085-7811823
(*Kildysart & Coolmeen
(Kilfidane)*, Killaloe)

McDonnell, Charles, Very Rev,
Adm
Westport, Co Mayo
Administration Kilmeena
(*Westport*, Tuam)

McDonnell, Colum (OSM)
Servite Priory, Benburb,
Dungannon,
Co Tyrone BT71 7JZ
Tel 028-37548241

McDonnell, Eunan (SDB)
Salesian College,
Maynooth Road, Celbridge,
Co Kildare
Tel 01-6275058/60

McDonnell, Francis, Very Rev
Canon
c/o Parochial House,
83 Terenure Road East,
Dublin 6
(Dublin, retired)

McDonnell, James (CSSp)
Blackrock College,
Blackrock, Co Dublin
Tel 01-2888681

McDonnell, Joseph (SSC)
Bursar, St Columban's,
Dalgan Park,
Navan, Co Meath
Tel 046-9021525

McDonnell, Leo, Very Rev
Cathedral House,
Cathedral Place, Limerick
Tel 061-413315
(*St Michael's*, Limerick)

McDonnell, Paschal (OFM)
Franciscan Friary,
Rossnowlagh, Co Donegal
Tel 072-9851342

McDonnell, Patrick, Very Rev
Canon, PE
Our Lady of Lourdes
Presbytery,
Hardman's Gardens,
Drogheda, Co Louth
Tel 041-9831899
(*Drogheda*, Armagh)

McDonnell, Paudge, Very Rev,
PP
Annyalla, Castleblayney,
Co Monaghan
Tel 042-9740121
(*Clontibret*, Clogher)

McDonnell, Thomas (SPS)
St Patrick's, Kiltegan,
Co Wicklow
Tel 059-6473600

McDunphy, Aodhán (OCSO)
Mount Saint Joseph Abbey,
Roscrea, Co Tipperary
Tel 0505-25600

McEldowney, Michael, PEm
c/o Diocesan Offices,
St Eugene's Cathedral,
Francis Street,
Derry BT48 9AP
(Derry, retired)

McElhatton, Francis (SPS)
St Patrick's, Kiltegan,
Co Wicklow
Tel 059-6473600

McElhennon, Kevin, PP
14 Killyclogher Road,
Omagh, Co Tyrone BT79 0AX
Tel 028-82243375
(*Killyclogher (Cappagh)*,
Derry)

McElhill, Laurence, Very Rev,
PE
(priest in residence),
43B Glen Road,
Belfast BT11 8BB
(*St Teresa's*, Down & C.)

McElhinney, Brian, Very Rev,
PP
Lavey, Stradone, Co Cavan
Tel 049-4330125
(*Lavey*, Kilmore)

McElroy, James (SM)
Cerdon, Marist Fathers,
St Mary's Road, Dundalk,
Co Louth
Tel 042-9334019

McElvaney, Terence
Church Square,
Co Monaghan
Tel 047-82255
(Clogher, retired)

McElwee, Christopher (IC), CC
Parochial House,
Omeath, Co Louth
Tel 042-9375198
(*Carlingford and Clogherny*,
Armagh)

McEneaney, Owen J., Very
Rev, Adm
Parochial House,
Pettigo, Co Donegal
Tel 071-9861666
(*Pettigo*, Clogher)

McEnroe, Patrick, Very Rev, PP
Darver, Readypenny,
Dundalk, Co Louth
Tel 042-9379147
(*Darver and Dromiskin*,
Armagh)

McEntee, Seamus
St Mary's,
New Road, Clondalkin,
Dublin 22
(*Clondalkin*, Dublin)

McEntire, Peter J. (CSSp)
Holy Spirit Missionary
College,
Kimmage Manor, Dublin 12
Tel 01-4064300

McErlean, Martin, Very Rev,
PP
Parochial House,
Castletown-Kilpatrick,
Navan, Co Meath
Tel 046-9055789
(*Castletown-Kilpatrick*,
Meath)

McEveney, Feargus (OFM)
Guardian,
Franciscan Friary,
Rossnowlagh, Co Donegal
Tel 072-9851342

McEvoy, A. (SDB)
Bursar, Salesian College,
Maynooth Road, Celbridge,
Co Kildare
Tel 01-6275058/60

McEvoy, Francis, Very Rev, PP,
VF
Parochial House,
Crookstown, Athy,
Co Kildare
Tel 059-8624109
(*Moone*, Dublin)

McEvoy, John, (SSC)
c/o St Columban's,
Dalgan Park, Navan
Co Meath
Tel 046-9021525

McEvoy, John, Very Rev, PP
Goresbridge, Co Kilkenny
Tel 059-9775180
(*Paulstown*, Kildare & L.)

McEvoy, Joseph, Very Rev, PP
Parochial House, Moynalty,
Kells, Co Meath
Tel 046-9244305
(*Moynalty*, Meath)

McEvoy, P. J., Very Rev, PP
Francis Street, Edenderry,
Co Offaly
Tel 046-9731296
(*Edenderry*, Kildare & L.)

McEvoy, Seamus, Very Rev
Dean, Adm
Seir Kieran,
Clareen, Birr, Co Offaly
Tel 0509-31080/086-2634093
(*Seir Kieran*, Ossory)

McEvoy, Seán, Very Rev
(elsewhere in the Diocese)
c/o Ara Coeli,
Armagh, BT61 7QY
Tel 028-37522045
(Armagh)

McFaul, Daniel, CC
5 Strathroy Road, Omagh,
Co Tyrone, BT79 7DW
Tel 028-82251055
(*Killyclogher (Cappagh)*,
Derry)

McFlynn, Gerard
18 Maresfield Gardens,
London NW3 5SX
(Down & C.)

McGahan, Noel, Very Rev, PP
25 Augher Road, Clogher,
Co Tyrone BT76 0AD
Tel 028-85549604
(*Clogher*, Clogher)

McGarry, Leo J. (CSSp)
Holy Spirit
Missionary College,
Kimmage Manor,
Dublin 12
Tel 01-406 4300

McGarvey, Patrick, Very Rev,
PP
Fanavolty, Kindrum,
Letterkenny, Co Donegal
Tel 074-9159007
(*Tamney (Clondavaddog)*,
Raphoe)

McGaughey, Sylvius (CP)
St Paul's Retreat,
Mount Argus, Dublin 6W
Tel 01-4992000

McGauran, Francis, Very Rev
Cuilmore, Strokestown,
Co Roscommon
(Elphin, retired)

McGavigan, Micheál, CC
St Brigid's, Carnhill,
Derry BT48 8HJ
Tel 028-71351261
(*The Three Patrons*, Derry)

McGee, Brendan, Dean, PE
St Patrick's Presbytery,
199 Donegall Street,
Belfast BT1 2FL
Tel 028-90324597
(*St Patrick's*, Down & C.)

McGee, Edward, BA, BD
St Mary's University College,
191 Falls Road,
Belfast 12 6FE
Tel 028-90327678
Resident Priest,
St Malachy's College,
Antrim Road,
Belfast BT15 2AE
Tel 028-90748285
(Down & C.)

McGee, Joseph (MSC)
Provincial Leader,
65 Terenure Road West,
Dublin 6W
Tel 01-4906622

McGeehan, Paul, CC
Glencolmcille, Co Donegal
Tel 074-9730888
(*Carrick (Glencolmcille)*,
Raphoe)

McGeever, Patrick (CSSp)
Rockwell College,
Cashel, Co Tipperary
Tel 062-61444

McGeough, Thomas, Very Rev,
PE
34 The Village,
Moorehall Lodge,
Ardee, Co Louth
Tel 041-6857556
(Armagh, retired)

McGettigan, Denis, Very Rev
Canon, PP
Raphoe, Lifford,
Co Donegal
Tel 074-9145647
Chaplain, Deele College,
Raphoe, Co Donegal
Tel 074-9145277
(Raphoe, Raphoe)

McGettrick, William (CSsR)
Chairperson, Diocesan
Commission for Religious,
Tel 028-90325668

McGill, Maurice (MHM)
Rector, St Joseph's,
Mill Hill Missionaries,
Waterford Road, Kilkenny
Tel 056-7721482

McGillicuddy, Cornelius
Sacred Heart Residence,
Sybil Hill Road, Killester,
Dublin 5
(Dublin, retired)

McGilloway, Joseph (OSB)
Glenstal Abbey, Murroe,
Co Limerick
Tel 061-386103

McGing, Aidan (CM)
Phibsboro, St Peter's,
Dublin 7
Tel 01-8389708/8389841

McGinley, Séamus, Very Rev,
PP
Parochial House,
Beragh, Omagh
Co Tyrone BT79 OSY
Tel 028-80758206
(Beragh, Armagh)

McGinn, Emlyn, CC
Parochial House, 3 Convent
Road,
Cookstown, Co Tyrone BT80
8QA
Tel 028-86763293
(Cookstown (Desertcreight
and Derryloran), Armagh)

McGinn, Patrick, Very Rev,
Adm
St Joseph's Presbytery,
Park Street, Monaghan
Tel 047-81220
(Monaghan, Clogher)

McGinnity, Gerard, Very Rev,
PP
Parochial House,
Knockbridge, Dundalk,
Co Louth
Tel 042-9374125
(Knockbridge, Armagh)

McGinnity, Michael, PP
St Malachy's Presbytery,
24 Alfred Street,
Belfast BT2 8EN
Tel 028-90321713
(St Malachy's, Down & C.)

McGirr, Austin, Very Rev, PP,
VF
Parochial House,
4 The Crescent, Portstewart,
Co Derry BT55 7AB
Tel 028-70832534
(Portstewart, Down & C.)

McGirr, Dermot, CC
48 Brook Street, Omagh
Co Tyrone, BT78 5HE
Tel 028-82242092
(Omagh (Drumragh), Derry)

McGlynn, Colm (OSM), Very
Rev
Provincial, Servite Priory,
Benburb, Dungannon,
Co Tyrone BT71 7JZ
Northern Ireland
Tel 028-37548241

McGlynn, Fergus, CC
43 Chestnut Grove,
Ballymount Road,
Dublin 24
Tel 01-4515570
(Kilnamanagh-Castleview,
Dublin)

McGlynn, Patrick (CSSp)
Holy Spirit Missionary
College, Kimmage Manor,
Dublin 12
Tel 01-406 4300

McGlynn, Thomas, Very Rev,
PP
143 Andersonstown Road,
Belfast BT11 9BW
Tel 028-90615702/028-
90603951
(St Agnes', Down & C.)

McGoldrick, Brian, PP
Doneyloop, Castlefin,
Lifford, Co Donegal
Tel 074-9146183
(Doneyloop, Derry)

McGoldrick, John
(priest in residence)
Parochial House,
56 Minterburn Road,
Laireakean, Caledon,
Co Tyrone BT68 4XH
Tel 028-37568288
(Aughnacloy (Aghaloo),
Armagh)

McGoldrick, Michael (OCD)
Provincial,
53 Marlborough Road,
Donnybrook, Dublin 4
Tel 01-6617163/6601832

McGoldrick, Neil, PP
Parochial House, Fahan,
Lifford, Co Donegal
Tel 074-9360151
(Fahan (Burt, Inch and
Fahan), Derry)

McGoldrick, Patrick, CC
Parochial House, Moville,
Co Donegal
Tel 074-9382102
(Moville (Moville Lower),
Derry)

McGonagle, Hugh, CC
Pilgrimage Director (Lourdes),
7 Elm Park, Ballinode, Sligo
Tel 071-9143430
(Sligo, Calry St Joseph's,
Elphin)

McGonagle, James, Very Rev,
Adm, VF
Parochial House, Culdaff,
Co Donegal
Tel 074-9379107
(Culdaff, Derry)

McGoohan, Ultan, CC
The Presbytery, Cavan
Tel 049-4331404/4332269
(Cootehill, Kilmore)

McGorty, Roger (MHM)
(elsewhere in Ireland)

McGourty, Michael, Very Rev,
PP
Irvinestown, Enniskillen,
Co Fermanagh BT94 1EY
Tel 028-68628600
(Irvinestown, Clogher)

McGovern, Ciarán, Very Rev,
PP
Newtownforbes, Co Longford
Tel 043-3346805
(Newtownforbes, Ardagh &
Cl.)

McGovern, Felim
The Presbytery, Cavan
Tel 049-4331404
(Kilmore, retired)

McGovern, John, Very Rev, Adm
St Joseph's Presbytery,
52 Kincora Park, Lifford,
Ennis, Co Clare
Tel 065-6822166/
086-3221210
(Abbey Cluster (Ennis),
Killaloe)

McGovern, Patrick (SMA)
African Missions,
Blackrock Road, Cork
Tel 021-4292871

McGovern, Terence, CC
Chapel Lane,
Droichead Nua, Co Kildare
Tel 045-433979
(Droichead Nua/Newbridge,
Kildare & L.)

McGovern, Thomas
30 Knapton Road,
Dun Laoghaire, Co Dublin
Tel 01-2804353
(Opus Dei)

McGowan, Michael, PC
7 St Patrick's Crescent,
Rathcoole, Co Dublin
Tel 01-4589210
(Saggart, Dublin)

McGowan, Thomas, Co-PP
Parochial House,
Garristown, Co Dublin
Tel 01-8354138
(Garristown, Dublin)

McGrady, Feargal, Very Rev,
PP
St Anne's Parochial House,
Kingsway, Finaghy,
Belfast BT10 0NE
Tel 028-90610112
(St Anne's, Down & C.)

McGrane, Camillus (OSM), CC
25/27 Hermitage Downs,
Marley Grange,
Rathfarnham, Dublin 16
Tel 01-4944295
(Marley Grange, Dublin)

McGrath, Aidan (OFM)
Secretary General,
Curia Generalizia dei Frati
Minori,
Via S. Maria Mediatrice 25,
00165 Roma, Italy

McGrath, Brendan (OFM)
Guardian, Adam & Eve's
4 Merchant's Quay, Dublin 8
Tel 01-6771128

McGrath, Brian (CSsR)
St Joseph's, Dundalk,
Co Louth
Tel 042-9334042/9334762

McGrath, Conor, CC
St Joseph's Presbytery,
56 Greystone Road,
Antrim BT41 1JZ
Tel 028-94429103
(Antrim, Down & C.)

McGrath, Francis, CC
The Parochial House,
Achill Sound, Achill,
Co Mayo
Tel 098-45109
(Achill, Tuam)

McGrath, Francis (OFM)
Franciscan Friary, Ennis,
Co Clare
Tel 065-6828751

McGrath, Francis (SMA)
Temporary diocesan work in
Ireland

McGrath, John, Very Rev, PP
Mullinahone, Thurles,
Co Tipperary
Tel 052-9153152
(Mullinahone, Cashel & E.)

McGrath, Joseph, Rt Rev Mgr, VG
Parochial House, Boherquill, Lismacaffney, Mullingar, Co Westmeath
(*Streete*, Ardagh & Cl.)

McGrath, Joseph, Rt Rev, PP, VG, VF
New Ross, Co Wexford
Tel 051-447080
(*New Ross*, Ferns)

McGrath, Matthew, Venerable, PP
St Michael's Street, Tipperary Town,
Tel 062-51536
(*Tipperary*, Cashel & E.)

McGrath, Michael, CC
St Mary's, Carrick-on-Shannon, Co Leitrim
Tel 071-9620347
(*Carrick-on-Shannon*, Ardagh & Cl.)

McGrath, Sean (SSC)
St Columban's, Dalgan Park, Navan, Co Meath
Tel 046-9021525

McGrath, Thomas, Very Rev
Cois Tra, Chapel Road, Duncannon, Co Wexford
(Ferns, retired)

McGrath, Tom (MHM), PP
Labasheeda, Co Clare
Tel 065-6830126
(*Kilmurray McMahon*, Killaloe)

McGrattan, Dominic, CC
St Patrick's Presbytery, 199 Donegall Street, Belfast BT1 2FL
Tel 028-90324597
(*St Patrick's*, Down and C.)

McGree, Thomas, CC
Durrow, Portlaoise, Co Laois
Tel 057-8736155/
087-7619235
(*Durrow*, Ossory)

McGreevy, Gerard, Very Rev
Canon, PE
Magherarney, Smithboro, Co Monaghan
Tel 047-57011
(Clogher, retired)

McGregor, Augustine (OCSO), Rt Rev
Retired Abbot,
Mount Melleray Abbey, Cappoquin, Co Waterford
Tel 058-54404

McGregor, Bede (OP)
St Malachy's, Dundalk, Co Louth
Tel 042-9334179/9333714

McGroarty, Damien
(elsewhere in the diocese)
c/o Diocesan Office, Letterkenny
(Raphoe)

McGroarty, Liam
c/o Archbishop's House, Drumcondra, Dublin 9
Tel 01-8379253
(Dublin)

McGroarty, William, CC
Parochial House, Letterkenny, Co Donegal
Tel 074-9121021

McGrory, James
Armagh Regional Marriage Tribunal, 15 College Street, Armagh BT61 9BT
Tel 028-37524537
(Derry)

McGuckian, Alan, (SJ)
Superior,
Peter Faber House, 28 Brookvale Avenue, Belfast BT14 6BW
Tel 028-90757615

McGuckian, Bernard (SJ)
Vice-Rector and Minister, Clongowes Wood College, Clane, Co Kildare
Tel 045-868663/868202

McGuckian, Michael (SJ)
Rector, St Ignatius Community & Church, 27 Raleigh Row, Salthill, Galway
Tel 091-523707

McGuckien, Kevin, Very Rev, PP
Director of Vocations, Parochial House, 23 Hannahstown Hill, Belfast BT17 0LT
Tel 028-90614567
(*Hannahstown*, Down & C.)

McGuckin, Felix, Very Rev
5 Oriel Road, Antrim BT41 4HP
Tel 028-94428086
(*Antrim, St Comgall's*, Down & C.)

McGuckin, Terence (CP)
Holy Cross Retreat, Ardoyne, Crumlin Road, Belfast BT14 7GE
Tel 028-90748231

McGuckin, Patrick, Very Rev, PE
79 Reclain Road, Galbally, Dungannon, Co Tyrone BT70 2PG
Tel 028-87759692
(Armagh, retired)

McGuigan, Seán, CC
Parochial House, 3 Convent Road, Cookstown, Co Tyrone BT80 8QA
Tel 028-86763293
(*Cookstown (Desertcreight And Derryloran)*, Armagh)

McGuinness, Austin (SSC)
Chaplain,
St Joseph's, Trim, St Columban's, Dalgan Park, Navan, Co Meath
Tel 046-9021525
(on special work)

McGuinness, Brendan, Very Rev, PP
Bekan, Claremorris, Co Mayo
Tel 094-9380203
(*Bekan*, Tuam)

McGuinness, Chris, (SPS), CC
Parochial House, Glenavy Road, Crumlin, Co Antrim BT29 4LA
Tel 028-94452941
(*Glenavy and Killead*, Down & C.)

McGuinness, David
St Joseph's Catholic Church, 134 Prince Avenue, Athens, Georgia 30601, USA
(Waterford & L.)

McGuinness, Joseph, Rt Rev Mgr, Adm
Chancellor,
Diocesan Office, Bishop's House, Monaghan
Tel 047-81019
Administration for St Patrick's Tyholland, Monaghan
Tel 047-85385
(*Tyholland*, Clogher)

McGuinness, Peter, Very Rev Canon, PE
3 Castleross Retirement Village, Carrickmacross, Co Monaghan
Tel 042-9690013
(Clogher, retired)

McGuire, Robert, CC
Galbally, Ballyhogue, Enniscorthy, Co Wexford
Tel 053-9247814/9247882
(*Bree*, Ferns)

McHale, Benny, CC
Athenry, Co Galway
Tel 091-844227
(*Athenry*, Tuam)

McHugh, Anthony, Very Rev, PP
Parochial House, 33 Crossgar Road, Saintfield, Ballynahinch, Co Down BT24 7JE
Tel 028-97510237
(*Saintfield and Carrickmannon*, Down & C.)

McHugh, Brendan, Very Rev, PE
Anniscliff House, 41 Moneysharvin Road, Maghera, Co Derry, BT46 SHZ
(Armagh, retired)

McHugh, Christopher, Very Rev, PP
Secretary of Primary Education,
Grange, Co Sligo
Tel 071-9163100
(*Cliffoney (Ahamlish)*, Elphin)

McHugh, Laurence (CSSp)
Holy Spirit Missionary College, Kimmage Manor, Dublin 12
Tel 01-4064300

McHugh, Patrick
Clontarf, Dublin 3
(Kilmore, retired)

McHugh, Patrick, Very Rev
22 Rosehill, Sligo
(Elphin, retired)

McHugh, Patrick, Very Rev Canon, PP
Castleblayney, Co Monaghan
Tel 042-9740027
(*Castleblayney (Muckno)*, Clogher)

McHugh, Patrick, Very Rev, PP
Director of Lourdes Pilgrimage,
Parochial House, Termon, Co Donegal
Tel 074-9139016(parish)/074-9125090(Lourdes office)
(*Termon*, Raphoe)

McHugh, Seán, PP
Teach an Sagairt, An Spidéal, Co na Gaillimhe
Tel 091-553155
(*An Spidéal*, Galway)

McHugh, Thomas, CC
Parochial House, 42 Abbey Street, Armagh BT61 7DZ
Tel 028-37522813
(*Armagh*, Armagh)

McIlraith, Cormac, Adm
52 Booterstown Avenue, Co Dublin
Tel 01-2882162
(*Booterstown*, Dublin)

McInerney, Declan, Very Rev, PP
Eyrecourt, Ballinasloe Co Galway
Tel 090-9675148
(*Eyrecourt, Clonfert and Meelick*), Clonfert)

McInerney, James (OFMConv)
Friary of the Visitation of the BVM,
Fairview Strand, Dublin 3
Tel 01-8376000

McIntyre, Raymond (SDB)
Salesian House,
45 St Teresa's Road,
Crumlin, Dublin 12
Tel 01-4555605

McKay, Brian (OCarm)
Prior,
Whitefriar Street Church,
56 Aungier Street, Dublin 2
Tel 01-4758821

McKay, Dermot, Very Rev, PP
51 Bay Road, Carnlough,
Ballymena,
Co Antrim BT44 0HJ
Tel 028-28885220
(*Carnlough*, Down & C.)

McKeever, Brendan (CP), PC
St Paul's Retreat,
Mount Argus, Dublin 6W
Tel 01-4992000
(*Mount Argus*, Dublin)

McKeever, Des (SPS)
St Patrick's, Kiltegan,
Co Wicklow
Tel 059-6473600

McKeever, John, CC
Parochial House,
St Patrick Street, Keady,
Co Armagh BT60 3TQ
Tel 028-37531246
(*Keady (Derrynoose)*,
Armagh)

McKeever, Joseph, Very Rev,
PP
9 Newry Road,
Crossmaglen, Newry,
Co Down BT35 9HH
Tel 028-30861208
(*Crossmaglen (Creggan
Upper)*, Armagh)

McKeever, Martin (CSsR)
Alphonsian Academy,
Via Merulana 31, CP 2458,
00185 Roma-PT158, Italy
Tel 0039-06494901

McKeever, Michael, CC
Director of Knock
Pilgrimage,
Church Hill, Letterkenny,
Co Donegal
Tel 074-9137057
Ard Adhamhnáin,
Letterkenny, Co Donegal
Tel 074-9121208
(*Termon*, Raphoe)

McKenna, Dermot (SJ)
Milltown Park, Sandford
Road, Dublin 6
Tel 01-2698411/2698113

McKenna, Hugh (OFM)
Provincial, Franciscan Friary,
4 Merchant's Quay,
Dublin 8
Tel 01-6742500

McKenna, John F., CC
Scotshouse, Clones,
Co Monaghan
Tel 047-56016
(*Killeevan (Currin, Killeevan
and Aghabog)*, Clogher)

McKenna, John, Very Rev
Canon, PP
Trillick, Omagh,
Co Tyrone BT78 3RD
Tel 028-89561350
(*Trillick*, Clogher)

McKenna, Joseph
(Birmingham Diocese)
Shannagh Nursing Home,
Belleek, Co Fermanagh
(Clogher, retired)

McKenna, Joseph (SM)
St Peter's Nursing Home,
Castlebellingham Village,
Co Louth

McKenna, Owen (SMA)
SMA House,
82 Ranelagh Road,
Ranelagh, Dublin 6
Tel 01-4968162/3

McKenna, Padraig, CC
St Joseph's, Carrickmacross,
Co Monaghan
Tel 042-9661231
(*Carrickmacross*, Clogher)

McKenna, Patrick, CC
Teconnaught,
2 Drumnaconagher Road,
Crossgar BT30 9AN
Tel 028-44830342
(*Crossgar (Kilmore)*, Down &
C.)

McKenna, Patrick, Very Rev,
PP, VF
503 Ormeau Road,
Belfast BT7 3GR
Tel 028-90642446
(*Holy Rosary*, Down & C.)

McKenna, Robert, Very Rev,
PE, AP
Parochial House,
26 Newtown Road,
Camlough, Newry,
Co Down BT35 7JJ
Tel 028-30830237
(*Bessbrook (Killeavy Lower)*,
Armagh)

McKenna, Seamus (IC)
Rosmini House, Dunkereen,
Innishannon, Co Cork
Tel 021-4776268/4776923

McKenna, Seamus, BA, HDE
Cork Regional Marriage
Tribunal,
The Lough, Cork
Tel 021-4963653
(Kerry)

McKeon, Austin, Rt Rev Mgr,
PP
Tulsk, Castlerea,
Co Roscommon
Tel 071-9639005
(*Tulsk (Ogulla and Baslic)*,
Elphin)

McKeon, Seamus, Very Rev, PP
Aughnacliffe, Co Longford
Tel 043-6684118
(*Colmcille*, Ardagh & Cl.)

McKeown, Donal, Most Rev,
DD
Bishop of Derry,
Diocesan Offices,
St Eugene's Cathedral,
Francis Street,
Derry BT48 9AP
Tel 028-71262302
(Derry)

McKeown, Noel (OP)
St Catherine's, Newry,
Co Down BT35 8BN
Tel 028-30262178

McKeown, Phelim, Very Rev,
PP
Parochial House,
Kilsaran,
Castlebellingham,
Dundalk, Co Louth
Tel 042-9372255
(*Kilsaran*, Armagh)

McKevitt, Brian (OP)
St Mary's Priory, Tallaght,
Dublin 24
Tel 01-4048100

McKiernan, Fintan, Very Rev,
PP
56 Mary Street, Derrylin,
Co Fermanagh, BT92 9LA
Tel 028-67748315
(*Derrylin*, Kilmore)

McKiernan, Peter, Very Rev,
PP
Crosskeys, Co Cavan
Tel 049-4336102
(*Denn*, Kilmore)

McKiernan, Thomas
Rosskeeragh, Belturbet,
Co Cavan
(Kilmore, retired)

McKinlay, Denis, Very Rev, PP
Parochial House,
91 Main Street,
Castlewellan,
Co Down BT31 9DH
Tel 028-43778259
Administration Kilcoo
(*Castlewellan (Kilmegan)*,
Kilcoo, Down & C.)

McKinley, Patrick, Very Rev
(Moderator)
68 Maplewood Road,
Springfield, Tallaght,
Dublin 24
(*Springfield*, Dublin)

McKinney, Anthony (OCarm)
Gort Muire, Ballinteer,
Dublin 16
Tel 01-2984014

McKinney, Liam, CC, VF
Parochial House,
9a Newry Road,
Crossmaglen, Newry,
Co Down BT35 9HH
Tel 028-30868698
(*Crossmaglen (Creggan
Upper)*, Armagh)

McKinstry, Gordon
12 The Meadows,
Randalstown,
Co Antrim BT41 2JB
(Down & C., retired)

McKittrick, Brian, CC
The Presbytery, Celbridge,
Co Kildare
Tel 01-6274971
(*Celbridge*, Dublin)

McLaughlin, Brian (CSSp)
Holy Spirit Missionary
College, Kimmage Manor,
Dublin 12
Tel 01-4064300

McLaughlin, Con, PP
Barrack Hill, Carndonagh,
Lifford, Co Donegal
Tel 074-9374104
Director,
Inishowen Pastoral Centre,
Carndonagh, Co Donegal
Tel 074-9374103
(*Carndonagh (Donagh)*,
Derry)

McLaughlin, Eamonn, CC
Parochial House,
Letterkenny, Co Donegal
Tel 074-9121021
(*Letterkenny (Conwal and
Leck)*, Raphoe)

McLaughlin, George, PEm
Chez Nous, Drumawier,
Greencastle, Co Donegal
(Derry, retired)

McLaughlin, Kevin (OMI)
An Tobar, Ardbraccan,
Navan, Co Meath

McLaughlin, Michael, Very
Rev, AP
Airfield, Inch, Ennis,
Co Clare
Tel 065-6839332
(*Inch and Kilmaley*, Killaloe)

McLaughlin, Pat (CSsR), CC
St Gerard's,
722 Antrim Road,
Newtownabbey,
Co Antrim BT36 7PG
Tel 028-90774833
(*St Gerard's*, Down & C.)

McLaughlin, Peter, PP
143 Melmount Road,
Sion Mills, Strabane,
Co Tyrone BT82 9EX
Tel 028-81658264
(*Sion Mills*, Derry)

McLaughlin, Pius (OFM)
Vicar, Franciscan Friary,
Rossnowlagh,
Co Donegal
Tel 072-9851342

McLaverty, Anthony, Very
Rev, CC
470 Falls Road,
Belfast BT12 6EN
Tel 028-90321102
(*St John's*, Down & C.)

McLaverty, George, Very Rev
518 Donegall Road,
Belfast BT12 6DY
(Down & C., retired)

McLoone, Francis, Very Rev,
PP
Killymard, Co Donegal
Tel 074-9721929
(*Killymard*, Raphoe)

McLoughlin, Christopher, Very
Rev Canon
(priest in residence,
Tourlestrane Parish)
c/o Kilmactigue, Aclare,
Co Sligo
Tel 071-9181007
(Achonry, retired)

McLoughlin, Eamonn, CC
Parochial House,
Letterkenny, Co Donegal
Tel 074-9121021
(*Letterkenny (Conwal and
Leck)*, Raphoe)

McLoughlin, Eugene (SMA),
CC
SMA House,
Claregalway, Co Galway
Tel 091-798880

McLoughlin, Eugene, Very Rev
Canon, PP, VF
Parochial House,
Roscommon
Tel 090-6626298
(*Roscommon*, Elphin)

McLoughlin, Joseph (CSsR)
Mount Saint Alphonsus,
Limerick
Tel 061-315099

McLoughlin, Joseph (SAC), CC
The Presbytery, Corduff,
Blanchardstown, Dublin 15
Tel 01-8215930
(*Corduff*, Dublin)

McLoughlin, Michael, Very
Rev, PP
Moycullen, Co Galway
Tel 091-555106
(*Moycullen*, Galway)

McLoughlin, Patrick (CSsR), CC
722 Antrim Road,
Newtownabbey,
Co Antrim BT36 7PG
Tel 028-90774833/4
(*St Gerard's*, Down & C.)

McLoughlin, Terence (OP)
St Mary's, The Claddagh,
Co Galway
Tel 091-582884

McLoughney, Paudie (SPS)
St Patrick's, Kiltegan,
Co Wicklow
Tel 059-6473600

McMahon, Andrew, CC
Adult Faith Development,
70 North Street, Lurgan
Co Armagh BT67 9AH
Tel 028-38323161
(*Shankill, St Paul's (Lurgan)*,
Dromore)

McMahon, Anthony, PP
Carhuligane, Mullagh,
Ennis, Co Clare
Tel 065-7087012/
086-8243801
(*Mullagh (Kilmurray-
Ibrickane)*, Killaloe)

McMahon, James (OSB)
Glenstal Abbey, Murroe,
Co Limerick
Tel 061-386103

McMahon, John, Very Rev, PP
Knockbride, Bailieboro,
Co Cavan
Tel 042-9660112
(*Knockbride*, Kilmore)

McMahon, Joseph (OFM)
Adam & Eve's,
4 Merchant's Quay,
Dublin 8
Tel 01-6771128

McMahon, Joseph, Very Rev,
PP, BA, BD, HDE
Scariff, Co Clare
Tel 061-924035/087-2665793
(*Feakle & Killanena-
Flagmount, Scariff
(Moynoe)*, Killaloe)

McMahon, Padraig, Very Rev,
Adm
Cathedral House, Mullingar,
Co Westmeath
Tel 044-9348338/9340126
(*Mullingar*, Meath)

McMahon, Patrick, CC
Bridgetown, Co Clare
Tel 061-377158
(*Killaloe*, Killaloe)

McMahon, Paul (SSC)
Belfast (on compassionate
leave)

McMahon, Richard (CSsR)
St Patrick's, Esker, Athenry,
Co Galway
Tel 091-844007

McMahon, Richard (CSsR), CC
Kiltulla, Athenry,
Co Galway
Tel 091-848208
(*Kiltulla and Attymon*,
Clonfert)

McMahon, Seamus (SM)
Australia

MacManus, Clement (CSsR)
St Joseph's, Dundalk,
Co Louth
Tel 042-9334042/9334762

McManus, Brendan (SJ)
Peter Faber House,
28 Brookvale Avenue,
Belfast BT14 6BW
Tel 028-90757615

McManus, Frank, Very Rev,
PP,
19 Ardvarney Road,
Ederney, Enniskillen,
Co Fermanagh BT93 0DG
Tel 028-68631315
(*Ederney (Cúl Máine)*,
Clogher)

McManus, John, Very Rev
(SPS), PP
Ballyleague, Lanesboro,
Co Longford
Tel 043-21171
(*Ballagh (Cloontuskert,
Kilgefin and Curraghroe)*,
Elphin)

McManus, John, Very Rev
On leave
(Down & C.)

McManus, Kevin (OSA), PP
St John's Priory,
Thomas Street, Dublin 8
Tel 01-6770393

McManus, Michael, CC
Drum, Athlone,
Co Roscommon
Tel 090-6437125
(*Athlone, SS Peter and
Paul's*, Elphin)

McManus, Patrick (SSC)
St Columban's, Dalgan Park,
Navan, Co Meath
Tel 046-9021525

McManus, Patrick, Very Rev
(Moderator)
34 Dollymount Grove,
Clontarf, Dublin 3
Tel 01-8057692/087-2371089
(*Clontarf, St Anthony's, St
John's, Dollymount*, Dublin)

McManus, Patrick J., Rt Rev
Mgr
Kilnaleck, Co Cavan
Tel 049-4336118
(Kilmore, retired)

McManus, Thomas, Very Rev,
PP
Corlough, Belturbet,
Co Cavan
Tel 049-9523122
(*Corlough and Drumreilly*,
Kilmore)

McManus, Tommy (OSA)
St Augustine's Priory,
Washington Street, Cork
Tel 021-4275398/4270410

McMenamin, Joseph (White
Fathers)
Promotion Director,
Cypress Grove, Templeogue,
Dublin 6W
Tel 01-4055526

McMenamin, William, Very
Rev Canon, PE
'St Columba's'
Meeting House Street,
Raphoe, Co Donegal
Tel 074-9144834
(Raphoe, retired)

McMorrow, Maurice, Very
Rev, PP
Ballinaglera,
Carrick-on-Shannon,
Co Leitrim
Tel 071-9643014
(*Ballinaglera*, Kilmore)

McMullan, Anthony (OP)
Prior, St Magdalen's,
Drogheda, Co Louth
Tel 041-9838271

McMullan, Brendan, Very Rev
26 Willowbank Park,
Belfast BT6 0LL
Tel 028-90794440
(Down & C., retired)

McMullan, Kevin, Very Rev
418 Old Park Road,
Belfast BT14 6QF
Tel 028-90748148
(Down and C., retired)

McNaboe, Desmond
(OFMCap)
Capuchin Friary,
Holy Trinity,
Fr Mathew Quay, Cork
Tel 021-4270827

McNally, Albert, Very Rev, PP,
VF
6 Hillside Avenue,
Dunloy BT44 9DQ
(Down and C., retired)

McNally, Brendan, Very Rev,
PE
Moorehall Lodge Village,
Ardee, Co Louth
Tel 041-6855117
(Armagh, retired)

McNally, James, Very Rev, PE
212 Staffordstown Road,
Toomebridge,
Co Antrim BT41 3QT
Tel 028-79650260
(Armagh, retired)

McNamara, Austin, Very Rev,
PP
Parochial House, Ballyhahill,
Co Limerick
Cathedral Place, Limerick
Tel 069-82103
(*Loughill/Ballyhahill*,
Limerick)

McNamara, Brian
Main Street, Derrylin,
Co Fermanagh BT92 9LA
(Kilmore, retired)

McNamara, Cormac (SM), PP
The Presbytery,
78A Donore Avenue,
Dublin 8
Tel 01-4542425
(*Donore Avenue*, Dublin)

McNamara, David (CSsR)
Mount Saint Alphonsus,
Limerick
Tel 061-315099

McNamara, Donal, Very Rev
Canon, PP, VF
St Munchin's, Clancy Strand,
Limerick
Tel 061-455635
(*St Munchin's and St Lelia's*,
Limerick)

McNamara, Frank, Very Rev,
PE
Newbrook Nursing Home,
Mullingar, Co Westmeath
(Meath, retired)

McNamara, Gerard, Very Rev,
PP
Ballyduff Upper,
Co Waterford
Tel 058-60227
(*Ballyduff*, Waterford & L.)

McNamara, Gerard, Very Rev
Bulgaden, Kilmallock,
Co Limerick
(Limerick, retired)

McNamara, John (OCD)
St Joseph's Carmelite
Retreat Centre,
Termonbacca,
Derry BT48 9XE
Tel 028-71262512

McNamara, John, Very Rev,
Adm
Parochial House,
Our Lady's Nativity Parish,
Old Hill, Leixlip,
Co Kildare
Tel 01-6245597
(*Leixlip*, Dublin)

McNamara, Kevin (MSC), CC
Gneeveguilla, Rathmore,
Co Kerry
Tel 064-7756188
(*Rathmore*, Kerry)

McNamara, Leslie
Director, Limerick Diocesan
Pastoral Centre,
Cathedral House,
Cathedral Place, Limerick
Tel 061-414624
(*St John's*, Limerick)

McNamara, Liam, Very Rev
Canon, AP
Tipperary Town
Co. Tipperary
Tel 062-82664
(*Solohead*, Cashel & E.)

McNamara, Martin (MSC)
Woodview House,
Mount Merrion Avenue,
Blackrock, Co Dublin
Tel 01-2881644

McNamara, Martin, Very Rev,
PP
Kiltulla, Athenry,
Co Galway
Tel 091-848021
(*Kiltulla and Attymon*,
Clonfert)

McNamara, Oliver, CC
Annaghdown, Co Galway
Tel 091-791142
(*Corrandulla (Annaghdown)*,
Tuam)

McNamara, Robert
Chaplain, Legion of Mary,
Annunciata House,
15 Fr Griffin Road, Galway
Tel 091-524222
(*Galway*)

McNamara, Thomas (SMA)
Religious Formation
Programme,
Loretto House, Dublin

McNamara, Walter (CSSp)
Holy Spirit Missionary
College, Kimmage Manor,
Dublin 12
Tel 01-4064300

McNamee, Ambrose (OCD)
The Abbey, Loughrea,
Co Galway
Tel 091-841209

McNamee, Paul
c/o Bishop's House,
Dublin Road, Carlow
(Kildare & L.)

McNeice, Damian, PC
4 Claremont Drive, Ballygall,
Dublin 11
Tel 01-8087553
(*Ballygall*, Dublin)

McNeice, Dermot (OSM)
Servite Priory, Benburb,
Dungannon,
Co Tyrone, BT71 7JZ

McNeill, Peter, Very Rev, PP
58 Ballydrumman Road,
Ballyward, Castlewellan,
Co Down BT31 9UG
Tel 028-40650207
(*Drumgooland, Dromara*,
Dromore)

McNelis, Denis, Very Rev, PP,
VF
Parochial House, Laytown,
Co Meath
Tel 041-9827258
(*Laytown-Mornington*,
Meath)

McNerney, John
Chaplains' Residence,
St Stephen's, UCD, Belfield,
Dublin 4
Tel 01-7164789
(Dublin)

McNicholas, Gerard (SSC)
St Columban's
Retirement Home,
Dalgan Park, Navan,
Co Meath
Tel 046-9021525

McNulty, James J. (CSSp)
Holy Spirit Missionary
College, Kimmage Manor,
Whitehall Road, Dublin 12
Tel 01-4064300

McNulty, Thomas, CC
Parochial House,
Grange, Carlingford,
Co Louth
Tel 042-9376577
(*Armagh*, Armagh)

McPartland, Jimmy, Very Rev,
Co-PP
1 Brookfield Road, Tallaght,
Dublin 24
Tel 01-4590894
(*Brookfield*, Dublin)

McPhillips, James, Very Rev,
PP
Drumary, Derrygonnelly,
Co Fermanagh BT93 6HW
Tel 028-68641207
(*Derrygonnelly (Botha)*,
Clogher)

McQuaid, Macartan, Very Rev
Canon
Chaplain, Emyvale,
Co Monaghan
Tel 087-2454705
(*Donagh, Errigal Truagh*,
Clogher)

McQuillan, Ignatius, Rt Rev
Mgr, PEm
(priest in residence)
60 Glenmore Park,
Belt Road, Derry BT47 2JZ
Tel 028-91291758
(Derry, retired)

McShane, Dermot, Very Rev,
PE
St John's Point,
Dunkineeley, Co Donegal
(Raphoe, retired)

McShane, Philip (OP)
St Mary's Priory,
Tallaght, Dublin 24
Tel 01-4048100

McSorley, Gerard, Rt Rev Mgr,
PE
Ballybay, Co Monaghan
Tel 042-9741031
(*Ballybay*, Clogher)

McSweeney, Eustace
(OFMCap)
Vicar, Capuchin Friary,
Station Road, Raheny,
Dublin 5
Tel 01-8313886

McSweeney, Myles
(priest in charge)
St Joseph's Presbytery,
Mayfield, Cork
Tel 021-4501861
(*St Joseph's (Mayfield)*, Cork
& R.)

McSweeney, Patrick T., Very
Rev Canon, PE
Nazareth House, Mallow,
Co Cork
Tel 022-21561
(Cloyne, retired)

McTiernan, Jim (White
Fathers)
Cypress Grove, Templeogue,
Dublin 6W
Tel 01-4055263/4055264

McTiernan, John, Very Rev, PP
Drumahaire, Co Leitrim
Tel 071-9164143
(*Drumahaire and Killargue*,
Kilmore)

McTiernan, Sean (SPS)
St Patrick's, Kiltegan,
Co Wicklow
Tel 059-6473600

McVeigh, Joseph
(priest in residence)
Tattygar House,
4 Tattygar Road,
Lisbellaw,
Co Fermanagh BT94 5GQ
Tel 028-66385232
(*Enniskillen*, Clogher)

McVeigh, Martin, Very Rev, PP
Parochial House,
Clogherhead,
Drogheda, Co Louth
Tel 041-9822438
(*Clogherhead*, Armagh)

McVeigh, Patrick, Very Rev
3 Broughshane Road,
Ballymena,
Co Antrim BT43 7DX
(Down & C., retired)

McVerry, Peter (SJ)
Arrupe Community,
217 Silloge Road,
Ballymun, Dublin 11
Tel 01-8420886
(Zam-Mal)

McWilliams, Luke, Very Rev,
PP
Parochial House,
28 Chapel Road,
Ballymena BT44 0RS
Tel 028-21771240
(*Cushendall*, Down and C.)

McWilliams, Patrick, Very Rev,
PP
103 Roguery Road,
Moneyglass, Toomebridge,
Co Antrim BT41 3PT
Tel 028-79650225
(*Duneane*, Down & C.)

Meade, Bernard (CM)
St Paul's College, Raheny,
Dublin 5
Tel 01-8318113

Meade, John (CSSp)
Rockwell College, Cashel,
Co Tipperary
Tel 062-61444/087-9450163

Meade, Michael, Very Rev PP
Parochial House,
Summerhill, Co Meath
Tel 046-9557021
(Summerhill, Meath)

Meagher, Charles (SSC)
St Columban's, Dalgan Park,
Navan, Co Meath
Tel 046-9021525

Meagher, John (OSA)
St Augustine's,
Taylor's Lane,
Ballyboden, Dublin 16
Tel 01-4241000

Medina, Nelson (OP)
St Saviour's,
Upper Dorset Street,
Dublin 1
Tel 01-8897610

Meehan, Conleth, CC
6 Allen Park Road,
Stillorgan, Co Dublin
Tel 01-2880545
(Mount Merrion, Dublin)

Meehan, Dermot, Very Rev,
PP
Swinford, Co Mayo
Tel 094-9252952
(Swinford (Kilconduff and
Meelick, Achonry)

Meehan, Dominic, CC
Templemore, Co Tipperary
Tel 0504-31492
(Templemore, Cashel & E.)

Meehan, Francis (SMA)
African Missions,
Blackrock Road, Cork
Tel 021-4292871

Meehan, Frank, Very Rev, PP
Shinrone, Co Offaly
Tel 0505-47167/087-2302413
(Shinrone, Killaloe)

Meehan, Patrick (SM)
Cerdon, Marist Fathers,
St Mary's Road, Dundalk,
Co Louth
Tel 042-9334019

Meehan, Patrick (SSC)
St Columban's Retirement
Home, Dalgan Park,
Navan, Co Meath
Tel 046-9021525

Meehan, Séamus, Very Rev, PE
Main Street, Dungloe,
Co Donegal
Tel 074-9521895
(Raphoe, retired)

Meehan, William, Very Rev,
PP
St Mary's, Clonmel,
Co Tipperary
Tel 052-6122954
(Clonmel, St Mary's,
Waterford & L.)

Mehigan, Donal (OP)
Holy Cross, Sligo, Co Sligo
Tel 071-9142700

Mejida, Timothy
Parochial House,
Rathmolyon, Co Meath
Tel 046-9555212
(Enfield, Meath)

Melican, Michael (IC)
Rector,
Rosminian House of Prayer,
Glencomeragh House,
Kilsheelan, Co Tipperary
Tel 052-6133181

Melican, P. J. (SPS)
St Patrick's, Kiltegan,
Co Wicklow
Tel 059-6473600

Mellett, Stan (CSsR), CC
Ballyfermot Assumption
Parish, 197 Kylemore Road,
Ballyfermot, Dublin 10
Tel 01-6264789
(Ballyfermot, Dublin)

Melody, Sean, Very Rev, PP
Sacred Heart Presbytery,
21 The Folly, Waterford
Tel 051-873759
(Sacred Heart, Waterford &
L.)

Mernagh, Michael (OSA)
St John's Priory,
Thomas Street, Dublin 8
Tel 01-6770393/0415/0601

Mernagh, Patrick, CF
McKee Barracks,
Blackhorse Avenue, Dublin 7
(Ferns)

Merrigan, Liam, Very Rev, PP
Drogheda Road,
Monasterevin, Co Kildare
Tel 045-525346
(Kildare & L.)

Meskell, Derek (CSsR)
Mount Saint Alphonsus,
Limerick
Tel 061-315099

Mhamwa, Thaddeus, PC
128 Roselawn Road,
Blanchardstown, Dublin 15
Tel 01-8219014
(Blanchardstown, Dublin)

Millar, George (SVD)
Maynooth, Co Kildare
Tel 01-6286391/2

Mills, Dermot (OMI)
52a Bulfin Road, Dublin 8
Tel 01-4531660
(Inchicore, St Michaels,
Dublin)

Milton, Raymond, Very Rev,
PP
Knockcroghery,
Co Roscommon
Tel 090-6661127
(Knockcroghery (St John's),
Elphin)

Minniter, Anthony, Very Rev,
PP
Ballindereen, Kilcolgan,
Co Galway
Tel 091-796118
(Ballindereen, Galway)

Minogue, James, Very Rev, AP
Castleconnell, Co Limerick
Tel 061-377166/087-6228674
(Castleconnell, Killaloe)

Mitchell, Francis, Very Rev,
Adm
Tuam, Co Galway
Tel 093-24250
(Tuam (Cathedral of the
Assumption), Tuam)

Mitchell, James, Rev Dr
No 2 St Mary's College
House, Shantalla Road,
Galway
Tel 091-588750
(Galway, retired)

Mitchell, Kilian (OPraem)
Abbey of the Most Holy
Trinity and St Norbert,
Kilnacrott, Ballyjamesduff,
Co Cavan
Tel 049-8544416

Mockler, John
11 Chestnut Gardens, Boher
Buí,
Newcastle West, Co Limerick
(Newcastle West, Limerick)

Mohan, Mark, PP
Parochial House,
Ballivor, Co Meath
Tel 046-9546488
(Ballivor, Meath)

Mohan, Richard, Rt Rev Mgr,
PP
Parochial House, Clones,
Co Monaghan
Tel 047-51048
(Clones, Clogher)

Moley, John, Very Rev
24 Mallard Road,
Downpatrick,
Co Down BT30 6DY
(Down & C., retired)

Mollin, Matthew, Very Rev, PE
4 St Finbar, Maryfield,
Chapelizod, Co Dublin
Tel 01-6268851
(Meath, retired)

Molloy, Francis, Very Rev
Lurgan, Co Armagh
(Dromore, retired)

Molloy, John, PP
Toomevara,
Co Tipperary
Tel 067-26023
(Toomevara, Killaloe)

Molloy, John (SSC)
St Columban's,
Dalgan Park, Navan,
Co Meath
Tel 046-9021525

Molloy, Michael (SSC)
St Columban's, Dalgan Park,
Navan, Co Meath
Tel 046-9021525

Molloy, Michael, Very Rev, PP
The Presbytery, Moore
Ballydangan, Athlone,
Co Roscommon
Tel 090-9673539
(Moore, Tuam)

Molloy, Patrick (MHM)
Rector, St Joseph's House,
50 Orwell Park, Rathgar,
Dublin 6
Tel 01-4127700

Moloney, Bernard
Cahir Road, Cashel,
Co Tipperary
Tel 062-61443
(Cashel, Cashel & E.)

Moloney, Brendan, Very Rev,
PP
Silvermines, Nenagh,
Co Tipperary
Tel 067-25864
(Silvermines, Killaloe)

Moloney, Dermot, Rt Rev
Mgr, PE, VG
5 Gold Cave Crescent,
Tuam, Co. Galway
Tel 093-52946
(Tuam, retired)

Moloney, Gerard (CSsR), PC
Marianella, 75 Orwell Road,
Dublin 6
Tel 01-4067212
Editor, Redemptorist
Communications,
Liguori House,
75 Orwell Road, Dublin 6
Tel 01-4067100/01-4922488

Moloney, Henry (CSSp)
Holy Spirit Missionary
College, Kimmage Manor,
Dublin 12
Tel 01-4064300

Moloney, Joseph, Very Rev, PE
Grove House, Vicar Street,
Tuam, Co Galway
(Tuam, retired)

Moloney, Leonard (SJ)
Headmaster,
Clongowes Wood College,
Clane, Co Kildare
Tel 045-868663/868202

Moloney, Michael, CC
Kiltegan, Co Wicklow
Tel 059-6473211
(Rathvilly, Kildare & L.)

Moloney, Raymond (SJ)
Milltown Park,
Sandford Road, Dublin 6
Tel 01-2698411/2698113

Molony, Raymond T., Very Rev Canon
Presbytery No. 2,
Thormanby Road,
Howth, Co Dublin
Tel 01-8322092
(Dublin, retired)

Monaghan, Stephen (CM), Very Rev
Phibsboro, St Peter's,
Dublin 7
Tel 01-8389708/8389841

Monahan, Finian (OCD)
The Abbey, Loughrea,
Co Galway
Tel 091-841209

Monahan, Fintan
Diocesan Secretary,
Archbishop's House, Tuam,
Co Galway
Tel 093-24166
(Tuam)

Monahan, Patrick, CC
'Renvyle', Corrig Avenue,
Dun Laoghaire, Co Dublin
Tel 01-2802100
(Dun Laoghaire, Dublin)

Monahan, Paul (SMA)
SMA House,
82 Ranelagh Road,
Ranelagh, Dublin 6
Tel 01-4968162/3

Monahan, Thomas (OP)
Provincial Bursar and Secretary,
Provincial Office, St Mary's,
Tallaght, Dublin 24
Tel 01-4048118/4048114

Mongan, Gerard, CC
2 Station Road, Dungiven,
Co Derry BT47 4LN
Tel 028-77741256
(Dungiven, Derry)

Monks, Frank (MI)
Superior,
St Camillus, Killucan,
Co Westmeath
Tel 044-74115

Monson, Eamon (SAC)
St Benin's, Dublin Road,
Shankill, Co Dublin
Tel 01-2824425
(Shankill, Dublin)

Montades, Rudy (SVD), CC
The Presbytery, City Quay,
Dublin 2
Tel 01-6773706
(City Quay, Dublin)

Montague, Paul, Very Rev, Adm
Ard Easmuinn, Dundalk,
Co Louth
Tel 042-9334259
(Dundalk, Holy Redeemer,
Armagh)

Mooney, Desmond, CC
6 Derrymacash Road,
Lurgan,
Craigavon, BT66 6LG
Tel 028-38341356
(Moyraverty (Craigavon),
Seagoe (Derrymacash),
Dromore)

Mooney, Oliver, Very Rev
Newry, Co Down
(Dromore, retired)

Mooney, Patrick, Very Rev, PP
Parochial House,
Glenamaddy, Co Galway
Tel 094-9659017
Administration for
Williamstown (Templetoher)
(Glenamaddy (Boyounagh),
Williamstown
(Templetoher), Tuam)

Moore, David, Very Rev, PP
62A Main Street, Pomeroy,
Co Tyrone, BT70 2QH
Tel 028-87757867
(Pomeroy, Armagh)

Moore, Edward, Very Rev, PE
Marian House, Sallins, Naas,
Co Kildare
(Kildare & L., retired)

Moore, Eoin (OCarm)
Terenure College, Terenure,
Dublin 6W
Tel 01-4904621

Moore, Gerard, Co-PP
The Presbytery,
St Mary's Parish,
Sandyford, Dublin 18
Tel 01-2858933
(Sandyford, Dublin)

Moore, James, CC
Cloyne Diocesan Centre,
Cobh, Co Cork
Tel 021-4811430
Rushbrooke, Cobh, Co Cork
Tel 086-8694744
(Cobh, St Colman's
Cathedral, Cloyne)

Moore, James, Very Rev, PP
Fintona, Omagh,
Co Tyrone BT78 2NS
Tel 028-82841907
(Fintona, Clogher)

Moore, Kevin, Very Rev
(Moderator)
Apartment No. 1, St
Sylvester's Church,
Malahide, Co Dublin
Tel 01-8451244
(Malahide, Dublin)

Moore, Michael (CSSp)
Rockwell College, Cashel,
Co Tipperary
Tel 062-61444

Moore, Paschal, Very Rev, PP
Piltown, Co Kilkenny
Tel 051-643112/087-2408078
(Templeorum, Ossory)

Moore, Patrick (SPS)
St Patrick's, Kiltegan,
Co Wicklow
Tel 059-6473600

Moore, Patrick B., Very Rev, PE
Sandy Corner, Sallymount,
Wicklow, Co Wicklow
(Dublin, retired)

Moore, Patrick, Very Rev, PP
Duagh, Listowel, Co Kerry
Tel 068-45102
(Duagh, Kerry)

Moore, Patrick, Very Rev, PP, VF
Parochial House,
Castlepollard,
Co Westmeath
Tel 044-9661126/
087-2510855
(Castlepollard, Meath)

Moore, Seamus, Very Rev, PE
8 Herbert Avenue, Dublin 4
Tel 01-2692501
(Dublin, retired)

Moore, Sean (CSsR)
Clonard Monastery,
1 Clonard Gardens,
Belfast, BT13 2RL
Tel 028-90445950

Moore, Seán, Very Rev, PP
Parochial House,
290 Monaghan Road,
Middletown,
Co Armagh BT60 4HS
Tel 028-37568406
(Middletown (Tynan),
Armagh)

Moorhead, John, Very Rev, PP
Parochial House, Eglish,
Birr, Co Offaly
Tel 057-9133010
(Eglish, Meath)

Morahan, Kieran (SMA)
SMA House, Claregalway,
Co Galway
Tel 091-798880

Morahan, Leo, Very Rev, PE
2 The Beeches, Louisburg,
Co Mayo
Tel 098-66869
(Galway, retired)

Moran, Benedict (OP), Very Rev, PP
Dominican Community,
St Aengus's, Balrothery,
Tallaght, Dublin 24
Tel 01-4624038
(Tallaght, Tymon North,
Dublin)

Moran, James (SJ)
Vice-Superior,
35 Lower Leeson Street,
Dublin 2
Tel 01-6761248

Moran, John F., CC
192 Navan Road, Dublin 7
Tel 01-8387902
(Dublin, retired)

Moran, Lorcan, Very Rev, PP
Ballycallan, Co Kilkenny
Tel 056-7769564/
086-8550521
(Ballycallan, Ossory)

Moran, Martin, Very Rev Canon, PP, VF
Rosscahill, Co Galway
Tel 091-550106
(Rosscahill (Killanin),
Galway)

Moran, Noel, Very Rev
Lahard, Milltown, Co Kerry
(Kerry, retired)

Moran, Patrick, CC
47 Westland Row, Dublin 2
Tel 01-6761270
(Westland Row, Dublin)

Moran, Willie (OCD)
Prior,
The Abbey, Loughrea,
Co Galway
Tel 091-841209

Morely, Paul, CC
Holy Family Presbytery
Newington Avenue,
Belfast BT15 2HP
Tel 028-90743119
(Holy Family, Down and C.)

Morgan, Francis (OCSO)
Our Lady of Bethlehem Abbey,
11 Ballymena Road,
Portglenone, Ballymena,
Co Antrim BT44 8BL
Tel 028-25821211

Morgan, Liam, CC
Sallins Road, Naas,
Co Kildare
Tel 045-897260
(Naas, Kildare & L.)

Moriarty, Cathal (SPS)
Councillor, St Patrick's
Kiltegan, Co Wicklow
Tel 059-6473600

Moriarty, Declan
Sacred Heart Residence,
Sybil Hill Road, Raheny,
Dublin 5
(Dublin, retired)

Moriarty, Frank, Very Rev
Adare, Co Limerick
Tel 061-396177
(Limerick, retired)

Moriarty, James, Most Rev, DD
Retired Bishop of Kildare
and Leighlin,
68 Clontarf Road, Dublin 3
Tel 01-8054738
(Kildare & L.)

Moriarty, John (CSSp)
Holy Spirit Missionary
College, Kimmage Manor,
Dublin 12
Tel 01-4064300

Morris, Anthony (OP)
Holy Cross, Sligo,
Co Sligo
Tel 071-9142700

Morris, Colm, PEm
Muff, Co Donegal
Tel 074-9384407
(Derry, retired)

Morris, Donal, Very Rev, Adm
Loughglynn,
Castlerea, Co Roscommon
Tel 094-9880007
(Loughglynn and Lisacul,
Elphin)

Morris, Fintan, CC
Caim, Enniscorthy,
Co Wexford
Tel 053-9255149
(Ballindaggin, Ferns)

Morris, John, Very Rev, PP
Solohead, Co Limerick
Tel 062-47614
(Solohead, Cashel & E.)

Morrissey, Michael (OCarm),
CC
Carmelite Presbytery,
Idrone Avenue, Knocklyon,
Dublin 16
Tel 01-4941204/4944986
(Knocklyon, Dublin)

Morrissey, Robin, Very Rev, PP
Churchtown, Mallow,
Co Cork
Tel 022-23385
(Churchtown (Liscarroll),
Cloyne)

Morrissey, Thomas (SJ)
Manresa House,
Dollymount, Dublin 3
Tel 01-8331352

Morrow, James (CSSp)
Holy Spirit Missionary
College, Kimmage Manor,
Dublin 12
Tel 01-4064300

Moss, Michael (FDP)
Sarsfield House,
Sarsfield Road, Ballyfermot,
Dublin 10
Tel 01-6266193/6266233

Mothersill, Joseph (OCarm)
Prior, Gort Muire, Ballinteer,
Dublin 16
Tel 01-2984014

Motherway, Nicholas (SPS)
St Patrick's, Kiltegan,
Co Wicklow
Tel 059-6473600

Mowbray, Alan (SJ), PC
Gonzaga Jesuit Community,
Sandford Road, Dublin 6
Tel 01-4972943
(Milltown, Dublin)

Mowles, Alan (SDB)
Salesian House,
45 St Teresa's Road,
Crumlin, Dublin 12
Tel 01-4555605

Moynihan, James, CC
Murrintown, Wexford
Tel 053-9139136
(Piercestown, Ferns)

Moynihan, Michael, Very Rev,
PP
Glengarriff, Co Cork
Tel 027-63045
(Glengarriff (Bonane), Kerry)

Moynihan, Noel (CSSp)
Holy Spirit Missionary
College,
Kimmage Manor, Whitehall
Road, Dublin 12
Tel 01-4064300

Muckian, Patrick (SM)
Philippines

Mulcahy, Brian (CP)
St Paul's Retreat,
Mount Argus, Dublin 6W
Tel 01-4992000

Mulcahy, James, Very Rev, PE
St John's Pastoral Centre,
John's Hill, Waterford
Tel 051-858306
(Waterford & L., retired)

Mulcahy, Joseph (SPS)
St Patrick's, Kiltegan,
Co Wicklow
Tel 059-6473600

Mulcahy, Kevin, CC
Ballymacoda, Co Cork
Tel 024-98110
(Ballymacoda and
Ladysbridge, Cloyne)

Mulcahy, Pat, Very Rev, PP
Lorrha, Nenagh,
Co Tipperary
Tel 0909-747009/
087-6329913
(Dunkerrin, Killaloe)

Mulcahy, Richard, Rt Rev
30 Knapton Road,
Dun Laoghaire, Co Dublin
Tel 01-2804353
(Opus Dei)

Mulcahy, Thomas (MSC)
'Croí Nua', Rosary Lane,
Taylor's Hill, Galway
Tel 091-520960

Mulcahy, Timothy (OP), CC
St Dominic's,
St Dominic's Road,
Tallaght, Dublin 24
Tel 01-4510620
(Tallaght, Dodder, Dublin)

Muldowney, Peter, Very Rev,
PP
Mooncoin, Co Kilkenny
Tel 051-895123/086-9131080
(Mooncoin, Ossory)

Mulhall, Brendan (CSsR)
Clonard Monastery,
1 Clonard Gardens,
Belfast BT13 2RL
Tel 028-90445950

Mulherin, Jim (OSM), PP
Church of the Divine Word,
Marley Grange,
25–27 Hermitage Downs,
Rathfarnham, Dublin 16
Tel 01-4944295/4941064
(Marley Grange, Dublin)

Mulhern, Kevin (SMA)
Dromantine College,
Dromantine, Newry,
Co Down BT34 1RH
Tel 028-30821224

Mulholland, Patrick, Very Rev,
PP
Parochial House, Portaferry,
Co Down BT22 1RH
Tel 028-42728234
(Portaferry, Down & C.)

Mulkerins, Bernard (SSC)
Director,
St Columban's Retirement
Home, Dalgan Park, Navan,
Co Meath
Tel 046-9021525

Mulkerrins, Michael, Very Rev
Canon, PE
Curate's Residence,
Renmore, Galway
Tel 091-757859
(Galway, retired)

Mullaly, Kevin
8 Finglaswood Road,
Finglas West, Dublin 11
Tel 01-8238354
(Blanchardstown, Dublin)

Mullan, Aidan, PP
19 Chapel Road, Dungiven,
Derry BT47 4RT
Tel 028-77741219
(Dungiven, Derry)

Mullan, Joseph, Very Rev, PP
49 Rathgar Road, Dublin 6
Tel 01-4971058
(Rathgar, Dublin)

Mullan, Kevin, PP
257 Dooish Road,
Drumquin, Omagh,
Co Tyrone BT78 4RA
Tel 028-82831225
(Drumquin (Langfield),
Derry)

Mullan, Michael, PEm
300 Drumsurn Road,
Limavady,
Co Derry BT49 0PX
Tel 028-77762165
(Derry, retired)

Mullan, Patrick, PP
Stella Maris House, Eglinton,
Co Derry BT47 3EA
Tel 028-71810240
(Faughanvale, Derry)

Mullane, Denis, Very Rev, PP
Templeglantine, Co Limerick
Tel 069-84021/069-81010
(Templeglantin,
Tournafulla/Mountcollins,
Limerick)

Mullaney, Michael
Ballycahill, Thurles,
Co Tipperary
Tel 0504-26080
(Holy Cross, Cashel & E.)

Mullan, Joseph, PP
49 Rathgar Road,
Dublin 6
Tel 01-4970039/0872326254
(Rathgar, Dublin)

Mullen, John (IC)
Clonturk House,
Ormond Road,
Drumcondra, Dublin 9
Tel 01-6877014

Mullen, Pearse (SSCC) CC
Sacred Heart Presbytery,
St John's Drive,
Sruleen, Clondalkin,
Dublin 22
(Sruleen, Dublin)

Mulligan, Ben, Very Rev, PE
(priest in residence)
42 Corke Abbey, Little Bray,
Co Wicklow
Tel 01-2720224
(Dublin, retired)

Mulligan, Declan, Very Rev, PP
Parochial House, 5 Aghalee
Road,
Aghagallon, Craigavon,
Co Armagh BT67 0AR
Tel 028-92651214
(Aghagallon and
Ballinderry, Down & C.)

Mulligan, John (SM)
Cois Abhainn,
More Hall Lodge, Co Louth

Mulligan, Larry (OFM)
Vicar, Franciscan Friary,
Clonmel, Co Tipperary
Tel 052-6121378

Mulligan, Rory (SM)
Norway

Mulligan, Thomas, Very Rev,
PP
Attymass, Ballina, Co Mayo
Tel 096-45095
(Attymass, Achonry)

Mulligan, Vincent (OMI)
Oblate House of Retreat,
Inchicore, Dublin 8
Tel 01-4534408/4541805

Mullin, Henry (CSSp)
Holy Spirit Missionary
College, Kimmage Manor,
Dublin 12
Tel 01-4064300

Mullin, Joseph, Very Rev
Canon, PP, VF
Lisoneill, Lisnaskea,
Enniskillen,
Co Fermanagh BT92 0JE
Tel 028-67721342
(Lisnaskea (Aghalurcher),
Clogher)

Mullin, Seamus, Very Rev
Canon, AP
Miltown Malbay, Co Clare
Tel 065-7084003
(*Miltown Malbay*, Killaloe)

Mullins, Anthony, Very Rev
Canon, PP
Dromin, Killmallock,
Co Limerick
Tel 063-31962
(*Dromin & Athlacca*,
Limerick)

Mullins, Melvyn,
192 Sundrive Road,
Dublin 12
Tel 01-4536988
(*Clogher Road*, Dublin)

Mullins, Michael, Very Rev, PP
St Anne's Presbytery,
Convent Hill, Waterford
Tel 051-855819
(*Ballybricken*, Waterford &
L.)

Mullins, Patrick (OCarm)
Provincial Office and
Carmelite Community,
Gort Muire, Ballinteer,
Dublin 16
Tel 01-2984014

Mullins, Patrick, Very Rev, PP
Cummer, Tuam,
Co Galway
Tel 093-41427
(*Cummer (Kilmoylan and
Cummer)*, Tuam)

Mulloy, Frank (CSSp)
Holy Spirit Missionary
College,
Kimmage Manor, Whitehall
Road, Dublin 12
Tel 01-4064300

Mulvaney, Martin, Very Rev,
PP
Drumlion,
Carrick-on-Shannon,
Co Roscommon
Tel 071-9620415
(*Croghan*, Elphin)

Mulvany, Seamus, Very Rev,
PP
Parochial House,
Tubberclaire-Glasson,
Athlone, Co Westmeath
Tel 090-6485103
(*Glasson*, Meath)

Mulvey, Anthony (CSsR)
St Joseph's, Dundalk,
Co Louth
Tel 042-9334042/9334762

Mulvey, Patrick, Very Rev
25 Thomastown Road,
Dun Laoghaire, Co Dublin
(Dublin, retired)

Mulvihill, Anthony, Very Rev
Ballymarkham, Quin,
Co Clare
(Limerick)

Mulvihill, Eamonn, Very Rev,
PP
Fenit, Tralee, Co Kerry
Tel 066-7136145
(*Spa*, Kerry)

Mulvihill, William, PP
Parochial House,
Monasterboice,
Co Louth
Tel 041-9822839
(*Monasterboice*, Armagh)

Mulvilhill, Michael (CSSp)
Holy Spirit Missionary
College, Kimmage Manor,
Dublin 12
Tel 01-4064300

Mundow, Sean, Rev
The Presbytery, Chapelizod,
Dublin 20
Tel 01-6264645/087-8195073
(*Chapelizod*, Dublin)

Munnelly, Patrick, Very Rev,
PP
Ardagh, Ballina, Co Mayo
Tel 096-31144
(*Ardagh*, Killala)

Munster, Ramon, Very Rev
Canon, PP
Bundoran, Co Donegal
Tel 071-9841290
(*Bundoran*, Clogher)

Murney, Peadar, Very Rev
Canon
25 Thomastown Road,
Dun Laoghaire, Co Dublin
Tel 01-2856660
(Dublin, retired)

Murphy O'Connor, Kerry,
Venerable Archdeacon, PP
The Presbytery,
Turner's Cross, Cork
Tel 021-4312466
(*Turner's Cross*, Cork & R.)

Murphy, Aidan, Very Rev, PP,
VF
Parochial House,
Termonfechin, Drogheda,
Co Louth
Tel 041-9822121
(*Termonfechin*, Armagh)

Murphy, Alphonsus, Very Rev,
PE
Carbury, Co Kildare
Tel 046-9553020
(Kildare & L., retired)

Murphy, Anthony (MHM)
(elsewhere in Ireland)

Murphy, Bernard (CFR)
St Patrick Friary,
64 Delmege Park, Moyross,
Limerick
Tel 061-458071

Murphy, Bernard (OCarm), PP
Carmelite Priory,
56 Aungier Street, Dublin 2
Tel 01-4758821
(*Whitefriar Street*, Dublin)

Murphy, Brendan, Very Rev
Gortboy, Newcastle West,
Co Limerick
(Limerick, retired)

Murphy, Brian (OSB)
Glenstal Abbey, Murroe,
Co Limerick
Tel 061-386103

Murphy, Canice (OP)
St Saviour's, Bridge Street,
Waterford
Tel 051-875061

Murphy, Colm (SSC)
Luxeuil, France

Murphy, Colm, Very Rev, PP
Clongeen, Foulksmills,
Co Wexford
Tel 051-565610
(*Clongeen*, Ferns)

Murphy, Colum
Cathedral Presbytery,
38 Hill Street,
Newry, BT34 1AT
Tel 028-30262586
(*Newry Pastoral Area*,
Dromore)

Murphy, Conor (OMI)
170 Merrion Road,
Ballsbridge, Dublin 4
Tel 01-2693658

Murphy, Cornelius (SMA)
SMA House, Wilton, Cork
Tel 021-4541069/4541884

Murphy, Cyril (SSC)
St Columban's,
Dalgan Park, Navan,
Co Meath
Tel 046-9021525

Murphy, Daniel
National Centre for Liturgy,
Maynooth, Co Kildare
Tel 01-7083478
(Cloyne)

Murphy, Daniel (SMA)
African Missions,
Blackrock Road, Cork
Tel 021-4292871

Murphy, David
Chaplain, Cork Prison,
Tel 021-4518820/087-
6836567

Murphy, David, CC
Caroreigh, Taghmon,
Co Wexford
Tel 053-9134113
(*Taghmon*, Ferns)

Murphy, Denis (OP)
(leave of absence)
St Catherine's, Newry,
Co Down BT35 8BN
Tel 028-30262178

Murphy, Denis, Very Rev, Adm
Tolerton, Ballickmoyler,
Carlow
Tel 056-4442126
(*Doonane*, Kildare & L.)

Murphy, Edmund (OP)
Newbridge College,
Droichead Nua, Co Kildare
Tel 045-487200

Murphy, Edward, Very Rev
Canon, PE
Newtownbutler, Enniskillen,
Co Fermanagh BT92 8JJ
Tel 028-67738640
(*Newtownbutler*, Clogher)

Murphy, Enda
Pastoral Services,
Kilmore Diocesan Pastoral
Centre, Cullies, Cavan
Tel 049-4375004

Murphy, Eoin, AP
25 The Haven, Glasnevin,
Dublin 9
Tel 086-8831791
(*Ballymun Road*, Dublin)

Murphy, Francis, Very Rev, PP
Kilmuckridge, Gorey,
Co Wexford
Tel 053-9130116
(*Kilmuckridge (Litter) and
Monamolin*, Ferns)

Murphy, Gabriel, Very Rev, PP
Keash, Ballymote, Co Sligo
Tel 071-9183334
(*Keash (Drumrat)*, Achonry)

Murphy, George, Very Rev
Canon, PP
Minane Bridge, Co Cork
Tel 021-4887105
(*Tracton Abbey*, Cork & R.)

Murphy, James (CSSp)
Holy Spirit Missionary
College, Kimmage Manor,
Dublin 12
Tel 01-4064300

Murphy, James (CSsR)
Mount Saint Alphonsus,
Limerick
Tel 061-315099

Murphy, James (SJ)
Irish Jesuit Provincialate,
Milltown Park,
Sandford Road, Dublin 6
Tel 01-4987333

Murphy, James, CC
St Brigid's, Rosslare,
Co Wexford
Tel 053-9132118
(*Tagoat*, Ferns)

Murphy, James, Very Rev, PP
St Canice's Presbytery,
Dean Street, Kilkenny
Tel 056-7752991/
087-2609545
(*St Canice's*, Ossory)

Murphy, Jason
(priest in residence)
Killoughter, Redhills,
Co Cavan
Tel 047-55021
(*Belturbet (Annagh)*,
Kilmore)

Murphy, Jeremiah (SAC), Very Rev
Provincial, 'Homestead',
Sandyford Road,
Dundrum, Dublin 16
Tel 01-2956180/2954170

Murphy, Jerry (SSC)
St Mary's, Tang,
Ballymahon,
Co Longford
Tel 0906-432214

Murphy, Jerry, CC
St Mary's, Tang,
Ballymahon, Co Longford
Tel 090-6432214
(*Drumraney*, Meath)

Murphy, John (OSA)
St Augustine's,
Taylor's Lane,
Ballyboden, Dublin 16
Tel 01-4241000

Murphy, John, Co-PP
St Anne's, Strand Road,
Portmarnock, Co Dublin
Tel 01-8461081
(*Portmarnock*, Dublin)

Murphy, John, Rt Rev Mgr
(priest in residence)
18 Rock Road, Lisburn,
Co Antrim BT28 3SU
Tel 028-92648244
(*Hannahstown*, Down & C.)

Murphy, John
(On sabbatical)
Bailieborough Road,
Virginia, Co Cavan
(Kilmore)

Murphy, John (OMI)
Oblate House of Retreat,
Inchicore, Dublin 8
Tel 01-4534408/4541805

Murphy, Joseph (CSSp)
17 St Brigid's Park,
Blacklion, Greystones,
Co Wicklow
Tel 01-2874888

Murphy, Joseph (OFMCap)
Holy Trinity,
Fr Mathew Quay, Cork
Tel 021-4270827

Murphy, Joseph, Very Rev Mgr
Secretariat of State,
(Section for Relations with States),
00120 Vatican City
Tel 0039-0669883193
(Cloyne)

Murphy, Kyran (SPS)
Assistant Regional Leader,
St Patrick's, Kiltegan,
Co Wicklow
Tel 059-6473600

Murphy, Laurence (SJ)
Manresa House,
Dollymount, Dublin 3
Tel 01-8331352

Murphy, Malachy, PP
Parochial House,
25 Priestbush Road,
Whitecross,
Co Armagh BT60 2TP
Tel 028-37507214
(*Whitecross (Loughilly)*,
Armagh)

Murphy, Martin (IC)
Rosminian House of Prayer,
Glencomeragh House,
Kilsheelan, Co Tipperary
Tel 052-33181

Murphy, Martin (SSC)
St Columban's, Dalgan Park,
Navan, Co Meath
Tel 046-9021525

Murphy, Martin, Very Rev, PP
Drom, Thurles,
Co Tipperary
Tel 0504-51196
(*Drom and Inch*, Cashel & E.)

Murphy, Michael
Presbytery No 1, Treepark Road,
Kilnamanagh, Dublin 24
Tel 01-4523805/086-2408188
(*Kilnamanagh-Castleview*,
Dublin)

Murphy, Michael (OFMCap)
Holy Trinity,
Fr Mathew Quay, Cork
Tel 021-4270827

Murphy, Michael J., Venerable Archdeacon
No. 1 Cathedral Place,
Killarney, Co Kerry
(Kerry, retired)

Murphy, Michael, CC
Robeen, Hollymount,
Co Mayo
Tel 094-9540026
(*Robeen*, Tuam)

Murphy, Michael, Very Rev Canon, PP
Ballyphehane, Co Cork
Tel 021-4965560
(*Ballyphehane*, Cork & R.)

Murphy, Mícheál, Very Rev, PP, VF
11 Ashgrove, Mountmellick,
Co Laois
Tel 057-8679302
(*Mountmellick*, Kildare & L.)

Murphy, Noel (CSSp)
Rockwell College, Cashel,
Co Tipperary
Tel 062-61444

Murphy, Noel, CC
14 Springfield Drive,
Dooradoyle, Limerick
Tel 061-304508
(*St Paul's*, Limerick)

Murphy, Pádraig, Very Rev, PP
Parochial House,
Ravensdale, Dundalk,
Co Louth
Tel 042-9371327
(*Lordship (And Ballymascanlon)*, Armagh)

Murphy, Patrick (CSSp)
Holy Spirit Missionary
College, Kimmage Manor,
Dublin 12
Tel 01-4064300

Murphy, Patrick, Very Rev, PP
Parochial House, Mohill,
Co Leitrim
Tel 071-9631024
(*Mohill (Mohill-Manachain)*,
Ardagh & Cl.)

Murphy, Patrick, Very Rev
Fatima Home, Oakpark,
Tralee, Co Kerry
(Kerry, retired)

Murphy, Patrick, Very Rev, PP
Templetuohy, Thurles,
Co Tipperary
Tel 0504-53114
(*Templetuohy*, Cashel & E.)

Murphy, Paul, CC
St Peter's Presbytery,
10 Fair Street,
Drogheda, Co Louth
Tel 041-9838239
(*Drogheda*, Armagh)

Murphy, Paul (OFMCap)
Provincial Office,
12 Halston Street, Dublin 7
Tel 01-8733205

Murphy, Paul F., Very Rev, CF
Chaplain's House,
Dún Uí Mhaoilíosa
Renmore, Galway
Tel 091-751156
(Waterford & L.)

Murphy, Paul, Very Rev, PP
St John's Presbytery,
New Street, Waterford
Tel 051-874271
(*St John's*, Waterford & L.)

Murphy, Peadar, Very Rev, PP
Aghabullogue, Co Cork
Tel 021-7334035
(*Aghabullogue*, Cloyne)

Murphy, Peter
National Chaplain,
Accord Catholic Marriage
Care Service,
Columba Centre,
Maynooth, Co Kildare
Tel 01-5053107
(Dublin)

Murphy, Peter, Very Rev, PP, VF
Parochial House,
Hale Street, Ardee,
Co Louth
Tel 041-6850920
(*Ardee & Collon*, Armagh)

Murphy, Pierce, Very Rev
(priest in residence)
Borris, Co Carlow via
Kilkenny
Tel 059-9773128
(*Borris*, Kildare & L.)

Murphy, Seán, Very Rev, PP
Miltown Malbay, Co Clare
Tel 065-7084129
(*Miltown Malbay*, Killaloe)

Murphy, Thomas, Very Rev Canon, PE
Ballyragget, Co Kilkenny
Tel 056-8833123/
086-8130694
(*Ballyragget*, Ossory)

Murphy, Thomas
Tara Winthrop Private Clinic,
Nevinstown Lane,
Pinnock Hill,
Swords, Co Dublin
(Dublin, retired)

Murphy, Timothy, Very Rev, PP
The Presbytery, Main Street,
Blessington, Co Wicklow
Tel 045-865442
Permanent Deacon
Porterstown-Clonsilla
(*Blessington, Porterstown-Clonsilla, Valleymount*,
Dublin)

Murphy, Vincent (SJ)
Clongowes Wood College,
Clane, Co Kildare
Tel 045-868663/868202

Murphy, William, Most Rev, DD
Retired Bishop of Kerry
No. 2 Cathedral Place,
Killarney, Co Kerry
Tel 064-6631168
(Kerry)

Murray, Brendan (SSC)
St Columban's, Dalgan Park,
Navan, Co Meath
Tel 046-9021525

Murray, Brendan, Very Rev Canon
(priest in residence)
Apt 13 Downview Manor,
Belfast BT15 4JL
(*Holy Family*, Down & C.)

Murray, Declan (SJ)
Superior, Crescent College
Comprehensive,
Dooradoyle, Limerick
Tel 061-229655

Murray, Denis, Very Rev, PP
Carrigallen, Co Leitrim,
via Cavan
Tel 049-4339610
(*Carrigallen*, Kilmore)

Murray, Dermot (SJ)
Clongowes Wood College,
Clane, Co Kildare
Tel 045-868663/868202

Allianz (ⅲ)

Murray, Donal, Most Rev, DD
Bishop Emeritus, Former
Bishop of Limerick,
Diocesan Office,
Social Service Centre,
Henry Street, Limerick
Tel 061-315856
(Limerick)

Murray, Francis, Very Rev, PP
Ferbane, Co Offaly
Tel 090-6454380
(Ferbane High Street and
Boora, Ardagh & Cl.)

Murray, Gerard, (SMA)
African Missions,
Blackrock Road, Cork
Tel 021-4292871

Murray, James
9 Hillcrest Manor,
Templeogue, Dublin 6W
(Dublin, retired)

Murray, James (OCarm)
Provincial Office and
Carmelite Community
Gort Muire, Ballinteer,
Dublin 16
Tel 01-2984014

Murray, James, CC
Director of ACCORD,
Carraroe, Sligo,
Co Sligo
Tel 071-9162136
(Sligo, St Anne's, Elphin)

Murray, John, CC
Castlebar, Co Mayo
Tel 094-901253/21844
(Castlebar (Aglish,
Ballyheane and Breaghwy),
Tuam)

Murray, John, Very Rev, PP
Parochial House, 54 St
Patrick's Avenue,
Downpatrick, Co Down,
BT30 6DN
Tel 028-44612443
(Downpatrick, Down & C.)

Murray, Liam, Adm
St Mary's, Athlone,
Co Westmeath
Tel 090-6472088
(Athlone, Ardagh & Cl.)

Murray, Michael, CC
Belcarra, Castlebar, Co Mayo
Tel 094-9032006
(Balla and Manulla, Tuam)

Murray, Michael, Very Rev
c/o 73 Somerton Road,
Belfast, BT15 4DE
(Down & C., retired)

Murray, Patrick J., Very Rev,
PP
Maypole Hill, Dromore,
Co Down BT25 1BQ
Tel 028-92692218
(Dromore, Dromore)

Murray, Patrick (MHM)
St Joseph's House,
50 Orwell Park, Rathgar,
Dublin 6
Tel 01-4127700

Murray, Patrick (SAC)
Ashborough Lodge,
Milltown, Co Kerry

Murray, Placid (OSB)
Glenstal Abbey, Murroe,
Co Limerick
Tel 061-386103

Murray, Raymond, Rt Rev
Mgr, PE
60 Glen Mhacaha,
Cathedral Road,
Armagh BT61 8AF
Tel 028-37510821
(Armagh, retired)

Murray, Terence (OMI), Very
Rev, PP
Superior, The Presbytery,
Darndale, Dublin 17
Tel 01-8474547
(Darndale, Dublin)

Murray, Tom CC
Diocesan Offices,
St Michael's, Longford
Tel 043-3346432
(Longford (Templemichael,
Ballymacormack), Ardagh &
Cl.)

Murtagh, Brian (CSSp)
Spiritan Missionaries,
Ardbraccan, Navan,
Co Meath
Tel 046-9021441

Murtagh, Colm, Very Rev, PE
Parochial House, Kildalkey,
Co Meath
Tel 046-9546488
(Meath, retired)

Murtagh, Fintan (SSC)
St Columban's Retirement
Home, Dalgan Park, Navan,
Co Meath
Tel 046-9021525

Murtagh, Michael, Co-PP
2 St Mary's Terrace, Arklow,
Co Wicklow
Tel 0402-41505
(Arklow, Dublin)

Murtagh, G. Michael, Very
Rev, PP
Parochial House,
Old Chapel Lane, Dunleer,
Co Louth
Tel 041-6851278
(Dunleer, Armagh)

Murtagh, John
Newry, Co Down
(Dromore, retired)

Murtagh, Liam, Very Rev
33 Grace Park Road,
Drumcondra, Dublin 9
(Dublin, retired)

Murtagh, Michael (CSsR)
Superior,
Clonard Monastery,
1 Clonard Gardens,
Belfast, BT13 2RL
Tel 028-90445950

Murtagh, Michael, CC
5 St Mary's Terrace,
Arklow, Co Wicklow
Tel 0402-41505
(Arklow, Dublin)

Murtagh, Ray (SPS)
St Patrick's, Kiltegan,
Co Wicklow
Tel 059-6473600

Murtagh, William, Very Rev,
PE, AP
Parochial House,
Clogherhead, Drogheda,
Co Louth
Tel 041-9822224
(Clogherhead, Armagh)

Murtha, Kieran (SSCC)
Cootehill, Co Cavan
Tel 049-5552188

Mushawasha, Martin, PC
80 St Mary's Road,
East Wall, Dublin 3
Tel 01-8560980
(East Wall-North Strand,
Dublin)

Mutunzi, Eladius Leonard, PC
Presbytery 2, 6 Old Hill,
Leixlip, Co Kildare
Tel 01-6243673
(Leixlip, Dublin)

Myers, David (IC)
Provincial, Clonturk House,
Ormond Road,
Drumcondra, Dublin 9
Tel 01-6877014

## N

Naikaruddy, Joseph
St Camillus, Killucan,
Co Westmeath
Tel 044-74196/74115

Nagle, Cathal
(Galway, retired)

Nagle, Joe (OFMCap)
Holy Trinity,
Fr Mathew Quay, Cork
Tel 021-4270827

Naikarakudy, Joseph (MI), CC
Chaplain,
Cathedral House, Mullingar,
Co Westmeath
Tel 044-9348338/9340126
(Mullingar, Meath)

Nallen, Michael, Very Rev, PP
Aughoose, Ballina, Co Mayo
Tel 097-87990
(Kilcommon-Erris, Killala)

Nallukunnel, Antony
(OFMConv), PP
Friary of the Visitation,
Fairview Strand, Dublin 3
Tel 01-8376000
(Fairview, Dublin)

Nally, John, Very Rev, PP
Parochial House,
Ballynacargy, Co Westmeath
Tel 044-9373923
(Ballynacargy, Meath)

Nash, Ger
Parochial House, Crusheen,
Ennis, Clare
Tel 065-6827113
(Crusheen, Killaloe)

Nash, Paul (OSB)
Glenstal Abbey, Murroe,
Co Limerick
Tel 061-386103

Nash, Tom (CSSp)
Community Leader,
Blackrock College,
Blackrock, Co Dublin
Tel 01-2888681

Naughton, John, Very Rev
Clonfert Avenue, Portumna,
Co Galway
(Clonfert, retired)

Naughton, Joseph (CSsR)
St Joseph's, Dundalk,
Co Louth
Tel 042-9334042/9334762

Naughton, Richard, Very Rev,
PP, VF
Mountain Lodge,
132 Dublin Road, Newry,
Co Down BT35 8QT
Tel 028-30262174
(Cloghogue (Killeavy
Upper), Armagh)

Naughton, Tom, CC
Charleville, Co Cork
Tel 063-81437
(Charleville, Cloyne)

Nawalaniec, Kazimierz, CC
Ballyphehane, Co Cork
Tel 021-4310835
(Ballyphehane, Cork & R.)

Nawrat, Lukasz (SDB)
Salesian College,
Pallaskenry, Co Limerick
Tel 061-393313

Neary, Donal (SJ), Very Rev,
PP, VF
The Presbytery,
Upper Gardiner Street,
Dublin 1
Tel 01-8363411
(Gardiner Street, Dublin)

Neary, Michael, Most Rev, DD
Archbishop of Tuam,
Archbishop's House, Tuam,
Co Galway
Tel 093-24166
(Tuam)

Nechikattil, Pius (SSP)
c/o Society of St Paul,
Moyglare Road,
Maynooth, Co Kildare
Tel 01-6285933

Needham, Gerard, Very Rev
Louisburgh, Co Mayo
(Tuam)

Neenan, Daniel, Rt Rev Mgr,
VG
1 Trinity Court,
Monaleen Road, Monaleen,
Limerick
Tel 061-330974/087-2208547
(Limerick)

Neeson, Patrick, Very Rev, PP
46 Blackstaff Road,
Ballycranbeg, Kircubbin,
Newtownards,
Co Down BT22 1AG
Tel 028-42738294
(Kircubbin (Ardkeen), Down
& C.)

Nellis, Christopher, Very Rev,
PP
Parochial House, Armoy,
Ballymoney,
Co Antrim BT53 8RL
Tel 028-20751205
(Armoy, Down & C.)

Nestor, Dermot, Very Rev, Co-
PP
Parochial House,
Nutgrove Avenue,
Dublin 14
Tel 01-2985916
(Churchtown, Dublin)

Neville, Alan (MSC)
Western Road, Cork
Tel 021-4804120

Neville, Anthony, CC
Claddaghduff, Co Galway
Tel 095-44668
(Inishbofin, Tuam)

Neville, James, Very Rev
Canon
Cedarville, Abbeyfeale,
Co Limerick
Tel 068-32884
(Limerick, retired)

Neville, Paddy (MHM)
St Joseph's House,
50 Orwell Park, Rathgar,
Dublin 6
Tel 01-4127700

Nevin, Henry, (SDS), CC,
Curate's House, Sea Park,
Lahinch, Co Clare
Tel 065-7081307
(Ennistymon, Galway)

Nevin, John (MHM)
St Mary's Parish,
25 Marquis Street,
Belfast BT1 1JJ
Tel 028-90320482/
01-4789093

Nevin, Michael G.
(priest in residence)
The Presbytery,
Harrington Street,
Dublin 8
Tel 01-4789093
(Harrington Street, Dublin)

Newell, Martin, Very Rev
Canon, AP
Claran, Co Galway
Tel 093-35436
(Headford (Killursa and
Killower), Tuam)

Newman, John, Very Rev, PP
Glanmire, Co Cork
Tel 021-4866307
(Glanmire, Cork & R.)

Neylon, Finbarr, CC
c/o Parish Office,
St John the Evangelist,
Greendale Road,
Kilbarrack, Dublin 5
Tel 01-8390433
(Kilbarrack-Foxfield, Dublin)

Neylon, Sean, Very Rev, PP
Taghmaconnell,
Ballinasloe,
Co Galway
Tel 090-9683929
(Taghmaconnell, Clonfert)

Ndugwa, Severinus, PC
No. 2 Presbytery,
St Canice's Parish,
Finglas, Dublin 11
Tel 087-8180097
(Finglas, Dublin)

Nguekam, Marino (CSSp)
Holy Spirit Missionary
College,
Kimmage Manor,
Whitehall Road,
Dublin 12
Tel 01-4064300

Nicholas, Michael (OFM)
Franciscan Friary,
Liberty Street, Cork
Tel 021-4270302

Niyoyita, Kizito (SJ)
Jesuit Community,
27 Leinster Road,
Rathmines, Dublin 6
Tel 01-4970250

Nizio, Lukasz, CC
The Presbytery,
11 Steelstown Road,
Derry BT48 8EU
Tel 028-71351718
(Our Lady of Lourdes,
Steelstown, Derry)

Njanackal, Rajeev Thomas, CC
Parochial House,
Brackenstown Road,
Swords, Co Dublin
Tel 01-8408926
(Brackenstown, Dublin)

Nohilly, Michael (SMA)
SMA House, Claregalway,
Co Galway
Tel 091-798880

Nohilly, Seamus (SMA)
Parochial House, Tubber,
Co Clare
Tel 091-633124/085-1443021
(Tubber (Kilkeedy), Killaloe)

Nolan, Brendan, Very Rev, PP
Our Lady's Island, Broadway,
Co Wexford
Tel 053-9131167
(Our Lady's Island &
Tacumshane, Ferns)

Nolan, Brian (CM)
41 Park View,
Dunard Road, Dublin 7

Nolan, Brian (CSsR)
Mount Saint Alphonsus,
Limerick
Tel 061-315099

Nolan, Damien
Director,
Ennis ACCORD Centre,
7 Carmody Street Business
Park, Ennis, Co Clare
Tel 1850-585000
Parish: 1a Laghtagoona,
Corofin, Co Clare
Tel 065-6837178/
086-8396636
(Corofin, Killaloe)

Nolan, Francis
Director, Accord,
St John's Pastoral Centre,
Castle Street, Tralee,
Co Kerry
Tel 066-7122280
St John's Presbytery,
Tralee, Co Kerry
Tel 066-7122522
(Tralee, St John's, Kerry)

Nolan, Martin (OSA)
St Augustine's,
Taylor's Lane,
Ballyboden, Dublin 16
Tel 01-4241000

Nolan, J. Michael, Rt Rev Mgr
26 Harmony Avenue,
Donnybrook, Dublin 4
(Dublin, retired)

Nolan, J., Very Rev
36 Ashfield, Greenville,
Listowel, Co Kerry
(Kerry, retired)

Nolan, James, Very Rev, PP
Davidstown, Enniscorthy,
Co Wexford
Tel 053-9233382
(Davidstown and
Courtnacuddy, Ferns)

Nolan, John P., Very Rev, PP
Duncannon, New Ross,
Co Wexford
Tel 051-389118
(Duncannon, Ferns)

Nolan, Mark-Ephrem M.
(OSB), Very Rev Dom
Prior,
Benedictine Monks,
Holy Cross Monastery,
119 Kilbroney Road,
Rostrevor,
Co Down BT34 3BN
Tel 028-41739979

Nolan, Martin (OSA)
St John's Priory,
Thomas Street,
Dublin 8
Tel 01-6770393

Nolan, Martin (SMA)
Dromantine College,
Dromantine, Newry,
Co Down BT34 1RH
Tel 028-30821224

Nolan, Placid (OP)
Holy Cross, Tralee,
Co Kerry
Tel 066-7121135/29185

Nolan, Robert, Very Rev, PP
Adamstown, Enniscorthy,
Co Wexford
Tel 053-9240512
(Adamstown, Ferns)

Nolan, Rory, CC
The Presbytery, Carlow
Tel 059-9131227
(Cathedral, Carlow, Kildare
& L.)

Nolan, Seán, Very Rev, PP
St Joseph's, Emyvale,
Monaghan
Tel 047-87152
(Errigal Truagh, Clogher)

Nolan, Simon (OCarm)
Gort Muire, Ballinteer,
Dublin 16
Tel 01-2984014

Nolan, Tod, Very Rev, PP
Killererin, Barnderg,
Tuam, Co Galway
Tel 093-49222
(Killererin, Tuam)

Noonan, Bernard, Rt Rev Mgr,
PP, VG
Moate, Co Westmeath
Tel 090-6481180
(Moate and Mount Temple,
Ardagh & Cl.)

Noonan, James (OCD)
Avila Carmelite Centre,
Bloomfield Avenue,
Morehampton Road,
Dublin 4
Tel 01-6430200

Noonan, James (SPS), CC
Foynes, Co Limerick
Tel 069-65165
(Shanagolden and Foynes,
Limerick)

Noonan, Joseph, Very Rev, PP
Adare, Co Limerick
Tel 061-396172/
087-2400700
(Adare, Limerick)

Noonan, Mark (CM), Very Rev
Phibsboro,
St Peter's, Dublin 7
Tel 01-8389708/8389841

Noonan, Michael, Very Rev,
PE
Portarlington, Co Laois
Tel 057-8623431
(Kildare & L., retired)

Noonan, Michael, Very Rev,
PP
The Presbytery, Raheen,
Limerick
Tel 061-301112/
087-6796217
(*Mungret/Crecora*, Limerick)

Noone, Cletus (OFM)
Franciscan Friary,
Ennis, Co Clare
Tel 065-6828751

Noone, Martin G., Very Rev,
VF
(Moderator)
St Mary's Prebytery,
Willbrook Road,
Rathfarnham, Dublin 14
Tel 01-4954554
Director, Lourdes Pilgrimage
Office, Holy Cross College,
Clonliffe Road, Dublin 3
Tel 01-8376820
(*Rathfarnham*, Dublin)

Noone, Sean
The Presbytery,
Pollathomas,
Co Mayo
(Dublin, retired)

Noone, Thomas, Very Rev, PP
69 Griffith Avenue,
Dublin 9
Tel 01-8332864
(*Marino*, Dublin)

Norman, James, PC
Dun Bhríd,
64 Orwell Park Rise,
Dublin 6W
Tel 01-8376027
(*Willington*, Dublin)

Norris, Thomas, Dr
Spiritual Director,
Pontificio Collegio,
Irlandese, Via dei Santi
Quattro 1,
00184, Rome, Italy
(Ossory)

Norton, Gerard (OP)
Prior, St Mary's Priory,
Tallaght, Dublin 24
Tel 01-4048100

Norton, Michael, Very Rev, PE
Rosbercon, New Ross,
Co Wexford
Tel 051-420333/
087-2580496
(*Rosbercon*, Ossory)

Nugent, Andrew (OSB)
Glenstal Abbey, Murroe,
Co Limerick
Tel 061-386103

Nugent, Eugene M.,
Archbishop, DCL
Apostolic Nunciature,
Villa Roma, Ivandry BP 650,
101 Antananarivo,
Madagascar
(Killaloe)

Nugent, William (CSSp)
Holy Spirit Missionary
College,
Kimmage Manor,
Dublin 12
Tel 01-4064300

Nulty, Denis, Most Rev, DD
Bishop of Kildare and
Leighlin,
Bishop's House, Carlow
Tel 059-9176725
(Kildare & L.)

Nwaogwugwu, Cornelius (CM)
St Vincent's College,
Castleknock,
Dublin 15
Tel 01-8213051

Nwakuna, Hyacinth (CSSp)
Blackrock College,
Blackrock,
Co Dublin
Tel 01-2888681
(*Blackrock*, Dublin)

Nyhan, Charles, CC
Cork Road, Carrigaline,
Co Cork
Tel 021-4371860
(*Carrigaline*, Cork & R.)

Nyland, P. J. (SDB)
Rector, Salesian House,
Warrenstown, Drumree,
Co Meath
Tel 01-8259894

# O

Ó Baoighill, Padraig, PP
Derrybeg, Letterkenny,
Co Donegal
Tel 074-9531310
Séiplineach,
Pobalscoil Ghaoth Dobhair,
Derrybeg, Letterkenny,
Co Donegal
Tel 074-9531040
(*Gweedore*, Raphoe)

Ó Baoill, Donnchadh, CC
Bun-a-leaca, Letterkenny,
Co Donegal
Tel 074-9531155
(*Gweedore*, Raphoe)

Ó Bréartúin, Liam S. (OCD)
53/55 Marlborough Road,
Dublin 4
Tel 01-6601832

Ó Brolcháin, Cormac (CSSp)
Blackrock College,
Blackrock, Co Dublin
Tel 01-2888681

Ó Cairbre, Padraig (SJ)
Director of Retreat
House/Vice-Rector,
Manresa House,
Dollymount, Dublin 3
Tel 01-8331352

Ó Ceallaigh, Fiachra (OFM),
Most Rev, DD, VG
Titular Bishop of Tre
Taverne and former
Auxiliary Bishop of Dublin,
Franciscan Friary, La Verna,
Gormanston, Co Meath
01-8412203
(Dublin)

Ó Ceannahbáin, Colm, Very
Rev, PE
An Tulach,
Baile na hAbhann
(Tuam)

Ó Cochláin, Pádraig, Very Rev,
PP
5 The Lawn, Finglas,
Dublin 11
Tel 01-8341894
(*Finglas*, Dublin)

Ó Cochláin, Seosamh, SP
c/o Diocesan Office,
Redemption Road, Cork
(Cork & R., retired)

Ó Conaire, Gearóid (OFM)
Adam & Eve's, 4 Merchant's
Quay, Dublin 8
Tel 01-6771128

Ó Conaire, Máirtín (OCD), PP
Kilronan,
Aran Islands, Co Galway
Tel 099-61221
(*Aran Islands*, Tuam)

Ó Conghaile, Eamon, CC
Tiernea, Lettermore,
Co Galway
Tel 091-551133
(*Carraroe (Kileen)*, Tuam)

Ó Cuill, Pádraig (OFMCap)
Capuchin Friary,
Church Street, Dublin 7
Tel 01-8730599

Ó Cuinn, Conall (SJ)
35 Lower Leeson Street,
Dublin 2
Tel 01-6761248

Ó Cuív, Liam, Very Rev, Co-PP
Blakestown, Clonsilla,
Dublin 15
Tel 01-8210874
(*Blakestown*, Dublin)

Ó Dálaigh, Micheál, Very Rev
Dean, AP
The Presbytery,
Curraheen Road, Cork
Tel 021-4343535
(*Curraheen Road*, Cork & R.)

Ó Dálaigh, Tadhg (MSC)
Woodview House,
Mount Merrion Avenue,
Blackrock, Co Dublin
Tel 01-2881644

Ó Dochartaigh, Michael, Very
Rev
Ard an Aonaigh,
Killarney, Co Kerry
(Kerry, retired)

Ó Dochartaigh, Tadhg, Very
Rev, PP
Firies, Killarney, Co Kerry
Tel 066-9764122
(*Firies*, Kerry)

Ó Domhnaill, Ruairí
Director of Vocations,
77 Lakelands,
Naas, Co Kildare
Tel 045-897470
(Kildare & L.)

Ó Donnchadha, Gearoid
'An tSaoirse', Fenit, Tralee,
Co Kerry
(Kerry, retired)

Ó Dúill, Piaras (OFMCap)
Capuchin Friary,
Church Street, Dublin 7
Tel 01-8730599

Ó Dúill, Séamus (SDS)
Ard Mhuire, Kilmoon,
Lisdoonvarna, Co Clare
Tel 086-1030261
(retired)

O Duláine, Connla (SJ)
St Ignatius Community &
Church, 27 Raleigh Row,
Salthill, Galway
Tel 091-523707

Ó Fatharta, Pádraig (SPS)
St Patrick's, Kiltegan,
Co Wicklow
Tel 059-6473600

Ó Fearghaill, Fergus, DSS
Carlow College,
College Street, Carlow
Tel 059-9153200
(Kildare & L.)

Ó Fearraí, Cathal, Very Rev,
PP, VF
Ballyshannon, Raphoe
Tel 071-9851295
(*Ballyshannon (Kilbarron)*,
Raphoe)

Ó Fiannachta, Pádraig, Rt Rev
Mgr
An Diseart, Green Street,
Dingle, Co Kerry
(Kerry, retired)

Ó Galláchóir, Nigel, CC
Dungloe, Co Donegal
Tel 074-9522194
Chaplain,
Rosses Community School,
Dungloe, Co Donegal
Tel 074-9521122
(*Dungloe (Templecrone and
Lettermacaward)*, Raphoe)

Ó Gallchóir, Colm, Very Rev,
PP
Killybegs, Co Donegal
Tel 074-9731030
(*Killybegs*, Raphoe)

Ó Gallchóir, Seán, Very Rev, PP
Tory Island, Co Donegal
Tel 074-9135214
(*Gortahork*, Raphoe)

Ó Giolláin, Leon (SJ)
Chaplain's Room,
St Stephen's, UCD,
Belfield, Dublin 4
John Sullivan House,
House of Formation,
27 Leinster Road,
Rathmines, Dublin 6
Tel 01-5242134

Ó Griofa, Gearóid, Very Rev, PP
Gort, Co Galway
Tel 091-631055
(Galway)

Ó hÍcí, Liam, PP
Ovens, Co Cork
Tel 021-4871180
(*Ovens*, Cork & R.)

Ó hAodha, Donncha
Nullamore,
Richmond Avenue South,
Dublin 6
Tel 01-4971239
(Opus Dei)

Ó hIceadha, Tomás, Very Rev, AP
Ballyferriter West,
Tralee, Co Kerry
Tel 066-9156499
(*Ballyferriter*, Kerry)

Ó hÓbáin, Eanna (OCarm), Very Rev, PP
Carmelite Presbytery,
Idrone Avenue,
Knocklyon, Dublin 16
Tel 01-4941204
(*Knocklyon*, Dublin)

Ó Huallacháin, Maelísa (OFM)
Franciscan House of Studies,
Dún Mhuire,
Seafield Road, Killiney,
Co Dublin
Tel 01-2826760

Ó Lainn, Máirtín, Very Rev
Carraroe, Co Galway
(Tuam, retired)

Ó Laoide, Caoimhín (OFM)
Guardian,
Franciscan Friary,
Ennis, Co Clare
Tel 065-6828751

Ó Loingsigh, Micheál, Very Rev, PP
Grenagh, Co Cork
Tel 021-4886128
(*Grenagh*, Cloyne)

Ó Longaigh, Seán, Very Rev, PP
Askeaton, Co Limerick
Tel 061-392249
(*Askeaton and Ballysteen*, Limerick)

O Maidín, Uinseann (OCSO)
Mount Melleray Abbey,
Cappoquin, Co Waterford
Tel 058-54404

Ó Máille, Padraig (SPS)
St Patrick's, 21 Leeson Park,
Dublin 6
Tel 01-4977897

Ó Maoldhomhnaigh, Conn, MA
Vice-President and Chaplain,
Carlow College,
College Street, Carlow
Tel 059-9153200
(Kildare & L.)

Ó Mathúna, Tadhg, Very Rev Canon, AP
2 Parochial House,
Blackrock, Cork
Tel 021-4358025
(*Blackrock*, Cork & R.)

Ó Murchú, Ailbe (OFM)
Guardian, Franciscan Friary,
Lady Lane, Waterford
Tel 051-874262

Ó Murchú, Daithí, CC
8 The Links, Knocknacarra,
Galway
Tel 091-590077
(*St John the Apostle*, Galway)

Ó Murchú, Tomás, SP
Riverstick, Kinsale, Co Cork
Tel 021-4771332
(*Clontead*, Cork & R.)

Ó Murchú, Diarmuid (MSC)
Formation House,
56 Mulvey Park, Dundrum,
Dublin 16
Tel 01-2951856

Ó Riain, Diarmaid (OFM)
Franciscan Friary,
Multyfarnham,
Co Westmeath
Tel 044-9371114/9371137

Ó Ríordáin, John J. (CSsR)
Mount Saint Alphonsus,
Limerick
Tel 061-315099

Ó Sabhaois, Ciaran (OCSO)
Mount Saint Joseph Abbey,
Roscrea, Co Tipperary
Tel 0505-25600

Ó Siochrú, Colm R.
Our Lady's Manor,
Bulloch Castle, Dalkey,
Co Dublin
(Dublin, retired)

Ó Súilleabháin, Pádraig (MSC), PP
Parish House, Leap,
Skibbereen, Co Cork
Tel 028-33177
(*Leap-Glandore*, Cork & R.)

Ó Tuathaigh, Antoin
c/o Diocesan Office,
Social Service Centre,
Henry Street, Limerick
(Limerick, retired)

O'Boyle, Aidan
Chicago
(Killala)

O'Boyle, Eugene
Hospital Chaplain,
The Monastery, Chapel
Street, Castlebar, Co Mayo
(Tuam)

O'Boyle, John, Rt Rev Mgr
Director, Diocesan Resource Centre,
Bishop Street,
Tuam, Co Galway
Tel 093-52284
(Tuam)

O'Boyle, Kevin, (SSC)
St Columban's, Dalgan Park,
Navan, Co Meath
Tel 046-9021525

O'Boyle, Paul, Very Rev, PP
Clane, Naas, Co Kildare
Tel 045-868249
(*Clane*, Kildare & L.)

O'Bric, Ailbe, Very Rev, PP
Clerihan, Clonmel,
Co Tipperary
Tel 052-6135118
(*Clerihan*, Cashel & E.)

O'Brien, Anthony (OCSO)
Mount Saint Joseph Abbey,
Roscrea, Co Tipperary
Tel 0505-25600

O'Brien, Anthony, Very Rev, PP
Carrigtwohill, Co Cork
Tel 021-4883236
(*Carrigtwohill*, Cloyne)

O'Brien, Augustine (MSC)
'Croí Nua', Rosary Lane,
Taylor's Hill, Galway
Tel 091-520960

O'Brien, Ben (OSA)
Duckspool House,
Abbeyside, Dungarvan,
Co Waterford
Tel 058-23784

O'Brien, Brendan J. (CSSp)
Holy Spirit Missionary
College, Kimmage Manor,
Dublin 12
Tel 01-4064300

O'Brien, Christopher, Very Rev, PE
Haroldstown, Tobinstown,
Tullow, Co Carlow
Tel 059-9161633
(Armagh, retired)

O'Brien, Daniel (MSC)
Myross Wood Retreat
House, Leap, Skibbereen,
Co Cork
Tel 028-33118

O'Brien, Donal, Very Rev, PP
Episcopal Vicar for the
Gaeltacht
Ballyvourney, Co Cork
Tel 026-45042
(*Ballyvourney*, Cloyne)

O'Brien, Eamon, Very Rev
No. 5 Hopecroft,
Main Street,
Glenavy BT29 4LN
(Down & C., retired)

O'Brien, Eamonn
Church Road, Croom,
Co Limerick
Tel 061-397213/087-0767521
(*Croom*, Limerick)

O'Brien, Eamonn, Very Rev, PE
Newbrook Nursing Home,
Mullingar, Co Westmeath
(Meath, retired)

O'Brien, Francis, Very Rev, PP
81 Castle Street,
Ballymoney,
Co Antrim BT53 6JT
Tel 028-27662003
(*Ballymoney and Derrykeighan*, Down & C.)

O'Brien, Gerard, Very Rev, PP
Bornacoola,
Carrick-on-Shannon,
Co Leitrim
Tel 071-9638229
(*Bornacoola*, Ardagh & Cl.)

O'Brien, Gregory, Very Rev, PP
2 Rossmore Road,
Templeogue, Dublin 6W
Tel 01-4508432
(*Willington*, Dublin)

O'Brien, Humbert (OP)
St Magdalen's, Drogheda,
Co Louth
Tel 041-9838271

O'Brien, James
Sacred Heart Residence,
Sybil Hill Road, Killester,
Dublin 5
(Dublin, retired)

O'Brien, James, Rt Rev Mgr
Congregation for Divine
Worship and the Discipline
of the Sacraments,
Vatican City 00120, Italy
Tel 003906-69884551
(Cloyne)

O'Brien, James, Very Rev, AP
Feakle, Co Clare
Tel 061-924035/087-2665793
(*Feakle & Killanena-Flagmount*, Killaloe)

O'Brien, John (OFM)
Franciscan Friary,
Liberty Street, Cork
Tel 021-4270302

O'Brien, John (SMA)
Superior, SMA House,
82 Ranelagh Road,
Ranelagh, Dublin 6
Tel 01-4968162/3

O'Brien, John Scroope, Very Rev, Adm
Parochial House,
211 Navan Road, Dublin 7
Tel 01-8681436
(*Navan Road*, Dublin)

O'Brien, John, Very Rev, PP
Borris, Co Carlow via
Kilkenny
Tel 059-9773128
(*Borris*, Kildare & L.)

O'Brien, John, Very Rev, PP
Parochial House, Oristown,
Kells, Co Meath
Tel 046-9054124
(*Oristown*, Meath)

O'Brien, John Joseph (SAC)
Pallottine College, Thurles,
Co Tipperary
Tel 0504-21202

O'Brien, Jordan (OP), Very
Rev, PP
Prior, St Saviour's,
Glentworth Street, Limerick
Tel 061-412333
(*St Saviour's*, Limerick)

O'Brien, Joseph (OP), Very Rev
Prior, St Dominic's, Athy,
Co Kildare
Tel 059-8631573

O'Brien, Joseph, Very Rev
Canon, PP
Abbey, Tuam, Go Galway
Tel 093-43510
(*Abbeyknockmoy*, Tuam)

O'Brien, Kennedy (SJ)
Minister, Gonzaga College,
Sandford Road, Dublin 6
Tel 01-4972943

O'Brien, Kieran (OSA)
Duckspool House
(Retirement Community),
Abbeyside, Dungarvan,
Co Waterford
Tel 058-23784

O'Brien, Kieran, Very Rev,
Adm, VF
Killarney, Co Kerry
Tel 064-6631014
(*Killarney*, Kerry)

O'Brien, Leonard, Rt Rev Mgr,
PE
O'Rahilly Street, Clonakilty,
Co Cork
(Cork & R., retired)

O'Brien, Liam, Very Rev, PP
Sneem, Co Kerry
Tel 064-6645141
(*Sneem*, Kerry)

O'Brien, Liam (MSC)
Woodview House,
Mount Merrion Avenue,
Blackrock, Co Dublin
Tel 01-2881644

O'Brien, Lorcan, Rt Rev Mgr,
Adm
Parochial House, Stillorgan
Road, Dublin 4
Tel 087-2408975
(*Donnybrook*, Dublin)

O'Brien, Martin, Very Rev, PP
Newline, Tulla, Co Clare
Tel 065-6835117/087-
2504075
(*Tulla*, Killaloe)

O'Brien, Michael
St Anne's Presbytery,
Convent Hill, Waterford
Tel 051-855819
(*Ballybricken*, Waterford &
L.)

O'Brien, Michael (MHM)
(Residing elsewhere in
Ireland)

O'Brien, Ned (SAC)
Provincial House,
'Homestead',
Sandyford Road, Dundrum,
Dublin 16
Tel 01-2956180/2954170

O'Brien, Pat (SPS), CC
Curate's House, Prosperous,
Co Kildare
Tel 045-868187
(*Prosperous*, Kildare & L.)

O'Brien, Pat, Very Rev, PP
Caherlistrane, Co Galway
Tel 093-55428
(*Caherlistrane
(Donaghpatrick and
Kilcoona)*, Tuam)

O'Brien, Patrick, Very Rev
Canon
No 9 Bungalow,
Chambersland,
New Ross, Co Wexford
(Ferns)

O'Brien, Paul (OSA)
St John's Priory,
Thomas Street, Dublin 8
Tel 01-6770393/0415/0601

O'Brien, Peter, Very Rev
Kilfian, Killala, Co Mayo
Tel 096-32420
(Killala)

O'Brien, Sean (MHM)
St Joseph's House,
50 Orwell Park, Rathgar,
Dublin 6
Tel 01-4127700

O'Brien, Terence (MSC), Very
Rev, PP
Sacred Heart Parish,
Western Road, Cork
Tel 021-4804120
(*Sacred Heart*, Cork & R.)

O'Brien, Thomas (MSC)
Western Road, Cork
Tel 021-4804120

O'Brien, Timothy, Very Rev, PP
Carrigatoher, Nenagh,
Co Tipperary
Tel 067-31231/087-
6548331/087-2623922
(*Portroe (Castletown Arrha)*,
*Youghalarra*, Killaloe)

O'Brien, Valentine (CSSp)
Holy Spirit Missionary
College, Kimmage Manor,
Dublin 12
Tel 01-4064300

O'Byrne, Christopher, Rt Rev
Mgr Canon, PE, AP
Parochial House,
12 Aughrim Road,
Magherafelt,
Co Derry BT45 6AY
Tel 028-79634038
(*Magherafelt and Ardtrea
North*, Armagh)

O'Byrne, Christopher, Very
Rev, PP
Lawrencetown, Ballinasloe,
Co Galway
Tel 090-9685613
(*Lawrencetown and
Kiltormer*, Clonfert)

O'Byrne, Gerard, Very Rev, PP
Rathangan, Co Kildare
Tel 045-524316
(*Rathangan*, Kildare & L.)

O'Byrne, Hugh, Very Rev, PP
Blackwater, Enniscorthy,
Co Wexford
Tel 053-9127118
(*Blackwater*, Ferns)

O'Byrne, John, AP
St Mary's, Athlunkard
Street, Limerick
Tel 085-7491268
(*St Mary's*, Limerick)

O'Byrne, John Bosco (OFM)
Franciscan Friary,
Liberty Street, Cork
Tel 021-4270302

O'Byrne, Michael, Very Rev,
PP
Kilmeaden, Co Waterford
Tel 051-384117
(*Portlaw*, Waterford & L.)

O'Byrne, Paddy, CC
Presbytery No 2,
Church Grounds
Tel 01-2882257
(*Kilmacud-Stillorgan*,
Dublin)

O'Byrne, Patrick, PE, CC
Daingean, Co Offaly
Tel 057-9344161
(*Daingean*, Kildare & L.)

O'Byrne, Patrick, Co-PP
No. 2 The Presbytery,
Mountview,
Blanchardstown, Dublin 15
Tel 01-8216380
(*Mountview*, Dublin)

O'Byrne, Patrick J., CC
188 Lower Kilmacud Road,
Kilmacud, Co Dublin
Tel 01-2981955
(*Mount Merrion*, Dublin)

O'Byrne, Thomas, Very Rev, PP
Myshall, Co Carlow
Tel 059-9157635
(*Clonegal, Myshall*, Kildare
& L.)

O'Byrne, William, Very Rev, PP
Kill, Co Kildare
Tel 045-878008
(*Kill*, Kildare & L.)

O'Callaghan, Flor (OSA)
St Augustine's Priory,
Dungarvan,
Co Waterford
Tel 058-41136

O'Callaghan, Benedict
(OCarm), Very Rev, PP
Ballyhale, Co Kilkenny
Tel 056-7768686
(*Ballyhale*, Ossory)

O'Callaghan, Ciarán (CSsR)
Vicar-Superior,
Marianella/Liguori House,
75 Orwell Road, Dublin 6
Tel 01-4067100

O'Callaghan, Denis, Rt Rev
Mgr, PE
Mallow, Co Cork
Tel 022-21112
(Cloyne, retired)

O'Callaghan, Donal
Muintir Mhuire, Ballybutler,
Ladysbridge, Co Cork
Tel 024-98852
(Cloyne)

O'Callaghan, Edward (OFM)
Vicar, Franciscan Friary,
Liberty Street, Cork
Tel 021-4270302

O'Callaghan, Enda (SJ)
St Ignatius Community &
Church, 27 Raleigh Row,
Salthill, Galway
Tel 091-523707

O'Callaghan, Flor (OSA), Very
Rev, PP
St Augustine's,
Taylor's Lane,
Ballyboden, Dublin 16
Tel 01-4944966
(*Ballyboden*, Dublin)

O'Callaghan, John (OSB)
Glenstal Abbey, Murroe,
Co Limerick
Tel 061-386103

O'Callaghan, Kevin, Rt Rev
Mgr, AP, VG, VF
The Presbytery, Lissarda,
Co Cork
Tel 021-7336053
(*Kilmurry, Ovens*, Cork & R.)

O'Callaghan, Martin, Very Rev
Prof
c/o 73 Somerton Road,
Belfast BT15 4DE
(Down & C., retired)

O'Callaghan, Peadar, Very
Rev, PE
Suimhneas, Charleville,
Co Cork
Tel 086-8054040
(Cloyne, retired)

O'Caoimh, Tomás
St Brendan's,
Tralee, Co Kerry
Tel 066-7125932
(*Tralee, St Brendan's*, Kerry)

O'Carroll, Caimin, Very Rev
Canon, AP
Barefield, Ennis, Co Clare
Tel 065-6821190/
087-2521388
(*Doora and Kilraghtis*,
Killaloe)

O'Connell, Ciaran, Very Rev
Mgr
Rector,
Pontifical Irish College,
Via Dei SS. Quattro 1,
00184, Roma, Italy

O'Carroll, Dermot (CP)
St Gabriel's Retreat,
The Graan, Enniskillen,
Co Fermanagh
Tel 028-66322272

O'Carroll, Gerard (SPS)
St Patrick's, Main Street,
Knock, Co Mayo
Tel 094-9388661

O'Ciarain, Peadar
Sons of Divine Providence,
Orione House,
13 Lower Teddington Road,
Hampton, Wick,
Kinston-upon-Thames,
KT1 4EU
(Dublin, retired)

O'Connell, Alphonsus (OCSO)
Mount Melleray Abbey,
Cappoquin, Co Waterford
Tel 058-54404

O'Connell, Anthony, Very Rev
5 Parkside, Stoneybatter,
Wexford
(Ferns, retired)

O'Connell, Chrysostom (OCSO)
Our Lady of Bethlehem
Abbey,
11 Ballymena Road,
Portglenone, Ballymena,
Co Antrim BT44 8BL
Tel 028-25821211

O'Connell, Con (MSC)
Woodview House,
Mount Merrion Avenue,
Blackrock, Co Dublin
Tel 01-2881644

O'Connell, Conal (SSC)
St Columban's, Dalgan Park,
Navan, Co Meath
Tel 046-9021525

O'Connell, David, CC
The Bungalow,
St Mary & St John,
Ballincollig, Co Cork
Tel 021-4877161
(*Ballincollig*, Cork & R.)

O'Connell, Gerard, CC
Irremore, Listowel, Co Kerry
Tel 068-40244
(*Lixnaw*, Kerry)

O'Connell, James (SM), Very
Rev, Adm
Holy Family Parish, Dundalk,
Co Louth
Tel 042-9336301
(*Dundalk, Holy Family*,
Armagh)

O'Connell, James, Very Rev,
PP
Stradbally, Co Laois
Tel 057-8625132
(*Stradbally*, Kildare & L.)

O'Connell, Jim (MHM)
Vice-Rector and Editor of
Advocate, St Joseph's,
Mill Hill Missionaries,
Waterford Road, Kilkenny
Tel 056-7721482

O'Connell, Jimmy (SM), Adm
Superior, Holy Family Parish,
Parochial House, Dundalk,
Co Louth
Tel 042-9336301
(*Holy Family*, Armagh)

O'Connell, John, Very Rev, AP
Moyne, Thurles,
Co Tipperary
Tel 0504-45129
(*Templetuohy*, Cashel & E.)

O'Connell, John, Very Rev, PE
53 Ardmore Wood,
The Presbytery,
Herbert Road, Bray,
Co Wicklow
Tel 01-2867309
(Dublin, retired)

O'Connell, John, Very Rev, PE
Caragh, Naas, Co Kildare
Tel 045-875602
(Kildare & L., retired)

O'Connell, John (Seán) (CSSp)
Holy Spirit Missionary
College, Kimmage Manor,
Dublin 12
Tel 01-406 4300

O'Connell, Liam (SJ)
Assistant Provincial,
Irish Jesuit Provincialite,
Milltown Park,
Sandford Road, Dublin 6
Tel 01-4987333
Jesuit Curia Community,
Loyola House,
Milltown Park,
Sandford Road, Dublin 6
Tel 01-2180276

O'Connell, Martin (SPS)
St Patrick's, Kiltegan,
Co Wicklow
Tel 059-6473600

O'Connell, Michael (MSC)
MSC Mission Support
Centre, PO Box 23,
Western Road, Cork
Tel 021-4545704/4543988

O'Connell, Pat (CSsR)
Marianella, 75 Orwell Road,
Dublin 6
Tel 01-4067100

O'Connell, Patrick (MHM)
Vice-Rector,
St Joseph's House,
50 Orwell Park, Rathgar,
Dublin 6
Tel 01-4127700

O'Connell, Philip, Very Rev, PE
32 Knockmoyle Est,
Tralee, Co Kerry
(Kerry, retired)

O'Connell, Raymond (OSM),
Very Rev
Servite Priory, Benburb,
Dungannon,
Co Tyrone, BT71 7JZ
Tel 028-37548241

O'Connell, Seamus, PEm
St Patrick's College,
Maynooth, Co Kildare
Tel 01-6285222
(Derry, retired)

O'Connell, T. J.
Kent, England
Tel 0044-1843-299340
(Clonfert)

O'Connell, Terence
142 Mayorstone Park,
Limerick
(Limerick, retired)

O'Connell, Tomás, CC
Cathedral Presbytery,
Thurles, Co Tipperary
Tel 0504-22229/22779
(*Thurles, Cathedral of the
Assumption*, Cashel & E.)

O'Connell, Vincent (CSSp)
Holy Spirit Missionary
College, Kimmage Manor,
Whitehall Road, Dublin 12
Tel 01-4064300

O'Conor, Joseph, PEm
17 Ashbourne View,
Omagh,
Co Tyrone BT78 1HN
Tel 028-82244806
(Derry, retired)

O'Connor, Alphonsus (OCSO)
Mellifont Abbey, Collon,
Co Louth
Tel 041-9826103

O'Connor, Anthony, Very Rev,
PP
Kilmacow, via Waterford,
Co Kilkenny
Tel 051-885269/087-2517766
(*Kilmacow*, Ossory)

O'Connor, Benjamin
c/o Cloyne Diocesan Centre,
Cobh, Co Cork
Tel 021-4811430
(Cloyne)

O'Connor, Bernard (SSC)
St Columban's Retirement
Home, Dalgan Park, Navan,
Co Meath
Tel 046-9021525

O'Connor, Brendan
Ely University Centre,
10 Hume Street, Dublin 2
Tel 01-6767420
(Opus Dei)

O'Connor, Charles (OMI)
170 Merrion Road,
Ballsbridge, Dublin 4
Tel 01-2693658

O'Connor, Christopher (MHM)
St Joseph's House,
50 Orwell Park, Rathgar,
Dublin 6
Tel 01-4127700

O'Connor, Christopher, Very
Rev Dean, PE
Craughwell, Co Galway
Tel 091-846124
(Galway, retired)

O'Connor, Columba (OSA)
Duckspool House
(Retirement Community),
Abbeyside, Dungarvan,
Co Waterford
Tel 058-23784

O'Connor, Dan (MSC)
Carrignavar, Co Cork
Tel 021-4884044

O'Connor, Daniel J., Rt Rev
Mgr, PC
St Mary's, Irishtown Road,
Dublin 4
Tel 01-6697429
(*Ringsend*, Dublin)

O'Connor, Daniel, Very Rev
Canon, PE
The Presbytery, Dungarvan,
Co Waterford
Tel 058-42381
(Waterford & L., retired)

O'Connor, Daniel (MHM)
St Joseph's House,
50 Orwell Park,
Rathgar, Dublin 6
Tel 01-4127700

O'Connor, Declan, Very Rev
Canon, PP, VF
Listowel, Co Kerry
Tel 068-21188
(*Listowel*, Kerry)

O'Connor, Denis, (CSsR) CC
32 Auburn Drive,
Dublin 15
Tel 01-8214003
(*Castleknock*, Dublin)

O'Connor, Dermot (CSsR)
St Patrick's, Esker, Athenry,
Co Galway
Tel 091-844007

O'Connor, Dermot (SJ)
Irish Jesuit Provincialate,
Milltown Park,
Sandford Road, Dublin 6
Tel 01-4987333

O'Connor, Dominic (OP)
St Dominic's, Athy,
Co Kildare
Tel 059-8631573

O'Connor, Donal, PP
The Presbytery, Beaufort
Co Kerry
Tel 064-6644128
(*Beaufort*, Kerry)

O'Connor, Eamonn, Very Rev,
PP
Rooskey,
Carrick-on-Shannon,
Co Roscommon
Tel 071-9638014
(*Kilglass*, Elphin)

O'Connor, Edward (SMA)
Vice-Superior,
African Missions,
Blackrock Road, Cork
Tel 021-4292871

O'Connor, Erill, Very Rev
Canon
14 Clare Road,
Drumcondra, Dublin 9
(Dublin, retired)

O'Connor, Fergus (Opus Dei),
Very Rev, PP
31 Herbert Avenue,
Dublin 4
Tel 01-2692001
(*Merrion Road*, Dublin)

O'Connor, Frank, CC
St John's Cathedral,
Cathedral House,
Cathedral Place, Limerick
Tel 061-414624/087-2589279
(*St John's*, Limerick)

O'Connor, Gerard, PP
Aglish, Cappoquin,
Co Waterford
Tel 024-96287
(*Aglish*, Waterford & L.)

O'Connor, Gerry (CSsR), CC
52 Elmdale Park,
Dublin 10
Tel 01-6233813
(*Cherry Orchard*, Dublin)

O'Connor, James (CSsR)
Mount Saint Alphonsus,
Limerick
Tel 061-315099

O'Connor, John (SAC), Very
Rev, PP
Provincial Secretary,
St Benin's, Dublin Road,
Shankill, Co Dublin
Tel 01-2824425
(*Shankill*, Dublin)

O'Connor, John C., Very Rev
c/o Lisbreen,
73 Somerton Road,
Belfast BT15 4DE
(Down & C., retired)

O'Connor, John (OSA)
Duckspool House,
Abbeyside, Dungarvan,
Co Waterford
Tel 058-23784

O'Connor, John, J. (OSA)
Bursar for Orlagh and
Ballyboden
Orlagh Retreat Centre,
Old Court Road, Dublin 16
Tel 01-4930932/4933315

O'Connor, Kevin
Oblate House of Retreat,
Inchicore, Dublin 8
Tel 01-4534408/4541805

O'Connor, Laurence, Very Rev,
PP
Bunclody, Enniscorthy,
Co Wexford
Tel 053-9377319
(*Bunclody*, Ferns)

O'Connor, Liam (OCSO)
Mount Saint Joseph Abbey,
Roscrea, Co Tipperary
Tel 0505-25600

O'Connor, Martin, Very Rev,
PP
Ballindine, Co Mayo
Tel 094-9364423
Administration For
Crossboyne and Taugheen
(*Ballindine (Kilvine)*, Tuam)

O'Connor, Michael (CSSp), CC
Presbytery No. 2,
Church Grounds,
Kill Avenue, Dun Laoghaire,
Co Dublin
Tel 01-2140863
(*Kill-O'-The-Grange*, Dublin)

O'Connor, Michael G. (CSsR)
Mount Saint Alphonsus,
Limerick
Tel 061-315099

O'Connor, Michael, Very Rev
c/o St John's Pastoral Centre,
John's Hill, Waterford
(Waterford & L.)

O'Connor, Muiris, Very Rev,
VF
Pastoral Area Assignment,
Askeaton, Co Limerick
(Limerick)

O'Connor, Oliver (SVD)
1 & 3 Pembroke Road,
Dublin 4
Tel 01-6680904

O'Connor, Padraig, Very Rev
Canon, PP, VF
Mountbellew, Ballinasloe,
Co Galway
Tel 090-9679235
(*Moylough and
Mountbellew*, Tuam)

O'Connor, Pat (CSsR)
Clonard Monastery,
1 Clonard Gardens,
Belfast, BT13 2RL
Tel 028-90445950

O'Connor, Patrick, Very Rev,
PP, VF
Parochial House, Athboy,
Co Meath
Tel 046-9432184
(*Athboy*, Meath)

O'Connor, Peter, Very Rev
The Presbytery
Chapel Green, Rush,
Co Dublin
Tel 01-8437208
(*Rush*, Dublin)

O'Connor, Peter, Very Rev,
Co-PP
The Presbytery, Baldoyle,
Dublin 13
Tel 01-8322060
(*Baldoyle*, Dublin)

O'Connor, Philip, Very Rev, PP
Parochial House, Dysart,
Mullingar, Co Westmeath
Tel 044-9226122
(*Dysart*, Meath)

O'Connor, Richard
Villa Maria Assunta, Via
Aurelia Antica 284,
00-165, Roma, Italia
(Kerry)

O'Connor, Seamus (SSC)
St Columban's, Dalgan Park,
Navan, Co Meath
Tel 046-9021525

O'Connor, Sean
St John's Presbytery,
Kilkenny
Tel 056-7756889
(*St John's*, Ossory)

O'Connor, Thomas, DD
St Patrick's College,
Maynooth, Co Kildare
Tel 01-6285222
(Meath)

O'Connor, Tom, CC
Dublin Road, Portlaoise,
Co Laois
Tel 057-8692153
(*Portlaoise*, Kildare & L.)

O'Connor, Tom (OSCam)
St Camillus,
South Hill Avenue,
Blackrock, Co Dublin

O'Connor, Tom (SPS)
St Patrick's, Kiltegan,
Co Wicklow
Tel 059-6473600

O'Conor, Joe (SPS)
St Patrick's, Kiltegan,
Co Wicklow
Tel 059-6473600

O'Conor, Patrick (SSC), CC
Mulrankin, Co Wexford
Tel 053-9135166
(*Kilmore*, Ferns)

O'Cuilleanáin, Fionnbarra
(SMA)
African Missions,
Blackrock Road, Cork
Tel 021-4292871

O'Cuiv, Shan
Team Assistant, c/o The
Presbytery, Clonburris,
Clondalkin, Dublin 22
Tel 01-4573440
(*Clondalkin/Rowlagh/
Neilstown/Deansrath/
Bawnogue*, Dublin)

O'Dea, Donal (SSC)
St Columban's, Dalgan Park,
Navan, Co Meath
Tel 046-9021525

O'Dea, Egbert (OFM)
The Abbey, 8 Francis Street,
Galway
Tel 091-562518

O'Dea, Francis, Very Rev, PP
Knockacraig,
Dromcollogher, Co Limerick
Tel 087-2443106
(*Dromcollogher/Broadford*,
Limerick)

O'Dea, Tom
Ballynacally, Co Clare
Tel 065-6838135/
086-8107475
(*Ballynacally*, Killaloe)

O'Doherty, Bartie (SPS)
St Patrick's, Kiltegan,
Co Wicklow
Tel 059-6473600

O'Doherty, Colm, PP
16 Castlefin Road,
Castlederg,
Co Tyrone BT81 7BT
Tel 028-81671393
(*Castlederg*, Derry)

O'Doherty, Daniel, Very Rev,
PE
Ballyheerin, Fanad,
Co Donegal
(Raphoe, retired)

O'Doherty, Donal, Very Rev
Mgr, PE
Holy Cross,
Upper Kilmacud Road,
Dundrum, Dublin 14
Tel 01-2985264
(Dublin, retired)

O'Doherty, Kevin (SPS)
St Patrick's, Kiltegan,
Co Wicklow
Tel 059-6473600

O'Doherty, Kevin, Very Rev,
PE
Nazareth House,
Fahan, Co Donegal
(Raphoe, retired)

O'Doherty, Kieran, Very Rev,
PP, VF
34 Moneysharvin Road,
Swatragh, Maghera,
Co Derry BT46 5PY
Tel 028-79401236
(*Swatragh*, Derry)

O'Doherty, Michael, Very Rev
Canon
No. 1 Lynch Heights,
Sun Hill, Killorglin,
Co Kerry
(Kerry, retired)

O'Doherty, Oliver, Very Rev
The Presbytery,
Church Road, Nenagh,
Co Tipperary
(Killaloe, retired)

O'Doherty, Seán, Very Rev
Canon, PP
Durrow, Portlaoise, Co Laois
Tel 057-8736156
(Durrow, Ossory)

O'Donnell, Anthony (SMA)
African Missions,
Blackrock Road, Cork
Tel 021-4292871

O'Donnell, Brian, CC
157 Glen Road, Maghera,
Co Derry BT46 5JN
Tel 028-79642359
(Maghera, Derry)

O'Donnell, Chris
Director, Limerick Diocesan
Pastoral Centre,
St Michael's Courtyard,
Denmark Street, Limerick
Tel 061-400133
(Limerick)

O'Donnell, Christopher
(OCarm)
Terenure College, Terenure,
Dublin 6W
Tel 01-4904621

O'Donnell, Cornelius, Very
Rev
Rathcormac, Fermoy,
Co Cork
Tel 025-36286
(Cloyne, retired)

O'Donnell, Desmond (OMI)
Oblate House of Retreat,
Inchicore, Dublin 8
Tel 01-4534408/4541805

O'Donnell, Edward (SJ)
Gonzaga College,
Sandford Road, Dublin 6
Tel 01-4972943

O'Donnell, Edward, Very Rev,
PP
42 Derryvolgie Avenue,
Belfast BT9 6FP
Tel 028-90665409
(St Brigid's, Down & C.)

O'Donnell, Gerard, Very Rev
On leave
Station Road, Ballina,
Co Mayo
(Killala)

O'Donnell, Hugh (OFM)
Assistant, St Fergal's,
Killarney Road,
Bray, Co Wicklow
Tel 01-2860980
(Bray (Ballywaltrim), Dublin)

O'Donnell, Hugh (SDB)
Rinaldi House,
72 Sean McDermott Street,
Dublin 1
Tel 01-8363358

O'Donnell, James, Very Rev,
PP
Killenaule, Co Tipperary
Tel 052-9156244
(Killenaule, Cashel & E.)

O'Donnell, James, Rt Rev Mgr,
AP
Macroom, Co Cork
Tel 026-41042
(Macroom, Cloyne)

O'Donnell, John
9 Rockview, Blacklion,
Co Cavan
(Kilmore, retired)

O'Donnell, Joseph, CC
Director of Vocations,
Parochial House,
Mountcharles, Co Donegal
Tel 074-9735009
(Inver, Raphoe)

O'Donnell, Louis (OSA)
St John's Priory,
Thomas Street, Dublin 8
Tel 01-6770393

O'Donnell, Michael (MSC)
MSC Mission Support
Centre,
PO Box 23, Western Road,
Cork
Tel 021-4545704

O'Donnell, Owen, Very Rev,
PE
Parochial House, Dunamore,
Cookstown, Co Tyrone
Tel 028-86751216
(Armagh, retired)

O'Donnell, P.J.
c/o Diocesan Office,
Social Service Centre,
Henry Street, Limerick
(Limerick, retired)

O'Donnell, Pat, Very Rev, PP
Rathmore, Co Kerry
Tel 064-7758026
(Rathmore, Kerry)

O'Donnell, Terence (IC)
Clonturk House,
Ormond Road,
Drumcondra, Dublin 9
Tel 01-6877014

O'Donoghue, Brendan, Very
Rev Canon, AP
12 Tullyglass Square,
Shannon, Co Clare
Tel 061-361257/086-8308153
(Shannon, Killaloe)

O'Donoghue, Fergus (SJ)
Parish Chaplain,
The Presbytery,
Upper Gardiner Street,
Dublin 1
Tel 01-8363411
(Gardiner Street, Dublin)

O'Donoghue, James (MHM),
CC
St Mary's, Marquis Street,
Belfast BT1 1JJ
Tel 028-90320482
(St Mary's, Down & C.)

O'Donoghue, James
Chaplain Mid Western
Hospital,
37 Gouldavoher Estate,
Dooradoyle, Limerick
Tel 087-8383525
(Cashel & E.)

O'Donoghue, James, CC
Kilsheelan, Clonmel,
Co Tipperary
Tel 052-6133292
(Kilsheelan, Waterford & L.)

O'Donoghue, Jim (MHM)
St Mary's Parish,
25 Marquis Street,
Belfast BT1 1JJ
Tel 028-90320482
(St Mary's, Down & C.)

O'Donohoe, Joseph (OPraem)
(elsewhere in Ireland)
c/o Abbey of the Most Holy,
Trinity and St Norbert,
Kilnacrott Abbey,
Ballyjamesduff,
Co Cavan
Tel 049-8544416

O'Donoghue, Neil, CC
Ard Easmuinn, Dundalk,
Co Louth
Tel 042-9334259
(Dundalk, Holy Redeemer,
Armagh)

O'Donoghue, Neville (SM)
St Columba's,
Church Avenue, Ballybrack,
Co Dublin
Tel 01-2858301

O'Donoghue, Patrick
119 Grace Park Manor,
Drumcondra, Dublin 9
(Dublin)

O'Donoghue, Patrick, CC
129 Túr Uisce, Doughiska,
Galway
Tel 091-756823
(Good Shepherd, Galway)

O'Donoghue, Patrick, CC
Oliver Villa, Mount Crozier,
Cobh, Co Cork
Tel 021-4201623
(Cobh, St. Colman's
Cathedral, Cloyne)

O'Donoghue, Patrick, Most
Rev
Bishop Emeritus of
Lancaster, Nazareth House,
Mallow, Co Cork
Tel 022-21561
(Cloyne)

O'Donoghue, Paul, CC
The Lough Presbytery,
St Finbarr's West, Cork
Tel 021-4322633
(The Lough, Cork & R.)

O'Donohue, Vincent, Very Rev
Canon, PE
18 Kilcrea Park,
Magazine Road, Co Cork
Tel 021-4856881
(Cloyne, retired)

O'Donovan, Chris
The Presbytery, Skibbereen,
Co Cork
Tel 028-22878/22877
(St Patrick's Cathedral,
Skibbereen, Rath and the
Islands, Cork & R.)

O'Donovan, Colman, Very Rev
Canon, PE
1 Youghal Road, Midleton,
Co Cork
Tel 021-4621617
(Cloyne, retired)

O'Donovan, Dan, CC
Creagh, Ballinasloe,
Co Galway
Tel 090-9645080
(Ballinasloe, Creagh &
Kilclooney, Clonfert)

O'Donovan, Ignatius (OSA)
St Augustine's Priory,
O'Connell Street,
Limerick,
Tel 061-415374

O'Donovan, James, Very Rev
Canon, PP
Ballinlough, Cork
Tel 021-4292296
(Ballinlough, Cork & R.)

O'Donovan, John, CC
The Presbytery,
Dunmanway, Co Cork
Tel 028-8845000
(Dunmanway, Cork & R.)

O'Donovan, John, Very Rev,
PP
Parochial House,
Hattons Alley,
Blackpool, Cork
Tel 021-4501022
(Blackpool/The Glen, Cork &
R.)

O'Donovan, Michael, Very
Rev, PP
The Presbytery, Caheragh,
Co Cork
Tel 028-31126
(Caheragh, Cork & R.)

O'Donovan, Padraig (SSC)
(priest in charge)
67-68 Castle Dawson,
Rathcoffey Road, Maynooth,
Co Kildare
Tel 01-6286036
Regional Vice-Director,
Dalgan Park, Navan,
Co Meath
Tel 046-9021525

O'Donovan, Pat, CC
Parochial House, Tirelton,
Macroom, Co Cork
Tel 026-46012/086-2578065
(Kilmichael, Uibh Laoire,
Cork & R.)

O'Donovan, Raymond (OP)
Newbridge College,
Droichead Nua, Co Kildare
Tel 045-487200

O'Donovan, Tadhg CC
Midleton, Co Cork
Tel 087-6292192
(Midleton, Cloyne)

O'Donovan, William, Very
Rev, PP
Conna, Mallow, Co Cork
Tel 058-59138
(Conna, Cloyne)

O'Dowd, Gabriel, CC
The Presbytery,
St Margaret's, Finglas,
Dublin 11
Tel 01-8341009
(Finglas, Dublin)

O'Dowd, Sean (SPS), CC
Deerpark Road, Athlone,
Co Westmeath
Tel 090 6490575
(Athlone, SS Peter and
Paul's, Elphin)

O'Driscoll, Aidan, Rt Rev Mgr,
Adm
The Presbytery, Clonakilty,
Co Cork
Tel 023-8833165
(Ballyroe, Clonakilty and
Darrara, Cork & R.)

O'Driscoll, Eamonn (OFM)
Vicar, Franciscan Friary,
Multyfarnham, Co
Westmeath
Tel 044-9371114/9371137

O'Driscoll, Fachtna (SMA)
Superior General,
Generalate, Via della
Nocetta 111,
00164 Rome, Italy
Tel 06-6616841

O'Driscoll, Kieron, PP
Barrett's Hill, Ballinhassig,
Co Cork
Tel 021-4885104
(Ballinhassig, Cork & R.)

O'Driscoll, Liam, Very Rev
Canon, Adm
Church of the Most Precious
Blood, Clogheen, Co Cork
Tel 021-4392122
(Clogheen (Kerry Pike), Cork
& R.)

O'Driscoll, Martin, Very Rev,
PP, Adm
Parochial House,
Inchigeelagh, Co Cork
Tel 026-49838
(Kilmichael, Cork & R.)

O'Driscoll, Michael
Bushmount, Clonakilty,
Co Cork
Tel 023-33991
(Cork & R., retired)

O'Driscoll, Neil (SJ)
(Residing elsewhere)
St Francis Xavier's,
Upper Gardiner Street,
Dublin 1
Tel 01-8363411

O'Driscoll, P.J., CC
Monument Hill, Fermoy,
Co Cork
Tel 087-6490381
(Fermoy, Cloyne)

O'Driscoll, Paul, Very Rev,
Adm
Parochial House,
Castledermot, Co Kildare
Tel 059-9144164
(Castledermot, Dublin)

O'Driscoll, Philip
23 Barclay Court, Blackrock,
Co Dublin
Tel 01-2883329
(Dublin, retired)

O'Duill, Seamus (SDS)
Ard Mhuire, Kilmoon,
Lisdoonvarna, Co Clare
Tel 086-1030261

O'Dúill, Fergal (LC)
Vocations Director,
Leopardstown Road,
Foxrock, Dublin 18
Tel 01-2955902
Chaplain, Clonlost Retreat
and Youth Centre,
Killiney Road, Killiney,
Co Dublin
Tel 01-2350064

O'Dwyer, Christy, Rt Rev Mgr,
PP
Diocesan Archivist,
Bohereenglas, Cashel,
Co Tipperary
Tel 062-61127
(Cashel, Cashel & E.)

O'Dwyer, John, Very Rev
Dean, PE
20 Cloonarkin Drive,
Oranmore, Co Galway
Tel 091-484501
(Galway, retired)

O'Dwyer, Michael (SAC), CC
9 Seaview Lawn, Shankill,
Co Dublin
Tel 01-2822277
(Shankill, Dublin)

O'Dwyer, Michael, Very Rev,
PP
Parochial House,
15 Moy Road, Portadown,
Co Armagh BT62 1QL
Tel 028-38350610
(Portadown (Drumcree),
Armagh)

O'Dwyer, Richard (SJ)
Irish Jesuit Provincialate,
Milltown Park,
Sandford Road, Dublin 6
Tel 01-4987333

O'Dwyer, Sean, Very Rev, PE
Clonmel Road, Cahir,
Co Tipperary
Tel 087-4184213
(Waterford & L., retired)

O'Farrell, Ambrose (OP)
47 Leeson Park, Dublin 6
Tel 01-6602427

O'Farrell, Anthony (CSSp)
Holy Spirit Missionary
College, Kimmage Manor,
Dublin 12
Tel 01-406 4300

O'Farrell, Donal (SSC)
St Columban's Retirement
Home,
Dalgan Park, Navan,
Co Meath
Tel 046-9021525

O'Farrell, Edward (CSSp), Adm
(pro-tem)
55 Fernhill Road, Greenhills,
Dublin 12
Tel 01-4504040
c/o Church of the Holy
Spirit, Kimmage Manor,
Whitehall Road, Dublin 12
Tel 01-4064377
(Greenhills, Kimmage
Manor, Dublin)

O'Farrell, Martin, Very Rev,
Co-PP
Aghadoe, Kinsaley Lane,
Malahide, Co Dublin
Tel 01-8461767
(Kinsealy, Dublin)

O'Farrell, Patrick, Very Rev, PP
Lisdowney, Ballyragget,
Co Kilkenny
Tel 056-8833138/
087-2353520
(Lisdowney, Ossory)

O'Farrell, Peter, CC
Cobh, Co Cork
Tel 021-4855983
(Cobh, St Colman's
Cathedral, Cloyne)

O'Fearraigh, Brian, CC
Derrybeg, Letterkenny
Tel 074-9531947
Séiplíneach, Pobalscoil
Chloich Cheannfhaola,
Falcarragh, Letterkenny,
Co Donegal
Tel 074-9135424/9135231
(Gweedore, Raphoe)

O'Flaherty, Séan, Rt Rev Mgr,
PE
Parkmore, Castlegar,
Galway
Tel 091-764764
(Galway, retired)

O'Flynn, Ciaran (SPS)
On temporary diocesan
work

O'Flynn, Finbarr, CC
Dungourney, Co Cork
Tel 021-4668406
(Imogeela (Castlemartyr),
Cloyne)

O'Flynn, Michael (CSsR)
St Patrick's, Esker, Athenry,
Co Galway
Tel 091-844007

O'Flynn, Silvester (OFMCap)
Guardian, Capuchin Friary,
Ard Mhuire, Creeslough,
Letterkenny, Co Donegal
Tel 074-9138005

O'Flynn, Thomas (OP)
St Mary's Priory, Tallaght,
Dublin 24
Tel 01-4048100

O'Gara, Francis (OCarm)
Terenure College, Terenure,
Dublin 6W
Tel 01-4904621

O'Gorman, Charles, Very Rev,
PP
Blacklion, Co Cavan
Tel 071-9853012
(Killinagh and Glangevlin,
Kilmore)

O'Gorman, Daniel, CC
Holycross House, Moyglass,
Fethard, Co Tipperary
Tel 052-6131343
(Killenaule, Cashel & E.)

O'Gorman, Eamonn, Very Rev,
PP
Ballyragget, Co Kilkenny
Tel 087-2236145
(Ballyragget, Ossory)

O'Gorman, John, Very Rev, PP
Menlough, Ballinasloe,
Co Galway
Tel 090-9684818
(Menlough (Killascobe),
Tuam)

O'Gorman, Kevin (SMA)
St Patrick's College,
Maynooth

O'Gorman, Maurice, Very Rev,
PP
Clashmore, Co Waterford
Tel 024-96110
(Clashmore, Waterford & L.)

O'Gorman, Patrick, Very Rev,
PP
Golden, Co Tipperary
Tel 062-72146
(Golden, Cashel & E.)

O'Gorman, Tom, Adm
Cloughleigh Presbytery,
1 Shallee Drive,
Cloughleigh, Ennis, Co Clare
Tel 065-6840715/
087-2285355
(Abbey Cluster (Ennis),
Killaloe)

O'Grady, Desmond (SJ)
Gonzaga College,
Sandford Road, Dublin 6
Tel 01-4972943

O'Grady, James, Very Rev, PP
Headford, Co Galway
Tel 093-35448
(Tuam)

O'Grady, Michael, CC
Pro-Cathedral House,
83 Marlborough Street,
Dublin 1
Tel 01-8745441
(Pro-Cathedral, Dublin)

O'Grady, Nicholas (CP)
St Paul's Retreat,
Mount Argus, Dublin 6W
Tel 01-4992000

O'Grady, Peter (OFM)
The Abbey, 8 Francis Street,
Galway
Tel 091-562518

O'Grady, Vincent (CSSp)
Holy Spirit Missionary
College, Kimmage Manor,
Dublin 12
Tel 01-406 4300

O'Hagan, Eugene, Very Rev,
Lisbreen, 73 Somerton Road,
Belfast BT15 4DE
Tel 028-90776185
(Down & C.)

O'Hagan, Francis, PP
71 Duncrun Road,
Bellarena, Limavady,
Co Derry BT49 0JD
Tel 028-77750226
(Magilligan, Derry)

O'Hagan, Hugh J., Very Rev,
PP
Parochial House,
31 Ballynafie Road,
Ahoghill BT42 1LF
Tel 028-25871351
(Ahoghill, Down & C.)

O'Hagan, Mark, Very Rev,
Adm
St Patrick's Presbytery,
Roden Place, Dundalk,
Co Louth
Tel 042-9334648
(Dundalk, St Patrick's,
Armagh)

O'Hagan, Martin, Very Rev, PP
71 North Street,
Newtownards,
Co Down BT23 4JD
Tel 028-91812137
(Newtownards, Down & C.)

O'Hagan, Patrick, PP
Parochial House, Moyville,
Co Donegal
Tel 074-9382057
(Moville (Moville Lower),
Derry)

O'Halloran, Giles (OSA)
Bursar and Sub-Prior,
St John's Priory,
Thomas Street, Dublin 8
Tel 01-6770393

O'Halloran, James (SDB)
Rinaldi House,
72 Sean Mc Dermott Street,
Dublin 1
Tel 01-8363358

O'Halloran, Raphael (SSS)
Blessed Sacrament Chapel,
20 Bachelors Walk, Dublin 1
Tel 01-8724597

O'Halloran, Richard, CC
Portlaw, Co Waterford
Tel 051-387227
(Portlaw, Waterford & L.)

O'Halloran, Tom, Very Rev
Borrisokane, Co Tipperary
Tel 067-27105
(Killaloe)

O'Hanlon, David, CC
Parochial House,
Summerhill, Co Meath
Tel 046-9557021
(Summerhill, Meath)

O'Hanlon, Denis, Very Rev, PP
Lisgoold
Tel 021-4642363
(Lisgoold, Cloyne)

O'Hanlon, Denis Luke (OCSO)
Mount Melleray Abbey,
Cappoquin, Co Waterford
Tel 058-54404

O'Hanlon, Donal (SSC)
St Columban's, Dalgan Park,
Navan, Co Meath
Tel 046-9021525

O'Hanlon, Francis, Very Rev,
PP
Shannonbridge, Athlone,
Co Westmeath
Tel 090-9674125
(Shannonbridge, Ardagh &
Cl.)

O'Hanlon, George, Very Rev
Canon
(priest in residence)
62 Coolkeeran Road,
Armoy, Ballymoney,
Co Antrim BT53 8XN
Tel 028-20751121
(Loughguile, Down & C.)

O'Hanlon, Gerard (SJ)
25 Croftwood Park,
Cherry Orchard, Dublin 10
Tel 01-6267413

O'Hara, Emmet (SAC)
Pallottine College, Thurles,
Co Tipperary
Tel 0504-21202

O'Hara, Vincent (OCD)
Prior,
Avila Carmelite Centre,
Bloomfield Avenue,
Morehampton Road,
Dublin 4
Tel 01-6430200

O'Hare, Martin (SMA), CC
African Missions,
Blackrock Road, Cork
Tel 021-4292871

O'Hare, Paddy (SM)
France

O'Hare, Peter, Very Rev, PP
16 Rossglas Road, Killough,
Co Down BT30 7QQ
Tel 028-44841221
(Killough (Bright), Down &
C.)

O'Hea, James (SMA)
African Missions, Blackrock
Road, Cork
Tel 021-4292871

O'Hea, Jarlath (OCarm)
Whitefriar Street Church,
56 Aungier Street, Dublin 2
Tel 01-4758821

O'Herlihy, Pat (SSC)
No. 2 Presbytery,
Our Lady Crowned Church,
Mayfield Upper, Cork
Tel 021-4508610

O'Higgins, Kevin (SJ)
(residing elsewhere)

O'Holohan, John (SJ)
St Francis Xavier's,
Upper Gardiner Street,
Dublin 1
Tel 01-8363411

O'Hora, Gerard, Very Rev, VF
Cathedral Presbytery,
Ballina, Co Mayo
Tel 096-71365
(Ballina, Killala)

O'Horo, Michael, Very Rev, PP
Skreen, Co Sligo
Tel 071-9166629
(Skreen and Dromard,
Killala)

O'Kane, David, PP
9 Church Street, Claudy,
Co Derry BT47 4AA
Tel 028-71337727
(Claudy (Cumber Upper &
Learmount), Derry)

O'Kane, Hugh (SMA), CC
(priest in residence)
53 Ballinlea Road,
Ballycastle,
Co Antrim BT54 6JL
Tel 028-20762498
(Ballintoy, Down & C.)

O'Kane, James, Very Rev, PE,
CC
21 Knocknacarry Avenue,
Cushenden,
Co Antrim BT44 0NX
Tel 028-21761269
(Cushendun, Down and C.)

O'Kane, Patrick, PP
1 Aileach Road,
Ballymagroarty,
Derry BT48 0AZ
Tel 028-71267070
(Holy Family,
Ballymagroarty, Derry)

O'Kane, Peter
Director, Diocesan Pastoral
Centre, 164 Bishop Street,
Derry BT48 6UJ
Tel 028-71362475
(Derry)

O'Kane, Peter, Very Rev, PP
Parochial House, Strangford,
Co Down BT30 7NL
Tel 028-44881206
(Kilclief and Strangford,
Down & C.)

O'Keefe, Fergus (SJ)
St Francis Xavier's,
Upper Gardiner Street,
Dublin 1
Tel 01-8363411
Spiritual Director,
Lay Retreat Association of
Saint Ignatius,
Milltown Park, Dublin 6
Tel 01-7072203

O'Keefe, Martin
Knock, Co Mayo
(Tuam, retired)

O'Keeffe, Anthony (OFMCap)
St Francis Capuchin Friary,
Rochestown, Co Cork
Tel 021-4896244

O'Keeffe, Anthony, Very Rev
Canon, PP, VF
Shanagolden, Co Limerick
Tel 069-60112/087-4163401
(Shanagolden and Foynes,
Limerick)

O'Keeffe, Gerard (OP)
St Dominic's, Athy,
Co Kildare
Tel 059-8631573

O'Keeffe, John (OFM)
Collegio S. Isidoro,
Via degli Artisti 41,
00187 Roma, Italy
Tel 0039-06-4885359

O'Keeffe, John, Very Rev, PP
Birdhill, Killaloe,
Co Tipperary
Tel 061-379172/087-2421678
(Newport, Cashel & E.)

O'Keeffe, John (SJ)
Campion House Residence,
28 Lower Hatch Street,
Dublin 2
Tel 01-6383990

O'Keeffe, John (SMA)
SMA House, Wilton,
Cork
Tel 021-4541069/4541884

O'Keeffe, Joseph
42 Nessan Court,
Church Road, Raheen,
Limerick
Tel 061-309151/086-3333539
(Limerick)

O'Keeffe, Joseph, Very Rev, PP
Burnfort, Mallow, Co Cork
Tel 022-29920
(Mourne Abbey, Cloyne)

**Allianz ⑪**

O'Keeffe, Laurence, Very Rev, PP
Clifden Villa, Clifden,
Co Kilkenny
Tel 056-7726560/
087-2258443
(*Clara*, Ossory)

O'Keeffe, Martin (OMI)
Mazenod House,
Churchfield, Knock,
Co Mayo
Tel 094-9388940

O'Keeffe, Patrick (CSsR)
St Patrick's, Esker,
Athenry, Co Galway
Tel 091-844007

O'Keeffe, Thomas, Very Rev
Assistant, 20 Glen Avenue,
The Park, Cabinteely,
Dublin 18
Tel 01-2853643/086-2646270
(Dublin, retired)

O'Keeffe, Martin (OMI)
Mazenod House,
Churchfield,
Knock, Co Mayo

O'Kelly, Francis (SSC)
St Columban's, Dalgan Park,
Navan, Co Meath
Tel 046-9021525

O'Kelly, Michael A., Very Rev, Co-PP
39 Oakton Park, Ballybrack,
Co Dublin
Tel 01-2827282
(*Loughlinstown*, Dublin)

O'Laoghaire, Sean, Very Rev, PE
Gowran Abbey Nursing Home, Gowran,
Co Kilkenny
(Kildare & L., retired)

O'Leary, Aidan (OSA)
St Augustine's Priory,
Grantstown, New Ross,
Co Wexford
Tel 051-561119

O'Leary, Alan, Very Rev, PP
The Presbytery, Schull,
Co Cork
Tel 028-28898
(*Goleen*, Cork & R.)

O'Leary, Anthony (CP)
St Gabriel's Retreat,
The Graan, Enniskillen,
Co Fermanagh
Tel 028-66322272

O'Leary, Brian (SJ)
Milltown Park,
Sandford Road, Dublin 6
Tel 01-2698411

O'Leary, Celestine (OCSO)
Mount Melleray Abbey,
Cappoquin, Co Waterford
Tel 058-54404

O'Leary, Con (SMA)
African Missions,
Blackrock Road, Cork
Tel 021-4292871

O'Leary, Finbarr
Lislevane, Bandon,
Co Cork
Tel 023-8846171
(*Barryroe*, Cork & R.)

O'Leary, Gerald, Very Rev, PP
Horeswood, Campile,
Co Wexford
Tel 051-388129
(*Horeswood and Ballykelly*, Ferns)

O'Leary, Gerard, CC
(Milltown, Kerry)

O'Leary, Gerard, Very Rev
(on study leave)
'The Firs', Grange,
Kilmallock, Co Limerick
(Limerick)

O'Leary, John, Very Rev, PE, AP
Parochial House,
Moore Hall, Ardee,
Co Louth
Tel 041-6850920
(*Ardee & Collon*, Armagh)

O'Leary, Joseph
1-38-16 Ekoda, Nakanoku,
Tokyo, 16J0022 Japan
(Cork & R.)

O'Leary, Noel (SMA), Very Rev, PP
St Joseph's, Blackrock Road,
Co Cork
Tel 021-4293325/
021-4616327
(*St Joseph's (Blackrock Road)*, Cork & R.)

O'Leary, Oscar (OFM)
Franciscan Friary,
Liberty Street, Cork
Tel 021-4270302

O'Leary, Timothy, Very Rev Canon, CC,
Mitchelstown, Co Cork
Tel 025-84088
(*Mitchelstown*, Cloyne)

O'Leary, Timothy, Very Rev, PP
Glenroe, Kilmallock,
Co Limerick
Tel 063-86040
(*Glenroe and Ballyorgan*, Limerick)

O'Leary, Oscar (OFM)
Franciscan Friary,
Liberty Street, Cork
Tel 021-4270302

O'Loan, Fergus (OCarm)
Gort Muire, Ballinteer,
Dublin 16
Tel 01-2984014

O'Looney, Michael (CSSp)
Holy Spirit Missionary
College, Kimmage Manor,
Dublin 12
Tel 01-4064300

O'Loughlin, Declan
Diocesan Advisor for
Religious Education (Post-Primary),
Parochial House,
30 Newline, Killeavy, Newry,
Co Down BT35 8TA
Tel 028-30889609
(Armagh)

O'Loughlin, Michael (SSC)
43 Moyland, Shanballa,
Loughville, Lahinch Road,
Ennis, Co Clare
Tel 065-6845321

O'Loughlin, Peader (SSC)
St Columban's, Dalgan Park,
Navan, Co Meath
Tel 046-9021525

O'Loughlin, Peter, Very Rev, PP
Kilmihil, Co Clare
Tel 065-9050016/
086-8250016
(*Kilmihil*, Killaloe)

O'Madagáin, Murchadh, Rev Dr
310 Sarasota Street, Venice,
Florida, FL 34285, USA
Tel 001-239-4504345
(Galway)

O'Mahony, Anthony, CC
The Presbytery, Bandon,
Co Cork
Tel 023-8865067
(*Bandon*, Cork & R.)

O'Mahony, Ambrose (OFM)
Franciscan Friary,
Liberty Street, Cork
Tel 021-4270302

O'Mahony, Bartholomew, Very Rev Canon, PP
Woodlawn,
Model Farm Road,
Ballineaspaig, Co Cork
Tel 021-4346818
(*Ballineaspaig*, Cork & R.)

O'Mahony, Brendan (OFMCap)
Holy Trinity,
Fr Mathew Quay, Cork
Tel 021-4270827

O'Mahony, Colm (OSA)
St Augustine's Priory,
Shop Street,
Drogheda, Co Louth
Tel 041-9838409

O'Mahony, Damien, CC
1 Kilmorna Heights,
Ballyvolane, Cork
Tel 021-4550425
(*Blackpool/The Glen*, Cork & R.)

O'Mahony, Dan Joe (OFMCap)
Capuchin Friary,
Church Street, Dublin 7
Tel 01-8730599

O'Mahony, Dan, Very Rev, PP
Cloonacool, Tubbercurry,
Co Sligo
Tel 071-9185156
(*Tubbercurry*, Achonry)

O'Mahony, Denis, Very Rev Canon
Killeagh, Farranfore,
Co Kerry
(Kerry, retired)

O'Mahony, Denis, Very Rev, PP
Abbeydorney, Co Kerry
Tel 066-7135146
(*Abbeydorney*, Kerry)

O'Mahony, Dermot, Most Rev Dean, DD
Titular Bishop of Tiava;
former Auxiliary Bishop of Dublin,
19 Longlands, Swords,
Co Dublin
Tel 01-8401596
(Dublin)

O'Mahony, Donal, Very Rev Canon, PP
Cloyne, Co Cork
Tel 021-4652597
(*Cloyne*, Cloyne)

O'Mahony, George, Very Rev, PP
Ballincollig, Co Cork
Tel 021-4871206
(*Ballincollig*, Cork & R.)

O'Mahony, John K., Very Rev Canon, AP
The Presbytery, Kinsale,
Co Cork
Tel 021-4773700
(*Kinsale*, Cork & R.)

O'Mahony, Joseph, CC
Macroom, Co Cork
Tel 026-41092
(*Macroom*, Cloyne)

O'Mahony, Kieran (OSA)
Augustinian Retreat Centre,
Old Court Road,
Dublin 16
Tel 01-4930932

O'Mahony, Michael, PP
Ballinspittle, Co Cork
Tel 021-4778055
(*Courceys*, Cork & R.)

O'Mahony, Nicholas, Rt Rev Mgr, PP
Diocesan Administrator of
Waterford and Lismore,
Parochial House, Tramore,
Co Waterford
Tel 051-381525
(*Tramore*, Waterford & L.)

O'Mahony, Pat (SMA), CC
St Patrick's Presbytery,
Rochestown Road, Cork
Tel 021-4892363
(*Douglas*, Cork & R.)

O'Mahony, Patrick (SMA)
Temporary diocesan work in Ireland

O'Mahony, Stephen, Very Rev, PP
Bohola
Claremorris, Co Mayo
Tel 094-9384115
(*Bohola*, Achonry)

O'Mahony, Stephen, Very Rev, PE
Liscarroll, Mallow, Co Cork
Tel 022-48128
(*Cloyne*, retired)

O'Mahony, Thomas, Very Rev, PP
Parochial House, Skryne,
Tara, Co Meath
Tel 046-9025152
(*Skryne*, Meath)

O'Malley, Donough, Very Rev Canon, PP
St Mary's,
Athlunkard Street, Limerick
Tel 061-414092/086-2586908
(*St Mary's*, Limerick)

O'Malley, Eoin (OSM)
Servite Priory, Benburb,
Dungannon,
Co Tyrone BT71 7JZ

O'Malley, Michael
c/o Archbishop's House,
Tuam
(Tuam)

O'Meara, Denis, Very Rev Canon
Beechwood House Nursing Home, Newcastlewest,
Co Limerick
(Cashel & E., retired)

O'Meara, Donagh
Ballyheafey, Killaloe,
Co Clare
Tel 061-376766/087-2322140
(Killaloe)

O'Meara, Michael, Very Rev, PP
Kinnity, Birr, Co Offaly
Tel 057-9137021/
087-7735977
(*Kinnitty*, Killaloe)

O'Meara, Noel (CSSp)
Holy Spirit Missionary College, Kimmage Manor,
Dublin 12
Tel 01-4064300

O'Melia, Joseph (OMI)
Oblate House of Retreat,
Inchicore, Dublin 8
Tel 01-4534408/4541805

O'Moore, Maurice, Very Rev Canon, PE
6 Richmond Avenue,
Monkstown, Co Dublin
Tel 01-2802186
(Dublin, retired)

O'Neill, Angelus (OFMCap)
Capuchin Friary,
Church Street, Dublin 7
Tel 01-8730599

O'Neill, Arthur
1B Willow Court,
Druid Valley, Cabinteely,
Dublin 18
Tel 087-2597520
(*Cabinteely*, Dublin)

O'Neill, Charles
Colmanswell, Charleville,
Co Limerick
Tel 063-89459
(Limerick, retired)

O'Neill, Daniel (MSC)
Carrignavar, Co Cork
Tel 021-4884044

O'Neill, Daniel (SMA)
SMA House, Claregalway,
Co Galway
Tel 091-798880

O'Neill, Donal, Very Rev, Adm
The Presbytery, Killgarvan,
Co Kerry
Tel 064-6685313
(*Kilgarvan*, Kerry)

O'Neill, Eugene, CC
5 Plater's Hill,
Coalisland,
Co Tyrone BT71 4JZ
Tel 028-87740302
(*Coalisland*, Armagh)

O'Neill, Eugene, Very Rev, PP
Parochial House,
4 Irish Street, Killyleagh,
Co Down BT30 9QS
Tel 028-44828211
(*Crossgar (Kilmore)*, Down & C.)

O'Neill, Fergal, CC
Portroe, Nenagh,
Co Tipperary
067-23105/087-6615975
(*Portroe (Castletown Arrha)*,
Killaloe)

O'Neill, Francis, Very Rev, PP
Ballyclough, Mallow,
Co Cork
Tel 022-27650
(*Ballyclough*, Cloyne)

O'Neill, Gerard (SDB)
Chaplain,
Collins Barracks, Cork

O'Neill, Hugh (SJ)
Milltown Park,
Sandford Road, Dublin 6
Tel 01-2698411/2698113

O'Neill, Ian, Very Rev, PP
Parochial House,
Claregalway, Co Galway
Tel 091-798104
(*Claregalway*, Galway)

O'Neill, Joe, CC
Curate's House, Prosperous,
Co Kildare
Tel 045-868187
(*Prosperous*, Kildare & L.)

O'Neill, John, Very Rev Canon, PP, VF
Lisvernane, Aherlow
Co Tipperary
Tel 062-56155
(*Galbally*, Cashel & E.)

O'Neill, Kevin, Rt Rev Mgr, BA, MSc Ed
President, Carlow College,
College Street, Carlow
Tel 059-9153200
(Kildare & L.)

O'Neill, Kevin (SSC)
No 3 and 4,
Ma Yau Tong Village,
Po Lam Road,
Tseung Kwan O,
Kowloon, Hong Kong, SAR

O'Neill, Larry (SPS)
St Patrick's, Kiltegan,
Co Wicklow
Tel 059-6473600

O'Neill, Míceál (OCarm)
Centro Internazionale S. Alberto,
Via Sforza Pallavicini 10,
00193 Roma, Italia

O'Neill, Niall (SJ)
Crescent College Comprehensive,
Dooradoyle, Limerick
Tel 061-480920

O'Neill, Pat
Ruan, Co Clare
Tel 065-6827799/
086-2612124
(*Dysart & Ruan*, Killaloe)

O'Neill, Peter (SSC)
House Superior,
St Columban's, Dalgan Park,
Navan, Co Meath
Tel 046-9021525

O'Neill, Roger, CC
New Ross, Co Wexford
Tel 051-447081
(*New Ross*, Ferns)

O'Neill, Seamus (SPS)
St Patrick's, Kiltegan, Co Wicklow
Tel 059-6473600

O'Neill, Seamus (SSC)
20 Tobermore Road,
Moykeenan, Draperstown,
Co Derry BT45 7HG
Tel 048-79627206

O'Neill, Sean, PP
Parochial House,
1 Rockstown Road,
Carrickmore, Omagh,
Co Tyrone BT79 9BE
Tel 028-80761207
(*Termonmaguirc
(Carrickmore, Loughmacrory
& Creggan)*, Armagh)

O'Rahelly, Edmond V., Very Rev, PP
Ballina, Killaloe, Co Clare
Tel 061-376178
(*Ballina*, Cashel & E.)

O'Regan, Kevin, Very Rev, PP
Ascension Presbytery,
Gurranabraher, Cork
Tel 021-4303655
(*Gurranabraher*, Cork & R.)

O'Regan, Liam, Very Rev Canon, AP
'Carraigin', Moneygourney,
Douglas, Cork
Tel 021-4363998
(*Douglas*, Cork & R.)

O'Regan, Robert (SMA)
African Missions,
Blackrock Road, Cork
Tel 021-4292871

O'Reilly, Anthony
Newry, Co Armagh
(Kerry)

O'Reilly, Arthur P., CC
285 Foreglan Road,
Dungiven,
Co Derry BT47 4PJ
Tel 028-71338261
(*Banagher*, Derry)

O'Reilly, Bernard (OCarm)
Carmelite Priory, Moate,
Co Westmeath
Tel 090-6481160/6481398

O'Reilly, Brian (SVD)
Provincial,
133 North Circular Road,
Dublin 7
Tel 01-8386743

O'Reilly, Brian, Very Rev, PP
Kilmacud-Stillorgan
Tel 087-7414857
Mount Merrion
Tel 01-2881271/01-2783804
(*Kilmacud-Stillorgan, Mount Merrion*, Dublin)

O'Reilly, Colm, Most Rev, DD
Retired Bishop of Ardagh
and Clonmacnois,
Deanscurragh, Longford
Tel 043-3347831
(Ardagh & Cl.)

O'Reilly, Damian, Very Rev Canon, Adm
Pro-Cathedral House,
83 Marlborough Street,
Dublin 1
Tel 01-8745441
(*Pro-Cathedral*, Dublin)

O'Reilly, Desmond
Our Lady of Lourdes, 1951
North Avenue,
Sacramento, CA 95838 USA
(Dublin)

O'Reilly, Hugh (CSSp)
Holy Spirit Missionary College, Kimmage Manor,
Dublin 12
Tel 01-4064300

O'Reilly, James (SPS)
Sally's Bridge,
Crettyard, Carlow

O'Reilly, John (OP), CC
St Mary's Priory,
The Claddagh, Galway
Tel 091-582884
(*St Mary's*, Galway)

O'Reilly, John, PP
Piercestown, Co Wexford
Tel 053-9158851
(*Piercestown*, Ferns)

O'Reilly, Joseph (IC)
Cottrell Lodge,
16A Ormond Road,
Drumcondra, Dublin 9
Tel 01-8572234
Provincial,
1 Grace Park Gardens,
Drumcondra, Dublin 9
Tel 01-8378314/8368730

O'Reilly, Kieran (SMA), Most
Rev, DD
Archbishop Designate of
Cashel and Emly,
Archbishop's House, Thurles,
Co Tipperary
Tel 0504-21512
(*Cashel & E.*)

O'Reilly, Leo, Most Rev, DD
Bishop of Kilmore,
Bishop's House, Cullies,
Co Cavan
Tel 049-4331496
(*Kilmore*)

O'Reilly, Martin, CC
Parochial House, Killanny,
Carrickmacross,
Co Monaghan
Tel 042-9661452
(*Killanny*, Clogher)

O'Reilly, Myles (SJ)
Rector,
Gonzaga College,
Sandford Road, Dublin 6
Tel 01-4972943

O'Reilly, Oliver, CC
Parochial House, Shercock,
Co Cavan
Tel 042-9669127
(*Bailieboro (Killann)*,
Kilmore)

O'Reilly, Paddy (OSA)
Parochial House,
St Helena's Drive, Dublin 11
Tel 01-8343444/086-8279504
(*Rivermount*, Dublin)

O'Reilly, Paddy (SPS)
St Patrick's, Kiltegan,
Co Wicklow
Tel 059-6473600

O'Reilly, Peter, Rt Rev Mgr
1 Darling Street, Enniskillen,
Co Fermanagh BT74 7DP
Tel 028-66322627
(*Enniskillen*, Clogher)

O'Reilly, Peter, Very Rev
on study leave
(Dublin)

O'Reilly, Seamus, Very Rev,
(SPS), Adm
Parochial House,
111 Causeway Street,
Portrush, Co Antrim BT56
8JE
Tel 028-70823388
(*Portrush*, Down & C.)

O'Reilly, Thomas, Very Rev,
Adm
Clonaslee, Co Laois
Tel 057-8648030
(*Clonaslee*, Kildare & L.)

O'Riordan, Anthony (SJ), Very
Rev, PP
134 Cosgrave Park,
Moyross, Limerick
Tel 061-451783/087-9286945
(*Corpus Christi*, Limerick)

O'Riordan, Anthony (SVD)
133 North Circular Road,
Dublin 7
Tel 01-8386743

O'Riordan, Daniel, Rt Rev
Mgr, PP
The Presbytery, Castleisland,
Co Kerry
Tel 066-7141241
(*Castleisland*, Kerry)

O'Riordan, David, Very Rev,
PP
Ladysbridge, Co Cork
Tel 021-4667173
(*Ballymacoda and
Ladysbridge*, Cloyne)

O'Riordan, Eugene (SMA)
African Missions,
Blackrock Road, Cork
Tel 021-4292871

O'Riordan, Jeremiah, Very
Rev, PP
Donoughmore, Co Cork
Tel 021-7337023
(*Donoughmore*, Cloyne)

O'Riordan, John C. (CSSp),
Most Rev
Holy Spirit Missionary
College, Kimmage Manor,
Dublin 12
Tel 01-4064300

O'Riordan, John P. (CSsR), CC
Mahon Parish,
2 The Presbytery,
Mahon, Cork
Tel 021-4515460
(*Mahon*, Cork & R.)

O'Riordan, Jude (OFM)
Adam & Eve's,
4 Merchant's Quay,
Dublin 8
Tel 01-6771128

O'Riordan, Martin
Lisgoold, Co Cork
Tel 021-4642543
(Cloyne, retired)

O'Riordáin, John J. (CSsR)
Redemptorists,
Mount St Alphonsus,
Limerick
Tel 061-315099

O'Rourke, Brendan (CSsR)
Superior, St Patrick's, Esker,
Athenry, Co Galway
Tel 091-844007
Provincial Vicar,
Liguori House,
75 Orwell Road, Rathgar,
Dublin 6
Tel 01-4067100

O'Rourke, Denis (SPS)
Bursar General, St Patrick's,
Kiltegan, Co Wicklow
Tel 059-6473600

O'Rourke, John (OP)
Holy Cross, Tralee, Co Kerry
Tel 066-7121135/29185

O'Rourke, John, Very Rev, AP
Gortnahoe, Thurles,
Co Tipperary
Tel 056-8834128
(*Gortnahoe*, Cashel & E.)

O'Rourke, Kevin (SJ)
St Francis Xavier's,
Upper Gardiner Street,
Dublin 1
Tel 01-8363411

O'Rourke, Kieran, Very Rev,
PP
Looscaun, Woodford,
Co Galway
Tel 090-9749100
(*Woodford*, Clonfert)

O'Rourke, Pat (SMA)
Superior,
Dromantine College,
Dromantine, Newry,
Co Down BT34 1RH
Tel 028-30821224

O'Rourke, Pat (LC), CC
The Prebytery,
St Patrick's Road,
Wicklow Town,
Co Wicklow
(*Wicklow*, Dublin)

O'Rourke, Sean
15 Seaview Park, Shankill,
Co Dublin
(Dublin, retired)

O'Saorai, Padraig
Woodlands House Nursing
Home, Trim Road, Navan,
Co Meath
(Dublin, retired)

O'Shaughnessy, Anthony,
Adm
73 Newtown Park, Leixlip,
Co Kildare
Tel 01-6244637
(*Confey*, Dublin)

O'Shaughnessy, Sean (CSSp)
Holy Spirit Missionary
College, Kimmage Manor,
Dublin 12
Tel 01-4064300

O'Shaughnessy, Thomas F.,
73 Annamoe Road,
Dublin 7
Tel 01-8385626
(*Cabra*, Dublin)

O'Shea, A. B., Very Rev, PP
Sooey, Coola, via Boyle,
Co Sligo
Tel 071-9165144
(*Riverstown*, Elphin)

O'Shea, Colum P. (SMA)
Superior, African Missions,
Blackrock Road, Cork
Tel 021-4292871

O'Shea, Donagh (OP)
St Mary's Priory, Tallaght,
Dublin 24
Tel 01-4048100

O'Shea, Fintan (OFM)
3 The Millhouse, Steelworks,
Foley Street, Dublin 1

O'Shea, Henry (OSB)
Glenstal Abbey, Murroe,
Co Limerick
Tel 061-386103

O'Shea, John, Very Rev
Canon, PP, VF
Convent Street, Abbeyfeale,
Co Limerick
Tel 068-31157/087-9708282
(*Abbeyfeale*, Limerick)

O'Shea, Kieran, CC
St Canice's Presbytery,
Granges Road, Kilkenny
Tel 056-7752994/
086-8272828
(*St Canice's*, Ossory)

O'Shea, Martin, Rt Rev Mgr,
Co-PP
23 Clare Road, Drumcondra,
Dublin 9
Tel 01-8378552
(*Drumcondra*, Dublin)

O'Shea, Maurice, Very Rev, PE
6 Beechpark Lawn,
Castleknock, Dublin 15
(Dublin, retired)

O'Shea, Michael, PP
Fedamore, Kilmallock,
Co Limerick
Tel 061-390112
(*Fedamore*, Limerick)

O'Shea, Michael, Very Rev, PP
The Presbytery,
12 School Street, Wexford
Tel 053-9122055
(*Wexford*, Ferns)

O'Shea, Philip, Very Rev, PE
Ballinakill, Garyhill,
Co Carlow
Tel 059-9727425
(Kildare & L., retired)

O'Shea, Thomas, Very Rev, CC
Ballylinan, Athy, Co Kildare
Tel 059-8625261
(*Arles*, Kildare & L.)

O'Siochru, Colm
Our Lady's Manor, Bulloch Castle,
Dalkey, Co Dublin
(Dublin, retired)

O'Sullivan, Alan (OP)
Black Abbey, Kilkenny,
Co Kilkenny
Tel 056-7721279 .

O'Sullivan, Andrew
(Moderator)
Parochial House,
St Mary's Parish,
Sandyford, Dublin 18
Tel 01-2956317
(Sandyford, Dublin)

O'Sullivan, Anthony, Very Rev, PP
Brosna, Co Kerry
Tel 068-44112
(Brosna, Kerry)

O'Sullivan, Billy, CC
The Presbytery, Turner's Cross, Cork
Tel 021-4313103
(Turner's Cross, Cork & R.)

O'Sullivan, Brendan, CC
The Presbytery, Longford
Tel 043-3346465
(Longford, Ardagh & Cl.)

O'Sullivan, Brian, PE
The Cottage, Glengara Park,
Glenageary,
Co Dublin
Tel 01-2360681
(Dublin, retired)

O'Sullivan, Brian (OSA)
Bursar, Via Piemonte 60,
00187 Rome, Italy
Tel 00396-4203121

O'Sullivan, Denis (SMA)
SMA House, Wilton, Cork
Tel 021-4541069/4541884

O'Sullivan, Denis, Very Rev, PE
Monasterevin, Co Kildare
Tel 045-525351
(Kildare & L., retired)

O'Sullivan, Desmond L. (CSSp)
Holy Spirit Missionary College, Kimmage Manor,
Dublin 12
Tel 01-4064300

O'Sullivan, John (MSC)
Woodview House,
Mount Merrion Avenue,
Blackrock, Co Dublin
Tel 01-2881644

O'Sullivan, John (OSA)
St Augustine's,
Taylor's Lane,
Balyboden, Dublin 16
Tel 01-4241000

O'Sullivan, John K.
97 Kincora Avenue,
Clontarf, Dublin 3
(Dublin, retired)

O'Sullivan, John, Very Rev
6 Ferngrove Avenue,
Aghagallon,
Craigavon BT67 0HA
(Down & C., retired)

O'Sullivan, Kieran, Very Rev, PP
Adrigole, Bantry, Co Cork
Tel 027-60006
(Adrigole, Kerry)

O'Sullivan, Leo (OSA)
St Augustine's,
Taylor's Lane,
Ballyboden, Dublin 16
Tel 01-4241000

O'Sullivan, Leo (SPS)
St Patrick's, Kiltegan,
Co Wicklow
Tel 059-6473600

O'Sullivan, Louis
Our Lady's Manor,
Bullock Castle, Dalkey,
Co Dublin
(Dublin, retired)

O'Sullivan, Michael (OSA)
St Augustine's,
Taylor's Lane,
Ballyboden, Dublin 16
Tel 01-4241000

O'Sullivan, Michael (SJ)
John Austin House,
135 North Circular Road,
Dublin 7
Tel 01-8386768

O'Sullivan, Michael (White Fathers)
c/o Cypress Grove,
Templeogue, Dublin 6W
Tel 01-4055263/4055264

O'Sullivan, Noel, Very Rev Dr, PP
St Patrick's College,
Maynooth, Co Kildare
(Cork & R.)

O'Sullivan, Owen (OFMCap)
Capuchin Friary,
Church Street, Dublin 7
Tel 01-8730599

O'Sullivan, Padraig, Co-PP
St Columba Parish House,
New Road, Clondalkin,
Dublin 22
Tel 01-4640441
(Clondalkin/Rowlagh/Neilstown/Deansrath/Bawnogue, Dublin)

O'Sullivan, Patrick, Very Rev (MSC), Adm
Leap, Co Cork
Tel 028-33177
(Kilmacabea, Cork & R.)

O'Sullivan, Patrick, Very Rev, PP
'Elm View', Roxboro Road,
Limerick
Tel 061-410846/087-2237501
(Our Lady Queen of Peace, Limerick)

O'Sullivan, Paul (OCD)
St Teresa's,
Clarendon Street, Dublin 2
Tel 01-6718466/6718127

O'Sullivan, Séan, Very Rev, PP
New Parochial House,
Monkstown, Co Cork
021-4863267
(Monkstown, Passage West, Cork & R.)

O'Sullivan, Ted, Very Rev Canon, PP
Parochial House, Douglas
Co Cork
Tel 021-4891265
(Douglas, Cork & R.)

O'Sullivan, Timothy, Very Rev
Villa Maria, Farnanes, Co Cork
(Cork & R., retired)

O'Toole, Brian (CSSp)
St Mary's College,
Rathmines, Dublin 6
Tel 01-4995760
Manager, Spiritan Mission Resource & Heritage Centre,
Kimmage Manor, Dublin 12

O'Toole, Colmcille (OCSO)
Mount Saint Joseph Abbey,
Roscrea, Co Tipperary
Tel 0505-25600

O'Toole, Patrick (CSSp)
Spiritan Community,
Ballintubber, Castlerea,
Co Roscommon
Tel 094-9655226

O'Toole, Peter Baptist (OFM)
Franciscan Friary,
Lady Lane, Waterford
Tel 051-874262

O'Toole, Sean
The Presbytery, Avoca,
Co Wicklow
Tel 0402-32153
(Dublin, retired)

O'Toole, Thomas, Very Rev, PP
Glenmore,
Via New Ross, Co Kilkenny
Tel 051-880213/087-2240787
(Glenmore, Ossory)

Odia, Cyril (SDB), CC
72 Sean McDermott Street,
Dublin 1
Tel 01-8363358
(Sean McDermott Street, Dublin)

Ogbonna, Magnus (MSP) CC
St Patrick's Presbytery,
Roden Place, Dundalk,
Co Louth
Tel 042-9334648
(Dundalk, St Patrick's, Armagh)

Olden, Michael, Rt Rev Mgr, PE
'Woodleigh',
Summerville Avenue,
Waterford
Tel 051-874132
(Waterford & L., retired)

Olin, Richard (CSSp)
Community Leader, St Mary's College,
Rathmines, Dublin 6
Tel 01-4995760

Olivoni, Alberto (SMA)
African Missions,
Blackrock Road, Cork
Tel 021-4292871

Omolade, Anthony
Presbytery, Silloge Road,
Ballymun, Dublin 11
Tel 01-8421551
(Ballymun/Silloge, Dublin)

Orr, Thomas, CC
Ballycanew, Gorey,
Co Wexford
Tel 053-9427184
(Camolin, Ferns)

Otwey-Buabeng, Joseph Raymond
Team Assistant,
32 Earlsfort Road, Lucan,
Dublin 22
Tel 01-6212560
(Lucan South, Dublin)

Owen, John (SVD)
1 & 3 Pembroke Road,
Dublin 4
Tel 01-6680904

Owens, Finnian (OCSO)
Our Lady of Bethlehem Abbey,
11 Ballymena Road,
Portglenone, Ballymena,
Co Antrim BT44 8BL
Tel 028-25821211

Owens, Peter, Very Rev, PP
Parochial House,
8 Minorca Place,
Carrickfergus,
Co Antrim, BT38 8AU
Tel 028-93363269
(Carrickfergus, Down & C.)

Oxley, Paul (SSC)
Bursar General, No 3 and 4,
Ma Yau Tong Village,
Po Lam Road,
Tseung Kwan O, Kow Loon,
Hong Kong, SAR

**P**

Paradiyil, Tomy (OSCam)
St Camillus, 11 St Vincent Street North,
Dublin 7
Tel 01-8300365

Park, Stefan (OSA), CC
Kill, Cootehill, Co Cavan
Tel 049-5553218
(Kilsherdany and Drung, Kilmore)

Parker, Thomas (SSC)
St Columban's Retirement
Home, Dalgan Park, Navan,
Co Meath
Tel 046-9021525

Parokkaran, Martin (OCarm),
CC
Carmelite Presbytery,
Idrone Avenue, Knocklyon,
Dublin 16
Tel 01-4941204
(Knocklyon, Dublin)

Parsons, Anthony (OCD)
The Abbey, Loughrea,
Co Galway
Tel 091-841209

Parys, Bart (SVD)
1 & 3 Pembroke Road,
Dublin 4
Tel 01-6680904

Pathackal, Abraham George,
CC
30 Wheatfields Close,
Clondalkin, Dublin 22
Tel 01-6263920
Team Assistant for Rowlagh
and Quarryvale
(Neilstown, Rowlagh and
Quarryvale, Dublin)

Patton, Gerard, Very Rev
43 Head Road, Kilkeel,
Co Down BT34 4HX
(Down & C., retired)

Pecak Marek, CC
(priest in residence)
Midleton, Co Cork
Tel 021-4634027
(Midleton, Cloyne)

Peelo, Adrian (OFM)
Old Mission San Luis Rey,
4050 Mission Avenue,
Oceanside,
CA 92057-6497 USA

Pentony, Liam, Very Rev, PE,
CC
Parochial House, Dromiskin,
Dundalk, Co Louth
Tel 042-9382877
(Darver and Dromiskin,
Armagh)

Peoples, William, Very Rev, PP
Donegal Town,
Co Donegal
Tel 074-9721026
(Donegal Town, Raphoe)

Pepper, Pierre, CC
Banagher, Co Offaly
Tel 090-6454309
(Cloghan and Banagher,
Ardagh & Cl.)

Perrotta, John (FDP)
Sarsfield House,
Sarsfield Road,
Ballyfermot, Dublin 10
Tel 01-6266193/6266233

Perry, Jim (SVD)
Maynooth, Co Kildare
Tel 01-6286391/2

Perumayan, Antony, CC
Guardian of the Syro-
Malabar Catholics,
St Paul's Presbytery,
125 Falls Road,
Belfast BT12 6AB
Tel 028-90325034
(St Paul's, Dublin)

Peters, James (CSSp)
Kimmage Manor,
Whitehall Road, Dublin 12
Tel 01-4064300

Peyton, Patrick, Very Rev
Canon, PP
Parochial House, Collooney,
Co Sligo
Tel 071-9167235
(Collooney (Kilvarnet),
Achonry)

Phair, John, Very Rev, PP
Kilnavart, Ballyconnell,
Co Cavan
Tel 049-9526126
(Templeport, Kilmore)

Philip, John (OSCam)
Chaplain,
Mater Hospital, Dublin
11 St Vincent St North,
Dublin 7

Philomin, Leo, Very Rev (OMI),
Co-PP
The Presbytery, Darndale,
Dublin 17
Tel 086-7954706
(Darndale-Belcamp, Dublin)

Pierce, Patrick (IC)
Rosminian House of Prayer,
Glencomeragh House,
Kilsheelan, Co Tipperary
Tel 052-6133181

Piert, John, Very Rev Canon,
PC
The Presbytery,
Johnstown, Arklow,
Co Wicklow
Tel 0402-31112
(Arklow, Dublin)

Plasek, Dariusz
Polish Chaplain,
Cathedral Presbytery,
Ennis, Co Clare
Tel 065-6824043/087-
7051257
(Abbey Cluster (Ennis),
Killaloe)

Planell, Francis
Harvieston,
Cunningham Road, Dalkey,
Co Dublin
Tel 01-2859877
(Opus Dei)

Plower, Thomas (MSC)
Church of the Resurrection,
Headford Road, Galway
Tel 091-762883
(Tirellan, Galway)

Plunkett, Oliver, Very Rev, PP
7 Crescent Avenue, Limerick
(St Joseph's, Limerick)

Poland, James, Very Rev
Rostrevor, Co Down
(Dromore, retired)

Pollock, James (IC)
Faughart Parish, St Brigid's,
Kilcurry,
Dundalk, Co Louth
Tel 042-9334410

Ponkattill, Manoj, CC
The Presbytery,
St Martin de Porres Parish,
Aylesbury, Dublin 24
Tel 01-4510160
(Tallaght, Oldbawn, Dublin)

Poole, John (OMI)
Oblate House of Retreat,
Inchicore, Dublin 8
Tel 01-4534408/4541805

Poole, Joseph (CSSp)
Community Leader,
Spiritan Community,
Ballintubber, Castlerea,
Co Roscommon
Tel 094-9655226

Porter, Michael, PP
Parochial House,
447 Victoria Road,
Ballymagorry, Strabane,
Co Tyrone BT82 0AT
Tel 028-718802274
(Leckpatrick, Derry)

Powell, Eric (SDS)
Room 420,
Our Lady's Manor,
Bullock Castle,
Dalkey, Co. Dublin
Tel 01-2718043

Powell, Gerald, Very Rev, PP
4 Holymount Road, Gilford,
Craigavon,
Co Armagh BT63 6AT
Tel 028-40624236
(Tullylish, Dromore)

Powell, Oliver
Gort Ard University
Residence,
Rockbarton North, Galway
Tel 091-523846
(Opus Dei)

Power, Anthony, CC
35 Grange Park Avenue,
Raheny, Dublin 5
Tel 01-8480244/0863905205
(Grange Park, Dublin)

Power, Brian, Very Rev, PP
Dunmore East,
Co Waterford
Tel 051-383127
(Killea (Dunmore East),
Waterford & L.)

Power, Gregory, Very Rev, PE
St Mary's, Clonmel,
Co Tipperary
Tel 052-6182690
(Waterford & L., retired)

Power, Jackie (OSA)
St Augustine's,
Taylor's Lane,
Ballyboden, Dublin 16
Tel 01-4241000

Power, Joseph, Very Rev, PP
Kilrush, Bunclody,
Enniscorthy, Co Wexford
Tel 053-9377262
(Kilrush and Askamore,
Ferns)

Power, Liam, Very Rev, PP
30 Viewmount Park,
Waterford
Tel 051-873073
(St Joseph and Benildus,
Waterford & L.)

Power, Nicholas, Very Rev
Canon
Moorfield, Rathaspeck,
Co Wexford
(Ferns, retired)

Power, Patrick (OFM), PP
Provincial Delegate,
St Anthony's Parish (English-
Speaking Chaplaincy),
23/25 Oudstrijderslaan,
1950 Kraainem, Belgium
Tel 0032-2-7201970

Power, Robert, Very Rev, Adm
Ardfinnan, Clonmel,
Co Tipperary
Tel 052-7466216
(Ardfinnan, Waterford & L.)

Power, Seamus, Very Rev, PE
19 Halcyon Place,
Park Village,
Castletroy, Limerick
(Limerick, retired)

Power, Thomas J., (MSC) PP
The Presbytery, Killinarden,
Tallaght, Dublin 24
Tel 01-4522251
(Killinarden, Dublin)

Prendergast, Patrick, Very
Rev, PP
Glenties, Co Donegal
Tel 074-9551117
(Glenties, Raphoe)

Prendergast, Joseph (CSSp)
Kimmage Manor,
Whitehall Road, Dublin 12
Tel 01-4064300

Prendiville, James, CC
The Presbytery, Hollywood
(via Naas), Co Wicklow
Tel 045-864206
(Ballymore Eustace, Dublin)

Prendiville, William (OSA)
St Augustine's Priory,
O'Connell Street, Limerick
Tel 061-415374

Price, Cathal
(priest in residence)
54 Foxfield St John, Dublin 5
Tel 01-8323683
(Kilbarrack-Foxfield, Dublin)

Prior, Dermot, Very Rev, PP
Virginia, Co Cavan
Tel 049-8547063
(*Virginia (Lurgan)*, Kilmore)

Prior, Paul
Director of Formation,
St Patrick's College,
Maynooth, Co Kildare
(Kilmore)

Przanowski, Krzysztof, CC
Polish Chaplaincy,
St Mary's Athlone,
Co Westmeath
Tel 090-6472088
(*Athlone*, Ardagh & Cl.)

Purcell, Denis
Mount Carmel, Callan,
Co Kilkenny
(Ossory)

Purcell, Eamon
67a Abbey Court,
Fr Russell Road, Dooradoyle,
Limerick
(Limerick)

Purcell, Francis, Very Rev
St John's Presbytery,
Kilkenny
Tel 056-7721072/
086-6010001
(*St John's*, Ossory)

Purcell, James, CC
Rosegreen, Cashel,
Co Tipperary
Tel 062-61713
(*Cashel*, Cashel & E.)

Purcell, Richard (OCSO), Rt
Rev Dom
Pontifical Commissary,
Mount Saint Joseph Abbey,
Roscrea, Co Tipperary
Tel 0505-25600

Purcell, William
Director of Vocations,
St Kieran's College, Kilkenny
Tel 056-7721086
St Mary's Cathedral,
Kilkenny
Tel 056-7721253/
087-6286858
(*St Mary's*, Ossory)

Pyburn, Daniel, Very Rev, PP
The Presbytery, Dromore,
Bantry, Co Cork
(*Caheragh*, Cork & R.)

---

### Q

Queally, Peter (CSSp)
Rockwell College, Cashel,
Co Tipperary
Tel 062-61444

Queally, Peter, AP
Oileán Cléire, Baltimore,
Co Cork
Tel 028-39103
(*Rath and the Islands*, Cork
& R.)

Quealy, Patrick, Very Rev
Canon, PE
Care Choice Dungarvan,
The Burgery,
Dungarvan, Co Waterford
Tel 058-40200
(Waterford & L., retired)

Quigley, Seán, PC
48 Aughrim Street, Dublin 7
Tel 01-8386176
(*Aughrim Street*, Dublin)

Quigley, Thomas, Very Rev, PP
Latton, Castleblayney,
Co Monaghan
Tel 042-9742212
(*Latton*, Clogher)

Quinlan, Brendan, Co-PP
Presbytery, Church Grounds,
Laurel Lodge, Castleknock,
Dublin 15
Tel 01-8208144
(*Laurel Lodge-*
*Carpenterstown*, Dublin)

Quinlan, John (SMA)
African Missions,
Blackrock Road, Cork
Tel 021-4292871

Quinlan, Leo, Very Rev
42a Strand Street, Skerries,
Co Dublin
(Dublin, retired)

Quinlivan, Brendan
(On sabbatical)
Director of Communications,
c/o Cathedral House,
Ennis, Co Clare
Tel 065-6869094/087-
2736310
(Killaloe)

Quinn, Brian, Very Rev, PP
Ballyraine, Letterkenny,
Co Donegal
Tel 074-9127600
(*Aughaninshin*, Raphoe)

Quinn, Denis, CC
The Presbytery,
Kimberley Road, Greystones,
Co Wicklow
Tel 01-2877025
(*Greystones*, Dublin)

Quinn, Denis, Very Rev, PP
Falcarragh, Co Donegal
Tel 074-9135196
(*Falcarragh*, Raphoe)

Quinn, Desmond (SSC)
St Columban's, Dalgan Park,
Navan, Co Meath
Tel 046-9021525

Quinn, Edward (OMI), Co-PP
The Presbytery, Darndale,
Dublin 17
Tel 01-8474547
(*Darndale-Belcamp*, Dublin)

Quinn, Frank (IC)
Mission Secretary,
Clonturk House,
Ormond Road,
Drumcondra, Dublin 9
Tel 01-6877014

Quinn, James, Canon, CC,
Adm
Taugheen, Claremorris,
Co Mayo
Administration Taugheen
Tel 094-9362500
(*Crossboyne and Taugheen*,
Tuam)

Quinn, John (SDB)
Vice-Rector and Bursar,
Rinaldi House,
72 Sean McDermott Street,
Dublin 1
Tel 01-8363358

Quinn, John, Very Rev, Adm
West Barrs, Glenfarne,
Co Leitrim
Tel 071-9855134
(*Glenfarne*, Kilmore)

Quinn, John, Very Rev, PP
Gortletteragh,
Carrick-on-Shannon,
Co Leitrim
Tel 071-9631074
(*Gortletteragh*, Ardagh &
Cl.)

Quinn, Ken
General Hospital,
Co Wexford
Tel 053-9142233
(Ferns)

Quinn, Michael, Very Rev, PP
Carracastle,
Ballaghaderreen, Co Mayo
Tel 094-9254301
(*Carracastle*, Achonry)

Quinn, Michael, Very Rev, PP
Crosserlough, Co Cavan
Tel 049-4336122
(*Crosserlough*, Kilmore)

Quinn, Richard (CSSp)
11 Silchester Court,
Glenageary, Co Dublin
Tel 01-2806375

Quinn, Séamus, Very Rev, PP
Parochial House,
Belcoo East, Belcoo
Co Fermanagh BT93 5FJ
Tel 028-66386225
(*Arney (Cleenish)*, Clogher)

Quinn, Sean, Very Rev, PE, AP
Parochial House,
Dillonstown, Dunleer,
Co Louth
Tel 041-6863570
(*Togher*, Armagh)

Quinn, Seán, Very Rev, PP
Parochial House,
Louth Village, Dundalk,
Co Louth
Tel 042-9374285
(*Louth*, Armagh)

Quinn, Stephen
Carmelite Priory,
Boars Hill, Oxford OX1 5HB
(Down & C., retired)

Quinn, Tadhg, Very Rev, PP
St John the Apostle,
Knocknacarra, Galway
Tel 091-590059
(*St John the Apostle*,
Galway)

Quirke, Brendan (OSA)
St Augustine's,
Taylor's Lane,
Ballyboden, Dublin 16
Tel 01-4241000

Quirke, Ciary (SJ)
Manresa House,
Dollymount, Dublin 3
Tel 01-8331352

Quirke, Denis, Very Rev
Fatima Home,
Oakpark, Tralee, Co Kerry
(Kerry, retired)

Quirke, Gerard, Very Rev, PP
Ballingarry, Thurles,
Co Tipperary
Tel 052-9154115
(*Ballingarry*, Cashel & E.)

---

### R

Rabbitte, Peter, Very Rev
Canon, PP, VF
The Cathedral, Galway
Tel 091-563577
(*Cathedral*, Galway)

Radley, William, Very Rev, PP
St Agatha's Parish Centre,
Headford, Killarney,
Co Kerry
Tel 064-7754008
(*Glenflesk*, Kerry)

Rafferty, Colm (SSC)
126 Grove Road, Swatragh,
Co Derry BT46 5Q2
Tel 028-79401209

Rafferty, James (CM)
99 Cliftonville Road,
Belfast BT14 6JQ
Tel 028-90751771

Rafferty, Terence, Very Rev
c/o Bishop's House
(Dromore)

Rafter, Roger (SAC)
Pallottine College, Thurles,
Co Tipperary
Tel 0504-21202

Raftery, Eamon (SMA)
St Vincent's College,
Castleknock, Dublin 15
Tel 01-8213051

Raftery, Gregory
An Der Tiefenriede 11, 3000,
Hanover 1, Germany
(Galway)

Raftery, Thomas (CSSp)
Templeogue College,
Dublin 6W
Tel 01-4903909

Raftice, Robert, Very Rev
Canon
St Joseph's Home,
Ferrybank, Waterford
Tel 051-833006/086-0614682
(Ossory, retired)
Raleigh, Patrick (SSC)
Regional Director,
St Columban's, Dalgan Park,
Navan, Co Meath
Tel 046-9021525
Ralph, Joseph (OP)
St Catherine's,
Newry, Co Down BT35 8BN
Tel 028-30262178
Ramsbottom, Pat, Very Rev,
PE
Gorman's Cottage,
Cooleragh, Co Kildare
Tel 045-890744
(Kildare & L., retired)
Randles, James A., Very Rev
Canon, PE
Sacred Heart Residence,
Sybil Hill Road,
Raheny, Dublin 5
(Dublin, retired)
Reaume, Michael (SM)
St Columba's,
Church Avenue, Ballybrack,
Co Dublin
Tel 01-2858301
Reburn, Frank, Co-PP
11 Millview Court,
Malahide, Co Dublin
Tel 01-8451902
(Malahide, Yellow Walls,
Dublin)
Reche, Charles-Benoit
St Patrick Friary,
64 Delmege Park,
Moyross, Limerick
Tel 061-458071
Reddan, Michael (SVD)
Donamon Castle,
Roscommon
Tel 090-6662222
Reddan, Michael (SVD)
The Presbytery, John's Mall,
Birr, Co Offaly
Tel 057-9121757/
087-7599789
(Birr, Killaloe)
Redmond, Noel (CSSp)
Templeogue College,
Dublin 6W
Tel 01-4903909
Redmond, Richard, CC
(Ballyduff) The Square,
Ferns, Enniscorthy,
Co Wexford
Tel 053-9366162
(Ferns, Ferns)
Redmond, Stephen (SJ)
Milltown Park,
Sandford Road, Dublin 6
Tel 01-2698411/2698113

Redmond, Tim (SPS)
Editor, Africa,
St Patrick's, Kiltegan,
Co Wicklow
Tel 059-6473600
Reedy, Patrick (CSSp)
Templeogue College,
Dublin 6W
Tel 01-4903909
Regan, Christopher (OFM)
Franciscan Friary,
Liberty Street, Cork
Tel 021-4270302
Regan, Harry
Presbytery 1,
Church Grounds,
Kill Avenue, Dun Laoghaire,
Co Dublin
Tel 01-2800901
(Dublin, retired)
Regan, James (SPS)
St Patrick's, Kiltegan,
Co Wicklow
Tel 059-6473600
(retired)
Regan, Michael, Very Rev, PP
Carraig na bhFear, Co Cork
Tel 021-4884119
(Carraig na Bhfear, Cork &
R.)
Regula, Robert (OP), CC
St Mary's Priory, Tallaght,
Dublin 24
Tel 01-4048100
(Tallaght, St Mary's, Dublin)
Reid, Desmond (CSSp)
Templeville Road,
Dublin 6W
Tel 01-4903909
Reidy, Denis, Very Rev Mgr,
PE
Teach on tSagairt,
Main Street,
Carrigtwohill, Co Cork
Tel 021-4533776
(Cloyne, retired)
Reidy, Raymond (SPS), CC
Church of the Resurrection,
Fethard Road, Clonmel,
Co Tipperary
Tel 052-6123239
(Clonmel, SS Peter & Paul,
Waterford & L.)
Reihill, Seamus (SPS)
St Patrick's, Kiltegan,
Co Wicklow
Tel 059-6473600
Reilly, Anthony, Very Rev, PP
Parochial House,
Palmerstown, Dublin 20
Tel 01-6266254
(Palmerstown, Dublin)
Reilly, Eamon (OMI)
Oblate House of Retreat,
Inchicore, Dublin 8
Tel 01-4534408/4541805

Reilly, John, Very Rev, PP
Lahardane, Ballina, Co Mayo
Tel 096-51007
(Lahardane, Killala)
Reilly, Liam, CC
St Patrick's Presbytery,
Ballina, Co Mayo
Tel 096-71360
(Ballina (Kilmoremoy),
Killala)
Reilly, Martin (SPS)
c/o St Patrick's,
Kiltegan, Co Wicklow
Tel 059-6473600
Reilly, Matthew (SSC)
St Columban's, Dalgan Park,
Navan, Co Meath
Tel 046-9021525
Reilly, Michael, Very Rev, PP
Lanesboro, Co Longford
Tel 043-3321166
(Lanesboro, Ardagh & Cl.)
Reilly, Michael, Very Rev, PP
Parochial House,
Bunninadden, Ballymote,
Co Sligo
Tel 071-9183232
(Bunninadden (Kilshalvey,
Kilturra and Cloonoghill),
Achonry)
Reilly, Michael, Very Rev, PP,
VF
Belmullet, Co Mayo
Tel 097-81426
(Belmullet, Killala)
Reilly, Michael, Very Rev
Canon, PP
Castlegar, Galway
Tel 091-751548
(Castlegar, Galway)
Reilly, Patrick (OPraem), CC
13 Seaview Park, Portrane,
Co Dublin
Tel 01-8436099
(Donabate, Dublin)
Reilly, Peter J., Very Rev, Adm
Presbytery 1,
Ballycullen Avenue,
Firhouse, Dublin 24
Tel 01-4599855
(Firhouse, Dublin)
Reilly, William
Casilla 09-01-5825,
Guayaquil, Ecuador
(Killala)
Reilly, William, Very Rev
Knock, Inverin, Co Galway
Tel 091-593122
(Spiddal/Knock, Tuam)
Relihan, Patrick
Pontificio Collegio Irlandese,
Via dei Santi Quattro, 1,
00184, Rome
Tel 0039-06-772631
(Cloyne)

Revatto, Geoffrey (SSC)
St Columban's Retirement
Home, Dalgan Park, Navan,
Co Meath
Tel 046-9021525
Revatto, Thomas (SSC)
St Columban's Retirement
Home, Dalgan Park, Navan,
Co Meath
Tel 046-9021525
Reynolds, Brian (OP), CC
Droichead Nua, Co Kildare
Tel 045-431394
(Droichead Nua/Newbridge,
Kildare & L.)
Reynolds, Gerard (CSsR)
Clonard Monastery,
1 Clonard Gardens,
Belfast BT13 2RL
Tel 028-90445950
Reynolds, Kenneth (OFMCap)
St Francis Capuchin Friary
Rochestown, Co Cork
Tel 021-4896244
Reynolds, Kevin (MHM) Very
Rev, Adm
Ahascragh, Ballinasloe,
Co Galway
Tel 090-9688617
Reynolds, Michael B. (CSSp)
Holy Spirit Missionary
College, Kimmage Manor,
Dublin 12
Tel 01-4064300
Reynolds, Patrick (CSsR), CC
The Presbytery,
103 Cherry Orchard Avenue,
Dublin 10
Tel 01-6267930
(Cherry Orchard, Dublin)
Reynolds, William (SJ)
Clongowes Wood College,
Clane, Co Kildare
Tel 045-868663/868202
Rice, Gerard, Very Rev, PE
Moyglare Nursing Home,
Maynooth, Co Kildare
(Meath, retired)
Rice, Patrick, Very Rev Canon,
PE
Little Sisters of the Poor,
Holy Family Residence,
Roebuck Road, Dundrum,
Dublin 14
(Dublin, retired)
Rice, Séamus, Very Rev, PE
4 Ballymacnab Road,
Armagh BT60 2QS
Tel 028-37531620
(Armagh, retired)
Rice, Tony (CSsR)
Formator, St Joseph's,
Dundalk, Co Louth
Tel 042-9334042/9334762
Richardson, William
Archbishop's House,
Dromcondra, Dublin 9
Tel 8373732
(Dublin)

**Allianz (ⅲ)**

Rigney, Liam, Very Rev, PP, PhD
Parochial House,
Moyglare Road, Maynooth,
Co Kildare
Tel 01-6286220/087-2607377
(*Maynooth*, Dublin)

Riordan, Michael, Very Rev Canon
Mount Desert,
Lee Road, Cork
(Cork & R., retired)

Riordan, Patrick (SJ)
Irish Jesuit Provincialate,
Milltown Park,
Sandford Road, Dublin 6
Tel 01-4987333

Riordan, Raymond
Chaplain,
St Finbarr's Hospital,
Douglas Road, Cork
Tel 021-4966555

Riordan, Tom, Very Rev
Willow Lawn,
Ballinlough, Cork
(Cork & R., retired)

Roban, Myles (SSC)
10 Belfield Springs,
Enniscorthy, Co Wexford
Tel 053-9237770

Roberts, Donal, Very Rev Canon, PP, VF
Macroom, Co Cork
Tel 026-21068
(*Macroom*, Cloyne)

Robinson, Denis (CSSp)
Holy Spirit Missionary
College, Kimmage Manor,
Dublin 12
Tel 01-4064300

Robinson, Denis, CC
The Presbytery,
Mourne Road, Dublin 12
Tel 01-4556199
(*Mourne Road*, Dublin)

Robinson, John, Very Rev, PP
Borris-in-Ossory, Portlaoise,
Co Laois
Tel 0505-41148/087-2431412
(*Borris-in-Ossory*, Ossory)

Roche, Donal (OP)
St Mary's Priory, Tallaght,
Dublin 24
Tel 01-4048100

Roche, Donal, Very Rev, Adm
The Abbey,
Wicklow, Co Wicklow
Tel 0404-67196
(*Wicklow*, Dublin)

Roche, Joseph, Very Rev, PP
Parochial House, Ardrahan,
Co Galway
Priest in charge, Kilchreest
Tel 091-635164
(*Ardrahan & Kilchreest*,
Galway)

Roche, Luke, Very Rev, PP
Castlemaine, Co Kerry
Tel 066-9767322
(*Castlemaine*, Kerry)

Roche, Simon (OP)
St Mary's, Pope Quay, Cork
Tel 021-4502267

Rochford, Seamus, Very Rev, AP
Emly, Co Tipperary
Tel 062-57103
(*Emly*, Cashel & E.)

Rodgers, Jack (SPS)
St Patrick's, Kiltegan,
Co Wicklow
Tel 059-6473600

Rodgers, J. J., Very Rev
Killanena, Co Clare
Tel 061-925265
(Killaloe, retired)

Rodgers, Michael (SPS)
Tearmann Spirituality
Centre, Brockagh,
Glendalough,
Co Wicklow
Tel 0404-45208

Rodgers, Peter (OFMCap)
Capuchin Friary,
Church Street, Dublin 7
Tel 01-8730599

Rodrigues Da Silva, Edvaldo (CSSp)
Holy Spirit Missionary
College, Kimmage Manor,
Whitehall Road, Dublin 12
Tel 01-4064300

Rodriguez, Paulino (MSC)
(Peru) c/o Parish Office,
Herbert Road, Bray,
Co Wicklow
Tel 01-2868413
(*Bray Holy Redeemer*,
Dublin)

Rogan, Edward, Very Rev, AP
Enniscrone, Ballina,
Co Mayo
Tel 096-36164
(*Kilglass*, Killala)

Rogan, Sean, Very Rev Canon, PE
(priest in residence)
Parochial House,
121 Dublin Road, Kilcoo,
Co Down BT34 5HP
Tel 028-40630314
(*Kilcoo*, Down & C.)

Rogers, Patrick (CP)
St Paul's Retreat,
Mount Argus, Dublin 6W
Tel 01-4992000

Rogers, Thomas, Very Rev, PP
Holy Family Presbytery,
Luke Wadding Street,
Waterford
Tel 051-37527
(*Holy Family*, Waterford &
L.)

Rohan, Joseph, CC
Ballycotton, Midleton,
Co Cork
Tel 021-4647899
(*Cloyne*, Cloyne)

Ronayne, James, Very Rev, PP, VF
Clifden, Co Galway
Tel 095-21251
(*Clifden (Omey and
Ballindoon)*, Tuam)

Rooney, Joseph
(priest in residence)
45 Ballyholme Esplanade,
Bangor,
Co Down BT20 5NJ
Tel 028-91465425
(*Bangor*, Down & C.)

Rooney, Joseph, JCL
Office of the Armagh
Regional Marriage Tribunal,
511 Ormeau Road,
Belfast BT7 3GS
Tel 028-90491990
(Down & C.)

Rooney, Joseph (SM)
Superior, Chanel
Community,
Coolock, Dublin 5
Tel 01-8477133

Rooney, Noel, Very Rev, PP
279 Sunset Drive,
Cartron Point, Sligo
Tel 071-9142422
Chaplain,
Ballinode Vocational School,
Sligo
Tel 071-9147111
(*Sligo, Calry St Joseph's*,
Elphin)

Rosario, Francis Sunil, PC
c/o Parish Office
Tel 01-8560980

Rosario, Ripon (SJ)
John Sullivan House
56/56A Mulvey Park,
Dundrum, Dublin 14
Tel 01-298397

Rosbotham, Gabriel, CC
Crossmolina, Chapel Road,
Co Mayo
Tel 096-31344
(*Crossmolina*, Killala)

Rosney, Arnold, CC
5 Drumgeely Avenue,
Shannon, Co Clare
Tel 061-471513/087-8598710
(*Shannon*, Killaloe)

Ross, Jim (SM)
Fiji

Ross, Michael (SDB)
Salesian House,
45 St Teresa's Road,
Crumlin, Dublin 12
Tel 01-4555605

Rothery, Colin, Adm
Parochial House,
49 Seville Place, Dublin 1
Tel 01-8741625
(*North Wall-Seville Place*,
Dublin)

Router, Michael, Very Rev, PP, VF
St Anne's, Bailieboro,
Co Cavan
Tel 042-9665117
(*Bailieboro (Killann)*,
Kilmore)

Rowan, Kevin, Co-PP
St Mary's Presbytery,
Willbrook Road,
Rathfarnham, Dublin 14
Tel 01-4932390
(*Rathfarnham*, Dublin)

Ruane, Noel S. (SVD)
1 & 3 Pembroke Road,
Dublin 4
Tel 01-6680904

Ruddy, Michael (SSCC), PP
Sacred Heart Presbytery,
St John's Drive, Clondalkin
Dublin 22
Tel 01-4570032
(*Sruleen*, Dublin)

Rushe, Patrick, Very Rev Adm, VF
Dundalk Institute of
Technology,
Dublin Road, Dundalk,
Co Louth
Tel 042-9370224
(Armagh)

Russell, Thomas (OFM)
Franciscan Friary, Clonmel,
Co Tipperary
Tel 052-6121378

Russell, William, Adm
Enniscouch,
Rathkeale, Co Limerick
Tel 069-63490/087-2272825
(*Rathkeale*, Limerick)

Ryan, Aidan, Very Rev, PP
Ballinahown, Athlone,
Co Westmeath
Tel 090-6430124
(*Ballinahown, Boher &
Pollough (Lemanaghan)*,
Ardagh & Cl.)

Ryan, Aloysius (OCarm)
Carmelite Priory,
White Abbey, Co Kildare
Tel 045-521391

Ryan, Anthony, Very Rev, PP
Doon, Co Limerick
Tel 061-380165
(*Doon*, Cashel & E.)

Ryan, Bill (OFMCap)
Capuchin Friary,
Ard Mhuire, Creeslough,
Letterkenny, Co Donegal
Tel 074-9138005

Ryan, Conor, Very Rev Canon, PP, VF
Castlefarm, Hospital,
Co Limerick
Tel 061-383108
(*Hospital*, Cashel & E.)

Ryan, Damian, Very Rev, PP
Manister, Croom, Co Limerick
Tel 061-397335
(*Manister*, Limerick)

Ryan, Daniel J.
c/o Archbishop's House,
Thurles, Co Tipperary
(Cashel & E., retired)

Ryan, Denis, PE
1 Rossmore Road,
Dublin 6W
(Dublin, retired)

Ryan, Derek (CSsR)
Santa Maria dei Monti
Mission, Furancungo,
Mozambique, Africa
c/o Marianella/
Liguori House,
75 Orwell Road, Rathgar,
Dublin 6
Tel 01-4067100

Ryan, Dermot, Dr
President,
St Kieran's College, Kilkenny
Tel 056-7721086/
086-6097483
(Ossory)

Ryan, Eugene (SSC)
St Columban's, Dalgan Park,
Navan, Co Meath
Tel 046-9021525

Ryan, Fergal, Very Rev, PP
Cahirdaniel, Co Kerry
Tel 066-9475111
(*Cahirdaniel*, Kerry)

Ryan, Fergus (OP)
Convent of SS Xystus and Clement
Collegio San Clemente,
Via Labicana 95,
00184 Roma
Tel 0039-06-7740021

Ryan, Gerard (CSSp)
Holy Spirit Missionary
College, Kimmage Manor,
Whitehall Road, Dublin 12
Tel 01-4064300

Ryan, James (OFMCap)
Capuchin Friary,
Ard Mhuire, Creeslough,
Letterkenny, Co Donegal
Tel 074-9138005

Ryan, James, Rt Rev Mgr, AP
Bohermore, Cashel,
Co Tipperary
Tel 062-61353
(*Cashel*, Cashel & E.)

Ryan, James, Very Rev
(priest in residence)
Cleariestown, Co Wexford
Tel 053-9139110
(Ferns, retired)

Ryan, John, Very Rev, PP
Aghinagh, Coachford,
Co Cork
Tel 026-48037
(*Aghinagh*, Cloyne)

Ryan, John J., Very Rev, AP
Garryspillane, Kilmallock,
Co Limerick
Tel 062-53189
(*Knocklong*, Cashel & E.)

Ryan, Joseph (OSCO)
Superior, Mellifont Abbey,
Collon, Co Louth
Tel 041-9826103

Ryan, Joseph, Very Rev, Co-PP
41 Cremore Heights,
St Canice's Road, Glasnevin,
Dublin 11
Tel 01-8573776
(*Ballygall*, Dublin)

Ryan, Liam (OSA)
Prior, St Augustine's Priory,
O'Connell Street, Limerick
Tel 061-415374

Ryan, Liam, Very Rev, DD
Cappamore, Co Tipperary
(Cashel & E., retired)

Ryan, Liam, Very Rev Canon,
PE, VF
Holycross, Thurles,
Co Tipperary
(Cashel & E., retired)

Ryan, Martin (CSsR)
Marianella/Liguori House,
75 Orwell Road, Rathgar,
Dublin 6
Tel 01-4067100

Ryan, Martin (OCarm)
Prior, Carmelite Priory,
Moate, Co Westmeath
Tel 090-6481160

Ryan, Michael
c/o Archbishop's House,
Thurles, Co Tipperary
Tel 0504-21512
(Cashel and E.)

Ryan, Michael (SSC)
112 The Sycamores,
Freshford Road, Kilkenny
Tel 086-8977569

Ryan, Michael, Rt Rev Dom
(OCSO)
Abbot, Bolton Abbey,
Moone, Co Kildare
Tel 059-8624102

Ryan, Michael, Rt Rev Mgr,
PP, VG
Castlecomer, Co Kilkenny
Tel 056-4441262/
086-3693863
(*Castlecomer*, Ossory)

Ryan, Michael J., Very Rev, PE
Clonmel Road, Cahir,
Co Tipperary
Tel 052-7443004
(Waterford & L., retired)

Ryan, Noel (SPS)
St Patrick's, Kiltegan,
Co Wicklow
Tel 059-6473600

Ryan, Patrick (OCSO)
Mount Melleray Abbey,
Cappoquin, Co Waterford
Tel 058-54404

Ryan, Patrick, Very Rev, PP
The Presbytery, Eadestown,
Naas, Co Kildare
Tel 045-862187
(*Eadestown*, Dublin)

Ryan, Patrick J. (CSSp)
Holy Spirit Missionary
College, Kimmage Manor,
Dublin 12
Tel 01-4064300

Ryan, Patrick J. (MHM)
St Joseph's House,
50 Orwell Park, Rathgar,
Dublin 6
Tel 01-4127700

Ryan, Seamus, Very Rev, PE
148B Blackditch Road,
Ballyfermot, Dublin 10
Tel 01-6265695
(Dublin, retired)

Ryan, Thomas, Very Rev, CC
Gleneden,
North Circular Road,
Limerick
Tel 061-329448/087-2997733
(*Our Lady of the Rosary*,
Limerick)

Ryan, Thomas, Very Rev, PP
5 Derravaragh Road,
Caherdavin Park, Limerick
Tel 061-452790
(*Christ the King*, Limerick)

Ryan, Thomas J., Very Rev
Canon, AP, VF
Bohergar, Brittas,
Co Limerick
Tel 061-352223
(*Murroe and Boher*, Cashel
& E.)

Ryan, Tom, Very Rev, PP
Director, Lourdes
Pilgrimage,
Shannon, Co Clare
Tel 061-361257
Parish:
SS John & Paul Presbytery,
4 Dun na Rí, Shannon,
Co Clare
Tel 061-364133/087-2349816
(*Shannon*, Killaloe)

Ryan, William, Very Rev
Canon, PP, VF
Parochial House,
Dungarvan, Co Waterford
Tel 058-42374
(*Dungarvan*, Waterford & L.)

Rybansky, Eugene
Team Assistant and Chaplain
to Slovakian Community,
The Presbytery,
2 River Valley Heights,
Swords, Co Dublin
Tel 01-8404162
(*River Valley*, Dublin)

Ryder, Andrew (SCI)
Sacred Heart Fathers,
Fairfield, 66 Inchicore Road,
Dublin 8
Tel 01-4538655

Ryder, John, PEm
16 Whitehouse Park,
Buncrana Road, Derry
(Derry, retired)

## S

Sammon, Francis (SJ), CC
156B Rathgar Road,
Dublin 6
Tel 01-4966042
(*Rathgar*, Dublin)

Sanda, Krzysztof (SCHR)
St Malachy's Presbytery,
24 Alfred Street,
Belfast BT2 8EN
Tel 028-90321713
(*St Malachy's*, Down & C.)

Sandham, Denis (MI)
(Chaplain to Beaumont
Hospital)
Superior, St Camillus,
South Hill Avenue,
Blackrock, Co Dublin
Tel 01-2882873

Scallon, Kevin (CM)
Ministry to Priests,
Phibsboro,
St Peter's, Dublin 7
Tel 01-8389708

Scallon, Paschal (CM), Very
Rev, Co-PP
St Peter's, Phibsboro,
Dublin 7
Tel 01-8389708
(*Phibsborough*, Dublin)

Scanlan, Charles
Ballinwillin, Lismore,
Co Waterford
Tel 058-54282
(Waterford & L.)

Scanlan, Liam V. (SPS)
St Patrick's, Kiltegan,
Co Wicklow
Tel 059-6473600

Scanlan, Patrick, Very Rev, PP
Castletownroche, Co Cork
Tel 022-26188
(*Castletownroche*, Cloyne)

Scanlon, Columba (OFM)
Adam & Eve's,
4 Merchant's Quay,
Dublin 8
Tel 01-6771128

Scanlon, Michael, Very Rev, PP
Cloghan, Birr, Co Offaly
Tel 090-6457122
(*Cloghan and Banagher*,
Ardagh & Cl.)

Scanlon, Thomas (CP)
Passionist Formation
Community,
7 Hills Mews,
Florence Road,
London W5 3RG

Schmitz, Matthew (LC)
Dublin Oak Academy,
Kilcroney, Bray,
Co Wicklow
Tel 01-2863290

Schroedel, Lawrence (CFR)
St Patrick Friary,
64 Delmege Park, Moyross,
Limerick
Tel 061-458071

Scott, Michael (SDB)
Salesian House,
45 St Teresa's Road,
Crumlin, Dublin 12
Tel 01-4555605

Scott, Philip (OCSO)
Our Lady of Bethlehem
Abbey,
11 Ballymena Road,
Portglenone, Ballymena,
Co Antrim BT44 8BL
Tel 028-25821211

Screene, Michael (MSC)
Leader, 'Croí Nua',
Rosary Lane,
Taylor's Hill, Galway
Tel 091-520960

Scriven, Richard, Very Rev, PP,
VF
The Rower, Inistioge,
Co Kilkenny
Tel 087-2420033
(*Inistioge*, Ossory)

Scully, Anthony, CC
St Brigid's Presbytery,
Brittas Bay, Co Wicklow
Tel 0404-47177
(*Kilbride and Barndarrig*,
Dublin)

Scully, Brendan (OFM)
Associate Pastor,
St Anthony's Parish (English-
Speaking Chaplaincy),
23/25 Oudstrijderslaan,
1950 Kraainem, Belgium
Tel +0032-2-7201970

Scully, Michael (SSC)
St Columban's, Dalgan Park,
Navan, Co Meath
Tel 046-9021525

Scully, Thomas (OMI)
Oblate House of Retreat,
Inchicore, Dublin 8
Tel 01-4534408/4541805

Seaver, Patrick, CC
4 Glenview Terrace,
Farranshone, Limerick
Tel 061-328838
(*St Munchin's and St Lelia's*,
Limerick)

Seery, Michael, Very Rev, PP
Parochial House,
115 Omagh Road,
Ballygawley,
Co Tyrone BT70 2AG
Tel 028-85568208
(*Ballygawley (Errigal
Kieran)*, Armagh)

Semla, Mariusz, CC
Tamney, Letterkenny,
Co Donegal
Tel 074-9159015
(*Tamney (Clondavaddog*,
Raphoe)

Serrage, Michael (MSC)
Formation House,
56 Mulvey Park, Dundrum,
Dublin 16
Tel 01-2951856

Sexton, Frank (OSA)
St Augustine's Priory,
Washington Street, Cork
Tel 021-4275398/4270410

Sexton, John
(priest in residence)
Killargue, Drumahaire
Co Leitrim
Tel 071-9164131
(*Drumahaire and Killargue*,
Kilmore)

Sexton, Pat, Very Rev
5 Cottage Gardens,
Station Road, Ennis,
Co Clare
Tel 065-6840828/087-
2477814
(Killaloe, retired)

Sexton, Peter (SJ)
House 27, Trinity College,
Dublin 2
Tel 01-8961260
(Dublin)

Sexton, Sean, Very Rev, PP
Kilnamona, Ennis, Co Clare
Tel 065-6829507/
087-2621884
(*Kilnamona (Inagh),* Killaloe)

Sexton, Tom (OSA)
St Augustine's Priory
Washington Street, Cork
Tel 021-4275398/4270410

Seymour, Tom, Very Rev
Church Road, Nenagh,
Co Tipperary
Tel 067-31831/087-2889055
(Killaloe, retired)

Shanahan, John, Very Rev, PP
Valentia Island, Co Kerry
Tel 066-9476104
(*Valentia*, Kerry)

Shanahan, Tom (OCD)
The Abbey, Loughrea,
Co Galway
Tel 091-841209

Shannon, Declan, CC
St Mary's, Athlone,
Co Westmeath
Tel 090-6472088
(*Athlone*, Ardagh & Cl.)

Shannon, Richard, CC
7 Cardiff Castle Road,
Finglas West, Dublin 11
Tel 01-8343928
(*Finglas West*, Dublin)

Sharkey, Liam
Ballyweelin, Rosses Point, Co
Sligo
(Elphin, retired)

Sharkey, Lorcan, Very Rev, PP
Cloghan, Lifford,
Co Donegal
Tel 074-9133007
(*Cloghan*, Raphoe)

Shaughnessy, Bernard, CC
Coolarne, Turloughmore,
Co Galway
Tel 091-797626
(*Lackagh*, Tuam)

Sheary, Patrick (SJ)
Irish Jesuit Provincialate,
Milltown Park,
Sandford Road, Dublin 6
Tel 01-4987333

Sheedy, Michael, Very Rev, PP
Toler Street, Kilrush,
Co Clare
Tel 065-9051093
(*Kilrush*, Killaloe)

Sheehan, Anthony, CC
5 Lavallin Drive,
Whitechurch, Co Cork
Tel 021-4200184
(*Blarney*, Cloyne)

Sheehan, Joseph (CSSp)
Holy Spirit Missionary
College, Kimmage Manor,
Dublin 12
Tel 01-4064300

Sheehan, Martin, Very Rev,
Adm
St Joseph's, Lauragh,
Killarney, Co Kerry
Tel 064-6683107
(*Tuosist*, Kerry)

Sheehan, Michael, CC
Parochial House,
11 Moy Road, Portadown,
Co Armagh BT62 1QL
Tel 028-38332218
(*Portadown (Drumcree)*,
Armagh)

Sheehan, Michael, Very Rev,
Adm
St Patrick's Presbytery,
199 Donegall Street,
Belfast BT1 2FL
Tel 028-90324597
(*St Patrick's*, Down & C.)

Sheehan, Niall
Portadown, Co Armagh
(Dromore, retired)

Sheehan, Patrick (MSC)
Woodview House,
Mount Merrion Avenue,
Blackrock, Co Dublin
Tel 01-2881644

Sheehan, Patrick, Very Rev
Canon
'Shalom', Rossbeigh,
Glenbeigh, Co Kerry
(Kerry, retired)

Sheehan, Patrick, Very Rev, PP
The Presbytery,
Bell Steel Road, Poleglass,
Belfast BT17 0PB
Tel 028-90625739
(*The Nativity*, Down & C.)

Sheehan, Rory, Very Rev, PP
Netherley Lodge,
130 Upper Dunmurry Lane,
Belfast BT17 0EW
Tel 028-90616300
(*Our Lady Queen of Peace,
Kilwee*, Down & C.)

Sheehan, Ted
Cathedral Presbytery, Cork
Tel 021-4304325
(*Cathedral of St Mary & St
Anne*, Cork & R.)

Sheehy, James (SSC)
Dungarvan, Co Waterford
(retired)

Sheehy, Richard, Very Rev
(Moderator)
50 Cremore Road, Glasnevin,
Dublin 9
Tel 01-8373455
(*Glasnevin*, Dublin)

Sheeran, James, Very Rev, Co-
PP, CC
The Presbytery,
Kilmacanogue,
Bray, Co Wicklow
Tel 01-2862110
(*Bray, St Peter's,
Enniskerry/Kilmacanogue*,
Dublin)

Sheerin, Michael, Very Rev, PP
Parochial House,
Lobinstown, Navan,
Co Meath
Tel 046-9053155
(*Lobinstown*, Meath)

Sheil, Michael (SJ)
Rector,
Clongowes Wood College,
Clane, Co Kildare
Tel 045-868663/868202

Shelley, Padraig, CC
Tullow, Co Carlow
Tel 059-9152159
(*Tullow*, Kildare & L.)

Shen-yi Hssii, Matthew (SJ)
John Sullivan House,
56/56A Mulvey Park,
Dundrum, Dublin 14
Tel 01-2983978

**Allianz ⑪**

Sheppard, Jim, Very Rev
189 Carrigenagh Road,
Ballymartin, Kilkeel,
Co Down BT34 4GA
(Down & C., retired)

Sheridan, Christopher CC
7 Bayside Square East,
Sutton, Dublin 13
Tel 01-8322964
(Bayside, Dublin)

Sheridan, Daniel, Very Rev, PP
Killeshandra, Co Cavan
Tel 049-4334179
(Drumlane, Kilmore)

Sheridan, Eamon (SSC), PP
St Joseph's, Balcurris,
Dublin 11
Tel 01-8423865
(Balcurris, Dublin)

Sheridan, James (CP)
St Paul's Retreat,
Mount Argus, Dublin 6W
Tel 01-4992000

Sheridan, John-Paul
St Patrick's College,
Maynooth, Co Kildare
Tel 01-7083600
(Ferns)

Sheridan, Paddy, CC
Robeen, Hollymount,
Co Mayo
Tel 094-9540026
(Robeen, Tuam)

Sheridan, Patrick (CP)
St Paul's Retreat,
Mount Argus, Dublin 6W
Tel 01-4992000

Sherlock, Vincent, Very Rev,
PP
Diocesan Communications
Officer, Kilmovee,
Ballaghaderreen,
Co Mayo
Tel 094-9649137
(Kilmovee, Achonry)

Sherry, Richard, Rt Rev Mgr,
DD, PE
Presbytery 2,
Stillorgan Road,
Donnybrook, Dublin 4
Tel 01-2692102
(Dublin, retired)

Shevlin, James, Very Rev, PE
21 Village Green, Omeath,
Co Louth
(Armagh, retired)

Shibanada, Julius
Church of the Sacred Heart,
Donnybrook, Dublin 4
(Donnybrook, Dublin)

Shiel, Patrick, Very Rev
74 Mount Drinan Avenue,
Kinsealy Downs,
Swords, Co Dublin
(Dublin, retired)

Shiels, Michael, CC
Presbytery 1,
St Canice's Parish,
Finglas, Dublin 11
Tel 01-8341051
(Finglas, Dublin)

Shiels, Joseph (SSC)
(Derry, retired)

Shine, John, Rt Rev Mgr Dean,
AP
Priest's Road, Tramore,
Co Waterford
Tel 051-381531
(Tramore, Waterford & L.)

Shine, Larry (CSSp)
St Paul's Church
Kilmurray, Castlerea,
Co Roscommon
Tel 094-9651789
(Elphin)

Shire, Joseph, Very Rev, PP
Ballyagran, Kilmallock,
Co Limerick
Tel 063-82028/063-
98287/087-6924563
(Ballyagran and Granagh,
Kilmallock, Limerick)

Shortall, Bryan (OFMCap), PP
Guardian,
Capuchin Friary,
Church Street, Dublin 7
Tel 01-8730599
(Halston Street and Arran
Quay, Dublin)

Shortall, Michael, PC
87 Beechwood Lawns,
Rathcoole, Co Dublin
Tel 01-4587187
(Saggart, Dublin)

Shorten, Kieran (OFMCap)
Capuchin Friary,
Church Street, Dublin 7
Tel 01-8730599

Sikora, Krzysztof (SVD)
Donamon Castle,
Roscommon
Tel 090-6662222
Polish Chaplain,
Knock Shrine, Co Mayo
Tel 094-9388100
(Tuam)

Silke, John J., Very Rev Dean,
PhD
'Stella Maris', Portnablagh,
Co Donegal
Tel 074-9136122
(Raphoe, retired)

Silke, Leo (SMA)
SMA House, Wilton, Cork
Tel 021-4541069/4541884

Simpson, Michael, CC
St Kevin's Presbytery,
Pearse Street,
Sallynoggin, Co Dublin
Tel 01-2854667
(Sallynoggin, Dublin)

Sinnott, John, Very Rev, PP
56 Auburn Road, Killiney,
Co Dublin
Tel 01-2856660
(Johnstown-Killiney, Dublin)

Sinnott, John, Very Rev, PP
Enniscorthy, Co Wexford
Tel 053-9388559
(Ballindaggin, Ferns)

Sinnott, Michael (SSC)
St Columban's, Dalgan Park,
Navan, Co Meath
Tel 046-9021525

Sinnott, Patrick
Chaplain, St John's Hospital,
Enniscorthy, Co Wexford
Tel 053-9233228
(Ferns)

Sinnott, Peter J., CC
No. 3 Presbytery,
Castle Street, Dalkey,
Co Dublin
Tel 01-2859212
(Dalkey, Dublin)

Sinnott, Thomas (MHM)
Midlands Prison,
Dublin Road,
Portlaoise, Co Laois
Tel 057-8672222
(Kildare & L.)

Sisti, Louis (SAC)
Pallottine College,
Thurles, Co Tipperary
Tel 0504-21202

Siwek, Rafal, CC
The Presbytery, Cavan
Tel 049-4331404/4332269
(Cavan, Kilmore)

Skelly, Oliver, Very Rev, PP
Parochial House, Coole,
Co Westmeath
Tel 044-9661191
(Coole, Meath)

Slater, Albert, CC
Keenagh, Ballina,
Co Mayo
Tel 096-53018
(Crossmolina, Killala)

Slater, David (OSA)
St Augustine's,
Taylor's Lane,
Ballyboden, Dublin 16
Tel 01-4241000

Slattery, John, Very Rev
30 Meadow Ville,
Burke's Hill,
Birr, Co Offaly
Tel 087-3388899
(Killaloe, retired)

Slattery, Martin, Very Rev, AP
Apt 5, Luke Wadding Suites,
Adelphi Wharf, Waterford
Tel 051-311561
(Trinity Within and St
Patrick's, Waterford & L.)

Slattery, Sean, Very Rev
Limerick
(Clonfert, retired)

Sleeman, Simon (OSB)
Glenstal Abbey, Murroe,
Co Limerick
Tel 061-386103

Slevin, Paschal (OFM)
Franciscan House of Studies,
Dún Mhuire, Seafield Road,
Killiney, Co Dublin
Tel 01-2826760

Slevin, Peter (CM), Very Rev
President/Superior,
St Vincent's College,
Castleknock, Dublin 15
Tel 01-8213051

Sloan, Robert, CC
139 Andersonstown Road,
Belfast BT11 9BW
Tel 028-90613724
(St Agnes', Down & C.)

Smith, Adrian (SM), Most Rev
Archbishop
Honiara, Solomon Islands

Smith, David (MSC)
Woodview House,
Mount Merrion Avenue,
Blackrock, Co Dublin
Tel 01-2881644

Smith, Declan, Very Rev, PP
Parochial House, Taghmon,
Mullingar, Co Westmeath
Tel 044-9372140
(Taghmon, Meath)

Smith, Desmond (SMA)
Rathduff, Ballina, Co Mayo
Tel 096-21596
(Backs, Killala)

Smith, Kevin (OPraem), Rt Rev
Abbey of the Most Holy
Trinity and St Norbert,
Kilnacrott, Ballyjamesduff,
Co Cavan
Tel 049-8544416

Smith, Martin (SPS), CC
1 Green Road, Carlow
Tel 059-9142632
(Cathedral, Carlow, Carlow)

Smith, Michael, Most Rev,
DCL, DD
Bishop of Meath,
Bishop's House,
Dublin Road, Mullingar,
Co Westmeath
Tel 044-9348841
(Meath)

Smith, Philip, Very Rev, PP
Parochial House, Ballymore,
Mullingar, Co Westmeath
Tel 044-9356212
(Ballymore, Meath)

Smith, Sean, Very Rev Canon,
CC
The Presbytery,
Newtownmountkennedy,
Co Wicklow
Tel 01-2819253
(Kilquade, Dublin)

Smith, Terence (CSSp)
Holy Spirit Missionary
College, Kimmage Manor,
Dublin 12
Tel 01-4064300

Smith, Terry (OPraem)
Abbey of the Most Holy
Trinity and St Norbert,
Kilnacrott Abbey,
Ballyjamesduff,
Co Cavan
Tel 049-8544416

Smyth, Brendan, Very Rev, PP
Holy Trinity Presbytery,
26 Norglen Gardens,
Belfast BT11 8EL
Tel 028-90590985/6
(Holy Trinity, Down & C.)

Smyth, Derek, CC
2 Kill Lane, Foxrock,
Dublin 18
Tel 01-2894734
(Foxrock, Dublin)

Smyth, Edmund (OCD)
Prior, Karmel,
53/55 Marlborough Road,
Donnybrook, Dublin 4
Tel 01-6601832

Smyth, James (SJ)
St Francis Xavier's,
Upper Gardiner Street,
Dublin 1
Tel 01-8363411

Smyth, Malachy (SSC)
Communications
Co-ordinator,
St Columban's,
Dalgan Park, Navan,
Co Meath
Tel 046-9021525

Smyth, Michael (MSC)
'Croí Nua', Rosary Lane,
Taylor's Hill, Galway
Tel 091-520960

Smyth, Patrick (OCarm)
Carmelite Priory,
White Abbey, Co Kildare
Tel 045-521391

Smyth, Patrick J. (SSC)
St Columban's,
Dalgan Park, Navan,
Co Meath
Tel 046-9021525

Smyth, Terry (OPraem)
Abbey of the Most Holy
Trinity and St Norbert,
Kilnacrott,
Ballyjamesduff, Co Cavan
Tel 049-8544416

Solma, Martin (SM)
Provincial, Provincial
Headquaters,
4425 West Pine Boulevard,
St Louis, MO 6308-2301,
USA
Tel 001-314-533-1207

Somers, James (SDB)
Salesian House,
45 St Teresa's Road,
Crumlin, Dublin 12
Tel 01-4555605

Somers, P. J. (SDB)
Curragh Camp, Co Kildare
Tel 045-441277
(Curragh Camp, Kildare & L.)

Spelman, Joseph, Rt Rev Mgr
Sacred Heart Residence,
Sybil Hill Road
Raheny, Dublin 5
Tel 01-8332308
(Achonry, retired)

Spence, Michael, Very Rev
Diocesan Seminary,
120 Cliftonville Road,
Belfast BT14 6LA
(Down & C.)

Spencer, Paul Francis (CP)
St Paul's Retreat,
Mount Argus, Dublin 6W
Tel 01-4992000

Spillane, Joseph (SPS)
St Patrick's, Kiltegan,
Co Wicklow
Tel 059-6473600

Spillane, Martin
Chaplain,
Tralee General Hospital,
Co Kerry
Tel 066-7126222
(Kerry)

Spillane, Martin (SPS)
On temporary diocesan
work

Spring, Finbarr (OSA)
St Augustine's Priory,
Dungarvan,
Co Waterford
Tel 058-41136

Spring, Noel, Very Rev, PP
Ballybunion, Co Kerry
Tel 068-27102
(Ballybunion, Kerry)

Sri Waluyo, Franciscus
Xaverius (SSCC)
Provincialate,
Coudrin House, 27
Northbrook Road, Dublin 6
Tel 01-6473756

St John, Paul (SVD), CC
162 Walkinstown Road,
Dublin 12
Tel 01-4501372
(Walkinstown, Dublin)

Stack, Thomas, Very Rev Mgr,
PE
Apt 4, Maple Hall (adjoining
church),
Milltown Road, Dublin 6
Tel 01-2697613
(Dublin, retired)

Stafford, Patrick, Very Rev, PP
Glynn, Enniscorthy,
Co Wexford
Tel 053-9128115
(Glynn, Ferns)

Standún, Padraic, PP
Carna, Co Galway
Tel 091-595452
(Carna, Tuam)

Stankard, Edward, Rt Rev
Mgr, PP
Cappatagle, Ballinasloe,
Co Galway
Tel 091-843017
(Cappatagle & Kilrickle,
Clonfert)

Stanley, Cathal
Dominic Street, Portumna,
Co Galway
Tel 090-9759182
(Clonfert, retired)

Stanley, Gerard, Very Rev, PP
Parochial House, Rathkenny,
Co Meath
Tel 046-9054138
(Rathkenny, Meath)

Stanley, Paddy (SM), CC
Holy Family Parish,
Parochial House,
Dundalk, Co Louth
Tel 042-9336301
(Dundalk, Holy Family,
Armagh)

Stansfield, Oliver, (IC)
(priest in residence)
Parochial House, Omeath,
Co Louth
Tel 042-9375198
(Carlingford and Clogherny,
Armagh)

Stapleton, Christy
c/o Diocesan Office,
Balinalee Road, Longford
(Ardagh & Cl.)

Stapleton, Jim (CSSp)
Holy Spirit Missionary
College, Kimmage Manor,
Dublin 12
Tel 01-4064300

Stapleton, John, Very Rev, PP
Killeigh, Co Offaly
Tel 057-9344161
(Killeigh, Kildare & L.)

Stapor, Tomasz (SJ) (PME)
Jesuit Community,
27 Leinster Road,
Rathmines, Dublin 6
Tel 01-4970250

Starken, Brian (CSSp), Co-PP
Parish of St Ronan's
Deansrath, Clondalkin,
Dublin 22
Tel 01-4570380
(Bawnogue/Deansrath,
Dublin)

Starkey, Hugh, Very Rev
Canon
40 Minerstown Road,
Downpatrick,
Do Down BT30 8LR
(Down & C., retired)

Staunton, Brendan (SJ), PC
Pro-Cathedral House,
83 Marlborough Street,
Dublin 1
Tel 01-8745441
(Pro-Cathedral, Dublin)

Staunton, Fachtna (MHM)
St Joseph's House,
50 Orwell Park,
Rathgar, Dublin 6
Tel 01-4127700

Staunton, Patrick (OCarm)
Assistant Provincial,
Provincial Office and
Carmelite Community,
Gort Muire, Ballinteer,
Dublin 16
Tel 01-2984014

Staunton, Ray (SM)
Chanel College, Coolock,
Dublin 5
Tel 01-8480655/8480896

Steblecki, Hilary (OFM)
Vicar, Franciscan Friary,
Killarney, Co Kerry
Tel 064-6631334/6631066

Steed, Bernard (SSC)
St Columban's, Dalgan Park,
Navan, Co Meath
Tel 046-9021525

Steen, Brendan (CM)
St Paul's College, Raheny,
Dublin 5
Tel 01-8318113

Stenson, Alex, Rt Rev Mgr, PP
Parish priest of Artane and
Killester,
126 Furry Park Road,
Dublin 5
Tel 01-8333793
(Artane, Killester, Dublin)

Stevenson, Liam, Very Rev
Canon, PP, VF
6 Scarva Road, Banbridge,
Co Down BT32 3AR
Tel 028-40662136
(Seapatrick (Banbridge),
Dromore)

Stevenson, Patrick, Very Rev,
PP
The Presbytery, Crosshaven,
Co Cork
Tel 021-4831218
(Crosshaven, Cork & R.)

Stewart, John, Very Rev
27F Windsor Avenue,
Belfast BT9 6EE
(Down & C., retired)

Stokes, John, Very Rev
44 Carlton Court, Swords,
Co Dublin
(Dublin, retired)

Stone, Tom (OCD)
Avila, Bloomfield Avenue,
Morehampton Road,
Dublin 4
Tel 01-6430200

Allianz (ⅲ)

Strain, Paul, Very Rev, Adm
Holy Family Presbytery,
Newington Avenue,
Belfast BT15 2HP
Tel 028-90743119
(*Holy Family*, Down & C.)

Stritch, Denis, Very Rev, PP
Meelin, Newmarket,
Co Cork
Tel 029-68007
(*Rockchapel and Meelin*,
Cloyne)

Stuart, Gerard, Very Rev, PP
Parochial House, Ratoath,
Co Meath
Tel 01-8256207
(*Ratoath*, Meath)

Stuart, William (IC)
Clonturk House,
Ormond Road,
Drumcondra, Dublin 9
Tel 01-6877014

Sugrue, Patrick (CSsR)
Mastergeeha, Killarney,
Co Kerry
(retired)

Sullivan, Donal (IC)
Clonturk House,
Ormond Road,
Drumcondra, Dublin 9
Tel 01-6877014

Sullivan, Kevin
St John's Parish Centre,
Castle Street, Co Kerry
Tel 066-7122522
(*Tralee, St John's*, Kerry)

Sullivan, Paul (OCD)
St Teresa's,
Clarendon Street, Dublin 2
Tel 01-6718466/6718127

Sullivan, Shane, CC
Tuam, Co Galway
Tel 093-24250
(*Tuam (Cathedral of the
Assumption)*, Tuam)

Supple, Michael D., Very Rev
Canon
Holy Family Residence,
Roebuck Road,
Dundrum, Dublin 14
(Dublin, retired)

Surlis, Tómas Very Rev, DD
President, St Nathy's
College,
Ballaghaderreen,
Co Roscommon
Tel 094-9860010
(Achonry)

Susai, Jega (SVD)
Donamon Castle,
Roscommon
Tel 090-6662222

Swan, Colum, Very Rev, PE
32 Cherrygrove, Naas,
Co Kildare
Tel 045-856274
(Kildare & L., retired)

Swan, William, CC
St Aidan's, Enniscorthy,
Co Wexford
Tel 053-9235777
(*Enniscorthy, Cathedral of St
Aidan*, Ferns)

Sweeney, Dennis (IC)
Clonturk House,
Ormond Road, Drumcondra,
Dublin 9
Tel 01-8374840

Sweeney, Desmond, Very Rev,
PE
17 Meadowvale, Ramelton
Tel 074-9151085
(Raphoe, retired)

Sweeney, Donal, (OP), Very
Rev, PP, Prior
St Mary's Priory, Tallaght,
Dublin 24
Tel 01-4048100
(*Tallaght, St Mary's*, Dublin)

Sweeney, Eugene, Very Rev,
PP, VF
Parochial House,
17 Eagralougher Road,
Loughgall,
Co Armagh BT61 8LA
Tel 028-38891231
(*Loughgall*, Armagh)

Sweeney, Gerard (SMA)
SMA House, Claregalway,
Co Galway
Tel 091-798880

Sweeney, Gerard, PP
41 Moyle Road,
Newtownstewart,
Co Tyrone BT78 4AP
Tel 028-81661445
(*Newtownstewart*, Derry)

Sweeney, Hugh, Very Rev, PP
Glenswilly, New Mills,
Letterkenny, Co Donegal
Tel 074 9137020
(*Glenswilly*, Raphoe)

Sweeney, James, Very Rev, PP
Director of Fatima
Pilgrimage,
Bruckless, Co Donegal
Tel 074-9737015
(*Buckless (Killaghtee)*,
Raphoe)

Sweeney, John (SAC)
Pallottine College, Thurles,
Co Tipperary
Tel 0504-21202

Sweeney, Michael, Very Rev,
AP
Glenvar, Letterkenny,
Co Donegal
Tel 074-9150014
(*Rathmullan (Killygarvan &
Tullyfern)*, Raphoe)

Sweeney, Oliver, Very Rev, PP
Poulfur, Fethard-on-Sea,
New Ross, Co Wexford
Tel 051-397048
(Ferns)

Sweeney, Owen, Rt Rev Mgr,
Canon
Sacred Heart Residence,
Sybil Hill Road, Killester,
Dublin 5
(Dublin, retired)

Sweeney, Patrick, PC
13 Home Farm Road,
Drumcondra, Dublin 9
Tel 01-8377402
(*Ballymun Road*, Dublin)

Sweeney, Raymond, Very Rev,
PP
Ballymacward, Ballinasloe,
Co Galway
Tel 090-9687614
(*Ballymacward & Gurteen
(Ballymacward &
Clonkeenkerril)*, Clonfert)

Swinburne, Robbie (SDB),
Very Rev, PP
Salesian House, Milford,
Castletroy, Limerick
Tel 061-330268
(*Our Lady Help of Christians*,
Limerick)

Symonds, Paul
2/4 Broughshane Road,
Ballymena,
Co Antrim BT43 7DX
Tel 028-25641515
(Down & C., on leave)

Syzmoniak, Radoslaw (SChr),
CC
c/o Parish Office,
4 Killyman Road,
Dungannon,
Co Tyrone BT71 6DH
Tel 028-87726893
(*Dungannon (Drumglass,
Killyman and Tullyniskin)*

Szalwa, Marian (SCJ), PC
Parochial House,
St John Vianney,
Ardlea Road, Dublin 5
Tel 01-8474123
(*Ardlea*, Dublin)

Szymczyk, Tomasz (SJ)
St Francis Xavier's,
Upper Gardiner Street,
Dublin 1
Tel 01-8363411

## T

Taaffe, Eugene, Very Rev, PP,
VF
Apt 2, The Presbytery,
Dublin Road, Balbriggan,
Co Dublin
Tel 01-6903391
(*Balbriggan*, Dublin)

Taaffe, Patrick, AP
3 Cottage Garden,
Station Road, Ennis,
Co Clare
Tel 065-6891983/
086-1731070
(*Abbey Cluster (Ennis)*,
Killaloe)

Talbot, Denis, Very Rev
Canon, AP
Galbally, Co Tipperary
Tel 062-37929
(*Galbally*, Cashel & E.)

Talbot, Liam (SDS)
70 Charlestown Park,
Dublin 11
Tel 01-8626255

Talty, Robert (OP)
St Mary's, Pope Quay, Cork
Tel 021-4502267

Tanham, Gerard, Very Rev, PP,
VF
Parochial Place,
1 Stanhope Place,
Athy, Co Kildare
Tel 059-8631781/
087-2311947
(*Athy*, Dublin)

Tarpey, Richard, Very Rev
Canon, PE
Ennistymon, Co Clare
Tel 065-7071346
(Galway, retired)

Tarrant, Joseph, CC
On sabbatical
(Kerry)

Taylor, Leonard, Very Rev
Rathlee, Easkey, Co Sligo
(retired)

Taylor, Liam
St Patrick's, Ormonde Road,
Kilkenny
Tel 056-7764400/
086-8180954
(*St Patrick's*, Ossory)

Taylor, Paul, CC
Presbytery, Main Street,
Celbridge, Co Kildare
Tel 01-6275874/086-3524530
(*Celbridge*, Dublin)

Teehan, Willie, Very Rev, PP
Director of ACCORD,
Nenagh Centre, Loreto
House,
Kenyon Street, Nenagh,
Co Tipperary
Tel 067-31272
Parish
Templederry, Co Tipperary
Tel 0504-52988/087-2347927
(*Killanave and Templederry*,
Killaloe)

Temgo, Michel Simo (SCJ), CC
Parochial House,
St John Vianney,
Ardlea Road, Dublin 5
Tel 01-8474173
(*Ardlea*, Dublin)

Terry, John, Very Rev Canon, PE
Terriville, Ballylanders, Cloyne, Co Cork
Tel 021-4646779
(Cloyne, retired)

Thankachan Njaliath, Paul
Chaplain for Pastoral Care of the Syro Malabar Community in the Dublin Diocese, based in Tallaght
Tel 01-4510166
(Dublin)

Thennatil, Vinod Kurian (IC), CC
Parochial House, Kilcurry, Dundalk, Co Louth
Tel 042-9334410/9333235
(Faughart, Armagh)

Thettayil, Polachan (IC)
Rosmini House, Dunkereen, Innishannon, Co Cork
Tel 021-4776268/4776923

Thomas, Biju, CC
Parochial House, 42 Abbey Street, Armagh BT61 7DZ
Tel 028-37522802
(Armagh, Armagh)

Thompson, Declan (SPS), CC
Muinebheag, Co Carlow
Tel 059-9723886
(Muinebheag/Bagenalstown, Kildare & L.)

Thompson, Peter (SMA)
Vice Superior and Bursar, Dromantine College, Dromantine, Newry, Co Down BT34 1RH
Tel 028-30821224

Thorne, Bernard (OSM)
Servite Priory, Benburb, Dungannon, Co Tyrone BT71 7JZ
Northern Ireland
Tel 028-37548241

Thornton, Gerard (MSC), PP
Parish House, Union Hall, Skibbereen, Co Cork
Tel 028-34940
(Castlehaven, Cork & R.)

Thornton, Paul, Adm
Parochial House, Brackenstown Road, Swords, Co Dublin
Tel 01-8401661
(Brackenstown, Dublin)

Thornton, Richard J. (CSSp)
Blackrock College, Blackrock, Co Dublin
Tel 01-2888681

Threadgold, Jeremiah
Sacred Heart Residence, Sybil Hill Road, Killester, Dublin 5
(Dublin, retired)

Thynne, Eoin, Rt Rev Mgr, HCF
Head Chaplain, Defence Forces, McKee Barracks, Blackhorse Avenue, Dublin 7
Tel 01-8042637
(Dublin)

Tiernan, Paschal (OP)
Dominican Community, St Mary's Priory, Tallaght, Dublin 24
Tel 01-4048100

Tiernan, Peter, Very Rev, PP
Cloone, Co Leitrim
Tel 071-9636016
(Aughavas And Cloone, Ardagh & Cl.)

Tierney, Celsus, CC
Holy Cross Abbey, Holy Cross, Thurles, Co Tipperary
Tel 0504-43118
(Holy Cross, Cashel & E.)

Tierney, Philip (OSB)
Glenstal Abbey, Murroe, Co Limerick
Tel 061-386103

Tighe, James, Very Rev
Elphin, Co Roscommon
Tel 071-9635131
(Elphin, retired)

Tighe, Paul, Rt Rev Mgr
Secretary of the Pontifical Council for Social Communications, Vatican City
(Dublin)

Timmons, Declan (OFM), CC
The Abbey, 8 Francis Street, Galway
Tel 091-562518
(Francis Street, Galway)

Timoney, Charles (White Fathers)
Provincialate, Cypress Grove Road, Templeogue, Dublin 6W

Timoney, Gerald, Very Rev Canon, PE
Irvinestown, Enniskillen, Co Fermanagh BT94 1GD
Tel 028-68621329
(Irvinestown, Clogher)

Timothy, Malcolm (OFM)
Vicar, Franciscan College, Gormanston, Co Meath
Tel 01-8412203

Timpu, Eugene
Sean McDermott Street, Dublin 1
Tel 086-3266467
(Sean McDermott Street, Dublin)

Tinkasiimire, Rustico, PC
10 Finglaswood Road, Finglas West, Dublin 11
Tel 01-8341284
(Finglas West, Dublin)

Toal, Donal (SMA), Very Rev
SMA House, 82 Ranelagh Road, Ranelagh, Dublin 6
Tel 01-4968162/3

Tobin, Martin, Very Rev, PP
Clogh, Castlecomer, Co Kilkenny
Tel 056-4442135/086-2401278
(Clogh, Ossory)

Tobin, Michael (OFMCap)
Capuchin Friary, Friary Street, Kilkenny
Tel 056-7721439

Tobin, Richard (CSsR)
St Joseph's, Dundalk, Co Louth
Tel 042-9334042/9334762

Toland, Liam, Very Rev, CC
29 Killough Road, Downpatrick, Co Down BT30 6PX
Tel 028-44612443
(Downpatrick, Down & C.)

Toman, Gary
The Chaplaincy, 28 Elmwood Avenue, Belfast BT9 6AY
Tel 028-90669737
(Down & C.)

Toner, Michael C., Very Rev, PP
Parochial House, 124 Eglish Road, Dungannon, Co Tyrone BT70 1LB
Tel 028-37549661
(Eglish, Armagh)

Toner, Terence, Very Rev, PP
Parochial House, Kilmessan, Co Meath
Tel 046-9025172
(Kilmessan, Meath)

Toner, William (SJ)
25 Croftwood Park, Cherry Orchard, Dublin 10
Tel 01-6267413

Tonge, Ivan, Very Rev, PP
St Patrick's, 2 Cambridge Road, Dublin 4
Tel 087-2726868
(Ringsend, Dublin)

Tonna, Paul (SJ) (MAL)
St Ignatius Community & Church, 27 Raleigh Row, Salthill, Galway
Tel 091-523707

Toomey, Michael
Priest's Road, Tramore, Co Waterford
Tel 051-386642
(Tramore, Waterford & L.)

Touhy, Séamus (OP)
St Mary's Priory, Tallaght, Dublin 24
Tel 01-4048100

Towey, Thomas, Very Rev, PP
Ballisodare, Co Sligo
Tel 071-9167467
(Ballisodare, Achonry)

Townsend, Mark, Very Rev, PP
Daingean, Co Offaly
Tel 057-9362006
(Daingean, Kildare & L.)

Tracey, Finbarr (SVD)
133 North Circular Road, Dublin 7
Tel 01-8386743

Tracey, Liam (OSM)
Prior, Church of the Divine Word, Marley Grange, 25-27 Hermitage Downs, Rathfarnham, Dublin 16
Tel 01-4944295/4941064

Travers, Charles, Rt Rev Mgr, CC
1 Convent Court, Roscommon
Tel 090-6628917
(Roscommon, Elphin)

Travers, John (SMA)
Dromantine College, Dromantine, Newry, Co Down BT34 1RH
Tel 028-30821224

Travers, Vincent (OP)
Provincial, Provincial Office, St Mary's, Tallaght, Dublin 24
Tel 01-4048118/4048114

Treacy, Bernard (OP), Very Rev
Superior, 47 Leeson Park, Dublin 6
Tel 01-6602427

Treacy, John, CC
14 Heathervue Road, Riverview, Knockboy, Waterford
Tel 051-843207
(SS Joseph and Benildus, Waterford & L.)

Treacy, Pat, Co-PP
Curates House, Convent Hill, Roscrea, Co Tipperary
Tel 0505-21370/087-9798643
(Cronan Cluster (Roscrea), Killaloe)

Treanor, Martin, Very Rev, PP
Inniskeen, Dundalk, Co Louth
Tel 042-9378105
(Inniskeen, Clogher)

Treanor, Noel, Most Rev, DD
Bishop of Down and Connor, Lisbreen, 73 Somerton Road, Belfast, Co Antrim BT15 4DE
Tel 028-90776185
(Down & C.)

Treanor, Oliver
St Patrick's College,
Maynooth, Co Kildare
Tel 01-6285222
(Down & C.)

Tremer, Gerard, Very Rev, PP, Adm
Parochial House,
1 Convent Road,
Cookstown,
Co Tyrone BT80 8QA
Administration Coagh
Tel 028-86763370
(*Coagh, Cookstown*, Armagh)

Troy, Michael (OCarm)
Prior, Terenure College,
Terenure, Dublin 6W
Tel 01-4904621

Troy, Ulic (OFM)
Guardian, Franciscan
College, Gormanston,
Co Meath
Tel 01-8412203

Tuffy, Patrick, Very Rev
Culleens, Co Sligo
(Killala, retired)

Tully, Andrew, CC
Ballyjamesduff, Co Cavan
Tel 049-8544410
(*Castlerahan and Munterconnaught*, Kilmore)

Tumilty, Stephen (OP)
St Catherine's, Newry,
Co Down BT35 8BN
Tel 028-30262178

Tuohy, David (SJ)
Dominic Collins' House
Residence,
129 Morehampton Road,
Dublin 4
Tel 01-2693075

Tuohy, Thomas (SM)
Mount St Mary's, Milltown,
Dundrum Road, Dublin 14
Tel 01-2697322

Turbitt, Hugh
c/o Diocesan Office,
St Michael's, Longford
(Ardagh & Cl.)

Turley, Paul (CSsR)
Clonard Monastery,
1 Clonard Gardens,
Belfast BT13 2RL
Tel 028-90445950

Twohig, David (OCarm)
Whitefriar Street Church,
56 Aungier Street, Dublin 2
Tel 01-4758821

Twohig, Terence (SSC)
St Columban's Retirement
Home, Dalgan Park, Navan,
Co Meath
Tel 046-9021525

Twohig, Vivian, Very Rev, PP
Mullagh, Loughrea,
Co Galway
Tel 091-843119
(*Mullagh and Killoran*, Clonfert)

Twomey, Bernard (OSA)
St Catherine's, Meath Street,
Dublin 8
Tel 01-4543356
(*Meath Street and Merchant's Quay*, Dublin)

Twomey, Christopher
(OFMCap)
St Anthony's Capuchin
Friary, 43 Dublin Street,
Carlow
Tel 059-9142543

Twomey, Donal (SPS)
St Patrick's, Kiltegan,
Co Wicklow
Tel 059-6473600

Twomey, John (Jack)
(OFMCap), PP
Priorswood,
St Francis of Assisi,
Dublin 17
Tel 01-8474469
(*Priorswood*, Dublin)

Twomey, Kieran, Very Rev, PP
1 Parochial House,
Blackrock, Cork
Tel 021-2410519
(*Blackrock*, Cork & R.)

Twomey, Patrick, Very Rev
Canon, PE
Bellevue, Mallow, Co Cork
Tel 022-55632
(Cloyne, retired)

Twomey, Vincent, D. (SVD)
Maynooth, Co Kildare
Tel 01-6286391/2

Tynan, Joseph, CC
Ballydavid, Littleton,
Thurles, Co Tipperary
Tel 0504-44317
(*Moycarkey*, Cashel & E.)

Tyndall, David
Chaplain,
Cathal Brugha Barracks,
Rathmines, Dublin 6
Tel 8046484
(Dublin)

Tyrrell, Gerard
Chaplaincy for Deaf People,
40 Lower Drumcondra Road,
Dublin 9
Tel 01-8305744
(Dublin)

Tyrrell, Patrick (SJ)
(Temporarily outside
Ireland) Irish Jesuit
Provincialate, Milltown Park,
Sandford Road, Dublin 6
Tel 01-4987333

Tyrrell, Paul, Co-PP
41 St Agnes' Road, Crumlin,
Dublin 12
Tel 01-6600075
(*Crumlin*, Dublin)

## U

Udogbo, Samuel (CSSp)
Rockwell College, Cashel,
Co Tipperary
Tel 062-61444

Ugwu, Stephen (OCD)
Avila, Bloomfield Avenue,
Morehampton Road,
Dublin 4
Tel 01-6430200

Uwah, Innocent
The Presbytery,
12 Coarse Moor Park,
Straffan, Co Kildare
Tel 01-6012197/085-1404355
(*Celbridge*, Dublin)

## V

Van de Poll, Jan (SJ) (NER)
Manresa House,
Dollymount, Dublin 3
Tel 01-8331352

Van Gucht, Koenraad (SDB)
Salesian College, Maynooth,
Celbridge, Co Kildare
Tel 01-6275058/60

Varghese, Joseph, CC
Parochial House,
32 Chapel Road,
Waterside, Derry BT47 2BB
Tel 028-71342303
(*Waterside (Glendermott)*, Derry)

Vaughan, Aidan (OFMCap), CC
Ascension Presbytery,
Gurranabraher, Cork
Tel 021-4303655
(*Gurranabraher*, Cork & R.)

Vaughan, Denis
45 The Oaks,
Maryborough Ridge,
Douglas, Cork
(Cloyne, retired)

Vinduska, Aaron (LC)
Leopardstown Road,
Foxrock, Dublin 18
Director,
Faith and Family Centre,
Dal Riada House,
Avoca Avenue, Blackrock,
Co Dublin
Tel 01-2889317

## W

Wadding, George (CSsR)
Liguori House,
75 Orwell Road, Dublin 6
Tel 01-4067100

Wade, Thomas (SMA), Very
Rev, PP
St Joseph's,
Blackrock Road, Cork
Tel 021-4292871
(*St Joseph's (Blackrock Road)*, Cork & R.)

Wafer, Andy (SSCC)
Coudrin House,
27 Northbrook Road,
Dublin 6
Tel 01-6473755/01-6686590

Waldron, Kieran, Very Rev
Canon, PE
Devlis, Ballyhaunis, Co Mayo
Tel 094-9630246
(Tuam, retired)

Waldron, Paul, Very Rev, Adm
Holy Family Presbytery
Luke Wadding Street,
Waterford
Tel 051-350023
(*Trinity Within and St Patrick's*, Waterford & L.)

Waldron, Peter, Very Rev
Canon, PP
Keelogues, Ballyvary,
Co Mayo
Tel 094-9031009
(*Keelogues*, Tuam)

Walker, David (OP), PP
Superior and Parish Priest,
Convento dos Padres
Dominicanos Irlandeses,
Praceta Infante D. Henrique,
No. 34, 1-Dto,
Rua do Murtal, San Pedro
Do Estoril
2765-531 Estoril, Portuagal
Tel +351-21-4673771
(Lisbon)

Wall, David (SSC)
St Columban's, Dalgan Park,
Navan, Co Meath
Tel 046-9021525

Wall, John, Very Rev, Co-PP
Parochial House, Enniskerry,
Co Wicklow
Tel 01-2863506/087-2660821
(*Enniskerry/Kilmacanogue*, Dublin)

Wall, John, Very Rev, PP
Annaduff,
Carrick-on-Shannon,
Co Leitrim
Tel 071-9624093
(*Annaduff*, Ardagh & Cl.)

Wall, Michael
Chaplain,
Mary Immaculate College
of Education
Tel 061-204331
(Limerick)

Wall, Michael
Sacred Heart Residence,
Sybil Hill Road,
Raheny, Dublin 5
(Dublin, retired)

Wallace, Laurence, Very Rev,
PP, VF
Muckalee, Ballyfoyle,
Co Kilkenny
Tel 056-4441271/
087-2326807
(Muckalee, Ossory)

Walsh, Aidan (OFMConv)
Friary of the Visitation of
the BVM,
Fairview Strand, Dublin 3
Tel 01-8376000
(Fairview, Dublin)

Walsh, Brendan, Very Rev, PP
Causeway, Co Kerry
Tel 066-7131148
(Causeway, Kerry)

Walsh, David (SPS)
St Patrick's, Kiltegan,
Co Wicklow
Tel 059-6473600

Walsh, Des, Very Rev Canon,
PP
Turloughmore, Co Galway
Tel 091-797114
(Lackagh, Tuam)

Walsh, Donal, Very Rev
Tinnahinch,
Graiguenamanagh,
Co Kilkenny
Tel 059-9725550
(Ossory, retired)

Walsh, Eamonn, Most Rev,
DD, VG
Titular Bishop of Elmham
and Auxiliary Bishop of
Dublin,
Head of the Office for
Clergy, Naomh Brid,
Blessington Road,
Tallaght, Dublin 24
Tel 01-4598032
(Dublin)

Walsh, Francis, Rt Rev Mgr, PC
Pro-Cathedral House,
83 Marlborough Street,
Dublin 1
Tel 01-8745441
(Pro-Cathedral, Dublin)

Walsh, Gearóid, Very Rev
Castletownbere, Co Cork
Tel 027-70849
(Allihies, Castletownbere,
Kerry)

Walsh, James, Very Rev, AP
Parochial House, Kilmeena,
Westport, Co Mayo
Tel 098-41270
(Kilmeena, Tuam)

Walsh, Jarlath (SMA)
SMA House, Wilton, Cork
Tel 021-4541069/4541884

Walsh, John (OP)
St Dominic's, Athy,
Co Kildare
Tel 059-8631573

Walsh, John, Very Rev
Lourdes House, Childers
Road, Limerick
Tel 061-467676
(Our Lady Of Lourdes,
Limerick)

Walsh, John, Very Rev, PE
Rath, Portlaoise, Co Laois
Tel 057-8626401
(Kildare & L., retired)

Walsh, John, Very Rev, PP
The Presbytery,
Farranree, Cork
Tel 021-4393815/4210111
(Farranree, Cork & R.)

Walsh, John, Very Rev Canon,
PP
Parochial House, Aghamore,
Ballyhaunis, Co Mayo
Tel 094-9367024
(Aghamore, Tuam)

Walsh, John R., CC
Parochial House,
Buncrana, Co Donegal
Tel 074-9361393
(Buncrana, Derry)

Walsh, Joseph, CC
Templemore, Co Tipperary
Tel 0504-31684
(Templemore, Cashel & E.)

Walsh, Joseph (OFM)
Adam and Eve's,
4 Merchant's Quay,
Dublin 8
Tel 01-6771128
(Upperchurch, Cashel & E.)

Walsh, Kevin, CC
Parochial House, Sallins,
Co Kildare
Tel 045-897150
(Naas, Sallins, Kildare & L.)

Walsh, Laurence (OCSO), Dom
Prior,
Mount Saint Joseph Abbey,
Roscrea, Co Tipperary
Tel 0505-25600

Walsh, Liam (OP)
St Saviour's,
Upper Dorset Street,
Dublin 1
Tel 01-8897610

Walsh, Michael, Very Rev, PP
Parochial House, Kilcormac,
Co Offaly
Tel 057-9135989
(Kilcormac, Meath)

Walsh, Michael F., Very Rev,
PE
Ballinarrid, Bonmahon,
Co Waterford
Tel 051-292992
(Waterford & L., retired)

Walsh, Nicky (SPS)
St Patrick's, Kiltegan,
Co Wicklow
Tel 059-6473600

Walsh, Pádraig, Very Rev, PP
St Brendan's, Tralee,
Co Kerry
Tel 066-7125932
(Tralee, St Brendan's, Kerry)

Walsh, Pat
Priests House, Aliohill,
Enniskeane, Co Cork
(Cork & R., retired)

Walsh, Patrick (CSsR)
Mount Saint Alphonsus,
Limerick
Tel 061-315099

Walsh, Patrick J., Most Rev,
DD
Bishop Emeritus of Down
and Connor,
6 Waterloo Park North,
Belfast BT15 5HW
Tel 028-90778182
(Down & C.)

Walsh, Paul (CSSp)
Holy Spirit Missionary
College, Kimmage Manor,
Whitehall Road, Dublin 12
Tel 01-4064300

Walsh, Paul (SM)
London

Walsh, Pearse, Adm
The Presbytery, City Quay,
Dublin 2
Tel 01-6773073
(City Quay, Dublin)

Walsh, Richard (OP), Prior
St Saviour's, Bridge Street,
Waterford
Tel 051-875061

Walsh, Sean (IC)
Clonturk House,
Ormond Road,
Drumcondra, Dublin 9
Tel 01-6877014

Walsh, Tomás (SMA), AP
Cathedral Presbytery, Cork
Tel 021-4304325
(Cathedral of St Mary & St
Anne, Cork & R.)

Walsh, William (CSSp)
Holy Spirit Missionary
College, Kimmage Manor,
Dublin 12
Tel 01-4064300

Walsh, William, Most Rev, DD
Retired Bishop of Killaloe,
'Camblin', College View,
Clare Road, Ennis, Co Clare
Tel 065-6842540
(Killaloe, retired)

Walsh, William, Very Rev, PP
8 Merval Crescent,
Clareview, Limerick
Tel 061-453026
(Our Lady of the Rosary,
Limerick)

Walshe, Adrian, CC
Castleblayney,
Co Monaghan
Tel 042-9740637
(Castleblayney (Muckno),
Clogher)

Walshe, Stephen (CSSp), CC
St Anne's, Sligo
Tel 071-9145028
(Sligo, St Anne's, Elphin)

Walshe, Thomas, Very Rev, PP
Rosenallis, Portlaoise,
Co Laois
Tel 057-8628513
(Rosenallis, Kildare & L.)

Walton, James, Very Rev, PP
Ballybricken, Grange,
Killmallock, Co Limerick
Tel 061-351158
(Ballybricken, Cashel & E.)

Walwa, Robert
15 Connawood Drive, Bray,
Co Wicklow
Tel 01-2829467
(Bray, St Peter's, Dublin)

Ward, Alan, CF
Chaplain,
Finner Army Camp,
Ballyshannon, Co Donegal
Tel 071-9842294
(Clogher)

Ward, Bonaventure (OFM)
Franciscan Friary,
Lady Lane, Waterford
Tel 051-874262

Ward, Conor, Rt Rev Mgr
17 Prospect Lawn, The Park,
Cabinteely, Dublin 18
Tel 01-2850294
(Cabinteely, Dublin)

Ward, John M., Very Rev, PE
1 Chestnut Grove,
Ballymount Road,
Kingswood Heights,
Dublin 24
Tel 01- 4515824
(Dublin, retired)

Ward, Pat, Very Rev, PP
Burtonport, Co Donegal
Tel 074-9542006
(Burtonport, Raphoe)

Ward, Paul, Very Rev, PP
Parochial House,
1 Bayside Square North,
Sutton, Dublin 13
Tel 01-8323150
(Bayside, Dublin)

Ward, Peter (CSsR)
Clonard Monastery,
1 Clonard Gardens,
Belfast BT13 2RL
Tel 028-90445950

Warrack, Colin (SJ)
Gonzaga College,
Sandford Road, Dublin 6
Tel 01-4972943

Warren, Ray (OMI), Very Rev
Provincial,
Oblates of Mary Immaculate
House of Retreat,
St Anne's,
Goldenbridge Walk,
Inchicore, Dublin 8
Tel 01-4540841/4542955

Waters, Ignatius (CP)
St Paul's Retreat,
Mount Argus, Dublin 6W
Tel 01-4992000

Watters, Brian, CC
79 Ivanhoe Avenue,
Carryduff, Belfast BT8 8BW
Tel 028-90817410
(Drumbo, Down & C.)

Wawrzaszek, Bogdan, CC
Curate's House, Kilcock,
Co Kildare
Tel 01-6287277
(Kilcock, Kildare & L.)

Weakliam, David (OCarm),
Terenure College, Terenure,
Dublin 6W
Tel 01-4904621

Welsh, Oscar (SMA)
African Missions,
Blackrock Road, Cork
Tel 021-4292871

Whearty, Roderick
St Fiacre's Gardens,
Bohernatownish Road,
Loughboy, Kilkenny
Tel 056-77701730
(St Patrick's, Ossory)

Whelan, Brian, CC
The Presbytery,
12 School Street, Wexford
Tel 053-9122055
(Wexford, Ferns)

Whelan, Edward, PE, CC
Ballon, Co Carlow
Tel 059-9159329
(Ballon, Kildare & L.)

Whelan, Gerard (SJ)
(Temporarily outside
Ireland)
Irish Jesuit Provincialate,
Milltown Park,
Sandford Road, Dublin 6
Tel 01-4987333

Whelan, John (OSA)
St Augustine's Priory, St
Augustine's Street, Galway
Tel 091-562524

Whelan, Joseph, Very Rev, Co-
PP
Parochial House,
Our Lady Queen of Peace,
Putland Road, Bray,
Co Wicklow
Tel 01-2865723
(Bray, Putland Road, Dublin)

Whelan, Marc (CSSp)
Provinical Leader,
Temple Park,
Richmond Avenue South,
Dublin 6
Tel 01-4975127/4977230

Whelan, Martin, CC
Diocesan Secretary,
Diocesan Office,
The Cathedral, Galway
Tel 091-563566
18 University Road, Galway
Tel 091-524875/563577
(Cathedral, Galway)

Whelan, Michael
c/o Archbishop's House,
Tuam
(Tuam)

Whelan, Michael (MSC)
Western Road, Cork
Tel 021-4804120

Whelan, Patrick, Very Rev, PP
St Patrick's Presbytery,
Forster Street, Galway
Tel 091-567994
(St Patrick's, Galway)

Whelan, Patrick A. (CSSp)
Holy Spirit Missionary
College, Kimmage Manor,
Dublin 12
Tel 01-4064300

Whelan, Seamus (SPS)
St Patrick's, Kiltegan,
Co Wicklow
Tel 059-6473600

Whelan, Tom (CSSp)
Holy Spirit Missionary
College, Kimmage Manor,
Dublin 12
Tel 01-4064300
Rector and Acting President,
Milltown Institute of
Theology and Philosophy,
Milltown Park,
Sandford Road, Dublin 6
Tel 01-2776300

Whelan, Tom, CC
Curate's House,
Castleconnell, Co Limerick
Tel 061-219482/087-2730299
(Castleconnell, Killaloe)

White, Brian, CC
Grianán Mhuire,
Main Street, Blackrock,
Dundalk, Co Louth
Tel 042-9322244
(Haggardstown and
Blackrock, Armagh)

White, David, Very Rev, PP
Parochial House,
182 Garron Road,
Glenariffe,
Co Antrim BT44 0RA
Tel 028-21771249
(Glenariffe, Down & C.)

White, Jerry (SSCC), CC
Sacred Hearts Community,
Tanagh, Cootehill, Co Cavan
Tel 049-5552188
(Rockcorry (Ematris),
Clogher)

White, Laurence, Very Rev,
Co-PP
186 Clontarf Road, Dublin 3
Tel 01-8333394/086-4143888
(Clontarf, St Anthony's,
Dublin)

White, Patrick
Training and Development
Officer,
Youth Link Training Offices,
Farset Enterprise Park,
683 Springfield Road,
Belfast BT12 7DY
Tel 028-90323217
(Down & C.)

White, Séamus, CC
Parochial House,
6 Circular Road,
Dungannon,
Co Tyrone BT71 6BE
Tel 028-87722631
(Dungannon (Drumglass,
Killyman and Tullyniskin),
Armagh)

White, Thomas, Most Rev
Abbey Nursing Home,
Gowran, Co Kilkenny
Tel 056-7726500
(Ossory, retired)

Whiteford, Kieran, Very Rev,
PP
Parochial House,
Loughinisland, Downpatrick,
Co Down BT30 8QH
Tel 028-44811661
(Loughinisland, Down & C.)

Whitmore, Fintan Brennan
(OH)
Director of Pastoral Care,
St John of God Hospitallar
Ministries, Hospitallar
House, Stillorgan, Co Dublin
Tel 01-2771504
(Dublin)

Whitney, Ciaran, Very Rev, PP,
VF
Chaplain, Post-Primary
School, Strokestown,
Co Roscommon
Tel 071-9633041
Parish: Strokestown,
Co Roscommon
Tel 071-9633027
(Strokestown, Elphin)

Whittaker, Michael, Very Rev,
PP
The Presbytery, Enfield,
Co Meath
Tel 046-9541282
(Enfield, Meath)

Whooley, Eoin, Very Rev, PP
Lislevane, Bandon,
Co Cork
Tel 023-8846914
(Barryroe, Cork & R.)

Whyte, Daniel, Very Rev
53 Marlo Park,
Bangor,
Co Down BT19 6NL
Tel 078-12184624
(Down & C., retired)

Wickham, Anthony, Very Rev,
PP
Clondrohid, Macroom,
Co Cork
Tel 026-41014
(Clondrohid, Cloyne)

Williams, John (OSA)
St Augustine's,
Taylor's Lane,
Balyboden, Dublin 16
Tel 01-4241000

Williams, Patrick, Archdeacon,
PE
6 Gort an Clochair, Kilkee,
Co Clare
(Tuam, retired)

Wilson, Desmond
6 Springhill Close,
Belfast BT12 7SE
Tel 028-90326722
(Down & C., retired)

Wilson, John Rt Rev Mgr,
Adm
Parochial House,
Ballymore Eustace, Naas
Co Kildare
Tel 045-864114
(Ballymore Eustace, Dublin)

Winkle, Patrick, CC
Youghal, Co Cork
Tel 024-92270
(Youghal, Cloyne)

Winter, William, Very Rev PP
Banteer, Co Cork
Tel 029-56010
(Banteer (Clonmeen),
Cloyne)

Woods, Daniel, Very Rev, PP
Kilcommon, Co Tipperary
Tel 062-78103
(Kilcommon, Cashel & E.)

Woods, Michael, Very Rev, PP
Parochial House,
40 Market Street,
Tandagree,
Co Armagh BT62 2BW
Tel 028-38840442
(Tandragee (Ballymore and
Mullaghbrack), Armagh)

Woods, Thomas
Edenville, Kinlough,
Co Leitrim
(Kilmore, retired)

Woods, Thomas, Rt Rev Mgr,
DD
Newbrook Nursing Home,
Mullingar,
Co Westmeath
(Meath, retired)
Woolen, Nigel, Adm (pro-tem)
Newport, Co Mayo
(*Newport (Burrishoole)*,
Tuam)
Wozniak, Josef (SC), CC
68 North Street, Lurgan,
Co Armagh BT67 9AH
Tel 028-38323161
(*Shankill, St Paul's & St
Peter's (Lurgan)*, Dromore)
Wright, Colum, Very Rev, PP
10 Oaklands,
Loughbrickland,
Co Down BT32 3NH
Tel 028-40623264
(*Aghaderg, Donaghmore*,
Dromore)
Wrobel, Kazimierz, CC
St Anne's, Sligo
(*Sligo, St Anne's*, Elphin)
Wynne, Owen (SCI)
Sacred Heart Fathers,
Fairfield, 66 Inchicore Road,
Dublin 8
Tel 01-4538655

## X

Xianbin, Anthony Xiao
Chaplain to the Chinese
Community, The Presbytery,
51 Home Farm Road,
Dublin 9
Tel 085-7417168
(*Drumcondra*, Dublin)

## Y

Yilma, Gobezayehu
Getachew, PC
287 South Circular Road,
Rialto, Dublin 8
Tel 01-4533490
(*Dolphin's Barn/Rialto*,
Dublin)
Young, Gerard, CC
Presbytery No 3,
Most Sacred Heart Parish,
St Joseph's Road, Dublin 7
Tel 01-8386571
(*Aughrim Street*, Dublin)
Young, Joseph
21 Marian Avenue,
Janesboro, Limerick
Tel 061-405835
(Limerick)
Young, Richard (OCD)
St Joseph's, Berkeley Road,
Dublin 7
Tel 01-8306356/8306336
Young, Robert, Very Rev, PP
The Presbytery, Kinsale,
Co Cork
Tel 021-4774019
(*Kinsale*, Cork & R.)
Younge, Patrick (OFM)
Guardian, The Abbey,
8 Francis Street, Galway
Tel 091-562518

## Z

Zacharek, Maciej, CC
Our Lady of Lourdes
Presbytery,
Hardman's Gardens,
Drogheda, Co Louth
Tel 041-9831899
(*Drogheda*, Armagh)
Zaggi, Douglas, PC
12 Coarsemoor Park,
Straffan, Co Kildare
Tel 01-6012303
(*Celbridge*, Dublin)
Zimnoch, Piotr, CC
50 Brook Steet, Omagh,
Co Tyrone BT78 5HE
(*Omagh (Drumragh)*, Derry)
Zuribo, Aloysius, CC
2 Carrigmore Place, Saggart,
Co Dublin
Tel 01 4589209/087-9706309
(*Newcastle, Saggart/
Rathcoole/Brittas*, Dublin)

# PARISH INDEX

*Where a parish has an alternative or historical name, both names are given e.g. Arney/Cleenish.*
*In such cases the parish appears in the list in each form,*
*i.e. Arney/Cleenish and Cleenish/Arney.*

## A

| | | |
|---|---|---|
| Abbeydorney | *Kerry* | 192 |
| Abbeyfeale | *Limerick* | 234 |
| Abbeygormican & Killoran/Mullagh & Killoran | *Clonfert* | 118 |
| Abbeyknockmoy | *Tuam* | 95 |
| Abbeylara | *Ardagh* | 106 |
| Abbeyleix | *Kildare* | 203 |
| Abbeyside | *Waterford* | 264 |
| Achill | *Tuam* | 95 |
| Achonry | *Achonry* | 102 |
| Adamstown | *Ferns* | 178 |
| Adare | *Limerick* | 234 |
| Addergole & Liskeevey/ Milltown | *Tuam* | 97 |
| Addergoole/ Lahardane | *Killala* | 211 |
| Adrigole | *Kerry* | 192 |
| Aghaboe | *Ossory* | 251 |
| Aghabullogue | *Cloyne* | 122 |
| Aghada | *Cloyne* | 122 |
| Aghaderg | *Dromore* | 167 |
| Aghagallon & Ballinderry | *Down* | 154 |
| Aghaloo/ Aughnacloy | *Armagh* | 28 |
| Aghalurcher/ Lisnaskea | *Clogher* | 113 |
| Aghamore | *Tuam* | 95 |
| Aghanagh/ Ballinafad | *Elphin* | 172 |
| Aghavea- Aghintaine/ Brookeboro | *Clogher* | 112 |
| Aghaviller | *Ossory* | 251 |
| Aghinagh | *Cloyne* | 122 |
| Aghyaran/ Termonamongan | *Derry* | 142 |
| Aglish | *Waterford* | 264 |
| Aglish, Ballyheane & Breaghwy/ Castlebar | *Tuam* | 96 |
| Ahamlish/Cliffoney | *Elphin* | 172 |
| Ahascragh/ Ahascragh & Caltra | *Elphin* | 172 |
| Ahoghill | *Down* | 154 |
| Allen | *Kildare* | 203 |
| Allihies | *Kerry* | 192 |
| Anacarty | *Cashel* | 85 |
| Annaclone | *Dromore* | 167 |
| Annacurra | *Ferns* | 178 |
| Annaduff | *Ardagh* | 106 |
| Annagh/Ballyhaunis | *Tuam* | 96 |
| Annagh/Belturbet | *Kilmore* | 223 |

| | | |
|---|---|---|
| Annaghdown/ Corrandulla | *Tuam* | 96 |
| Annagry | *Raphoe* | 258 |
| Annascaul | *Kerry* | 192 |
| An Spidéal | *Galway* | 186 |
| Antrim | *Down* | 154 |
| Aran Islands | *Tuam* | 95 |
| Ardagh | *Killala* | 210 |
| Ardagh & Carrickerry | *Limerick* | 234 |
| Ardagh & Moydow | *Ardagh* | 106 |
| Ardara | *Raphoe* | 258 |
| Ardboe | *Armagh* | 28 |
| Ardcarne/Cootehall | *Elphin* | 172 |
| Ardcath | *Meath* | 242 |
| Ardee & Collon | *Armagh* | 28 |
| Ardfert | *Kerry* | 192 |
| Ardfield & Rathbarry | *Cork & Ross* | 132 |
| Ardfinnan | *Waterford* | 264 |
| Ardglass & Dunsford | *Down* | 155 |
| Ardkeen/Kircubbin | *Down* | 156 |
| Ardlea | *Dublin* | 42 |
| Ardmore | *Derry* | 142 |
| Ardmore | *Waterford* | 265 |
| Ardpatrick | *Limerick* | 234 |
| Ardrahan | *Galway* | 186 |
| Ardstraw East/ Newtownstewart | *Derry* | 144 |
| Ardstraw West & Castlederg/ Castlederg | *Derry* | 143 |
| Ardtrea/Moneymore | *Armagh* | 30 |
| Ardtrea North & Magherafelt | *Armagh* | 30 |
| Arklow | *Dublin* | 42 |
| Arles | *Kildare* | 203 |
| Armagh | *Armagh* | 27 |
| Armoy | *Down* | 154 |
| Arney/Cleenish | *Clogher* | 112 |
| Arran Quay & Halston Street | *Dublin* | 48 |
| Artane | *Dublin* | 42 |
| Ashbourne- Donaghmore | *Meath* | 242 |
| Ashford | *Dublin* | 42 |
| Askea | *Kildare* | 203 |
| Askeaton/Ballysteen | *Limerick* | 234 |
| Athboy | *Meath* | 242 |
| Athea | *Limerick* | 234 |
| Athenry | *Tuam* | 95 |
| Athleague/Athleague & Fuerty | *Elphin* | 172 |
| Athlone | *Ardagh* | 106 |
| Athlone, SS Peter & Paul's | *Elphin* | 172 |
| Athy | *Dublin* | 42 |
| Attymass | *Achonry* | 102 |
| Aughadown | *Cork & Ross* | 132 |
| Aughagower | *Tuam* | 96 |
| Aughaninshin | *Raphoe* | 258 |

| | | |
|---|---|---|
| Aughaval/Westport | *Tuam* | 95 |
| Aughavas & Cloone | *Ardagh* | 106 |
| Aughnacloy/Aghaloo | *Armagh* | 28 |
| Aughnamullen East | *Clogher* | 112 |
| Aughnamullen West/Latton | *Clogher* | 113 |
| Aughnish/ Ramelton | *Raphoe* | 259 |
| Aughrim | *Dublin* | 42 |
| Aughrim/Aughrim & Kilmore | *Elphin* | 172 |
| Aughrim & Kilconnell | *Clonfert* | 117 |
| Aughrim Street | *Dublin* | 42 |
| Avoca | *Dublin* | 43 |
| Ayrfield | *Dublin* | 43 |

## B

| | | |
|---|---|---|
| Backs | *Killala* | 210 |
| Badoney Lower/ Gortin | *Derry* | 143 |
| Badoney Upper/Plumbridge | *Derry* | 144 |
| Bagenalstown/ Muinebheag | *Kildare* | 204 |
| Bailieboro/Killann | *Kilmore* | 223 |
| Balally | *Dublin* | 43 |
| Balbriggan | *Dublin* | 43 |
| Balcurris | *Dublin* | 43 |
| Baldoyle | *Dublin* | 43 |
| Balla & Manulla | *Tuam* | 96 |
| Ballagh/Cloontuskert, Kilgefin & Curraghroe | *Elphin* | 172 |
| Ballaghaderreen/ Castlemore & Kilcolman | *Achonry* | 101 |
| Ballaghameehan | *Kilmore* | 223 |
| Ballina | *Cashel* | 85 |
| Ballina/Kilmoremoy | *Killala* | 210 |
| Ballinabrackey | *Meath* | 242 |
| Ballinafad/Aghanagh | *Elphin* | 172 |
| Ballinaglera | *Kilmore* | 223 |
| Ballinahinch | *Cashel* | 85 |
| Ballinahown, Boher & Pollough/ Lemanaghan | *Ardagh* | 106 |
| Ballinakill | *Clonfert* | 117 |
| Ballinakill | *Kildare* | 203 |
| Ballinakill/Letterfrack | *Tuam* | 97 |
| Ballinameen/ Kilnamanagh & Estersnow | *Elphin* | 172 |
| Ballinamore/ Oughteragh | *Kilmore* | 223 |
| Ballinascreen/ Draperstown | *Derry* | 142 |

| | | |
|---|---|---|
| Ballinasloe, Creagh Kilclooney | Clonfert | 117 |
| Ballincollig | Cork & Ross | 132 |
| Ballindaggin | Ferns | 178 |
| Ballindereen | Galway | 186 |
| Ballinderry | Armagh | 28 |
| Ballindine/Kilvine | Tuam | 96 |
| Ballineaspaig | Cork & Ross | 132 |
| Ballingarry | Cashel | 85 |
| Ballingarry & Granagh | Limerick | 234 |
| Ballinhassig | Cork & Ross | 132 |
| Ballinlough | Cork & Ross | 132 |
| Ballinlough/ Kiltullagh | Tuam | 96 |
| Ballinora | Cork & Ross | 132 |
| Ballinrobe | Tuam | 96 |
| Ballinskelligs/Prior | Kerry | 192 |
| Ballinteer | Dublin | 43 |
| Ballintemple | Kilmore | 223 |
| Ballintober & Ballymoe/ Ballintubber | Elphin | 172 |
| Ballintoy | Down | 154 |
| Ballintra/Drumholm | Raphoe | 258 |
| Ballintubber/ Ballintober & Ballymoe | Elphin | 172 |
| Ballisodare | Achonry | 102 |
| Ballivor | Meath | 242 |
| Ballon | Kildare | 203 |
| Ballyadams | Kildare | 203 |
| Ballyagran & Colmanswell | Limerick | 234 |
| Ballybane | Galway | 185 |
| Ballybay/Tullycorbet | Clogher | 112 |
| Ballyboden | Dublin | 43 |
| Ballybrack/Killiney | Dublin | 43 |
| Ballybricken | Cashel | 85 |
| Ballybricken | Waterford | 264 |
| Ballybrown/ Patrickswell | Limerick | 235 |
| Ballybunion | Kerry | 192 |
| Ballycallan | Ossory | 251 |
| Ballycastle/ Kilbride & Doonfeeny | Killala | 210 |
| Ballycastle/Ramoan | Down | 154 |
| Ballyclare & Ballygowan | Down | 154 |
| Ballyclough | Cloyne | 122 |
| Ballycroy | Killala | 211 |
| Ballycullane | Ferns | 178 |
| Ballydesmond | Kerry | 192 |
| Ballydonoghue | Kerry | 192 |
| Ballyduff | Waterford | 265 |
| Ballyfermot | Dublin | 43 |
| Ballyfermot Upper | Dublin | 43 |
| Ballyferriter | Kerry | 192 |
| Ballyfin | Kildare | 203 |
| Ballyforan/Dysart & Tisrara | Elphin | 172 |
| Ballygalget | Down | 154 |
| Ballygall | Dublin | 43 |
| Ballygar/Killian & Killeroran | Elphin | 172 |
| Ballygarrett | Ferns | 178 |
| Ballygawley/Errigal Kieran | Armagh | 28 |
| Ballyhahill/Loughill | Limerick | 235 |
| Ballyhale | Ossory | 251 |
| Ballyhaunis/Annagh | Tuam | 96 |
| Ballyhea | Cloyne | 122 |
| Ballyheigue | Kerry | 192 |
| Ballylanders | Cashel | 85 |
| Ballylongford | Kerry | 192 |
| Ballylooby | Waterford | 265 |

| | | |
|---|---|---|
| Ballymacelligott | Kerry | 192 |
| Ballymacoda & Ladysbridge | Cloyne | 122 |
| Ballymacormack, Templemichael/ Longford | Ardagh | 106 |
| Ballymascanlon & Lordship | Armagh | 30 |
| Ballymacward & Gurteen/ Ballymacward & Clonkeenkerril | Clonfert | 117 |
| Ballymahon/Shrule | Ardagh | 106 |
| Ballymena/Kirkinriola | Down | 154 |
| Ballymoney & Derrykeighan | Down | 154 |
| Ballymore | Meath | 242 |
| Ballymore Eustace | Dublin | 43 |
| Ballymore & Mayglass | Ferns | 178 |
| Ballymore & Mullaghbrack/ Tandragee | Armagh | 31 |
| Ballymote/Emlefad & Kilmorgan | Achonry | 102 |
| Ballymun/Sillogue | Dublin | 43 |
| Ballymun Road | Dublin | 43 |
| Ballynacally/ Clondegad | Killaloe | 217 |
| Ballynacargy | Meath | 242 |
| Ballynahinch/ Magheradroll | Dromore | 167 |
| Ballyneale & Grangemockler | Waterford | 265 |
| Ballyovey/Partry | Tuam | 97 |
| Ballyphehane | Cork & Ross | 132 |
| Ballyphilip/ Portaferry | Down | 156 |
| Ballyporeen | Waterford | 265 |
| Ballyragget | Ossory | 251 |
| Ballyroan | Dublin | 44 |
| Ballyscullion/ Bellaghy | Derry | 142 |
| Ballyshannon/ Kilbarron | Raphoe | 258 |
| Ballysokeary | Killala | 211 |
| Ballyvaughan | Galway | 186 |
| Ballyvourney | Cloyne | 122 |
| Ballywaltrim/Bray | Dublin | 45 |
| Baltinglass | Kildare | 203 |
| Balyna | Kildare | 203 |
| Banagher | Derry | 142 |
| Banbridge/Seapatrick | Dromore | 167 |
| Bandon | Cork & Ross | 132 |
| Bangor | Down | 154 |
| Bannow | Ferns | 178 |
| Banogue | Limerick | 234 |
| Bansha & Kilmoyler | Cashel | 85 |
| Banteer/Clonmeen | Cloyne | 122 |
| Bantry | Cork & Ross | 132 |
| Barndarrig & Kilbride | Dublin | 49 |
| Barryroe | Cork & Ross | 133 |
| Bawnogue | Dublin | 44 |
| Bayside | Dublin | 44 |
| Beagh/Gort | Galway | 186 |
| Bearna | Galway | 186 |
| Beaufort/Tuogh | Kerry | 192 |
| Beaumont | Dublin | 44 |
| Beauparc | Meath | 242 |
| Beechwood Avenue | Dublin | 44 |
| Bekan | Tuam | 96 |
| Bellaghy/ Ballyscullion | Derry | 142 |
| Belleek-Garrison/Inis Muighe Samh | Clogher | 112 |
| Belmullet | Killala | 211 |
| Belturbet/Annagh | Kilmore | 223 |

| | | |
|---|---|---|
| Bennekerry | Kildare | 203 |
| Beragh | Armagh | 28 |
| Bere Island & Castletownbere | Kerry | 192 |
| Berkeley Road | Dublin | 44 |
| Bessbrook/Killeavy Lower | Armagh | 28 |
| Birr | Killaloe | 216 |
| Blackpool/The Glen | Cork & Ross | 133 |
| Blackrock | Cork & Ross | 133 |
| Blackrock | Dublin | 44 |
| Blackwater | Ferns | 178 |
| Blakestown | Dublin | 44 |
| Blanchardstown | Dublin | 44 |
| Blaris/Lisburn | Down | 156 |
| Blarney | Cloyne | 122 |
| Blessington | Dublin | 44 |
| Bluebell | Dublin | 44 |
| Bodyke & Ogonnelloe/ Kilnoe & Tuamgraney | Killaloe | 217 |
| Boher & Murroe | Cashel | 86 |
| Boherbue/Kiskeam | Kerry | 192 |
| Boherlahan & Dualla | Cashel | 85 |
| Bohermeen | Meath | 242 |
| Bohernabreena | Dublin | 44 |
| Bohola | Achonry | 102 |
| Bonane/Glengarriff | Kerry | 193 |
| Bonniconlon/ Kilgarvan | Achonry | 102 |
| Bonnybrook | Dublin | 44 |
| Booterstown | Dublin | 44 |
| Bornacoola | Ardagh | 106 |
| Borris | Kildare | 203 |
| Borris-in-Ossory | Ossory | 251 |
| Borrisokane | Killaloe | 216 |
| Borrisoleigh | Cashel | 85 |
| Botha/Derrygonnelly | Clogher | 112 |
| Bournea/ Couraganeen | Killaloe | 216 |
| Boyle | Elphin | 172 |
| Boyounagh/ Glenamaddy | Tuam | 96 |
| Brackenstown | Dublin | 44 |
| Braid | Down | 155 |
| Bray/Ballywaltrim | Dublin | 45 |
| Bray/Holy Redeemer | Dublin | 45 |
| Bray, Putland Road | Dublin | 45 |
| Bray, St Peter's | Dublin | 45 |
| Bree | Ferns | 178 |
| Bright/Killough | Down | 156 |
| Broadford | Killaloe | 217 |
| Broadford/ Dromcollogher | Limerick | 234 |
| Brookeboro/Aghavea-Aghintaine | Clogher | 112 |
| Brookfield | Dublin | 45 |
| Brosna | Kerry | 192 |
| Bruckless/Killaghtee | Raphoe | 258 |
| Bruff/ Meanus/Grange | Limerick | 234 |
| Bruree/Rockhill | Limerick | 235 |
| Bulgaden/ Martinstown | Limerick | 234 |
| Bullaun, Grange & Killaan/New Inn & Bullaun | Clonfert | 118 |
| Bunclody | Ferns | 178 |
| Buncrana/Desertegney & Lower Fahan | Derry | 142 |
| Bundoran/Magh Ene | Clogher | 112 |
| Bunninadden/Kilshalvey, Kilturra & Cloonoghill | Achonry | 102 |
| Burgess and Youghal/ Youghalarra | Killaloe | 216 |

| | | | | | | | | |
|---|---|---|---|---|---|---|---|---|
| Burren/St Mary's | *Dromore* | 167 | Carrigart/Meevagh | *Raphoe* | 258 | Clane | *Kildare* | 203 |
| Burriscarra & | | | Carrigtwohill | *Cloyne* | 122 | Clara | *Meath* | 242 |
| Ballintubber | *Tuam* | 96 | Carron & New Quay | *Galway* | 186 | Clara | *Ossory* | 251 |
| Burrishoole/Newport | *Tuam* | 97 | Cashel | *Cashel* | 85 | Clare Abbey/ | | |
| Burt, Inch & | | | Cashel/ | | | Clarecastle | *Killaloe* | 215 |
| Fahan/Fahan | *Derry* | 143 | Newtowncashel | *Ardagh* | 107 | Clare Island/Inishturk | *Tuam* | 96 |
| Burtonport/ | | | Castlebar/Aglish, | | | Clarecastle/ | | |
| Kincasslagh | *Raphoe* | 258 | Ballyheane & | | | Clare Abbey | *Killaloe* | 215 |
| Butlerstown | *Waterford* | 265 | Breaghwy | *Tuam* | 96 | Claregalway | *Galway* | 186 |
| Buttevant | *Cloyne* | 122 | Castleblayney/ | | | Claremorris/ | | |
| | | | Muckno | *Clogher* | 112 | Kilcolman | *Tuam* | 96 |
| | | | Castlebridge | *Ferns* | 178 | Clarinbridge | *Galway* | 186 |
| | | | Castlecomer | *Ossory* | 251 | Clashmore | *Waterford* | 265 |
| **C** | | | Castleconnell | *Killaloe* | 217 | Claudy/Cumber | | |
| | | | Castleconnor | *Killala* | 211 | Upper & | | |
| Cabinteely | *Dublin* | 45 | Castlederg/Ardstraw | | | Learmount | *Derry* | 143 |
| Cabra | *Dublin* | 45 | West & Castlederg | *Derry* | 143 | Cleariestown and | | |
| Cabra West | *Dublin* | 45 | Castledermot | *Dublin* | 45 | Rathangan | *Ferns* | 179 |
| Caheragh | *Cork & Ross* | 133 | Castledockrell & | | | Cleenish/Arney | *Clogher* | 112 |
| Caherconlish | *Cashel* | 85 | Marshallstown | *Ferns* | 179 | Clerihan | *Cashel* | 85 |
| Caherlistrane/ | | | Castlegar | *Galway* | 186 | Clifden/Omey & | | |
| Donaghpatrick & | | | Castlegregory | *Kerry* | 192 | Ballindoon | *Tuam* | 96 |
| Kilcoona | *Tuam* | 96 | Castlehaven | *Cork & Ross* | 133 | Cliffoney/Ahamlish | *Elphin* | 172 |
| Cahir | *Waterford* | 265 | Castleisland | *Kerry* | 192 | Clogagh & | | |
| Cahirciveen | *Kerry* | 192 | Castleknock | *Dublin* | 45 | Timoleague | *Cork & Ross* | 134 |
| Cahirdaniel | *Kerry* | 192 | Castlelyons | *Cloyne* | 122 | Clogh | *Ossory* | 251 |
| Callan | *Ossory* | 251 | Castlemagner | *Cloyne* | 122 | Cloghan/Kilteevogue | *Raphoe* | 258 |
| Camolin | *Ferns* | 178 | Castlemaine | *Kerry* | 192 | Cloghan & Banagher/ | | |
| Camross | *Ossory* | 251 | Castlemartyr/ | | | Gallen & Reynagh | *Ardagh* | 106 |
| Camus/Strabane | *Derry* | 144 | Imogeela | *Cloyne* | 123 | Clogheen | *Waterford* | 265 |
| Cappagh | *Limerick* | 234 | Castlemore & | | | Clogheen/Kerry Pike | *Cork & Ross* | 133 |
| Cappagh/Killyclogher | *Derry* | 143 | Kilcolman/ | | | Clogher | *Clogher* | 112 |
| Cappamore | *Cashel* | 85 | Ballaghaderreen | *Achonry* | 101 | Clogher Road | *Dublin* | 45 |
| Cappatagle & Kilrickle/ | | | Castlepollard | *Meath* | 242 | Clogherhead | *Armagh* | 28 |
| Killalaghtan & | | | Castlerahan & | | | Cloghogue/Killeavy | | |
| Kilrickile | *Clonfert* | 117 | Munterconnaught | *Kilmore* | 223 | Upper | *Armagh* | 28 |
| Cappawhite | *Cashel* | 85 | Castlerea/Kilkeevan | *Elphin* | 172 | Clonakilty & Darrara | *Cork & Ross* | 133 |
| Cappoquin | *Waterford* | 265 | Castletara | *Kilmore* | 223 | Clonard | *Ferns* | 178 |
| Caragh | *Kildare* | 203 | Castletown | *Dublin* | 45 | Clonaslee | *Kildare* | 203 |
| Carbury | *Kildare* | 203 | Castletown | *Ossory* | 251 | Clonbroney | *Ardagh* | 106 |
| Carlingford & | | | Castletown | | | Clonbullogue | *Kildare* | 203 |
| Clogherny | *Armagh* | 28 | Arrha/Portroe | *Killaloe* | 216 | Clonbur/Ross | *Tuam* | 96 |
| Carna/Moyrus | *Tuam* | 96 | Castletown- | | | Clonburris | | |
| Carnaross | *Meath* | 242 | Geoghegan | *Meath* | 242 | (see Clondalkin) | *Dublin* | 45 |
| Carndonagh/Donagh | *Derry* | 142 | Castletown-Kilpatrick | *Meath* | 242 | Clonca/Malin | *Derry* | 144 |
| Carnew | *Ferns* | 178 | Castletownbere & | | | Clondahorkey/ | | |
| Carnlough | *Down* | 155 | Bere Island | *Kerry* | 192 | Dunfanaghy | *Raphoe* | 258 |
| Carracastle | *Achonry* | 102 | Castletownroche | *Cloyne* | 122 | Clondalkin | *Dublin* | 45 |
| Carraig na bhFear | *Cork & Ross* | 133 | Castleview- | | | Clondavaddog/ | | |
| Carraroe/Kileen | *Tuam* | 96 | Kilnamanagh | *Dublin* | 49 | Tamney | *Raphoe* | 259 |
| Carrick/ | | | Castlewellan/ | | | Clondegad/ | | |
| Glencolmcille | *Raphoe* | 258 | Kilmegan | *Down* | 155 | Ballynacally | *Killaloe* | 217 |
| Carrick-Finea/ | | | The Cathedral/ | | | Clondrohid | *Cloyne* | 123 |
| Drumlumman South | | | St Peter's | *Down* | 153 | Clonduff/Hilltown | *Dromore* | 167 |
| & Ballymachugh | *Ardagh* | 106 | Cathedral | *Galway* | 185 | Clonegal | *Kildare* | 203 |
| Carrick-on-Shannon/ | | | Cathedral, Carlow | *Kildare* | 203 | Clones | *Clogher* | 112 |
| Kiltoghert | *Ardagh* | 106 | Cathedral of St Mary | | | Clonfeacle/Moy | *Armagh* | 30 |
| Carrick-on-Suir | *Waterford* | 265 | & St Anne | *Cork & Ross* | 132 | Clonfert, Donanaghta | | |
| Carrickbeg | *Waterford* | 265 | Cathedral of the | | | & Meelick/ | | |
| Carrickedmond & | | | Assumption/Tuam | *Tuam* | 95 | Eyrecourt, | | |
| Abbeyshrule/ | | | Causeway | *Kerry* | 193 | Clonfert & Meelick | *Clonfert* | 118 |
| Taghshiney, | | | Cavan/Urney & | | | Clongeen | *Ferns* | 178 |
| Taghshinod & | | | Annagelliff | *Kilmore* | 223 | Clonguish/ | | |
| Abbeyshrule | *Ardagh* | 106 | Celbridge | *Dublin* | 45 | Newtownforbes | *Ardagh* | 107 |
| Carrickfergus | *Down* | 155 | Chapelizod | *Dublin* | 45 | Clonlara/Doonas & | | |
| Carrickmacross/ | | | Charlestown/ | | | Truagh | *Killaloe* | 217 |
| Machaire Rois | *Clogher* | 112 | Kilbeagh | *Achonry* | 102 | Clonleigh/Lifford | *Derry* | 144 |
| Carrickmore/ | | | Charleville | *Cloyne* | 122 | Clonmacnois/ | | |
| Loughmacrory/ | | | Cherry Orchard | *Dublin* | 45 | Shannonbridge | *Ardagh* | 107 |
| Creggan/ | | | Christ the Redeemer, | | | Clonmany | *Derry* | 143 |
| Termonmaguirc | *Armagh* | 31 | Lagmore | *Down* | 153 | Clonmeen/Banteer | *Cloyne* | 122 |
| Carrigaholt & Cross/ | | | Christ the King | *Limerick* | 234 | Clonmel, St Mary's | *Waterford* | 265 |
| Kilballyowen | *Killaloe* | 215 | Churchtown | *Dublin* | 45 | Clonmel, St Oliver | | |
| Carrigaline | *Cork & Ross* | 133 | Churchtown/ | | | Plunkett | *Waterford* | 265 |
| Carrigallen | *Kilmore* | 223 | Liscarroll | *Cloyne* | 122 | Clonmel, SS Peter | | |
| | | | City Quay | *Dublin* | 42 | & Paul's | *Waterford* | 265 |

| | | |
|---|---|---|
| Clonmellon | Meath | 242 |
| Clonmore | Kildare | 203 |
| Clonoe | Armagh | 28 |
| Clonoulty | Cashel | 85 |
| Clonrush/ Mountshannon | Killaloe | 217 |
| Clonskeagh | Dublin | 46 |
| Clontarf, St Anthony's | Dublin | 46 |
| Clontarf, St John's | Dublin | 46 |
| Clontead | Cork & Ross | 133 |
| Clontibret | Clogher | 112 |
| Clontuskert | Clonfert | 117 |
| Cloonacool/ Tubbercurry | Achonry | 102 |
| Cloone/Cloone-Conmaicne | Ardagh | 106 |
| Cloontuskert, Kilgefin & Curraghroe/ Ballagh | Elphin | 172 |
| Clostoken & Kilconieran (Kilconickny, Kilconieran & Lickerrig) | Clonfert | 117 |
| Cloughbawn & Poulpeasty | Ferns | 178 |
| Cloughjordan | Killaloe | 216 |
| Cloughprior & Monsea/Puckane | Killaloe | 216 |
| Cloverhill/Oran | Elphin | 172 |
| Cloyne | Cloyne | 123 |
| Coagh | Armagh | 28 |
| Coalisland | Armagh | 29 |
| Cobh, St Colman's Cathedral | Cloyne | 122 |
| Coleraine | Down | 155 |
| Coleraine/Dunboe, Macosquin & Aghadowey | Derry | 143 |
| Collinstown | Meath | 242 |
| Collon & Ardee | Armagh | 28 |
| Collooney/Kilvarnet | Achonry | 102 |
| Colmcille | Ardagh | 106 |
| Conahy | Ossory | 252 |
| Confey | Dublin | 46 |
| Cong & Neale | Tuam | 96 |
| Conna | Cloyne | 123 |
| Conwal & Leck/ Letterkenny | Raphoe | 258 |
| Cookstown/ Desertcreight & Derryloran | Armagh | 29 |
| Coolaney/Killoran | Achonry | 102 |
| Coolcappa | Limerick | 234 |
| Coole/Mayne | Meath | 243 |
| Cooleragh & Staplestown | Kildare | 204 |
| Cooley | Armagh | 29 |
| Coolmeen & Kildysart/ Kilfidane | Killaloe | 217 |
| Coolock | Dublin | 46 |
| Cooraclare/ Kilmacduane | Killaloe | 215 |
| Cootehall/Ardcarne | Elphin | 172 |
| Cootehill/Drumgoon | Kilmore | 223 |
| Corcaghan/Kilmore & Drumsnat | Clogher | 112 |
| Corduff | Dublin | 46 |
| Corlough & Drumreilly | Kilmore | 223 |
| Corofin | Killaloe | 216 |
| Corpus Christi | Down | 153 |
| Corpus Christi | Limerick | 234 |
| Corrandulla/ Annaghdown | Tuam | 96 |

| | | |
|---|---|---|
| Couraganeen/ Bournea | Killaloe | 216 |
| Courceys | Cork & Ross | 133 |
| Craanford | Ferns | 178 |
| Craigavon/ Moyraverty | Dromore | 167 |
| Cratloe | Limerick | 234 |
| Craughwell | Galway | 186 |
| Crecora/Mungret | Limerick | 235 |
| Creggan Lower/Cullyhanna | Armagh | 29 |
| Creggan Upper/ Crossmaglen | Armagh | 29 |
| Creggs/Glinsk & Kilbegnet | Elphin | 172 |
| Croagh & Kilfinny | Limerick | 234 |
| Croghan/Killukin & Killummod | Elphin | 172 |
| Croom | Limerick | 234 |
| Crossabeg & Ballymurn | Ferns | 178 |
| Crossboyne & Tagheen | Tuam | 96 |
| Crosserlough | Kilmore | 223 |
| Crossgar/Kilmore | Down | 155 |
| Crosshaven | Cork & Ross | 133 |
| Crossmaglen/Creggan Upper | Armagh | 29 |
| Crossmolina | Killala | 211 |
| Crumlin | Dublin | 46 |
| Crusheen/Inchicronan | Killaloe | 216 |
| Cúl Máine/Ederney | Clogher | 113 |
| Culdaff | Derry | 143 |
| Culfeightrin | Down | 155 |
| Cullyhanna/Creggan Lower | Armagh | 29 |
| Culmore | Derry | 143 |
| Cumber Upper & Learmount/Claudy | Derry | 143 |
| Cummer/ Kilmoylan & Cummer | Tuam | 96 |
| Curragh Camp | Kildare | 204 |
| Curraha | Meath | 243 |
| Curraheen Road | Cork & Ross | 133 |
| Currin, Killeevan & Aghabog/ Killeevan | Clogher | 113 |
| Curry | Achonry | 102 |
| Cushendall | Down | 155 |
| Cushendun | Down | 155 |
| Cushinstown | Ferns | 178 |

**D**

| | | |
|---|---|---|
| Daingean | Kildare | 204 |
| Dalkey | Dublin | 46 |
| Danesfort | Ossory | 252 |
| Darndale/Belcamp | Dublin | 46 |
| Darver & Dromiskin | Armagh | 29 |
| Davidstown & Courtnacuddy | Ferns | 179 |
| Deansrath | Dublin | 46 |
| Delvin | Meath | 243 |
| Denn | Kilmore | 223 |
| Derriaghy | Down | 153 |
| Derry City/Templemore St Eugene's & Templemore St Columba's | Derry | 142 |
| Derrygonnelly/Botha | Clogher | 112 |
| Derrylin/Knockninny | Kilmore | 224 |
| Derrymacash/Seagoe | Dromore | 168 |
| Derrynoose/Keady | Armagh | 29 |

| | | |
|---|---|---|
| Desertcreight & Derryloran/ Cookstown | Armagh | 29 |
| Desertegney & Lower Fahan/Buncrana | Derry | 142 |
| Desertmartin/Desert-martin & Kilcronaghan | Derry | 143 |
| Devenish/Irvinestown | Clogher | 113 |
| Dingle | Kerry | 193 |
| Dollymount | Dublin | 46 |
| Dolphin's Barn/Rialto | Dublin | 46 |
| Dominick Street | Dublin | 46 |
| Donabate | Dublin | 46 |
| Donacavey/Fintona | Clogher | 113 |
| Donagh | Clogher | 113 |
| Donagh/Carndonagh | Derry | 142 |
| Donagheady/ Dunamanagh | Derry | 143 |
| Donaghmede-Clongriffin-Balgriffin | Dublin | 47 |
| Donaghmore | Armagh | 29 |
| Donaghmore | Dromore | 167 |
| Donaghmore/ Knockea | Limerick | 234 |
| Donaghmore/ Killygordon | Derry | 143 |
| Donaghmoyne | Clogher | 113 |
| Donaghpatrick & Kilcoona/ Caherlistrane | Tuam | 96 |
| Donegal Town/Tawnawilly | Raphoe | 258 |
| Doneraile | Cloyne | 123 |
| Doneyloop/Urney & Castlefinn | Derry | 143 |
| Donnybrook | Dublin | 47 |
| Donnycarney | Dublin | 47 |
| Donore | Meath | 243 |
| Donore Avenue | Dublin | 47 |
| Donoughmore | Cloyne | 123 |
| Doon | Cashel | 85 |
| Doonane | Kildare | 204 |
| Doonas & Truagh/Clonlara | Killaloe | 217 |
| Doonbeg/Killard & Kilkee | Killaloe | 215 |
| Doora & Kilraghtis | Killaloe | 215 |
| Douglas | Cork & Ross | 133 |
| Downpatrick | Down | 155 |
| Drangan | Cashel | 85 |
| Draperstown/ Ballinascreen | Derry | 142 |
| Drimoleague | Cork & Ross | 133 |
| Drogheda, Holy Family | Meath | 243 |
| Drogheda, St Mary's | Meath | 243 |
| Drogheda | Armagh | 27 |
| Droichead Nua/Newbridge | Kildare | 204 |
| Drom & Inch | Cashel | 85 |
| Dromara | Dromore | 167 |
| Dromard | Ardagh | 106 |
| Dromcollogher/ Broadford | Limerick | 234 |
| Dromin & Athlacca | Limerick | 234 |
| Dromintee | Armagh | 29 |
| Dromod/Waterville | Kerry | 194 |
| Dromore | Clogher | 113 |
| Dromore | Dromore | 167 |
| Dromore-West/ Kilmacshalgan | Killala | 211 |
| Dromtariffe | Kerry | 193 |

Allianz (ⅲ)

| | | |
|---|---|---|
| Drumachose, Tamlaght, Finlagan & part of Aghanloo/ Limavady | Derry | 144 |
| Drumahaire & Killargue | Kilmore | 224 |
| Drumaroad & Clanvaraghan | Down | 155 |
| Drumbo | Down | 155 |
| Drumcliff/ Maugherow | Elphin | 172 |
| Drumcondra | Dublin | 47 |
| Drumconrath | Meath | 243 |
| Drumcree/ Portadown | Armagh | 31 |
| Drumgath/ Rathfriland | Dromore | 167 |
| Drumglass, Killyman & Tullyniskin/ Dungannon | Armagh | 28 |
| Drumgooland | Dromore | 167 |
| Drumgoon/Cootehill | Kilmore | 223 |
| Drumholm/Ballintra | Raphoe | 258 |
| Drumkeerin/ Inishmagrath | Kilmore | 224 |
| Drumlane | Kilmore | 224 |
| Drumlish | Ardagh | 106 |
| Drumlumman North/ Mullahoran & Loughduff | Ardagh | 107 |
| Drumlumman South & Ballymachugh/ Carrick-Finea | Ardagh | 106 |
| Drumoghill/ Raymochy | Raphoe | 258 |
| Drumquin/Langfield | Derry | 143 |
| Drumragh/Omagh | Derry | 144 |
| Drumraney | Meath | 243 |
| Drumrat/Keash | Achonry | 102 |
| Drumshanbo/ Murhaun | Ardagh | 106 |
| Duagh | Kerry | 193 |
| Dublin Airport (see Swords) | Dublin | 47 |
| Duleek | Meath | 243 |
| Dun Laoghaire | Dublin | 47 |
| Dunamaggan | Ossory | 252 |
| Dunamanagh/ Donagheady | Derry | 143 |
| Dunboe, Macosquin & Aghadowey/ Coleraine | Derry | 143 |
| Dunboyne | Meath | 243 |
| Duncannon | Ferns | 179 |
| Dundalk, Holy Family | Armagh | 27 |
| Dundalk, Holy Redeemer | Armagh | 27 |
| Dundalk, St Joseph's | Armagh | 27 |
| Dundalk, St Patrick's | Armagh | 27 |
| Dunderry | Meath | 243 |
| Dundrum | Dublin | 47 |
| Dundrum & Tyrella | Down | 155 |
| Duneane | Down | 155 |
| Dunfanaghy/ Clondahorkey | Raphoe | 258 |
| Dungannon/ Drumglass, Killyman & Tullyniskin | Armagh | 28 |
| Dungarvan | Waterford | 265 |
| Dungiven | Derry | 143 |
| Dungloe/ Templecrone & Lettermacaward | Raphoe | 258 |

| | | |
|---|---|---|
| Dunhill | Waterford | 265 |
| Duniry & Abbey/Duniry & Kilnelehan | Clonfert | 117 |
| Dunkerrin | Killaloe | 216 |
| Dunlavin | Dublin | 47 |
| Dunleer | Armagh | 29 |
| Dunloy & Cloughmills | Down | 155 |
| Dunmanway | Cork & Ross | 133 |
| Dunmore | Tuam | 96 |
| Dunmore East/Killea | Waterford | 265 |
| Dunsford & Ardglass | Down | 155 |
| Dunshaughlin | Meath | 243 |
| Durrow | Ossory | 252 |
| Dysart | Meath | 243 |
| Dysart & Ruan | Killaloe | 216 |
| Dysart & Tisrara/ Ballyforan | Elphin | 172 |

**E**

| | | |
|---|---|---|
| Eadestown | Dublin | 47 |
| Easkey | Killala | 211 |
| East Wall-North Strand | Dublin | 47 |
| Edenderry | Kildare | 204 |
| Edenmore | Dublin | 47 |
| Ederney/Cúl Máine | Clogher | 113 |
| Edgeworthstown/ Mostrim | Ardagh | 106 |
| Effin/Garrienderk | Limerick | 234 |
| Eglish | Armagh | 29 |
| Eglish | Meath | 243 |
| Elphin/Elphin & Creeve | Elphin | 172 |
| Ematris/Rockcorry | Clogher | 113 |
| Emlefad & Kilmorgan/ Ballymote | Achonry | 102 |
| Emly | Cashel | 85 |
| Emo | Kildare | 204 |
| Enfield | Meath | 243 |
| Ennis, Cathedral | Killaloe | 215 |
| Ennis, Christ the King | Killaloe | 215 |
| Ennis, St Joseph's | Killaloe | 215 |
| Enniscorthy, Cathedral of St Aidan | Ferns | 178 |
| Enniskeane & Desertserges | Cork & Ross | 133 |
| Enniskerry/ Kilmacanogue/part of Bray Grouping | Dublin | 47 |
| Enniskillen | Clogher | 113 |
| Ennistymon | Galway | 186 |
| Errigal/Garvagh | Derry | 143 |
| Errigal Kieran/ Ballygawley | Armagh | 28 |
| Errigal Truagh | Clogher | 113 |
| Esker-Doddsboro-Adamstown | Dublin | 47 |
| Eskra | Clogher | 113 |
| Eyeries | Kerry | 193 |
| Eyrecourt, Clonfert & Meelick/Clonfert, Donanaghta & Meelick | Clonfert | 118 |

**F**

| | | |
|---|---|---|
| Fahan/Burt, Inch & Fahan | Derry | 143 |

| | | |
|---|---|---|
| Fahy & Quansboro/ Fahy & Kilquain | Clonfert | 118 |
| Fairview | Dublin | 47 |
| Fairymount/Tibohine | Elphin | 172 |
| Falcarragh | Raphoe | 258 |
| Farranree | Cork & Ross | 133 |
| Faughanvale/ Faughanvale & Lower Cumber | Derry | 143 |
| Faughart | Armagh | 29 |
| Feakle & Killanena-Flagmount | Killaloe | 217 |
| Fedamore | Limerick | 235 |
| Feenagh & Kilmeedy | Limerick | 235 |
| Fenagh | Ardagh | 106 |
| Ferbane High Street & Boora/Tisaran & Fuithre | Ardagh | 106 |
| Fermoy | Cloyne | 122 |
| Ferns | Ferns | 179 |
| Ferrybank | Ossory | 252 |
| Fethard | Cashel | 85 |
| Finglas | Dublin | 47 |
| Finglas West | Dublin | 48 |
| Fintona/Donacavey | Clogher | 113 |
| Firhouse | Dublin | 48 |
| Firies | Kerry | 193 |
| Fohenagh & Kilgerrill/ Fohenagh & Killure | Clonfert | 118 |
| Forkhill/ Mullaghbawn | Armagh | 31 |
| Fossa | Kerry | 193 |
| Fourmilehouse/ Kilbride | Elphin | 172 |
| Foxford/Toomore | Achonry | 102 |
| Foxrock | Dublin | 48 |
| Foynes & Shanagolden | Limerick | 235 |
| Francis Street | Dublin | 48 |
| Frankfield-Grange | Cork & Ross | 133 |
| Frenchpark/ Kilcorkey & Frenchpark | Elphin | 172 |
| Freshford | Ossory | 252 |

**G**

| | | |
|---|---|---|
| Galbally | Cashel | 85 |
| Gallen & Reynagh/ Cloghan & Banagher | Ardagh | 106 |
| Galloon/ Newtownbutler | Clogher | 113 |
| Galmoy | Ossory | 252 |
| Gardiner Street | Dublin | 48 |
| Garrienderk/Effin | Limerick | 234 |
| Garristown | Dublin | 48 |
| Gartan & Termon/ Termon | Raphoe | 259 |
| Garvagh/Errigal | Derry | 143 |
| Geevagh | Elphin | 172 |
| Glanmire | Cork & Ross | 133 |
| Glantane | Cloyne | 123 |
| Glanworth & Ballindangan | Cloyne | 123 |
| Glasnevin | Dublin | 48 |
| Glasson–Tubberclaire | Meath | 243 |
| Glasthule | Dublin | 48 |
| The Glen/Blackpool | Cork & Ross | 133 |

| | | |
|---|---|---|
| Glenamaddy/ | | |
| Boyounagh | *Tuam* | 96 |
| Glenariffe | *Down* | 155 |
| Glenarm/ | | |
| Tickmacreevan | *Down* | 155 |
| Glenavy & Killead | *Down* | 155 |
| Glenbeigh | *Kerry* | 193 |
| Glenbrien & Oylegate | *Ferns* | 179 |
| Glencolmcille/ | | |
| Carrick | *Raphoe* | 258 |
| Glendalough | *Dublin* | 48 |
| Glendermott/ | | |
| Waterside | *Derry* | 144 |
| Glenfarne | *Kilmore* | 224 |
| Glenflesk | *Kerry* | 193 |
| Glengarriff/Bonane | *Kerry* | 193 |
| Glenmore | *Ossory* | 252 |
| Glenravel/Skerry | *Down* | 155 |
| Glenroe & Ballyorgan | *Limerick* | 235 |
| Glenswilly/Glenswilly | | |
| & Templedouglas | *Raphoe* | 258 |
| Glenties/Iniskeel | *Raphoe* | 258 |
| Glin | *Limerick* | 235 |
| Glinsk & Kilbegnet/ | | |
| Creggs | *Elphin* | 172 |
| Glounthaune | *Cork & Ross* | 133 |
| Glynn | *Ferns* | 179 |
| Golden | *Cashel* | 85 |
| Goleen | *Cork & Ross* | 133 |
| Good Shepherd | *Galway* | 185 |
| Gorey | *Ferns* | 179 |
| Gort/Beagh | *Galway* | 186 |
| Gortahork/ | | |
| Tory Island | *Raphoe* | 258 |
| Gortin/Badoney | | |
| Lower | *Derry* | 143 |
| Gortletteragh | *Ardagh* | 107 |
| Gortnahoe | *Cashel* | 86 |
| Gowran | *Ossory* | 252 |
| Graignamanagh | *Kildare* | 204 |
| Graiguecullen | *Kildare* | 204 |
| Granard | *Ardagh* | 107 |
| Grange/ | | |
| Bruff/Meanus | *Limerick* | 234 |
| Grange Park | *Dublin* | 48 |
| Greencastle | *Derry* | 143 |
| Greencastle | *Down* | 153 |
| Greenhills | *Dublin* | 48 |
| Greenlough/Tamlaght | | |
| O'Crilly | *Derry* | 143 |
| Grenagh | *Cloyne* | 123 |
| Greystones | *Dublin* | 48 |
| Gurranabraher | *Cork & Ross* | 133 |
| Gurteen/Kilfree & | | |
| Killaraght | *Achonry* | 102 |
| Gweedore | *Raphoe* | 258 |

**H**

| | | |
|---|---|---|
| Hacketstown | *Kildare* | 204 |
| Haddington Road | *Dublin* | 48 |
| Haggardstown & | | |
| Blackrock | *Armagh* | 29 |
| Halston Street & | | |
| Arran Quay | *Dublin* | 48 |
| Hannahstown | *Down* | 155 |
| Harold's Cross | *Dublin* | 48 |
| Harrington Street | *Dublin* | 48 |
| Hartstown | *Dublin* | 49 |
| Headford/Killursa & | | |
| Killower | *Tuam* | 96 |
| Hilltown/Clonduff | *Dromore* | 167 |

| | | |
|---|---|---|
| Hollyhill/ | | |
| Knocknaheeny | *Cork & Ross* | 134 |
| Holy Cross | *Cashel* | 86 |
| Holy Cross | *Down* | 153 |
| Holy Family | *Down* | 153 |
| Holy Family | *Waterford* | 264 |
| Holy Family, | | |
| Ballymagroarty | *Derry* | 142 |
| Holy Family | *Limerick* | 233 |
| Holy Rosary | *Down* | 153 |
| Holy Trinity | *Down* | 153 |
| Holy Trinity | | |
| Cathedral/Trinity | | |
| Within & | | |
| St Patrick's | *Waterford* | 264 |
| Holywood | *Down* | 155 |
| Horeswood & | | |
| Ballykelly | *Ferns* | 179 |
| Hospital | *Cashel* | 86 |
| Howth | *Dublin* | 49 |
| Huntstown | *Dublin* | 49 |

**I**

| | | |
|---|---|---|
| Imogeela/ | | |
| Castlemartyr | *Cloyne* | 123 |
| Inagh/Kilnamona | *Killaloe* | 217 |
| Inch & Kilmaley | *Killaloe* | 217 |
| Inchicore, Mary | | |
| Immaculate | *Dublin* | 49 |
| Inchicore, | | |
| St Michael's | *Dublin* | 49 |
| Inchicronan/ | | |
| Crusheen | *Killaloe* | 216 |
| Inis Muighe | | |
| Samh/Belleek- | | |
| Garrison | *Clogher* | 112 |
| Inishbofin | *Tuam* | 96 |
| Inishmagrath/ | | |
| Drumkeerin | *Kilmore* | 224 |
| Iniskeel/Glenties | *Raphoe* | 258 |
| Inistioge | *Ossory* | 252 |
| Inniscarra | *Cloyne* | 123 |
| Innishannon | *Cork & Ross* | 133 |
| Inniskeen | *Clogher* | 113 |
| Inver | *Raphoe* | 258 |
| Iona Road | *Dublin* | 49 |
| Irvinestown/ | | |
| Devenish | *Clogher* | 113 |
| Iskaheen/Iskaheen & | | |
| Upper Moville | *Derry* | 143 |
| Islandeady | *Tuam* | 96 |

**J**

| | | |
|---|---|---|
| James's Street | *Dublin* | 49 |
| Jobstown | *Dublin* | 49 |
| Johnstown-Killiney | *Dublin* | 49 |
| Johnstown | *Meath* | 243 |
| Johnstown | *Ossory* | 252 |

**K**

| | | |
|---|---|---|
| Kanturk | *Cloyne* | 123 |
| Keadue, Arigna & | | |
| Ballyfarnon/ | | |
| Kilronan | *Ardagh* | 107 |
| Keady/Derrynoose | *Armagh* | 29 |
| Keash/Drumrat | *Achonry* | 102 |

| | | |
|---|---|---|
| Keelogues | *Tuam* | 96 |
| Kells | *Meath* | 243 |
| Kenagh/Kilcommoc | *Ardagh* | 107 |
| Kenmare | *Kerry* | 193 |
| Kerry Pike/Clogheen | *Cork & Ross* | 133 |
| Kilanerin & Ballyfad | *Ferns* | 179 |
| Kilballyowen/ | | |
| Carrigaholt & | | |
| Cross | *Killaloe* | 215 |
| Kilbarrack-Foxfield | *Dublin* | 49 |
| Kilbarron/ | | |
| Ballyshannon | *Raphoe* | 258 |
| Kilbarron & | | |
| Terryglass | *Killaloe* | 216 |
| Kilbeacanty/ | | |
| Peterswell | *Galway* | 186 |
| Kilbeagh/ | | |
| Charlestown | *Achonry* | 102 |
| Kilbeg | *Meath* | 243 |
| Kilbeggan | *Meath* | 243 |
| Kilbehenny | *Cashel* | 86 |
| Kilbride/ | | |
| Fourmilehouse | *Elphin* | 172 |
| Kilbride/Leenane | *Tuam* | 97 |
| Kilbride & Barndarrig | *Dublin* | 49 |
| Kilbride & Doonfeeny/ | | |
| Ballycastle | *Killala* | 210 |
| Kilbrittain | *Cork & Ross* | 133 |
| Kilbroney/Rostrevor | *Dromore* | 167 |
| Kilcar | *Raphoe* | 258 |
| Kilchreest | *Galway* | 186 |
| Kilcleagh & | | |
| Ballyloughloe/Moate | | |
| & Mount Temple | *Ardagh* | 107 |
| Kilclief & Strangford | *Down* | 155 |
| Kilcloon | *Meath* | 243 |
| Kilcock | *Kildare* | 204 |
| Kilcolman | *Killaloe* | 216 |
| Kilcolman/ | | |
| Claremorris | *Tuam* | 96 |
| Kilcommoc/Kenagh | *Ardagh* | 107 |
| Kilcommon | *Cashel* | 86 |
| Kilcommon/ | | |
| Roundfort | *Tuam* | 97 |
| Kilcommon-Erris | *Killala* | 211 |
| Kilconduff & | | |
| Meelick/Swinford | *Achonry* | 102 |
| Kilconly & Kilbannon | *Tuam* | 96 |
| Kilcoo | *Down* | 155 |
| Kilcooley & | | |
| Leitrim/Leitrim & | | |
| Ballyduggan | *Clonfert* | 118 |
| Kilcorkey & | | |
| Frenchpark/ | | |
| Frenchpark | *Elphin* | 172 |
| Kilcormac | *Meath* | 244 |
| Kilcornan | *Limerick* | 235 |
| Kilcullen | *Dublin* | 49 |
| Kilcummin | *Kerry* | 193 |
| Kildalkey | *Meath* | 244 |
| Kildallan & Tomregan | *Kilmore* | 224 |
| Kildare | *Kildare* | 204 |
| Kildimo & Pallaskenry | *Limerick* | 235 |
| Kildorrery | *Cloyne* | 123 |
| Kildress | *Armagh* | 29 |
| Kildysart & Coolmeen/ | | |
| Kilfidane | *Killaloe* | 217 |
| Kileen/Carraroe | *Tuam* | 96 |
| Kilfarboy/Miltown | | |
| Malbay | *Killaloe* | 217 |
| Kilfenora | *Galway* | 186 |
| Kilfian | *Killala* | 211 |
| Kilfidane/Kildysart | | |
| & Coolmeen | *Killaloe* | 217 |
| Kilfinane | *Limerick* | 235 |

| | | |
|---|---|---|
| Kilfree & Killaraght/ | | |
| Gurteen | Achonry | 102 |
| Kilgarvan | Kerry | 193 |
| Kilgarvan/ | | |
| Bonniconlon | Achonry | 102 |
| Kilgeever/Louisburgh | Tuam | 97 |
| Kilglass | Killala | 211 |
| Kilglass/Kilglass & | | |
| Rooskey | Elphin | 172 |
| Kilglass & | | |
| Rathreagh/ | | |
| Legan & | | |
| Ballycloghan | Ardagh | 107 |
| Kilglass & | | |
| Rooskey/Kilglass | Elphin | 172 |
| Kilgobinet | Waterford | 265 |
| Kilkee & Doonbeg/ | | |
| Killard | Killaloe | 215 |
| Kilkeedy/Tubber | Killaloe | 216 |
| Kilkeel/ | | |
| Upper Mourne | Down | 155 |
| Kilkeevan/Castlerea | Elphin | 172 |
| Kilkerley | Armagh | 29 |
| Kilkerrin & Clonberne | Tuam | 96 |
| Kill | Kildare | 204 |
| Killaghtee/Bruckless | Raphoe | 258 |
| Killala | Killala | 211 |
| Killalaghtan & | | |
| Kilrickle/ | | |
| Cappatagle & | | |
| Kilrickle | Clonfert | 117 |
| Killaloe | Killaloe | 217 |
| Killanave & | | |
| Templederry | Killaloe | 217 |
| Killanena-Flagmount | | |
| & Feakle | Killaloe | 217 |
| Killanin/Rosscahill | Galway | 186 |
| Killann/Bailieboro | Kilmore | 223 |
| Killanny | Clogher | 113 |
| Killard/Doonbeg & | | |
| Kilkee | Killaloe | 215 |
| Killarney | Kerry | 192 |
| Killascobe/Menlough | Tuam | 97 |
| Killashee | Ardagh | 107 |
| Killasnett/ | | |
| Manorhamilton | Kilmore | 224 |
| Killasser | Achonry | 102 |
| Killaveney & | | |
| Crossbridge | Ferns | 179 |
| Killavullen | Cloyne | 123 |
| Killcluney | Armagh | 30 |
| Killea/Dunmore East | Waterford | 265 |
| Killeagh | Cloyne | 123 |
| Killeavy Lower/ | | |
| Bessbrook | Armagh | 28 |
| Killeavy | | |
| Upper/Cloghogue | Armagh | 28 |
| Killedan/Kiltimagh | Achonry | 102 |
| Killeedy | Limerick | 235 |
| Killeentierna | Kerry | 193 |
| Killeeshil | Armagh | 30 |
| Killeevan/Currin, | | |
| Killeevan & | | |
| Aghabog | Clogher | 113 |
| Killeigh | Kildare | 204 |
| Killenaule | Cashel | 86 |
| Killenummery & | | |
| Ballintogher/ | | |
| Killenummery & | | |
| Killery | Ardagh | 107 |
| Killererin | Tuam | 96 |
| Killeshandra | Kilmore | 224 |
| Killesher/Kinawley | Kilmore | 224 |
| Killester | Dublin | 49 |
| Killian & | | |
| Killeroran/Ballygar | Elphin | 172 |
| Killimer & Kilrush | Killaloe | 215 |
| Killimor & | | |
| Tiranascragh/ | | |
| Killimorbologue & | | |
| Tiranascragh | Clonfert | 118 |
| Killimordaly & | | |
| Killtulagh/ | | |
| Kiltulla & | | |
| Attymon | Clonfert | 118 |
| Killinagh & | | |
| Glangevlin | Kilmore | 224 |
| Killinarden | Dublin | 49 |
| Killiney/Ballybrack | Dublin | 43 |
| Killinkere | Kilmore | 224 |
| Kill-O'-The-Grange | Dublin | 49 |
| Killoe | Ardagh | 107 |
| Killoran/Coolaney | Achonry | 102 |
| Killorglin | Kerry | 193 |
| Killough/Bright | Down | 156 |
| Killucan | Meath | 244 |
| Killukin & | | |
| Killummod/ | | |
| Croghan | Elphin | 172 |
| Killursa & | | |
| Killower/Headford | Tuam | 96 |
| Killybegs | Raphoe | 258 |
| Killyclogher/ | | |
| Cappagh | Derry | 143 |
| Killygarvan & | | |
| Tullyfern/ | | |
| Rathmullan | Raphoe | 259 |
| Killygordon/ | | |
| Donaghmore | Derry | 143 |
| Killyleagh | Down | 156 |
| Killymard | Raphoe | 258 |
| Kilmacanogue/ | | |
| Enniskerry/part of | | |
| Bray Grouping | Dublin | 47 |
| Kilmacabea | Cork & Ross | 133 |
| Kilmacduane/ | | |
| Cooraclare | Killaloe | 215 |
| Kilmacow | Ossory | 252 |
| Kilmacrennan | Raphoe | 258 |
| Kilmacshalgan/ | | |
| Dromore-West | Killala | 211 |
| Kilmactigue/ | | |
| Tourlestrane | Achonry | 102 |
| Kilmacud-Stillorgan | Dublin | 49 |
| Kilmaine | Tuam | 96 |
| Kilmainhamwood & | | |
| Moybologue | Kilmore | 224 |
| Kilmalinogue & | | |
| Lickmolassey/ | | |
| Portumna | Clonfert | 118 |
| Kilmallock | Limerick | 235 |
| Kilmeen | Tuam | 97 |
| Kilmeen & | | |
| Castleventry | Cork & Ross | 133 |
| Kilmeena | Tuam | 97 |
| Kilmegan/ | | |
| Castlewellan | Down | 155 |
| Kilmessan | Meath | 244 |
| Kilmichael | Cork & Ross | 133 |
| Kilmihil | Killaloe | 216 |
| Kilmore & | | |
| Kilmore Quay | Ferns | 179 |
| Kilmore | Kilmore | 224 |
| Kilmore/Crossgar | Down | 155 |
| Kilmore | Armagh | 30 |
| Kilmore & Drumsnat/ | | |
| Corcaghan | Clogher | 112 |
| Kilmore Road West | Dublin | 49 |
| Kilmore-Erris | Killala | 211 |
| Kilmoremoy/Ballina | Killala | 210 |
| Kilmovee | Achonry | 102 |
| Kilmoylan & | | |
| Cummer/Cummer | Tuam | 96 |
| Kilmuckridge/Litter | | |
| & Monamolin | Ferns | 179 |
| Kilmurray- | | |
| Ibrickane/Mullagh | Killaloe | 217 |
| Kilmurry | Cork & Ross | 133 |
| Kilmurry McMahon | Killaloe | 216 |
| Kilnadeema & | | |
| Aille/Kilnadeema | | |
| & Kilteskill | Clonfert | 118 |
| Kilnamanagh- | | |
| Castleview | Dublin | 49 |
| Kilnamanagh & | | |
| Estersnow/ | | |
| Ballinameen | Elphin | 172 |
| Kilnamartyra | Cloyne | 123 |
| Kilnamona/Inagh | Killaloe | 217 |
| Kilnoe & Tuamgraney/ | | |
| Ogonnelloe & | | |
| Bodyke | Killaloe | 217 |
| Kilquade | Dublin | 50 |
| Kilrane & St Patrick's | Ferns | 179 |
| Kilrea & Desertoghill/ | | |
| Kilrea | Derry | 143 |
| Kilronan/Keadue, | | |
| Arigna & | | |
| Ballyfarnon | Ardagh | 107 |
| Kilrossanty | Waterford | 265 |
| Kilrush & Askamore | Ferns | 179 |
| Kilsaran | Armagh | 30 |
| Kilshalvey, Kilturra & | | |
| Cloonoghill/ | | |
| Bunninadden | Achonry | 102 |
| Kilsheelan | Waterford | 265 |
| Kilsherdany & Drung | Kilmore | 224 |
| Kilskeery/Trillick | Clogher | 114 |
| Kilskyre | Meath | 244 |
| Kiltane | Killala | 211 |
| Kilteely | Cashel | 86 |
| Kilteevogue/Cloghan | Raphoe | 258 |
| Kiltimagh/Killedan | Achonry | 102 |
| Kiltoghert/ | | |
| Carrick-on- | | |
| Shannon | Ardagh | 106 |
| Kiltoom/Kiltoom & | | |
| Cam | Elphin | 172 |
| Kiltormer & Oghill/ | | |
| Lawrencetown & | | |
| Kiltormer | Clonfert | 118 |
| Kiltrustan, | | |
| Lissonuffy & | | |
| Cloonfinlough/ | | |
| Strokestown | Elphin | 173 |
| Kiltubrid | Ardagh | 107 |
| Kiltulla & Attymon/ | | |
| Killimordaly & | | |
| Killtulagh | Clonfert | 118 |
| Kiltullagh/Ballinlough | Tuam | 96 |
| Kilvarnet/Collooney | Achonry | 102 |
| Kilvine/Ballindine | Tuam | 96 |
| Kilworth | Cloyne | 123 |
| Kimmage Manor | Dublin | 50 |
| Kinawley/Killesher | Kilmore | 224 |
| Kincasslagh/ | | |
| Burtonport | Raphoe | 258 |
| Kingscourt | Meath | 244 |
| Kinlough & Glenade | Kilmore | 224 |
| Kinnegad | Meath | 244 |
| Kinnitty | Killaloe | 216 |
| Kinsale | Cork & Ross | 134 |
| Kinsealy | Dublin | 50 |
| Kinvara | Galway | 186 |
| Kircubbin/Ardkeen | Down | 156 |
| Kirkinriola/Ballymena | Down | 154 |
| Kiskeam/Boherbue | Kerry | 192 |

| | | |
|---|---|---|
| Knock | Tuam | 97 |
| Knock/Spiddal | Tuam | 97 |
| Knockaderry & Cloncagh | Limerick | 235 |
| Knockainey | Cashel | 86 |
| Knockanore | Waterford | 265 |
| Knockavilla | Cashel | 86 |
| Knockbride | Kilmore | 224 |
| Knockbridge | Armagh | 30 |
| Knockcroghery/St John's | Elphin | 172 |
| Knocklong | Cashel | 86 |
| Knocklyon | Dublin | 50 |
| Knockmitten (see Clondalkin) | Dublin | 46 |
| Knocknagoshel | Kerry | 193 |
| Knocknaheeny/ Hollyhill | Cork & Ross | 134 |
| Knockninny/Derrylin | Kilmore | 224 |
| Kyle & Knock | Killaloe | 216 |

**L**

| | | |
|---|---|---|
| Lackagh | Tuam | 97 |
| Lacken | Killala | 211 |
| Ladysbridge & Ballymacoda | Cloyne | 122 |
| Lahardane/ Addergoole | Killala | 211 |
| Lanesboro/Rathcline | Ardagh | 107 |
| Langfield/Drumquin | Derry | 143 |
| Laragh | Kilmore | 224 |
| Larkhill-Whitehall-Santry | Dublin | 50 |
| Larne | Down | 156 |
| Lattin & Cullen | Cashel | 86 |
| Latton/ Aughnamullen West | Clogher | 113 |
| Laurel Lodge-Carpenterstown | Dublin | 50 |
| Lavey | Kilmore | 224 |
| Lavey/ Termoneeny & part of Maghera | Derry | 143 |
| Lawrencetown & Kiltormer/Kiltormer & Oghill | Clonfert | 118 |
| Laytown-Mornington | Meath | 244 |
| Leckpatrick/Leckpatrick & part of Donagheady | Derry | 144 |
| Leenane/Kilbride | Tuam | 97 |
| Legan & Ballycloghan/ Kilglass & Rathreagh | Ardagh | 107 |
| Leighlin | Kildare | 204 |
| Leitrim & Ballyduggan/ Kilcooley & Leitrim | Clonfert | 118 |
| Leixlip | Dublin | 50 |
| Lemanaghan/Ballina-hown, Boher & Pollough | Ardagh | 106 |
| Letterfrack/Ballinakill | Tuam | 97 |
| Letterkenny/ Conwal & Leck | Raphoe | 258 |
| Lettermore | Galway | 186 |
| Lifford/Clonleigh | Derry | 144 |
| Limavady/Drumachose, Tamlaght, Finlagan & part of Aghanloo | Derry | 144 |

| | | |
|---|---|---|
| Lisburn/Blaris | Down | 156 |
| Liscannor | Galway | 186 |
| Liscarroll/ Churchtown | Cloyne | 122 |
| Lisdoonvarna & Kilshanny | Galway | 186 |
| Lisdowney | Ossory | 252 |
| Lisgoold | Cloyne | 123 |
| Lismore | Waterford | 265 |
| Lisnaskea/ Aghalurcher | Clogher | 113 |
| Lissan | Armagh | 30 |
| Listowel | Kerry | 193 |
| Litter/Kilmuckridge & Monamolin | Ferns | 179 |
| Little Bray (see Bray, St Peter's) | Dublin | 50 |
| Lixnaw | Kerry | 193 |
| Lobinstown | Meath | 244 |
| Longford/ Templemichael, Ballymacormack | Ardagh | 106 |
| Longwood | Meath | 244 |
| Lordship & Ballymascanlon | Armagh | 30 |
| Lorrha & Dorrha | Killaloe | 216 |
| The Lough | Cork & Ross | 134 |
| Lough Gowna & Mullinalaghta/ Scrabby & Colmcille East | Ardagh | 107 |
| Loughgall | Armagh | 30 |
| Loughglynn/Lough-glynn & Lisacul | Elphin | 172 |
| Loughguile | Down | 156 |
| Loughill/ Ballyhahill | Limerick | 235 |
| Loughilly/Whitecross | Armagh | 31 |
| Loughinisland | Down | 156 |
| Loughlinstown | Dublin | 50 |
| Loughmore | Cashel | 86 |
| Loughrea, St Brendan's Cathedral | Clonfert | 117 |
| Louisburgh/Kilgeever | Tuam | 97 |
| Louth | Armagh | 30 |
| Lower Mourne | Down | 156 |
| Lucan | Dublin | 50 |
| Lucan South | Dublin | 50 |
| Lurgan, St Paul's, Shankill | Dromore | 168 |
| Lurgan, St Peter's, Shankill | Dromore | 168 |
| Lurgan/Virginia | Kilmore | 224 |
| Lusk | Dublin | 50 |
| Lusmagh | Clonfert | 118 |

**M**

| | | |
|---|---|---|
| Machaire Rois/Carrick-macross | Clogher | 112 |
| Macroom | Cloyne | 123 |
| Magh Ene/Bundoran | Clogher | 112 |
| Maghera | Derry | 144 |
| Maghera/Newcastle | Down | 156 |
| Magheracloone | Clogher | 113 |
| Magheradroll/ Ballynahinch | Dromore | 167 |
| Magherafelt & Ardtrea North | Armagh | 30 |
| Magheralin | Dromore | 167 |
| Magilligan | Derry | 144 |
| Mahon | Cork & Ross | 134 |

| | | |
|---|---|---|
| Mahoonagh | Limerick | 235 |
| Malahide | Dublin | 50 |
| Malin/Clonca | Derry | 144 |
| Mallow | Cloyne | 123 |
| Manister | Limerick | 235 |
| Manorhamilton/ Killasnett | Kilmore | 224 |
| Marino | Dublin | 50 |
| Marley Grange | Dublin | 50 |
| Marshallstown and Castledockrell | Ferns | 179 |
| Martinstown/ Bulgaden | Limerick | 234 |
| Maugherow/ Drumcliff | Elphin | 172 |
| Mayfield/St Joseph's | Cork & Ross | 134 |
| Mayne/Coole | Meath | 243 |
| Maynooth | Dublin | 50 |
| Mayo Abbey/ Mayo & Rosslea | Tuam | 97 |
| Mayobridge/ St Patrick's | Dromore | 167 |
| Meadowbrook | Dublin | 51 |
| Meanus/ Bruff/Grange | Limerick | 234 |
| Meath Street & Merchants Quay | Dublin | 51 |
| Meelick & Kilconduff/ Swinford | Achonry | 102 |
| Meelick & Eyrecourt, Clonfert/ Clonfert, Donanaghta & Meelick | Clonfert | 118 |
| Meelick/Parteen | Limerick | 235 |
| Meelin & Rockchapel | Cloyne | 124 |
| Meevagh/Carrigart | Raphoe | 258 |
| Mell | Armagh | 30 |
| Mellifont | Armagh | 30 |
| Melmount/Mourne | Derry | 144 |
| Menlough/Killascobe | Tuam | 97 |
| Merchants Quay & Meath Street | Dublin | 51 |
| Merrion Road | Dublin | 51 |
| Mervue | Galway | 185 |
| Middle Killeavy/Newry | Armagh | 30 |
| Middletown/Tynan | Armagh | 30 |
| Midleton | Cloyne | 123 |
| Milford | Cloyne | 124 |
| Millstreet | Kerry | 193 |
| Milltown | Dublin | 51 |
| Milltown | Kerry | 193 |
| Milltown | Meath | 244 |
| Milltown/Addergole & Liskeevey | Tuam | 97 |
| Miltown Malbay/Kilfarboy | Killaloe | 217 |
| Mitchelstown | Cloyne | 124 |
| Moate & Mount Temple/Kilcleagh & Ballyloughloe | Ardagh | 107 |
| Modeligo | Waterford | 265 |
| Mohill/Mohill-Manachain | Ardagh | 107 |
| Monagea | Limerick | 235 |
| Monageer | Ferns | 179 |
| Monaghan | Clogher | 112 |
| Monaleen | Limerick | 235 |
| Monamolin & Kilmuckridge/ Litter | Ferns | 179 |
| Monasterboice | Armagh | 30 |
| Monasterevan | Kildare | 204 |
| Moneymore/Ardtrea | Armagh | 30 |
| Monkstown | Cork & Ross | 134 |
| Monkstown | Dublin | 51 |

Allianz (ⅲ)

| | | |
|---|---|---|
| Mooncoin | Ossory | 252 |
| Moone | Dublin | 51 |
| Moore | Tuam | 97 |
| Mostrim/Edge-worthstown | Ardagh | 106 |
| Mount Argus | Dublin | 51 |
| Mount Merrion | Dublin | 51 |
| Mountbellew & Moylough | Tuam | 97 |
| Mountcollins/Tournafulla | Limerick | 235 |
| Mountmellick | Kildare | 204 |
| Mountnugent | Meath | 244 |
| Mountrath | Kildare | 204 |
| Mountshannon/Clonrush | Killaloe | 217 |
| Mountview | Dublin | 51 |
| Mourne/Melmount | Derry | 144 |
| Mourne Abbey | Cloyne | 124 |
| Mourne Road | Dublin | 51 |
| Moville/Moville Lower | Derry | 144 |
| Moy/Clonfeacle | Armagh | 30 |
| Moycarkey | Cashel | 86 |
| Moycullen | Galway | 186 |
| Moygownagh | Killala | 211 |
| Moylough & Mountbellew | Tuam | 97 |
| Moynalty | Meath | 244 |
| Moynalvey | Meath | 244 |
| Moyraverty/Craigavon | Dromore | 167 |
| Moyrus/Carna | Tuam | 96 |
| Moyvane | Kerry | 193 |
| Muckalee | Ossory | 252 |
| Muckno/Castleblayney | Clogher | 112 |
| Muinebheag/Bagenalstown | Kildare | 204 |
| Muintir Bháire | Cork & Ross | 134 |
| Mulhuddart | Dublin | 51 |
| Mullagh | Kilmore | 224 |
| Mullagh/Kilmurray-Ibrickane | Killaloe | 217 |
| Mullagh & Killoran/Abbeygormican & Killoran | Clonfert | 118 |
| Mullaghbawn/Forkhill | Armagh | 31 |
| Mullahoran & Loughduff/Drumlumman North | Ardagh | 107 |
| Mullinahone | Cashel | 86 |
| Mullinavat | Ossory | 252 |
| Mullingar, Cathedral of Christ the King | Meath | 242 |
| Multyfarnham | Meath | 244 |
| Mungret/Crecora | Limerick | 235 |
| Murhaun/Drumshanbo | Ardagh | 106 |
| Murragh & Templemartin | Cork & Ross | 134 |
| Murroe & Boher | Cashel | 86 |
| Myshall | Kildare | 204 |

**N**

| | | |
|---|---|---|
| Naas | Kildare | 205 |
| Narraghmore | Dublin | 51 |
| The Nativity | Down | 153 |
| Naul | Dublin | 51 |
| Navan | Meath | 242 |

| | | |
|---|---|---|
| Navan Road | Dublin | 51 |
| Neilstown | Dublin | 51 |
| Nenagh | Killaloe | 217 |
| New Inn | Cashel | 86 |
| New Inn & Bullaun/Bullaun, Grange & Killaan | Clonfert | 118 |
| New Ross | Ferns | 179 |
| Newbawn & Raheen | Ferns | 179 |
| Newbridge | Armagh | 31 |
| Newbridge/Droichead Nua | Kildare | 204 |
| Newcastle | Dublin | 51 |
| Newcastle/Maghera | Down | 156 |
| Newcastle & Fourmilewater | Waterford | 265 |
| Newcastle West | Limerick | 235 |
| Newmarket | Cloyne | 124 |
| Newmarket-on-Fergus | Killaloe | 216 |
| Newport | Cashel | 86 |
| Newport/Burrishoole | Tuam | 97 |
| Newry | Dromore | 167 |
| Newry/Middle Killeavy | Armagh | 30 |
| Newtown | Waterford | 266 |
| Newtownards | Down | 156 |
| Newtownbutler/Galloon | Clogher | 113 |
| Newtowncashel/Cashel | Ardagh | 107 |
| Newtown-cunningham/Killea | Raphoe | 258 |
| Newtownforbes/Clonguish | Ardagh | 107 |
| Newtownpark | Dublin | 52 |
| Newtownstewart/Ardstraw East | Derry | 144 |
| Nobber | Meath | 244 |
| North Wall-Seville Place | Dublin | 52 |
| North William Street | Dublin | 52 |

**O**

| | | |
|---|---|---|
| O'Callaghan's Mills | Killaloe | 217 |
| Ogonnelloe & Bodyke/Kilnoe & Tuamgraney | Killaloe | 217 |
| Ogulla & Baslic/Tulsk | Elphin | 173 |
| Oldcastle | Meath | 244 |
| Omagh/Drumragh | Derry | 144 |
| Omey & Ballindoon/Clifden | Tuam | 96 |
| Oran/Cloverhill | Elphin | 172 |
| Oranmore | Galway | 186 |
| Oristown | Meath | 244 |
| Oughteragh/Ballinamore | Kilmore | 223 |
| Oughterard | Galway | 186 |
| Oulart | Ferns | 179 |
| Our Lady Help of Christians | Limerick | 234 |
| Our Lady of Lourdes | Limerick | 233 |
| Our Lady of Lourdes, Steelstown | Derry | 142 |
| Our Lady of the Rosary | Limerick | 233 |
| Our Lady Queen of Peace | Limerick | 233 |
| Our Lady Queen of Peace, Kilwee | Down | 153 |

| | | |
|---|---|---|
| Our Lady's Island & Tacumshane | Ferns | 179 |
| Ovens | Cork & Ross | 134 |
| Oylegate & Glenbrien | Ferns | 179 |

**P**

| | | |
|---|---|---|
| Pallasgreen | Cashel | 86 |
| Palmerstown | Dublin | 52 |
| Parke/Turlough | Tuam | 97 |
| Parteen/Meelick | Limerick | 235 |
| Partry/Ballyovey | Tuam | 97 |
| Passage West | Cork & Ross | 134 |
| Patrickswell/Ballybrown | Limerick | 235 |
| Paulstown | Kildare | 205 |
| Peterswell/Kilbeacanty | Galway | 186 |
| Pettigo | Clogher | 113 |
| Phibsborough | Dublin | 52 |
| Piercestown | Ferns | 179 |
| Plumbridge/Badoney Upper | Derry | 144 |
| Pobal/Tempo | Clogher | 114 |
| Pomeroy | Armagh | 31 |
| Portadown/Drumcree | Armagh | 31 |
| Portaferry/Ballyphilip | Down | 156 |
| Portarlington | Kildare | 205 |
| Porterstown-Clonsilla | Dublin | 52 |
| Portglenone | Down | 156 |
| Portlaoise | Kildare | 205 |
| Portlaw | Waterford | 266 |
| Portmarnock | Dublin | 52 |
| Portroe/Castletown Arrha | Killaloe | 216 |
| Portrush | Down | 156 |
| Portstewart | Down | 156 |
| Portumna/Kilmalinogue & Lickmolassey | Clonfert | 118 |
| Poulpeasty & Cloughbawn | Ferns | 178 |
| Powerstown | Waterford | 266 |
| Prior/Ballinskelligs | Kerry | 192 |
| Priorswood | Dublin | 52 |
| Pro-Cathedral | Dublin | 42 |
| Prosperous | Kildare | 205 |
| Puckane/Cloughprior & Monsea | Killaloe | 216 |

**Q**

| | | |
|---|---|---|
| Quin | Killaloe | 215 |

**R**

| | | |
|---|---|---|
| Rahan | Meath | 244 |
| Raheen | Kildare | 205 |
| Raheny | Dublin | 52 |
| Ramelton/Aughnish | Raphoe | 259 |
| Ramoan/Ballycastle | Down | 154 |
| Ramsgrange | Ferns | 179 |
| Randalstown | Down | 156 |
| Ransboro/Strandhill | Elphin | 173 |
| Raphoe | Raphoe | 259 |
| Rasharkin | Down | 156 |

| Parish | Diocese | Page |
|---|---|---|
| Rath & the Islands | Cork & Ross | 134 |
| Rathangan & Cleariestown | Ferns | 179 |
| Rathangan | Kildare | 205 |
| Rathaspic, Russagh & Streete/ Rathowen | Ardagh | 107 |
| Rathcline/Lanesboro | Ardagh | 107 |
| Rathcormac | Cloyne | 124 |
| Rathdowney | Ossory | 252 |
| Rathdrum | Dublin | 52 |
| Rathfarnham | Dublin | 52 |
| Rathfriland/ Drumgath | Dromore | 167 |
| Rathgar | Dublin | 52 |
| Rathgormack | Waterford | 266 |
| Rathkeale | Limerick | 235 |
| Rathkenny | Meath | 244 |
| Rathmines | Dublin | 52 |
| Rathmore | Kerry | 193 |
| Rathmullan/ Killygarvan & Tullyfern | Raphoe | 259 |
| Rathnure & Templeudigan | Ferns | 179 |
| Rathowen/ Rathaspic, Russagh & Streete | Ardagh | 107 |
| Rathowen & Streete | Ardagh | 107 |
| Rathvilly | Kildare | 205 |
| Ratoath | Meath | 244 |
| Raymochy/ Drumoghill | Raphoe | 258 |
| Renmore | Galway | 185 |
| Rhode | Kildare | 205 |
| Rialto/Dolphin's Barn | Dublin | 52 |
| Ring & Old Parish | Waterford | 266 |
| Ringsend | Dublin | 52 |
| River Valley | Dublin | 52 |
| Riverchapel, Courtown Harbour | Ferns | 179 |
| Rivermount | Dublin | 52 |
| Riverstown | Elphin | 172 |
| Robeen | Tuam | 97 |
| Rochfortbridge | Meath | 244 |
| Rockchapel & Meelin | Cloyne | 124 |
| Rockcorry/Ematris | Clogher | 113 |
| Rockhill/Bruree | Limerick | 235 |
| Rolestown-Oldtown | Dublin | 53 |
| Rosbercon | Ossory | 252 |
| Roscommon | Elphin | 173 |
| Roscrea | Killaloe | 216 |
| Rosenallis | Kildare | 205 |
| Roslea | Clogher | 114 |
| Rosmuc | Galway | 186 |
| Ross/Clonbur | Tuam | 96 |
| Rosscahill/Killanin | Galway | 186 |
| Rosscarbery & Lissavaird | Cork & Ross | 134 |
| Rosses Point | Elphin | 173 |
| Rostrevor/Kilbroney | Dromore | 167 |
| Roundfort/ Kilcommon | Tuam | 97 |
| Roundstone | Tuam | 97 |
| Roundwood | Dublin | 53 |
| Rowlagh and Quarryvale | Dublin | 53 |
| Rush | Dublin | 53 |

**S**

| Sacred Heart | Cork & Ross | 134 |
| Sacred Heart | Down | 153 |
| Sacred Heart | Waterford | 264 |
| Sacred Heart Church | Galway | 185 |
| Saggart/Rathcoole/ Brittas | Dublin | 53 |
| Saintfield & Carrickmannon | Down | 156 |
| Sallins | Kildare | 205 |
| Sallynoggin | Dublin | 53 |
| Salthill | Galway | 185 |
| Sandyford | Dublin | 53 |
| Sandymount | Dublin | 53 |
| Saul & Ballee | Down | 156 |
| Saval | Dromore | 167 |
| Scariff/Moynoe | Killaloe | 217 |
| Schull | Cork & Ross | 134 |
| Scrabby & Colmcille East/Lough Gowna & Mullinalaghta | Ardagh | 107 |
| Seagoe/Derrymacash | Dromore | 168 |
| Sean McDermott Street | Dublin | 42 |
| Seapatrick/Banbridge | Dromore | 167 |
| Seir Kieran | Ossory | 252 |
| Seville Place-North Wall | Dublin | 52 |
| Shanagolden & Foynes | Limerick | 235 |
| Shandrum | Cloyne | 124 |
| Shankill/ St Paul's, Lurgan | Dromore | 168 |
| Shankill/St Peter's, Lurgan | Dromore | 168 |
| Shankill | Dublin | 53 |
| Shannon | Killaloe | 216 |
| Shannonbridge/ Clonmacnois | Ardagh | 107 |
| Shinrone | Killaloe | 216 |
| Shrule | Galway | 186 |
| Shrule/Ballymahon | Ardagh | 106 |
| Silloge | Dublin | 53 |
| Silloge/Ballymun | Dublin | 43 |
| Silvermines | Killaloe | 217 |
| Sion Mills | Derry | 144 |
| Sixmilebridge | Killaloe | 216 |
| Skerries | Dublin | 53 |
| Skerry/Glenravel | Down | 155 |
| Skibbereen, St Patrick's Cathedral | Cork & Ross | 132 |
| Skreen & Dromard | Killala | 211 |
| Skryne | Meath | 245 |
| Slane | Meath | 245 |
| Slieverue | Ossory | 252 |
| Sligo, St Anne's | Elphin | 172 |
| Sligo, Calry St Joseph's | Elphin | 172 |
| Sligo, St Mary's | Elphin | 172 |
| Sneem | Kerry | 193 |
| Solohead | Cashel | 86 |
| Spa | Kerry | 193 |
| Spiddal/Knock | Tuam | 97 |
| Springfield | Dublin | 53 |
| Sruleen | Dublin | 53 |
| St Agnes' | Down | 153 |
| St Anne's | Down | 153 |
| St Anthony's | Down | 153 |
| St Augustine's | Galway | 185 |
| St Bernadette's | Down | 154 |
| St Brigid's | Down | 154 |
| St Canice's | Ossory | 251 |
| St Columba's & St Eugene's Cathedral/ Templemore/ Derry City | Derry | 142 |
| St Colmcille's | Down | 153 |
| St Finbarr's South | Cork & Ross | 134 |
| St Francis | Galway | 185 |
| St Gerard's | Down | 154 |
| St James's/ Whiteabbey | Down | 154 |
| St John's | Down | 154 |
| St John's | Ossory | 251 |
| St John's | Waterford | 264 |
| St John's/ Knockcroghery | Elphin | 172 |
| St John's Cathedral | Limerick | 233 |
| St John the Apostle | Galway | 185 |
| St Johnston/ Taughboyne | Raphoe | 259 |
| St Joseph's | Galway | 185 |
| St Joseph's | Limerick | 233 |
| St Joseph's/ Blackrock Road | Cork & Ross | 134 |
| St Joseph's/Mayfield | Cork & Ross | 134 |
| St Luke's | Down | 154 |
| St Malachy's | Down | 154 |
| St Mary's | Down | 153 |
| St Mary's | Galway | 185 |
| St Mary's | Limerick | 233 |
| St Mary's | Ossory | 251 |
| St Mary's/Burren | Dromore | 167 |
| St Mary's, Creggan | Derry | 142 |
| St Mary's on the Hill | Down | 154 |
| St Matthew's | Down | 154 |
| St Michael's | Down | 154 |
| St Michael's | Limerick | 233 |
| St Mullins | Kildare | 205 |
| St Munchin's & St Lelia's | Limerick | 233 |
| St Nicholas | Limerick | 234 |
| St Oliver Plunkett | Down | 154 |
| St Patrick's | Cork & Ross | 134 |
| St Patrick's Cathedral, Skibbereen | Cork & Ross | 132 |
| St Patrick's | Down | 153 |
| St Patrick's | Galway | 185 |
| St Patrick's | Limerick | 233 |
| St Patrick's | Ossory | 251 |
| St Patrick's/ Mayobridge | Dromore | 167 |
| St Paul's | Down | 154 |
| St Paul's | Limerick | 233 |
| St Paul's | Waterford | 264 |
| St Peter's/ The Cathedral | Down | 153 |
| St Peter's/ Warrenpoint | Dromore | 167 |
| St Saviour's | Limerick | 233 |
| St Saviour's | Waterford | 264 |
| St Senan's, Enniscorthy | Ferns | 179 |
| St Teresa's | Down | 154 |
| St Vincent de Paul | Down | 154 |
| St Vincent's, Sunday's Well | Cork & Ross | 134 |
| Stamullen | Meath | 245 |
| Strabane/Camus | Derry | 144 |
| Stradbally | Kildare | 205 |
| Stradbally | Waterford | 266 |
| Straide/ Templemore | Achonry | 102 |
| Strandhill/Ransboro | Elphin | 173 |
| Stranorlar | Raphoe | 259 |
| Strathfoyle/ Strathfoyle, Enagh Lough | Derry | 144 |
| Streete & Rathowen | Ardagh | 107 |
| Strokestown/ Kiltrustan/ Lissonuffy & Cloonfinlough | Elphin | 173 |
| SS Joseph & Benildus | Waterford | 264 |
| SS Peter's & Paul's | Cork & Ross | 134 |

Allianz (ili)

| | | |
|---|---|---|
| Summerhill | Meath | 245 |
| Suncroft | Kildare | 205 |
| Sutton | Dublin | 53 |
| Swatragh | Derry | 144 |
| Swinford/ Kilconduff & Meelick | Achonry | 102 |
| Swords | Dublin | 53 |

**T**

| | | |
|---|---|---|
| Taghmaconnell | Clonfert | 118 |
| Taghmon | Ferns | 179 |
| Taghmon | Meath | 245 |
| Taghshiney, Taghshinod & Abbeyshrule/ Carrickedmond & Abbeyshrule | Ardagh | 106 |
| Tagoat | Ferns | 179 |
| Tallaght, Dodder | Dublin | 54 |
| Tallaght, Oldbawn | Dublin | 54 |
| Tallaght, St Mary's | Dublin | 54 |
| Tallaght, Tymon North | Dublin | 54 |
| Tallanstown | Armagh | 31 |
| Tallow | Waterford | 266 |
| Tamlaght O'Crilly/ Greenlough | Derry | 143 |
| Tamney/ Clondavaddog | Raphoe | 259 |
| Tandragee/ Ballymore & Mullaghbrack | Armagh | 31 |
| Tarbert | Kerry | 193 |
| Tarmonbarry | Elphin | 173 |
| Taughboyne, St Johnston | Raphoe | 259 |
| Tawnawilly/ Donegal Town | Raphoe | 258 |
| Templeboy | Killala | 211 |
| Templecrone & Lettermacaward/ Dungloe | Raphoe | 258 |
| Templeglantine | Limerick | 235 |
| Templemartin & Murragh | Cork & Ross | 134 |
| Templemichael, Ballymacormack/ Longford | Ardagh | 106 |
| Templemore | Cashel | 86 |
| Templemore/Derry City, St Eugene's Cathedral & St Columba's | Derry | 142 |
| Templemore/Straide | Achonry | 102 |
| Templeogue | Dublin | 54 |
| Templeorum | Ossory | 252 |
| Templeport | Kilmore | 224 |
| Templetoher/ Williamstown | Tuam | 97 |
| Templetown & Poulfur | Ferns | 179 |
| Templetuohy | Cashel | 86 |
| Tempo/Pobal | Clogher | 114 |
| Terenure | Dublin | 54 |
| Termon/Gartan & Termon | Raphoe | 259 |

| | | |
|---|---|---|
| Termonamongan/ Aghyaran | Derry | 142 |
| Termoneeny and part of Maghera/ Lavey | Derry | 143 |
| Termonfechin | Armagh | 31 |
| Termonmaguirc/ Carrickmore, Loughmacrory & Creggan | Armagh | 31 |
| The Three Patrons | Derry | 142 |
| Thomastown | Ossory | 252 |
| Thurles, SS Joseph and Brigid | Cashel | 85 |
| Thurles, Cathedral of the Assumption | Cashel | 85 |
| Tibohine/ Fairymount | Elphin | 172 |
| Tickmacreevan/ Glenarm | Down | 155 |
| Timoleague & Clogagh | Cork & Ross | 134 |
| Tinryland | Kildare | 205 |
| Tipperary | Cashel | 86 |
| Tirellan | Galway | 186 |
| Tisaran & Fuithre/Ferbane High Street & Boora | Ardagh | 106 |
| Togher | Armagh | 31 |
| Togher | Cork & Ross | 134 |
| Toomevara | Killaloe | 217 |
| Toomore/Foxford | Achonry | 102 |
| Tory Island/ Gortahork | Raphoe | 258 |
| Touraneena | Waterford | 266 |
| Tourlestrane/ Kilmactigue | Achonry | 102 |
| Tournafulla/ Mountcollins | Limerick | 235 |
| Tracton Abbey | Cork & Ross | 134 |
| Tralee, St Brendan's | Kerry | 193 |
| Tralee, St John's | Kerry | 193 |
| Tramore | Waterford | 266 |
| Travelling People | Dublin | 54 |
| Trillick/Kilskeery | Clogher | 114 |
| Trim | Meath | 245 |
| Trinity Within & St Patrick's/ Holy Trinity Cathedral | Waterford | 264 |
| Tuam/Cathedral of the Assumption | Tuam | 95 |
| Tuamgraney & Kilnoe/ Ogonnelloe & Bodyke | Killaloe | 217 |
| Tubber | Meath | 245 |
| Tubber/Kilkeedy | Killaloe | 216 |
| Tubbercurry/ Cloonacool | Achonry | 102 |
| Tulla | Killaloe | 217 |
| Tullaherin | Ossory | 252 |
| Tullamore | Meath | 245 |
| Tullaroan | Ossory | 252 |
| Tullow | Kildare | 205 |
| Tullycorbet/Ballybay | Clogher | 112 |
| Tullyfern & Killygarvan/ Rathmullan | Raphoe | 259 |

| | | |
|---|---|---|
| Tullylish | Dromore | 167 |
| Tulsk/Ogulla & Baslic | Elphin | 173 |
| Tuogh/Beaufort | Kerry | 192 |
| Tuosist | Kerry | 193 |
| Turlough/Parke | Tuam | 97 |
| Turner's Cross | Cork & Ross | 134 |
| Two-Mile-House | Kildare | 205 |
| Tydavnet | Clogher | 114 |
| Tyholland | Clogher | 114 |
| Tynagh | Clonfert | 118 |
| Tynan/Middletown | Armagh | 30 |

**U**

| | | |
|---|---|---|
| Uibh Laoire | Cork & Ross | 134 |
| University Church | Dublin | 54 |
| Upper Mayfield | Cork & Ross | 134 |
| Upper Mourne/Kilkeel | Down | 155 |
| Upperchurch | Cashel | 87 |
| Urlingford | Ossory | 252 |
| Urney & Annagelliff/Cavan | Kilmore | 223 |
| Urney & Castlefinn/ Doneyloop | Derry | 143 |

**V**

| | | |
|---|---|---|
| Valentia | Kerry | 194 |
| Valleymount | Dublin | 54 |
| Virginia/Lurgan | Kilmore | 224 |

**W**

| | | |
|---|---|---|
| Walkinstown | Dublin | 54 |
| Warrenpoint/ St Peter's | Dromore | 167 |
| Watergrasshill | Cork & Ross | 134 |
| Waterside/ Glendermott | Derry | 144 |
| Waterville/ Dromod | Kerry | 194 |
| Westland Row | Dublin | 42 |
| Westport/Aughaval | Tuam | 95 |
| Wexford | Ferns | 178 |
| Whiteabbey/ St James's | Down | 154 |
| Whitecross/ Loughilly | Armagh | 31 |
| Whitefriar Street | Dublin | 54 |
| Whitehouse | Down | 154 |
| Wicklow | Dublin | 54 |
| Williamstown/ Templetoher | Tuam | 97 |
| Willington | Dublin | 54 |
| Wilton, St Joseph's | Cork & Ross | 134 |
| Windgap | Ossory | 253 |
| Woodford | Clonfert | 118 |

**Y**

| | | |
|---|---|---|
| Yellow Walls, Malahide | Dublin | 54 |
| Youghal | Cloyne | 124 |
| Youghalarra/ Burgess & Youghal | Killaloe | 216 |

# GENERAL INDEX

## A

Abbots, Mitred, 17
ACCORD, 19
Achonry, Diocese of, 100-3
Adoration Sisters, Belfast, 302
Adorers of the Sacred Heart of Jesus of
Montmartre, 291
*Africa*, 313
*African Missionary* (SMA), 313
Aid to the Church in Need, 303
Aiken Barracks, Dundalk, 317
Aiséirí, Ferns, 182
Alcoholics Anonymous, Limerick, 239
Alexian Brothers (CFA), 290
*Alive!*, 313
All Hallows College, Drumcondra, 76
Alpha Ireland, 303
America, Irish chaplaincy in, 319
An Clochán Retreat Centre, 67
Apostolate of Eucharistic Adoration, 303
Apostleship of Prayer incorporating
Eucharistic Youth Movement (CYM),
303
Apostleship of the Sea, 303
Apostolic Nuncio, Britain, 332
Arbour Hill Prison, 56, 317
Ardagh and Clonmacnois, Diocese of,
104-9
Ardfert Retreat Centre, 301
Armagh, Archdiocese of, 25-34
charitable and other societies, 34,
educational institutions, 33, parishes,
27-31, religious orders and
congregations, 32-3
Armagh Regional Marriage Tribunal, 316
Association for Church Archives of
Ireland, 303
Association of Papal Orders in Ireland,
303
Association of Primary Teaching Sisters,
304
Augustinians (OSA), 271, 299
Avila Carmelite Centre, Morehampton
Road, Dublin, 300

## B

Banóglaigh Catoilicí na hÉireann, 304
*Being One*, 313
Benedictines (OSB), 272, Sisters, 291
Benedictine Monks of Perpetual
Adoration of the Most Holy Sacrament
(OSB), 272
Bishops, of Ireland, 16-17
Bishops, Synod of, Rome, 14
Blessed Sacrament Congregation (SSS),
272
Blessed Sacrament Sisters, 291
Blowick Centre, Navan, 302
Bon Sauveur Sisters, 291
Bon Secours Sisters (Paris), 292
Brigidine Sisters, 292
Britain, Archbishops and Bishops, 332-4
Britain, The Irish Chaplaincy in, 307

Brothers, Religious, 290-1
Brothers of Charity, 290
*Bulletin of St Vincent de Paul*, 313

## C

Camillians (OSCam), 272, 299
Capuchins (OFMCap), 272-3
Caritas Christi, 297
Carlow College, 208
Carmelite Retreat Centre, Derry, 300
Carmelite Sisters, 292
Carmelite Sisters for the Aged and
Infirm, 292
Carmelites (OCarm), 273-4, 299
Carmelites (OCD), 274
Casement Aerodrome, Baldonnel, 55,
317
Cashel, Archdiocese of, and Diocese of
Emly, 83-8
Castlerea Prison, 317
Cathal Brugha Barracks, Dublin, 55, 317
CatholicIreland.net, 304
Catholic Boy Scouts of Ireland, 304
Catholic Communications Office, 304
Catholic Guides of Ireland, 304
Catholic Historical Society of Ireland, 304
Catholic Men and Women's Society of
Ireland, 304
Catholic Nurses Guild of Ireland, 304
Catholic Primary School Management
Association (CPSMA), 304
Catholic Protection and Rescue Society of
Ireland (CPRSI) *see* Cúnamh, 306
Catholic Youth Care, 301
CEIST, 304
Central Catholic Library, 304-5
Chaplains, 317-19 *see also* under
individual institutions
Charismatic Renewal Movement, 305
Charity of Jesus and Mary Sisters, 292
Charity of Nevers Sisters, 292
Charity of Our Lady Mother of Mercy
Sisters, 292
Charity of St Paul the Apostle Sisters, 292
Charity of the Incarnate Word Sisters,
292
Christian Brothers (CFC), 290
Christian Education, Religious of, 296
Christian Life Communities, 305
Christian Renewal Centre, Newry, 300
Christian Retreat Centres, 292
ChurchServices.tv, 305
Church of Ireland, 324, Archbishops and
Bishops, 325
Church Resources, 305
*Church of Ireland Gazette*, 313
Cistercian Order (OCSO), 274, Sisters, 292
Clarissan Missionary Sisters of the Blessed
Sacrament, 292
Clogher, Diocese of, 110-15
Clonfert, Diocese of, 116-19
Cloverhill Remand Prison, 317
Cloyne, Diocese of, 120-6
Collins Barracks, Cork, 317
Columba Community, 141, 297, 302

Comboni Missionaries (MCCJ), 274
Communion and Liberation, 305
Concern Worldwide, 305
Conference of Religious of Ireland, 305
Congregation of the Most Holy
Redeemer (CSsR), 284-5
Congregation of Our Lady of Charity of
the Good Shepherd, 294
Congregation of the Passion (CP), 284
Congregation of the Sacred Hearts of
Jesus and Mary (SSCC), 275
Congregation of the Sisters of Mercy,
293
Congregation of the Sisters of Nazareth,
296
Congregations, Rome, 13
Cork & Ross, Diocese of, 131-9
Cork Prison, 317
Cork Regional Marriage Tribunal, 316
Council for Clergy of the Irish Episcopal
Conference, 23
Council of Irish Adoption Agencies,
305
Council of Management of Catholic
Secondary Schools, 305-6
Cross & Passion Congregation, 293
CROSSCARE, 41
Cumann Ceol Eaglasta na hÉireann (Irish
Church Music Association), 307
Cumann na Sagart, 306
Cumann na Séiplíneach Scoile (School
Chaplains Association), 311
Cúnamh, 306
CURA, 306
Curia, Roman, The, 13-14
Curragh Camp, 317
Custume Barracks, Athlone, 317

## D

Daughters of Charity of St Vincent de
Paul, 293
Daughters of the Cross of Liège, 293
Daughters of the Heart of Mary, 293
Daughters of the Holy Spirit, 293
Daughters of Jesus, 293
Daughters of Mary and Joseph, 293
Daughters of Our Lady of the Sacred
Heart, 293
Daughters of Wisdom (La Sagesse), 293
*Daystar*, 313
De La Salle Brothers (FSC), 291
Defence Forces Chaplaincy Service, 317
Derry, Diocese of, 140-6
Dialogue Ireland Trust, 306
Disciples of Divine Master Sisters, 293
Divine Word Missionaries (SVD), 275, 299
*Doctrine and Life*, 313
Dominican Biblical Institute, 299
Dominican Contemplatives, 293
Dominican Order (OP), 275-6
Dominican House of Study, Dublin, 299
Dominican Pastoral Centre, Cork, 301

Dominican Retreat Centre, Tallaght, 300
Dominican Sisters, 293
Dowdstown House, Meath, 302
Down and Connor, Diocese of, 151-60
Dromantine Retreat and Conference Centre, Newry, Co Down, 300
Dromore, Diocese of, 165-9
Drumalis Retreat Centre, Co Antrim, 300
Dublin, Archdiocese of, 39-78, parishes, 42-54, religious orders and congregations, 58-76
Dublin City University, 55
Dublin Regional Marriage Tribunal, 316

## E

Ecclesiastical address, forms of, 335
Ecumenics, Irish School of, 299, 308
Education, Special Institutes of, 299
Elphin, Diocese of, 170-5
Emly, Diocese of, see Cashel, Archdiocese of, 83-88
Emmanuel House of Providence, Co Galway, 301
Emmaus, Swords, Co Dublin, 300
England and Wales, Bishops' Conference of, 332-3
Episcopate, Irish, 16-17
Equestrian Order of the Holy Sepulchre of Jerusalem, Lieutenancy of Ireland, 306
Equipes Notre-Dame (Teams of Our Lady), 306
ERST, 306
Esker Retreat House, Co Galway, 301
Europe, Irish Chaplaincy in, 319
Evangelical Catholic Initiative, 306-7

## F

Family and Media Association, 307
Family of Adoration Sisters, 293
Family of God, The, 307
Far East, The, 313
Father Mathew Union, 307
Ferns, Diocese of, 176-182
Finner Army Camp, Ballyshannon, 114, 317
Focolare Movement, 307
Foilseacháin Ábhair Spioradálta, 314
Franciscan Brothers (OSF), 291
Franciscan Friars of the Renewal (CFR), 278
Franciscan Missionaries of the Divine Motherhood, 293
Franciscan Missionaries of Mary, 294
Franciscan Missionaries of Our Lady, 294
Franciscan Missionaries of St Joseph, 294
Franciscan Missionary Sisters for Africa, 294
Franciscan Order (OFM), 276-8, 299
Franciscan Order (OFMConv), 278
Franciscan Sisters of the Immaculate Conception, 294
Franciscan Sisters of Littlehampton, 294
Franciscan Sisters, 294
Furrow, The, 314

## G

Galway, Kilmacduagh and Kilfenora, Dioceses of, 183-9

Galway Regional Marriage Tribunal, 316
General Information, 320-3
Glencomeragh House of Prayer, 301
Glenstal Abbey Monastic Guest House, Murroe, 302
Gormanston Camp, Co Meath, 317
Greek Orthodox Church in Ireland, 324, 326

## H

Handmaids of the Sacred Heart of Jesus, 294
Hierarchy, Irish, 16-17
Holy Child Jesus, Society of the, 294
Holy Cross Monastery, 302
Holy Faith Sisters, 294
Holy Family of Bordeaux Sisters, 294
Holy Family of Saint Emilie de Rodat Sisters, 294
Holy Spirit Congregation (CSSp), 278-9
Houses of Study, 299

## I

IMU Mission Institute, 299
Infant Jesus Sisters, 294
Inter-Church Centre, Belfast, 324
Inter-Church Meeting, Irish, 308
Intercom, 313
International Military Pilgrimage to Lourdes, 317
Ireland's Cardinals, 328
Irish Biblical Association, 307
Irish Catholic, 314
Irish Chaplaincy in Britain, The, 307, 318
Irish Church Music Association (Cumann Ceol Eaglasta na hÉireann), 307
Irish College, Paris, 307
Irish Council of Churches, 307, 324
Irish Episcopal Council for Emigrants, 307
Irish Episcopal Commission for Liturgy, 307
Irish Episcopal Conference, 17
Irish Hospitalité of Our Lady of Lourdes, 308
Irish Missionary Union (IMU), 308
Irish Pilgrimage Trust, The, 308
Irish School of Ecumenics, 299, 308
Irish School of Evangelisation (ISOE) 78, 308
Irish Theological Association, 308
Irish Theological Quarterly, 314

## J

James Stephens Barracks, Kilkenny, 317
Jesuits (SJ), 279-81
Jesuit Communication Centre, 308
Jesus and Mary, Congregation of, 294
Jesus Caritas Fraternity of Priests, 308
John Paul II Centre, Killarney, 302

## K

Kairos Communications Ltd, 309
Kerry, Diocese of, 190-6
Kildare and Leighlin, Diocese of, 201-8
Kilfenora, Diocese of, see under Galway
Killala, Diocese of, 209-12
Killaloe, Diocese of, 213-20
Kilmacduagh, Diocese of, see under Galway
Kilmore, Diocese of, 221-6
Knights of St Columbanus, 309
Knock Shrine Pilgrimages, 309

## L

La Retraite Sisters, 294
La Retraite Hermitage, 302
La Sainte Union des Sacres Coeurs, 294
La Salle Pastoral Centre, Portlaoise, 301
La Verna, Drumshanbo, 302
La Verna Retreat Centre, Co Donegal, 300
L'Arche Workshops, Kilkenny, 255
Lay Fraternity of Blessed Charles de Foucauld, 309
Lay Secular Institutes, 297
Legion of Mary, 309
Legionaries of Christ (LC), 60, 281
Life in the Eucharist Team, 309
Limerick, Diocese of, 231-9
Limerick Diocesan Pastoral Centre, 302
Limerick Prison, 318
Little Company of Mary, 294
Little Sisters of the Assumption, 295
Little Sisters of the Poor, 295
Liturgy, Irish Episcopal Commission for, 307
Liturgy, National Centre for, 310
Loreto Sisters (IBVM), 295
Lough Derg, St Patrick's Purgatory, 115, 309
Loughan House, Co Cavan, 225, 318
Lutheran Church in Ireland, 324

## M

McKee Barracks, Dublin, 55, 317
Maghaberry Prison, Co Antrim, 318
Magilligan Prison, Co Derry, 318
Malta, Order of, 310
Manresa House, Dublin, 300
Maria Legionis, 314
Marianists (SM), 281
Marie Auxiliatrice Sisters, 295
Marie Reparatrice Sisters, 295
Marino Institute of Education, 76
Marist Brothers (FMS), 291
Marist Fathers (SM), 281-2, Sisters, 295
Marriage Encounter, 309
Marriage Tribunals, 316
Mater Dei Institute of Education, 76, 299
Meath, Diocese of, 240-8
Medical Missionaries of Mary, 295
Medical Missionaries of Mary, 314
Methodist Church in Ireland, 324, 326
Midlands Prison, 205, 318
Mill Hill Missionaries (MHM), 282
Milltown Institute of Theology and Philosophy, 76, 298
Milltown Studies, 314

Missionaries of Africa (White Fathers), 282, 299
Missionaries of Charity, 295
Missionaries of the Sacred Heart (MSC), 282-3
Missionary Francisan Sisters of the Immaculate Conception, 295
Missionary Sisters of the Assumption, 295
Missionary Sisters of the Holy Cross, 295
Missionary Sisters of Our Lady of Apostles, 295
Missionary Sisters Servants of the Holy Spirit, 295
Missionary Sisters of St Columban, 295
Missionary Sisters of St Peter Claver, 295
Missionary Sisters of the Holy Rosary, 295
Monastery of St Catherine of Siena, Louth, 301
Moravian Church, Irish District, 324
Mount St Anne's, Co Laois, 301
Mountjoy Prison, Dublin, 57, 318
Mountjoy Women's Prison/Dóchas, 57, 317
Myross Wood House, Leap, 283

N

Nano Nagle Centre, 301
National Association of Christian Brothers Past Pupils Unions, 309
National Association Executive of Primary Diocesan Advisors, 309
National Association of Healthcare Chaplains, 310
National Centre for Liturgy, 310
National Chaplaincy for Deaf People, 310
National Marriage Appeal Tribunal, 316
National Mission Council of Ireland, 310
Naval Base, Haulbowline, Co Cork, 317
New Liturgy, 314
Non-Subscribing Presbyterian Church, 324
Non-Subscribing Presbyterian Magazine, 314
Norbertine Canons (OPraem), 283
Notre Dame des Missions, 295

O

Obituary List, 320-3
Oblates of Mary Immaculate (OMI), 283, 299
Offices, Roman Curia, 13-14
Opus Dei, 270
Order of Malta Ambulance Corps, 310
Ordinations, 323
Organisations and Societies, 303-13
Orlagh Retreat Centre, 300
Ossory, Diocese of, 249-255
Our Lady of Bethlehem Abbey, Portglenone, 302
Our Lady of Sion Sisters, 295
Our Lady of the Cenacle, 295
Our Lady's Choral Society, Dublin, 78

P

Pallottines (SAC), 283-4
Papal Nuncio, 15
Passionists (CP), 284
Passionist Retreat Centre, 300
Pastoral Centres, 301-2
Patrician Brothers (FSP), 291
Pax Christi – International Catholic Movement for Peace (Irish Section), 310
Peace in Christ, Kilkenny, 301
People's Eucharistic League, 310
Perpetual Adoration Sisters, 295
Pioneer, 314
Pioneer Total Abstinence Association of the Sacred Heart, 311
Pontifical Councils, Rome, 13-14
Pontifical Irish College, Rome, 298
Poor Clares, 295-6
Poor Servants of the Mother of God, 296
Portlaoise Prison, 318
Prelatures, Personal, 270
Presbyterian Church in Ireland, 324, 326
Presbyterian Herald, 314
Presentation Brothers (FPM), 291
Presentation of Mary Sisters, 296
Presentation Sisters, 296
Prisons and Places of Detention in Ireland, Chaplaincy, 317-18
Private Retreats, 302
Proceedings of the Irish Biblical Association, 314
Provinces, Diocesan, 24
Purcell House, All Hallows College, Drumcondra, 301

Q

Queen's University, Belfast, 156

R

Radharc Trust, The, 311
Raphoe, Diocese of, 256-61
Reality, 314
Redemptoris Mater Archdiocesan Missionary House of Formation, 299
Redemptoristines, 296
Redemptorists (CSsR), 284-5, 299
Regional Marriage Tribunals, 316
Regnum Christi, 311
Religious of Christian Education, 296
Religious of Ireland, Conference of, 305
Religious Brothers, Communities of, 290-1
Religious Life Review, 314
Religious News Network (RNN), 311
Religious Orders and Congregations, 271-97, see also under individual dioceses
Religious Periodicals, 313-15
Religious Press Association, 311
Religious Sisters, Communities of, 291-7
Religious Sisters of Charity, 296
Religious Society of Friends, 324
Renmore Barracks, Galway, 317
Retreat Houses, 300-1
Retreats, Private, 302

Review of Irish Episcopal Conference, 8-12
Roman Curia, 13-14
Roman Pontiffs, The, 336-8
Romanian Orthodox Church in Ireland, 326
Rosminian House of Prayer, Glencomeragh, Kilsheelan, Co Tipperary, 301
Rosminians (IC), 285
Rosminians (Sisters of Providence), 296
Rostrevor Christian Renewal Centre, 300
Russian Orthodox Church in Ireland, 324

S

Sacred Heart Fathers (SCJ), 286
Sacred Heart Messenger, 314
Sacred Heart Society, 296
Sacred Hearts of Jesus and Mary, 296
Sacred Hearts of Jesus and Mary (Picpus), 296
Sagart, An, 314
St Aidan's Monastery of Adoration, Ferns, 302
St Anthony Brief, The, 315
St Anthony's Retreat Centre, Dundrean, 300
St Benedict's Priory Retreat House, The Mount, Cobh, 300
St Bricin's Hospital, Dublin, 317
St Catherine of Siena Monastery, Drogheda, 301
St Clare Sisters, 296
St Columban's Missionary Society (SSC), 286-7
St Columbanus, Knights of, 309
St John of God Brothers (OH), 291
St John of God Sisters, 296, 301
St John's Pastoral Centre, Waterford, 302
St Joseph of Annecy Sisters, 296
St Joseph of the Apparition Sisters, 297
St Joseph of Chambery Sisters, 297
St Joseph of Cluny Sisters, 297
St Joseph of Lyon Sisters, 297
St Joseph of the Sacred Heart Sisters, 297
St Joseph's Advocate, 315
St Joseph's Young Priests Society, 311
St Kieran's College, Kilkenny, 254
St Louis Sisters, 297
St Macartan's College, Monaghan, 115
St Malachy's College, Belfast, 160
St Mary's University College, 160
St Mary Madeleine Postel Sisters, 297
St Martin Magazine, 315
St Patrick's College, Drumcondra, 55, 76
St Patrick's College, Maynooth, 76, 298
St Patrick's College, Thurles, 88
St Patrick's Institution, Dublin, 318
St Patrick's Missionary Society (SPS), 287-8
St Patrick's Purgatory, Lough Derg, 115
St Paul, Society of (SSP), 290
St Paul de Chartres Sisters, 297
St Peter's Diocesan College, Wexford, 181
St Vincent de Paul, Society of, 312
St Vincent de Paul Night Shelter, Dublin, 78
Salesian Bulletin, The, 314
Salesian Sisters of St John Bosco, 296
Salesians (SDB), 288, 299
Salvation Army, 324

Salvatorians (SDS), 288
Saotharaithe Ógra Críostaí (Young
   Christian Workers), 312-13
Sarsfield Barracks, Limerick, 236, 317
School Chaplains Association (Cumann
   na Seiplineach Scoile), 311
Scotland, Hierarchy of, 333-4
Scouting Ireland, 311
Scripture in Church, 314
Secretariat of State, Rome, 13
Secular Franciscan Order, 311
Seminaries, 298
Servite Priory, Benburb Centre,
   Co Tyrone, 301
Servitium Christi, 297
Servites (OSM), 288-9
Seville Lodge Trust, 302
Sheaf, The, 314
Shelton Abbey, Arklow, 57, 318
Sisters, Religious, 291-7
Societies, 303-13
Society of African Missions (SMA), 289
Society of Jesus (SJ), Jesuits, 279-81
Society of Mary (SM), Marianists, 281
Society of Mary (SM), Marist Fathers,
   281-2
Society of Madonna della Strada, 297
Society of St Paul (SSP), 290
Society of St Vincent de Paul, 78, 312
Sons of Divine Providence (FDP), 290
Special Institutes of Education, 299
Spirituality, 315
Spiritual Family, The Work of Christ
   Familia Spiritualis Opus (FSO), The, 297
Statistics, 329-31
Stella Maris Retreat Centre, Co Dublin,
   301
Studies, 315

T

Tallaght Rehabilitation Project, 300
Teach Chaoimhín, Glendalough, 301
Teach Lorcain, Glendalough, 301
Teams of Our Lady, Equipes Notre-Dame,
   306
Teresian Association, The, 312
Threshold, 78
Timire An Chroí Naofa, 315
Tobar Mhuire, Passionists, Co Down, 300
Training Unit, Dublin, 318
Trócaire, 312
Tribunals, Rome, 13
Trinity College, Dublin, 55
Tuam, Archdiocese of, 93-9

U

Ukrainian Apostolic Eparchy, 333
United States of America, Irish
   Chaplaincy, 319
Universe Catholic Weekly, The, 315
University College, Cork, 135
University College, Dublin, 55
University Hospital, Galway, 187
University of Ulster, Coleraine, 156
University of Ulster, Jordanstown, 156
Ursulines, 297
Ursulines of Jesus, 297

V

Veritas Communications, 312
Veritas Company Ltd, 312
Veritas Publications, 312
Verna, La, Drumshanbo, 302
Verna, La, Retreat Centre, Co Donegal,
   300
Viatores Christi, 312
Vincentians (CM), 290
Visitation Sisters, 297
Vocations Ireland, 312
Volunteer Mission Movement, 312

W

Waterford and Lismore, Diocese of,
   262-9
Waterford and Lismore Diocesan Pastoral
   Centre (St John's), 269
Wheatfield Prison, Clondalkin, 57, 318
Whiteoaks Rehabilitation Centre,
   Donegal, 302
World Missions, Ireland, 312

Y

Young Christian Workers (Saotharaithe
   Ógra Críostaí), 312-3
Young Offenders' Centre, Hydebank, 318